CONTEMPORARY. CURRENT. *Complete.*

A PPLIED
C URRENT
T OPICAL
I NNOVATIVE
V ISUAL
E VIDENCE BASED

With its signature active learning approach, **Child Development: An Active Learning Approach, Third Edition,** is the most interactive introduction to child development today.

APPLIED

Learning Questions: Each chapter opens with questions that help guide students as they read. At the end of the chapter, the questions are linked to the summary for review.

Test Your Knowledge: In *Student-on-the-Street* videos, *True/False Questions* from the chapter quizzes are posed to students on their campuses, and the authors comment on the students' answers.

Check Your Understanding: Each section of a chapter concludes with a set of questions that lets students check on their mastery of the material before moving on to the next topic.

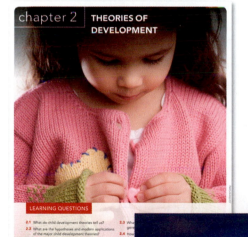

CURRENT

Authors provide the latest content, including a focus on *neuroscience, diversity,* and *culture*.

TOPICAL

The topical organization allows students to *engage in depth* with each topic to see continuities and discontinuities of development.

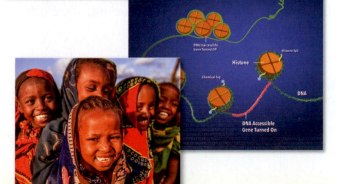

INNOVATIVE

Active Learning exercises throughout the narrative turn reading into an active process.

VISUAL

Abundant *illustrations, charts, photos,* and *videos* bring concepts to life.

Active Learning videos: Demonstrations Videos are available for many of the **Active Learning** activities that involve interviewing or conducting an activity with a child or adolescent.

Development In Action videos: Professionals in the field of child development discuss various topics from the book, and videos taped in child care settings show children engaged in a number of the activities described in the text.

EVIDENCE-BASED

Journey of Research features trace the evolution of ideas in the field, enhancing the focus on deep learning, critical thinking, and analysis.

Active LEARNING

Developing Body Awareness

Offer to play a variation of the game Simon Says with a child between ages 3 and 8. Tell the child that he or she should do the actions exactly as "Simon says." Begin by having the child do the movements with you. As you say "Simon says touch your nose" or "Simon says touch your knees," do the action along with the child. Do this with about 10 body parts. Then just give the directions and allow the child to do the

ACTIVE LEARNING VIDEO ▲
Two-year-old Sabrina demonstrates her developing sense of body awareness.

JOURNEY OF *Research*

The History of Research on Genetics

The modern study of genetics began in 1866 when Gregor Mendel published a paper outlining a number of the principles that guide the transmission of genetic information from one generation to another. However, it took until 1900 before the significance of his work was recognized (Lane, 1994). The basic principles of inheritance that he described came to be known as Mendelian inheritance. Although Mendel was able to describe the way in which characteristics of pea plants were passed on from one generation to the next, he did not know about genes or how they work.

⑤SAGE coursepacks

Our Content Tailored to your LMS

SAGE coursepacks for instructors makes it easy to import our quality instructor materials and student resources into your school's learning management system (LMS). Intuitive and simple to use, SAGE coursepacks allow you to integrate only the content you need without an access code.

sagepub.com/coursepacks

BOOST COMPREHENSION. BOLSTER ANALYSIS.

SAGE Premium Video Helps Your Students Do Both.

Included with the interactive eBook!
Use bundle ISBN: **978-1-5063-8126-8**.

Assessment questions for **SAGE Premium Video** offer high-quality video assignments and test students on comprehension, analysis, and application.

PRAISE FOR
Child Development

"[Test Your Knowledge is] very engaging and effective. **ATTENTION GRABBER**. The questions/your answers stick with you as you read the chapter allowing one to either confirm or change their thinking."

—Aaliyah Baker, *Cardinal Stritch University*

"I really like the **LEARNING GOALS** and the end-of-chapter summaries. With so much content, it is helpful to have a reminder of the **MOST IMPORTANT POINTS** from the chapter at the end."

—Amy M. Claridge, *Central Washington University*

"I really appreciated the *Active Learning* exercises! Wow. These are probably the best that I have seen for these. I also appreciated the **FOCUS ON CAREERS**, as well as being a good consumer of research…. I was especially impressed with the *Test Your Knowledge* openers. I could envision myself using these for each chapter as a **DISCUSSION STARTER** in class."

—Tara M. Stoppa, *Eastern University*

"The *Active Learning* sections are particularly engaging. I believe students will really enjoy doing these on their own, and it is also something that I can facilitate in the classroom…. The *Test Your Knowledge* section is also a favorite of mine. This is an **ENGAGING** and **USEFUL** tool to help students focus their learning…My students would enjoy a text that encourages such deep and effective interaction—less passive reading—and **PUSHES CRITICAL THINKING**.

—Dawn N. Hicks Tafari, *Winston-Salem State University*

"There are a lot of examples, activity suggestions for students, and questions to get students thinking about the material…. The content is **EVIDENCE BASED** and **UP TO DATE**, and research studies are explained in a way students can understand."

—Amy M. Claridge, *Central Washington University*

child
DEVELOPMENT
THIRD EDITION

Dedicated to the memory of my father, Julian Levine. –LL

With gratitude to Jeff and Liz, Gabi and Madi, for all that they have taught me. –jm

child DEVELOPMENT

AN ACTIVE LEARNING APPROACH

THIRD EDITION

LAURA E. LEVINE
Central Connecticut State University

JOYCE MUNSCH
California State University, Northridge

Los Angeles | London | New Delhi
Singapore | Washington DC | Melbourne

FOR INFORMATION:

SAGE Publications, Inc.
2455 Teller Road
Thousand Oaks, California 91320
E-mail: order@sagepub.com

SAGE Publications Ltd.
1 Oliver's Yard
55 City Road
London, EC1Y 1SP
United Kingdom

SAGE Publications India Pvt. Ltd.
B 1/I 1 Mohan Cooperative Industrial Area
Mathura Road, New Delhi 110 044
India

SAGE Publications Asia-Pacific Pte. Ltd.
3 Church Street
#10-04 Samsung Hub
Singapore 049483

Acquisitions Editor: Lara Parra
Development Editor: Cheri Dellelo
Associate Editor: Lucy Berbeo
eLearning Editor: Morgan Shannon
Editorial Assistant: Zachary Valladon
Production Editor: Olivia Weber-Stenis
Copy Editor: Gretchen Treadwell
Typesetter: C&M Digitals (P) Ltd.
Proofreader: Sally Jaskold
Indexer: Michael Ferreira
Cover Designer: Gail Buschman
Marketing Manager: Katherine Hepburn

Printed in Canada.

Library of Congress Cataloging-in-Publication Data

Names: Levine, Laura E., author. | Munsch, Joyce, author.

Title: Child development : an active learning approach / Laura E. Levine, Emerita Central Connecticut State University, Joyce Munsch, Emerita, California State University, Northridge.

Description: Third edition. | Los Angeles : SAGE, [2017] | Includes bibliographical references and index.

Identifiers: LCCN 2016034251 | ISBN 978-1-5063-3069-3 (pbk. : alk. paper)

Subjects: LCSH: Child psychology. | Child development.

Classification: LCC BF721 .L5225 2017 | DDC 155.4—dc23 LC record available at https://lccn.loc.gov/2016034251

This book is printed on acid-free paper.

16 17 18 19 20 10 9 8 7 6 5 4 3 2 1

Brief Contents

Detailed Contents

Christopher Futcher/E+/Getty Images

3. How We Study Development   64

Cliff Moore / Science Source/ Getty Images

6. Physical Development: The Brain and the Body   176

Gandee Vasan/Stone/Getty Images

PART III. COGNITIVE DEVELOPMENT   223

7.   Theories of Cognitive Development   224

Laura Levine

Will & Deni McIntyre/Corbis Documentary/
Getty Images

8. Intelligence and Academic Achievement   270

9. Language Development   312

JGI/Jamie Grill/Blend Images/Getty Images

PART IV. SOCIAL AND EMOTIONAL DEVELOPMENT 357

10. Emotional Development and Attachment 358

KidStock / Blend Images / Getty Images

11. Identity: The Self, Gender, and Moral Development   404

©iStockphoto.com/mikeuk

14.   Activities, Media, and the Natural World   540

Fuse/Corbis/Getty Images

15. Health, Well-Being, and Resilience   578

Steve Glass / Getty Images

List of Features

JOURNEY OF RESEARCH

TEST YOUR KNOWLEDGE

Preface

This third edition of *Child Development: An Active Learning Approach* continues to reflect our primary goal of creating significant learning experiences for students who want to understand children. In this topically organized book we provide the field's most current, evidence-based knowledge about important issues in child development. A topical approach has the advantage of allowing students to better see the continuities and discontinuities in development without the necessity of reintroducing each topic area with each new age group studied.

Our intent in writing this book is not to provide an encyclopedia of facts about child development. Rather, we aim to create a narrative that connects ideas and research in meaningful ways. We believe that this narrative style is the best way to engage students in the learning process.

We also believe that learning is an active process. Therefore, we have created activities spread throughout the book designed to encourage students to engage in an active journey to discover the principles and to understand the findings from the field of child development. We also provide opportunities throughout the book for students to learn about how our understanding of child development has evolved through the scientific process to reach our current state of knowledge.

The topical coverage and pedagogical features in this book have been conceived and carefully executed to help students discover the excitement of studying child development and to equip them with tools they can use long after they take this class.

PHILOSOPHICAL APPROACH

EMPHASIS ON LEARNING HOW TO LEARN

Long after they leave the classroom, students who interact with children and adolescents will need to find information to answer questions that arise. We want to encourage students' independent pursuit of knowledge about child development so we provide tools that will help them do that. They are introduced to the use of databases including PsycInfo, as well as the Internet, as research tools. Activities in the text suggest ways in which students can conduct their own research and independently find information on topics that interest them.

CRITICAL THINKING SKILLS

When students look for answers to questions they have about child development, they need to be able to critically evaluate the information they find. In Chapter 1, we talk about how to be a smart consumer of information on development, including how to evaluate information found on the Web. In addition, the true/false questions that appear at the beginning of each chapter and again alongside the relevant material throughout the chapter continuously challenge students to reflect on what they believe about child development and to evaluate the sources of those beliefs. The instructor teaching site and student webpage provide access to research articles that students can explore independently to add to their understanding of specific topics. This ability to critically evaluate ideas about children and their development will be beneficial to students who plan to go on for graduate study, those who will work directly with children and families in professional careers, and those who will use these ideas when caring for their own children.

FOCUS ON WHAT CONSTITUTES EVIDENCE

We help students realize that although there is a place for "what I think" and for individual examples, the strength of a social science rests on marshalling convincing evidence within an agreed upon framework. Chapter 3 introduces students to basic concepts about research, and these ideas regarding what constitutes scientific evidence are also reinforced and developed throughout the book.

PEDAGOGICAL FEATURES

This book actively engages students to provide them with a solid foundation in theories, research, and the application of information related to child and adolescent development. Features intended to engage students are often included in textbooks as "add-ons," but our active learning philosophy is at the heart of all of the pedagogy provided throughout this book. As educators, we know that students must *act* on the material presented in a course to make it their own. We all try to do this in a number of ways in our classrooms, but for the student, reading a textbook is a solitary and often passive process. To help guard against this passivity, we use the key pedagogical features described in the following sections to capture students' interest and turn reading into an active process.

CHALLENGING MISCONCEPTIONS

One of the challenges in teaching a course in child development is to help students give up some of the intuitive ideas or simplistic thinking they have about child development. Many students enter courses on child and adolescent development confident that they already know most of what they need to know about development and that this is "all just common sense," but experienced instructors know that some of the most important information in their courses is, in fact, counterintuitive. Unfortunately, students' long-held ideas and beliefs are often quite difficult to change, and students can complete a course in child development with many of their misconceptions intact. To combat this tendency, we ask students to begin each chapter by testing their initial knowledge of topics contained in that chapter. Unexpected or surprising answers to these questions draw the students into the chapter to find information related to their misconceptions. In addition, the activities throughout the book encourage students to seek out further information and to learn to evaluate that information rather than accepting what they hear without question.

ACTIVE LEARNING

A variety of learning activities in the text complement and enhance the ideas presented in each chapter. Activities might involve asking students: (a) to reflect on their own experiences while growing up (and perhaps compare those experiences to the experiences of classmates), (b) to immediately test their understanding of a concept, (c) to conduct an observation or interview with a child, if possible, or to watch a SAGE-created video that illustrates the activity in the text, (d) to carry out a simple firsthand experience and reflect on what they've learned from it, or (e) to seek out information that goes beyond the text through the use of library resources or the Internet. Each of these activities is designed to consolidate student learning through personal experiences that illustrate the ideas presented in the book.

JOURNEY OF RESEARCH

It is not unusual for students of child and adolescent development to expect that by the end of the semester, they will have simple answers to a number of very complex questions. Of course, we can seldom provide these simple answers. Instead, we need to help students understand that the science of child development is an ongoing endeavor and that we continue to build and add to our understanding each day. Although it is important that students learn about our current best knowledge, this information is more meaningful when students understand it in the context of our evolving ideas about a given topic. To help students better understand this material, we keep the focus of the text on the current state of knowledge and use the Journey of Research feature to provide the historical contextual information on the topic. This helps students understand that what they learn today in their class may be information that changes—sometimes substantially—in the future as our body of knowledge grows. This is, after all, how the scientific process works.

LEARNING OBJECTIVES AND SELF-TESTING REVIEW

Increasingly, research has been demonstrating that the best way for students to retain information they are learning, and also to transfer that knowledge to new situations, is by testing their understanding for themselves. Other study approaches such as re-reading, highlighting, and even summarizing have not been found to be as effective as self-testing (Carpenter, 2012). For example, students who try to remember that *chien = dog* by repeating it over and over will not remember this new French word as well as those who study *chien = ?* On the student webpage that accompanies this text, we provide chapter quizzes as well as flash cards for students to test themselves. However, we believe it is important to provide this opportunity within the book as well. Therefore, we begin each chapter with a set of "Learning Questions" and have organized our review at the end of the chapter using these same questions to elicit brief answers. There is also a set of questions at the end of each section of the chapter that allows students to "Check Your Understanding" before they move on to the next topic. Students can test themselves in all these ways, promoting greater retention of what they are learning and increasing the likelihood that they will be able to apply this knowledge in useful ways.

GRAPHICS AND ARTWORK

Because many individuals are visual learners and because child development is a field rich in imagery, each chapter contains photos and graphics to illustrate important concepts in a memorable way. Many of the photos in the text include questions embedded in their captions that prompt the student to think further about the topic.

KEY TOPICS

NEUROSCIENCE

To reflect the burgeoning interest in the field of neuroscience and its implications for child development, we devote part of the chapter on physical development to recent research on brain development and behavior. In addition, we have included new and updated information on brain function where it is relevant throughout the book. This information is presented in clear language that makes it appropriate for the student of child development who may not have a strong background in biology.

DIVERSITY AND CULTURE

Issues of diversity and culture are introduced at the beginning of the text. These concepts are then integrated into each topic area to give the broader picture of how each aspect of development is influenced by the many different circumstances that constitute children's lives around the world.

DEVELOPMENTAL PSYCHOPATHOLOGY

Coverage of topics related to psychopathology or developmental differences gives students a better understanding of the continuum of human behavior. However, rather than confine information on psychopathology to a single chapter, we have integrated these topics where they give students a deeper understanding of how these differences relate to the spectrum of development of all children.

WHAT'S NEW IN THE THIRD EDITION

CHAPTER 1

- New section on *Getting the Most From Your Textbook* introduces students to the features they can use throughout the book

- The section on *Finding and Assessing Information About Development* and *Active Learning: Evaluating Information on the Web* have been moved from Chapter 3 to this chapter, so students are immediately provided with information about being a good consumer of information on development

- Information on the pedagogical features is now interspersed through the chapter rather than appearing in the opening paragraph to make it more meaningful to students

- New example of social policy: WIC

- New coverage of positive psychology

- New information on ages and stages

- Expanded section on culture

CHAPTER 2

- New *Active Learning*: Comparing Psychoanalytic Theories

- Strengthened focus on developmental issues by omitting general discussion of Freud and *Active Learning*: Free Associations

- New figures:
  - o Figure 2.1: Id, ego, and superego
  - o Figure 2.3: Illustration of positive reinforcement and negative reinforcement
  - o Figure 2.4: Punishment and Extinction
- New modern applications of classical conditioning
- Added coverage of applied behavioral analysis (ABA) and functional behavioral assessment in modern applications of operant conditioning; collaborative learning and dynamic assessment to modern applications of Vygotsky's theory
- New discussion of developmental cognitive neuroscience; updated information on culture and developmental theory
- Dynamic systems theory enhanced as a major heading with expanded coverage

CHAPTER 3

- New Figure 3.1: The Scientific Method
- Revised description of the difference between reliability and validity, including a new example; new coverage of the concept of random sampling, ethnography and microgenetic research designs
- New Table 3.1: A comparison of research methods and Table 3.3: Comparison of Developmental Research Designs
- Expanded and clarified discussion of the distinction between research methods and research design
- Increased coverage of a variety of physiological measures
- Added discussion of the pitfalls of anecdotal evidence

CHAPTER 4

- New *Active Learning* features: Assessing Genetic Risk, Concordance Rates
- Strengthened the focus of this chapter on the interaction of genes and environment by moving the information on culture to Chapter 1
- New Figure 4.1: Human chromosomes as spectral karyotypes
- New discussion of mutations and single nucleotide polymorphism (SNP); new discussion of identifying genes
- Updated information on generalist genes
- New Table 4.2: Who should receive genetic counseling?
- Updated figures illustrating amniocentesis and CVS
- New coverage of commercial genetic tests, ethical considerations in genetic testing, adoption studies, and new research showing environmental effects on genetic expression using twin studies
- Updated information on studies of identical twins reared apart
- Updated discussion of canalization; new information about inheritance of epigenetic change, stress and epigenetic changes

CHAPTER 5

- Coverage of new topics including:
  - prenatal ultrasound
  - preconception health care
  - the emotional toll of infertility
  - environmental toxins as a pregnancy risk
  - abusive head trauma and shaken baby syndrome
  - the Neonatal Behavioral Assessment Scale
  - mirror neurons in the newborn
  - the impact of the Zika virus on a pregnancy
  - prenatal exercise for women
  - depression with peripartum onset
- New information on the sex ratio of conceptions and births, the 2015 outbreak of rubella, the effect of maternal smoking on asthma risk among children, consequences of the legalization of recreational and medical marijuana, the impact of endocrine disruptors, paid and unpaid parental leave
- Expanded information on miscarriage and its emotional consequences, prematurity and low birth weight; new description of prenatal ultrasounds
- Updated information and statistics on
  - Choice of birth settings
  - maternal diseases during pregnancy
  - international maternal mortality rates
  - infant mortality rates
  - number of cesarean births
  - out-of-hospital births
  - effects of prenatal alcohol use

CHAPTER 6

- New *Active Learning* feature: School Lunches
- Added coverage of brain development during early and middle childhood and adolescence
- New sections on Body Awareness, Motor Disability: Developmental Coordination Disorder
- Updated information on neuronal development, autism spectrum disorder
- New research on the impact of the Back to Sleep program on motor skill development; more coverage of motor skill development in early and middle childhood
- Updated information on teen pregnancy, the HPV vaccine

- New Figure 6.12: Estimated new HIV diagnoses among youth ages 13 to 24 in the United States, by race/ethnicity and sex

- New coverage of food allergies, prepubescence

- Expanded coverage of nutrition in early and middle childhood and adolescence

- New information on media use and obesity

- Updated information about anorexia and bulimia

- Updated and expanded information on neurological research on autism; information on autism spectrum disorder (ASD) has been updated to reflect the criteria in DSM-5

- New information on the possible role of folate in autism, the HPV vaccine for boys, the role of endocrine disruptors in pubertal timing

CHAPTER 7

- New *Active Learning* feature: Metacognition

- *Journey of Research* feature: Is Object Permanence Learned or Innate appear in the section on the theory of core knowledge with new information about the assessment of object permanence

- New Table 7.2: Six substages of the sensorimotor period

- New coverage of Piaget's concept of intuitive thought; expanded coverage of Piaget's stage of formal operations, including scientific thinking

- New information on social media and the imaginary audience, and the context of the imaginary audience in adolescence; new example of scaffolding in education

- Expanded discussion of postformal operations, private speech

- Updated information about ADHD to reflect changes in DSM-5

- New information about the impact of early attention span, distracted driving by teens, memory in toddlers, false memory in adults; new example of developmental changes in encoding processes

- Expanded coverage of memory in adolescence, executive function skills in childhood, cognitive flexibility, inhibitory control, and planning

- New coverage of processing capacity, executive function in adolescence, neurocognitive development as evidence for Piaget's theory

CHAPTER 8

- Major reorganization of the chapter with new headings to more clearly differentiate coverage of defining/assessing intelligence, variations in intellectual ability, learning in the school context, and group differences in academic achievement

- Added coverage of new research on the neurological basis of intelligence and intrinsic and extrinsic motivation

- New Figure 8.3: *Percentage distribution of children ages 3–21 served under the Individuals with Disabilities Education Act (IDEA), Part B, by disability type*; new Figure 8.4: *The three-ring conception of giftedness*; new Figure 8.5: *The gender gap in undergraduate enrollment*

- Expanded and updated information on IQ testing, including new coverage of WISC-V

- Updated statistics and information on intellectual disability and specific learning disorders to reflect changes in DSM-5

- Updated research on the long-term developmental outcomes for children with specific learning disorders

- Addition of Renzulli's three-ring model of giftedness

- Expanded information on creativity, including a distinction between big-C and small-c creativity and how to encourage creativity in a classroom setting

- Descriptive information on Head Start reorganized with more emphasis on program outcomes; new information on Early Head Start

- Updated information on the impact of class size, teacher expectancy, and statistics on the possible "boy problem" in schools

- New information on the impact of media on girls' attitudes toward math and science

- New discussion of implicit associations and gender stereotypes

- New statistics throughout the chapter on academic outcomes

- Updated and expanded information on school dropouts and high school graduates

- New section on *College-Bound Students*

CHAPTER 9

- New Table 9.1: *Five aspects of language*

- New discussion of morphology

- New information about cognitive processing theory and statistical learning

- New information about cochlear implants

- Coverage of literacy reorganized to be separate from oral language development

- Updated coverage of SES and language development and of differences in parental communication within SES groups

- New information about the earliest age when infants recognize words

- New Table 9.3: *Milestones of Language Development*

- New Table 9.2: *A comparison of 4 theories of language development*

- New information on the impact of using sign language with babies, acquisition of nouns and verbs in infancy across cultures, and development of humor

- New discussion of development of discourse skills in middle childhood

- New information about how school-age children learn to read and updated coverage of the reading performance of U.S. children

- New Table 9.5: Writing skills in three different language groups

- New information about the impact of the physical act of writing on spelling ability; blogging and writing skills among teens; bilingual children and their vocabulary development

- New section on *Culture, identity and bilingualism*

- Updated coverage of bilingual education and children learning English as a second language
- Updated information on communication disorders and dyslexia

CHAPTER 10

- New information on the use of emoji in electronic messages, emotional display rules and cultural differences
- Expanded coverage of Rothbart's theory of temperament
- Added coverage on *emotion coaching* and *emotion dismissing* parents
- New and updated information on children's fears
- Additional information on anxiety disorders to reflect changes in DSM-5
- Updated information on depression and suicide in adolescence, oppositional defiant disorder and conduct disorder
- New discussion of disruptive mood dysregulation disorder (DMDD)
- Reorganized coverage of attachment
- New information on the relationship between attachment status and physiological responses to stress
- Updated and expanded information on the role of fathers in attachment relationships
- Coverage of attachment to nonparental caregivers revised to focus specifically on attachment issues
- Updated research on cross-cultural studies of attachment
- Updated information on children's use of a secure base script to get help in times of distress
- Coverage of attachment disorders has been updated to reflect changes in DSM-5

CHAPTER 11

- Added discussion of cultural differences in infant mirror self-recognition
- New information on parents' use of personal pronouns and the child's name to promote pronoun use
- New information on culture and autobiographical memory, identity status and family relationships in adolescence, and cultural variations in identity status in adolescence
- New description of Harter's five dimensions of self-esteem
- New information on school and adolescent self-esteem
- New sections on *Media, Self-Concept, and Self-Esteem* and the *Gender Self-Socialization Model*, and *Transgender, Transsexual and Gender Nonconforming Children and Teens*
- New information about the experiences of LGBT youth
- New coverage of the debate about bathroom use by transgender people, the role of innate processes in moral development, social domain theory of moral development, service learning and morality

CHAPTER 12

- Several updated or revised *Active Learning* features
- New information about theory of mind in infancy
- New discussion of developmental trends in theory of mind, relationship between development of theory of mind and siblings
- New information on culture and theory of mind
- New information about recess and obesity
- New discussion of discovery learning,
- New coverage of AAP guidelines concerning recess in schools
- Updated Figure 12.5: Bullying at school
- New information on peer status that distinguishes popular-prosocial children from popular-antisocial children, and rejected-aggressive children from rejected-withdrawn children
- Updated and expanded information on peer pressure and children's resistance to it
- Updated statistics on bullying and peer violence

CHAPTER 13

- New discussion of family systems theory
- Updated Figures 13.1: Children's household living arrangements and Figure 13.2: Statistics on the rise in number of unmarried mothers in the U.S.
- New Figure 13.3: A cohort comparison of divorce risk and Table 13.1: Your chances of divorce may be much lower than you think
- Updated Figure 13.6: Workforce participation by U.S. mothers
- New Figure 13.7: Growth in the number of stay-at-home fathers in the United States.
- New Figure 13.9: Paid maternity leave, 2015
- Statistical information on family structure is focused to deal more specifically on children's current living arrangements
- New information on the impact of divorce on infants, young children, and preschoolers;
- impact of caring for grandchildren on elderly grandparents
- Expanded discussion of foster care, including new information on foster care for young children
- Chapter now more clearly distinguishes between family structure and function
- New information on managing the stress associated with balancing work and family, the differential effect of maternal employment on adolescents in different socioeconomic statuses.
- Information on parenting styles has been updated to use the terminology *disengaged parents;* updated and expanded info on the consequences of various parenting styles; expanded information on the impact of culture on parenting style outcomes; new discussion of coparenting

CHAPTER 14

- New *Active Learning* feature: Encouraging Children and Teens to Engage with Nature
- New section on *The World of Work*
- Updated information on latchkey children
- Updated discussion of participation in sports and other activities, sports injuries, and concussion
- New information on the role of coaches
- Updated information on electronic media use
- New information on mobile media use
- New information on social media and texting
- Updated information on children and the natural world
- New section on *"Selfies" and narcissism*
- New figure illustrating changes in media use with age
- New figures illustrating types of media used and gender differences in media use
- Updated information on positive youth development
- Updated information on natural mentors

CHAPTER 15

- Two new *Active Learning* features: Finding Local Sources of Support, Keeping a Sleep Diary
- Updated information on common childhood illnesses
- New information on the dangers of parental refusal to vaccinate children
- Expanded coverage of HPV and the HPV vaccine; updated information on childhood cancer
- New Table 15.2: Childhood mental disorders
- Updated statistics and graphics regarding fatal and nonfatal accidental injuries
- smoking, drinking, and use of illicit drugs
- New information on e-cigarettes and vaporizers
- New discussion of substance use disorder
- New information on the effect of stress on infant brain development
- Added research on the effect of moving poor families to better neighborhoods
- New information on the risk of skin cancer from exposure to harmful ultraviolet rays
- New information on the hygiene hypothesis and the role of diet in asthma
- New coverage of the Adverse Childhood Experiences scale
- New information on the consequences of emotional and psychological abuse
- New information on opioid use by teens

- New section on *Sleep Deficit*
- New coverage of lead poisoning from water in Flint, Michigan and around the nation
- Updated Figure 15.5: Unintentional injury deaths among U.S. children
- Updated information about the rate of child poverty
- New coverage of the Moving to Opportunity program
- New coverage of Head Start Trauma Smart program
- New information on the operation of Child Protective Services
- New information on sex trafficking

ANCILLARIES

SAGE edge offers a robust online environment you can access anytime, anywhere, and features an impressive array of free tools and resources to keep you on the cutting edge of your learning experience.

<u>**SAGE edge for Students**</u> provides a personalized approach to help you accomplish your coursework goals in an easy-to-use learning environment.

- Mobile-friendly **eFlashcards** strengthen your understanding of key terms and concepts
- Mobile-friendly practice **quizzes** allow you to independently assess your mastery of course material
- A complete online **action plan** includes tips and feedback on your progress and allows you to individualize your learning experience
- **Learning objectives** reinforce the most important material
- EXCLUSIVE! Access to full-text **SAGE journal articles** that have been carefully chosen to support and expand on the concepts presented in each chapter

<u>**SAGE edge for Instructors**</u> supports your teaching by making it easy to integrate quality content and create a rich learning environment for students.

- **Test banks** provide a diverse range of pre-written options as well as the opportunity to edit any question and/or insert your own personalized questions to effectively assess students' progress and understanding
- **Sample course syllabi** for semester and quarter courses provide suggested models for structuring your courses
- Editable, chapter-specific **PowerPoint® slides** offer complete flexibility for creating a multimedia presentation for your course.
- EXCLUSIVE! Access to full-text **SAGE journal articles** that have been carefully selected to support and expand on the concepts presented in each chapter
- **Multimedia content** includes original SAGE videos that appeal to students with different learning styles
- **Lecture notes** summarize key concepts by chapter to help you prepare for lectures and class discussions

ACKNOWLEDGMENTS

We are very grateful to our team at SAGE Publications for their help in creating this third edition. We appreciate all the effort put into this project by the members of our editorial team: Lara Parra, Reid Hester, Lucy Berbeo, Olivia Weber-Stenis, Gretchen Treadwell, Morgan Shannon, and Zachary Valladon. We appreciate the efforts of our marketing director Katherine Hepburn. Special thanks go to Cheri Dellelo, who not only guided us through this third revision, but also brought us together in the first place.

We want to thank the children and staff of the Associated Students' Children's Center and the Child and Family Studies Center at the California State University at Northridge for their participation in filming videos to accompany the text, as well as the children and parents who took part in filming the Active Learning demonstration videos with us.

Thanks go to the following individuals who reviewed the manuscript:

Aaliyah Baker, Cardinal Stritch University

Cassendra M. Bergstrom, University of Northern Colorado

Elizabeth M. Blunk, Texas State University

Adam M. Brown, St. Bonaventure University

Jan Charone-Sossin, Pace University

Amy M. Claridge, Central Washington University

Jessamy E. Comer, Rochester Institute of Technology

Cristina B. Davy, UMASS Lowell

Amy Dombach, Felician College

Shawn Edwinson, Sacramento City College

Claire Etaugh, Bradley University

Emily A. Farris, University of Texas of the Permian Basin

Hemalatha Genapathy-Coleman, Indiana State University

J. Sue Gruber, Wright State University

Glenna Gustafson, Radford University

Bert Hayslip Jr., University of North Texas

Shawnee M. Hendershot, Pittsburg State University

Dana D. Horn, Henderson State University

Lisa Huffman, Cameron University

Pamela M. Ludemann, Framingham State University

Paulina Multhaupt, Macomb Community College

Michael T. Paff, Iona College

Maria Pagano, New York City College of Technology, City University of New York

Dongxiao Qin, Western New England University

Jill Rinzel, University of Wisconsin-Waukesha

Tara M. Stoppa, Eastern University

Dawn N. Hicks Tafari, Winston-Salem State University

Stacy D. Thompson, Southern Illinois University Carbondale

Kristie Veri, William Paterson University

Karl F. Wheatley, Cleveland State University

As always, we are grateful to our families and friends for their continuing support, as well as their ideas and stories that have contributed to the creation of this book.

About the Authors

Laura E. Levine received her PhD in developmental and clinical psychology from the University of Michigan. After working with children and families at the Children's Psychiatric Hospital and in private practice in Ann Arbor for 10 years, she moved to Connecticut and was a stay-at-home mother of her two children for 6 years. She returned to academia in 1994 and taught child psychology and life span development for 20 years at Central Connecticut State University, where she is currently an emeritus professor of the Department of Psychological Science. She has received three university teaching awards, and her research on the social development of young children and on the relation between media use and attention difficulties has appeared in journals such as *Developmental Psychology*, the *Journal of Applied Developmental Psychology*, *Infant Mental Health Journal*, *Infant and Child Development*, *Computers and Education*, and *CyberPsychology, Behavior, and Social Networking*.

Dr. Levine has been very active in promoting excellence in college teaching. She was involved in the creation of the Center for Teaching Excellence at Central Connecticut State University and served on the board of the Connecticut Consortium to Enhance Learning and Teaching. She created numerous programs for faculty both at her university and at regional and national conferences. Her work on the scholarship of teaching and learning can be found in *New Directions for Teaching and Learning, College Teaching*, and the *International Journal for the Scholarship of Teaching and Learning*.

Joyce Munsch received her PhD in human development and family studies from Cornell University. She was a faculty member in human development and family studies at Texas Tech University for 14 years, where she also served as associate dean for research in the College of Human Sciences for 2 years. In 2002, Dr. Munsch went to California State University at Northridge as the founding chair and professor in the Department of Child and Adolescent Development. She currently is an emeritus professor in the department.

Dr. Munsch's research focused on adolescent stress and coping and social networks. Her work has been published in the *Journal of School Psychology*, *Adolescence, The Journal of Early Adolescence*, the *Journal of Research on Adolescence*, and the *American Journal of Orthopsychiatry*. Throughout her career, Dr. Munsch administered grants that supported community-based programs. She was the codirector of the Early Head Start program at Texas Tech University and co–principal investigator for three Texas Youth Commission (Department of Juvenile Justice) grants. At Cal State Northridge, she administered the Jumpstart program for over 10 years. Her commitment to community service learning was recognized in 2005 when she was awarded the CSUN Visionary Community Service Learning Award. In 2012, her service to the County of Los Angeles was recognized by a commendation from the County Board of Supervisors. At

Texas Tech, she was the College of Human Sciences nominee for the Hemphill-Wells New Professor Excellence in Teaching Award, the Barnie E. Rushing Jr. Faculty Distinguished Research Award, the El Paso Energy Foundation Faculty Achievement Award, and the President's Excellence in Teaching Award; she also received the Kathryn Burleson Faculty Service Award and the College of Human Sciences Outstanding Researcher Award.

PART I

UNDERSTANDING DEVELOPMENT:
Why and How We Study Children
and Adolescents

Christopher Futcher/E+/Getty Images

chapter 1 | ISSUES AND THEMES IN CHILD DEVELOPMENT

1.1 Who needs to have a good understanding of child development and why?

1.2 What are the domains of child development and some recurring themes and issues in the field?

1.3 What are the contexts for child development?

1.4 How can you be a smart consumer of information about development?

Master these objectives using an online action plan at **edge.sagepub.com/levine3e**

Take a moment to think about why you want to learn about children, adolescents, and their development. You may enjoy the interactions you have with children and want to understand them better, or your career goal may involve working with children or adolescents. Perhaps you want to better understand yourself or those you know by exploring how childhood has affected who you have become. Your interest may be more scientific, with a focus on understanding the research that explains the processes of development. Your particular goal will influence how you approach the information in this book.

We have presented the information and designed the activities within this book to stimulate your thinking in all these ways. We want to share with you the excitement that we feel about the topic of child and adolescent development and to pique your curiosity so that you will want to learn even more about it. By the time you have finished reading this book, you will have a solid foundation in a number of important topics related to development. It is our hope that this will motivate you to continue learning about children and their development long after you have completed this course.

In this first chapter, we introduce some of the basic concepts of child and adolescent development. We first look at why people study children, and present some ways that people use knowledge about children to promote positive development. If you are curious about how *you* might apply this knowledge in a future career, the Active Learning feature in this section will lead you through the process of researching careers that require a solid understanding of child and adolescent development. We then discuss some of the basic themes related to how development occurs and introduce you to the different contexts that influence children's lives. Finally, we provide strategies and guidelines that will enable you to differentiate reliable information from other material you may encounter as you study child development.

WHY STUDY CHILD DEVELOPMENT?

1.1 Who needs to have a good understanding of child development and why?

Many people are interested in studying child development because the topic itself is fascinating and important. Others want information they will be able to use in their role as a parent. Many students know that they will be able to use the information in a future career as a professional who works with children or a policymaker who shapes social policy affecting children and families. These are all great reasons to study child development, and we will explore them all in this chapter.

UNDERSTANDING THE PROCESS OF DEVELOPMENT

One reason why students are interested in studying child development is that experiences in childhood shape who we become as adults. Examining that process helps us to understand the role that infancy, childhood, and adolescence play in forming our abilities, beliefs, and attitudes. Researchers who study children as they develop over long periods of time have provided ample evidence that early traits, behaviors, and experiences are related to

Thinkstock

Conscientiousness. What long-term outcomes might result from this child's willingness to work hard?

many adult outcomes. One well-known example of this is a study of gifted children begun by Lewis Terman in 1921 (Friedman & Martin, 2011). Although Terman died many years ago, others are still mining his data to answer questions about life span development. One finding is that those children who were rated high in the quality Terman called conscientiousness or social dependability had many positive outcomes in adulthood, including a reduction of 30% in the likelihood they would die in any particular year (Friedman et al., 1995). How does earlier conscientiousness link with these later outcomes? The connection is partially explained by the fact that conscientious individuals were less likely to smoke and drink alcohol to excess, both of which are predictive of a shorter life span. Some have hypothesized that conscientious people have better marriages, while others think they may be better prepared to handle the emotional difficulties they encounter (Friedman et al., 1995). Ongoing research is continuing to explore the full complexity of these connections.

Although the earliest stages of development are clearly important for later development and functioning, Charles Nelson (1999), neuroscientist and developmental psychologist, has argued that the first 3 years of life are no more important than later periods. He likens early development to building a house. A solid foundation is essential, but the ultimate shape and function of the house depends on adding the walls, the roof, the pipes, and all the rest. Nelson's focus is on the development of the brain, but his comments could apply to many other areas of

child development. He says that while the basic form of the brain is set down within the first years of life, it is continually affected by the experiences we have later in life. An example of this principle comes from research by Alan Sroufe and his colleagues, who found that the nature of infants' secure relationship with their mother was an important predictor of their ability to have close romantic relationships in adulthood. However, the nature of their peer relationships through middle childhood also related to later romantic relationships (Raby et al., 2015; Sroufe, Egeland, Carlson, & Collins, 2005). Experiences early in life have consequences for functioning later in life but experiences all along the path to adulthood also contribute to an adult's psychological functioning.

USING OUR KNOWLEDGE OF CHILD DEVELOPMENT

A second reason to study child development is to be able to use this information to improve the lives of children and adolescents. An understanding of how children think, feel, learn, and grow, as well as how they change and stay the same, is essential to the ability to foster positive development. This understanding can help parents and family members, professionals who work with children and families, and people who create and carry out social policies and programs that affect children and their families to do this.

Parents and Family Members

A solid understanding of child development can help all parents do their best in this important role. Many parents read books, search websites, and browse magazines designed to help them understand their children so they can become better parents. How useful any of these sources of information will be to an interested parent depends largely on how well the information in them is grounded in scientific research.

Parents' understanding of their children's needs and abilities at each stage of development helps them provide the appropriate amount and type of support and stimulation to foster their children's growth and development, but for some parents, knowledge about child development is even more crucial. For example, teen parents are more likely than older parents to lack knowledge about what to expect from their children at different ages. They are likely to talk to and play less with their infants, and to use physical punishment to discipline their children (Mann, Pearl, & Behle, 2004). When teen parents learn about child development, their frustration decreases and they have more realistic expectations for their children, their ability to empathize with their children increases, and they better understand how to discipline their children without resorting to physical punishment.

Another high-risk group that can benefit from parenting interventions is incarcerated parents. When one group of incarcerated parents took part in a program called the Family Nurturing Program, many showed the same kind of gains as those found among teenagers. They became more empathic and less punitive and developed more realistic expectations for their children (Palusci, Crum, Bliss, & Bavolek, 2008).

Programs to support parents. Incarcerated parents have been helped by programs such as The Family Nurturing Program. Such programs help parents maintain a relationship with their children while they are physically separated from them and also help the parents learn how to promote positive development in their children.

Child Development Professionals

You may be interested in studying child development because you see yourself in a future career that involves working with children and families. In different ways and at different levels, people in all the helping professions are engaged in the identification and prevention of problems, in providing interventions when problems do occur, and in promoting positive development for all children and teens.

Community organizers, community psychologists, and outreach workers are a few of the professionals that focus on preventing problems before they emerge. Child therapists and family therapists are two types of professionals who help families address existing problems. In child therapy, the therapist meets individually with the child, while family therapists see

Careers in child development. Knowledge about child development is essential to people working in many different careers (including pediatricians, teachers, social workers, counselors, therapists, lawyers, and nurses). If you are interested in a career working with children, there are many opportunities available to you.

other family members together with the child. Social workers, psychologists, marriage and family therapists, and child psychiatrists also provide these and other types of interventions to families. Promoting the optimal development of children and adolescents is a primary goal of professionals who work in the fields of education and health care, and of mental health professionals, youth service workers, and representatives of community organizations who run a variety of programs for children. A strong foundation in the study of child development helps each of these various professionals find and use ways to support and encourage children and adolescents to reach their full potential.

We recognize that students today are interested in knowing where their education can eventually lead them and are hungry for information about future careers. If you are taking this course because you are considering a career related to child development, how much do you know about the career you are thinking about entering? You can assess your current knowledge about a career related to child development by completing **Active Learning: How Much Do You Know About Careers in Child Development?**

Active LEARNING

How Much Do You Know About Careers in Child Development?

If you are interested in a career that includes working with children, begin by completing the table below with what you currently know about the career you would like to enter when you finish your education. If you haven't settled on a career yet, simply choose one that currently holds some interest for you. Even if you feel you have very little information on a particular topic, take your best guess at every answer.

Next, use the *Occupational Outlook Handbook* (U.S. Bureau of Labor Statistics, 2015b) to find current information on your career. At the Bureau of Labor Statistics website at www.bls.gov, type "Occupational Outlook Handbook" into the search box or select it from the drop-down menu under "Publications." There also is likely a copy of the Bureau of Labor Statistics *Occupational Outlook Handbook* in your campus library. Select the career you are interested in from the alphabetic drop-down menu, or type the name of your career in the search box on the page. For each career, you will find information on the following:

- **What people in this career do**—duties and responsibilities.

- **Work environment**—where people in this career work and conditions affecting their employment.

- **How to become a professional in this field**—the education and training required both for entry into the field and for advancement within this career. You will also find information about any certifications or licenses required to work in this profession, and the skills and personal qualities required for success on the job.

- **Pay**—average salaries earned in this career.

- **Job outlook**—how many people are currently employed in this career and whether the demand for this profession is increasing or decreasing.

- **Similar occupations**—additional information about careers related to the one you are researching. For instance, if you think you would like to be a child psychologist, here you can find that related careers include being a counselor, social worker, special education teacher, or recreation worker. If you click on any of these links, it will take you to the page in the *Occupational Outlook Handbook* that provides all the information about that alternative career.

- **Contacts for more information**—links to professional organizations that support and advocate for people working in that career. The organization webpages are rich sources of information about each career, and you should look at one or two of them before you finish exploring this page.

Although the *Occupational Outlook Handbook* lists hundreds of occupations, you won't find every conceivable job title. For instance, *child life specialist* and *early interventionist* are not yet in the handbook, but you can find information about a related career to begin your search. Child life specialists do work similar to what a counselor does, but they work in the specialized setting of a hospital, and their clients are children with chronic illnesses and life-threatening conditions and their families.

Name of the career you researched: _____

Does it appear in the *Occupational Outlook Handbook* (OOH)? _____ Yes _____ No

(If "no," name the related career you researched): _____

Topic	Your Current Knowledge	Information From the OOH
Educational level required for entry into this career (for example, high school diploma, associate's degree, bachelor's degree, master's degree, PhD, or other advanced degree)		
Educational level required for advancement in this career		
Important day-to-day work responsibilities (that is, what one does each day in this career)		
Work setting (for example, office, school, hospital), and how much travel is required (if any)		
Median annual earnings		
Demand (for example, is the demand for this career expected to increase or decrease over the next 10 years, and by how much?)		

Another very useful website to examine if you are specifically interested in a career in the field of psychology is the American Psychological Association's site. You can find career information at www.apa.org/careers/resources/guides/careers.aspx

Policymakers

As a society, we have a stake in promoting the well-being of all our citizens, including our children. Our ideas and programs designed to accomplish this constitute our **social policy** on these issues. Research on child development can guide and inform the people who make these policies. For example, Walter Gilliam (2008), director of the Edward Zigler Center in Child Development and Social Policy at Yale University, found that preschool children in Connecticut were more than 3 times as likely to be expelled as children in Grades K–12. His research also showed that when a mental health consultant was available to help teachers

Social policy Policies that to are intended to promote the welfare of individuals in a society.

Digital Vision/Thinkstock

Making social policy. Social policy that affects children and families is made at the highest levels of the federal government down to local school boards and neighborhood councils. Interested citizens also take part when they write letters to elected officials, sign petitions, work for causes they support, and vote.

Tracy A. Woodward/The Washington Post via Getty Images

The Women, Infants and Children Program. This pregnant woman can use vouchers from the WIC program at this farmer's market to ensure a nutritious diet essential for healthy prenatal development.

develop ways to handle problem behaviors, far fewer children were expelled. He took his findings to legislators to advocate for a solution. As a result, half of the states now provide early childhood mental health consultation (Perry, 2014). Consider how many young children are being better served because of the research and advocacy of Dr. Gilliam.

Another example of social policy in action is the Special Supplemental Nutrition Program for Women, Infants, and Children (WIC), which provides supplemental food and nutrition education for low-income, nutritionally at-risk women, infants, and children up to 5 years of age. Good nutrition during a woman's pregnancy helps to ensure the healthy development of her baby, and good nutrition during early childhood is associated with a number of positive outcomes throughout a child's life. Although these are important program outcomes, the WIC program cost almost $6.2 billion in 2015 (U.S. Department of Agriculture, 2016). When the budget for an expensive program such as this one is up for renewal, lawmakers look to experts in the field for research evidence of the program's effectiveness that can justify the expenditure.

Research on WIC has found that participation in the program is associated with a reduced risk of having a low birth weight baby or one who is born prematurely, and an increased probability that a mother will breastfeed her infant (Rossin-Slater, 2015). As you will learn in Chapter 5, both prematurity and low birth weight are associated with a number of negative developmental outcomes. The lifetime financial savings from lower levels of medical intervention needed as a result of the increased birth weight of the children born to WIC participants results in a favorable cost-benefit ratio for the program (Rossin-Slater, 2015). Information such as this helps policymakers evaluate the effectiveness of the program and make modifications to it, if necessary. **Active Learning: Social Policy Affecting Children and Adolescents** provides some additional information about the type of issues social policy organizations have focused on in recent years.

Active LEARNING

Social Policy Affecting Children and Adolescents

A number of organizations in the United States provide legislators and private citizens with information related to child development that is important to the country. Their goal is to help bring about changes in social policy based on solid research. You may want to visit their websites to retrieve reports that interest you.

The mission of the *Annie E. Casey Foundation* (2015a) is to "advance research and solutions to overcome the barriers to success, help communities demonstrate what works and influence decision makers to invest in strategies based on solid evidence" (para. 2). From its home page at www.aecf.org, click on one of the headings (Kids, Families, Communities, or Leaders) and it will take you to a page that lists reports, blogs, and policy statements related to that topic. One of the most widely used resources from the foundation is its annual *Kids Count* report which provides up-to-date statistics on children's health, education, and well-being. From this page, you can create your own state-by-state report using these data.

The mission of the *Future of Children* (2010) is "to translate the best social science research about children and youth into information that is useful to policymakers, practitioners, grant-makers, advocates, the media, and students of public policy" (para. 1). You will find the website at futureofchildren.org. This organization publishes two issues of its journal each year, each devoted to a single topic. Recent issues have included promoting children's health, military children and families, and postsecondary education in the United States.

The Society for Research in Child Development is a professional organization with almost 6,000 members in the United States and around the world. It periodically produces policy briefs on a variety of topics related to child development. Go to its home page at www .srcd.org and use the drop-down menu under Publications to select Social Policy Report. On that page, you will find a list of their recent reports.

There is a wealth of information at each site. Visit at least one site now and identify a topic or two that interest you, review the information available, and make a mental note to visit these sites again when you are looking for up-to-date information for a course paper.

As citizens, we bear a responsibility to vote and to speak out for the well-being of our children. The more we understand about their needs, the more effective we will be in advocating on their behalf and supporting the policies we believe will best serve them.

CHECK YOUR UNDERSTANDING

1. What are some reasons for studying child development?
2. Who is likely to benefit from being knowledgeable about child development?
3. What is the relationship between social policy and research on child development?

UNDERSTANDING HOW DEVELOPMENT HAPPENS

1.2 **What are the domains of child development and some recurring themes and issues in the field?**

Understanding everything about children's development is certainly a daunting task. To make it more manageable we organize the material in several ways. One way to do this is to divide information into the different domains of development: physical, cognitive, and social-emotional. Within each of these domains we need to keep our focus on the developmental process, so we also organize information by the ages and stages of life. There also are

Domains of development. When we study development, we look at changes in the physical, cognitive, and social-emotional development of children and adolescents.

a number of issues that have been debated in the field of child development over the years. We briefly introduce several of those ideas here, but we will revisit them in more detail at various points throughout the book.

DOMAINS OF DEVELOPMENT

When studying development, we often distinguish between three basic aspects or domains of development: physical, cognitive, and social-emotional. **Physical development** includes the biological changes that occur in the body, including changes in size and strength, as well as the integration of sensory and motor activities. Neurological, or brain, development has become a major area for research in the domain of physical development. **Cognitive development** includes changes in the way we think, understand, and reason about the world. It includes the accumulation of knowledge as well as the way we use that information for problem solving and decision making. **Social-emotional development** includes all the ways we learn to connect to other individuals and interact effectively with them, understand our emotions and the emotions of others, and express and regulate our emotions.

Although it is useful to make distinctions between these domains, it is important to understand that they continually interact with each other. For instance, during puberty adolescents undergo dramatic physical changes over a short period of time, but these changes also affect social development. As adolescents grow to look more like adults and less like children, adults begin to treat them more like adults, giving them new responsibility and expecting greater maturity from them. These opportunities, in turn, contribute to the cognitive development of adolescents as they learn from their new experiences. In a similar way, when infants learn to walk and can get around on their own, their relationship

Physical development Biological changes that occur in the body and brain, including changes in size and strength, integration of sensory and motor activities, and development of fine and gross motor skills.

Cognitive development Changes in the way children think, understand, and reason as they grow older.

Social-emotional development Changes in the ways we connect to other individuals and express and understand emotions.

with caregivers changes. The word *no* is heard much more frequently, and infants need more careful supervision because they now can get themselves into dangerous situations. And of course, infants' enhanced ability to explore the environment gives them many new opportunities to learn about the world in ways that advance their cognitive development.

AGES AND STAGES

As we describe each of the domains of development, we examine how changes occur at the different ages and stages during childhood and adolescence: infancy, toddlerhood, early childhood, middle childhood, and adolescence. These terms are used to identify broad periods of development that have behaviors or characteristics that set that stage apart from the other stages.

During *infancy* (the first year of life), children are totally dependent on their caregivers for their physical care, but they already can use all of their senses to begin exploring their world and during this period they begin developing the motor skills they will need to explore it further. They also form a strong emotional attachment to their caregivers and lay the foundation for learning language. *Toddlers* (ages 1-3) continue developing their motor skills and can explore their physical world more actively. Language develops at an astonishing rate during this period, and toddlers begin showing independence and autonomy from their caregivers as they learn to do things for themselves. In *early childhood* (ages 3-6), children are learning about the physical and social world through play. As peers become more important, young children are learning the skills necessary to understand how other people think and feel. During *middle childhood* (ages 6-12), children develop the intellectual ability to think in a more ordered and structured way and school becomes a major context for development. At this stage, children begin developing a clearer sense of self and an understanding of who they are and what makes them unique. Play and peers are essential parts of their lives. The physical changes associated with puberty mark the transition from childhood into *adolescence* (ages 12-18). As their bodies undergo the physical changes that move them toward adulthood, adolescents are able to think and reason at a more abstract level and they develop a stronger sense of who they are and who they want to become. Family remains important to them, but peer relationships take on a greater importance than they had before.

THEMES IN THE FIELD OF CHILD DEVELOPMENT

We all have our own ideas about children. You brought some of your own with you when you entered this class. Stop for a few minutes and think of a couple of sentences or phrases that capture what you believe to be true about how child development occurs. Do you believe that if you spare the rod you will spoil the child? Or that as the twig is bent, so grows the tree? Do you think that children are like little sponges? Or that they grow in leaps and bounds? Each of these bits of folk wisdom touches on an issue that has been debated within the field of child development. We briefly discuss several of those issues here but we will revisit them at various points throughout the book.

Nature and Nurture

Throughout history the question of whether our behavior, thoughts, and feelings result from **nature**, our genetic inheritance, or from **nurture**, the influence of the environment, has shaped our understanding of why we act certain ways and how we can influence human behavior. The controversy was originally described as nature *versus* nurture. For example, let's say you are an aggressive (or shy, or outgoing . . .) person. Researchers wanted to find out whether you became aggressive because you were "born that way," with your genes determining the outcome, or whether you learned to be aggressive because of what you saw or experienced in your environment. People initially argued for one side or the other, but in more recent times it has become clear that any developmental outcome is a mixture of both.

Nature The influence of genetic inheritance on development.

Nurture The influence of learning and the environment on children's development.

Sandro Di Carlo Darsa/PhotoAlto/Corbis

Quantitative change and qualitative change. As children grow, there are quantitative changes that are evident in this photo (for example, they grow taller and weigh more), but there are also qualitative changes that are less easy to see (for example, they move from one cognitive stage to the next).

Researcher D. O. Hebb said that asking whether behavior is due to nature or to nurture is similar to asking whether the area of a rectangle is due to its length or its width (Meaney, 2004). Just as both length and width are necessary to determine area, genes and environment interact to determine behavioral development. More recent research has continued to show how nature and nurture are inextricably intertwined in surprising and complex ways. We have left behind the era of nature versus nurture and entered the era of nature through nurture in which many genes, particularly those related to traits and behaviors, are expressed only through a process of constant interaction with their environment (Meaney, 2010; Stiles, 2009). We discuss these ideas further in Chapter 4.

Continuous Versus Stagelike Development

Is development a series of small steps that modify behavior bit by bit, or does it proceed in leaps and bounds? In Chapter 2 and throughout the rest of the book, you will learn about some theories in the field of child development that describe development as a series of stages children move through, similar to the "leaps" described previously. In these theories, each stage has characteristics that distinguish it from the stages that come before and after. Other theories, however, describe processes that change development in small increments and, therefore, are described as *continuous* theories.

Another way to think about how we describe the process of development is to differentiate between quantitative and qualitative change. **Quantitative changes** are changes in the amount or quantity of what you are measuring. For instance, as children grow they get taller (they add inches to their height), they learn more new words (the size of their vocabulary grows), and they acquire more factual knowledge (the amount of information in their knowledge base increases). However, some aspects of development are not just the accumulation of more inches or words. Instead, they are **qualitative changes** that alter the overall quality of a process or function, and the result is something altogether different. Walking is qualitatively different from crawling, and thinking about abstract concepts such as justice or fairness is qualitatively different from knowing something more concrete, such as the capitals of all 50 states. **Stage theories** typically describe qualitative changes in development, while **incremental theories** describe quantitative changes. Both types of change occur, and that is why we don't have just one theory that describes all aspects of development. Some theories are more appropriate for describing certain types of changes than others.

Stability Versus Change

How much do we change during the process of development? As we grow, develop, and mature, are we basically the same people we were at earlier ages, or do we reinvent ourselves along the way? We find evidence of both stability and change as we look at development. For instance, characteristics such as anxiety (Weems, 2008), shyness (Dennissen, Asendorpf, & van Aken, 2008; Schmidt & Tasker, 2000), and aggressiveness (Dennissen et al., 2008; Kokko & Pulkkinen, 2005) tend to be relatively stable over time. However, what does change is the way in which these characteristics are expressed. For example, young children hit, kick, or throw things when they are angry, but school-age children may express

Quantitative changes Changes in the amount or quantity of what you are measuring.

Qualitative changes Changes in the overall nature of what you are examining.

Stage theories Theories of development in which each stage in life is seen as qualitatively different from the ones that come before and after.

Incremental theories Theories in which development is a result of continuous quantitative changes.

FIGURE 1.1

Patterns of stability and change. By looking at individual differences in patterns of change over time, the researchers who carried out this study were able to see that children who started the study with low or moderate levels of aggression showed little change in their level of aggressive behavior as they got older (those represented by the bottom two lines), while children who started at high levels of aggression changed over time (those represented by the top line).

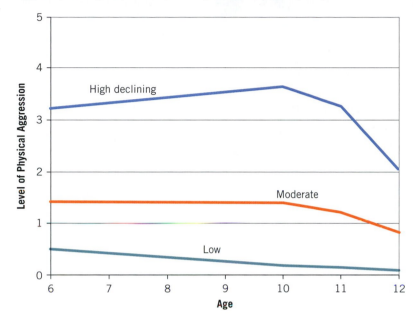

SOURCE: Kokko, Tremblay, Lacourse, Nagin, & Vitaro (2006).

their aggression through teasing, taunting, and name-calling (Kokko & Pulkkinen, 2005), and adolescents may attack each other through social means (for example, spreading rumors or excluding others from social activities).

Figure 1.1 shows the results of a study of aggressive behavior in children aged 6 to 12. Kokko, Tremblay, Lacourse, Nagin, and Vitaro (2006) identified three different patterns of stability or change in this behavior, shown by the three lines in the figure: (1) The "low" group starts at a low level and remains at a low level through the period of time studied; (2) the "moderate" group starts at a moderately high level at age 6 and stays close to that level over the period studied; (3) the "high-declining" group starts at a relatively high level but ends at a considerably lower level, although still significantly higher than the other two groups. As you look at Figure 1.1, do you wonder what factors contributed to change in a pathway or to its stability? That would be a logical thing to think about next because such information could help us develop interventions to change pathways that can eventually lead to problem behavior.

Individual Differences

Scientific research strives to identify general principles that describe average or typical patterns. We want to be able to make general statements about what usually happens. But you cannot spend much time observing children or adolescents without recognizing how different each one is from all the others. Our study of children needs to deal with both aspects of development—those aspects that are universal and shared by all or almost all individuals, and those in which we differ from each other.

Throughout this book you will learn about general conclusions drawn from research. Although these are true as general statements, there also are numerous exceptions that give us insights we would not have otherwise. For example, children who grow up in poverty with

©iStockphoto.com/Susan Chiang

Individual differences. Characteristics of individual children, such as age, gender, or ethnic background, can affect the developmental process, so outcomes that apply to one child will not necessarily apply to another. This means we must always be mindful of individual differences.

Equifinality The principle by which different developmental pathways may result in the same outcome.

Multifinality The principle by which the same pathways may lead to different developmental outcomes.

Developmental psychopathology An approach that sees mental and behavioral problems as distortions of normal developmental processes rather than as illnesses.

parents who cannot effectively care for them are at risk for a number of developmental and mental health problems, but a small group manages to thrive in the face of great difficulty. By looking at these children, we can identify factors that help protect a child from some developmental risks.

While we can make a number of valid general statements about how development proceeds, the developmental pathway of any given individual is difficult to predict. *Different* pathways can result in the *same* outcome, a process known as **equifinality** (*equi* = equal, *finality* = ends). For example, depression may result from biological and genetic processes, but it also can result from early traumatic experiences. However, it is also true that the *same* pathway can lead to *different* outcomes, known as **multifinality** (Cicchetti & Toth, 2009). For example, children who are victims of abuse can have many different long-term outcomes that can include depression but also resiliency and healing. Individual characteristics of a child or an adolescent, including the child's gender, age, ethnic or racial background, and socioeconomic status, are just some of the characteristics that may influence the specific outcome in any given situation.

This understanding of individual differences has changed the way we view behavioral and emotional disorders. In the field of **developmental psychopathology**, psychological disorders are now seen as distortions of normal developmental pathways (Cicchetti & Toth, 2009; Sroufe, 2009). Accordingly, in this book we include these disorders in our discussions of typical development. For example, language disorders appear with the discussion of typical language development, and attention deficit disorder appears in the section in which we describe typical development of attention. Thinking about atypical development this way may help reduce the stigma associated with mental disorders because it helps us see them as variations in development rather than as illnesses.

The Role of the Child in Development

Are you the person you are today because you *chose* to be that person, or did someone else *make* you who you are? How you think about that question pretty much sums up the issue of an active child versus a passive one. Some theories presume that forces in the environment shape the development of the child. The clearest example of this way of thinking is called *learning theory* or *behaviorism*. As you will see in Chapter 2, this approach explores the way systematic use of rewards and punishment affects the likelihood that a child will—or won't—behave in certain ways. You may agree with this point of view if you think children are like sponges that absorb whatever they are exposed to or like lumps of clay that parents shape into the type of children they want.

However, other theories in child development give children a much more active role in shaping their own development. For example, Jean Piaget developed a theory of cognitive development based on the idea that children actively explore their environment and in the process create their own theories about how the world works. Another influential theorist, Lev Vygotsky, proposed that learning is a collaborative process in which the child seeks to solve problems while more experienced people provide just enough help to allow the child to continue learning independently. Sandra Scarr and Kathleen McCartney (1983) described a process of active **niche-picking** in which people express their genetic tendencies by actively seeking out environments they find "compatible and stimulating" (p. 427).

As with some of the other issues we have already discussed, maybe the answer to this issue isn't one or the other, but rather some combination of both. Richard Lerner (2002) succinctly captured the idea that children are affected by and also affect their environments when he said that children are both the products *and* the producers of their own development. Characteristics of individual children evoke different reactions from the people with whom the children interact, and these reactions provide feedback in a way that can change the children. For example, the way peers respond to obese children is different from the way they respond to children who are not overweight (Zeller, Reiter-Purtill, & Ramey, 2008). These reactions feed back to children and affect their level of self-esteem, which, in turn, will affect their future interactions with peers.

Positive Psychology

In recent years, a very important shift has occurred in the field of psychology. For many years, the field has used what has been called a *disease model* (Seligman & Csikszentmihalyi, 2000). The primary focus was on understanding the cause of problems in people's lives and finding ways to restore their functioning and well-being. Beginning in the late 1990s, psychologists began to think more about people's strengths rather than their weaknesses, and to look for ways to foster optimal outcomes for all individuals, not just those who were struggling. Rather than fixing what was broken, the goal of positive psychology is to nurture what is best in the individual (Seligman & Csikszentmihalyi, 2000). Using this approach, researchers have identified a number of human strengths including courage, optimism, interpersonal skills, perseverance, and insight that allow all people not only to survive, but to flourish.

The influence of positive psychology on the study of child development is most clearly seen in the **positive youth development** movement. The framework for positive youth development is based on a set of developmental assets that support optimal development for all children, not just those who are at risk. These assets allow the child to cope with challenges, but also to take advantage of opportunities. We have already said several times in this chapter that you will learn about ways to support optimal development and foster positive growth. Research inspired by the positive youth development perspective appears in many topics throughout the book, including creativity, school achievement, positive parenting, play, stress and coping, and resilience. Chapters 14 and 15 provide detailed information on the impact of activities on youth development and the role of positive experiences in fostering resilience in the face of challenge.

Integrating Themes and Issues

Each of the themes and issues presented here cuts across many of the specific topics that you will study. Each also has been the subject of discussion and debate for many years. For that reason, we are not searching for a single best way to understand the complex process of child development. Rather, each of these issues is a lens through which we can view the process. Themes help us tie together the disparate pieces of information that come to us through our research. As you continue to read this book, think about the ways you conceptualize development. As your understanding grows, continue to ask yourself what you believe about development, but also think critically about *why* you hold these beliefs. You should expect your ideas to undergo some significant changes as your understanding of this process grows.

CHECK YOUR UNDERSTANDING

1. What are the differences between physical, cognitive, and social-emotional development?
2. Why is the relationship between nature and nurture relevant to the study of child development?
3. Contrast quantitative and qualitative changes that occur in development.

Niche-picking The process by which people express their genetic tendencies by finding environments that match and enhance those tendencies.

Positive youth development An approach to finding ways to help all young people reach their full potential.

CONTEXTS OF DEVELOPMENT

1.3 What are the contexts for child development?

Children around the world are similar to one another in many ways, but the way development occurs varies widely depending on the context in which a child grows up. *Context* is a very broad term that includes all the settings in which development occurs. Children develop in multiple contexts that include family, schools, communities, and cultures. Throughout this book you will learn about these different contexts and the way they influence various aspects of children's development.

FAMILY

Families are the primary context for development for most children. Families today take many different forms, but whether they are nuclear families, single-parent families, stepfamilies, or adoptive families, they all serve one important function: They are responsible for the **socialization** of their children. They instill the norms, values, attitudes, and beliefs of their **culture** so that children grow up to be positive, contributing members of their society. In Chapter 13, we discuss the effect of different family forms on child development, and also examine the ways that families link children and adolescents to the other contexts that influence their development.

Some families have more resources than others and some have less, and these differences affect children's development. **Socioeconomic status (SES)** is a combined measure of a family's income and parental education and occupation (Bradley & Corwyn, 2002). In general, a higher SES allows a family to have more resources to support healthy child development. Beginning before the child is born, low SES parents have less access to good prenatal care, and their babies are more likely to be born prematurely or at low birth weight and to develop other long-term health problems. Children who spend time living in poverty are found on average to have lower academic performance than those who do not. This makes sense if you consider that parents with more resources are able to provide books, educational experiences, and other activities that a family with few resources cannot. In addition, poorer nutrition and less access to health care affect the growing brain and body, influencing a child's ability to learn. Finally, families with few resources are more likely to experience highly stressful events, such as loss of income, relocation, divorce and separation, and violence (Bradley & Corwyn, 2002). Children's response to stress such as this, especially when it is repeated, puts severe strains on their ability to develop optimally. You will learn about the effects of a family's socioeconomic status as a context for children's development as you read about development throughout this book.

SCHOOL

In most countries, school is another important context for development. During the school year, children ages 6 to 17 spend 6 to 7 hours a day at school (Juster, Ono, & Stafford, 2004). Within this context, children learn academic skills, such as reading, writing, and arithmetic and older children and adolescents are prepared for higher education or entry into the workforce, but schools also play a role in socializing children to become good citizens. In recent years, schools have increasingly taken on functions other than educating children. Today schools provide nutritious meals, some health care, and social services for their students (de Cos, 2001). School also is where most children and adolescents make friends, and sometimes become the victims of bullies. You can see from this description why we will talk about schools as a developmental context when we are talking about physical, cognitive, and social-emotional development. You will learn more about the role that schools play in fostering academic achievement in Chapter 8.

Socialization The process of instilling the norms, attitudes, and beliefs of a culture in its children.

Culture The system of behaviors, norms, beliefs, and traditions that form to promote the survival of a group that lives in a particular environmental niche.

Socioeconomic status A person's social standing based on a combined measure of income, education, and occupation.

COMMUNITY

The characteristics of the community in which children live impact many aspects of development (Narine, Krishnakumar, Roopnarine, & Logie, 2013). Economic adversity in a community will affect the range and quality of support services available to children and their families. The quality of neighborhood schools affects the educational opportunities and out-of-school activities that are available. Whether a neighborhood is safe or not affects the amount of time children might spend outside their homes and the kinds of things they do with this time. The amount of noise in the environment can physically harm their hearing or disrupt their learning and social interaction with others (Shield & Dockrell, 2003). Community environments can promote healthy development, or they can expose children to environmental pollutants, including air that is unhealthy to breathe, water that is unsafe to drink, and toxins that can cause physical and neurological damage.

CULTURE

The general findings from research on development are modified not only by individual differences, but also by group differences, such as those between different cultures. For example, a very strict parenting style would likely have a different effect on children raised in a culture that views strictness as a sign of love and care than in one that views the same behavior as a sign the parent doesn't like the child. Matsumoto and Juang (2004) point out that culture is a way of describing similarities within one group of people and differences between groups of people. These similarities within a group may include customs, language, beliefs, values, and many other characteristics that can differentiate one group from another. Culture emerges from a group's *environmental niche* or their place in their particular environment. Culture forms to promote the survival of the group in its niche by improving the ability of the group to meet the demands of an environment. For example, a desert society will have different rules and traditions than a society located on rich farmland.

Throughout the book we draw on cross-cultural studies to illustrate both research that finds similarities across cultures, which suggests there is a universal process at work, and research that illustrates important differences between cultures. Much of what you will read

Cultural differences. Which of these photos fits your idea of how to raise a child? Culture affects what we expect parents to do. In Western society, young children generally do not take care of infants. In some African societies, talking directly to young children is seen as ridiculous.

is based on research carried out in Western, developed countries, but increasingly the study of child development seeks to understand children within the context of their own cultures. One of the important changes in the field of child development in recent years has been a deeper, richer appreciation of this diversity.

Despite this increasing awareness, it is still easy to slip into the assumption that the way we do things is the right way and that other ways are wrong. For example, Robert LeVine and colleagues (1994) showed U.S. mothers videos of mothers from the Gusii people in Kenya. The U.S. mothers were appalled that 5- and 6-year-old children in these videos were put in charge of their infant siblings and that mothers did not praise their children. On the other hand, when he showed tapes of the U.S. mothers to the Gusii mothers, they were appalled that mothers did not nurse their babies immediately when they cried and they could not understand why U.S. mothers talked to their babies when the babies clearly could not understand them.

To understand a culture other than our own, we must understand its environmental context and its values. Infant mortality is a major problem for the Gusii, so the protection and health of infants is the primary concern. Mothers in this culture soothe and calm their babies by nursing them often to prevent the stress of crying. Health is also an issue in the United States but can usually take a backseat to our emphasis on engaging and teaching infants. Stimulating the infant's cognitive development is a priority, so talking to babies, offering toys, and interacting are important. Neither of these approaches is right or wrong. Both are responsive to the realities of the environment in which they occur, usually in a way to best promote the well-being of the children.

When we look at parenting practices in other cultures, we need to guard against labeling those practices as deficient when in reality they are simply different from practices that are more familiar to us. For an example of how we may misinterpret the actions and intentions of people whose culture is different from our own, see **Active Learning: Cultural Competence and Grief.**

Active LEARNING

Cultural Competence and Grief

Joanne Cacciatore (2009) recounts an experience she had with a family that had just suffered the unexpected death of an 18-month-old son. Although two sets of grandparents and the young child's parents were present, no one except one of the grandfathers would talk with a representative of the medical examiner's office. When the grandfather did talk with her, he stayed at least 4 feet away and did not make eye contact. He steadfastly insisted that no autopsy be performed on the child's body, even though the law required one in cases of sudden child deaths in his state. The family sat in the medical examiner's office for almost 2 hours in silence, with little or no show of emotion. When they finally were asked whether they wanted to have some time with the dead child to say their good-byes, they adamantly refused.

How would you interpret this family's behavior? What circumstances could account for it? How does it fit with your cultural beliefs regarding the way a family grieves for the death of a young child? Does their behavior seem typical, atypical, or pathological to you?

Answer: This case involved a Native American family and their behaviors were completely expected and normal for some families in their culture. In this culture it is the proper role of the grandfather to be the spokesman for the family. Native Americans may not make sustained eye contact when talking to others even when they are dealing with personal grief. Because this culture values listening, it is not unusual for its members to remain silent even while sitting together. Autopsies are usually prohibited, as is postmortem contact with the deceased. In the cultural context of this family, their behavior was appropriate, respectful, and in keeping with their traditions and beliefs (Cacciatore, 2009). However, we also need to remember that within any culture there is a range of individual differences. Other Native American families who are more assimilated to Western culture might not adhere to all these cultural traditions and may have behaved very differently in this situation.

Cultural differences in feeding. Babies in individualistic cultures are often encouraged to try to feed themselves, but babies in collectivist cultures are more likely to be fed in a way that emphasizes that eating is an opportunity to enjoy family closeness. Do you see how these different cultural values are reflected in these pictures?

One way in which cultures vary is along the continuum from **individualism** to **collectivism.** U.S. culture is based on values of rugged individualism. Our heroes often are those who are self-made and managed to rise from deprived circumstances to become successful. In other cultures, the emphasis is more on an obligation to those around you: your family or your group, however you define it.

Cultural values are expressed in overt behaviors such as how we greet people, but there are also much more subtle ways in which culture guides not only our behaviors but the ways in which we think or experience our feelings. How is such subtle cultural information taught to children? Certainly there are some cultural expectations that are taught explicitly to them. For example, we might say to a child "Look at me when I'm speaking to you" versus "Be careful to show respect and look down when addressing your elders." However, much cultural information is conveyed in less obvious ways. For example, in many cultures around the world, the value of connection to others is communicated even in infancy because babies are constantly kept close to the mother's body, sleeping with the mother, while she anticipates the baby's needs. In cultures that value individualism, babies are expected to sleep through the night in their own bed and are praised for soothing themselves when they cry (Greenfield, Keller, Fuligni, & Maynard, 2003).

Robin Harwood studied middle-class mothers in Connecticut and in Puerto Rico. She was interested in how the individualistic values of American society and the more collectivist values of Puerto Rican society might be taught even to infants through the way that their mothers interacted with them. With this in mind, Harwood and her colleagues set out to see whether the feeding practices of mothers in the two cultures would reflect these different value systems (Miller & Harwood, 2002). Think about the scene you expect to see when a mother feeds her 1-year-old baby. If you were born in the United States, most likely you have an image of the baby sitting in a high chair. The mother spoon-feeds the baby but often lets the baby take the spoon to begin learning to feed herself (usually with messy and somewhat hilarious results, as shown in the leftmost photo on this page). She may also put some "finger food," like dry cereal, on the tray for the baby to take on her own. Contrast this picture with that of the typical Puerto Rican mother and baby. This mother spoon-feeds the baby to make sure that the baby eats well, the feeding remaining under her control and not the baby's, as shown in the photo at the right. What is the subtle message that each mother is giving to her

Individualism The cultural value that emphasizes the importance of the individual with emphasis on independence and reliance on one's own abilities.

Collectivism The cultural value that emphasizes obligations to others within your group.

baby from her earliest days of life? The American mother is saying, "Be independent. Learn to do things on your own separately from me. We will watch and praise you." The Puerto Rican mother is saying, "Be close to family. Listen to and cooperate with your parents. Enjoy your food in the context of family love and expectations for proper behavior." Thus, cultural values are translated directly into parenting techniques. Babies are learning the values of their culture even with their first bites of food.

CHECK YOUR UNDERSTANDING

1. What is the primary context for most children's development?
2. How does socioeconomic status affect a child's development?
3. How does culture affect childrearing?

BEING A SMART CONSUMER OF INFORMATION ABOUT DEVELOPMENT

1.4 How can you be a smart consumer of information about development?

Information about children and child development is everywhere—in books, magazines, and television programs, at home, and online. How can you judge the quality of the information you see, both in this course and elsewhere? You will be better able to do this if you become an informed consumer of information about development.

KNOWING YOUR SOURCES

Information about child development is readily available, but not all of it is true or reliable. How do you know you are getting information from someone who is knowledgeable about the field and who is providing information that is objective and unbiased?

Your campus library owns many journals, books, and professional publications in the field of child development, and you can trust these to be reliable sources of information. You can probably access many of them through your library's electronic databases. For students in child and adolescent development, the PsycINFO and Education Resources Information Center (ERIC) databases are probably of greatest interest. PsycINFO contains nearly 4 million records that include peer-reviewed journals, books, and dissertations from the 17th century to the present (American Psychological Association, n.d.). ERIC is sponsored by the U.S. Department of Education and has more than 1.4 million bibliographic records of journal articles and other education-related materials, including conference papers and reports (Institute of Education Sciences, n.d.). In these databases, you can find abstracts of articles (brief summaries of the research done and the conclusions drawn from it) and information that will allow you to locate the complete articles.

Peer review A process by which professional peers critique research and make suggestions for improvement prior to its publication or dissemination.

The reason you can have confidence in the information you find in professional journals is that many of them use a **peer review** process to determine which articles they will publish. After an article is submitted to a journal, it is reviewed by professionals knowledgeable about the topic of the research. These research peers tell the journal editors whether they think the article should be published and often make suggestions to improve it. This process ensures that the information you take from a peer-reviewed journal has passed professional scrutiny before it ever got into print.

However, when you turn to the Internet to find information and use a search engine such as Google or Yahoo! you need to provide your own scrutiny and use good judgment. Remember that anyone can post information on the web, so the author of a web page does not necessarily have any particular expertise. The information may simply be wrong, or it may be opinion masquerading as fact. This is especially a risk when you are researching a controversial topic. Commercial sites may provide some amount of legitimate information, but often their real intent is to sell you a product (Piper, 2000).

Although the Wikipedia website is popular with college students, anyone can write an article or edit an existing post on the site. An author does not have to have any expertise on a topic to post an entry. For these reasons, Wikipedia is *not* considered a reliable source of information for most purposes. If you do use a site like this, use it as a starting point only for background information, and be sure to expand your search to include other professional sources of information. Many Wikipedia entries include a bibliography of professional books and articles that may help send you in the right direction to find scientific information on the topic you are researching.

Many libraries currently use Jim Kapoun's guidelines for evaluating webpages you want to use for research. You can use these guidelines to evaluate a webpage that interests you by completing **Active Learning: Evaluating Information on the Web.**

Active LEARNING

Evaluating Information on the Web

Begin this activity by picking a topic related to child development that you would like to know more about. For example, what is the effect of violent video games on children's level of aggression, or how does parental divorce affect teens' romantic relationships? Find a website devoted to this topic through a search engine such as Google and evaluate it using the criteria below.

Name of the site you found: _____

URL: _____

1. Accuracy of Web Documents • Who wrote the page and can you contact him or her? • What is the purpose of the document and why was it produced? • Is this person qualified to write this document?	
2. Authority of Web Documents • Who published the document and is it separate from the "Webmaster"? • Check the domain of the document, [and ask] what institution publishes this document? • Does the publisher list his or her qualifications?	
3. Objectivity of Web Documents • What goals/objectives does this page meet? • How detailed is the information? • What opinions (if any) are expressed by the author?	
4. Currency of Web Documents • When was it produced? • When was it updated? • How up-to-date are the links (if any)?	
5. Coverage of Web Documents • Are the links (if any) evaluated, and do they complement the documents' theme? • Is the site all images or a balance of text and images? • Is the information presented/cited correctly?	

SOURCE: Kapoun (1998, July/August). Reprinted by permission of the author.

(Continued)

(Continued)

What is your overall evaluation of the accuracy and helpfulness of this site? _____
_____

Next, log on to PsycINFO through your campus library website and search for the same research topic. Be sure to enter specific search terms for the topic you've chosen, not a full sentence or phrase; for example, enter *video games* on one line and *aggression* on the next rather than entering *effect of video games on aggression* on one line. Chances are your search will return many, many published articles. If it doesn't, try changing one or more of your search terms. For instance, if you searched for *teenagers,* you could try searching for *adolescents.* Choose one or two of the articles that you find that give you electronic access to the full text of the articles and look over the information.

What are advantages and disadvantages of using the Internet versus PsycINFO for finding information on child development? How much do you trust the information in each? What gives you confidence in the results you found?

BECOMING A CRITICAL THINKER

As you learn about child development, don't hesitate to look for answers to your own questions. No single book can contain all the information you need on any topic, so seek out divergent opinions on topics that intrigue you. Expose yourself to a wide range of ideas. You will probably find some that make sense to you and some that are harder to accept, but keep an open mind and don't stop asking questions and learning. Just be sure you turn to credible sources of information as you go through this process. As you learn more about research methods in Chapter 3, you will become better able to examine the evidence behind the ideas you find rather than just relying on what someone else has said.

Remember that a science is an organized body of knowledge that is accumulated over time so it is always changing and growing. Throughout the book you will find features called the **Journey of Research**. In these features there will be a brief historical sketch of how some important ideas in the field have developed over the years. Our current understanding of a topic will make more sense to you when you understand the origin of those ideas.

As new ideas come into existence, old ideas fall out of favor as they are replaced with better information. For instance, autism was once attributed to (or perhaps we should say "was blamed on") mothers who were cold and rejecting toward their children, but today research on autism focuses on differences in the structure and functioning of the brain in autistic children as an underlying cause. The fact that an idea has been around for a long time—or that many people endorse it—does not necessarily mean it is true. Remember that for a very long time, everyone believed that the earth was flat. Likewise, just because an idea is new doesn't necessarily mean it is better than what we believed before. New research findings need to be tested and replicated, or produced again by others, before we can gain confidence that they are accurate and reliable. The best suggestion here is to be open to new ideas but to be cautious about jumping on a bandwagon until there is good evidence that the bandwagon is going in the right direction. If new ideas cannot be replicated, they are not a fact—they are a fluke!

GUARDING AGAINST GENERALIZATIONS

As you learn about child development, it is easy to assume others have had experiences the same as or similar to yours with the same or similar consequences. Your own experiences are meaningful and real. They all become part of what has made you the person you are today and help shape the person you will be tomorrow. That fact is never in question, but your experiences may not represent the average or typical experience of other people. Trying to generalize from one particular experience to general statements is always dangerous. Likewise, when we conduct research we cannot necessarily generalize findings based on one population to another population that might have different characteristics.

The opposite of this is also true. When you read about conclusions drawn from research, they may not describe what your personal experiences were, but this does not mean the research is invalid. Rather it reminds us that research describes the outcome for groups, not for every individual within a group. When we say men are more physically aggressive than women, for instance, it does not mean every man is more aggressive than any woman, only that on average there is a difference between the groups, and within the groups there is a good deal of individual variability.

AVOIDING PERCEPTUAL BIAS

Sometimes students think that child development is just common sense and that they already know everything they need to know. Unfortunately, it isn't that simple. We can't rely on folk wisdom, or ideas that are widely accepted but have not been scientifically tested, to tell us what we need to know about development. Having such preconceived ideas can also affect how you process new information. As you read this book, it will be easier for you to remember the facts you encounter that fit well with what you already believe to be true, and to forget or ignore those that don't. This tendency to see and understand something based on the way you expected it to be is called a **perceptual bias** and it can affect your learning. That is one reason we will use common misconceptions to begin each chapter. Testing your knowledge about the topics in the chapter *before* you begin reading will make you more aware of information in the chapter that will challenge your initial ideas. You will want to spend a little more time and effort making sure you understand this information.

Active Learning: Testing Your Knowledge of Child Development provides a selection of questions that appear in the chapters that follow. You can take a few minutes here to test your current knowledge about these topics. Pay special attention to the information that challenges the ideas that you are bringing with you to this class. We hope you will look forward to learning more about any of these answers that do not correspond to your current beliefs as you read this book.

Perceptual bias The tendency to see and understand something in the way you expect it to be.

Active LEARNING

Testing Your Knowledge of Child Development

1. **T ☐ F ☐** Each human being has hundreds of thousands of genes that make him or her a unique individual.

2. **T ☐ F ☐** Research has shown that exposing a fetus to extra stimulation (for example, playing music near the woman's stomach) can stimulate advanced cognitive development.

3. **T ☐ F ☐** Humans use only 10% of their brain.

4. **T ☐ F ☐** Children who are gifted or talented often pay a price for their giftedness because they are likely to be socially or emotionally maladjusted.

5. **T ☐ F ☐** It is perfectly fine to use baby talk with infants.

6. **T ☐ F ☐** There is not a very strong relationship between your moral values and beliefs and what you will actually do when making a decision about how you should behave.

(Continued)

(Continued)

7. T ☐ F ☐ Adolescents today are much less likely to be victims of violence while in school than they were 20 years ago.

8. T ☐ F ☐ A good deal of parent–adolescent conflict is normal in families with adolescents.

9. T ☐ F ☐ The incidence of stepfamilies in the United States has not changed much from 1900 to today.

10. T ☐ F ☐ Adults who were abused as children are likely to become abusive parents themselves.

Answers:

1. **False.** The Human Genome Project has mapped all the genes that make up a human being and they only found 20,000 to 25,000 genes, not the 100,000 or more that they had expected to find (Chapter 4).

2. **False.** Although a fetus is able to hear and even respond to sounds prior to birth, there is no evidence that auditory stimulation beyond the level provided by the natural prenatal environment has any extra cognitive benefits (Chapter 5).

3. **False.** Neurologist Barry Gordon, who studies the brain, finds the notion that we use only 10% of our brain ridiculous. He says, "It turns out . . . that we use virtually every part of the brain, and that [most of] the brain is active almost all the time" (Boyd, 2008, para. 5) (Chapter 6).

4. **False.** Gifted children have generally been found to be socially and emotionally well-adjusted and to feel positive about their gifts and abilities (Chapter 8).

5. **True.** The way adults often talk to babies—in a high-pitched voice, with a great deal of exaggeration, and in a singsong rhythm—is actually well suited to the hearing capabilities and preferences of a baby. Babies pay attention to us when we talk this way, and doing it will not delay their language development (Chapter 9).

6. **True.** Although we like to think that our behavior always reflects our values and ethics, in real-world situations there are many other factors that influence what we actually do (Chapter 11).

7. **True.** In 1992, the rate of violent victimization of teens was 53 students per 1,000, while in 2014 the rate had dropped to 14 students per 1,000 (Chapter 12).

8. **False.** A lot of parent–adolescent conflict does occur in *some* families, but conflict is not overwhelming or pervasive in most families (Chapter 13).

9. **True.** The incidence (or likelihood of occurrence) of stepfamilies is similar in these two periods of time, but the reason for their creation has changed. Today stepfamilies come about primarily due to divorce, while in the past they were due to death of one of the parents or marital desertion (Chapter 13).

10. **False.** This is one of the most serious misunderstandings about child abuse. About 30% of abused children perpetuate the cycle by repeating abuse when they themselves become parents, but the majority do not. They successfully break the cycle when they reach adulthood (Chapter 15).

How did you do? Many of these questions represent common beliefs, so it wouldn't be surprising if you got a number of them wrong. The purpose of these quizzes is not to make you feel badly about what you do or don't know, but rather to point out that many ideas that we have about child development that sound like "common sense" don't agree with what research has shown to be the case. We hope your results make you eager to learn more about these topics, but remember to pay extra attention to those ideas that contradict your preconceived ideas.

GETTING THE MOST FROM YOUR TEXTBOOK

You are making a substantial investment of time and money when you buy a textbook for a course. For that reason, you will want to be sure that you get the most you possibly can from your book.

We have already told you that you will want to use the **True/False Quiz** that begins each chapter to identify important ideas that challenge your initial level of understanding, and the **Journey of Research** to put current ideas into a historical context that shows the evolution of our thinking on a given topic. But there is another feature of this text that is designed specifically to support your learning. Each chapter begins with a set of **Learning Questions** that point to the major topics covered in the chapter. These can act as guideposts that will help focus your learning. When you complete each section of the chapter, you will find a set of review questions that will **Check Your Understanding**. Use these questions as an opportunity to make sure you have a good understanding of that topic before moving on to the next one. When you have finished a chapter, the **Chapter Summary** repeats the Learning Questions and summarizes the most relevant information on each topic.

We all learn best when we can relate new ideas to our own experiences. To facilitate opportunities for this type of learning, we provide a variety of **Active Learning** features. Throughout this book, you will find activities that help you feel or think the way a child feels or thinks, or to reflect on your own experiences while you were growing up. Other activities allow you to carry out simple experiments or observations with children and adolescents to see for yourself examples of the behaviors we are describing. There are videos available for most of the Active Learning features that involve children that will show you how the activity is done, whether you plan to do it yourself or simply want to see how it is done. You will also find some activities that help you test your understanding of the material presented, some that are designed to help you learn how to find the kind of information you will need when you are working with children, and others that involve interviewing parents about their experiences. Each of us constructs our understanding of any new information in a unique way. All of these activities are designed to help you relate the text material to your own life, view development from many different perspectives, and gain new insight into various aspects of development. We hope that all these opportunities help you develop a deep understanding of the material so that your new knowledge will stay with you far beyond the end of your course and influence how you understand and interact with children and adolescents in the future.

CHECK YOUR UNDERSTANDING

1. How does peer review assure readers that scientific information is valid and reliable?
2. What does it mean to be a critical thinker?
3. What is perceptual bias?

CONCLUSION

We hope this chapter has made you eager to learn more about child development. Now that you have been introduced to some of the basic concepts in the field, you are ready to explore these concepts more deeply. As you read this book, we want you to take an active role in your own learning process. By using the activities we have provided, you will be able to examine your current beliefs about children and adolescents and then move to new levels of understanding that you can continue to build upon.

Our understanding of the nature of child development has important consequences for our ability to foster children's positive growth. There are so many interesting and important topics in the pages that follow that it is difficult to pick just a few to highlight, but they include understanding what can be done to help ensure a healthy pregnancy for both mother and infant, developing educational practices that help children across a wide range of abilities to thrive in their classrooms, and learning about the new and exciting findings from the field of neuroscience that are helping us to understand how the brain works. We look at what promotes healthy development as well as what threatens it and the protective factors that can buffer those negative effects. We also discuss how all of this unfolds in the increasingly diverse world in which children live.

CHAPTER SUMMARY

Test your understanding of the content.
Take the practice quiz at **edge.sagepub.com/levine3e**

The chapter summary at the end of each chapter is designed in a question/answer format so you can test yourself to see what you have learned. While looking at each question, cover the answer and try to answer it yourself. Then see how the answer corresponds to your own understanding. Self-testing is a very effective way to study and learn.

1.1 Who needs to have a good understanding of child development and why?

Informed parents and family members are better able to understand their children's needs and abilities at each stage of development, which helps them respond appropriately to their children and provide the amount and type of stimulation that supports their children's growth and development. Professionals in a variety of careers, including pediatricians, teachers, social workers, counselors, therapists, lawyers, nurses, and people in many other careers, all draw on child development knowledge in their work. Policymakers who are responsible for shaping **social policy** are guided in their decision making by knowledge of how it will affect children and families. Citizens who are knowledgeable about child development can advocate or vote for policies that promote positive child development.

1.2 What are the domains of child development and some recurring themes and issues in the field?

Physical development consists of the biologically based changes that occur as children grow. **Cognitive development** consists of the changes that take place in children's thinking and learning. **Social-emotional development** consists of the changes that occur in children's understanding and expression of emotions as well as their ability to interact with other people. These domains continually interact with each other to shape development. Development is divided into stages that include infancy, toddlerhood, early childhood, middle childhood, and adolescence. Themes in the study of development include debate about the relative contribution of **nature** and **nurture** to development, whether change is incremental (quantitative) or stagelike (qualitative), and how much stability versus change occurs over time. In addition, different developmental pathways may result in the same outcome (**equifinality**), and the same developmental pathways may result in different outcomes (**multifinality**). Examining less adaptive processes and outcomes is the domain of **developmental psychopathology**. Another theme centers on whether

children play an active role in their own development or are passive recipients of external influences. Through the process of **niche-picking**, people express their genetic tendencies by seeking out compatible environments. Positive psychology looks at people's strengths rather than weaknesses and seeks to foster optimal development. In child development, this perspective is reflected in the **positive youth development** movement.

1.3 What are the contexts for child development?

The contexts for development include a child's family, as well as their schools, communities, and culture. Family is the primary context for development for most children and is responsible for their **socialization**. Family resources, including their **socioeconomic status (SES)**, make a significant impact on the experiences a child will have. Characteristics of the school a child attends and the community in which the child lives affect every aspect of development. Although we see cultural differences in how parents raise their children, one approach is not better than another because each culture prepares children to be successful in the context of their particular environment. Cultures vary along the continuum of **individualism** and **collectivism.**

1.4 How can you be a smart consumer of information about development?

Know that your sources are knowledgeable and objective. Be sure your information is based on scientific evidence that has been replicated in studies conducted by more than one researcher. Look for convergence from many different sources of information and think critically about them. Don't generalize from a single example, but also don't reject the results of research because your individual experiences don't agree with the research findings. Try to be objective so that you don't fall prey to **perceptual bias** that just confirms what you already expected. Finally, examine your preconceptions carefully to determine what is scientifically based fact and what is unproven folk wisdom. To get the most from your textbook, use all of the features in it.

KEY TERMS

Strengthen your understanding of these key terms with
mobile-friendly eFlashcards at **edge.sagepub.com/levine3e**

Cognitive development   10

Collectivism   19

Culture   16

Developmental psychopathology   14

Equifinality   14

Incremental theories   12

Individualism   19

Multifinality   14

Nature   11

Niche-picking   15

Nurture   11

Peer review   20

Perceptual bias   23

Physical development   10

Positive youth development   15

Qualitative changes   12

Quantitative changes   12

Social policy   7

Social-emotional development   10

Socialization   16

Socioeconomic status   16

Stage theories   12

Give your students the SAGE edge!

SAGE edge offers a robust online environment featuring an impressive array of free tools and resources for review, study, and further exploration, keeping both instructors and students on the cutting edge of teaching and learning. Learn more at **edge.sagepub.com/levine3e**

chapter 2

THEORIES OF DEVELOPMENT

JGI/Blend/Getty

TEST YOUR KNOWLEDGE

Test your knowledge of child development by deciding whether each of the following statements is *true* or *false*, and then check your answers as you read the chapter.

▲ **VIDEO: Watch as students answer some of these questions and the authors respond.**

1. **T ☐ F ☐:** Research cannot tell us whether a theory is true or false.

2. **T ☐ F ☐:** The bulk of your personality is fixed and established by the time you enter adolescence.

3. **T ☐ F ☐:** Freud's theory is based on outdated ideas so it is not relevant to the field of child development today.

4. **T ☐ F ☐:** The best way to establish and maintain a behavior is to reward people every time they exhibit the behavior that you are interested in.

5. **T ☐ F ☐:** The best way to stop an undesirable behavior in a child is to punish a child for doing it.

6. **T ☐ F ☐:** Children can learn basic math concepts better through games of pick-up sticks and group-based arithmetic games than paper-and-pencil lessons.

7. **T ☐ F ☐:** Darwin's concept of the "survival of the fittest" means that the strongest animal is most likely to survive.

8. **T ☐ F ☐:** Infants must have skin-to-skin contact with their mother within the first few hours after birth for *bonding*, or love, to develop.

9. **T ☐ F ☐:** The best way to study children is through carefully controlled experiments in a laboratory setting.

10. **T ☐ F ☐:** A good theory should be universal, applying to all children in all situations.

Correct answers: (1) T, (2) F, (3) F, (4) F, (5) F, (6) T, (7) F, (8) F, (9) F, (10) F

When we observe and work with children and adolescents, we want to make sense out of what we see. The explanations that we develop about why children behave in certain ways become theories. In this chapter, we describe why we need theories to guide our work with children. We then describe some of the basic characteristics of different theories, such as whether children develop through small incremental steps or through large leaps. We next discuss some of the major theories that have influenced how we understand child development today. Some of these theories have their origins in the late 19th or early 20th century, but each also has modern applications that we have included in this chapter. Because no theory is a static "truth" that never changes, we will see how ideas about children and adolescents have developed over time in response to society's changes. We will also look at new research providing evidence that either supports or refutes theoretical ideas. We present these theories here as a broad introduction to the variety of ideas that lie behind modern research and practice with children; however, you will read much more about these theories as they are applied to specific topics discussed in the rest of this book.

BASIC PRINCIPLES AND APPLICATIONS

2.1 What do child development theories tell us?

Why do we need to have a theory in order to understand children? In this section, we discuss this question and then describe two ways in which developmental theories differ in their explanations of how children grow and change.

WHY THEORIES OF DEVELOPMENT ARE IMPORTANT

To advance our understanding of why and how children develop the way they do, it is not enough simply to observe children. When we systematize and organize the ideas that come from those observations, we develop a model that allows us to predict how children will behave in the future. This model is called a **developmental theory**. Although we all have our own personal theories about various aspects of human behavior, the theories that we use to build a scientific understanding about child and adolescent development must be public and testable. Theories in any science serve two important functions: They help us *organize* the knowledge that we already have and they help us *make predictions* that we then can investigate and test.

> **Developmental theory** A model of development based on observations that allows us to make predictions.

For example, a parent might react very differently to an infant's continual crying depending on his understanding of what this crying means. If he subscribes to the theory of behaviorism, he might believe that picking up the crying baby will reward that behavior and make the baby cry more in the future. However, if he subscribes to the theory of ethology, he might believe that crying is a behavior that signals the baby needs comfort and if that need is met, the baby will eventually cry less.

Now that we have stated opposing theoretical ideas, we can examine research that tests those ideas. St. James-Roberts (2007) reviewed research on two types of parenting: *demand parenting*, in which babies were reliably picked up when they cried (based upon an ethological approach), and *structured parenting*, in which standard bedtimes and routines were put in place and some crying was acceptable (based upon a behavioral approach). (Note that no one simply left babies to cry uncontrollably!) In his review, St. James-Roberts found evidence that supports each of these theoretical ideas. Demand parenting resulted in babies crying less during the first 3 months of life but continuing to cry at night after that age. This supports the idea that quickly responding to a crying infant meets the infant's needs, as ethological theory would suggest. However structured parenting resulted in more crying during the first 3 months but reduced crying at night thereafter. This supports the idea from behavioral theory that responding quickly will establish a pattern that reinforces the crying itself. As we see in this example, the answers to questions based on theories are often not a clear yes or no. Instead, they point the way to further questions that we can examine through further research. St. James-Roberts and colleagues used the results of these research findings to develop an intervention program to help improve infant sleep (Hiscock et al., 2014).

As this research suggests, most theories can never be proven beyond a shadow of any doubt, but the scientific process does allow us to gather evidence that supports or opposes the truth of these ideas. For example, some say Darwin's theory of evolution is not a proven fact, and technically this is true. However, the enormous body of evidence that supports its ideas outweighs the evidence against it. Consequently, evolutionary theory is widely accepted in scientific circles today. On the other hand, other theories have come and gone as evidence piled up that did not fit with the predictions they made. For example, at one time, we thought inadequate early mothering was the cause of the severe mental illness known as schizophrenia (Ambert, 1997), but as research continued, it became clear that the more

> T ☐ F ☐ Research cannot tell us whether a theory is true or false. **True**

likely culprit in the development of schizophrenia is a combination of genetic endowment and environmental influence (Boksa, 2008). As our understanding advanced, the theory that mothers' behavior was the cause for this mental disorder disappeared.

HOW DO DEVELOPMENTAL THEORIES DIFFER?

As you will remember from Chapter 1, development has to do with both stability and change over time, so each developmental theory must address the issues of how and why change happens and why some aspects of behavior remain the same.

How Does Change Happen?

As we saw in Chapter 1, some theories describe development as a series of quantitative changes that happen little by little, smoothly over time, such as growing physically inch by inch. Other theories describe development as a series of qualitative changes that occur at certain ages and alter the nature of the child or adolescent in significant ways. These qualitative theories are called stage theories, because each stage in life is seen as different from the ones that come before and after. One way to understand the difference between the two types of change is to consider the development of memory. Children can remember more and more as they get older (quantitative change), but they may suddenly increase their memory capacity when they develop a new way of encoding information into memory (qualitative change).

Why Does Change Happen?

Developmental change may be driven by biological processes inside each person, by environmental events that affect each person, or by an interaction of the two. Development is also affected by the way we make sense out of our experiences. One of the important ways developmental theories differ from each other is the relative weight they attach to internal and external influences on development. In the next section, we describe some of the central theories that have been influential in our thinking about children's development. As you read about each theory, keep two questions in mind:

1. How does the theory describe development? Does change occur quantitatively, in small steps, or qualitatively, in distinct stages?

2. What drives development? Is development the product of biological processes, environmental influences, or a combination of both?

CHECK YOUR UNDERSTANDING

1. What two functions do theories serve in science?
2. What is the relationship between theory and truth?
3. What are two ways in which theories of development differ from each other?

THEORIES OF CHILD AND ADOLESCENT DEVELOPMENT

2.2 What are the hypotheses and modern applications of the major child development theories?

As we begin this description of developmental theories, it is important for you to understand that theoretical ideas do not exist in a vacuum. Leading theorists developed their ideas while living and participating in a particular culture at a particular point in historical time, and their ideas about child development reflect these influences. However, each of these theories has been tested over time, retaining the concepts and principles that continue to be useful, and losing or changing those that don't. In different ways, each of these theories has helped to shape the type of questions we ask, the type of research we conduct, and the interpretation we place on our findings.

PSYCHOANALYTIC THEORY

We begin our discussion of theories with **psychoanalytic theory** (*psyche* = the mind; *analysis* = looking at the parts of the mind individually to see how they relate) because it was the first theory to describe stages of development through childhood. In this theory, developed by Sigmund Freud (1856–1939), biological urges move each person through a series of stages that shape the personality. Although psychoanalytic theory has been very controversial throughout its existence, many of its concepts have become part of our assumptions about how the mind works. Furthermore, Freud has been recognized as one of the 100 most influential people of the 20th century (Gay, 1999).

Freud theorized that our personality is made up of three parts: the id, the ego, and the superego. According to Freud, we are all born with an **id**, which consists of our basic instinctual drives. Infants have no way to control their drives. They want *what* they want *when* they want it. An infant is not going to wait politely for you to get off the phone when she is feeling very hungry. She is going to cry and demand food because she has a strong need to satisfy this basic drive. The id operates on what Freud called the **pleasure principle** because it seeks immediate gratification for all its urges.

As children grow older, they begin to become aware of the reality of the world around them and begin to develop the ability to think and control their emotions. This ability to negotiate between basic drives and the real world is the job of the **ego**. As the ego develops, the child is still motivated by her basic drives, but she now is able to interact in the real world to get her needs met. Even though she is hungry, she now realizes that if she waits until her father is off the phone and asks politely, she may be more likely to get the cookie she wants. This way of dealing with our wants and desires is known as the **reality principle**.

Finally, sometime between the ages of 5 and 7, the child begins to incorporate moral principles that work against the drive-motivated functioning of the id. These moral principles are maintained by the **superego**. Freud believed that children do not have any internal sense of guilt that guides their actions until they develop a superego. Whereas a younger child might simply take a cookie when hungry, an older child will be able to control herself and resist the temptation because she knows that taking a cookie when she isn't supposed to is wrong. Figure 2.1 illustrates how the id, ego, and superego function.

Sigmund Freud's Psychosexual Stages

Freud believed our most basic drive is the sex drive. If you believe that biologically the goal of our lives is to pass on our genes, then you might agree with Freud that the sex drive is central to everything else. Along with this, Freud believed that many of our thoughts and feelings about sexuality are hidden in our **unconscious mind**, the part of our mind of which we are unaware. He outlined five stages in child and adolescent development, which he called **psychosexual stages**. At each of these stages, sexual energy is invested in a different part of the body, and gratification of the urges associated with those areas of the body is particularly pleasurable. He labeled these stages the oral, anal, phallic, latency, and genital stages. He believed that the way in which gratification of urges is handled during each of these stages determines the nature of an adult's personality and character. Satisfying the urges at each stage allows the individual to positively resolve the needs of that stage and to move on to the next. On the other hand, failing to meet one's needs in any of the stages can result in psychological disturbance in adulthood. We next describe these stages and Freud's ideas about the effects later in life if development during these stages does not go well.

Psychoanalytic theory Freud's theory in which the way we deal with biological urges moves us through a series of stages that shape our personalities.

Id According to psychoanalytic theory, the part of personality that consists of the basic drives, such as sex and hunger.

Pleasure principle The idea that the id seeks immediate gratification for all of its urges to feel pleasure.

Ego The part of the personality that contends with the reality of the world and controls the basic drives.

Reality principle The psychoanalytic concept that the ego has the ability to deal with the real world and not just drives and fantasy.

Superego Freud's concept of the conscience or sense of right and wrong.

Unconscious mind The part of the mind that contains thoughts and feelings about which we are unaware.

Psychosexual stages Freud's idea that at each stage sexual energy is invested in a different part of the body.

FIGURE 2.1

Id, ego, and superego. In Freud's theory, the id is the part of the personality that wants immediate gratification of all its desires. The ego has the job of finding a realistic way to satisfy those needs. The superego is the part that contains the moral guides and restrictions on those desires.

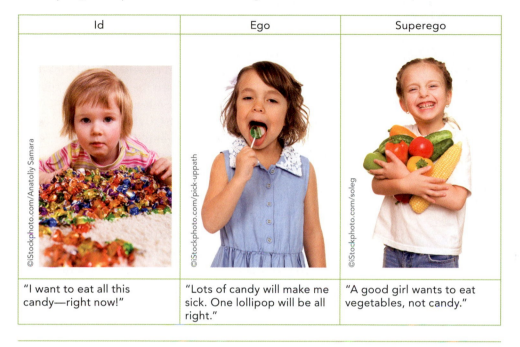

Id	Ego	Superego
"I want to eat all this candy—right now!"	"Lots of candy will make me sick. One lollipop will be all right."	"A good girl wants to eat vegetables, not candy."

The **oral stage** lasts from birth to about 18 months of age. Children in the oral stage derive a great deal of satisfaction from activities that stimulate their mouth, lips, or tongue. This is why young children often immediately put anything they get their hands on into their mouth. Freud developed the idea that someone can get "stuck" or fixated in one of the first three psychosexual stages during early childhood. A child can get fixated if his needs are not adequately met at a stage or if he receives so much gratification that he is not willing to move on to the next stage. Later in life, that person will then exhibit characteristics of the stage he fixated on (Freud, 1953). For example, an individual who is fixated in the oral stage may want to continue to try to satisfy his oral urges by overeating or smoking. Many of us have some remnants of this stage as we chew on our fingers or pencils; however, a fixation is really only a concern when it interferes with adaptive functioning in some critical way.

The **anal stage** lasts from 18 months to 3 years. At this age the pleasure center moves to the anus, and issues of toilet training become central. Although many of us squirm to think of the anus as a pleasure center, we have only to listen to the "poopy talk" of young children to see the hilarity it brings about. The task of the child at this age is to learn to control his bodily urges to conform to society's expectations. A person who is fixated at this stage may become overcontrolled (referred to as *anal compulsive*) as an adult (Freud, 1959). For this person, everything must be in its proper place to an extreme degree. Conversely, someone might become *anal explosive*, creating "messes" wherever he goes.

The **phallic stage** lasts from 3 to 6 years of age. Sexual energy becomes focused on the genitals. Boys and girls develop what has been called "the family romance." Boys imagine marrying their mother when they grow up and girls imagine marrying their father. To move on to the next psychosexual stage, children must learn to give up these desires and begin to identify with the parent of the same sex.

Oral stage Freud's first stage in which the infant's sexual drive is centered on the mouth area.

Anal stage Freud's second stage during which toddlers' sexual energy is focused on the anus.

Phallic stage Freud's third stage in which children 3 to 6 years of age overcome their attraction to the opposite-sex parent and begin to identify with the same-sex parent.

Latency stage Freud's fourth stage, involving children ages 6 to 12, when the sex drive goes underground.

Freud's latency stage. Does this picture of girls interacting with girls and boys interacting with boys remind you of your own experience in elementary school?

Erik Erikson. Erikson was a psychoanalyst who focused more on the role of social issues in development than Freud and who introduced stages of life development that continued through adulthood.

Genital stage Freud's fifth and final stage in which people 12 and older develop adult sexuality.

Psychosocial stages Erikson's stages based on a central conflict to be resolved involving the social world and the development of identity.

T ☐ **F** ☐ The bulk of your personality is fixed and established by the time you enter adolescence. **False**

The **latency stage** occurs between 6 and 12 years of age. *Latent* means inactive, and Freud (1953) believed that during this time the sex drive goes underground. Children move from their fantasies in the phallic period of marrying their parent to a new realization that they must take the long road toward learning to become a grown-up. The sex drive provides energy for the learning that must take place but the drive itself is not expressed overtly. Children transfer their interest from parents to peers (Freud, 1965). At this age, children who had cross-sex friendships often relinquish them as boys and girls learn the meaning of "cooties" and each sex professes disgust for the other.

This separation of the sexes begins to change at about age 12, when young adolescents enter the **genital stage**. At this point, sexual energy becomes focused on the genital area, and a more mature sexual interest occurs between peers.

Erik Erikson's Psychosocial Stages

Many followers of Freud further developed aspects of his theory, but one of the most influential was Erik Homburger Erikson (1902–1994). Erikson believed that issues of the ego are more important than those linked with the id and instinctual drives. He believed that the development of identity is the central issue for children and adolescents. At each stage in his theory a conflict arises rooted in the social experiences typical at that stage of development. For this reason, Erikson's theory is said to describe **psychosocial stages** (as opposed to Freud's psycho*sexual* stages). The way in which we resolve the conflict at each stage lays the groundwork for the next stage of our development.

For example, Erikson believed that infants have to establish trust in the world around them, so he called the developmental issue for infants *trust versus mistrust*. Infants are totally dependent on the adults who care for them. When their caregivers are dependable and reliably meet the infant's needs, the infant learns to trust the world and feel safe and secure in it. However, when caregivers are inconsistent in providing care or are emotionally unavailable to the infant, she develops a sense of mistrust in the world. These early experiences can color the way the individual approaches social relationships later in development. In a similar way, each subsequent developmental stage presents a different developmental conflict. The way infants resolve the issue of trust versus mistrust sets the stage for the way they will go on to deal with issues of *autonomy versus shame and doubt* as they become more independent from their parents in the next stage.

Of course none of us have a completely positive or completely negative set of experiences; therefore, we can think of the two possible outcomes of each stage as two sides of a seesaw, with one side higher than the other but both actively in play. For example, we will all have some trust and some mistrust in our relationships; it is the balance of the two that lays the foundation for later development.

The other important aspect of Erikson's theory is that he believed development does not stop in adolescence. He went beyond Freud's stages to add three stages of adulthood. He was the first theorist to recognize that we continue to grow and develop throughout our lives. Erikson's eight psychosocial stages are described briefly in comparison to Freud's psychosexual stages in Table 2.1. You can use this table to carry out **Active Learning: Comparing Psychoanalytic Theories** to review these two theories.

Active LEARNING

Comparing Psychoanalytic Theories

Use Table 2.1 to test your understanding and memory of the stages of Freud and Erikson.

1. Review Freud's Psychosexual Stages in Columns 2 and 3 to be sure you understand the description of each one.

2. Take a sheet of paper and cover all the columns except Column 1, Ages. Try to recall the name for Freud's stages that correspond to each age through adolescence.

3. Study Erikson's Psychosocial Stages in Columns 4 and 5 to understand the issues in each stage.

4. Cover Columns 4 and 5 and try to recall the name of Erikson's stages that correspond to each of Freud's stages.

5. Cover all but Column 1 and try to recall both Freud's and Erikson's stages that correspond to each age group.

TABLE 2.1

A comparison of Freud's and Erikson's stages of development.

Ages	Freud's Psychosexual Stages		Erikson's Psychosocial Stages	
Infancy	Oral	Pleasure is focused on the mouth and "taking in."	Trust versus mistrust	Infant develops trust in maternal care and in one's ability to cope or a sense of hopelessness.
Toddlerhood	Anal	Pleasure is focused on the anal region and control of one's own body and its products.	Autonomy versus shame and doubt	Toddler develops more independence and self-control or a lack of confidence.
Early Childhood	Phallic	Pleasure is focused on the genital area; development of the "family romance."	Initiative versus guilt	Child exhibits exuberant activity or overcontrol.
Middle Childhood	Latency	Sexual energy goes underground as child focuses on peers and learning.	Industry versus inferiority	Child learns the tasks of society or develops a sense of inadequacy.
Adolescence	Genital	Sexual energy reaches adult level, with focus on intimate relationships.	Identity versus role confusion	Adolescent integrates previous experiences to form an identity or feels confusion about his or her role in society.
Early Adulthood			Intimacy versus isolation	One develops an ability to form close relationships or fears and avoids relationships.
Middle Adulthood			Generativity versus stagnation	One guides the next generation or is preoccupied with one's own needs.
Later Adulthood			Ego integrity versus despair	One achieves a sense of meaning in life or feels one's life has not been worthwhile and fears death.

SOURCES: Compiled from Kahn (2002) and Erikson (1963).

Modern Applications of Psychoanalytic Theory

Despite the controversy that has surrounded Freud's psychoanalytic theory, ideas that come from it are still very influential, particularly in relation to the study of the development of mental and emotional disorders (Fonagy, Target, & Gergely, 2006). Many psychotherapists continue to use therapy based on Freud's idea that inner conflicts from earlier life experiences, especially early trauma, form the basis for later psychological symptoms, and bringing those inner conflicts from the unconscious mind into consciousness will be therapeutic.

Erikson's ideas about the effect of social experiences on development have influenced contemporary child care practices and our understanding of the way development occurs as a series of interrelated experiences. For instance, we urge new parents to be sensitive and responsive to their infants as a way to establish a sense of trust, as Erikson described. We better understand the challenge of adolescence when we see it as a struggle to establish a coherent sense of individual identity (Meeus, van de Schoot, Keijsers, & Branje, 2012). Erikson's theoretical ideas have been used in the treatment of children with emotional disturbances to provide a framework for understanding the central issues that children deal with at different ages (Turns & Kimmes, 2014) and as a framework for parenting advice (Fletcher & Branen, n.d.).

Erikson's ideas also have remained influential because they reflect the way we think about development today, as outlined in Chapter 1. The role Erikson gives to the influence of culture, the environment, and social experiences on development fits well with our current interest in understanding the contexts in which development occurs. His portrayal of the child as an active participant in shaping his or her own development and the incorporation of both change (as reflected in different crises in each of the stages) and stability (as seen in the idea that later stages continue to be influenced by the resolution of earlier issues) also dovetails with our current thinking.

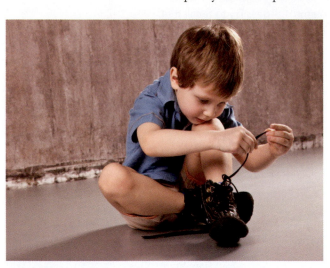

iStock

Toddlerhood: Autonomy versus shame and doubt. According to Erik Erikson, toddlers are learning to do things for themselves and their caregivers must be patient with the child's early attempts to master these tasks. With support and encouragement from adults, young children develop a sense of autonomy or being able to do things on their own. However, when adults are overly critical or impatient, the child can feel shame and doubt in their abilities.

CHECK YOUR UNDERSTANDING

1. What are the three parts of the personality according to Freud?
2. What drive does Freud say is most important for human development?
3. How do the stages in the theories of Freud and Erikson differ?

LEARNING THEORIES

A very different school of thought about how children develop is offered by the learning theories. Whereas psychoanalytic theory focuses on internal processes of the mind, the learning theories focus on observable behavior. These theories are based on the link between the stimulus (an event in the external environment) and the response of the child. In the following sections, we describe the theories known as behaviorism (which is based on principles of classical conditioning and operant conditioning) and social cognitive theory (which is based on principles of modeling and imitation).

John B. Watson and Classical Conditioning

Behaviorism The theory developed by John B. Watson that focuses on environmental control of observable behavior.

John B. Watson (1878–1958) is the father of the theory known as **behaviorism.** Unlike other psychologists in the early 1900s, he was not interested in studying the impact of internal factors such as genetic influences and the workings of the mind on human development

(Buckley, 1989). Instead, he concentrated on what he could see: behavior, or what people *do*. The modern academic field of psychology was just emerging, and psychologists in America were trying hard to establish the field as an experimental science, with testable predictions based on observable phenomena rather than unseen concepts such as Freud's unconscious mind.

Watson studied the ways in which the environment influences human behavior. He subscribed to a notion put forth by great philosophers including Aristotle and John Locke that we are born a "blank slate" or *tabula rasa*, ready to be drawn on by environmental experiences. He felt so strongly about this that he made the following statement:

> Give me a dozen healthy infants, well-formed, and my own specified world to bring them up in and I'll guarantee to take any one at random and train him to become any type of specialist I might select—doctor, lawyer, artist, merchant-chief and, yes, even beggar-man and thief, regardless of his talents, penchants, tendencies, abilities, vocations, and race of his ancestors. I am going beyond my facts and I admit it, but so have the advocates of the contrary and they have been doing it for many thousands of years. (Watson, 1928, p. 104)

One way in which we learn from our environment, according to Watson, is through a process called **classical conditioning**, illustrated in Figure 2.2. In this process, a particular stimulus or event in the environment is paired with another stimulus over and over again. The first stimulus, known as the *unconditioned stimulus*, provokes a natural response, known as the *unconditioned response*. For example, Ivan Pavlov (1849–1936), a Russian physiologist who was studying reflexes and the processes of digestion, presented food to hungry dogs in his lab. In response, the dogs salivated, just as you would if you were hungry and walked by a bakery. The food is the unconditioned stimulus because it elicits a natural or unconditioned

Classical conditioning The process by which a stimulus (the unconditioned stimulus) that naturally evokes a certain response (the unconditioned response) is paired repeatedly with a neutral stimulus. Eventually the neutral stimulus becomes the conditioned stimulus and evokes the same response, now called the conditioned response.

FIGURE 2.2

Classical conditioning. This figure shows the steps in the process of classical conditioning.

BEFORE CONDITIONING

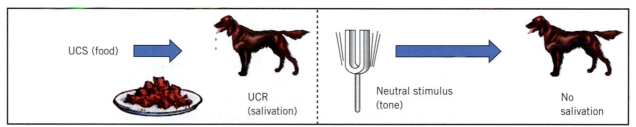

An unconditioned stimulus (UCS) produces an unconditioned response (UCR).

A neutral stimulus produces no salivation response.

DURING CONDITIONING   **AFTER CONDITIONING**

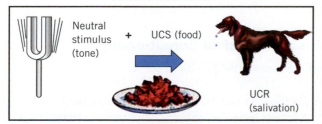

The unconditioned stimulus is repeatedly presented just after the neutral stimulus. The unconditioned stimulus continues to produce an unconditioned response.

The neutral stimulus alone now produces a conditioned response (CR), thereby becoming a conditioned stimulus (CS).

response, salivation. Then Pavlov made a distinctive noise, such as ringing a bell, immediately before he presented the food. At first the bell did not provoke salivation from the dogs, so it was considered a neutral stimulus. However, over time, as Pavlov continued to ring the bell before presenting the food, the dogs began to associate the sound of the bell with the food, so the animals had *learned* something about the bell, and it now became a *conditioned stimulus*. Finally, Pavlov presented only the bell and found that the dogs continued to salivate just as if the food had been presented. Salivation to a formerly neutral stimulus, such as the ringing of a bell, is known as a *conditioned response* (Pavlov, 1927).

In a well-known experiment with a 9-month-old infant known only as Little Albert, Watson applied the idea of classical conditioning by demonstrating that he could use it to condition fear in a human infant (Watson & Rayner, 1920). (Clearly, this type of research would be considered unethical today and would not be conducted unless strict safeguards were implemented to assure the infant's safety and well-being.) Watson found that Little Albert, like many infants, was frightened by a sudden loud sound so the noise was an unconditioned stimulus and would bring about fear as an unconditioned response. When Watson first showed Little Albert a white rat, the child was curious but not afraid of the animal, so the rat was initially a neutral stimulus because it did not produce a fear response. However, Watson then made the loud clanging noise at the same time that he presented the white rat to the infant. He did this numerous times over a number of days, and Little Albert soon began to cry as soon as he saw the white rat. Eventually Watson stopped making the loud sound, and yet every time he showed Little Albert the white rat, which by now had become a conditioned stimulus, the infant continued to show fear, which now was a conditioned, or learned, response.

Aside from the obvious ethical questions about conducting research like this with an infant, there are also many questions about the scientific quality and meaning of the research that Watson carried out with Little Albert. Other people who subsequently carried out this type of classical conditioning with other infants were unable to replicate the results that Watson had described (e.g., Bregman, 1934). Even in Watson and Rayner's (1920) own description, there were times when Little Albert did not show much fear of the rat or of the other stimuli such as a rabbit and a dog to which he supposedly had generalized his fear.

Despite questions about Watson's experiment, classical conditioning has become an accepted principle of learning. It's easy to think of examples in everyday life. A child who gets sick after eating asparagus may later find that just seeing asparagus makes him feel queasy. The sick feeling has become classically conditioned to the sight of that vegetable. On the other hand, a child who visits fast food restaurants may associate that type of food with the fun she has at the play areas provided and subsequently crave that food (Petrovich & Gallagher, 2007). To check whether you understand the steps of the classical conditioning process, try **Active Learning: Understanding the Process of Classical Conditioning.**

Active LEARNING

Understanding the Process of Classical Conditioning

Read the following paragraph and then answer the questions below.

Every time your roommate leaves the room he says "Goodbye!" and loudly slams the door, making you flinch. After this happens a number of times, your roommate says to you "Gotta go now. Goodbye!" and you realize that you are flinching even before you hear the door slam. Can you identify all the elements in this classical conditioning paradigm listed below?

Unconditioned stimulus (the stimulus that naturally is tied to a response that you can't control):

_____

Unconditioned response (the response that is automatic):

_____

Conditioned stimulus (the stimulus that is paired with the unconditioned stimulus):

_____

Conditioned response (the response you have learned):

_____

Answer: Originally, the unconditioned stimulus always produces the unconditioned response. In this case, the slamming door made you flinch so the slam is the unconditioned stimulus and the flinch is the unconditioned response. However, over time the slam has been paired with your roommate saying "Goodbye!" You didn't originally flinch when he said it, so goodbye was originally a neutral stimulus. With repeated pairings with the slamming door, goodbye has become a conditioned stimulus, your flinch has become a conditioned response, and you begin to flinch when your roommate says "Goodbye!"

Classical conditioning has been used to explain **phobias**, the irrational fear of something specific that is so severe that it interferes with day-to-day functioning. Think of things in your everyday environment that could elicit a phobic response. They include dark places (nyctophobia), spiders (arachnophobia), snakes (ophidiophobia), and great heights (acrophobia). From an evolutionary perspective, it makes sense that humans have an instinctual fear of things that could harm or even kill them. These fears are so strong that even things associated with them that could not possibly harm you can elicit the fear response. For example, if you have a snake phobia, you might refuse to go outdoors because there could be a snake lurking there. One of the dangers of this type of learning is that once the conditioned (or learned) response has been established, people understandably avoid the stimulus that produces the unpleasant response so they don't have the opportunity to find out that they really have nothing to fear.

Phobia An irrational fear of something specific that is so severe that it interferes with day-to-day functioning.

Modern Applications of Classical Conditioning

Modern psychologists have used classical conditioning to treat phobias by exposing patients to their feared situations in a controlled way. This idea began long ago when Mary Cover Jones (1924) followed Watson's experiment with Little Albert with a study of a 2-year-old boy who seemed to have the exact phobias of rats, rabbits, and other objects that Watson claimed he had conditioned into Little Albert. Jones was able to undo these fears

Virtual reality treatment for fear of flying. Virtual exposure to the feared experience helps many overcome phobias. How would a behaviorist explain why this procedure works?

by *deconditioning* the child; she presented him with candy at the same time a rabbit was brought to him and encouraged imitation when he saw another child holding the rabbit. Today people who are being deconditioned are first trained in relaxation techniques. Next they are exposed to the object or situation they fear in a series of gradual steps from least frightening to most frightening, and they use their relaxation techniques to reduce their anxiety at each step.

More recently, virtual reality therapy, a technique that uses computer simulation of real interactive environments, has been used for treating children with anxiety disorders to expose them to feared stimuli in a gradual way that they can tolerate. Although the amount of research on this approach has been limited, it has been shown to be helpful for children with school phobias and phobias of spiders (Bouchard, 2011; Bouchard, Weiderhold, & Bossé, 2014).

B. F. Skinner and Operant Conditioning

B. F. Skinner (1904–1990) further developed the theory of behaviorism by introducing the idea of **operant conditioning.** While studying rat behavior at Harvard, he noticed that the rats were affected not by what came before their behavior, as was true of classical conditioning, but by what came *after* (Vargas, 2005). He concluded that spontaneous behaviors are controlled by the environment's response to them.

In the vocabulary of operant conditioning, a **reinforcement** is anything that follows a behavior and increases the likelihood that the behavior will continue or happen again. Reinforcement can be planned, like the candies some parents give to toddlers when they use the potty, or unplanned, like nodding and smiling when someone is talking to you. As long as you smile and nod, the person is likely to continue to talk with you because he finds the way you are responding to him pleasant and rewarding. Positive reinforcement occurs when you get something you like and want. It is easy to think of examples of positive reinforcement: a gold star on a good paper, getting your allowance for keeping your room clean, or watching your favorite TV program after you have finished studying for your upcoming test. **Negative reinforcement** occurs when something disagreeable is removed. You can think of the word *negative* as a minus sign, taking something away, rather than as something bad. Do you wear your seat belt when you drive? You should simply because it helps keep you safe, but car manufacturers weren't sure that was enough of an incentive, so they installed an obnoxious buzzer that won't turn off until you buckle your belt. Getting away from that annoying sound is an example of negative reinforcement. Buckling your seat belt is reinforced and, therefore, likely to increase when the annoying sound goes away. Please note that both positive and negative reinforcement cause a behavior to happen *more*. Figure 2.3 illustrates the comparison between positive reinforcement and negative reinforcement.

Skinner described several concepts related to reinforcement that help us understand how the process works. One is the process of **shaping behavior.** Obviously you can't reinforce a behavior if that behavior doesn't occur, so shaping is a way that lets you build that behavior in a series of steps. For example, you cannot reinforce positive peer interaction with a child who does not interact with his peers. However, Skinner developed the idea, based on his work with pigeons, that behavior could slowly be "shaped" through reinforcement of behaviors that progressively get more and more like the behaviors desired. In this way he was able to train pigeons to engage in complex behaviors like playing ping-pong. To use shaping with a child who does not interact with peers, you could begin by rewarding the child when the child is simply near another child. The next step might be that the child is reinforced only when he looks at the other child, and finally the reinforcement might only be provided when he speaks while looking at the child. Eventually, the reward would be contingent only on true interaction with a peer.

Operant conditioning The process that happens when the response that follows a behavior causes that behavior to happen more.

Reinforcement A response to a behavior that causes that behavior to happen more.

Negative reinforcement In operant conditioning, a response that makes a behavior more likely to happen again because it removes an unpleasant stimulus.

Shaping behavior Reinforcing behaviors to become progressively more like the desired behavior.

Joe Raedle/Photonica World/Getty Images

The effects of reinforcement. Many people spend hours at casino slot machines. The fact that they win often but not every time makes this behavior very persistent.

FIGURE 2.3

Illustration of positive reinforcement and negative reinforcement

Positive Reinforcement

Positive reinforcement makes a behavior more likely to continue. Awarding a trophy for academic performance will make it more likely that this boy will continue to work hard in school.

Negative Reinforcement

Negative reinforcement also makes a behavior more likely to continue. Listening to a crying baby is difficult. When this mother finds that holding her baby stops the crying she is likely to continue to hold her baby.

If reinforcement increases the likelihood that a behavior will occur, you might think that the most effective way to establish and maintain a behavior would be to reinforce a child every time she performs that behavior. However, although continual reinforcement does a great job of establishing a behavior, when the reinforcement stops the behavior is likely to stop as well. Skinner found that less frequent reinforcement is more effective for maintaining a behavior. Imagine that you found a slot machine that gave you a payoff each time you pulled the handle. You would quickly learn to keep putting coins into that machine. But what if the machine then suddenly stopped paying off? How quickly would you abandon this behavior that never produced a reward? That is why games of chance reward you in an unpredictable way. They keep you motivated to continue playing in the hope that the next try will produce a big reward. Now think about how you would study if you knew you were going to have a quiz that would give you points toward your final grade every 2 weeks. Compare that to how your study habits would change if you knew you would have quizzes but didn't know when they would be given. Which schedule would result in more consistent study habits? With regularly scheduled quizzes, you may be likely to cram all of your studying in a day before the exam. However, if your reinforcement for getting a good grade

T ☐ F ☐ The best way to establish and maintain a behavior is to reward people every time they exhibit the behavior that you are interested in. **False**

Punishment Administering a negative consequence or taking away a positive reinforcement to reduce the likelihood of an undesirable behavior occurring.

depends on "pop quizzes" that are unpredictable, your best strategy is to study at a steady pace so you are always ready.

You can test the effects of reinforcement by trying **Active Learning: Reward Yourself!**

Active LEARNING

Reward Yourself!

Of course you already know that reading your textbook helps boost your grades (and presumably increases your learning). Although grades themselves are a form of reinforcement, they are quite long-term, and many people need a more immediate reinforcer to do what is needed to achieve them. If you are someone who does not stay current with your class readings, set up a reinforcement program for yourself. First, keep track of how many pages of reading you are currently doing in a week. Next, choose a reward you know to be effective for you and keep track of your progress when you consistently reward your reading. For example, see how many pages you should be reading during a given week. For every 5 or 10 pages that you read, give yourself a treat, such as listening to one or two of your favorite songs. Again, keep track of the number of pages you are reading during a week. Did you end up reading more when you gave yourself a reinforcement that depended upon your behavior?

Extinction In operant conditioning, the process by which a behavior stops when it receives no response from the environment.

T ☐ F ☐ The best way to stop an undesirable behavior in a child is to punish a child for doing it. **False**

TRUE/FALSE VIDEO ▲

If reinforcement increases the likelihood of a response, **punishment** is intended to decrease it. Punishment consists of administering an undesirable consequence (such as a spanking) or taking away a desired consequence (such as "no dessert because you didn't eat your dinner") in response to an unwanted behavior. However, Skinner (1953) believed that a more effective way to control behavior is to ignore undesirable behavior rather than punish it. This is a process that Skinner called **extinction.** People don't usually continue doing something that has no reward or payoff for them. As the undesirable behavior decreases, alternative desired behavior should be rewarded so it replaces the undesirable one. For example, a teacher might ignore a squabble between two children (thereby denying them attention from the teacher) but later compliment them on their positive play behaviors. As the time spent in positive play increases, there should be less and less opportunity for squabbling. Figure 2.4 illustrates the comparison between extinction and two types of punishment.

One reason why punishment doesn't always work the way we expect it to is because what we consider punishment may be something different for the child. For example, a child may be looking for *any* response from a parent; therefore, even yelling or spanking may unintentionally reinforce the undesirable behavior because the child is getting the parental attention that she wants. You will read more about the problems associated with the use of punishment in Chapter 13.

Modern Applications of Operant Conditioning

Operant conditioning has been used as a classroom management strategy for many years. Students may be given tokens, stickers, or checkmarks on a classroom chart to reward good behavior. At some point these tokens can be redeemed for gifts, privileges, or special activities (Landrum & Kauffman, 2006). An approach called **applied behavior analysis (ABA)** uses operant conditioning techniques with children in special populations, particularly those with autism spectrum disorder, to increase adaptive behavior and decrease maladaptive behavior (Myers & Plauche Johnson, 2007).

Applied behavior analysis (ABA) Application of principles of behaviorism to change behavior of individuals with a range of difficulties, including autism spectrum disorder.

FIGURE 2.4

Punishment and Extinction

Punishment 1: Negative consequence This boy receives a scolding for misbehaving.	 ©iStockphoto.com/didesign021
Punishment 2: Removal of a reward This girl didn't eat her dinner, therefore she doesn't receive a dessert.	 Ingram Publishing/Getty Images
Extinction: Ignoring temper tantrums leads to a decrease in their occurrence.	 ©iStockphoto.com/Leigh Schindler

ABA begins when therapists observe children to determine the reinforcements that are helping to maintain undesirable behavior, a process called **functional behavioral assessment** (Anderson, Rodriguez, & Campbell, 2015). Next the therapist will identify the problematic behavior and note where, when, and how often it occurs and then identify the rewards or reinforcements the child is getting from this behavior. See Figure 2.5 for an example of a chart used in this process. The therapist sets a new goal and implements changes to work

Functional behavioral assessment Identification of reinforcements that are maintaining undesirable behavior in order to change them and reduce the behaviors.

FIGURE 2.5

Applied Behavior Analysis (ABA) programs. Practitioners of ABA use charts such as this one to keep track of what comes before and what comes after a behavior they are trying to change. Once they see the triggers for the behavior or the reinforcement it receives, they can design a program to change these patterns.

ABC Chart

Student _____

Targeted Behavior _____

Time/Date	Setting	Antecedent (include activity, staff, setting, etc.)	Behavior (include intensity and duration)	Consequence (include staff, setting, and sequence of events)	Staff Initials

toward that goal. This could involve ignoring the problematic behavior or punishing it, if necessary, while rewarding an alternative desired behavior in its place (Neitzel & Bogin, 2008). For example, a child might be annoying peers in a classroom because it gets him sent to detention where he doesn't have to do his class work. In this case, the way this behavior was being dealt with was unintentionally rewarding the misbehavior by getting the student out of doing his work. The intervention might be that the classroom teacher ignores the misbehavior whenever possible so the behavior isn't reinforced or there are negative consequences for it, such as being required to do something else the child doesn't like to do when he is not doing his class work. At the same time, the child would receive reinforcement for appropriate behaviors, such as when the child is paying attention to his work. This procedure has been used successfully with autistic children to improve IQ, language, and sociability (Lablanc, Richardson, & McIntosh, 2005; Simpson et al., 2005), as well as to reduce behavioral problems in children with multiple disabilities (O'Mea, 2013).

Albert Bandura and Social Cognitive Theory

Albert Bandura, who was originally trained as a behaviorist, was dissatisfied with some of the ideas that grew out of behaviorism because it is difficult or impossible to identify either stimuli or reinforcements for the entire range of human behavior we see (Pajares & Schunk, 2002). Bandura proposed that, in addition to classical and operant conditioning, we learn through imitation. He believed that people can learn new behaviors simply by watching others rather than by receiving direct reinforcement of their own behaviors from the environment (Bandura, 1986). With these ideas, he had returned to the view, rejected by both Watson and Skinner, that internal mental processes (cognition) play an important role in human learning and human behavior. For this reason, he called his theory a *social cognitive learning theory* because the learning occurs from watching other people (social) but is also processed in one's mind (cognitive).

According to Bandura, imitation has four parts: (1) attention to a model, (2) mental representation or memory of that model's actions, (3) motoric ability to reproduce the action, and (4) the motivation to imitate the action (Grusec, 1992). Let's rephrase that to help you better understand the process: You need to notice what someone else is doing (attention) and then be able to remember what you saw (mental representation) and actually be able to do the same thing yourself (motoric response) if or when you want to (motivation). If all these conditions are in place, you will be able to repeat or imitate the behavior that you saw someone else model.

Bandura's earliest work was designed to show how children learn by direct observation. In his classic experiment, one group of children observed an adult on television act aggressively to a Bobo doll (a large inflated figure of a clown that is weighted on the bottom), hitting it, kicking it, throwing it, and striking it with a toy hammer (Bandura, Ross, & Ross, 1963). These children and another group of children who had not seen the video were then brought individually into a room containing the Bobo doll and other toys. The children who had seen the adult attacking the Bobo doll were much more likely to hit, kick, or throw the doll or strike it with a hammer. In contrast, the children who hadn't seen the adult model attacking the Bobo doll never carried out these aggressive acts. This should not be surprising to anyone who has watched children on a playground doing karate chops like Teenage Mutant Ninja Turtles or other characters they have seen on TV and in movies. Furthermore, Bandura found that the children exposed to the adult model were also aggressive to the doll in ways they had not seen, such as shooting it with a toy gun. Bandura concluded that observation of a model may provoke a more generalized response based on the children's cognitive understanding of what was happening. In this case, they saw the adult hit the Bobo doll, but they also understood that the general idea was to be aggressive to the doll.

Bandura's later development of his theory placed greater emphasis on the cognitive, or thinking, aspects of behavior development and specifically on thinking about our own ability to have control in our lives. Over time the name of his theory changed to eliminate *learning*, because this term was connected with the idea of conditioning, which is associated with environmental control of our behavior. Bandura renamed his theory **social cognitive theory** to emphasize that thought has social origins but is then processed through our own individual cognitive interpretations.

Social cognitive theory The theory that individuals learn by observing others and imitating their behavior.

Albert Bandura

Bandura's experiment on modeling. What did this boy and girl learn by watching the adult in the film at the top?

Self-efficacy A belief in our ability to influence our own functioning and life circumstances.

Modern Applications of Social Cognitive Theory

The emphasis in social cognitive theory on the role of cognition in determining motivation to perform a behavior has led to Bandura's more recent research that is focused on **self-efficacy** or "the core belief that one has the power to influence one's own functioning and life circumstances" (Bandura, Caprara, Barbaranelli, Pastorelli, & Regalia, 2001, p. 125). These beliefs play a crucial role in understanding motivation because they are powerful predictors of which goals we will pursue (Pajares, 2005). We tend to pursue tasks at which we believe we can succeed and to avoid ones at which we believe we will fail. The concept of self-efficacy has found wide applications in a variety of situations that involve people's decision to make changes in their lives. Health self-efficacy (the belief that you can make decisions or change behaviors that impact your health and well-being) has been associated with positive lifestyle changes in adolescents who are HIV-positive, patients in cardiac rehabilitation, and adults suffering from osteoporosis (Jones, Renger, & Kang, 2007). Coping self-efficacy has been associated with recovery from posttraumatic stress disorder in victims of natural disasters, military combatants, and victims of sexual or criminal assault (Benight & Bandura, 2004). Perhaps the most important application of the idea of self-efficacy has been in the area of education. Students with a sense of self-efficacy work harder and longer at academic tasks, tackle more difficult tasks, and have a greater sense of optimism that they will succeed (Pajares, 2002; Phan & Ngu, 2016).

CHECK YOUR UNDERSTANDING

1. According to behaviorism, what is the most important influence on human behavior?

2. How are classical and operant conditioning similar and how are they different?

3. What is the basic learning principle of social cognitive theory?

THEORIES OF COGNITIVE DEVELOPMENT

Cognition is a broad term that has to do with processes of the mind, including thinking and learning. In this section, we introduce theories that describe cognitive processes and how they develop. We will examine them further in Chapter 7, where we discuss cognitive development.

Jean Piaget's Cognitive Developmental Theory

Jean Piaget (1896–1980) was a Swiss scientist whose theory has been very influential in the way we think about child development. Like Freud, Piaget was honored by *Time* magazine as one of the 100 most influential people of the 20th century (Papert, 1999). Piaget studied children's thinking through what he called the *clinical method*. He encouraged children to talk freely in response to his interview questions and learned about their thoughts from a detailed analysis of what they said (Piaget, 1955/1973).

Piaget believed we are constantly adapting to our environment by organizing the world in ways we can understand. When we take in new information we try to connect it with what we already know; however, when we cannot connect it we change our understanding in order to accommodate the new information. Take the example of a little boy who goes to the zoo and sees an elephant for the first time. He turns to his mother and says, "Look, it's a big doggy with two tails." This child has the concept of *dog* but not *elephant* so he tries to fit this new experience into one of his existing concepts. He does his best to make sense out of seeing an animal with both a trunk and a tail. Will he always think the elephant is a strange dog? Of course not, because an adult or older child will point out the unique features of elephants, such as their long trunks. The child can now add a new concept, elephant, to what he knows.

Like Freud and Erikson, Piaget believed that children change in qualitative ways from one age period to the next. The stages that he described were based on the way he believed children thought about and understood the world at each age level. In his theory, children are not just less knowledgeable than adults; rather, they think in qualitatively different ways at each developmental stage. Piaget described four stages of cognitive development: sensorimotor, preoperational, concrete operations, and formal operations. We describe these stages when we examine Piaget's theory in more depth in Chapter 7.

Modern Applications of Piaget's Theory

Criticism of Piaget's theory has focused largely on the methodology he used and his conclusions about when children enter each of the stages in his theory, but his greatest contribution to our understanding of cognitive development may lie in his concept of **constructivism** (Newcombe, 2011). Piaget understood that we do not operate like video cameras, taking in what is around us passively and indiscriminately. Instead, he believed that we are active learners, always working to construct our understanding of the world. Piaget saw children as being like "little scientists," always actively experimenting on the world to increase their understanding of it.

Piaget's ideas have had a great impact on educational practices, taking the focus away from rote learning of facts and instead promoting children's active approach to constructing their own learning. Many teachers use Piaget's ideas as the basis for their teaching style (Hinde & Perry, 2007), and research in this area is ongoing. For example, Constance Kamii and her colleagues (Kamii, Rummelsburg, & Kari, 2005) gave low-socioeconomic status, low-achieving students in first grade math-related activities to explore (for example, pick-up sticks and group-based arithmetic games) instead of traditional math assignments (for example, "What is 2 + 2?"). At the end of the year, these students scored higher on tests of mental arithmetic and logical reasoning than did similar students who had received teacher-directed, pencil-and-paper instruction.

Lev Vygotsky's Sociocultural Theory

Lev Semyonovich Vygotsky (1896–1934), a Russian psychologist, had somewhat different ideas about cognitive development. He emphasized the importance of the social world and of culture in promoting cognitive growth, rather than looking at children as independent learners who actively explore the environment on their own (Vygotsky, 1978). According to Vygotsky (1986), learning first takes place in the interaction between people. The individual then internalizes that learning, and it becomes a part of one's own, independent thinking.

Vygotsky believed that looking at what the child is capable of learning in interaction with a skilled helper is a better indicator of his level of cognitive development than just testing what he already knows. He was more interested in what the child could become than in how the child currently functioned (Wertsch, 1985). He believed the teacher must first determine what a child knows, and stay close to what the child already knows when helping the child take the next step. In Vygotsky's concept, adults help the "construction" of the child's understanding by providing guidance and support until they can step back when the child fully understands. For example, if you have a jack-in-the-box and want to play with a 6-month-old baby, you will likely just turn the handle for her and watch her

Accommodating new information. This boy might think this elephant is a big dog the first time he sees it, but he will soon learn it is a new type of animal and will accommodate his thinking to include the category of elephant.

©iStockphoto.com/microgen

Constructivism The idea that humans actively construct their understanding of the world, rather than passively receiving knowledge.

T ☐ F ☐ Children can learn basic math concepts better through games of pick-up sticks and group-based arithmetic games than paper-and-pencil lessons. **True**

reaction. When the child is 2 years old, you might hold her hand on the handle so she can learn to turn it. When she is 3, you might just give her the toy and watch unless she needed some help like a reminder of what to do. Your input is no longer needed. You will learn more about Vygotsky's ideas in Chapter 7.

Modern Applications of Vygotsky's Theory

Like Piaget's theory, Vygotsky's ideas have had a powerful influence in the field of education. One specific educational practice that developed out of Vygotsky's ideas is known as **dynamic assessment**. In this approach, instead of testing what a child knows or can do at one particular time, the instructor asks a question to assess the child's understanding of a concept. When a child answers the question incorrectly, the instructor starts with the most indirect help, such as a suggestion that the child think about whether he has seen a problem like this before. If this help is not enough, the adult will increase the level of direction, potentially ending by giving and explaining the correct answer. Some children will only need the small suggestion, while others need a more direct approach (Poehner, 2007).

Another educational strategy that has grown out of Vygotsky's theoretical ideas is **collaborative learning**. This occurs when a student works with another person or as a part of a group toward a common goal, such as a project or an assignment. The members of the group usually are at different levels of ability or understanding, and through the process of working together they learn from each other. We discuss this and other educational strategies based on Vygotsky's theory in more detail in Chapter 8.

Information Processing

Whereas Piaget and Vygotsky provide more global concepts about cognition and its development, information processing theory breaks down the way we understand and use information into steps, such as acquiring information, storing it, and retrieving it (Robinson-Riegler & Robinson-Riegler, 2008). The earliest approach to information processing described cognition as a series of linear steps: first we pay attention to something, then we process, or think about it, then we store it in memory where we can later retrieve and use it. This has been referred to as the **stores model** and is based on a view of the mind as similar to a computer. However, the more we learn about cognition, the more complex it appears to be.

A more current model is called the **connectionist** or **neural network model**. Rather than representing memory or learning as the transfer of information sequentially from one storage box to another, this newer way of thinking about information processing more closely reflects the way that nerve cells (neurons) in the brain operate through multiple simultaneous connections with other neurons throughout the brain. Using this model, information is processed through concept nodes that are interconnected by links (see Figure 2.6). For example, when we see a white duck, different concept nodes may be activated. One node can represent a specific concept (*white*), one can represent a higher-order concept (*duck*), and one can represent a superordinate concept (*bird*) (Robinson-Riegler & Robinson-Riegler, 2008). The concept nodes are analogous to nerve cells in the brain, and the links are connections between individual neurons. When information is stored in memory, it becomes a new node that is connected to other nodes in the network. Although each node is connected in some way to other pieces of information in our memory, the strength of these connections can vary, and learning involves changing the strength of these connections. When input comes into the system (for example, the sight of a bird in flight), certain nodes are activated. If the links between those nodes are strong enough, the output is a concept (in this case, *bird*).

Information processing theory examines different aspects of cognitive development in detail. Unlike Piaget, who saw qualitative changes occurring in the way children think

Dynamic assessment
A testing procedure that uses a test-intervene-test procedure to assess the examinee's potential to change.

Collaborative learning
An educational strategy that allows groups of students who are at different ability levels to work together on a common goal.

Stores model The idea that information is processed through a series of mental locations (sensory to short-term to long-term memory "stores").

Connectionist or **neural network model** In this model of memory, the process is envisioned as a neural network that consists of concept nodes that are interconnected by links.

FIGURE 2.6

Neural network model of memory. Neural networks are a newer way of thinking about information processing. Concepts are made up of information (or *nodes*) and the links that connect that information to represent a concept. The width of the links in this figure represents the strength of each connection. For instance, the concept of obesity has a strong connection with ideas about the cause of the condition, but a weaker connection to ideas about the cost of the problem to society.

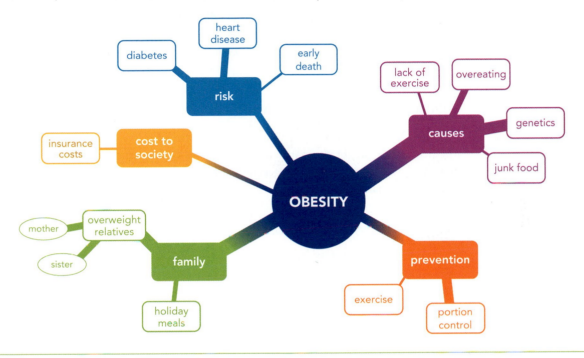

as they move from one stage to another, information processing looks at the gradual development of cognitive processes. For example, we know that children remember more the older they get, but what changes occur in the way they think to allow this to happen? In Chapter 7 you will read about recent research that examines development of attention, memory, and other processes through which we make sense of our world. You will also find related topics throughout the book. For example, the topic of social cognition, or how thinking is applied to social situations, appears in Chapter 12 where we discuss social development.

Modern Applications of Information Processing

Information processing theory has led to an enormous amount of research on growth and changes in cognitive processes during childhood and adolescence. One new development in the study of cognitive development is the ability to link cognitive processes with brain changes through the use of functional and structural imaging technologies. Current technologies allow researchers to link specific cognitive processes with changes in both the structure and the function of the brain and nervous system. This area of study, known as **developmental cognitive neuroscience,** allows us to understand how the developing brain both promotes and limits certain cognitive abilities. For example, the ability to think in an abstract way, rather than dealing only with the concrete world around us, develops throughout adolescence. Brain imaging studies have shown changes during adolescence in the activation of parts of the brain that deal with aspects of abstract thought (Dumontheil, 2014). Such studies support the idea that the immaturity of the adolescent brain limits cognitive abilities. Therefore, teachers, judges, and others should not expect teens to operate at the same level

Developmental cognitive neuroscience The study of the relation between cognitive development and the development of the brain.

as adults. You will learn more about brain development and its relation to cognitive development in Chapters 6 and 7.

CHECK YOUR UNDERSTANDING

1. According to Piaget, how do children construct their knowledge of the world?
2. How does dynamic assessment of children's abilities differ from traditional types of assessment?
3. How do the stores model and the connectionist model of information processing differ?

EVOLUTIONARY THEORIES

Charles Darwin's theory of evolution is based on the idea that living things that adapt to their environment, not necessarily the ones that are the biggest or strongest, are more likely to pass on their genes to the next generation. His focus was primarily on physical characteristics, but his basic idea that human behavior that has adaptive value will persist is central to the theories of ethology and sociobiology.

Ethology

Konrad Lorenz (1903–1989) is considered the father of modern **ethology,** which is the study of the adaptive value of animal and human behavior in the natural environment (Tinbergen, 1963). As a zoologist studying animal behavior in Munich, Germany, Lorenz found that ducks and geese would *immediately* follow their mothers after they were born. This automatic behavior, called **imprinting,** is adaptive because the mother provides her offspring with food and protection from predators. If a newborn animal didn't do this, it would be unlikely the animal would survive to pass along its genes to the next generation. Some researchers attempted to apply the idea of imprinting to human behavior by claiming that infants must have skin-to-skin contact with their mother within the first few hours after birth for bonding, or love, to develop. Like many direct applications of animal behavior to humans, this has turned out not to be the case. Although animal behavior can give us some ideas about human behavior, the direct application of one to the other is usually too simplistic. Although there is no evidence for the concept of bonding in human beings, ethological principles contributed to our understanding of the slower, less automatic development of attachment between infant and mother during the first year of life. You will learn more about attachment in Chapter 10. For an example of animal behavior that does correspond more clearly to human behavior, see **Active Learning: Rough-and-Tumble Play.**

T ☐ F ☐ Darwin's concept of the "survival of the fittest" means that the strongest animal is most likely to survive. **False**

T ☐ F ☐ Infants must have skin-to-skin contact with their mother within the first few hours after birth for *bonding,* or love, to develop. **False**

TRUE/FALSE VIDEO ▲

Konrad Lorenz and imprinting. Konrad Lorenz observed the behavior of geese (left) and demonstrated the presence of imprinting by removing the mother goose immediately after the babies were born and substituting himself. The goslings then followed him as if he was their mother (right).

Active LEARNING

Rough-and-Tumble Play

One example of a similarity between animal behavior and human behavior is the existence of rough-and-tumble play, which appears in many species. Rough-and-tumble (R&T) play consists of "vigorous behaviours such as wrestling, grappling, kicking and tumbling that would appear to be aggressive except for the playful context" (Pellegrini & Smith, 1998, p. 579). It is not the same as real aggression because all parties know that the goal is not to hurt anyone. Children often laugh while engaging in R&T play. Children, especially boys, all around the world take part in this type of play (Smith, 2010). If you were an ethologist, how would you explain this behavior? Think about what adaptive value the behavior might have for the participants either at the time that it happens or in the future. Remember your own experiences with rough-and-tumble play to add your own thoughts and feelings to your understanding of the behavior.

Rough-and-tumble play. How would an ethologist explain the presence of rough-and-tumble play in many species and in human societies around the world? How do we know this is play and not real fighting?

Answer: There have been several ethologically based explanations for rough-and-tumble play. One explanation is that it is practice for later aggressive and defensive behavior in adulthood, because this type of activity develops muscles and endurance (Pellegrini, 1987). Another possible explanation, found more with adolescents than younger children, is that R&T play is used to establish dominance (Fry, 2005; Pellegrini, 2003). Just as chickens develop a "pecking order," teens can use R&T play to find out who is stronger and more skilled without needing to have a real fight.

Sociobiology

In 1975, biologist Edward O. Wilson introduced the field of **sociobiology**, which examines the role that principles of evolution play in the development of social behavior and culture. One example of what sociobiologists study is the impact of kinship on relationships. According to sociobiology, people are more likely to protect, help, and give to relatives than to other people because they share some of their genes with biological family members, and therefore they have a stake in making sure family members survive to pass on the genes they share (Pollet, 2007).

Modern Applications of Evolutionary Theory

Evolutionary approaches such as ethology and sociobiology have contributed to a newer approach known as *evolutionary developmental psychology* which applies the principles and

Ethology The study of the adaptive value of animal and human behavior in the natural environment.

Imprinting In ethology, the automatic process by which animals attach to their mothers.

Sociobiology The application of principles of evolution to the development of social behavior and culture.

ideas of evolutionary theory specifically to questions of how and why children develop as they do (Blasi & Bjorklund, 2003; Causey, Gardiner, & Bjorklund, 2008). Ideas taken from evolutionary theory have influenced research on several important topics in the field of child development, including aggression, altruism, attachment, and social dominance hierarchies. Explanations from evolutionary theory help us understand how each of these behaviors helps us adapt to our environment. Children's behavior is seen as an adaptation to the environment in two ways: (1) What children do is adaptive because it is a preparation for adult life, and (2) what children do is adaptive at their own stage of development and in their specific life circumstances.

One example of research based on an evolutionary developmental approach has focused on the onset of puberty in girls. The timing of when girls enter puberty is affected by many factors but is largely controlled by their genes. However, research has shown that girls enter puberty at earlier ages when their parents have a high level of conflict with little support or satisfaction in their marriage, when their father is absent or severely dysfunctional, or when they have an insecure relationship with their mother at age 15 months (Belsky, Houts, & Fearon, 2010; Saxbe & Repetti, 2009; Tither & Ellis, 2008). Evolutionary developmental psychologists point to the idea that a girl with a dysfunctional childhood may not be able to count on reaching adulthood successfully; therefore, early puberty is an adaptation to her environment that may ensure that she will be able to pass on her genes by enabling her to get pregnant earlier in life.

CHECK YOUR UNDERSTANDING

1. What role does adaptation play in the theory of evolution?
2. How do the processes of animal imprinting and human attachment differ?
3. According to sociobiology, why are you more likely to help a family member than a stranger?

ECOLOGICAL THEORY

Cornell University

Urie Bronfenbrenner. Urie Bronfenbrenner developed ecological theory to explain the importance of the context in which children develop.

T ☐ F ☐ The best way to study children is through carefully controlled experiments in a laboratory setting. **False**

We tend to think of the study of ecology as focusing on plants and animals and their relationships to the environment, but in the 1970s, Urie Bronfenbrenner (1917–2005) applied the idea of the interaction of organisms with their environment to the field of developmental psychology to create a theory of human ecology. Using this framework, he defined development as a function of the "interaction between the developing organism and the enduring environments or contexts in which it lives out its life" (Bronfenbrenner, 1975, p. 439). Bronfenbrenner believed that you cannot understand the life course of an individual without understanding how that person interacts with all the different facets of his environment. He also believed that this is a dynamic process. All aspects of the environment affect the individual, and the individual affects all aspects of his environment.

Bronfenbrenner emphasized the importance of understanding the individual, not on her own or with one or two other people, but rather within all of these contexts. His theory is, in part, a criticism of some of the techniques of experimental psychology, in which children are tested in the laboratory with an experimenter and perhaps a parent, and the results are then assumed to reflect how the child would act in a natural setting. He developed the concept of *ecological validity,* the idea that research findings should be able to generalize to real-world settings. For example, a laboratory may be an excellent place to look at reactions in a well-controlled experimental setting, but it is not necessarily a good way to look at the everyday interactions of parent and child (Bronfenbrenner, 1977).

Bronfenbrenner (1977, 1986) proposed that individuals grow and develop within a nested set of influences that he divided into five systems—the microsystem, mesosystem, exosystem, macrosystem, and chronosystem—as shown in Figure 2.7 on page 55. These systems are embedded one within the other, each influencing the other in a back-and-forth fashion. The relationship between the systems also changes over time as the child grows and develops.

The **microsystem** includes the face-to-face interactions that a person has in her immediate settings, such as home, school, or friendship groups. The interaction between a mother and a child forms a microsystem, as does the interaction between a child and a peer, or between a pair of siblings. The **mesosystem** brings together two settings that contain the child. For example, when parents meet and talk to a child's teacher, the home setting interacts with the school setting and this interaction influences her progress at school. The **exosystem** consists of settings that the child never enters (that is, ones that are *external* to the child) but that affect the child's development nevertheless. For example, even if the child never goes to a parent's workplace, what happens in that setting can have an effect on the child. A job that is so demanding that it leaves a parent exhausted at the end of the day affects how the parents will interact with their children when they come home. The **macrosystem** consists of cultural norms that underlie the institutions and activities that make up someone's everyday life. For example, the macrosystem in the United States includes the ideology of democracy, as well as the value that is placed on individual achievement. The **chronosystem** consists of the events that take place at different times in a child's life, as well as the time in history in which the child lives. For example, parental divorce affects a 2-year-old child much differently than a teenager. Also, the current experience of parental divorce, when it has become more common, is different than it would have been in 1940 when it was a relatively rare occurrence (Bronfenbrenner, 1986).

It will be easier for you to remember the various systems that make up ecological theory if you are able to recognize examples of each of them. **Active Learning: Examples of Ecological Systems** gives you a chance to do this.

Microsystem In ecological theory, the face-to-face interaction of the person in her immediate settings, such as home, school, or friendship groups.

Mesosystem The interaction among the various settings in the microsystem, such as a child's school and home.

Exosystem Settings that the child never enters but that affect the child's development nevertheless, such as the parents' place of work.

Macrosystem Cultural norms that guide the nature of the organizations and places that make up one's everyday life.

Chronosystem In ecological systems theory, the dimension of time, including one's age and the time in history in which one lives.

Active LEARNING

Examples of Ecological Systems

Match each description below with the correct level of the ecological system that it represents. The levels are the microsystem, mesosystem, macrosystem, exosystem, and chronosystem.

Example	System Level
1. The number of mothers with children under the age of 5 who were employed outside the home doubled between 1970 and 1990.	
2. A child's parents go to school for a parent–teacher conference so they can find out how their child is doing.	
3. Native American parents raise their children to avoid interpersonal conflicts and to cooperate with others to work for the greater good.	
4. The child's preschool teacher shows the child how to stack two blocks on each other.	

(Continued)

(Continued)

Example	System Level
5. New parents in Germany are entitled to 47 weeks of paid parental leave after the birth of their baby.	
6. A parent gets a promotion and a big raise, but that also means that he will need to work longer hours.	
7. Parents invite a teen's group of friends to their house to watch some movies.	
8. Fathers today take a more active role in parenting than fathers did in the past.	
9. A teenager and his best friend make plans for how they will spend time together on the weekend.	
10. A new mother spends some time with her friends, who tell her that she is too worried about caring for her baby and she should just relax and enjoy being a mother.	

Answers: (1) chronosystem, (2) mesosystem, (3) macrosystem, (4) microsystem, (5) macrosystem, (6) exosystem, (7) mesosystem, (8) chronosystem, (9) microsystem, (10) exosystem

Modern Applications of Ecological Theory

Ecological theory has expanded the range and number of characteristics that researchers include to more fully understand a child's development within the context of many different aspects of life. For example, Brophy-Herb, Lee, Nievar, and Stollak (2007) used ecological theory as a basis for understanding the development of social competence in preschoolers. Instead of looking at single factors like socioeconomic status or family stress as predictors of children's social competence, they examined an intersecting and nested array of factors that they believed would have an influence on social competence. These included individual characteristics of the child (age, sex, and level of stress); family characteristics (whether the parents were married or divorced, level of stress, and socioeconomic status); teacher behavior (classroom teaching style); and classroom climate (warmth, organization, and number of children with behavior problems). One of the findings illustrates the complexity of the research done with an ecological approach. Although they found that children with more stress in their lives were rated as having lower social competence, the nature of the child's classroom modified this relationship. A child experiencing high stress was more likely to have lower social competence in a classroom in which many children had behavioral problems than a stressed child in a classroom where few other children had behavior problems.

Another legacy of human ecology is the application of theory to social policy. A human ecologist believes that all levels of society affect human development. The logical extension of this belief is to become involved in the creation of social policy, including legislation and programs at all levels of government. Bronfenbrenner himself was active in the creation of Head Start, a program that was designed to help disadvantaged children by providing interventions at several different levels. Head Start not only provides an excellent educational program for children but also helps their families by providing help with financial, social, educational, and psychological difficulties they might be experiencing. It also works hard to create links between the classroom setting and the child's home.

FIGURE 2.7

Bronfenbrenner's ecological systems model. Think of the various systems in the ecological systems model as a set of nested environments, but with interactions both within a level and across levels. All of these interconnected systems change as a function of time, as represented by the chronosystem.

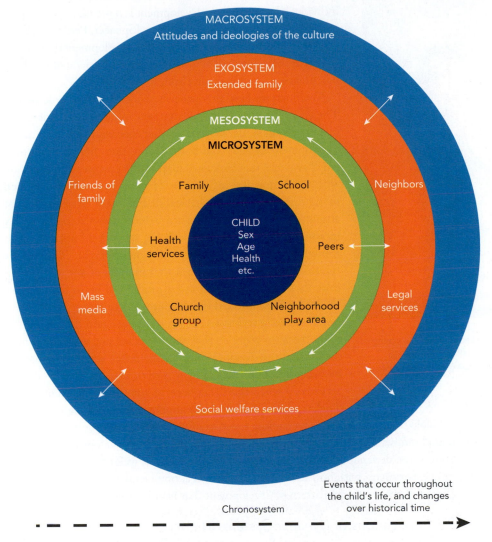

SOURCE: Kopp & Krakow, 1982. Reprinted with permission of the publisher.

1. Why is it important to understand children within the context of the world around them?

2. What are the five systems that make up Bronfenbrenner's ecological system?

3. Why does ecological theory play an important role in shaping social policy?

DYNAMIC SYSTEMS THEORY

In the past 30 years, the study of children's development has become increasingly sophisticated. Esther Thelen (1941–2004) introduced the idea that development is a complex process that involves the dynamic interaction of a multitude of systems, including individual biology, environmental influences, the way we control ourselves and interact with others, and how we think about, or represent, our experiences in our minds (Sameroff, 2010). Within an

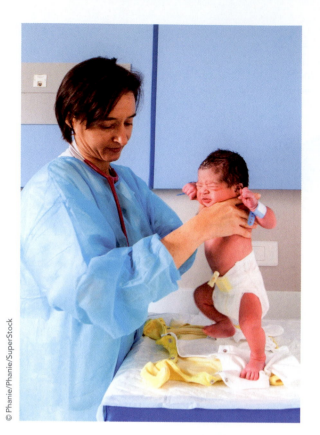

© Phanie/Phanie/SuperStock

The stepping reflex. The stepping reflex is present in young infants. If you support their weight and allow their feet to touch a flat surface, they will raise and lower their legs as though they are walking.

Dynamic systems theory
The theory that all aspects of development interact and affect each other in a dynamic process over time.

individual, any one system, such as the visual perception system, interacts with other systems, such as the motor system, to respond to experiences in the environment. **Dynamic systems theory** states that all these different aspects of development interact and affect each other over time in unique ways for each individual. In this theory, development is more like a jazz improvisation than a written piece of music (Spencer, Perone, & Buss, 2011). As the child seeks solutions for developmental problems that arise, each element adjusts to every other element resulting in a unique pattern for each child.

To illustrate how this process works, we can look at how Thelen applied the theory of dynamic systems to the development of motor skills. Whereas earlier theories had linked motor development to body and brain maturation, her research provided evidence that biological maturation operates in interaction with environmental influences (Spencer et al., 2006). Thelen found that the nature of physical development was flexible, not absolute. For example, newborn babies have a stepping reflex in which they appear to be walking when held upright, even though they cannot support their own weight. This reflex typically disappears at about 2 to 3 months of age, and it was initially thought that this was a product of brain maturation. However, Thelen found that babies who seem to have lost their initial stepping reflex will begin stepping again if placed up to their chests in water so that their legs are not so heavy, which means that the disappearance of this reflex is not driven solely by brain development (Thelen, 1989). Infants stop "stepping" reflexively when their legs become too heavy for them to lift. Thelen posited that the development of real walking is not just a matter of biological maturation but a coming together of many different experiences, bodily growth, and motivation. She showed that each infant explores and develops these abilities in different ways, depending on such individual characteristics as weight and activity level. Each child experiments with how to do things, and each action he takes influences what the next action will be, creating a pattern of development that is unique to that person.

Modern Applications of Dynamic Systems Theory

Dynamic systems theory was first applied to physical development, where it became a framework for interventions with children who have motor challenges, such as cerebral palsy. These challenges had previously been seen primarily as issues that involved the maturation of the nervous system, and the goal of therapy was to replace abnormal muscle tone and posture with normal posture (Darrah, Law, & Pollock, 2001). Therapists now recognize that children with motor dysfunction may discover solutions on their own for their challenges. Dynamic systems theory has led therapists to consider characteristics of the child, including the nervous system, the musculoskeletal system, and the child's motivation or readiness, the environment, and the nature of the task itself when planning an intervention (Perry, 1998; Sauve & Bartlett, 2010).

In recent years, dynamic systems theory has been used to promote the understanding of many different aspects of child development, including cognitive development. This theory helps us to understand that influences between systems do not go in just one direction. The brain affects the body, but the body also affects the brain in an ongoing dialogue that continues over time (Spencer, Austin, & Schutte, 2012). For example, adults were shown one of the following photos of a pitcher and asked to press a button to answer the question "Is this a pitcher?" They responded more quickly when the button for the "yes" response was on the same side of their body as the handle for the pitcher (Thelen & Smith, 2006). People recognize an object more quickly when the response they make is compatible with their action on the object (picking up the pitcher). Action and visual perception are thus connected and influence one another. Dynamic systems theory continues to show surprising interactions among the many aspects of human functioning and human experience.

©iStockphoto.com/jurisam
Can Stock Photo Inc./Arcady

CHECK YOUR UNDERSTANDING

1. How is human development similar to a jazz improvisation?
2. How does dynamic systems theory show that motor activity influences the activity of the brain?

OVERVIEW AND HISTORICAL CONTEXT OF THEORIES

You can review the developmental theories described in this chapter using Table 2.2. To have a broader historical understanding of how some of these theories developed, read **Journey of Research: Theories in Historical and Cultural Context.**

TABLE 2.2

Developmental theories. Briefly review the theories that have been described in this chapter along with the descriptions of how change happens. As you recall from Chapter 1, change can be quantitative, also called continuous, or it can be qualitative, also called stagelike. Then look at each theory's idea of why change happens. Is it due to biology, the environment, or a combination of these?

Theory	Quantitative or qualitative change	Biology and/or environment
Psychoanalytic Theory	Qualitative: Freud has 5 stages Erikson has 8 stages	Biology drives development and is affected by environmental experiences.
Behaviorism	Quantitative	Environment drives development.
Piaget's Cognitive Theory	Qualitative: Piaget has 4 stages	Biology drives development, and the environment shapes it.
Vygotsky's Cognitive Theory	Quantitative	Environment, in the form of culture and social influence, drives development.
Information Processing	Quantitative	Biology and environment interact.
Evolutionary Theories	N/A	Biology underlies adaptation to the environment.
Ecological Theory	Quantitative	A nesting of environmental influences is also affected by a child's biology.
Dynamic Systems Theory	Quantitative	Biological growth interacts with environmental experiences.

JOURNEY OF *Research*

Theories in Historical and Cultural Context

What follows is not a complete review of the history of developmental theories, but it illustrates well the ways in which historical and social contexts influence the nature of theories. Each of these theories continues to influence our study of child and adolescent development to this day, although they are not equally influential.

Freud's psychoanalytic theory. Some aspects of Freud's theory may seem quaint or even a bit strange to us today because they are based on beliefs about human sexuality that reflect the culture at the time in which Freud lived—the Victorian era in Germany during the late 19th century. This was a time in history when sexuality was treated as something private or even shameful. Sex was seen as a necessary evil for procreation within a marriage, and sex for pleasure was frowned upon (Goodwin, 2005).

In this context, Freud interpreted the mental disorders that he was seeing in his patients as the product of some sexual trauma—real or imagined—in their early experiences. He reasoned that if you cannot accept sexual feelings or thoughts, they will be pushed down into the unconscious, only to resurface from time to time in ways that disrupt your functioning (Goodwin, 2005). While this explanation may have made sense in the context of the Victorian era, it may have less relevance in cultures where sexual impulses are seen as a normal expression of our humanity.

John B. Watson and behaviorism. Behaviorism came to prominence in America in the early part of the 20th century, at a time when psychology was moving away from Freud's focus on what was going on inside a person's mind (either the conscious or the unconscious part of it) and toward a focus on what was observable—the person's behavior (Crain, 2005; Goodwin, 2005). In 1913, Watson published an article titled "Psychology as the Behaviorist Views It" in which he described psychology as a "purely objective experimental branch of natural science" (Watson, 1994, p. 248) with a goal of predicting and controlling behavior. His research with Little Albert reflected these goals.

Watson also was influenced by the work of a contemporary Russian physiologist, Ivan Pavlov, and came to believe that all one needed to do to understand development was to understand the stimulus-response relations that controlled it (Lerner, 2002). In his 1928 book, *Psychological Care of Infant and Child*, Watson applied behaviorist learning principles to child rearing. For instance, he warned parents that being too affectionate toward their children would make the children irresponsible, dependent, and unsuccessful in later life. The book was quick to find an audience because, at this point in history, parents wanted to benefit from this new, more scientific approach to understanding behavior.

Although behaviorist psychology dominated American psychology until the middle of the 20th century, it was not widely influential in Europe, where ideas from cognitive theorists such as Piaget and Vygotsky shaped scientific thinking about child development (Goodwin, 2005).

Jean Piaget and cognitive developmental theory. Today Jean Piaget is recognized as one of the most influential theorists in the field of development. However, he lived and worked in Europe and when his work was first published in the 1920s and 1930s, it received a cool reception in America (Whitman, 1980). While American psychology was moving in a more rigorous scientific direction, Piaget was conducting research using open-ended clinical interviews with children. In the middle of an interview, he might suddenly change the questions he was asking to pursue something that the child had said that caught his interest

(Piaget, 1969). He also spent a great deal of time observing the spontaneous behavior of children, including his own three children. His research did not contain statistics to back up his conclusions and he used abstract concepts as explanations (Lerner, 2002). By the 1960s, however, a reaction was developing to strict behaviorist approaches and their reduction of human behavior to a set of stimulus-response connections. American psychologists had become more open to new ideas like *humanistic psychology,* which emphasizes a person's conscious ability to make choices, and *ecological psychology,* which examines behavior within multiple contexts. In this new climate, Piaget's ideas were now embraced for the richness with which they described children's ways of understanding their world.

Urie Bronfenbrenner and ecological systems theory. Another reflection of the growing dissatisfaction with the direction in which psychology was going came from Urie Bronfenbrenner in an article written in 1977 for the journal *American Psychologist.* In it, Bronfenbrenner criticized what he saw as a narrow focus on collecting data for data's sake and a reliance on experimental designs that were so carefully controlled that they resulted in highly artificial situations that had little resemblance to the real life of children. His concern was captured in his statement that "it can be said that much of contemporary developmental psychology is the science of the strange behavior of children in strange situations with strange adults for the briefest possible periods of time" (Bronfenbrenner, 1977, p. 513). Rather than seeing the environment as something that needs to be controlled, Bronfenbrenner believed that we must study behavior as it occurs embedded within a nest of environments and settings because each of these has its own impact on the process.

The 1960s and 1970s were a time of great change in American society, and part of this change was a new appreciation of the pluralism and diversity of people's experiences. Bronfenbrenner's ecological systems theory used a more holistic approach to draw attention to the immediate, as well as the distant, influences on development (Lerner, 2002). The challenge for researchers today is to find ways to study the incredible complexity of multiple, interacting influences on development. The result of doing this, however, is a richer, more complete understanding of the process of human development.

If you stop and think for a moment about how the world you live in today influences the way you think about children and how they develop, you will realize that our culture and our experiences so color our worldview that we might not even be aware of those influences unless we make a conscious effort to think about them. In the next section, you will see how the technological advances that have marked the beginning of the 21st century have influenced our current ideas about child development.

THE IMPACT OF BIOLOGY AND CULTURE ON CHILD DEVELOPMENT THEORY AND RESEARCH

We have described many of the major theories that drive research on children's development. In this section, we describe two major factors that are not theories, but still play a very large role in the type of research carried out in the field of child development. All aspects of development interact with our basic biology, including our brain and its development and our genes. We first describe the impact that new technological advances have had on our understanding of the role of biology in development. The second factor is the major role that culture plays in determining the goals and practices that bring about specific outcomes for children around the world.

NEUROPSYCHOLOGY AND BEHAVIORAL GENETICS

2.3 What are neuropsychology and behavioral genetics?

Neuropsychology
The study of the interaction of the brain and behavior.

Behavioral genetics Research to determine the degree of genetic basis for a behavior, a trait, or an ability.

Neuropsychology, the study of the interaction of the brain and behavior, and **behavioral genetics,** the study of the interaction of genes and behavior, are on the cutting edge of research in the field of child development. Using new brain imaging technology and research methods, researchers are able to see the structure and functioning of our brains as they never have before, and whole genome sequencing can be used to identify specific genes. These new capabilities have produced an avalanche of research that connects the brain and specific genes with different aspects of children's development. The earliest approaches to studying both genes and the brain assumed that biology determined behavior. However, the more we learn about the functioning of both the brain and genes, the clearer it becomes that the effects go in both directions. Biology has an impact on behavior, but the environment also affects our biological functioning. The brain's development, to some extent, depends on an individual's experiences. The development of connections between nerve cells, the coating of the nervous system, and the neurochemistry of the brain are all shaped in part by what a person does. For example, when you intensely study a foreign language, you increase the amount of grey matter in your brain. It appears that the cognitive control you use to switch from one language to another is reflected in changes in particular parts of the brain (Li, Legault, & Litcofsky, 2014). Likewise, environmental events also affect the expression of genes. For example, research has shown that when children experience child abuse the expression of certain genes can be changed. These changes may account for the higher reactivity of these individuals to stress later in their lives (Essex et al., 2013; Lester et al., 2011). You will learn more about the interaction of genes and behavior in Chapter 4, and more about neuropsychology in Chapter 6. Examples of these topics appear throughout this book.

CHECK YOUR UNDERSTANDING

1. How has new technology changed research in the fields of neuropsychology and behavioral genetics?

2. How do children's life experiences affect the development of their brain?

T ☐ F ☐ A good theory should be universal, applying to children in all situations. **False**

DEVELOPMENTAL THEORY IN A CULTURAL CONTEXT

2.4 How does culture influence theories of child development?

Developmental theories reflect cultural values. Sub-Saharan African theories of child development emphasize children's connection to their community rather than the more individualistic approach of most Western theories.

iStock/Bartosz Hadyniak

Although some of the theories we have described take cultural differences into account, all were developed by European or American theorists and most are based on research with Western, middle-class families (Kärtner, 2015). If we assume all societies must conform to Western values, we forget that different ideas and behaviors may be more adaptive for children growing up in different contexts and environments. To understand the diversity of development, we must take into account the indigenous theories, or ethnotheories, of child development that guide the way children are raised in a variety of cultures.

Many of the theories we've described in this chapter focus on the development of the individual. However, as we said in Chapter 1, a focus on individual identity as well as individual needs and achievements is largely a Western value. Developmental theory in many non-Western cultures focuses instead on the role of the individual in the context of the social group. For example, Nsamenang and Lo-oh (2010) explain that in sub-Saharan Africa, the overarching theory of development "positions the child not in his or her sovereignty but as socially integrated in a human community" (p. 386). This means that children are seen primarily as participants in their cultural communities, rather than as autonomous individuals. To illustrate, compare

Erik Erikson's stages described earlier in this chapter to the following stages of development described by Nsamenang (2015) for African culture: the neonatal period, social priming, social apprenticeship, social entrée, social internment, adulthood, old age/death, and ancestral and spiritual selfhoods. Social priming might compare to Erikson's stage of autonomy versus shame and doubt, and social apprenticeship might compare to Erikson's stage of identity versus role confusion. In African culture, the issues focus on how the child moves into competence in the social world, while Erikson's stages focus on the goal of individual identity for the child.

Even within Western cultures, goals can differ. In a study of seven Western countries, parents from all the countries included "sociable," "loving," "active," and "strong-willed" in their description of their child. However, U.S. parents also included "intelligent" and "independent," while Italian parents were more likely to describe their child as "even-tempered" and "simpatico," indicating more social and emotional competence (Harkness, Johnston Mavridis, Ji Liu, & Super, 2015). As we described in Chapter 1, these cultural values are transmitted from parent to child from birth through adolescence.

Theories are shaped by the culture in which they exist. We've described a number of theories that relate to cognitive development. Intelligence and cognitive development are seen as valuable in their own right in Western cultures. However, in many African cultures, responsibility is a higher goal, and intelligence is interpreted within the context of an individual's ability to carry out responsibilities in the household. The focus of African theories would likely be quite different from those developed in Western countries.

CHECK YOUR UNDERSTANDING

1. How does culture play a role in theories of child development?
2. How do a culture's values shape the conceptualization of the stages children go through?

CONCLUSION

Studying these theories should help you understand the source of most of the rest of the ideas presented in this book. By exploring the big questions of why and how we develop from childhood through adolescence, we gain a deeper understanding of our observations and interactions. Although you might be tempted to say "I agree" or "I don't agree" with any particular theory, it is important to base your opinions on reasoned arguments that can be tested. Whether you accept one theory or another should ultimately depend on the evidence that supports or refutes each one. In the next chapter, we examine how psychologists carry out research to help us move toward a better understanding of human development.

CHAPTER SUMMARY

Test your understanding of the content.
Take the practice quiz at **edge.sagepub.com/levine3e**

2.1 What do child development theories tell us?

Theories of development give us a model that allows us to predict how children will behave. Some theories propose that development occurs in stages, while others see development as a continuous process. Theories also differ in their emphasis on biological, environmental, and personal mechanisms that bring about growth and development.

2.2 What are the hypotheses and modern applications of the major child development theories?

a. Psychoanalytic theories. In Freud's **psychoanalytic theory**, sexual drive shifts from one area of the body to another as the child develops, forming the basis for five **psychosexual stages**. Erik Erikson believed the social world and the development of identity were driving forces for development through eight

psychosocial stages. Freud's theory has application in understanding and treating mental and emotional disorders. Erikson's theory has helped us understand the influence of social experiences on development.

b. Behaviorism. The theory of **behaviorism** states that the environment determines development. In **classical conditioning** an unconditioned stimulus is paired with a neutral stimulus. After repeated pairings, the neutral stimulus elicits a conditioned response. In **operant conditioning** something that follows a behavior affects the likelihood of that behavior happening again. **Reinforcement** increases the behavior, while **punishment** and **extinction** decrease it. Classical conditioning has been used in the treatment of phobias. Operant conditioning has been used for classroom management and in **applied behavior analysis.**

c. Social cognitive theory. Bandura's **social cognitive theory** emphasizes the importance of imitation as a learning process. It has been applied in the study of **self-efficacy.**

d. Theories of cognitive development. Piaget's theory of cognitive development states that we are always trying to organize our understanding of the world by fitting new information into our current understanding, or accommodating new information by changing our concepts to fit that information. The idea that children actively construct their understanding of the world has significantly influenced the field of education. Vygotsky emphasized the role of social interaction and believed adults or more skilled peers build children's knowledge through interaction. His theory has been applied through the use of **dynamic assessment** and **collaborative learning** in educational settings. Two models of the theory of information processing are the **stores model** that likens the mind to a computer and portrays mental processing as a linear progression of steps, and the **connectionist** or **neural network model** that describes mental processing as a network of concept nodes that are interconnected by links similar to the connections between neurons in the brain. These models have helped us understand cognitive processes and are helping us learn about the structure and function of the brain.

e. Evolutionary theories. **Ethology** is the study of animal and human behavior in relationship to their adaptation to the natural environment. **Sociobiology** examines the role that genes play in influencing human social behavior that evolved to promote adaptation to the environment. Evolutionary theories help us understand how our behaviors help us to adapt to our environment.

f. Ecological theory. Bronfenbrenner proposed that individuals grow and develop within a nested set of influences that he divided into five systems: **microsystem, mesosystem, exosystem, macrosystem,** and **chronosystem.** His theory has been applied in research that considers multilevels of influence on behavior and development, and in developing effective social policy.

g. Dynamic systems theory. **Dynamic systems theory** examines the way all aspects of development— biological, cognitive, and social-emotional — influence one another. It has found application in interventions for motor development problems.

2.3 **What are neuropsychology and behavioral genetics?**

Neuropsychology is the study of the brain and behavior. **Behavioral genetics** is the study of genes and behavior. Both the brain and genes are influenced and shaped by an individual's experiences.

2.4 **How does culture influence theories of child development?**

All cultures have their own theories about how children develop. To understand what is most adaptive within a particular context and environment, we must always keep in mind the realities of children's lives in different settings.

KEY TERMS

Strengthen your understanding of these key terms with mobile-friendly eFlashcards at **edge.sagepub.com/levine3e**

Give your students the SAGE edge!

SAGE edge offers a robust online environment featuring an impressive array of free tools and resources for review, study, and further exploration, keeping both instructors and students on the cutting edge of teaching and learning. Learn more at **edge.sagepub.com/levine3e**

chapter 3 | HOW WE STUDY DEVELOPMENT

LEARNING QUESTIONS

3.1 What is the scientific method and how is it used to study development?

3.2 What are the different types of research designs used to study development?

3.3 What must we consider when interpreting and communicating the results of a study?

3.4 What special precautions must be used when our research participants are children?

Master these objectives using an online action plan at **edge.sagepub.com/levine3e**

TEST YOUR KNOWLEDGE

Test your knowledge of child development by deciding whether each of the following statements is *true* or *false*, and then check your answers as you read the chapter.

1. **T ☐ F ☐:** We know that watching television causes children to have shorter attention spans because many teachers report that this is what they see in the children in their classrooms.

2. **T ☐ F ☐:** If we conduct research by interviewing students in a large high school, we can assume that our findings will apply to any adolescent who is the same age as the ones we have studied.

3. **T ☐ F ☐:** When conducting research by doing an observation, it is important that the person who is doing the observation does not know the purpose of the research.

4. **T ☐ F ☐:** If observations are carefully done, you will be able to determine the causes of the behavior you are observing.

5. **T ☐ F ☐:** Children's memories are good enough to allow them to give reliable eyewitness testimony.

6. **T ☐ F ☐:** Studying a single individual intensively is a valid scientific methodology.

7. **T ☐ F ☐:** An experiment always consists of a situation set up by researchers to test specific hypotheses.

8. **T ☐ F ☐:** Even if research consistently finds that mothers who talk to their children a great deal have children with high self-esteem, we should not conclude that frequent conversations with parents build self-esteem in children.

9. **T ☐ F ☐:** Research has found that boys who watch a lot of violence on TV are more aggressive, but you know someone who watches a lot of violence and you see that he is not at all aggressive. This disproves the research.

10. **T ☐ F ☐:** Once we have established that the results of our research are statistically significant, we can be confident they will have an impact on real-world situations.

Correct answers: (1) F, (2) F, (3) T, (4) F, (5) T, (6) T, (7) F, (8) T, (9) F, (10) F

▲ **VIDEO: Watch as students answer some of these questions and the authors respond.**

I n this chapter, we look at how researchers study children and adolescents to add to our understanding of growth and development. As we said in Chapter 2, we all have some intuitive beliefs about development, often based on our own life experiences, but theories must be subjected to rigorous scientific testing to determine whether or not they are valid. This can be done in a number of ways, which means that there isn't one best way to study development. Rather, we look for the most appropriate method to investigate the particular topic we want to examine.

We take you through the steps of the scientific method: developing a hypothesis, choosing who to study, and figuring out how to measure the concepts you want to explore. For each step you will find an **Active Learning** feature that allows you to apply what you are learning and check your understanding of the concepts as they are presented. After we have taken you through the scientific research process, we discuss how to make sense of the results of a research project and then describe the important process of communicating results to a wider audience so that they become part of the ongoing scientific conversation. Finally, we focus on the importance of protecting the welfare of children and adolescents who take part in this research.

Scientific method The process of formulating and testing hypotheses in a rigorous and objective manner.

Basic research Research that has the primary goal of adding to our body of knowledge rather than having immediate direct application.

THE SCIENTIFIC METHOD

3.1 What is the scientific method and how is it used to study development?

Child development is one of many disciplines that uses the **scientific method** to add to its body of knowledge. This approach helps us organize the information that we currently have and generate new ideas that extend our understanding. It also is a self-correcting process because the findings from our current research guide our future efforts. We begin by asking a question (often based on our observations or theoretical ideas), next we identify the factors or elements that need to be examined to answer that question, and then we put our question to the test. Based on what we find, we can accept or reject the premise on which the original question was based (Salkind, 2004). Each of these steps is described in more detail in the remainder of this chapter.

BASIC AND APPLIED RESEARCH

The primary goal of much research is to add to our understanding of the phenomena we are interested in and to help us refine our theories. This type of research is called **basic research** because whether the results have any immediate application is not the primary concern. On the other hand, there is research that clearly intends to help us make changes that will affect people's lives. This is called **applied research** because its goal is to solve immediate problems or improve the human condition. Applied research might look at different parenting styles, classroom practices, or health care policies with the goal of improving what we do. Of course, this is not a black-or-white situation. We often find that basic research lays a foundation for later applied research.

Testing a hypothesis. Does watching television affect children's ability to stay on task and to stay focused when they need to? Research by Levine and Waite (2000) has tried to answer this question.

Applied research Research that has the primary goal of solving problems or improving the human condition.

Hypothesis A prediction, often based on theoretical ideas or observations, that is tested by the scientific method.

T ☐ F ☐ We know that watching television causes children to have shorter attention spans because many teachers report that this is what they see in the children in their classrooms. **False**

DEVELOPING HYPOTHESES

Because the field of child development is grounded in science, we rely on the scientific method to build our understanding of it. Figure 3.1 illustrates this process. This process often starts with our observations. If you spend any amount of time watching children, whether you are looking at their moment-to-moment behavior or at how they grow, change, and develop over time, you probably will have some questions about what you see. Theories, such as those you read about in the last chapter, are developed to answer the questions that arise from our observations. From these theories we develop predictions about what children will think, feel, and do in certain situations. These predictions are called **hypotheses.**

No matter how much sense a particular hypothesis seems to make, it still needs to be tested. The methods described later in this chapter are some of the ways that we test hypotheses. If we cannot find a way to subject a hypothesis to a test, it has little or no scientific value and is little more than speculation. For example, you may believe that watching too much television can cause children to have a short attention span, but until this belief is tested and supported by research, it remains just a hypothesis. We use an example of research that was designed to test this hypothesis in the set of activities called **Active Learning: The Scientific Method** that appear throughout this chapter. You can begin these activities by trying **Active Learning: The Scientific Method—Forming a Hypothesis**.

iStock

FIGURE 3.1

The Scientific Method. This figure shows each of the steps in the scientific method. Using this method, we refine our current theories and point to the questions that will guide our future research.

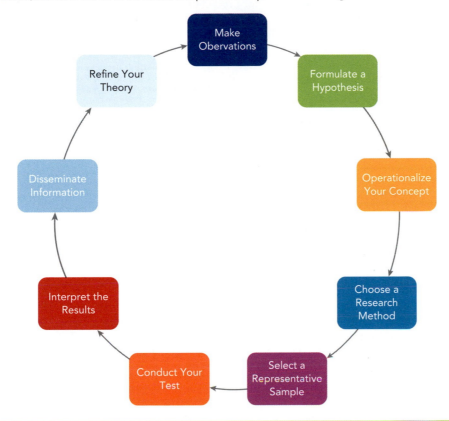

Active LEARNING

The Scientific Method—Forming a Hypothesis

Research articles most often begin with an abstract that briefly summarizes the entire article.

1. First read the following abstract of an article by Levine and Waite published in 2000.

Abstract

To evaluate the common assumption that television viewing is related to attentional difficulties in school, 70 fourth and fifth grade students recorded a "television diary" for one week and reported their preferred television shows. Parents estimated their child's television viewing time and reported their child's preferred shows. Assessment of attentional difficulties included teacher ratings, parent ratings, standardized tests, and classroom observations. It was found that the amount of television a child viewed was significantly related to teacher ratings of attentional difficulties, but not to parent ratings, classroom observations, or a standardized test. Type of shows viewed did not relate to any attentional outcome variable. There was a clear relationship between fourth and fifth grade children's ability to pay attention in school, as assessed by their teacher, and the amount of time they spent watching television.

(Continued)

(Continued)

2. After reading this abstract, look again at the first sentence. Write down what you believe to be the major hypothesis, or prediction, of this study.

Hypothesis: _____

Answer: In the first section of their paper, in which the authors review what other researchers have found that leads to their own hypothesis, they state: "The major hypothesis of this study is that for children in later elementary school the amount of television viewed will be related to ADHD behaviors," especially as shown in the classroom" (Levine & Waite, 2000, p. 667). In other words, the authors are predicting that the more television children watch, the more difficulty they will have maintaining their attention. Note for now that the hypothesis says "will be related to" and not "will cause." We will return to this point when we discuss experimental and correlational research designs later in the chapter.

OPERATIONALIZING CONCEPTS

Operationalize To define a concept in a way that allows it to be measured.

Variable A characteristic that can be measured and that can have different values.

To test a hypothesis, we first need to find some way to turn the concept into something we can see and measure. In scientific terms, we **operationalize** the concepts we want to study. These concepts are then referred to as **variables**, that is, concepts or characteristics that can be measured and can have different values. However, this process is not as simple as it may sound. Suppose you are interested in studying aggression. You probably think that aggression is one of those things that you would recognize if you saw it, but would you? It might be fairly

Operationalizing "aggression." Aggression can take different forms. How would you operationalize the concept of aggression in order to study it objectively?

straightforward if we only considered hitting, kicking, or pinching someone as the way we operationalize aggression, but that would only tap into *physical aggression*. Maybe we should add *verbal aggression*, such as name-calling, swearing, and screaming to our list. But isn't it also pretty hurtful when someone spreads rumors about you or tries to turn other people against you? These are examples of a type of indirect aggression called *relational aggression*.

Measures of any or all of these types of aggression might be included in our operationalization of the concept. The point is that you must make clear what you are including in your definition of aggression and what you are not. **Active Learning: The Scientific Method—Operationalizing Concepts** gives you a chance to see for yourself how difficult this step of the scientific process can be.

Active LEARNING

The Scientific Method—Operationalizing Concepts

Continuing with our example, Levine and Waite (2000) were looking at the relationship between television viewing and children's attentional behavior. To operationalize "television viewing," they had the children keep diaries of their television viewing for one week and asked the children's parents to estimate how much television their children watched. Thus, they operationalized television viewing as the amount of television watched in a week. This is a pretty straightforward way to operationalize "television viewing," but it is more difficult to decide how to operationalize "attentional behavior." These authors operationalized this concept by observing children in their classrooms for 15-minute periods during which they recorded behaviors such as the child being "off task, fidgeting, [making] inappropriate vocalizations, playing with an object, and being out of seat" (Levine & Waite, 2000, p. 672, adapted from Barkley, 1991).

Think about how you would operationalize each of the following concepts if you wanted to measure them as a part of your research. Be very clear in your descriptions of each type of behavior you include so someone else who is looking at the same behaviors could place the behaviors into the same categories. For example, if you wanted to observe aggression, you might first choose a specific aspect of aggression, such as physical aggression. You would then need to define this in behavioral terms. You might define physical aggression as any action that causes physical pain to another child. Then you would describe the specific behaviors you would record during your observation, such as hitting, biting, and pinching.

Following these steps, operationalize the following concepts, as you might observe them in adolescents:

- Self-esteem
- Stress
- Affection

Compare your list with those of other students in your class and discuss the following:

- How much overlap is there in the behaviors each student identified as part of the operationalization of the concept?
- Is the description of each behavior clear and unambiguous?
- Do the categories of behavior described cover the entire range of the concept or only a portion of that range?
- How would you measure each of your indicators? For example, will you use observation, self-report of the participants, the reports of others, or physiological measurement?

Reliability and Validity

Reliability The ability of a measure to produce consistent results.

Validity The ability of a research tool to accurately measure what it purports to measure.

Two essential characteristics of any measure used in scientific research are **reliability** and **validity.** A measure is *reliable* when it produces the same or similar results each time it is used. There might be *some* variation from one occasion to another, but a measure would not be very useful in research if it gave you widely different values each time you used it.

We also need to be sure that our measures accurately reflect the construct or characteristic in which we are interested. A measure is considered *valid* if it measures what it says it is going to measure. For example, in **Active Learning: The Scientific Method—Operationalizing Concepts,** you might have defined self-esteem for an adolescent as a feeling of being proud of one's self for one's achievements. You might then have tried to measure this concept by asking questions such as "Are you proud of your accomplishments?" and "Do you ever feel bad about yourself when you are not able to do something well?" It certainly appears that these questions would be a valid measure of the concept you are trying to assess, so this is called *face validity*. However, there are many other ways to see whether your questionnaire is a valid measure of self-esteem, such as seeing whether it gives similar results to another valid test of the same concept.

It is important to note how reliability and validity are related to each other. Just because a test is reliable does not necessarily mean that it also is valid. Suppose we told you that we had developed a new way to measure intelligence based upon your shoe size. This likely would be a very reliable measure because each time we measured your feet, we would get the same value. The size of your feet doesn't change a lot from day to day. However, do you think this would be a valid way to measure intelligence? Certainly not, because there isn't any reason to think that foot size is related in any meaningful way to your cognitive abilities. Measures that are used in scientific research need to be both reliable and valid.

SAMPLING AND REPRESENTATIVE SAMPLES

Generalize To draw inferences from the findings of research on a specific sample about a larger group or population.

Population A set that includes everyone in a category of individuals that researchers are interested in studying (for example, all toddlers, all teenagers with learning disabilities).

Representative sample A group of participants in a research study who have individual characteristics in the same distribution that exists in the population.

We want our research to do more than say something about the particular children or adolescents who take part in our research. We want to be able to **generalize** our results to larger populations, but this step must be done carefully. For example, if we conducted research at kindergartens in suburban public schools, we should not mistakenly assume that our findings apply equally to children from social, economic, or ethnic backgrounds that are very different from those of the children we studied. We might not find the same results if our research involved children from low-income families enrolled in a Head Start program or children from higher-income families enrolled in an expensive private school.

To understand the process of sampling, we need to distinguish between a **population** and a sample. A population includes everyone in the category we are interested in studying or learning more about. All toddlers, all elementary school children with dyslexia, or all adolescent females—each represents a population. But thinking about these groups, it is clear that including an entire population in any research study is impossible, so we need to select a sample from that population. Because we want to generalize the findings from a particular study to the population, a sample should reflect the characteristics of the population of interest and this is called a **representative sample.** There are at least two ways to do this. First, you can select your participants randomly from the population you want to study. If the selection is truly random, by chance the group of people you select should have the characteristics of the group as a whole. Second, if you know the characteristics of the population, you can choose your participants in a way that matches that set of characteristics. If you want to generalize your findings to all toddlers, for instance, you need to include boys and girls in the age range you are interested in and include demographic characteristics (for example, socioeconomic characteristics, ethnic and racial diversity, types of family structure) in proportions that are similar to the general population.

If our sample does not mirror the characteristics of the population (for example, if it primarily includes Anglo children from middle-class two-parent families), we would need to be careful to generalize our results only to children with the same characteristics as the sample.

T ☐ F ☐ If we conduct research by interviewing students in a large high school, we can assume that our findings will apply to any adolescent who is the same age as the ones we have studied. **False**

When you read research that is published in professional journals, you'll see how careful researchers are to specify how widely their conclusions can be applied, and they often call for additional research that will extend their work to a broader cross section of participants. Representative sampling is used in all types of research, whether the researchers conduct surveys, questionnaires, observations, or experiments.

In Chapter 1, we warned against generalizing from your own experiences to the experience of other people. You cannot rely on your personal experience or an isolated example from someone else's experience in place of scientific evidence based on research using representative sampling. If a friend were to tell you that his grandfather had begun smoking at age 16 and lived to be 97 years old, would you take that as evidence that smoking is not harmful to your health? In light of the overwhelming evidence of the harmful effects of smoking on health, this type of *anecdotal evidence* should not carry much weight in your decision making.

An example of what can happen when population sampling is *not* done correctly comes from research on air bags in automobiles. Research clearly shows that air bags save lives, but it also shows that they are not equally effective for all drivers and passengers. Although air bags can help prevent crash fatalities, they also can cause a range of injuries that include corneal abrasions, aortic ruptures, abdominal injuries, and fractures of the forearms (Segui-Gomez, 2000). The problem comes from the fact that the force of the deployment of the airbag was initially determined using crash test dummies that were the size of the average American male. Generalizing from findings of what made air bags most effective for the average man to the population as a whole resulted in air bag systems that actually placed women and children at greater risk for nonfatal injuries. Fortunately, research is now being conducted with female-size and child-size crash dummies to collect new data that will help manufacturers develop air bags that are more effective for everyone (Shaver, 2012). **Active Learning: The Scientific Method—Sampling** allows you to look closely at the sample used by Levine and Waite (2000), think about the characteristics of the sample used in this research, and decide to which groups of children the results of this study can be generalized.

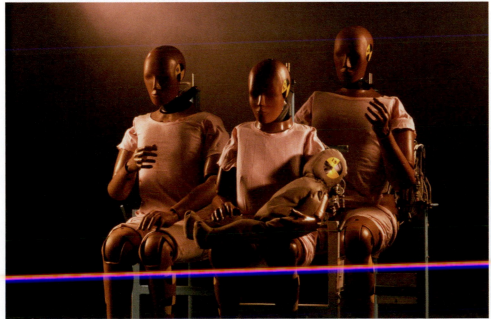

One size does not fit all. Automotive engineers originally designed air bags to protect the "average" American man. Today they realize that passengers come in all shapes and sizes and what works for an average-size man doesn't work well for others.

Andy Sacks/Stone/Getty Images

Active LEARNING

The Scientific Method—Sampling

Returning again to the research on television and attention, we can look at how Levine and Waite (2000) selected the sample for their research. Read the following description of the children who took part in the study:

> Seventy fourth and fifth grade students participated in the study. There were 33 girls and 37 boys. Children's ages ranged from 8 years 6 months to 11 years 9 months. . . . The children came from four public schools: two schools were urban, one was suburban, and one was rural. Fifty children were White, non-Hispanic; three were Hispanic, two were African American, one was Asian, one was identified as "other" and not specified. Thirteen parents chose not to report the child's ethnicity. The sample was primarily middle and working class. (p. 670)

From this description of the sample, describe the population to which the results of this study might apply. To which populations should we not generalize the results from this sample?

Answer: The research results can apply to both boys and girls who are about 8 to 12 years old. The children can be from urban, suburban, or rural settings. The results will apply primarily to White middle- and working-class children but not to minority children, who were not represented in numbers large enough to allow conclusions to be drawn about them.

METHODS AND MEASURES

Once researchers have developed their hypothesis, operationalized the concepts within it, and chosen their sample, they must decide how they will gather the data for their study. We will describe some of the ways commonly used to study children and adolescents, including observations, self-report measures, standardized tests, physiological measures, archival records, case studies, and ethnography. Each method has both advantages and disadvantages (see Table 3.1), and that is one of the reasons why we can't say that any one method is better than the others. Researchers choose the method that is most likely to answer the questions that guide the research.

TABLE 3.1

A comparison of research methods.

Method	Advantages	Disadvantages
Observations	Rich source of information	Can be confused with interpretation
	Can observe behavior as it naturally occurs	Potential observer bias
	Can be conducted in a laboratory to gain control in the situation	Can produce large amounts of raw data that must be coded and analyzed
	Can lead to new hypotheses	The presence of an observer may change the behavior being observed
		Cannot identify the causes of behavior

Method	Advantages	Disadvantages
Surveys, Questionnaires	Gathers information quickly and efficiently Can be used to gather information on many different topics	Must precisely word questions Can include misleading or biased questions Respondent may not answer honestly Respondent may not be able to accurately recall or report on behavior Respondent may provide a socially desirable answer rather than a truthful one
Interviews (structured and clinical)	Can be a first-person or a third-person account	No second observer to verify the information
Standardized Tests	Can assess many qualities or characteristics Allow an individual to be compared to the average performance of a group	Must periodically update norms Performance tests must be scored and interpreted by trained examiner May be biased against certain groups
Physiological Measures	Can gather data that don't require language or an active response from participants Responses are difficult to fake	Requires expensive equipment that can be difficult to maintain Interpretation of data is not always clear
Archival Data	Large amounts of data may be available Economical regarding time and money	No control over the variables collected or the sample characteristics
Case Studies	Source of rich information and hypotheses for future research Can utilize multiple methods Can investigate situations it would be unethical to intentionally create	Cannot generalize information to a larger population Time intensive Possible observer bias
Ethnography	Can provide a rich, detailed look at cultural groups	May change the behavior of group members Time intensive Risk of observer bias

Observations

We can learn a great deal about anything we are interested in—including development—by making careful observations. Scientific observations differ from our casual, everyday observations of the world because they need to be both systematic and objective and must be carefully planned and executed if they are going to be valid.

To understand more about the difference between objective observation and subjective interpretation, try **Active Learning: Observation or Interpretation?**

Active LEARNING

Observation or Interpretation?

A narrative description is a complete, step-by-step description of a child's behavior. It is important to learn to separate this objective description from interpretations that unintentionally read a meaning or cause into the behavior. To better understand this distinction, observe a child for about 15 to 30 minutes (or you can observe anyone if a child is not readily available). Divide the pages you use into two columns. In the left column, write down what you see the child do. For example:

(Continued)

(Continued)

Observation: Annie stands in the doorway and looks into the room. She buries her head in her father's leg and holds on.

Later, in the right column, give your interpretation of the behaviors. For example:

Interpretation: Annie seemed shy about entering the room and turned to her father for comfort.

Your interpretations should be about the child's behavior and not a summary statement about what the child "is like," because the child may appear to be different at another time. For example, don't write that Annie is a shy child. Maybe she doesn't feel well that day but usually bounces into the room with no fear. It takes many observations to make any kind of general statement about a child.

Try the following exercise to practice. Write down what you see in this set of photos under Observation and then write down how you would interpret what you see in the column for Interpretation. In each case you will describe what the child is actually doing and what their face looks like in the Observation section. Only in the Interpretation section will you write what you think is the meaning of what you see. For example, is the boy in the third photo looking angry, sad, or devious? Each of these would be a different interpretation of the expression on the child's face.

	Observation	Interpretation
Thinkstock/Creatas		
Thinkstock		
©iStockphoto.com/djedzura		

If the researchers conducting the observations are testing their own hypotheses, there is a risk that they might see or pay more attention to things that tend to support those hypotheses and overlook things that don't. This tendency is called **observer bias.** Having more than one observer code the observations helps assure us that the observations are objective rather than subjective. Another safeguard against observer bias is to use observers who don't know the specific hypothesis that is being tested (that is, observers who are "blind" to the hypothesis), so that it cannot influence their perception of the events they are observing.

Observations can be made in a setting where the behavior of interest naturally occurs, or they can be made in a setting that offers more control over circumstances, such as a research laboratory. One advantage of doing observations in naturally occurring settings is that we get to see children behaving as they normally do within the social relationships that are a part of their everyday lives, and we see them in situations that have real emotional significance for them (Dunn, 2005). However, moving observations into a laboratory gives researchers greater control over the situation and allows them to create a specific set of conditions in which to conduct their observations. You will read about some of the early influential work in the field of child development that used observation as its methodology in **Journey of Research: Doing Observational Research.**

> **T ☐ F ☐** When conducting research by doing an observation, it is important that the person who is doing the observation does not know the purpose of the research. **True**

Observer bias The tendency for an observer to notice and report events that the observer is expecting to see.

JOURNEY OF *Research*

Doing Observational Research

The scientific study of child development is relatively recent, but parents have been keeping records of their children's growth and development for their own enjoyment for a very long time. In the 1800s, educated parents often kept what were called *baby biographies* of their children. In 1877 Charles Darwin, a renowned scientist of the day, took the notable step of publishing some observations he had made of his own son in the scientific journal *Mind.* In this article, Darwin described his observations regarding early reflexive behaviors in the infant, as well as later voluntary movement. He also noted incidents of anger, fear, pleasure, and affection in his son. The fact that a noted scientist found these observations worthy of publication in a journal gave the study of children's development a legitimacy that it hadn't had before.

Years later, one of the most influential developmental theorists, Jean Piaget, made extensive, detailed observations of his three children, and these observations formed the basis of a number of his writings on cognitive development (see, for example, Piaget, 1952/1963). Although Piaget did not conduct his observations using the guidelines we have described (for instance, there was only one observer, he was testing his own hypotheses, and was observing children in whom he was emotionally involved), his observations helped him to develop his theory that has subsequently been tested by other researchers with more modern methods.

At about this same time, Roger G. Barker and Herbert F. Wright were studying 119 children living in a Midwestern town using a methodology they called *ecological psychology.* In one of the publications resulting from their work, it took the authors 435 pages to record and interpret a single 14-hour observation of one 7-year-old boy (Barker & Wright, 1951). It took a team of eight observers, each making 1-minute observations, to record this information—a very labor-intensive process, to say the least. Today video cameras have largely replaced paper-and-pencil recordings, and are used by both child development researchers and proud parents to record children's behavior. However, the goal of observational research remains the same: to capture the full, rich range of behavior as it naturally occurs.

Making a detailed record of everything that happens in a stream of behavior can make researchers aware of aspects of behavior that they have not noticed before and can be a good source of new hypotheses for future research. Both of these are advantages of doing observational studies. However, recording everything that happens even in a fairly short period of time produces a tremendous amount of raw data that need to be analyzed and reduced before useful information emerges.

For this reason, researchers often structure their observations in ways that allow them to be more focused. **Checklists** can be used to assess many aspects of children's development, including social skills, physical skills, language development, and problem behaviors. When observing the child, the researcher simply marks the presence or absence of each item on the checklist. For example, a checklist of gross motor skills might include the behaviors walking, jumping, and hopping. The observer would ask the child to do each of these and check it off if he can accomplish it or the observer can simply observe the child's behavior and record what she sees. A checklist provides a quick way to look at a child's development in relation to what other children of the same age can do. Also, the observer may use the checklist to keep track of children's progress as they grow and develop. As a result, checklists are often used in educational, medical, and other settings that require quick, efficient assessment of a child's level of functioning.

Although observations are very useful sources of information about behavior, there are some limitations when using this method. First, the goal is to capture behavior as it naturally occurs, but the mere presence of an observer might change the way that people behave. Fortunately, children usually adapt to the presence of an observer without too much difficulty. Although they are initially curious and might ask questions about what the observer is doing, the lure of getting back to what they were doing (such as playing with their friends) is usually far stronger. Another limitation of observational research is that it does not tell us directly about the causes of behavior because the observer does not have enough control over the situation to make this determination. For example, if you observe a child who stays on the sidelines while other children are playing and refuses to interact with the other children, there are many possible explanations for this behavior. From the observation alone, it is impossible to tell whether this is the behavior of a child who simply is not very social, a temporary reaction to something that occurred earlier in the day, or an indication of an adjustment problem for the child. Based on these observations, the researcher might formulate a hypothesis to explain the child's behavior, but additional research would need to be conducted to determine the cause of the observed behavior.

Self-Report Measures

Another way to gather information relatively quickly and efficiently is to use self-report measures such as **surveys, questionnaires,** and **interviews**. However, the usefulness of the information gathered from self-report measures largely depends on the accuracy of the answers they produce. Having questions that are precise, well-written, and understandable is essential to the validity of this research. You may have had the experience of trying to complete a survey in which the questions were unclear or difficult to answer. In that case, it wouldn't matter how much you wanted to give accurate information; you wouldn't be able to do so. Of course, another possibility is that the person taking the survey is unwilling or unable to give complete or accurate responses. And sometimes people give the answer they think the researcher is looking for or give answers that they think make them look good in the eyes of the researcher (a problem that is called *social desirability*). For example, students being surveyed about their drug and alcohol use may downplay the amount they use so they will not look deviant to the researcher. You can see how social desirability becomes a challenge for researchers who are investigating a sensitive topic, such as sexuality, drugs, or prejudice.

Typically, each survey participant responds to the same questions, presented in the same order. These questions might be open-ended (for example, "What do you do when you are spending time with your friends?" or "What is your favorite subject in school?") or may use

Checklist A prepared list of behaviors, characteristics, or judgments observers use to assess a child's development.

T □ F □ If observations are carefully done, you will be able to determine the causes of the behavior you are observing. **False**

Survey A data collection technique that asks respondents to answer a common set of questions.

Questionnaire A written form of a survey.

Interview A data collection technique in which an interviewer poses questions to a respondent.

a forced-choice format (for example, "How many hours a week do you watch television? (a) less than 1 hour, (b) between 1 and 3 hours, (c) between 3 and 6 hours, or (d) 6 hours or more"). To better understand how poorly worded or otherwise misleading questions can keep a participant from providing complete and truthful answers, read **Journey of Research: Children's Eyewitness Testimony.**

JOURNEY OF *Research*

Children's Eyewitness Testimony

An important illustration of how the way a question is asked can affect the response that you get comes from research on children's eyewitness testimony. Think for a minute about the subtle difference between asking someone "Did you see that?" and asking her "Didn't you see that?" The first alternative suggests that there can be one of two legitimate answers ("Yes, I saw that" or "No, I didn't see that"), but the second alternative implies that you may have missed something that someone else saw. The pressure is to respond to the second question by saying "Of course I saw that." Although you may feel that you would respond to such a question by simply saying what you did or didn't see, regardless of how the question was phrased, a child is more likely to be swayed by the question itself.

Prior to the 1990s, there had been relatively little research on children's ability to accurately recall events so that they could serve as eyewitnesses, but in the 1990s there were some high-profile cases of alleged child abuse that placed children in the witness seat. Under relentless and often suggestive questioning, the children described horrible abuse they had allegedly suffered at the hands of adults who were caring for them. Based on this testimony, several of the defendants received jail sentences. However, these charges were later dismissed or the plaintiffs were released from prison because of the improper way that evidence had been gathered. Here is an example of the type of improper questioning that was used in the notorious McMartin Preschool case in which seven teachers were accused of sexually abusing several hundred young children:

Interviewer: Can you remember the naked pictures?

Child: (Shakes head "no")

Interviewer: Can't remember that part?

Child: (Shakes head "no")

Interviewer: Why don't you think about that for a while, okay? Your memory might come back to you.

(Interview Number 111, p. 29, as cited in Garven, Wood, Malpass, & Shaw, 1998)

We now know that even young children are able to accurately recall events and can give reliable eyewitness testimony (Odegard & Toglia, 2013). However, when the questions they are asked are misleading, they are subjected to repeated questioning, or the interviewer makes overt suggestions about what has happened, we cannot trust children's answers (Ceci & Bruck, 1995; Krähenbühl & Blades, 2006). It is clear from the way the interviewer in the McMartin case kept repeating the question and refused to take the child's denial that there had been naked pictures that this interviewer had a particular answer in mind and wanted the child to give that answer. Suggesting that a memory "might come back" implies that the event is something that happened but has been forgotten, rather than allowing the possibility that it never happened at all. Because children are limited in their ability to understand and interpret language, we need to be particularly careful about the wording of questions when designing surveys, questionnaires, and interviews for them.

T ☐ F ☐ Children's memories are good enough to allow them to give reliable eyewitness testimony. **True**

Clinical interview An interview strategy in which the interviewer can deviate from a standard set of questions to gather additional information.

Usually an interviewer asks everyone who is interviewed the same set of questions, but sometimes the interviewer might want to ask additional follow-up questions or ask the respondent to expand on her original answers or provide examples. In this case, a **clinical interview** allows the researcher greater flexibility.

In addition to his naturalistic observations of children which we described earlier, Piaget used clinical interviews to refine his theoretical ideas. In the following example, Piaget used a clinical interview to learn about children's sense of morality. In one pair of stories, he asked the children he was interviewing to compare the actions of two girls. The first girl, Marie, wants to surprise her mother by sewing her a nice present. She doesn't really know how to use the scissors and ends up cutting a big hole in her own dress. The second girl, Margaret, takes her mother's scissors while her mother is out. She doesn't really know how to use them and makes a little hole in her own dress. Piaget would then ask a series of questions to determine which girl the children considered to be naughtier:

P: Which one is the naughtiest?

C: The one who made the big hole.

P: Why did she make this hole?

C: She wanted to give her mother a surprise.

P: That's right. Then which of the little girls was nicest?

C: (hesitation)

P: Say what you think.

Standardized test A test that is administered and scored in a standard or consistent way for all examinees.

C: The one who made the little hole is the nicest.

P: If you were the mother . . . which would you have punished most?

C: The one who made a big hole.

(Piaget, 1965, p. 127)

Although this interview has some standard questions like "Which one is the naughtiest?", many of the other questions are unique, based on a particular child's responses.

A variation on the self-report approach is to rely on a second party, like a parent, teacher, or care provider, to give the information on the target child. This is a particularly important way to collect data on infants and children who are too young to respond to an interviewer's questions. The more time the people being interviewed spend with the child and the more familiar they are with the child's behavior, the more likely it is that they will be able to provide high-quality information. For example, parents have been asked to describe the antisocial and acting-out behavior of their adopted adolescents (Klahr, Rueter, McGue, Iacono, & Burt, 2011), and teachers have been asked to rate the social-emotional competence of their students (Merrell, Cohn, & Tom, 2011).

Standardized Tests

Tests can provide information on a wide range of topics relevant to understanding development. You are probably familiar with **standardized tests** such as IQ tests and achievement tests. In Chapter 8, we have a great deal of

How naughty is this? Using a clinical interview, Piaget asked children who is naughtier: a child who makes a big hole in her dress while trying to make her mother a present or a child who makes a small hole in her dress while playing with scissors she shouldn't have. What would you say?

information about the use of standardized tests in educational settings. Researchers standardize a test by administering it to large groups of children to establish **norms** for the test. This provides an expected range of scores, and individuals who later take the same test will have their results compared to this norming group. By comparing an individual child's performance to the appropriate age norms, we can determine whether that child is performing at the same level as the average child of the same age or is performing above or below average.

Many of these tests are paper-and-pencil tests that can be administered to groups of children all at the same time, but some of them are called *performance tests* because they require the child to do something (for example, assemble a puzzle, build a tower of blocks). Someone who has been trained to administer and interpret the test, such as a school psychologist, works one-on-one with the child to administer a performance test.

Standardized testing has been a controversial topic for many years. Much of this controversy has centered on the validity of the tests, that is, whether they are actually measuring what they say they are measuring. A related controversy has surrounded how standardized test results are interpreted and used. Early wide-scale use of intelligence tests during World War I and World War II found that native-born Americans scored better on the tests than immigrants, immigrants from Northern and Western Europe scored better than ones from Southern and Eastern Europe, and Black Americans received the lowest scores of all (Glaser, 1993). The controversy centered on whether the differences in test scores reflected inherent differences in mental abilities between these groups, or whether the tests were biased in some way that put certain groups at more of a disadvantage than other groups. This became known as the *cultural test bias hypothesis* (Reynolds, 2000).

College entrance tests such as the Scholastic Assessment Test (SAT), formerly known as the Scholastic Aptitude Test, or the American College Testing (ACT) program have received the same types of criticisms. Critics have claimed that they are biased in a way that discriminates against certain groups of students. On average, men score higher than women on these tests, Asians/Asian Americans/Pacific Islanders and Whites score higher than Mexican Americans/Latinos or African Americans, and students from families with higher incomes score higher than students from families with lower incomes (College Board, 2008; FairTest, 2010).

Careful selection of norming samples that include all the segments of the population who will use the test helps to reduce testing bias. It is also important that the test developers be culturally sensitive so they do not use language or describe specific situations in the test that will be familiar to some test takers but not to others. In recent years a number of psychometric reviews have come to the conclusion that "well-constructed, reliable, well-standardized psychological tests are not biased against native-born American racial or ethnic minorities" (Reynolds, 2000, p. 145; see also Balkin, Heard, Lee, & Wines, 2014) and that any content bias is usually quite small. However, in response to concerns about possible bias in SAT/ACT results, over 850 colleges have stopped using them in admission decisions or have made them optional (FairTest, 2016; Hiss & Franks, 2014). Because educational decisions that are made based on standardized test scores have such important consequences for individuals, organizations such as the American Psychological Association and the American Educational Research Association recommend that decisions never depend upon a single test score.

In addition to using standardized tests to determine whether children are "on track" regarding their development, tests are also useful for assessing the effectiveness of programs and interventions. For example, the effectiveness of a summer enrichment program that paired talented young adolescents from limited-opportunity backgrounds with high school students or college-aged students was assessed using standardized tests of mathematics and reading skills (Laird & Feldman, 2004). In another program evaluation, a standardized test of math ability was used to assess the effectiveness of a 6-week classroom intervention conducted in Head Start classrooms designed to promote emergent math skills in preschool children (Arnold, Fisher, & Doctoroff, 2002).

Norm The average or typical performance of an individual of a given age on a test.

Physiological Measures

It is not always easy to gather the types of data we need to answer important questions about development, but today a number of physiological measures are helping us get those answers. *Electroencephalograms (EEGs)* measure electrical activity in the brain (Dupler, 2014). *Functional magnetic resonance imaging (fMRI)* measures blood flow in the brain to show which parts of the brain are active (UC San Diego Center for Functional MRI, 2016). The photos on the facing page show the information we get from these measures. *Event-related potentials (ERPs)* measure the brain's electrical response to meaningful sensory stimuli. Other physiological responses that have been measured include the activity of sweat glands to measure arousal, the dilation of the eye to indicate heightened interest, an increased heart rate to reflect information processing demands, and changes in breathing patterns to indicate anxiety or stress (Sowden & Barrett, 2006).

These measures have been in the forefront of research on information processing, as well as in studies of brain dysfunction in conditions such as ADHD and autism. They also provide important information on facets of human functioning related to the central nervous system, emotions, stress, cognitive processes, personality, and intelligence (Sowden & Barrett, 2006). Because physiological measures enable us to measure what is going on inside an individual without needing to rely on verbal communication, they have been particularly important in research involving infants and young children who can't answer questions because they either are not speaking at all yet, or their language ability is so limited that they can't understand and follow complex instructions or provide complex verbal responses to questions.

One advantage of using physiological measures in research is that the responses are not under the conscious control of the individual, so they cannot easily be faked or presented in a way intended to make them socially desirable (Blascovich, 2004). Most of these measures are noninvasive, meaning that nothing needs to be placed inside the body to collect the data. For instance, the photo on this page shows a type of cap with electrodes embedded in it that is used to record brain activity in an infant. A cap is placed snugly on the child's head, but is not at all painful for the child. A weak electrical current then passes from the cap through the bones of the skull to record brain activity.

As an example of how physiological measures have been used, researchers looked at how 12-month-old infants reacted to stimuli in the environment when their caregivers reacted to an event in a positive, negative, or neutral way (de Haan, 2007). By measuring event-related potentials, they found that the infants paid more attention to the stimuli when their caregivers reacted in a negative way than when the caregivers reacted in a neutral or positive way. In an evolutionary sense, it makes sense that infants would pay more attention to things that their caregivers found unpleasant or distressing.

Research using fMRIs to scan the brains of children diagnosed with autism spectrum disorder has found that the part of the brain that controls face recognition is underactive in these children (Kalb, 2005). As you may know, children with autism often do not make eye contact with others and show little or no interest in social relationships. By using physiological measures, researchers have been able to understand more about the processes that underlie certain behaviors. Building on these findings, they are now developing interventions that can teach face recognition skills to autistic children. In one such program, children use computerized games to choose a face appearing on the screen that matches a target face or to connect three different views of the same face (Tanaka

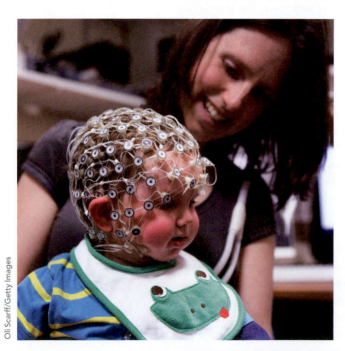

Measurement of brain function. This infant's brain activity is being measured by means of a specially designed "electrode hat."

Oli Scarff/Getty Images

et al., 2010). After 20 hours of training, the participants were better able to recognize mouth features and eye features in faces.

Archival Records

Researchers don't always collect their own data. They may use **archival records** (or secondary data) that others have collected, sometimes for a different reason. For instance, a researcher might use historical diaries, letters, or photographs to gain insight into what childhood was like in the past. Reports and statistics collected by the U.S. government provide a historical snapshot of many topics relevant for a developmental researcher. In this book, you will read about research on child abuse, adolescent pregnancy, and many health conditions affecting children and adolescents that are based on government reports. Medical records and school records are other sources of archival data that are relevant to understanding a child's development.

One of the most ambitious sources of archival data related to child development is the Panel Study of Income Dynamics (PSID). Data collection from a nationally representative sample of over 18,000 individuals began in 1968 and has continued on a yearly basis since then (PSID, 2015a). Through in-person interviews with parents and children younger than age 18 and telephone interviews with those over the age of 18, information was gathered on a number of family, school, and neighborhood characteristics that are linked to the physical health, emotional well-being, cognitive development, and social relationships of the children (PSID, 2015b). Because data collection of this scope requires a great deal of time, money, and effort, making archival data available to many researchers is more cost-effective than having each researcher collect data individually. More than 3,000 peer-reviewed publications are based on the data in this archive (PSID, 2015a). However, a limitation of using archival data is that the researcher has no control over the variables that are available for analysis, nor any choice in the characteristics of the sample, although in large and diverse data sets, researchers can often create a sample that is relevant to their research interests.

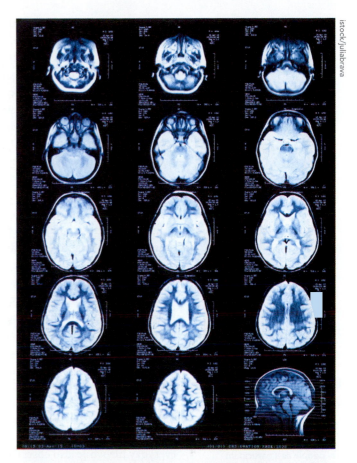

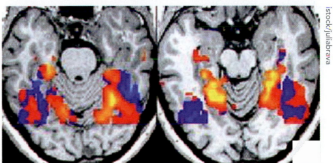

MRIs and fMRIs. The MRI image (top) shows pictures of successive sections through the brain from the back to the front. The fMRI image (bottom) shows where the blood is flowing through the brain when the person thinks about an activity and actually does that activity.

Case Studies

A **case study** takes a comprehensive and intensive look at a single individual or a small group of individuals. This intense focus allows the researcher to look at a topic in much greater depth than would be possible in a study involving a large number of participants. As part of the case study, the researcher can use a variety of the methods we have already discussed, including observations, clinical interviews, psychological tests and assessments, or archival data. Case studies have been used to investigate widely different research questions, such as the psychological challenges faced by a child with a severe mental disorder called psychosis (Green, Fazio-Griffith, & Parson, 2015), the problems encountered by a blended family

Archival records Data collected at an earlier date that are used for research purposes.

Case study An in-depth study of a single individual or small group of individuals which uses multiple methods of study.

(Zeleznikow & Zeleznikow, 2015), and the coping mechanisms of an adolescent with HIV-positive parents (Lowe, 2007).

Individuals who are subjects of case studies are often exceptional in some way, which is what makes them interesting subjects for this type of examination. Their life experiences often include situations that we would never intentionally create for a child just so we could study them. For example, one well-known case study in child development involved Genie, a young girl who had been raised in conditions of horrible deprivation. After Genie was removed from her abusive family, a group of researchers worked to rehabilitate her and in the process kept detailed case notes on her attempts at recovery. You will learn more about the story of Genie in Chapter 9 when we discuss language development. Sigmund Freud also published several papers based on case studies of his patients, including a young boy with a pathological fear of horses and a young man suffering from an obsessive fantasy (Kahn, 2002).

Earlier in this chapter, we talked about the need to guard against observer bias when doing observational research. Because of the close relationship that can develop between the researcher and the subject of a case study, it is particularly important that the researcher strive to remain objective in his observations and interpretation of data. Despite this challenge, case studies offer us an in-depth picture of development because they can bring together information from multiple sources using multiple methods. Although the findings from case studies do not generalize to a wide segment of the population, they can be a rich source of new hypotheses that can be explored by future research with other more typical or representative groups of individuals.

Ethnography

Ethnography is a research technique adapted from the field of anthropology in which a researcher lives with a group of people as a participant observer, taking part in the group's everyday life while also observing and interviewing the people in the group. Ethnography is a type of qualitative research that begins with observations and then uses those observations to generate hypotheses to help explain the behavior observed (Morgan, 2014). It does not manipulate variables, nor is it designed to test hypotheses. The primary goal of this approach is to use observations to understand how people make sense of their world and the experiences in it (Merriam, 2009). This technique is especially helpful when studying children in different cultures as it allows the researcher to see the whole context of the children's development. For example, Samantha Punch (2012) lived in an area of Bolivia in order to study children's development in a poor, rural community, and when Sudhir Venkatesh (2008) wanted to administer questionnaires to gang members in inner-city Chicago, he ended up living among them for almost 10 years. This resulted in a rich account of their lives in a book titled *Gang Leader for a Day: A Rogue Sociologist Takes to the Streets.*

Although ethnographies give us a rich picture of a cultural group by someone who is embedded in that group for an extended period of time, researchers must consider the fact that their presence may change the behavior of the individuals in the group that they are observing. This can become a threat to the validity of the conclusions drawn from the study. Another threat to the validity of the study is that the researchers' own biases may affect how they interpret what they see, so they must always guard against observer bias. A researcher's personal safety could be placed in jeopardy in some research settings, and ethnographic researchers must be willing to commit to the considerable amount of time needed to carry out this type of study.

Active Learning: The Scientific Method—Measures will help you review some of the types of measures we have just discussed by asking you to recognize examples.

T ☐ F ☐ Studying a single individual intensively is a valid scientific methodology. **True**

Ethnography A qualitative research technique in which a researcher lives with a group of people as a participant observer, taking part in the group's everyday life while observing and interviewing people in the group.

Michael Nichols/National Geographic Creative

Ethnography. This ethnographic researcher entered into the everyday life of this group of people to gain a rich picture of all aspects of their environment.

Active LEARNING

The Scientific Method—Measures

Now let's examine the types of measures used in the study on television viewing and attention problems by Levine and Waite (2000). In the abstract of the article, the authors state that "70 fourth and fifth grade students recorded a 'television diary' for one week and reported their preferred television shows. Parents estimated their child's television viewing time and reported their child's preferred shows. The assessment of attentional difficulties included teacher ratings [the ADD-H Comprehensive Teachers Rating Scale], parent ratings [the Distractibility/Hyperactivity scale (DI) of the Parenting Stress Index], standardized tests [the Stroop color and word test], and classroom observations" (Levine & Waite, 2000, p. 667).

For each type of measure listed below, put an X in front of the measure if it was used in this research (leave blank if it wasn't used). If a method was used, describe what type of data was collected using this measure.

_____ observations _____

_____ self-report measures _____

_____ standardized tests _____

_____ physiological measures _____

_____ archival records _____

_____ case studies _____

_____ ethnographic studies _____

_____ other types of measures _____

REPLICATION OF RESULTS

Our confidence that our conclusions are valid is strengthened if results are replicated or repeated in subsequent research. We can do this by repeating the research using other groups that are the same or similar to the group we originally studied, or by extending the research to new groups to determine whether the conclusions can be generalized to new situations. We also expect that other researchers will be able to replicate our results by conducting their own independent research and coming to the same or similar conclusions (Makel, Plucker, & Hegarty, 2012).

Replication of results is at the core of the scientific method. As we discussed in Chapter 1, if results cannot be reproduced by others the finding is just a fluke. Yet most research is published because it shows something new, so replications are often not accepted for publication. In the past several years, there has been a movement to change this. The Association for Psychological Science (n.d.) has provided an outlet for publications that is dedicated to replications in order to "emphasize findings that are robust, replicable and generalizable" (para. 2).

CHECK YOUR UNDERSTANDING

1. Explain what it means to say that a measure is reliable and valid.
2. Explain the importance of having a representative sample in research.
3. What are the advantages and disadvantages of using observations, standardized tests, and case studies to collect data?

HOW RESEARCH IS DESIGNED

3.2 What are the different types of research designs used to study development?

We have talked about a variety of methods used to gather information about development. You can think of research methods and measures as the tools we use to collect the data we are interested in. In this next section, we describe research designs, which are the roadmap or blueprint we use to structure our research. The design we choose tells us what will be done and when and how we will do it. You will learn the differences between experimental and correlational research designs and the strengths and limitations of each. We also describe the types of developmental research designs used in research with children and adolescents.

EXPERIMENTAL RESEARCH DESIGNS: IDENTIFYING THE CAUSES OF BEHAVIOR

Experimental research design occupies a central place in the study of child development because it allows us to *identify the causes* of behavior. With research that is not based on an experimental design, we can speculate about the causes, but we do not have enough control over the situation to make a firm determination. However, when a researcher designs an experiment, the goal is to control as many aspects of the experimental situation as possible in order to draw conclusions about the causes of the outcome.

Experiments can take different forms and can include one, two, or more groups of participants, but these are the essential features you will find in an **experimental research design**:

- The **experimental group** is the group that receives the special treatment of interest to the researcher.

- The **control group** does not receive the special treatment and provides a baseline against which the experimental group can be compared.

- The participants are randomly assigned to either the experimental or the control group. Because this assignment is made by chance, the two groups will likely start out being very similar to each other, without any systematic differences that could affect the outcome of the experiment. To get a **random assignment** to groups, you could simply flip a coin for each participant, with all "heads" going into one group and all "tails" into the other; or you could put all the names in a hat and pull them out one by one, alternately assigning them to one group or the other.

Experimental research design A research design in which an experimental group is administered a treatment and the outcome is compared with a control group that does not receive the treatment.

Experimental group The group in an experiment that gets the special treatment that is of interest to the researcher.

Control group The group in an experiment that does not get the special treatment and provides a baseline against which the experimental group can be compared.

Random assignment Assigning participants to the experimental and control groups by chance so that the groups will not systematically differ from each other.

- The **independent variable** is the special treatment the researcher hypothesizes will make a difference between the experimental and control groups at the end of the experiment. The assumption is that the independent variable is the cause of any change we observe following the experiment.

- The **dependent variable** is the outcome of interest to the researcher. We measure it at the end of the experiment to see whether manipulating the independent variable has produced the expected effect.

Independent variable The variable in an experiment that the researcher manipulates.

Dependent variable The outcome of interest to the researcher that is measured at the end of an experiment.

If we look at an example of experimental research, this terminology will have more meaning for you. A recent study looked at the impact of attending Head Start on cognitive development and several social-behavioral outcomes for preschool children, including social skills, positive approaches to learning, and aggressive behavior (Zhai, Brooks-Gunn, & Waldfogel, 2014). All children were eligible to enroll in Head Start but there were not enough spaces for all of them. The children who were randomly chosen to participate in the Head Start program became the experimental group and the other children who could not be enrolled became the control group. Remember, the experimental group is the group receiving the special treatment that the researchers are interested in studying, and the control group does not receive the treatment. What is different between the two groups is the independent variable (in this case, whether the child attended Head Start or not). At the beginning of the experiment, the researchers made sure that the children in the two groups were matched on a number of characteristics to be sure that the groups were as similar as possible. This gives us confidence that any difference found at the end of the experiment is due to what the researchers did, rather than to an initial difference between the groups. The dependent variable is the outcome of interest to the researchers and what is measured and compared between the groups at the end of the experiment. In this study, the outcome measures were the children's cognitive and social-behavioral development.

By the end of first grade, the researchers found that the children who attended Head Start had better cognitive scores and parent-reported behavioral development than the children who did not attend Head Start. Because the two groups of children were similar at the start of the experiment, and because the only relevant difference between the groups during the intervention was whether the children attended Head Start or not, the researchers could conclude that participating in Head Start was the *cause* of the difference they observed at the end of the experiment.

Table 3.2 shows the steps in this process and can help you understand how they relate to each other.

TABLE 3.2

The experimental process. This table shows how an experiment (in this case an experiment to study the effect of attending Head Start) is conducted, starting with a sample of the population of interest to the researcher and ending with results that can be interpreted.

Step 1: Select a Sample	Step 2: Random Assignment	Step 3: Pretest	Step 4: Treatment	Step 5: Posttest	Step 6: Compare Results
A representative group of children is chosen for the study.	Children are randomly assigned to groups.	Pretest establishes groups are the same.	Independent variable is administered to the experimental group.	Dependent variable is measured for both groups.	Researcher determines whether results support hypothesis.
Sample	Experimental Group	Cognitive and social-behavioral development test scores	Attend Head Start	Cognitive and social-behavioral development test scores	Experimental group scores > control group scores
	Control Group	Cognitive and social-behavioral development test scores	Do not attend Head Start	Cognitive and social-behavioral development test scores	

Active Learning: Experimental Research Design provides an opportunity to review the terminology used in experiments and to check that you can recognize each element when you see it in the description of an experiment.

Active LEARNING

Experimental Research Design

You can test your understanding of experimental research design by identifying the components of an experiment in this example taken from a study by Beth Hennessey (2007) that was designed to build social competence in a sample of school-age children.

A total of 154 fourth graders in eight classrooms participated in the study. Students completed the Social Skills Rating System in the fall and again in the spring and the teachers rated their students' social competence at both times. During the year, half of the teachers in each school implemented the Open Circle Program, a social skills training program that "encourages students, teachers and administrators to learn and practice communication, self-control and social problem-solving skills" (Hennessey, 2007, p. 349), while the other half did not use the Open Circle Program. Based on the teachers' reports, Hennessey concluded that the students who were in the classrooms that used the Open Circle Program training showed greater improvement in their social skills and problem-solving behavior than students who did not receive this training.

From the description of this experiment, identify the following:

Experimental group _____

Control group _____

Independent variable _____

Dependent variable _____

Because we can control many aspects of a situation that might affect the outcome of an experiment, we presume that we understand the cause of any changes that we find in the results. However, it is still possible that some other variable or condition that we haven't taken into account is responsible for the outcome. For this reason, it is essential that experiments be carefully planned and carefully executed. It also may have occurred to you by now that, as appealing as using the experimental method might be to researchers, it cannot be used to answer many of the questions that are of great interest to us as developmentalists. There are many situations that we could never ethically create as an experiment. For example, if we want to study the effect of peers on children's social development, we couldn't intentionally keep some children from having friends just so we could see how their development differs from children who do have friends.

Natural or "Quasi" Experiments

Sometimes a situation occurs without a researcher creating it, and we can use that situation as a **natural or "quasi" experiment** to test a hypothesis. In West Africa, administrators in private schools can decide which discipline techniques they will use in their schools. Some choose to use corporal punishment, such as slapping children on the head or pinching them when they misbehave. Other administrators choose to use nonphysical child management techniques (Talwar & Lee, 2011). Researchers used this naturally occurring situation to examine the effect of these two different school environments on children's willingness to lie about their misbehavior.

Children from both types of schools listened to a researcher play with a toy while they had their back turned to her. The researcher then said she needed to leave the room for a while and told the child not to turn around to look at the toy while she was gone. When she returned, she asked the child if he or she had looked at the toy in her absence. Although the majority of the children from both types of schools peeked, many more of the children from the schools that used physical punishment denied what they had done. In other words, they lied about the fact that they had peeked. The researchers concluded that the punitive school environment gave children the motivation to lie as a means of self-protection.

Similar to experiments conducted in a laboratory, researchers in this study controlled as many variables as possible with the exception of the variable they were interested in studying. Both schools were located in the same city and enrolled students from similar socioeconomic backgrounds. Students from the two schools also scored at a similar level on some standardized tests of cognitive ability. The relevant variable that differed between them was the discipline practices of the school they attended, so this was the independent variable in this study. The likelihood that they would lie about their misbehavior was the dependent variable measured at the end of the experiment.

One drawback in a natural experiment is that it is more difficult to rule out other factors that may affect the results. For example, in a true experiment, some teachers would be randomly assigned to use physical punishment and a comparable sample of teachers would be assigned to use nonphysical punishment. You can clearly see why this research could only be done as a natural experiment. What teacher would agree to hit a child when that teacher did not believe in using physical punishment in a classroom? However, because this was a natural experiment, it is possible that teachers who were drawn to the school that used physical punishment differed from those who went to the other school in other ways that made them less approachable to students. Therefore, it is possible that it is the teacher's personality or some other difference in the school environment that is responsible for the outcome rather than simply the use of physical punishment.

> **T ☐ F ☐** An experiment always consists of a situation set up by researchers to test specific hypotheses. **False**

Natural or "quasi" experiment Research in which the members of the groups are selected because they represent different "treatment" conditions.

Correlational research design Research design that measures the strength and direction of the relationship between two or more variables that are not created by the experimenter.

©iStockphoto.com/Stephanie Frey

CORRELATIONAL DESIGNS

The second way we can test hypotheses is to examine the relationship between two or more variables using a **correlational research design.** This design is used to look at

What did you do? When young children were left alone in a room and told not to peek at a toy while the researcher was out, most could not resist temptation and peeked. When they were later asked if they had looked, children from schools that relied on physical punishment for discipline were more likely to lie about what they did. Physical discipline gave the children an incentive to be deceptive about their misbehavior.

Positive correlation
A correlation in which increases in one variable are associated with increases in another variable.

Negative correlation
A correlation in which increases in one variable are associated with decreases in another variable.

how two or more naturally occurring variables relate to each other; researchers do not create an independent variable as they would in an experimental research design. When we look at correlations, we are interested in two things: the *strength* of the relationship and the *direction* of the relationship. Figure 3.2 illustrates these aspects of correlations. The first is the direction of the relationship. Correlations can be *positive* or *negative*. In a **positive correlation,** the value of one variable increases as the value of the second variable increases. For example, lifetime earnings are positively correlated with the number of years in school. As years completed in school go up, so do lifetime earnings. (We hope you find that to be good news.) In a **negative correlation,** as the value of one variable increases, the value of the second variable decreases. For example, the more often people brush their teeth, the fewer cavities they are likely to have.

The second characteristic of correlations is the strength of the relationship between two variables. This can range from a correlation of +1.0 (a perfect positive correlation) to a correlation of −1.0 (a perfect negative correlation). You would realistically never expect to find a perfect correlation between variables related to development. Many correlations in development research are in the moderate range of +.15 to +.40. As a correlation moves down from +1 or −1, the relationship gets weaker and weaker. When a correlation reaches zero, it means that there is no relationship between the two variables. For example, the correlation between people's shoe size and their IQ would probably be close to zero because there is no reason to think that these characteristics are related to each other in any systematic way. You can test your understanding of the direction and magnitude of correlations by completing **Active Learning: Positive and Negative Correlations.**

Active LEARNING

Positive and Negative Correlations

A school counselor uses three different tests to assess children's aptitude for math so she can advise the school about the best placement for each child. After testing 400 children, she measures each child's actual performance in math classes and correlates it with the results of the three tests. She finds the following correlations between test scores and the children's math performance:

Test 1: −.85

Test 2: +.35

Test 3: +.65

Which test should she keep as the best predictor of how a child is going to do in math, and why is that test the best predictor?

SOURCE: Adapted from Chew (2006).

Answer: The correct answer is Test 1. Although the correlation is negative, it is the strongest relationship between the test and math performance because the number (-.85) is the one closest to -1.0. To use this information correctly, however, the counselor needs to remember that students with high scores on this aptitude test are likely to perform *poorly* in math classes because this is a *negative correlation*. As the value of test scores went up, the value of their actual performance in math class went down.

FIGURE 3.2

Examples of correlations. In these graphs, each dot represents one individual's scores on Variables 1 and 2. Lines that slope upward indicate a positive correlation, and ones that slope downward indicate a negative correlation. The spread of the data points around each line shows how strong the correlation is. The closer the points are to falling on a straight line, the stronger the correlation.

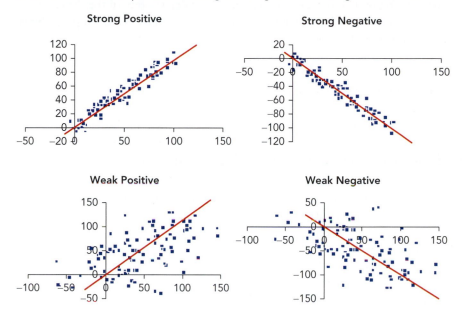

SOURCE: Adapted from Columbia University (2015).

Let's think about how you can use information from correlational data. If you read an article in your local newspaper that said, "Study finds that mothers who talk to their children a great deal have children with high self-esteem," could we correctly conclude that frequent conversations with their children will build self-esteem? We could not. Correlational research tells us that there is a relationship between two variables (in this case, mothers' conversations and children's self-esteem), but we do not know what, if anything, was controlled in the study. A third variable that wasn't even measured by the correlational research might be responsible for the relationship we observed. For instance, it may be that the mothers who talked a lot to their children were also ones who gave their children a lot of praise and positive feedback. In this case, it wouldn't be the *amount* of what they said that mattered as much as the *nature* of what they said. There are a lot of correlational studies in the developmental literature, and we know a good deal about a topic when we understand the relationship between two variables, but we must use caution when interpreting correlational findings because the fact that two things occur together does *not* mean that one of them necessarily caused the other. In Chapter 1, you were advised to be a careful consumer of information about development. If you know that when there is a correlation between two variables it is not the same thing as saying that one causes the other, it will make you a better consumer of information you might hear on television or read on the Internet.

Why would a researcher choose to use a correlational design rather than to conduct an experiment? One reason would be that doing a correlation is a much simpler procedure. You simply need to collect the data for the two variables you are interested in. You could even use archival data collected by someone else. That is why correlational information can be used as a starting point for research with an experimental design. For instance, based on the correlational finding described previously, we could develop an intervention that trains mothers to use more positive statements in their conversations with their children. Within an experimental research design, we could then compare their children to other children whose

TRUE/FALSE VIDEO ▲

T ☐ F ☐ Even if research consistently finds that mothers who talk to their children a great deal have children with high self-esteem, we should not conclude that frequent conversations with parents build self-esteem in children.
True

mothers talk to them the same amount but who use fewer positive statements. If the amount of conversation is the same for both groups of mothers, but the mothers who use more positive statements have children with higher self-esteem, we can then correctly conclude that positive statements (not just the amount of conversation) are a cause of higher self-esteem in children.

Before moving on to our next topic, check your understanding of the different types of methods used in child development research by completing **Active Learning: The Scientific Method—Research Designs.**

Active LEARNING

The Scientific Method—Research Designs

Look again at the abstract of the article by Levine and Waite (2000) found in **Active Learning: The Scientific Method—Forming a Hypothesis** near the beginning of this chapter. In it you have enough information to answer these questions:

1. Does this study use an experimental or a correlational research design? Here is a hint: Did the experimenters randomly assign children to different groups who then received different treatments?

2. Can the researchers conclude that television viewing causes children to have attention problems? Why or why not?

Answers: 1. The children were not randomly assigned to groups. The researchers looked at the relationship between the amount of television they watched and their attentional difficulties (that is, they correlated these two measures). They did not directly manipulate the amount of television that the children watched, so this research is a correlational research design, not an experimental design. **2.** The answer again is no. Because this is a correlational design, the researchers cannot conclude anything about causation. They can only state that television viewing is related to attention difficulties. Just as we described earlier, it is possible (and some have argued for this point of view) that children who have attention difficulties are more likely to watch a lot of television because it holds their attention more effectively than other activities, so we can't be sure which variable is the cause and which is the effect. It is also possible that a third variable, such as parental depression or neglect, might cause both increased television viewing and attention problems so we cannot talk about the causes of the behaviors we observed in this research.

DEVELOPMENTAL DESIGNS

If we define development as "change with age," there are several ways to examine the changes that occur as children grow and develop. As we look at these designs, we will find that each has its own advantages and disadvantages, but that each also has a place in answering the complex questions we have about development.

Longitudinal Research

Longitudinal design
A research design that follows one group of individuals and gathers data from them at several points in time.

A **longitudinal design** follows one group of individuals and gathers data from them at several points in time. The biggest advantage that comes with doing a longitudinal study is that it gives us the clearest picture of how the variables we are interested in change as a function of age.

To illustrate, Côté, Tremblay, Nagin, Zoccolillo, and Vitaro (2002) conducted a longitudinal study of 1,569 children and adolescents from kindergarten through sixth grade. Teachers rated each child on several behaviors once a year over this period. The results from this longitudinal study found that the risk for developing a conduct disorder in adolescence was highest among the boys who maintained a high level of hyperactivity over time. Figure 3.3 shows the results from this study.

FIGURE 3.3

Longitudinal study of hyperactivity. In this study, four patterns of hyperactivity were found for boys over time. Almost 17% never showed hyperactivity, 35.8% had decreasing levels of hyperactivity, 10.9% had slightly increasing but low levels, and 36.5% remained hyperactive from age 6 through 12. Boys who showed a consistently high level of hyperactivity were at greater risk of developing a conduct disorder than those who had lower levels.

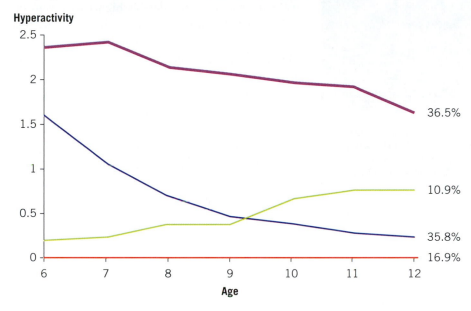

SOURCE: Côté, Tremblay, Nagin, Zoccolillo, & Vitaro (2002).

NOTE: The trajectory in bold purple represents the risk trajectory.

Although longitudinal research provides unique and valuable information, it can be a difficult method to use. Stop for a moment and decide for yourself what would be some of the challenges of following and testing more than 1,500 students each year for 7 years. It should be clear to you that this was a very ambitious research effort.

Because you need to track your study participants across a period of time, it is inevitable that some of the participants who begin a longitudinal study will not complete all the waves of data collection. The loss of participants from a sample over the course of a longitudinal study is called **attrition.** If all participants had an equal risk of dropping out of the study before its completion, this would reduce the size of your sample and reduce your ability to detect differences among the participants, but it might not otherwise jeopardize the validity of your research. However, all students are *not* at an equal risk of dropping out. Some children and adolescents are more likely than others to move, to be unavailable when one or more of the data collections occur, or simply to decide to withdraw from the study. For instance, it would be more difficult to retain children who are poorer, less healthy, or more trouble-prone because they are more likely to be absent from school more often or may move more frequently and change schools.

To the extent that it is children with these characteristics who are more likely to drop out, the final sample is less representative than it was when the study began. Although we may have started with a representative sample, over time **sample bias** will creep into our longitudinal study. If the most trouble-prone children are the ones most likely to drop out, the children who remain in the study at the end may be functioning at a higher level in any number of ways compared to the children who were lost from the sample, and this would inflate our final estimate of the children's abilities or level of functioning.

If you have ever watched the national college basketball play-offs (the NCAA "March Madness"), you have an idea of how sample bias creeps into a longitudinal study. You

Attrition The loss of participants over the course of a longitudinal study.

Sample bias Changes in the makeup of the sample in a longitudinal or sequential study that make the sample less representative over time.

Andy Lyons/Getty Images Sport/Getty Images

Sample bias. Just as the weakest players and teams are eliminated early during the NCAA basketball play-offs, the research participants with the most problems in their lives are more likely to drop out of a longitudinal study over time. This creates bias in the sample by the end of the study.

could measure the average basketball skill level across all the players on the 64 teams that begin the competition. However, during the play-offs, teams are defeated and drop out of the competition. If you based your final estimate of the level of basketball skill of the players on the teams that made it through to the Final Four, your estimate would be considerably higher than your original estimate because the teams with the weaker players have been eliminated. The same thing happens as more children with greater challenges in their lives drop out of longitudinal research, and the longer the period of time covered by the study, the greater this risk becomes.

To answer the question that we asked earlier about the challenges of doing longitudinal studies such as the one conducted by Côté and colleagues (2002), you probably realize that it takes a good deal of time and money and a large number of research personnel to conduct a study of a large group of individuals across multiple waves of data collection. Many researchers do not have the resources they would need to conduct this type of research.

Other challenges of doing longitudinal studies include the fact that researchers are locked into using one set of measures, even if better alternatives come along during the course of the study. If researchers change measures during the study and find changes in the level of the outcomes they are measuring, they cannot be sure whether the change was due to the fact that the participants were older or whether the new measure was actually measuring something slightly different than the original measure. In addition, if the same or similar measures are used repeatedly, it is possible that there is a practice effect and a participant's response will be influenced by how that individual answered questions at an earlier point in the study. Despite these concerns, however, longitudinal research still provides a very powerful way to look at developmental change, and that is why it is widely used.

Cross-Sectional Research

Cross-sectional design
A research design that uses multiple groups of participants who represent the age span of interest to the researcher.

A **cross-sectional design** is an approach that uses multiple groups of participants who represent the age span of interest to the researcher. If you were interested in developmental changes between elementary and middle school, you could use groups of participants who were 8 years old, 10 years old, and 12 years old and collect data from all the groups at about the same time. Then, by comparing the results between groups, you could construct a picture of the changes that occur over that period of development. Because all of the data collection occurs at the same time, you can efficiently collect data from a large number of participants in a relatively quick, cost-effective manner. You don't need to wait years between your data collection points. Obviously participant dropout and sample bias is not an issue because there is only a single data collection. However, there are some drawbacks of using a cross-sectional design. Based on cross-sectional research, you will know that children of different ages show differences on the outcome you measured, but you won't know *why*. We presume that it is age changes that are responsible, but we need to be careful when making these presumptions.

One of the challenges in doing cross-sectional research is that the different age groups in the study must be as similar as possible on any variable that might affect the study's outcome. Here is an extreme example to make this point clear: Imagine you are interested in how self-esteem changes during the transition from elementary to middle school. To examine these changes, you study a group of 8-year-old students who attended a public elementary school in a disadvantaged neighborhood, a group of 10-year-old students from a private school with a religious affiliation, and a group of 12-year-old students from a suburban public school. Even if you found differences in self-esteem between the groups, could you correctly interpret them as age-related changes or changes associated with school transitions? Clearly you couldn't. Because the groups came from such widely different school settings (and, therefore, it is likely that they differ from each other in a variety of ways in addition to age), you could not make any valid interpretation of these data. The differences that may exist between groups used in actual cross-sectional research would be much more subtle than those in this example, but any difference between the groups that is not recognized and accounted for by the research can be a threat to the validity of the conclusions drawn from this type of research.

Finally, cross-sectional research can be affected by what is known as the **cohort effect.** A cohort is a group of people born at about the same point in historical time. A cohort effect becomes a concern in cross-sectional research when the age range represented by the different groups is large enough that the participants in the groups come from different birth cohorts or when some

Cohort effect. When groups in cross-sectional research come from different cohorts (or birth groups), it is important not to interpret differences we observe as due to age if they may actually represent differences in cohort life experiences. This child may know more about computers than his grandfather, but it is because he has had more experience using them, not because people forget how to use computers as they get older.

aspect of the environment has changed significantly between the groups in the study. We use the term *baby boom generation* to describe people born between the mid-1940s and the mid-1960s; *Gen Xers* were born between the early 1960s and the late 1970s; and *millennials* were born between the late 1970s and about 1995. You can easily see how members of each of these cohorts would have had different experiences while growing up that would make them different in a number of ways. For example, millennials grew up with computers, but baby boomers never saw a personal computer until they were adults. If we were to measure competence in computer use, we would likely find that the millennials are more skilled than the baby boomers. However, we could not conclude that as people get older they become less skilled at using a computer. The difference we see is likely due to a different set of life experiences, *not* to a loss of computer skills with increasing age. This is an important point to keep in mind because researchers who conduct cross-sectional research want to conclude that differences seen between age groups in cross-sectional research are due to developmental changes, and not to something else.

> **Cohort effect** Differences between groups in a cross-sectional or sequential study that are attributable to the fact that the participants have had different life experiences.

Sequential Research

Finally, **sequential designs** bring together elements of cross-sectional research and longitudinal research. This design uses several groups of people of different ages who begin their participation in the study at the same time (just as cross-sectional research does) and follows the groups over a period of time (just as longitudinal research does). What makes this method unique is that there is overlap between the groups on their ages at one point in the testing.

For example, if we were interested in looking at children's health over the age range from birth until age 20, we could begin by assessing four different groups: infants, 5-year-olds, 10-year-olds, and 15-year-olds. If we repeated our assessment 5 years later (when the infants were 5 years old, the 5-year-olds were 10, etc.), we then would have two different groups that had been assessed at age 5. Because we only needed to follow the groups for 5 years, we would have reduced the risk of participants dropping out of the research study to below what it would have been in a 20-year study (and therefore reduced sample bias). We also would have reduced the time, money, and personnel needed to conduct the study compared to a 20-year-long study of children's health. Finally, if there were any cohort differences between the groups, those effects would have become apparent in the results when we compared the results of the group that ended the study at a given age to the results of the group that started the study at that age.

Although some advantages are gained through the use of sequential research, you still need to construct the cohort groups so that they are as much alike as possible at the start of

> **Sequential design** A research design that uses multiple groups of participants and follows them over a period of time, with the beginning age of each group being the ending age of another group.

the study, and you still need to be able to track and reassess the groups at regular intervals, so sample attrition and practice effects are still potential problems.

Microgenetic Research

Microgenetic design
A research design that involves frequent observations of participants during a time of change or transition.

A fourth type of developmental research design is a **microgenetic design.** In this case, the term *genetic* refers to the *genesis* or beginning of a behavior, not to the action of our genes. *Micro* refers to the fact that this approach looks at small, moment-to-moment changes that eventually lead to larger developmental change. This is a particularly good way to look at naturally occurring behaviors in a social context (Lavelli, Pantoja, Hsu, Messinger, & Fogel, 2005).

To use a microgenetic design, an individual or small group of individuals are observed frequently during the time that a change is expected to happen. The frequency of the observations allows researchers to see changes that otherwise would be missed by designs that rely on less frequent observations. The full picture of developmental change that results describes not only what happens and when it happens, but also the process by which the change occurs (Fogel, 2011). For example, Spencer and colleagues (Spencer, Vereijken, Diedrich, & Thelen, 2000) used this design to study the emergence of reaching behavior in infants by observing four infants on a weekly basis between the ages of 3 and 30 weeks. They found that infants could reach out and grasp a toy they wanted between 12 and 22 weeks of age. They also found that an infant needed to have certain component skills in their behavioral repertoire before they could reach for an object, but that these skills did not necessarily appear in the same order for each infant. This illustrates why microgenetic designs are a good way to study individual differences. The fact that different infants took different pathways to reaching would have been lost if the researchers used another type of design.

Microgenetic designs also are particularly good at answering one of the questions introduced in Chapter 1: the question of how much stability versus change there is in development. A microgenetic design identifies new behaviors (the change elements) that build upon earlier ones (the stable elements) to shape the trajectory of development.

As with any research design, there are advantages and disadvantages of microgenetic research. Participating in this type of research requires a strong commitment on the part of the participants. In one study, parents brought infants to a laboratory for observation every week for a full year (Lavelli et al., 2005). However, this level of commitment to a study also means that parents and children become true collaborators in the research process. We also need to recognize that because the design requires repeated testing, some of the change we observe may be due to a practice effect. Because of the intensive nature of the observations, this is a time-consuming and expensive approach. And, while it produces a great deal of data that is rich and informative (Flynn, Pine, & Lewis, 2006), it also means that all that data must be analyzed and reduced before it can yield an understandable set of conclusions. This can be a daunting task.

In summary, while other developmental research designs give us a snapshot of what is happening at different points in development, the microgenetic approach gives us insight into the *process* of change as it is actually happening (Flynn et al., 2006). The number of microgenetic studies has increased in recent years and its use appears to be growing.

Table 3.3 summarizes the characteristics, advantages, and disadvantages of the four developmental research designs we have described.

CHECK YOUR UNDERSTANDING

1. Explain why an experiment can identify the causes of behavior while a correlational study cannot.
2. Describe the advantages of using a longitudinal design and a cross-sectional design.
3. Describe the advantages of a sequential design over longitudinal and cross-sectional designs.
4. Describe the advantages of a microgenetic design over typical longitudinal and cross-sectional ones.

TABLE 3.3

Comparison of developmental research designs.

	Longitudinal Designs	Cross-Sectional Designs	Sequential Designs	Microgenetic Designs
Sample Size	Large	Large	Large	Small
Length of Study	Long-term, typically from months to years	Short (all children participate at about the same time)	Relatively long	Typically brief, but with very frequent observations
Advantages	Captures the continuity of development	Quicker, easier, less expensive than longitudinal studies	Can detect cohort effects Less time-consuming and expensive than longitudinal designs Lower risk of attrition and threat of sample bias	Captures both stability and change Good for studying individual differences Can identify factors that promote or hinder developmental change Produces rich, informative data
Disadvantages	Requires multiple points of data collection Expensive, time-consuming Risk of attrition and threat of sample bias	Requires that groups are carefully matched on a number of characteristics Potential cohort effects	Requires that groups are carefully matched Requires multiple points of data collection	Requires strong commitment from participants May create a practice effect Time intensive and expensive Great deal of data to reduce and analyze

INTERPRETING AND COMMUNICATING THE RESULTS OF A STUDY

TRUE/FALSE VIDEO ▲

3.3 **What must we consider when interpreting and communicating the results of a study?**

After we conduct research, we must still interpret the results. The accuracy of our final understanding of what a study shows is greatly affected by how the data are interpreted, but two people could look at the results of a study and interpret them in a different way. In reaching our conclusions, we must be careful not to generalize beyond the characteristics of the sample that participated in the research. We also need to remember that conclusions drawn from research—even very carefully conducted research—are generalizations that apply to groups of individuals. As you learned in Chapter 1, there is a great deal of diversity among individuals within any group. Research tells us about what is average or typical for a group of people, so the fact that some individuals fall outside that range does not invalidate the general conclusion.

To help us correctly interpret our studies, results of research are tested using various statistical methods. If you were evaluating the effectiveness of a new program intended to improve social problem-solving skills, you would hypothesize that at the end of the experiment the students who participate in the program will have better social problem-solving skills than a similar group of students who don't participate in the program. Tests of statistical significance give us confidence that results from research are not accidents or chance occurrences.

However, even if the results of a research study are statistically significant, you still might wonder whether the findings make any difference in the real world. Just because a study finds

T ☐ F ☐ Research has shown that boys who watch a lot of violence on TV are more aggressive, but you know someone who watches a lot of violence and you see that he is not at all aggressive. This disproves the research. **False**

that differences between two groups are statistically significant (that is, they did not happen by chance), it does not necessarily mean that the difference is large or important. A real-life example of this distinction comes from research on the relationship between birth order and intelligence (Kristensen & Bjerkedal, 2007). An analysis of the IQ test scores of over 250,000 young men in the Norwegian military service found that the scores of the first-born men in the sample were higher than the scores of second-born men at a statistically significant level of .05 (meaning there are only 5 chances in 100 that this is a chance finding). But before any first-born readers of this text begin celebrating their intellectual superiority over their siblings, you need to know that the difference in test scores between the two groups was only 2.82 points. Although these results are statistically significant, it is not likely that a difference of less than 3 IQ points will have any practical significance in the lives of these men. Results that are statistically significant do not always translate into something that has consequences in the real world. Increasingly, researchers are also reporting **effect sizes,** which are a statistical measure of how large the difference is between groups that are being compared. While the significance level tells us that there is a difference, the effect size tells us how big that difference is (Sullivan & Feinn, 2012). Sometimes a statistical procedure called **meta-analysis** is used to combine data from different studies to determine whether there is a consistent pattern of findings across studies. We will discuss the results from meta-analyses on several important topics throughout this book.

After researchers have confidence in the conclusions drawn from their research, they share that information with others. In Chapter 1, we described the peer review process that articles go through before they are published in journals. A similar process precedes the presentation of research information at professional meetings. This process gives others who are knowledgeable about the topic the opportunity to critique the way that the research was conducted and identify any possible flaws in the logic or problems with the methodology, analysis, or interpretation of the findings before those findings are shared with others.

Researchers also make their information available to the public, government agencies, private organizations, and policymakers who can use this information in ways that benefit children and families. In Chapter 1, you read about the importance of sharing findings with policymakers so they can be translated into public policy. Most university websites feature research currently being conducted by their faculty and students. Think of how often you see new findings from the field of child development covered as a story on the evening news or in a local newspaper or national magazine. All of these avenues help disseminate research findings to a wider audience than just the scientific community.

T ☐ F ☐ Once we have established that the results of our research are statistically significant, we can be confident they will have an impact on real-world situations. **False**

Effect size A statistical measure of how large the difference is between groups being compared.

Meta-analysis A statistical procedure that combines data from different studies to determine whether there is a consistent pattern of findings across studies.

CHECK YOUR UNDERSTANDING

1. Why must we be careful when we generalize the results from any one study?
2. What is the difference between statistical significance and effect size?

ETHICS IN RESEARCH WITH CHILDREN AND ADOLESCENTS

3.4 What special precautions must be used when our research participants are children?

Any research with human participants must ensure their safety and well-being. U.S. Department of Health and Human Services (2005a) regulations provide specific protections for research participants. They may be exposed to only minimal risks during their participation, and any potential risk must be weighed against the anticipated benefits from the research. They must be informed of the purpose of the research and its risks and benefits and must freely agree—without coercion—to participate; they have the right to withdraw from participation at any point. Finally, the privacy of participants must be protected, and the data collected must be treated as confidential.

Because of their particular vulnerability, children are given additional protections when they participate in research. The Society for Research in Child Development (SRCD, 2012) has developed specific guidelines that include:

- the expectation that no physical or psychological harm will be done to children who participate in research.

- the expectation that the researcher will use the least stressful research procedures possible.

- the necessity to obtain consent from both the children and their parents for the child's participation. If children are not old enough to give consent because they do not necessarily understand the full significance of the research, they still must assent if they are old enough to do that.

- the right of children and families to freely choose to participate in the research and to be able to terminate participation at any point if they want to.

- the responsibility of the researcher to inform parents of any threats to the child's well-being that they become aware of during the course of the research and to arrange for assistance for the child.

It is only with the help and cooperation of children and families that the field of child development can continue to build its understanding. They are truly participants in this process.

CHECK YOUR UNDERSTANDING

1. What does the U.S. Department of Health and Human Services require as ethical guidelines for research with human participants?
2. What additional considerations come from the Society for Research on Child Development for research involving children?

CONCLUSION

In this chapter, you received a broad introduction to the various ways that researchers add to our knowledge base in child and adolescent development. Each approach has advantages and disadvantages, so no one approach is the best choice in all situations. Instead we strive to find an approach or method that is appropriate for the type of research we are conducting. Beyond that, as information accumulates over time, we build our confidence in our findings and conclusions. This is particularly true when different methods have been used by different researchers but the information they find fits together into a coherent picture.

CHAPTER SUMMARY

Test your understanding of the content.
Take the practice quiz at **edge.sagepub.com/levine3e**

3.1 What is the scientific method and how is it used to study development?

The **scientific method** is the way we add knowledge to our understanding of child development. It begins with observations, which generate **hypotheses.** After we **operationalize** the concepts in our hypotheses, we select a **representative sample** from the **population** that participates in the research. Any measures that we use must have good **reliability** and **validity**. Research can be conducted using **observation, checklists** of behaviors, or by asking children (or people who know them well) to report on behaviors. Self-report measures include **surveys, questionnaires,** and **interviews** (including **clinical interviews**). We also gather data by using **standardized tests,** physiological measures, or **archival records.** Sometimes a **case study** is conducted to intensively study a single individual who is of interest or the researcher conducts an **ethnographic study** to study a different culture.

3.2 What are the different types of research designs used to study development?

Research designs are the roadmap or blueprint that we use to structure our research. We can use an **experimental design,** or a **correlational design,** and we can use one of several developmental designs: **longitudinal, cross-sectional, sequential,** or **microgenetic designs**. In an experimental design, participants are randomly assigned to either the **experimental group** or the **control group.** The **independent variable** is the treatment given to the experimental group but not to the control group. At the conclusion of the experiment, the **dependent variable** is measured for both groups and compared. If there is a difference, we can conclude that the independent variable caused the change. Because the researcher has a great deal of control over what happens during the experiment, the results can help determine the causes of the behavior we observe. A **correlational research design** measures the strength and direction of the relationship between two variables. Although a correlation indicates that two variables are related, it cannot tell us what causes the relationship. In a **longitudinal design,** a single group of study participants is followed for a period of time and is tested or assessed repeatedly. In a **cross-sectional design,** several groups of participants of different ages are assessed at the same time and compared to get a picture of how changes occur as a function of age. A **sequential design** follows several groups over time, with overlap in the ages of the participants at the times of each test. In a **microgenetic design,** the researcher makes frequent, detailed observations of the participants around the time that a developmental transition is expected to occur.

3.3 What must we consider when interpreting and communicating the results of a study?

The results of a study must be interpreted with caution, being careful not to **generalize** them beyond the characteristics of the sample used in the research or to draw conclusions that go beyond the scope of the study. We need to remember that the results apply to groups, not individuals, so there will be individuals who are exceptions to the study results. Finally, we can assess the statistical significance of the findings using tests of probability, but finding statistical significance does not necessarily mean that the results will have real-world or practical significance. **Effect size** gives a statistical measure of how large the difference is between groups that are being compared. Through publication in research journals and presentations at professional meetings, researchers disseminate their findings. They also make their findings available to the public, governmental agencies, private organizations, and policymakers.

3.4 What special precautions must be used when research participants are children?

All research must protect the physical and psychological safety and well-being of all participants, and children in particular. Researchers must minimize any risk to them, and protect their confidentiality. If children are old enough to understand the nature of the research, they are asked to provide informed consent that is freely given. Children (or their parents) have the right to withdraw from participation in the study at any point and researchers are obligated to rectify any threats to the children's well-being that they detect.

KEY TERMS

Strengthen your understanding of these key terms with
mobile-friendly eFlashcards at **edge.sagepub.com/levine3e**

Applied research   66
Archival records   81
Attrition   91
Basic research   66
Case study   81
Checklist   76
Clinical interview   78
Cohort effect   93
Control group   84
Correlational research design   87
Cross-sectional design   92
Dependent variable   85
Effect size   96
Ethnography   82
Experimental group   84
Experimental research design   84
Generalize   70
Hypotheses   66
Independent variable   85
Interview   76
Longitudinal design   90

Meta-analysis   96
Microgenetic design   94
Natural or "quasi" experiment   87
Negative correlation   88
Norm   79
Observer bias   75
Operationalize   68
Population   70
Positive correlation   88
Questionnaire   76
Random assignment   84
Reliability   70
Representative sample   70
Sample bias   91
Scientific method   66
Sequential design   93
Standardized test   78
Survey   76
Validity   70
Variable   68

Give your students the SAGE edge!

SAGE edge offers a robust online environment featuring an impressive array of free tools and
resources for review, study, and further exploration, keeping both instructors and students on
the cutting edge of teaching and learning. Learn more at **edge.sagepub.com/levine3e**

practice
AND
apply
WHAT YOU'VE LEARNED

edge.sagepub.com/levine3e

Blend Images/KidStock/Brand X/Getty
Randy Faris/Corbis/VCG/Corbis/Getty
ERproductions Ltd/Blend Images/Getty
Tanya Constantine/Blend Images/Getty

PART II

BIOLOGICAL BEGINNINGS AND PHYSICAL DEVELOPMENT

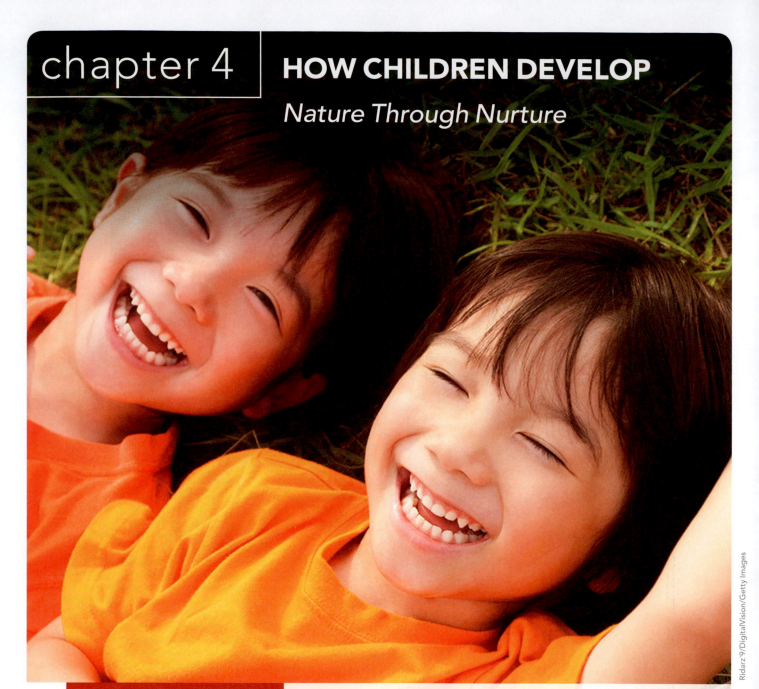

chapter 4

HOW CHILDREN DEVELOP

Nature Through Nurture

LEARNING QUESTIONS

4.1 How has the study of genetic inheritance changed in the last century?

4.2 How do genes and chromosomes function?

4.3 How do genetic disorders develop, and what role do genetic testing and counseling play in identifying, preventing, and treating these disorders?

4.4 How do we study the relationship between our genetic inheritance and our traits and behavior?

4.5 How do genes and the environment interact?

Master these objectives using an online action plan at **edge.sagepub.com/levine3e**

TEST YOUR KNOWLEDGE

Test your knowledge of child development by deciding whether each of the following statements is *true* or *false*, and then check your answers as you read the chapter.

1. **T ☐ F ☐:** When a child is conceived, it is the mother's genetic material that determines the gender of the child.

2. **T ☐ F ☐:** Each human being has hundreds of thousands of genes that make him or her a unique individual.

3. **T ☐ F ☐:** Two parents with brown eyes can still have a child with blue eyes.

4. **T ☐ F ☐:** Carrying one recessive gene for sickle-cell anemia can be beneficial for an individual.

5. **T ☐ F ☐:** Every gene in the body has one specific function.

6. **T ☐ F ☐:** Males are more likely to have a genetic disorder than females.

7. **T ☐ F ☐:** Mike is a talented pianist. Because both of his parents are musicians, genes must have determined that Mike would also have musical talent.

8. **T ☐ F ☐:** Genes have been found to play a role in the development of almost all behaviors that have been studied.

9. **T ☐ F ☐:** Identical twins reared apart are more similar on many personality characteristics than fraternal twins reared together.

10. **T ☐ F ☐:** The experiences you have in your life can change the structure of your genes.

Correct answers: (1) F, (2) F, (3) T, (4) T, (5) F, (6) T, (7) F, (8) T, (9) T, (10) F

▲ **VIDEO: Watch as students answer some of these questions and the authors respond.**

Genes are the basic unit of our biological inheritance from our mother and father. In this chapter, we examine what we know about the effects of genes on children's development. We begin with a brief historical view of the study of genetics. We then describe genes and how they work and examine how they impact development. Finally, we discuss the interaction of genes and environment to show that nature (genes) and nurture (environment) are inextricably tied together so we cannot attribute most aspects of development separately to one or the other.

THE STUDY OF GENETICS AND BEHAVIOR

4.1 **How has the study of genetic inheritance changed in the last century?**

There is a long history associated with the *nature versus nurture controversy*, based on the idea that certain human attributes will be directed by our genes (nature) or by our experiences in our environment (nurture). As discussed in Chapter 1, recent research has revealed a much more complex interaction between genes and environment in determining who we are. We now know that the way in which many genes are expressed is greatly influenced by the experiences that each individual has in the environment (Meaney, 2010; Stiles, 2009).

The ongoing task of scientific research in the field of genetics is to expand knowledge of how genes interact with the environment to make us who we are. To begin to understand some of the surprising and even shocking history of genetics research, read **Journey of Research: The History of Research on Genetics.**

JOURNEY OF *Research*

The History of Research on Genetics

The modern study of genetics began in 1866 when Gregor Mendel published a paper outlining a number of the principles that guide the transmission of genetic information from one generation to another. However, it took until 1900 before the significance of his work was recognized (Lane, 1994). The basic principles of inheritance that he described came to be known as Mendelian inheritance. Although Mendel was able to describe the way in which characteristics of pea plants were passed on from one generation to the next, he did not know about genes or how they work.

At this same point in history, Francis Galton, following certain principles of evolutionary theory developed by his cousin Charles Darwin, concluded that just as pea plants could be bred to have certain characteristics, so could desirable traits be bred into human beings. He called this concept eugenics. This process would involve reproduction by "superior" human beings and sterilization of inferior ones. Galton's idea became so influential that, beginning in 1907, 30 states in the United States passed laws allowing for the forced sterilization of about 60,000 people considered to be "criminals, idiots, rapists, and imbeciles" (Watson, 2003, p. 27). The terms *idiot* and *imbecile* in those days were not just name-calling. They indicated levels of performance on IQ tests. As the Nazis came to power in Germany in the 1930s, they enthusiastically adopted a policy that embraced eugenics. They began with sterilization but then moved to mass murder of all those deemed unfit to reproduce for a multitude of reasons. This came to include annihilation of entire ethnic groups in the service of creating a pure "Aryan race" (Watson, 2003).

As a result of the excesses of the eugenics movement, genetics research came to be seen as suspect. It was not until the 1950s that James Watson and Francis Crick discovered the basic secrets of genetic structure and function. Their finding allowed scientists to understand the exact process that underlies the genetic transmission first described by Mendel almost 100 years earlier. In 1990, with James Watson as its first director, the Human Genome Project undertook the ambitious goal of mapping all of the human genes (National Human Genome Research Institute, 2010). In 2003, exactly 50 years after Watson and Crick's discovery, a mapping of the entire sequence of DNA that makes up the human genome was completed (National Human Genome Research Institute, 2016).

As you can see from the Journey of Research, there have been two ways in which scientists have approached the study of genes and biological inheritance. Before they knew about the existence of genes in the body, they examined the effects of genetic inheritance by observing the inheritance of certain characteristics from one generation to the next. Later in this chapter, we will look at research surrounding **behavioral genetics** based on looking at similarities and differences between individuals who have the same genes (identical twins) and individuals who are adopted so that they share genes with two birth parents, but share environmental influences with adoptive parents and siblings.

Behavioral genetics
Research to determine the degree of genetic basis for a behavior, a trait, or an ability.

The second way to study genes began when Watson and Crick discovered the biological structure and function of genes. To understand the way that genes impact child development, we begin here with a description of genes and how they work which emerges from the study of **molecular genetics**.

Molecular genetics Research focused on the identification of particular genes to identify how these genes work within the cell.

CHECK YOUR UNDERSTANDING

1. What did Mendel study and how does it relate to our current understanding of genetics?
2. What did the Human Genome Project accomplish?
3. How do molecular genetics and behavioral genetics differ?

MOLECULAR GENETICS: CHROMOSOMES, GENES, AND DNA

4.2 How do genes and chromosomes function?

Our genetic inheritance begins at conception. A woman's egg cells and a man's sperm cells each contain half our genetic material, organized into 23 **chromosomes**. When a father's sperm penetrates a mother's egg during **fertilization**, the fertilized egg that results is called a **zygote**. When fertilization occurs, the chromosome strands from the sperm join those from the egg to form 23 matched pairs in which genes with the same function pair up. As you can see in Figure 4.1, in 22 of these pairs of chromosomes (called *autosomes*) the two chromosomes look very similar. Note, however, that the chromosomes in the 23rd pair can be the same or different. These two chromosomes have been named the X chromosome and the Y chromosome. Because women have two X chromosomes, the eggs they produce can only contain an X chromosome in the 23rd position. Because men have an X and a Y chromosome, the sperm they produce can contain either an X or a Y chromosome in this position. When the egg and the sperm unite, it is the father's contribution of either an X or a Y chromosome that determines the sex of the child. A conception with an X chromosome from both parents is a female. One with an X chromosome from the mother and a Y chromosome from the father is a male.

To understand the basic units of genetic inheritance, first look at Figure 4.2. You see in this figure that chromosomes are found in the nuclei of each cell. Chromosomes are composed of chains of DNA (deoxyribonucleic acid). These chains twirl around each other in a *double helix* that looks much like a winding staircase with a banister, as shown in Figure 4.2. The basic building blocks of life are the four nitrogenous bases that make up DNA: guanine (G), adenine (A), thymine (T), and cytosine (C) (Klug, Cummings, Spencer, & Palladino, 2016). The complete sequence of these bases that make up the genetic instructions in an organism is called the **genome.** Within the sequence of bases are areas that work together to provide the codes needed to assemble proteins, which are the molecules within cells that create the structure and function of the body. These areas on the chromosomes are called genes.

When the Human Genome Project, which was mentioned in the *Journey of Research,* completed mapping all the genes that make a human being, one of the biggest surprises was that the total came to only about 25,000 genes, not the 100,000 or more that researchers had expected to find (U.S. Department of Energy Genome Programs, 2012). If the number of genes alone governed how complex and sophisticated we are as a species, then it would appear that we are only a little more complicated than plants, mice, or fruit flies. Even rice

Chromosomes The strands of genes that constitute the human genetic endowment.

Fertilization The union of a father's sperm and a mother's egg to produce a zygote.

Zygote A fertilized egg.

T ☐ F ☐ When a child is conceived, it is the mother's genetic material that determines the gender of the child. **False**

Genome The complete sequence of bases that make up the genetic instructions of an organism.

T ☐ F ☐ Each human being has hundreds of thousands of genes that make him or her a unique individual. **False**

FIGURE 4.1

Human chromosomes. This image shows a full set of 23 pairs of chromosomes. This set represents a male so there is an X-chromosome and a Y-chromosome in the 23rd position. For a female there would be two X-chromosomes in the 23rd position.

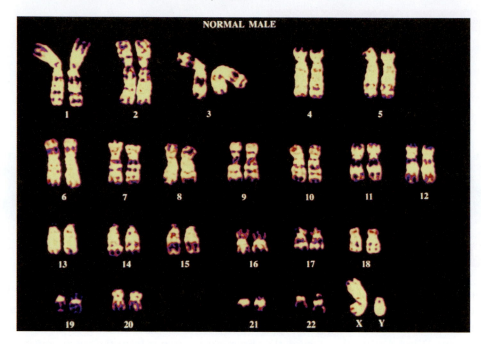

SOURCE: Biophoto Associates/Science Source/Getty Images.

has between 46,000 and 55,600 genes! (National Human Genome Research Institute, 2007). Something other than simply the number of genes must account for the large differences between species.

We also now know that only 2% of the entire human genome is needed to make up those 25,000 genes (Plomin, 2013). The other 98% of the genome was long considered to be "junk" that had no effect, but this idea also is changing rapidly. With new technology, scientists are now able to use whole-genome sequencing to study the entire human genome (Plomin, 2013). Some of the areas formerly considered to have no function have been found to play an important role in regulating the way the 25,000 active genes are expressed (Zhang et al., 2013).

Although most of the genes in the human genome have been identified, we are still a long way from knowing exactly what each actually does (U.S. Department of Energy Genome Programs, 2008). Think of genes as simply a set of instructions, such as you might get when you purchase a new cell phone with many unfamiliar features. If you read and follow the instructions, you will be able to perform all the functions built into the cell phone. However, if you don't, you may never use some of them. In a similar way, genes may either be read or ignored, with consequences for the aspects of human structure and functioning to which they are related. We will learn more about the ways in which genes are either expressed or how their instructions remain silent later in this chapter.

A gene is made up of the four bases, as a sentence is made up of words. A sentence can contain all kinds of information and instructions. Likewise, a gene contains information and instructions for the body to make a protein (Jorde, Carey, Bamshad, & White, 2006). The trick to identifying a particular gene is finding the sequence of G, A, T, and C that gives the body directions to create a certain protein. To better understand this process, look at the following sentence:

FIGURE 4.2

What are genes? Genes are segments of DNA, which is made up of the bases guanine, adenine, cytosine, and thymine. Genes are found on chromosomes, which are located within the nucleus of every cell. In the double helix molecule that makes up DNA, the base adenine always pairs with the base thymine, and the base guanine always pairs with the base cytosine. This "alphabet" of only four letters produces strings of bases that write the instructions for all the cells in our body.

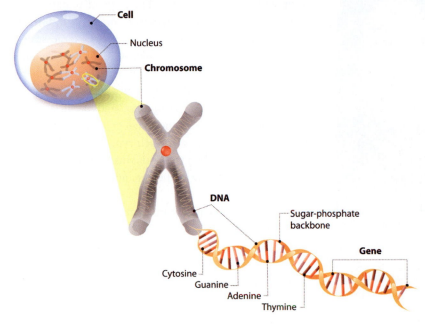

SOURCE: ttsz/Getty Images Plus.

Gotothegrocerystorepickupmilkcomehome

One way to divide this would be as follows:

Got oth egro

Ceryst orepick upm

Ilk comeho me

We all know this is wrong and makes no sense. You would really divide this sequence of letters into three meaningful instructions:

Go to the grocery store.

Pick up milk.

Come home.

In a similar way, scientists have taken sequences of bases such as ATCATCTTTGGTGTT and figured out which sequences give clear instructions to produce proteins.

All human beings share 99.5% of their genome; the remaining one-half of 1% is what contributes to our differences (National Human Genome Research Institute, 2012). Changes that can occur in the structure of genes, called **mutations**, also differentiate among human beings. We can inherit mutations from our parents, but we each have approximately 175 new mutations that are unique to us as individuals (Plomin, 2013). Most are inconsequential because they make no difference to our growth and development, but evolution of the species depends on the occurrence of mutations that turn out to be adaptive. Adaptive mutations are therefore handed down

Mutations Changes in the formation of genes that occur as cells divide.

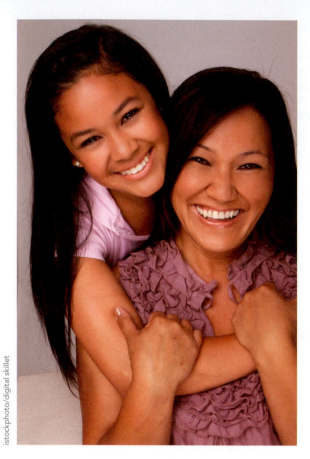

Gene dominance. Do you look as similar to one of your parents as this girl does to her mother? Inheritance of dominant genes from one parent or the other can result in striking resemblances.

Nucleotide An organic molecule that contains one of the four bases with a phosphate group and a sugar molecule.

Dominant genes Genes that are usually expressed in the phenotype.

Recessive genes Genes that are generally not expressed in the phenotype unless paired with another recessive gene.

Genotype The genes that are present at a particular location on the chromosome.

Phenotype The genetically-based characteristics that are actually shown in one's body.

from generation to generation (Wolters Kluwer Health, 2009). However, other mutations are harmful and have been linked to diseases such as cystic fibrosis and disorders such as autism and schizophrenia (Plomin, 2013). Mutations can occur in several different ways. A mutation can consist of variations in a single **nucleotide**, which is a combination of one of the four bases with a phosphate group and a sugar molecule. This type of mutation is referred to as a single nucleotide polymorphism, or SNP (Grigorenko & Dozier, 2013). Mutations can also consist of large-scale changes in the order of nucleotides in a gene. Groups of nucleotides can be inserted, deleted, or there can be variations in the number of copies of groups of nucleotides that appear in a gene. These various mutations can affect between one and thousands of nucleotides.

Let's return to our sentence analogy to illustrate the nature of these types of mutations. In each type of mutation described as follows, you can see that the initial instruction has been changed in some important way so the outcome will be quite different:

Single nucleotide polymorphism (SNP):

PICK UP MILK becomes PACK UP MILK

Change in the number of copies:

PICK UP MILK becomes PICK UPUPUPUPUP MILK

Insertion:

PICK UP MILK becomes PICK UP NO MILK

Deletion:

PICK UP MILK becomes PICK MILK

With this very basic understanding of how genes operate within the cell, we will now discuss how genes are translated into our physical appearance and our behaviors.

MENDELIAN INHERITANCE: DOMINANT AND RECESSIVE GENES

You may have been told that you look very much like your father or exactly like your mother. How can this be, when you received an equal number of chromosomes from each parent? When eggs and sperm are formed, the chromosomes in each "unzip" along the double helix so they each contain half the genetic material usually found in a cell. When egg and sperm combine at conception, chromosomes from each parent pair up and the genes from one parent are zipped up to similar genes from the other parent. Each gene from the father is paired with a gene from the mother. Traditional Mendelian genetics tells us that each pair of genes is made up of some combination of **dominant** and **recessive genes**. The genes that are present at a particular location on the chromosome are called the **genotype**. The information contained in the dominant genes is what is usually expressed in the person's body. What we see when we look at a person's bodily traits and characteristics is called the **phenotype**. The information from a recessive gene is usually not expressed in the phenotype unless the gene is paired with another recessive gene.

FIGURE 4.3

Genetic transmission of eye color (dominant and recessive genes).

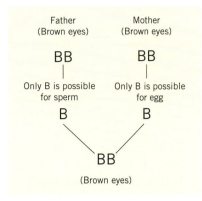

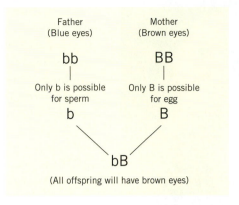

Both parents have only dominant genes for brown eyes, so that is the only genetic information they can pass to their children. All their children will have brown eyes.

The father only has recessive genes for blue eyes, so that is all he can pass along to his child. The mother only has dominant genes for brown eyes, so that is all she can pass along. Each child will have one gene for blue eyes and one gene for brown eyes, so all the children will have brown eyes.

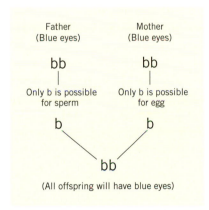

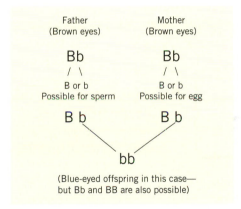

Both parents only have recessive genes for blue eyes. They both have blue eyes and can only pass genes for blue eyes to their children, so all their children will have blue eyes.

Each parent has both a dominant gene for brown eyes and a recessive gene for blue eyes (so both have brown eyes). However, if each passes along a recessive gene for blue eyes, the child will have blue eyes, but if either parent passes along a gene for brown eyes, the child will have brown eyes.

To use a simple example, brown (B) eye color is dominant over blue (b) eye color. It is not really as simple as this, but we will tell you more about what makes this process more complex after we work through this example. If your mother has brown eyes because she has two genes for brown eyes in her genotype, that is the only information she can pass along to her children. If your father has blue eyes, he *must* have two recessive genes for blue eyes. In this case, the only possible genetic combination you and your siblings can inherit is one dominant gene for brown eyes and one recessive gene for blue eyes. This also means that brown eyes will be expressed as the phenotype of all the children in your family. However, you will still carry in your genotype the one recessive gene for blue eyes that you received from your father. And if you have a child with someone who has brown eyes but who also carries one recessive gene for blue eyes, you will have a blue-eyed child if those two recessive genes are paired in the child. See Figure 4.3 to better understand how this might happen.

T ☐ F ☐ Two parents with brown eyes can still have a child with blue eyes.
True

Transmission of eye color. Although this mother has brown eyes, she must carry the recessive gene for blue eyes in her genotype. When her daughter received this recessive gene from her mother and another recessive gene for blue eyes from her father, she ended up with blue eyes.

T ☐ F ☐ Carrying one recessive gene for sickle-cell anemia can be beneficial for an individual. **True**

Although eye color is frequently used to illustrate the idea of dominant and recessive genes, you may have already realized that it isn't that simple. People also have green eyes, gray eyes, and hazel eyes. Although brown as an eye color is dominant over any of these alternatives, green, gray, and hazel eyes have their own dominance hierarchies. Also, the color of some people's eyes is bright and clear, and the color of other people's eyes is soft and washed out. This is because there are modifier genes that can influence the intensity of eye color. You may even know someone who has one blue eye and one brown eye. But while the genetic process is more complicated than our example indicates, the way dominant and recessive genes work is still central to an understanding of genetic inheritance.

Whether you have blue eyes or brown eyes is not crucial to your future development. Other types of gene pairings are, however, because some genetic disorders are caused by two recessive genes pairing up with each other. One such disease is *sickle-cell anemia,* which is found in 1 of every 500 African Americans. Sickle-cell anemia is a painful and destructive disease in which the shape of red blood cells is distorted. Normal red blood cells are smooth and round, but sickle cells look like the letter *C* (National Heart, Lung, and Blood Institute [NHLBI], 2007). Normal red blood cells have a large surface area which enables them to transport oxygen throughout the body, but sickle cells are not able to do this effectively. They are also hard and tend to clump together, restricting the blood flow into smaller blood vessels, as shown in Figure 4.4. This failure to transport oxygen to where it is needed results in pain and can eventually cause damage to the organs (NHLBI, 2007). We discuss genetic disorders more fully later in this chapter.

You may wonder why such maladaptive genes have not disappeared from the human gene pool, but there is a good evolutionary reason for this. It turns out that, although having two such recessive genes is harmful, having *one* of these recessive genes may be protective in certain environments. The recessive gene for sickle-cell anemia, which is carried in the genotype of about 1 in 10 African Americans, appears to protect people from malaria (Wolters Kluwer Health, 2009). The first hint that this might be true came from the

FIGURE 4.4

Sickle-cell anemia. Normal red blood cells move freely through the blood vessels (A). Sickle-shaped red blood cells stick together and block the normal flow of blood, depriving the organs of needed oxygen (B).

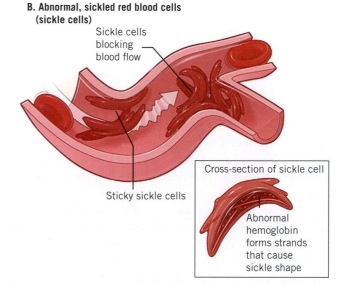

A. Normal red blood cells

Normal red blood cell (RBC)

RBCs flow freely within blood vessel

Cross-section of RBC

Normal hemoglobin

B. Abnormal, sickled red blood cells (sickle cells)

Sickle cells blocking blood flow

Sticky sickle cells

Cross-section of sickle cell

Abnormal hemoglobin forms strands that cause sickle shape

SOURCE: National Heart, Lung and Blood Institute (2007).

observation that the areas in Africa in which this gene is found in the population are almost identical to the areas in which malaria is a major problem. With these protective advantages, individuals with these recessive genes are more likely to survive to pass them on to the next generation (Sabeti, 2008). However, similar to our example with blue eye color, if two people who carry the recessive gene have children, there is a 1-in-4 chance that their children will inherit two recessive genes and suffer from sickle-cell anemia. For a better idea about how disorders can result from recessive genes, try to answer the questions in **Active Learning: Understanding the Inheritance of Tay-Sachs Disease**.

Active LEARNING

Understanding the Inheritance of Tay-Sachs Disease

Tay-Sachs is a terrible genetic disease that results in progressive neurological deterioration and death of an infant, usually by age 5. The highest occurrence of this illness happens among Ashkenazi Jews, whose ancestors came from Eastern Europe (Wolters Kluwer Health, 2009), and elevated levels are also found in French Canadians (Martin, Mark, Triggs-Raine, & Natowicz, 2007). There is a recessive gene that is responsible for Tay-Sachs, and there is a simple blood test that can locate that gene. Answer the questions below to enhance your understanding of how a recessive gene works:

1. A woman decides to be tested for the Tay-Sachs gene and finds that she is a "carrier" of Tay-Sachs. That means that she has the gene for the disease. Does she have to worry that she will get Tay-Sachs herself? What, if anything, does she have to worry about?

2. Can you determine the likelihood that any child she has will inherit Tay-Sachs disease, or do you need other information to do this?

3. Her husband decides also to be tested and finds that he does not carry the Tay-Sachs gene. What is the likelihood now that this couple will have a child who has this disease?

4. What if her husband finds that he, too, is a carrier? Now what is the likelihood that a child of theirs will have Tay-Sachs?

*This is the only combination that will result in the child having Tay-Sachs because both parents are contributing a recessive gene for the disease. Therefore, there is a 1-in-4 (or 25%) chance that the child will get the disease. Furthermore, each time this couple conceives a child, there will always be a 25% chance that the child will have the disease.

Father	Mother		
		Tay-Sachs (ts) gene (recessive)	Normal (N) gene (dominant)
Tay-Sachs (ts) gene (recessive)	ts/ts*	N/ts	
Normal (N) gene (dominant)	N/ts	N/N	

Tay-Sachs disease when both parents are carriers:

Answers: 1. The woman does not have to worry that she will get the disease herself. In the case of a carrier, she "carries" the gene but does not experience its effects. The dominant gene in this gene pair will determine the outcome, or phenotype, of the person. 2. We cannot know the likelihood of her child developing Tay-Sachs without knowing the genotype of the father of the baby. If he is a carrier, he could pass a recessive gene for the condition on to his children. A baby must inherit the recessive Tay-Sachs gene from both the mother and the father to get the disease. 3. If the husband is not a carrier, there is no chance that the child will have Tay-Sachs because the baby must have two Tay-Sachs genes, one from the mother and one from the father. Any children from this couple will inherit one dominant gene from the father that will protect them from having this condition. 4. Look at the chart below (referred to as a Punnett square) that shows the possible pairings of a mother's and a father's genes to see what the likelihood is of a child having this

Pair-bonding. This type of vole mates for life. How could you turn them into animals that have no special mate?

As we have shown, a single gene pair can be responsible for deadly disorders. Furthermore, at least with animals, one single gene pair also can be linked with behaviors that appear to be quite complex. For example, in a small animal called a vole, one particular gene determines whether an animal is monogamous or "plays the field." There are many types of voles in the wild. While the prairie vole chooses a partner for life, the meadow vole mates with whoever is available. Scientists discovered that the gene that produces the hormone vasopressin differs in these two types of voles. When they switched that gene between the two types of voles, the monogamous prairie vole became a wanderer, and the wandering meadow vole immediately began to direct his mating energies toward one female only and gave up his wandering ways (Lim et al., 2004). It is unlikely that we will find a single gene that determines such complex behavior in human beings. However, in recent research in Sweden, it was found that men with a certain form of the vasopressin gene are more likely than other men to have trouble with long-term, committed relationships (Walum et al., 2008). Clearly, human genes will interact with cultural expectations to determine practices such as monogamy or polygamy. However, it is interesting to begin to uncover in the animal world the role of some genes that are similar to those found in humans.

ONE BEHAVIOR, MANY GENES; ONE GENE, MANY EFFECTS

Certain disorders, such as sickle-cell anemia and Tay-Sachs, are the result of a single recessive gene pair. However, as we noted previously, most human behaviors are unlikely to be the result of only one gene. **Polygenic inheritance** means many different genes may interact to promote any particular trait or behavior (McGuffin, Riley, & Plomin, 2001). In addition, they may interact with our environmental experiences in ways we describe later in this chapter. Therefore, the occurrence of any trait or ability is likely to be multifactorial; that is, it depends on many factors, including a number of genes interacting with one another and with various aspects of the environment. In addition, any one gene may influence a variety of outcomes. This is referred to as **pleiotropic effects.** For example, one gene might be implicated in aggression but might also be active in regulating heart rate (Rowe, 2003).

A specific type of pleiotropic effect occurs when some genes or combination of genes seem to have a general effect on many related abilities. These have been labeled **generalist genes** (Kovas & Plomin, 2007). For example, genetic analyses have shown that the same genes that influence abilities in reading also influence abilities in language and math (Haworth et al., 2009). Researchers believe they will find a set of many genes, each having a small effect, that together exert a general effect on a range of cognitive abilities (Trzaskowski, Shakeshaft, & Plomin, 2013). Instead of looking for one gene that determines mathematical ability, scientists now look for groups of many genes, each contributing a small amount to mathematical and other learning abilities. The more of these genes that are active, the greater the person's learning ability (Kovas & Plomin, 2007). Therefore, although scientists have identified the functions of some individual genes, we must be careful not to oversimplify the findings that emerge as research continues.

Polygenic inheritance Numerous genes that may interact together to promote any particular trait or behavior.

T ☐ F ☐ Every gene in the body has one specific function. **False**

Pleiotropic effects The many different influences any single gene may have.

Generalist genes Genes that affect many, apparently distinct cognitive abilities.

CHECK YOUR UNDERSTANDING

1. What are chromosomes?
2. What is polygenic inheritance?
3. What are pleiotropic effects?

GENETIC DISORDERS

4.3 How do genetic disorders develop, and what role do genetic testing and counseling play in identifying, preventing, and treating these disorders?

We have discussed some of the outcomes in human functioning in which genes play a role. Now we focus on situations in which genes contribute to disorders that interfere with healthy functioning of the human mind and body. We describe three types of genetic disorders: single gene disorders, chromosome disorders, and multifactorial inheritance disorders.

SINGLE GENE DISORDERS

Some genetically based disorders result from a single gene. In **Active Learning: Understanding the Inheritance of Tay-Sachs Disease,** you saw that Tay-Sachs is one of these. Others are phenylketonuria (PKU) and cystic fibrosis. Phenylketonuria is a condition in which the child cannot digest a common protein in the human diet. This condition can result in intellectual disability (de Groot, Hoeksma, Blau, Reijngoud, & van Spronsen, 2010). In cystic fibrosis, the child's body produces a thick, sticky mucus that clogs the lungs, making the child vulnerable to pulmonary infections. It is also associated with nutritional deficiencies (Ratjen & Döring, 2003).

Single-gene disorders can occur in two ways: (1) An individual can inherit a pair of recessive genes that carry the instructions for that disorder, or (2) mutations can occur as cells divide so that some of the bases that give the instructions to create proteins are out of order or missing. In the case of cystic fibrosis, the genetic cause of the disorder is a missing sequence (or what we had called a *deletion* earlier in this chapter) in a specific gene called the CFTR gene. The normal sequence of one part of this gene is ATCATCTTTGGTGTT. If the three bases highlighted here are missing on one chromosome, the person will not develop cystic fibrosis. However, the child will develop the disease if he inherits this mutation from both parents (U.S. National Library of Medicine, 2015).

Many genetic disorders are coded on recessive genes, but most of the time the recessive gene is paired with a dominant gene that does not carry this disorder, so the information in the dominant gene protects the individual from developing the disorder. One student put this succinctly: "If one gene is screwed up, you have a backup." As long as the dominant gene is doing its job, the dysfunctional gene will likely not be noticed. However, in one situation a recessive gene will be expressed because there is no second gene to create a pair. As you can see in the photo on this page, the Y chromosome is much smaller than the X chromosome and contains only 70 to 200 genes, the fewest of all the chromosomes. By comparison, the X chromosome contains 900 to 1400 genes (U.S. National Library of Medicine, 2010a; 2010b). In addition, only some of the genes on the Y chromosome are active. Thus when an X chromosome pairs with a Y chromosome to create a boy, some of the X chromosome's active genes will not find a partner on the Y chromosome. In those cases, the genes will be expressed whether they are normally recessive or dominant. The outcome is an increased vulnerability in boys to the effects of recessive genes on the X chromosome that cause such problems as red-green color blindness, hemophilia, and Duchenne muscular dystrophy (Jorde et al., 2006). Disorders that result from genes on the X or Y chromosomes or from the number of X and

Single gene disorders Genetic disorders caused by a single recessive gene or mutation.

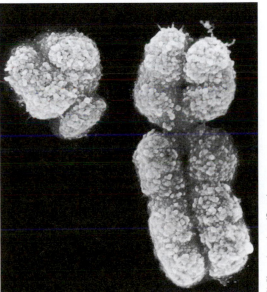

X and Y chromosomes. Do you see the potential problem when the X chromosome and the Y chromosome pair up? Large portions of the X chromosome (the one on the right) do not have a partner on the Y chromosome (the one on the left), and therefore any recessive gene on the X chromosome without a partner will appear in the male's phenotype. If the recessive gene is the source of a genetic problem, the man is vulnerable to it.

BioPhoto Associates/Getty Images

T ☐ F ☐ Males are more likely to have a genetic disorder than females. **True**

FIGURE 4.5

Chromosomes for Down syndrome. Compare these chromosomes from someone with Down syndrome with those in Figure 4.1. Did you notice the extra copy of the 21st chromosome? This is referred to as *trisomy* because there are three chromosomes instead of two.

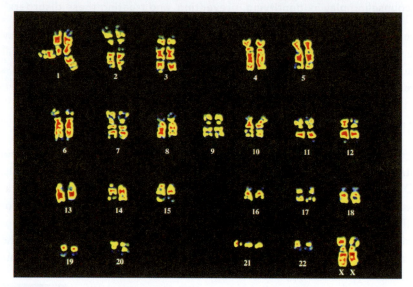

SOURCE: Biophoto Associates/Photo Researchers, Inc.

Chromosome disorders
Disorders that result when too many or too few chromosomes are formed or when there is a change in the structure of the chromosome caused by breakage.

Down syndrome. This girl has facial features that are typically associated with Down syndrome, including small upturned eyes, small ears, and a flat facial profile.

Richard Bailey/Corbis Documentary/Getty Images

Y chromosomes are referred to as *sex-linked disorders*. As you will learn in the next section, having more or less than two sex chromosomes can have significant effects on development.

CHROMOSOME DISORDERS

Genetic disorders can also occur at the level of the chromosome. **Chromosome disorders** occur when one of the 23 pairs of chromosomes contains some number of chromosomes other than two. For example, Figure 4.5 shows the chromosomal configuration of an individual with Down syndrome. In the 21st position, there are three chromosomes, rather than two. In another condition, Turner's syndrome, there is only a single chromosome in the 23rd position in a female. Any deviation from the 46 chromosomes that are normally contained in 23 pairs will result in a chromosome disorder. Because a single chromosome contains a large number of genes, any deviation—whether an addition or a loss—results in a number of characteristics being affected.

The second way a chromosome disorder occurs is when there is a change in the structure of the chromosome caused by breakage (National Human Genome Research Institute, 2011a). When sections of chromosomes break apart, they may not come back together in their original form. Some sections may be turned around backward or may even link to a different chromosome. Both of these types of abnormality may occur by chance, but the second type also can be passed along to a child by a parent who has this type of chromosomal pattern. Table 4.1 describes three conditions that are caused by chromosomal abnormalities.

TABLE 4.1

Chromosomal abnormalities.

Disorder	Chromosomal description	Symptom description	Treatments
Down Syndrome	One extra 21st chromosome	Intellectual disability; typical facial features; poor muscle tone; possible problems with heart, digestion, and hearing	Physical, occupational, speech, and educational therapy; medical intervention as needed
Klinefelter Syndrome	An extra X chromosome in men (XXY in the 23rd position)	Infertility; small genitals; enlarged breasts; reduced facial, armpit, and pubic hair; possible autoimmune disorders	Testosterone therapy; medical and educational intervention as needed
Turner Syndrome	A missing X chromosome in women (XO in the 23rd position)	Short stature; webbing of the neck; lack of development of ovaries resulting in lack of sexual maturation at puberty	Estrogen replacement therapy; possible growth hormone administration; other medical care as needed

SOURCES: National Human Genome Research Institute (2011a; 2011c, 2013a, 2013b).

MULTIFACTORIAL INHERITANCE DISORDERS

Multifactorial inheritance disorders result from the interaction of many genes that also interact with environmental influences. Many disorders, including depression, alcoholism, schizophrenia, and autism, appear to have some genetic input. However, it is likely they result from the interaction of many genes that also interact with environmental influences. There are currently no genetic tests for this type of multifactorial problem (National Human Genome Research Institute, 2011c), but individuals can take preventative steps when they know from their family history that they are at higher risk of developing a disorder. For example, an individual with a number of cases of alcoholism in the family may choose to avoid alcohol. Someone whose family has a high level of depression may learn to identify those symptoms early to get appropriate treatment if needed.

Multifactorial inheritance disorders Disorders that result from many genes in interaction with environmental influences.

GENETIC COUNSELING AND TESTING

People become particularly concerned about genetics when they are about to start a family. In each pregnancy, any couple statistically has a 3% chance of having a child with a genetically based disorder (Centers for Disease Control and Prevention [CDC], 2008a). Based on these low odds, there is usually no reason for genetic counseling. However, in some cases individual risk is higher, and such individuals may want to seek out a genetic counselor to help them assess the type and amount of risk. See Table 4.2 for a description of couples who are at an increased risk of conceiving a child with a genetic disorder or birth defect, and who thus might consider having genetic counseling.

Genetic counseling and testing can occur before or during a pregnancy. Counselors ask about the couple's own medical histories and their families' history of diseases and genetic disorders and may recommend certain tests. Blood tests can identify the presence of single recessive genes that are more common in certain populations, such as those for Tay-Sachs disease (Ashkenazi Jews), sickle-cell anemia (African Americans or Africans), and thalassemia, a blood disorder associated with reduced production of hemoglobin (Southeast Asians, Taiwanese, Chinese, Filipinos, Italians, Greeks, or Middle Easterners; American Medical Association, 2008). As we saw in **Active Learning: Understanding the Inheritance of Tay-Sachs Disease,** couples should be concerned about these possible disorders only if both partners carry the recessive gene for the condition.

TABLE 4.2

Who should receive genetic counseling?

The March of Dimes organization recommends that the following individuals consult with a genetic counselor:

- Those who have, or are concerned that they might have, an inherited disorder or birth defect.
- Women who are pregnant or planning to be after age 35.
- Couples who already have a child with intellectual disability, an inherited disorder, or a birth defect.
- Couples whose infant has a genetic disease diagnosed by routine newborn screening.
- Women who have had babies who died in infancy or three or more miscarriages.
- People concerned that their jobs, lifestyles, or medical history may pose a risk to outcome of pregnancy. Common causes of concern include exposure to radiation, medications, illegal drugs, chemicals, or infections.
- Couples who would like testing or more information about genetic conditions that occur frequently in their ethnic group.
- Couples who are first cousins or other close blood relatives.
- Pregnant women whose ultrasound examinations or blood testing indicate that their pregnancy may be at increased risk for certain complications or birth defects.

SOURCE: March of Dimes (2015). Used with permission.

During pregnancy, several tests can identify some possible genetic abnormalities in the developing fetus. For example, tests of the mother's blood, such as the *alpha-fetoprotein test,* can uncover abnormalities in hormone levels that signal the possibility of spina bifida, a neural tube defect that affects the development of the brain and spinal cord, or Down syndrome (Larson, 2002). However, the alpha-fetoprotein test is not a diagnostic test; it is a screening tool that may indicate that further testing should be done. Further testing can be carried out to identify chromosome disorders as well as some single gene disorders, such as sickle-cell anemia. However, there are many other genetic and nongenetic factors that are not assessed by these tests.

Another prenatal test, as shown in Figure 4.6, is **amniocentesis,** in which a long, thin needle is inserted through the mother's abdomen and into the amniotic sac that surrounds the fetus. Cells from the skin surface of the developing embryo are routinely shed into the amniotic fluid that surrounds the embryo. When fluid from the sac is withdrawn, it contains fetal cells that can be analyzed for genetic abnormalities. In **chorionic villus sampling (CVS),** cells are obtained from the microscopic projections called *villi* found on the outside layer of the embryonic sac, called the **chorion.** These cells can be obtained either through the abdomen by using a needle to extract cells directly from the chorion or through the vagina and cervix by using a thin tube to remove cells from the placenta. The cell sample is then analyzed (Jorde et al., 2006). Because all of the structures that support the pregnancy (including the placenta, the amniotic sac, and the chorion) are products of the conception, the cells they contain have the same genetic makeup as the embryo, and that is why they can be tested for genetic problems. CVS is performed at 10 to 11 weeks of gestation, while amniocentesis cannot be performed until 15 to 17 weeks. The risk of miscarriage resulting from the procedure itself is slightly higher for CVS than for amniocentesis, but the parents receive information about any possible genetic problems earlier in the pregnancy (Jorde et al., 2006).

There are a number of ways an individual can take a preliminary look at his or her own genetic vulnerabilities. Several of these ways are discussed in **Active Learning: Assessing Genetic Risk.**

Amniocentesis A test to look for genetic abnormalities prenatally, in which a physician uses a long, thin needle to extract amniotic fluid, which is then tested.

Chorionic villus sampling (CVS) A test to look for genetic abnormalities prenatally, in which a small tube is inserted either through the vagina and cervix or through a needle inserted in the abdomen, and a sample of cells is retrieved from the chorion for testing.

Chorion The outer fetal membrane that surrounds the fetus and gives rise to the placenta.

FIGURE 4.6

Genetic testing. During amniocentesis (shown on the left), a physician uses a sonogram to show a picture of the fetus in the amniotic sac and then uses a long, thin needle to extract about 4 teaspoons of amniotic fluid. Fetal cells floating in the fluid can be tested for genetic problems. In chorionic villus sampling (shown in the figure on the right), a small tube, or catheter, is inserted either through the vagina and cervix or through a needle inserted in the abdomen, and a sample of cells from the chorion (which has the same genetic makeup as the fetus) is retrieved for testing.

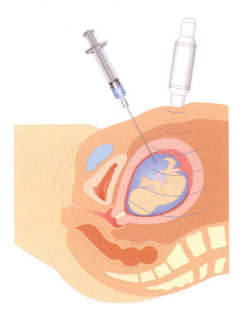
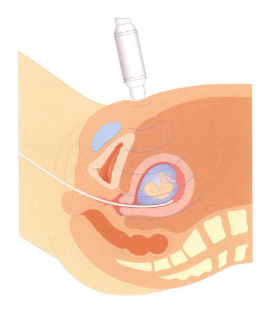

SOURCE: Dorling Kindersley/Getty Images.

Active LEARNING

Assessing Genetic Risk

Knowing which genetic conditions affect your family members will make you aware of your own possible genetic vulnerabilities. To begin assessing your genetic risk, you can simply collect information about genetic conditions that have affected your blood relatives. These include cancer, diabetes, heart disease, high blood pressure, stroke, and alcoholism (National Society of Genetic Counselors, n.d.). Along with the condition, also record the age at which the condition appeared in each of your relatives. The likelihood of developing these conditions increases with age, so you will need to periodically update your information. Because health issues are a sensitive subject and some family members may be reluctant to share information, be careful about how you approach this topic.

Another way to assess genetic risk is through Internet assessment tools. A number of well-established medical risk calculators are available online at no cost. You can use a search engine to find the Framingham Risk Assessment Tool available through the National Institutes of Health to assess your risk of developing heart disease or suffering a heart attack, or My Health Advisor from the American Diabetes Association to help you assess your risk of developing diabetes. If you do use an Internet assessment tool, however, be sure the source is a legitimate health authority and not just a company trying to sell you a product or service.

(Continued)

(Continued)

You may have heard of commercial genetic tests that promise to help you assess your genetic risk of developing certain diseases or conditions. For these tests, you purchase a testing kit online, provide the company with a saliva sample or swab from the inside of your cheek, and receive a report that outlines your individual genetic risks (often expressed as "high", "low," or "average") for a variety of possible disorders or characteristics, as well as some strategies that can help to reduce the risk. However, currently the Centers for Disease Control recommends that you only take these tests on the advice of a doctor and in a medical setting. Only 12 out of 1,000 such tests have been approved by the Food and Drug Administration and none of these are home tests (Hatfield, 2016).

Ethical Considerations in Genetic Testing

Questions about privacy and the use of genetic screening results raise many ethical questions for genetic research, particularly when children are the subjects (National Human Genome Research Institute, 2011b). For example, the American Academy of Pediatrics (AAP) notes several objections to the suggestion that more extensive prenatal genetic screening be offered to all pregnant women (Beaudet, 2013). One is the likelihood of false positive results (that is, results indicating a problem where none exists), which can cause parents enormous anxiety and could force them to make reproductive decisions with enormous impact on their families based on erroneous information. A second issue is the need to ensure the privacy of the findings from such tests. There is great concern that employers, insurers, and others might gain access to these records and use them to discriminate against individuals with genetic disorders by denying them insurance or employment.

To help navigate the legal and ethical pitfalls of genetic testing, the American Academy of Pediatricians (AAP) Committee on Bioethics (2001) has recommended that all newborn genetic screening tests meet these guidelines: "1) identification of the genetic condition must provide a clear benefit to the child; 2) a system must be in place to confirm the diagnosis; and 3) treatment and follow-up must be available for affected newborns" (p. 1452). In addition, the American Association of Pediatrics recommends that testing for conditions that develop in adulthood, such as breast cancer and Huntington's disease, should not be carried out until a child is old enough to make his or her own informed decision about having the test, especially when earlier identification of the condition would not lead to a better outcome through early interventions.

Parents and others considering genetic testing must be educated about the risks, including possible stigmatization, discrimination, and psychological harm, before making their decision (AAP Committee on Bioethics, 2001). There is much to be gained from genetic research and testing, but we should proceed carefully in order to avoid harm, especially to children.

TREATMENT OF GENETIC DISORDERS

Given the toll that genetic disorders take on individuals, we continue to search for ways to treat these conditions. One approach is to try to correct the genetic defects themselves, but this is difficult to do with the state of our current knowledge. A different approach is to alter the environment in ways that can reduce or eliminate the damaging effect of the genetic disorders.

Gene therapy Treatment of genetic disorders through implanting or disabling specific genes.

Although **gene therapy**, the treatment of genetic disorders through the implantation or disabling of specific genes, is not yet available for humans, scientists are working on ways to use all of our new knowledge about genes to prevent and treat human disorders. Research is under way to use viruses that are genetically altered to "infect" cells with healthy genes to replace disordered ones (U.S. Department of Energy Genome Programs, 2012). Using a different technique, researchers also have been able to localize and then disable certain problematic genes. For example, researchers at Leiden University Medical Center in the Netherlands were able to block the action of a gene implicated in the development of Duchenne muscular dystrophy (Grady, 2007). Although the results to date have been modest, the idea that we may be able to intervene at the level of genes is intriguing. Gene therapy that is currently being conducted only on an experimental basis is one of the exciting avenues of research in the field of molecular genetics (National Cancer Institute, 2006).

The second approach to controlling the effects of gene-based disorders involves making changes in the individual's environment. For example, we have long known that the effects of the genetic disorder phenylketonuria (PKU) can be prevented by removing phenylalanine from the diet of those newborns found to carry the two recessive genes for it (Plomin, DeFries, Craig, & McGuffin, 2003). Remember that a child who has PKU has inherited recessive genes that cannot produce an enzyme that is essential in the digestion of phenylalanine, a common protein that is found in foods such as beef, poultry, fish, eggs, milk products such as yogurt and cheese, and wheat products (de Baulny, Abadie, Feillet, & de Parscau, 2007). When phenylalanine is only partially digested because of the missing enzyme, harmful substances are produced that can damage the child's brain and central nervous system, resulting in intellectual disability (de Groot et al., 2010). Once again, it is not the gene itself that causes the problem, but rather the interaction of the gene with the newborn's intake of food containing phenylalanine. By eliminating the phenylalanine from the diet of an infant through the use of a special formula, the harmful effects are eliminated (Schuett, 2008). Because the brain is growing so rapidly during the early years, it is particularly vulnerable to these damaging toxic effects, but the National Institute of Child Health and Human Development (2006) recommends that people with PKU maintain a diet low in phenylalanine throughout their lives to prevent the appearance of symptoms. That diet primarily includes fruits, vegetables, and low-protein grain products. In the future, perhaps we will be able to provide early intervention for babies with other identifiable genes that cause behavioral disorders.

CHECK YOUR UNDERSTANDING

1. How do single-gene disorders occur?
2. What causes chromosome disorders such as Down syndrome?
3. What is amniocentesis?
4. What are some risks of genetic testing?

BEHAVIORAL GENETICS

4.4 How do we study the relationship between our genetic inheritance and our traits and behavior?

With some understanding of how genes function, we now look at the question of how behavior is related to the genes we inherit. The scientific study of behavioral genetics began before we had knowledge of which specific genes might affect specific behaviors, and, in spite of the fact that scientists have identified the genes that make up the human genome, we are still a long way from knowing what most of our genes actually do and how our behaviors relate to gene functioning. Although molecular genetics, which focuses on identifiable individual genes, has become a major area of research in recent years, the more traditional approach of behavioral genetics continues to provide important information. When researchers find a

TRUE/FALSE VIDEO ▲

T ☐ F ☐ Mike is a talented pianist. Because both of his parents are musicians, genes must have determined that Mike would also have musical talent. **False**

Heritability A measure of the extent to which genes determine a particular behavior or characteristic.

genetic association for a particular human characteristic, molecular genetics can then be used to identify specific genes that may be involved in producing that characteristic.

Behavioral genetics begins with the study of a particular behavior. Historically, researchers have used several approaches to try to separate the relative influence of genes and environment on individual differences in that behavior. You might think that simply noting how similar children are to their parents could tell us how much of a particular behavior has genetic roots, but genetic influences and environmental settings are often intertwined in complex ways. For example, imagine walking into the home of a new friend and discovering that this friend is a very talented pianist. You then find out that both parents in this family perform with a local choir and their youngest child is a gifted violinist. What would you conclude about the source of this musical talent? Did the children in this family inherit genes for their musical ability, or did they learn about music from the experiences that their parents have provided for them? In this situation, there is no way to know which has happened. In fact, it's likely that both genes and environment have had an effect, but, scientifically, it is impossible to sort out which factor had what effect.

In theory, we might solve this problem by taking children from musical families and placing them in families that are not musical to see what happens. If musical ability is produced by genes, these children will still develop this talent. If it is produced by environmental influences, they will not necessarily be musical. Obviously, it is highly unethical to do anything like this with human beings, so psychologists have had to look for natural situations that might provide the same information. Three types of studies have been carried out that take advantage of such natural situations: (1) studies of adopted children, (2) comparisons of identical and fraternal twins, and (3) studies of identical twins who were adopted in infancy and reared by different families. The goal of this type of research is to establish the level of **heritability**, a measure of the extent to which genes determine a particular behavior or characteristic.

STUDIES OF ADOPTED CHILDREN

One way to try to determine heritability is to study adopted children. Children who are adopted have birth parents from whom they inherit their genes and adoptive parents who provide the environment in which they grow up. To look at the relative contribution of genes and environment on a particular developmental outcome, researchers must have information about both the adoptive parents and the biological parents. They then look at the **concordance rate**, or the degree to which a trait or an ability of one individual is similar to that of another, between children and their biological and adoptive parents. A higher concordance rate between child and birth parents shows the influence of the genes on that characteristic, while a higher concordance rate between child and adoptive parent shows the influence of the environment.

A variation on this approach has been to examine the similarity between parents and their adopted children as compared to their similarity to their biological children within the same family. One example of this type of research was carried out to examine the heritability of general cognitive ability. Petrill and Deater-Deckard (2004) found a modest correlation between mothers' scores on the Stanford-Binet Intelligence Scale and their biological children's scores, but essentially no correlation with their adoptive children's scores. This would indicate that the genes the mother passed on to her biological child contributed to the similarity in their IQ, while the environment provided to the adoptive child did not have much influence.

STUDIES COMPARING IDENTICAL AND FRATERNAL TWINS

Another approach to measuring the relative influence of genes and environment has capitalized on the fact that there are two types of twins. Fraternal or nonidentical twins are formed

Concordance rate The degree to which a trait or an ability of one individual is similar to that of another; used to examine similarities between twins and among adopted children and their biological and adoptive parents.

FIGURE 4.7

Genetic similarities between monozygotic and dizygotic twins. The difference in the degree of gene similarity of dizygotic and monozygotic twins as shown in this figure has been used by researchers to study the effects of genes on many human characteristics.

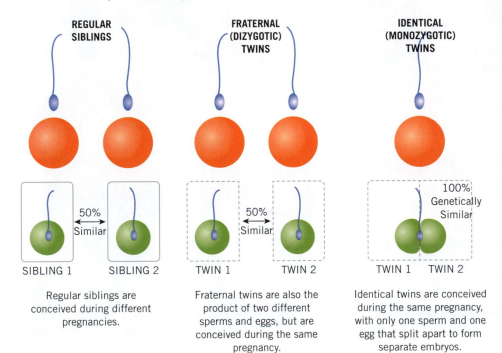

REGULAR SIBLINGS	FRATERNAL (DIZYGOTIC) TWINS	IDENTICAL (MONOZYGOTIC) TWINS

SIBLING 1 50% Similar SIBLING 2

TWIN 1 50% Similar TWIN 2

100% Genetically Similar TWIN 1 TWIN 2

Regular siblings are conceived during different pregnancies.

Fraternal twins are also the product of two different sperms and eggs, but are conceived during the same pregnancy.

Identical twins are conceived during the same pregnancy, with only one sperm and one egg that split apart to form separate embryos.

when a mother's ovary releases two eggs during a menstrual cycle, and each is fertilized by a different sperm. The resulting twins are referred to as **dizygotic (DZ) twins**, because they develop from two (di-) fertilized eggs (zygotes). They are only as genetically similar to each other as any other pair of siblings. Because they have about half their genes in common (see Figure 4.7), they don't have an identical appearance. In fact, DZ or *fraternal twins* do not even have to be the same sex. Because each egg is fertilized by a different sperm, one sperm can be carrying an X chromosome while the other is carrying a Y chromosome in the 23rd position. The tendency to have dizygotic twins is genetically related so some families are more likely to have them than others.

The second way twins develop occurs when a single egg is fertilized by a single sperm to form a zygote. The zygote begins replicating and producing additional cells, but early in this process, for reasons that we don't really understand, the ball of cells splits into two (Gilbert, 2000). Each ball of cells continues to develop prenatally to become one of two *identical twins*, referred to as **monozygotic (MZ) twins** because they are the product of a single (mono) fertilized egg (zygote). Because monozygotic twins both have the same set of genetic material (including the information on chromosome pair 23), they are always the same sex and look much alike. This type of twinning occurs by chance, so the tendency to have MZ twins does not run in families.

It has always been a puzzle why identical twins can have small differences in their basic appearance or develop different genetically based disorders. Scientists had previously assumed that the environment was responsible for these differences. However, recently researchers have discovered that even identical twins have small differences in the arrangement of their genes, and these differences may result in observable and sometimes significant differences (Bruder et al., 2008).

Now that you understand the genetic difference between identical and fraternal twins, you can understand how scientists have been able to look at concordance rates between twins

Dizygotic (DZ) twins Twins formed when a woman produces two ova or eggs, which are fertilized by two sperm; genetically DZ twins are as similar as any siblings.

Monozygotic (MZ) twins Formed when a woman produces one egg that is fertilized by one sperm and the resulting ball of cells then splits to form two individuals with the same genes.

Twins and triplets. Identical twins are always the same gender, but fraternal twins can be the same gender or different. Triplets can be identical or fraternal or a set of identical twins with a fraternal sibling.

to try to identify which behaviors or personality traits are linked with genetic inheritance. If identical twins, who share almost all their genes, are more similar to each other (that is, they have a higher concordance rate) on a trait such as shyness than are fraternal twins, who share only half their genes, the researchers conclude that genes play a role in determining whether someone is shy. One example of this type of research looked at the causes of alcoholism. Pagan et al. (2006) followed twins, both identical and fraternal, from adolescence through early adulthood. They found the age at which the twins began using alcohol was no more similar between identical twins than between fraternal twins, but identical twins were more similar to each other in terms of the amount they drank and whether they became problem drinkers in late adolescence and early adulthood. This finding provides evidence that genes play less of a role in when teens begin to drink, but they play a stronger role at later ages in the development of problem drinking.

More recent research with twins has examined the role of specific aspects of the environment rather than looking only at the effects of similarity in genes. For example, Kendler, Gardner, and Dick (2011) found that the genetic effects on alcohol use in adolescence were stronger when parental monitoring of their teens was low and when alcohol was easily available. This means that identical twins were more similar to each other in alcohol use than nonidentical twins in these situations. Genetic effects were much more limited when parents kept a watchful eye on their child and the peer environment did not promote alcohol use. In this case, there was little difference in concordance rate between identical and nonidentical twins. This research is helping to further clarify the interaction of genes and environment to show that genes do not necessarily determine our destiny and to identify the role of specific aspects of the environment.

Although behavioral genetics has shown that almost all behaviors studied have some genetic input, different traits and behaviors are more or less heritable (Dick & Rose, 2004). It is useful to discover which traits and behaviors are *highly* likely to develop from genetic input because this will aid in the search for the specific genes responsible. On the other hand, we also want to know which aspects of the environment influence the development of behavior so we can promote those environments associated with positive outcomes.

STUDIES OF IDENTICAL TWINS REARED APART

The third type of study is a natural experiment that combines twin and adoption research. This type of experiment looks at identical and fraternal twins who were adopted into separate families and measures how similar each individual is to his or her twin. If, for example, identical twins who are raised in different homes are more similar to each other on a certain characteristic than fraternal twins who are raised in the same home, it suggests that genes are the stronger influence on the characteristic being studied.

The study of twins reared apart began as early as the 1920s, even before scientists could genetically determine which twins were monozygotic and which were dizygotic. For example, Newman (1932) identified six pairs of identical twins raised apart on the basis of their palm and finger prints and compared them to 50 pairs of identical twins reared together. He found expected similarities in basic physical features, but strong environmentally based differences in intelligence, temperament, and even weight and height.

The largest modern study of this unique population is the Minnesota Study of Twins Reared Apart (Segal, 2012). The Minnesota study began with the discovery of the "Jim twins," Jim Lewis and Jim Springer. Although reared apart for 39 years, they showed startling similarities. Media coverage at that time focused on the anecdotal coincidences, such as their first marriages to women named Linda and the second to women named Betty, and their sons' names (James Alan and James Allan), but the research team focused on a series of tests carried out with the Jim twins and subsequently with 81 pairs of MZ twins and 56 pairs of DZ twins. This research has reached the conclusion that identical twins reared apart are about as similar to each other on aspects of their personality, interests, and social attitudes as identical twins reared together, and more similar than fraternal twins reared together (Lehman, 2005; Segal, 2012).

This research would appear to provide strong evidence for the powerful influence of genes on many characteristics. However, there is much ongoing controversy about these findings. Joseph (2001) makes the case that many of these separated twins actually knew each other. Some were even adopted by relatives who lived in the same area and some were raised together for a number of years before they were separated. That would mean that the environments for the twins were really very similar. However, Segal (2012) counters this argument by pointing out that the twin pairs in the Minnesota twins study were separated earlier and for a longer period of time than twins in previous studies and therefore provide better evidence of genetic input into a variety of characteristics.

Another criticism of this research raised by Joseph (2001) is that the similarities between twins might be due to similarities in age, sex, race, and ethnicity, and similar level of attractiveness, because each of these characteristics is likely to make people similar to each other even though there is no genetic relationship between them. He suggested that the twins' level of similarity should be compared to the similarity between pairs of unrelated strangers who have all of these characteristics in common. Although research that includes all of these characteristics has not been done to date, Segal (2013) did study people who were unrelated but looked alike in order to determine whether appearance elicits similar responses from others, which then would affect the personality and self-esteem of the individuals in these created pairs. She found that dizygotic twins raised apart and raised together were much more similar to each other than unrelated look-alikes. Remember that dizygotic twins share half of their genes in common, while the unrelated look-alikes should not have any substantial

number of genetic similarities. From this, she concluded that the personality similarities found between identical twins in the Minnesota study are due to genes or possibly to other factors, but not to appearance. The controversies surrounding research on twins reared apart are ongoing.

Check your understanding of the use of concordance rates in twin studies by carrying out **Active Learning: Concordance Rates.**

Active LEARNING

Concordance Rates

Twin and adoption studies use concordance rates, that is, the likelihood that two people will be similar to each other on some characteristic, to assess the likelihood that genes influence the characteristic. Check your understanding of what concordance rates indicate by examining the following evidence and deciding what conclusions you would reach.

1. In a Danish population-based twin study of autism spectrum disorder (ASD), the following concordance rates were found for monozygotic and for dizygotic twins:

   If one MZ twin was diagnosed with ASD, the likelihood was 95.2% that the other would also be diagnosed with ASD.

   If one DZ twin was diagnosed with ASD, the likelihood was 4.3% that the other would also be diagnosed with ASD (Nordenbæk, Jørgensen, Kyvik, & Bilenberg, 2014).

What would you conclude from this about the role of genes in the development of ASD?

2. In a study of types of emotional attachment to the mother, MZ and DZ 3-year-old twins were assessed to determine whether they had secure or insecure attachment.

   If one MZ twin was securely attached, the likelihood that the other was securely attached was 70%.

   If one DZ twin was securely attached, the likelihood that the other was securely attached was 64% (O'Connor & Croft, 2001).

What would you conclude from this about the role of genes in the development of secure attachment?

Answers: 1. These findings indicate a strong role of genes in the development of ASD because twins with identical genes are more similar than twins with only half of their genes in common. **2.** These findings indicate only a small or no role for genes in the development of secure attachment because twins with identical genes were only slightly more similar to each other in the quality of their attachment than those with only 50% of their genes in common.

CHECK YOUR UNDERSTANDING

1. Why do genetics researchers study adopted children?

2. What does a concordance rate measure?

3. What could explain many of the striking similarities reported between identical twins separated at birth?

THE INTERACTION OF GENES AND ENVIRONMENT

4.5 **How do genes and the environment interact?**

We have now seen how genes work within our bodies at the molecular level, and we have looked at the ways in which scientists seek to discover which behaviors, traits, and abilities are linked to our genetic inheritance. As scientists have learned more about specific genes and how they function, it has become clear that the influence genes have on behavior is affected by the experiences people have, especially early in life.

HOW THE ENVIRONMENT SHAPES GENE EXPRESSION

Our understanding of genetic inheritance has become much more complex since the time of Mendel. We now know that genes can act differently in a variety of circumstances. One of the major findings in recent research on genes is that the environment can influence gene expression. Two ways in which this happens are through *canalization* and *epigenesis*.

Canalization

There is considerable variability in how strongly genes affect different traits or characteristics. Although some characteristics seem to be relatively impervious to environmental factors, others are much more easily influenced. The degree to which the expression of a gene is influenced by the environment is captured in the concept of **canalization** proposed by Conrad Hal Waddington (1942). One way to visualize this concept is to imagine a bowling alley. Anyone who has ever gone bowling knows that throwing the bowling ball down the alley can result in hitting any, all, or none of the pins at the end of the alley. However, if you add a device that limits where the ball can go, every time the bowler throws the ball it will hit the same pin or pins. When describing gene expression, genes that are deeply canalized are like the bowling ball with the device that directs it to the same pin or pins every time.

Genes for deeply canalized traits have a self-righting tendency that produces the expected developmental outcome under all but the most extreme environmental conditions (Black, Hess, & Berenson-Howard, 2000). For example, across a wide range of environmental conditions, almost all infants reach the early motor milestones, like sitting up and walking. In contrast, genes that are not deeply canalized are like the bowling ball that can hit any, all, or none of the pins. Intelligence is a trait that is not deeply canalized and is therefore much more variable in its outcome than walking or sitting. Because this genetic pathway is *less* constrained or less deeply canalized, it is *more* influenced by the characteristics of the child's environment. Children raised in the relatively enriched environment of middle- and upper-income status are likely to express the levels of intelligence provided by their genetic inheritance. However, genetic inheritance plays a smaller role for children raised in low-income families. The relative environmental deprivation they experience limits their ability to express genes for high intelligence and restricts them to a narrower range of outcomes (Turkheimer, Haley, Waldron, D'Onofrio, & Gottesman, 2003). The concept of canalization gives us insight into the complex interaction between our genetic endowment and the influence of the environment.

Canalization The degree to which the expression of a gene is influenced by the environment.

Behavioral Epigenetics

What determines how individual genes are influenced by environmental experiences? One answer comes from **epigenetics**, which is the study of the chemical reactions that activate

Epigenetics A system by which genes are activated or silenced in response to events or circumstances in the individual's environment.

FIGURE 4.8

Epigenetics. Chemical tags can be activated or silenced by an individual's experiences. The tags allow certain genes to be read or cause them to be hidden. The basic structure of the DNA does not change, but the expression of the gene does. In this figure, chemical tags (blue) determine whether DNA (green) winds tightly around histones or unwinds, permitting the expression of genes.

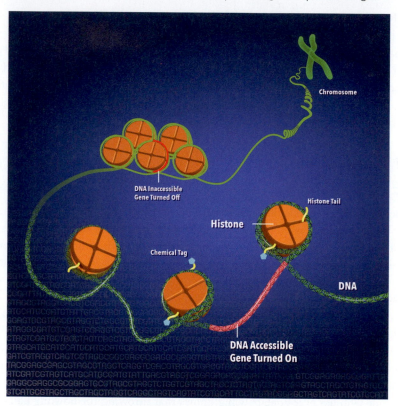

SOURCE: Courtesy of the National Human Genome Research Institute.

and deactivate parts of the genetic material of an organism, as well as the factors that influence these chemical reactions (Zhang & Meaney, 2010). Behavioral epigenetics has been described as the bridge between nature and nurture (Zhang & Meaney, 2010). All living things have chemical tags that can turn a gene's activity on or off (see Figure 4.8). While the structure of the genes remains the same, the way each gene is expressed may be very different depending on where and when these chemical tags are "turned on" or expressed.

What is most important is that the tags can be influenced by events or circumstances in the individual's environment. Behavioral epigenetics has demonstrated how early life experiences can literally get "under the skin" by activating or silencing certain genes (Szyf & Bick, 2013).

One example of how behavioral epigenetics works has been demonstrated by Michael Meaney, a researcher at McGill University, who studied rat mothers and their offspring. He and his colleagues found that rat babies reared by mothers who ignored them and did not touch them were more fearful and stressed by environmental events later in their lives, shown both by the babies' behavior and by the levels of stress hormones they produced. These researchers were able to link this behavior with a particular gene that was active in babies reared by nurturing mothers but which had been "turned off" in the neglected babies.

To be sure that this effect was due to the mother's behavior and not to her genes, the researchers switched babies between nurturing and non-nurturing mothers at birth, and the results were the same. In those babies who had been reared by non-nurturing mothers, the gene had been "turned off" by these early experiences even though their biological mothers were very nurturing (Diorio & Meaney, 2007). In an evolutionary sense, it appears that

T ☐ F ☐ The experiences you have in your life can change the structure of your genes. **False** baby rats that do not experience adequate mothering "reprogram" their genes. The result of this reprogramming is that the babies respond more quickly to stress. The evolutionary advantage is that their increased responsiveness enables them to respond quickly when facing danger, rather than waiting for unresponsive mothers to protect them.

Similar results have been found in humans. Turlecki and Meaney (2016) reviewed 40 studies (13 animal studies and 27 human studies) on the relation between early stress and later epigenetic markers in children's genomes. The human studies examined a history of trauma in early childhood, including child abuse and parental death. They found strong evidence for the effect of early stress on changes in the epigenome in parts of the brain that control reactions to stress. Individuals with these changes are more reactive even to lower levels of stress and more prone to depression and anxiety as a result.

Epigenetic response to stress. Highly stressful events early in life, such as the death of a parent, can result in changes in the individual's epigenome that contribute to a higher incidence of depression and anxiety later in life.

The effects of stress early in life on the epigenome also depend on the particular versions of genes the individual is born with. For instance, researchers have found that humans have one of two versions of a gene on the X chromosome that determines how much of an enzyme called monoamine oxidase-A (MAO-A) is produced in their bodies. There is some evidence that individuals with less MAO-A tend to be more aggressive. You might think that this is evidence that some forms of aggression are genetically determined, and you would be partially right. However, in a longitudinal study in New Zealand, not all boys with the version of the gene that produces lower levels of MAO-A turned out to be aggressive. (Only boys were studied because it is more complicated to study girls, who have *two* X chromosomes.) Boys with this version of the gene who *also* experienced abuse during their childhood were much more likely to become aggressive adults. The environmental trigger of abuse early in life "turned on" the negative effects of the lower level of MAO-A (Caspi et al., 2002). Those boys with the other version of the gene were much less likely to become aggressive, whether they experienced child abuse or not. Table 4.3 shows the relationship between the genetic inheritance and environmental experiences in producing higher levels of aggression. This finding was confirmed in several subsequent studies (Kim-Cohen et al., 2006; Reif et al., 2007), and similar results have been found for different genes relating to depression and posttraumatic stress disorder (Binder et al., 2008; Caspi et al., 2003).

TABLE 4.3

Interaction of genes and environment. This table shows the outcome when boys have different versions of the gene that produces MAO-A in relation to their early life experiences. When they have the predisposing gene *and* they experience child abuse, they are more likely to be highly aggressive as adults.

		Version of Gene That Produces MAO-A	
		Gene producing low levels of MAO-A	Gene producing average levels of MAO-A
Experience of Child Abuse	Yes	Higher average levels of aggression	Typical levels of aggression
	No	Typical levels of aggression	Typical levels of aggression

Aggression is also addressed in a study of adults who had been adopted at birth. Cadoret, Yates, Troughton, Woodworth, and Steward (1995) found that these adults were more likely to be aggressive if their biological parents had shown antisocial behavior problems *and* their experience with their adoptive parents had been difficult, for example, if there had been a divorce or substance abuse in their adopted family. Again, a specific combination of genes and environmental experiences was necessary to produce the aggressive behavior. Based on studies such as these, it appears certain genes can make individuals more or less susceptible to environmental effects (Dick & Rose, 2004).

Can epigenetic changes be handed down to the next generation? When a woman has a baby, any epigenetic changes to the chemical tags that turn on or off certain of *her* genes are usually wiped clean. That is, infants start with a fresh slate and build their own epigenetic pattern as they grow and develop (Daxinger & Whitelaw, 2012). However, there is evidence that some epigenetic changes may actually be passed down to the developing fetus. In animal research, prenatal exposure to certain chemicals can have epigenetic effects on the animal that appear in its great-grandchildren even if they were never exposed to the chemical (Skinner, Haque, Nillson, Bhandari, & McCarrey, 2013). Scientists are just beginning to extend this research to human development.

Complexities in the Study of Gene-Environment Interaction

Another example of the type of recent research designed to show the interaction of genes and environment has focused on the timing of the onset of puberty, especially for girls, that was described in Chapter 2. Puberty is triggered by the action of certain genes and its individual timing is in part inherited. If your mother entered puberty at an early age, you are also more likely to experience puberty early (Belsky et al., 2007; Ellis & Essex, 2007). However, a variety of environmental factors also appear to turn on the genes for puberty.

There is evidence that girls are more likely to enter puberty earlier when they experience a difficult early family life and when their fathers are absent (Ellis & Essex, 2007; Posner, 2006). Although this finding appears to represent an environmental effect on the timing of puberty, it is possible that a purely genetic explanation may be adequate. One particular gene associated with aggression in men (the X-linked AR gene) also can be inherited by a daughter. However, we know that the principle of pleiotropism says that genes may have more than one outcome. In girls, this same gene is not associated with aggression but instead acts to trigger early puberty. Therefore, a father with this gene is more likely to be aggressive and have more interpersonal conflict, likely creating a more difficult family life, but this also means his daughter may inherit this gene from him that can trigger early puberty. It is not the father's aggression that turned on the gene for puberty, but rather inheritance of the gene itself that both promotes aggression in the father and turns on early puberty in the daughter (Posner, 2006). This is another example of the complexity that awaits us as we try to fully understand the interaction of genes and the environment.

HOW GENES SHAPE THE ENVIRONMENT

So far we have described the way genes affect physical and biological processes and the way the environment influences the expression of genes to produce various developmental outcomes. A third developmental mechanism occurs when genes influence the nature of the environment in which they exist.

Sandra Scarr (1992) proposed that one way to think about how genes shape the environment is to see them as passive, active, or evocative. With a **passive gene-environment interaction**, genes don't have to do much to be expressed because the children are born into a family that provides them with both their genes and an environment that encourages the expression of those genes. For example, actress Gwyneth Paltrow probably inherited genes for creativity from her famous mother Blythe Danner, who has had a long successful acting career. However, it is also likely that her mother provided an environment that supported her

Passive gene-environment interaction A situation in which a child's family shares his own genetically determined abilities and interests.

daughter's talent as she grew up. Paltrow has gone on to win both an Academy Award and an Emmy for her acting skills.

With an **active gene-environment interaction**, genes become a driving force for children to seek out experiences that fit their genetic endowments (Rowe, 2003). For example, a child with genes that promote risk-taking may be drawn like a magnet to snowboarding, bungee jumping, or whatever is offered that provides a physical and risky challenge. On the other hand, a child with a genetic predisposition to be timid will seek out activities that are solitary and not overly stimulating or exciting. In Chapter 1, when we discussed the active role that children play in their own development, we called this type of gene effect *niche-picking*. You find the part of your environment (the niche) in which you feel most comfortable, and you actively make this choice (Feinberg, Reiss, Neiderhiser, & Hetherington, 2005).

Finally, with an **evocative gene-environment interaction**, genes cause children to act in a way that draws out or "evokes" certain responses from those around them. For example, individuals with certain forms of a gene related to the production of the hormone oxytocin were more outgoing and less shy compared to individuals with a different form of the same gene. Researchers found that the more friendly behavior exhibited by these individuals evoked a positive response from people in their social world, resulting in a higher level of social support and more friends (Creswell et al., 2015).

It is important to realize that all genes operate in all three of these ways. A child who has inherited genes for musicality and has a musical family may also actively seek out musical experiences outside of the family and this behavior evokes certain responses from people such as music teachers who further promote the child's musical interests and abilities. Our genes play out their influence in our environment, but they also have an important role in creating our environment.

Larry Busacca/WireImage/Getty Images

Like mother, like daughter. Well-known actress Gwyneth Paltrow grew up learning from her famous actor-mother Blythe Danner. Paltrow likely received both genes and environmental influences that set her on her path to a successful career in acting.

Active gene-environment interaction When one's genetic endowment becomes a driving force for children to seek out experiences that fit their genetic endowments.

Evocative gene-environment interaction When children's genetic endowment causes them to act in a way that draws out or "evokes" certain responses from those around them.

CHECK YOUR UNDERSTANDING

1. What does the concept of canalization describe?
2. What is epigenetics?
3. What are the differences between a passive gene-environment interaction, an active gene-environment interaction, and an evocative gene-environment interaction?

CONCLUSION

All human beings begin with the combination of the genes of their two parents. However, we are then born into an environment that shapes the way those genes will be expressed. As we have seen, our genetic inheritance also shapes the environment we will experience. We are a long way from understanding all of the complex interaction between our genetic inheritance and our experiences in our environment. As we continue in our study of child development, we will examine the way our physical, cognitive, language, emotional, and social development are shaped both by our genetic inheritance and by the environmental context of our lives.

CHAPTER SUMMARY

Test your understanding of the content.
Take the practice quiz at **edge.sagepub.com/levine3e**

4.1 How has the study of genetic inheritance changed in the last century?

In the 19th century, Mendel studied the transmission of genetic information from one generation to the next, but genes and their structure were not discovered until the 1950s by Watson and Crick. In 2003 the Human Genome project mapped all the genes that make up a human being.

4.2 How do genes and chromosomes function?

Chromosomes are made of chains of **genes,** which consist of the **nucleotide** bases guanine, adenine, thymine, and cytosine. The order of these bases gives a cell the instructions for producing different proteins. Genes are generally paired up, with half of each pair coming from each parent. A **genotype** is the genes a person has for a particular characteristic and a **phenotype** is the genetically based characteristics that we can see. **Dominant genes** are expressed in the phenotype regardless of the gene they are paired with, but **recessive genes** are expressed only if they are paired with another recessive gene, or if they are carried on the X chromosome of a male child with no matching gene on the Y chromosome. Each trait or behavior can be produced by the interaction of many genes, a process called **polygenic inheritance.** In addition, any one gene may have many different influences, called **pleiotropic effects.** Disorders such as cystic fibrosis result when **mutations** occur in a gene.

4.3 How do genetic disorders develop, and what role do genetic testing and counseling play in identifying, preventing, and treating these disorders?

Single-gene disorders, such as sickle-cell anemia and Tay-Sachs disease, result when an individual inherits a pair of recessive genes that carry that disorder. **Chromosome disorders** such as Down syndrome occur when a child receives the wrong number of chromosomes, or when there is a change in the structure of the chromosome caused by breakage. **Multifactorial inheritance**

disorders, such as depression and alcoholism, result from the interaction of many genes that also interact with environmental influences. Genetic counseling helps parents assess the risk their child might have for certain conditions. During pregnancy the *alpha-fetoprotein test,* **amniocentesis,** and **chorionic villus sampling** can assess genetic defects. Important ethical considerations regarding genetic testing include the possibility of false positive results for prenatal tests, causing unnecessary worry for parents, and the need to maintain the confidentiality of test results to avoid discrimination in employment or availability of health insurance. **Gene therapy** that can change defective genes is still in the experimental stage, but the symptoms of certain gene disorders can be controlled through environmental changes.

4.4 How do we study the relationship between our genetic inheritance and our traits and behavior?

Studies of **concordance rates** between adopted children and their birth parents and their adoptive parents, twin studies comparing the concordance rate between **monozygotic** and **dizygotic twins,** and studies of identical twins reared apart have examined the relative contributions of genes and environment on children's behavior.

4.5 How do genes and the environment interact?

Canalization is the degree to which genes are affected by environmental variations. **Epigenetics** is a system through which chemical tags activate or silence gene activity in response to events or circumstances in the individual's environment. Genes can also affect the nature of an individual's environment. In a **passive gene-environment interaction,** children are born into a family that shares and promotes their own genetically determined abilities and interests. In an **active gene-environment interaction,** children seek out experiences on their own that fit their genetic endowments. In an **evocative gene-environment interaction,** children's genetically based tendencies to act in certain ways draw out or evoke certain responses from those around them.

KEY TERMS

**Strengthen your understanding of these key terms with
mobile-friendly eFlashcards at edge.sagepub.com/levine3e**

Active gene-environment interaction   129
Amniocentesis   116
Behavioral genetics   104
Canalization   125
Chorion   116
Chorionic villus sampling (CVS)   116
Chromosomes   105
Chromosome disorders   114
Concordance rate   120
Dizygotic twins   121
Dominant genes   108
Epigenetics   125
Evocative gene-environment interaction   129
Fertilization   105
Gene therapy   118
Generalist genes   112

Genome   105
Genotype   108
Heritability   120
Molecular genetics   105
Monozygotic twins   121
Multifactorial inheritance disorders   115
Mutations   107
Nucleotide   108
Passive gene-environment interaction   128
Phenotype   108
Pleiotropic effects   112
Polygenic inheritance   112
Recessive genes   108
Single gene disorders   113
Zygote   105

Give your students the SAGE edge!

SAGE edge offers a robust online environment featuring an impressive array of free tools and resources for review, study, and further exploration, keeping both instructors and students on the cutting edge of teaching and learning. Learn more at **edge.sagepub.com/levine3e**

chapter 5

PRENATAL DEVELOPMENT, THE NEWBORN, AND THE TRANSITION TO PARENTHOOD

LEARNING QUESTIONS

5.1 What happens during the three stages of prenatal development?

5.2 What are some health issues and risks that can affect a pregnancy?

5.3 What happens during the process of labor and delivery?

5.4 What are some of the risks to the newborn's well-being?

5.5 How do new parents cope with the transition to parenthood?

Master these objectives using an online action plan at **edge.sagepub.com/levine3e**

TEST YOUR KNOWLEDGE

Test your knowledge of child development by deciding whether each of the following statements is *true* or *false*, and then check your answers as you read the chapter.

1. **T ☐ F ☐:** As many as half of all conceptions never implant in the woman's uterus.

2. **T ☐ F ☐:** A mother and her infant can have different blood types.

3. **T ☐ F ☐:** There are differences in the structure of male brains and female brains that can be observed prenatally.

4. **T ☐ F ☐:** Research has shown that exposing a fetus to extra stimulation (for example, playing music near the woman's stomach) can stimulate advanced cognitive development.

5. **T ☐ F ☐:** The amount of alcohol that a woman consumes while she is pregnant doesn't matter because all amounts of alcohol are equally harmful to the infant.

6. **T ☐ F ☐:** Adolescents who were exposed to marijuana prenatally are more likely to use marijuana than adolescents who were not exposed.

7. **T ☐ F ☐:** Infants who are born to women with HIV are almost certain to have the disease themselves.

8. **T ☐ F ☐:** An infant who is born prematurely will have developmental problems and lag behind other children of the same age.

9. **T ☐ F ☐:** The United States has the highest rate of infant mortality among nations with a similar level of economic well-being.

10. **T ☐ F ☐:** Following the birth of a baby, couples today pretty much share household and child care responsibilities equally.

Correct answers: (1) T, (2) T, (3) T, (4) F, (5) F, (6) T, (7) F, (8) F, (9) T, (10) F

▲ **VIDEO: Watch as students answer some of these questions and the authors respond.**

From the moment a sperm unites with an egg in the process of fertilization, the complicated and amazing process of development begins. As you learned in Chapter 4, that moment determines the genetic makeup of the new individual, but from that very moment the fertilized egg, or zygote, also begins interacting with the environment. What happens in the prenatal environment of a woman's womb over the next 9 months can have a tremendous effect on the course of development. As you'll see in this chapter, the process has some safeguards built into it that help ensure that the newborn is healthy and fully ready to enter the world, but the system is not perfect, and the number of potential threats is substantial. Fortunately, we know a great deal today about ways to help a mother get through her pregnancy without complications and how to help the newborn get off to the best possible start in life. In this chapter, we describe the process of prenatal development. We also look at the experience of birth from the perspective of the parents and the infant, and see how the couple handles the transition to becoming a family.

PRENATAL DEVELOPMENT

5.1 What happens during the three stages of prenatal development?

We begin by looking at the process of prenatal development, describing how, over the period of 9 months, a single fertilized cell develops into a fully formed and functional newborn. We also look at how assistive reproductive technology can help couples who are dealing with infertility.

THE THREE STAGES OF PRENATAL DEVELOPMENT

Ovum An unfertilized egg.

Ovulation The release of a mature egg from an ovary.

The prenatal journey begins when a follicle in a woman's ovary matures and releases an **ovum** (or egg) during her monthly menstrual cycle in the process called **ovulation.** The ovum begins to travel down the fallopian tube toward the uterus. This is where fertilization occurs when the egg is penetrated by one of the approximately 300 million sperm that are released into the woman's reproductive system during an act of intercourse.

You'll remember from Chapter 4 that if the sperm that unites with the egg is carrying a Y chromosome in the 23rd position, the conception is a male, but if it is carrying an X chromosome, the conception is a female. Although the ratio of male to female conceptions has been a topic of debate for a number of years, the best current evidence available has established that there are an equal number of male and female conceptions (Orzack et al., 2015). However, by the time the babies are born, the number of males exceeds the number of females, although the exact ratio varies from one country to another (World Fact Book, 2015). More male than female fetuses are lost in the early weeks of a pregnancy and again near the end, but the overall rate of loss during the prenatal period is higher for female fetuses. The reasons for these differential losses are not clear. In some countries, the selective abortion of female fetuses increases the male-to-female ratio even more and accounts for some of the country-to-country difference.

Prenatal development is divided into three stages of very different lengths. We next describe what happens in each of these stages in detail.

The Germinal Stage (Conception to 2 Weeks)

Germinal stage The prenatal stage that lasts from conception to 2 weeks postconception.

The first stage of prenatal development, called the **germinal stage,** begins when the sperm penetrates the egg. Once a zygote or fertilized egg has been created, the outside thickens so that no other sperm will be able to enter the egg. The newly created zygote continues its journey through the fallopian tube, and the process of cell division begins (see Figure 5.1). It takes about 15 hours for that single cell to become 2 cells, and then the process continues with 2 cells becoming 4, 4 becoming 8, and so on, until there is a ball of 32 cells at 4 to 5 days following conception. Most pregnancies consist of a single conception, but about 3.3% of pregnancies result in the birth of twins (Martin, Hamilton, & Osterman, 2012). Other multiples, such as triplets or higher-order births such as quadruplets, are considerably rarer, accounting for only 124 out of every 100,000 births (Martin, Hamilton, Osterman, Curtin, & Mathews, 2013).

Blastocyst A hollow ball of cells that consists of the inner cell mass (which becomes the embryo) and an outer ring of cells (which becomes the placenta and chorion).

Inner cell mass A solid clump of cells in the blastocyst, which later develops into the embryo.

Trophoblast The outer ring of cells in the blastocyst that later develops into the support system for the pregnancy.

As the number of cells continues to proliferate, the solid ball of cells becomes a hollow ball called a **blastocyst** with a solid group of cells called the **inner cell mass** at one end and an outer ring of cells called the **trophoblast** (see Figure 5.2). The inner cell mass will go on to become the embryo and part of the amnion that surrounds the embryo, and the outer ring of cells will become the support system for the pregnancy, which includes the placenta and the chorion. We describe these structures and their functions when we discuss the next stage of prenatal development.

FIGURE 5.1

The germinal stage. In the week following the fertilization of the ovum, the newly formed zygote travels down the fallopian tube, and the developing blastocyst implants in the lining of the uterus.

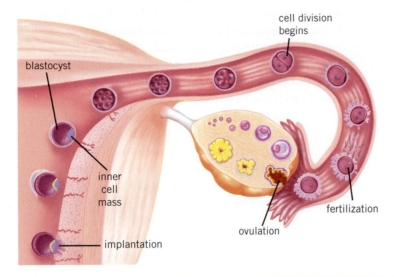

When the blastocyst reaches the uterus, it is ready to implant in the lining of the uterus. During the woman's menstrual cycle, her hormones have prepared the lining for just this purpose. The cells in the trophoblast secrete an enzyme that digests some of the lining so that the blastocyst can securely embed itself there. If the ball of cells fails to implant for any reason, it passes out of the woman's body without her even realizing there had been a conception. This is not an uncommon occurrence. In fact, it is estimated that between 30% and 50% of conceptions fail to implant and do not survive (Moore, Persaud, & Tochia, 2013). After implantation, fingerlike extensions from the outer layer of the trophoblast grow into the uterus, and a connection between the embryo and the mother is established (Galan & Hobbins, 2003). Once an outside source of nourishment is available, the blastocyst can really begin to grow in size.

T ☐ F ☐ As many as half of all conceptions never implant in the woman's uterus.
True

FIGURE 5.2

Development of the blastocyst. As the zygote continues to replicate and divide, a solid ball of cells forms. The cells fold over themselves and form a hollow ball of cells called the blastocyst, which contains the inner cell mass (which becomes the embryo) and an outer ring of cells called the trophoblast (which becomes the support system for the pregnancy).

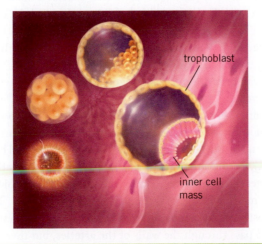

Infertility The inability to conceive within 1 year of frequent, unprotected sex.

Couples who engage in unprotected sex can expect to conceive a child within 1 year, so failure to conceive within that length of time may mean that **infertility** is a problem for the couple. About 12% of married women in the United States have difficulty either getting pregnant or carrying a pregnancy to term (RESOLVE: The National Fertility Association, 2014). One-third of the cases are attributable to female factors, one-third are attributable to male factors, and in the remaining cases the cause is mutual or cannot be determined. One of the most important factors in infertility is maternal age. Women in the United States are waiting longer to have children, and today 20% don't have their first child until the age of 35 or older (Centers for Disease Control and Prevention [CDC], 2013b). About one-third of these women will have a problem with fertility.

Infertility can take a heavy emotional toll on a couple. It has been described as an "emotional rollercoaster" (Read et al., 2014, p. 390) because periods of hope are followed by periods of disappointment, and this continues month after month. Couples often feel isolated and even stigmatized by their situation and may come to see themselves as defective in some way. Because women often do much of the emotional work in a relationship, they may set aside their own needs while they try to protect their husbands from feelings of failure. Men, in turn, often worry about the financial cost of the fertility treatments that are available to the couple. For example, the average cost of a single in vitro fertilization cycle in the United States is $12,400, and this cost often is not covered by insurance (RESOLVE: The National Fertility Association, 2014). About 1% of infants born in the United States are conceived using assisted reproductive technology (CDC, 2014a).

Embryonic stage The prenatal stage that lasts from 2 weeks to 2 months postconception.

Embryo The developing organism from conception to the end of the second month of a pregnancy.

Amnion The inner fetal membrane that surrounds the fetus and is filled with amniotic fluid.

Fetus The developing organism from the end of the eighth week postconception until birth.

Placenta The organ that supports a pregnancy by bringing oxygen and nutrients to the embryo from the mother through the umbilical cord and carrying away fetal waste products.

Despite the emotional toll of infertility, less than one-third of infertile couples seek counseling, but when they do, it is important that they receive the specific type of support that they need (Read et al., 2014). For one couple that might be emotional support to help them deal with what they see as an unforeseen and uncontrollable event in their lives, for another it might be information about the options they have, and another couple may need both types of help.

The Embryonic Stage (2 Weeks to 2 Months)

The **embryonic stage** begins at about 2 weeks postconception and lasts until 8 weeks. At this point the conception is called an **embryo.** The support system that is developing for the pregnancy includes two fetal membranes as well as the placenta and umbilical cord. You can think of the membranes as two sacs, one inside the other. The *chorion* is the outer one, and the connection that it establishes with the uterus gives rise to the placenta. The inner one, called the **amnion,** surrounds the developing embryo and is filled with amniotic fluid to cushion and protect the embryo (later called a **fetus**).

The **placenta** performs the essential functions of bringing oxygen and nutrients to the developing embryo from the mother through the umbilical cord and carrying away fetal waste products. As shown in Figure 5.3, this transfer between the mother and the embryo occurs *without* any intermingling of the blood of the mother and the embryo (Cunningham et al., 2014). If you look carefully at the figure, you'll see that when the fetal arteries enter the spaces in the placenta, they spiral around within the spaces and then return to the fetus as a closed loop. They do *not* directly connect to the maternal arteries or veins. This is why a mother and her child can have different blood types. The two blood systems remain separate throughout the pregnancy.

Because the concentration of oxygen and nutrients in the fetal blood is lower than in the maternal blood, these substances move from the maternal blood through the artery walls where they are picked up by the fetal blood in the placenta and carried back to the developing fetus. In a similar way, the waste products that are in high concentration in the fetal blood move through the artery wall into the spaces, where the maternal blood picks them up to transport back to the mother for disposal through her organ systems. This transport system can prevent some substances from moving from the mother to the fetus because their molecules are too large to pass through the walls of the arteries, but there are many substances that are potentially damaging to the developing embryo that unfortunately *can* move across

T ☐ F ☐ A mother and her infant can have different blood types. **True**

FIGURE 5.3

Functions of the placenta. It is within the placenta that oxygen and nutrients in the maternal blood are picked up by the fetal blood, and waste products carried in the fetal blood are released into the maternal blood to be disposed of by the mother's body.

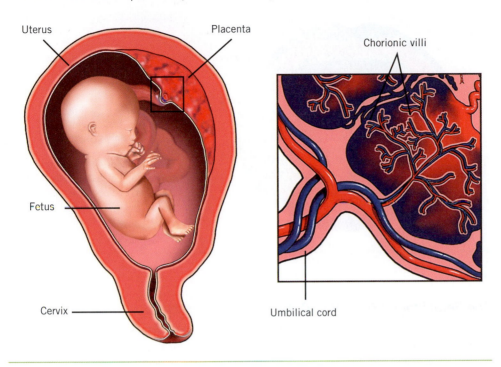

the placenta and enter the fetal blood system. We discuss some of these substances, such as alcohol and nicotine, a little later in the chapter.

During the embryonic stage, the inner cell mass differentiates into three layers, each of which goes on to develop into different organs and structures. This differentiation is shown in Figure 5.4. All of the major organ systems of the body are laid down in a process called **organogenesis** (meaning the *genesis* or beginning of the organs). Because development occurs rapidly within a very short period of time, this is a **critical period** for development. Anything in the prenatal environment that disrupts the process at this point can cause damage that is both severe and irreversible.

During the prenatal period, development starts from the head region and progresses down through the body. This is called **cephalocaudal development** (*cephalus* means "head" and *caudal* means "tail"). This means that throughout the pregnancy, but especially in the early months, the upper half of the embryo (and later the fetus) is more advanced than the lower half. At 9 weeks of age, the head represents about half of the entire length of the fetus because the brain is developing so rapidly that it outpaces the rest of the body.

Some women have a prenatal **ultrasound** between 6 and 10 weeks of the pregnancy. During the test, high-frequency sound waves pass through the woman's uterus and bounce off of the baby. The returning sounds create a video image showing the embryo's size, shape, and position in the womb. The test is often repeated midpregnancy at about 20 weeks. At that point, the test can confirm that the baby is growing at the expected rate, and the physician can check for any physical abnormalities, confirm if there is more than one fetus, determine whether other aspects of the pregnancy appear to be normal, and visually determine the sex of the baby, if the parents want that information. Because an ultrasound is a medical procedure, the American Congress of Obstetricians and Gynecologists (2013) recommends that the test be performed only when there is a specific medical reason for it, so women with low-risk pregnancies may not have this test performed at all.

Organogenesis The process in prenatal development by which all of the major organ systems of the body are laid down.

Critical period A period of time during which development is occurring rapidly and the organism is especially sensitive to damage, which often is severe and irreversible.

Cephalocaudal development A principle whereby development proceeds from the head region down through the body.

Ultrasound A prenatal test that uses high-frequency sound waves to create an image of the developing embryo's size, shape and position in the womb.

FIGURE 5.4

Differentiation of the inner cell mass. The cells in the inner cell mass differentiate into three different types of cell, each of which goes on to have a different function. The description to the right of the figure explains what each layer becomes as the embryo develops.

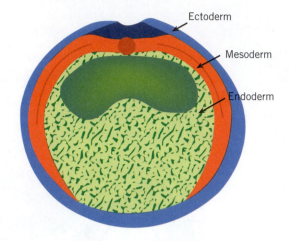

Ectoderm

Mesoderm

Endoderm

Ectoderm → skin, sense organs, brain, and spinal cord

Mesoderm → muscles, blood, bones, and circulatory system

Endoderm → respiratory system, digestive system, liver, and pancreas

The Fetal Stage (Week 9 to Birth)

Fetal stage The prenatal stage that lasts from Week 9 postconception until birth.

From the beginning of the third month until the baby is born is the **fetal stage** of prenatal development. This stage is characterized by the continued growth of the fetus and a remarkable increase in size and weight. All of the organ systems need to complete their development and become functional so that the newborn will be capable of surviving independently of the mother after birth.

One particularly significant event during this period is the transformation of the genitalia of the fetus into male or female genitalia. Although the biological sex of the embryo is determined at conception by the chromosomal information carried in the sperm, up until this point in the pregnancy, the internal and external appearance of male and female embryos has been the same (McClure & Fitch, 2005). In a male fetus, at 9 weeks the testes begin to produce the male hormone *androgen,* and that hormone alters the development of the genitalia from that point on (McClure & Fitch, 2005). In a female fetus, the genitalia continue along their developmental pathway, and a female reproductive system is laid down.

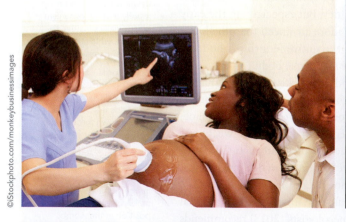

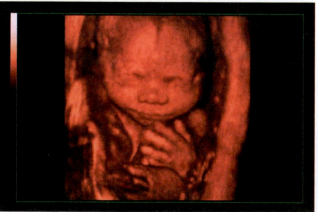

Prenatal testing. This technician is performing a prenatal ultrasound for this couple. Ultrasounds can produce a 3-D image of the developing embryo and fetus that shows some birth defects that would not be apparent on a standard ultrasound. This image is one of a typically developing fetus.

©iStockphoto.com/monkeybusinessimages

Photo By BaSIP/UIG Via Getty Images

Hormones produced prenatally not only shape the physical development of the fetus; they also influence the development of the brain (Hines, 2006). By the 26th week of the pregnancy, we can observe anatomical differences in brain structure of male and female fetuses (Achiron, Lipitz, & Achiron, 2001). For instance, the two hemispheres of the male brain are more symmetrical than the hemispheres of the female brain, there is more grey matter and less white matter in the female brain, and the concentration of grey matter in the neocortex is higher in female brains (Good et al., 2001). However, we should remember that there are many more similarities than differences between male and female brains, and many other factors, such as experiences later in life, also affect the formation and function of boys' and girls' brains.

At about 10 weeks, fetal breathing movements begin, although there is no air in the amniotic sac to breathe. Instead, fetuses breathe in and then expel amniotic fluid. Between Week 12 and Week 16, most women will begin to feel the movement of the fetus. At first it feels like a light fluttering, but as time goes on, the movement becomes more and more marked. By a gestational age of 20 weeks, fetuses have been recorded moving more than 50 times in a single 50-minute session (DiPietro et al., 2004). Fetal movement continues to decline from this point until the baby is born. At 32 weeks, the fetus spends between 90% and 95% of its time sleeping (Hopson, 1998), but it still develops quite a repertoire of activities prior to birth.

Although the fetus is protected from extreme stimulation within its uterine environment, it is not isolated from the sensory world. The cutaneous senses (or "skin senses" such as touch and pain) and the proprioceptive senses (the ones that detect motion or the position of the body) are the first to develop. The cutaneous senses are followed by the chemical senses such as smell and taste and the vestibular senses (the sense of equilibrium and balance). The last to develop are the auditory and visual senses (Lecanuet, Graniere-Deferre, & DeCasper, 2005). The intrauterine environment provides at least some stimulation for all these senses and by the time the baby is born, all the senses are functional to some extent (Hopkins & Johnson, 2005). For instance, sounds from the world outside the womb travel through the mother's abdomen to provide auditory stimulation. Amniotic fluid contains chemosensory molecules that stimulate the smell and taste receptors, and movement of the fetus stimulates the vestibular senses (Lecanuet et al., 2005). What we see throughout the prenatal period is a great deal of continuity as systems develop and later become functional. This prepares the newborn to begin interacting with—and responding to—the environment almost immediately after birth.

We now even have evidence that some simple forms of learning can occur before birth. For instance, recent research has found newborns respond differently to vowel sounds that were part of the native language they were exposed to in utero than to sounds that they were not exposed to (Moon, Lagercrantz, & Kuhl, 2013). These are all signs of an intact and functional central nervous system, but we should not presume that prenatal differences in stimulation are related to later differences in cognitive functioning (Lecanuet et al., 2005). Research that has documented prenatal sensory capabilities has led to the development and marketing of a variety of gadgets that make claims about their ability to stimulate neural growth or facilitate learning, memory, thinking, and even social interaction. However, this shows a lack of understanding of what this research really means. Stimulation that goes beyond what is normally provided to the developing fetus is *not* necessarily better and could even be harmful. The normal prenatal environment provides enough stimulation at this point in development (Lecanuet et al., 2005).

T ☐ F ☐ There are differences in the structure of male brains and female brains that can be observed prenatally. **True**

Unnecessary prenatal stimulation. Although there are commercial devices that claim to provide extra beneficial stimulation to the developing child while in utero, there is no scientific support for this practice. Everyday sounds in the mother's environment provide all the stimulation that is necessary.

T ☐ F ☐ Research has shown that exposing a fetus to extra stimulation (for example, playing music near the woman's stomach) can stimulate advanced cognitive development. **False**

There are many other common beliefs about pregnancy that have been handed down from generation to generation. Test yourself by answering the questions in **Active Learning: Old Wives' Tale or Scientific Fact?** to see which of these ideas have a scientific basis and which do not.

Active LEARNING

Old Wives' Tale or Scientific Fact?

Throughout this book we ask you to test your common sense or intuitive knowledge of development against what we know about it scientifically. There are probably more old wives' tales about pregnancy than about any other period in development. Which of the following statements about pregnancy are true, and which are false?

1. T ☐ F ☐: If your belly is pointy, you are having a boy, but if it spreads out from side to side, you are having a girl.

2. T ☐ F ☐: If you raise your arms above your head, the umbilical cord could strangle your baby.

3. T ☐ F ☐: A pregnant woman shouldn't get a flu shot.

4. T ☐ F ☐: When you are pregnant, you are eating for two.

5. T ☐ F ☐: You shouldn't dye your hair while you are pregnant.

6. T ☐ F ☐: For each baby, you will lose a tooth.

7. T ☐ F ☐: Having sex while you are pregnant will hurt the baby.

8. T ☐ F ☐: Women may have difficulty concentrating in the first 3 months of a pregnancy.

9. T ☐ F ☐: Pregnant women have a special glow.

10. T ☐ F ☐: Your hair will fall out after your pregnancy.

SOURCES: Alcañiz (1997-2016); Gardephe & Ettlinger (1993); Kam (2014); KidsHealth (2008).

Answers:

1. False. The shape of a pregnant woman's belly is not related to the gender of her baby. It depends more upon the woman's body build.

2. False. A woman's movements do not affect the movement of the umbilical cord. If a baby is born with the cord wrapped around his or her neck, it is because of the fetus' prenatal movement in the uterus, not the mother's movements during her pregnancy.

3. False. Being pregnant suppresses a woman's immune system, giving her a higher risk of becoming severely ill or even dying if she gets the flu. A flu shot protects her and her unborn baby during the pregnancy, and helps protect the newborn from the flu after birth.

4. True. A pregnant woman does eat for two, but the second person she is eating for probably weighs 8 pounds or less. That means that an additional 300 calories a day on average are all the extra calories she will need.

5. False. The chemicals in hair dye are absorbed into the skin in only minimal amounts and are not harmful to the pregnancy, although the strong smell of some products could make some women feel nauseated. Women who are concerned can avoid coloring their hair in their first trimester or using dyes that contain ammonia.

6. False. You need 50% more calcium in your diet while you are pregnant, but if your dietary intake is not adequate, it will come from your bones, not your teeth.

7. False. The baby is protected within the amniotic sac, so sexual activity should not affect it. However, because membranes can rupture later in a pregnancy, using a condom near the end of a pregnancy to guard against infection is a good precaution.

8. True. Fatigue, morning sickness, and preoccupation with the pregnancy itself can make a woman forgetful early in her pregnancy.

9. True. The woman's body produces a great volume of blood to support the pregnancy, which results in more blood flow in the vessels and an increase in oil gland secretions. This could be responsible for the "glow" that we associate with pregnancy.

10. True. Hormones secreted during a pregnancy cause hair to grow faster and fall out less, but the hormonal changes that follow the birth of the baby can cause a significant amount of hair to fall out as the body readjusts.

HEALTH AND RISKS IN PREGNANCY

5.2 What are some health issues and risks that can affect a pregnancy?

In this section, we describe some of the things that a woman can do to help ensure her health and the well-being of her baby during a pregnancy. In addition to getting early and continuing prenatal care and being careful about her diet and exercise, a woman needs to avoid a number of potentially harmful substances, such as tobacco and alcohol. We discuss the ways in which these substances are particularly damaging to the developing fetus during critical periods of development.

THREE TRIMESTERS OF PREGNANCY

The three stages of prenatal development that we just described tell us what is happening to the developing infant during the 9 months of the pregnancy. However, from the point of view of the pregnant woman, those 9 months are divided in a different way, into 3-month periods called trimesters, each of which has its own characteristics.

During the first trimester it may not be apparent to other people that the woman is pregnant, but changes in the level of her hormones may cause certain effects, including fatigue, breast tenderness, and *morning sickness*, a nausea that often subsides as the day progresses. In the second trimester, most women start to feel better and the pregnancy begins to become apparent as the fetus grows larger. The woman now is able to feel the fetus moving inside of her. These first fetal movements are called the *quickening*. In the third trimester, the fetus continues to grow, and the woman becomes more tired and uncomfortable (Chye, Teng, Hao, & Seng, 2008). At the end of this time, she will experience the fetus dropping lower within her, as it begins to get into position to begin the birth process.

MISCARRIAGE

It is not an uncommon occurrence for a pregnancy to result in a **miscarriage** or **spontaneous abortion**, which is the natural loss of a pregnancy before 20 weeks gestational age of the fetus (U.S. National Library of Medicine, 2016b). It is estimated that 50% to 80% of miscarriages that occur in the first trimester of a pregnancy are caused by chromosomal abnormalities and not by anything the woman has done (Simpson, 2007), but in many cases the cause is unknown. However, when medical professionals are able to identify a cause, it is easier for women to come to terms with the loss and knowing the cause relieves some of the initial distress (Nikčević & Nicolaides, 2014).

With early miscarriages, the woman may not realize that she has been pregnant, but for women who know they are pregnant and who miscarry a wanted pregnancy, there is a real sense of loss that should be acknowledged. Women use a number of coping strategies to deal with the loss of a pregnancy (Van, 2012). Talking with another woman who has herself

Miscarriage (or spontaneous abortion) The natural loss of a pregnancy before the fetus reaches a gestational age of 20 weeks.

experienced a miscarriage can be particularly helpful. Not only is there a feeling of shared understanding, but if the other woman has subsequently carried a pregnancy to term, it provides reassurance and a sense of hope in the situation. Partners or others who feel they don't know what to say or do should be aware that "just being there" is an important and effective way to help the grieving process (Van, 2012, p. 82). Recurrent miscarriage affects only 1% to 3% of couples (Alijotas-Reig & Garrido-Gimenez, 2013), so most women who have a miscarriage can take comfort from the fact that they will most likely be able to have a child through a future pregnancy.

Abortion A medical procedure that uses medicine or surgery to remove an embryo or fetus and placenta from a woman's uterus.

In some cases, a woman may choose to terminate a pregnancy by having an induced **abortion**, a medical procedure that uses medicine or surgery to remove an embryo or fetus and placenta from a woman's uterus (U.S. National Library of Medicine, 2016a). Worldwide, about 20% of pregnancies end in abortion (Sedgh et al., 2012). In the United States, some of the major reasons women give for having an abortion are financial difficulty, lack of support from a partner, and the need to care for other children (Biggs, Gould, & Foster, 2013). Although this is a difficult choice to make, research has shown that most women feel most anxious *before* the event. Although they may feel some grief and sadness afterwards, the predominant feeling is relief (Weitz, Moore, Gordon, & Adler, 2008). The American Psychological Association's Task Force on Mental Health and Abortion concluded that adult women with an unplanned pregnancy who have an abortion during the first trimester have no worse psychological outcome than those who deliver the baby (American Psychological Association [APA], 2014). However, negative reactions to abortion are more likely if the woman has little support for the procedure, has had previous mental health problems, and if the pregnancy was wanted.

MATERNAL HEALTH AND WELL-BEING

The things that help to protect the health and well-being of a woman at any point in her life are also the things that help to ensure a healthy pregnancy. A good diet, an appropriate amount of exercise, an adequate amount of sleep, and stress management all have a role to play in this process.

Even before a woman gets pregnant, preconception care can reduce or prevent many threats to her or her baby (Mehta-Lee, Bernstein, Harrison, & Merkatz, 2013). She can stop smoking, drinking, or using illicit or recreational drugs, and maintain a healthy diet and an appropriate amount of physical activity. In consultation with her physician, the woman should evaluate whether any over-the-counter or prescription medications that she uses should be reduced or eliminated and discuss possible health risk factors in her workplace or home environment.

Imagemore Co, Ltd./Getty Images

Prenatal Care. Regular visits to a doctor throughout a woman's pregnancy are essential to good prenatal care. The presence of the expectant father at such visits helps him understand the importance of his role as a father-to-be.

Once a woman becomes pregnant, seeing a physician on a regular basis, beginning early in the pregnancy, is one of the best things she can do to avoid problems later on. Women who do not receive prenatal care are 3 times more likely to give birth to a low-weight baby and 5 times more likely to have an infant that dies (Child Trends, 2015b). In the United States, women typically see their doctors once every 4 weeks for the first 28 weeks of their pregnancy, and then see them every 2 weeks until they are a month away from their due date, when they move to having weekly visits. Women with chronic health conditions, such as diabetes, asthma, or allergies, may need to see their health care provider more frequently or may be referred to a physician who specializes in high-risk pregnancies who can help them manage their medications during their pregnancy.

Although the United States spends about twice as much per person on health care as any other country (Peter J. Peterson Foundation, 2013), U.S. maternal and infant health are *not* the best in the world (Central Intelligence Agency, 2014; Heisler, 2012). Each year nearly 1 million American women give birth without having received adequate medical attention during their pregnancy (Health Resources and Services Administration, n.d.). Black and Native American women are more than twice as likely as White women to receive late or no prenatal care (Child Trends, 2015b).

A 2014 worldwide comparison of maternal death rates found that the United States ranked 60th in the world, with 18.5 maternal deaths per 100,000 live births. This is triple the rate found in the United Kingdom and 8 times the rate of Iceland, the country with the lowest maternal mortality rate (Almendrala, 2014). Many of the deaths result from complications of conditions such as heart disease, diabetes, obesity, or kidney problems that begin during the woman's pregnancy or are exacerbated by it. This is one reason why adopting a healthy lifestyle both before and during pregnancy and getting early and consistent prenatal care are so very important.

Maternal Diet

A well-balanced diet is essential for both a mother and her baby during a pregnancy. However, the developing baby is so small relative to the size of the mother that an average of 300 extra calories a day is all that is needed to support prenatal growth (Katz, 2003), with fewer calories required early in the pregnancy and more required nearer to the time for delivery. The recommended weight gain for women who begin their pregnancy at a normal weight is 25 to 35 pounds (Katz, 2003). Women who are

Healthy eating while pregnant. Healthy eating is always important, but it is particularly important while you are pregnant. The mother's diet provides all of the nutrients that her developing child needs. Avoiding foods that can be harmful is equally essential.

underweight can safely gain a bit more, and women who are overweight should gain less, although this is *not* a good time to severely restrict the number of calories eaten. The goal is a newborn who weighs between 7 and 8 pounds (Olds, London, & Ladewig, 2002). In cases where a mother is malnourished because of a severely restricted diet, the negative consequences can be severe and long-lasting, affecting the future health of the infant, as well as cognitive skills, problem-solving abilities, developmental levels, and behavioral functioning (Boulet, Schieve, & Boyle, 2011; Kessenich, 2003; Sudfeld et al., 2015).

Because pregnant women need to have an adequate amount of vitamins and minerals, doctors usually prescribe a multivitamin or prenatal vitamin. Folic acid, one of the B vitamins, plays an important role in preventing defects of the brain and spinal cord, so women who are planning on becoming pregnant should be sure their diet contains an adequate amount of this essential vitamin even before they become pregnant (Chye et al., 2008). Folate is found in foods such as beans, leafy green vegetables, and orange juice, but it also is available as a food supplement. Doctors also may recommend iron or calcium supplements (Katz, 2003).

There are some foods that should be avoided during a pregnancy because of risks associated with them. For instance, certain fish including shark and swordfish may have high levels of mercury or industrial pollutants (U.S. Department of Health and Human Services [USDHHS], 2016). Other foods to avoid include soft cheeses such as Brie, feta, or queso fresco; raw cookie dough or cake batter; raw or undercooked fish (including sushi) and shellfish; unpasteurized juice, cider, or milk; and raw or undercooked sprouts. Although there has been some concern about a relationship between caffeine consumption and preterm birth, a recent meta-analysis failed to support this concern (Maslova, Bhattacharya, Lin, & Michels,

© Can Stock Photo Inc./szefei

Yoga while pregnant. Moderate exercise while a woman is pregnant can be beneficial to her health and the health of her baby. It relieves some of the discomforts of being pregnant, while keeping the mother fit and strong. It also helps to prepare her body for labor and delivery.

2010). Moderate caffeine consumption equivalent to 1 or 2 cups of coffee per day is usually considered safe (Morgan, Koren, & Bozzo, 2013). However, because caffeine also can come from tea, chocolate, and soda, and bottled water and energy drinks may contain caffeine even though it is not listed on their labels, these foods also should be included when calculating daily caffeine consumption.

Exercise

An appropriate level and type of exercise is beneficial to pregnant women in ways similar to the way it benefits everyone else. A woman should always consult her physician about her particular situation, but women who were physically active before they became pregnant can usually continue moderate levels of the same activity after they become pregnant, although they will have to adapt their routines to their changing bodies. Pregnancy hormones make joints and muscles more flexible, a woman's center of gravity shifts as her belly gets bigger, and, of course, she weighs more (American Pregnancy Association, 2015). Exercise needs to be modified to accommodate these physical changes. For women who have not been physically active before, walking can be a good activity during pregnancy. Low impact activities, such as yoga, are better activity choices than ones that involve a chance of falling or too much bouncing or jumping.

Exercise relieves some of the normal discomforts associated with a pregnancy, such as backaches or fatigue, and improves mood and sleep quality (American Pregnancy Association, 2015; Mayo Clinic, 2015b). It also can help prevent excessive weight gain and strengthens and prepares the woman's body for labor. As a precaution, women should stay well hydrated and not get overheated while exercising (American Pregnancy Association, 2015).

TERATOGENS

Teratogens Agents that can disrupt prenatal development and cause malformations or termination of the pregnancy.

A number of factors can have a negative impact on prenatal development. Agents that can cause malformations in an embryo or a fetus are broadly referred to as **teratogens**. They include diseases that a mother has or contracts during her pregnancy (such as rubella, Zika, syphilis, or HIV), things that the mother ingests (such as alcohol, medication, or drugs), and toxins in the environment (such as mercury in the foods she eats or exposure to environmental pollution). Because there are so many potential teratogens, we can only talk briefly about some of the most common ones in this chapter.

Each teratogen has a specific effect on the developing embryo or fetus and can result in a structural abnormality, such as a small or malformed head or limbs, or a functional deficit, such as hearing loss or intellectual disability. The nature and magnitude of the effect depends on *when* in the prenatal period the fetus or embryo is exposed to the teratogen, the *amount* or dosage of the exposure, and the *length of time* the exposure continues. For example, an exposure that could end a pregnancy if it occurred early in the germinal stage might produce serious physical defects if it occurred during the embryonic stage, but result in much less severe defects if it occurred late in the fetal stage. Figure 5.5 shows the sensitive periods for the impact of various teratogens on development.

The effect of a woman contracting rubella (or German measles) at different points in her pregnancy provides a good illustration of this point. Although rubella is a relatively rare disease in the United States where most children are vaccinated against it, the World Health Organization (2014) estimates that worldwide 110,000 babies are born with the symptoms of a prenatal rubella infection each year. Exposure in the first 11 weeks of the pregnancy results

FIGURE 5.5

Sensitive periods in prenatal development. Each organ system has a period in prenatal development when it is particularly sensitive to disruption by teratogens. This figure shows those sensitive or critical periods of development.

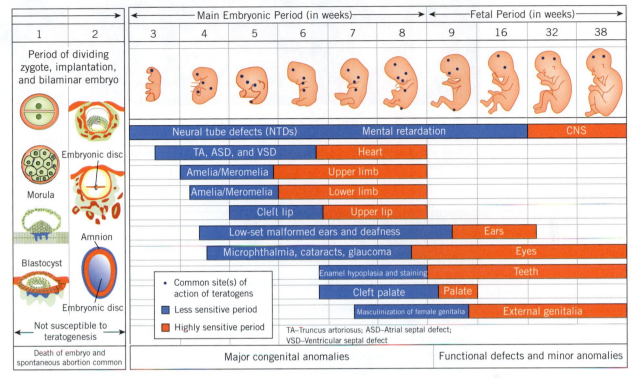

SOURCE: Moore & Persaud (2003).

in significant problems with vision, hearing, and the functioning of the heart in 90% of the cases, but exposure later in the pregnancy results in 20% of infants born with congenital defects (Reef & Redd, 2008).

Alcohol

Alcohol should not be a part of a pregnant woman's diet. When a pregnant woman drinks an alcoholic beverage—whether it is beer, wine, or hard liquor—the alcohol in it enters her bloodstream and circulates through her system until her liver can break it down over the next couple of hours so it can be passed from her body. During that time, because the concentration of alcohol in the woman's bloodstream is higher than the concentration in the fetal blood, the alcohol crosses the placenta and does damage to the developing embryo or fetus. The relatively small size of the embryo, together with the fact that vital organ systems may be in critical stages of development, helps explain why even a small amount of alcohol can be a problem. The effect of alcohol on a 120-pound woman is different from the effect on a 1- or 2-pound fetus.

The most clear-cut effect of alcohol on a pregnancy is seen in children born to women who have consumed large quantities of alcohol throughout their pregnancy or who have had occasional bouts of binge drinking (defined as having 5 or more drinks at one time). Either pattern of drinking can result in **fetal alcohol syndrome (FAS),** which includes physical characteristics such as abnormal facial features, small stature, and a small head, and functional problems with learning, memory, and attention span, as well as trouble controlling behavior and regulating emotions (CDC, 2014f). FAS represents the extreme end of a continuum of problems known as **fetal alcohol spectrum disorders (FASDs),** which includes any subset of characteristics of FAS at varying levels of severity. Our understanding of how alcohol affects a pregnancy is described with more detail in **Journey of Research: Understanding the Effects of Alcohol on a Pregnancy.**

Fetal alcohol syndrome (FAS) A condition in the child resulting from heavy or binge consumption of alcohol during a pregnancy; associated with characteristic facial features, small stature, and a small head, as well as cognitive deficits and trouble controlling behavior and regulating emotions.

Fetal alcohol spectrum disorders (FASDs) A range of impairments in a child resulting from consumption of alcohol during a pregnancy.

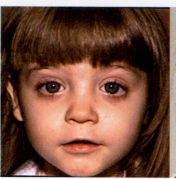
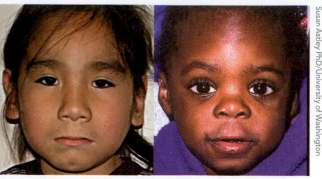

Susan Astley PhD/University of Washington

Facial characteristics of children with fetal alcohol syndrome. These photos show some of the facial features that are characteristic in children with fetal alcohol syndrome, including a smooth ridge between the nose and upper lip, a thin upper lip, wide-spaced eyes, underdeveloped ears, and a short nose with a flat bridge.

JOURNEY OF *Research*

Understanding the Effects of Alcohol on a Pregnancy

As far back as ancient Greece and Rome, people suspected that alcohol could have a negative impact on pregnancies (Calhoun & Warren, 2006). However, concern did not appear in the medical literature until the 1700s, when a group of physicians in England described alcoholic women giving birth to children who were "weak, feeble, and distempered" (Calhoun & Warren, 2006, p. 169). In 1899, an English deputy medical examiner noted that alcoholic mothers had an increased risk of having a child who died at birth. However, these early observations linking alcohol and birth defects were largely ignored by the medical community until a group of French researchers published a paper in the 1960s describing some commonly occurring problems noted in the offspring of a group of 100 women who drank heavily during their pregnancy (Calhoun & Warren, 2006). In the 1970s, British researchers identified the shared anomalies among children born to chronic alcoholic mothers, concluded that alcohol was the cause of these anomalies, and coined the term *fetal alcohol syndrome* (Calhoun & Warren, 2006). As interest in this topic took hold, research examined other factors that contributed to the problems seen in children born to alcoholic mothers. In addition to drinking, these women likely were doing other things that negatively affected their pregnancy. For instance, they may have smoked, been malnourished, received no prenatal care, or had untreated medical conditions.

As public concern continued to grow, the U.S. Food and Drug Administration issued a bulletin in 1977 that discouraged "binge" or "chronic, excessive" drinking during pregnancy (Bobo, Klepinger, & Dong, 2006, p. 1062). A decade later, the federal Alcoholic Beverage Labeling Act was passed requiring that alcoholic beverages carry a warning that they should not be consumed during a pregnancy because of the risk of birth defects. Several health initiatives since then have tried to inform women of this danger. In 2005, the Surgeon General updated a 1981 advisory that suggested that pregnant women "*limit* [emphasis added] the amount of alcohol they drink" by saying that "*no amount* [emphasis added] of alcohol consumption can be considered safe during a pregnancy" and warning women that alcohol can damage the fetus at any stage in a pregnancy (USDHHS, 2005b).

How successful have our efforts been to educate women about the dangers of drinking while pregnant? Between 2006 and 2010, 1 in 13 pregnant women (7.6%) reported using alcohol in the past 30 days and, among those women, 1 in 5 reported binge drinking (Marchetta et al., 2012). Although accurate numbers are difficult to obtain, the American

Academy of Pediatrics estimates that there may be as many as 40,000 infants born each year in the United States with FASDs (AAP, n.d.). Given that prenatal exposure to alcohol is considered the leading preventable cause of birth defects and intellectual disability in the United States (Williams, Smith, and the Committee on Substance Abuse, 2015), these figures are discouraging.

Recently, several large studies conducted by European researchers have challenged the idea that complete abstinence is required (McCarthy et al., 2013; Skogerbø et al., 2013), but it is difficult to identify all of the effects of alcohol on brain and cognitive development. The failure of these researchers to detect harm attributable to maternal alcohol consumption does not necessarily mean that none has happened. A recent study in South Africa illustrates how difficult it is to detect these effects by comparing children with FASD to those who did not have any symptoms. While some mothers who had consumed alcohol while pregnant had children who were not identified as having FASD (that is, no symptoms were detected), these researchers found that the more drinking mothers in this sample had done, the more symptoms of FASD their children were likely to have (May et al., 2013). Drinking during the first trimester raised the likelihood of FASD 12 times, while drinking throughout pregnancy raised the risk 65 times.

No study has claimed that heavy alcohol consumption during pregnancy is safe, and the Centers for Disease Control and Prevention (2014e) and the American Academy of Pediatrics (as cited in Williams, Smith, and the Committee on Substance Abuse, 2015) continue to caution women that there is no known safe amount of alcohol consumption during a pregnancy.

T ☐ F ☐ The amount of alcohol that a woman consumes while she is pregnant doesn't matter because all amounts of alcohol are equally harmful to the infant. **False**

Any effects of prenatal exposure to alcohol are permanent and irreversible. Stopping drinking at any point in a pregnancy prevents further damage, but it does *not* reverse the harm that has already been done. Although intervention programs can help improve the functioning of children born with FAS and FASDs, this is a completely preventable condition and, in this case, an ounce of prevention is worth more than a pound of cure. Because so much development occurs in the weeks before a woman realizes she is pregnant and because nearly one half of all pregnancies in the United States are unplanned (Finer & Zolna, 2011), abstaining from alcohol if a woman is sexually active even before she becomes pregnant is a good idea.

TRUE/FALSE VIDEO ▲

Tobacco

Another totally preventable source of developmental risk is maternal smoking and exposure to secondhand smoke during a pregnancy (CDC, 2007; Rogers, 2009). The more a woman smokes, the greater her risk of having a baby with low birth weight (Rogers, 2009). What causes this effect? As a woman smokes, the level of carbon monoxide in her blood increases and this reduces the capacity of her blood to carry oxygen to the fetus. Because the nicotine in the smoke constricts the blood vessels, this further limits the flow of oxygen and nutrients through the placenta and, because nicotine tends to suppress appetite, pregnant smokers eat less. All these factors contribute to the growth retardation that is so strongly associated with babies born to smokers.

Smoking also has been associated with an increased risk of miscarriage, premature birth, and sudden infant death (Shea & Steiner, 2008) and is a major contributor to later developmental problems for the child. A systematic review of 40 years of published studies found a positive association between maternal smoking and defects of the heart, musculoskeletal system, face and eye, and gastrointestinal system, and malformation of the genitals (Hackshaw, Rodeck, & Boniface, 2011). Behavioral effects that have been found include attention deficit hyperactivity disorder (ADHD), conduct disorders, and learning disabilities (Rogers, 2009; Shea & Steiner, 2008; Slotkin, 2008).

While smoking has decreased among the general population over the last couple of decades, it decreased at a slower rate among young women ages 19 to 29 than among other groups, and in 2010, about 10% of pregnant women still reported smoking during the last 3 months of their pregnancy (CDC, 2014i). The good news is that when women stop smoking, even as late as the second trimester of their pregnancy, the weight and body measurements of their infants are comparable to those of infants whose mothers were nonsmokers (American Congress of Obstetricians and Gynecologists [ACOG], 2010, reaffirmed 2015).

Babies born to mothers who smoke during their pregnancy appear to undergo withdrawal symptoms similar to those seen in babies born to mothers addicted to illicit drugs (Law et al., 2003), and maternal smoking during a pregnancy is a strong predictor of whether or not adolescents begin smoking and become addicted themselves (Abreu-Villac, Seidler, Tate, Cousins, & Slotkin, 2004). Even when women stop smoking while they are pregnant or breastfeeding, many resume shortly thereafter (Xu, Wen, Rissel, & Baur, 2013), exposing children to smoke in their home environment. Even *thirdhand smoke*, the residue found in dust, carpets, and many other surfaces in a household where people smoke, may affect infants who spend time playing with toys at floor level (Winickoff et al., 2009). For these reasons, it would be beneficial to both mother and infant to find ways to make a smoke-free environment a long-term lifestyle change rather than a brief adaptation to the pregnancy itself.

Prescription and Over-the-Counter Drugs

It is difficult to make general statements about the use of prescription medications or over-the-counter drugs because the potential effect of drugs on a pregnancy depends on the specific type of medication that is used, when in the pregnancy it is taken, for how long it is used, and its dosage. If a woman wants to use over-the-counter medications to relieve the discomfort of colds, headaches, or nausea, she should discuss this decision with her physician first so they can weigh the potential benefits against the possible risks for the fetus. Because most herbal remedies and food supplements have not been tested by the U.S. Food and Drug Administration for safety, it is best to avoid these completely while pregnant. To see how safe your own medications would be for a pregnant woman, try **Active Learning: Safety of Medications During Pregnancy**.

Active LEARNING

Safety of Medications During Pregnancy

Do you know whether the medications that are in your medicine cabinet right now are safe for use during pregnancy? Make a list of all your medications (both prescription and over-the-counter), vitamins, and herbal supplements, and check their safety.

You can visit your campus library where you'll find reference books such as the *Physicians' Desk Reference* (*PDR*) (PDR Staff, 2016). The *PDR* contains the information that you usually get from the insert that comes with your prescription, including any warnings or contraindications for the drug's use. Separate volumes of the *PDR* deal specifically with nonprescription

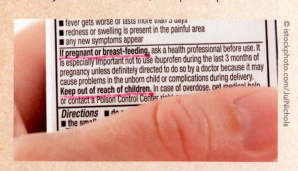

Medications and pregnancy. A woman should be very careful about what medications she uses during her pregnancy. The labeling on the medication itself may provide a warning about use during pregnancy, but the Physicians' Desk Reference also contains information about safety.

drugs, dietary supplements, and herbal medicines. Some of these volumes may be available to you electronically through the PDR Network website.

You also can search the Internet by typing the name of a specific drug and the word *pregnancy* to see if there are any advisories against its use. If you do this, however, please be sure that you pay attention to the credentials of the site you are using. Sites maintained by the Centers for Disease Control and Prevention, the National Institutes of Health, or the American Congress of Obstetricians and Gynecologists will give you information you can trust.

After you complete your search, take some time to think about what a pregnant woman would need to consider when weighing the benefits resulting from the use of these medications and supplements against the potential risk to her pregnancy and developing fetus.

Medication is most likely to be harmful in the early weeks of the pregnancy during that critical period in development, but there are some medications that should never be used during a pregnancy. Common drugs like Accutane (used to treat acne; Honein, Paulozzi, & Erickson, 2001), Soriatane (used to treat the skin condition of psoriasis; Stiefel Laboratories, 2008), and thalidomide (used to treat multiple myeloma, complications of AIDS, and leprosy; Ito et al., 2010) all can result in severe birth defects.

When a woman has a chronic condition such as asthma, diabetes, or high blood pressure, continuing to take her medication may be necessary during her pregnancy. For example, women who are diabetic have an increased risk of miscarriage, preterm births, and some birth defects if they do not effectively control their glucose level while they are pregnant (Cunningham et al., 2014). For women living with AIDS, the National Institutes of Health (2014) recommend that they continue using antiretroviral drugs during pregnancy because it lowers the risk of passing HIV to the unborn child. For other drugs, such as antidepressants, the findings about the effects on the fetus have been mixed (Mayo Clinic, 2015). For these reasons, pregnant women with chronic conditions need to work closely with their physicians to balance the benefits of continuing their medications with the potential risks of their use.

Illegal Drugs

It is difficult to conduct research on the effect of illegal drugs on a human pregnancy because it is difficult to get accurate information from mothers who are using illegal substances about the amount or type of drugs they use, or the length of time they have used them. It also is difficult to disentangle the effect of the drugs themselves from the effect of other things that might be going on that negatively affect the pregnancy. A woman who is using illegal drugs may be less likely to see a doctor during her pregnancy or to take good care of herself in other ways. Despite these difficulties, there has been a good deal of research on the effect of marijuana and cocaine on pregnancies in recent years.

Infants who are exposed to cocaine prenatally are significantly more likely to be born prematurely, to be born at a low birth weight, or to be small for their gestational age (Gouin, Murphy, Shah, & Knowledge Synthesis Group on Determinants of Low Birth Weight and Preterm Births, 2011). These newborns show signs of withdrawal for several weeks after they are born and prenatal exposure can affect the way they interact with their parents after birth. Infants rely on crying to signal to their caregivers that they are distressed, but infants who are prenatally exposed to cocaine are less clear in the signals they send (Field, 2007) so it is more difficult for their parents to care for them adequately.

At the height of the cocaine epidemic in the United States, there was concern about how our society would be able to meet the needs of infants damaged prenatally by cocaine exposure. However, as longitudinal data have accumulated, the developmental impacts have been less severe than originally anticipated (Bandstra, Morrow, Mansoor, & Accornero, 2010). We now know that many of the problems initially thought to be a consequence of prenatal cocaine exposure are, in fact, related to other risk factors such as the poor quality of infants' early environment (Frank, Augustyn, Knight, Pell, & Zuckerman, 2001).

Marijuana is the most commonly used illicit drug among pregnant women in the United States (Metz & Stickrath, 2015). Concern within the medical community about its use has increased as more states have legalized marijuana for recreational or medicinal use. Despite these changes at the state level, marijuana continues to be classified as a Schedule 1 drug by the federal government and, therefore, continues to be considered "illicit." Although it does have some recognized medical uses, both the American Medical Association (CBS News, 2015) and the American Congress of Obstetricians and Gynecologists (2015) have advised pregnant women and nursing mothers to avoid it. The American Congress of Obstetricians and Gynecologists recommends that doctors ask pregnant women about their use of marijuana along with questions about their use of alcohol and tobacco, urge them to discontinue its use while pregnant and nursing, and to use alternative medicines when necessary. The American Medical Association has recently called for point-of-sale warning labels on marijuana, similar to those used on alcoholic beverages and tobacco products to warn pregnant women about the risk of using the product.

The psychoactive ingredient in marijuana crosses the placenta barrier during pregnancy and also is found in breastmilk of users. The deficits that have been identified in their offspring include learning disabilities and memory impairment in young children; impulsivity and hyperactivity, inattention, and poor problem-solving skills in school-age children; and hyperactivity, inattention, and lack of self-control and emotional regulation in adolescents (Wu, Jew, & Lu, 2012). One weakness in our current understanding of the impact of prenatal marijuana exposure is that the concentration of TCH, the active compound in marijuana, is much higher today than when many earlier studies were done. That means our current understanding of its effects may actually underestimate the long-term effects of the drug.

Animal studies have found evidence that there are changes in the sensitivity of the specific brain circuits that are involved in the reward system of the brain, potentially making this substance even more reinforcing for adult animals with this prenatal history (Malanga & Kosofsky, 2003). Several longitudinal studies with humans have found that prenatal maternal use of marijuana predicted the likelihood of adolescents beginning to use the drug themselves (Porath & Fried, 2005), lowered the age at which they initiated use, and increased the frequency of use (Day, Goldschmidt, & Thomas, 2006). A pregnancy is often an opportunity for a woman to decrease or even discontinue her substance use, but many resume use following the birth of their infant, although at a lower level (Bailey, Hill, Hawkins, Catalano, & Abbott, 2008; Koniak-Griffin, Spears, & Stein, 2010). A recent analysis found that it was the youngest mothers who were most likely to resume use (De Genna, Cornelius, Goldschmidt, & Day, 2015). As you will learn in Chapter 15, in recent years, attitudes toward marijuana have become more positive among young people and they increasingly do not see the drug as harmful. This suggests that in the future children with a possible neurological sensitivity to marijuana because of their prenatal exposure to the drug also will have role models who are engaging in this behavior. Although the effects of marijuana use may be subtle, "even subtle effects can have both short-term and long-term implications" for a child's development (Huizink & Mulder, 2006, p. 36), so women need to think carefully about these implications before using recreational drugs while pregnant.

Diseases

There are a number of diseases and medical conditions that can have a detrimental effect on a pregnancy. In this section, we will discuss several common ones. To begin with, screening for sexually transmitted infections (STIs) is a routine part of prenatal care. Some sexually transmitted infections, such as syphilis and HIV, can cross the placenta and infect the baby

T ☐   F ☐

Adolescents who were exposed to marijuana prenatally are more likely to use marijuana than adolescents who were not exposed.

True

FIGURE 5.6

Number of pediatric AIDS cases in the United States, 1985–2013. "Perinatal transmission" includes the transmission of the virus that causes AIDS from mother to child during pregnancy, labor and delivery, or breastfeeding. With the use of antiretroviral medications during pregnancy, the rate of transmission has decreased dramatically in recent years. Continued treatment of infected infants after birth further reduces the number who go on to develop AIDS.

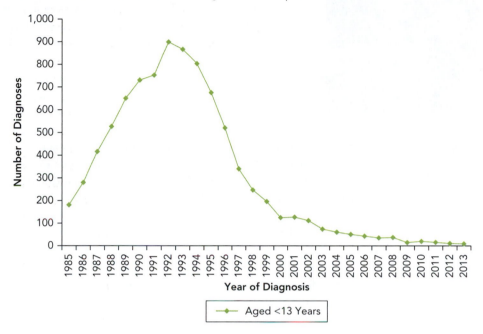

NOTE: Data have been adjusted for reporting delays and missing risk-factor information.

SOURCE: National Center for HIV/AIDS, Viral Hepatitis, STD & TB Prevention (n.d.).

prenatally, while others, such as gonorrhea, genital herpes, and chlamydia, are present in the birth canal and can infect the baby during the birth process (USDHHS, 2015). Fortunately, bacterial infections such as chlamydia, gonorrhea, and syphilis can be treated and cured with antibiotics during the pregnancy (CDC, 2008b). Although viral STIs such as genital herpes and HIV cannot be cured, antiviral medication can reduce the symptoms and their effect on the developing fetus (CDC, 2009).

The virus that causes HIV can be transmitted in several ways. It can cross the placental barrier and be transmitted from mother to baby during the pregnancy, but it also can be passed along when the baby is delivered vaginally or through the mother's breast milk after the baby is born. That is why it is recommended that HIV-positive mothers deliver their babies through a planned cesarean section and not breastfeed their infants (AIDSinfo, 2015). Taking antiviral medication while pregnant lowers the viral load in the woman's blood and, if the baby also is treated with anti-HIV medication after birth, the infection risk for the infant drops to less than 1% (CDC, 2015d). Figure 5.6 illustrates the dramatic decline that has occurred in perinatally acquired pediatric AIDS in the United States in recent years with the use of these medications.

Neonatal herpes is another maternal infection that can have devastating consequences for an infant. Infants who are born with the disease and do not respond to treatment are at risk for neurological damage, intellectual disability, or death (American Social Health Association [ASHA], 2015). Fortunately, the risk of an infant contracting herpes is usually low. An estimated 25% to 30% of pregnant women have genital herpes, but the infection rate for their babies is 0.1% (that is, one-tenth of 1%) (ASHA, 2015). However, the risk can be as high as 30% to 50% if the woman acquires the disease late in her pregnancy because in that

T □ F □ Infants who are born to women with HIV are almost certain to have the disease themselves. **False**

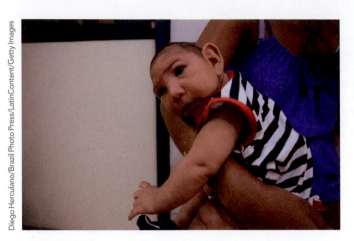

Diego Herculano/Brazil Photo Press/LatinContent/Getty Images

Microcephaly. Exposure to the Zika virus during pregnancy is associated with infants born with microcephaly, an abnormally small brain. Depending on the severity of the condition, microcephaly is associated with seizures, intellectual disability, vision and hearing problems, and a range of developmental delays. Pregnant women need to protect themselves and their babies by avoiding being bitten by infected mosquitos whenever possible and by practicing safe sex with partners who may carry the virus.

case her body does not have enough time to develop antibodies that protect against the virus (CDC, 2015c). Ninety percent of the cases of herpes in infants are transmitted to the infant as the infant passes through the birth canal. Consequently, if a mother has active genital herpes at the time she goes into labor, the infant is usually delivered by cesarean section (CDC, 2015c). Neonatal herpes also can be transmitted after the baby is born, often through kissing by an adult with an active oral herpes infection (ASHA, 2015), so it is just good common sense to avoid that kind of contact.

A newly recognized threat to a healthy pregnancy is Zika, a disease caused by a virus transmitted by an infected mosquito. Zika also can be sexually transmitted from a man who has the infection to his partner (CDC, 2016l). Doctors have known about the virus since the 1940s, but a 2015 epidemic of babies born in Brazil with microcephaly drew the world's attention to it. In healthy adults, the infection is mild, usually lasts less than a week, and may cause a fever, rash, muscle pain, or headaches, or may produce no symptoms at all (CDC, 2016i). However, when a pregnant woman is bitten by an infected mosquito, the virus is transmitted through the placenta where it disrupts fetal brain development, resulting in *microcephaly*, a birth defect in which the newborn's head is abnormally small (Kleber de Oliveira et al., 2016). Depending on the severity of the condition, microcephaly is associated with seizures, intellectual disability, vision and hearing problems, and a range of developmental delays (CDC, 2016d). There still is a great deal that we do not know about this disease, but in addition to microcephaly, radiologists in Brazil have found changes in the size of the spaces in the brain that are filled with cerebrospinal fluid, loss of both white matter and grey matter, abnormalities of the brainstem, and calcification of brain tissue (Soares de Oliveira-Szejnfeld et al., 2016).

The best advice for pregnant women is to avoid being bitten by mosquitos and to use condoms with partners who may be infected with the virus. It is very difficult for health agencies to predict how quickly any virus will spread, but the virus has been detected in a number of countries, including several areas in the United States, and it places potentially millions of people at risk. Private companies and federal agencies are working to develop a vaccine but, because vaccines must be shown to be safe and effective before they are approved for use in humans, a vaccine for the general public is likely still years away (Weisberg, 2016).

Maternal Stress

Whenever we are under stress, our body produces stress hormones, and one of those hormones, cortisol, can pass through the placenta to the fetus. High levels of maternal stress hormones during a pregnancy have been associated with a slower growth rate in the fetus and lower birth weight and with temperamental difficulties in infants (Wadhwa, 2005). As we have seen for other conditions, the exact effects of prenatal stress and maternal cortisol production depend on the nature, timing, and duration of exposure. Several studies have shown that maternal stress early in the prenatal period has a greater impact on fetal growth, length of gestation, infant reactivity to stress, and cognitive development at 12 months of age (Wadhwa, 2005; Davis & Sandman, 2010; Davis, Glynn, Waffarn, & Sandman, 2011). Pregnant women can help to control their stress levels through the healthy practices we have already discussed, including eating a healthy diet, getting enough rest, and exercising on a regular basis.

Environmental Toxins

There are a number of environmental toxins in our homes and workplaces that have the potential to harm a developing fetus (Sahin & Gungor, 2010; Wilson, 2014). If a pregnant woman needs to use household cleaning products, insect repellants, pesticides, and solvents, she should carefully follow the usage warnings that appear on the product labels. Whenever possible, products that are toxic should be replaced by ones that do not contain ingredients shown to be toxic to humans. Women who live in older homes can be exposed to lead in paints that were used before 1978 or from old lead pipes in household plumbing. Living in an urban area or near heavily traveled roads also can expose a woman to air pollutants. To avoid exposure to radiation, pregnant women need to avoid exposure to X-rays, for example during dental exams. They also need to consider whether they are being exposed to harmful substances in their workplace and talk with their employer and physician about ways to reduce or eliminate the exposure.

Maternal stress. Pregnancy brings with it some unique stresses, but excessive stress from any source can affect the fetus because stress hormones cross through the placenta. What are some of the things a pregnant woman could do to manage her level of stress?

Some chemicals are identified as **endocrine disruptors** because they interfere with the functioning of the hormonal system in our bodies (National Institute for Environmental Health Sciences, 2016). These chemicals can interfere with the normal functioning of cells. When transmitted through the placenta, they affect the development of the part of the brain that controls metabolism and have been associated with an increased risk of certain cancers, abnormal growth patterns, and neurodevelopmental delays in children (World Health Organization, 2016). Women need to educate themselves about the sources of these chemicals and avoid them when possible.

Endocrine disruptors
Chemicals that interfere with the functioning of the hormonal systems of the body.

We conclude this section of the chapter by saying that there are a number of factors that can adversely affect prenatal development, but there is much that a pregnant woman can do to help ensure the health and well-being of her baby. The goal of any pregnancy is to have a healthy baby, and fortunately this is exactly what happens in most cases. Although the risks are real and we need to guard against them whenever possible, there also is a great resiliency in the developing child. And, as we point out throughout this book, what happens to the child after birth has a huge impact on the eventual developmental outcome. Children who are born with birth defects or developmental deficits can benefit greatly from growing up in a nurturing, supportive environment, and early intervention can do a great deal to help these children develop to their fullest potential.

CHECK YOUR UNDERSTANDING

1. What can a mother expect during each of the three trimesters of her pregnancy?
2. What are the risks to the baby of maternal smoking and drinking during a pregnancy?
3. What other factors can pose a risk to the developing embryo or fetus?

THE BIRTH EXPERIENCE

5.3 What happens during the process of labor and delivery?

After months of waiting, the parents-to-be are understandably excited—and perhaps a bit apprehensive—when labor finally begins. How long the process will take and the woman's

Jose Luis Pelaez Inc Blend Images/Newsroom

FIGURE 5.7

Stages of labor. As this figure shows, during the first stage of labor, the frequency and intensity of contractions increase to thin out and open the cervix. In the second stage, the infant is delivered, and in the third stage the placenta is discharged from the woman's body.

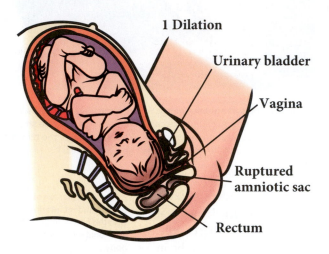

1 Dilation

Urinary bladder

Vagina

Ruptured amniotic sac

Rectum

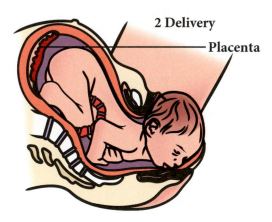

2 Delivery

Placenta

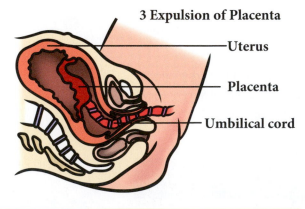

3 Expulsion of Placenta

Uterus

Placenta

Umbilical cord

Cervix The narrow, lower end of the uterus.

Early labor The first phase in the first stage of labor in which contractions are usually not painful but the cervix begins to thin out and dilate.

subjective experience of the birth can be quite variable from one woman to the next. Figure 5.7 shows what occurs at each of the three stages of labor, which are described in this next section.

LABOR AND DELIVERY

First Stage: Early and Active Labor

Earlier in the pregnancy the woman may have felt some sensations caused by tightening of the uterine muscles called *Braxton Hicks contractions,* which can begin as early as the sixth week of pregnancy but aren't noticeable until midpregnancy. They usually are infrequent, painless, and sporadic (Cunningham et al., 2014), but as the woman gets closer to her due date, the contractions begin to soften and thin out the **cervix**, the narrow lower end of the uterus. This prepares it for true labor. We will look at each of the three stages of labor in detail.

For first-time mothers, the first stage of labor usually lasts between 10 and 20 hours, although it could go on for days. So much happens during this stage that it is divided into three phases. During **early labor**, true contractions begin. At first they last about 30 to 60 seconds and come every 5 to 20 minutes. At this point, the contractions themselves are usually not very painful, and most women can safely remain at home, taking part in light activities or using the time to get some rest, if possible. The contractions begin to thin out (or *efface*) and open up (or *dilate*) the cervix. As the cervix opens, a mucus plug is discharged from the vagina.

When the cervix has dilated to 4 centimeters, the second phase called **active labor** begins, and the contractions become longer, stronger, and more frequent (Cunningham et al., 2014). The cervix continues dilating, but now at a more rapid pace. When contractions last 1 minute and are coming about every 5 minutes, the woman should get to the hospital or birthing center (ACOG, 2007). It is during this phase that women may feel they need some pain medication or will want to use the breathing and relaxation strategies they learned during childbirth classes. About half of American women use an epidural, a regional anesthesia that decreases sensation in the lower half of the body, to give some pain relief (American Pregnancy Association, 2016). On average, this second phase of labor lasts between 3 and 8 hours.

Once the cervix has dilated to 7 centimeters, the woman enters the third phase called **transition** because it marks the movement into the second stage of labor (Cunningham et al., 2014). This is the shortest, but also the most difficult, phase of labor, lasting on average between 15 minutes and 3 hours. Contractions now come in very rapid succession and last up to 90 seconds each, with little or no pause between them. For about three-quarters of women, the amniotic sac that surrounded and protected the fetus ruptures (that is, her "water breaks") near the end of this phase.

Second Stage: Pushing

When the cervix has fully dilated to 10 centimeters, the second stage of labor begins. The uterine contractions now begin to push the baby down through the birth canal. Many women feel a strong urge to push with each contraction. About 11% of vaginal deliveries in the United States involve an episiotomy, a surgical incision from the back of the vagina to the anus to allow the baby to exit the birth canal without tearing the tissue, but the medical necessity of this procedure has recently been called into question and its use has declined considerably in the last 10 years (Friedman, Ananth, Prendergast, D'Alton, & Wright, 2015; Melo, Katz, Coutinho, & Amorim, 2014). Once the baby's head emerges from the birth canal, the health care provider will clear the baby's airways and check the position of the umbilical cord. Fairly rapidly one shoulder and then the other are delivered, and the rest of the baby's body quickly follows. If everything is going normally, the baby may be placed on his mother's stomach while the umbilical cord is clamped and cut.

Third Stage: Delivering the Placenta

Now the uterus begins to contract again to expel the placenta. This generally occurs without any pain or discomfort to the mother, and this stage lasts only 5 to 10 minutes (ACOG, 2007). The contraction of the uterus helps close off the blood vessels where the placenta separated from the uterus to prevent further bleeding. If an episiotomy has been performed, the doctor will close that incision at this time.

Birthing Options

Today, there are a wide range of birthing options available. Women can choose a birth setting, the type of professional assistance they receive, and a birthing technique. Deciding which is the best depends on a woman's personal preferences and her medical condition, but she also needs to consider the benefits and possible risks of each alternative.

When a woman gives birth in a hospital, she has access to medical professionals and medical technology, including access to pain medications, but hospitals are sometimes seen as impersonal settings in which the woman gives up much control over the circumstances of the birth. There also has been concern that medical interventions are overused when births occur in a hospital setting. A birth center provides a more home-like atmosphere and gives the woman greater autonomy during her labor. Birth centers are staffed by certified nurse-midwives, rather than obstetricians (Bouchez, 2008). While a birth center will have standard medical equipment, the staff does not perform surgical procedures such as epidurals or cesarean deliveries and does not induce labor or administer drugs.

The number of U.S. women who are choosing to give birth outside of a hospital has been increasing in recent years, but still only represents about 1.5% of births (CDC, 2014b). Home births have generally been considered safe, in large part because only women with low-risk pregnancies are choosing this option. When a woman plans a home birth, it is important that the midwife who attends the birth is a certified nurse midwife who has the professional training necessary to safely oversee the delivery and who knows when it is necessary to transport the woman to a medical center. Being attended by someone who lacks such credentials could put both mother and newborn at risk (Tuteur, 2016).

In addition to physicians and midwives, **doulas** and birth coaches may support a woman during labor. Unlike a physician or midwife, a doula does not directly assist in the birth process but rather is a trained, knowledgeable companion who is present to support the woman through her pregnancy, labor, and delivery. The support a doula provides has been associated with lower rates of cesarean section and forceps deliveries, less use of epidurals and other pain medications, shorter labors, greater satisfaction with birth experiences, and fewer low birthweight babies (Green & Hottelling, 2014; Gruber, Cupito, & Dobson, 2013). One possible explanation of these benefits is that the doula's presence reduces the amount of stress hormones the woman produces during her labor. A husband, partner, relative, or close friend who has attended childbirth preparation classes with the woman can act as a birth coach.

Active labor The second phase in the first stage of labor in which contractions become longer, stronger, and more frequent and the cervix dilates to 4 centimeters.

Transition The third phase in the first stage of labor in which contractions come in rapid succession and last up to 90 seconds each, with little or no pause between them, and which ends when the cervix has dilated 10 centimeters.

Doula A trained, knowledgeable companion who supports a woman during her labor and delivery.

Birthing options. Women have some choice about where and how they give birth. The birth can take place in a hospital, in a birthing center, or at home. Some births take place in a tub of water. The birth can be assisted by a physician, midwife, or doula. What do you think are advantages or disadvantages of each of these alternatives?

A coach does specific things to help the woman relax and to make her more comfortable during her labor, and provides emotional support during the process.

One of the most dramatic recent changes in American childbirth has been the number of children born by cesarean delivery, in which the baby is delivered through an incision the doctor makes in the woman's lower abdomen. In 2014, 32.2% of all U.S. births were cesarean births (see Figure 5.8) (Hamilton, Martin, Osterman, Curtin, & Mathews, 2015). Cesarean deliveries were once the result of medical necessity, but at least part of the recent increase has been for nonmedical reasons that include maternal choice, more conservative medical

FIGURE 5.8

Rates of Cesarean births, 2013–2014. In 2014, almost one-third of U.S. infants were born by cesarean delivery, a 2% decline from the previous year. Non-Hispanic Black women, Asian or Pacific Islanders, and Hispanic women have the highest rates of cesarean deliveries.

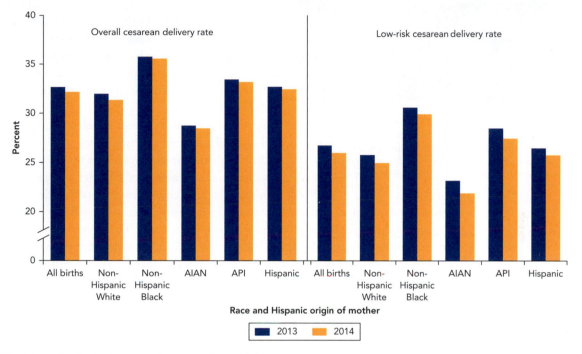

NOTE: API = Asian or Pacific Islander; AIAN = American Indian or Alaska Native.

SOURCE: Hamilton, Martin, Osterman, & Curtin (2015).

practice guidelines that call for surgical intervention sooner, and physicians' fear of litigation. In an evaluation of the benefits and risks of elective cesareans compared to a planned vaginal delivery, a panel of experts convened by the National Institutes of Health concluded that when a woman chooses to have a caesarean birth, her wishes should be honored if there are no medical contraindications and the known risks and benefits have been discussed with her (Viswanathan et al., 2006).

In non-Western cultures, the birth process may be quite different from what we have described. For example, an Ifaluk woman, who lives in Micronesia on one of two tiny islands in the Pacific Ocean, gives birth in a birth house, accompanied by a midwife and her female relatives (Le, 2000). When the baby is ready to be born, the woman kneels on a mat and helps the baby out by herself. She must try not to show distress or pain, in accord with the Ifaluk value of remaining calm at all times. If there are complications, the other women will help. After the baby is born, the woman's mother helps by holding the baby and then bathes the baby in the ocean. This is a sharp contrast to the Western, hospital-based approach to childbirth.

THE NEWBORN

You probably have heard stories about labor and delivery from the perspective of the mother, but have you ever wondered how this is experienced by the baby? It can seem pretty traumatic. The newborn rapidly goes from a warm, quiet, and dark prenatal environment into a bright, noisy, and cold postnatal environment. In this section, we look at how newborns are routinely handled following their birth and at some of the capabilities they bring with them that get them off to a good start.

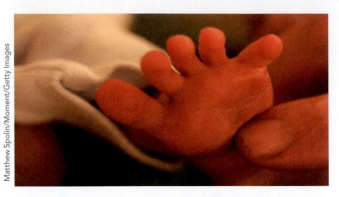

The Babinski reflex. The condition of a newborn is assessed by the Apgar Scale to determine whether any intervention is needed. Part of that assessment includes a test of the newborn's reflexes. For instance, when the sole of the newborn's foot is stroked from the top to the heel, the baby's toes fan out. In an adult, the toes curl inward.

Apgar Scale An assessment of a newborn's overall condition at 1 minute and 5 minutes after birth that is based on the newborn's activity level, pulse, grimace, appearance, and respiration.

The Baby's Birth Experience

Fortunately, babies are physiologically well prepared to handle the stress of being born. For one thing, the skull of a baby is composed of separate plates that overlap and compress during the birth process, allowing the head to elongate so it can fit through the birth canal. The mother's production of stress hormones during labor triggers the production of stress hormones in the baby which prepare the lungs to begin breathing, send additional blood to the baby's brain and vital organs, and make the baby alert right after the birth (Weiss, 2014).

As soon as the baby's head is delivered, the doctor or midwife will use a rubber syringe to clear away any material in the mouth and air passages. After the baby emerges, the umbilical cord is clamped and cut after it stops pulsing. The baby's weight, head circumference, and length are measured and a few drops of an antibiotic are placed in the baby's eyes to prevent infection from any organisms that were in the birth canal (Ben-Joseph, 2014). The baby's overall condition is assessed using the **Apgar Scale** at 1 minute and again at 5 minutes after birth. The newborn receives 0, 1, or 2 points for its *A*ctivity level, *P*ulse, *G*rimace (reflexive responses to a stimulus such as a mild pinch), *A*ppearance, and *R*espiration. A total score of 7 to 10 points is the normal range, and these newborns receive routine care, with their status reassessed at 5 minutes. A score in the range of 4 to 6 indicates that some intervention is needed. This might involve additional suction to help the baby breathe, massage, or administration of oxygen. A score of 3 or less means that immediate lifesaving intervention is needed (Bregman, 2005).

A more extensive tool sometimes used to assess infants from birth through the age of 3 months who are at developmental risk is the Neonatal Behavioral Assessment Scale. The scale consists of 18 observations that describe the newborn's capacities and adaptation to the environment. These include the newborn's ability to adapt to levels of light and sound in the environment, the quality of the newborn's muscle tone, activity level, alertness and responsiveness, and ability to be consoled when distressed. This information can help new parents to understand the unique characteristics of their infant so they can better meet the infant's needs (The Brazelton Institute, n.d.; Nugent, 2013).

Shortly after birth, the baby will be given a bath. Because newborns can easily become cold, they are wrapped in a blanket and a cap is placed on their heads. They are also given a vitamin K shot to help their blood clot properly and sometime before they leave the hospital, a few drops of blood will be drawn to test for PKU and other genetic and biochemical disorders (March of Dimes, 2008b).

Infant States

Infant states Different levels of consciousness used to regulate the amount of stimulation an infant receives; states range from crying to deep sleep.

As you learned earlier in this chapter, all of the newborn's senses begin developing during the prenatal period and become functional before birth. Although newborns can hear, see, taste, smell, and respond to touch, they have a limited capacity to process information from the environment so they have a set of **infant states** to help them regulate the level of stimulation they receive. Moving through these states keeps the sensory input at a level the newborn can process. Infant states have been organized into two sleep states (quiet sleep and active sleep) and four awake states (drowsy, quiet alert, active alert, and crying) that reflect different levels of activity and alertness (March of Dimes, 2003).

Most newborns experience a period of *quiet alertness* shortly after they are born. Their eyes are open and they are attentive to what is going on around them, but their bodies are very still and their breathing is regular. This is a wonderful opportunity for parents to begin the process of bonding with their infant. For the newborn, this initial period of quiet alertness is usually followed by a state of quiet sleep.

Infant states. Infants continually move through a series of states that allow them to regulate the amount of stimulation that they receive. Can you see how this is an adaptive way for an infant to meet his or her needs for rest, stimulation, and physical care?

Newborns typically sleep 16 to 18 hours a day (Hanrahan, 2006). About half this time is spent in REM (rapid eye movement) sleep, which is the light sleep in which dreams occur, and half is spent in regular sleep, which ranges from drowsiness in which the eyes open and close to a quiet sleep in which the infant is quiet and doesn't move. Because infant stomachs are so small, babies wake up to eat about every 3 or 4 hours throughout the day and the night (Hanrahan, 2006).

A topic related to infant sleeping that has been controversial is cosleeping (Sobralske & Gruber, 2009). Although sharing a family bed is a common practice in many cultures around the world, the American Academy of Pediatrics (AAP) has been critical of this practice because of its relationship with sudden infant death syndrome (SIDS) and other sleep-related causes of infant death (AAP, 2011c). While bed sharing facilitates breastfeeding and enhances the development of attachment to the mother, the AAP recommends that infants sleep close to their parents (perhaps in a crib in the parents' room), but not in the same bed.

The last state on the continuum is *crying*, which is the way that infants signal that they need something. The amount of time that infants cry increases to an average of 2.6 hours a day at 6 weeks of age, but decreases after that time (Hiscock, 2006). Sensitively responding to infants' needs can help this state pass.

Some infants smoothly transition from one state to another, but others move rapidly or unexpectedly from one state to another. Some signal what they need in a way that is clear and easy for parents to interpret so they can promptly respond, and others are much more difficult for new parents to "read." How much time is spent in each state changes as the infant grows, with more time in the quiet alert and active alert states and less in sleep, but the goal remains the same: to allow the infant to control the amount of sensory input from the environment while providing opportunities for rest, learning, and interaction with the infant's caregivers. Over those early weeks, most parents and infants are able to get in sync with each other so things go relatively smoothly. That doesn't mean, however, that there won't be plenty of nights with too little sleep for the new parents and times when they worry about how well they and their infant are doing.

Mirror neurons. Mirror neurons may give infants the ability to imitate simple actions that they see others do. This baby is responding to her mother opening her mouth. Try this for yourself with a young infant. How do you think you would feel when an infant responds to you by doing what you just did?

Mirror Neurons

You might be surprised if you stuck out your tongue at a newborn to see that he may stick his tongue out at you. Newborns are capable of imitating simple facial expressions (Nagy, Pilling, Orvos, & Molnar, 2013) but until recently, scientists had little idea how infants could do this. In the 1990s, a team of Italian researchers studying the brains of macaque monkeys discovered what are now called *mirror neurons* (Ferrari & Rizzolatti, 2013). The same neurons fired if the monkey put something in its own mouth, or if the monkey saw the researcher put something in the researcher's mouth. Brain imaging studies with humans found that the same regions of the brain are activated for both experienced and observed motor movement and emotional expression. Just as we automatically open our mouths as we feed babies or laugh when we hear others laugh (which is why laugh tracks are added to television shows), newborns also imitate some of our actions automatically. This is a powerful way in which they are brought into the social world. They learn from us, and we enjoy seeing ourselves reflected in our infants.

CHECK YOUR UNDERSTANDING

1. What happens during each of the three stages of labor?
2. How do the roles of a midwife and a doula differ?
3. What are typical experiences of a newborn in the delivery room?
4. Why do infants have different states they go through?

RISKS TO THE NEWBORN'S HEALTH AND WELL-BEING

5.4 What are some of the risks to the newborn's well-being?

Babies enter the world equipped in many ways to begin their journey of development and to interact with the people who will love and care for them along the way, but the journey is easier for some newborns than others. In this section we examine some of the challenges that newborns can face in those early months of life.

PREMATURITY AND LOW BIRTH WEIGHT

Premature (or preterm) A birth that occurs before a gestational age of 37 weeks.

Low birth weight A full-term infant who weighs less than 5 pounds, 8 ounces.

A number of factors can place a newborn at risk, but being born prematurely or being born at a low birth weight are significant risk factors. These conditions typically co-occur. That is, infants who are born early weigh less than those who are born full term. Saying that an infant is **premature** or **preterm** are alternative ways of saying that the infant was born before a gestational age of 37 weeks (U.S. National Library of Medicine, 2016c). Determining that a baby has a **low birth weight** is a function of the gestational age of the infant. For babies

Jennie Woodcock/Reflections/Corbis/Getty

TABLE 5.1

Prematurity and low birth weight. This table shows the criteria that are used to determine levels of prematurity and low birth weight. Although at times it is important to know how early an infant arrived and at other times it is important to know the infant's birth weight, these two conditions usually co-occur. When an infant is born early (or preterm), it is almost always the case the infant also will have a less than normal birth weight.

Degree of prematurity	Gestational age	Birth weight
Full-term	Over 37 weeks	
Preterm	Less than 37 weeks	
Very preterm	Less than 32 weeks	
Extremely preterm	Less than 28 weeks	
Normal birth weight (NBW)		Greater than 2,500 g (5.5 lbs)
Low birth weight (LBW)		Less than 2,500 g (5.5 lbs)
Very low birth weight (VLBW)		Less than 1,500 g (3.25 lbs)
Extremely low birth weight (ELBW)		Less than 1,000 g (2 lbs 3 oz)

SOURCE: Specialist Schools and Academies Trust (2011).

born at full term (37-42 weeks of gestation), a weight of less than 5 pounds, 8 ounces is considered low birth weight. Babies who are born smaller in size than would be normal for their gestational age are described as *small for gestational age* and are particularly at risk. Being small for gestational age is an indication that some circumstance in the prenatal environment restricted the infant's physical development. Table 5.1 shows the criteria for identifying different levels of prematurity and low birth weight.

The underlying causes of premature births are complex and not always well understood (USDHHS, 2015d), but we have identified several factors that increase the risk. Giving birth to twins, triplets, or more babies at one time is one factor because multiples are more likely to be born prematurely. We have already discussed unhealthy maternal behaviors such as smoking, drinking, or using drugs while pregnant. Being obese or underweight, or having untreated medical conditions such as high blood pressure or diabetes also are responsible for some premature and low-birth-weight births (Browne, 2005; Denney, Culhane, & Goldenberg, 2008). In other cases, there is an abnormality in the woman's reproductive system, such as a placenta that prematurely separates from the uterus or a cervix that opens too soon.

After increasing from the 1980s through 2006, the number of preterm births in the United States declined between 2007 and 2014 (Hamilton, Martin, Osterman, & Curtin, 2015; Martin, Osterman, & Sutton, 2010). Preliminary estimates for 2014 place the rate at 9.6%. Any decrease is significant because premature infants are at risk of suffering from a number of neurological and developmental problems. Beyond the human cost, prematurity also carries a large financial cost. According to the March of Dimes (2014), in 2013 the average medical cost for the first year of life of a healthy, full-term baby was $5,085, compared to a cost of $55,393 for a baby born before 37-week gestation or one weighing less than 2,500 grams, or 5.5 pounds, at birth.

We have made great strides in recent years in our ability to care for premature newborns. Medical technology today increases their chances of both survival and healthy development. The modern neonatal intensive care unit (NICU) has roots that reach back over 100 years. Read **Journey of Research: From Child Hatchery to Modern NICU** to understand the progress that has been made.

JOURNEY OF *Research*

From Child Hatchery to Modern NICU

One of the first attempts to improve the survival rates of premature infants was an incubator developed by obstetrician Étienne Stéphane Tarnier in the 1880s (Sammons & Lewis, 1985). It consisted of a wooden box with sawdust-filled walls. The box was divided into two compartments. Half of the bottom compartment was left open to allow for circulation of air, and the other half held stone bottles filled with hot water to control the temperature. As the air circulated into the upper compartment, which contained the infant, it passed over a wet sponge to pick up moisture. A chimney in the top compartment allowed the air to pass over the infant and exit into the room (Neonatology on the Web, 2007). In addition to controlling heat and humidity and isolating sick infants from healthy ones (Sammons & Lewis, 1985), the incubator was "so simple that any village carpenter can make it, and cheap enough to be within the means of all but the most destitute" (Neonatology on the Web, 2007, para. 3).

In 1896, Martin A. Couney supervised a display of incubators with six premature infants in them at the Berlin World's Fair in an exhibit named "Kinderbrutanstalt" or "child hatchery." This exhibit was such a commercial success (yes, people were willing to pay admission to see these wonders) that Couney repeated it at other expositions around the world until the 1940s (Snow, 1981). The doctor himself did not profit from these admission charges. Instead, the money was used to cover the cost of the intensive nursing care he provided for the infants. He did provide excellent care to these infants and even claimed to have saved an infant as small as 1.5 pounds (Snow, 1981).

In the 1940s, the care of premature infants increasingly moved into the hands of medical specialists, and neonatology, the medical specialty that deals with newborn infants, emerged as a recognized medical specialty. Because physicians at that time believed that parents were the primary source of dangerous infections and that premature infants could easily be overstimulated, parents were routinely excluded from the nursery. This practice continued until the early 1970s (Davis, Mohay, & Edwards, 2003), but today parents are an important part of the team that cares for a premature infant. They are encouraged to participate in the care and feeding of their infant, to ask questions so they understand the complicated medical interventions that may be sustaining their infant, and to get close to their infant to begin building a bond.

Today, we know that touch and stimulation at a level that is appropriate for the capacity of the premature infant is beneficial, not harmful. Parents might even be encouraged to provide **kangaroo care**, a practice where the baby is placed in skin-to-skin contact with the parent's bare chest or breasts and draped with a blanket. Kangaroo care is associated with improved temperature regulation (Park et al., 2014), greater weight gain (Bera et al., 2014; Samra, El Taweel, & Cadwell, 2013), and stronger attachment between mother and infant (Gathwala, Singh, & Balhara, 2008). Studies on the effect of systematic massage on premature infants have shown that three 15-minute sessions provided for a period of 10 days can result in a 47% greater weight gain compared to infants who don't receive massage (Field, Diego, & Hernandez-Reif, 2007). Take a look at the photos on the next page to see how far we have come from that first sawdust-filled box.

Kangaroo care A practice where the baby is placed in skin-to-skin contact with the parent's bare chest or breasts and draped with a blanket.

Premature infants are not yet able to regulate their bodily functions in the same way that a full-term infant can, so the NICU monitors the functioning of the infant and compensates for things that the infants cannot yet do for themselves. For instance, premature infants do not have a layer of body fat that helps them regulate body temperature and fluid loss, so incubators provide constant levels of heat and moisture. They may not yet have a sucking reflex or

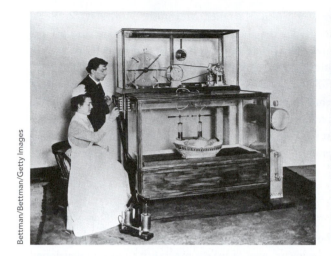
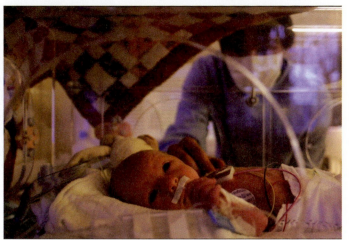

Neonatal intensive care—then and now. We have come a long way from the original sawdust-filled box that served as an early incubator. Modern care for premature infants carefully controls their environment and continually monitors their bodily functions, but even in this intensive medical environment, human touch is an important part of the care.

gag reflex, so they need special feeding procedures. Their immature central nervous system can easily be overwhelmed by stimuli, so the light level is kept low, noise is minimized, and the infants are handled slowly and gently (VanderBerg, 2007). Overall the staff in the NICU need to be particularly sensitive toward infants who cannot signal what they need (Bowden, Greenberg, & Donaldson, 2000; VanderBerg, 2007).

Modern NICUs are very successful at saving even very small, fragile babies. The survival rate for premature babies born at very low birth weight of less than 1500 grams, or about 3.3 pounds, is approximately 90%, and for infants born at extremely low birth weight of less than 1000 grams, or about 2.2 pounds, the rate is still between 50% and 70% (Volpe, 2009). The question that remains is whether there is a point at which a premature infant is so small and the chance of survival is so low that the humane thing to do is to provide comfort care rather than trying to save the life of the infant. Comfort care provides for the basic needs of the infant but stops short of using heroic measures that might cause additional pain and suffering without being likely to prolong the life of the infant.

Despite our best efforts, prematurity accounts for more than 70% of neonatal deaths (Williamson et al., 2008), but most premature infants do survive and for them there is a wide range of developmental outcomes. A consistent finding from numerous studies is that low-birth-weight and premature infants are at an increased risk of cognitive impairment and academic failure as they grow up (Hill, Brooks-Gunn, & Waldfogel, 2003; Jepsen & Martin, 2006). They also can have sensory or motor impairments or be medically fragile. Those who are born the earliest are the ones who are at greatest risk (Cunningham et al., 2014; Dombrowski, Noonan, & Martin, 2007; Tyson et al., 2008), but even among very premature infants born at 25 weeks, 20% survive with no significant health problems (Cunningham et al., 2014).

To have good developmental outcomes, however, premature infants and their parents need access to comprehensive services that start early in development and are delivered consistently over time (Hill et al., 2003). Even under the best of circumstances, caring for a premature infant places extraordinary demands on a parent, so parents need to stay motivated to use the services and to follow through on the recommendations made by professionals who work with their child. For this reason, how the parents view their infants and the expectations they have for them are crucial.

If parents see their premature infant in a negative way and have low expectations for their child, they may unconsciously treat the infant in ways that actually hinder the child's development. This way of perceiving a premature infant is called a *prematurity stereotype,* and both mothers of premature infants and mothers of full-term infants may see premature

T ☐ F ☐ An infant who is born prematurely will have developmental problems and lag behind other children of the same age. **False**

infants in a stereotypically negative way (Stern, Karraker, McIntosh, Moritzen, & Olexa, 2006). When mothers watched videotapes they had been told showed premature infants and full-term infants, the premature infants were rated as being less physically mature in appearance, less sociable, less cognitively competent, and less behaviorally mature. However, all the videotapes actually showed full-term infants. When the researchers labeled the infant in the video as "premature," the behavior of a full-term infant was seen in a less favorable way simply because of the label and the preconceptions that came with it (Stern et al., 2006). For this reason, it is important that we help parents of premature infants understand that their infants can have good developmental outcomes so that they can see and appreciate the progress that their children make.

INFANT MORTALITY

Infant mortality The rate of infant death within the first year of life.

Infant mortality is a measure of the number of infants who die in the first year of life. In general, developed countries have far lower rates of infant mortality than less developed countries, but even within the more developed world, there are differences in how effective each country is at preventing infant death. Figure 5.9 shows the infant mortality rates for a number of developed countries. Note where the United States ranks in this figure: The United States has the highest rate of infant mortality among countries with a similar level of economic well-being (Peterson-Kaiser Health System Tracker, 2015).

In the United States, an average of 6.1 babies out of 1,000 live births die within the first year and these rates vary significantly by race. In 2009, the infant mortality rate for non-Hispanic Black women was 12.4 deaths per 1,000 live births compared to 5.3 deaths for non-Hispanic White women (MacDorman, 2013). The difference was largely attributable to the large number of premature births to non-Hispanic Black women. A bit of good news is the fact that

T ☐ F ☐ The United States has the highest rate of infant mortality among nations with a similar level of economic well-being. **True**

FIGURE 5.9

Infant mortality rates around the world: 2013. This figure shows international infant mortality rates per 1,000 live births in 2013. The United States has the highest rate among countries with a similar gross domestic product, a measure of a country's economic well-being.

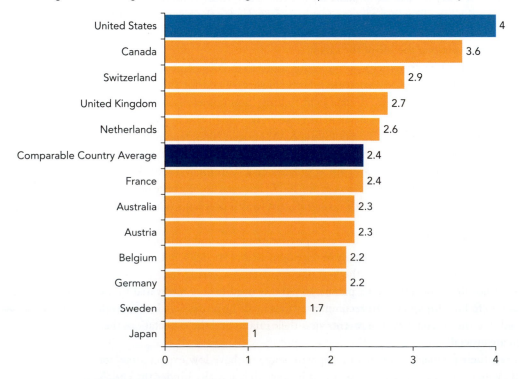

SOURCE: Peterson-Kaiser Health System Tracker (2015).

between 2005 and 2011, the U.S. infant mortality rate decreased by 12%, with the biggest decrease among the highest-risk group, non-Hispanic Black infants (MacDorman, Hoyert, & Mathews, 2013).

SUDDEN INFANT DEATH SYNDROME (SIDS)

Having an infant die unexpectedly is a parent's worst nightmare. **Sudden infant death syndrome (SIDS)**, or the unexpected death of an apparently healthy infant, is the leading cause of death for children between the ages of 1 month and 1 year, with deaths peaking between the ages of 1 month and 4 months (Task Force on Sudden Infant Death Syndrome, 2011).

Of course, we want to understand the cause of SIDS, but there probably never will be a simple explanation because it is likely that some combination of factors is responsible. These factors include a physical vulnerability in the infant (for example, some abnormality in the part of the brain that controls breathing, a brain chemical imbalance, or a bacterial infection), some stressor in the environment (for example, secondhand smoke, overheating the infant with too much clothing, or an overheated room), and a critical time in early development when the centers of the infant's brain that normally control breathing are still immature and may not trigger reflexive breathing when needed (Mayo Clinic, 2009).

Because the list of risk factors that have been identified for SIDS is quite long and because some of them are not under the control of the parent, it may seem that there is little that a concerned parent can do, but that conclusion would be wrong. There are several strategies that are both simple and effective. Putting an infant down to sleep on his or her back has done a great deal to reduce the incidence of SIDS (National Institutes of Health, 2015). Babies can still have "tummy time" when they are awake and someone is watching them, but this is not how they should be put to sleep. Other simple but effective precautions are to use a firm mattress for the infant, keep blankets and pillows out of the infant's sleep area, and do not allow smoking in the home. While doing these things does not guarantee that an infant will be safe, they are smart and easy things to do to lower an infant's risk.

When parents lose an infant to SIDS, they feel overwhelming grief and possibly a great deal of guilt. The fact that there is so much that we don't understand about SIDS makes the loss particularly difficult. First Candle (2015), a national nonprofit organization that supports infant health and survival, provides resources for parents who have lost a baby to SIDS, as well as for siblings and others who are affected by this sudden loss.

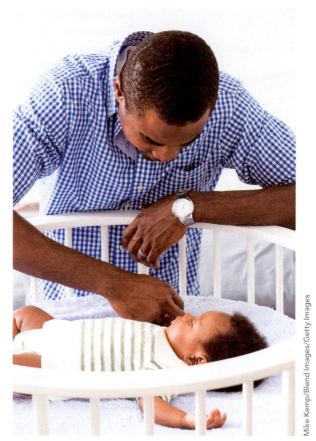

Mike Kemp/Blend Images/Getty Images

Back to sleep. The "back to sleep" program (the recommendation that parents place an infant on his or her back to sleep on a firm surface) has greatly reduced the incidence of sudden infant death syndrome in the United States.

Sudden infant death syndrome (SIDS) The death of an apparently healthy infant; the rate of SIDS peaks between the ages of 1 month and 4 months.

ABUSIVE HEAD TRAUMA AND SHAKEN BABY SYNDROME

Sometimes an adult who is frustrated with a baby may shake the baby hard, causing the baby's brain to bounce against the inside of the skull. This causes bruising, bleeding, or swelling in the brain that can result in permanent brain damage or even death. Also, because babies' heads are large in proportion to their bodies and their neck muscles are weak, they can suffer whiplash, much like what you might experience in a car accident. Among the symptoms of shaken baby syndrome are decreased alertness, extreme irritability or other changes in behavior, lethargy or sleepiness, poor feeding or lack of appetite, and vomiting. In more severe cases, an infant might even lose consciousness, suffer seizures, or stop breathing (Kaneshiro & Zieve, 2011).

Prolonged episodes of crying for no apparent reason are not uncommon among young infants, but these times can be very stressful for a new parent. The incidence of shaken baby syndrome is highest between 2 and 3 months of age, when this crying is at its peak (Parks, Annest, Hill, & Karch, 2012). It is important for all caregivers to know that although they may feel anger at a baby, they should never act on that anger. Learning techniques for self-control can prevent potentially abusive behavior. These may include simply putting the baby down, getting some help with child care, and verbally expressing frustration or anger to a supportive person. If these negative feelings occur frequently, counseling or parenting classes can be helpful. The risk for infants being abused at the hands of their caregivers is discussed in more detail in Chapter 15.

CHECK YOUR UNDERSTANDING

1. What are some risks to the newborn's health and well-being?
2. How are premature infants cared for?
3. How can the risk of sudden infant death syndrome be reduced?
4. What effects does shaking a baby have?

THE TRANSITION TO PARENTHOOD

5.5 How do new parents cope with the transition to parenthood?

Becoming a parent is one of life's most important transitions. At the moment a baby is born, so is a new parent. Think about some of the major transitions you've had in your life. Whether it is moving from elementary school to middle school, getting your first paying job, moving out of your parents' home to live on your own, or coming to college, any major transition brings with it some amount of stress and requires coping and adjustment for you to handle it successfully. Becoming a parent affects all aspects of your life including your sense of identity, your relationships with your partner and others, and your career, so it is not surprising that becoming a parent involves a good deal of stress.

A number of years ago, a sociologist named Jessie Bernard (1972) suggested that how men and women experience their marriage is so different that rather than "their marriage," we could talk about "his marriage" and "her marriage." Perhaps the same can be said of the couple's experience with the birth of their child. For this reason, we look at the experience of new mothers and then of new fathers before we look at how the birth of a child affects a couple.

BECOMING A MOTHER

It is a common misunderstanding to think that after a baby is born, a new mother automatically follows her instincts and knows just what to do. In fact, many first-time mothers are not necessarily comfortable with breastfeeding, changing diapers, or soothing a crying baby. Women around the world must learn how to be mothers, and there is a myriad of ways in which this happens. For most women, the way they themselves were mothered as a child often provides a model of what a mother should be like. New mothers also frequently turn to their own mothers, other new mothers, relatives, child care professionals, and books or websites on child care for support and advice (Walker, 2005). However, when a woman receives conflicting advice from different sources, it adds to her stress rather than relieving it.

Mothers report that when this happens, they fall back on their own instincts or experiences, or they use the baby's cues to guide their decisions (Walker, 2005).

Women are happiest about the transition to becoming a mother when they have had a choice about whether to have a child; have support from a partner, family, and others; and have adequate resources to support the child (Lips, 2006). However, pregnancy, childbirth, and child rearing are experiences that will touch on the full range of human emotion. In a society that idealizes mothers as being totally self-sacrificing, all-giving nurturers, women who struggle with the normal array of mixed feelings may have an added burden of feeling guilty that they are not living up to this ideal if they are sad or anxious following the birth of their baby. Fortunately, new mothers get some help during this transition from their biology. Nurturing behavior gets a boost from hormones such as oxytocin and prolactin, which are at elevated levels in expectant and new mothers (Bower, 2005; Brunton & Russell, 2008; Lim & Young, 2006). Oxytocin promotes the formation of a bond between mother and infant and a desire to be physically close, while prolactin promotes caregiving behaviors.

The rapid hormonal changes that occur following a birth, along with the other stresses that new mothers experience, frequently result in the "baby blues." The symptoms of the baby blues include mood swings, sadness, loss of appetite, trouble sleeping, and irritability. Often a little time, together with some rest and help with caring for the newborn, is enough to alleviate the symptoms. A more severe form of the baby blues is **depression with peripartum onset,** which has replaced the term *postpartum depression* in the most recent update of the *Diagnostic and Statistical Manual of Mental Disorders* (DSM-5) of the American Psychiatric Association (2013). Depression with peripartum onset is a more accurate term because the peripartum period includes the last month of pregnancy and the first couple of months after birth. Half of women who experience depression at this time begin to experience symptoms before the baby is born. Symptoms can include depression, loss of interest in things that had been pleasurable, lack of energy, trouble concentrating, feelings of guilt or worthlessness, and also severe anxiety or even panic attacks. When these symptoms are severe enough that they interfere with the woman's ability to function, she should consult with her doctor because there are effective treatments available. The most common approaches to treating depression following the birth of a child include antidepressant medications and counseling or psychotherapy (Logsdon, Wisner, & Shanahan, 2007).

Depression with peripartum onset A major depression that occurs in the last month of pregnancy or the first couple of months after birth.

Just as there are cultural differences in the birth process, there are some differences in what happens after birth. To continue our cross-cultural comparison with the Ifaluk mother's experience, the new Ifaluk mother will never be left alone in the first 10 days following the birth of her baby and she is not expected to do any work for the first 3 months of the baby's life. Other women, usually relatives, cook and take care of household tasks while the mother rests (Le, 2000). By contrast, women in Western society may have only limited social support. After they return from the hospital, their partners often return to work, leaving the new mother alone with her newborn for most of the day. Visitors are more interested in the newborn than the new mother, and women with young infants often feel uncomfortable or unwelcome in social settings such as restaurants or coffee shops. Even if there are community resources available, a new mother may not know what they are or where to find them. Consequently, new mothers can feel a profound sense of isolation (Kendall-Tackett, 2014). The other common experience for women today is to feel pressure to quickly return to work. Later in this chapter, we discuss paid parental leave for both mothers and fathers. Without an adequate amount of paid leave, many mothers feel torn between their desire to devote themselves completely to the care of their infant and the need to return quickly to work.

Philip Game/Alamy

Childbirth experiences in Micronesia. When an Ifaluk mother has a child, she receives support from others in her community who help care for her and her child as she recovers from childbirth.

BECOMING A FATHER

Changes begin to occur for a man from the time when he learns that he is about to become a father. Most of these changes are psychological and emotional, but some men experience physiological symptoms described as a *sympathetic pregnancy*. Anthropologists have observed a phenomenon called **couvade** (from the French word *couver*, meaning "to hatch") in men from different cultures around the world (Brennan, Marshall-Lucette, Ayers, & Ahmed, 2007). In *ritualistic couvade,* the man might feign contractions and labor pains at the same time that the mother is in labor. In the developed world, a fairly common type of *psychosomatic couvade* occurs in which men experience a variety of physical symptoms associated with pregnancy, including weight gain, nausea, indigestion, backaches, mood swings, and food cravings. In international studies, the estimate of incidence varies greatly, from 11% to 97%, but it is clear that this is a phenomenon that occurs in a significant number of men (Brennan et al., 2007).

An expectant father expresses his emotional investment in the pregnancy by nurturing and caring for his partner. He can help her choose a healthy diet, encourage her to get enough rest and an appropriate amount of exercise, and support her as she deals with the emotional and physical changes of pregnancy. Having good information about what is happening to his partner and learning how to provide tangible assistance can help an expectant father prepare for his transition into fatherhood (Boyce, Condon, Barton, & Corkindale, 2007). Many men accompany their partners to childbirth classes and prepare for the birth process, but many also report that they feel marginalized and even unnecessary in these classes, which focus largely on the woman and her experience (Kowlessar, Fox, & Wittkowski, 2015).

Choosing to actively participate in the birth of their baby by being present during labor and in the delivery room is another way men express their empathy for their partner. However, the actual experience may fall short of their expectations (Bartlett, 2004; Poh, Koh, & He, 2014; Reed, 2005). In a review of the literature, Bartlett (2004) concluded that many men feel coerced to participate in the process and that their most outstanding memory of the birth is the pain that their partner was experiencing. They also report feeling unprepared for their role as labor coach (especially younger men and first-time fathers) and feeling that they were not needed or even were in the way during the delivery. Despite these feelings, many men are overcome with a powerful and perhaps unexpected rush of emotions following the birth of their baby (Poh et al., 2014; Reed, 2005). Those early moments and the opportunity to see and hold their newborn become rich rewards for the new father.

It is still true in some cultures that fathers and other men are strictly prohibited from taking part in the birth experience and early care of the baby. Ifaluk men are only allowed to see their newborn from a distance while the mother and baby stay in the birth house for the first 10 days. During this time, the father has two responsibilities: to provide the mother with fish to eat and to make a cradle for the baby. On the other hand, the Ifaluk mother hands over the responsibility of caring for the child to the father when the child is 2 years old, and he becomes the major caretaker for the next 2 to 3 years (Le, 2000). Clearly, the expectations for a new father can differ enormously from one culture to another.

We mentioned earlier that mothers get help with their transition to parenthood through some hormonal changes. Interestingly, there also is evidence that hormonal changes in men may be linked with fathering behavior (Gettler, McDade, & Kuzawa, 2011). Storey, Walsh, Quinton, and Wynne-Edwards (2000) studied expectant couples who were living together and found that immediately before their baby's birth both men and women had higher than

Couvade A sympathetic pregnancy in which a man experiences a variety of symptoms associated with pregnancy or childbirth while his partner is pregnant.

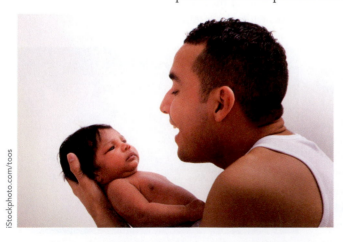

iStockphoto.com/toos

A new father is born. The transition to becoming a new father can be a powerful experience for men. A father's role today involves much more than being the breadwinner for the family. Fathers can be sensitive and nurturant caregivers for their newborn infants.

normal levels of prolactin and cortisol, and following the birth both also showed lowered levels of testosterone, the hormone that is often linked with aggressive behavior. The pattern of increasing and decreasing hormones of the father was similar to that of his partner in each couple. For men, this pattern of hormone change was strongest in those who experienced the pregnancy-like symptoms of couvade described earlier.

BECOMING A FAMILY

In their classic book *The Transition to Parenthood* (1994), Jay Belsky and John Kelly say that while men and women become parents at the *same time*, they don't become parents in the *same way*. They identified a number of issues that surface for new parents (Belsky & Kelly, 1994) and more recent research has identified a similar set of concerns. These issues include fatigue and exhaustion (especially in the early weeks after the birth and especially for the mother), as well as feelings of anxiety, depression, and self-doubt about parental competence. Women worry about changes in their physical appearance, and men worry about providing for their family financially (Halle et al., 2008). Both worry about the increase in household responsibilities and changed relationships with in-laws and both find sources of gratification, including the fact that they find the new baby to be irresistible. If you have spent time with new parents, you have probably noticed that it is difficult to get them to talk about anything else.

TRUE/FALSE VIDEO ▲

How to divide the additional work that comes from having a baby in the household often becomes a sore point for the couple. One reason is that men and women may use a different yardstick to measure their contribution to this workload. If men compare what they do around the house and time spent caring for the newborn (that is, changing diapers, feeding the infant, getting up during the night) against what their fathers did, their contribution is significant in comparison. Between 1965 and 2011, the amount of time that men spent in child care tripled (Parker & Wang, 2013). However, in most cases, men's contribution still is only about half what their partners are doing (see Figure 5.10). During this same period of

T ☐ F ☐ Following the birth of a baby, couples today pretty much share household and child care responsibilities equally. **False**

FIGURE 5.10

Division of labor between U.S. mothers and fathers, 1965 and 2011. Although fathers have increased their involvement with their children significantly since 1965, they still spend much less time with them than mothers do.

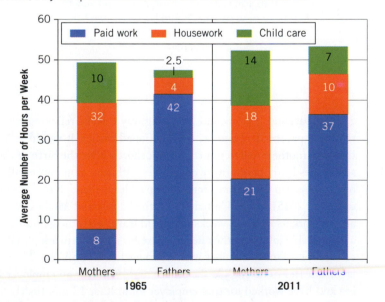

SOURCES: Bianchi, Robinson, & Milkie (2006); Parker & Wang (2013).

NOTE: Based on adults ages 18 to 64 with their own child(ren) under age 18 living in the household.

time, the amount of time women spent in child care increased almost 50% (Parker & Wang, 2013). Using this yardstick to measure the parents' relative contribution to child care, new mothers can end up feeling unhappy and disgruntled. Despite the idealized notion that new parents will equally share the responsibility of parenting, a traditional gender division of labor following the birth of a baby often continues to exist. Fathers assume the role of helper, while mothers assume the role of primary caregiver (Fox, 2001; Gjerdingen & Center, 2005; Kotila, Schoppe-Sullivan, & Kamp Dush, 2013).

Active Learning: Easing the Transition to Parenthood can help you better understand the types of support that can help parents transition into their new roles by exploring the range of services that are available to parents in different circumstances.

Active LEARNING

Easing the Transition to Parenthood

Use the Internet to research the services or types of supports that would be available to new parents living in your community in each of the following circumstances. For each service or support, note whether or not parents need to pay for the services and whether the provider of the service or support is a professional (for example, a nurse or a parent educator) or a nonprofessional (for example, an experienced parent).

- An older married couple with a premature infant
- A single mother with a healthy, full-term infant
- An unmarried couple with a low-birth-weight infant

Searching online for early intervention programs and the name of your state or community should lead you to some useful information. Can you think of any way that the delivery of services for these new parents could be improved?

Paid parental leave would go a long way toward relieving some of the financial stress that new parents feel and, as we mentioned earlier, it would relieve some of the pressure that new mothers feel to return to work shortly after the birth of their infants. Although we sometimes hear about private companies with very generous family leave policies, only 12% of employees in the private sector have paid leave through their employers (U.S. Department of Labor, 2015). In the United States, the Family and Medical Leave Act (FMLA) of 1993 allows workers up to 12 weeks of unpaid leave, with the guarantee of return to the same or a comparable job when they need to care for a newborn, adopt, take a child into foster care, or care for a family member with a serious health problem. Note, however, that this leave is *unpaid* and to be eligible the parent must work for an employer with at least 50 employees and have worked for that employer for at least 12 months (U.S. Department of Labor, 2015). That means that only 40% of the U.S. workforce is covered by this federal legislation (Lewis, Stumbitz, Miles, & Rouse, 2014). There are only three states—California, Rhode Island, and New Jersey—that currently mandate some paid leave for their citizens (National Partnership for Women and Families, 2016).

FIGURE 5.11

Cross-country comparison of paid parental leave. Compared to other industrialized countries, the United States lags far behind in the amount of paid maternal and paternal leave that is available to new parents. In addition, only 40% of the American workforce is covered by federal legislation that provides unpaid leave to them.

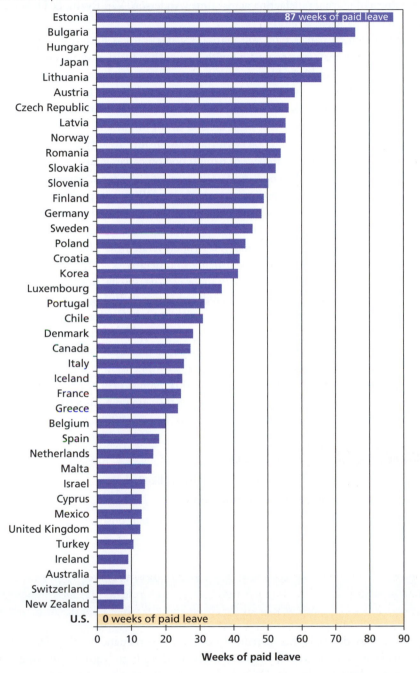

NOTE: Includes maternity leave, paternity leave, and parental leave entitlements in place as of April 2015. Estimates based on a "full-rate equivalent," calculated as total number of weeks of any paid leave available to a new parent, multiplied by average rate of earnings reimbursement for those weeks of leave.

SOURCE: Livingston (2016).

The International Labour Organization has described the provision of benefits to mothers in the United States as "very underdeveloped" compared to other countries (Lewis et al., 2014, p. 22). The United States also lags far behind other economically developed countries in terms of paid leave for new fathers. Figure 5.11 shows an international comparison of paid parental leave.

In light of the considerable amount of stress associated with becoming a new parent, it is not surprising that there are a number of studies that report a significant decrease in marital satisfaction following the birth of a baby (Hansen, 2012; Luhmann, Hofmann, Eid, & Lucas, 2012; Pinquart & Teubert, 2010; Twenge, Campbell, & Foster, 2003). However, this is not a universal finding. Some couples report increased marital satisfaction and happiness or a stable pattern of marital satisfaction across time (Anderson, Van Ryzin, & Doherty, 2010; Dush, Taylor, & Kroeger, 2008).

Recent research on parenthood and marital satisfaction has moved in the direction of identifying the circumstances associated with a smooth transition to parenthood versus a rocky one (Holmes, Sasaki, & Hazen, 2013). First, having realistic expectations for how parenthood will change new parents' lives helps them adjust to this transition (Holmes et al., 2013). For instance, as we have already noted, if a new mother expects that both parents will equally share the extra work created by an infant and this expectation is not fulfilled, it can lead to dissatisfaction with the relationship. Reality can also fall short of expectations with regard to the impact of parenthood on career goals, energy level, money pressures, relationships with friends and family, and more. Second, personal goals usually need to change following the transition to parenthood. When new parents can find a good fit between the individual's life goals and the opportunities offered by parenthood, they are happier. For instance, in one study, new mothers who reported a decline in achievement-related goals and an increase in family- and motherhood-related goals following the transition to parenthood had a greater sense of well-being (Salmela-Aro, 2012). Third, the father's involvement in child care is associated with more positive satisfaction trajectories for both parents (Agache, Leyendecker, Schäfermeier, & Schölmerich, 2014).

When looking at the research on marital satisfaction, it is important to remember that a family is a system, and for most couples it is likely that any decline in satisfaction with their marriage is offset by other satisfactions that the couple gets from taking on their new role as parents. For instance, becoming a parent adds a new dimension to one's sense of personal identity (Lee, MacDermid, Dohring, & Kossek, 2005; Nomaguchi & Milkie, 2003; Reeves, 2006) and most parents feel very good about the job they are doing as a parent and feel very good about how their child is developing (Wenger & Fowers, 2008).

CHECK YOUR UNDERSTANDING

1. What are a new mother's experiences typically like?
2. How do men typically adjust to fatherhood?
3. How does the birth of a baby affect the parents' relationship?

CONCLUSION

In this chapter, we described the incredible journey that is prenatal development. This journey took us from a single fertilized cell to a newborn ready to begin interacting with the environment and the people in it. Despite many risks, the vast majority of pregnancies end with the birth of a healthy, well-functioning baby, and in spite of the difficulties parents encounter along the way, most would, and do, choose to do it all over again. In the chapters that follow, we look at the physical, cognitive, social, and emotional development that takes place as the newborn moves through childhood and then adolescence. In the next chapter, we focus on the processes of physical development.

CHAPTER SUMMARY

Test your understanding of the content.
Take the practice quiz at **edge.sagepub.com/levine3e**

5.1 What happens during the three stages of prenatal development?

During **ovulation**, a woman's ovary releases an egg or ovum. If the ovum is fertilized by a sperm, the resulting single cell multiplies until it becomes a hollow ball of cells called a **blastocyst,** which implants in the lining of the uterus. This is the **germinal stage** of prenatal development, from conception to 2 weeks postconception. Couples for whom **infertility** is a problem have a number of treatments and interventions available to help them conceive. In the **embryonic stage,** from 2 weeks to 2 months postconception, the number of cells increases until they form an **inner cell mass** that becomes the **embryo,** and a surrounding ring of cells that becomes the support system that includes the **placenta.** The developing embryo is vulnerable to **teratogens,** which can disrupt the process of **organogenesis.** In the third stage, the **fetal stage,** from week 9 to birth, the fetus grows in size and weight, and all the organ systems become functional.

5.2 What are some health issues and risks that can affect a pregnancy?

Some pregnancies result in a **miscarriage.** In many cases, the cause is unknown. Seeing a physician for early and regular prenatal visits helps ensure that a pregnancy progresses normally. A pregnant woman also needs to eat a healthy diet, get an appropriate amount of exercise, and should limit her intake of caffeine and avoid drinking alcohol (which could result in **fetal alcohol syndrome** or **fetal alcohol spectrum disorders**) and smoking (which is associated with low-birth-weight babies and premature deliveries, as well as developmental problems later in childhood). Use of illegal drugs threatens a pregnancy directly and is associated with a number of other unhealthy behaviors. Medical marijuana, other prescription drugs, and over-the-counter drugs should only be used in consultation with the woman's physician. Any preexisting illnesses (such as a sexually transmitted infection) should be treated and new infections that can be transmitted through the placenta (such as rubella and Zika) must be avoided. Pregnant women should try to reduce their stress level as much as possible because stress hormones can cross the placenta. Pregnant women also need to avoid exposure to environmental toxins.

5.3 What happens during the process of labor and delivery?

Labor occurs in three stages: In the first stage (which consists of **early labor, active labor,** and **transition**), contractions dilate and efface the cervix. In the second stage, the infant is born. In the third stage, the placenta is delivered. About one-third of U.S. babies are born by cesarean section. The newborn is prepared to deal with the physical stress of being born and can be assessed using the **Apgar Scale** or the Neonatal Behavioral Assessment Scale. The senses of a full-term newborn are functional but the newborn has limited ability to process this information so the infant has different **infant states** (quiet sleep, active sleep, drowsy, quiet alertness, active alertness, and crying) that help keep sensory stimulation at a level that the newborn can process. **Mirror neurons** enable the newborn to mimic simple actions and facial expressions.

5.4 What are some of the risks to the newborn's well-being?

Prematurity and **low birth weight** are significant risk factors for the newborn. Premature infants are not able to regulate their bodily functions but modern neonatal intensive care units (NICUs) are equipped to care for these infants. Most can have good developmental outcomes with appropriate early intervention. However, **infant mortality** rates in the United States are higher than in many other industrialized countries. When a seemingly healthy infant dies unexpectedly, it is called **sudden infant death syndrome (SIDS).** Not smoking while pregnant and after the birth, as well as placing the infant on his or her back to sleep on a firm mattress, are two simple things that help reduce this risk. Although there are some benefits of infants cosleeping with parents, the American Academy of Pediatrics recommends against it to reduce the possibility of SIDS. Parents should never shake a baby because it can cause **shaken baby syndrome.**

5.5 How do new parents cope with the transition to parenthood?

Many women feel they are expected to be "perfect" mothers," but it takes time for a new mother to learn how to care for her newborn. Hormonal changes in both the mother and father help prepare them to do this. Some new mothers suffer from the "baby blues," which are relatively mild and short-term, but others experience **depression with peripartum onset** which is more severe and requires intervention. Men may feel undervalued and unprepared for their role during labor and delivery or when caring for the newborn. Although new fathers today contribute more to child care than they did in the past, they still do not contribute at the same level as new mothers. New parenthood can negatively affect the quality of the couple's relationship, but both parents tend to find the postpartum period both exhilarating and exhausting as being a parent becomes part of their identity.

KEY TERMS

Strengthen your understanding of these key terms with mobile-friendly eFlashcards at edge.sagepub.com/levine3e

Abortion   142
Active labor   155
Amnion   136
Apgar Scale   158
Blastocyst   134
Cephalocaudal development   137
Cervix   154
Couvade   168
Critical period   137
Depression with peripartum onset   167
Doula   155
Early labor   154
Embryo   136
Embryonic stage   136
Endocrine disruptors   153
Fetal alcohol spectrum disorders (FASDs)   145
Fetal alcohol syndrome (FAS)   145
Fetal stage   138
Fetus   136

Germinal stage   134
Infant mortality   164
Infant states   158
Infertility   136
Inner cell mass   134
Kangaroo care   162
Low birth weight   160
Miscarriage (or spontaneous abortion)   141
Organogenesis   137
Ovulation   134
Ovum   134
Placenta   136
Premature (or preterm)   160
Sudden infant death syndrome (SIDS)   165
Teratogens   144
Transition   155
Trophoblast   134
Ultrasound   137

Give your students the SAGE edge!

SAGE edge offers a robust online environment featuring an impressive array of free tools and resources for review, study, and further exploration, keeping both instructors and students on the cutting edge of teaching and learning. Learn more at **edge.sagepub.com/levine3e**

practice AND apply

WHAT YOU'VE LEARNED

edge.sagepub.com/levine3e

chapter 6 | PHYSICAL DEVELOPMENT
The Brain and the Body

LEARNING QUESTIONS

6.1 How are the brains of children and adolescents similar to and different from the brains of adults? What disorders are linked with the structure and function of the brain?

6.2 How do the senses develop during infancy?

6.3 How do children's bodies change from infancy through adolescence?

6.4 What factors influence and shape motor development?

6.5 What role does nutrition play in development?

Master these objectives using an online action plan at **edge.sagepub.com/levine3e**

TEST YOUR KNOWLEDGE

Test your knowledge of child development by deciding whether each of the following statements is *true* or *false,* and then check your answers as you read the chapter.

1. **T** ☐ **F** ☐: Humans use only 10% of their brains.

2. **T** ☐ **F** ☐: Newborn babies form synapses (the connections between nerve cells) in their brains at the rate of a hundred new connections each second.

3. **T** ☐ **F** ☐: Children who practice the violin every day for many years become better at playing the violin in part because their activity makes physical changes in the structure of their brains.

4. **T** ☐ **F** ☐: There is good cause for alarm about the increase in the incidence of autism spectrum disorder in recent years.

5. **T** ☐ **F** ☐: Infants are born with a preference for the foods common in their culture.

6. **T** ☐ **F** ☐: Adolescent girls who go through puberty earlier than their peers are happier than girls who go through puberty later.

7. **T** ☐ **F** ☐: In the United States, 90% of adolescents between the ages of 15 and 19 have had sex at least once.

8. **T** ☐ **F** ☐: Keyboarding is less effective than writing in cursive for promoting reading, writing, and cognitive skills.

9. **T** ☐ **F** ☐: The rate of childhood obesity appears to have finally leveled off in the United States.

10. **T** ☐ **F** ☐: The most effective way to prevent eating disorders is to give adolescents information about how harmful these behaviors can be to the adolescent's body.

Correct answers: (1) F, (2) F, (3) T, (4) F, (5) T, (6) F, (7) F, (8) T, (9) T, (10) F

▲ **VIDEO: Watch as students answer some of these questions and the authors respond.**

I n this chapter, we present some of the central issues in regard to the physical development of infants, children, and adolescents. However, as we look at physical development it is important to remember that it affects and is affected by all other areas of development. For example, infants who experience a high level of stress (emotional) because of abuse or neglect are found to have higher levels of stress hormones later in life (physical), which may result in hypervigilance, which is the tendency to watch for and anticipate danger in the environment (cognitive) (Gunnar, 2007). Keeping in mind the fact that human beings are not just the sum of their parts, we present separate chapters on the basic building blocks of development—physical, cognitive, and social-emotional development—but we do so with the awareness that we cannot really separate the effects of one "building block" from those of the others. We will remind you of these reciprocal influences as we discuss each one.

We begin by looking at how the brain develops, including some information on disorders associated with brain development. We then discuss how our senses develop. Next we show how the body grows from infancy through the sexual maturation of adolescence, and examine how we move from the physical helplessness of newborns to the highly developed motor skills we see in children and adolescents. In the final section, we describe the critical role that nutrition plays in supporting healthy growth.

BRAIN DEVELOPMENT

6.1 How are the brains of children and adolescents similar to and different from the brains of adults? What disorders are linked with the structure and function of the brain?

We begin our study of brain development by addressing two common misconceptions. The first is the well-known myth that humans use only 10% of their brains. As we describe the parts and the functions of the brain in the following sections, it should become clear to you that we use *all* parts of our brains (Boyd, 2008). The second misconception is that what we *think* has little to do with how our bodies function and that our body's functioning has little to do with our thoughts. Not only will you be learning about the impact of the brain on the body's activities, but you will also learn about the impact the body has on the brain and the effect that experience has on the development of *both* body and brain. To see one of the surprising ways in which the brain and the body interact, try **Active Learning: Brain and Body.**

T ☐ F ☐ Humans use only 10% of their brains. **False**

Active LEARNING

Brain and Body

Sit comfortably in a chair. Cross your right leg over your left (at the knee or ankle). Circle your right foot to the right (in a clockwise direction). Now, using your right hand, draw a number "6" in the air. Were you able to keep your foot circling to the right? A few people can, but most people cannot. This is easy to do using your right foot and your *left* hand, so the problem lies in the fact that the left side of your brain controls the right side of your body and seems to be able to go in only one direction at a time. You know that your body is physically capable of doing both actions, but your brain may not let you do both at the same time.

STRUCTURES OF THE BRAIN

The brain is an organ of the body made up of a number of different parts. We can examine the brain from two perspectives: from side to side and from back to front. As you can see in the photo of the brain on the facing page, the brain is divided down the middle into two halves, or **hemispheres**. Some parts of the brain are found on both sides, and some are found only on one side. For example, the motor cortex that controls the body's movements is similar on both sides, but the language centers of the brain appear on the left side for up to 95% of right-handed people and 75% of lefties (Somers et al., 2015). The two sides of the brain communicate with each other through the structure that joins them, called the **corpus callosum**. Although the two sides have some distinct functions, there is no such thing as being totally right-brained or left-brained. Both halves of our brains are involved in complex ways in almost everything we do. For example, although much of language is processed on the left side, specific aspects of language, such as humor and the emotional tone of what you say, are found in the right hemisphere (Kinsbourne, 2009).

Hemispheres The two halves of the brain.

Corpus callosum The band of fibers that connects the two hemispheres of the brain.

We get a different view of the brain when we look at it from the side as shown in Figure 6.1. The parts, or lobes, of the brain have some distinct functions; however, most aspects of human functioning involve many parts of the brain in coordination with one another. For example, the occipital lobe is known to control vision but the parietal, temporal, and frontal lobes also play a role in vision (Merck Manual, 2008).

Look at Figure 6.1 to identify the parts of the brain in this image and the functions they perform.

- The *brain stem* is the most primitive part of the brain and controls basic survival functions such as breathing, heart rate, and sleep.

- The *cerebellum* is located at the top of the brain stem and receives information from the sensory systems, spinal cord, and other parts of the brain to coordinate balance and voluntary movement.

- The *cerebrum* or *cortex* accounts for about two-thirds of the brain's mass and handles the higher functions of thought and action. The cerebrum includes many different parts, including

  o the *occipital lobe*, which processes vision;

  o the *temporal lobe*, which processes auditory information and enables us to understand language;

  o the *parietal lobe*, which processes sensory input and is where taste, temperature, and touch are integrated or processed; and

  o the *frontal lobe*, which processes complex thoughts, planning, movement, language, and impulse control.

The *amygdala* and the *hippocampus* shown in Figure 6.2 are located deep inside the brain. The amygdala contributes to our emotions and moods, and the hippocampus processes and stores memory (Bear, Connors, & Paradiso, 2007; Sprenger, 2013).

Although this is a good description of some of the functions that we currently know are associated with different areas of the brain, brain research is one of the most active areas in the field of child development, so our understanding of brain functions and development will undoubtedly continue to change as research continues.

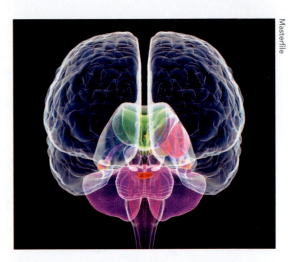

The two hemispheres of the human brain. Although the two hemispheres of the brain may look similar, some brain functions are handled mainly by one side, other functions are handled mainly by the other side, and some are handled by both. The corpus callosum (shown in green in this picture) connects the two hemispheres so they can communicate with each other.

FIGURE 6.1

Side view of the human brain. This figure shows important structural features of the human brain and the functions associated with each of them. Figure 6.2 shows two important structures, the amygdala and hippocampus, which are buried deep in the interior portion of the brain.

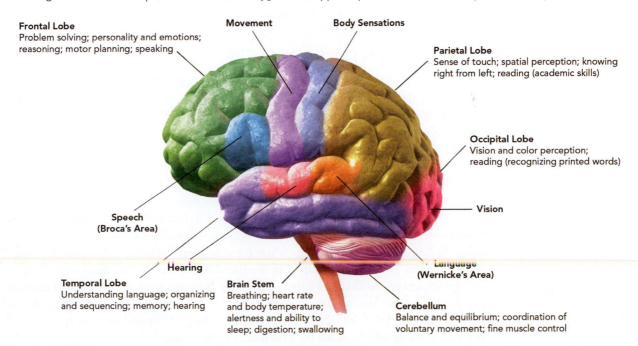

Frontal Lobe
Problem solving; personality and emotions; reasoning; motor planning; speaking

Movement

Body Sensations

Parietal Lobe
Sense of touch; spatial perception; knowing right from left; reading (academic skills)

Occipital Lobe
Vision and color perception; reading (recognizing printed words)

Vision

Speech (Broca's Area)

Language (Wernicke's Area)

Hearing

Temporal Lobe
Understanding language; organizing and sequencing; memory; hearing

Brain Stem
Breathing; heart rate and body temperature; alertness and ability to sleep; digestion; swallowing

Cerebellum
Balance and equilibrium; coordination of voluntary movement; fine muscle control

FIGURE 6.2

Amygdala and hippocampus. These brain structures lie deep inside the brain. The amygdala is responsible for our emotions and moods, and the hippocampus processes and stores long-term memory.

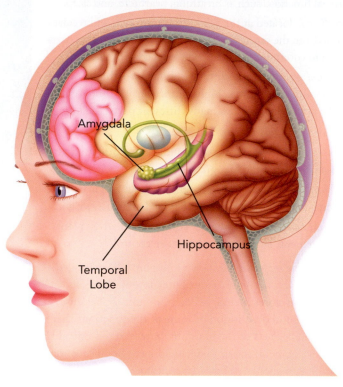

Amygdala

Hippocampus

Temporal
Lobe

SOURCE: BSIP/UIG/Universal Images Group/Getty.

As we continue our discussion of the brain, this overview should help you think about how different aspects of physical development link back to the different parts of the brain and the functions they control. In future chapters you will learn more about the cognitive, language, and emotion centers of the brain and their functions.

DEVELOPMENTAL PROCESSES

The brain is changing and developing from infancy through adolescence. In this section, we describe the development of the connections between nerve cells, called synapses, as well as the development of the myelin sheath that coats the nerve cells. You may be surprised to learn that your personal experiences as you grow up affect the way your brain forms connections between synapses and develops the myelin sheath.

Neurons and Synaptic Connections

The human brain is made of approximately 86 billion nerve cells, called **neurons** (Azevedo et al., 2009). Each nerve cell sends messages via special chemicals called **neurotransmitters** to other nerve cells through extensions of the cell called **axons** and receives messages through receptors called **dendrites**. The place where the axon from one neuron meets the dendrite of another neuron is called the **synapse**, as illustrated in Figure 6.3. Just about everything we do depends on communication between nerve cells. Neurotransmitters are released from one cell and bring their "message" to the second cell. Adults have approximately 1 quadrillion of these synaptic connections (Kasthuri & Lichtman, 2010). Neurons and their synaptic connections make up what is called the **grey matter** of the brain.

Infants are born with almost all the neurons they will ever have; however, they have relatively few synapses or connections between them. As a result, babies have fewer inborn

Neurons The cells that make up the nervous system of the body.

Neurotransmitters Chemicals that transmit nerve impulses across a synapse from one nerve cell to another.

Axons The parts of a nerve cell that conduct impulses away from the cell body.

Dendrites The portions of a neuron that receive impulses from other neurons.

Synapse The place where the axon from one neuron meets the dendrite of another neuron.

Grey matter The neurons and synapses that make up the brain.

FIGURE 6.3

Neurons and synapses. Two nerve cells (neurons) are connected to each other when the axon of one reaches the dendrite of the other at the synapse (shown at the left). At the synapse, chemicals called *neurotransmitters* are released from one cell and bring their "message" to the second cell (shown at the right).

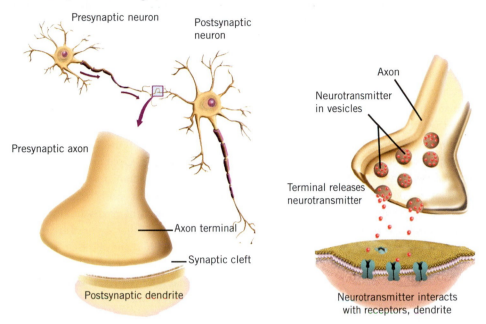

SOURCE: Garrett, B. *Brain & Behavior: An Introduction to Biological Psychology.* © 2009 SAGE.

behavior patterns than other animals, and this makes them more open to learning from their environment. The experiences they have actually shape the development of synaptic connections and the formation of their brains (Rosenzweig, Breedlove, & Watson, 2005). The development of new synapses is referred to as **synaptogenesis.** After a baby is born, new synapses may be formed at the rate of more than *1 million* connections *per second* (Greenough, Black, & Wallace, 1987). One reason why infants' brains are more active than adults' brains is because they are so busy forming these connections (Gopnik, Meltzoff, & Kuhl, 1999).

By the time children enter early childhood, synaptogenesis in the areas of the brain responsible for vision, hearing, and language has already greatly diminished, but production in the prefrontal cortex, in the very front of the frontal lobe, is just reaching its peak and this process will not be complete until late adolescence or early adulthood.

Plasticity of the Brain

The ability of the infant brain to change in form and function is referred to as **plasticity.** If you, as an adult, had half of your brain (one hemisphere) removed, the result would be catastrophic. You would lose movement in the opposite side of your body, and you would lose the functions handled in that hemisphere. However, until about age 4 or 5, children who have had one hemisphere removed to treat an otherwise untreatable condition, such as severe epilepsy, can recover almost full function (Eliot, 1999). In one study of children who had an entire temporal lobe removed, there was no significant decline in the group's overall IQ following the surgery (Westerveld et al., 2000). Even when the surgery involved the left temporal lobe (the part of the brain associated with language), there was no loss of verbal intelligence and nonverbal intellectual functioning actually improved significantly. This occurs because the brain at this young age has enough plasticity for brain cells that were originally intended to serve one function (for example, controlling movement) to turn into cells that control another function instead (for example, language). In the study by Westerveld et al. (2000), the small group of children who did experience significant decline following surgery tended to be the oldest children in the group because plasticity decreases with age.

T ☐ F ☐
Newborn babies form synapses (the connections between nerve cells) in their brains at the rate of a hundred new connections each second. **False**

Synaptogenesis The development of new synapses.

Plasticity The ability of an immature brain to change in form and function.

Pruning The deterioration and disappearance of synapses that are not used.

At various times within the first years of life, babies' brains produce so many new synaptic connections that the density of connections is greater than that found in the adult brain (Blakemore & Choudhury, 2006). However, many of these connections do not survive. In a process called **pruning**, synaptic connections that are not used deteriorate and disappear. Just as you prune away dead branches on a tree to strengthen it, this process of pruning away unused synapses strengthens the brain. Rather than being a terrible loss, this process makes the brain much more efficient. For example, unlike adults, newborn infants can distinguish between all speech sounds in any language. However, during their first year of life, they are exposed only to the specific sounds in the particular language they hear each day. This strengthens the synapses for those sounds, but those synapses that were not used because the infant never hears those sounds are pruned away. This increases the infant's ability to discriminate the sounds in the language the baby is hearing (Blakemore & Choudhury, 2006), and by the end of that time, babies can no longer distinguish between language sounds that are found only in languages they don't regularly hear.

The process of pruning follows a "use it or lose it" principle. Greenough et al. (1987) described two ways that this happens: experience-expectant mechanisms and experience-dependent mechanisms. **Experience-expectant brain development** occurs because our brain *expects* certain events to happen. For example, in the normal course of events, our eyes will be exposed to light. When these expected events occur, the pathways that are used are retained. In their classic experiments with kittens, Hubel and Wiesel (1965) showed that if this does not happen, the eye still develops normally, but the part of the brain that processes visual information does not function. Kittens with one eye closed for a period of time after birth were never able to develop vision in that eye, even when the eye was later open. This is why children who have an eye that has considerably less vision or doesn't coordinate with the other eye (a condition called *amblyopia* or "lazy eye") must have intervention early in their lives or they may lose effective vision in that eye as the brain "turns it off."

Experience-expectant brain development Development that occurs when we encounter experiences that our brain expects as a normal event.

Experience-dependent brain development Development that occurs in response to specific learning experiences.

Experience-dependent brain development is much more individual and depends on each person's particular experiences. In addition to unused synapses being pruned away, new synapses can develop in response to stimulation. For example, Elbert, Pantev, Wienbruch, Rockstroh, and Taub (1995) studied the brains of violinists. If you pretend to play the violin, the fingers of your left hand move all around, pressing on the strings to produce different notes, while the fingers of your right hand usually stay in one position, holding the bow. Elbert et al. found that the area of the right side of the brain that controls the left hand has many more synaptic connections than the same area of the left side of the brain in violinists. It is unlikely that these people are born this way, making them more likely to become violinists. Instead, the constant use of the fingers of the left hand to move and hold the appropriate strings on the violin further develops that part of the right side of the brain.

T ☐ F ☐ Children who practice the violin every day for many years become better at playing the violin in part because their activity makes physical changes in the structure of their brains. **True**

Myelination of Neurons

So far we have discussed the development of synapses through the process of synaptogenesis, but for messages to be sent successfully, another necessary process in the development of the nervous system is **myelination**. For neurons to work efficiently, they need to be coated with a fatty substance known as myelin, as shown in Figure 6.4. This coating of the axons that connect the neurons constitutes the **white matter** of the brain.

Myelination The process of laying down a fatty sheath of myelin on the neurons.

White matter The myelin-coated axons that connect neurons in the brain.

Picture an electrical cord between the wall socket and your lamp. How does the message travel from your light switch to turn on the lamp on your desk? Within the electrical cord is a metal wire that carries the electrical current. If bare wire were used with no insulation, not only would you get a shock when you touched it, but your light would not work very well. Only some of the current, not all of it, would be likely to arrive at its destination. For that reason, an electrical cord is always insulated with some material that cannot carry an electric current so that all of the current goes to its destination. In a similar fashion, the neurons in the nervous system are insulated with myelin so that the message the neurotransmitters send will be received most effectively.

FIGURE 6.4

The myelin sheath. The myelin sheath is a fatty coating that wraps around the nerves to ensure that the messages sent along a neuron are delivered efficiently. In this figure, the axon is shown in blue with the myelin sheath wrapped around it. A cross section is shown here so you can see how the coating wraps around the axon.

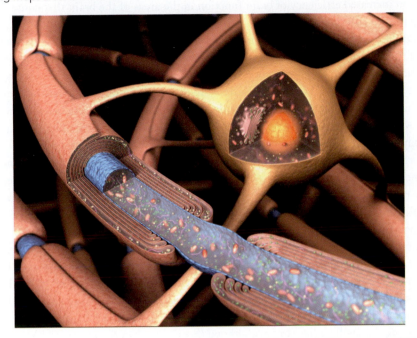

When babies are born, just as the synaptic connections are not complete, so too the myelin sheath does not yet cover all of the nerves in the nervous system. The process of producing synaptic connections, pruning away those that are not being used, and myelinating the connections that are left will continue throughout childhood and adolescence. Myelination begins in the lower centers at the base of the brain and continues through the higher centers of the cortex (Deoni et al., 2011). As researchers learn more about the normal progression of myelination, they are also likely to find evidence of abnormal processes that may contribute to such disorders as autism and schizophrenia (Deoni et al., 2011).

We have already learned that synaptogenesis is affected by our experiences through the process of experience-dependent brain development. There is also evidence that myelination is affected by our experiences. Bengtsson et al. (2005) compared brain development in children who spent long hours practicing piano to that in children who did not play piano. Their evidence indicates that the extra stimulation that certain neurons experience when children are practicing results in more myelination of those neurons, including those in the corpus callosum, which connect the two hemispheres of the brain. The corpus callosum is involved in the ability to coordinate movements of your two hands at the same time. In this study, children who played piano had increased brain efficiency, and this increased ability continued into adolescence.

Brain Development Through Childhood and Adolescence

As we've said, the brain continues to develop through childhood and adolescence. Specific brain structures that experience growth during middle childhood include the frontal lobe, the parietal lobe, and the corpus callosum. The growth of the corpus callosum is important because the increasing connectivity and coordination between different areas of the brain contribute to the improvement of motor skills, visual-spatial skills, and coordination (American Psychological Association Division of Educational Psychology, 2014). Ongoing synaptic pruning in middle childhood allows children to use fewer and more select regions of the brain to complete the tasks they are performing and this allows them to perform tasks more efficiently (Mah & Ford-Jones, 2012). For example, compare the way a 6-year-old pitcher throws a ball to a batter to the way a 12-year-old does the same thing. Compared to the younger child, the older child's throw is more precise and purposeful, and this is based in part on increased efficiency of brain function in the areas of the brain that control motor function.

In early adolescence, there is another overproduction of synapses, this time in the frontal lobes of the brain. Until this overproduction of synaptic connections is pruned away, it results in inefficiency of thought. For instance, when children and adolescents were shown a picture of a face (for example, a sad face) and heard a word that might or might not match that expression ("happy" or "sad"), it took longer for the 11- and 12-year-old participants to correctly decide whether the image and word matched than it did either younger or older participants in the study (McGivern, Andersen, Byrd, Mutter, & Reilly, 2002). The decrease in early adolescent performance was attributed to the proliferation of synapses at this age, and the increased efficiency in later adolescence was attributed to the synaptic pruning that had occurred.

The normal pruning process is complete in some areas of the brain by age 12, but in others, especially the prefrontal cortex, the process is not complete until well into adolescence or early adulthood (Blakemore & Choudhury, 2006; Giedd, 2004; Gogtay et al., 2004). Because the prefrontal cortex is the part of the brain that controls judgment and planning and regulates impulse control, the tendency of some adolescents to act on their emotions without thinking through a situation may be related to the immaturity of this system in their brain. Because the connections between the centers for reasoning and the centers for emotions, such as the amygdala, are still developing during adolescence, their emotional responses are less tempered by reasoning than will be the case in adulthood (Society for Neuroscience, 2007).

Our understanding of the immaturity of the adolescent brain has had consequences for adolescents who are in the judicial system. In a landmark case in 2005, the Supreme Court overturned the death sentence of Christopher Simmons, who had murdered an elderly woman when he was 17. This decision effectively made it illegal to execute people who committed crimes before the age of 18. It was affected by the argument entered into evidence by the American Society for Adolescent Psychiatry that although adolescents may know right from wrong, they are less able to control their impulses, are more influenced by their peers, and are less able to think through the consequences of their actions because of the immaturity of their brain development, in particular, the prefrontal cortex, which controls these functions (Dittmann, 2005; Lehmann, 2004).

The number and type of changes that occur in adolescence may make the brain especially vulnerable to the effect of neurotoxins (such as alcohol and other drugs) during this period of development (Squeglia, Jacobus, & Tapert, 2009). For instance, use of alcohol and marijuana during adolescence has been shown to affect both the structure and the functioning of the brain. Heavy drinking is associated with impaired performance on tests of memory, attention, spatial skills, and executive functioning, and marijuana use is associated with decreases in several aspects of cognitive functioning, including learning. Furthermore, these deficits are seen in adolescents who are not currently using substances, suggesting that they are the result of long-term changes in the brain. Any cognitive deficits that result at this time in development have potential consequences for future academic, occupational, and social functioning as the adolescent moves into early adulthood.

DISORDERS RELATED TO BRAIN DEVELOPMENT

With the use of functional magnetic resonance imaging (fMRI), researchers today are able to examine the connectivity between different areas of the brain as early as the second trimester of a pregnancy. Research conducted by Moriah Thomason and her colleagues is giving us new insight into the order and timing of connections that allow different parts of the brain to communicate with each other (Thomason et al., 2015). This line of research could lead to very early diagnosis of brain disorders and better interventions and therapies for children with such conditions.

When brain development does not occur as expected, or when there is damage to the brain at any point, a number of disorders may result. We discuss here three very different types of outcome: cerebral palsy, autism spectrum disorder, and schizophrenia. We discuss cerebral palsy because specific brain abnormalities are known to cause this disorder. We include autism and schizophrenia in this section on the brain because, although their precise cause (or causes) remains elusive, there now is almost universal agreement that there is an underlying biological explanation connected with brain development.

Assistive technology for cerebral palsy. Computer technology that is available today can enable a young person with cerebral palsy to participate in classroom activities and communicate his thoughts and feelings, even though he has limited physical mobility.

Cerebral Palsy

Cerebral palsy is an umbrella term that describes a group of brain-based disorders affecting a person's ability to move and maintain balance and posture. People with cerebral palsy may experience difficulties with muscle tone, coordination, movement, and speech. The condition is caused by abnormal development of the brain or damage to it, either prenatally, during birth, or after birth up to age 3 (Abdel-Hamid, Ratanawongsa, Zeldin, & Bazzano, 2015; National Institute of Neurological Disorders and Stroke [NINDS], 2015). Approximately 800,000 children and adults in the United States live with one or more symptoms of cerebral palsy (NINDS, 2015), and the prevalence rate has remained largely unchanged over the past 40 years (Abdel-Hamid et al., 2015).

Risk factors for cerebral palsy include premature birth, low birth weight, conception of two or more fetuses, maternal exposure to toxins or infections, and lack of oxygen during the birth process (Abdel-Hamid, 2011). While some children are profoundly affected and will need total care throughout their lives, others show only mild impairment and require little or no special assistance. Although this condition does not get progressively worse, early intervention and therapy can be beneficial because it can help prevent or delay the onset of secondary problems. Medications can help control seizures and muscle spasms, surgery can lengthen muscles and tendons that are too short to function, and physical therapy can help the child build necessary skills. An exciting new avenue of research is investigating the use of a drug that allows the regrowth of the myelin coating on nerve cells in the brain (Fancy et al., 2011). When a lack of oxygen disrupts the nerve cells' ability to create myelin, those cells die and this can lead to cerebral palsy. Research with mice discovered a drug that allows the myelin to regrow and repair the damage and, although this research is far from being ready to use in humans, it offers hope for a new pharmaceutical treatment of this type of brain injury. There are also new technologies that let children with cerebral palsy use even limited head movements to operate a computer that has a voice synthesizer, which can transform their motions into spoken language.

Cerebral palsy A chronic condition that appears early in development and primarily involves problems with body movement and muscle coordination.

Autism Spectrum Disorder

In 2013, the American Psychiatric Association (APA) issued the fifth revision of its *Diagnostic and Statistics Manual* (DSM-5). The DSM-5 contains the descriptions, symptoms, and other criteria used by clinicians, researchers, and mental health professionals across the country to diagnose mental disorders. One of the most important changes in this edition involved the diagnosis of autism spectrum disorder. Previously, individuals could be diagnosed in one of four separate categories of autism which included Asperger's syndrome, a less severe condition

Autism spectrum disorder
A disorder characterized by pervasive impairment in social communication and interaction and by restricted or repetitive behaviors, interests, or activities. Severity is classified by how much support the individual needs to function effectively.

in which individuals often had good language and cognitive skills. Currently, autism spectrum disorder is classified by severity, but it is not divided into different types.

Autism spectrum disorder (ASD) involves a pervasive impairment in social communication and interaction, and restricted or repetitive behaviors, interests, or activities (APA, 2013). The degree of impairment can run from mild to severe, with severity determined by how much support the individual needs to function effectively. Some children with autism have few words and respond only to focused, direct approaches from other people, while those with less severe symptoms may speak normally, but cannot successfully maintain the normal back and forth of conversation (APA, 2013). The individual shows symptoms in early childhood, even if the condition is not recognized and diagnosed until later in development.

Over the years, a number of possible causes of ASD have been proposed, including ones with a biological basis and others with an environmental cause. **Journey of Research: Searching for the Cause of Autism Spectrum Disorder** describes the history of our understanding of this disorder. Today research into the neurological basis of autism spectrum disorder and other similar developmental disorders is one of the most exciting and active areas in the field of child development.

JOURNEY OF *Research*

Searching for the Cause of Autism Spectrum Disorder

In an early description of autism spectrum disorder, the psychiatrist Leo Kanner (1949) identified the cause as parental coldness, marked by a mechanical attention to the child's needs that lacked any genuine warmth. From this perspective, the infant's aloofness and withdrawal were seen as an adaptive response to an almost intolerable situation. As a result of Kanner's description, the psychological literature from the 1940s through the early 1970s was filled with references to "refrigerator mothers" (Frith, 2003). Today inadequate parenting has been eliminated as a possible cause of ASD as more contemporary research has focused on possible biological causes, including genetics and neurological differences.

Strong evidence for a possible genetic cause comes from the observation that ASD runs in families. According to the Centers for Disease Control and Prevention (2016b), if one identical twin has ASD, the other twin will have the same diagnosis about 36% to 95% of the time, depending on the particular study, while if one nonidentical twin has ASD, the other twin will be affected 0% to 31% of the time. Another genetic difference is that boys are 4.5 times more likely than girls to be diagnosed with ASD (CDC, 2016b).

A different line of research has searched for possible environmental causes (or triggers) of autism spectrum disorder. You may have heard of research that looked at the role of mercury used as a preservative in the measles-mumps-rubella (MMR) vaccine given to infants. In 1998, the British medical journal *Lancet* published a study that appeared to find a link between ASD and this vaccine (Wakefield et al., 1998). Since that time numerous research studies have been conducted to investigate this possible link, but the scientific consensus today is that the clinical evidence does not support the idea that immunizations are a cause for ASD (CDC, 2012b; National Research Council, 2011). For example, in Montreal, Canada, when the mercury compound that was the suspected cause of ASD was removed from the vaccine, there was no corresponding decrease in the incidence of ASD (Fombonne, Zakarian, Bennett, Meng, & McLean-Heywood, 2005).

In 2016, a group of researchers from Johns Hopkins University presented a paper at a professional meeting that reported an increased risk of autism in children born to women who had high levels of folate in their blood at the time of their delivery (Hamblin, 2016). The media latched on to the information and headlines and newscasts widely reported on this potential risk. However, as you know from Chapter 5, an adequate amount of folate plays an important role in preventing neural tube and spinal defects during pregnancy. Since receiving all this attention, the researchers have expressed concern that people are misinterpreting their research. At this point, the source of the high level of folate in the affected women is not known. It might come from supplements a woman has taken during her pregnancy, but it also could come from naturally occurring folate in her diet or a problem she has with metabolizing the folate she takes in from any source. For this reason, the researchers do not want pregnant woman and those planning for a pregnancy to discontinue using folate as recommended by their physicians.

Other environmental factors such as air pollution, nutritional factors, and environmental toxins all continue to be investigated. However, the major area of research being carried out today is the link between ASD and brain function and structure. We describe this research next.

The three active avenues of neurological research that hold great promise for a better understanding of the causes of autism include studies of brain structure, brain functioning, and the connectivity between different parts of the brain. We will look briefly at each of these lines of research.

Among the studies of *brain structure*, imaging studies have found enlargement of the amygdala, the area of the brain that is active in emotional experience and expression, in the brains of young children with ASD. This research found that the larger the amygdala, the more difficulty the person had with social relationships (Sparks et al., 2002). Another structural difference involves total brain volume. The brains of young children who have been diagnosed with ASD have greater brain volume than typically developing children, at least until early adolescence when a crossover occurs. Beyond that point, the brain volume of typically developing adolescents exceeds that of adolescents diagnosed with autism, as shown in Figure 6.5 (Lange et al., 2015). This line of research continues to

FIGURE 6.5

Brain volume comparison of children with autism and typically developing children. One of the structural differences in the brain of children diagnosed with autism (blue line) is that their total brain volume is greater than that of typically developing children (green line) early in development, but in early adolescence the groups reverse and typically developing children have the greater total brain volume from that point. These lines represent the growth curve that best represents all the individual results shown around them. New technologies continue to give us greater insight into structural and functional differences in the neurology of children with autism spectrum disorders.

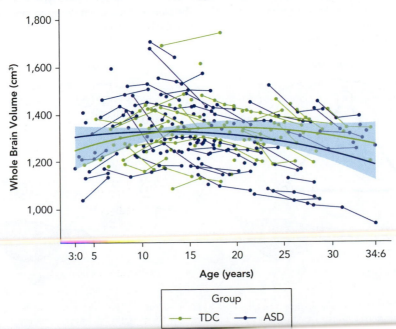

Source: Lange et al. (2015).

look for specific parts of the brain associated with different symptoms of autism, such as problems with social interaction or repetitive behaviors (Ha, Sohn, Kim, Sim, & Cheon, 2015).

A second line of neurological research looks for *functional differences* in children diagnosed with ASD. Findings include the fact that it takes more effort for children with autism to interpret a speaker's intention during social communication and this is linked to hyperactivation of certain parts of the brain. However, for some other cognitive tasks children with ASD have lower activation of the brain than other children (Ha et al., 2015). Children with ASD have been shown to have deficits in working memory that may affect language skills (Schuh & Eigsti, 2012), and they have an impaired ability to analyze the emotions in facial expressions (Ha et al., 2015). There is evidence that the brains of typically developing infants respond differently when they see faces than when they see objects, but the brains of infants with ASD do not seem to respond differently, which may indicate that they do not differentiate people from objects (McCleery, Akshoomoff, Dobkins, & Carver, 2009).

The third line of neurological research has examined *connectivity* between brain regions. This research has found that instead of having efficient, strong connections among specific neurons, children with ASD have less efficient connections among many more neurons (Müller et al., 2011). You can see this illustrated in Figure 6.6. This overabundance is a result of a slowed process of pruning away synapses that are not used (Tang et al., 2014). As we have mentioned, failing to do this results in less efficient transmission of information. Recent research that used electroencephalograms (EEGs) with children younger than those in studies employing fMRIs has found the same overconnectivity previously seen in older children (Uddin, 2015). This research is important because it may help us find a sensitive and reliable biomarker for autism that could become part of an early identification process.

Accurately estimating the prevalence of autism spectrum disorder (ASD) is not easy, but there has been a steady increase in this estimate in the United States in recent years

FIGURE 6.6

Atypical brain connectivity: Autism. This figure shows the pattern of connectivity in a typical brain in comparison to those in the brain of a person with autism. The blue lines represent strong connections, while the orange lines represent weak connections. Note that the brain of an autistic person has more connections than is typical, but they are much weaker.

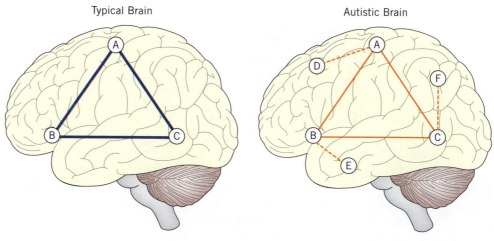

SOURCE: Akhgarnia (2011).

(see Table 6.1). By the most recent estimate from the Centers for Disease Control and Prevention, 1 in 68 children has been identified with ASD, an estimated prevalence that is 30% higher than in 2008 and a staggering 120% higher than the estimate in 2002.

When we try to understand the increase in number of cases of ASD, it is important to think about how we recognize and diagnose the disorder. At least part of the increase may be attributable to improved case finding in recent years (Gernsbacher, Dawson, & Goldsmith, 2005). That would mean that even if the real incidence of ASD hasn't increased, we may be doing a better job of identifying (and, therefore, being able to count) children with the disorder. Also, the criteria we use to diagnose ASD has broadened over the years (Gernsbacher et al., 2005). As the definition became more inclusive, we would expect that more children would be identified. We also continue to develop reliable ways to diagnose autism at younger and younger ages. Today 18% of all diagnoses are made for children under the age of 3, and diagnoses made as early as 18 months are considered valid and stable (Chawarska, Lin, Paul, & Volkmar, 2007; Lord et al., 2006). However, as we continue our efforts to identify all cases of autism and as we make identification at younger and younger ages, it also is possible that our statistics include some children who are mistakenly identified as autistic. In fact, a recent study found that 13% of children diagnosed with autism were no longer consider autistic upon further testing (Blumberg et al., 2016). All of these factors taken together probably contribute to the increase in the number of cases diagnosed in recent years.

Of course, any increase in the true incidence of ASD would be a cause for concern, but the fact that we are now identifying more children who might otherwise have been overlooked and not receive early and comprehensive intervention services is not necessarily a bad thing.

T ☐ F ☐ There is good cause for alarm about the increase in the incidence of autism spectrum disorder in recent years. **False**

TABLE 6.1

Prevalence of autism spectrum disorder. The prevalence of autism spectrum disorder in the United States continues to increase. The most recent estimate from the Centers for Disease Control and Prevention is that 1 in every 68 American children has this disorder, a 120% increase since 2002.

Identified Prevalance of Autism Spectrum Disorder ADDM Network 2000–2012 Combining Data from All Sites				
Surveillance Year	Birth Year	Number of ADDM Sites Reporting	Prevalence per 1,000 children (Range)	This is about 1 in X children . . .
2000	1992	6	6.7 (4.5–9.9)	1 in 150
2002	1994	14	6.6 (3.3–10.6)	1 in 150
2004	1996	8	8.0 (4.6–9.8)	1 in 125
2006	1998	11	9.0 (4.2–12.1)	1 in 110
2008	2000	14	11.3 (4.8–21.2)	1 in 88
2010	2002	11	14.7 (5.7–21.9)	1 in 68
2012	2004	11	14.6 (8.2–24.6)	1 in 68

SOURCE: Centers for Disease Control and Prevention (2016b).

Under the Individuals with Disabilities Education Act (IDEA), all states have specialists trained to work with young children diagnosed with ASD (National Institute of Mental Health [NIMH], 2009). After being assessed by a team of specialists, a child's strengths and weaknesses can be identified and an effective treatment plan designed to target the symptoms. Together with the family, the team develops an Individualized Family Service Plan (IFSP) describing the services to be provided to the family, not just the child, and this plan is reviewed at least once every 6 months.

Reuters/Chip East

Art by Stephen Wiltshire. Stephen Wiltshire draws pictures like these entirely from memory, showing the unusual abilities sometimes found in people with ASD. When we describe autism as a "spectrum" this is exactly what we mean — that people with this disorder show a wide range of levels of functioning.

The optimal intervention consists of at least 2 years of intensive intervention during the pre-school years (NINDS, 2008). We know that early intensive behavioral intervention can bring about substantial improvement in IQ and adaptive behavior (skills needed for everyday life) for many autistic children, although some will need ongoing close supervision and care throughout their lives. In a few rare cases, children with ASD can even show extraordinary abilities in a limited area of expertise. For example, Stephen Wiltshire was diagnosed with autism at age 3 and didn't learn to speak until 9 years of age, yet his amazing renderings of cityscapes are now shown around the world, and he has been honored for his contribution to the art world by Queen Elizabeth II (Stephen Wiltshire Gallery, 2012).

Schizophrenia A psychotic disorder marked by disorganized thinking, hallucinations, and delusions.

Schizophrenia

Some disorders of the brain do not appear until adolescence. **Schizophrenia** is a very rare but serious mental disorder that affects between 0.3% and 0.7% of the population (APA, 2013). It is related to both structural and functional differences in many regions of the brain (Ren et al., 2013). Diagnosis requires two or more of the following symptoms: delusions (unrealistic, fixed beliefs such as believing that you are being pursued by the CIA), hallucinations (most commonly, hearing voices that are not there), disorganized speech, very disorganized or catatonic behavior (lack of reaction to the environment), or negative symptoms (for example, reduced expression of emotion and reduction in self-motivated behavior), which must be present for at least 1 month. Symptoms often first appear in late adolescence, but the onset can be much later into the mid-30s (APA, 2013).

In the very rare cases when children and younger teens develop this disorder, it is referred to as *early-onset schizophrenia* (McDonell & McClellan, 2007). However, although schizophrenia may not be diagnosed until adolescence, in many cases the disorder is preceded either by a gradual deterioration in social and cognitive functioning or by ongoing difficulties in these areas (Quee et al., 2014). After the symptoms of schizophrenia develop, functioning in these areas continues to decline, resulting in difficulty with social, academic, and occupational functioning (Tandon et al., 2013; McClellan & Stock, 2013).

Although we do not understand all the causes of schizophrenia, it is clear that genes play a large role, as shown by research with twins. If one identical twin is schizophrenic, there is a 40% to 60% chance the other will be as well, while a fraternal twin has only a 5% to 15% chance of sharing this condition with a twin (McClellan & Stock, 2013). Prenatal disruption of brain development by factors such as the mother's experience of starvation or influenza increases the possibility the child will develop schizophrenia (Brown & Susser, 2008; Limosin, Rouillon, Payan, Cohen, & Strub, 2003), as does early head injuries for those with a genetic vulnerability (Abdel-Malik, Husten, Chow, & Bassett, 2003). There also is a growing body of evidence that adolescent marijuana use can increase the risk of schizophrenia for some teens who are more vulnerable to the disorder because of genetic predisposition, a dysfunctional environment, and other factors that are not yet entirely clear. For this reason, parents, teachers, and health care providers should be aware of the possibility and look for a decline in school performance and odd behavior in teens who are using marijuana (Evins, Green, Kane, & Murray, 2012).

Schizophrenia is a chronic disorder with little likelihood of a cure. Treatment includes medication, together with work with the adolescent's family to promote understanding of the disorder, and training for the individual in social skills, life skills, and problem solving skills, together with specialized education programs (McClellan & Stock, 2013; Volkmar & Tsatsanis, 2002).

CHECK YOUR UNDERSTANDING

1. What are the roles of neurons and synapses?
2. What is the difference between experience-expectant and experience-dependent brain development?
3. What role does myelination play in brain development?
4. How are cerebral palsy, autism spectrum disorder, and schizophrenia related to brain development?

DEVELOPMENT OF THE SENSES

6.2 How do the senses develop during infancy?

A central function of the brain is to take in and make sense of our experiences. The first step in that process is the use of our senses to connect us to the world. In this section, we focus on the very beginning of sensory development to show how the development of the senses in infancy brings infants into the social world.

In the early days of the field of psychology, William James (1890/1990) described the world of the infant as "one great blooming, buzzing confusion" (p. 462), and the idea that newborns were unable to make sense of their world persisted for years. Today we know this statement seriously underestimates the capabilities of newborns to receive information about the world through all their senses in an organized way and to respond to that information. Although all the senses begin developing during the prenatal period and become functional before birth, some are more advanced in their development than others. There is no doubt the newborn can hear, see, taste, smell, and respond to touch. We look here at how each of the senses develop during infancy and how they connect the infant to other people.

VISION

Although newborns are capable of focusing their eyes, their vision is much worse than normal adult vision. It is difficult to measure the **visual acuity** of young infants (or the ability to see things in sharp detail), but one estimate is that at birth, acuity is around 20/400 to 20/800 (meaning that the infant can see at 20 feet what an adult with normal vision could see at 400 to 800 feet). By 1 month, acuity has improved to 20/200 to 20/400, and by 6 months it is 20/25 to 20/30. Until they are about 3 months old, infants can focus on objects

visual acuity The ability to see things in sharp detail.

that are 8 to 10 inches in front of them (American Optometric Association, 2013; University of Calgary, n.d.). That is one reason why we often put our faces close to infants when we are talking to them—they don't see us clearly until we get that close. They will not develop adult levels of visual acuity until sometime between 6 months and 3 years (Slater, Field, & Hernandez-Reif, 2007).

However, from birth, infants are attracted to looking at the faces of people around them, especially their mother. In addition, they tend to concentrate on areas of high contrast—that is, where darkest dark meets lightest light. At first this may mean they scan the parent's hairline, but at 2 months of age, infants concentrate attention on the eyes, where the white of the eye surrounds a darker center (Farroni, Menon, & Johnson, 2006; Ramsey-Rennels & Langlois, 2007). Think about how you would feel when holding a baby who looks you directly in the eye. Many parents respond with the feeling that "this baby *knows* me." This is surely an adaptive way babies attract others to interact with them. In fact, research has shown that mothers are more likely to continue to interact warmly with their infants when they are looking their mothers in the eye (Nomikou, Rohlfing, & Szufnarowska, 2013).

HEARING

Hearing becomes functional while the fetus is still in the womb, and one sound fetuses hear loudly is their mother's voice. Kisilevsky and colleagues (2003) have shown that even prenatally, fetuses will respond differently to the sound of their mother's voice than to the voice of another woman. A tape recording of the infant's mother reading a poem out loud or a tape recording of another woman reading the same poem were played close to the woman's stomach near the end of her pregnancy. When the fetuses heard their mothers' voices, their heart rate accelerated, but when they heard a stranger speaking, their heart rate decelerated, as though they were paying attention and trying to figure out who was speaking. The fact that the same poem elicited two different responses depending upon who was speaking tells us that the fetuses can discriminate between them. In other research that compared the preference of newborns for their mother's voice versus their father's voice, there was a clear preference for listening to the mother's voice (Lee & Kisilevsky, 2014).

These two studies look at different aspects of hearing: what we pay attention to and what we prefer to listen to. When a stimulus is presented repeatedly, we tend to lose interest in it, but if the stimulus changes, it recaptures our attention. This is a process known as *habituation*, which you will learn about in Chapters 7 and 8. The first study showed that fetuses are familiar with the sounds of their own mother's voice, but the novelty of another person's voice grabs their attention. The second study shows that given two options, newborns have a preference for their mother's voice over their father's. Whether this is because of differences in their familiarity with the voices or the characteristics of them (for example, male voices are deeper) is not known at this time.

In addition to voices, fetuses hear the mother's heartbeat and sounds of digestion, as well as other outside sounds. In fact, in the first few months after birth many babies seem to need a certain level of noise to go to sleep, perhaps because they were used to that level of noise before they were born. Many parents resort to leaving a vacuum cleaner running or putting the baby near a running clothes dryer to provide a level of background sound. Teddy bears that have built-in "heart sounds" also can help soothe babies.

SMELL

Babies are born with a functioning sense of smell and show preference for some smells over others. By 4 days of age, even bottle-fed infants show a preference for the smell of breast milk (Marlier & Schaal, 2005). They also know their mother's smell from very early in their lives (Lipsitt & Rovee-Collier, 2012) and research has shown that babies who are being breast-fed recognize their mother's scent within the first 2 weeks of life (Vaglio, 2009). Babies are even soothed by the scent of clothes that their mother has been wearing (Sullivan & Toubas, 1998).

TASTE

Infants prefer sweet taste and react negatively to salty, sour, and bitter tastes (Bezerra, Russo, & Alves, 2013; Rosenstein & Oster, 2005). Mother's milk is sweet, so this draws the baby to the food and to the mother. Sweet taste is widely used to calm infants and reduce their pain response when they must undergo a painful procedure (Harrison, Beggs, & Stevens, 2012). In addition, mother's milk, as well as amniotic fluid, can carry chemosensory molecules from the foods the mother eats, imparting the flavor from that food (Fifer, Monk, & Grose-Fifer, 2004). This means that babies are introduced to the tastes of their local foods even before birth, and there is evidence that early experience with particular tastes becomes acceptance or preference for such tastes later in life (Mennella, Griffin, & Beauchamp, 2004).

©iStockphoto.com/bo1982

Taste preferences. A mother's amniotic fluid can carry chemosensory molecules from food that she eats. These molecules, in turn, can stimulate the fetus's smell and taste receptors before birth. After an infant is born, the infant's food environment continues to reinforce those cultural tastes and smells.

T ☐ F ☐ Infants are born with a preference for the foods common in their culture. **True**

TOUCH

Touch can be very soothing. In one study, babies who were held in skin-to-skin contact with their mothers cried less when given a slightly painful medical procedure (in this case, it was a heel stick to extract a small amount of blood) (Gray, Watt, & Blass, 2000). Many adults who have had a massage know how relaxing it can be. Infant massage is part of the everyday experience of babies in many parts of the world. In India, Uganda, and Bali, for example, babies are given a massage with oil after their bath and before they are put to bed (Field, 2014). Tiffany Field (2014) and her colleagues have found that infant massage improves growth and effectively soothes babies of all ages, even premature ones. Massage with children can be helpful in improving conditions that range from anxiety (Field, 2010) to HIV (Diego, Hernandez-Reif, Field, Friedman, & Shaw, 2001). The research by Field and her colleagues appears to show that not only can massage make you feel better, but it also can improve your body's ability to fight off the effects of disease.

CROSS-MODAL TRANSFER OF PERCEPTION

So far we have described how infants perceive the world through their individual senses. However, the senses also have to work together. For example, if you closed your eyes and touched an apple, when you opened your eyes and someone showed you an apple and an orange, you would know you had just touched the apple and not the orange by simply looking at the two. In other words, your perception of "apple" crosses from the tactile mode to the visual mode.

Infants, even from birth, show some aspects of cross-modal transfer of perception, but their abilities are limited in a number of ways. They can visually recognize something they have only touched and not seen (as in the apple example above), but they cannot recognize by touch something they have just seen but not previously touched (Sann & Streri, 2007). These abilities are strengthened as infants grow older and have more experience with seeing, touching, hearing, smelling, and tasting many things in their world.

Many toys designed for young children incorporate features that let them use their senses to explore the world. **Active Learning: How Toys Stimulate Babies' Senses** lets you identify some of these features for yourself in a popular type of infant's toy.

Active LEARNING

How Toys Stimulate Babies' Senses

This toy can be held by any of the handles, all of which have different textures. When a baby shakes it, it makes a soft chiming sound. Find at least five different ways in which this toy provides appropriate sensory stimulation for a baby.

Possible answers: 1. The high contrast between black and white attracts babies' eyes to the bull's eye on top. **2.** Different textures develop the sense of touch. **3.** The sound it makes stimulates hearing. **4.** Babies are attracted to faces, so they will be drawn to the butterfly's face. **5.** It is entirely soft and therefore safe for a baby to use. **6.** Babies can hold the cube by its handles with two hands, helping with coordination.

To review, we have seen that infants prefer to look at faces, naturally "look you in the eye," recognize their mother's voice, and prefer her scent and the taste of her milk. Clearly from the minute we are born, we are well equipped to enter a social world, and we are prepared to form relationships with those who take care of us. Although true attachment will not develop until later in the first year of life, as we discuss in Chapter 10, infants prefer the special people who care for them, and they have inborn mechanisms that draw these people into relationships with them.

CHECK YOUR UNDERSTANDING

1. How does each of the senses develop during infancy?
2. How do infant sensory preferences connect infants to their caregivers?
3. What is cross-modal transfer of perception?

BODY GROWTH AND CHANGES

6.3 How do children's bodies change from infancy through adolescence?

In this section, we discuss how bodily proportions change from the large head and small body of the infant to adult proportions. During middle childhood, bones lengthen, muscles strengthen, and baby teeth are replaced with adult ones. Finally, we discuss the major changes that happen to the body during puberty as children move into sexual maturity.

CHANGING BODILY PROPORTIONS

Of course all babies are beautiful, but beyond that they share some physical characteristics that draw us to them. When they are born, the comparative proportions of their heads and bodies are very different from those of older children and adults. A baby's head is very large in comparison to his small, helpless-looking body. If you do the activity described in **Active Learning: Head-to-Body Proportions** with a young child, you will see for yourself how short the child's arms are in comparison to the size of her head.

Active LEARNING

ACTIVE LEARNING VIDEO ▲

Three children at different developmental stages demonstrate head-to-body proportions.

Head-to-Body Proportions

Take your right hand and reach over your head to touch your left ear. No problem, right? Now ask a toddler or preschooler to do the same thing, helping her if necessary. How far does the child's hand get over her head? Most likely the child's arm will not reach the opposite ear because her head is much larger in relation to the rest of her body than the head of an adult is to his body.

As children mature, their arms and legs lengthen, and the rest of the body catches up in size to the head. This fact has been used in some countries as a rough test of the child's readiness to attend school. In one area of Tanzania, where there were inadequate birth records to document children's ages, this test was used to determine the level of children's physical maturation and therefore their readiness to start school (Beasley et al., 2000).

To prepare for this activity, or, if you do not have access to a child, you can watch the video of this Active Learning.

In addition to a large head, infants also have large eyes, a small nose and mouth, and relatively fat cheeks. There may be an evolutionary reason for this appearance. It makes babies appear cute, and we are attracted to taking care of them (Vance, 2007). This attraction is even stronger for women who have larger amounts of reproductive hormones in their system (Sprengelmeyer et al., 2009). A secret that few parents will reveal is that some aspects of baby care can be very unpleasant because they must deal with all kinds of bodily fluids, smells, and being up half the night, but as a new mother once wrote: "It's a good thing God made babies so cute; otherwise you would send them right back to the hospital!" We protect and nurture our babies in spite of the difficulties of caring for them in part because of the effect that their bodily proportions have on us.

Growth during infancy and until age 2 is very rapid. The average infant doubles her birth weight by about 5 months of age, and triples it by her first birthday. During this same time,

Moodboard/Cultura/Getty Images

Infant facial features. Do you recognize in this photo the facial features we find so endearing in infants? An infant's large head, round face, and big eyes are characteristics that attract us and motivate us to care for the infant.

the infant will add about 10 inches or 50% to her length at birth. If the same rate of growth applied to the average 11- or 12-year-old, it would be terrifying, but after the second birthday, growth slows. Two-year-olds are approximately half the height they will be in adulthood, so to predict a child's adult height, you could double the height of that 2-year-old. However, a better indicator would be to look at the height of family members. Assuming adequate nutrition, height is highly genetic, so it is very likely that a child's eventual height will fall somewhere within the range of the height of her close relatives.

As children's rate of growth slows in early childhood, their trunk and limbs catch up in size with the earlier growth of their head so their bodily proportions change and become more similar to those of an adult. Figure 6.7 shows how the size of the head relative to the body changes between birth and 15-1/2 years of age. The growth centers found at ends of bones will remain soft until sometime in adolescence, when the ends will harden and growth will stop.

During early childhood, the proportion of body fat and muscle in the body also is changing. The layer of subcutaneous fat in a 5-year-old is only about one-half the thickness of the layer of fat in a 9-month-old infant, so young children lose the chubbiness we associate with infants (Huelke, 1998). Both boys and girls lose fat and gain muscle during early childhood, but in slightly different proportions. By the time they are 5 years old, girls have slightly more fat than boys, and boys have slightly more muscle (Sakai, Demura, & Fujii, 2012).

Children settle down into a steady growth rate in middle childhood, adding on average a little over 2 inches in height each year, and gaining about 6.5 pounds (American Academy of Pediatrics, 2004). Although growth charts usually show growth curves as a smooth and continuous function, growth typically occurs in growth spurts of about 24 hours, followed by days or weeks of no growth (Adolph & Berger, 2006).

Adolescent growth spurt
The period of rapid increase in height and weight that occurs in early adolescence.

As children approach adolescence, growth hormones work together with sex hormones (particularly estrogen for adolescent females and testosterone for adolescent males) to produce another period of rapid increase in height in both girls and boys known as the **adolescent growth spurt.** Girls, on average, begin their growth spurt at about 9 to 10 years of age, and boys typically start about 2 years later (Malina, Bouchard, & Oded, 2004). At the peak of the adolescent growth spurt, a young person can add 4 inches in height in a single year. This pubertal growth spurt ends by about age 15 for girls and age 16 or 17 for boys. **Active Learning: Your Growth in Childhood** guides you in looking back at your own physical development during childhood.

Active LEARNING

Your Growth in Childhood

Families often keep track of their children's growth. See whether your family kept a baby book detailing your growth in the early years. If your parents later marked your growth on a wall, look at the rate of change over time. Were there some periods of more rapid growth compared to other times in your life? If possible, compare these changes to those of your siblings or of your friends or classmates. At what points were girls taller than boys? When did this change?

FIGURE 6.7

Changing bodily proportions. As children move through early childhood, their head, which was disproportionately large in infancy, grows less rapidly than their trunk and lower extremities resulting in body proportions that look more like those of an adult.

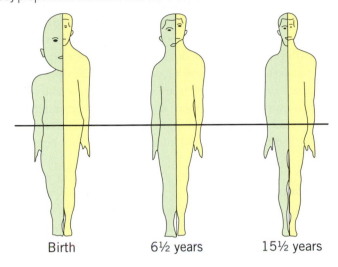

Birth   6½ years   15½ years

SOURCE: Burdi, Huelke, Snyder, & Lowrey (1969).

TEETH

As the body grows and proportions change, the face changes as well. One factor in this change is the development of teeth. Babies are usually born toothless (a fact that most nursing mothers appreciate), but within the first year, baby teeth emerge. However, these baby teeth will not last very long. Permanent teeth begin to push up through the gums, loosening their baby teeth. It is a very exciting development for children when, at about age 6, they lose their first baby tooth. Their molars (the teeth in the back of their mouth) don't normally loosen until around ages 10 to 12. Why do we lose our first teeth? Unlike bones, teeth do not grow. Instead, our bodies develop much larger teeth under the gums that eventually push out and replace the smaller ones.

SEXUAL DEVELOPMENT

Prepubescence refers to the years immediately before puberty when hormonal changes begin. The earliest events in the pubertal sequence occur in middle childhood, sooner than many people realize. The pubertal changes and range of ages at which they typically occur are shown in Figure 6.8. At some point between ages 5 and 9, the adrenal glands increase production of androgens in both boys and girls. These hormones will later be linked to the growth of facial hair and increased muscle mass in boys and to the growth of pubic and armpit hair in both boys and girls. A few years later, estrogen produced by the girl's ovaries will trigger changes in the growth of her uterus, vagina, and breasts and will cause fat to accumulate in the distribution pattern typical of females. Estrogen is also necessary to support the girl's menstrual cycles, which can begin as early as age 10.

Losing baby teeth. Do you remember feeling as excited about losing your baby teeth as this girl appears to be? Notice that her two bottom teeth are new ones coming in and are larger than the others.

Prepubescence The period before puberty when

Puberty The physical changes that occur in adolescence and make an individual capable of sexual reproduction.

Primary sex characteristics Physical characteristics directly involved in reproduction.

Menarche A girl's first menstrual period.

Spermarche The beginning of production of viable sperm.

Secondary sex characteristics Physical characteristics associated with gender that do not directly affect the sex organs.

Puberty, the physical changes that occur in adolescence and make an individual capable of sexual reproduction, begins (and therefore also ends) earlier for girls than for boys. During puberty, primary and secondary sex characteristics develop. **Primary sex characteristics** involve changes that occur in the organs necessary for reproduction—the vagina, ovaries, and uterus of the female, and the testes and penis of the male. For females, this process culminates in **menarche** (the first menstrual flow or *period*) and the beginning of ovulation. For males, it culminates in **spermarche,** or the ability to produce viable sperm. Characteristics that are associated with gender but do not directly involve the sex organs are **secondary sex characteristics**. Breast development in females, deepening of the voice in males, and growth of pubic and underarm hair in both genders are examples of secondary sex characteristics. They are important outward signs to others that a child is becoming physically mature. These changes often affect the way that both peers and adults interact with a young person. As young people look less like children and more like adults, they tend to be treated more like adults.

The Timing of Puberty

Many factors, including diet, health, body type, weight, and racial background, affect the timing of puberty. Heredity also plays a role because daughters often go through puberty at about the same age their mothers did (Ersoy, Balkan, Gunay, & Egemen, 2005). There also are some consistent racial and ethnic differences for both boys and girls. On average, African American girls and boys mature earlier than Hispanic children who develop earlier than non-Hispanic White children (Herman-Giddens et al., 2012; Herman-Giddens, 2013).

Girls from families with more social and economic resources reach menarche 3 months to 3 years before girls from disadvantaged families, perhaps because of better diet and better overall health in more well-to-do families (Parent et al., 2003). Chemicals found in the environment called *endocrine disruptors* also may play a role in the timing of puberty because of their effect on the hormonal (or endocrine) system of the body. You read about the effects these chemicals have on prenatal development in Chapter 5. Endocrine disruptors include a wide range of chemicals that are found in our food and drinking water, as well as in air, soil, house dust, and various household and commercial chemicals (Meeker, 2012). They have been implicated in lowering the age of puberty, as have hormones in the milk and meat that we eat (Daniel & Balog, 2009). Interestingly, some studies have found that the same chemicals associated with early puberty in girls are associated with delayed puberty in boys (Meeker, 2012).

Another individual characteristic that affects pubertal timing is body fat. A critical level of body fat is necessary for girls to maintain regular menstrual periods. That is why women who are anorexic, or who exercise so strenuously that their reserves of body fat drop to extremely low levels, may have irregular periods or stop menstruating altogether. Although the relationship is not as well established for boys, there is some evidence that body mass index also is related to the timing of puberty for boys, but again evidence points to the opposite result. For boys, being overweight may *delay* the onset of puberty, although the reason for this delay is still unclear (Solorzano & McCartney, 2010; Kaplowitz, 2008).

In a small percentage of girls, the earliest physical changes in the pubertal sequence, such as the beginning of breast buds and appearance of pubic hair, have been reported as early as 6 or 7 years of age (Nield, Cakan, & Kamat, 2007). This occurrence is known as **precocious puberty** (Parent et al., 2003). Rare medical conditions, such as brain tumors or exposure to endocrine disruptors, can be responsible for these early changes, but in most cases the girls are simply the earliest-maturing girls in their peer group (Kaplowitz, 2008).

Because the physical changes of puberty have such a profound effect on how others see the young person, undergoing these changes relatively earlier—or considerably later—than age-mates can have a significant impact on development. Early maturing boys tend to have a positive self-image and feel good about themselves in a number of ways, including being more self-confident and seeing themselves as independent. Because boys who mature

Precocious puberty A condition in which pubertal changes begin at an extraordinarily early age (as young as 6 or 7 years of age).

FIGURE 6.8

The pubertal sequence. During puberty, sexual development occurs in a set sequence of changes, the timing and speed of which vary from person to person. This chart shows a typical sequence and normal range of development for the milestones of sexual development.

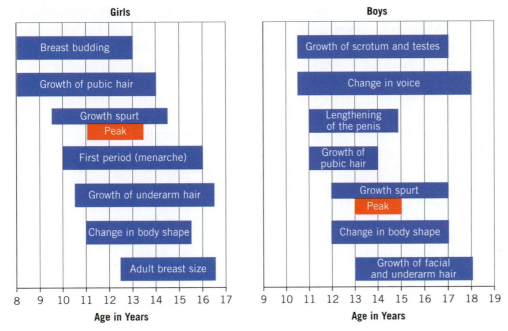

SOURCE: Reprinted with permission from the Merck Manual Home Health Handbook, edited by Robert Porter. Copyright 2013 by Merck Sharp & Dohme Corp., a subsidiary of Merck & Co, Inc, Whitehouse Station, NJ.

earlier are taller and heavier than their peers in early adolescence, they are more likely to be athletes and this gives them a lot of status in the peer group (Hyde & Gengenbach, 2007). However, early maturing boys tend to spend their time with older peers because their physical development is a better match with that of older adolescents, and this can expose them to behaviors they are not ready to handle (Goldstein, 2011; Mendle, Turkheimer, & Emery, 2007). For instance, they are also more likely than their on-time peers to begin using drugs or alcohol (Faden, Ruffin, Newes-Adeyi, & Chen, 2010; Westling, Andrews, Hampson, & Peterson, 2008). These risks are even greater for early-maturing adolescents growing up in disadvantaged neighborhoods or with parents who are harsh or inconsistent in their discipline (Ge, Brody, Conger, Simons, & Murry, 2002). It has been easy to think that the relative psychological immaturity of early maturers or their association with older peers is responsible for the problematic behaviors we see. However, it is possible that it is child characteristics that existed before the onset of puberty that are responsible for the chance of a young person engaging in risky behaviors. In support of this idea, there is evidence from longitudinal research that boys who experience early puberty also had greater behavioral difficulties and poorer psychosocial adjustment earlier in their childhood (Mensah et al., 2013).

Late-maturing boys, on the other hand, have a more negative self-concept and are more likely to feel inadequate and rejected. Consequently, they may suffer from depression (Kaltiala-Heino, Kosunen, & Rimpela, 2003) or engage in alcohol or substance use as a way of compensating for their low social status (Weichold, Silbereisen, & Schmitt-Rodermund, 2003).

When a girl physically matures earlier than the other girls her age, it often sets her apart and isolates her from them. It might even inspire a bit of jealousy or envy (Reynolds & Juvonen, 2011). Attention from boys (especially older boys) can make these girls targets of peer rumors and gossip (Reynolds & Juvonen, 2011). Early-maturing girls have an

T ☐ F ☐ Adolescent girls who go through puberty earlier than their peers are happier than girls who go through puberty later. **False**

experience more anxiety in social situations because of their increased self-consciousness (Blumenthal et al., 2011). Furthermore, because girls physically mature on average about 2 years before boys do, boys the same age may be intimidated by a girl who is becoming a woman in front of their eyes (Reynolds & Juvonen, 2011).

Similar to what we saw with early maturing boys, this social isolation from age-mates might drive the early-maturing girl to spend time with older adolescents (Weichold et al., 2003). A physically mature but chronologically young adolescent girl may be particularly susceptible to peer pressure to drink, smoke, or be sexually active because she does not yet have the cognitive maturity to know whether, when, and how to say no—and to stick to it (Weichold et al., 2003).

It is girls who mature at the same time as their age-mates who appear to have the advantage. They fit in comfortably with girls their own age and also with most of the boys, and they find support from a peer group that is dealing with the same issues and concerns they have. Girls who mature slightly later than average do not gain weight when their early-developing peers do so they remain relatively thin, which fits well with the cultural stereotype of what an attractive young woman should look like. Consequently, these girls tend to have positive body images (Mendle et al., 2007).

The good news regarding pubertal timing is that by the end of high school, almost all adolescents have undergone the physical changes of puberty, and a distinction between early and late maturers no longer has much meaning (Natsuaki, Biehl, & Ge, 2009). Unless the differences in timing of physical maturation have been responsible for other risky behaviors that become problematic in and of themselves (Copeland et al., 2010; van Jaarsveld, Fidler, Simon, & Wardle, 2007), adolescents are again on a pretty level playing field in this regard. **Active Learning: Timing of Puberty** helps you reflect on your own experiences as you went through puberty.

Active LEARNING

Timing of Puberty

Think back to when you went through puberty. (Some of you, especially boys, may still be experiencing some of these changes such as growth in height and increase in facial hair.) Do you remember your changes occurring before, after, or at the same time as those of your peers? When you compared yourself with others, were those comparisons favorable or not, and why? You might want to discuss your experiences with others to find out more about the range of ways in which adolescents experience puberty and variations in its timing, as well as the possible impact of these differences on adolescent development.

TRUE/FALSE VIDEO ▲

T ☐ F ☐ In the United States, 90% of adolescents between the ages of 15 and 19 have had sex at least once. **False**

Risks of Sexual Maturation: Pregnancy and STDs

After adolescents go through puberty, males can produce viable sperm, and females can become pregnant. For most adolescents, their growing interest in the opposite sex eventually leads to romantic relationships, and for some of those adolescents, it also leads to the decision to become sexually active. In 2015, in the United States, 41% of all high school students reported that they had had sexual intercourse at least once (CDC, 2015j). However, U.S. teens are waiting longer to become sexually active than they have in the past. Sexually inexperienced teens report not having sex because it is against their religion or morals, they did not want to become pregnant, or they hadn't yet found the right person (Guttmacher

FIGURE 6.9

Declining teen birthrate. The teen birthrate in the United States has continued to decline in recent years, reaching a historically low level in 2014.

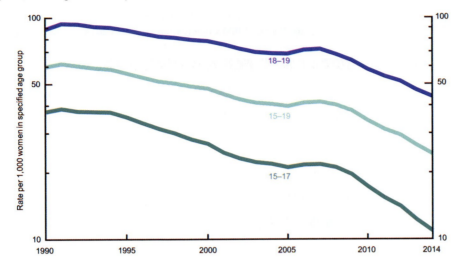

SOURCE: Hamilton, Martin, Osterman, & Curtin (2015).

Institute, 2014). When adolescents do become sexually active, their decision carries with it the risks of becoming pregnant and of contracting a sexually transmitted infection.

Teen pregnancy. In 2014, the teen birthrate in the United States reached a historic low of 24.2 births per thousand teens age 15–19, a rate 61% lower than in 1991 (see Figure 6.9; Hamilton, Martin, Osterman, & Curtin, 2015). Although the rates for Black and Hispanic teens are more than double the rate for non-Hispanic White teens, all groups have decreased during this time. Almost the entire decline in pregnancies among older teens (18 and 19 years of age) can be attributed to an increased use of contraceptives. Among younger teens, about one-quarter of the decline was due to reduced levels of sexual activity, and the remainder to increased reliance on contraception (Guttmacher Institute, 2014). As you can see from Figure 6.10, despite the decline, the adolescent pregnancy rate in the United States is still considerably higher than in other Western and industrialized nations (World Data Bank, 2015; Hamilton & Ventura, 2012).

What accounts for this difference between countries? U.S. teens and European teens have similar levels of sexual activity, but European teens are more likely to use contraception than their U.S. counterparts and to use more effective methods (Guttmacher Institute, 2014). Schalet (2011) attributed the lower rates of adolescent births and abortions among adolescents in the Netherlands to several cultural differences. Dutch adolescents are less likely than American adolescents to grow up in poverty, and poverty is one risk factor for early childbearing. They also are more likely to have been educated on the use of contraception and to encounter fewer barriers if they want contraception or abortion services than American adolescents. Another important cultural difference is that Dutch parents are more accepting of adolescent sexuality in the context of a committed relationship which makes it easier for their adolescents to ask for advice or assistance when they need it. Schalet (2011) has argued that giving adolescents a sense of sexual autonomy gives them a greater sense of control over their sexuality and enables them to make better decisions.

Why is it so important to continue to work toward reducing the rate of teen pregnancy even further? This is because having a child during the teen years has implications for the mother, her child, and society. Only half of young women who give birth during high school go on to graduate, compared with 90% of those who do not give birth, and failure to graduate leads to lower incomes and higher rates of poverty. The children of teen mothers suffer more

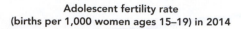

FIGURE 6.10

International comparison of teen birthrate. The adolescent birthrate in the United States is much higher than in other industrialized countries. What accounts for this large difference?

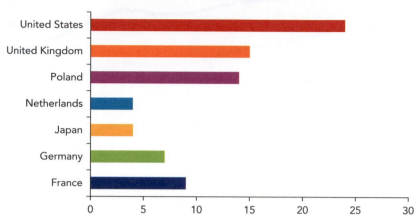

Adolescent fertility rate
(births per 1,000 women ages 15–19) in 2014

SOURCE: World Data Bank (2015).

Teen pregnancy. This teen mother is unusual because she is attending college. Only half of teens who give birth while still in high school will finish high school.

health problems. They also are more likely to be put in jail during their teen years, to be unemployed, and daughters of teen mothers are more likely to give birth themselves during their teen years. The cost to society of these problems plus increased foster care placement for the children of teenage mothers is estimated to be at least $9.4 billion a year (CDC, 2016a).

Approaches to reducing teen pregnancy in the United States have included school-based clinic services, mentoring and role-modeling programs, self-esteem initiatives, and opportunity development programs. Child Trends, a nonprofit and nonpartisan research center, assessed a wide range of interventions and found that the most successful ones included sex education and HIV education, engaged teens in school-based and outside activities, or were early childhood programs that lifted children's abilities and aspirations (Manlove et al., 2002). Allen, Seitz, and Apfel (2007) have suggested that the only effective approach will target the whole person instead of trying to deal with adolescents as a "bundle of sexual urges to be controlled" (p. 197). They suggest that we need to find ways to build competencies that protect the adolescent not only from risky sexual activity but also from a range of other risky behaviors.

Sexually transmitted infection (STI) An infection caused by a microorganism that is transmitted by direct sexual contact.

Sexually transmitted disease (STD) A pathology that can result from a sexually transmitted infection.

STIs and STDs. Teens who are sexually active also risk contracting a **sexually transmitted infection (STI)** or a **sexually transmitted disease (STD).** Although these terms are sometimes used interchangeably, a sexually transmitted infection is caused by a microorganism passed from one individual to another through intimate contact, while a sexually transmitted disease is the pathology that can result from such an infection (Shuford, 2008). The CDC (2013c) estimates that there are about 19 million *new* sexually transmitted diseases each year, and almost half occur in young people between the ages of 15 and 24 (see Figure 6.11). Of course, many cases go undiagnosed and are never reported. It might surprise you to learn that

FIGURE 6.11

Rates of STIs in different populations. Adolescents and young adults are at greater risk of contracting a number of sexually transmitted infections than the general population, as shown by these figures from the Centers for Disease Control and Prevention.

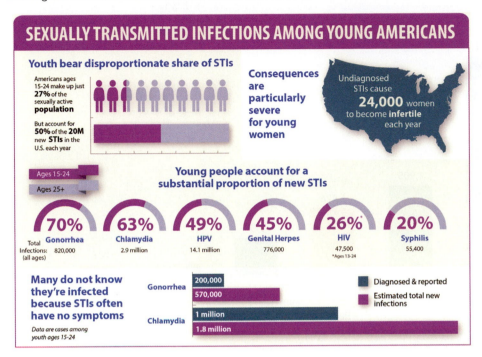

SOURCE: CDC (2013c).

prevalence is high even among adolescents who have only recently become sexually active (26%) and those who had only a single sexual partner (20%) (Forhan et al., 2009).

Many STIs do not produce symptoms that make the individual aware he or she should seek medical treatment, and some may not require treatment. For instance, 90% of new cases of an HPV (human papillomavirus) infection clear without treatment within 2 years (National Cancer Institute, 2010). However, these infections can go on to produce cancerous cells. An estimated 12,000 women are diagnosed with cervical cancer annually and 4,000 die from it (National Cancer Institute, 2010).

In June 2006, the Food and Drug Administration approved a vaccine that can prevent the types of HPV most likely to lead to cervical cancer. Since the vaccine was introduced, the prevalence of those types of HPV declined 56% among teen girls between ages 14 and 19 (Reagan-Steiner et al., 2015). Unfortunately, despite the evidence of its effectiveness, voluntary vaccination rates remain relatively low. In 2014, 40% of females between ages 13 and 17 had received the three doses required for full protection (CDC, 2015l). Increasing the rate to 80% (a target other countries have met) would prevent 50,000 girls from developing cervical cancer during their lifetime (CDC, 2015a). The most frequent reasons given by parents for not having their daughters vaccinated were parents' belief that their daughters did not need the vaccine or were not sexually active, or the parents felt they did not have enough information to make an informed decision (Wong et al., 2011). However, 13% of teens become sexually active before age 15 (Guttmacher Institute, 2012). Because early vaccination is important for full protection, parents need to be realistic in deciding if and when they will have their adolescent daughters vaccinated. The Centers for Disease Control and Prevention (2015f) also recommend the vaccine for boys, preferably when they are 11 or 12 years old. Each year over 9,000 men develop cancers related to the HPV virus.

Other commonly occurring STIs include bacterial infections like chlamydia, gonorrhea, and syphilis. Each can be treated and cured, but if left untreated they can lead to serious

FIGURE 6.12

Estimated new HIV diagnoses among youth ages 13 to 24 in the United States, by race/ethnicity and sex in 2014. Young men are at greater risk of being newly infected with HIV than young women, and this risk is substantially greater for young Black men. Inadequate sex education, particularly for gay and bisexual men, low rates of HIV testing, and low rates of condom use are all contributing factors to this high infection rate.

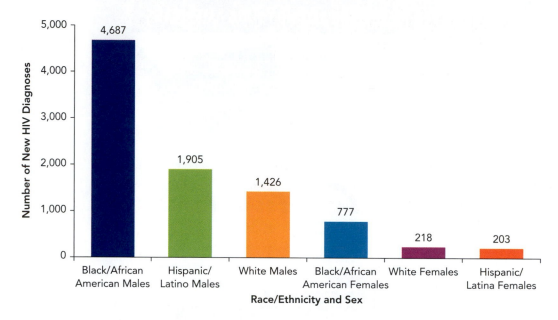

NOTE: Subpopulations representing 2% or less of the overall U.S. epidemic are not represented in this chart.

SOURCE: CDC (2016f).

complications, including infertility and death in the case of syphilis (CDC, 2014h; Guttmacher Institute, 2012). Although adolescents 14 and older can obtain treatment for STIs without parental consent in all 50 states, they may not know where to get the care they need, may not be able to afford it, or may be afraid that if they get treatment, their treatment will not remain confidential (Forhan et al., 2009).

It is a different story with viral infections, such as HIV/AIDS, hepatitis B, and herpes, which can be treated but not cured (Guttmacher Institute, 2012). In 2014, young people between the ages of 13 and 24 years of age accounted for an estimated 22% of the new HIV infections (CDC, 2016f). Eighty percent of this group were gay and bisexual males. However, when we talk about the number of cases of AIDS among adolescents, we need to remember this infection takes about 10 years to develop. Even if an individual is infected while an adolescent, symptoms may not become evident until the person is in his or her 20s, so the eventual rate of HIV infections may be considerably higher. Estimates are that 44% of young people infected with HIV do not know they are infected (CDC, 2016f). Figure 6.12 shows how the rate of new infections differs by the race/ethnicity and sex of the young person. Despite the progress we have made in developing drugs that help extend the life of infected individuals, AIDS is still an epidemic.

CHECK YOUR UNDERSTANDING

1. How do bodily proportions change from infancy through middle childhood?
2. What physical changes happen during prepubescence?
3. What are the consequences of early and late puberty for boys and girls?
4. Why are teen pregnancy and birth rates higher in the United States than in other developed countries?

MOTOR DEVELOPMENT

6.4 **What factors influence and shape motor development?**

As children's bodies grow and change, their physical abilities are also developing. In this section, we examine the development of motor skills. We begin with a description of babies' first movements: the reflexes. We then describe how the myelination of the nervous system plays a large role in determining the sequence in which motor milestones are achieved. Finally, we discuss other factors, such as physical activity, that influence the development of motor skills in older children and adolescents.

INFANT REFLEXES

Newborns can't move around on their own and they don't have much control over their limbs, but from the time they are born they have a set of involuntary, patterned motor responses called **reflexes** that are controlled by the lower brain centers. These help them respond to some of the stimuli in their environment.

Reflexes Patterned, involuntary motor responses that are controlled by the lower brain centers.

The reflexes are hardwired into the newborn's nervous system, so they don't need to be learned. As the higher centers of the brain develop and take over from the lower centers in the first few months of life, most of these reflexes disappear on a predictable timetable (see Table 6.2) and are replaced by voluntary and intentional actions. For instance, if you gently touch a newborn's cheek, she will reflexively turn in the direction of the touch which puts her in position to nurse. It doesn't take very long, however, for even a young infant to learn the signals indicating that she is about to be fed. At that point, she will begin to turn in the direction of her caregiver as soon as she senses that it is mealtime, but this now is a voluntary action.

TABLE 6.2

Newborn Reflexes

Reflex	Description	When This Reflex Disappears
Sucking Reflex	When something touches the roof of the baby's mouth, her lips close, and she will suck reflexively.	About 2 months
Crawling Reflex	When the baby is placed on his tummy, his legs will make crawling motions even though he is not able to move forward.	About 2 months
Moro Reflex (or Startle Reflex)	When a baby loses support and feels like she is falling or hears a loud sound, she will flail her arms and legs outward. Most babies will cry when startled and then will pull their limbs back in.	About 3 months
Stepping Reflex	If the baby's weight is supported but his feet touch the ground, he will lift and set his feet in a "walking" motion.	About 3 months
Tonic Neck Reflex	When a baby is placed on her back and her head is turned to the side, she will stretch out the arm and leg in the direction she is facing and pull inward the opposite arm and leg, often called a "fencer's pose."	About 4 months
Babinski Reflex	When the side of a baby's foot is stroked, his big toe points up and the other toes will fan out.	About 4 months
Rooting Reflex	If the baby's cheek is gently stroked, she will turn in the direction of the touch and begin to suck with her mouth.	About 4 months
Palmar Grasp	When the baby's palm is touched with another's index finger, he will clench the finger.	About 6 months
Gag Reflex	The baby's reflexive gag helps prevent choking.	This reflex does not disappear.
Blinking Reflex	The baby will blink when the eye is touched or exposed suddenly to bright light.	This reflex does not disappear.

Cephalocaudal development of motor skills. The cephalocaudal direction of myelination results in infants gaining control of their bodies in sequence from the head down to the toes. The effects of the cephalocaudal direction of myelination are illustrated in the following photo series.

Ross Whitaker/The Image Bank/ Getty Images

© iStockphoto.com/Michael Mattner

1. Head and neck: Parents of newborn infants must be careful to support the baby's head, but as myelination proceeds downward, babies become able to hold up their head independently.

2. Neck and shoulders: A newborn placed on his stomach will remain in that position, but as myelination moves down the neck, the baby will be able to raise his head to see the world.

3. Shoulders: As the shoulders come under control, the baby will reach the next milestone: rolling over (from stomach to back and from back to stomach).

Jonas Unruh/E+/Getty Images

4. Arms and chest: With control of this region, the baby will be able to use his arms to push up from his stomach to survey a larger area around him. However, his legs are still flat to the floor.

5. Hips: When the hips and back come under the baby's control, she can now begin to sit up, at first with support and then independently.

6. Thighs: With control of the legs, babies can pull their legs underneath them and begin to crawl. Often babies will initially crawl backward, in part because their control of their arms is greater than their control of their legs (Greene, 2004).

7. Lower legs: With control traveling from the thighs to the lower part of the legs, babies begin to pull up on furniture to a standing position.

JGI/Jamie Grill/Blend Images/Getty Images

David Young-Wolff/The Image Bank/Getty Images

8. Feet: Control of the feet is needed to walk independently. At first babies walk with feet wide apart and hands raised to help with balance. As they gain more control of their feet and toes and better balance, their gait becomes more like that of an adult.

©iStockphoto.com/Julie Fairman, ©iStockphoto.com/dustin steller

Proximodistal development of motor skills. Look at how you hold your pen or pencil. Which fingers do you use, and how do you use them? Compare how your hand works to how these children are able to use their hands. Why do you think that preschoolers are often given "fat crayons" to use instead of pens?

Reflexes and voluntary behavior are not entirely distinct types of response. There is a continuum that represents different mixes of reflexive and voluntary behavior that we see as motor development proceeds (Anderson, Roth, & Campos, 2005). However, if a reflex is missing or fails to disappear when it should, this can be an indication of a neurological problem, and the infant should be assessed by a doctor.

DEVELOPMENT OF MOTOR SKILLS

Children are developing both **gross motor skills**, which involve the large muscle groups of the body (for example, the legs and arms) and **fine motor skills**, which involve small movements, mostly of the hands and fingers, but also of the lips and tongue. Conscious motor activity is largely controlled by the motor cortex, located in the rear portion of the frontal lobe. The motor cortex runs across the top of the brain, from ear to ear.

Myelination of Motor Neurons

The brain connects through the spinal cord to all of the neurons in the body. As we discussed previously, the nervous system works more efficiently when neurons have been coated with the fatty substance known as myelin. This is true not only for the neurons in the brain but also for the motor neurons in the body. Myelination of motor neurons is far from complete at birth. This fatty coating, the myelin sheath, is set down in the nervous system in the body in two directions: from the head downward (in a *cephalocaudal* direction, from head to tail) and from the torso out to the extremities of the fingers and toes (in a **proximodistal** direction, from the center of the body out toward the extremities). Infants gain control of their bodies in a sequence that reflects these patterns of myelination. We see this sequence of motor milestones in the information that many parents joyfully record in their baby books.

The proximodistal direction of myelination, from the central axis of the body out to the extremities, results in the following steps in motor development:

1. Torso: Babies will roll over, using control of their chest and shoulders.

2. Arms: Control of the arms begins with the ability to swipe at objects infants see. They become able to use their arms to push up from the ground, which eventually develops into crawling.

Gross motor skills Skills that involve the large muscle groups of the body—for example, the legs and arms.

Fine motor skills Skills that involve small movements, mostly of the hands and fingers, but also of the lips and tongue.

Proximodistal Development that proceeds from the central axis of the body toward the extremities.

3. Hands: When infants begin to purposefully grasp objects, they scoop objects with all their fingers up against their palms, in what is called the *palmar grasp.*

4. Fingers: As they gain control of their fingers, babies can use thumb and forefinger to pick up things as small as Cheerios. This is called the *pincer grasp.* Only later can they control the rest of their fingers to be able to use a *tripod grasp,* using thumb, forefinger, and middle finger to hold a pencil.

Motor skills interact with other areas of infant development. In a classic study, Eleanor Gibson related the development of crawling with the development of depth perception. She created what she called the *visual cliff,* a Plexiglas covered table shown in Figure 6.13 that gives the illusion that one side drops off from table level to floor level while actually keeping a baby safe from falling (Gibson & Walk, 1960). She found that about 4 to 6 weeks after babies learn to crawl they begin to refuse to crawl over the visual cliff. She argued that babies developed an awareness and fear of heights as a result of learning to crawl and experiencing the ups and downs that come with mobility. However, in more recent years, Adolph, Kretch, and Lobue (2014) have argued that infants' avoidance of the cliff is due to their growing ability to perceive the relationship between their own body and the environment. Once they begin to crawl, that experience increases infants' awareness of their own body and how it relates to the world around it so they know when they can master climbing down a cliff and when it is too high for them. When babies first begin to walk they must learn this all over again. Initially they walk right over the cliff (Kretch & Adolph, 2013).

The new ability to move around has other effects as well. Infants can now try to stay near their parents as attachment develops; they can explore more freely which increases learning; and they can get into more trouble which means that parents and others will do more to control their behavior.

Motor Development in Older Children

Both fine and gross motor skills show considerable development during early childhood and throughout the school years. Table 6.3 summarizes some of the changes typically shown between the ages of 3 and 10 years.

Fine motor skills enable the 3-year-old to hold a crayon using her fingers rather than her fist, to build a tower of blocks, and to use scissors to cut paper. Four-year-olds begin to feed and dress themselves, and color inside the lines (American Academy of Pediatrics, 2009a). During the school years, the development of fine motor skills is reflected in improvements in handwriting, both printing and cursive, and in the detail and complexity children incorporate into their drawings. Many children also now enjoy activities that rely on fine motor skills and good eye-hand coordination, such as beading, sewing, building models, and playing complex video games.

New gross motor skills for 3- and 4-year-olds typically include running, jumping, hopping, and riding a tricycle. When children begin school, their gross motor skills are still relatively undeveloped, but by fifth or sixth grade, most have made great strides and their motor skills are almost as coordinated as those of an adult. They are increasingly able to control and coordinate parts of their body, and their flexibility, balance, reflexes, and strength all improve. Because the ligaments in their limbs are not yet firmly attached to the bones, children in middle childhood are quite flexible compared to children of other ages (Cain, 2005). For all these reasons, many enjoy participating in physical activities such as group and individual sports that depend on gross motor skills.

As children have become increasingly skilled at keyboarding, there has been a debate within the educational community about whether they still need to learn cursive writing. Some advocates make the philosophical argument that cursive is a skill all educated people

FIGURE 6.13

The visual cliff. Four to six weeks after they learn to crawl, infants begin to avoid crossing the apparent "cliff" in this apparatus designed by Eleanor Gibson to assess infants' depth perception.

Mark Richard/Photo Edit

should possess, but there also is brain research to support the idea that cursive writing affects brain functioning in a way that keyboarding does not. Think about the difference between shaping a complex series of curves, loops, and slants as you form a written sentence versus what is involved when you copy the same sentence by striking keys on a keyboard. Writing in cursive activates different circuits in the brain than keyboarding (Klemm, 2013) and the use of the fine motor skills and eye-hand coordination required by cursive writing promotes reading, writing, and cognitive skills (James & Engelhardt, 2012). William Klemm (2013), an advocate for cursive writing, has said it benefits brain development similar to the way learning to play a musical instrument does, but while not everyone can afford to take music lessons, everyone can use paper and pencil to write.

Physical activity is important for motor development of children at all ages. As schools cut back on recess time, it becomes even more important for families to ensure that their children are running, biking, and playing actively for their long-term health and the development of their muscles. The CDC (2015e) recommends that children take part in 60 minutes of exercise per day, including aerobic, muscle-strengthening, and bone-strengthening activities. These activities do not need to include intensive involvement in sports, unless a child loves sports. Walking to school, riding a bike, or raking leaves can all be sources of healthful exercise. Physical activity is related not only to optimal functioning of children's muscles but also to optimal functioning of their brains (Bear et al., 2007; Chaddock-Heyman, Hillman, Cohen, & Kramer, 2014; Hillman, Buck, Themanson, Pontifex, & Castelli, 2009). The message, then, is for children to walk away from the TV, computer, and video games and go outside to play.

T ☐ F ☐
Keyboarding is less effective than writing in cursive for promoting reading, writing, and cognitive skills. **True**

DEVELOPMENT IN ACTION VIDEO ▲

BODY AWARENESS

As young children gain more control over their bodies by walking, running, and hopping, and as they increase their ability to pick up and manipulate objects, they also develop their sense of

TABLE 6.3

Motor skill development. Children between the ages of 3 and 10 develop a wide range of fine motor and gross motor skills. As you review the developmental milestones in this table, think about the ways in which they enable children to interact more effectively with the environment while at the same time making them more independent.

Age	Fine Motor/Visual Perception	Gross Motor Skills
3 Years	• Picks up blocks • Places shapes in holes • Turns pages of a book • Paints at an easel	• Stands on one foot • Walks backwards and sideways • Jumps down from a step • Kicks a large ball with force
4 Years	• Holds a pencil in adult way • Copies a square accurately • Brings thumbs into opposition with each finger in turn • Colors inside lines	• Pedals a bicycle • Hops on the spot and along • Bounces a large ball • Runs smoothly
5–6 Years	• Picks up and replaces minute objects • Has good control when writing and drawing with pencils and paint brushes • Prefers to use dominant hand • Copies a square and triangle • Copies letters V, T, H, O, X, L, A, C, U, Y • Writes a few letters spontaneously • Draws a person with six or more body parts and facial features • Cuts out a simple picture • Draws a house with door, windows, roof, and chimney • Starts to color neatly within outlines • Counts fingers on one hand with index finger of the other hand • Prints first name	• Walks easily on a narrow line • Skips on alternate feet • Stands on one foot (right or left) for 8-10 seconds • Hops 7 to 10 feet forward on each foot • Catches a beanbag without trapping it against the body • Throws a beanbag onto a target 5 out of 10 times • Rides a two-wheeled bike without stabilizers • Walks downstairs alternating feet
6–7 Years	• Prints all numbers 1–9 without a model to copy (some may be reversed) • Prints first and last name • Discriminates left from right • Has good control over pencil, with change in direction • Threads small beads onto a cord confidently • Uses scissors to cut more complex shapes • Ties own shoelaces	• Catches a tennis ball two-handed, away from the body • Aims and throws accurately • Stands on either leg for 15–20 seconds • Walks along a narrow line on tiptoes • Jumps repeatedly with feet together • Skips with alternating feet
7–10 Years	• Prints all numbers and letters (without reversing any) • Becomes competent in cursive handwriting • Manipulates and places pegs competently in a peg board with either hand • Manipulates scissors competently	• Stands and balances on either leg for 30 seconds and beyond • Walks along a narrow line heel to toe • Hops repeatedly on either leg with controlled landing

SOURCES: Adapted from Bailey (2005) and Lammas & Poland (2014). Reprinted with permission from the authors.

Proprioception The sense of knowing where the parts of one's body are located in space without the need to look at them.

body awareness. Feedback from receptors in our joints, muscles, and ligaments travels to the part of the brain that controls movement to give us a sense of where the different parts of our body are in space without our needing to look at them. This sense is called **proprioception.** We usually are not aware of this type of information unless we consciously think about it. Were you thinking about where your feet were before you read that last sentence? Probably not. But you will need this information if you decide to stand up right now and walk across the room.

Young children must learn how to use this feedback to move effectively through their environment and control their motor activity. Until they do, their movement may appear clumsy or awkward, or they may have difficulty judging how much force or strength they need to accomplish a task. Children develop body awareness naturally as a part of their normal activity, but parents and caregivers can enhance this development with some of the simple games young children love to play. Simon Says ("Simon says do this. . . . Do this. . . . Do this") or the Hokey Pokey allow children to consciously move specific parts of their body and gain a sense of where they are in relationship to the rest of their body. Many people have enjoyed asking a toddler, "Where is your nose? Where are your ears?" and children delight in showing they know the answer. Body awareness also can be facilitated by structured activities, such as introducing children to simple forms of yoga (Wenig, 2007). Yoga can help children develop strength, flexibility, coordination, and body awareness while engaging in a relaxing and noncompetitive physical activity.

You can observe the development of body awareness in young children for yourself with the activity described in **Active Learning: Developing Body Awareness.**

Active LEARNING

ACTIVE LEARNING VIDEO ▲

Two-year-old Sabrina demonstrates her developing sense of body awareness.

Developing Body Awareness

Offer to play a variation of the game Simon Says with a child between ages 3 and 8. Tell the child that he or she should do the actions exactly as "Simon says." Begin by having the child do the movements with you as you say "Simon says touch your nose" or "Simon says touch your knees." Do this with about 10 body parts. Then just give the directions and allow the child to do the actions on his or her own without a model. Finally, ask the child to keep following the directions but with eyes closed. Body awareness is a sense of where your body is in space even when you can't see it, and this last task is much harder for a young child. Note how many errors the child makes in the three conditions. Does he or she have more difficulty touching different parts of the body with eyes closed? If you have a chance to try this activity with children of different ages, do you see differences in their ability to do the tasks as they get older? As always, if the game becomes difficult or frustrating for the child, thank him or her for playing with you and end the game.

To prepare for this activity, or, if you do not have access to a child, you can watch the video of this Active Learning.

MOTOR DISABILITY: DEVELOPMENTAL COORDINATION DISORDER

Developmental coordination disorder (DCD) A condition in which delays in reaching motor milestones interfere with daily living or academic performance.

Although we expect to see some variability in the ages at which children reach motor milestones, ... called developmental coordination disorder (DCD) in which delays in reaching these milestones interfere with daily living or academic performance (APA, 2013). It is usually first noticed when a young child has a significant delay in reaching milestones like sitting up, walking, jumping, or standing on one foot, or has problems with fine motor skills such as writing, using scissors, or tying shoelaces. Over time, these difficulties can interfere with a child's social development because the child may not be able to play with other children. They can also affect academic performance once children begin school. Although these problems first appear in the early years of life, the diagnosis is generally not made until age 5 because of the wide range of ages at which children normally develop different motor skills.

About 6% of school-aged children have this condition, and it is more common in boys (APA, 2013). Possible causes include biological factors such as prenatal malnutrition (Davidson, 2003) or abnormalities in the neurotransmitter or receptor systems in the central nervous system (Barnhart, Davenport, Epps, & Nordquist, 2003). The condition can be improved with physical education and daily exercise that help the brain and body work together, but in some cases occupational therapy or physical therapy is necessary to help children master daily self-help activities (Barnhart et al., 2003; Tokolahi, 2014).

CHECK YOUR UNDERSTANDING

1. What is the difference between gross motor and fine motor skills?
2. How does the process of myelination affect the order in which motor skills develop?
3. How can you promote body awareness in young children?
4. What is developmental coordination disorder?

NUTRITION

6.5 What role does nutrition play in development?

Growth and development rely to a large extent on healthy nutrition for infants, children, and adolescents. In this section, we discuss how to get babies off to a healthy start and how to provide a healthy diet for children and teens. We also describe problems with nutrition, from malnourishment to obesity to eating disorders.

BREAST-FEEDING

A number of national agencies and organizations, including the Centers for Disease Control and Prevention and the American Academy of Pediatrics, as well as international agencies including the United Nations Children's Fund (UNICEF) and the World Health Organization (WHO), have strongly advocated for breast-feeding infants because of the benefits associated with it. Table 6.4 summarizes some of those benefits, for both the mother and her infant.

Colostrum The thick, yellowish substance filled with antibodies and nutrients that is produced from a woman's breasts after she gives birth before milk is produced.

When a woman begins breast-feeding, her breasts initially produce a thick, yellowish substance called **colostrum** which is rich in nutrients to fuel the newborn's early growth and antibodies that help protect the newborn from infection (USDHHS, 2014). Colostrum is very easy for the newborn to digest. In the next 3 to 5 days, the mother's body will begin producing breast milk which will appear thin and watery compared to the colostrum, but which contains the right balance of fat, sugar, water, and protein for the newborn. The antibodies provided through colostrum and the mother's milk not only help the infant fight off infections, but may also promote earlier development of the infant's own immune system (Jackson & Nazar, 2006).

TABLE 6.4

Benefits of breast-feeding. Research has identified a number of benefits of breast-feeding for both mothers and infants. Despite these numerous benefits, many U.S. mothers do not continue to breast-feed for as long as recommended by the American Academy of Pediatrics.

	Benefits for Mothers	Benefits for Infants
Conclusive Evidence	• Lower risk of type 2 diabetes[1,3,5] • Lower risk of high cholesterol[5] • Delayed resumption of menstruation with exclusive breast-feeding and predominant breast-feeding*[1] • Lower risk of ovarian cancer[1,3,5] and certain types of breast cancer[3,5] • Lower risk of cardiovascular disease[5] • Uterus returning to pre-pregnancy shape • Lower blood pressure[4,5] and less reactive to stress[4] • Reduced maternal obesity in later life[5]	• Fewer respiratory illnesses, ear infections, and gastrointestinal diseases[2,3] • Lower risk of allergies[2], asthma[3], and eczema[3] • Reduced rate of sudden infant death syndrome (SIDS)[2,3] • Lower rates of childhood obesity[3] • Reduced adolescent and adult obesity[2] • Lower rates of diarrhea, especially where sanitation is poor[2,3] • Less vomiting[3] • Lower risk of childhood leukemia[3] • Lower rates of Type 2 diabetes[3]
Inconclusive Evidence	• Bone mineral density[1] • Postpartum weight change[1] • Maternal depression[1]	• Cognitive development and educational attainment[6]

*Women should not rely on breast-feeding as a substitute for contraception.

SOURCES: Chowdhury et al. (2015)[1]; Jackson & Nazar (2006)[2]; USDHHS (2014)[3]; Tu, Lupien, & Walker (2005)[4]; Schwarz & Nothnagle (2015)[5]; Sajjad et al. (2015)[6].

The American Academy of Pediatrics (2012) recommends that babies be exclusively breast-fed until 6 months of age, with other foods gradually supplementing it between 6 months and 1 year. Mothers are urged to wait to introduce solid foods into an infant's diet because doing this too early has been associated with development of allergies later in the child's life (Nwaru et al., 2010). While the number of American women who breast-feed their infants has risen in recent years, many do not continue to breast-feed for the recommended length of time. For example, in 2011, 79% of new mothers began breast-feeding, but the number dropped sharply to 49% at 6 months, and 27% by 12 months (CDC, 2014c).

For infants in poor and developing countries, the consequences for being breast-fed are even more significant. A systematic review of breast-feeding and infant mortality concluded that in developing countries infants between birth and 5 months of age who were not breast-fed were 14 times more likely to die than infants that were exclusively breast-fed (Sankar et al., 2015). In these countries where the water is often contaminated and sanitation is poor, UNICEF (2015) claims that optimal levels of breast-feeding could save more lives than any other preventive intervention.

Although the benefits of breast-feeding for many aspects of physical health are well-established, there remains a debate about the impact on children's later cognitive development (Ip et al., 2007; Tawia, 2013). Because breast milk provides ideal nutrition for the newborn and promotes overall healthier development, it is logical to think that these factors would positively impact cognitive development. However, early research that came to this conclusion has been criticized because mothers who choose to breast-feed differ from those who don't. They tend to be older, more educated, have higher incomes, and are more likely to be married or have a partner (Dennis, 2002; Li, Darling, Maurice, Barker, & Grummer-Strawn, 2005;

Persad & Mensinger, 2008). Each of these demographic characteristics also is associated with better cognitive outcomes for children. That means that women who breast-feed their infants would be more likely to have brighter children, regardless of whether they breast-fed their infants or not.

A more recent study found a statistically significant effect for breast-feeding on measured intelligence in children ages 7 to 16 even after controlling for the mother's demographic characteristics (Kanazawa, 2015). In this case, each month of breast-feeding was associated with an increase of .16 IQ points, or a total of 3.86 IQ points if the mother breast-fed for the full 2 years recommended by the World Health Organization. To put this finding in perspective, we remind you of the distinction made in Chapter 3 between statistical significance and practical significance. While these results are statistically significant, a question remains about what impact a less than 4-point increase in IQ test scores has on a child's cognitive development.

In light of the questions raised about the magnitude of some of the benefits attributed to breast-feeding (Jung, 2015), there has been some backlash against the heavy promotion of breast-feeding as the only good choice a new mother can make. Critics feel that this promotional campaign has resulted in blaming or shaming women who can't or don't breast-feed. We know there are some circumstances under which breast-feeding is not recommended. You learned in Chapter 5 that HIV can be transmitted from an infected mother to her infant through breast milk, and when a woman is undergoing chemotherapy or using antibiotics, antianxiety medications, or antidepressants, these substances also can be passed to an infant through her breast milk (American Academy of Pediatrics Committee on Drugs, 2001). Therefore, in these instances, a woman should not breast-feed. For many more women, however, the decision is influenced by more practical considerations, such as the woman's need to return to work. In these cases, formula does provide all the nutrients necessary for typically developing infants, although it does not provide the immunity that breast milk provides.

The debate is not so much about a choice between breast-feeding or bottle-feeding as it is between *breast-feeding* and *breast milk*. Breast-feeding gives women a wonderful opportunity to form a strong attachment to their infant in the process, but one clear advantage of bottle-feeding is that fathers also can participate in feeding the infant. However, it does not need to be formula in those bottles. Mothers can pump breast milk to be used later for bottle-feeding, and that breast milk will provide all the nutritional benefits and healthful immunity it offers. Work places can also do more to support a woman's decision to breast-feed (Gartner et al., 2005; Skafida, 2012) by providing private settings where mothers can pump milk for their babies. Providing training and support for breast-feeding while a woman is in the hospital would also support a woman's intention to breast-feed (Ogbuanu et al., 2009).

In conclusion, whether breast milk comes from the breast or is given to the baby from a bottle, it provides all the nutrition, as well as some immunity to a range of infections and diseases, that are needed for healthy development. Babies who are not breast-fed can still receive good nutrition from formula. Each new mother makes this decision based on her personal circumstances and her understanding of the options available to her.

HEALTHY EATING

You may remember learning about the food pyramid in elementary or high school. In 2012, the U.S. Department of Agriculture (USDA) replaced that image with a new logo, called "My Plate," which graphically shows us the proportion of fruits, vegetables, grains, protein, and dairy that should make up a healthy meal. As Figure 6.14 shows, fruits and vegetables should make up half of the plate. The USDA also recommends that we cut back on solid fats, added sugars and salt, and be sure that at least half of the grains we consume are whole grain.

Children who get off to a good start with a diet that contains a variety of healthy foods benefit throughout childhood and adolescence and into adulthood, but a healthful diet is particularly necessary to support the periods of rapid growth that occur in infancy and again at the start of adolescence.

A national survey in which American parents reported on what their infants and toddlers ate found that most are eating a healthy diet with more fruits and vegetables and fewer desserts, sweetened drinks, and salty foods than those who were interviewed 6 years earlier. However, many were still not receiving enough fiber from fruit, vegetables, legumes, and whole grains, and were receiving too much salt and saturated fat (Butte et al., 2010). All of these are risk factors for heart disease and high cholesterol later in life. In addition to healthy food choices, there are some other foods that pose a special risk for young children and should not be part of their diet. Unpasteurized milk or juices made from unwashed fruits can contain harmful bacteria. Honey can contain the botulinum organism, and raw eggs can contain salmonella. Adults also need to be particularly careful about giving young children firm, round foods such as popcorn, whole grapes, or hot dogs because these foods are approximately the size of a child's airway and can lodge in the child's throat and cause choking (American Academy of Pediatrics, 2006b).

Between 4% and 8% of children suffer from one or more food allergies (Branum & Lukacs, 2009; Gupta et al., 2011), with the incidence peaking among 3- to 5-year-olds (Gupta et al., 2011). Although any food can cause an allergic reaction, 90% of childhood allergies are caused by just 6 common foods: milk, eggs, peanuts, tree nuts (such as walnuts or cashews), soy, and wheat (American Academy of Pediatrics, 2013). Most allergic reactions to food are not serious or life-threatening, but they can be (Sicherer et al., 2010). In one study, slightly more than a third of the children with allergies had a history of severe reactions (Gupta et al., 2011). Although *anaphylaxis,* a severe reaction to an allergen that affects many systems in the body, is rare, preschool children are more likely to experience a severe reaction than older children. To help prevent allergy-related problems, many preschools have "no-share" food policies regarding food that can be brought into the classroom.

Healthy eating continues to be important as children enter middle childhood, but as they get older, they have more autonomy over what they eat because more of their food is consumed away from home. The good news is that the diets of most American children do a good job of meeting their nutritional needs (Clark & Fox, 2009), but the shortcomings described previously for infants' and toddlers' diets continue to be a problem for older children and for adolescents (Child Trends, 2013b; Volkarsky, 2010).

The root of some of these nutritional problems lies with the kind of foods favored by school-aged children. Hamburgers, cheeseburgers, and pizza contribute substantial amounts of fat and sodium to the diet, and whole milk and ice cream contribute saturated fat. On a typical day, one-third of American children and over 40% of American adolescents consume food or beverages from a fast-food restaurant (Poti, Duffey, & Popkin, 2014). Meals from these restaurants tend to be high in calories, total fat, saturated fat, sugar, and sodium; they are also low on nutritious foods such as milk, fruits, and vegetables (other than potatoes) (Bowman, Gortmaker, Ebbeling, Pereira, & Ludwig, 2004; Powell & Nguyen, 2013). Although eating fast food contributes to high rates of obesity in the United States, recent research has found that it is the quality of the *remainder* of the child's diet that is more strongly associated with weight status and dietary outcomes (Poti et al., 2014). Educating children during middle childhood about wise food choices can help ensure that the quality of their diet improves, rather than deteriorates, as they move through the elementary school years.

A number of American schoolchildren eat one or more meals a day at school. In 2012 and 2013, about 13.2 million children participated in the School Breakfast Program on a typical

FIGURE 6.14

Choose My Plate. The "My Plate" logo from the U.S. Department of Agriculture helps you see the proportions of different types of food that make up a healthy meal.

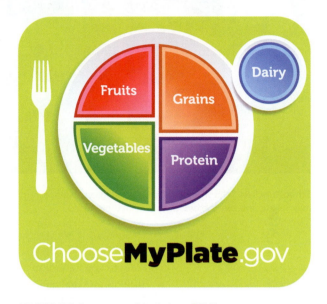

SOURCE: U.S. Department of Agriculture (2012).

Baerbel Schmidt/Stone/Getty Images

School lunches. School lunches can offer children healthy alternatives that help to improve the overall quality of their diets.

day, and 85% received a free or reduced-price breakfast (Food Research and Action Center, 2010). Eating breakfast improves attention and memory (Rampersaud et al., 2005), with the benefit being greater for children who otherwise have poorer diets (Hoyland, Dye, & Lawton, 2009; Kristjansson et al., 2007). However, a primary reason why school breakfast programs are associated with better academic performance is not what you might expect. Children who eat their breakfast at school have better attendance than those who don't, so when we try to interpret the impact of a school breakfast program on students' cognitive performance, at least part of that effect may be attributable to their better school attendance rather than to the nutritional value of the meal itself (Hoyland et al., 2009; Kristjansson et al., 2007).

On a typical day, even more U.S. children (30.7 million) participate in the school lunch program, with about 70% receiving free or reduced-price lunches. Children who participate are more likely than those who don't to consume low-fat milk, fruits, and vegetables and less likely to consume less healthy items like dessert and snacks (Condon, Crepinsek, & Fox, 2009). Some real challenges remain, however. For one thing, many elementary schools give children only 20 minutes for lunch, hardly enough time to wait in line to get their food and enjoy a nutritious meal, and many school kitchens do not have the space or equipment to prepare many of its foods from scratch. Try **Active Learning: School Lunches** to find out about the choices that children make from the foods currently offered by their schools.

Active LEARNING

ACTIVE LEARNING VIDEO ▲

These children discuss the lunches in their schools. What do they think would make their school lunches more nutritious?

School Lunches

Talk to a couple of elementary school-aged children who regularly get their lunch from their school cafeteria. It doesn't matter whether they purchase their lunch or get it through the school lunch program. Ask them what they like and don't like about the lunches, whether they usually get low-fat milk or 100% fruit juice with their meals, and whether they usually eat any fruit or vegetables. Ask the children you talk to what they would do to improve the foods they are served. You can then decide whether their suggestions would make the meals more nutritious or not. For instance, they might say they would prefer white bread to the whole wheat bread their cafeteria uses, but this would not be a more nutritious change. Compare what you find to what your classmates find when they interview children of different ages. Do different factors influence children's food decisions as they get older?

To prepare for this activity, or, if you do not have access to a child, you can watch the video of this Active Learning.

As adolescents spend more time away from their parents, they make more of their own choices about what to eat. Parents may not provide all the teenager's food, but it still is important that they continue to encourage healthy eating. Parental encouragement is associated with greater consumption of fruits and vegetables and lower consumption of fast foods (Bauer, Laska, Fulkerson, & Neumark-Sztainer, 2011).

MALNOURISHMENT

An estimated 19 million children in developing countries suffer from severe malnutrition, and the younger children are, the greater the effect of malnutrition on their growth (Management of Acute Malnutrition in Infants Project, 2009). The lack of nutrients affects brain development as well as other aspects of physical health and growth. If the infant survives malnourishment, and many do not, the effects are irreversible and can last a lifetime even if they get plenty of food later in life. In a study in Barbados, adults who had been malnourished as infants were more likely to have ongoing attention deficits and conduct problems that began in childhood but continued through adulthood (Galler et al., 2012a; Galler et al., 2012b).

We often associate malnourishment with children who live in third world countries or countries being torn apart by war, but it exists to some extent in every country, including the United States. However, a much greater threat in the United States than malnutrition is **undernutrition,** a deficiency of calories or of one or more essential nutrients. A paradoxical situation called **food insecurity** exists for people who do not always have access to the nutritious food needed to meet their basic needs (Franklin et al., 2012). When food is not consistently available, adults and children may adopt the strategy of overeating when it *is*. This pattern of feast and famine can result in weight gain over time. It is estimated that 1 in 7 American households experience food insecurity. Low-income, ethnic minority, and female-headed households are at the greatest risk, and adolescents may be even more vulnerable than younger children (Franklin et al., 2012). Food insecurity is associated with higher rates of illness, lower academic achievement, and more aggression, withdrawal, and emotional distress (Ashiabi & O'Neal, 2008).

Undernutrition A deficiency of calories or of one or more essential nutrients.

Food insecurity A situation in which food is often scarce or unavailable, causing people to overeat when they do have access to food.

OBESITY AND BEING OVERWEIGHT

Being overweight or obese has serious negative consequences for children. For one thing, overweight children are likely to become overweight adolescents who in turn become overweight adults (Malina, Bouchard, & Oded, 2004; Singh, Mulder, Twisk, van Mechelen, & Chinapaw, 2008), and we know children who are overweight or obese have an increased risk of developing a number of life-threatening health conditions, including type 2 diabetes and asthma (Black, Smith, Porter, Jacobsen, & Koebnick, 2012; Brüske, Flexeder, & Heinrich, 2014; Long, Mareno, Shabo, & Wilson, 2012). The American Diabetes Association (2008) estimates that 1 in 3 children born in 2000 will develop diabetes in their lifetime, and this ratio climbs to 1 in 2 for minority children. The long-term effects of **obesity** (being 20% or more over an individual's ideal weight) include elevated blood pressure, increased levels of cholesterol, and even some cancers (Malina et al., 2004). In addition to the tremendous personal cost of diabetes to the affected individuals, total economic cost in the United States in 2012 was $245 billion (American Diabetes Association, 2013).

The good news is that after years of national attention to the problem of childhood obesity, we finally appear to be making some progress. After years of increasing rates of obesity, the percentage of children ages 2 to 19 considered obese has not increased in the last 10 years (CDC, 2015b), and recent statistics have found a decrease in the rate of obesity among 2- to 5-year-old children (CDC, 2015b). The exact reasons for the decline are hard to identify, but lower consumption of sugary beverages, more nutritious meals and snacks at child care centers, more emphasis on physical activity, and increased rates of breast-feeding may all be

Obesity Being 20% or more over an individual's ideal weight.

TRUE/FALSE VIDEO ▲

T ☐ F ☐ The rate of childhood obesity appears to have finally leveled off in the United States.
True

making a contribution. Although there was no comparable decrease in other age groups in this study, we can hope that as these young children move from early childhood into middle childhood, they will sustain this progress.

Minority and low-income children continue to be at a disproportionately high risk of being obese, but their parents are often in denial about their children's weight. In a study of low-income mothers by Rich and colleagues (2005), all the participating children were at or above the 95th percentile in weight for their height (which is considered obese), but 81% of their parents said their child was healthy and 50% were not concerned about their child's weight. Parents often explained their lack of concern by saying the child would simply grow out of it, was tall or big-boned, or looked just fine. Unfortunately, overweight children do not typically grow out of the problem, so results such as these remind us how important it is to understand parents' perspectives on a situation if we want to design interventions to change their behavior. Parents not only need to have information about childhood obesity, but they also need to be motivated to use it to improve their children's health (Weatherspoon, Venkatesh, Horodynski, Stommel, & Brophy-Herb, 2013).

EATING DISORDERS

At the other end of the spectrum are eating disorders that are associated with children and adolescents being severely underweight. Although there are a number of eating disorders, the dramatic nature of anorexia nervosa and bulimia nervosa keeps them in the forefront of our attention. **Anorexia nervosa** is a condition in which individuals intentionally restrict their food intake to a point that it may become life-threatening. Despite their thinness, anorexics still see themselves as grossly overweight and remain fearful of gaining weight. This condition takes a terrible toll on the young person's overall health. A number of changes can easily be seen, including thinning hair, brittle nails, a yellowing of the skin, and the growth of fine downy hair on the face, arms, and back, but many anorexics experience more serious hidden changes, including gastrointestinal and cardiovascular problems, and osteoporosis. As we said earlier in this chapter, a woman's body needs a certain level of body fat to sustain her periods so as a young woman's level of body fat falls, she either will fail to begin menstruating, or her menstrual periods will become erratic or cease altogether. Because anorexia can be life-threatening, hospitalization may be required, but hospitalization often occurs late in the process after a great deal of physical damage has already been done. Although some programs have had success with helping the anorexic regain weight, relapses following treatment are common, and mortality from anorexia is higher than for other psychiatric disorders (Arcelus, Mitchell, Wales, & Nielsen, 2011).

Bulimia nervosa is an eating disorder that is characterized by eating binges in which enormous amounts of food are consumed, followed by self-induced vomiting or the excessive use of laxatives to get rid of the food. Individuals with bulimia base their self-esteem largely on their weight and feel out of control during binge eating (APA, 2013). Many cases of bulimia go undetected because the goal of bulimics is to maintain their weight rather than lose a great deal of weight and much of the behavior associated with bulimia is secret behavior.

Anorexia nervosa A condition in which individuals become obsessed with their weight and intentionally restrict food intake to a point that it may become life threatening.

Bulimia nervosa An eating disorder characterized by eating binges, followed by purging (for example, self-induced vomiting or the excessive use of laxatives) to get rid of the food.

JGI/Jamie Grill/Blend Images/Getty Images

The pressure to be thin. The cultural ideal of thinness makes an impact on even very young girls. In a 2007 study, 40% of 9- and 10-year-olds claimed they were on some kind of a diet to help them lose weight (Agras, Bryson, Hammer, & Kraemer, 2007).

The prevalence of bulimia among young women is estimated at 1% to 1.5% and the prevalence of anorexia is estimated at 0.4%. Both of these disorders are much less common in men (APA, 2013). Participating in activities where weight is a continuing issue (such as gymnastics or dance for females and wrestling for males) can put both girls and boys at risk.

There are no simple explanations for what causes eating disorders. Both anorexia and bulimia can begin with normal dieting and concerns about weight that reflect the emphasis our culture places on thinness. Research based on twin studies has found some evidence for a genetic link, and children with an anxiety disorder or who demonstrate obsessional behavior are at increased risk of developing anorexia (APA, 2013). Girls who mature earlier than other girls are at risk because their early physical maturation is associated with being heavier than their peers (Berger et al., 2009; Tyrka, Graber, & Brooks-Gunn, 2000). Psychological factors such as depression and low body esteem also are predictive of developing eating disorders in both boys and girls (Gardner et al., 2000; Keel & Forney, 2013). Another possible cause is a dysfunctional family dynamic. However, it is difficult to know whether any family dysfunction we see in families of anorexics is a cause of the disorder or a result of the stress of having a child with this problem (Sim et al., 2009). You will learn more about the role that media plays in promoting disordered eating in Chapter 14.

In a review of programs designed to *prevent* eating disorders (rather than to treat them once they occur), Stice and Shaw (2004) found that the most effective programs were ones that target high-risk groups of adolescents rather than the general population of adolescents. They also found that older adolescents benefited more than younger ones, perhaps because the risk of developing an eating disorder increases after age 15. It may surprise you to learn that programs that focus on providing information to adolescents about the harmful effects of disordered eating were ineffective at producing a change in the adolescent's behavior. Rather, it was programs that focused on changing maladaptive attitudes (such as seeing a thin body as the ideal body type or feeling very dissatisfied with your own body) and maladaptive behaviors (such as fasting or overeating) that were the most effective.

T ☐ F ☐ The most effective way to prevent eating disorders is to give adolescents information about how harmful these behaviors can be to the adolescent's body. **False**

CHECK YOUR UNDERSTANDING

1. What are some benefits of breast-feeding for mothers and babies?
2. How does eating breakfast affect children's performance in school?
3. What are the effects of food insecurity on healthy eating habits?
4. Identify recent trends in obesity and being overweight in American children.
5. How are the symptoms of anorexia nervosa and bulimia nervosa different?

CONCLUSION

The healthy development and functioning of the human body is central to all aspects of human experience. We have seen in this chapter that physical development relates to many aspects of emotional, social, and cognitive development. In the next chapters, we look at these areas, with the clear understanding that all of these aspects of development are linked to what we have studied in this chapter: brain function, sensory development, physical changes such as those in puberty, and the health of the body.

Test your understanding of the content.
Take the practice quiz at **edge.sagepub.com/levine3e**

6.1 How are the brains of children and adolescents similar to and different from the brains of adults? What disorders are linked with the structure and function of the brain?

Human brains are divided into two **hemispheres,** which are connected by the **corpus callosum.** Each area of the brain handles some specialized functions. The brain is made up of **neurons.** Although infants have billions of neurons, they have relatively few **synapses** that connect them. In early brain development, **synaptogenesis** forms connections between neurons, and **myelination** improves the efficiency of the neural impulses. Cells in a young brain have a **plasticity** that allows them to take over new functions if some part of the brain is damaged. Unused synapses are pruned, but when an individual encounters typical experiences, **experience-expectant brain development** occurs and those synaptic connections are retained. When an individual encounters unique experiences, **experience-dependent brain development** occurs and new synapses are formed. Brain development continues through adolescence, especially the development of the prefrontal cortex. There is another round of overproduction and pruning of synapses in adolescence.

Cerebral palsy is a condition that involves problems with body movement and muscle coordination resulting from damage to the brain prenatally, at birth, or shortly thereafter. **Autism spectrum disorder** (ASD), which is characterized by pervasive impairment in social communication and interaction and by restricted or repetitive behaviors, interests, or activities, may be caused by different patterns of brain development (for example, failure to prune unnecessary synapses or different patterns of connectivity). It is not caused by poor parenting. The increased incidence of ASD may be the result of some combination of better case finding, earlier diagnosis, misdiagnosis, and a true increase in the disorder. **Schizophrenia** is a very rare but serious mental disorder related to both structural and functional differences in many regions of the brain. Symptoms include delusions, hallucinations, disorganized speech, very disorganized or catatonic behavior, and reduced expression of emotion and self-motivated behavior. When children and younger teens develop this disorder, it is referred to as early-onset schizophrenia.

6.2 How do the senses develop during infancy?

Although an infant's **visual acuity** is initially poor, it develops to adult levels by 6 months to 3 years after birth. Infants focus on their parents' eyes, seemingly inviting interaction. Hearing is well developed at birth, and infants have shown a preference for their mothers' voices, which they heard while still in the womb. The infant's sense of smell also is highly developed at birth, and infants prefer sweet tastes to other tastes. Both smell and taste preferences are shaped by exposure to chemosensory molecules prenatally, so after birth infants prefer smells and tastes associated with the foods their mothers ate. Infants are sensitive to touch, which promotes development and well-being. Infants show cross-modal transfer of perception.

6.3 How do children's bodies change from infancy through adolescence?

Infants grow very rapidly in the first few years of life, and then the rate of growth slows substantially until the child experiences the **adolescent growth spurt.** The child's body proportions change to become more similar to adult body proportions. When adolescents go through **puberty,** they become capable of reproducing. Girls experience **menarche,** and boys experience **spermarche.** Both **primary sex characteristics** and **secondary sex characteristics** develop. The timing of puberty has an impact on an individual's social, emotional, and cognitive development. Maturing early has some advantages for boys and disadvantages for girls, but both early maturing boys and early maturing girls can be at risk of being drawn into risky behavior if they associate with older peers. Adolescents who are sexually active are at risk of a pregnancy or getting a **sexually transmitted disease.** The adolescent pregnancy rate has decreased in recent years, but still is higher than in other developed countries.

6.4 What factors influence and shape motor development?

Infants are born with a set of **reflexes,** but reflexes are fairly quickly replaced with voluntary movement as the nervous system matures. Children gain control over both **fine motor skills** and **gross motor skills,** and these skills develop following the *cephalocaudal* and **proximodistal** principles (moving from the head to the tail, and from the center of the body to the extremities) in the pattern of myelination of motor neurons. **Proprioception** helps children develop body awareness. Some children have a **developmental coordination disorder.** Motor development is shaped by a complex interaction of genes, maturation, and environmental experiences. Throughout development, children and adolescents benefit from physical activity.

6.5 What role does nutrition play in development?

Breast-feeding helps an infant get off to a good start and has benefits for the nursing mother as well, but levels of breast-feeding in the United States are not as high as is

recommended. Although children in the United States tend to have healthy diets, they eat too much sugar, fat, and sodium and too few fruits, vegetables, and have too little fiber in their diets, which has consequences for their health. Children in the United States are more likely to suffer from **undernutrition** than malnutrition. When an adequate diet is not always available, people may experience **food insecurity** and overeat when food is available. **Obesity** is a major health risk because it is associated with diabetes and other health problems, but the rate of childhood obesity may be leveling off. At the other extreme, some children and adolescents experience eating disorders, such as **anorexia nervosa** or **bulimia nervosa.**

KEY TERMS

Strengthen your understanding of these key terms with
mobile-friendly eFlashcards at **edge.sagepub.com/levine3e**

Adolescent growth spurt   196
Anorexia nervosa   218
Autism spectrum disorder   186
Axons   180
Bulimia nervosa   218
Cerebral palsy   185
Colostrum   212
Corpus callosum   178
Dendrites   180
Developmental coordination disorder (DCD)   211
Experience-dependent brain development   182
Experience-expectant brain development   182
Fine motor skills   207
Food insecurity   217
Grey matter   180
Gross motor skills   207
Hemispheres   178
Menarche   198
Myelination   182
Neurons   180
Neurotransmitters   180

Obesity   217
Plasticity   181
Precocious puberty   198
Prepubescence   197
Primary sex characteristics   198
Proprioception   210
Proximodistal   207
Pruning   182
Puberty   198
Reflexes   205
Schizophrenia   190
Secondary sex characteristics   198
Sexually transmitted disease (STD)   202
Sexually transmitted infection (STI)   202
Spermarche   198
Synapse   180
Synaptogenesis   181
Undernutrition   217
Visual acuity   191
White matter   182

Give your students the SAGE edge!

SAGE edge offers a robust online environment featuring an impressive array of free tools and resources for review, study, and further exploration, keeping both instructors and students on the cutting edge of teaching and learning. Learn more at **edge.sagepub.com/levine3e**

practice
AND
apply

WHAT YOU'VE LEARNED

edge.sagepub.com/levine3e

PART III

COGNITIVE DEVELOPMENT

chapter 7

THEORIES OF COGNITIVE DEVELOPMENT

Laura Levine

TEST YOUR KNOWLEDGE

Test your knowledge of child development by deciding whether each of the following statements is *true* or *false*, and then check your answers as you read the chapter.

1. **T** ☐ **F** ☐: The primary difference between how young children and adults think about and understand the world is the difference in the amount of information they know.
2. **T** ☐ **F** ☐: If a young child drops an object from her high chair over and over again, she is probably just asserting herself and testing her parents' patience.
3. **T** ☐ **F** ☐: We describe preschoolers as egocentric because they are selfish.
4. **T** ☐ **F** ☐: Infants appear to have an intuitive understanding of how gravity works.
5. **T** ☐ **F** ☐: Four-year-olds who are better able to maintain focused attention are more likely to complete college at age 25.
6. **T** ☐ **F** ☐: Adolescents are able to study efficiently while listening to a favorite TV show because by this age their attentional processes are so well developed they can split their attention between multiple activities.
7. **T** ☐ **F** ☐: Attention-deficit/hyperactivity disorder is a disorder of childhood, but fortunately children outgrow the symptoms with age.
8. **T** ☐ **F** ☐: The primary cause of attention-deficit/hyperactivity disorder is poor parenting.
9. **T** ☐ **F** ☐: Few people have clear memories of what happened in their lives before the age of 3.
10. **T** ☐ **F** ☐: Older children and adults are less likely than younger children to think they remember something they never actually saw.

Correct answers: (1) F, (2) F, (3) F, (4) T, (5) T, (6) F, (7) F, (8) F, (9) T, (10) F

▲ **VIDEO: Watch as students answer some of these questions and the authors respond.**

When we study cognitive development, we are acknowledging that changes occur in how we think and learn as we grow. The difference between how children think and how adults think is more than the difference in how much they know. There are differences in the very way that they think about and understand their experiences. In this chapter, you will learn about the theories and research that contribute to current understanding of how children's cognitive abilities develop. You were briefly introduced to the theories of Piaget, Vygotsky, and information processing in Chapter 2. In this chapter, we look into these three theories in more depth and examine some of the research that supports or challenges their ideas. We also introduce you to a new theory called the *theory of core knowledge*.

PIAGET'S THEORY OF COGNITIVE DEVELOPMENT

7.1 What are Piaget's four stages of cognitive development and what occurs during each one?

Jean Piaget (1896–1980) was a student of biology before he studied psychology and child development. By age 10, he had already published his first article in the field of biology based on his study of an albino sparrow (McKeachie & Sims, 2004). By the time he was 21, he had published over 20 articles on the subject of mollusks, such as snails and slugs (Singer & Revenson, 1996). Piaget's godfather was concerned that Piaget's life was too narrowly focused on one thing so he introduced the young man to the study of philosophy. Piaget then became interested in the philosophical question of how we come to know and understand our world, an area of study referred to as *epistemology*. His approach to studying the development of the human mind was a synthesis of ideas drawn from his earlier interest in biology and this new interest in philosophy. On the one hand, he looked at human beings as biological organisms, who must adapt successfully to their environment, just as snails and clams do. On the other hand, he looked at the more unique characteristics of the human mind, with its capacity for reflection and understanding, and wondered how it all worked. As we will see, both approaches contributed to the theory of **genetic-epistemology** (*genetic* from biology, *epistemology* from philosophy) that he developed.

Genetic-epistemology
Piaget's theory that cognitive development of knowledge is based on both genetics (from biology) and epistemology (a philosophical understanding of the nature of knowledge).

Many developmental researchers have claimed that Piaget revolutionized the study of children's cognitive development (Flavell, Miller, & Miller, 2002). Although his theory has received criticism and has undergone revision over the years, it provides a set of basic principles of cognitive development that guides much research today. They include the following ideas:

- Intelligence is an active, constructive, and dynamic process.
- Mistakes children make in their thinking are usually meaningful because the mistakes reflect the nature of their thought processes at their current stage of development.
- As children develop, the structure of their thinking changes, and these new modes of thought are based on the earlier structures (Flavell et al., 2002).

Schema A cognitive framework that places concepts, objects, or experiences into categories or groups of associations.

We first discuss Piaget's basic ideas about how cognitive development occurs and then describe his four stages of development. Piaget believed that we are always actively trying to make sense of our experiences in order to adapt successfully to our environment and ensure our survival. By "making sense" he meant organizing our experiences into **schemas**, cognitive frameworks that place concepts, objects, or experiences into categories or groups of associations. Each person has a unique way of organizing experiences based on the schemas she has developed. **Active Learning: Organizing by Cognitive Schema** gives you a chance to explore different ways to organize a single set of objects depending on which schemas you use.

Active LEARNING

Ly Wylde Photography/Moment Select/Getty Images

Organizing by Cognitive Schema

Look at this photo of footwear. Before you read any further, list as many ways to organize or categorize these shoes as you can. In Piaget's terms, each of these ways of organizing the shoes might indicate a schema that you have for footwear.

Did you categorize the shoes by type, by color, or by wearer? What other categories did you use?

Often, when we have a new experience, it immediately makes sense to us because we can fit it into a schema we already have. For example, a child may have a new kind of sandwich that she easily understands is a kind of food similar to foods she's had before. When we can fit new experiences easily into our preexisting schemas, we engage in what Piaget called **assimilation**. However, let's say that this child has never seen crab served in its shell. If the child is served something that is this different from the foods she is familiar with, she may not connect it with her schema for food. Piaget would say that she is thrown into a state of confusion, or **disequilibrium**, by the experience. People generally find the uncertainty of disequilibrium uncomfortable, so they try to make sense out of what they are seeing in order to return to a comfortable state through a process Piaget referred to as **equilibration**. When we need to change our schemas to fit new experiences, we use **accommodation** because we are *accommodating* or changing the way we think about something in order to understand the new information. In this case, if a parent can convince the child to try eating the crab, she may discover that it is a delicious food, and she accommodates her existing schema for food by including crab in it and equilibrium is restored.

Disequilibirum. Never having eaten crab before, it does not yet fit into this boy's schema for food. If he tries it and likes it, his disequilibrium will be resolved.

Assimilation Fitting new experiences into existing mental schemas.

Disequilibrium A state of confusion in which your schemas do not fit your experiences.

Equilibration An attempt to resolve uncertainty to return to a comfortable cognitive state.

PIAGET'S STAGES OF COGNITIVE DEVELOPMENT

As a result of his research and his conversations with children, Piaget believed that children think in a different way than adults do; that is, not only do children have less information or less skill in thinking (quantitative differences), but more important, there are qualitative differences, meaning that children think in a particular way that is unique to their developmental level. Based on detailed observations of children, Piaget identified four stages from infancy through adolescence, each representing different qualities of thought (see Table 7.1). Each stage is built on the abilities acquired during the previous one, but each has features that are new and unique to that stage. We describe these stages in some detail, along with activities you can do to understand firsthand how children think at each age level. Although Piaget set out the ages for each stage, you should think of these as approximations. Some children reach them sooner or later than others. What he felt was most important is that these stages could only occur in the order he described. Children could not jump from

T ☐ F ☐ The primary difference between how young children and adults think about and understand the world is the difference in the amount of information they know. **False**

Accommodation Changing mental schemas so they fit new experiences.

TABLE 7.1

Piaget's stage theory. Piaget believed that children's thinking changes in qualitative ways as they move through the four stages of cognitive development.

Stage	Age	Description
Sensorimotor	Birth–2 years	Infants understand the world through the information they take in through their senses and their actions on it.
Preoperational	2–7 years	Young children can use mental symbols but do not yet think logically, and their thinking is egocentric.
Concrete Operations	7–12 years	Children now think logically, but their thinking is concrete, not abstract.
Formal Operations	12 years and older	Adolescents can think both logically and abstractly.

TABLE 7.2

Six substages of the sensorimotor stage. These substages give a general idea of what Piaget described during the first 2 years of life, but even Piaget did not see them as clear and separate stages.

Substage	Age	Characteristics	Examples
1. Use of Reflexes	0–1 month	Automatic reflexes	Infant makes sucking motion with mouth when stroked on the cheek.
2. Primary Circular Reactions	1–4 months	Adaptation of reflexes to the environment	Infant adjusts sucking to accommodate a new pacifier.
3. Secondary Circular Reactions	4–8 months	Repetition of actions that make interesting events last	Infant swings arm and happens to hit bell; infant repeats this action many times.
4. Coordination of Reactions and Application to New Situations	8–12 months	Action schemas applied to new objects	Infant taps bell and it rings; infant tries tapping a new object in the same way.
5. Tertiary Circular Reactions	12–18 months	Intentional discovery of new means to explore the environment	Toddler rings bell and discovers hitting bell with a stick also makes it ring.
6. Invention of New Means of Exploration Through Mental Combinations	18–24 months	Use of mental activity to guide exploration	Toddler sees cracker on table and pulls chair over to climb up and get it.

SOURCE: Adapted in part from Piaget (1952).

sensorimotor thinking to formal operations and then back to concrete operations. The path of development only moves in one direction.

Sensorimotor stage
Piaget's first stage in which infants learn through their senses and their actions on the world.

Sensorimotor Stage (Birth to 2 Years)

The first stage in Piaget's theory is the **sensorimotor stage**. As the name of this stage implies, Piaget believed infants organize their world by means of their senses and their physical action on it. Although Piaget described six substages of the sensorimotor period, he believed that "the facts remain so complicated and their sequence can be so rapid that it would be dangerous to separate these stages too much" (Piaget, 1952, p. 331). Therefore, we summarize these substages briefly in Table 7.2, and present in more detail four general trends in development within the sensorimotor period: (1) from reflexes to goal-directed activity, (2) from the body to the outside world, (3) development of object permanence, and (4) from motor action to mental representation.

From reflexes to goal-directed activity. As we learned in Chapter 6, all infants are born with reflexes, which are automatic, patterned behaviors that are not learned but are built into the nervous system. However, Piaget said that learning begins even in the first month of life as infants begin to adapt these reflexes to the environment. For example, the sucking reflex is usually evoked when the lips are touched. However, the infant soon begins to suck before his lips are touched, perhaps when he is placed in his mother's arms. In this way, even these automatic behaviors begin to accommodate to the environment (Piaget, 1962).

Between 1 and 4 months, infants begin to use reflexes in different ways. When the reflex results in a pleasurable experience, the infant repeats it over and over again. For example, when the infant somehow gets his thumb in his mouth, it begins what Piaget called a **circular reaction**. The action produces a good feeling, which prompts the infant to continue the action, and the good feeling continues to stimulate the action, in a circular

Circular reaction An infant's repetition of a reflexive action that results in a pleasurable experience.

fashion. When the baby's thumb falls out of his mouth, he has to rediscover the action that will place it back where it feels good (Piaget, 1962). Between 4 and 8 months, infants begin to use intentional actions to prolong interesting sights, and Piaget referred to these as *secondary circular reactions*. The different circular reactions the infant is developing are examples of **motor schemas**. Infants organize their understanding of the world through their action on it. We all know that if you give an 8-month-old any object, the first thing she will do is put it in her mouth. She is using this sucking or mouthing schema as her way of using her senses to organize her understanding of the world: Can I suck on this object? How does it taste? How does it feel in my mouth?

Between 8 and 12 months, infants combine the motor schemas they have already developed to begin solving problems. Instead of just repeating actions over and over they have a goal in mind and use motor schemas such as grasping, hitting, and mouthing in combinations to reach that goal. At the next stage, usually between the ages of 12 and 18 months, infants develop new behaviors that allow them to achieve their goals, referred to as *tertiary circular reactions*. Although they still repeat actions over and over, now they do it with planned variations designed to "see what happens when I do *this!*" For example, any parent knows the stage babies go through when they continually drop things on purpose. If you watch carefully, you'll see that each time the child does this, the action is likely to be a little different as he experiments with "What happens when I drop it this way? What happens when I drop it and Mommy is there? What happens when I drop it and she's not there?" This can be very frustrating for parents, but Piaget saw it as an example of the active experimentation that children engage in at all ages.

From the body to the outside world. When babies are very young, their major interest is meeting their bodily needs for food, sleep, and comfort. As they grow, their attention is increasingly focused on the world around them. Their vision and coordination improve and they begin to apply circular reactions to objects outside of their own bodies. For example, if a baby kicks her legs and sees that the mobile hanging over her crib moves in response, she repeats the kicking over and over until she tires of the excitement of the response she can create in the world.

Development of object permanence. Piaget believed newborns do not understand that objects (or people for that matter) exist outside of their own action on them; that is, infants lack **object permanence**. An infant grasping a toy experiences "grasping a toy," not "I, a separate entity, am grasping this toy, which also has an existence of its own" (Fast, 1985). While the child is grasping the toy, it is part of his experience, but when he is not, the toy does not exist for him. As the infant develops new means of exploration, he learns that he can grasp the toy and also chew on it and also look at it. When he applies *several* motor schemas to an object, the motor schemas become detached from the object itself. The toy is no longer just "something I grasp," but "a thing separate from my actions on it." Finally, by the end of the sensorimotor stage, the child understands that objects exist independently and act according to their own rules (Fast, 1985). **Active Learning: Testing Object Permanence** will walk you through the procedures Piaget used to assess object permanence in infants.

Motor schema Infants' understanding of the world through their action on it.

T □ F □ If a young child drops an object from her high chair over and over again, she is probably just asserting herself and testing her parents' patience. **False**

Object permanence The understanding that objects still exist when an infant does not see them.

What happens if I drop it this way? This infant is curious to see what happens when dropping things in different ways. Do they bounce, do they splat, does Mommy come and pick it up?

Active LEARNING

Testing Object Permanence

Piaget (1954) devised a series of experiments called the **A-not-B task** to test infants' understanding of object permanence. You can carry out this test if you have access to a child between 6 months and age 2 or you can look at the video that accompanies this Active Learning. If others in your class test children of different ages within this age range, you can compare results to see how object permanence changes during this period of time. You will need to have an interesting toy or object that is safe for an infant to have (that

A-not-B task A test for object permanence in which an object is hidden under cloth A and then moved under cloth B.

ACTIVE LEARNING VIDEO ▲

The major developmental milestone of object permanence is explored with two infants: 7-month-old Nicho and 10-month-old Damian.

is, nothing the child can choke on or that is otherwise unsafe to put in the mouth) and two cloths to cover the objects. There are three steps to the series of experiments Piaget carried out:

1. Put two cloths side by side on the table between you and the child. Show the child the toy and be sure he is interested in it and is watching you. Then hide the toy under one of the cloths. Observe and record whether the child searches for the toy.

2. If the child searches and finds the toy, begin Step 2 by hiding it again under the same cloth. Then, while the baby is still watching, move the toy from under the first cloth to under the second cloth. Observe and record where the baby searches.

3. If the child finds the toy the second time, repeat Step 2 but try to move the toy from the first cloth to the second without letting the child see what you are doing. Observe and record where the child searches.

Does the child you are testing show through his behaviors that he understands that objects continue to exist even if he can't see them? Is he tricked when you move the toy?

To prepare for this activity, or, if you do not have access to a child, you can watch the video of this Active Learning.

In Piaget's experiments, young infants would not search at all when an object was hidden. It was as if they believed that the toy simply disappeared when it was hidden. At an older age, they would search under the first cloth, but if the toy was moved under a second cloth, they would continue to search in the first location or give up even if they clearly saw the experimenter move the object under the second cloth. This is known as the *A-not-B error* because the infant continues to look in the first location, *A*, and does not switch to the second location, *B*, where the object is now hidden. A third stage occurs when infants find the object after seeing the object moved from *A* to *B*, but not when they don't see the switch. Finally, when infants have true object permanence, they will find the object even if they did not see it moved. There is no question in the baby's mind that the toy still exists even though he can no longer see it, and he will search until the toy is recovered.

From action to mental representation. Piaget believed that infants understand the world through motor schemas, such as grasping, sucking, and shaking. Motor schemas are quite

Doug Goodman/Photo Researchers, Inc.

The development of object permanence. How does the concept of object permanence explain why this baby loses interest in the toy dog when it is hidden?

different from the kinds of cognitive schemas that you used earlier in **Active Learning: Organizing by Cognitive Schema**. Piaget theorized that ultimately these motor schemas would become the basis for internal, cognitive representations of the world. He believed that children's first thoughts are mental representations of the actions they have been performing. In other words, the motor schemas are internalized, and the infant can *think* of them instead of actually *doing* them. Piaget (1963) provides the following example of the planning that can now occur: His daughter Jacqueline, at the age of 1 year and 7 months, tried to put a chain necklace into a matchbox. Over and over, she tried to put one end of the chain in, then the next part, and then the next. However, each time the first part would fall out as she was trying to put the rest in, and she remained unsuccessful. Piaget reported that his other daughter Lucienne at an older age used her new abilities to think ahead rather than to just act. With the same objective of putting the necklace into the matchbox, she rolled the necklace into a ball and successfully placed it into the box. Instead of the trial-and-error approach of her sister at a younger age, Lucienne was able to think about an effective way to accomplish this goal and then did it.

Preoperational Stage (2 to 7 Years)

Piaget defined his second stage by what it lacks: operations. For Piaget, **operations** are mental actions that follow systematic, logical rules. When children are *pre*operational, they do not think in a logical way (perhaps this is why we do not have them start formal schooling until late in this stage). However, we first discuss the new and positive change during this period: the ability to use symbols.

According to Piaget, the major accomplishment of the **preoperational stage** is the ability to represent actions mentally rather than physically. Toddlers can think about and refer to objects that are not in their immediate vicinity because they can represent them in their minds. They can *tell* you about an apple they ate yesterday, unlike the infant who must *show* you an actual apple. A symbol is anything that represents something that is not present, but symbols at this age are still very concrete. Abstract symbols, such as a balance scale representing the concept of justice, are still outside of the comprehension of the preoperational child. Three ways in which children demonstrate their ability to use symbols are through their fantasy play, use of language, and drawings.

In fantasy play, children use objects or themselves and other people to represent something that is not there. While they are actually holding a banana, in their mind they are imagining that it is a telephone and they can pretend to talk to someone at the other end of the line, who is also a figment of their imagination. The imaginary companion is another example of the use of symbols in fantasy play. Some children create an entire

Operations Mental actions that follow systematic, logical rules.

Preoperational stage Piaget's second stage of development, in which children ages 2 to 7 do not yet have logical thought and instead think magically and egocentrically.

Allen Donikowski/Moment/Getty Images

Symbolic representation. When a young child develops the ability to use symbols, a squiggle can represent anything he wants it to be.

them that their imaginary friend must have a seat at the dinner table and be served his own food. For Piaget, the development of language is important because it shows that children can use symbols. Whenever we say a word, we are representing something that is not there. Look at this word: *APPLE*. You will notice that it is not round, and if you were to lick the page in your textbook, you will find that it isn't sweet. It isn't even red, but you knew the object in the real world that it stood for when you first read it. Finally, children demonstrate the use of symbols whenever they make a drawing of something, even if that drawing is not recognizable by someone else. Two-year-olds demonstrate that they understand the representative nature of pictures because a toddler who is shown a picture of a banana does not try to eat it. Instead the child understands that the picture only represents a real banana (Preissler & Bloom, 2007).

While the use of symbols is a major step forward and liberates children from the immediate physical world, Piaget also placed considerable emphasis on the limitations of children's thought at this age. We next describe three limitations that characterize preoperational thought: intuitive thought, egocentrism, and the inability to conserve.

Intuitive thought. Beginning around age 3, many children enter the "why" stage. They have some understanding of what are seeing and experiencing, and now they ask "why?" about anything and everything as they try to figure out the world around them. Piaget (1955/1973) believed young children are beginning to put together logical explanations but are still influenced more by what they perceive than by logical reasoning. He called this initial reasoning **intuitive thought**. Preoperational children may base their conclusions on a set of unrelated facts, or they may assume that things that just happen to occur at about the same time cause each other. For example, an angry child might accuse an innocent bystander of doing him harm by reasoning, "You were there when I fell, so it's your fault that I hurt myself." We wouldn't expect a 2- or 3-year-old child to explain the movement of the planets, or the changing of the seasons, but children are curious about many natural phenomena in the world. In their effort to understand what they see in nature, magical explanations may be the best that children can do.

Egocentrism. Piaget believed that young children find it difficult to see the world from another person's point of view, especially if that point of view differs from their own. Piaget called this **egocentrism** (*ego* means "I" or "self"). Be careful in understanding this term. It is not the same as selfishness or egotism (thinking *you* are the *greatest*), although young children often have plenty of each of those characteristics as well. It really means that the child's mind is insufficiently developed to allow her to understand that someone else's perspective could be different from her own. The result may be a "selfish" child who grabs toys from others, but the reason is that the child cannot yet understand that someone else wants the same toy just as much as she does. It is important for adults to set appropriate limits on children's behavior at this age, but it is equally important to help the child become aware of the thoughts and feelings of others to overcome behavior that otherwise appears to be willfully selfish.

In the youngest preoperational children, egocentrism can be found even in terms of what they think someone else sees. For example, if someone on the phone asks a child how old she is, the child may hold up two fingers to indicate 2 years old, thinking that if she can see her fingers, then the person at the other end of the line can, too. Piaget's famous "three mountains task," illustrated in Figure 7.1, was used to assess egocentrism. Children were shown a

Intuitive thought
According to Piaget, the beginning forms of logic developing during the preoperational stage.

Egocentrism The inability to see or understand things from someone else's perspective.

T ☐ F ☐
We describe preschoolers as egocentric because they are selfish.
False

FIGURE 7.1

Piaget's three mountains task. In Piaget's three mountains task, a child who is egocentric believes that the teddy bear always sees the same view that she herself sees.

large model of three mountains (remember they lived in Switzerland where mountains were very familiar to them) on a table (Piaget & Inhelder, 1956). With the child standing on one side of the table, an adult shows her pictures of the mountains that show what they look like as viewed from each side of the table and asks her what a doll would see from each side of the table. Regardless of where the doll was, 4-year-old children reported that the doll saw the same view that they themselves saw. In other words, they did not differentiate between their own point of view and that of others. Egocentrism may be expressed in other ways. For example, if you ask a 3-year-old what to get Mommy for her birthday, he may reply "a toy truck!" If he likes it, he believes that she must like it as well. Egocentrism makes it difficult for children to understand that other people see, feel, think, and understand things differently than they do.

Conservation. An important cognitive skill that preoperational children have not yet acquired is **conservation**. Preschool children do not understand that the quantity of something (amount, volume, mass) remains the same regardless of changes in its appearance. If you were to take a lump of clay and flatten it into a pancake, you would realize that you still had the same amount of clay because you haven't added or removed any of it. However, preoperational children would be fooled by the change in the appearance of the clay and might think that the new shape had more or less clay than the original lump.

Piaget believed that one reason why preschool children are fooled when the shape of the clay changes is because they can only focus on one aspect of a problem at a time, a cognitive limitation he called **centration**. For instance, when preoperational children see water in several glasses, they only notice the height of the water and decide that the glass with the highest level has more water in it regardless of the width of the different glasses. They would be fooled by the height of the water, even if they had seen you pour the water from the tall thin glass into the short fat one. Later, when children are in the stage of concrete operations, they begin to **decenter** and are able to think about more than one aspect of this situation at a time. In this stage, children understand that they need to consider both the level of the water and the width of the container and they are able to come to the correct solution more easily. See **Active Learning: Conservation** for tests you can carry out with preschool and school-age children to understand more about the development of conservation.

Conservation The understanding that a basic quantity of something (amount, volume, mass) remains the same regardless of changes in appearance.

Centration Focusing on only one aspect of a situation.

Decenter The ability to think about more than one aspect of a situation at a time.

Active LEARNING

Conservation

To see the development of conservation, have a preschool child (age 3 to 5) and/or a school-age child (age 6 to 10) carry out the following tasks. Be sure to ask the preschooler the questions first if you are testing the two children at the same time.

1. **Conservation of volume** (see Figure 7.2a).

   Equipment: two identical transparent containers and a third transparent container that is a different shape.

   Fill the two identical containers with the same amount of water. Show these to the child and ask, "Do these containers have the same amount of water, or does one container have more than the other?" Be sure to adjust the amount of water until the child agrees that the containers have the same amount. Then tell the child to watch while you pour

FIGURE 7.2A

Piaget's conservation of volume, mass, and number tasks. These illustrations show you the types of transformations that occur when you are testing a child's ability to use reversibility and decentration to solve conservation problems.

Conservation of volume

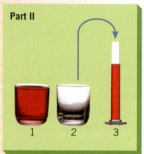

the water from one of the identical containers into the third container. Ask the child, "Now do these two containers have the same amount of water, or does one container have more than the other?" If the child answers that one has more, ask which one. For each child, be sure to ask *why* he or she thinks that they are the same (if that's what the child said) or why he or she thinks that one has more than the other (if that was the child's response). Their explanation of their belief is the most important part of this experiment.

2. **Conservation of mass** (see Figure 7.2b).

   Equipment: clay (you can use play dough, if you prefer).

   Make two identical balls of clay. Show them to the child and ask, "Do these two pieces of clay have the same amount of clay, or does one have more than the other?" Be sure to adjust the amount of clay until the child agrees that

FIGURE 7.2B

Conservation of mass

the two pieces have the same amount. Then take one ball and, with the child watching, roll it into a long tube. Ask the child, "Now, do these two pieces of clay have the same amount of clay, or does one have more than the other?" Be sure to ask each child *why* he or she thinks the two pieces of clay have the same amount or why one has more than the other, depending on how the child answered.

3. **Conservation of number** (see Figure 7.2c).

Equipment: eight identical items, such as pennies or cookies.

Make two rows of four items parallel to each other. Ask the child, "Does this row have the same number of pennies [or cookies] as this other row?" If the child does not agree they are the same, show the child by counting that each has four, and then ask again. Once the child has agreed that the rows are the same, move the pennies or cookies in one row so that they are much farther apart. Then ask the child, "Now, are there the same number of pennies [or cookies] in these two rows, or does one have more than the other?" Again, be sure to ask the child to explain his or her answer.

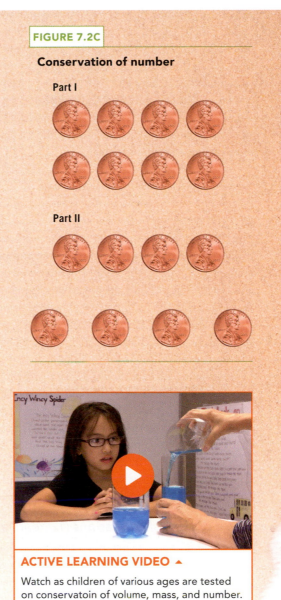

FIGURE 7.2C

Conservation of number

Part I

Part II

If the child you have tested is fooled by the change in the appearance of the liquid, the clay, or the row of objects, that child is still in the preoperational stage and cannot yet conserve volume, mass, or number. If the child is not fooled, he or she has developed the ability to conserve and is in concrete operations. Some children may show conservation for some of the tests but not for all. These children are in a transitional state, moving from preoperational to concrete operational thinking.

ACTIVE LEARNING VIDEO ▲

Watch as children of various ages are tested on conservatoin of volume, mass, and number.

To prepare for this activity, or, if you do not have access to a child, you can watch the video of this Active Learning.

To conclude, the preoperational stage is marked by an advance to symbolic thinking, but children's thinking at this stage is tied to what they see rather than what they reason out with the use of logic. Their perception is still tied to their own point of view, although they gradually begin to realize that others may see and understand the world differently than they do. Many of the limitations found in preoperational children are overcome in the next stage, called concrete operations.

Stage of Concrete Operations (7 to 12 Years)

The third stage in Piaget's theory is **concrete operations**. Children in the stage of concrete operations can think logically but the limitation of this period is that thinking is concrete

Concrete operations The third stage in Piaget's theory in which children between 6 and 12 years of age develop logical thinking but still cannot think abstractly.

rather than abstract. For example, how would you explain the saying "Don't put all your eggs in one basket"? As an abstract thinker, you might say, "Don't count on only one plan to work out. Have some backup plans." But a concrete thinker might say: "When you go to the store, take two baskets and put half your eggs in one and half in the other." Concrete thought is very much in the here and now. This is probably why we don't start teaching subjects that involve abstract thinking such as political science or philosophy to children until they are at least in middle school. Two cognitive advances that enable concrete operational thinking are reversibility and classification. Once children develop these cognitive skills, they are also able to solve conservation problems.

Reversibility is the ability to reverse mental operations. This ability allows a child to overcome the pull toward perceptual bias when making judgments about conservation tasks. For example, if the contents of a short, wide glass are poured into a tall, thin glass, the water level will be higher in the second glass. As we described earlier, this may cause the child to think the second glass contains more water. However, a child who understands reversibility realizes that if you reverse the procedure and pour the water back into the short glass, the amount will still be the same. If you carried out **Active Learning: Conservation** with a child in the stage of concrete operations, the child may have used reversibility to explain why they knew that the two glasses still had the same amount of water.

Changes in **classification** skills between the preoperational and concrete operational stage can be demonstrated through the game of "20 Questions." In this game, a child must ask a series of "yes" or "no" questions to figure out what the other person is thinking about. When playing 20 Questions, the first question an adult or older child is likely to ask is something like "Is it alive?" This is a highly efficient question because this eliminates a very large number of potential items: everything that is or is not alive. Children in the concrete operational stage will continue to work their way down from larger to smaller categories (for example, "Is it an animal?" or "Is it a plant?"), but children in the preoperational stage may start with very specific questions like "Is it a cat?" or "Is it my chair?" These children do not yet understand that individual objects can fit into larger categories. For Piaget, logical operations allow the child to understand that everything fits into larger and larger categories.

Stage of Formal Operations (12 Years and Older)

Thinking undergoes an important qualitative change as children enter adolescence. In middle childhood, children were able to think logically about concrete events but were not yet able to think about abstract or hypothetical concepts. Piaget's stage of **formal operations** is marked by the development of abstract thinking. Being able to think abstractly means teenagers no longer take literally a statement such as "Don't count your chickens before they hatch." They understand this does not refer to actual chickens. More important, in the stage of formal operations, teens can think about broad abstract concepts such as democracy rather than just concrete concepts, such as counting votes in an election. A younger child can think about *doctors* and *nurses*, but someone in formal operations can think about the *field of medicine* (LeHalle, 2006).

Piaget (1999) said that by the age of about 12 children begin to reason logically about hypothetical possibilities, rather than only about the concrete world. He called this new ability **hypothetico-deductive reasoning**. It has also been referred to as **scientific thinking** because it is the type of thinking scientists use when they set out to test a hypothesis. In adolescence, hypothetico-deductive reasoning allows individuals to generate new hypotheses that they can test to answer questions. In order to test their hypotheses, they must use deductive reasoning, a form of logic in which a general principle leads to a logical conclusion. Piaget believed that someone with formal operations is able to follow a logical process even if it does not fit reality. For example:

1. Brown cows give chocolate milk.

2. This is a brown cow.

3. Therefore, it gives chocolate milk.

Reversibility The ability to reverse mental operations.

Classification The ability to organize objects into hierarchical conceptual categories.

Formal operations Piaget's fourth stage in which people 12 and older think both logically and abstractly.

Hypothetico-deductive reasoning The ability to form hypotheses about how the world works and to reason logically about these hypotheses.

Scientific thinking The type of thinking that scientists use when they set out to test a hypothesis.

Obviously this is a false premise leading to a false conclusion, but the logical process behind it is sound. A concrete thinker would not be able to separate herself from reality to reach the logical conclusion, and would instead proclaim that no cows give chocolate milk. Piaget believed formal operations allow adolescents to step back from the concrete reality to reason in this more abstract, purely logical way.

Formal operational thought also includes the ability to generate many possible solutions to a problem and test them before making a decision in order to discover which one is correct. Measuring the effects of any specific variable requires holding all the other variables constant. To see one way in which Piaget tested this ability, you can try **Active Learning: Formal Operations**.

Active LEARNING

ACTIVE LEARNING VIDEO ▲

How systematic are these teens in attempting to study scientifically the answer to what makes the pendulum swing faster or slower?

Formal Operations

Piaget tested children of various ages on what he called the "pendulum problem." He provided each child with a pendulum, consisting of an object hanging from a string, and asked the child to figure out what determines how fast the string swings back and forth.

To carry out this activity yourself, find a length of string and attach an object to the end of it. Suspend the object so it can swing freely. Have available lighter and heavier objects and longer and shorter strings. Make a list of what you think might cause the string to swing quickly or slowly. Then write down the step-by-step process by which you would try to figure out which of the possibilities is the answer. If you have access to children of different ages, you can also do this with them, having each one generate her own list of possible causes and asking how she would test them. To prepare for this activity, or, if you do not have access to a child, you can watch the video of this Active Learning.

Some possible answers to what determines how fast the string goes back and forth that you or the child might come up with are the weight at the end of the string, the length of the string, the strength of the initial push, and the height from which the weight is dropped.

In order to test these possibilities, young children would simply try different combinations in an almost random fashion. For example, they might put a heavier weight on a longer string and then put a lighter weight on a shorter string, and in the process of trying different combinations they might stumble on the right answer. However, the hypothetico-deductive reasoning that appears in the stage of formal operations allows teens to approach this problem in a scientific way. They will think of possible answers to the problem and then test these specific hypotheses in a systematic way by controlling all the variables but the tested one. To learn the effect of the weight at the end of the string, they will vary the weight while keeping the length of the string, the strength of the initial push, and the height from which the weight is dropped the same. If varying the weight does not make a difference, they will test the strength of the initial push, and so on through all the possibilities. Did you (or a child you tested) carry out systematic experiments to determine the answer?

Have you figured out the answer to the pendulum problem? You can see the answer below.

Answer: It is the length of the string that determines how fast it goes back and forth.

When teens develop the ability to carry out the scientific process, they are able to take an idea or hypothesis and look at evidence to decide whether there is scientific support for it or not. However, just because they have the ability to think at this higher level does not mean that they always do. Kuhn (2009) states that we develop two systems of thought, one based on experience and the other on analysis. Effortless, intuitive thinking based on experience causes many people to make judgments without reflecting on all the possibilities. For example, Jonas plays violent video games but believes that he himself is not an aggressive person. On this basis, he disagrees with research on large samples of teenagers showing that those who play these games are more likely than others to be aggressive. This is an example of putting personal experience above scientific thinking. Jonas would be thinking analytically if he found scientific evidence that opposed or modified the first finding, for example a study in which boys who were aggressive before playing violent video games became more aggressive after playing, but non-aggressive boys did not become more aggressive. Argument and counterargument, based on evidence, is the essence of the scientific process and develops only with formal operational thinking.

Piaget believed that not everyone reaches the stage of formal operations and that many people remain concrete thinkers all their lives. In one study in England, 14-year-old students tested on the pendulum task in 1976 were compared with 14-year-olds tested in 2007 (Shayer & Ginsburg, 2009). At both times, the majority of 14-year-olds did not reach the level of formal operations on this task, but the percent who did declined over this time period from 23% to 10% for boys and from 25% to 13% for girls. There is some evidence that achieving this level of thought is not the product of maturation but rather is dependent on whether an individual's education trains him or her to develop it (Artman, Cahan, & Avni-Babad, 2006). Formal operational thinking continues to develop through adolescence, so it may be that students who do not show formal operational thinking will develop this level of thought later in their development. However, they may never develop formal operational thinking.

One consequence of this ability to think hypothetically is that teens may become idealistic because they now can imagine what *could be* rather than simply what *is*. Idealism can motivate them to engage in activities in which they are committed to a larger goal. It can also cause them to question adult authority, for example, by confronting rules. They realize that even though there is a rule, it doesn't mean it always has to be that way. Other alternatives are just as reasonable and logical, and they may want to fight for these alternatives.

Imaginary audience The belief that one is the center of other people's attention much of the time.

The imaginary audience. This girl likely assumes that others are looking as closely at her appearance as she is. Is her "audience" real or imaginary?

Adolescent egocentrism. As you recall, Piaget described young children in the preoperational stage as egocentric because they are unable to see things from the perspective of people other than themselves. David Elkind proposed that there is a resurgence of egocentrism in early adolescence, making it difficult for young teens to see the world from others' perspectives. However, this egocentrism is different from that of the preoperational child. According to Elkind, adolescent egocentrism is expressed through what he has called the *imaginary audience* and the *personal fable* (Alberts, Elkind, & Ginsberg, 2007).

When Elkind refers to an **imaginary audience**, he means that young teens believe they are the center of other people's attention in the same way that they are the center of their own attention. Teens may refuse to go to school because their hair looks bad, or they may become self-conscious about the way their body looks. In the young teen's mind, everyone at school will also be very aware of his or her perceived flaws, although it is more likely that most other teens are more concerned about how they themselves look than they are about how other people look. Although the "audience" is often seen as harsh and judgmental, it can also be positive: "Sometimes when I see a good-looking girl/boy, I think that they are looking at me in a very admiring way" (Alberts et al., 2007, p. 75). Of course, social media has brought the concept of the imaginary audience to a new level. Teens can present themselves online, and imagine that hundreds or thousands of people are interested in them (Cingel & Krcmar, 2014).

Elkind developed the Imaginary Audience Scale to measure this aspect of adolescent egocentrism (Elkind & Bowen, 1979). The following is an item from that scale:

Instructions: Please read the following stories carefully and assume that the events actually happened to you. Place a check next to the answer that best describes what you would do or feel in the real situation.

You are sitting in class and have discovered that your jeans have a small but noticeable split along the side seam. Your teacher has offered extra credit toward his/her course grade to anyone who can write the correct answer to a question on the blackboard. Would you get up in front of the class and go to the blackboard, or would you remain seated?

_____Go to the blackboard as though nothing had happened.

_____Go to the blackboard and try to hide the split.

_____Remain seated.

(Elkind & Bowen, 1979)

The first answer reflects a willingness to be exposed to an imaginary audience. The second reflects more discomfort, and the third reflects the most discomfort with exposing yourself to an imaginary audience. Elkind and Bowen (1979) found that the highest scores on this scale, indicating acute awareness of an imaginary audience, were found in eighth graders, a time when adolescents are particularly sensitive about their appearance, but research since that time has found that preoccupation with the imaginary audience and self-consciousness continue to increase throughout adolescence (Takishima-Lacasa, Higa-McMillan, Ebesutani, Smith, & Chorpita, 2014). Not surprisingly, thoughts about an imaginary audience may fluctuate for individuals depending on the life events they face (Galanaki, 2012). For instance, young teens entering a new school might worry more about what others are thinking about them and imagine that other students are looking closely at them.

A **personal fable** is a belief held by teenagers that their experiences are unique and different from those of everyone else. For example, a girl whose boyfriend has broken up with her may think, "My mother could never understand what I am going through. She could never have felt a love like I felt." While such thoughts may be harmless, the personal fable can become the basis of risky behaviors (Alberts et al., 2007). For instance, a teen may understand the effect of alcohol on reaction time but still believe that he is such a good driver that "I can drive drunk and nothing will happen to me." Or a teen might understand the risks of unprotected sex but still feel that "I won't get pregnant—that only happens to other people."

Martin and Sokol (2011) proposed that the imaginary audience and personal fable represent more than the egocentric focus on the self that we associate with adolescence. They also can be seen as adaptations that help the adolescent deal with some of the important developmental tasks of this stage of life. Adolescents encounter many new interpersonal situations and are understandably concerned about how they are perceived in those situations. The imaginary audience gives adolescents the chance to imagine what might happen in these situations and to anticipate some ways to handle them. The personal fable, with its focus on the uniqueness of individual, helps prepare the young person for the individuation (or separation of the self) from his or her family that typically comes as the adolescent moves into young adulthood.

Personal fable The belief (often held by teenagers) that you are in some way unique and different from all other people.

Postformal operations
The cognitive ability to consider multiple perspectives and bring together seemingly contradictory information.

Is Formal Operations the Final Stage?

Piaget's studies led him to the conclusion that the stage of formal operations was the final, highest stage of mental development. However, some theorists believe cognitive development can continue to another stage called **postformal operations**.

In the stage of postformal operations, the individual comes to understand that knowledge is not absolute; that is, there is not always one and only one right answer. Through this process, an individual can consider multiple perspectives and reconcile seemingly contradictory information (Labouvie-Vief, 2006). For example, people who agree with the following statements are indicating that they think at the postformal operational level: "I see that a given dilemma always has several good solutions," "There are many 'right' ways to define any life experience; I must make a final decision on how I define the problems of life," and "I am aware that I can decide which reality to experience at a particular time, but I know that reality is really multi-level and more complicated" (Cartwright, Galupo, Tyree, & Jennings, 2009, p. 185). Clearly the complexity of thought in this stage goes beyond the logical, abstract processes proposed by Piaget in the stage of formal operations.

CRITIQUE OF PIAGET'S WORK

Although Piaget's observations and experiments demonstrate aspects of children's behaviors that have been replicated many times, some researchers have argued that Piaget drew incorrect conclusions from his results. Two of the criticisms focus on the age at which Piaget says each of the cognitive abilities emerges and on the critical issue of whether cognitive abilities develop together in qualitative stages or separately in a series of small steps. The third major criticism has centered on whether the stages Piaget described are universal or culturally determined.

Ages and Stages

One criticism of Piaget's work is that the tasks he developed actually tested more than the concept he intended to test. For example, Piaget believed that *seriation,* or the ability to put objects in order by height, weight, or some other quality, does not appear until the stage of concrete operations. In support of this conclusion, you would find that if you give a younger child many sticks of different lengths to put in order by height, he would likely be unable to do so accurately However, if you were to give this same child three sticks to put in order, he may be able to do so with no difficulty. Piaget's critics claim, therefore, that young children are capable of seriating, but are unable to do so when their cognitive abilities are overwhelmed by complexities of the task that are irrelevant to the basic ability. In this case, being unable to compare a multitude of sticks may have overcome the child's basic ability to seriate. There have been many other similar studies demonstrating that younger children are capable of more than Piaget found if the tests are simplified in some way.

You'll remember from Chapter 1 that the issue of whether development proceeds through a series of small steps or in leaps and bounds is a central issue for all developmental theories. Piaget's theory organized cognitive development into stages that reflect qualitatively new ways of thinking, but some critics have claimed that these stages do not really exist as distinct entities. For instance, Mareschal and Shultz (1999) describe development of the ability to seriate as a series of small steps: the child can arrange 2, then 3, then 4 sticks as he gets older. This would indicate that the ability develops gradually rather than as the result of a major reorganization in the way the child thinks when he enters concrete operations. However, Jerome Kagan (2008) has argued that infants' early abilities that look like the abilities Piaget has described in older children are not necessarily the same thing. For example, a young infant reflexively grabs an object put in her hand and one could argue that this grabbing is the precursor of the grabbing a toddler does when she wants a toy someone else is holding. However, even though one behavior looks like the other, they are clearly different in meaning. Kagan argues that claiming a toy as "mine!" requires a major reorganization of cognitive function that is significantly different from the earlier level of reflexive action. This point of view supports Piaget's idea that cognitive development is organized in qualitatively different stages.

How Universal Is Cognitive Change?

Piaget believed that the stages he described would apply to all children around the world. When his ideas were initially tested in a variety of cultures, researchers simply used Piaget's exact methods (Maynard, 2008). This research found Piaget's stages in these cultures but they emerged at later ages than Piaget suggested. For this reason, early research described the progress of children in non-Western cultures in negative ways, such as "lagging," or "slow" (Maynard, 2008, p. 58). This turns out to be a good example of cultural insensitivity, as researchers were applying the measures developed in their own culture to assess children who grew up in a different culture.

Were these delays really an indication that non-Western children moved through the stages of cognitive development more slowly, or were they simply an artifact of how they were being tested? To answer this question, cross-cultural researchers attempted to adapt Piagetian tasks in ways that made them more culturally relevant for use in non-Western cultures. For example, Saxe and Moylan (1982) adapted Piaget's conservation of length task for use with children from Papua New Guinea. To assess the children's understanding of conservation of length, the researchers used both bamboo sticks of different lengths (material that is similar to the way this task is done in Western settings) and string bags (which are common items in the everyday life of the children in New Guinea). Among children who did not attend Westernized schools, there was no developmental change in their understanding of the stick task with increasing age, but

Culture and cognitive abilities. This girl from Zinacantán in Chiapas, Mexico, will learn to weave extremely intricate patterns that require concrete operations to understand. Researchers have not always looked at culturally defined abilities such as these to determine the level of children's cognitive development.

there clearly was a developmental trend for the string bag task that showed evidence of a growing understanding of conservation. Other research done in a culturally sensitive way found that children reached the Piagetian cognitive milestones at about the age his theory predicted. These findings support Piaget's claim of universal change.

Controversy continues to surround Piaget's work, and there are many modern theorists who see him only as a historical figure with little relevance to modern research (Desrochers, 2008). However, there are many others who see his work as the foundation for much of our current understanding of children's cognitive development.

We next describe an approach to understanding cognitive development that emerged out of research that was critical of Piaget's ideas, called the *theory of core knowledge*. This approach presents evidence that early cognitive abilities are determined biologically rather than through interaction with the environment as Piaget had claimed.

CHECK YOUR UNDERSTANDING

1. What is the difference between accommodation and assimilation in Piaget's theory?

2. Describe the major cognitive advances in each of Piaget's four stages of cognitive development.

3. How do the personal fable and the imaginary audience affect development during adolescence?

4. What criticisms have been made of Piaget's theory?

THEORY OF CORE KNOWLEDGE

7.2   **What is the premise of the theory of core knowledge?**

Would you be surprised by any of the following?

1. A ball that was buried in the sand in one location is pulled out of the sand in a different location.

2. You see one doll in a case. Someone then hides the case, and you see that person add one other doll. When the case is later opened, there are three dolls in it; in other words, 1 + 1 = 3.

3. You see a block pushed to the end of a small platform and then beyond the edge so that most of it is not supported, and yet it does not fall, as shown in Figure 7.3.

Violation of expectation
Research based on the finding that babies look longer at unexpected or surprising events.

Theory of core knowledge
The theory that basic areas of knowledge are innate and built into the human brain.

T ☐ F ☐ Infants appear to have an intuitive understanding of how gravity works.
True

These are just a few of the scenarios that have been presented to babies within the first year of life to determine their understanding about the nature of objects and how they function. Researchers believe that babies look longer at something they don't expect to see. Would you look longer at someone with a hat on his head or someone with an octopus on his head? Based on this **violation of expectation** paradigm, researchers have found that babies look longer at the events described here than they do at expected events (for example, 1+1=2 dolls), even before their first birthday (Baillargeon, Needham, & DeVos, 1992; Newcombe, Sluzenski, & Huttenlocher, 2005).

From the three examples mentioned, it appears that (1) infants understand that objects remain in the same place unless moved, an indication that they have a form of object permanence; (2) they have a basic concept of number, at least up to three; and (3) they have a basic understanding of the effects of gravity. Many other competencies have been explored and found so early that researchers claim they are innate abilities, and this conclusion is the groundwork for the theory of core knowledge.

The **theory of core knowledge** is a modern theory based on the idea that humans are born with innate cognitive systems for understanding the world (Spelke & Kinzler, 2007). These basic systems are not developed from experience, but rather represent core knowledge that appears to be built into the human brain. This theory is a direct challenge to Piaget's ideas that children construct even very basic knowledge about the nature of objects and people through experience. Although researchers who subscribe to the theory of core

FIGURE 7.3

Do infants understand gravity? Even babies are surprised when they see an object seemingly defying gravity, as in the last frame below.

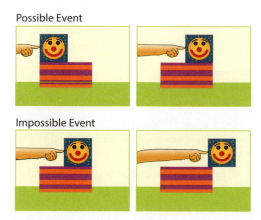

Possible Event

Impossible Event

knowledge claim that infants are born with certain basic knowledge, there are some differing ideas about what exactly comprises that set of knowledge. Spelke and Kinzler (2007) present evidence for four areas of core knowledge:

1. Knowledge that an object moves as a cohesive unit—it does not contact another object unless they are close to each other, and it moves on a continuous path.

2. Knowledge that agents (people) act purposefully toward a goal—infants also know that objects are not acting with a goal "in mind" in the same way that people do.

3. Knowledge (within limits) of number, as experienced in all modalities—for example, *hearing* a number of tones or *seeing* a number of objects. This understanding is not exact and gets less precise as the number gets larger. The knowledge of number also includes a basic understanding of addition and subtraction.

4. Knowledge of spatial relationships—this includes how to use the shape of one's environment to find out where one is when one becomes disoriented.

Spelke (2000) argues that these earliest core understandings of the world provide the basis for the learning that then occurs as children develop.

The idea that these basic forms of knowledge are innate and built into the brain is an ongoing area of controversy. For example, although Spelke and Kinzler (2007) argued that infants know from birth that people but not objects act with intention, other researchers have provided some evidence that these abilities are learned very early but are not innate. Woodward (2009), for instance, found that infants are more likely to understand other people's intentions in reaching for objects after they themselves have learned to intentionally reach for an object. She argues that they learn from their own actions about how to interpret the actions of other people.

The ongoing research in this area is a wonderful example of the scientific process, as evidence and counter-evidence help us refine our understanding of the early stages of cognitive development. **Journey of Research: Is Object Permanence Learned or Innate?** describes some of the research that has examined the question of whether babies are born knowing that objects continue to exist even when they cannot be seen or whether this knowledge is learned.

JOURNEY OF *Research*

Is Object Permanence Learned or Innate?

Research on object permanence carried out from a Piagetian perspective has found a developmental progression as his theory would predict. Infants younger than 7 months do not search for a hidden object, at a slightly older age they will retrieve an object that is partially hidden, and finally by 8 to 10 months of age, they can retrieve an object that is totally hidden (Moore & Meltzoff, 2008).

However, according to the theory of core knowledge, infants are *born* with "persistence"—that is, an understanding that objects persist through time and space (Baillargeon, 2008). In other words, they are born with object permanence. Piaget's critics have pointed out that the way he tested for object permanence—retrieving an object from under a cover—requires much more than understanding that the object continues to exist when it cannot be seen. Infants also must be able to remember where the object was, plan for its retrieval, and have the motor skills to reach out and grasp the object (Baillargeon, Li, Ng, & Yuan, 2009).

(Continued)

(Continued)

How can we look for evidence of object permanence without relying on these other abilities? When modern researchers have used more sophisticated techniques that reduce the difficulty of the task, they report evidence of object permanence (or persistence) at much younger ages. For example, researchers can use computer software to track where a baby is looking. Based on the idea that infants will look longer at events that surprise them, researchers have found that babies look longer at events that violate an expectation of object permanence. Baillargeon, Spelke, and Wasserman (1985) showed 4-month-old babies a toy. A screen was then placed in front of the toy and tipped slowly backward. In the real world, the screen would hit the toy and stop tipping. Some babies saw exactly that (the expected outcome), but some babies saw the screen continue to tip all the way back, as if it were going right through the toy (an unexpected outcome). Babies in the unexpected outcome condition looked significantly longer than those in the expected outcome condition. Therefore, it appeared that babies knew the object should still be there even though they couldn't see it and should have stopped the screen from tipping backward.

This line of research has continued to be controversial. Sirois and Jackson (2012) have questioned whether longer looking time is really a measure of surprise. Instead they examined changes in the dilation of infants' pupils during the same task as the one Baillargeon developed. Pupils dilate in response to how much light is present, but they also get larger in response to interest, arousal, and the amount of information being processed. In their research with 10-month-old infants, Sirois and Jackson found no change in pupil size when it appeared to the infant that the screen was going right through the toy. Their interpretation of the results reported by other researchers was that longer looking time actually reflected the infant's interest in other factors, such as the movement of the screen, not surprise indicating object permanence. Using this interpretation, they concluded there was no evidence for object permanence in these infants.

The ongoing research on object permanence is a good illustration of the way we have used new techniques to try to answer longstanding questions in our field. It also reminds us that the conclusions we draw from research depend upon the way we interpret the results we find.

Before leaving the discussion of the theory of core knowledge, it is important to note that some have concluded that the approach proposed by this theory is "woefully inadequate to fully explain adult human functioning" (Cole & Cagigas, 2010, p. 131). They argue that culture plays a central role in shaping the nature of cognition, as it develops from its earliest beginnings to its adult form. In the next section, we look at one theory of cognitive development that centers on the idea that culture shapes how our thoughts develop.

CHECK YOUR UNDERSTANDING

1. What are four areas of core knowledge that have been identified?
2. What is violation of expectation and what does it tell us about how infants understand the world?
3. How does the theory of core knowledge differ from Piaget's theory of cognitive development?

VYGOTSKY'S SOCIOCULTURAL THEORY OF COGNITIVE DEVELOPMENT

7.3 What are the basic processes described by Vygotsky's sociocultural theory?

Lev Vygotsky (1896–1934) lived in Russia during the time of the communist revolution. Marxist principles played an important role in shaping his study of the human mind. The principles included a focus on the process of development, collective activities, and the importance of understanding development within its cultural and historical context (Gielen & Jeshmaridian, 1999).

Although Vygotsky had supported much of the ideology of the communist government, his work was banned in his home country during his lifetime in favor of the "reflexology" of Pavlov, which denied the importance of the mind and its inner processes (Trevarthen, 1991). As a result, Vygotsky's work did not become available in the West until 1962, when his book *Thought and Language* was published in English. Since then his ideas have become very influential in the study and application of cognitive theory and have had a particularly profound effect in the field of education.

In contrast to Piaget, who saw the child as an active but largely independent learner, Vygotsky believed all learning and ideas begin in the social world. Consequently, learning is culturally based, because all people are situated within their own culture. The tools, language, and actions of a particular culture are transmitted to children and serve to shape their cognitive abilities (Gauvain & Parke, 2010). Central to Vygotsky's theory is the idea that children learn through the process of social collaboration with someone who is more knowledgeable than they are. Vygotsky described three ways in which children's ideas are shaped by their interactions with a more experienced person: the zone of proximal development, scaffolding, and private speech.

THE ZONE OF PROXIMAL DEVELOPMENT (ZPD)

Vygotsky began his work as a psychologist by working with children who had physical and mental impairments. At first he simply tested children's mental abilities. However, he soon developed the idea that children should be tested twice: the first time performing on their own and the second time performing with a little help from an adult. This technique assesses the child's readiness to learn, as well as the child's actual level of achievement. The difference between what the child can do independently and what the child can do with the help and guidance of a more skilled adult or peer is what Vygotksy (1978) called the **zone of proximal development**, or ZPD. ZPD has become the basis for dynamic assessment of children that focuses on what the child can do with a little guidance.

Zone of proximal development According to Vygotsky, this is what a child cannot do on her own but can do with a little help from someone more skilled or knowledgeable.

SCAFFOLDING

Scaffolding is what an adult does to move a child through the ZPD to achieve knowledge. A scaffold is the structure that goes up around a building so that workers can stand on it to create or improve the building. Vygotsky uses this term to describe the way adults and older children form a cognitive structure around a child that they can use to move the child to fuller understanding. When that is achieved, the scaffolding is no longer needed and comes down; in other words, the child can now carry out the task independently.

Scaffolding The idea that more knowledgeable adults and children support a child's learning by providing help to move the child just beyond his current level of capability.

To better understand scaffolding, think about teaching a child to tie her shoes. For an infant, you would simply do it for her. For a 2-year-old, you might hold her hands and do it with her. For a preschooler, you might show her the "bunny ears" approach, in which the child forms two loops and circles one around the other, maybe with a song or rhyme that goes with the process. By age 6 or 7, you can teach the child how to wrap one string around and through the other. The amount and type of help you provide at each of these steps is the scaffold that supports the child's learning. Finally, no scaffolding is necessary when the child can perform this task on her own. Teaching in this way is a sensitive process of helping the child achieve what is just out of reach and then stepping back when the child can do it alone. When we present learning opportunities that are far beyond the child's current level, the child cannot benefit from our instruction. If we continue to present opportunities that the child has already mastered, this also fails to advance the child's understanding. It is when we get it just right—in the zone that is just a little beyond the child's current level—that our instruction is effective and learning occurs.

In the following example, a teacher demonstrates effective scaffolding in teaching her kindergarten class about a new book they are about to read. See what techniques you see that exemplify the strategy of scaffolding:

Ms. Palmer: Now, we are going to talk about shoes, because that's what our book's going to be about. Before we are going to start talking about shoes, we need to talk about what happens when we come to a word we don't know. What are you going to do if you come to a word you don't know, Declan?

Declan: Sound it out.

Ms. Palmer: Sound it out, very good. Now, I need to ask you a question, Declan. This word is in our book. (Teacher writes "slippers" on a small white board.) Can you guys figure that word out? Someone tell me what that is? I like what I hear you doing, Declan. I like what Riley's doing, too.

Students: (The children make various attempts to decode the word "slippers.")

Ms. Palmer: Very good, this is the word "slippers." But more importantly, what Ms. Palmer heard you doing was . . . I did not see you going like this s-l-i-pp-e-r-s. You didn't try to sound each letter, right? No, I heard Declan go "sliii." And I heard Riley going, "errrs." Do you know what you guys were doing and you probably don't even realize it? Do you know? Riley?

Riley: We were chunking.

Ms. Palmer: You were chunking! You guys are so awesome. You were chunking. My favorite way of sounding out. So when it's a longer word, we need to find chunks that we know. Very good. There are going to be different types of shoes in here. (Ankrum, Genest, & Belcastro, 2014, pp. 43-44)

You might have seen that Ms. Palmer introduced a problem (what to do with new words), then invited a student to contribute what he already knew about how to deal with that problem (sounding it out). She then had the students try this strategy and picked out the strategy she wanted them to use (chunking). However, instead of just telling them what to do, she invited them to figure out what they had been doing with a little help from her. Did you see any other aspects of scaffolding in this example?

PRIVATE SPEECH

Private speech is an essential component of the learning process for Vygotsky. He stated that the child hears what others say to him and then he says it in some form to himself.

Private speech Talking to oneself, often out loud, to guide one's own actions.

Scaffolding is what the *adult* does, but private speech is what the *child* does to change external interactions into internal thoughts. For example, an adult might scaffold a child's attempts to put together a jigsaw puzzle by saying, "First try to find the pieces with one flat side to put on the outside edge of the puzzle." You may then hear the child saying to himself, "Flat pieces, find flat pieces." The child is talking to himself to guide his own actions. Vygotsky and others have shown that the more difficult the task, the more children talk to themselves in this way (Aro, Poikkeus, Laakso, Tolvaned, & Ahonen, 2015; Duncan & Cheyne, 2002; Fernyhough & Fradley, 2005). Gradually this private (or self-directed) speech becomes inner, unvocalized speech, and finally it becomes thought. Research has shown that young children who talk to themselves in this way are able to carry out difficult tasks more successfully than those who do not talk to themselves as they work (Berk, Mann, & Ogan, 2006).

Children also use private speech in situations that do not involve learning a new skill. Many children talk to themselves during fantasy play and before they go to bed. Nelson (2015) studied this "crib speech" in a young girl called Emily. One night Emily was recorded saying the following while alone in her bed:

> . . . we're all going to get out of the car, go into nursery school, and Daddy's going to give us kisses, then go, and then say and then we will say goodbye, then he's going to work and we're going to play at nursery school. Won't that be funny? Because sometimes I go to nursery school cause it's a nursery school day . . . (as cited in Nelson, 2015, p. 173).

Emily is representing her experiences using language and Nelson argues that this helps her understand the world around her. Just as adults might jot down reminder notes to themselves, children go over their experiences and represent them through speech while alone. Emily is remembering what she's been told and anticipating what will happen the next day, helping her to structure her activities in a way that makes sense to her.

Vygotsky saw cognition and learning as existing within the context of culture and history, not as an independent function within each human being. By contrast, in the next section we describe information processing, a theory that focuses on the variety of internal cognitive processes that are connected with individual brain function.

Scaffolding learning. These children are at different stages in learning to swim. According to Vygotsky's theory, each of these adults is providing the appropriate amount of scaffolding or help so the children can move on to being able to do things on their own.

thinkstock/comstock

©iStockphoto.com/Iuliia Sokolovska

1. What is the zone of proximal development?
2. How does scaffolding function in Vygotsky's view of cognitive development?
3. What role does private speech play in children's learning?

INFORMATION PROCESSING

7.4 How do attention, memory, executive function, and metacognition develop through childhood and adolescence?

Information processing has become one of the major contemporary approaches to the study of cognitive development. One problem with presenting information processing theory concisely is that there are many different approaches and the evidence from thousands of research studies does not yet fit into a single neat framework that would explain it all (Fogel, 2002). In this section, we talk about the processes that allow us to take in information, manipulate it in our minds, and think about how we are doing so. These processes include attention, memory, executive function, and metacognition.

ATTENTION

When someone is told to "Pay attention!" it means that person should focus her mental processes on one thing (maybe a teacher's words) and not on another (maybe her friends' conversation). Paying attention involves tuning in to certain things while tuning out others (**selective attention**) and maintaining focus over time (**sustained attention**; Fan et al., 2009). In this section, we examine how these aspects of attention develop in infancy, childhood, and adolescence. We then look at what happens when attention does not function as it should in children who have attention-deficit/hyperactivity disorder.

Attention in Infancy

What attracts infants' attention? For one thing, we know that infants will look longer at something they haven't seen before. This preference for novelty helps infants learn as much as they can about the world by focusing their attention on what is new. The other side of this attraction to novelty is that infants lose interest in what they have seen before, a process known as **habituation**. For example, if you enter a room that has a noisy air conditioner, you will probably be very aware of the sound at first. After a while, however, you would habituate to the sound, and no longer pay any attention to it. In the laboratory, habituation has been used to assess many aspects of cognition that infants obviously cannot tell us about in words. In the habituation procedure, a researcher shows an object to an infant over and over again and records how long the infant looks each time the object is presented. Normally, the infant will lose interest over time and will decrease the amount of time spent looking. The rate of habituation is how quickly the infant decreases the length of time spent looking with repeated showings.

As infants get older and their ability to process information becomes more efficient, they habituate to familiar stimuli more quickly (Colombo & Mitchell, 2009). The rate at which babies habituate is somewhat predictive of later cognitive abilities, but Colombo and Mitchell (2009) conclude that rate of habituation itself does not indicate intelligence; rather, habituation is a basic ability that is essential for the development of higher level learning.

Although sustained attention decreases as infants become familiar with a simple object and this happens more quickly as infants get older, sustained attention *increases* in older

Selective attention Tuning in to certain things while tuning out others.

Sustained attention Maintaining focus over time.

Habituation The reduction in the response to a stimulus that is repeated.

infants when they are shown more complex stimuli, such as a Sesame Street video, and this change continues on through preschool (Courage, Reynolds, & Richards, 2006). Think about completing a three-piece jigsaw puzzle over and over again. Clearly you would quickly lose interest. However, if you were given a complex puzzle to solve, your interest might grow with each new aspect of the puzzle that you noticed. This difference has also been found for infant attention.

Attention in Childhood

As children grow, they are increasingly capable of directing and sustaining their attention. However, as anyone who has worked in a preschool can tell you, some children can sit in circle time and pay attention, and others have great trouble doing so. Individual differences in the ability to focus and sustain attention have consequences for later development. In a longitudinal study, parents rated their 4-year-old child's attention span and persistence. Children who were better able to maintain focused attention and who persisted even when faced with difficulties had higher math and reading achievement at age 21 and a greater chance of college completion by age 25 (McClelland, Acock, Piccinin, Rhea, & Stallings, 2013).

Although individual differences in attention may in part be genetic (Posner, Rothbart, & Sheese, 2007), they are also influenced by the child's experiences. For example, attention in preschool children has been linked to differences in parenting that are related to the families' economic circumstances. Low-income mothers are likely to experience more parenting stress and tend to provide less stimulation and support to their children. These differences in parenting are related to more impulsivity and less sustained attention in 5-year-olds, and these characteristics, in turn, are related to lower cognitive, academic, and social competence (Dilworth-Bart, Khurshid, & Vandell, 2007). Focused and sustained attention is thus an important building block for future academic success.

Helen Neville and her colleagues (2013) also found that low-income preschoolers had less effective selective attention; that is, they were less able to ignore distracting stimuli than children from families with more resources. Neville developed a training program for these children focused on games that allowed them to practice attention skills. Her program also trained parents to promote their child's attention skills. After 8 weeks, she found positive changes in the way these children's brains functioned and also in their language skills, nonverbal IQ, social skills, and problem behaviors. Parents benefitted from the program too, showing reduced stress and greater ability to maintain conversations with their children.

The ability to sustain attention and avoid distractions (selective attention) increases greatly when children move into middle childhood and has been linked to achievement in both math and reading (Anobile, Stievano, & Burr, 2013; Franceschini, Gori, Ruffino, Pedrolli, & Facoetti, 2012). As children become more skilled in these areas, attention is also shaped by **automaticity**, the process by which skills become so well practiced that we can do them without much conscious thought. As cognitive skills become more automatic, they free up **processing capacity** (the amount of information the mind can actively deal with at one time) that can be used for other tasks. Think of a time when you were learning a complex skill like driving a car with a standard transmission. When you were first learning this skill, you needed to focus all your attention on what you were supposed to do and when you were supposed to do it. However, as you became more skilled, these actions became more automatic and you did not need to think consciously about each step (Diamond, 2006). We see this process at work in the way children learn to count or to

Automaticity The process by which skills become so well practiced that you can do them without much conscious thought.

Processing capacity The amount of information an individual can think about at one time.

Inattention and distractibility. Difficulty with the ability to focus and sustain attention on what is happening in the classroom puts a child at a significant disadvantage.

recognize words. At first, these cognitive tasks take a good deal of effort on the child's part, but over time they become so automatic they no longer take as much processing capacity. For example, children move from focusing their attention on the laborious process of sounding out letters to focus instead on reading words and entire sentences for comprehension.

Attention in Adolescence

When you sit down to read this book or do other academic work, do you have music on, answer text messages, and/or have TV running in the background? If so, you are like many students who have become so confident in their ability to control their attention that they believe that they can attend to several things at the same time, a process called **multitasking**. However, research does not support this belief. In fact, our brain can carry out only one thinking activity at a time. When we multitask, we really are switching back and forth between tasks. In doing so, we often lose track of our original task and miss whatever is occurring while we make these switches.

Multitasking Doing several different activities at the same time, often involving several forms of media.

One area of great concern is that teens often believe they can use electronic media successfully while driving, switching their attention from the road to their device and back again, but recent studies have shown that teens who talk on cell phones while driving have delayed reaction times to events on the road, weave between lanes, and are much more likely to have an accident. Teens who text message while driving increase their chances of being in an accident even more (Drews, Yazdani, Godfrey, Cooper, & Strayer, 2009). In fact, reaction time for people who either talk or text on a cell phone while driving is slower than the reaction times of drunk drivers (Strayer, Drews, & Crouch, 2006), yet 49% of young adults report they have texted while driving (Tison, Chaudhary, & Cosgrove, 2011). Of course, teens are not the only ones texting and driving. Adults are guilty of modeling this type of dangerous behavior when they use technology while driving. In most states, texting while driving is now against the law (Governors' Highway Safety Association, 2014). All drivers should be aware that texting typically involves taking their eyes off the road for 5 seconds. This means that at a speed of 55 miles per hour, they are covering the length of a football field, essentially with their eyes closed (CDC, 2016c).

Jason Doiy/E+/Getty Images

Texting and driving. Although many teens think they can multitask while driving, research shows their reaction times are slower than that of drunk drivers.

TRUE/FALSE VIDEO ▲

T ☐ **F** ☐
Adolescents are able to study efficiently while listening to a favorite TV show because by this age their attentional processes are so well developed they can split their attention between multiple activities.
False

Use of electronic media can also interfere with schoolwork for teens. In one experimental study, adolescents were assigned to one of two groups. One group did homework with soap operas on TV in the background, and the other group did homework without background TV. Those with the TV on took longer to do their work because they were distracted by the programs, and even though the two groups spent the same amount of time actually looking at their homework, the students with TV remembered and understood less when they were tested on it (Pool, Koolstra, & van der Voort, 2003). Pool et al. (2003) argue that the distraction of TV interfered with the students' ability to integrate all the information from the homework. Consequently, they ended up with a much more superficial understanding of the material and remembered less. Research on study habits has shown that the students who do the worst on their exams are those who study with many distractions: music, television, using e-mail, and/or talking with friends (Gurung, 2005). This finding has been confirmed in neurological research. It appears that when we try to do two things at once, we do not use the part of the brain designed for deep processing of information. Instead we use a different part designed for more superficial, rapid processing (Foerde, Knowlton, & Poldrack, 2006).

See the effects of multitasking for yourself by trying **Active Learning: Studying and Distractions.**

Active LEARNING

Studying and Distractions

1. Set a goal of reading 10 pages of this textbook when you are likely to have distractions. Note the time that you start reading. Write down the time you finish reading the 10 pages. Subtract your starting time from your ending time.

2. Now find a time and place to read 10 more pages of this textbook where you are reasonably certain not to be interrupted and will not to be tempted to interrupt yourself. Write down the time you start reading and the time you finish the 10 pages. Subtract to find out how long it took you.

3. Compare the results of studying both ways. Was one way more efficient than the other?

Bowman, Levine, Waite, and Gendron (2010) found that students who were interrupted with instant messages while reading a textbook online took much longer to do the same amount of reading than students who were not interrupted even when the amount of time spent on the distractions was subtracted from the total reading time. If you are used to studying with the television, computer, and cell phone on, look at your results and decide for yourself whether the interruptions made you slower. You may want to consider putting off your other activities until you have finished studying. The end result is likely to be more efficient studying and more free time for you.

Attention-Deficit/Hyperactivity Disorder

For some children the ability to focus and sustain attention is so compromised that it interferes with their ability to carry out everyday tasks. They may be diagnosed with **attention-deficit/hyperactivity disorder** (ADHD), defined in the DSM-5 as "a persistent pattern of inattention and/or hyperactivity-impulsivity that interferes with functioning or development" (APA, 2013, p. 59). About 5% of children are diagnosed with ADHD and boys are twice as likely as girls to receive this diagnosis (APA, 2013).

There are three patterns of symptoms: predominantly hyperactive-impulsive, predominantly inattentive, or a combination of both. A child with a hyperactive-impulsive presentation always seems to be in motion, fidgets, has trouble staying on task, can't wait for others to finish before speaking, and does everything quickly and without much apparent thought. This is more than a child with high energy. The child cannot control his impulsive behavior which interferes with his ability to function effectively on a day-to-day basis. A child with an inattentive presentation has difficulty with both sustained and selective attention. The child is easily distracted, has trouble getting organized, has trouble following directions, continually loses things, and often shifts from one task to another without completing any of them (APA, 2013). A child with a combined presentation shows symptoms of both inattention and hyperactivity-impulsivity.

Some of this might sound to you like a description of fairly typical behavior seen in an elementary classroom, but the behavior must be extreme and create significant impairment

© Bob Daemmrich/Alamy

The limits of attention. Teens believe that they can do homework effectively while they do many other activities at the same time. However, the evidence from research shows this is not true.

Attention-deficit/ hyperactivity disorder (ADHD) A disorder marked by extreme difficulty with inattention, impulsivity, or a combination of both.

FIGURE 7.4

Incidence of ADHD. According to parents' reports, their children's level of inattentiveness remained the same from early childhood through adolescence, but hyperactivity and impulsivity declined with age. Can you think of reasons why older children and adolescents might show less hyperactivity and impulsivity as they get older?

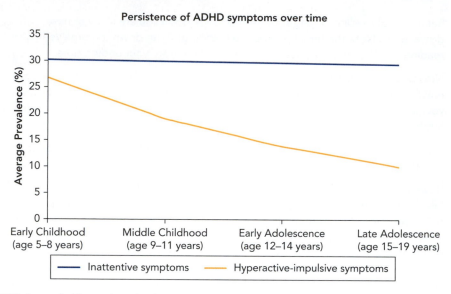

Persistence of ADHD symptoms over time

SOURCE: Centers for Disease Control and Prevention (2015i).

T ☐ F ☐ Attention-deficit/ hyperactivity disorder is a disorder of childhood, but fortunately children outgrow the symptoms with age. **False**

TRUE/FALSE VIDEO ▲

in the child's daily life in more than one setting, such as at home and in school, or in school and with peers, to receive this diagnosis (APA, 2013). Although the symptoms can change or lessen in severity as the child gets older, ADHD cannot be cured and is likely to continue into adulthood. If it is not diagnosed and treated, it can continue to cause problems in many aspects of the adult's life (Barkley, 2008). Figure 7.4 shows parents' reports of their children's ADHD symptoms as they grew from early childhood to late adolescence. While the level of inattentiveness remained the same in these children, the amount of hyperactivity and impulsiveness declined as they got older. A young child with ADHD might express hyperactivity by running around uncontrollably, while a teen might express the same tendency through fidgeting or restlessness—behaviors that are more controlled and less apparent to others. However, there still are consequences for teens with ADHD. The risk of accidents is higher at all ages for children with ADHD, but it is especially elevated when a teen with ADHD gets behind the wheel of a car. Teens with untreated ADHD are also more likely to develop substance use disorders (APA, 2013).

What causes ADHD? Both twin studies and adoption studies support the likely role of genetics, with some specific genes playing a part in the development of behaviors associated with ADHD. Differences in brain structure and function also have been identified (Frank-Briggs, 2011; Steinhausen, 2009). Structurally, the brain volume of hyperactive children has been found to be 5% smaller than that of children who are not hyperactive. Functionally, there are differences in the neurotransmitters that help with focusing attention and controlling impulses, and there is reduced communication between the posterior part of the brain which retrieves previously learned information and the front part of the brain which applies the information to a current situation (Semrud-Clikeman, 2014). Numerous environmental factors also have been investigated (ADHD Educational Institute, 2012). These include prenatal factors such as maternal use of alcohol or tobacco or exposure to other environmental toxins, and adverse family living conditions as the child grows up. As we know from Chapter 4, genetic and neurobiological factors can interact with environmental factors in complex ways and they can produce differences in the specific symptoms of ADHD, their severity, and course of development.

The American Academy of Pediatrics (2011) recommends that treatment of ADHD include the use of an approved medication, together with behavioral therapy which helps parents provide structure in their child's environment and positive reinforcement for good behavior. A variety of medications are used to treat ADHD, with stimulants such as Ritalin and Adderall being used most frequently. Although the exact way medication helps regulate behavior is not known, it appears to alter neural activity in the prefrontal cortex, which ordinarily inhibits behavior (Rubia, Alegria, & Brinson, 2014).

Because this combination of medication and behavioral therapy has been effective in increasing attention, improving impulse control, reducing task-irrelevant behavior, and reducing disruptive behavior, it is widely used in school-age populations (Smith & Shapiro, 2015). Although there is less research on the use of medication to treat ADHD symptoms in teens and adults than in children, the existing studies support the continued effectiveness of these medications beyond childhood (Prince, Wilens, Spencer, & Biederman, 2015; Vaughan et al., 2012). Some critics have charged that we rely too heavily on medication and that ADHD is being overdiagnosed, but other professionals attribute the increase in the number of children with this diagnosis to better identification of those who otherwise would have gone unrecognized and, therefore, untreated.

Some families use complementary or alternative therapies such as dietary modification or nutritional supplements as part of their child's treatment, but little or no scientific evidence supports the effectiveness of these approaches (Ballard, Hall, & Kaufmann, 2010; Karpouzis & Donello, 2012). Eliminating sugar from a child's diet has produced no behavioral improvement in ADHD symptoms, and eliminating food additives has had only small effects. Dietary interventions are not even mentioned in the American Academy of Pediatrics (2011a) practice guideline for treating ADHD.

We have, however, dispelled the idea that poor parenting causes ADHD (Kutscher, 2008). The challenging behavior shown by children with ADHD no doubt can disrupt effective parenting, so parents need to learn how to deal effectively with the child's behavior, but the parents' behavior is more likely a response to the child's characteristics rather than a cause of them.

MEMORY

Now that we have examined issues in the development of attention, we move on to the next step in information processing: memory. After we have paid attention to something, we must move it into memory if we want to use that information in the future. In this section, we describe the development of memory from infancy through adolescence, looking at how memory processes change as a function of age.

In Chapter 2, we introduced the stores model of information processing that describes how input to our sensory systems moves through a series of steps, illustrated in Figure 7.5. As information comes in through our senses, it is retained for a very brief period of time in its raw form. This is known as **sensory memory**. In this fraction of a second the information either moves along to the next step or is lost. Information that moves along then enters **working (or short-term) memory**. The capacity of short-term memory is limited, and information can be retained for only a brief time *unless* the information is processed. Working memory processes short-term memories using **encoding processes** and these processes help to move them along into **long-term memory**, which is thought to be capable of permanent storage. Figure 7.5 illustrates the stores model of information processing.

Memory in Infancy

How do we know whether infants can remember? In her classic work on infant memory, Carolyn Rovee-Collier (1999) had infants lie in a crib under a mobile with attractive toys

---

T ☐ F ☐ The primary cause of attention-deficit/hyperactivity disorder is poor parenting. **False**

Sensory memory The capacity for information that comes in through our senses to be retained for a very brief period of time in its raw form.

Working (or short-term) memory The memory system that stores information for only a brief time to allow the mind to process information and move it into long-term memory.

Encoding processes The transformation processes through which new information is stored in long-term memory.

Long-term memory The capacity for nearly permanent retention of memories.

FIGURE 7.5

The stores model of memory. This model of information processing shows information moving through a set of locations or "stores" to end up in long-term storage where it can later be retrieved and used by working memory.

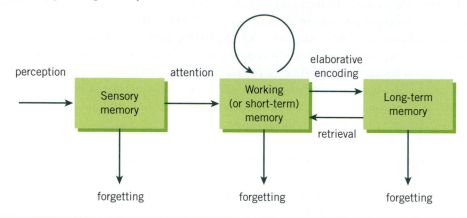

hanging on it. She then tied a ribbon from the baby's ankle to the mobile so that when the baby kicked, it would make the mobile shake in a pleasing way. Each baby learned to kick to move the mobile. The babies were then brought back into this situation, some after one day, some after several days, and some after a week or longer. If the baby remembered the mobile, she would kick right away. If not, she would have to learn all over again how to make the mobile move. Using this and another paradigm appropriate for somewhat older babies, Rovee-Collier found that 3-month-olds could remember what they needed to do for 1 week and 18-month-olds could remember for 13 weeks.

One limitation of infant memory is that infants are much more likely to remember something when they are in the same circumstances as when they first encountered it (Hayne, 2004). You may have had a similar experience when you see your professor or a classmate in the supermarket or the gym and you do not recognize that person in such a different context. Infants appear to have this difficulty to a much greater degree than older children and adults. However, just as your memory may return when the person reminds you how you know them, infants can recover memory with just a little reminder. In Rovee-Collier's research, when the experimenter shook the mobile briefly, 3-month-old infants remembered what to do after 1 month, 4 times as long as they could remember without the reminder (Bearce & Rovee-Collier, 2006).

Memory gradually increases between ages 1 and 2. Bauer and Leventon (2013) taught 13-, 16-, and 20-month-olds to imitate specific actions. The 13-month-olds could not remember these actions for even 1 month unless they were given reminders. The 16- and 20-month-olds could remember them for 1 month, but not for 3 months unless they were given reminders.

Infantile amnesia An adult's inability to remember experiences that happened before they were about 3 years of age.

T ☐ F ☐ Few people have clear memories of what happened in their lives before the age of 3. **True**

Infantile amnesia. Close your eyes for a minute and try to think of the earliest memory you can call to mind. Some people can remember particularly salient events that occurred before they were 3 years of age, such as an injury that led to treatment in the hospital (Peterson, 2002), but most people cannot recall events before age 3 because of what has been called **infantile amnesia**. This does not mean that infants cannot remember things that have happened to them because we have already seen that they can. Rather, it appears that later in life it becomes difficult to remember what happened in that earlier period of time.

Various explanations have been proposed for the occurrence of infantile amnesia. One explanation involves physical changes occurring in the brain. As we've seen, the brain is far from complete when an infant is born. Two areas that are necessary for memory processes are the hippocampus and the prefrontal cortex. Important parts of these two areas only become functional between 20 and 24 months of age (Bauer, 2007). We will see that memory continues to develop as these areas of the brain continue to develop throughout childhood and adolescence. A related hypothesis is that it is very rapid production of new neurons in the hippocampus during this period that interferes with the formation of stable memories (Akers et al., 2014; Josselyn & Frankland, 2012).

Other explanations have relied on psychological or cognitive explanations. Courage and Howe (2004) have argued that before infants have a clear sense of self, their memories are not organized into a coherent story of their own lives. It is much harder to remember random events than those that tie together in a meaningful way. Rovee-Collier (1999) has argued that we are generally better at remembering something if we use the same processes to retrieve that memory that we used earlier to store it. Infants use nonverbal processes because they have not yet developed language, so when older children and adults try to use their usual verbal methods, they are not able to recall the earlier nonverbally processed events.

One interesting study illustrated how verbal and nonverbal processes affect our memory differently. Toddlers were shown a demonstration of how a "Magic Shrinking Machine" could turn large toys into smaller ones (Simcock & Hayne, 2002). The toddlers were allowed to turn the crank themselves to make this happen. Most of the toddlers who were originally tested this way did not yet have enough language to describe what had happened. When they were brought back either 6 months or 1 year later, they had developed adequate vocabulary to describe the event, but they could not do so, even when shown the device and toys again. However, when they were allowed to use the Magic Shrinking Machine, they remembered just what to do and how it worked. Their nonverbal memory remained, but because the events had never been coded into verbal memory, they were unable to remember them with words to tell others. It appears that we can remember things from infancy nonverbally through our emotions and actions, but we can't talk about them with others. It has been argued that only when we can talk about events do we remember them in conscious thought (Fogel, 2002). In fact, when mothers talk with young children about their past experiences, their children are more likely to retain memories from early life when they are adolescents (Jack, MacDonald, Reese, & Hayne, 2009). When children develop the ability to remember the events of their lives in a coherent way, called **autobiographical memory**, they begin the narrative of their lives that forms the basis for the development of self-concept. In Chapter 11, we discuss how autobiographical memory relates to identity development.

Do they remember? Rovee-Collier's research has shown that infants can learn to kick to make a mobile move in an interesting way. When they are in the same situation even days or weeks later, they will remember how to do this.

Autobiographical memory
A coherent set of memories about one's life.

Memory in Childhood

Major changes are occurring in working memory as children develop. Working memory holds short-term memories while using them to solve problems and to move them into long-term memory (Tulsky et al., 2013). To illustrate, when you are given a string of numbers and then asked to say them backwards, you must remember the numbers at the same time that you are reversing their order. Working memory is what allows you to hold those numbers in memory at the same time as you think about how to arrange them in reverse order. The working memory of young children has a very limited capacity. The average 5-year-old can hold one or two pieces of information in his mind at a time (Alloway, 2010). In a practical way, this means that "put your book in your cubby, and come sit at the table" may be all the information he can handle in working memory at once, but the capacity of working memory steadily increases from age 4 to age 11 (Alloway, Gathercole, & Pickering, 2006; Gathercole, Pickering, Ambridge, & Wearing, 2004). To see one of the ways that working memory has been assessed in children, try **Active Learning: Working Memory**.

Active LEARNING

Working Memory

To see how working memory has been assessed in children (Gaillard, Barrouillet, Jarrold, & Camos, 2011), get a piece of paper large enough to cover a page in this book and cut a hole about ¼ inch tall and 1 inch wide about halfway down the paper. Line up the left edge of the opening so that you can see the START button in the window. Slide the paper down so you can see the first letter in the line below. Read the letter out loud and then quickly move down to the next row and add 1 to each number appearing in that row, stating each result out loud. Continue with each letter and series of numbers, covering the letters after you have read them out loud. When you reach STOP at the end of the series, try to recall the letters you read in the order they were presented.

Gaillard et al. (2011) report that third graders remembered on average two letters, while sixth graders remembered between three and four. How effective were you at keeping the letters in mind briefly while you carried out the addition? If you found this task difficult, it is because the brain has difficulty processing information (adding numbers), while at the same time maintaining memory for a new stimulus (the letters). When attention is diverted from the letters to perform the addition, the memory trace decays (Gaillard et al., 2011).

START

G

7 2 5

R

3 6 7

M

1 4 5

V

3 8 2

C

9 1 6

STOP

Information processing speed The efficiency with which one can perform cognitive tasks.

Encoding processes and information processing speed. One factor underlying the growth in working memory is a general increase in **information processing speed** which is how quickly we can perform cognitive tasks (Demetriou, Christou, Spanoudis, & Platsidou, 2002; Kail & Ferrer, 2007). Processing speed has generally been found to increase throughout childhood and adolescence, and these changes have been linked to changes in the overall structure of the brain (Erus et al., 2015). As processing speed increases, children can rehearse and retrieve information more efficiently so memory is increased (Ferguson & Bowey, 2005).

A second factor is that children develop encoding strategies that help them store and retrieve information, and these strategies improve in complexity and efficiency as children get older (Ghetti & Angellini, 2008). Children younger than 5 or 6 usually do not use a deliberate strategy to try to remember something even when they are taught to do so. By 5 to 6 years of age, they still do not use these strategies spontaneously, but they can use them when they are taught to do so. By age 7, children begin to use active strategies to maintain memory (Camos & Barrouillet, 2011), and spontaneous use grows throughout middle childhood (Schneider, 2002). However, the age of acquisition and use of these strategies varies enormously between individual children (Schneider, Kron, Hünnerkopf, & Krajewski, 2004). When 6-year-olds were asked how they memorized a group of pictures, their answers reflected these differences. While one child used an active encoding strategy: "I looked carefully and I repeated: red, blue, brown," another had no strategy: "I looked at them, and I remembered them . . . I just looked at them" (Visu-Petra, Cheie, & Benga, 2008, p. 101).

One encoding process that even young children use is the creation of mental **scripts** that help them remember what to do in a familiar situation (Nelson, 2014). Children as young as 3 might have a script for going out to lunch at a fast-food restaurant (and may act out that scenario in play with their friends), but older children, adolescents, and adults also use scripts. A school-age child might have a script for going to a friend's house for a sleepover, or a teenager might have one for how to behave the first time he meets a friend's parents.

Simply repeating information (the process of **rehearsal**) is another strategy that children, adolescents, and adults all use to improve memory. While this can be effective, if you can group information together while you learn it, you are more likely to be able to retrieve and use it later. If you are trying to remember words from a list that contains the words *horse, wrench, rose, hammer, pig, cow, tulip, saw,* and *lily*, you can group items into conceptual categories. Horses, pigs, and cows are animals; hammers, saws, and wrenches are tools; roses, tulips, and lilies are flowers. Another way to encode these words would be by the setting in which you find these items: a farm for the animals, a workshop for the tools, a garden for the flowers. Using strategies such as these improves children's recall, but younger children may not be able to recognize which aspects of the information they can use to encode information in this way.

Another encoding process is called **elaboration**. The idea here is to create extra connections that can tie bits of information together. You can do this through the use of images or sentences. For instance, if you need to remember to buy lemons on the way home, you could picture yourself walking to the parking lot wearing lemons on your feet instead of shoes. As you walked to the parking lot after your classes, this odd picture should easily come to mind to remind you to buy lemons.

See **Active Learning: Encoding Processes** to try different ways to encode information into memory.

Scripts Memory for the way common occurrences in one's life, such as grocery shopping, take place.

Rehearsal Repeating information to remember it.

DEVELOPMENT IN ACTION VIDEO ▲

Elaboration A memory strategy that involves creating extra connections, like images or sentences, that can tie information together.

Active LEARNING

Encoding Processes

Imagine that you need to memorize the following list of words:

| Seashell | Soccer | Beach | Skiing |
| Baseball | Sand | Basketball | Seagull |

How would you try to do it? Some possible strategies you might use include (a) repeating the words over and over, (b) dividing the list into those words that start with *s* and those that start with *b*, (c) dividing the list into sports- and beach-related words, (d) making a sentence or two using the words, and (e) imagining a picture that includes what each word represents.

Repetition	Initial Sound	Concept	Sentence	Imagery
Seashell	*S sound*	*Sports*	I took my *baseball* and my *basketball* to the *beach*. I sat on the *sand* and played with a *seashell* as I watched a *seagull* fly by. It was so hot that I wished I were *skiing* or even playing *soccer* instead.	Create pictures in your mind that include several images in each (a boy on a *beach* holding a *baseball* in one hand and a *basketball* in the other with a *seagull* sitting on his head).
Baseball	Seashell	Baseball		
Soccer	Soccer	Soccer		
Sand	Sand	Basketball		
Beach	Skiing	Skiing		
Basketball	Seagull	*Beach*		
Skiing	*B sound*	Seashell		
Seagull	Baseball	Sand		
	Beach	Beach		
	Basketball	Seagull		

Which of these approaches do you think would work best for you? Choose one and give yourself 30 seconds to memorize this new list of words. Then cover this list and test yourself. How effective was the technique you used?

Classroom	Penguin	Paper	Cardinal
Parakeet	Canary	PowerPoint	Computer

All of these ways of trying to remember a list of words are examples of encoding processes (and they are also techniques you may want to consider using when memory is required in your studying).

Adults foster memory development in children when they talk with them about their activities. If a parent asks a child what she did at school that day and has a conversation about it, the child will be more likely to form memories. Another way to promote memory is through music. You can probably remember the words to a song you have not heard for years when the first few notes are played. Music helps form powerful memories, which is one reason we teach children using songs. You likely know the alphabet song that has been used to help generations of children remember their letters.

Knowledge base. As children and adolescents learn more about the world, they build their knowledge base. This has implications for memory because it becomes easier to store away and recall information when you can make many connections between new information and previously learned information. Several research studies have found that children who are already experts in a subject are able to remember more information related to the subject of their expertise than children who are not experts, and increasing children's knowledge base on a particular subject results in better memory for new, related information (Blasi, Bjorklund, & Soto, 2003; Schneider, 2015).

You have seen this effect in action if you know a child or an adolescent who has a strong interest in a particular topic and has become an expert in that subject. Children who become fascinated with dinosaurs or baseball statistics, or who know everything imaginable about Harry Potter, quickly digest any new information they encounter on their favorite subject and can begin using that new information immediately with little effort. You can also see this process at work in the course on child development that you are currently taking. Your professor for this course will be able to integrate new information about child development into his or her knowledge base more quickly and with less effort than you are likely to be able to do. By the end of the course, however, your expanding knowledge base will allow you to understand and integrate any new information on child development more effectively than you could have before you studied this topic.

False memories. Have you ever been told that a memory for something that you thought had happened to you had actually happened to your sister or friend? How reliable are our memories? **False memories** occur for both adults and children. There are several different types of false memories. One type is memory of an event that never happened. Research has shown that it can be fairly easy to create the type of false memory in young children in which they think they have experienced something that never happened. In one study, children were told to imagine that they were taking a hot-air balloon ride and to think in detail about what it was like (Ceci, Bruck, & Loftus, 1998). They were then asked whether this had really happened to them. They were given similar instructions to remember in detail other events, some of which had really happened to them and some of which had not. The researchers repeated this for 11 weeks, and gradually children began to agree that they had in fact gone on a hot-air balloon ride. On the 12th week, another researcher interviewed each child, telling the child that the previous researcher had said some things that were not true. When the child was asked which things had really happened, many still remembered having taken the fictional balloon ride.

Sheer Photo, Inc/Getty Images

Building a knowledge base. This boy has built a large knowledge base about coins of the world. If he were given new coins to add to his collection, he would be able to remember these coins much more quickly than someone who does not have this background information.

Younger preschoolers were more likely to make these mistakes than older preschoolers. However, even adults are vulnerable to creating false memories through suggestion. When adults were given false feedback about a questionnaire they had filled out about food experiences they had had in childhood, their behavior and preferences were affected. In one study, participants were told that they had gotten sick on egg salad when they were children, and in a second study participants were told that they loved asparagus as children when they first ate it. In both cases, these suggestions were then experienced as memories by many of these adults and the memory affected their actual preference for these foods (Geraerts et al., 2008; Laney, Morris, Bernstein, Wakefield, & Loftus, 2008).

False memories Memory for something you thought happened but did not.

Another type of false memory, called *false recognition,* is created when we remember the gist of what we experienced rather than the specific details (Brainerd & Reyna, 2004). **Active Learning: Creating False Memories** will give you a chance to develop this type of false memory.

Active LEARNING

Creating False Memories

After you read these instructions you will see two lists of words. Cover the list of words on the right. Read the list on the left-hand side of the page, then cover that list, and look at the list on the right side. Circle the words on the second list that you saw in the first list.

(Continued)

(Continued)

desk	blackboard
pen	pen
blackboard	school
eraser	orange
PowerPoint	teacher
teacher	desk
student	grandfather

STOP: Don't read any further until you've tried this activity. Then look at the discussion written upside down below.

Did you mistakenly identify "school" as one of the words that you saw? If you did, you had a false memory, based on the fact that you knew that all of the words you initially saw were related to the concept of school. Therefore, you mistakenly "remembered" school as one of the words that you had seen in the first list.

> T ☐ F ☐ Older children and adults are less likely than younger children to think they remember something they never actually saw. **False**

Although you might think that younger children would be more likely to come up with false memories than older children or adults, this is not always the case. In tests such as the one used in **Active Learning: Creating False Memories**, older children are more likely to mistakenly identify a new related word as one they had seen in a previous list of words because they are more likely to remember that the words related to a particular category, while younger children remember the specific words because they do not think of them as belonging to a larger category. Brainerd and Reyna (2004) describe this as the **fuzzy trace theory**. They believe that there are two ways in which we remember. One is a planful, strategic way, such as the use of strategies we described earlier. The other is an intuitive, automatic way that they describe as a fuzzy trace memory in which we remember the gist but not all the details. Although children and adults of all ages use both types of memory, young children are more likely than older children or teens to have very specific, verbatim memories (e.g., "that's the same red coat you wore the last time!"), while older children are more likely to have extracted the meaning of an event and then remember the gist of the event rather than each detail (for example, "we had a great time at that party!").

Fuzzy trace theory The theory that there are two memory systems: a systematic, controlled memory for exact details, and an automatic, intuitive memory for the gist, or meaning, of events.

Memory in Adolescence

It appears that both long-term and working memory reach peak capacity at age 11 or 12 and do not change much after that (Bauer et al., 2013; Thaler et al., 2013). What does change through adolescence is the way the brain manages working memory. The prefrontal cortex of the brain continues to develop through adolescence, and this area of the brain is central to working memory in adults. However, when working on a memory task, younger teens are more likely to use both the prefrontal cortex and the hippocampus. By age 18, teens use only the prefrontal cortex, as adults do (Finn, Sheridan, Kam, Hinshaw, & D'Esposito, 2010). We can only speculate about the effects of using two areas of the brain versus the more efficient use of just the prefrontal cortex. Using two different parts of the brain may help younger teens be more open to storing information in different types of situations. While this may help them accumulate new knowledge, it also may make them less efficient at storing specific information (Finn et al., 2010).

EXECUTIVE FUNCTION

Executive function is the ability of the brain to coordinate attention and memory and control behavioral responses for the purpose of attaining a certain goal (Blair, Zelazo, & Greenberg, 2005). Although its exact definition and components are subject to much debate, this form of top-down cognitive control includes control of attention and working memory, speed

Executive function The ability of the brain to coordinate attention and memory, and control behavioral responses for the purpose of attaining a certain goal.

of information processing, cognitive flexibility, inhibitory control, and planning (Boelema et al., 2013; Weintraub et al., 2013).

Executive Function in Childhood

Executive function provides the basis for learning academic skills and may even predict school success more accurately than IQ (Blair & Razza, 2007). The ability to regulate your behavior is crucial to your ability to function well in a classroom setting (Ponitz, McClelland, Matthews, & Morrison, 2009). This includes being able to pay attention, follow directions, and inhibit irrelevant behavior. Children with more advanced executive functioning are able to learn basic language, literacy, and arithmetic skills more quickly (Bull & Lee, 2014; Viterbori, Usai, Traverso, & De Franchis, 2015). **Active Learning: Executive Function** gives you an opportunity to do a simple assessment of several aspects of executive function in young children, including attention, working memory, cognitive flexibility, and inhibitory control.

Active LEARNING

ACTIVE LEARNING VIDEO ▲

Watch as children of different ages demonstrate the concept of executive function.

Executive Function: Head-Shoulders-Knees-Toes

One aspect of executive function is the ability to control your own behavior. The ability to inhibit an automatic response in order to carry out the correct response in a particular situation is important for learning. You can make a simple assessment of these skills by playing "Head-Shoulders-Knees-Toes" with one or more preschool children between the ages of 3 and 6.

Tell the child you are going to play a game in which he or she should follow your directions when you say "touch your head" or "touch your toes." Give the child several opportunities to do this while mixing up the order of your directions, something like this: Touch your head, touch your toes, touch your toes, touch your head, touch your head, touch your toes. After you have established that the child can follow your directions, tell the child, "Okay, now let's be silly. When I tell you to touch your head, you should touch your toes. When I tell you to touch your toes, you should touch your head." Again give the child a set of directions, observing how easy or difficult it is for the child to inhibit the original response and shift to the contrary response.

Repeat the activity, using the instructions to "touch your shoulders" and "touch your knees."

If you can do this with children of different ages, or compare your results with others, you will see how much these executive functions develop in a relatively short period of time. While 3-year-olds will find it difficult to pay attention to your instructions, inhibit their first tendency to do what you say rather than doing the opposite, and remember the directions, 6-year-olds are likely to find it easy and fun.

To prepare for this activity, or, if you do not have access to a child, you can watch the video of this Active Learning.

Children are best able to develop executive function skills when their home and school provide organized and predictable environments. Children have higher levels of executive function when their parents are warm, stimulate the child's learning, and scaffold their learning by prompting, praising, and elaborating their work (Fay-Stammbach, Hawes, & Meredith, 2014). On the other hand, when children experience chaotic or threatening environments, executive function may suffer. If you think about a time when you were highly stressed, you may remember finding it difficult to think clearly about what you should do. When children experience continuing high levels of stress while their brains are developing, the effect on the brain may last longer than the stress itself. For example, children who have experienced abuse and neglect early in life generally have lower executive function ability (National Scientific Council on the Developing Child, 2005/2014). Also, the stress of living in poverty increases the risk of difficulties with executive function that have been linked to ADHD and other disorders including impulse control and attention problems (Raver, Blair, & Willoughby, 2013; Weintraub et al., 2013).

The good news is that intervention can improve these abilities. In one program called Tools of the Mind, young children were encouraged to tell themselves out loud what they were supposed to do to carry out extended dramatic play, and they were given aids to memory and attention. Children in this program were later found to have greater executive function ability, which correlated with greater academic skills, than a comparable group of children who did not take part in the program (Diamond, Barnett, Thomas, & Munro, 2007).

We next take a closer look at three specific abilities that underlie executive function: cognitive flexibility, inhibitory control, and planning.

Cognitive flexibility The ability to switch focus as needed to complete a task.

- **Cognitive flexibility** is the ability to switch focus as needed to complete a task. Researchers at the National Institutes of Health have recently developed a set of tests to assess executive function across the life span. The task used to assess cognitive flexibility is the Dimensional Change Card Sort, in which children are asked to sort cards by one criterion (such as shape) and then switch to another (such as color) (Zelazo et al., 2013). See Figure 7.6 for an illustration of this type of test. Three-year-olds find it very difficult to change from one task to the other but this type of cognitive flexibility improves through middle childhood.

Inhibitory control The ability to stay on task and ignore distractions.

- **Inhibitory control** is the ability to stop more automatic behaviors to do what is needed to carry out a task correctly. For example, one simple task used to assess inhibitory control is to ask children to tap a hammer twice after an adult has tapped it once and tap it once after the adult has tapped it twice. The child must overcome the automatic tendency to imitate what the adult has done in order to carry out the correct action. In an ethnically diverse sample, children's performance on this task was assessed at age 4 and their performance predicted their math achievement in first grade (Ng, Tamis-LeMonda, Yoshikawa, & Sze, 2015).

- Planning is another central aspect of executive function. Planning includes thinking through a task ahead of time and then evaluating the outcomes as you proceed through the task, changing what you are doing as necessary. This has often been assessed with the use of the game "Tower of Hanoi," shown in Figure 7.7. In this task, the goal is to move all the disks to the right-hand rod by moving one disk at a time and never putting a larger disk on top of a smaller disk. Simpler versions of this task have fewer disks to move. When working on the Tower of Hanoi task, adolescents spend a longer time than younger children thinking about the problem before they begin moving pieces and are quicker to solve the problem using fewer moves (Asato, Sweeney, & Luna, 2006).

FIGURE 7.6

The Dimensional Change Card Sort task measures cognitive flexibility. In the task below, children are shown the blue rabbit and the red boat and told to match a series of pictures by color first (the red rabbit goes with the red boat) and then subsequently on shape (the red rabbit goes with the blue rabbit). Being able to shift from one set of instructions to the other is an indication of cognitive flexibility.

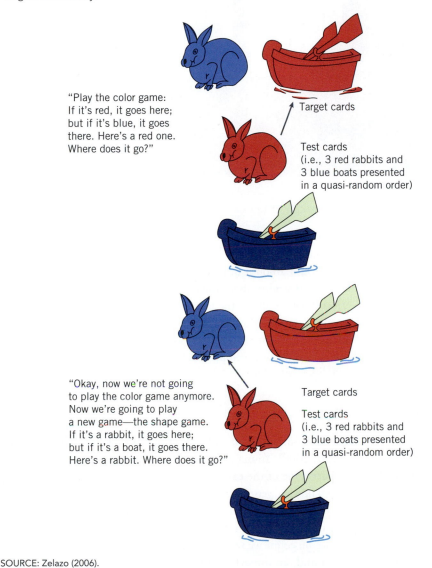

"Play the color game: If it's red, it goes here; but if it's blue, it goes there. Here's a red one. Where does it go?"

Target cards

Test cards (i.e., 3 red rabbits and 3 blue boats presented in a quasi-random order)

"Okay, now we're not going to play the color game anymore. Now we're going to play a new game—the shape game. If it's a rabbit, it goes here; but if it's a boat, it goes there. Here's a rabbit. Where does it go?"

Target cards

Test cards (i.e., 3 red rabbits and 3 blue boats presented in a quasi-random order)

SOURCE: Zelazo (2006).

Executive Function During Adolescence

Executive function continues to develop during adolescence. As we know, teenagers are prone to engage in risky behavior, and the immaturity of executive function may be one reason. As with working memory, brain development underlies some of the limitations we see. Further myelination and synaptic pruning, concepts you learned about in Chapter 6, continue to occur in the prefrontal cortex, the area most responsible for executive function, throughout adolescence (Blakemore & Choudhury, 2006). In addition, it appears that in teens the reward system, which is mediated by the neurotransmitter *dopamine*, is heightened while the control system in the brain is still developing (Luna, Paulsen, Padmanabhan, & Geier, 2013; Wahlstrom, White, & Luciana, 2010). Therefore, for a teen, an invitation to

FIGURE 7.7

The Tower of Hanoi. How many moves would it take you to get all of these disks to the right-hand pole without ever putting a larger disk on top of a smaller one?

take part in risky behavior is more tempting for the reward it offers and less controlled by an understanding of the consequences.

Some have argued that a certain amount of risk taking in adolescents is important for the development of autonomy and learning about the larger world (Wahlstrom et al., 2010). Risk taking has positive effects when it allows the teen to try new and exciting experiences, such as taking a trip to a foreign country. However, the obvious downside is the temptation to engage in activities, such as experimenting with drugs or driving too fast, that endanger the teen's safety. As with many aspects of development, finding the right balance is the key to positive development.

METACOGNITION

Metacognition The ability to think about and monitor one's own thoughts and cognitive activities.

Theory of mind The ability to understand self and others as agents who act on the basis of their mental states, such as beliefs, desires, emotions, and intentions.

Metacognition is the process of thinking about and regulating your own thoughts and cognitive activities (Vrugt & Oort, 2008). Young children are not very aware of thinking as a process in which they take part. One of the earliest abilities they develop is called **theory of mind**, the ability to understand that people, including themselves, experience and act on mental states such as beliefs, emotions, and intentions. This ability is a first step in developing the more mature process of metacognition, which includes understanding how mental states are linked to performance on cognitive tasks (Lecce, Demicheli, Zocchi, & Palladino, 2015). We discuss theory of mind, an important underpinning for social understanding, more fully in Chapter 12 in the context of social development.

To understand metacognition, think about what happens when you are studying for an exam in one of your courses. You might start by assessing how much you already know about a subject. That helps you determine how much time it will take you to prepare. Next you can consider which strategies you will use to prepare for your exam. You would most likely choose a different approach when studying for an English literature exam than when studying for a chemistry final. To gauge how much more you need to do or to reevaluate the strategies you are using, you continue to evaluate your level of understanding as your studying progresses. After you get your grade on the exam, you can evaluate the effectiveness of the strategies that you used so that you can use this information the next time you need to prepare for an exam to do it more effectively or more efficiently. Each decision that you make when directing your own learning is an indication of your level of understanding of how cognition and memory work (Winn, 2004).

The process of developing metacognitive skills that began in early childhood continues to develop in middle childhood. In one study, when children in third and fifth grade were presented various pieces of new material to learn, they were able to report accurately whether they learned each one (Metcalfe & Finn, 2013). When given the opportunity to choose to study some of the material again, the fifth graders chose items they said they hadn't learned well, while the third graders just chose randomly. It appears that metacognitive knowledge is developing during this time, but the ability to apply it appropriately is slower to develop.

As adolescents get older they get better at evaluating their own learning accurately (Weil et al., 2014). Studies with students from middle schools and college have all shown that students' performance can improve when they better understand how their cognitive processes work (Cano & Cardelle-Elawar, 2004; Gaskins & Pressley, 2007). Try **Active Learning: Metacognition** to see how you can improve your own performance by becoming more aware of your cognitive processes.

Active LEARNING

Metacognition

Planning, monitoring, and evaluating are three essential aspects of metacognition for students. For your next class session, answer the following questions before, during, and after the class.

Planning (before class)	Monitoring (during class)	Evaluating (after class)
What are the goals of this class session going to be?	What insights am I having as I experience this class session? What confusions?	What was today's class session about?
What do I already know about this topic?	Am I writing down questions that arise for me during the class?	What did I hear today that is in conflict with my prior understanding?
How could I best prepare for this class session?	Do I find this interesting? How could I make this material personally relevant?	How did the ideas of today's class session relate to previous class sessions?
Where should I sit and what should I be doing (or not doing) to best support my learning during this class?	Can I distinguish important information from details? If not, how will I figure this out?	What do I need to do now to get my questions answered and my confusions clarified?
What questions do I already have about this topic that I want to find out more about?		What did I find most interesting about class today?

SOURCE: Adapted from Tanner (2012).

Did you find that carrying out these steps helped you to think more deeply about your learning process? This type of thinking is metacognition. Students who are aware of their own thinking in this way tend to learn more effectively than those who go about learning in a haphazard way.

COMPARING FOUR THEORIES OF COGNITIVE DEVELOPMENT

7.5 How do the theories by Piaget and Vygotsky and the theories of core knowledge and information processing differ and how are they similar?

In this chapter, we have presented four theories of cognitive development that may seem quite different from one another. In fact, there are major differences, but there are also important similarities. See Table 7.3 for a brief summary of some of the basic aspects of each theory. All four of these theories describe children's cognitive abilities and limitations as they move through development, and all focus on the processes through which more advanced understanding emerges from earlier, less adequate understanding (Meadows, 2006). In this final section of the chapter, we highlight some of the differences between the theories, and also discuss some of the ways in which the different theories may work together to promote our understanding of cognitive development.

One of the ways that Piagetian theory and information processing differ is that Piaget proposed stages based on qualitative changes in the way children think, while information processing focuses on the step-by-step, quantitative changes that occur. However, new technology has allowed researchers to examine brain function related to working memory and executive function and relate their findings to some of Piaget's stage changes. For example, using an fMRI to measure blood flow in the brain, Houdé et al. (2011) found that children who were capable of conservation of number (they still knew there were the same number of

TABLE 7.3

A comparison of four cognitive theories.

	Piaget's Genetic Epistemology Theory	Theory of Core Knowledge	Vygotsky's Sociocultural Theory	Information Processing Theory
Stages or Continuous Development	Stages are central to this theory.	Development is continuous.	Development is continuous.	Development is continuous.
Role of Innate Knowledge	Biological maturation interacts with environmental experiences.	Many aspects of knowledge are innate.	Learning is social, and innate knowledge plays only a small role.	Brain function is central, but innate knowledge is not.
Role of Environmental Influence	Environment interacts with genetic unfolding.	Core aspects of knowledge are built upon by experiences in the environment.	The environment and culture are central to cognitive development.	Brain function interacts with environmental experiences to produce cognitive development.

coins even if the coins in one row were moved apart) were activating parts of their brain that had to do with number concept and with inhibition, an aspect of executive function. The researchers explained that conservation required the ability to use numbers, but also the ability to inhibit a tendency to equate longer length with more objects. Their research supported Piaget's stage theory by providing evidence of changes in both brain function and abilities described by the information processing approach. This example demonstrates how information processing principles may work to flesh out more fully the general ideas that Piaget had proposed by examining the underlying mechanisms that lead to the changes he described.

Piaget and Vygotsky both subscribed to the constructivist point of view. That means that both believed that children are not passive recipients of knowledge but rather construct their understanding, building on what they already know. The difference between the theories is the source of the child's knowledge. Piaget saw knowledge as coming from the child's own actions on the environment, but Vygotsky argued that knowledge is constructed through our interactions with others and is embedded in one's social, cultural, and historical surroundings. For Vygotsky, language shapes thought, but for Piaget, language was primarily a way to express thought.

The theory of core knowledge differs from the other theories because it argues that some basic information and understanding are built into the human brain. Piaget, Vygotsky, and information processing theories all argue that knowledge is built from the interaction of the mind with life experience and that infants do not have certain types of basic information already present at birth (Cohen, Chaput, & Cashon, 2002).

Ongoing research will continue to help determine which aspects of each of these theories describe the different processes of cognitive development most accurately.

CHECK YOUR UNDERSTANDING

1. How can information processing enhance our understanding of Piaget's theory?
2. How do Piaget and Vygotsky apply constructivism in their theories?
3. How does the theory of core knowledge differ from the three other theories?

CONCLUSION

We have examined four different approaches to understanding how children's and adolescents' ability to think and to learn changes as they grow. Brain maturation and life experiences influence each other, and both contribute to how cognitive development occurs. In this chapter, we focused on the processes of development that are found in all children. In the next chapter, we look at a specific aspect of cognition: intelligence. The study of intelligence is focused much less on the mechanisms by which all children develop. Instead, the focus is on individual differences and what they mean for children's performance in school and in life.

CHAPTER SUMMARY

Test your understanding of the content.
Take the practice quiz at **edge.sagepub.com/levine3e**

7.1 What are Piaget's four stages of cognitive development and what occurs during each one?

Piaget described cognitive development as a process of **assimilation**, taking in new information and linking it to **schemas** we already have, and **accommodation**, changing those schemas when new information doesn't fit. These processes lead to qualitative changes in the way children think that he described in four stages: the **sensorimotor stage,** the **preoperational stage,** the **stage of concrete operations,** and the **stage of formal operations.** Infants understand the world through their actions on it, but young children in the preoperational stage develop the ability to represent the world symbolically through mental representation. These young children still have a number of limitations in their thinking, including **intuitive thinking, egocentrism,** and lack of **conservation.** Older children in concrete operations begin to think logically. However, it is not until adolescence and the stage of formal operations that thinking becomes both logical and abstract. Adolescent egocentrism gives rise to the **imaginary audience** and the **personal fable.**

7.2 What is the premise of the theory of core knowledge?

The **theory of core knowledge** states that humans are born with areas of knowledge that are innate and built into the human brain. There are some differing ideas about what that knowledge is, but it may include basic understanding of how objects and agents move, the nature of number, and spatial relationships.

7.3 What are the basic processes described by Vygotsky's sociocultural theory?

Vygotsky believed that all learning is based on social interaction that develops out of the cultural context in which children develop. Children have certain capabilities, but to learn they must be helped to move just beyond their current level of understanding. The difference between what they can do on their own and what they can do only with assistance is called the **zone of proximal development (ZPD). Scaffolding** is what an adult does to move the child through the ZPD to full independent achievement. Children use **private speech** to move information that comes from other people to inner thought.

7.4 How do attention, memory, executive function, and metacognition develop through childhood and adolescence?

a. Attention involves tuning in to certain things while tuning out others (**selective attention**) and maintaining focus over time (**sustained attention**). Infants pay more attention to something that is novel and will spend more time paying attention to complex stimuli than simple stimuli. **Processing speed,** or the speed and accuracy with which we can handle information, increases, and **automaticity** makes us able to do certain familiar tasks without too much conscious thought. Although teens think they can pay attention to several things at the same time, or **multitask,** research indicates that they will need more time to do something when distracted and will process the information more superficially. A child or an adolescent with extreme difficulties sustaining attention and/or controlling impulsive behavior may be diagnosed with **attention-deficit/hyperactivity disorder (ADHD).** Treatment may involve behavioral intervention with the family and school as well as medication.

b. Infant memory is nonverbal, so older children and adults have difficulty recalling experiences that happened before the age of 3, referred to as **infantile amnesia.** When children develop language they begin to use **encoding processes** within working memory to hold on to information so it can be used. These include **scripts, rehearsal,** and **elaboration.** New information becomes easier to remember as children build a knowledge base. **False memories** can occur in young children, who may be very suggestible, but older children and teens also develop false memories because they remember the gist, or meaning, of an event rather than remembering the specifics of the experience.

c. **Executive function** is that aspect of brain organization that coordinates attention and memory and controls behavioral responses for the purpose of attaining a certain goal. Three important aspects of executive function are **cognitive flexibility, inhibitory control,** and planning.

d. **Metacognition** is the ability to think about and monitor one's own thoughts and cognitive activities. Adolescents become much more proficient in using metacognition than younger children.

7.5 How do the theories of Piaget and Vygotsky and the theories of core knowledge and information processing differ and how are they similar?

Information processing theory describes quantitative changes while Piaget's theory describes qualitative changes. However, cognitive processes described by information processing theory can be used to explain the changes that occur when children move from one Piagetian stage to the next. Piaget and Vygotsky differ in their emphasis on individual or social origins of cognitive development, but both theories take a constructivist point of view. The theory of core knowledge states that some basic aspects of knowledge are innate and built into the human brain, while the other three theories describe development as an interaction of brain maturation and environmental experience.

KEY TERMS

Strengthen your understanding of these key terms with
mobile-friendly eFlashcards at **edge.sagepub.com/levine3e**

Give your students the SAGE edge!

SAGE edge offers a robust online environment featuring an impressive array of free tools and resources for review, study, and further exploration, keeping both instructors and students on the cutting edge of teaching and learning. Learn more at **edge.sagepub.com/levine3e**

chapter 8 | INTELLIGENCE AND ACADEMIC ACHIEVEMENT

Will & Deni McIntyre/Corbis Documentary/Getty Images

LEARNING QUESTIONS

8.1 How do we define and measure intelligence?

8.2 What are examples of some cognitive deficits and intellectual gifts?

8.3 What are some issues that affect learning within the school environment?

8.4 How do gender, ethnicity/race, and socioeconomic status affect academic achievement?

Master these objectives using an online action plan at **edge.sagepub.com/levine3e**

TEST YOUR KNOWLEDGE

Test your knowledge of child development by deciding whether each of the following statements is *true* or *false*, and then check your answers as you read the chapter.

1. **T ☐ F ☐:** The best way to measure intelligence is to measure how much information someone knows.

2. **T ☐ F ☐:** A person's level of measured intelligence primarily depends upon the genes that he or she has inherited.

3. **T ☐ F ☐:** Five times more children with autism receive services within the schools than children with a specific learning disorder or an intellectual disability.

4. **T ☐ F ☐:** Children who are gifted or talented often pay a price for their giftedness because they are likely to be socially or emotionally maladjusted.

5. **T ☐ F ☐:** The smarter you are, the more likely it is that you will also be creative.

6. **T ☐ F ☐:** Placing high-, average-, and low-performing students together in groups to collaborate on a project benefits all the children in the group equally.

7. **T ☐ F ☐:** Students who repeat a grade substantially improve their performance on their second attempt.

8. **T ☐ F ☐:** Most students who drop out of high school go on to eventually complete their high school education.

9. **T ☐ F ☐:** Throughout elementary school and into high school, girls frequently earn better grades in math than boys.

10. **T ☐ F ☐:** The best way to improve a child's academic performance is to believe in the child and let him know that you have faith in his ability to succeed.

Correct answers: (1) F, (2) F, (3) F, (4) F, (5) F, (6) F, (7) F, (8) T, (9) T, (10) F

▲ **VIDEO: Watch as students answer some of these questions and the authors respond.**

Many of the theories we discussed in Chapter 7 focus on the universal processes of cognitive development—that is, the experiences and abilities that all children have. There is another tradition in the study of cognitive development that focuses more on individual differences in cognitive abilities, or what makes us different from one another rather than what makes us similar. This is the perspective that has guided the study of intelligence. In this chapter, we first look at how intelligence has been defined and measured. We then look at variations in intellectual development that include intellectual disabilities and giftedness. Although intelligence is one factor related to success in school, we examine other factors that have an impact on students' academic achievement, including characteristics of the classroom, its teachers, and school policies. We look at those students who go on to college and those who do not and examine what some of their opportunities and challenges are. We end the chapter with a discussion of group differences in academic achievement, including the impact of gender, ethnicity, race, and socioeconomic status.

DEFINING AND ASSESSING INTELLIGENCE

8.1 How do we define and measure intelligence?

In this section, we look at various ways that researchers and theorists have defined intelligence and the ways they have measured it. This discussion includes our understanding of how both nature and nurture contribute to its development. We also review some of the neurological research that is exploring the relationship between brain structure and function and various aspects of intelligence.

DEFINING INTELLIGENCE

How do we define intelligence? Is there one factor that underlies all intelligence, or is intelligence made up of a number of independent abilities? How we answer these questions affects how we measure intelligence. Before reading further, try **Active Learning: Defining Intelligence** to see how *you* would define intelligence.

Active LEARNING

Defining Intelligence

How do you know when someone is intelligent? Is it based on things they are able to do? Is it the amount of information they can remember? Or is it the way they manage their life in the world? Write down three of your ideas about what makes someone intelligent.

Next think about how you would measure the kind of abilities you included in your definition of intelligence. Design a test to measure just one of the abilities you described. If possible, discuss these ideas with others in your class. Did you find that you have similar concepts of intelligence, or were there large differences?

If you found differences, you are in good company. In 2007, two researchers compiled a list of more than 70 different informal definitions of intelligence (Legg & Huter, 2007). Although it has been difficult for psychologists to agree on just what constitutes intelligence, all the definitions that we use involve much more than the amount of knowledge a person has as the criteria for being intelligent, so any valid assessment must look at more than how much a person knows.

T ☐ F ☐ The best way to measure intelligence is to measure how much information someone knows. **False**

Intelligence Those qualities that help us adapt successfully so that we achieve our goals in life.

Perhaps part of the difficulty in agreeing on a definition of intelligence is that we often try to define intelligence as though it were a "thing" when it really is more like a process (Willis, Dumont, & Kaufman, 2011). A simple but useful definition proposed by Robert Sternberg (2012) is that **intelligence** is "the ability to adapt to the environment, to think and learn, and to understand oneself and others" (p. 209). "Adapt", "think," and "understand" are all processes, so this definition suggests that these are things that intelligent people can do.

The second part of the difficulty is that we need to decide whether intelligence is one ability or many. The idea of a single general intelligence called *g*, which underlies all cognitive abilities, has a history that goes back to the very early days of intelligence testing (Gould, 1996). If we look at a number of different measures of intelligence or cognitive abilities, those measures are often at least moderately correlated with each other. That suggests that there is some factor that they have in common. In the early 1900s, Charles Spearman proposed that this was the *g*, or general factor that underlies intelligence. However, other researchers who accept the idea of a general intelligence factor also believe that different abilities (called *s* or specific factors) lie within that general ability. For example, the Wechsler Intelligence Scale for Children (WISC-V), a widely used intelligence test, gives a full scale IQ score, but also has five composite index scores: verbal comprehension, visual-spatial, working memory, fluid reasoning, and processing speed (Weschler, 2014).

Intelligence testing. Intelligence tests are very challenging for the test taker because they are designed to determine the limits of one's ability.

Another way in which *g* has been subdivided is into fluid intelligence and crystallized intelligence. **Fluid intelligence** allows us to solve novel problems for which we have little training and is measured both by how effectively we solve the problems and by how quickly we solve them. **Crystallized intelligence**, on the other hand, is a measure of the knowledge we already have that we can draw on to solve problems (Cattell, 1963). Research on brain function has supported the idea that these two separate types of intelligence exist. Performance on tasks requiring fluid intelligence has been linked with activity in the prefrontal cortex in the brain, while tasks requiring crystallized intelligence rely on specific frontal and posterior temporal and parietal areas of the brain (Nisbett et al., 2012).

There are other psychologists who believe that there is no generalized intelligence that underlies all mental abilities. In the 1950s, J. P. Guilford proposed a theory of intelligence that identified 120 distinct abilities (Cianciolo & Sternberg, 2004). More recently, researchers such as Howard Gardner and Robert Sternberg have described intelligence as a much smaller collection of separate and independent abilities, which we later describe in more detail. Thinking of intelligence as a collection of abilities suggests that someone can be strong in one area and weak in another because each type of intellectual ability operates somewhat independently.

Fluid intelligence Intelligence that allows us to quickly and effectively solve novel problems for which we have little training.

Crystallized intelligence What we already know and can draw on to solve problems.

MEASURING INTELLIGENCE

To understand more about how intelligence has been conceptualized and measured in the field of education, read **Journey of Research: The History of Intelligence Tests**.

JOURNEY OF *Research*

The History of Intelligence Tests

The modern history of intelligence testing begins in the early 1900s when Alfred Binet and Theodore Simon were asked by the Minister of Public Instruction in Paris to create a test that would help them identify students with mental difficulties in order to develop alternative teaching strategies to help these students do well in school (Wasserman, 2012).

(Continued)

(Continued)

Before this time, students who were judged to be mentally deficient were simply kicked out of school. For example, Thomas Edison's teacher thought he was "addled," so he was not allowed to continue in the classroom and was taught at home (Detterman & Thompson, 1997, p. 1082).

Binet made modest claims for his test. It was designed to reflect a child's level of performance on tasks similar to those required in school (van der Veer, 2007). An individual child's mental achievements were compared with those of other children of the same age who were performing well in school, and the comparison determined the child's **mental age**. For instance, if a 10-year-old child could do all the things 10-year-olds generally do, her mental age (MA) would be 10, but another 10-year-old might only perform at the level of a typical 8-year-old (MA = 8), and another might achieve at the level of a typical 12-year-old (MA = 12). Those who perform below the expected level for their age would be identified as needing an alternative form of instruction to be successful in school.

Lewis Terman, a psychologist at Stanford University, standardized Binet's test on a sample of children in the United States and adapted it for use in U.S. schools. However, Terman began scoring the test not as a mental age, but as a single number representing the child's general level of intelligence, called the **intelligence quotient or IQ**. At that time, the IQ score was calculated by dividing a child's mental age by her chronological age and then multiplying by 100. For example, if a 10-year-old scored at the 10-year-old level, her IQ score would be 10 (her mental age) divided by 10 (her chronological age) multiplied by 100, 10/10x100 or IQ = 100. However, if another 10-year-old scored at the 12-year-old level, her IQ would be 12/10 x 100 = 120 (Wasserman, 2012).

Eventually researchers became concerned about using mental age as the basis for the IQ score, so in place of the ratio IQ developed by Terman, David Wechsler developed IQ tests for adults and children that were based on a **deviation IQ** (Wasserman, 2012). To determine a deviation IQ, an intelligence test is first administered to a very large sample of individuals of all ages to establish the norms for the test, or expected scores for that population. For each specific age, the expected mean score is arbitrarily set to 100, with a standard deviation from the average score of 15 points. That ensures that most people will fall between 100 – 15 = 85 and 100 + 15 = 115 (see Figure 8.1). Note that as you move farther away from the average (that is, the greater the deviation), the fewer and fewer people score at those more extreme levels.

When children take the WISC-V, their score is compared only to those scores found for other children of their same age. For example, Joe scored higher than the majority of 10-year-olds, which gave him an IQ score of 120. However, it is no longer said that he scored at the level of a 12-year-old (that is, that he had a mental age of 12). Instead, the deviation IQ score of 120 means that he has scored higher than many other children who are 10 years old. Look at where an IQ score of 120 falls in Figure 8.1.

As mentioned earlier, WISC-V measures five factors that contribute to the total IQ. Each of these measures derives from a child's performance on subtests that assess different abilities. It would not be appropriate for us to provide actual items from the Wechsler tests, but the following examples are similar to ones that are used today or they are from previous versions of the test that are no longer used (see Table 8.1 and Figure 8.2). These will give you an idea of the nature of these tests.

As research on brain functioning has dramatically increased in recent years, a number of tests that measure neurological functioning related to intelligence have been developed. Each measures a specific ability related to intelligence. These tests must be interpreted by

Mental age The age level at which a child is performing on a test of mental ability.

Intelligence quotient or IQ Originally a measure of intelligence calculated based on the ratio of a child's mental age to chronological age, largely replaced now by the deviation IQ.

Deviation IQ A measure of intelligence that is based on the individual's deviation from the norms for a given test.

FIGURE 8.1

Normal curve (distribution of IQ scores). IQ tests are designed so that the scores of most people fall near the midpoint (an IQ score of 100). As you move farther away from the center, there are fewer and fewer people with extremely high or extremely low scores.

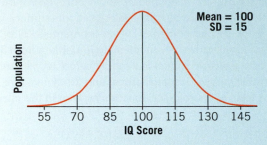

Mean = 100
SD = 15

Population

55 70 85 100 115 130 145
IQ Score

TABLE 8.1

Wechsler Intelligence Scale for Children (WISC). These are examples of subtests within the WISC and questions similar to those found on the actual test.

Arithmetic	If 4 toys cost 6 dollars, how much do 7 cost?
Vocabulary	What does "debilitating" mean?
Comprehension	Why are streets usually numbered in order?
Block Design	Use blocks to replicate a two-color design.
Similarities	In what way are "dogs" and "rabbits" alike?
Digit Span	Remember progressively longer lists of numbers.

FIGURE 8.2

Matrix Reasoning

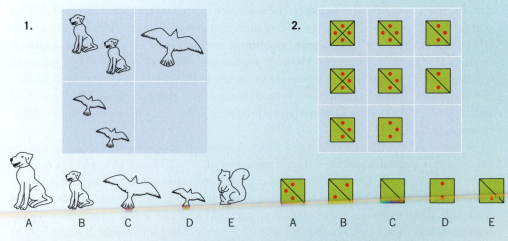

SOURCE: Sample IQ items from Gottfredson (1998). Reprinted by permission of the author.

Answers to Matrix Reasoning Items: 1. A; 2. D

(Continued)

(Continued)

a trained neuropsychologist and are most often used to diagnose or confirm a diagnosis of a cognitive deficit or to identify the location of an abnormality in the central nervous system (Malik & Turner, 2015). They are typically used as part of a battery of assessments that include clinical reports, a physical examination, and reports from individuals familiar with the child. An example of an assessment used in educational settings would be the NEPSY-II (which stands for the second edition of A Developmental NEuroPSYchological Assessment), which assesses neurocognitive functioning in children from 3 to 16 years of age in the areas of attention, executive function, language, memory, learning, sensorimotor functioning, social perception, and visuospatial processing (Korkman, Kirk, & Kemp, 2016). You will learn more about tests of neurological functioning later in this chapter.

Standardized Testing and Alternative Testing Methods

Most tests of intelligence are standardized tests because they are always administered and scored in the same way. There are a number of advantages to using standardized tests. The validity, reliability, and norms for the tests have been established by the developers of the tests. Because an individual test taker is compared to same-age peers, these tests can identify children who need services or interventions. They also can identify the child's areas of strength and weakness and can be used to track changes in these strengths and weaknesses over time (Flanagan, Mascolo, & Hardy-Braz, 2009). Of course, there also are criticisms of standardized IQ testing. In Chapter 3, we discussed the concern that the tests may be biased against certain groups of students, but also noted that there is a large body of psychometric research that has failed to find evidence in today's intelligence tests to support this concern (see reviews of this literature by Reynolds, 2000; also Balkin et al., 2014). Another concern is the fact that test results can be influenced by a number of factors that are not relevant to the test such as how the child is feeling when she takes the test, the child's motivation to do well on the test or not, or poor testing conditions such as a noisy testing room.

In response to criticisms of standardized testing and with a desire to be able to create appropriate and specific educational plans for children, alternative forms of testing have been developed. One approach that we described in Chapter 2 is based on Vygotsky's ideas about how children learn through scaffolding by adults. *Dynamic assessment* attempts to measure the child's potential for change when the examiner intervenes and assists the child. This potential can be measured by the number of hints that are needed for a child to solve a problem he has previously failed or a second assessment of the child's ability after the assistance is removed (Lidz, 2003). The goal of dynamic assessment is to eliminate factors that influence a child's performance that are not relevant to the test itself, such as confusion on the child's part about what he or she is supposed to do. Dynamic assessment is intended to supplement rather than replace standardized testing by providing additional information on the child's potential for change (Flanagan et al., 2009).

Authentic assessment A testing procedure that focuses on the process used in solving complex, real-life problems rather than the product that results from the process.

A second alternative to standardized testing is **authentic assessment**. The content of the assessment is quite different from items typically used in intelligence tests and is a reaction to concerns regarding the fixed format of standardized tests. Instead an authentic assessment presents complex problems that resemble real-life skills, such as ones required in the workplace (Powers, 2005). For example, a young child might be asked to respond to a story starter, such as "The best day in my life was. . . ." or an older child would describe how he would get to a grocery store to do a week's worth of shopping that included food from all four food groups and necessary toiletries and cleaning supplies. This approach is appropriate for student populations that are difficult to assess using standardized methods, including disabled students, very young children, and gifted students.

While the role of the examiner in a standardized test is to administer the test in the exact same way to all individuals without interfering with the testing procedure in any way, examiners for dynamic assessments and authentic assessments are active participants in the testing process itself. The examiners must have specialized training in the administration of the test, and the test is given to only one child at a time. For these reasons, these tests are not widely used.

Infant Intelligence

The way that we assess intelligence in infants and very young children is another example of alternative testing. Assessing intelligence in infants is difficult because we rely heavily on language in our tests of older children but infants cannot understand test instructions or provide verbal responses. For those reasons, most tests of infant intelligence assess physical, motor, sensory, and/or early language development. Although these

Testing infant intelligence. This examiner is administering the Bayley Scales of Infant Development to this young child. These scales assess the cognitive, motor, and early language development of the infant and can be used to assess the infant's developmental status, not intellectual ability. Parent questionnaires also provide information on social-emotional development and adaptive behavior.

tests can identify intellectual disability and developmental delays based on a neurological impairment, they are not reliable predictors of later cognitive functioning (Aldrich, 2001).

Newer approaches to assessing intelligence in young children are based upon measures of information processing abilities. The techniques that are used were described in Chapter 7. They include measures of infant attention, attraction to novelty, and habituation to a repeated stimulus. An infant's response to novelty and habituation to familiar stimuli appear to be particularly important predictive factors for later intelligence (Bornstein, Hahn, & Wolke, 2013; Fagan, Holland, & Wheeler, 2007; Kavšek, 2004). These information processing abilities have been related to both later global intelligence and specific cognitive abilities. For instance, attention, processing speed, and memory in infancy have been found to predict general intelligence at age 11 (Rose, Feldman, Jankowski, & Van Rossem, 2012). A preference for novelty has been associated with both general intelligence and several specific cognitive abilities (Fagan et al., 2007). Infants' ability to regulate themselves (for example, to settle back to sleep after a brief disruption), which can be a measure of executive control, is also an important predictor of intelligence measured at age 6 (Canals, Hernández-Martínez, Esparó, & Fernández-Ballart, 2011).

What explains the continuity of intellectual development when infant intelligence is assessed using information processing abilities and executive control functions? Memory, processing speed, the ability to pay attention to new stimuli and habituate to familiar ones, and to regulate emotions are all characteristics that help infants learn from their environment. For instance, an infant who is attracted to novel elements in the environment is better equipped to learn as he encounters new experiences, and this ability continues to support new learning as the infant moves into childhood and later into adolescence and adulthood.

The Nature-Nurture Controversy and Intelligence

Over the years, views on the relative influence of genes and environment on intelligence have swung back and forth. The first large-scale use of intelligence tests was during World War I, when a large number of soldiers were given tests to determine if they were fit for military service (Boake, 2002). A deeply flawed analysis of the scores of army recruits led to the conclusion that immigrants from Northern Europe were more intelligent than those from Southern Europe. This misinterpretation later contributed to the passage of a law in 1924 that severely limited immigration from a number of countries in which people had been found by these tests to have a lower IQ (Gould, 1996), and eventually led to the eugenics

Photograph by Stephen Ausmus, U.S. Department of Agriculture, Agricultural Research Service

movement described in Chapter 4. The movement was based on the idea that intelligence is linked with certain genes and people with those genes should be encouraged to have children so they can pass on their genes, while those whose genes are linked to lower levels of intelligence should not. The horrors perpetrated by the Nazis in World War II in the name of eugenics brought an end to the influence of the eugenics movement in the United States.

The controversy over whether intelligence is due to nature or nurture resurfaced in 1994 when Herrnstein and Murray published their book *The Bell Curve: Intelligence and Class Structure in American Life* in which they presented what they considered to be evidence of (in the words of critic Stephen Jay Gould, 1996, p. 34) "permanent and heritable differences" in IQ among individuals and, more specifically, among different racial groups. Much of the controversy arose from the book's declaration that any inherited differences were *permanent*.

The book stirred up so much controversy that the American Psychological Association set up a task force to respond to its claims (Neisser et al., 1996). This task force concluded that racial differences do exist on IQ scores but the size of these differences were "well within the range of effect sizes that can be produced by environmental factors" (Neisser et al., 1996, p. 94) and that "there is certainly no . . . support for a genetic interpretation" (p. 97). In short, the task force concluded that differences are more likely to be related to environmental issues than to inborn, genetic ones that are somehow connected with race. Later in this chapter, we look at poverty, a significant factor in a child's environment, and its effects on intelligence and academic achievement.

After reading Chapter 4, you know that the question of whether intelligence comes from genes *or* the environment probably is not the most helpful one to ask. Given what we know about how genes and environment interact, we can be pretty sure that both have an influence on something as complex as intelligence. The evidence is clear that genes do play some role. Davies et al. (2011) examined the genotype of almost 4,000 people and found evidence that a combination of a number of genes was predictive of 40% to 50% of the variance (or differences between people) in intelligence in adulthood. This shows that IQ is related to genetic inheritance. But note, it also means that the remaining 50% to 60% of the variation in IQ is due to factors other than genes. A review of a number of studies found that monozygotic (or identical) twins who have almost 100% of their genes in common but who have been raised in different families are more similar to each other on IQ scores than dizygotic (or fraternal) twins who share only 50% of their genes but live in the same family (Plomin & Petrill, 1997). These authors came to the conclusion that the influence of genes on general intelligence is "significant and substantial" (p. 56), but they also pointed out that although this is *what is*, it does not have to be *what could be*. Although there is a clear genetic input to IQ, this does *not* mean that IQ cannot also be changed by the influences of the environment.

It appears that the amount of variance in IQ scores attributable to genes and the amount attributable to environment may vary by a family's socioeconomic status. When researchers looked separately at children in families of low socioeconomic status (SES) and those in families of middle to high SES in the United States, they found that most of the variability in IQ for low SES children is due to environmental influences, while IQ scores are largely determined by genes in higher SES groups (Turkheimer, Haley, Waldron, D'Onofrio, & Gottesman, 2003). In a study of infants, mental ability was unrelated to genetic inheritance at age 10 months, but by 2 years of age genes played a large role for infants raised in high SES families, and a negligible role for those raised in low SES families (Tucker-Drob, Rhemtulla, Harden, Turkheimer, & Fask, 2011). These studies suggest that when children are raised in situations that provide them with adequate resources and supports, they express the level of intelligence provided to them by their genetic inheritance; however, when they grow up in deprived environments they may not be able to reach that level.

So while it is likely that there are differences in genetic potential among individuals or groups of individuals, intelligence is one of those characteristics that we described in Chapter 4 as not very deeply canalized. This means that whatever the genetic starting point, the environment has a substantial impact on the eventual outcome or end point for this characteristic.

T ☐ F ☐ A person's level of measured intelligence primarily depends upon the genes that he or she has inherited. **False**

We also said that many important traits are polygenic because many genes work together in combination to produce the trait, and intelligence is one of those traits. When many genes work in concert there is a wide range of potential outcomes (or what we call a **range of reaction**). Where any individual ends up within that range is determined by the quality of the environment and her experience in it, as well as other characteristics of the individual, such as her level of motivation or how hard she is willing to work to attain her goals. Although genes may roughly set an upper and lower limit, experience, especially educational experiences, influences how much of that potential is fulfilled. This is clearly seen in children from lower SES families who are adopted by middle-class families. These children are generally found to score about 12 points higher on IQ tests than nonadopted siblings or other children adopted into lower SES families (Nisbett et al., 2012).

One argument against the idea that IQ is innate and unchangeable comes from the fact that the scoring of IQ tests needs to be readjusted at regular intervals because test performance has been going up since the beginning of the 20th century. The norms for IQ tests have been adjusted by about one-third of an IQ point per year to make sure that 100 remains the average score (Loehlin, Horn, & Willerman, 1997).

There has been a debate about what these changes, known as the **Flynn effect** after Dr. Robert Flynn (2007) who first described it, really mean. Do these increases in scores mean that we are all more intelligent than previous generations? Flynn himself argues that fluid intelligence *has* increased over time because society has developed an increasing need for this type of thinking. For example, while abstract thinking is required for success in modern society, it may not have been essential in a farming society in the early part of the 1900s. Although Binet's initial idea of measuring intelligence was to *predict* how children will do in school, there is clear evidence that the very act of going to school increases intelligence, and more children are going to school for more years now than in the past (Nisbett et al., 2012).

Neuroscience and Intelligence

Neuroscientists who study intelligence and the brain must deal with several basic questions. First, as we discussed at the beginning of this chapter, the definition of intelligence is not clear-cut: Is it one general ability or is it a combination of many different abilities? Second, is intelligence related to structures of the brain or to the function of the brain? If it is due to structures, researchers would look at the different parts of the brain, but if it is due to functions they would examine the synaptic connections between parts of the brain. Finally, as you learned when you read Chapter 6, the brain is formed not only by biological maturation, but also as a result of the experiences that an individual has. Therefore, differences in the brain between people with high and low intelligence may be programmed by genes, may result from life experiences, or may be an interaction of both.

A recent meta-analysis of studies that relate the brain to intelligence concluded that there are differences in both function and structure of the brain between individuals with high and low intelligence as measured by IQ tests (Basten, Hilger, & Fiebach, 2015). At present, research indicates that both the structure and the connectivity of the frontal and parietal areas of the brain form the basis for intelligence. This is known as the Parieto-Frontal Integration Theory (P-FIT) (Basten et al., 2015; Nikolaidis et al., 2016). As you learned in Chapter 6, sensory information is taken in through the parietal region and is then processed in the frontal region of the brain. This research is still in its early stages but there already is evidence that other, subcortical regions may also be involved in intelligence.

There is also evidence that the brain develops differently during childhood and adolescence for people with different levels of intelligence. For children with higher intelligence, development of white matter, or myelination, takes place over a longer period of time, resulting in more myelination by age 3. This increased level of myelination strengthens neural networks and better supports later development (Deoni et al., 2016). In addition, the cortex of the brain is a sheet of neurons that varies in thickness in different areas, reflecting different amounts of neurons. In children with higher intelligence, the cortex gets thicker more quickly and over a longer period of time. This development is then followed by a period of more vigorous

Range of reaction The range of potential outcomes for any given genotype.

Flynn effect The increase in intelligence test scores that has occurred over time, necessitating the renorming of the tests.

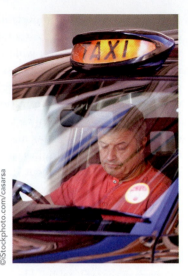

Mika/Corbis/Getty Images

©iStockphoto.com/pojoslaw

©iStockphoto.com/casarsa

What do these people have in common? Recent studies of people who have mastered complex tasks, from playing a violin to juggling or driving a taxi through the streets of London, have found changes within the structures of their brain related to these activities.

pruning of synaptic connections during adolescence (Shaw et al., 2006). It appears that intelligence is linked with more robust development of the brain during childhood, allowing for more efficiency of brain function as unnecessary connections are pruned away in adolescence.

All of this new knowledge does not resolve the question of whether nature or nurture determines brain development and intelligence. In Chapter 6, when you learned about *experience-dependent brain development*, you learned that violinists develop more synaptic connections in the right side of their brains which control the movements of their left hand (Elbert et al., 1995). Along the same lines, other research has detected changes in the white matter in the brain in people who master complex physical tasks such as juggling (Scholz, Klein, Behrens, & Johansen-Berg, 2009) and increases in grey matter in taxi drivers who train for 3 to 4 years to commit to memory the intricate layout of 25,000 London streets (Woolett & Maguire, 2011). Also, the density of the grey matter in the portion of the left hemisphere of the brain primarily responsible for language increases in people who are bilingual, with the amount of density increasing as their proficiency in the second language increases (Mechelli et al., 2004).

Research connecting life experiences to brain structure is some of the most powerful information that reminds us of how nature and nurture work together to shape developmental outcome. Individuals with a greater volume of grey matter may initially be drawn to more cognitively complex activities, but participating in those activities then stimulates the production of additional grey matter (Toga & Thompson, 2005). In Chapter 1, we described this process as *niche-picking*. People express their genetic tendencies by seeking out environments that are a good fit with those tendencies. It is the environment that helps us reach the potential set by our genetics.

IQ Scores and Academic Achievement

As we described in the **Journey of Research: The History of Intelligence Tests**, Binet's initial goal in developing his test was to help identify children who could benefit from appropriate interventions. Although an intelligence test gives us an estimate of an individual child's performance relative to other children of the same age, it tells us very little about what kind of help a child who is performing below expectations needs. Consequently, other tests have been developed to more specifically identify what is interfering with a child's learning. It takes more than an IQ score to identify a child who has a learning disorder or attention-deficit/hyperactivity disorder. While an intelligence test may be part of the assessment, we do not rely on it alone for a diagnosis. You will learn more about how we identify children with a specific learning disorder and plan interventions for them later in this chapter.

On the other hand, intelligence tests do a relatively good job of predicting academic achievement for typically developing children. Many studies have found a moderately strong correlation between scores on standardized tests of intelligence and various school performance measures (Duckworth, Quinn, & Tsukayama, 2012; Farmer, Floyd, Reynolds, & Franzler, 2014; Rohde & Thompson, 2007). They usually explain about half of the variance (or difference) between individuals.

What else should we be looking at? One important factor is test-taking motivation. Can you honestly say that you have worked your very hardest on every test that you have ever taken? Performing well requires effort, and you need to be motivated to exert that effort. Many people will admit that they have not put their maximum effort into every testing situation.

When we talk about motivation, we often distinguish between intrinsic and extrinsic motivation. **Intrinsic motivation** comes from inside the person because the person finds an activity or task interesting or enjoyable. It is something you want to do. **Extrinsic motivation,** on the other hand, depends on receiving some incentive or reward from the environment. In a classroom setting, working hard on an assignment because you feel proud of yourself when you succeed at a challenging task is an example of intrinsic motivation. Working hard on that assignment because you want the good grade your teacher will give you is extrinsic motivation.

You might not be surprised to learn that when students are offered a monetary incentive for doing well on a standardized IQ test, test scores increase, with students who initially had lower baseline scores showing even more improvement than students who initially performed at a higher level (Duckworth, Quinn, Lynam, Loeber, & Southamer-Loeber, 2011). The monetary incentive does not increase what the children know, but it increases their motivation to perform at their highest level of ability on the test. Of course, if the testing material is too difficult for a particular student, no amount of external motivation is going to enable the student to do well on it.

Another factor that may predict academic performance better than intelligence tests is self-control. In a study by Duckworth and Seligman (2005), 164 children were given IQ tests at the beginning of the eighth grade and several measures of self-control, including receiving a dollar bill in an envelope which they were told they could either keep or return at the end of the week to receive $2. For these children, willingness to wait to receive the $2 reward (evidence of self-control) was twice as predictive of grades in school as their IQ scores. The standardized tests used to assess intelligence don't typically measure factors like self-control.

More recent research has found that while IQ scores predicted changes over time in scores on standardized tests better than a measure of self-control, self-control predicted changes in report card grades better than IQ scores (Duckworth et al., 2011). This finding can be understood when we realize that both IQ tests and other standardized tests rely upon questions that tap into what is learned both in schools and outside of schools. On the other hand, getting good grades depends upon knowledge obtained in school and on behaviors that largely rely on self-control, such as paying attention in class, behaving in positive ways, and getting homework done on time (Duckworth et al., 2012). This means that if we are interested in the predictive power of our tests, the tests we use must be directly related to the outcome we are trying to predict.

We will return to the topic of academic achievement later in this chapter after we discuss other ways that intelligence has been conceptualized and measured.

ALTERNATIVE VIEWS OF INTELLIGENCE

Many critics of intelligence testing have argued that the kinds of abilities tested by most IQ tests are not the only ones that are related to success in modern society and that there is no one type of intelligence that underlies all others (that is, there is no g factor). Two of the most influential alternative contemporary theories are Gardner's theory of multiple intelligences and Sternberg's triarchic theory.

Gardner's Theory of Multiple Intelligences

Howard Gardner proposed a **theory of multiple intelligences,** making the case that there are many different ways to express intelligence. He originally named seven types of intelligence but now includes two more, for a total of nine as shown in Table 8.2. However, he

Intrinsic motivation Motivation that comes from inside the person, such as a feeling of pride for a job well done.

Extrinsic motivation Motivation that depends on receiving an incentive or reward from the environment.

Theory of multiple intelligences Gardner's idea that there are a number of different types of intelligence that are all relatively independent of each other.

Kevin Winter/Getty Images Entertainment/Getty Images

Musical savant. Derek Paravicini, who was born prematurely and weighed 1 pound, 8 ounces at birth, is blind, virtually unable to speak, and has severe learning difficulties. However, since the age of 2 he has shown extraordinary musical abilities.

states, ". . . . there is not, and there never can be, a single irrefutable and universally accepted list of human intelligences" (Gardner, 2011, p. 63), so presumably his list may change or continue to grow.

To support the idea of separate intelligences, Gardner looked for evidence that each specific type of intelligence resides largely in a different part of the brain that has a distinct way of processing information. For example, a brain injury can impair one type of intelligence while leaving others virtually unaffected. This means that following an injury to a specific part of the brain, a musician might lose the ability to speak but retain the ability to play music. Gardner (1975) argues that this supports the idea that these two intelligences (linguistic and musical) are relatively autonomous. As another example, we often see significant disparities of ability within a single individual. Gardner specifically points to special populations, such as savants or prodigies. Savants have low overall levels of attainment but have exceptional ability in a very specific domain (like calculating dates from a calendar or memorizing sports trivia). Likewise, prodigies may be rather unremarkable in most areas, while being extremely gifted in one specific area (like playing piano or learning foreign languages).

Some of Gardner's critics do not agree that there is strong evidence for nine different types of intelligence because there is some degree of correlation between them (Abbott & Burkitt, 2015). If they were truly independent, ability in one area would not correlate with ability in the others. For instance, Visser, Ashton, and Vernon (2006) chose a set of 16 tests (2 for each of eight intelligence domains in Gardner's theory) and administered them to 200 adults. They found that the tests of linguistic, logical/mathematical, spatial, naturalistic, and interpersonal intelligences were highly correlated, suggesting a strong loading on a *g* or general factor for intelligence. Perhaps not surprisingly, other abilities that depend more on sensory, motor, or personality factors, such as bodily-kinesthetic intelligence, were more independent and not strongly loaded on the general factor. These results would argue against multiple intelligences as separate and independent. Gardner's (2006) response was that many of the tests used in the Visser study have a strong logical and linguistic component, so it is not surprising that they are correlated.

Although we said in Chapter 6 that certain functions are localized in different areas of the brain, few human activities rely on a single type of ability. As one example, a game of chess requires logical thought to plan your moves, spatial skills to help you visualize the board, and interpersonal skills to determine the strategies that your opponent is likely to use (Torff, 1996). Although these may be separate abilities, they need to work together in the process of completing the game. Although Gardner (1999) at one point seemed optimistic that we would find neurological evidence to support his theory of separate intelligences, the evidence that we have to date shows the processing pathways in the brain are shared, not functionally isolated from each other (Waterhouse, 2006). Despite the lack of research-based support for this basic premise of multiple intelligences, Gardner's ideas have been widely accepted and implemented within the field of education (Armstrong, 2009; Gardner & Traub, 2010).

Ordinarily we expect new theories to be subjected to rigorous scientific examination, but Gardner's ideas appear to have entered the field without that level of testing. One explanation for this is the fact that this theory simply makes sense to many people. Waterhouse (2006)

TABLE 8.2

Gardner's multiple intelligences theory. These are brief descriptions of the nine types of intelligence described by Howard Gardner and some possible careers associated with each type.

Type of Intelligence	Description	Possible Careers
Linguistic	The ability to use language	Public speakers and writers
Musical	The ability to make music	Composers and musicians
Logical-Mathematical	The ability to reason about abstract concepts	Mathematicians and scientists
Spatial	The ability to see the world and then mentally manipulate or recreate what is seen	Engineers and artists
Bodily-Kinesthetic	The ability to use one's body effectively	Dancers and athletes
Interpersonal	Skill in interacting with other people	Sales representatives and politicians
Intrapersonal	The ability to understand one's own emotions and thoughts and express them	Actors and poets
Naturalist	The ability to distinguish and categorize natural phenomena	Weather forecasters and park rangers
Existential	The tendency to think about the ultimate questions of life and death	Philosophers and religious leaders

SOURCES: Gardner (1993); Gardner & Moran (2006).

attributes part of the appeal to the fact that the theory of multiple intelligences seems to be more democratic than standard psychometric testing. Traditional intelligence tests give a single estimate of a child's ability, whereas multiple intelligences offer the hope that every child will find some area of strength and distinctive talent.

We have included in Table 8.2 a brief definition of each of the nine types of intelligence currently in Gardner's theory, together with examples of careers that would be based on each of these strengths. In the preface to the most recent edition of his book *Frames of Mind: The Theory of Multiple Intelligence*, Gardner (2011) suggests that educators have to *individualize* their teaching by knowing the profile of their students and, to the extent that they can, teach in a way that brings out each child's capacities. In his words, they should *pluralize* the classroom by choosing the most important ideas or concepts to be taught and teaching them in multiple ways. After looking at this table, try **Active Learning: Applying Multiple Intelligences** to see how you would apply Gardner's ideas in an educational setting.

Active LEARNING

Applying Multiple Intelligences

Imagine you are trying to teach a classroom of second graders about arithmetic. You know that within this class there are children with each type of intelligence that Gardner has described. Design plans for how you would teach this material so that each child would understand. For example, a child with high musical intelligence might learn best from a song about addition. A child with high bodily-kinesthetic intelligence might need to hop a number of times to understand the same concept. Of course, in the real world, teachers cannot teach everything in nine different ways, but the theory of multiple intelligences suggests they can vary the ways they teach so that all children have a chance to learn using their own mental strengths.

Sternberg's Triarchic Theory

Robert Sternberg has also moved away from the idea that there is one underlying determinant of intelligence, *g*. He believes that intelligence is related not only to success in school but also to success in life. He has said that "one's ability to achieve success depends on capitalizing on one's strengths and correcting or compensating for one's weaknesses through a balance of analytical, creative and practical abilities" (Sternberg, 2002c, p. 448). According to Sternberg's **triarchic theory**, living a successful life entails using these three types of intelligence to interact in the best possible way with one's particular environment.

Sternberg describes **analytical intelligence** as the one closest to *g* and the one prized highly in most schools. **Creative intelligence** is the ability to generate ideas and to deal successfully with novelty. This type of intelligence is tested when children are asked to find as many possible solutions to a problem as they can rather than the one "correct" solution. This is sometimes referred to as **divergent thinking**. Sternberg (2003a) also suggests that the ideas we generate must have value. This means that to be creative we need both divergent thinking to produce new ideas and **convergent thinking** to narrow the alternative ideas down to the one that is most practical or likely to succeed. **Practical intelligence** relates to using abilities to solve everyday problems by changing ourselves or our behavior to better fit the environment, changing the environment, or moving to a different environment in which we can be more successful.

Sternberg's research has provided some support for the existence of these different types of intelligence (Sternberg, 2003b; Sternberg, Castejón, Prieto, Hautamäki, & Grigorenko, 2001). His recent research has examined how the assessment of what he calls the *theory of successful intelligence* can improve the prediction of success in college for undergraduate students (Sternberg, 2009). While the verbal and mathematical portions of the SATs, high school grade point average, and Sternberg's measures all were correlated with college grade point average, his measures doubled the predictive power of the SAT scores alone. Table 8.3 illustrates differences in teaching and assessment of learning in relation to each of these types of intelligence.

Sternberg's goal is to encourage the educational system to move beyond an emphasis on memory skills to promote and value analytical, creative, and practical abilities. As a child, Sternberg himself felt passed over because his abilities did not fall in the standard areas assessed by schools and IQ tests. He has made it his lifework to bring more understanding to those children whose abilities are different. We return to a discussion of Sternberg's theory and research later in the chapter when we discuss creativity.

Triarchic theory Sternberg's idea that intelligence represents a balance of analytical, creative, and practical abilities.

Analytical intelligence The type of intelligence that is the one closest to "g" or general intelligence and the one prized highly in most schools.

Creative intelligence The ability to generate ideas and to deal successfully with novelty (sometimes referred to as divergent thinking).

Divergent thinking The ability to find as many possible solutions to a problem as possible, rather than the one "correct" solution.

Convergent thinking Finding one correct solution for a problem.

Practical intelligence The ability to solve everyday problems by changing ourselves or our behavior to fit the environment better, changing the environment, or moving to a different environment in which we can be more successful.

TABLE 8.3

Prompts used to teach and test memorization versus Sternberg's three types of intelligence. Schools have traditionally placed an emphasis on memorization, but Sternberg emphasizes intellectual skills beyond memorization. This table shows the kinds of questions used for teaching and assessment of each type of intelligence.

Types of Intelligence	Prompts for Teaching and Testing
Memory (the type of intelligence often emphasized in school)	Recall, recognize, match, verify, repeat
Analytical (Sternberg)	Analyze, evaluate, explain, compare and contrast, judge
Creative (Sternberg)	Create, explore, imagine, suppose, synthesize
Practical (Sternberg)	Put into practice, use, implement, apply

SOURCE: Sternberg (2002b).

1. Why is it so difficult for us to define intelligence?

2. What are some alternative ways to measure intelligence?

3. What do we know about the relative contribution of genes and environment to intelligence?

4. What has neuroscience contributed to our understanding of intelligence and the brain?

5. What are two alternative views of intelligence that have been influential in the field of education?

VARIATIONS IN INTELLECTUAL ABILITY

8.2 What are examples of some cognitive deficits and intellectual gifts?

Children's intellectual abilities vary in many ways. Some fall at the lower range of general ability and are described as intellectually disabled, while others fall at the upper range and are described as gifted and talented. Within the average range of abilities, there are children who have specific learning disorders that limit their learning in particular ways. In this section we describe these three variations that affect children's academic progress. Look again at Figure 8.1 to remind yourself what the distribution of intelligence scores looks like.

INTELLECTUAL DISABILITY

According to the DSM-5, an **intellectual disability** is a type of intellectual impairment that begins early in life and includes deficits in intellectual, social, and adaptive functioning (APA, 2013). Between 1% and 3% of American children receive this diagnosis. At one time, we used a score of less than 70 on a standardized test of intelligence as the sole indicator of an intellectual disability. Today we recognize that intellectual disability includes difficulties in three areas of functioning—conceptual, social, and practical—and we are more interested in gauging how the disability affects the individual's everyday life than in relying on a single number for a diagnosis. Therefore, the child's ability to think clearly, to make and retain friendships, and to manage everyday activities and responsibilities are all examined before a diagnosis of intellectual disability is made (APA, 2013).

We discussed a number of causes of intellectual disability in earlier chapters, including genetic causes such as Down syndrome, and environmental causes such as fetal alcohol syndrome, extreme malnutrition, and exposure to toxins such as lead or mercury, but professionals are able to identify a specific reason for an intellectual disability in any individual child in only about 25% of cases (U.S. National Library of Medicine, 2015b). The more severe the intellectual disability, the more likely it is that the child also will have other disabilities, such as impaired vision, hearing loss, cerebral palsy, or a seizure disorder (CDC, 2005).

At one time, children with intellectual disabilities were simply excluded from school, but in 1975 federal legislation known as the Individuals with Disabilities Education Act (IDEA) was passed to ensure that children with disabilities received free and appropriate public education. The law has been revised several times, but the focus has remained to provide early intervention, special education, and related services to eligible children (National Dissemination Center for Children with Disabilities [NDCCD], 2011a).

Intellectual disability A type of intellectual impairment that begins early in life and includes deficits in intellectual, social, and adaptive functioning.

A great deal can be done to help children with intellectual disabilities reach their full developmental potential through intervention programs and special education. Infants and toddlers up to the age of 3 are eligible for early intervention services if they are experiencing delays in cognitive, physical, social, or emotional development, communication or adaptive development, or if they have a diagnosed condition that is likely to result in a developmental delay (NDCCD, 2011a). For children and youth between the ages of 3 and 21 years of age, special education and other services are available through the school system. While children who are intellectually disabled learn more slowly than children with average or above-average abilities, they are able to learn new skills that will improve the quality of their lives (The ARC, 2015).

SPECIFIC LEARNING DISORDER

Specific learning disorder (SLD) Persistent difficulty with learning that is substantially below the average and cannot be better explained by another problem. Specific areas of difficulty include reading, writing, and arithmetic.

Another condition related to cognitive ability covered by the provisions of the IDEA is a **specific learning disorder (SLD)**. DSM-5 describes one overarching category for specific learning disorder paired with what are called "specifiers" for difficulties within the various academic domains. This means that a child might be diagnosed as having a SLD with impairment in reading, writing, or arithmetic, or some combination of these three (International Dyslexia Association, 2014). The diagnosis requires persistent difficulty with performance that is substantially below the average on an appropriate test of skill that cannot be better explained by another problem, such as a vision or hearing problem or a motor disorder. Children who have a learning disorder are not intellectually disabled and have average to above-average general intelligence. The National Center for Learning Disabilities (NCLD, 2014) estimates that 2.4 million children in the United States have a specific learning disorder. We discuss specific learning disorders in general here, but will discuss those specifically related to written and spoken language in Chapter 9.

Some types of learning disorders appear to run in families, especially those related to reading and spelling deficits, which may indicate a genetic link for these disorders (Gargiulo, 2012). Other possible causes include prenatal exposure to toxins (such as maternal drinking or smoking), premature birth, shortage of oxygen during delivery, or head injuries after birth. Although the specific reason for a child's learning disorder is often not known, research on possible causes continues because a better understanding of causes will help us do a better job of preventing learning disorders or developing more effective interventions.

Although learning disorders have their roots in early development, they usually are not identified until children reach school age and need to begin developing their reading and writing skills. Children develop these abilities at different rates, so we should never jump to the conclusion that a child has a learning disorder if she is slower to read and write than other children. The child may need better instruction or more practice and time to develop these skills. However, if the child's difficulties persist, then it is time for the child's school to evaluate the child's performance.

Although a SLD cannot be cured, the effects of a learning disorder on a child's development can be reduced significantly with the proper educational support services. With help, children can work with their strengths and learn strategies to help them deal effectively with their condition. That is why the provision of special educational services is so important for these children. As Figure 8.3 shows, during the 2012-2013 school years, children with a specific learning disorder accounted for the largest proportion of students receiving services under IDEA legislation (Kena et al., 2015), almost 5 times the number of students receiving services for autism or intellectual disability. Collaboration among classroom teachers, support specialists, and parents is essential for an optimal outcome for these children.

However, even with support, children with learning disorders face more than academic challenges in the classroom, so parents and teachers need to be sensitive to other sources of stress in the child's life. Difficulties in meeting the day-to-day expectations in the classroom can have a negative effect on the child's self-esteem (Alexander-Passe, 2006; NCLD, 2014). Children with learning disabilities also may lack the interpersonal and social skills needed to make and keep

T ☐ F ☐ Five times more children with autism receive services within the schools than children with a specific learning disorder or an intellectual disability. **False**

friends (NCLD, 2014). Because children who are different from other children can become a target for bullies, teachers and other school personnel need to be vigilant to protect these children from harm to their physical well-being, self-esteem, and psychological well-being.

Children try to find ways on their own to cope with their challenges. Some underreact by trying to ignore their problems (Firth, Greaves, & Frydenberg, 2010) or withdraw from social interaction (NCLD, 2014), and others overreact by acting out (for example, becoming the class clown, being aggressive toward other children, or engaging in delinquent behavior) (Ahrens, Dubois, Lozano, & Richardson, 2010; Alexander-Passe, 2006). Although these are coping mechanisms that everyone may use from time to time, they are not productive ones. Withdrawing from a stressful situation may temporarily ease the anxiety, but it doesn't solve a problem. Acting up may get you attention, but it doesn't help you meet your challenges. Research conducted in Australia has shown that coping interventions can help adolescents with a learning disorder develop a stronger sense of control over their situation and increase their use of adaptive coping strategies (Firth, Frydenberg, & Greaves, 2008). When young people are proactive in dealing with their disability, set goals for themselves, are self-aware and emotionally stable, and have good social support, they can be highly successful (Goldberg, Higgins, Raskind, & Herman, 2003; Seo, Abbott, & Hawkins, 2008).

Problems that arise in the elementary school years can persist and become worse as children with learning disorders move into adolescence. Research that looked at how adolescents with dyslexia (an SLD that involves difficulty with written language) coped found some important and interesting gender differences (Alexander-Passe, 2006). This research found that girls were more likely to try to find ways to make themselves feel better about the situation. For instance, they might try to avoid the tasks at hand or to distract themselves from their problems by socializing with friends rather than studying. In contrast, boys were more likely to attack the situation directly in an attempt to deal with it. They showed persistence and hard work and tried to analyze their past attempts to figure out what went wrong and could be corrected in the future. Consequently, in this study, having a SLD had a greater effect on the academic and general self-esteem of girls than it had on the self-esteem of boys, and girls reported higher levels of depression.

In a recent review of 62 articles that looked at the long-term outcomes for children with a learning disorder, Sharfi and Rosenblum (2014) found that young adults with a learning

FIGURE 8.3

Percentage distribution of children ages 3–21 served under the Individuals with Disabilities Education Act (IDEA), Part B, by disability type: School year 2012–2013.

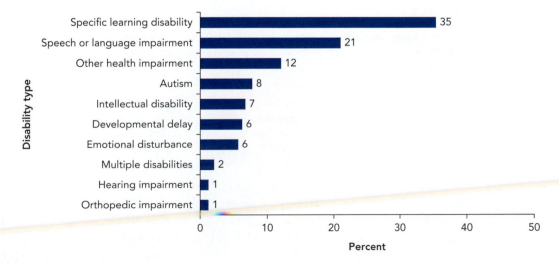

SOURCE: National Center for Education Statistics (2016).

disorder were less likely to attend a 4-year college, or if they did attend one, to graduate. After entering the workforce, they earned less than young adults without a learning disorder. However, on the positive side, those students who did graduate from college were employed at a level comparable to the general workforce population and had a similar level of salary and benefits. Having a learning disorder does not mean that children cannot achieve a great deal in their lives. A number of people with outstanding accomplishments in their fields have a learning disorder. You may know that actress Whoopi Goldberg, singer Solange Knowles, Olympic athlete Michael Phelps, and director Steven Spielberg each have a specific learning disorder (LD OnLine, 2008a, 2008b).

Many colleges offer support services, such as untimed tests or note-taking services, for students with an identified learning disorder. You may want to explore the services available on your campus for these students.

GIFTEDNESS

Gifted (or talented) children Children and youth who exhibit high performance capability in intellectual, creative, and/or artistic areas; possess an unusual leadership capacity; or excel in specific academic fields.

Three-ring model of giftedness A conception of giftedness as the intersection of above average intellectual ability, creativity, and task commitment.

The other end of the continuum of cognitive ability represents children who are functioning at a very high level and have an extraordinary amount of potential for their development. These children are identified as **gifted** or **talented**. It has been difficult to arrive at a single, generally accepted definition of giftedness (National Association for Gifted Children, 2013; Renzulli, 1998) and we continue to rely primarily on measures of intellectual ability as the defining characteristic, even though giftedness includes a wide range of human abilities, talents, and accomplishments (McClain & Pfeiffer, 2012). A conceptualization of giftedness that has attempted to broaden our definition has been proposed by Renzulli (1998; 2005) and is known as the **three-ring model of giftedness**. In this model, giftedness is seen as the intersection of above-average intellectual ability, creativity, and task commitment (see Figure 8.4). More recently, personal characteristics such as optimism, courage, physical and mental energy, and a sense of destiny have been added to the model (Sternberg, Jarvin, & Grigorenko, 2011).

These ideas are reflected in an approach to gifted education that is called a *talent development model* (Pfeiffer, 2012). We often think of giftedness as a quality of the individual that is "real" and permanent, as though children are born gifted or not. If that is true, there may not be much that we can expect educators to do to nurture or develop that talent. However, a talent development approach sees giftedness as a characteristic that

---

FIGURE 8.4

The three-ring conception of giftedness. Renzulli (1998) has proposed a model that places giftedness at the intersection of above-average ability, creativity, and task commitment.

SOURCE: Renzulli (1998).

can be supported, encouraged, and nurtured by the environment in order for intellectual ability and talent to be transformed into outstanding performance and innovation (Subotnik, Olszewski-Kubilius, & Worrell, 2011). The challenge for the schools has been to design programs that can accomplish this.

In contrast to the general agreement about the need to provide services to children with intellectual challenges, considerable debate and disagreement exist about the nature, amount, or type of services the educational system should provide to gifted children. When there has been some perceived threat to our country's status or well-being (such as the release of international statistics indicating that American children are lagging behind other nations in their academic achievement), there are calls for programs to support the development of our brightest chil-

Gifted and talented programs. Programs for gifted and talented students may provide added educational enrichment. This girl rides on a hoverboard powered by a leaf blower as a way to learn about Newton's laws of motion.

dren. When there is no such perceived threat, however, our traditional commitment to egalitarianism in our schools and a fear of possibly creating an elite class of students works against having programs for gifted and talented students (Reis, 2004). This concern has been heightened by the underrepresentation of Black and Latino students in programs for the gifted (Reis & Renzulli, 2010). When education budgets are tight, programs for the gifted are seen as a luxury that we can do without, yet the public generally supports programs for gifted and talented youngsters as long as they do not reduce the opportunities for average or below-average learners (Reis, 2004).

Programs for gifted and talented students take a variety of forms (Reis, 2004). They often use an **enrichment approach**, in which the curriculum is covered but in greater depth, breadth, or complexity than is done in a typical classroom. Teachers in these classes usually have a good deal of flexibility in how they structure the students' learning experience. However, many enrichment programs for gifted students take place after school, on Saturdays, or during the summer, and supplement the instruction the child receives in his or her regular classroom (Brody, 2005).

An **accelerated program** in the child's regular school allows the student to move through the standard curriculum but more quickly than is typical. Rather than moving at a pace that suits an entire class of students, the individual student moves ahead as the student shows mastery of the material. A student who is advanced in a particular subject (for example, mathematics) might take that subject with a class at a higher grade level but remain in his or her regular grade for other subjects, or the student may be allowed to skip an entire grade to accelerate his or her progress in all subjects. Accelerated approaches often encounter resistance based on the presumption that children who complete their secondary schooling early will not be ready emotionally or socially to move on to a university to complete their education. However, the majority of studies that have looked at gifted children enrolled in accelerated programs have failed to find negative social or emotional outcomes (Lehman & Erdwins, 2004; Plucker & Callahan, 2014; Sayler & Brookshire, 2004). Gifted students report that they feel positively about themselves (Plucker & Callahan, 2014), do not feel socially isolated from their peers (Sayler & Brookshire, 2004), and report high levels of life satisfaction (Gross, 2006). On the other hand, they often report that they were bored, uninterested, and frustrated prior to being accelerated and were more satisfied after enrolling in accelerated programs (Vialle, Ashton, Carlon, & Rankin, 2001).

Outside the school environment, parents of gifted or talented children can do a great deal to foster and encourage their children's talents. Parents can provide their children with a wide

Enrichment approach An educational approach for gifted children in which the curriculum is covered but in greater depth, breadth, or complexity than is done in a typical classroom.

Accelerated program A type of program that allows gifted students to move through the standard curriculum but more quickly than is typical.

TRUE/FALSE VIDEO ▲

T ☐ F ☐ Children who are gifted or talented often pay a price for their giftedness because they are likely to be socially or emotionally maladjusted. **False**

range of intellectual opportunities that keep the child engaged and challenged, but parents also need to protect their children from becoming overcommitted to too many activities or consumed by the need to be perfect in everything they do (Davidson Institute for Talent Development, 2004). Adults never should have such high expectations that they lose sight of the fact that gifted children are, after all, still children.

CREATIVITY AND INTELLIGENCE

Creativity Thinking that is novel and that produces ideas that are of value.

T ☐ F ☐ The smarter you are, the more likely it is that you will also be creative. **False**

Where does **creativity** fit into our understanding of intelligence? Can you be creative but not necessarily intelligent, or are creativity and intelligence so closely related that people who are high (or low) on one are also high (or low) on the other? A substantial number of studies have examined the relationship between creativity and intelligence and many have found that the correlation is positive but moderately low. The conclusion drawn from this research is that although a certain level of intelligence is necessary to be creative, high intelligence is not sufficient by itself and even children of relatively low intellect can generate multiple solutions for a problem (that is, they can be creative) (Kim, 2005; Jauk, Benedek, Dunst, & Neubauer, 2013). While traditional intelligence testing and many academic situations require children and adolescents to come up with one correct solution, called *convergent thinking*, creativity is based on an ability to see multiple solutions to a problem, called *divergent thinking*.

Most of the tests that measure creativity are based on the idea that you need to be able to be flexible in your thinking and to generate multiple solutions to a problem, including solutions that are unique or original. **Active Learning: Creativity Tests** allows you to explore your own creativity using some items adapted from tests of creativity.

Active LEARNING

Creativity Tests

The following items are similar to items used on various tests of creativity. Give yourself a specific amount of time (perhaps 1 or 2 minutes per question) and provide as many alternative answers as you can. You might want to do this activity with a small group of friends so you can observe whether there are substantial differences in how individuals perform on these tasks.

Word Fluency	Write as many words beginning with a given letter as you can in a specified amount of time.
Alternate Uses	Give as many possible uses as you can for a given item (for example, a brick or a bicycle tire).
Consequences	Give as many consequences as you can for a hypothetical situation (for example, what if we could live under water? What if animals could talk?).
Making Objects	Draw as many objects as you can using only a specific set of shapes (for example, one circle and two squares).
Decorations	Use as many different designs as possible to outline a common object.

Scoring of this type of test is often quite complex, so this activity is simply an opportunity to stimulate your creativity, not to assess the results. How quickly were you able to generate multiple answers that were highly original?

Today some psychologists distinguish between big-C creativity and small-c creativity (Fasko, 2006). If you have ever scribbled a phone number on the palm of your hand because there was no paper available or used duct tape to fix practically anything, you have shown **small-c creativity**, the type we use to solve everyday problem and adapt to change. By contrast, **big-C creativity** transforms a culture by impacting the very way people think or the way they live their lives (Csikszentmihalyi, 1998). For example, Picasso transformed the world of art and Steve Jobs transformed technology. Can the classroom environment support both types of creativity?

You'll remember that Robert Sternberg described three types of intelligence—analytical, practical, and creative—and believes that school should foster all three, but teaching that fosters creativity is lacking in most classrooms. It may be that teachers don't know how to teach it (Sternberg, 2003b; Pang, 2015), or they may feel that the recent emphasis on standardized testing does not leave enough time to incorporate creative learning opportunities into the class day (Hennessey, 2015; Pang, 2015). However, creativity can be integrated into classroom activities in some fairly simple ways. For instance, students who read a story could then be asked to think about the plot for a sequel to that story, or a history lesson could be followed by an opportunity to speculate on an alternative scenario, such as thinking about what America might be like if Columbus had not reached the new world (Hennessey, 2015). To stimulate creativity, children need to be encouraged to experiment and try new things, and to think about situations in fresh ways without being bound to old practices and ideas. They also need to be allowed to try and fail without becoming discouraged.

Justin Sullivan/Getty Images

Big-C creativity. Steve Jobs's transformation of our world through innovations in personal computing is an example of big-C creativity.

Small-c creativity The type of creativity we use in everyday life to solve problems and adapt to change.

Big-C creativity The type of creativity that transforms a culture by impacting the way we think or live our lives.

CHECK YOUR UNDERSTANDING

1. How is having an intellectual disability different from having a specific learning disorder?
2. What is the three-ring model of giftedness?
3. How are intelligence and creativity related to each other?

ACADEMIC ACHIEVEMENT: LEARNING IN THE SCHOOL CONTEXT

8.3 What are some issues that affect learning within the school environment?

Intelligence is one factor that influences how well an individual will learn both in school and in the rest of life. Although learning occurs in many contexts—at a child's home, in school, and in the neighborhood—in this chapter we focus on the school environment and its impact on student learning. You will read about the role of family and community in fostering academic achievement in later chapters. There are many issues related to academic achievement that play out within the classroom once the child enters school. We discuss several of these issues and highlight some of the complexities surrounding them.

AP Photo/Mark J. Terrill

High expectations. Extraordinary educators such as Erin Gruwell have been represented in movies, but you may know other educators whose high expectations have challenged you personally to excel.

CLASSROOM ENVIRONMENT

Outside their family home, children in developed societies spend the largest portion of their time in a school classroom. The most important structural feature in that environment is the teacher. The Center for Public Education (2005) has reviewed the literature on the effect of teacher quality on student achievement and reached these conclusions:

- Teacher quality is a more important influence on student performance than race, class, or the particular school the student is attending.

- The size of the effect is substantial, especially when these teachers work with disadvantaged students. For example, the achievement gain for African American students with an effective teacher was 3 times as large as the gain for White students.

- The effect of having high-quality teachers accumulates over the years.

- Content knowledge, experience, training and certification, and general cognitive skills are all important characteristics of effective teachers.

There have been some very powerful movie portrayals of real teachers who have transformed the lives of their students. In *Stand and Deliver*, a math teacher, Jaime Escalante, works after school, on weekends, and during vacations to help his predominantly Hispanic students from the Los Angeles barrio master calculus (Menéndez, 1988). In *Freedom Writers*, Erin Gruwell helps a group of gangbangers in a racially divided high school find meaning and hope for their lives through reading assignments and the daily journals that the students keep (LaGravenese, 2007). These teachers have been recognized for their inspirational work with students, but there are many teachers who quietly make a difference in the lives of their students every day. **Active Learning: Teacher-Heroes in Movies and Real Life** guides you to think about such teachers in your own life.

Active LEARNING

Teacher-Heroes in Movies and Real Life

Think about the most inspirational teacher you have ever had. What did that person do that was different from what other teachers did that made this person special to you? Was it something she did, something she said, or the way she seemed to feel about you that made a difference? If you have seen any inspirational movies about teachers, did you see any parallels between your experience and the teachers portrayed in the movies? What downside, if any, is there to these movies creating such high expectations in the mind of the public for what a really great teacher can do for students?

STUDENT-TEACHER RATIOS

Do you think that it matters how many students there are in a classroom? Surveys in naturally occurring school settings support the idea that smaller classes, particularly in the early grades, benefit students (Biddle & Berliner, 2002). The differences favoring small classes also emerge from experimental studies that assigned matched groups of children to large or small classes. The gains are similar for boys and girls, but the benefits are strongest for minority students, children from low-income families, and those attending inner-city schools (Whitehurst & Chingos, 2011).

Although we can say smaller classes are beneficial to certain children, it is important to understand *why* this happens. For instance, smaller classrooms in the early grades allow teachers to spend more time helping individual students establish effective work habits and positive attitudes toward school. When less time needs to be spent on classroom management, it frees up more time for academic instruction (Biddle & Berliner, 2002).

Small class size. Optimal learning occurs when well-trained, enthusiastic teachers can pay close attention to individual students in the early grades. Small class size gives them more opportunity to interact in this way with their students.

However, smaller teacher-to-student ratios by themselves do not ensure better instruction, and reducing class size is expensive. By one estimate made in 2011, reducing every class in the United States by just one student would cost more than $12 billion in educational funding (Whitehurst & Chingos, 2011). Perhaps those resources would be better spent on directly improving teacher preparation and qualifications. When teachers have high-quality interactions with their students that are based on warm and supportive relationships and actively engage their students in classroom activities, it positively affects student achievement (Guo, Connor, Tompkins, & Morrison, 2011). Again, while this is more likely to happen in a smaller classroom, simply having a smaller class does not guarantee it.

ABILITY GROUPING

The use of **ability grouping** in schools is another issue in education that has been controversial. This practice has also been called *streaming, tracking,* or *clusters* (Trautwein, Ludtke, Marsh, Koller, & Baumert, 2006). After a decline in the use of ability grouping from the 1960s through the mid-1990s, there has been a resurgence in their use in recent years (Loveless, 2013). The rationale behind this educational approach is that ability groups allow students to be taught at a level that is most appropriate for their current level of understanding. It is intended to allow high-performing students to advance more rapidly thus avoiding boredom and frustration as they wait for slower students to master the material, and to allow low-performing students to get the material at a slower pace that better matches their ability level. Critics, however, see this stratification as harmful to low-performing students because it can damage their self-esteem and create negative attitudes toward school and schoolwork (Ireson, Hallam, & Plewis, 2001). Other critics have charged that children in lower-ability tracks receive poorer-quality teaching and have a less supportive educational environment, which, in turn, contributes to their lower levels of academic achievement (Nomi, 2010).

In some schools, collaborative learning has replaced ability grouping. Collaborative learning, as described in Chapter 2, puts students with different ability levels together to work on a common goal, such as a project or an assignment. Students in collaborative learning groups show higher achievement, better self-esteem, and greater social competency than those in other instructional approaches (Curry, De Amicis, & Gilligan, 2011). They also report liking

Ability grouping An educational approach that places students of similar ability in learning groups so they can be taught at a level that is most appropriate for their level of understanding.

what they are studying more and are more likely to develop friendships with students from different ethnic backgrounds (Curry et al., 2011).

One explanation for why collaborative learning is beneficial is that complex tasks make greater demands on cognitive processing and dividing the cognitive load among multiple people is helpful (Kirschner, Paas, & Kirschner, 2009). For this reason, a collaborative approach would not be particularly beneficial for a simpler task that is within the cognitive processing abilities of any single individual. Of course, working in a group requires additional effort to maintain communication within the group and to integrate individual information into a final group solution, but these efforts are justified when a task is complex.

While ability grouping creates homogeneous groups of students who have a similar ability level, collaborative learning creates heterogeneous groups of students of varying ability levels. Proponents of collaborative learning maintain that all students in the group can benefit from this arrangement. They believe that high-achieving students benefit from the opportunity to explain concepts to the lower-achieving group members, while the low-achieving members of the group benefit by getting assistance, encouragement, and stimulation from the more advanced group members (Marsh et al., 2008). Do you see the Vygotskian principle of scaffolding here when children are learning from their interactions with more skilled peers?

However, research on this educational approach has found it to be more advantageous for low-performing students than for high-achieving ones (Nomi, 2010). High-ability students tend to achieve at a similar level regardless of whether their group is homogeneous or heterogeneous (Saleh, Lazonder, & De Jong, 2005). Perhaps it shouldn't surprise us that high-ability students do well in a variety of conditions. Although they perform better when they are grouped with other high-achieving students, there are benefits other than academic achievement that come along with their participation in a heterogeneous group, including the development of social and leadership skills and enhanced self-esteem (Neber, Finsterwald, & Urban, 2001).

GRADE RETENTION

When children have not mastered the material for a grade level, they may be retained in that grade for another year so that they can repeat the material. Sometimes, however, children who have not mastered grade-level material still are promoted to the next grade, a process that is known as **social promotion**. As the term implies, the primary motivation for doing this is to keep the child in a class with same-age peers so that the child is not perceived as a failure and does not become alienated from peers and from school (Lorence & Dworkin, 2006).

One consistent set of findings from research on grade retention is that some children are at greater risk than others of being retained. African American and Latino students are more likely to be retained than Anglo students (Cannon, Lipscomb, & Public Policy Institute of California, 2011; Frey, 2005; Jacobs & Lefgren, 2004), boys are retained at higher rates than girls (Cannon et al., 2011; Frey, 2005), and children from low-income families are more likely to be retained than children from more affluent families (Cannon et al., 2011; Frey, 2005). English-language learners are also at an increased risk (Cannon et al., 2011).

Research that looked at whether—or when—retention versus social promotion is beneficial to the child has produced mixed findings. Findings from several longitudinal studies in which retained students were compared to students who were promoted showed no significant benefits of retention and small to moderate effects that favor the students who were promoted over those who were retained (Moser, West, & Hughes, 2012; Silberglitt, Jimerson, Burns, & Appleton, 2006). Retained students also are more aggressive during adolescence and more likely to drop out of high school (Frey, 2005; Jimerson & Ferguson, 2007). Students who drop out of school are 5 times more likely to have been retained than those who graduate, although retention at earlier ages is less associated with dropping out than retention at older ages (David, 2008).

To understand the lack of support for grade retention, we should think about the purpose of retention. Students are retained because they have not mastered the material at a certain grade level. If that hasn't happened on a first attempt, should we think that simply exposing

T ☐ F ☐ Placing high-, average-, and low-performing students together in groups to collaborate on a project benefits all the children in the group equally. **False**

Social promotion Promoting a child who has not mastered grade-level material to keep the child in a class with same-age peers.

the student to the same information a second time will make the difference? Contrary to what we might expect, research has found that 50% of students who repeat a grade do no better on their second attempt and 25% actually do worse (Kenneady & Intercultural Development Research Association, 2004). As an alternative to grade retention, students might make up educational deficits through summer school or before- and after-school programs or extra help during the school day (David, 2008). When students do repeat a grade, they do better when they are given extra help and assistance during the school year while they repeat the grade (Lorence & Dworkin, 2006). If you have ever had to retake one of your college courses, you know that if you simply do again what you did the first time, it is likely that you will get the same results. However, if you change what you do or how you do it, you are more likely to have a better outcome. Although this makes sense, schools must be willing to spend the extra money that is necessary to provide additional help to students who are repeating a grade.

SCHOOL DROPOUTS AND HIGH SCHOOL GRADUATES

In Figure 8.5, we can see the significant improvement that has occurred in the high school dropout rate in recent years. The overall rate declined from 12% in the 1990s to about 7% in 2013 (Kena et al., 2015), with the steepest decline for Hispanic students. Another bit of good news here is that one study found that 63% of students who drop out of high school go on to eventually pass their GED (General Educational Development) test within 8 years of their original anticipated graduation date (Child Trends, 2010). However, these statistics still mean that over a million students do not graduate with their class (Rumberger, 2013).

> **T ☐ F ☐** Students who repeat a grade substantially improve their performance on their second attempt. **False**

> **T ☐ F ☐** Most students who drop out of high school go on to eventually complete their high school education. **True**

FIGURE 8.5

Dropout rates. The dropout rate has been steadily declining since the 1990s. This is especially important because employment today is much more dependent on high school completion than it was in the past. Note that the rate for Hispanics is inflated because it includes a large number of immigrants in this age group who never attended school in the United States.

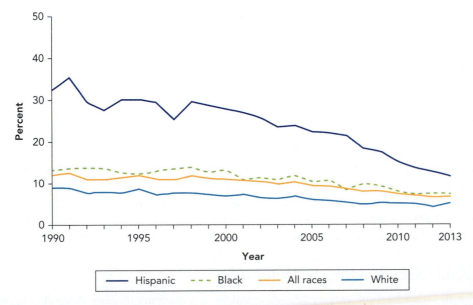

NOTE: The "status dropout rate" represents the percentage of 16- through 24-year-olds who are not enrolled in school and have not earned a high school credential (either a diploma or an equivalency credential such as a General Educational Development [GED] certificate). Data are based on sample surveys of the civilian noninstitutionalized population, which excludes persons in prisons, persons in the military, and other persons not living in households. Data for all races include other racial/ethnic categories not separately shown. Race categories exclude persons of Hispanic ethnicity.

SOURCE: Kena et al. (2015).

It is in everyone's interest to find ways to keep these students in school so they complete their education sooner rather than later.

Researchers have examined school records to determine whether there were developmental pathways that distinguished between high school graduates and dropouts (Hickman, Bartholomew, Mathwig, & Heinrich, 2008). The differences they discovered are what we might expect. Students who eventually dropped out of high school performed more poorly on standardized tests and received lower course grades than graduates, had higher levels of grade retention and absenteeism, and had more problem behaviors. What was more surprising was the origin of these differences. They began in kindergarten and persisted throughout elementary school, with the gap between future dropouts and their peers who would graduate on time widening as the students moved into middle school and continued into high school. These findings suggest that programs of early intervention even before children enter kindergarten do *not* start too early because the origins of eventual school dropout arise very early in a child's school career.

Although the dropout rate has declined, there still is reason to be concerned about it and to look for ways to reduce it further. Young people who do not complete high school are ill equipped for employment in today's marketplace. They are more likely to be unemployed than high school graduates, and when they are employed, they earn less and hold jobs with less occupational status (Child Trends, 2013a).

About one-third of students who graduate from high school do not go on to higher education (U.S. Bureau of Labor Statistics, 2015a). Critics feel that these high school students are being shortchanged by the school system because they are not adequately prepared for the transition from school to work. While a high school diploma is essential and college is desirable, these critics argue that lessons from Europe strongly suggest that "well-developed, high-quality vocational education programs provide an excellent pathway for many young people to enter the adult work force" (Symonds, Schwartz, & Ferguson, 2011, p. 38). The Harvard Graduate School of Education estimates that nearly half the 14 million jobs that will be created by 2018 will go to people with an associate's degree or occupational certificate (Symonds et al., 2011).

One reason U.S. students drop out of high school is that they do not see the connection between what they are studying and opportunities in the workplace (Symonds et al., 2011). European high school students who do not plan to go to college can choose to enter an apprentice program while in high school that provides "a multi-year sequence of work-based and school-based learning opportunities providing formal certification of participants' competence" at the end of their training (Hamilton & Hamilton, 1997, p. 1). Employers in Europe make this investment in training young people because they know they will have a highly qualified workforce available to them at the end of the training. There are few programs like this for students in the United States.

The School-to-Work Opportunities Act of 1994 created a program that facilitated the transition of non-college-bound students in the United States from high school into productive careers. Although these programs did not raise grades, they did reduce dropout rates and increase college enrollment. Despite positive initial outcomes, the program's funding expired in 2001 and was not renewed. Although the American Recovery and Reinvestment Act of 2009 provided some funding that might include school-to-work programs, it did not mandate the creation of these types of programs (America's Future Workforce, 2013).

COLLEGE-BOUND STUDENTS

Not all high school students are struggling and, in fact, many are thriving. According to the Federal Interagency Forum on Child and Family Statistics (2013), in 2009 three-quarters of high school graduates had completed Algebra II, over a third had taken a mathematics course in analysis/precalculus, and over two-thirds had taken at least one course each in biology and chemistry. During the 2009-2010 school year, over 1.8 million high school students took at least one advanced placement course (Aud, KewalRamani, & Frohlich, 2011).

About two-thirds of high school graduates enroll in college in the fall immediately following their high school graduation (National Center for Educational Statistics, 2013), but some of them are better prepared than others and this affects the likelihood that they will complete their college education. By one estimate, fewer than half of the students who take the SAT are prepared to succeed in college, a number that did not change between 2009 and 2013 (The College Board, 2013). Not being at this level of readiness can slow—or even derail—a student's college career. Although tests such as the SATs are good predictors of academic performance in college, high school grades are even better, especially for minority and first-generation students, so some colleges are dropping the SAT and ACT as a major admissions requirement (Hiss & Franks, 2014).

The transition from high school to college can be stressful. College students usually have a great deal more autonomy than high school students, and many are living away from home for the first time. Some students may not have all the academic preparation they need, and some do not yet have the skills and attitudes they need to be successful in college, including the ability to engage in critical thinking, having an inquisitive nature and a willingness to accept critical feedback, an openness to possible failure, and the ability to cope with ambiguous learning tasks (Venezia & Jaeger, 2013). While many older adolescents are capable of these things, as college students they may find it difficult to meet all these expectations.

Having the knowledge, motivation, and resources necessary to complete a college education are important because students who drop out of college often end up with significant education-related debt but none of the benefits they hoped for from a degree. Most college campuses devote considerable resources to their student support services. Efforts prior to college admission that help ensure students are well prepared for the demands of college, and helping students evaluate the fit between their needs and the characteristics of the campus they have chosen, can also help boost the likelihood of their success.

CHECK YOUR UNDERSTANDING

1. Explain why a smaller student-teacher ratio can be beneficial to students.
2. What is collaborative learning and which students benefit the most from it?
3. What must happen if grade retention is going to be beneficial for a student?
4. How could the educational system better prepare noncollege-bound students for the workforce?
5. Why is the transition from high to college stressful for many students?

GROUP DIFFERENCES IN ACADEMIC ACHIEVEMENT

8.4 How do gender, ethnicity/race, and socioeconomic status affect academic achievement?

So far, we have described some of the ways in which individual children and adolescents differ in their cognitive ability and looked at some of the issues within the school environment that affect students' academic achievement. In this section, we turn our attention to group differences—including gender, ethnic/racial identity, and socioeconomic status—that affect achievement.

GENDER AND ACADEMIC ACHIEVEMENT

There is a large body of research that has looked at the different experiences that boys and girls have in the classroom. There has been recent concern about the ways in which boys may be struggling to succeed in school, and a long-standing concern about the girls' lack of interest in courses in science, math, and technology. After looking at these concerns and attempts to improve the situations, we ask whether single-gender classrooms are a possible solution for both boys and girls.

Boys' Academic Achievement

A relatively recent concern within the school environment has been referred to as the "boy problem." Educational statistics suggest that it is becoming more difficult for boys than for girls to be successful in school. For instance, consider the following:

- In elementary school, girls outperform boys in reading and writing, more girls than boys participate in gifted and talented programs, boys are more likely than girls to be retained in grade, boys are 3 times more likely than girls to be in special education, and more boys than girls are suspended or expelled from school.

- In high school, girls have higher GPAs than boys and earn a greater proportion of As in their classes, and boys are more likely than girls to drop out of school.

- In college, more women than men enroll in postsecondary education (see Figure 8.6), women earn more bachelor's degrees, and more women plan to attend graduate school or professional school after completion of their bachelor's degrees (Fortin, Oreopoulos, & Phipps, 2015; National Center for Education Statistics, 2004; U.S. Department of Education, 2012).

Some of the blame for boys' poor performance has been placed on the curriculum because it emphasizes reading and writing, subjects where girls usually outperform boys; it uses books that don't interest or appeal to boys as much as they appeal to girls; and schools are cutting activities such as science labs, physical education, and recess that favor the experiential learning style of boys (Sax, 2007; Von Drehle, 2007). Consequently, there have been calls to

---

FIGURE 8.6

The gender gap in undergraduate enrollment. Since the 1990s, the number of women enrolled in degree-granting undergraduate programs has been greater than the number of men, and this gap is projected to continue to increase through 2020.

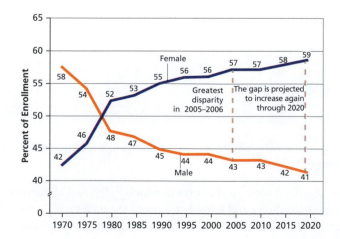

SOURCE: Aud, Hassar, et al. (2011).

create a more "boy-friendly" classroom (Martino & Kehler, 2006). Outside of school, boys are more likely to spend more time on activities like video games that don't require reading skills (Weis & Cerankosky, 2010), while girls are more likely to read for pleasure (Organisation for Economic Co-operation and Development, 2009).

Others have looked to biological differences between boys and girls to explain their different performance in the classroom. For example, the language centers in the brain of an average 5-year-old boy look more like the language centers in the brain of the average 3-year-old girl (Lenroot et al., 2007; Sax, 2007), which makes teaching reading to 5-year-old boys more difficult or perhaps even developmentally inappropriate. When boys are not able to succeed at these tasks, it causes frustration, and they tend to avoid these activities in the future.

However, when the issue of boys' school performance was carefully reexamined, the picture became more complicated. Sara Mead (2006) reanalyzed some of the statistics on school performance and came to the conclusion that boys from middle-class or upper-middle-class families are, in fact, performing *better* in school than they have in the past, but the same is not true for minority boys and boys from disadvantaged families (see also Froschl & Sprung, 2008). It appears that the "boy problem" may be restricted to these particular groups of boys. Of course, that does not mean that we shouldn't be concerned about their success. It simply means that we can be more focused in targeting our efforts. It also reminds us that, if we are concerned about differential performance in school, it is not enough to look only at differences between boys and girls. We also need to look at differences *within* groups of boys and *within* groups of girls because there is great diversity within each group.

Girls and the STEM Fields

While the concern about a possible "boy problem" in schools is a fairly recent one, there is a very long-standing concern about how to get girls more interested in science, technology, engineering, and math (the STEM disciplines). Figure 8.7 shows the percent of bachelor's degrees awarded to men and women in the STEM fields in 2004 and in 2014. Despite ongoing efforts to interest girls in the STEM disciplines, it appears that little has changed over this period of time.

FIGURE 8.7

Gender distribution of bachelor's degrees in science and engineering disciplines (2004, 2014). Are you surprised to see that women have not changed their level of participation in the STEM fields since 2004?

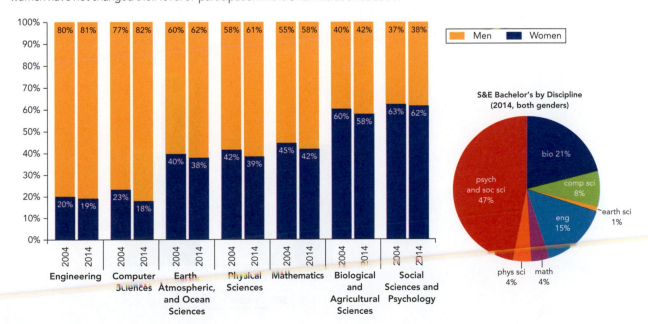

SOURCE: National Student Clearinghouse Research Center (2015).

For many years, this difference was attributed to girls' lower ability or their weaker interest in these subjects, but we now know that girls take just as many science and math classes in high school as boys and perform at a similar level in both areas (Hill, Corbett, & St. Rose, 2010; Planty, Provasnik, & Daniel, 2007). Mathematical ability as measured by standardized tests is not significantly different between boys and girls in elementary school or middle school (Ganley & Vasilyeva, 2011; Lindberg, Hyde, Peterson, & Linn, 2010; Scafidi & Bui, 2010), and girls frequently earn better grades in elementary and high school math classes than boys (Ganley & Vasilyeva, 2011; Kenney-Benson et al., 2006). Girls do, however, perform slightly poorer than boys on "high stakes math tests," including the SAT, ACT, and advanced placement tests (Hill et al., 2010, p. 5). Later we discuss the concept called *stereotype threat* that may help explain why girls perform as well as boys in class, but continue to perform below boys on these tests.

Despite our understanding that ability level does not clearly differentiate boys and girls, the idea that boys are better than girls at math persists (Else-Quest, Hyde, & Linn, 2010). Girls themselves buy into this misconception starting at young ages. As early as second grade, girls do not see math as a part of their self-concept (Cvencek, Meltzoff, & Greenwald, 2011). Muzzatti and Agnoli (2007) asked elementary school children about their beliefs about boys' and girls' ability to do well in math. In second grade, boys said that boys' ability was equal to that of girls, but girls said that girls' ability exceeded that of boys. In third grade, boys now said that boys' ability exceeded that of girls, and girls now thought that the ability of boys and girls was equal. However, by fourth grade, boys said that boys' ability exceeded girls' ability, and girls now agreed with them that boys were better at math. One consequence is that if girls whose math ability is equal to that of boys perceive themselves as less skilled, they will become less likely to choose a career they believe requires that skill (Correll, 2004; Hill et al., 2010).

Where do these ideas come from? In part, they come from girls' experiences in the classroom. Girls are sometimes treated in ways that subtly devalue their ideas and contributions,

FIGURE 8.8

Stereotype threat. When given a difficult test in math, women who were told that there were no gender differences for this test did better than men and better than women who heard instructions emphasizing that they were taking a test of mathematics ability, activating a stereotype threat for this group.

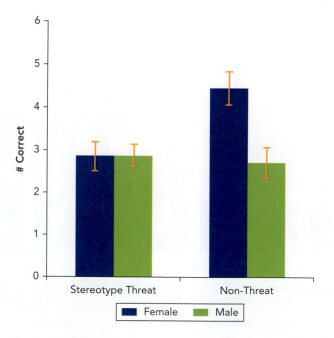

SOURCE: Good, Aronson, & Harder (2008).

especially in science and math classes. For example, when girls achieve at the same level as boys in math, teachers tend to attribute girls' success to hard work while they attribute boys' success to ability (Espinoza, da Luz Fontes, & Arms-Chavez, 2014). Many of today's female elementary school teachers grew up with stereotypical ideas about gender and math that resulted in high levels of math anxiety and they can unwittingly transmit these negative attitudes to their students. Girls, but not boys, who studied for 1 year in a classroom with one of these math-anxious teachers ended the year with more stereotyped ideas about math abilities and poorer math performance (Beilock, Gunderson, Ramirez, & Levine, 2010).

Girls and science. Young girls are as interested in science as boys. To sustain this interest, many programs have been developed to encourage girls to enter the fields of math and science.

How parents view their children's ability also is an important influence on how their children see their own abilities (Tiedemann, 2000). Like teachers, parents make different attributions for their sons' success in math compared to their attributions for their daughters' success. Similar to teachers, parents tend to attribute their daughters' success to the girls' hard work, but when boys are doing well, they attribute their sons' success to talent and effort (Jacobs, Davis-Kean, Bleeker, Eccles, & Malanchuk, 2005). This means that boys and girls get different messages about *why* they are successful. Which type of career would you want to pursue? One that you had to work hard at or one that you were good at?

The media also enforces ideas about gender differences and math. In one study, college women were shown either neutral commercials or commercials that promoted the stereotype that women are worse at math and science than men. When they were then asked to choose a career area, women who saw the stereotyped commercials were more likely to choose careers that did *not* involve math and science than those who saw the neutral commercial (Davies, Spencer, Quinn, & Gerhardstein, 2002).

The math anxiety that many girls experience, especially in testing situations, is linked to the idea of **stereotype threat**. The term was first used by Steele and Aronson (1995) to describe a situation in which individuals become anxious when they fear that they are going to confirm a negative stereotype about a group with which they identify. This notion suggests that when girls take a difficult math test, like the SAT, ACT, or advanced placement tests, they become anxious because they think they may prove the stereotype that girls are not good at math to be correct. Because anxiety decreases the working memory needed to carry out difficult math problems, girls' performance on the test goes down (Schmader, 2010). However, if the threat can be reduced, performance is restored. When university women were specifically told that a calculus test they were about to take had not shown gender differences in the past, their performance was even better than that of men in their class, as shown in Figure 8.8 (Good, Aronson, & Harder, 2008).

Girls are often unaware of the stereotypes they hold. Unconscious stereotypes have been assessed by **implicit association tests** (Greenwald, Poehlman, Uhlmann, & Banaji, 2009). You can try a brief version of this test provided in **Active Learning: Implicit Associations Test**. In a study conducted in 34 countries, implicit associations between science and gender predicted sex differences in science and math achievement in eighth grade students (Nosek et al., 2009), and girls as young as 9 already showed implicit gender-based stereotypes about math ability. Middle school girls showed stronger implicit association between gender and math ability than boys did and the strength of this association was related to intentions or preference to take math classes in the future and to achievement in math (Steffens, Jelenec, & Noack, 2010).

Stereotype threat The anxiety that results when individuals feel they are behaving in ways that confirm negative stereotyped expectations of a group with which they identify.

Implicit associations test A measure of a person's automatic, unconscious associations between different concepts.

Active LEARNING

Implicit Associations Test

Make cards with the following category words on them: *math, arts, female, male*. Next make cards with the following words: *math, poetry, algebra, art, geometry, dance, calculus, literature, equations, novel, female, woman, girl, she, lady, male, man, boy, he, sir.*

1. Put the category cards with the words *math* and *male* together on your left and the cards with *arts* and *female* together on your right. Put the rest of the cards in a pile in front of you.

2. As you pick up each card in the pile, decide whether to put it with the category cards on your left (math and male) or with the category cards on your right (arts and female). Time yourself as you sort all of the cards to the left or the right as you think they belong.

3. Now take back all the cards into a pile. Put the category cards with the words *math* and *female* on your left and the cards with *arts* and *male* on your right.

4. Again, time yourself as you sort the rest of the cards either left or right as you think they belong.

Did it take longer to do one of these sorts than the other? If you implicitly associate female with arts and male with math, it is easier and therefore quicker to sort each card in your pile into these combined categories than into the pairs associating the categories of math with female and arts with male. (Adapted from Greenwald & Nosek, 2001).

You can find an online version of this test at https://implicit.harvard.edu/implicit/

The one area of ability relevant to the STEM disciplines in which there are small but significant differences that favor boys is spatial relationships (see Figure 8.9), and it has been argued that this difference is wired into the brains of boys and girls before birth. However, we know from Chapter 6 that our brains continue to develop throughout childhood in response to our experiences. Training girls on spatial skills using computer games such as Tetris that are based on manipulation of shapes can produce large improvements in their abilities in this area (Terlecki, Newcombe, & Little, 2008) and specific training on spatial skills can erase gender differences in mental rotation in first graders (Tzuriel & Egozi, 2010). Although boys may have some initial genetic advantage in this area, training with girls can improve their performance significantly.

A good deal of effort has been put into breaking down stereotypes and encouraging girls to enter careers in the STEM fields. More than 400 intervention projects have been sponsored by the National Science Foundation and the American Association of University Women (AAUW) Educational Foundation (Darke, Clewell, & Sevo, 2002). One successful strategy is based on changing a student's **academic mindsets**, those deeply held beliefs that influence our behaviors in academic settings (Rattan, Savani, Chugh, & Dweck, 2015). Two crucial aspects of those mindsets are beliefs about whether intelligence is fixed or can be developed and whether the individual belongs in a particular setting (for instance, an advanced math class or a career as an engineer).

One successful intervention taught girls that the brain is like a muscle that strengthens when it is exercised, rather than something that is fixed and unchangeable. When girls received information that intelligence could be expanded and that the brain develops through our lifetime, the gender gap in performance on a standardized test in math disappeared (Good, Aronson, & Inzlicht, 2003). The dilemma when the second aspect of a

Academic mindsets
Deeply held beliefs that influence our behaviors in academic settings.

FIGURE 8.9

Mental rotation tasks. Items such as the one below are one of the few types of tests that consistently show higher performance for boys than girls.

Look at this object: Two of these four drawings show the same object. Can you find the two? Put a big X across them.

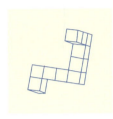 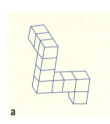  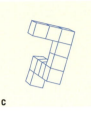 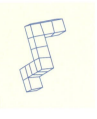

a   b   c   d

SOURCE: © American Psychological Association (1988).

Answer: a and c

mindset—the need to feel a sense of belonging in a situation—falls short is illustrated by one young woman who was interested in engineering as a career but stated, "It's intimidating being a girl who wants to go into the engineering field when it is definitely a male-dominated career" (Britsch, Callahan, & Peterson, 2010, p. 13). With few women professionals in these fields, girls lack models and mentors who can encourage them to pursue careers in the sciences (Blackwell, 2010; Else-Quest et al., 2010). If more women enter these professions, it will help to create the necessary sense that women belong in them, but we still have a long way to go to make this happen.

Single-Gender Classrooms

Many schools are trying to develop educational alternatives that will equally meet the needs of both boys and girls. One of those alternatives is single-gender classrooms. In 2006, the U. S. Department of Education allowed the development of single-gender classrooms or schools within the public school system (U.S. Department of Education, 2006). The hope is that single-gender classrooms can be structured to better fit the different educational needs of boys and girls. However, critics of this change say that there are many more similarities between the genders than there are differences between them (Paulson & Teicher, 2006). Another concern has been that single-gender classrooms do not give students the chance to learn to work and play with students of the other gender and in the long run this may harm their socioemotional development (Pahlke & Hyde, 2016). To date, most studies that

Klaus Vedfelt/Taxi/Getty Images

Single-gender classrooms. If girls and boys have different learning styles, they may do better in single-gender classrooms that are tailored to their needs. What do you think children gain—and lose—by being in a single-gender classroom?

have compared single-gender and mixed-gender educational settings have not shown benefits resulting from separating girls and boys (Brown & Ronau, 2012; Nisbett et al., 2012; Pahlke & Hyde, 2016).

ETHNIC, RACIAL, AND CULTURAL INFLUENCES ON SCHOOL ACHIEVEMENT

American schools have become increasingly diverse in recent years. For instance, in fall 2014 Latino, African American, and Asian students were more than half of the public school K-12 population (Maxwell, 2014). An achievement gap, sometimes substantial, exists between students from different ethnic, racial, and socioeconomic backgrounds, with White students on average outperforming minority students and children from families with higher socioeconomic status outperforming children from poorer families. While the achievement gap in both reading and mathematics between White and African American students and between White and Hispanic students has decreased in recent years, a gap still exists (Loeb, 2007).

Closing this gap has received a tremendous amount of attention from researchers, educators, and policymakers as we strive to ensure that all children receive the best educational opportunity they can. We'll look briefly at some of the explanations that have been offered for why there is an achievement gap and then at some of attempts to reduce it.

The first explanation is based on our expectations for different children. We all can find ourselves living up—or down—to the expectations that other people have for us. The same is true for children in the classroom, but when these **expectancy effects** influence the amount of effort that children expend on their schoolwork and that lack of effort lowers a child's academic achievement, there is good reason for concern.

In 1968, Robert Rosenthal and Lenore Jacobson conducted an experiment in which they intentionally manipulated teachers' expectations for the academic performance of some of their students. The researchers told the teachers that they were able to identify students who would be intellectual "bloomers" over the coming academic year and that teachers should expect to see significant intellectual growth in these children. The "bloomers" were, in fact, selected randomly from class lists, but by the end of the school year, total IQ scores of the "bloomers" were significantly higher than those of the other students who acted as controls for this experiment. Rosenthal and Jacobson (1968) claimed that changing the expectations that the teachers held for these students changed the teachers' behavior in a way that facilitated the intellectual growth in the children. Perhaps the teachers spent more time with these children, were more supportive and encouraging toward children who were about to "bloom," or gave them different learning opportunities than they gave the other children.

This research received a lot of attention within the fields of education and psychology and by the general public, but also generated a lot of debate. It offered a very optimistic message by suggesting an apparently simple way to improve academic performance—believe in the child and communicate that belief to him or her. Although some attempts to replicate the original findings have been successful, others have not (Spitz, 1999). While believing in a child's ability to succeed is important, those beliefs are only likely to be successful if faith in the child's ability is accompanied by a strong effort to help the child master the material he or she needs to learn.

The mechanism that underlies teacher expectancy effects is called a **self-fulfilling prophecy.** Your expectations cause you to predict (that is, to make a prophecy about) what will happen in the future. Those same expectations or beliefs may lead you to behave in ways that, in turn, help ensure that you find exactly what you had expected to find (Madon, Guyll, Willard, & Scherr, 2011). For instance, if you have low expectations for a child's performance, you may spend little time working with the child or encouraging the child, or you might be overly critical of what the child does. These behaviors deny the child an opportunity to learn and may even make the child dislike school and withdraw from classroom

Expectancy effects The effect that the expectations of others can have on one's self-perception and behavior.

TRUE/FALSE VIDEO ▲

T ☐ F ☐ The best way to improve a child's academic performance is to believe in the child and let him know that you have faith in his ability to succeed. **False**

Self-fulfilling prophecy The process by which expectations or beliefs lead to behaviors that help ensure that you fulfill the initial prophecy or expectation.

activities. The child also may incorporate how you see him into his own self-concept. He comes to see himself as a failure and gives up trying, so consequently he does poorly—just as you had expected—and your initial prophecy is fulfilled.

While teachers with egalitarian values may not be aware of unconscious assumptions they make, even they can have different expectations for their students based on the student's ethnicity (van den Bergh, Denessen, Hormstra, Voeten, & Holland, 2010). A number of studies have found the highest expectations for Asian American students, and more positive expectations for European American students than for either Latino or African American students (McKown & Weinstein, 2008; Tenenbaum & Ruck, 2007). Some children are more vulnerable than others to the negative impact of early teacher expectations. Children whose first-grade teachers underestimated their abilities did more poorly later in their schooling than their early test scores would have predicted and the effect was stronger for the children from low-income families (Sorhagen, 2013).

Despite our best efforts, differential expectations may exist, but we can put them into perspective. First, while the effect of self-fulfilling prophecies is statistically significant, the effect is relatively small. In a review of research carried out over the last 35 years, Jussim and Harber (2005) concluded that the effects of self-fulfilling prophecies account for only 5% to 10% of the variance observed in students' grades (see also Tenenbaum & Ruck, 2007), although the effect may be stronger for students from stigmatized social groups. Second, teachers are not the only source of influence on student achievement. Parents also play a significant role, especially for Latino students because family is so central to Latino values. Alfaro, Umaña-Taylor, and Bámaca (2006) found that academic support from teachers was important to both Latino boys and girls, but support from fathers was particularly important for boys and support from mothers was particularly important for girls. Although Latino parents hold educational aspirations for their children and adolescents that are similar to those of Anglo parents, unfortunately they sometimes feel that their involvement in their children's education is not welcomed by the school (Quiocho & Daoud, 2006). This is a perception that schools can work to change by being welcoming to all parents. There is good reason to make both teachers and parents aware of the potential effect their expectations have on their students' performance and to encourage them to use positive expectations to boost positive performance rather than negative expectations that could be harmful.

THE IMPACT OF POVERTY ON ACADEMIC ACHIEVEMENT

Poverty is a threat to the healthy growth and development of all children who grow up without adequate resources. According to recent statistics, 22% of American children— almost one in four—are growing up in poverty and live below the federal poverty threshold (Jiang, Ekono, & Skinner, 2015). In 2013, 32% of children in poor families were White, 24% were Black, and 35% were Hispanic (Jiang et al., 2015). Although many children who grow up in poverty go on to become adults who contribute positively to society, we know that the percentage is less than children growing up in more affluent circumstances (Shonkoff & Phillips, 2000). Childhood poverty is associated with difficulties for children in all areas of development, but the negative impact on cognitive functioning and academic achievement has been most clearly documented (McLoyd, 2000; Nikulina, Widom, & Czaja, 2010).

The list of problems associated with poverty that affect academic achievement is very long. It includes the following:

- Poor health due to the unavailability of health care, unsafe living conditions, and poor diet
- Lack of resources in the neighborhood, including structured after-school activities
- High rates of depression and posttraumatic stress disorder in both parents and children

Affluence and poverty. Compare these two scenes and think about what each setting provides for the children in it and what the consequences might be for the children's academic achievement.

- Anxiety linked to caring for a family in a dangerous neighborhood where loved ones may be lost to violence or children may witness frightening events

- High levels of stress that contribute to marital discord and instability

- Safety concerns that limit children's ability to explore their environment

- Poor schools with inadequate facilities

- Racism or other discrimination

- Segregation leading to a lack of opportunities and social exclusion (McLoyd, 2000; Ryan, Fauth, & Brooks-Gunn, 2006)

These factors interact with each other in complex ways. For instance, parents who are struggling with the stresses of poverty are less likely to provide educational stimulation and guidance in the home. They also have lower expectations for their children's achievement and, as we have already noted, teachers also are more likely to have low expectations for the achievement of students from impoverished families (Benner & Mistry, 2007; Sorhagen, 2013).

Children whose families have few economic resources show lower levels of cognitive development as early as 18 to 24 months of age (Ryan et al., 2006). By the time they enter kindergarten they are already significantly behind their middle-class peers in basic pre-academic skills in reading and arithmetic as shown in Figure 8.10 (Isaacs, 2012). When children begin school with skills at a low level, it becomes increasingly difficult to catch up, and school can become a source of frustration.

The Head Start program was developed in the 1960s to narrow the gap between children from different socioeconomic backgrounds so that economically disadvantaged children could enter school on par with their more advantaged peers. Most people think of Head Start as solely a preschool program, but it is much more than that. Poverty affects families, not just children, so Head Start was designed to help the whole family and the whole child. A caseworker helps each family find resources for the family's most pressing needs, children are given two nutritious meals each school day, and dental care and vision screening are provided. Parental involvement also is an essential part of the program. In Head Start, parents learn skills and attitudes that promote their active involvement in their children's educational experiences both at home and at school. When parents were actively involved with Head Start, their children's pre-academic skills were more likely to improve (Head Start, n.d.; Hindman & Morrison, 2011).

In 1994, Head Start was expanded to create the Early Head Start (EHS) program to serve pregnant women and children under 3. The services it offers vary according to the

FIGURE 8.10

Starting school at a disadvantage. This figure shows the likelihood of scoring Very Low (failing to be school ready) on several measures of school readiness by poverty status. Poor children not only start school at a disadvantage, but that disadvantage increases over time.

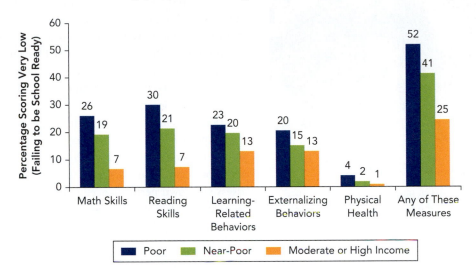

SOURCE: Isaacs (2012).

needs of the community, but it can include child care provided at a center or in a home, and weekly home visits to promote the parents' ability to support their children's development (U.S. Department of Health and Human Services, 2015a).

Research has been conducted on the effectiveness of Head Start and Early Head Start from the very beginning of the programs. It has found that children show some significant cognitive gains by the end of the program that prepare them for the transition into kindergarten, but these gains are typically modest and disappear at some point before the end of third grade (Love et al., 2005; Puma et al., 2012; U.S. Department of Health and Human Services, 2010). Needless to say, these findings are disappointing for a program with such ambitious goals, but we need to remember that Head Start is designed as an intervention for disadvantaged children who often are growing up in very difficult circumstances. In a continuing effort to improve the effectiveness of the programs, a recent federal mandate has increased the qualifications for teaching staff in Head Start and Early Head Start programs. As of September 30, 2013, at least half of Head Start teachers nationwide had to have a bachelor's degree or advanced degree in early childhood education or a closely related field. By 2014, Head Start had passed that goal, with 70.8% of its teachers meeting this qualification (National Head Start Association, 2014). We have already discussed the importance of teacher qualifications for the academic success of older children. The same is true for educators who work with the youngest students.

Research that has looked beyond the early elementary grades has looked at a wider range of outcomes than standardized test scores. When longitudinal research compared the school performance of children who had been in Head Start to that of children from a similar background who had not been in the program, the former Head Start children had fewer suspensions, expulsions, grade retentions, and special education placements. They were more likely to graduate from high school and attend college, and had higher incomes. They also were less likely as young adults to be dependent on welfare and less likely to have engaged in criminal behavior (Garces, Thomas, & Currie, 2002; Joo, 2010; Shonkoff & Phillips, 2000). In some cases, the effects were found for girls but not boys, or for White

Off to a good start. Head Start children, such as this boy, who come from low-income families receive a good beginning to their education through the help of teachers in the federal Head Start program.

children but not minority children, but the positive long-term effects were strongest for those children who came from the most disadvantaged backgrounds (Garces et al., 2002).

What might account for these long-term outcomes? One possible answer comes from a study of 132 Head Start children (the majority of whom were African American or Hispanic) that found significant improvement in executive function over the preschool year (Fuhs & Day, 2011). As you learned in Chapter 7, executive function includes the ability to inhibit behavior when you need to, to think flexibly and shift your attention from one task to another, to regulate your emotional responses, to monitor and assess your own performance, and to plan and organize the tasks you must accomplish. Do you see how developing this set of skills as a young student would help you succeed in school and avoid some problem behaviors? On average, Head Start children also show increases in cooperative behavior in the classroom (Head Start, 2007).

Head Start is intended to be an investment that helps children throughout their lives, and long-term research has found some ways that it has done that. The argument has been made that the money spent on Head Start (approximately $7,600 per child in 2010) reaps financial benefits that clearly outweigh the initial expense (Head Start, 2010). When you consider the cost involved when children require special education services, do not complete high school, or are involved in the criminal justice system, you can begin to see how an initial expenditure that helps prevent these outcomes is justified. The benefits from reducing special education placements and grade retention alone offsets between 40% and 60% of original program costs. James Heckman (2011), Nobel prize–winning economist, summarized his research on the effects of early intervention as follows:

> The logic is quite clear from an economic standpoint. We can invest early to close disparities and prevent achievement gaps, or we can pay to remediate disparities when they are harder and more expensive to close. Either way we are going to pay. And, we'll have to do both for a while. But, there is an important difference between the two approaches. Investing early allows us to shape the future; investing later chains us to fixing the missed opportunities of the past. (p. 47)

Motivated by arguments such as these, an extra $2.1 billion was added in 2009 to Head Start and Early Head Start funding through the American Recovery and Reinvestment Act.

CHECK YOUR UNDERSTANDING

1. In what ways may the school curriculum affect boys' achievement?

2. What is stereotype threat and how does it harm girls' performance on standardized tests?

3. What are the arguments for and against single-gender classrooms?

4. How do expectancy effects become self-fulfilling prophecies?

5. What short-term and long-term effects have been found for children who attend Head Start?

CONCLUSION

In Chapter 7, we looked at cognitive processes that determine how people think. In this chapter, we have looked at individual differences in how well people are able to use these skills, in other words, intelligence. Reaching consensus on how to define intelligence is difficult and the debate continues as to whether intelligence is one general factor, *g*, or many different abilities. Intelligence plays an important role in how children achieve in school, but other factors such as self-control and motivation are also central to academic achievement. The school environment, especially the teachers, affects how well children learn, but different groups of children have specific challenges. Whether a child has an intellectual disability, a specific learning disorders or is gifted, schools must provide support so that each child can achieve at the highest level possible. Low income and minority boys are more likely to struggle with school achievement, while girls are still avoiding careers in the STEM fields of science, technology, engineering, and math. Finally, the Head Start program that helps families in poverty before children enter school has made some strides in helping these children succeed in school and live better lives after they finish school.

CHAPTER SUMMARY

Test your understanding of the content.
Take the practice quiz at **edge.sagepub.com/levine3e**

8.1 How do we define and measure intelligence?

It has been difficult to agree on one definition of intelligence. One debate concerns whether there is one general underlying factor *g* (which can be divided into **fluid intelligence** and **crystallized intelligence**) or a set of relatively independent abilities or skills. Intelligence can be assessed using standardized testing or by alternative forms of testing such as dynamic assessment or **authentic assessment** and newer tests based on neurological functioning. Infant testing relies on measures related to information processing capabilities. There is also a debate over the relative contribution of genes (which set the **range of reaction**) and the environment (which affects where an individual falls in that range) to intelligence. Neuroscience is helping us understand the relationship of brain structure and function to intelligence. Although IQ tests predict a child's potential academic achievement, motivation and self-control may predict achievement equally well or better. Both **intrinsic motivation** and **extrinsic motivation** affect children's performance. Alternative theories of intelligence are Gardner's **theory of multiple intelligences** and Sternberg's **triarchic theory.**

8.2 What are examples of some cognitive deficits and intellectual gifts?

Children at the low end of the continuum of cognitive ability have an **intellectual disability.** Children with a **specific learning disorder** have average or above average intelligence, but difficulty in one of the academic domains. They may need help in finding positive ways to cope but many have good adult outcomes. **Giftedness** includes a range of abilities and talents that are encompassed by the **three-ring model of giftedness. Enrichment programs** and **accelerated programs** are designed for gifted children. **Creative intelligence** is not highly correlated with IQ, but brings together **divergent thinking** and **convergent thinking** to find unique solutions. We also can distinguish between **small-c creativity** and **big-C creativity.**

8.3 What are some issues that affect learning within the school environment?

Reducing class size is more beneficial for low-performing students than high-performing students, but all students benefit from having a well-qualified teacher who devotes time and attention to individual students. **Ability grouping** may be harmful to low-performing students, while **collaborative learning** is more beneficial for low-performing students than high-performing students. **Social promotion** moves children along even when they haven't mastered the material but grade retention does not clearly benefit students who are retained unless they receive additional help. The high school dropout rate in the United States has declined in recent years, yet racial and ethnic disparities continue to exist. Many dropouts do eventually earn a GED. Students who drop out usually have a long history of school-related problems. Students who graduate from high school but do not go on to college may not be well prepared for entrance into the workforce. Unlike the United States, European high schools offer apprenticeships that provide an alternative pathway to success for non-college-bound students. Two-thirds of U.S. high school graduates go on to higher education, but need to be prepared for the rigors of college to be successful.

8.4 How do gender, ethnicity/race, and socioeconomic status affect academic achievement?

Some attribute the possible "boy problem" with academic achievement to a classroom curriculum which is a better fit with the skills and interests of girls than boys, but others attribute it to maturational differences. This problem may be specific to minority and disadvantaged boys. Girls continue to be less likely than boys to take advanced math classes or prepare for careers in science, technology, engineering, or mathematics despite similar grades in math and sciences. **Stereotype threat** tied to math anxiety may contribute to girls' decisions. Teachers may also treat girls differently and teachers and parents may have lower expectations for girls. American schools have become increasingly diverse and an achievement gap exists between students from different ethnic, racial, and socioeconomic backgrounds. Teachers' **expectancy effects** may influence how they treat students for whom they have low expectations and can become a **self-fulfilling prophecy.** Fortunately, these beliefs have a relatively small effect on student grades. Children growing up in poverty generally have lower academic achievement than their more advantaged peers from very young ages. The Head Start program was designed to help disadvantaged young children get off to a good start in school by working with the family and the whole child. Initial research found that improvement in IQ scores for Head Start participants dissipated over a few years, but longitudinal research has found long-term benefits regarding academic achievement, fewer school and behavioral problems, and better adult outcomes.

KEY TERMS

Strengthen your understanding of these key terms with mobile-friendly eFlashcards at **edge.sagepub.com/levine3e**

Give your students the SAGE edge!

SAGE edge offers a robust online environment featuring an impressive array of free tools and resources for review, study, and further exploration, keeping both instructors and students on the cutting edge of teaching and learning. Learn more at **edge.sagepub.com/levine3e**

practice AND apply
WHAT YOU'VE LEARNED

edge.sagepub.com/levine3e

chapter 9 | LANGUAGE DEVELOPMENT

JGI/Jamie Grill/Blend Images/Getty Images

LEARNING QUESTIONS

9.1 What are five basic aspects of language?

9.2 What parts of the brain are specialized for language?

9.3 What are the basic theories about how children develop language?

9.4 How does language develop from before birth through adolescence?

9.5 How do children learn to read and write?

9.6 What are some consequences of being bilingual as a child? What types of education programs are used for children who do not speak English?

9.7 What types of language disorders can children have?

Master these objectives using an online action plan at **edge.sagepub.com/levine3e**

TEST YOUR KNOWLEDGE

Test your knowledge of child development by deciding whether each of the following statements is *true* or *false,* and then check your answers as you read the chapter.

1. **T ☐ F ☐:** Infants are born with a preference for listening to their native language.

2. **T ☐ F ☐:** A sensitive parent should be able to tell the difference between a baby who is crying because he is hungry and one who is crying because he is uncomfortable or lonely.

3. **T ☐ F ☐:** Teaching babies to use sign language will delay development of their spoken language.

4. **T ☐ F ☐:** It is perfectly fine to use baby talk with infants.

5. **T ☐ F ☐:** If a young child says "I goed outside," a parent should correct him by saying "No, you meant to say, 'I *went* outside.'"

6. **T ☐ F ☐:** Using flash cards and workbooks is the best way to ensure that a child develops early literacy skills.

7. **T ☐ F ☐:** About one in four eighth graders is reading below the basic level for their grade.

8. **T ☐ F ☐:** When young children use spelling that they have "invented" (rather than conventional spelling), it slows down their ability to learn how to spell correctly.

9. **T ☐ F ☐:** Students who do a lot of texting and those who do not text a lot do not differ from each other on their ability to spell or use Standard English.

10. **T ☐ F ☐:** When a young child learns two languages at the same time, the extra effort it takes to learn the second language slows down the child's general cognitive development.

Correct answers: (1) T, (2) F, (3) F, (4) T, (5) F, (6) F, (7) T, (8) F, (9) T, (10) F

▲ **VIDEO: Watch as students answer some of these questions and the authors respond**

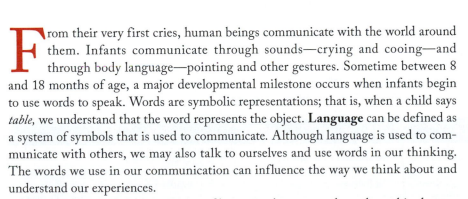

From their very first cries, human beings communicate with the world around them. Infants communicate through sounds—crying and cooing—and through body language—pointing and other gestures. Sometime between 8 and 18 months of age, a major developmental milestone occurs when infants begin to use words to speak. Words are symbolic representations; that is, when a child says *table,* we understand that the word represents the object. **Language** can be defined as a system of symbols that is used to communicate. Although language is used to communicate with others, we may also talk to ourselves and use words in our thinking. The words we use in our communication can influence the way we think about and understand our experiences.

Language A system of symbols used to communicate with others or in our thinking.

After defining some basic aspects of language that we use throughout this chapter, we look at the brain's role in processing and producing language. We then describe some of the theories that are used to explain the amazing process by which we develop the ability to understand and use language. After a description of the stages of language development—from a baby's first cries through the slang used by teenagers—we look at the topic of bilingualism. We examine how learning to speak more than one language affects a child's language development, how our educational system is trying to accommodate the increasing number of bilingual children in the classroom, and how bilingualism relates to cultural identity. Finally, we end the chapter with information about disorders that affect children's language development.

ASPECTS OF LANGUAGE

9.1   What are five basic aspects of language?

Phonology The study of the sounds of a language.

Phoneme The smallest distinct sound in a particular language.

Morphology The way words are formed from the sounds of a language and how these words are related to other words.

Morpheme The smallest unit in a language that has meaning.

Syntax The grammar of a language.

Semantics The study of the meanings of words.

Pragmatics The rules that guide how we use language in social situations.

There are five basic aspects of language that have been studied: phonology, morphology, syntax, semantics, and pragmatics (see Table 9.1). **Phonology** is the study of the sounds of a language. (To remember this term, think of the sounds that come from your *phone*, or the word cac*ophony*, meaning a lot of loud, annoying sounds.) A **phoneme** is the smallest distinct sound in a particular language. For example, *go* has two phonemes: *g* and *o*, and *check* has three phonemes: *ch*, *e*, and *ck* (National Reading Panel, 2000). Different languages have types of phonemes that are distinct. For instance, in Japanese, the length of a vowel can indicate a different word. The word *toko* means "bed," while *toko* with a long final *o* means "travel" (Sato, Sogabe, & Mazuka, 2010). In English, no matter how long we draw out the *a* in *cat*, it still means "cat." **Morphology** is the way words are formed from these sounds and how these words are related to other words. A **morpheme** is the smallest unit that has meaning in a language. For example, the word *cats* has two morphemes: *cat* and *s*. *Cat* refers to the animal, and *s* means more than one. **Syntax** is the grammar of a language—that is, how we put words in order and how we change words (for example, by changing *play* to *played* when we talk about the past) so they make sense to our listeners. **Semantics** is the meanings of words and sentences. **Pragmatics** is how we use language in social situations. We use language for different purposes, such as greetings, information, demands, and requests, and we also speak differently in different situations or with different people (American Speech-Language-Hearing Association, n.d.). You probably speak in different ways to your professor, to your friends, and certainly to a 2-year-old. In each case, you are using language in a different way. We also follow rules for conversations and telling stories. For example, we take turns in a conversation, waiting to hear what the other person says before speaking. When children develop the ability to communicate with language, they are developing all five of these areas. They must understand and form the sounds of the language they are learning. They must learn what words mean and how to put them together so they make sense, and they must learn when and how to use language to accommodate their listeners and to accomplish their goals. We consider all of these aspects as we describe language development.

TABLE 9.1

Five aspects of language. When children develop language, they are developing new abilities in each of these five aspects of language.

Aspects	Subject of study	Example
Phonology	The sounds of a language	Chat = *ch-a-t*
Morphology	The formation of words	Walked = *walk-ed*
Syntax	Grammar—how words are put together to make sense	She chatted while she walked.
Semantics	The meanings of words and sentences	Chat = talk in a friendly and informal way
Pragmatics	Use of language in different social situations	To a child: See the choo-choo! To an adult: The train is coming.

CHECK YOUR UNDERSTANDING

1. What are five aspects of language that researchers have examined?
2. What is the difference between a morpheme and a phoneme?

LANGUAGE AND THE BRAIN

9.2 **What parts of the brain are specialized for language?**

Of course, language originates in the brain and there are specific parts of the brain dedicated to language function. The brain's left hemisphere contains two areas that are central to language: Broca's area and Wernicke's area. As shown in Figure 9.1, **Broca's area**, which is active in the production of speech, is located near the motor center of the brain that produces movement of the tongue and lips (Gleason, 2005). A person with damage to this area will have difficulty speaking and as a consequence will use the fewest words needed to get his message across. For example, when a man with damage in Broca's area was asked about his upcoming weekend plans, he answered, "Boston. College. Football. Saturday" (Gleason, 2005, p. 17).

You can also see in Figure 9.1 that **Wernicke's area**, which helps us understand and create the meaning in speech, is located near the auditory center of the brain. Someone with

Broca's area The part of the brain that is involved in the physical production of speech.

Wernicke's area The part of the brain that has to do with understanding the meaning in speech.

FIGURE 9.1

Language centers of the brain. Broca's area (shown here in green), which controls speech production, is next to the motor cortex that controls movement. Wernicke's area (shown in light green), which controls language comprehension, is next to the auditory area that controls hearing.

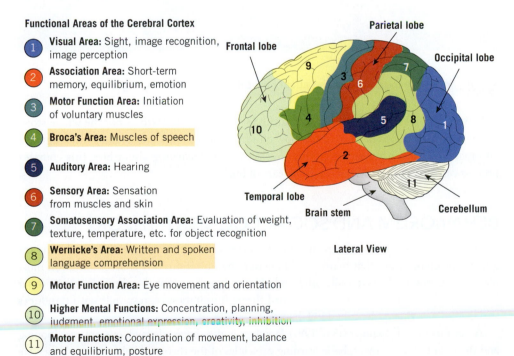

Functional Areas of the Cerebral Cortex

1. **Visual Area:** Sight, image recognition, image perception
2. **Association Area:** Short-term memory, equilibrium, emotion
3. **Motor Function Area:** Initiation of voluntary muscles
4. **Broca's Area:** Muscles of speech
5. **Auditory Area:** Hearing
6. **Sensory Area:** Sensation from muscles and skin
7. **Somatosensory Association Area:** Evaluation of weight, texture, temperature, etc. for object recognition
8. **Wernicke's Area:** Written and spoken language comprehension
9. **Motor Function Area:** Eye movement and orientation
10. **Higher Mental Functions:** Concentration, planning, judgment, emotional expression, creativity, inhibition
11. **Motor Functions:** Coordination of movement, balance and equilibrium, posture

damage to this area of the brain has no trouble producing words, but has difficulty making sense. For example, one patient with damage to Wernicke's area responded as follows to the question "What brings you to the hospital?"

> Boy I'm sweating, I'm awful nervous, you know, once in a while I get caught up, I can't mention the tarripoi, a month ago, quite a little, I've done a lot well, I impose a lot, while, on the other hand, you know what I mean, I have to run around, look it over, trebbin and all that sort of stuff. (Gardner, 1976, p. 68)

The capabilities of these two regions do not develop at the same time. Infants *understand* words before they can *say* them. Another way we describe this is to say comprehension of language precedes production of language. When you tell a 1-year-old to put a toy in a box, she will most likely *understand* you and might follow your directions, yet she is not likely to be able to *say* anything close to "put the toy in the box." This difference between **receptive language** and **expressive language** continues throughout life (Celce-Murcia & Olshtain, 2001). Even college students can understand a sophisticated or technical lecture in class, while their own speech and writing are likely to be less complex.

The brain is not a simple organ, and we continue to learn about its complexity. For instance, although language is primarily handled by the left hemisphere of the brain where Broca's and Wernicke's areas are, some aspects of language, such as recognition of the emotion in someone's words, are controlled by the right hemisphere (Gleason, 2005).

Receptive language The ability to understand words or sentences.

Expressive language The written or spoken language that we use to convey our thoughts, emotions, or needs.

CHECK YOUR UNDERSTANDING

1. What are the functions of Broca's area and Wernicke's area of the brain?

2. What is the difference between receptive and expressive language?

THEORIES OF LANGUAGE DEVELOPMENT

9.3 What are the basic theories about how children develop language?

Although brain development is a prerequisite for language, it clearly is not the whole story. There are many different ideas about how children learn to talk and understand language, and many controversies persist to this day. We are still learning about how this complex process can occur so quickly in the first years of life.

BEHAVIORISM AND SOCIAL COGNITIVE THEORY

If you were to take a survey of people on the street and ask them how children learn language, the chances are that many would answer "by imitation." Of course, imitation must play an important role. After all, children learn the language that they hear, not some other language. The idea that language is learned through imitation corresponds with Bandura's social cognitive theory described in Chapter 2.

According to B. F. Skinner (1957/1991), language is also shaped through operant conditioning and the use of reinforcement, basic learning principles of the theory of behaviorism. When we respond to a baby's babbling with a smile or some vocalization of our own, babies babble even more.

If we respond when a child says "cookie" with the desired cookie, it becomes more likely that she will use that word again the next time she wants a cookie. If we remember that reinforcement is anything that makes a behavior continue, then it is clear that we reinforce the development of a child's language in many ways. Consistent with these ideas, research has shown that the more mothers respond to their babies' vocalizations, the sooner their babies develop language (Tamis-LeMonda, Bornstein, & Baumwell, 2001).

In a direct test of the relative influence on language development of reinforcement (the mechanism described by behaviorist principles) and imitation (the mechanism described by social cognitive theory), children were shown a picture and heard an adult describe it by saying, "The elephant is pulled by the mouse." When the children were asked to talk about the picture, they were given a reward if they said, "The mouse pulls the elephant" (Østvik, Eikeseth, & Klintwall, 2012), yet they were still more likely to imitate what an adult said, even if they were explicitly rewarded for saying something different.

A mother-infant "conversation." Social cognitive theory emphasizes the importance of social interaction for language learning. As this mother talks to her infant, she models using language to communicate, and the infant wants to imitate his mother to continue the fun.

NATIVISM

In contrast to the ideas proposed by operant conditioning and social cognitive theory, both of which focus on interactions in the environment, Noam Chomsky (1968) developed a theory proposing that the human brain is innately wired to learn language, a theory known as **nativism**. He believes that children could not learn something as complex as human language as quickly as they do unless there is already a grammatical structure for language hardwired in their brains before they ever hear human language. He calls this **universal grammar**.

According to this theory, hearing spoken language triggers the activation of this structure which does more than just promote imitation. It allows a child to extract the principles and rules for the language from what they hear. For instance, nativists such as Chomsky point to the evidence that children will say things they have never heard, such as "The cats eated the mouses" rather than "The cats ate the mice." We *hope* that children have never heard adults say something like "eated" or "mouses," and therefore they could not just be imitating language they have heard. However, you can easily see that, although the first sentence is grammatically incorrect, in some respects it *could be* correct. In English we do add -*ed* for the past tense and -*s* for plurals, but we have exceptions to those rules, called irregular verbs or nouns. When children make this type of grammatical error, they are showing that they have learned a pattern, but they are applying it to words that don't follow that pattern.

This process of acting as if irregular words follow the regular rules is called **overregularization**. Children create these words from their own understanding of grammar. Chomsky believes that the basic principles of grammar are inborn and universal because they are hardwired in the brain. Clearly, we do not all speak the same language and the rules for grammar are not the same in all languages, so how can there be a universal grammar? Chomsky believes that the basic principles of language in the brain are similar to the basic principles that underlie the operation of the hard drive of your computer. Just as your computer's hard drive can run many different types of software, the language structures in your brain can process the specific characteristics of many different languages.

Nativism A theory of language development that hypothesizes that human brains are innately wired to learn language and that hearing spoken language triggers the activation of a universal grammar.

Universal grammar A hypothesized set of grammatical rules and constraints proposed by Chomsky that is thought to underlie all languages and that is hardwired in the human brain.

Overregularization A type of grammatical error in which children apply a language rule to words that don't follow that rule or pattern (for example, adding an *s* to make the plural of an irregular noun like *foot*).

INTERACTIONISM

Interactionism A theory of language development that proposes that the child's biological readiness to learn language interacts with the child's experiences with language in the environment to bring about the child's language development.

A third approach incorporates aspects of both behaviorism and nativism. According to **interactionism**, both children's biological readiness to learn language and their experiences with language in their environment come together to bring about language development. Just as we learned about how nature is expressed through nurture in Chapter 4, these theorists argue that both are equally necessary for the child to develop language and both must work together.

In addition, interactionism means that language is created socially, in the interaction between infant and adult. For example, adults naturally simplify their speech to young children not because they think "I need to teach this child how to speak" but because the child then understands and responds to what the adult is saying (Bohannon & Bonvillian, 2005). Research on mother–infant speech has found that mothers in a variety of cultures make many of the same modifications in their speech to infants, perhaps because these changes produce a good fit between the mother's speech and the infant's perceptual and cognitive capabilities (Gogate, Maganti, & Bahrick, 2015). To facilitate language development, adults will often repeat what children say but **recast** it into more advanced grammar. For example, a child might say, "More cookie," and the adult might respond, "Oh, do you want more cookies?" In the process, he is modeling a slightly higher level of language proficiency, which the child can then imitate. The child in this example might then say, "Want more cookies." Interactionism describes the development of a child's language as the result of the child's social engagement with others.

Recast Repeating what children say but in a more advanced grammar to facilitate language learning.

COGNITIVE PROCESSING THEORY: STATISTICAL LEARNING

Are social interaction and biological readiness enough to explain how children learn language? As our understanding of how the brain processes information has advanced, another view of language learning has emerged based on a process of "data crunching." It says that children take in and statistically process the language they hear (Hoff & Naigles, 2002). Proponents of this **cognitive processing theory** argue that infants are processing language even during the first year of life, before they can speak (Naigles et al., 2009). Therefore, their understanding of language is learned, not innate as Chomsky's theory asserts. Although the learning may be *motivated* by social interaction, cognitive processing theory asserts that the actual process of learning words and their meanings relies more on the computational ability of the human brain.

Cognitive processing theory The theory that learning language is a process of "data crunching," in which the actual process of learning words and their meanings relies on the computational ability of the human brain.

One basic question cognitive processing theory has addressed is how infants learn to differentiate words out of the stream of sounds they hear. Although we can see the spaces between words on a written page, these "spaces" are often not evident when we speak. For example, if you heard someone say, "Theelephantisdrinkingwater," how would you figure out that *elephant* is a separate word and *antis* is not? One answer is that infants' brains are constantly figuring out statistically how likely it is that certain sounds will follow each other. This likelihood is referred to as the **transitional probability** (Karuza et al., 2013). For example, when we hear *ele*, it is most often followed by *phant* or *vator*, so there is a high transitional probability between these syllables. However, the entire word *elephant* can be followed in a sentence by many different sounds, and any particular one has a low transitional probability. Researchers have used made-up words embedded in random syllables to see whether adults, children, and infants can differentiate the "words" from the rest of the utterance (Lew-Williams & Saffran, 2012). Take a look at the "sentence" below and see whether you can figure out what the "word" is:

Transitional probability The likelihood that one particular sound will follow another one to form a word.

Bupadapatubitutibubupadadutabapidabupada

Did you discover *bupada?* When people of all ages hear lengthy readings such as this, they are able to pick out the "words" even though they have no real meaning. When researchers applied this idea to the processing of discriminating words in a real but unfamiliar language (Italian), they found 8-month-olds were able to use conditional probabilities to differentiate between nonwords and words they had heard in a stream of conversation (Pelucchi, Hay, & Saffran, 2009). Infants were also likely to figure out the meaning of the words (Hay, Pelucchi, Estes, & Saffran, 2011; Lany & Saffran, 2010). Now, if you heard someone say *bupada* in addition to hearing the stream of sounds with *bupada* embedded within it, you would be much more likely to pick *bupada* out of the stream of sounds as a word, and researchers have found that infants too are helped to discriminate words when they hear them separately as well as in sentences (Lew-Williams, Pelucchi, & Saffran, 2011).

Table 9.2 provides a comparison of the basic processes of language development proposed by each of these four theories.

TABLE 9.2

A comparison of 4 theories of language development. Four theories of how children develop language provide four different mechanisms to explain the process.

Theory	How Language Is Acquired
Behaviorism/Social Cognitive Theory	Reinforcement/imitation
Nativism	Innate brain function
Interactionism	Biological readiness together with social stimuli
Cognitive Processing Theory	Statistical computation

CHECK YOUR UNDERSTANDING

1. How do behaviorism and social cognitive theory describe the way young children learn language?
2. How is nativism different from all the other theories of language development?
3. How do adults modify the way they speak to babies and what purpose does this serve?
4. How does cognitive processing theory explain how infants can pick individual words out of the stream of conversation?

STAGES OF LANGUAGE DEVELOPMENT

9.4   **How does language develop from before birth through adolescence?**

In this section, we describe the development of language. We purposely de-emphasize the ages at which these developments occur because children differ enormously in the rate at which they develop language. Table 9.3 gives an overview of some of the major developments from infancy through adolescence.

One major question about language development that remains controversial is whether there is a specific age beyond which children are not capable of developing language. To see how our thinking has changed on this issue, see **Journey of Research: Is There a Critical Period for Language Learning?**

TABLE 9.3

Milestones of language development. Children typically go through a series of milestones in their ability to understand language (receptive) and to speak it (expressive). Children can differ in when they reach these milestones, so we describe what happens at each stage, rather than identifying specific ages.

Stages	Milestones
Prenatal	• Capable of hearing spoken language
Infancy	• Distinguishing sounds in all languages—narrowing to the sounds in the infant's native language only • Shared attention with adults to promote language learning • Crying—differentiated for parents by intensity rather than the meaning of specific cries • Cooing—soft vowel sounds such as *ooh* and *aah* • Babbling—repeated syllables (*bababa*) leading to varied syllable combinations (*badagoo*) • Communicating through gestures
Toddlerhood	• Single words • Vocabulary burst—200–500 words by age 2 • Use of constraints to build vocabulary • Two-word combinations ("Mommy up!") • Telegraphic speech ("Me go home")
Early Childhood	• Adding morphemes to change words ("I walk*ed* to the store") • Egocentric speech—social speech that does not take the other person's point of view into account • Private speech—speech directed to the self that becomes internalized as thought
Middle Childhood	• Discourse skills—understanding the logic of a story • Metalinguistic ability—understanding that words are not the same as what they mean • Knowledge-telling style of writing
Adolescence	• Complex grammar • Slang • Knowledge-transforming style of writing

JOURNEY OF *Research*

Is There a Critical Period for Language Learning?

If there is a critical period during which children must learn language, then infants and children who are deprived of environmental stimulation and early facilitation of language learning may have difficulty with language that lasts their whole lives. Evidence for the existence of such a critical period for language learning comes from studies of children who were severely deprived during the early years of life. One famous case is that of a girl called Genie.

Throughout her childhood, Genie spent most of her time strapped to a chair in a back bedroom of her family home where she had little social contact or interaction with others. In 1970, the girl's situation came to the attention of welfare authorities in Los Angeles, and at age 13 Genie was removed from her home. At that point, her overall development was severely delayed, and she had little functional language. Genie provided a unique opportunity for scientists to examine the idea that there is a critical period for language development. At 13 she was already past the age when children normally develop language, but the developmentalists who worked with her used a variety of methods to promote her language development and carefully documented her progress. Although Genie eventually learned words, researchers concluded that she was unable to use grammar (Curtiss, 1977).

This conclusion has been reported over and over again as evidence for a critical period for language learning. However, Peter Jones (1995) reexamined the earlier reports of Genie's language learning and came to a different conclusion. Look at several things that Genie was able to say in 1974 and 1975:

"I want think about Mama riding bus."

"Teacher said Genie have temper tantrum outside."

"I do not have a toy green basket."

These sentences may not be perfect, but they show quite complex levels of grammatical construction. From this Jones (1995) concluded that Genie was able to develop language, and in particular grammar, even at her advanced age.

On the other hand, there is a case report of a woman called Chelsea who was incorrectly diagnosed as intellectually disabled until she was 31 years old, when it was discovered that she was deaf. She had lived with her family but received no education and no language input. When she was given hearing aids, she was able to learn words, but was never able to develop normal grammar. Here are some sentences she produced:

"banana the eat"

"Peter sandwich bread turkey" (Herschensohn, 2007, p. 91).

The importance of the window of opportunity for language learning is further illustrated by research on orphans who lived the first months of their lives in poorly equipped and poorly staffed orphanages in Romania where they suffered extreme deprivation. Those who were placed with foster families before age 2 had few problems with language development, whereas those who were adopted at an older age had marked language delays (Windsor et al., 2011). However, note that these children suffered language *delays*, not disorders likely to last throughout their lives. In a similar way, children who are born deaf but who receive cochlear implants have better language outcomes if the implantation occurs when they are younger (Nicholas & Geers, 2007). Early implantation appears to better preserve or restore the auditory system that supports language development in infants (National Institute on Deafness and Other Communication Disorders, 2013).

In the area of brain research, evidence has also shifted from the idea that language can be learned only early in life to the idea that it can be learned later as well, although it is more difficult at older ages. Researchers originally speculated that brain development was responsible for a critical period for language learning. Specifically, the original hypothesis was that certain parts of the brain worked most efficiently until a certain age, and then the restructuring of the neural connections forced the brain to use entirely different areas for learning language. However, recent research using brain imaging techniques has shown that individuals continue to learn language, including a second language, using the same parts of the brain that were used in first language learning (Stowe & Sabourin, 2005).

Clearly, language is learned most efficiently in early life, but we have moved away from the idea of a critical period beyond which language cannot develop. Instead we now think about a sensitive period when it is easiest to develop language.

PRENATAL DEVELOPMENT

Language learning appears to begin before birth. As we described in Chapter 6, during the last trimester of prenatal development, the fetus can hear its mother's voice as shown by changes in fetal heart rate and motor activity when the mother is speaking, and this prenatal exposure affects the infant's preferences for language after birth (Karmiloff & Karmiloff-Smith, 2001). This was demonstrated in a study in which pregnant women read passages from a specific book, such as Dr. Seuss's *The Cat in the Hat*, twice a day when they thought their fetus was awake (DeCasper & Spence, 1986). After the babies were born, those who had heard the story were more likely to try to elicit the sound of their mother reading *The Cat in the Hat* (rather than a new poem they had never heard before) by sucking a pacifier in a certain way. It appears that infants become familiar with and prefer "the rhythms and sounds of language" that they hear prenatally (Karmiloff & Karmiloff-Smith, 2001, p. 43). As a result, within the first few days of life, infants show a preference for the particular language their mother speaks, whether it is English, Arabic, Chinese or any other language. In addition, newborns who had heard their mothers regularly speak more than one language show a preference for both languages (Byers-Heinlein, Burns, & Werker, 2010). This prenatal awareness of language sets the stage for language learning once the baby is born. In one study, it was even shown that babies only 3 to 5 days old sound like the language they have been hearing when they cry. French babies cried from low pitch to high, while German babies cried from high pitch to low, mimicking the sounds of the language they heard (Mampe, Friederici, Christophe, & Wermke, 2009).

INFANTS' PREVERBAL COMMUNICATION

Infants communicate in a number of ways before they can say even one word. In this section, we describe the development of the earliest stages of communication: crying, cooing, and babbling.

Crying

Babies cry as soon as they are born. At first this is a reflexive behavior, not intentional communication from the infant. The process of communication begins when babies learn that crying can act as a signal that brings relief from whatever is bothering them because it motivates adults to do what it takes to make it stop.

Although babies cry for many reasons, there does not appear to be clear evidence that they have different cries for hunger, discomfort, or loneliness. Research shows only that parents differentiate the intensity and severity of crying, not the specific reason for the cry (Gustafson, Wood, & Green, 2000). Knowing this should bring relief to parents who may have been told that they should recognize *why* their baby is crying but realize they cannot.

Cooing

Between 2 and 4 months after birth, babies begin to make more pleasant sounds (Menn & Stoel-Gammon, 2005). The first sounds that infants are able to produce are soft vowel sounds, so they sound a bit like doves **cooing**. At this stage, they also begin to laugh, which is a great reward to parents. Infants at this stage begin to join in a prelanguage "conversation" as they take turns with parents (Tamis-LeMonda, Cristofaro, Rodriguez, & Bornstein, 2006). The baby coos; the parent talks back; the baby looks and laughs; the parent smiles and talks. In this way, babies begin to learn how to use language even before they can speak.

Babbling

Babies typically begin to make one-syllable sounds, such as *ba* and *da*, when they are 4 to 6 months old and begin to combine those sounds repetitively (*baba*, *gaga*) when they are 6 to 8 months old (Sachs, 2005). Among the most common consonant sounds are /b/,

T ☐ F ☐ Infants are born with a preference for listening to their native language. **True**

T ☐ F ☐ A sensitive parent should be able to tell the difference between a baby who is crying because he is hungry and one who is crying because he is uncomfortable or lonely. **False**

Cooing Soft vowel sounds, such as *ooh* and *aah*.

/d/, and /m/. At this point, parents get very excited, thinking that the baby means "daddy" when he says "dada" or "mommy" when he says "mama." Although it does not appear that these first vocalizations are meaningful, babies may start to learn they have meaning because of the way their parents respond to these sounds (Menn & Stoel-Gammon, 2005). It is interesting to note that in languages from around the world, even among those with no common origins, the words for *father—dada* (English), *abba* (Hebrew), and *baba* (Mandarin Chinese)—and *mother—mama* (English), *ahm* (Arabic), and *manah* (Greek)—start with the earliest sounds babies make.

Saying *bababa* changes to saying something like *daDAW ee der-BEH* as babbling begins to sound more and more like the language the baby is hearing (maybe the second phrase sounds like *the doggie under the bed*) and *not* like other languages. Although babies initially are able to make all the sounds in languages around the world, at this point a baby growing up with English will not produce the type of /r/ sounds used in French or Spanish because the baby is not hearing those sounds in the language environment. While the baby is making more sounds heard in her native language, she is making fewer sounds that do not appear in that language.

Now the feedback from hearing speech plays more of a role in language development than it did earlier. Deaf babies will babble early on, but at the age when hearing babies increase the variety of their sounds, deaf babies do not because they are not receiving this language input from their environment (Menn & Stoel-Gammon, 2005). On the other hand, deaf babies who are learning sign language appear to go through the same stages of language learning as hearing babies, in this case "babbling" with hand gestures instead of sounds.

©iStockphoto.com/Tanuki Photography

Why is this baby crying? Babies' cries do not communicate specific information, except intensity of pain or discomfort. The parent must figure out from experience why the baby would be crying at that particular time: Is it time for a nap, a feeding, or just some company?

PREVERBAL PERCEPTION OF LANGUAGE

We've already seen that infants respond to language even before they are born. It is also true that they are learning a great deal about language before they can say even one word. Babies younger than 6 months of age can distinguish the sounds made in all languages, but by 10 months, infants have lost some of that ability (Best & McRoberts, 2003). For example, Hindi has two distinct phonemes that both sound like "da" to English speakers. One is made the same way as in English, but the other is made with the tongue on the roof of the mouth. Babies in an English language environment can discriminate these two sounds until about 10 months of age, when they lose the ability to differentiate between these two sounds because they are not hearing them in their native language (Conboy & Kuhl, 2011). Asian infants can tell the difference between the English language sounds "ra" and "la," but Asian adults have a more difficult time because this distinction is not found in the language they speak (Kuhl, 2010).

The process by which infants narrow their perception to the specific sounds in the language they are hearing appears to be linked to their later language production. Infants who are better at discriminating sounds in their native language at 7 months have better language development during the second year of life, while infants who are better at discriminating sounds in a nonnative language at 7 months have more delayed language development (Kuhl, Conboy, Padden, Nelson, & Pruitt, 2005). It appears that part of learning a language depends on identifying the specific sounds that make up that language. Infants who develop this ability later also develop language at a later age.

HOW ADULTS FOSTER LANGUAGE DEVELOPMENT

Before we continue our description of the stages of language development, let's take a focused look at the role that adults play in fostering young children's language development. We first look at how parents' interaction with their infants and toddlers both verbally and through gestures promotes language development in these early years. We then look at the impact that the socioeconomic status of the parents has on how they talk with their children and how these differences impact children's language development.

Shared Attention, Gestures, and Sign Language

In the first months after birth, infants are focused mostly on their own bodies and on interaction with the people in their world. At about 6 months, they begin to develop more interest in the objects and events around them. At this point, caregivers begin to talk about what the infant sees as both infant and caregiver gaze at objects and events. When babies look or point at what they see, adults tend to label what it is for them (Goldfield & Snow, 2005). In fact, one researcher has referred to pointing as "the royal road," if not the only road, to language development (Butterworth, 2003, p. 9).

Pointing is just one of the gestures that children use to communicate. Infants use many gestures before they can speak, and continue to use them along with speech (Igualada, Bosch, & Prieto, 2015). Parents have begun to take advantage of this fact by introducing forms of sign language to infants. Nonverbal signs are representations that have meaning, just like words. Using signs can reduce frustration for both parent and child when the child can sign what she wants instead of crying. Some people fear babies will rely on these signs and it will delay the development of spoken language, but a recent study found no difference in infants' language development whether mothers signed with their babies or did not (Kirk, Howlett, Pine, & Fletcher, 2013). Furthermore, when adults use sign language it also encourages the kind of attentive and responsive parenting that promotes healthy development of infants in all areas of growth (Barnes, 2010).

Although most parents gesture as they talk to their infants, the amount and type of gesturing differs from parent to parent. Rowe and Goldin-Meadow (2009) found that parents in families of higher socioeconomic status (SES) use gestures with their infants to communicate a broader range of meaning than parents from families of lower SES. In turn, the children from the higher-SES families used more gestures to communicate meaning by 14 months of age, and this difference in gesturing at 14 months predicted differences in the size of the children's vocabulary at 4-1/2 years of age, when they were about to begin kindergarten. Gesturing may enhance language learning in several ways. First, when a child points to an object and a parent "translates" that gesture into a word by naming the object, that word enters the child's vocabulary sooner (Rowe & Goldin-Meadow, 2009). Just using gestures without parental naming also enhances vocabulary development. Iverson and Goldin-Meadow (2005) found that when children use a gesture, such as flapping their hands to signify a bird, the actual word *bird* tends to show up about 3 months later. The representation of the idea through gesturing may help the child learn the word meaning and eventually say and use the word.

T ☐ F ☐ Teaching babies to use sign language will delay development of their spoken language.
False

© age fotostock Spain, S.L./Alamy

What is this toddler saying? Toddlers use pointing as a way of communicating before they have words. We don't know what this child is pointing at, but his mother is sure to tell him all about it.

How many parental gestures a child may see also varies because there are cultural differences in the use of gestures. For example, Italians tend to use many more gestures than Americans when they speak, although gesturing seems to serve the same purpose in both populations (Iverson, Capirci, Volterra, & Goldin-Meadow, 2008). For both Italians and Americans, the child's use of gestures together with speech was predictive of the development of the next stage of language development: two-word utterances.

The rate at which children develop language is related to the nature of their interaction with their parents. Children develop language more quickly if their parents talk to them, but more specifically if their parents respond to their interests, for example by naming what they are actually looking at rather than something else. Parents and infants who develop the ability to engage each other in a dynamic way, following each other's leads from one focus of attention to the next, seem to foster language development most effectively.

Sign language for babies. Babies can gesture long before they can use words. They can learn to use signs such as this sign for "more" taken from American Sign Language to communicate what they want and need, and this does not delay their development of spoken language.

© Christina Kennedy/Alamy

Child-Directed Speech

In addition to naming objects, in many cultures adults begin to shape infants' developing language ability by talking to them as if they understood, even when it is clear that they do not. Adults carry on conversations with their infants, taking turns with whatever the baby responds. Karmiloff and Karmiloff-Smith (2001) provide the following illustration:

>Mother: Oh, so you're HUNgry, are you?
>(Baby kicks.)
>
>Mother: YES, you ARE hungry. WELL, we'll have to give you some MILK then, won't we?
>(Baby coos.)
>
>Mother: Ah, so Mommy was RIGHT. It's MILK you want. Shall we change your diaper first?
>(Baby kicks.)
>
>Mother: RIGHT! A clean diaper. THAT's what you want. GOOD girl. (p. 48)

This type of exchange provides the baby with early experience of the back-and-forth of dialogue that will be important in later speech, but we must be careful about concluding that what adults do is the *most* important factor for children's developing speech. Research with some cultures, such as the Gusii people of Kenya, shows that parents in these cultures speak to their babies much less often than American parents, but their infants still develop language. In fact, when LeVine and his colleagues (1994) instructed Gusii mothers to talk and play with their babies while they were videotaped, they complied but said "it was of course silly to talk to a baby" (p. 210). Another interesting variation is found among the Kaluli of Papua New Guinea. Although the Kaluli tend not to talk *to* their babies,

Laying the foundation for speech. This mother is laying the foundation for her infant's later speech. What is the infant learning about language from this interaction?

T ☐ F ☐ It is perfectly fine to use baby talk with infants. **True**

Child-directed speech Speech that is tailored to fit the sensory and cognitive capabilities of infants and children so that it holds their attention; includes speaking in a higher pitch with exaggerated intonation and a singsong rhythm and using a simplified vocabulary.

they hold up the babies to face people and speak *for* the baby (Feld & Shieffelin, 1998). Despite these different early experiences with language, Gusii children and Kaluli children become as proficient with their language as American children are with English. There are many roads to language competence, and we must be careful not to apply one standard to all people.

Think about the way you talk to babies or hear others do so. You are unlikely to approach a baby and say in a low, monotone voice, "Hello, baby, how are you today? I hope you are having a fine day." You would be much more likely to say, "Hel-LO, BAAAA-BEEEE. How are YOU today?" The special way that we talk to infants and young children was once referred to as *motherese*. However, since we have found that in most cultures, *all* adults, and children too, change the way they speak to infants and young children, this type of speech is now known as **child-directed speech** (Bryant & Barrett, 2007; Weisleder & Fernald, 2013).

Some people believe using child-directed speech is harmful to infants, teaching them the wrong way to speak, but the evidence is that what we naturally do in this way actually fosters language development (Rowe, 2008; Weisleder & Fernald, 2013). When we use child-directed speech we speak in a higher pitched voice, exaggerate our sounds, simplify our vocabulary, and talk in a singsong rhythm. These changes in our normal speech patterns are actually tailored to fit the sensory and cognitive capabilities of infants and children so that it holds their attention, resulting in more engagement between adult and child (Paul, Chawarska, Fowler, Cicchetti, & Volkmar, 2007). In addition, the musical quality of child-directed speech appears to promote early perception of the phonemes, or sounds, in a language (Lebedeva & Kuhl, 2010).

SES and Language Development

Although most parents talk with their infants, there are very large differences in the amount and quality of their child-directed speech, and these differences have consequences for the children's later development, including their readiness to enter school. In a classic study of children's language environment, Betty Hart and Todd Risley (1995) followed 42 families over a 2.5-year period, observing and recording their everyday conversation. Their sample consisted of families who were receiving welfare, working-class families, and families where the parent or parents held professional jobs. The difference in the amount of language that the children were exposed to was striking. On average, parents on welfare used 600 words an hour with their toddlers, working-class parents used 1,300 words, and parents with professional jobs used 2,100 words. By the time the children were 3 years old, children in professional families had been exposed to 8 million more words on average than children in welfare families. This cumulative effect is shown in Figure 9.2.

However, it is not just the number of words spoken that makes the difference in children's language development. The quality of the language spoken and the interactive, responsive nature of the communication are more important. Hart and Risley (1995) found that professional parents did not initiate verbal interactions with their children any more frequently than other parents, but they were more likely to respond to what their toddlers said and used more affirmative or encouraging statements and fewer prohibitions, such as "Stop that" or "Don't."

FIGURE 9.2

Differences in toddlers' vocabulary. The more words toddlers hear in their everyday life, the more they produce when they learn to speak. Children in families in which the parents are professionals hear significantly more words than children in working-class families or families on welfare, and this is reflected in the size of their vocabularies.

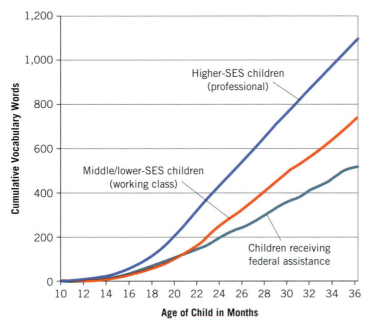

SOURCE: Hart & Risley (1995). Reprinted by permission of the publisher.

Differences in language development by a family's socioeconomic status start early and continue as children get older. By 18 months of age, children from disadvantaged families already show less comprehension of simple words than do their more advantaged peers (Fernald, Marchman, & Weisleder, 2013). Vasilyeva, Waterfall, and Huttenlocher (2008) followed children from 22 to 42 months of age and looked at the type of early sentences used by children whose parents had different levels of education. One group of parents had high school diplomas as their highest level of education, the second group of parents had college degrees, and the third group of parents had professional degrees (for example, a master's degree, a doctorate, or a professional degree in medicine or law). They found no differences in the children's use of *simple* sentences across groups. The children also did not differ in the age at which they started producing simple sentences or in the proportion of simple sentences that they used. However, differences later emerged in the acquisition and use of *complex* sentences. Children from more educated families began producing complex sentences earlier and used them more frequently. Figure 9.3 shows the different paths of development for these two types of sentences. The authors say that children with families from different educational backgrounds move further apart as they grow older, and other research has shown that the disparity continues beyond the preschool years.

However, the differences between SES groups are averages and disguise the fact that some working-class parents talk with their children as much and as well as affluent parents (Fernald & Weisleder, 2015). Even for children within the same SES groups, the amount and quality of language they experience affects their acquisition of language. In one study of low income Spanish-speaking families, large differences between families were recorded in the amount that adults spoke to their infants. Toddlers whose parents spoke to them more had a larger vocabulary at age 2 (Weisleder & Fernald, 2013). In fact, the quality of the parents'

FIGURE 9.3

Differences in the complexity of toddlers' sentences. There is little difference in the use of simple sentences among children from families with different levels of education (left). However, there are differences in the number of complex sentences these children produce (right).

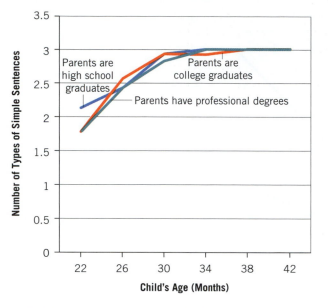

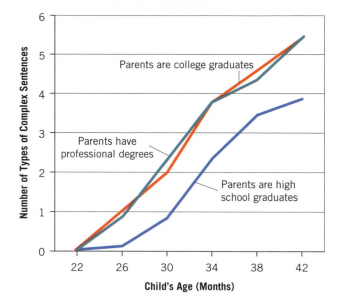

SOURCE: Vasilyeva, Waterfall, & Huttenlocher (2008).

verbal interactions with the child predicted the child's language development better than the family's SES.

Let us now return to our description of the stages of language development as we look at the acquisition of words and sentences.

TODDLERS' DEVELOPMENT OF WORDS AND SENTENCES

Babbling sometimes leads directly to babies' first words. The sounds they play with while babbling may be the sounds they use for the first words they say (Menn & Stoel-Gammon, 2005). Through their interactions with caregivers, infants begin to associate words with familiar objects and people. Remember that comprehension of language precedes the production of language. While infants begin to *understand* words between 6 and 9 months of age, they do not begin to *say* words, on average, until about 13 months (Bergelson & Swingley, 2012; Tamis-LeMonda et al., 2006). Babies may make up their first words and these words may not correspond to an adult word. For example, one baby referred to any motorized vehicle as a *gogo*, and *baba* meant water. When the family took him through a car wash, he created a new word combination out of these two made-up words to describe his experience. He called it a *baba-gogo*.

Growth of Vocabulary

At 1 year, babies typically have only a few words in their vocabulary, but by 2 years of age they generally have between 200 and 500 words (Fernald, Pinto, Swingley, Weinberg, & McRoberts, 2001). Although they initially learn new words slowly, over this second year of life they begin to learn them more quickly (Ganger & Brent, 2004). For some babies, the learning of new words explodes in what has been called a **vocabulary burst**, but for others the learning

Vocabulary burst The rapid growth of a child's vocabulary that often occurs in the second year.

is more gradual. This is one of those aspects of development where there is quite a wide range that falls within what would be considered normal. Later in this chapter, we describe some patterns of language development that fall outside this normal range and can indicate serious problems, but language delays are not uncommon or necessarily a sign of a disorder.

How do toddlers master their native language so quickly? First, during their second year, children begin to understand that words are symbols standing for objects in the world (Preissler & Carey, 2004). This realization provides a strong incentive for them to acquire and use language. Around the world, children typically add nouns to their vocabulary before they add verbs. Nouns are thought to be easier to learn because they refer to objects in the child's world and the child has realized that things should have names (Waxman et al., 2013). However, different languages express verbs in a variety of ways; for example, an English-speaker would likely always say "the girl *is* young," but speakers of many other languages would leave the verb out, knowing it is implied by the meaning of the rest of the sentence. Because verbs are handled in different ways, the ease with which children learn them varies depending on the language they are learning (Waxman et al., 2013).

A second way children build vocabulary is through the use of several assumptions and principles called **constraints** because they limit or constrain the alternatives the child considers when learning a new word. One of these constraints is the **whole object bias**. When a child sees a giraffe for the first time and someone points to the animal and says "giraffe," the child assumes the word describes the entire animal—not its strange, long neck; not its skinny legs; and not its brown spots. Children make this assumption even when the new object obviously has two parts to it, and even if one of the parts is more prominent than the other (Hollich, Golinkoff, & Hirsh-Pasek, 2007). Another constraint is the **mutual exclusivity constraint**. Children assume that there is one (and only one) name for an object. If they hear a novel word, they assume the new word describes an object that they do not already know the name for because the object wouldn't have two different names (Hansen & Markman, 2009). The **taxonomic constraint** leads children to assume that two objects that have features in common can have a name in common, but that each object also can have its own individual name (Markman, 1990). For example, both dogs and cats have four legs and a tail and are covered with fur so they are both *animals,* but they each have some unique characteristics that distinguish between them so they also can have their own individual name.

Two other mechanisms for learning new words are **syntactic bootstrapping**, in which children use syntax, or grammar, to learn the meaning of new words (Gutman, Dautriche, Crabbé, & Christophe, 2015) and **semantic bootstrapping** in which they use word meanings to learn grammatical categories (verbs or nouns) (Johnson & de Villiers, 2009). To "pull yourself up by your bootstraps" is an expression that means to solve a problem using your own resources. In this case, children use knowledge that they have in one domain of language (syntax) to help them learn another domain (semantics) (Karmiloff & Karmiloff-Smith, 2001). For instance, there are differences in the forms words take that help to determine whether they are nouns or verbs. If you were introduced to two new words—*klumfs* and *pribiked*—which would you think was a noun and which a verb? You know we add *-s* to nouns to form a plural in English, therefore that is a strong clue that *klumfs* is a noun. Likewise, a verb can have a past tense, so the *-ed* at the end of *pribiked* is a strong clue that this is a verb. Second, where a word appears in a sentence (its syntax) provides clues to word meaning. In English, the noun usually precedes the verb, so if someone told you that the "thrulm progisted the car," you could assume that *thrulm* is a noun and *progisted* is a verb. If someone told you that "you have a very *glickle* smile," you might guess that *glickle* is an adjective that modifies or describes your smile.

Young children also use verbs they know to learn new nouns. In one study, 15- and 19-month-olds were shown a picture of a small animal and a colorful abstract object. They then heard a conversation in which one person says "The *dax* is crying." When the 19-month-olds were shown the two original pictures again and were asked "Where is the *dax*?" they were likely to look at the animal rather than the abstract object. They

Constraints Assumptions language learners make that limit the alternative meanings that they attribute to new words.

Whole object bias An assumption made by language learners that a word describes an entire object, rather than just some portion of it.

Mutual exclusivity constraint An assumption made by language learners that there is one (and only one) name for an object.

Taxonomic constraint An assumption language learners make that two objects that have features in common can have a name in common, but that each object also can have its own individual name.

Syntactic bootstrapping The use of syntax to learn the meaning of new words (semantics).

Semantic bootstrapping The use of conceptual categories to create grammatical categories.

were more likely to do so than if they heard someone say "The *dax* is right here." Fifteen-month-olds did not look more at the animal, but by 19 months of age, children understand that only living things can cry, therefore the use of the verb "cry" helped them to figure out that the word *dax*, a made-up word, refers to the animal and not to an abstract design (Ferguson, Graf, & Waxman, 2014).

As children apply all these principles to their acquisition of new words, they can quickly learn new words, often based on a single exposure, in a process called **fast mapping**. The constraints allow the child to form an initial hypothesis, which can be tested in future situations that provide a basis for rapid acquisition of words (Pan, 2005). To see for yourself how constraints can help guide a young child's word learning, try **Active Learning: Using Linguistic Constraints**.

Fast mapping A process by which children apply constraints and their knowledge of grammar to learn new words very quickly, often after a single exposure.

Active LEARNING

Using Linguistic Constraints

You can use this activity to learn some novel "words" to see how a young child might experience learning them. In each situation, decide what you would say and name the linguistic constraint that you used to guide your decision.

1. You know that a bat is a long, thin object, and you know that a ball is small and round. If I ask you to hand me the glumph, which object in this picture do you pick up?

   Which constraint did you use to make your decision?

2. The creature with the pink hair is a lorum. When you have more than one lorum, what do you call them?

   How did you know what more than one lorum is called?

3. These are both floogles, but the green one is a flinger and the purple one is a flagger.

   What constraint helps you understand how these creatures are similar and how they are different?

4. This glumbug is dingling.

   How do you know which of these new words is a noun and which is a verb?

5. If I tell you this is a boblabo, am I naming the creature's beak, its wings, or something else?

   What constraint allows you to determine what the word boblabo *refers to?*

Creating Sentences

After children have acquired a number of words in their vocabulary, they enter a stage of language development in which there is enormous growth in both the understanding of word meanings and in the use of more sophisticated grammatical construction. At around a year and a half, children begin to combine words in phrases such as *Mommy up* or *All gone kitty*. This is the beginning of their use of grammar. At this stage, all children around the world use language in the same way, by including only the most basic information in what they say. For example, they may say, "Eat apple," but they cannot say, "I'm eating an apple" or "You ate the apple." For some children, one word, such as *allgone* or *more*, becomes a "pivot" word to which other words are attached, as in *allgone apple* and *allgone mommy*.

When children begin to put three or more words together, they use the simplest combination of words that convey the meaning they intend. In the days long before instant messaging and texting, people used to send telegrams. When you sent a telegram, you would pay by the word. Therefore, you would not say, "I am going to arrive at 11:00 p.m. at the train station;" instead you might send the message "Arriving station 11 p.m." You would leave out all the little, unnecessary words. When young children begin to put words together, they act as if they have to pay for each word, and they only use the ones necessary to get their point across. This has been referred to as **telegraphic speech.**

When children begin to combine three or more words, the ordering of the words in these simple sentences reflects the language they are hearing. For example, the order in sentences in English is very likely to be a subject, then a verb, and then the object of the verb: *The dog* (subject) *chased* (verb) *the cat* (object). English-speaking children find it difficult to produce and understand passive sentences in which this order is changed: *The cat was chased by the dog*. However, children who speak Sesotho, a language found in southern Africa, hear passive sentences frequently and can produce these forms as soon as they learn to speak (Demuth, 1990). You can try **Active Learning: The Impact of Word Order** to see whether a child you know understands passive sentences.

Telegraphic speech A stage in language development in which children only use the words necessary to get their point across and omit small words that are not necessary (for example, *Go bye-bye*).

Active LEARNING

The Impact of Word Order

First, you will need to take two pieces of paper and draw two pictures. On one piece of paper, draw a dog facing right and running. On the second piece of paper, draw a cat facing right and running. Ask a child between 3 and 10 years of age to arrange the pictures to show *The dog is chasing the cat*. Then ask the child to arrange the picture to show *The dog is chased by the cat*. Does the child understand that in the second sentence, which

(Continued)

(Continued)

is in the passive form, the cat is actually chasing the dog? If not, this shows that the child still understands language through the grammatical structure of subject-verb-object. Some 4-year-old English-speaking children can understand passive sentences, but many children in elementary school still have trouble with this form (Vasilyeva, Huttenlocher, & Waterfall, 2006). Compare your results with those of others in the class who tested children of different ages.

To prepare for this activity, or, if you do not have access to a child, you can watch the video of this Active Learning.

ACTIVE LEARNING VIDEO ▲
Younger children have difficulty understanding a passive sentence that switches word order, but this 7-year-old is not fooled.

One thing parents tend *not* to do with young children is to correct their grammar explicitly. The following story helps show what effect it might have if you were to spend much time correcting young children's grammar. In the 1970s, before the age of the computer, when people still wrote letters to each other, a young man carried on a correspondence with his girlfriend who was at a different college far away. Both of these young people were highly intellectual, as you will see. Each wrote love letters to the other. The recipient would then *correct the grammar* in the letter and send it back to the sender. You probably reacted quite negatively to this scenario, but why? Clearly, dealing with the grammar instead of the content of a love letter took all of the meaning—in this case, the romance—out of the exchange. In the same way, when a child is trying to tell us something, we respond to the content, not the form of what he is saying. When the child says, "Me go store," we answer, "Oh, are you going to the store?" We do not respond by saying "You should say, 'I am going to the store.'" If we did, the child would be totally confused. Karmiloff and Karmiloff-Smith (2001) provide the following example of what happened when a mother tried to correct her child's grammar:

Child: Daddy goed to work.

Mother: Yes, that's right. Daddy went to work.

Child: Daddy goed to work in car.

Mother: Yes, Daddy *went* in his car.

Child: Daddy goed his car very fast.

Mother: Ah ha, Daddy *went* to work in his car. Say *went* to work, not *goed*. Daddy *went* to work.

Child: Daddy wented to work. (p. 102)

As this example shows, sometimes even when we directly try to correct grammar, it doesn't work. Also, if you've ever had a parent correct your grammar while you were trying to tell him something important, you can understand a child's frustration when a parent responds to the form of a sentence rather than to the meaning of what is said.

T ☐ F ☐ If a young child says "I goed outside," a parent should correct him by saying "No, you meant to say, 'I *went* outside.'" **False**

LANGUAGE DEVELOPMENT IN EARLY CHILDHOOD

Young children become much more proficient in understanding and producing both vocabulary and grammar. By age 3, most children are putting together multiword sentences. Also, whereas younger children use only the basic forms of words, such as *I go store*, preschoolers begin to add morphemes. At the beginning of the chapter, we defined a morpheme as the smallest unit that has meaning in a language. A morpheme may be a word like *house*, *car*, or *alligator*, or it may be any part of a word that has meaning, such as *-ed*, which indicates past tense, or *-s*, which indicates a plural. As the preschooler learns to use morphemes appropriately, she no longer says "I walk home" but rather "I walked home" when she means the past tense. As we mentioned in the earlier section on nativist theory, when children learn to use these added morphemes, they often use them on words for which they don't work. Interestingly, they may use both the correct and the incorrect version, even in the same sentence: "I goed to the store and then went home."

Follow the directions in **Active Learning: Collecting a Language Sample** to look at the nature of a young child's language development.

Active LEARNING

Collecting a Language Sample

Take a 10- to 15-minute language sample of a child between the ages of 18 months and 4 years by watching the child while he or she is playing with another child or talking with an adult. Try to write down exactly what the child says. How many words does she put together: one, two, three, or more? Look at the stages of development we have described to see where this child fits in. If the child is using just single words, how does she make herself understood (for example, by using gestures)? If she does put words together, are they in the same order that we would find in adult grammar, or are there words that are left out (for example, *I am going to the store* becomes *I go store*)? Do the words the child uses have appropriate endings (for example, *kicked, playing, desks*)? Does the child overregularize and put these endings on irregularly formed words (for example, *wented, sitted*)? Compare your findings with those of others in your class who observed children older or younger than the child you observed.

ACTIVE LEARNING VIDEO ▲

Write down what these children say; do they use language patterns that are different from the way adults speak?

To prepare for this activity, or, if you do not have access to a child, you can watch the video of this Active Learning.

Although their use of language is rapidly increasing, preschoolers still have some limitations to their ability to communicate with others. Jean Piaget (1973) described the inability of young children to take the role of other people in their conversations as **egocentric speech**.

Egocentric speech A limitation of young children's communication due to their inability to take the perspective of other people into account.

For example, a child may say something like "I went to that place and saw someone going round and round." She does not realize that you have no idea what "that place" is or how someone can go "round and round" because she doesn't understand that you don't know everything that she knows. For Piaget, the explanation for egocentric speech is that children are not born social beings; they must learn to be social and to understand other people's points of view. When they do, their language becomes socialized, and communication is much more effective. Schematically, Piaget described the development of speech as follows:

Presocial speech   ⟶   Egocentric speech   ⟶   Socialized speech

Lev Vygotsky (1962) had a very different idea about what egocentric speech was. For Vygotsky, children are born social beings, so their speech is never "presocial." Instead, children always intend to communicate, but at some point their speech divides into two types: speech directed at other people and speech directed at oneself. In Chapter 7, we introduced the concept of *private speech,* or talking to oneself. Speech directed at other people continues to be communicative, but private speech becomes increasingly silent. Younger children talk to themselves out loud, for example, "I'm using the red crayon." Somewhat older children more often whisper or mutter to themselves when carrying out a task. Some children may even move their mouths silently. Vygotsky said that this speech becomes internalized eventually as silent speech ("saying it in my head") and then as thought. Schematically, Vygotsky described the development of speech as follows:

Social speech ⟶ Communicative speech
             ⟶ Egocentric or private speech ⟶ Inner speech or thought

Private speech does not end in early childhood. When confronted with a difficult task, about one-third of 17-year-olds were found to talk openly (10%) or covertly, such as mumbling or whispering (20%), to themselves (Winsler & Naglieri, 2003). Try **Active Learning: Private Speech** to see when even adults may still engage in private speech.

Active LEARNING

Private Speech

If you ever find yourself talking out loud when you are alone (that is, using private speech), think about what you are most likely to say to yourself. The chances are that what you will say is about tasks that you need to do, like "Oh . . . the psych assignment!" or "Almost forgot that!" These comments generally have to do with self-direction or organization. As adults, we usually do not vocalize in this way to ourselves, but when we are alone or attempting to do something difficult, we may.

Get a friend to help you with this activity and find a quiet place to do it. Your friend will need a desk or table to work on so he can write. Use a page from a book or a sheet of newspaper that he can write on. Tell him that you are looking at how accurately people can scan written material to find target letters. Tell him that he should "cross out the Ts, circle the Os, and square the Ls" (the latter means that he should draw a box around the letter L) on the page you give him. Repeat these instructions a couple of times to be sure he understands (you can say it like a little rhyme) and ask him to repeat it to you a time or two to further confirm his understanding, but do not let him write it down. Tell him that you will later count how many letters he was able to mark up correctly in 3 minutes.

After you are sure your friend understands the instructions, tell him that you will sit out of the way so that you don't distract him and you will tell him when to start and when to stop.

After 2 minutes, give him a 1-minute warning (to create a little more pressure on him). While he is working, listen carefully to hear whether he resorts to using private speech to help him perform the task. Kronk (1994) found that 37 out of 47 participants talked to themselves while working on a difficult cognitive task that she gave them, and that 46 out of 47 talked to themselves if others were working on the same task and talking to themselves.

LANGUAGE DEVELOPMENT IN MIDDLE CHILDHOOD

In middle childhood, in addition to refining and expanding vocabulary and grammar, children develop the ability to understand whether a story or information they are hearing makes logical sense, known as **discourse skills**. For example, they are able to identify the problem in the following sequence: "On her way she lost her purse. When she got to the store, she took out her purse and bought her favorite candy" (Language and Reading Research Consortium, 2015, p. 1954). When shown a story represented by pictures that are out of order, they are able to organize the pictures correctly to indicate what comes first and what comes later. They also develop the ability to make inferences from what they hear. For instance, if a teacher reads *Goldilocks and the Three Bears* to her class, a question that requires children to make an inference might be "Why did Goldilocks break baby bear's chair?" The children must draw on their knowledge of the size of babies and of girls to draw the conclusion that she was too big for the chair (Reading Rockets, 2015).

Another ability children develop at this age is the understanding that words are not the same as what they stand for. For example, a child might say he likes the word *brussel sprouts* because of how it sounds, even though he does not like the vegetable. This understanding is the basis for **metalinguistic abilities**, in which children begin to think about language and how to use it (Pan, 2005). Try **Active Learning: Metalinguistic Awareness** to see how older children start to appreciate words as words.

Discourse skills The ability to understand whether a story or information someone is hearing makes logical sense.

Metalinguistic abilities The abilities to think about and talk about language.

Active LEARNING

Metalinguistic Awareness

To see whether children at various ages understand that a word is not the same as what it refers to, try the following activity. Ask a child, "What are your favorite things?" and then ask, "What are your favorite words?" For each response to each question, ask why it is her favorite. Compare your child's responses with those of classmates who interviewed children at different ages. Preschoolers are not likely to differentiate words from the things they refer to. They are likely to say their favorite word is *lollipop* because such candies are delicious. Older children are more likely to

ACTIVE LEARNING VIDEO ▲

As children develop their understanding of language, they come to realize that words are not the same as what they stand for.

know the word is not the same as the thing. They may say they like the same word, *lollipop*, but their reason will be because they like the sounds it makes (Pan, 2005).

To prepare for this activity, or, if you do not have access to a child, you can watch the video of this Active Learning.

Peek-a-boo! Toddlers find peek-a-boo to be great fun. It is an early type of social humor.

These new metalinguistic abilities allow children to use language in new ways. For example, humor takes on a new dimension, as in this example:

KNOCK KNOCK

Who's there?

Lettuce.

Lettuce who?

Lettuce in, we're hungry!

As we can see from this example, many jokes require a fairly sophisticated understanding of language. You won't think the joke is funny unless you understand you have been tricked because the sounds for *lettuce* and *let us* are the same but the meanings are very different. This implies an understanding that words we say can sound alike but indicate very different things. Children with language impairments have much more difficulty understanding humor, especially when the joke relies on a word having multiple meanings (O'Mara & Waller, 2003). Table 9.4 describes and illustrates some of the changes in what children find funny as they get older. As you look at these stages, think about what cognitive advances are necessary for a child to move from one stage of humor to another.

School-age children develop the ability to use words to mean something beyond their literal meaning. For example, they can use a metaphor such as *school is a ball!* or *time is*

TABLE 9.4

Children's humor. What children find funny largely depends on their stage of cognitive development, but the sense that something is inappropriate or incongruous underlies most of what we find funny. These stages of the development of humor are adapted from the work of Paul McGhee.

Stage	Description	Example
Stage 0: Laughter Without Humor	Children smile and laugh but not in connection with humor.	Infant laughs when seeing another baby.
Stage 1: Laughter at the Attachment Figure	Children demonstrate an increasing awareness of their interpersonal surroundings and participate in social humor with a parent or other attachment figure.	Toddler plays peek-a-boo with parent, laughing each time her face is revealed.
Stage 2: Treating an Object as a Different Object	Children begin producing "jokes" nonverbally by performing incongruous actions.	Child holds a stuffed animal to his ear and talks into it as though it were a phone.
Stage 3: Misnaming Objects or Actions	Once children's vocabulary hits a critical point, they can extend their incongruity humor to misnaming objects or actions.	Child intentionally names objects incorrectly (for example, pointing to her nose and saying it is her ear).

Stage	Description	Example
Stage 4: Playing With Words	As children's verbal competence grows they may experiment with rhyming words, made-up silly words, and other humorous word play that does not directly link to concrete objects within their reach that strike them as funny.	A group of friends laughs when each one says "moose!"
Stage 5: Riddles and Jokes	Children begin to understand that humor has a meaning—that jokes must resolve from something absurd into something that makes cognitive sense. They often start memorizing riddles and jokes and using them as a means of initiating social interactions with peers and adults.	Child retells a knock-knock joke.
Stage 6: Funny Stories	Teens develop preference for spontaneous wit and amusing anecdotes over memorized jokes and riddles.	Teen recounts a real-life experience, emphasizing and exaggerating the silly elements; teen makes observations that point out the absurdity of an ostensibly serious situation.

Note that the appearance of a new type of humor does not displace the earlier types. For example, although adolescents prefer spontaneous wit to memorized jokes, both adolescents and adults can be amused by a clever pun or a well-told joke.

SOURCES: Adapted from McGhee (1979) and Cunningham & Scarlett (2004).

money. They also begin to use irony or sarcasm, in which the speaker means the opposite of what he is really saying. For example, Filippova and Astington (2010) asked school-age children to respond to a scenario in which Billy helps his mom empty the dishwasher and breaks a plate. His mom says, "You sure ARE a GREAT helper!" Although 5-year-olds did not understand that the mother was not really complimenting Billy, 7- and 9-year-olds understood the sarcasm.

THE LANGUAGE OF TEENAGERS

The language of teenagers can sound quite a bit different from that of many adults. In one sense, adolescent speech becomes more adult-like. Sentences are longer, and the grammar is more complex. Adolescents are also more likely to use slang or made-up words, especially when talking among themselves. They may do this for fun or to bond with a particular group, or simply to identify with being an adolescent. Swearing also reaches a peak in adolescence and seems to serve the same purposes (Jay & Janschewitz, 2012).

Teens often change the meaning of a word to its opposite: *That's dope* comes to mean *it's really good*. Shortcuts may be developed. The word *relationship* is shortened to *ship*. Adolescent slang sometimes catches on with the wider society and becomes part of how everyone talks (Brenoff, 2016; Ely, 2005). We were going to include a list of teen slang words here but realized that they would likely be outdated by the time this book was published. Instead, if you are not far beyond adolescence yourself, think about which words you use with your friends but not with older people like your parents. Do you have any idea about the origin of those words? Were you using other words when you were in high school or middle school? Is the slang you use particular to the area of the country in which you live or to a particular group to which you belong? Different regions of the country and different subgroups within the country develop their own particular slang. For instance, teens from Nebraska are less likely than teens from California to use slang pertaining to surfing.

LITERACY: READING AND WRITING

9.5   How do children learn to read and write?

Until now, our discussion of language has focused on spoken language. In this section, we introduce another very important aspect of language: the ability to understand and use written language. School is the context in which most children learn to read and write, but the groundwork for these skills is laid down throughout the preschool years.

READING

Emergent literacy The set of skills that develop before children begin formal reading instruction, that provide the foundation for later academic skills

Research on reading typically has looked at how a child acquires specific skills such as phonetics (or decoding sounds from letters) within the school context, but children also learn about reading, writing, and print material through informal processes, such as parents reading to children before they start school (Lonigan, Purpura, Wilson, Walker, & Clancy-Menchetti, 2013).

Emergent Literacy

In recent years, we have given increasing attention to **emergent literacy,** the set of skills that develop before children begin formal schooling and that provide the foundation for these academic skills. When a young child picks up a book, holds it right-side-up, and turns the pages, "reads" a story by looking at the pictures in a book, or picks up a pencil and scribbles on a paper, these are all emergent literacy skills. As in the development of spoken language, the heart of emergent literacy is the interaction between an adult and the child, in this case as the adult reads to the child or tells a story. From these shared experiences, the child develops an awareness of print, learns to recognize and name letters, becomes aware of the sounds associated with different letters, and learns new words (Irwin, Moore, Tornatore, & Fowler, 2012).

Reading to very young children does more than actually teaching them to read. Reading to children on a regular basis in the first 3 years of life has been linked to a higher level of both language development and cognitive development (Rodriguez et al., 2009; Rodriguez & Tamis-LeMonda, 2011). In 2014 the American Academy of Pediatrics put out a new policy statement recommending that physicians promote parents reading to their young children to develop language skills and create an interest in reading (O'Keefe, 2014). In 2009, half of U.S. children between 1 and 5 years of age were read to every day by members of their family

Dialogic reading. As this father reads to his daughter and asks her questions about the story, he actively engages her in the process and lays the groundwork for emergent literacy skills.

Jupiterimages/Creatas/Thinkstock

(U.S. Census Bureau, 2011b). This was true for 59% of children in families above the poverty level but only 45% of those below that level, so this is a group of parents who could benefit from knowing more about the importance of early reading.

Many adults love to read to children, but children should be active participants in the process. A technique known as **dialogic reading** is particularly effective in developing early literacy skills (Zevenbergen & Whitehurst, 2003). As the adult and child look at a picture book together, they actively talk about it. The adult engages the child in the process by asking questions and encouraging a dialogue about what is going on in the story. What is essential to this process, however, is that the partners then switch roles and the child becomes the storyteller and the adult becomes the active listener and answers the child's questions (Ghoting & Martin-Díaz, 2006; Institute of Education Sciences, 2007). Dialogic reading provides the essential dimension of active involvement and the practice, practice, practice that is required to develop a complex skill like reading.

Vygotsky's zone of proximal development helps explain why dialogic reading is such an effective technique. As you know, Vygotsky believed children learn best when adults (or more skilled peers) expose them to ideas that are just a bit beyond where they are in their own development. When an adult is successful at keeping the dialogue and questioning during dialogic reading within the child's zone of proximal development, the interactions build on the child's existing skills and move the child to the next level of understanding. Techniques such as word-and-picture flash cards and workbooks that emphasize drill and basic skills acquisition are popular with some parents, especially those with less education (Neuman, Kaefer, Pinkham, & Strouse, 2014). However, these techniques separate acquiring specific literacy skills from the rich context of reading and do not provide the same sort of sensitive feedback and interaction that dialogic reading can provide. While techniques such as flash cards have helped low-achieving children and children with cognitive disabilities (Browder et al, 2006), most children can benefit from informal reading-related activities (Gerard, 2004).

The basic technique in dialogic reading is the PEER strategy. During the interaction with the child, the adults *prompt* the child to talk about the story, *evaluate* the child's response, *expand* upon it, and encourage the child to *repeat* the expanded utterances (Zevenbergen & Whitehurst, 2003). If you are looking at a book with a picture of several animals, you might *prompt* the child to respond by saying, "Do you see a kitty here?" If the child says, "Here's a kitty," you can say, "Yes [*the evaluation*], and she is sitting next to a doggie [*the expansion*]." To complete the sequence, ask the child to *repeat*, "The doggie is sitting next to the kitty." The goal is to ask questions that encourage the child to think about what she is seeing and to build her language skills in answer to your questions. Follow the directions in **Active Learning: Using Dialogic Reading** to see how you can use this approach when reading with a child.

Dialogic reading A technique used to facilitate early literacy, in which an adult and a child look at a book together while the adult asks questions and encourages a dialogue, followed by switching roles so the child asks questions of the adult.

T ☐ F ☐ Using flash cards and workbooks is the best way to ensure that a child develops early literacy skills. **False**

Active LEARNING

Using Dialogic Reading

Using the techniques of dialogic reading is a skill and requires practice. Use this opportunity to read to a young child (preferably a child who is 3 or 4 years old). If you choose a book you are familiar with (perhaps a favorite book from your own childhood), you will know the story well enough that you can focus your attention on providing prompts for the child. You might want to create a little "cheat sheet" for yourself with the following prompts before you begin, because when you are first using dialogic reading, you will probably find yourself stumped from time to time about what kind of prompt to use next.

(Continued)

(Continued)

- *Completion prompts* involve leaving a blank at the end of a sentence that the child can fill in: "When the girl went to the store, she bought a _____."

- *Recall prompts* ask the child for information about what has already been read: "Where did the little girl want to go?" or "Why was Emma feeling sad?"

- *Open-ended prompts* ask the child to describe what is happening in a picture.

- *W-prompts* are the *w*-questions that reporters use when gathering information for a story—*what, where, when, why,* and *how* (not a *w* word, but still important for gathering information): "*What* is Keisha going to do next?" or "*Why* is Larry excited?"

- *Distancing prompts* take the child out of the storybook to make her think about the real world: "This dog looks a lot like the dog that we saw at Aunt Cindy's house last week. Do you remember that dog? What did you like about him?" (Zevenbergen & Whitehurst, 2003).

ACTIVE LEARNING VIDEO ▲

Adults can engage children in the reading process by using the principles of dialogic reading.

If you practice this technique, creating these opportunities for learning will become quite natural to you. Finding that *zone of proximal development* and pitching your comments and questions to a child at just the right level to advance the child's understanding is what many parents, and all good teachers, do all the time.

To prepare for this activity, or, if you do not have access to a child, you can watch the video of this Active Learning.

Learning to Read in School

Children begin to acquire the skills of conventional literacy as they move from kindergarten to first grade. **Journey of Research: What's the Best Way to Learn to Read?** describes the approaches and debates that have surrounded the nature of reading instruction over the years.

JOURNEY OF *Research*

Phonics (or basic skills) approach An approach to teaching reading that starts with basic elements like letters and phonemes and teaches children that phonemes can be combined into words before moving on to reading as a whole.

What's the Best Way to Learn to Read?

There has been quite a debate over the years about which approach is the best one to use to teach children how to read. The two broad approaches that have been widely used are the **phonics (or basic skills) approach,** which focuses on letter-sound relationships, and **whole language instruction,** which focuses on using reading materials that are inherently interesting to the child (Education Week, 2004).

Children traditionally learned to read using what today is called *authentic literature*, such as the Bible or literary classics. However, in the 1930s, American schools began using basal readers to teach reading. Basal readers relied on word recognition. They contained a limited vocabulary (a first-grade reader used only 300 words) and a great deal of repetition (Moran, 2000) so that students could easily learn to recognize all of the words. New words were added slowly and repeated frequently after they were introduced.

Perhaps you are familiar with another children's book that uses this same look-say approach. Theodor Seuss Geisel (better known to us as Dr. Seuss) was asked by his publisher to create a children's primer that used only 225 "new reader" vocabulary words. The result was the publication in 1957 of one of the most popular children's books, *The Cat in the Hat* (Dr. Seuss Enterprises, n.d.).

However, basal readers fell out of favor in the 1970s as phonics became the dominant approach to teaching reading (Carbo, 1996). The phonics approach is a *bottom-up approach* because it starts with basic elements like letters and phonemes and moves up to words before moving on to reading as a whole (Armbruster, Lehr, & Osborn, 2001). With this approach, children learn that words are composed of separate sounds or phonemes and that phonemes can be combined into words (for example, you would learn the sounds associated with the letters *c* and *a* and *t* before you would combine those sounds into the word *cat*). Children learn that words can be sounded out by breaking them down into their phonemes (Texas Education Agency, 2004). Remember that phonemes are not the same as letters. It is equally important that children be able to break down a word like *chat* into its phonemes *ch – a – t*. Phonics places the emphasis on building these skills through exercises and practice. The phonics approach has been shown to be effective with at-risk students when they are first learning to read (Moustafa, 2001), and phonological skills are considered by many to be the best predictor of children's success in learning to read (Bingham & Pennington, 2007).

In the 1990s, however, the whole language approach gained favor over phonics in the educational community (Pearson, 2004). The whole language approach is a *top-down approach* that emphasizes understanding the meaning of words from the context in which they appear (Armbruster et al., 2001). Advocates for a whole language approach draw a parallel between this way of learning to read and the way that children naturally learn spoken language (Armbruster et al., 2001). In a language-rich environment, children first learn individual words to represent objects, actions, or desires and then learn to put the individual words together into meaningful sentences. In this view, the purpose of reading is to extract meaning from the text rather than to decode individual letters, phonemes, and syllables (Ryder, Tunmer, & Greaney, 2008).

The whole language approach returned to an emphasis on authentic literature that had an inherent interest for children rather than on books built around teaching a set of reading skills. However, this change did not always sit well with teachers who knew that students benefited from reading instruction and who recognized that it was not enough to immerse students in literature and expect them to figure out the principles of reading on their own. Not only did reading suffer, but so did the students' mastery of subject content because many had difficulty reading textbooks (Pearson, 2004). By the end of the 1990s, the effectiveness of the whole language approach was being questioned, both by politicians who were emphasizing accountability in schools and by educators who were critical of the negative effect this approach had on students' performance in subjects other than reading.

In 1997, the National Institute of Child Health and Human Development, together with the U.S. Department of Education, convened a panel of reading experts who were charged to survey the scientific literature on reading. The panel conducted a meta-analysis of

Whole language instruction A way to teach reading that emphasizes understanding the meaning of words from the context in which they appear.

(Continued)

(Continued)

38 studies and reached the conclusion that there was "solid support for the conclusion that systematic phonics instruction makes a more significant contribution to children's growth in reading than do alternative programs providing unsystematic or no phonics instruction" (National Reading Panel, 2000, Section 2, p. 45). The report almost immediately came under criticism (see Camilli, Vargas, & Yurecko, 2003; Garan, 2001; Shanahan, 2004; Yatvin, 2002).

Where do we stand today? Although there still is controversy about which approach is best, there is increasing support for a **balanced reading approach** that combines elements of both the whole language and the phonics approaches (Donat, 2006). Children need "effective, early instruction in phonology and oral language; in word recognition and reading fluency; and in comprehension and writing skills" (Moats, 2007, p. 1). Children also need access to interesting books and the motivation to read them. In one international study, children whose schools had large libraries had significantly higher reading scores than those who did not (Krashen, 2009). One thing is for sure: More reading leads to better reading, so the more that students enjoy and take part in reading, the higher their level of reading will be. Basic instruction in phonics along with enjoyable and comprehensible books are likely to promote good reading.

Balanced reading approach An approach to teaching reading that combines elements of the whole language approach (which emphasizes comprehension and meaning) with elements of the phonics approach (which emphasizes decoding of words).

Phonological awareness The understanding that words are made up of a combination of individual sounds.

Learning to read depends on two basic skills: decoding written letters and understanding the words and sentences (Lonigan, 2006). As we've discussed, an environment rich in language helps children develop vocabulary and also the ability to read and comprehend what they are reading. However, decoding written letters is also essential. **Phonological awareness** is the understanding that words are made up of a combination of individual sounds. Children can learn about the sounds of words through rhyming games, playing with words that sound alike, and making up silly words. By age 4 or 5, children can learn that *hat* and *cat* rhyme, but neither one rhymes with the word *log*. Once children are capable of sounding out words they will develop a number of sight words they quickly recognize, and these words contribute to reading fluency and comprehension. Children who successfully learn to read find it enjoyable and do more of it, but for children who have difficulty with learning to read, a downward path develops when they avoid it and then never build up the practice necessary to read fluently. It is easier to prevent these problems than to overcome them later on, so the emergent literacy experiences we described earlier are important. Key emergent literacy skills that predict which preschoolers are likely to have an easier time learning to read include oral language, phonological awareness, and print knowledge, such as knowing how to hold a book and the direction in which the letters are read (Lonigan, 2006).

Results from the 2015 National Assessment of Educational Progress showed that both fourth- and eighth-grade students had higher reading scores than students in 1992. However, the last national assessment for twelfth graders in 2012 showed reading levels that did not differ from those found at the very first assessment in 1971. The bad news is that 24% of eighth graders and 28% of twelfth graders were reading below the basic level for their grade (National Center for Education Statistics [NCES], 2015b; The Nation's Report Card, 2012). These findings show that the majority of students are reading at least at grade level, but clearly there is more work to be done to help those who are not.

T ☐ F ☐ About one in four eighth graders is reading below the basic level for their grade. **True**

WRITING SKILLS

Even very young children love to take a crayon or marker and "write" a letter or story. The earliest writing skills (similar to what we saw for the development of reading skills) are basic:

TABLE 9.5

Writing skills in three different language groups. If you've learned to write in English, writing letters and words from left to right probably feels very normal and natural to you, but for children learning to write in these other languages, it feels normal and natural to write from right to left or from top to bottom.

Language Groups	Direction of Writing	What Each Symbol Represents	Number of Symbols in Alphabet	Example From the First Language Listed in Each Group
English, French, Spanish	Left to right	Each letter represents a sound.	26 26 27	I speak and write English. ———————→
Hebrew, Arabic, Persian/Farsi	Right to left	Each letter represents a consonant; added marks represent vowels.	22 28 32	אני מדבר ולכתוב בעברית. ←———————
Chinese, Japanese, Korean	Top to bottom, then right to left; or it can be written horizontally left to right	Each character represents a word or part of a word.	Thousands	我会说和写中文. ———————→ or 我会说和写中文. (vertical)

Children understand that writing moves from left to right (in English-speaking countries), from the top of the page down, and that it is meant to convey information. But the process of writing differs for different languages. Table 9.5 shows some of the ways that writing occurs around the world.

Remember from Chapter 6 that children develop their fine motor skills as they develop motor control that moves down their arms to their fingers. As their fine motor skills improve, they can begin to write recognizable letters. Figure 9.4 is an example of how writing skills develop in young English-speaking children. Children love being able to write their own names and often master this skill even before they enter school. As further fine motor development occurs, they can move on to more writing, including the ability to write in cursive. (You can refresh your memory about the controversy about the benefits of keyboarding vs. cursive writing in Chapter 6.)

Young children will sound out familiar words and they often begin to invent their own spelling of words based on how the words sound. The results may initially be incomprehensible—for example, a child might write *train* as *chran*—but this first writing is the basis for further learning about spelling and writing. Contrary to what some adults think, using invented spelling does not slow down or prevent a young child from learning conventional spelling. In fact, it can even help them with the task of learning to read (Sénéchal, Ouellette, Pagan, & Lever, 2012).

In the early elementary grades, children begin to learn and apply conventional spelling rules (such as adding the suffix -ed to a word to form the past tense) and to learn more

T ☐ F ☐ When young children use spelling that they have "invented" (rather than conventional spelling), it slows down their ability to learn how to spell correctly. **False**

FIGURE 9.4

Early writing. This writing sample from a prekindergarten child shows how much progress is made in just a few short months. Children take great pride in learning how to write their names.

This is how I write my name:	This is how I write my name:	This is how I write my name:
September 2007	December 2007	February 2008

SOURCE: Cox (2010). Reprinted with permission.

Knowledge telling A style of writing (typical of younger children) in which the writer proceeds with little or no evidence of planning or organization of ideas, with the goal of telling as much as she knows about a topic.

Knowledge transforming A type of writing in which the goal is to convey a deeper understanding of a subject by taking information and transforming it into ideas that can be shared with a reader.

TRUE/FALSE VIDEO ▲

T □ F □ Students who do a lot of texting and those who do not text a lot do not differ from each other on their ability to spell or use Standard English.
True

about the typical patterns of occurrence of certain letters in their written language (Kemp & Bryant, 2003). The eventual goal is for the process of spelling to become automatic so that the retrieval of information on how to spell a word is very quick and very accurate. There is some evidence that the physical process of writing itself helps children to memorize the way words are spelled (Bosse, 2015).

However, writing is more than correctly shaping letters on a piece of paper or stringing words together. We use writing to communicate our ideas, so writing also must include composition skills. Children in the early elementary grades may write about a topic by simply tying together a series of statements that describe the facts, but there is an important difference between this **knowledge telling** and the **knowledge transforming** that adolescents and adults do (Alamargot & Chanquoy, 2001). When you rely on knowledge telling, you show little or no evidence of planning or organization of ideas with the goal of telling as much as you know about the topic you are writing on. In knowledge transforming, however, the goal becomes to take information and transform it into *ideas* that you can share with your reader so that the reader understands and learns from them. It attempts to convey a deep understanding of the subject. However, the fact that teenagers are capable of doing this does not mean that they necessarily do it.

In recent years, electronic communication, such as texting, has influenced teens' written language. Teens report sending a median of 30 texts a day, with older teen girls between ages 15 and 17 sending 60 texts a day, far outdistancing any other form of daily communication they use (Pew Research Center, 2015). Because communicators try to make interactions as efficient as possible, they have developed shorthand methods, such as substituting the well-known *LOL* for *laugh out loud* and *u* for *you*. Although some have expressed concern that the continual use of texting abbreviations will negatively affect a young person's ability to spell or write Standard English, this does not appear to be the case (Varnhagen et al., 2010). When a group of college students who were regular users of "text speak" were compared to other college students who were not, there was no significant difference between the groups on tests of their literacy level or ability to correctly spell words they abbreviate when texting (Drouin & Davis, 2009). However, these shortcuts do occasionally sneak into students' written school papers, so it is important for students to learn when it is appropriate to use them and when it is not.

While teens who text or use other brief modes of communication do not do more writing than other teens, the situation is different in regard to blogging. About 28% of teens maintain a personal blog (Rideout, Foehr, & Roberts, 2010), and blogging appears to promote more writing among teens. Of those who have a blog, 47% write outside of school assignments for their own personal reasons, while only 33% of teens without blogs do so. In addition, 65% of bloggers believe writing is important for their later success, while only 53% of nonbloggers hold this belief (National Writing Project, 2014).

According to the most recent report of the National Assessment of Educational Progress (NAEP, 2012), in 2011, 20% of eighth graders and 21% of twelfth graders performed below the basic level in writing for their grade. University and business leaders alike are concerned about the number of high school graduates who do not have good writing skills. A survey by the National Commission on Writing (2004) gathered information from the human resource directors of 120 major U.S. companies. Half the respondents said they take writing into consideration when hiring an employee (especially salaried employees) and that an applicant who submits a poorly written application might not be considered for any position. They also reported that two-thirds of salaried employees have some responsibility for writing as part of their job and that communicating clearly plays a role in promotion and retention. One respondent to the survey succinctly said, "You can't move up without writing skills" (p. 3). The National Commission on Writing concluded that employees' writing deficiencies cost U.S. businesses as much as $3.3 billion a year. Although teens may have their own ways of talking and writing, when they enter the business world they need to have a good set of language and writing skills if they expect to be successful.

Teen communication. Many adolescents use their cell phones to text their friends. Although texting uses a lot of abbreviations and special terminology, it fortunately doesn't seem to interfere with adolescents' ability to use Standard English.

CHECK YOUR UNDERSTANDING

1. What skills are important when children begin to write?
2. What role does invented spelling play in learning to write?
3. Compare knowledge telling and knowledge transforming.
4. How has electronic communication affected teens' writing skills?

BILINGUALISM AND BILINGUAL EDUCATION

TRUE/FALSE VIDEO ▲

9.6 What are some consequences of being bilingual as a child? What types of education programs are used for children who do not speak English?

GROWING UP BILINGUAL

Learning to speak a language is a complex cognitive task, so learning to speak two different languages is even more cognitively complex. For this reason, parents sometimes wonder whether being bilingual is so demanding that it will hurt a child's overall cognitive development. Fortunately, this does not appear to be the case and there is evidence that in some ways bilingualism may actually enhance cognitive abilities. Many people around the world speak more than one language, and a growing body of research on bilingualism indicates that

T ☐ F ☐ When a young child learns two languages at the same time, the extra effort it takes to learn the second language slows down the child's general cognitive development. **False** parents do *not* need to worry about having their children learn two languages at the same time at an early age (Bialystok & Viswanathan, 2009; Kovács & Mehler, 2009).

There is no clear evidence that being bilingual negatively impacts the size of a child's vocabulary (De Houwer, Bornstein, & Putnick, 2014; Silvén, Voeten, Kouvo, & Lundén, 2014) and bilingual children reach language milestones at approximately the same age as monolinguals (Petitto et al., 2001). One advantage of learning a second language at a young age is that it makes it more likely that the child will speak it without a detectable accent and will be proficient at using the language (Huang, 2014). In addition, bilingual children and adults seem to have some cognitive advantage in the area of executive function. Barac and Bialystok (2012) reported that bilingual 6-year-old children demonstrated more skill than monolingual children on tasks that required the ability to inhibit a response when necessary and the ability to be cognitively flexible and to shift focus from one task to another. These abilities begin to develop much earlier in bilingual children. Differences in executive function even appear in preverbal infants who are from bilingual homes. After infants from monolingual and bilingual homes learned to anticipate an event based on a verbal clue, when the clue was changed, the infants from bilingual homes were able to more easily shift to a new response (Kovács & Mehler, 2009). Older bilingual children have an advantage in solving problems that require the child to ignore irrelevant or misleading information to solve the problem correctly, have greater mental flexibility and greater creativity, are better at scientific problem solving, and have better concept formation (Andreou & Karapetsas, 2004; Bialystok, 2001). They have metalinguistic skills that allow them to understand and think about language in a more advanced way, including having an understanding of the relative nature of language (for instance, they understand that the same object can be called by different names in different languages).

BILINGUAL EDUCATION

Thus far, we have described children who are already competent in two languages, but there are over 4.6 million children in the United States for whom English is not the first language, or the language spoken in their home or neighborhood. The vast majority of children in this country with limited English proficiency speak Spanish as their first language, followed by Vietnamese, Chinese, Hmong, and Arabic (U.S. Department of Education, 2015). When these children get to school, they are generally expected to understand and speak English. There has been much debate about what is the best way to help ensure that these bilingual learners will be successful in school. See **Journey of Research: Bilingual Education—Sink or Swim?** for a closer look at how our approach to teaching children who are learning English has developed over time.

JOURNEY OF *Research*

Bilingual Education—Sink or Swim?

Research on bilingual education is embedded in political, philosophical, and social contexts. How we have approached teaching children who are not native speakers of English has reflected the historical context at the time. At times, our educational system has accommodated bilingualism, at times there has been opposition to it, and at still other times it has been largely ignored (Menken & Solorza, 2014).

The earliest known bilingual education in this country occurred in the 17th century. The colony of Virginia needed Polish settlers to work on shipbuilding and glassworks, so they allowed them to set up bilingual schools in the colony (Goldenberg & Wagner, 2015). In the 18th and 19th centuries, immigrants often lived in their own communities and ran their own schools in which instruction was given in their native language (Public Broadcasting Service [PBS], 2001), but by the end of the 1800s, the tide had started to turn. For instance, Native Americans were forbidden to be taught in their native language, and laws were passed requiring that classes be taught in English. This trend was amplified when the United States entered World War I and concerns about the loyalty of non-English speakers provoked hostility against people who spoke German. Eventually this hostility became hostility against the use of any minority language in schools. By the mid-1920s, virtually all bilingual education in public schools had been eliminated (PBS, 2001).

The tide turned again, this time in favor of bilingualism, in the 1960s against a backdrop of desegregation in public schools, the civil rights movement (Crawford, 1995), and the sharp increase in the number of immigrants arriving in the country. By the mid-1960s, immigrant populations were increasingly demanding instruction in their native language and the incorporation of their culture into the curriculum. In response, the federal government passed the Bilingual Education Act of 1968, which provided $85 million over 3 years to create equal educational opportunity for nonnative speakers, even if that meant that different learning environments had to be provided for them (Petrzela, 2010). The legislation argued that children were being deprived of an education if they were taught in a language they did not understand (Cromwell, 1998). A second goal of this legislation was to recognize and respect nonnative students' cultures and the cultural pluralism in our society (Cromwell, 1998).

In the years that followed, the need for language services for children who were not native English speakers continued to grow. By the 1980s, 40% of the U.S. population consisted of minority-language speakers (PBS, 2001). Today an estimated 5 million children with limited English proficiency are enrolled in U.S. schools, and they are the fastest-growing segment of the school-age population (Uro & Barrio, 2013).

This increase in the number of nonnative speakers, together with a growing dissatisfaction about the progress that the students were making in learning English in bilingual classes, provoked another backlash that resulted in several pieces of state legislation in the 1980s and 1990s that again eliminated bilingual education or prohibited expenditures for classes in any language other than English (PBS, 2001). In 2001, the federal Office of Bilingual Education and Minority Language Affairs became the Office of English Language Acquisition, emphasizing the goal of learning English rather than promoting bilingualism (Goldenberg & Wagner, 2015).

In recent years, the pendulum has begun to swing back toward adopting bilingual programs. In addition to promoting English for nonnative speaking children, programs have been developed to promote native languages together with English. For instance, the Hawaiian Language Immersion program was established in 1987 and a new program in Montana will fund Native American language immersion programs (Goldenberg & Wagner, 2015). Many states are promoting bilingualism by awarding a Seal of Biliteracy to high school students who have studied and attained proficiency in two or more languages by the time they graduate high school. Currently 19 states and Washington DC offer this seal, and 14 more are considering it (Seal of Biliteracy, 2016). It is against this shifting backdrop of social change that research on bilingual education has been conducted.

Programs designed to teach English to children who are not native speakers have taken a variety of forms in the United States. Some of the most common types of programs are:

- **Immersion programs** in which the students are taught academic subjects in English, with teachers tailoring the language they use to the current language level of their students.

- **English as a second language (ESL) pull-out programs** in which students spend part of the day in a separate classroom designed specifically to teach English and there is no accommodation for their native language in their regular classrooms.

- **Transitional bilingual education programs** in which the students receive some instruction in their native language while they also receive concentrated instruction in learning English. The goal of transitional programs is to prepare the students to *transition* to regular classes in English as soon as possible, so they do not fall behind their peers in content areas such as math, science, and social studies.

- **Developmental bilingual programs** that build on students' skills in their native language while they learn English as a second language. Students initially receive instructions in the core subjects in their native language but receive instruction in art, physical education, and music in English. As soon as they have sufficient skills, English is used for their instruction in the core subjects as well. Students typically remain in these programs longer than in traditional transition programs, but they continue learning English throughout their time in the program.

- **Two-way immersion programs**, less frequently used than other alternatives, place children who are native speakers of English with children who are nonnative speakers. The children work together in a classroom where *both* majority and minority languages are used. This type of program requires highly trained and skilled teachers who can support the development of both languages for their students in a language-integrated classroom (Department of Education, 2013).

It has been difficult to determine which approach might be considered best or most effective. Many programs are not pure forms of the approaches we have just described, so it becomes difficult to compare and evaluate programs that are actually hybrids of several approaches (Guglielmi, 2008). The intended goal of such programs has shifted from time to time as well, so the assessment of program effectiveness must change with the goal. For instance, if the goal is to assimilate recent immigrants into the American language and culture, an immersion approach fits well with that goal. On the other hand, if the goal is to promote multiculturalism, a dual language approach fits well with that goal (Ginn, 2008). Rather than trying to find a one-size-fits-all solution, research needs to identify a range of educational approaches that can be tailored to the characteristics of the children in a specific community, while taking into account local needs and the resources available to support the language program.

CULTURE, IDENTITY, AND BILINGUALISM

When families immigrate to a different country, they bring their culture and their language with them. Although the vast majority of parents want their children to learn the new language in order to succeed in their adopted country, many parents also want their children to maintain the language of their country of origin, referred to as their *heritage language* (Krogstad & Gonzalez-Barrera, 2015). Having children and adolescents who speak the heritage language is one important way for them to identify with the culture of their family and it does not interfere with their proficiency in English (Tsai, Park, Liu, & Lau, 2012). Parents with a strong cultural identity are more likely to speak their heritage language with their children and, as a result, the children are more likely to be bilingual. However, the heritage

---

Immersion programs Programs in which English language learners are taught academic subjects in English.

English as a second language (ESL) pull-out programs Programs in which students are taught English in a separate classroom.

Transitional bilingual education programs Programs for English language learners in which students receive some instruction in their native language while they also receive concentrated instruction in learning English.

Developmental bilingual programs Programs in which English language learners receive instruction in core subjects in their native language until they have the language skills to be instructed in English.

Two-way immersion programs Programs in which children who are native speakers of English and children who are not work together in a classroom where both English and the children's other native language are used.

language can be easily lost. For example, only one-fifth of American-born children of Chinese immigrants speak Chinese well (Tsai et al., 2012).

Research has shown that use of the heritage language is greatly decreased by the third generation living in the new country even where there are large groups of immigrants from the same culture living together, such as Mexican Americans in Southern California (Rumbaut, Massey, & Bean, 2006). In 2014, 88% of Latino youth in the United States say they speak English very well and 37% reported that they speak only English at home (Krogstad, 2016). Most also believe that knowing Spanish is not necessary to keep their Latino identity. The majority of Latino teens report also speaking a combination language, known as Spanglish (Krogstad & Gonzalez-Barrera, 2015). One consequence of these changes is that children become unable to communicate with their grandparents who generally find it more difficult to learn English and with family members who stayed in their country of origin, making it harder to transmit cultural information, values, and make meaningful personal connections (Mejia & Carcamo, 2016). You will learn more about the development of ethnic identity in Chapter 11.

Bilingual classrooms. Many children in U.S. classrooms speak more than one language. The American educational system has adapted to this diversity through a variety of programs designed to teach English as a second language (ESL).

CHECK YOUR UNDERSTANDING

1. What cognitive advantages are associated with being bilingual?
2. Describe the various types of bilingual education programs.
3. How does the native language of immigrants relate to their ethnic identity?

LANGUAGE DISORDERS

9.7 What types of language disorders can children have?

When children have difficulty with language, it can affect them academically, socially, and emotionally. In this section, we describe four types of communication disorders. We then discuss the unique language difficulties encountered by children with autism spectrum disorder. Finally, we describe dyslexia, the specific learning disorder linked with written language.

COMMUNICATION DISORDERS

Children vary widely in the age at which they reach language milestones. However, when children begin school, teachers, and other school staff may recognize language-related problems that have gone unnoticed to that point or that need continued attention. The DSM-5 (APA, 2013) identifies several communication disorders that affect children's ability to listen, speak, and use language in their social communications and in school:

Language disorder A disorder in which a child's understanding and use of language is significantly below his nonverbal intelligence.

Speech sound disorder Difficulty producing or using sounds at an age-appropriate level.

Childhood-onset fluency disorder or stuttering Difficulty with fluency and time patterning of speech.

Social or pragmatic communication disorder Difficulty with appropriate use of both verbal and nonverbal communication.

- A **language disorder** causes both the child's understanding of language (receptive) and the ability to use language (expressive) to be substantially below norms for his age. The child has a limited vocabulary and has difficulty using tense correctly, recalling words, or producing sentences of the length and complexity expected of a child of that age. In addition, the child has difficulty describing an event or topic and holding a conversation.

- A **speech sound disorder** causes difficulty producing sounds or using sounds correctly for the child's age (for example, the child substitutes one sound for another). As a result, the child's speech is difficult to understand and this interferes with social and academic skills.

- A **childhood-onset fluency disorder or stuttering** is a disorder in which the child has difficulty with fluency and time patterning of speech. The child may repeat sounds or syllables, repeat whole words, pause within a word, or pause in speech.

- A **social or pragmatic communication disorder** results in difficulty with both verbal and nonverbal communication. The child does not use communication appropriately in different situations. For example, the child does not greet others, does not change the way she communicates to a young child or to an adult, has trouble taking conversational turns or explaining misunderstandings, and cannot understand humor or metaphors that rely on multiple meanings of the same word.

Any child (or adult, for that matter) might show any of these language problems from time to time, but we wouldn't consider this a disorder unless the problems are persistent, the child's language is substantially below that expected for a child of the same age, and the problem interferes with other aspects of the child's life, such as her ability to communicate with others or her performance in school. Because some studies have found that language disorders are associated with difficulties in parent-child interaction and in social-emotional development, it is important that we identify and treat them as early as possible so that secondary problems do not develop (Desmarais, Sylvestre, Meyer, Bairati, & Rouleau, 2008).

AUTISM SPECTRUM DISORDER

In Chapter 6, you learned about the criteria for a diagnosis of autism spectrum disorder (ASD). Language development plays a central role in diagnosing this disorder, so we continue the description of ASD that we began there with an examination of the communication aspects of the disorder. They include difficulties with verbal and nonverbal communication that range from a complete lack of speech to impaired use of speech for social interaction (APA, 2013).

One of the earliest indications that a child may have ASD is that the child does not reach early milestones in language development, such as using single words by 16 months or combining two words by 2 years of age. Some autistic children may not babble or make meaningful gestures, such as pointing to things that they want, or they may not respond to their name, but other children with ASD coo and babble normally although their language doesn't develop from that point forward. Some autistic children remain mute throughout their lives, but others develop some language, although they may do it at an unusually late age (between 5 and 9 years) (NIMH, 2009). The child may know a number of words (in some cases even having an unusually large vocabulary) but may use single words over and over again or be unable to combine the words he does have into meaningful sentences. Some autistic children have **echolalia**, a condition in which they repeat what they hear (like an echo). For example, a parent asks a child, "What do you want, Johnny?" and the child responds, "What do you want, Johnny?" rather than answering the parent's question. Any child may do this when they are first learning a language, but the echolalia persists for

Echolalia When children repeat what has been said to them instead of responding appropriately.

children on the autism spectrum. Autistic children also may reply to questions in a way that is not responsive. For instance, if you ask a child if he would like something to drink, he might count from one to five for you. Sometimes children on the autism spectrum respond in social situations with "scripts" for what they should say or do. For example, the autistic child may introduce herself by saying, "Hello, my name is Josephine," even though you have met this child many times before and know that her name is Josephine. She has learned that this is the polite way to respond when meeting someone so she always uses it.

Autistic children also have difficulty with many of the skills that are part of what goes on in our typical day-to-day conversations with other people. Try **Active Learning: Observing Conversation Skills** to sharpen your understanding of the skills necessary to carry on an effective conversation. These skills are part of what we called the *pragmatics of language* at the beginning of this chapter.

Active LEARNING

Observing Conversation Skills

You may not have thought about how many social skills we use when we engage in a conversation. All of these skills work together to give meaning to what we are saying and to ensure that we are actually communicating by exchanging information when we talk to each other.

Find some place where you can watch people who know each other engage in conversation. A cafeteria on your campus or a student study lounge would be good places to do this. If you do this activity in class, you can have some students be partners for this exercise by engaging in a conversation while other students conduct the observations. To reduce some of the awkwardness, give the students a topic to discuss. It can be something as simple as talking about the weather last week, something that has happened on your campus recently, or their opinions about whether we should ask for paper or plastic when we shop for our groceries (the topic doesn't matter very much, as long as it is not too controversial because we want to observe a conversation, not an argument).

As the participants talk, for 3 to 5 minutes try to carefully observe all the things that they do to sustain that conversation and to communicate effectively. When you have a list, compare it to the description of conversational clues that follow in the text. How many of them did you notice and include in your notes?

In the United States, conversation is often marked by eye contact between the individuals who are talking. They may smile and nod when they agree with each other or frown if they do not agree. What we say is usually tied to our facial expression and our body language because we are integrated human beings, and all those pieces go together in a way that makes sense. Most of the time, one person waits for the other person to finish talking before adding something to the conversation. They take turns speaking and usually don't interrupt or speak over the other person. They also try to keep the conversation going by adding new information to what has already been said or by asking questions about what the previous

Robin Nelson/PhotoEdit

Building language skills. This special education teacher is coaching an autistic boy to use sign language to compensate for the problems he has with spoken language.

speaker has said. They keep an appropriate distance between each other (and what is appropriate depends on the culture you are in and the intimacy of the relationship). Friends often sit closer together than strangers or classmates who are talking to each other. Facial expressions, gestures, and body language fit the topic of the conversation. If the speakers are joking, their faces reflect their amusement, and they may throw their heads back and laugh out loud. If they are discussing something distressing or serious, they may hunch over, bite their nails, or play with their fingers. If someone is sharing a concern or talking about a disappointment, the other person may reach out to touch his arm or back in consolation. If the topic changes from one thing to another, one of the speakers probably indicates that a new topic is being introduced into the conversation by saying something like "By the way . . ." or "What do you think about . . . ?" We also usually clearly indicate when the conversation is over by saying something like "I've got to get to class now" or "I'll see you later."

As you read through the previous paragraph, the content probably seemed very commonsense and familiar. It may have been *so* familiar that you didn't even make note of some of these things if you carried out the observation in the **Active Learning** feature. Now think for a moment how difficult it would be to have a conversation if the person you were speaking to didn't look you in the eye when you spoke, didn't respond to what you said or responded in a way that didn't relate to what you had just said, didn't show any facial expressions or use any gestures, or used expressions and gestures that were inappropriate for what he was saying (NIMH, 2009). These are all difficulties with the pragmatics of language that are frequently seen in autistic children.

When autistic children fail to develop language or gestures (such as sign language) to express what they want or need, they may resort to simply grabbing what they want or screaming (NIMH, 2009). As they grow up and increasingly realize they have difficulty understanding others and making themselves understood, they may become depressed or anxious (NIMH, 2009). Anger, depression, and anxiety are not symptoms of autism itself. They are secondary consequences of living with this disorder and the challenges it brings with it.

DYSLEXIA: A LANGUAGE-BASED LEARNING DISORDER

Dyslexia A learning disorder marked by difficulty reading as a result of problems with decoding written language.

As you learned in Chapter 8, *specific learning disorder* is a broad term that encompasses a number of different types of learning problems. According to the DSM-5, **dyslexia** is a language-based learning disorder in which there is a "pattern of learning difficulties characterized by problems with accurate or fluent word recognition, poor decoding, and poor spelling abilities" (APA, 2013, p. 67). In most cases, it does not involve reversing letters or seeing words jump around on a page, and it is not a problem with the child's vision. Problems with earlier language development precede the development of dyslexia for about half of the children with this disorder (Snowling, 2012). About 3% to 10% of school-age children have difficulties with decoding written language, the hall-mark of developmental dyslexia (Duff & Clarke, 2011).

The possibility that genes play a role in the development of dyslexia comes from studies suggesting specific learning disorders run in families and from twin studies. Children who have dyslexia are 4 to 8 times more likely to have parents or other close relatives who have the disorder, and monozygotic twins are more similar in their likelihood of having this diagnosis than are dizygotic twins (APA, 2013; Kovas et al., 2007). Other possible causes include damage experienced in the prenatal environment, an injury during the birth process, or a serious illness or injury shortly after birth. It is also possible for extremely poor nutrition or exposure to environmental toxins to play a role (National Institute of Child Health and Human Development, 2012).

Dyslexia is considered a neurodevelopmental disorder, meaning that the function and structure of the brain play a role in its development (APA, 2013). The brains of people with dyslexia are wired in such a way that they have difficulty processing the sounds of words. The left hemisphere of the brain is usually active when we read, but for individuals with dyslexia, the brain shows more activity in the right hemisphere (Breier et al., 2002). Because the right hemisphere is ordinarily used to process new or novel information, this suggests that dyslexics find reading to be more of a novel task than a familiar one (Semrud-Clikeman, 2014). Structurally, the connection between Broca's area of the brain, which aids speech production, and Wernicke's area, which supports our understanding of written or spoken language, is smaller in kindergartners who have poorer awareness of the sound of letters, a hallmark of dyslexia (Saygin et al., 2013; see also Boets et al., 2013).

Reading can be a struggle. Many children take great pleasure in being able to read, but for a child with a specific learning disorder, reading can be a day-to-day struggle. Children with an identified specific learning disorder such as dyslexia can receive special services in their schools.

It is important to identify children with this disorder before their avoidance of reading becomes firmly established. Training that is part of a comprehensive literacy curriculum can benefit many children with reading difficulties. Some evidence suggests that systematic training in phonics can improve a child's reading skills, although the size of the effect may not be large (Browder et al., 2006; Duff & Clarke, 2011), and even when reading accuracy improves, there may continue to be long-term problems with reading fluency and spelling (Snowling & Hulme, 2011).

CHECK YOUR UNDERSTANDING

1. What types of communication disorders are described in the DSM-5?
2. How does autism spectrum disorder affect a child's ability to use language and communicate?
3. What difficulties does a child with dyslexia have?

CONCLUSION

Language is essential to the human experience. We connect with other people and communicate our ideas, feelings, and needs with language. We also use language to understand the world. Infants and toddlers around the world seem to go through the same stages in learning language, and by age 3 or 4, most are able to speak fairly clearly to those around them. Language development does not end in preschool. All five aspects of language (phonology, morphology, syntax, semantics, and pragmatics) continue to develop and become more complex and sophisticated through adolescence. Children must also learn to decipher written language if they live in a literate society. Many children grow up speaking more than one language, and this appears to create some cognitive advantage. However, bilingual education has been promoted at times and rejected at other times throughout the history of this country. When children have difficulty with language development, as in the case of autism or a specific learning disorder, it is imperative that parents, teachers, and other professionals take all necessary steps to ensure that children achieve the highest level they can attain. Language is just one aspect of a child's cognitive development, but it is a central one in most societies around the world.

CHAPTER SUMMARY

Test your understanding of the content.
Take the practice quiz at **edge.sagepub.com/levine3e**

9.1 What are five basic aspects of language?

Language includes **phonology** (the sounds that make up the language), **morphology** (the way words are formed from these sounds and how these words are related to other words), **syntax** (the grammar of the language), **semantics** (the meanings of words), and **pragmatics** (how we use language in social situations to communicate).

9.2 What parts of the brain are specialized for language?

Broca's area is important for the production of speech, and **Wernicke's area** is important for understanding and making sense out of speech. However, other areas of the brain also contribute to aspects of language perception and production.

9.3 What are the basic theories about how children develop language?

Behaviorism emphasizes the role of reinforcement in the environment as a way to motivate and shape children's language development, while social cognitive theory emphasizes the role of imitation of the language that children hear. **Nativism** emphasizes the role of biology by explaining language development as a result of a **universal grammar** that gives our brains an inborn capacity to learn language. **Interactionism** brings these ideas together by stating that children's biological readiness to learn language must work together with their experiences with language in their environment to bring about language development. **Cognitive processing theory** emphasizes the "data crunching" capacity of the human brain, suggesting that infants statistically analyze the speech they hear in order to figure out language.

9.4 How does language develop from before birth through adolescence?

Children move through stages of language development, but there is a good deal of variability from child to child in the age at which each milestone appears. Even before birth, the fetus hears and discriminates the sounds of language. Before they can use words, infants communicate by crying, **cooing, babbling,** and gesturing. Infants and toddlers begin verbalizing by using one word at a time (usually nouns in English-speaking cultures) and then create primitive sentences when they put two words together. When children make sentences that contain only the essential words (for example, *Mommy ride car*), this is called **telegraphic speech. Fast mapping** allows children to add words rapidly to their vocabulary (often after a single exposure). Children build vocabulary through the use of several assumptions and principles called **constraints** as well as **syntactic bootstrapping** and **semantic bootstrapping.** Preschoolers make multiword sentences using grammar that is very close to that of adults, but they continue to make mistakes because they tend to apply rules in cases where the rules won't work (called **overregularization**). **Metalinguistic ability** develops as older children begin to think about language in and of itself. With this ability, they can understand that a word is different from what it represents. One outcome is that they are able to understand jokes that are based on changing word meanings. Adolescents' speech is more complex in grammar and in subject matter than children's speech, and it differs from adult speech in the use of slang.

9.5 How do children learn to read and write?

Emergent literacy refers to the set of skills that young children develop before formal instruction in reading.

Adults can use **dialogic reading** to talk with young children about the books they are reading together to build the child's language skills. Once children enter school, a **balanced reading approach** combines training in **phonological awareness** with word recognition, reading fluency, and comprehension. Young children move from scribbling to forming letters and then words. In school they may move from invented spelling to learning the rules of conventional spelling, until writing becomes an automatic process they don't have to think about. When writing, young children string ideas together with little organization, called **knowledge telling,** but adolescents become capable of writing to convey ideas and deeper understanding of a subject, called **knowledge transforming.**

9.6 What are some consequences of being bilingual as a child? What types of education programs are used for children who do not speak English?

Bilingual children do not generally have any difficulties associated with their use of two languages, and there is some evidence that they may have some advantages over monolingual children, such as showing more advanced executive functioning. The five types of bilingual education programs are (a) **immersion programs,** which teach students only in English; (b) **English as a second language (ESL) pull-out programs,** in which students spend part of the day in a separate classroom learning English and there is no accommodation for their native language in their regular classrooms; (c) **transitional bilingual education programs,** which teach students in their native language while providing concentrated instruction in learning

English; (d) **developmental bilingual programs,** which initially teach core subjects in the students' native language and other instruction in English, and then switch to all English as the students' skills develop; and (e) **two-way immersion programs,** in which children who are native speakers of English and children who are nonnative speakers work together in a classroom where *both* languages are used. In practice, however, programs seldom are pure examples of these types. Instead they may incorporate various elements of these program types into a unique program.

9.7 What types of language disorders can children have?

Communication disorders include a **language disorder** in which a child's receptive and expressive language is substantially below norms for the child's age, a **speech sound disorder** which causes difficulty producing sounds or using sounds correctly, a **childhood-onset fluency disorder** or **stuttering,** and a **social** or **pragmatic communication disorder** in which the child does not use communication appropriately in different situations. Children with autism spectrum disorder often have serious difficulties with speech that can range from a lack of any language, to **echolalia** (in which children repeat what is said to them instead of responding), to difficulties with using language appropriately in social situations. **Dyslexia** is a specific learning disorder in which children have difficulty distinguishing or separating sounds and as a consequence they experience problems when learning to spell and read written words.

KEY TERMS

Strengthen your understanding of these key terms with mobile-friendly eFlashcards at **edge.sagepub.com/levine3e**

Give your students the SAGE edge!

SAGE edge offers a robust online environment featuring an impressive array of free tools and resources for review, study, and further exploration, keeping both instructors and students on the cutting edge of teaching and learning. Learn more at **edge.sagepub.com/levine3e**

aldomurillo/E+/Getty Images
Jose Luis Pelaez Inc/Blend Images/Getty Images
M.Kolchins/Moment/Getty Images
Rob Lewine/Image Source/Getty Images

PART IV

SOCIAL AND EMOTIONAL DEVELOPMENT

chapter 10

EMOTIONAL DEVELOPMENT AND ATTACHMENT

KidStock / Blend Images / Getty Images

LEARNING QUESTIONS

10.1 What is emotion and how do biology and culture shape our emotions?

10.2 What is temperament?

10.3 How do children learn to regulate and control their emotions?

10.4 Describe how normal emotions develop and some emotional problems that children and adolescents experience.

10.5 What is attachment and why is it important for development?

10.6 What is an attachment disorder?

Master these objectives using an online action plan at **edge.sagepub.com/levine3e**

TEST YOUR KNOWLEDGE

Test your knowledge of child development by deciding whether each of the following statements is *true* or *false,* and then check your answers as you read the chapter.

1. **T ☐ F ☐:** Emotions are universal, so people all over the world understand each other's emotional expressions.

2. **T ☐ F ☐:** The temperament with you are born with is the one that will stay with you throughout your life.

3. **T ☐ F ☐:** Boys and girls are equally likely to try to peek as an adult wraps a present, even if they are told not to.

4. **T ☐ F ☐:** The best thing to do for an anxious child is to ignore the child's fears and let the child grow out of them.

5. **T ☐ F ☐:** Asking a teen whether he is thinking about committing suicide will make it more likely he will do it.

6. **T ☐ F ☐:** Programs that use a "tough-love" approach (for example, wilderness camps, boot camps) for adolescents with conduct problems have been highly successful at rehabilitating these young people.

7. **T ☐ F ☐:** When babies cry because a parent has left, it is evidence that they are too attached to their parents.

8. **T ☐ F ☐:** Mothers must have immediate contact with their babies after they are born if a secure attachment is to be formed.

9. **T ☐ F ☐:** If a child has developed an insecure attachment to a parent, that child can still become securely attached later in her life.

10. **T ☐ F ☐:** Teens who are securely attached to their friends are also likely to be securely attached to their parents.

Correct answers: (1) F, (2) F, (3) T, (4) F, (5) F, (6) F, (7) F, (8) F, (9) T, (10) T

▲ **VIDEO: Watch as students answer some of these questions and the authors respond.**

EMOTIONS: UNIVERSALITY AND DIFFERENCE

10.1 What is emotion and how do biology and culture shape our emotions?

Are you usually a pleasant and positive person, or do you struggle with feelings of sadness? Are you easily frightened, or are you unflappable? Are you calm and easygoing, or are you readily provoked to anger? In this section, we discuss both the biological underpinnings and the environmental influences that shape our expression, experience, and interpretation of emotions.

Eric O'Connell/The Image Bank/Getty Images

Watching scary movies. Scary movies arouse a number of emotional responses. Have you ever thought about why you cover (or partially cover) your eyes when you watch a scary movie? You are trying to control the amount of stimulation that you take in so you can keep it at a level that is arousing and fun but not too overwhelming.

WHAT IS EMOTION?

When you are sitting in a scary movie, you may experience a rapid heartbeat and a sense of tension, you may grip the arm of your friend next to you, and actually jump when the hidden menace jumps out at you. This experience of fear includes your body's physiological reaction, your interpretation of the situation, communication with another person, and your own actions, and these are all parts of what we call **emotion**. We all experience a range of emotions, from happy to sad, angry to afraid, and embarrassed to disgusted.

One way to understand the role emotions play in communication is to look at situations in which they are absent. See **Active Learning: Why We Use Emoticons and Emoji** to see what problems can arise when our electronic communication lacks emotional expression and how people have tried to solve them. You will also learn about some cultural differences in the expression of emotions.

Active LEARNING

Why We Use Emoticons and Emoji

Have you ever had an online conversation with someone, only to realize that you had misunderstood what she really meant to say? If someone writes, "I want to see you," how do you interpret that? Is this person saying that they long to see you, or are they preparing to scold you? What is missing from this message is any indication of how the sender is feeling. In 1982, a professor of computer science, Scott Fahlman (n.d.), proposed that we include this familiar character sequence " :-)" in online communication to distinguish sarcastic or silly comments from serious ones because people were badly misunderstanding each other. Using even a simple emoticon such as this, you would read "I want to see you :-)" very differently from "I want to see you >:-(." Emotions are necessary to make sure our meaning is communicated clearly. As we know, the emoticons and emoji that we use today have come a long way from that original text-based smiley face.

Western-style emoticons typically are written so that you need to tip your head to the left to see them, but other cultures have their own way of drawing emoticons that you may not recognize. Emoticons reflect cultural differences in how individuals understand other people's emotions. For example, when interpreting photographs of faces expressing different emotions, Westerners tend to scan the whole face, while East Asians focus on the eyes (Jack, Blais, Scheepers, Schyns, & Caldara, 2009). This difference is apparent when we compare the emoticons used in these two cultures:

East/West Differences in Emoticons		
Emotion	West	East
Happy	:-)	(^_^)
Sad	:-(	(;_;) or (T_T)
Surprised	:-o	(o.o)

Today's smartphone users are familiar with *emoji*, the picture characters that were developed in Japan and now appear in almost all social media. Emoji images also are intended to convey emotion and ensure that the meaning of a message is understood by the recipient. Although they were meant to have a standard meaning, they are not, in fact, universal. Emoji can have different overtones and meanings depending on an individual's culture and language.

The Unicode Consortium (1991-2015) is a nonprofit corporation that develops and maintains standards for emoji. Nevertheless, considerable confusion about the meaning of some emoji exists. How do you interpret these commonly used emoji? Imagine the breakdown in communication that would result if you confused what you thought these images meant with the Unicode Consortium standard meaning provided below.

Image A	Image B	Image C

SOURCES: Barbash (2015); Dahlgreen (2015).

Answers: Image A: This is the Unicode emoji for "sleepy face" (not "sad" or "unhappy," as many people think).
Image B: This emoji represents "face with a look of triumph" (not angry or fed up).
Image C: This emoji is "dizzy face" (not shocked, bored, or dead).

Because there is a physiological component in emotions, we might think that emotions are rooted in our biology and would be similar for all human beings, regardless of their cultural background. In fact, there is remarkable similarity around the world in the display and understanding of facial expressions that indicate basic emotions: happiness, sadness, fear, anger, interest, and disgust (Izard, 2007; Oatley, Keltner, & Jenkins, 2006). In addition, there is some evidence for the universality of more complex emotions, such as pride (Tracy & Robins, 2008). The argument has been made that **basic emotions** are automatic and unlearned because all infants demonstrate these basic emotions, and because particular neural systems in the brain are at least partially dedicated to the expression of each one (Izard, 2007).

Although some aspects of emotional expression may be universal, there is also considerable evidence that the way we display our own emotions and understand those shown by others are mediated in part by our culture, language, gender, temperament, and personality (Izard, 2007; Kayyal & Russell, 2013; Matsumoto, 2006). The cultural norms for when, how, and to whom emotions should, or shouldn't, be shown are known as **emotional display rules** (Engelmann & Pogosyan, 2013) and children learn early in development how to manage the display of their emotions in accordance with these norms. By middle childhood, most

Emotion The body's physiological reaction to a situation, your cognitive interpretation of the situation, communication to another person, and your own actions.

Basic emotions An automatic and unlearned set of emotions that arise early in development and have a biological basis.

T □ F □ Emotions are universal, so people all over the world understand each other's emotional expressions. **False**

Basic emotions. Because basic emotions have a physiological component, they are part of an infant's responses from the beginning. Basic emotions are universal, so you probably recognize these examples. If you need help, the first is meant to represent happiness, then anger, sadness, and disgust.

Emotional display rules Culturally determined norms for when, how, and to whom emotions should, or should not, be shown.

children understand and behave in ways that reflect the expectations of their culture. For instance, in the United States and many European countries, girls are expected to be more emotionally expressive than boys. They typically show higher levels of happiness, but also of sadness, fear, anxiety, shame, guilt, empathy, and sympathy (Brody & Hall, 2008; Chaplin & Aldao, 2013). On the other hand, the expression of anger and aggression is generally more accepted in these societies for boys than for girls (Rose & Rudolph, 2006).

One well-documented cultural difference involves the intensity of an emotional display. In general, it is more acceptable for people in individualistic cultures, such as the United States, to show their feelings openly than for people from collectivist cultures, such as Japan (Safdar et al., 2009). Knowing this, a Japanese person may interpret someone's small smile as indicating great happiness, while an American may interpret a broad grin as moderate happiness.

There also are cultural differences in which emotions can be shown. In European American cultures that value individuality and independence, displaying emotions such as pride and even anger are acceptable because both emotions support the value of the individual, while emotions such as guilt and shame, which devalue the individual, are less acceptable. By contrast, in East Asian cultures that value interdependence and harmony, the display of shame or guilt is acceptable because it shows that the individual wants to improve and is aware of how his or her behavior affects others, while the display of anger is not acceptable because it threatens relational harmony (DeLeersnyder, Boiger, & Mesquita, 2013; Safdar et al., 2009). When people immigrate to a new country, adapting to the display rules of their new country is part of the acculturation process (DeLeersnyder, Mesquita, & Kim, 2011). The longer they reside in a country, the more their emotional display patterns resemble those of their host nation.

Emotion schemas All the associations and interpretations that an individual connects to a certain emotion.

Temperament, described more fully later in this chapter, is another one of the filters through which we interpret our emotions. The feeling that a shy child might interpret as panic may be what a more adventurous child interprets as excitement. Cognition also plays a role. We develop ways of thinking about emotions, called **emotion schemas**, that affect how we experience and show emotions (Izard, 2007). You'll remember that a schema is a cognitive

Universal emotions. These girls from Myanmar in Southeast Asia (left) and from the Himba tribe in Namibia, Africa (right), would likely recognize each other's smiles as expressing the same emotion.

framework that organizes the world into categories and associations. When we experience sadness, we draw on a wealth of associations and memories to understand what we are feeling. For example, the idea that "big boys don't cry" is a powerful control on the expression of sadness that is activated for many boys and may make it difficult for them to get help or even to understand their own sad feelings. A boy in the United States who is hit by a baseball may automatically begin to cry, but his schema for crying includes "big boys don't cry." He decides "I cannot let myself cry," and his facial expression may then reflect anger at himself for experiencing this forbidden emotion. The expression of anger is more acceptable for boys in American culture than the expression of sadness. Behaving in a socially acceptable way then reinforces and strengthens the boy's schema of sadness.

DEVELOPMENT OF EMOTIONS: THE ROLE OF SELF AND OTHERS

As we said earlier, there are biological underpinnings to emotions that make their expression in some ways universal. However, children also learn about emotions from other people even before they develop any self-awareness. We first describe how children are affected by other people when they are learning about the emotions they are feeling through two processes: social referencing and empathy. We then discuss how the development of a clearer sense of self, which will be described in Chapter 11, enables them to experience self-conscious emotions such as guilt and shame.

Social Referencing

One way that we begin to understand our emotions is by looking at how others are reacting when we are uncertain about how we should react, a process called **social referencing**. Social referencing first develops between 9 and 12 months of age (Hennighausen & Lyons-Ruth, 2005). You may have seen a baby or young child start to laugh when other people are laughing, without any idea what they are laughing about. Or, when a child meets a new person, she is more likely to be friendly if she sees her mother smiling at that person.

In a replication of the visual cliff experiment described in Chapter 6, either an infant's mother or the infant's father encouraged their infant to come to them by crossing what

Social referencing Using the reaction of others to determine how to react in ambiguous situations.

appeared to be a steep drop-off, the visual cliff. Verbal and facial encouragement by either parent did not make a difference in the infant's show of anxiety or their likelihood of crossing the visual cliff. However, when the parents expressed anxiety as the infants approached the cliff, the infants responded to their fathers' level of anxiety by avoiding the visual cliff, but not the mothers'. The researchers concluded that fathers play a larger role in infants' social referencing in a physically hazardous situation, perhaps because fathers typically encourage more risk taking in their offspring. For that reason, the infant would be more sensitive to his cues in this situation (Möller, Majdandžic, & Bögels, 2014). Later in this chapter, we talk more about how parents respond to their child's emotions and the impact their reactions have on the child's emotional development.

Although this type of social referencing of emotions continues throughout our lives, as children get older, conversations with parents about what happens to them also help shape the way in which children understand and cope with their emotions. Parents who use more words to label and describe emotions have children who are more comfortable talking about their feelings. For example, for children with asthma, emotional well-being was related to their mothers' use of emotion words and explanations in their conversations with their children about the child's disease (Sales & Fivush, 2005).

Empathy

Empathy Sharing the feelings of other people.

Sharing other people's feelings, whether pain or pleasure, is the essence of **empathy**. As we saw in Chapter 5, infants imitate the actions of others from the earliest days of their lives. The same is true for emotions. If a baby hears another baby crying, he is quite likely to start crying himself (Geangu, Benga, Stahl, & Striano, 2010). Have you experienced something similar yourself? When you see someone crying on television or a movie, do you ever find your own eyes getting wet? Experiencing the feelings of others is a primitive form of empathy and is the basis for much human interaction. When we experience another's distress we are more likely to try to show **sympathy** by helping or comforting that person. We discuss empathy further when we talk about moral development in Chapter 11, but you can see how empathy is expressed in children by completing **Active Learning: Empathy and Sympathy**.

Sympathy Concern for others' welfare that often leads to helping or comforting them.

Active LEARNING

Empathy and Sympathy

You can carry out the following experiment designed by Carolyn Zahn-Waxler and her colleagues to look at empathy and sympathy in children (Robinson, Zahn-Waxler, & Emde, 1994). When you are with a child you know, pretend to hurt yourself. You can pretend to pinch your finger in a drawer, stub your toe, or experience some other noticeable but minor "hurt." Practice beforehand so you can react in a realistic way.

How does the child respond? Young children may ignore you, laugh, look hurt or cry themselves, or show sympathy by asking if you need a Band-Aid or if you are OK. Think about what each type of behavior means in terms of the child's ability to take another's point of view as well as empathizing with another's pain. As children get older, they move from showing personal distress when they empathize with you (for example, crying themselves) to being more oriented to your feelings and helping you feel better.

After you note the child's reaction, be sure to reassure the child that you now are feeling much better and do not hurt anymore. Also thank the child if he or she tried to help you.

If you were to search the literature for research on empathy in older children and adolescents, you would find much more research on adolescents who *lack* a sense of empathy than on those who have a well-developed sense of empathy. A lack of ability to empathize with others has been associated with adolescents who are sexually abusive, delinquent and antisocial, or bullies among their peers. One protection against this problem is a history of warm relationships with others. For instance, a secure attachment with parents is associated with higher levels of empathy (Murphy, Laible, Augustine, & Robeson, 2015; Panfile & Laible, 2012). As you will learn later in this chapter, attachment plays an important role in many aspects of a child's emotional development.

Empathy. Even young children can experience empathy and will attempt to soothe another person, as this girl is doing for her friend.

Self-Conscious Emotions

When we talk about emotions, we distinguish between basic (or primary) emotions and self-conscious (or secondary) emotions. Infants demonstrate the basic emotions within the first year of life (Izard, 2007), can recognize happiness when they see it in others before age 3, and recognize the other basic emotions by age 4 or 5 (Tracy, Robins, & Lagattuta, 2005). Secondary emotions such as pride, shame, and guilt develop later because they depend on an awareness of self that very young children do not yet possess. Secondary emotions require children to think about how an event affects their evaluation of themselves so that is why secondary emotions are also called **self-conscious emotions** (Tracy et al., 2005). Emotions such as embarrassment, guilt, and shame usually appear by the time a child is 3 years old.

While it is pretty easy to recognize differences between the basic emotions, the differences between the secondary emotions are more subtle and require more explanation. The distinction between guilt and shame is that one focuses on the self and the other focuses on the behavior. **Guilt** results when children think about a specific behavior they have done that they regret ("I did *something bad*"). When we feel guilty, it creates a sense of remorse so we often want to do something to make the situation better (Stuewig et al., 2015). **Shame** occurs when the focus is on an aspect of ourselves that we believe we cannot change ("*I* did something bad"). Shame has also been linked with personal failures, such as poor performance at school or in sports, whereas guilt is linked to moral issues, such as hurting others. Many researchers have claimed that children do not develop the cognitive abilities necessary to understand these emotions until well into middle childhood. Shame emerges at a younger age, but children begin to show guilt when they better understand the rules for their behavior and the mental states of others (Bafunno & Camodeca, 2013).

Berti, Garattoni, and Venturini (2000) found that 5-year-old Italian children were just as likely as older children to understand that guilt is caused by something one has done wrong and that it can be dealt with by trying to repair the damage done. However, the 5-year-olds also tended to believe that they only had to feel guilty if someone else was there to see what happened. If no one was there, then they would feel happy, not guilty. Older children's sense of guilt was not affected by whether someone else was there. In Chapter 11, we talk more about the process of moral development and how children internalize the values of their culture and feel guilt or shame if they violate these internalized standards, but for now you can see whether you are clear on this distinction by answering the question in **Active Learning: Shame and Guilt**.

Self-conscious emotions Emotions that depend on awareness of oneself, such as pride, guilt, and shame.

Guilt Feelings children have when they think about the negative aspects of something they have done, particularly moral failures.

Shame A feeling that occurs as a result of personal failure or when children attribute their bad behavior to an aspect of themselves that they believe they cannot change.

Active LEARNING

Shame and Guilt

Read the following scenario imagining that you are a child.

You are hurrying home one day to watch your favorite television program. You see your little brother outside. He is sitting on the sidewalk crying. He dropped a bag of marbles, and they are rolling all over the place. You don't stop to help him. You just keep on walking toward home.

Would you think, "I am a mean kid for not helping"? Or would you think "I did something bad by not helping"?

Which of these two responses would indicate guilt and which would indicate shame?

Answer: Ferguson, Stegge, Miller, and Olsen (1999) suggest that thinking you are a "mean kid" is indicative of shame, and feeling that "you did something wrong" is indicative of guilt.

CHECK YOUR UNDERSTANDING

1. What is emotion?
2. What are the basic emotions?
3. How does social referencing influence children's expressions of emotion?
4. How do empathy and sympathy differ?
5. What is the difference between shame and guilt?

TEMPERAMENT

10.2 What is temperament?

Temperament The general emotional style an individual displays in responding to events.

Although most of us will be frightened when we see a horror film, some people will be so terrified that they will never go to see another film like that again, while others will be scared but also excited by it and will take every opportunity to see more. **Temperament** is the general way in which we respond to experiences in the world, whether they are horror films, doing a class presentation, or being cut off in traffic. Although different experiences evoke different emotional responses, the concept of temperament implies that individuals have a general emotional style that guides their tendency to respond in certain ways to a variety of events in their environment. Some people are usually timid, fearful, and anxious; some are fearless and outgoing; and others are often aggressive and angry.

Some of these differences reflect characteristic ways we have learned to respond to our experiences, but parents report that their children were different from each other from the moment they were born; one child was quiet while the other was boisterous, or one was demanding while the other was content. There is some evidence that they are right, that we are born with a certain temperament based to some degree on our genetic inheritance (Goldsmith, Lemery, Aksan, & Buss, 2000; Rothbart, 2007).

TABLE 10.1

Temperament profiles. This table shows where children who are classified by Thomas and Chess as "easy," "slow to warm," or "difficult" fall on each of the nine dimensions of temperament that they describe.

Dimension of Temperament	Easy	Slow to Warm	Difficult
Activity Level	Varies	Low to moderate	Varies
Adaptability	Very adaptable	Slowly adaptable	Slowly adaptable
Approach/Withdrawal	Positive approach	Initial withdrawal	Withdrawal
Attention Span and Persistence	High or low	High or low	High or low
Distractibility	Varies	Varies	Varies
Intensity of Reaction	Low or mild	Mild	Intense
Quality of Mood	Positive	Slightly negative	Negative
Rhythmicity	Very regular	Varies	Irregular
Threshold of Responsiveness	High or low	High or low	High or low

SOURCE: Adapted from Chess, Thomas, & Birch (1965).

MEASURING TEMPERAMENT

There have been several different approaches to describing and measuring temperament, but one of the most influential was developed by Alexander Thomas and Stella Chess (Chess & Thomas, 1999; Thomas & Chess, 1977). Based on structured interviews with parents, they identified nine characteristics that contribute to a child's temperament: activity level, adaptability, approach or withdrawal, attention span and persistence, distractibility, intensity of reaction, quality of mood, rhythmicity (or regularity), and threshold of responsiveness. Any individual child can score high, low, or average on each of these characteristics, and combining this information produces three temperament profiles: an easy temperament, a difficult temperament, and a slow-to-warm temperament. Table 10.1 shows where children with each of these temperament profiles fall on each of these dimensions.

Infants with an **easy temperament** have a generally positive mood, adapt fairly easily to change, and are regular and predictable in their patterns of eating, sleeping, and elimination (Chess & Thomas, 1999). By contrast, infants with a **difficult temperament** have a more negative mood, are easily frustrated and slow to adapt to change, and have irregular patterns of eating, sleeping, and elimination. Children with difficult temperaments also tend to react more intensely to situations than children with easy temperaments. For these children, it is even more important that parents try to keep their environments regular and predictable and that changes be introduced gradually. The third temperament described by Chess and Thomas (1999) is the **slow-to-warm temperament**. The reaction of these children to new experiences is milder than the reaction of a difficult child, and that is true for both things they like and things they dislike. However, if they are given some time and are not pressured by adults, with repeated exposure to the new experience

Easy temperament A child's general responsiveness marked by positive mood, easy adaptation to change, and regularity and predictability in patterns of eating, sleeping, and elimination.

Difficult temperament A child's general responsiveness marked by more negative mood, intense responses, slow adaptation to change, and irregular patterns of eating, sleeping, and elimination.

Slow-to-warm temperament A general responsiveness marked by a slow adaptation to new experiences and moderate irregularity in eating, sleeping, and elimination.

they gradually come around on their own. Slow-to-warm children also are less irregular in their eating, sleeping, and elimination patterns than difficult children but are not as regular as easy children.

In their original study on children's temperament, Thomas and Chess (1977) found that easy children made up about 40% of their sample, difficult children made up 10%, and slow-to-warm children made up about 15%. The remaining 35% of the children could not be classified into one of these categories primarily because they displayed these characteristics in a different configuration or were not consistent in the type of behaviors they showed from one occasion to another. According to Chess and Thomas (1999), what is most important in determining the consequences of having one type of temperament versus another is the **goodness of fit** between the child's characteristics and the demands of the environment. For instance, if an infant doesn't like a lot of noise and crowds of people, a sensitive parent tries to avoid these situations or plans to take the infant into these situations only when she is well rested, fed, and comfortable (Sturm, 2004), thereby creating a good fit between the child's temperament and the environment she is in. The role that temperament plays in child development is discussed throughout this book. For example, later in this chapter, we find that infants' temperament relates to the nature of their attachment to their mother.

A second influential way of describing and measuring temperament comes from Mary Rothbart (1981). The research by Thomas and Chess grew out of their clinical work, but Rothbart placed a greater emphasis on the neurobiological bases of temperament (Zentner & Bates, 2008). She has defined temperament as biologically based differences in reactivity and self-regulation, but recognizes that these characteristics are influenced by experience and can show change over time (Rothbart & Bates, 2008). Her research with infants has identified three higher-order factors that comprise temperament: extraversion, negative emotionality/affect, and self-regulation. We will discuss the role that self-regulation in the form of *effortful control* plays later in this chapter. Effortful control is a characteristic of temperament that becomes increasingly important as children get older. Negative affect and the inability to self-regulate have been associated with both internalizing and externalizing problems later in development, including depression in adolescents (Verstraeten, Vasey, Raes, & Bijttebier, 2009) and attention-deficit/hyperactivity disorder (Auerbach et al., 2008).

STABILITY OF TEMPERAMENT

The question of whether the temperament with which we are born remains the basis for our emotional responses for the rest of our lives is a complicated one. Research shows a tendency for many children to maintain the same temperament over time (Carranza, Gonzalez-Salinas, & Ato, 2013; Casalin, Luyten, Vliegen, & Neurs, 2012; Neppl et al., 2010; Rothbart et al., 2000). However, there are also many children who change. Although children usually do not change from one extreme to another, smaller changes do occur (Carranza et al., 2013; Goldsmith et al., 2000).

Think about your own temperament. If you are shy now, were you also shy as a child? If you are outgoing now, have you been told that you were very friendly as a child? Were you shy until a certain age and then you changed to become more outgoing? Mary Rothbart and her colleagues have added to the work by Chess and Thomas with rigorous analyses of parent questionnaires about children's temperament (Rothbart, Ahadi, Hershey, & Fisher, 2001). To learn more about Rothbart's approach to describing temperament and to apply it to an understanding of your own temperament, interview your parents as suggested in **Active Learning: Temperament**.

Goodness of fit How well a child's temperamental characteristics match with the demands of the child's environment.

T ☐ F ☐ The temperament that you are born with is the one that will stay with you throughout your life. **False**

Active LEARNING

Temperament

Mary Rothbart and her colleagues developed some ideas about the dimensions of temperament different than those developed by Chess and Thomas. In their research, they found three basic dimensions: (1) extraversion, (2) negative emotion, and (3) self-control (Rothbart et al., 2001). Use these dimensions to interview your parents about what you were like as a young child. Here are some sample characteristics from Rothbart's *Children's Behavior Questionnaire* for each dimension. For each one, ask your parent whether that characteristic applied to you as an infant or toddler.

Extraversion: "Usually rushes into an activity without thinking about it"; "Gets so worked up before an exciting event that s(he) has trouble sitting still."

Negative emotion: "Has temper tantrums when s(he) doesn't get what s(he) wants"; "Has a hard time settling down for a nap."

Self-control: "Can lower his/her voice when asked to do so"; "When picking up toys or other jobs, usually keeps at the task until it's done."

Did you respond quickly to experiences, like grabbing an object you wanted right away, or did you move slowly into new situations? Were you able to calm yourself down when upset or angry? Do you feel that your parents' descriptions of you as a child still describe you now in any way? If you feel that your temperament has undergone some significant change, can you identify anything that initiated that change (for instance, becoming more outgoing after you had to move to a new school and make new friends)? These indicators of temperament seem to stay the same for some people, but they can change if experiences provide the impetus for those changes.

©iStockphoto.com/Nadezhda1906

Picture Partners/Photo Researchers, Inc.

Temperament. Children's temperament ranges from shy and retiring to outgoing and adventurous, and where a child falls on this continuum influences how that child interprets new experiences. Where would you place yourself? Have you always been that way?

REGULATION OF EMOTIONS AND SELF-CONTROL

10.3 How do children learn to regulate and control their emotions?

When children (and adults) can control the expression of their emotions, they are more likely to be able to use emotions in a positive way. One example of an adult who is not in control of his emotions is a person who experiences road rage. This person may chase after someone who has cut him off in traffic, putting himself and others at risk. This level of anger also harms the person's health because high levels of anger and aggression are related to a higher likelihood of heart disease (Suarez, 2004). If you have ever experienced road rage yourself, you can now think with a clearer, calmer head about what would have been a better way to deal with your feelings. In children, we see a similar inability to control rage when the child has a temper tantrum. Remember this parallel and your own health the next time someone cuts you off in traffic.

SELF-CONTROL AND SELF-REGULATION

Newborn infants have very little ability to regulate their own emotions. Until about the middle of their first year, the frontal lobe of an infant's brain is not developed enough to regulate emotional impulses in the way that it will later in life (Smith, Diaz, Day, & Bell, 2015). As a result, infants have little or no ability to modulate their reactivity to external events. All they know is what they are feeling and what they want at that very moment.

Some of an infant's first attempts at emotional regulation involve self-soothing behaviors, such as thumb sucking, holding a favorite "blankie," or by avoiding a feared or frustrating object by looking away (Eisenberg, Hofer, & Vaughan, 2007). They also learn to signal in a subtle way when they are being overstimulated. If you are playing with an infant and the infant suddenly yawns, stretches, and turns away, that is a way of letting you know that he is feeling overwhelmed by what is going on and that you need to reduce the amount of stimulation he is trying to process. Being sensitive to the infant's signals—whether they are signals that the infant is hungry, tired, or uncomfortable—helps the infant learn to regulate his own emotions because he comes to know that he doesn't need to get frantic to get a response from his caregivers.

Until the frontal lobe has developed enough to become the infant's "emotional manager" (Smith et al., 2015, p. 264), infants must rely on their caregivers to help regulate the amount of distress they experience. One way that adults do this is by providing an environment that has predictable routines. Parents don't need to be rigid about this, but regular times for meals, sleep, and play help keep an infant from becoming overly hungry, tired, or bored. You know from your own experience that it is more difficult to exercise self-control when you are feeling very tired or hungry. Parents and caregivers also can help infants calm down when

Regulating emotions. A driver in the throes of road rage looks a great deal like a young child having a temper tantrum. In both cases, the individual has failed to regulate and control their negative emotions.

they can't do this for themselves. Parents will often cuddle a distressed infant, carry her, or give her a pacifier (Dayton, Walsh, Oh, & Volling, 2015).

As children become toddlers, the important adults in their lives continue to be powerful models for how to regulate and control emotions and behaviors. On the other hand, if adults react to their own frustrations with negative outbursts, toddlers learn that such behavior is acceptable. Remaining calm and composed and expressing frustration in words before taking action models self-control rather than impulsive behavior for children. Parents and caregivers can also help by redirecting their child's behavior. For instance, if a toddler bites in frustration, parents can give him an alternative behavior that works. People who work with young children know that biting at this age is not unusual, and you frequently hear them say "Use your words" to remind children that they can express their frustration in other more acceptable ways. Aggression between children is very common in the preschool years (Dodge, Coie, & Lynam, 2006), but as they grow they learn ways to effectively control these negative emotions. That is why we are so concerned about children and adolescents who fail to do this.

John Gottman (2001) has described two ways that parents teach their children to deal with their emotions. He calls these styles **emotion coaching** and **emotion dismissing**. He begins with the premise that negative emotions are unpleasant and we need to find a way to deal with them. Parents who are emotion dismissing see emotions as toxic, and for that reason they want to protect their children from their feelings so these parents minimize the importance of emotions and instead try to distract or cheer up their child so that the negative emotion will pass. For instance, if a child gets hurt and is upset, an emotion dismissing parent might minimize it by saying "It's just a scratch. No big deal. It will get better." This type of response tells the child that he doesn't know what he is feeling or that what he is feeling is not legitimate. It is not that this parent doesn't care about the child, but rather that the parent wants to make the child feel better and sees ignoring the child's negative feeling as a way to do that. Emotion dismissing parents want their child to be happy, so they see negative emotions in their child as a sign that they have failed as parents. Because these parents don't use language that can describe a range of emotions, their children never learn how to express what they are feeling in words.

By contrast, emotion coaching parents help their children explore and understand their feelings. Although some emotions are negative, they understand that helping a child label her emotions and understand them can create an opportunity for the child to learn what she can do to deal with them. In this case, when a child is hurt (even if the injury is small), the

Emotion coaching A parental style that teaches children how to understand their emotions and deal with them.

Emotion dismissing A parental style that teaches children to ignore their feelings.

iStock/RapidEye

iStock/ibooo7

emotion coaching parent would legitimize the child's feelings by acknowledging that even a little scratch can hurt and that the child feels sad. Telling the child that it *doesn't* hurt does not accomplish the same thing. As children learn to label and understand their own emotions, it becomes easier for them to develop empathy and understand the emotions of others (Gottman, 2001). After the parent validates the child's feelings, there is the opportunity to go on to discuss what the child can do to make the situation better. Over time, children with emotion coaching parents become better at calming themselves after being upset.

A number of studies have tested the effectiveness of parent training programs based on these ideas and have shown the parent coaching strategies can be taught to parents of young children and that the increased use of these strategies results in the reduction of problem behaviors and an increase in empathy as reported by parents and by teachers (Havighurst, Wilson, Harley, & Prior, 2009; Lauw, Havighurst, Wilson, Harley, & Northam, 2014; Wilson, Havighurst, & Harley, 2014).

EFFORTFUL CONTROL AND DELAY OF GRATIFICATION

As you learned in Chapter 7, executive function is the coordinating function of the brain that allows us to choose our goals, initiate appropriate responses, inhibit inappropriate ones, monitor our success, and correct errors, if they occur (Zhou et al., 2007). The development of executive function has been linked

Emotion coaching. When a parent acknowledges what her child is feeling, the child better understands her own emotions and becomes better at calming herself when she is upset.

Effortful control The ability to consciously control one's behavior.

with **effortful control**, the ability to consciously control one's own behavior. In a well-known study, 4-year-old children were told that they could eat one marshmallow right away or they could wait and get two marshmallows (Eigsti et al., 2006). When tempted in this way, children who actively tried to inhibit their immediate impulse to grab that marshmallow and eat it by doing things such as sitting on their hands, looking away from the marshmallow, or whistling a tune were more able to wait than those children who concentrated on the marshmallow. **Active Learning: How Do Children Resist Temptation?** will show you how you can try this experiment with a child.

Active LEARNING

How Do Children Resist Temptation?

Walter Mischel and his colleagues found that children who exert active self-control at 4 years of age are more able to concentrate and tolerate frustration when they become teenagers (Eigsti et al., 2006). Although infants have little ability to delay gratification, by age 4 many children can use particular tactics to help themselves do so. Try the following task with a preschool child:

ACTIVE LEARNING VIDEO ▲

Look at all the ways these children actively try to avoid eating the marshmallow while they wait for a second one.

Equipment Needed

2 marshmallows (or other attractive reward)

A table and chair for the child

Procedure

1. You can do this activity with a boy or a girl between the ages of 3 and 5 years of age. In a room with no distractions (for example, no toys or books), seat the child at a table with one marshmallow (or other treat) on a plate.

2. Tell the child you have to leave the room for a little while. Ask whether the child would prefer to have one marshmallow or two marshmallows. Explain that if the child can wait until you come back, the child will receive two marshmallows. However, if the child feels unable to wait, the child can eat the one marshmallow but will not receive the second marshmallow. Be sure the child understands the instructions.

3. Leave the room and secretly observe the child for up to 10 minutes or return sooner if the child eats the marshmallow or if the child appears to be greatly distressed. Ideally you would have a one-way mirror. Otherwise find a way to be sure the child cannot see you watching. Observe if and how the child tries to stop himself or herself from eating the marshmallow. Does the child sit on his or her hands, look away from the marshmallow and around the room, sing to create a distraction, and so on? These are all observable ways that the child may try to exercise effortful control.

4. If the child waited and did not eat the marshmallow, give the child both marshmallows. If the child ate one of the marshmallows, then he or she does not receive the second marshmallow.

5. Be sure to tell the child how helpful he or she was and thank the child regardless of whether the child got one marshmallow or two.

6. Compare your results with those of others in your class. Did children who had more tactics to try to control themselves have more success in waiting until the time was up to receive the marshmallows? Were there differences depending on the ages of the children; for example, were 4-year-olds able to wait longer than 3-year-olds?

To prepare for this activity or if you do not have access to a child, watch the video of this Active Learning.

Young children who waited for the second marshmallow were more likely to distract themselves from the marshmallow by looking at or thinking about other things. When preschoolers were taught to *reframe* the temptation by thinking of the marshmallow as a cloud or a cotton ball rather than a treat, they were better able to wait for the larger reward (Mischel et al., 2011). You may be able to relate these findings to a similar situation you may have experienced. When you are at a party with lots of wonderful food, you may try to avoid overeating by moving away from where the food is being served and becoming involved in conversation so you aren't thinking about all that temptation.

As they get older, children become better able to delay gratification. McCabe and Brooks-Gunn (2007) looked at this topic by using **delay of gratification** tasks in a preschool classroom, rather than in a research laboratory. First, they asked children to wait to eat an M&M candy until the researcher blew a whistle, and then they placed the children in groups of four and repeated the procedure. They also asked the children, first individually and then as part of a group, not to peek as the researcher wrapped a present for them. Not surprisingly, they found that older children were better able to regulate their behavior and delay gratification than younger children, whether they were tested individually or as part of

Delay of gratification The ability to wait until later to get something desirable.

Resisting temptation. Being able to control yourself when faced with temptation is an important step in emotional development.

T ☐ F ☐ Boys and girls are equally likely to try to peek as an adult wraps a present, even if they are told not to. True

a group. Although girls waited longer than boys before peeking on the gift wrap task, there was no gender difference in the likelihood that they would peek at some point during the test period. Finally, the researchers note that there was *not* consistency across the different situations they tested. This highlights the fact that children's behavior is the result not only of the child's characteristics, but rather of the child's characteristics in the context of a particular environmental situation. Ask yourself honestly what situation would be so tempting that you too would peek even when you know you shouldn't.

LONG-TERM OUTCOMES OF SELF-CONTROL

Emotional intelligence The ability to understand and control one's emotions, to understand the emotions of others, and to use this understanding in human interactions.

The development of self-control in young children has a number of positive outcomes as children grow older because self-control plays an essential role in the development of emotional intelligence. **Emotional intelligence** involves understanding and controlling one's own emotions, understanding the emotions of others, and being able to use all of this understanding to navigate human interactions successfully. The type of emotion coaching described earlier in this chapter plays an important role in helping children develop this understanding and sensitivity (Greenberg, 2015). They learn how to better regulate their own emotions, and how to understand and empathize with the emotions of others. This is an ability that is separate and distinct from other cognitive abilities and does not differ for boys and girls (Mavroveli et al., 2009; Mavroveli & Sánchez-Ruiz, 2011).

Children who can regulate their emotions and behaviors are seen as more socially and academically competent, as more agreeable and more sympathetic, and as more resilient (Izard, 2007; McCabe & Brooks-Gunn, 2007; Mischel & Ayduk, 2004). They are also seen by their peers as kind, helpful, and as leaders (Mavroveli, Petrides, Sangareau, & Furnham, 2009). Emotional regulation is also linked to lower levels of problematic behavior (Sawyer, Miller-Lewis, Searle, Sawyer, & Lyngh, 2015) and several behavioral disorders that we discuss later in the chapter, including conduct disorder and oppositional defiant disorder (McCabe & Brooks-Gunn, 2007).

1. What is effortful control?
2. What are the age and gender differences in the ability to delay gratification?
3. What is emotional intelligence and why is it important to positive development?

NORMAL EMOTIONS AND EMOTIONAL PROBLEMS

10.4 Describe how normal emotions develop and some emotional problems that children and adolescents experience.

The experience and expression of emotions change as children grow older. In this section, we describe expected patterns of development for fear, sadness, and anger and then describe the difficulties that children may experience when they are unable to regulate their emotional responses. Difficulties with regulating emotion and using executive control strategies are associated with **externalizing (or other-directed) behaviors**, in which the children "act out" on the environment, and **internalizing (or self-directed) behaviors**, in which children experience painful emotions and may do things that are hurtful to themselves. Difficulties with fear, anxiety, sadness, and depression are generally associated with internalizing behaviors, while anger and aggression are most often associated with externalizing behavior. We also discuss some of the interventions that have been used to help children who have difficulty managing these emotions.

FEAR AND ANXIETY

There are some predictable age-related changes in what children fear. Fear of things like loud noises or novel items in the child's environment typically appears at around 7 months of age and, as the child moves through toddlerhood, fear of the dark or of the scary monsters in the closet is common. In a study by Muris, Merckelbach, Gadet, and Moulaert (2000) in the Netherlands, approximately three-quarters of the 4-year-old children interviewed reported that they experienced fears, worries, and scary dreams. Fear of separation from a parent peaks at 4 years of age, but decreases as the child gets older. While test performance anxiety is low among young children, this fear increases with age and becomes the top concern among 10- to 12-year old children (Ollendick, Grills, & Alexander, 2014).

In general, older children have fewer fears than younger ones. Repeated exposure to frightening experiences that really do no harm, a growing understanding of the physical world, and increases in the ability to use coping strategies all contribute to the decline in fearfulness among older children. There also is a tendency for girls to be more fearful and shy than boys (Cummings, Caporino, & Kendall, 2014), or at least more willing to show these emotions. What children fear can also depend upon the cultural background of the child (Ollendick et al., 2014). Relatively little research has looked at these differences, but the research that has been done finds more similarity than difference between African American and European American children. Among the differences, African American children have more fears that are concrete and grounded in reality (for instance, getting a shock from electricity or mean-looking dogs) compared to European American children who have more fears tied to performance (for instance, getting poor grades) or death and dead people (Ollendick et al., 2014). African American children also have a greater number of fears than European American children. Greater fearfulness has been shown to have a negative impact

Externalizing (or other directed) behaviors
Behaviors, such as aggressive or destructive behavior, in which the child or adolescent "acts out" on the environment.

Internalizing (or self-directed) behaviors
Behaviors in which a child's emotions are turned inward and become hurtful to themselves.

on children's self-concepts, with those who experience more fear being more likely to make negative self-statements (Ollendick et al., 2014).

The difference between fear and anxiety is not always clear, but fear is generally thought of as a response to a real event, whereas **anxiety** involves the anticipation of events that may or may not occur. Some level of fear and anxiety from time to time during development is normal, but when anxiety is so great that it interferes with everyday activities and creates a great deal of distress, it is considered an **anxiety disorder** (APA, 2013). While the exact cause of anxiety disorders is not known, heredity, temperament, stressful experiences, and/or biochemical factors all play a role. For example, individuals with generalized anxiety disorder report feeling their emotions more intensely than others, are more emotionally reactive to negative events that they experience, and feel less in control of their emotions (Newman, Llera, Erickson, Przeworski, & Castonguay, 2013). Functional magnetic resonance imagining (fMRI) has shown that the amygdala (the portion of the limbic system that plays an important role in the processing of emotions, especially fear) is hyperreactive in people with anxiety disorders and this hyperactivity makes it more difficult for individuals to control the experience of fear and anxiety. Although a vulnerability to anxiety may tend to run in families, the same genetic mix might or might not result in an anxiety disorder, depending upon the individual's life experiences (Vann, 2016).

Anxiety disorders are the most common mental disorder among teens, and the one that is diagnosed at the youngest age (Merikangas et al., 2010). Longitudinal studies of children with anxiety disorders have found that these conditions in childhood predict the development of emotional disorders in adolescence, so they should not be ignored with the assumption that they will simply disappear with age (Beesdo et al., 2009; Bittner et al., 2007).

The American Psychiatric Association (2013) recognizes a number of specific anxiety disorders. Some of the more commonly occurring ones in children and adolescents are summarized in Table 10.2. You are probably familiar with the anxiety disorder known as a *phobia*, an irrational fear of something specific that is so severe that it interferes with day-to-day functioning. Some common phobias among adults and children include fear of spiders, snakes, heights, flying, water, and public speaking. One approach that has been successful in helping children deal with their fears involves a process of *desensitization*, similar to what we described in Chapter 2 when we talked about using virtual reality to conquer classically conditioned fears. The child begins by constructing a list of fear-provoking situations from the least fearful to the most fearful, and the therapist then guides the child through the items, one by one, letting the child first guess what he thinks will happen before actually completing that step (Dingfelder, 2005). As the child works through his hierarchy of fears, the therapist uses the time to give the child suggestions that will be helpful in the future, such as suggesting that the child with a dog phobia ask a pet owner if her dog is friendly before approaching the dog. For many children, even a single session with a therapist can get the child through more than half of the steps in his hierarchy and many even complete the entire list (Dingfelder, 2005).

SADNESS AND DEPRESSION

Sadness is a normal reaction to experiences such as loss and disappointment. However, children who have difficulty regulating their sadness are more likely than others to develop depression in early adolescence (Feng et al., 2009). Depression can run the gamut from something that is relatively mild and short-lived to something that is persistent and quite severe. When we talk about a **major depression**, as described in the DSM-5, we are referring to one that is long-lasting and severe enough to affect the individual physically, emotionally, cognitively, and socially. Physically the person often has trouble sleeping (or may sleep all the time), feels tired, or loses her appetite. The person may be restless or feel very slowed down. Emotionally she may feel worthless and guilty. Cognitively, depression often interferes with a person's ability to concentrate, and in severe cases, there can be reoccurring thoughts of

Anxiety A vague fear of events that may or may not occur.

Anxiety disorder A level of anxiety that is severe, lasts a long time, and interferes with normal functioning.

T ☐ F ☐ The best thing to do for an anxious child is to ignore the child's fears and let the child grow out of them. **False**

Major depression A condition marked by feelings of worthlessness and hopelessness, a lack of pleasure, sleep and appetite disturbances, and possibly suicidal thoughts.

TABLE 10.2

Common anxiety disorders in children and adolescents.

Diagnosis	Description	Symptoms/Age of Onset
Phobia	An irrational fear of something specific that is so severe it interferes with day-to-day functioning.	Symptoms in children include crying, tantrums, clinging, and freezing up. Adolescents may experience extreme fear resulting in rapid heart rate, dizziness, and sweaty palms.
Generalized Anxiety Disorder	Vague but persistent worry that something bad is about to happen.	Onset in childhood is unusual but can begin in adolescence.
Panic Disorder	A sudden, intense feeling of terror and dread accompanied by physical sensations such as heart palpitations, chest pain, and nausea; fear of a reoccurrence can keep people from engaging in their regular activities.	Onset in childhood is unusual, but can begin in adolescence.
Separation Anxiety Disorder	A condition in which a child is fearful and nervous when away from a loved one, usually a parent or other caregiver, to whom the child is attached; the child cannot tolerate separations as appropriate for the child's age.	Symptoms can begin in early childhood and often involve avoidance of school.
Social Anxiety Disorder (Social Phobia)	Unusual or excessive fear of being scrutinized and evaluated in social situations.	Symptoms in children may include crying, tantrums, freezing up, clinging and failing to speak. Adolescents may go to extreme lengths to avoid social situations.

SOURCES: Anxiety and Depression Association of America (2014); APA (2013).

death. The person loses interest in things that she previously enjoyed. Children and adolescents may show more irritability than sadness (APA, 2013).

Depression in children prior to adolescence is relatively rare, affecting about 1% of children (Sadock & Sadock, 2008), although it can be diagnosed in children as young as 3 (Luby, 2010). The key to assessing depression in children this young is to use age-appropriate measures. For instance, a young child might not be able to talk directly about negative thoughts, but might show these thoughts in play (Luby, 2010). Assessment at this early age is important because preschool children who are depressed have a much higher likelihood of continuing to experience depression as they grow older (Luby, Si, Belden, Tandon, & Spitznagel, 2009). The incidence of a major depressive disorder increases to 11% among adolescents aged 13 to 18 (Avenevoli, Swendsen, He, Burstein, & Merikangas, 2015). Because a relationship has been found between depression in adolescence and a number of problematic behaviors later in development, it is important that we not ignore these symptoms or mistake them for typical adolescent moodiness. In a recent analysis of national data, researchers report that 75% of adolescents who experience a major depressive disorder will attempt suicide at some point in their lives (Nock et al., 2013). This information may make you wonder if depression has become an epidemic among adolescents, but a review of studies conducted over a 30-year period found no increase in the prevalence of adolescent depression across that time (Costello & Angold, 2011).

As you can see in Figure 10.1, the incidence of depression increases throughout adolescence, with adolescent girls being 3 times more likely than adolescent boys to have had a major depressive episode in the past year (National Institute of Mental Health, 2014). The number of adolescent girls who report feeling sad or hopeless is higher than the number for boys for all ethnic/racial groups (CDC, 2014k). To date, much of the research that has looked at depression in children and adolescents from ethnic minorities has found mixed results, but several large-scale studies have found no difference in rates of depression among different ethnic groups (Latzman et al., 2011; Twenge & Nolen-Hoeksema, 2002).

Adolescents who are depressed are at a substantially increased risk of also suffering from an anxiety disorder, the most common mental health disorder to co-occur with depression. Rates of co-occurrence can be as high as 75% (Cummings, Caporino, & Kendall, 2014). This high rate of co-occurrence can be explained by the substantial overlap in the symptoms used to assess each of the conditions, or by the fact that the disorders share a similar set of risk factors, such as a family history of the disorders, certain information processing biases, or a biological predisposition to them (Garber & Weersing, 2010). Another possibility would be that these disorders are linked in a sequence. Suffering with an anxiety disorder could be a contributing factor to later developing depression. Fortunately, both conditions respond to the same types of treatment. There are several medications that are effective in treating both conditions, and cognitive behavioral therapy, which is described in more detail later in this section, also has been used successfully with both.

A variety of explanations have been proposed to explain gender differences in depression. Because of the sharp increase in depression in females at midpuberty, researchers have looked for biological causes, but there is *not* a great deal of support for this hypothesis. However, girls' reaction to the physical changes associated with puberty, such as an increase in weight, has been linked with lower body satisfaction and higher levels of depression (Vogt Yuan, 2007). Another possible explanation for higher levels of depression in girls is that they are more likely than boys to experience multiple stress events during adolescence, including daily hassles and interpersonal problems (Shih, Eberhard, Hammen, & Brennan, 2006). Finally, girls and boys are socialized differently, with boys being allowed to express their frustration and anger by acting out, while girls are socialized to internalize these feelings in a way that may take a psychological toll on them in the form of depression. Girls also

FIGURE 10.1

Depression among U.S. adolescents by gender and ethnicity.

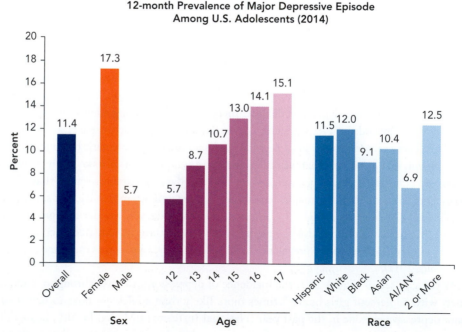

12-month Prevalence of Major Depressive Episode Among U.S. Adolescents (2014)

*AI/AN = American Indian/Alaska Native

SOURCE: National Institute of Mental Health (2014).

are more likely to try to cope with difficulties by ruminating about them; that is, they focus over and over again on their failures and the causes and outcomes of those failures. This coping style is much more likely to lead to depression than more positive ways of coping, such as focusing on positive aspects of events or distracting oneself with other activities (Papadakis, Prince, Jones, & Strauman, 2006).

Although chronic or severe depression is a serious emotional condition, it is one that is treatable. However, less than 40% of depressed teens receive treatment (Substance Abuse and Mental Health Services Administration [SAMHSA], 2009), often because symptoms are mistaken for "normal" adolescent moodiness. **Cognitive behavioral therapy**, in which a therapist helps the individual change maladaptive behaviors and also maladaptive thoughts in order to reach problem-focused goals can help a person change the way he thinks about and deals with his problems and can improve coping and social skills (Desrocher & Houck, 2013; Weersing & Brant, 2010). Although antidepressant medications are frequently used in the treatment of depression in adults, they may not work as well for adolescents and may even carry additional risks (Maughan, Collishaw, & Stringaris, 2013; Wolfe & Mash, 2006).

Teen depression. Although girls are more likely to experience depression in adolescence than boys, 10% of boys also go through this difficult emotional state.

Cognitive behavioral therapy A therapeutic approach based on changing maladaptive thoughts and behaviors to deal with problem-focused goals.

As noted earlier, depression can lead to suicide, the third leading cause of death among youth between the ages of 10 and 24 (CDC, 2015k). The risk is particularly high among teens who cope with negative emotions by suppressing them rather than finding a way to express how they feel (Kaplow, Gipson, Horwitz, Burch, & King, 2014). In addition to 4,600 teen deaths attributed to suicide each year, many more young people attempt to kill themselves. When high school students were surveyed about suicidal thoughts they had had in the previous year, 16% said they had seriously considered it, 13% reported having a plan, and 8% had made an attempt (CDC, 2015k). Although more girls than boys attempt suicide, boys are much more likely to actually die from a suicide attempt in part because boys are more likely to use guns while girls are more likely to use poison (including drug overdose), which allows for emergency treatment (CDC, 2015k). In fact, 81% of the suicides in the 10- to 24-year-old age group are male. Native American and Alaskan Native teens have the highest rate of suicide fatalities. Teens, especially girls, who have had a friend commit suicide are more likely to think about it and act on those thoughts themselves (Abrutyn & Mueller, 2014).

Because children and adolescents spend so much time in the school environment, schools are the logical context in which to implement programs to reduce the risk of suicide. Table 10.3 describes the major types of school-based interventions. Programs that are *universal* are ones that target everyone in a school with the goal of reducing risk factors or enhancing protective ones. *Selective programs* focus on subgroups that are considered to be at particular risk in the future. *Indicated interventions* are designed for individuals who have already expressed suicidal intentions and have made an attempt. Note that being at risk of suicide includes both having made an attempt and having thought about engaging in behaviors that could end one's life (Robinson et al., 2013).

Despite the widespread adoption of suicide awareness and prevention programs that claim to represent the best practices in the field, the overall evidence for their effectiveness is weak

TABLE 10.3

School-based suicide risk prevention and intervention programs.

Program Type*	Target Population	Description/Goals	Limitations
Awareness or Educational Programs	Universal (entire grade or school)	All students are exposed to an educational curriculum designed to make students more familiar with the signs and symptoms of suicide so they can recognize them in themselves or others.	Changes attitudes and knowledge but not behavior. A supportive network may not be available to individuals identified as suicide prone.
Screening Program	Universal or selective	All students or at-risk students are screened to identify those who should be referred for additional services.	Services must be available following screening. Screening may misidentify those who are or are not suicidal.
Gatekeeper Training	School staff	Teachers, administrators, and staff are trained to recognize the warning signs of suicide and to refer students for mental health services.	Services must be available. Training is more effective at changing attitudes than behavior.
Skills Training	Universal	Teachers, administrators, and staff learn skills, such as coping, problem solving, and decision making, that can reduce suicide intentions. Goal is to lower suicide risk factors.	Training does not target suicide specifically.

*Note that programs often are hybrid programs that combine different elements into a unique program designed for a particular school or district.

SOURCES: Katz et al. (2013); Robinson et al. (2013).

(Katz et al., 2013; Robinson et al., 2013). Each type of program has its own advantages and limitations as shown in Table 10.3.

Many people think that asking someone about suicidal thoughts will put ideas into that person's head, so they avoid talking about the subject with teens. The fact is that asking about suicide will not make it more likely that someone will think about it or do it and may be very important if help can then be found for the individual (SAMHSA, 2012). When a young person does commit suicide, friends and other peers often need help dealing with their reactions. Schools should have a plan in place that includes providing counseling to those requesting it. The American Foundation for Suicide Prevention (2011) provides a toolkit with a suggested statement that schools can use to help students understand what has happened. It says: "[Suicide] is usually caused by a mental disorder such as depression, which can prevent a person from thinking clearly about his or her problems and how to solve them. Sometimes these disorders are not identified or noticed; in other cases a person with a disorder will show obvious symptoms or signs. One thing is certain: there are treatments that can help. Suicide should never, ever be an option" (p. 15).

T ☐ F ☐ Asking a teen whether he is thinking about committing suicide will make it more likely he will do it.
False

TRUE/FALSE VIDEO ▲

ANGER AND AGGRESSION

Problems with aggression and impulsivity have been described as "the most persistent and common forms of childhood maladjustment" (Olson, Bates, Sandy, & Lanthier, 2000, p. 119). Fortunately, most children learn to control their anger as they get older, but a relatively small group shows a high level of aggression that persists (Campbell, Spieker, Burchinal, Poe, & NICHD Early Child Care Research Network, 2006; Cote, Vaillancourt, LeBlanc, Nagin, & Tremblay, 2006).

In a study of over 1,100 children, researchers identified trajectories of aggressive behavior between the time the children were 24 months old and when they were 9 years old, as shown in Figure 10.2 (Campbell et al., 2006). Most of the children displayed low or moderate levels of aggression as toddlers, and this level decreased across time. However, a small group of children showed high levels of aggression in toddlerhood that persisted through the ages

FIGURE 10.2

Changes in levels of aggression with age. At the start of this study of aggression, 2-year-olds differed in their scores on a measure of aggression. While initial levels were moderate to low for most toddlers, they were high for one group. Over time, the level decreased for most groups, but for the group that started at the highest level, levels remained high throughout the study to age 9.

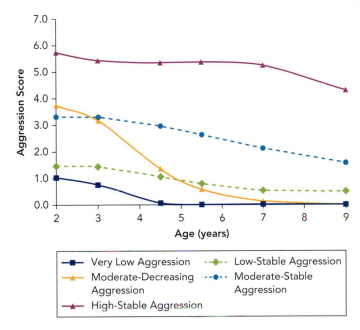

SOURCE: Campbell et al. (2006).

studied. When levels of aggression remain high, they are associated with academic problems, relationship problems, peer rejection, and even later criminal behavior (Olson et al., 2000). Aggression is a primary symptom in oppositional defiant disorder, disruptive mood dysregulation disorder (DMDD), and conduct disorder, so we next look at these disorders in more details.

Oppositional Defiant Disorder (ODD)

Being oppositional or defiant from time to time is one way children assert their need to be autonomous. However, when confrontation, defiance, and argumentativeness become part of a persistent pattern of behavior, the child may have a behavioral disorder known as **oppositional defiant disorder** or ODD. Oppositional defiant disorder includes three types of symptoms: angry/irritable mood, argumentative/defiant behavior, and vindictiveness (APA, 2013). Because symptoms include fairly common behaviors such as temper tantrums, argumentativeness with adults, refusal to comply with adult requests, and aggression toward peers, knowing when these behaviors have moved beyond the normal range to become disordered behavior is a challenge, but the frequency and severity of occurrence are considered when making a diagnosis.

It has been difficult to determine the cause of oppositional defiant disorder, but both the child's temperament and factors within the family environment play a role. Gerald Patterson and his colleagues at the Oregon Social Learning Center have described a pattern of interaction that frequently occurs in families with defiant children that they call a **coercive family environment** (Granic & Patterson, 2006). Coercive behavior forces someone else to do something that person doesn't want to do. The pattern starts when the child behaves in some way that irritates the parent, for instance jumping on the furniture, and the parent asks the child to stop. Instead of complying with this request, the child engages in some other coercive behavior like whining or throwing a temper tantrum that annoys the parent even

Oppositional defiant disorder A persistent pattern of behavior marked by defiant, disobedient, and hostile behavior toward authority figures.

Coercive family environment A pattern of family interaction in which parents and children mutually train each other so that the child becomes increasingly aggressive and the parents become less effective in controlling the child's behavior.

iStock/killerb10

Dealing with defiant behavior. It is normal for young children to assert themselves by being defiant from time to time, but it is how parents respond to this behavior that can lay the groundwork for later problems. Parents need to be firm and consistent in handling normal defiance.

Disruptive mood dysregulation disorder (DMDD) Severe and frequent temper tantrums that are out of proportion with the situation.

Conduct disorder A persistent pattern of behavior marked by violation of the basic rights of others or of major age-appropriate social norms or rules.

more. The child's behavior is so annoying that the parent gives up, perhaps with a statement like, "You never listen to anything you are told to do." In the child's mind, he has won this battle so it reinforces the child's coercive behavior. Likewise, when the parent gives up and the child stops crying or whining, the peace and quiet reinforces the parent's ineffective parenting. This sets up a pattern of confrontation, followed by opposition, followed by defeat for the parent and success for the child.

Oppositional defiant disorder typically is identified in preschool children (Shaw, Owens, & Giovannelli, 2001), but it can appear for the first time in early adolescence (McMahon & Kotler, 2006; Patterson, Dishion, & Yoerger, 2000). Early onset is associated with ineffective parenting and a difficult temperament in the child. Interventions that help parents provide structure in the home environment and establish daily routines can have some success in breaking the cycle, particularly if they begin before the child starts school (Egger, 2009; Shaw et al., 2001). In the case of late-onset oppositional defiant disorder, the adolescents typically have families who have done at least a marginally good job of setting limits and monitoring their child's behavior up to this point, but parental monitoring wanes in early adolescence and the influence of deviant peers becomes so strong that the adolescent is drawn into deviant behaviors (Patterson & Yoerger, 2002).

Disruptive Mood Dysregulation Disorder (DMDD)

Disruptive mood dysregulation disorder (DMDD) is first diagnosed in children between 6 and 10 years of age when they have "severe and recurrent temper outbursts that are grossly out of proportion in intensity or duration to the situation" three or more times per week (APA, 2013, p. 156). Children with DMDD are irritable and angry most of the time and in many different situations.

DMDD is a new diagnosis in the DSM-5 and there has been controversy over whether it is a unique and independent diagnosis (Mayes et al., 2015). Although it is considered more severe than oppositional defiant disorder, its two primary symptoms—irritable/angry mood and temper outburst—are ones shared with a number of other disorders. In a recent study that assessed DMDD symptoms in children 6 to 12 years of age and re-assessed the children eight years later, only 29% of children whose symptoms were a problem when first assessed remained a problem at the end of the study (Mayes et al., 2015). This new diagnostic category will need to continue to be scrutinized for its validity and usefulness to clinicians.

Conduct Disorder

An even more serious diagnosis is **conduct disorder**, which the DSM-5 describes as a "repetitive and persistent pattern of behavior in which the basic rights of others or major age-appropriate social norms or rules are violated" (APA, 2013, p. 469). The behaviors used to diagnose this condition include aggressiveness toward people and animals, property destruction, deceptiveness or theft, and serious rule violations, including frequently running away from home or being truant from school (McMahon & Kotler, 2006).

Rates of conduct disorder vary from less than 1% to 10% of the U.S. population (APA, 2013). Similar to what we saw in the case of oppositional defiant disorder, there is a childhood-onset type and an adolescent-onset type of conduct disorder (Moffitt & Caspi, 2005). The early-onset variety is associated with "inadequate parenting, neuro-cognitive problems, and temperament and behavior problems" (Moffitt & Caspi, 2001, p. 355), and is 10 times more likely to affect boys than girls. The adolescent-onset variety is associated with ethnic minority status and time spent with deviant peers (McMahon & Kotler, 2006) and there is a 5-to-1 ratio of males to females (Moffitt & Caspi, 2001).

Conduct disorder is one of the most difficult disorders to treat, but multisystemic treatment (MST) has shown some promise (Curtis, Ronan, & Borduin, 2004). Based on Bronfenbrenner's ecological theory, described in Chapter 2, this approach examines many levels of influence that may be contributing to the problem, including family, peers, school, and community. The therapist and family work together to build on strengths within the family and the community to overcome problems. In a meta-analysis of 11 studies, MST was found to make substantial improvements in family relations and to decrease children's aggression toward peers, involvement with other conduct-disordered youth, and overall criminality (Curtis et al., 2004).

Treatments such as MST that actively involve the family seem to work better than those that remove the child from the family, often to programs based on confrontation or "tough love" (Duffy, 2014). As intuitive and appealing as wilderness programs and boot camps may sound, they do not reduce recidivism and can actually be harmful to youth conduct (Cullen, Blevins, Trager, & Gendreau, 2005; Lyman & Barry, 2006). These group interventions put adolescents who have been delinquent together in a setting where they have the opportunity to share information about their crimes and learn from each other, When this happens, deviant peers actually reinforce each other's delinquent behavior (Duffy, 2014). Because the child or adolescent eventually needs to be able to function in his or her home, school, and community, treatment that keeps the family together as a unit makes achieving that goal more likely. Even if the adolescent were to acquire some positive skills as part of an out-of-home treatment program, if he or she returns to an environment that does not support those behavioral changes, they are not likely to persist.

Mauro Fermariello/Science Source

Conduct disorder. A conduct disorder involves aggression, a serious violation of another person's rights, or a major violation of societal rules. Age-inappropriate behavior such as drinking at this young age could be part of a pattern of behavior that indicates a potentially serious problem.

T ☐ F ☐ Programs that use a "tough-love" approach (for example, wilderness camps, boot camps) for adolescents with conduct problems have been highly successful at rehabilitating these young people. **False**

CHECK YOUR UNDERSTANDING

1. What is the difference between fear and anxiety?
2. Why is it dangerous to mistake a major depression for normal adolescent moodiness?
3. What role does a coercive family environment play in the development of an oppositional defiant disorder?
4. What is multisystemic treatment?

THE DEVELOPMENT OF SECURE ATTACHMENT

10.5 What is attachment and why is it important for development?

Love is one of the most important and formative of emotions. The first love that we develop is for those who care for us, usually our parents. The love in this relationship consists of an emotional bond, known as **attachment**, which is central to the well-being of infants and

Attachment An emotional bond to a particular person.

children as they grow. In this section, we look at how attachment develops, how it differs from person to person, and what its consequences are. Before continuing, try **Active Learning: Experiencing a Sense of Secure Attachment**.

Active LEARNING

Experiencing a Sense of Secure Attachment

In a quiet place, close your eyes and relax for a brief time. Keeping your eyes closed, try to remember a time in your life when you felt cared for, secure, and loved. If you are able to bring forth a memory, stay with it for a few minutes. Experience that feeling. Who are you with in this memory? What is happening? Now slowly open your eyes and return to the present. Reflect on your experience. How did you feel? Was there one person in particular who helped you feel that way? This activity is designed to elicit feelings connected with the experience of emotional attachment. These are feeling-memories that we may call on in times of stress. This exercise is not necessarily an easy one to do, so do not be alarmed if you were not able to call forth a memory.

Secure attachment A strong, positive emotional bond with a person who provides comfort and a sense of security.

Secure attachment is a strong, positive emotional bond with a particular person who provides comfort and a sense of security. If you are attached to someone, you are more likely to turn to that person for comfort when you are distressed. You are usually happy to see that person and may be unhappy about separations. This is a person with whom you can feel free to be yourself in the fullest sense. Although we talk quite a bit about the development of attachment in infants, attachment remains central to our well-being throughout our lives.

Journey of Research: The History of the Study of Attachment gives you more information about how our thinking about the roots of attachment has changed over the years.

Attachment across the life span. Attachment begins in infancy but continues throughout our lives.

JOURNEY OF *Research*

The History of the Study of Attachment

In the early to mid-1900s, both psychoanalytic and behavioral theorists developed ideas about how the bond between child and parent is formed. Both theories were based on the idea of **drive reduction**—that is, the idea that human behavior is determined by the motivation to satisfy basic needs, such as hunger. When we feel hungry, we are driven to seek out food, and our drive is reduced when we eat. In both theories, the development of a child's attachment to his mother is based on the mother's ability to satisfy such drives. Specifically, as the mother provides food to satisfy the infant's hunger drive, the infant learns to associate his sense of satisfaction, or drive reduction, with her presence and develops an attachment to her.

In the 1950s, new ideas about the nature of attachment appeared. In 1958, Harry Harlow published an article titled "The Nature of Love" in which he reported the results of his research with macaque monkeys. To test his ideas about how attachment forms, Harlow separated infant

Nina Leen/Time & Life Pictures/Getty Images

Harlow's monkeys. In his research, Harry Harlow (1958) found that monkeys preferred a soft cloth "mother," even if it did not provide food, over a wire "mother" that provided food through a bottle. How did this finding challenge the ideas of both psychoanalytic and behavioral theories of attachment?

Drive reduction The idea that human behavior is determined by the motivation to satisfy or reduce the discomfort caused by biological needs or drives.

monkeys from their mothers at birth and raised them with two surrogate mothers. One "mother" was a wire mesh tube, and the other was a wooden tube covered in sponge rubber with terry cloth wrapped around it so that it would be comfortable to touch. Half the monkeys were fed from a bottle protruding from the wire mother, and half were fed from the cloth mother.

What Harlow found was that infant monkeys spent the majority of their time clinging to the cloth mother regardless of which surrogate mother provided milk. When the infant monkeys were frightened by a loud, moving toy, they were more likely to run to the cloth mother for security. When they were placed in a new, unknown setting, they again preferred to cling to the cloth mother and eventually were able to explore the room, using it as a safe base to return to when they became frightened. When the cloth mother was absent, the babies were distressed and unable to explore the environment or play. Harlow came to believe that the primary function of nursing a baby might actually be to provide contact comfort with the mother and that it was this contact comfort that created the mother-infant attachment, not feeding as the behaviorists and psychoanalysts believed.

At about the same time, John Bowlby, a child psychiatrist trained in psychoanalysis, was exploring his observation that separations from parents had an enormous impact on

(Continued)

(Continued)

the psychological well-being of children seen in a psychiatric clinic (Ainsworth & Bowlby, 1989). Bowlby believed that Harlow's research with monkeys confirmed his suspicions that a psychoanalytic explanation for attachment was not adequate.

Bowlby also was intrigued by a new theory that was based on the observation of natural behavior of animals. Remember from Chapter 2 that Konrad Lorenz's theory of ethology proposed that genes produce certain behaviors and that, if these behaviors help the animals adapt successfully to their environment, those genes will be handed down from one generation to the next. In 1958, Bowlby set forth his new theory of attachment based on ethology. He argued that attachment is a biologically based, active behavior related to the infant's need for protection in order to survive. Bowlby believed that infant behaviors such as crying, smiling, sucking, clinging, and following are adaptive behaviors that promote the survival of the child by helping develop attachment between mother and child.

In what ways is attachment adaptive? First, because infants are dependent on an adult caregiver to provide all the things that keep them alive, it makes sense biologically that they would have behaviors built into their repertoire that are designed to keep an adult nearby. Crying, smiling, and following all serve this purpose. Second, when infants feel secure, they are able to explore their environment, checking back from time to time with a parent as a form of "emotional refueling," like a car that runs out of gas and needs to be filled up to continue on its travels (Mahler, Bergman, & Pine, 2000, p. 69). The child uses the parent as a **secure base for exploration** and because exploration is essential for human learning, these behaviors are adaptive.

In 1950, Mary Ainsworth joined Bowlby's research team (Ainsworth & Bowlby, 1989). Ainsworth was interested in assessing and classifying different types of emotional security. When she moved from England to Uganda in 1954, she began her research by observing mothers and their infants. These and subsequent observations led to the classification of four categories of attachment: secure attachment, anxious avoidant attachment, anxious ambivalent/resistant attachment, and disorganized/disoriented attachment. The basic theory outlined by Bowlby and Ainsworth remains the underlying model for most of the work on attachment being done today.

Secure base for exploration The use of a parent to provide the security that an infant can rely on as she explores the environment.

THE DEVELOPMENT OF ATTACHMENT: BOWLBY'S STAGES

As John Bowlby (1969) brought new ideas from Harlow's research and from ethological theory into his research on attachment, he described the following four stages in the early development of attachment:

1. **Preattachment** (birth to 6 weeks)

2. **Attachment in the making** (6 weeks to 6–8 months)

3. **Clear-cut attachment** (6–8 months to 18 months–2 years)

4. **Goal-corrected partnership** (also referred to as the *formation of reciprocal relationships*; 18 months on) (Ainsworth, Blehar, Waters, & Wall, 1978)

Preattachment (Birth to 6 Weeks)

From their earliest days, infants act in ways that attract others to care for them. It is very difficult to sit and do nothing when we hear a baby crying, especially if that baby is our

Preattachment The stage of development of attachment from birth to 6 weeks, in which infant sensory preferences bring infants into close connection with parents.

Attachment in the making The stage from 6 weeks to 6 to 8 months in which infants develop stranger anxiety, differentiating those they know from those they don't.

Clear-cut attachment The stage from 6 to 8 months to 18 months to 2 years, when an infant develops separation anxiety when a person he is attached to leaves him.

Goal-corrected partnership The stage of development of attachment from 18 months on, when toddlers create reciprocal relationships with their mothers.

own. Both new mothers and new fathers experience hormonal changes following childbirth that may increase their responsiveness to their baby's distress. Their body responds with more rapid heartbeats and other physiological responses that promote caregiving to their new babies (Feldman, Weller, Zagoory-Sharon, & Levine, 2007; Weisman, Zagoory-Sharon, & Feldman, 2014).

As we discussed in Chapter 6, the sensory preferences of the infant predispose them to social interactions with the world in general, and with their mothers in particular. Newborns can immediately imitate some facial expressions, they prefer to see faces rather than inanimate objects, they respond to voices, and most love to be touched and held. Their cry communicates their needs to those around them and draws others to care for them. Even at birth infants look at other people's eyes and begin to follow the direction in which someone is looking with their own gaze (Farroni, Massaccesi, Pividori, & Johnson, 2004).

First smiles. It is a wonderful reward for a new parent when an infant begins to smile at her mother, and fathers feel the same thrill. This is an early step in the process of forming a specific attachment to the infant's caregivers.

Attachment in the Making (6 Weeks to 6–8 Months)

Babies begin to smile at about 6 weeks of age. At first, these smiles seem almost random, but by about 2 months, babies clearly have developed a social smile directed specifically at people (Wörmann, Holodynski, Kärtner, & Keller, 2014). Very quickly, smiling becomes reserved for people the baby recognizes. A 3-month-old baby may look seriously at a stranger but begin to grin when he sees his mother. These early signs of recognition and responsiveness begin to lay a foundation of a special relationship with the familiar and important people in the baby's social world.

In many infants, this early discrimination of familiar from unfamiliar intensifies. If you have ever gone to babysit for a 6-month-old infant who has never met you before, you know what **stranger anxiety** means. Sometimes all the baby has to do is see a stranger and he begins wailing. In other cases, the baby may interact and smile as long as he is in his mother's arms, but if the stranger tries to hold him, the crying begins.

Clear-Cut Attachment (6–8 Months to 18 Months–2 Years)

In this stage, infants begin to move about on their own and become able to actively maintain contact with their caregiver. Infants now clearly discriminate between their attachment figures and strangers. During this stage, babies seek out their parents when stressed or afraid, and separation from parents, in and of itself, becomes frightening so infants protest when their parents leave. This distress is referred to as **separation anxiety**. An infant crying at the departure of someone who helps the infant feel secure does not indicate an excessive attachment to that person. It is quite a normal reaction. In addition, the parent becomes a secure base for exploration. When a parent is around and the infant can get to the parent, she is comfortable to explore her environment, but if the parent is absent, exploration may stop.

Stranger anxiety Fearfulness that infants develop at about 6 months of age toward people they do not know.

Separation anxiety Distress felt when separated from a parent.

T □ F □ When babies cry because a parent has left, it is evidence that they are too attached to their parents. **False**

You may recall a time when you felt homesick, perhaps on a school trip, at summer camp, or even when beginning college. Although you can control your emotions better than an infant, you still may have felt anxious about being on your own without the people who made you feel most comfortable. Did you call or text your parents or friends back home more frequently? In this situation, you can see that we continue to need the same "emotional refueling" we see in infants.

Goal-Corrected Partnership (18 Months On)

As the baby becomes a toddler, she becomes increasingly aware that her mother has goals and motives that are different from her own. At this point she realizes that she must create a partnership with her mother through their interaction. This partnership is based on the idea of two separate individuals interacting, each with an equal role in keeping the interaction going (Bowlby, 1969).

Toddlers are now able to form symbolic representations of the particular attachment relationships they have experienced (Bowlby, 1969). This concept, referred to as an **internal working model** of attachment, has helped psychologists understand how early attachment patterns contribute to the types of close relationships that children—and even adults—develop later in life. Based on past experiences with caregivers, an inner script develops, so in this sense children's future interactions are shaped by their past interactions. For example, a child who has been abused may expect aggression from others, and this expectation will shape how the child behaves when meeting new people. Abused children may respond to new people by provoking them to be angry, possibly re-creating the abuse situation the children previously experienced. This behavior may seem strange but can be understood as an attempt to reduce the uncertainty of the new situation and to control the child's fears by making the new situation one that the child can at least understand based on previous experiences. In a similar way—but with a very different outcome—children who have been warmly cared for come to expect that others will treat them positively, so these children themselves act in a warm and engaging way. Their own positive behaviors then elicit positive responses from others.

Although research supports the idea that internal working models are fairly stable over time, there also is evidence that they can be modified (Cobb & Davila, 2009). It takes time and patience to overcome the negative expectations a child with a negative working model of attachment has developed for new relationships, but it can be done.

SECURITY OF ATTACHMENT

As you read in **Journey of Research: The History of the Study of Attachment**, Mary Ainsworth worked with John Bowlby and further developed his ethological theory. Ainsworth was interested in looking at individual differences in the types of attachment that infants and mothers formed together, based on the degree of security the infant felt in that relationship. She developed a procedure known as the Strange Situation to classify types of attachment. The Strange Situation places an infant and mother in a series of situations that become increasingly stressful for the infant. Except for the first episode, each lasts 3 minutes unless the baby is crying, in which case the time period is cut short.

Attachment as a secure base for exploration. Securely attached children will play away from the parent, as long as they can go back from time to time for some "emotional refueling."

Hilary Helton/Photolibrary/Getty Images

Internal working model Mental representations of the particular attachment relationships that a child has experienced that shape expectations of future relationships

1. An observer brings mother and baby into a comfortable room equipped with a one-way mirror and immediately leaves.

2. Baby plays while mother responds naturally.

3. Stranger enters, and at the end of 3 minutes the mother leaves.

4. Baby is in the room with the stranger, who may interact with the baby.

5. Mother returns, stranger leaves, and at the end of 3 minutes the mother again leaves.

6. Baby is alone for 3 minutes.

7. Stranger enters and may interact with the baby.

8. Mother returns. (Ainsworth & Bell, 1970)

Partnership of mother and child. By 18 months children like this boy actively attempt to maintain an interaction with their mother, creating a goal-corrected partnership.

Based on her observations of infants' reactions during the **Strange Situation,** Ainsworth described four types of attachment: secure attachment, and three types of insecure attachment: anxious avoidant attachment, anxious ambivalent/resistant attachment, and disorganized/disoriented attachment. The two behaviors that Ainsworth found best identified the type of attachment relationship infants had with their mother were (1) the child's ability to be comfortable and explore a new setting while the mother was in the room, with the mother acting as a secure base for exploration; and (2) the child's response to the mother's return to the room, known as *reunion behavior,* as assessed by whether the child, who was stressed by the mother's departure, was able to use the mother after her return to calm down so the infant can return to playing. Interestingly, distress at separation itself was *not* a reliable indicator of type of attachment. Table 10.4 describes the typical infant and mother behaviors associated with each type of attachment.

Strange Situation Mary Ainsworth's experimental procedure designed to assess security of attachment in infants.

TABLE 10.4

Types of attachment. This table shows Ainsworth's four types of attachment with their associated behaviors in the Strange Situation and aspects of mothering that have been related to each type.

Type of Attachment	Security/ Organization	Safe Base for Exploration	Reunion With Caregiver	Early Mothering
Secure	Secure/organized	Explores freely with caregiver present	Seeks out caregiver and is easily soothed by caregiver	Responsive to infant's needs
Anxious Avoidant	Insecure/ organized	Explores with or without caregiver's presence	Does not seek out caregiver	Emotionally unavailable, dislikes neediness
Anxious Ambivalent/ Resistant	Insecure/ organized	Stays close to caregiver, doesn't explore freely	Both seeks and rejects contact with caregiver	May be attentive, but not in response to baby's cues or needs
Disorganized/ Disoriented	Insecure/ disorganized	May "freeze," explores in a disorganized fashion	May go to caregiver while looking away, shows a dazed expression or fear	Intrusiveness, maltreatment and/or emotional unavailability, or caregiver behavior is confusing or frightening

SOURCES: Ainsworth (1979); Shamir-Essakow, Ungerer, & Rapee (2005); Sroufe (2005); Sroufe, Egeland, Carlson, & Collins (2005).

Infants with secure attachment rely on their parent to respond to their needs, and turn to their parent when they are stressed. The baby's reliance on a trustworthy parent allows him to explore the environment, knowing that mother is there if help is needed. In contrast, infants with insecure attachment have learned that their parent is not as available to them and have adapted in one of two ways. In **anxious avoidant attachment**, the mother has been unresponsive to her infant, and the infant has learned not to rely on her help and support. This infant is not distressed when his mother leaves the room, is just as comfortable with the stranger as with his mother, and, when his mother returns to the room, does not rush to greet her. In **anxious ambivalent/resistant attachment**, the mother may interact positively with the infant, but she does not respond to the infant's cues. For example, she may ignore the baby when he is trying to get her attention but may interact when the baby is more interested in sleeping than interacting. In anxious ambivalent/resistant attachment, the infant is reluctant to move away from his mother to explore the room, is very distressed when his mother leaves the room, and will not let the stranger comfort him. However, when mother returns, the infant's behavior is described as "ambivalent" because he seems to want to approach his mother but also appears to be angry and resists the mother's attempt to pick him up (Bosma & Gerlsma, 2003).

Although the three types of attachment differ in level of security, or trust, in their relationships, all three are organized and coherent ways of responding to a particular situation. The fourth category, **disorganized/disoriented attachment**, describes infants whose behavior is unpredictable and odd and shows no coherent way of dealing with attachment issues (Hennighausen & Lyons-Ruth, 2010). This category is often linked with parental abuse or neglect and is connected with unmanageable fear. Think about how this pattern would develop. The very person to whom the baby would normally turn when afraid is the same person who is causing the fear. The babies don't know what to do or where to turn. They cannot organize their behavior because they do not have a predictable environment. They never know what to expect or what is expected of them.

ATTACHMENT AS A RELATIONSHIP

Attachment is based on the relationship between two people, each of whom has an impact on the nature of the relationship. The interaction of a particular child and a particular parent creates a unique relationship that is different from that of any other two people.

The Role of the Mother

What could affect the ability of a mother to be a sensitive, responsive caregiver to her baby? The factors are remarkably similar to those that help someone through any stressful situation. Mothers are more likely to respond positively to their babies when they have the following:

- A positive relationship with their partner

- Adequate economic resources

- Good psychological health

- A history of good care in their own childhood

- An infant who is easy to care for (Cox, Paley, Payne, & Burchinal, 1999; Crockenberg & Leerkes, 2003; Figueiredo, Costa, Pacheco, & Pais, 2009; Martins & Gaffan, 2000)

In 1979, two medical doctors, John Kennell and Marshall H. Klaus, vigorously promoted the importance of early attachment. Their research appeared to show that newborn human infants must experience close skin-to-skin contact with their mothers within a few hours after birth for the mothers to be able to form a bond with them. This research transformed

Anxious avoidant attachment An attachment classification in which the infant is not distressed when her mother leaves, is as comfortable with the stranger as with her mother, and does not rush to greet her mother when she returns.

Anxious ambivalent/resistant attachment An attachment classification in which the infant is reluctant to move away from his mother to explore and is very distressed when she leaves, but when she returns, he approaches her but also angrily resists her attempt to pick him up.

Disorganized/disoriented attachment An attachment classification in which behavior is unpredictable and odd and shows no coherent way of dealing with attachment issues, often linked with parental abuse or neglect.

the way that hospitals treated new mothers and their infants. Rather than being immediately separated after birth, newborns and their mothers were given an opportunity to interact. However, subsequent research failed to confirm the long-term effect of this type of early contact (Eyer, 1992; Figueiredo et al., 2009; Myers, 1984). For a healthy newborn, immediate skin-to-skin contact is wonderful for both mother and baby, but does not determine their emotional attachment to each other. In the case of premature infants, the normal attachment process can be disrupted by the extraordinary care that premature infants require, so taking infants out of the incubator to allow mothers to have skin-to-skin contact with their newborns does help to promote attachment and improves the baby's development through age 10 (Feldman, Rosenthal, & Eidelman, 2014).

> **T ☐ F ☐** Mothers must have immediate contact with their babies after they are born if a secure attachment is to be formed.
> **False**

The Role of the Father

Fathers have often been neglected in the research on infant attachment, but it has become clear that infants are capable of forming more than one relationship and that the unique relationship they develop with their fathers plays an important role in their lives (Palm, 2014). Some research has shown that fathers are more likely to react sensitively to their sons than their daughters and that baby boys are more likely than baby girls to be securely attached to their fathers (Schoppe-Sullivan et al., 2006). One possible explanation lays in the different types of interactions that mothers and fathers have with their infants. While mothers are frequently a source of security, fathers are more likely to be a stimulating playmate for their infants. There may be a better match between a father's active and stimulating play style and a son's attention pattern than is true for daughters (Palm, 2014). Other characteristics of the father are also important. Fathers who are more extraverted, who better understand the infant's state of mind, and who believe that they play an important role in their child's development are more likely to have a secure attachment with their children (Palm, 2014). However, both boy and girl infants form attachments to both parents during their first year. In about two-thirds of the cases, the attachment security category is the same for both parents (Lickenbrock & Braungart-Rieker, 2015). When an infant has a secure attachment to the father, the infant also is very likely to have a secure attachment with the mother, but the reverse is not necessarily the case. A secure attachment to the mother does not guarantee a secure attachment to the father (Kobak, Rosenthal, & Serwik, 2005).

The Role of the Infant

Infants, too, play a role in the type of attachment relationship formed with the parent. Each infant's temperament affects the way that parents respond to that child. Parents must adapt differently to infants who are highly active or irritable than to infants who are calm and placid. While you might expect that a baby who is irritable and temperamentally difficult would be harder for a parent to care for, resulting in more insecure attachment, this does not appear to be the case. Research has shown that for parents with adequate resources having an irritable baby can lead to *more* secure attachment (Gartstein & Iverson, 2014; Leerkes & Crockenberg, 2006). Perhaps mothers of irritable babies need to be even more attuned to their needs in order to soothe them, and some research has found that this can result in a more secure attachment relationship.

Ariel Skelley/Blend Images/Getty Images

Not "bonding," but . . . Although their research was flawed, the ideas of Kennell and Klaus (1979) about early bonding helped change hospital practices. This mother reflects the joy of being handed her newborn immediately after birth.

David Sacks/Lifesize/Thinkstock

Attachment to the father. Fathers as well as mothers can form strong attachments to their infants. The same characteristics—being sensitive and responsive to the infant's needs—are important for father-infant and mother-infant attachment.

Other infant characteristics such as being born prematurely or having neurological problems can affect the way attachment is first formed because it is more difficult for a mother, even a sensitive one, to read the signals from an infant with a developmental impairment (Brisch et al., 2005).

All Together Now

Researchers are increasingly looking at the complexity of the attachment relationship within the context of the family, society, and culture (Palm, 2014). They are looking at attachment as an ongoing relationship in which the characteristics and behaviors of the parent and the baby shape each other over time. For example, in one study, when infants in the first 6 months of life had a high level of intense and frequent crying, mothers were less likely to be highly sensitive to their infants by the time they were 6 months old. This combination of factors, in turn, led to the infant having an insecure attachment at 1 year of age (Sroufe, 2005). In other words, the baby's behavior affected the mother's ability to respond sensitively, and this interaction influenced the quality of the attachment relationship. To further complicate the picture, Crockenberg and Leerkes (2003) found that mothers were likely to be less sensitive to these infants only when they were already at risk because of poverty, inadequate social support, or a history of parental rejection. As we noted previously, mothers who were *not* at risk were often *more* engaged with their fussy babies.

A way to check your own understanding of the various factors that influence attachment is to see if you can use and apply that information. Try **Active Learning: Educating Parents** to see how you might apply what you have learned about attachment.

Active LEARNING

Educating Parents

Imagine that you are a parent educator. Given what you now know about the formation of attachment, plan a class for new parents to explain what attachment is and how they can promote a secure attachment in their baby. To help you get started, you will want to think about how you would define attachment for these new parents. What would you tell them about where attachment comes from and how stable it is? What are the best things a parent can do to help ensure their infants will develop a secure attachment? What are some things parents can do for themselves to help them become effective parents?

Parents don't have to be perfect to have a securely attached infant. There is enough resiliency in both infants and parents that most often the outcome is a positive one. As we've seen, development of secure attachment is influenced by both infant and parent, as well as by the circumstances in which the family finds itself. It is too easy to blame the mother when there are difficulties, so it is essential that we take the whole picture into account when evaluating an infant who is not developing an optimal attachment relationship.

Attachment to Nonparental Caregivers

Reading all of this information about mother-infant attachment may be making you wonder if mothers are the only ones who can or should take care of infants and young children. We've already pointed out that fathers also form significant attachment relationships with their infants. However, some parents are concerned that attachment to a child care provider will undermine the child's attachment to them. In 1991, the National Institute of Child Health and Human Development (NICHD) began a large, longitudinal research project at 10 locations across the United States designed to examine the effects of early child care on child development. Based on numerous studies that came from this project, the rather surprising conclusion was that many of the characteristics that were expected to affect the quality of an infant's attachment to parents, including the number of hours spent in care, the quality of the care itself, and the type of care, had very few significant effects (Friedman & Boyle, 2008). It appears that most children do not need exclusive contact with parents for a secure attachment to form.

DEVELOPMENT IN ACTION VIDEO ▲

In fact, for mothers who were sensitive caregivers, secure attachment was more strongly related to maternal sensitivity than to any characteristic of out-of-home care. For mothers who were insensitive caregivers, however, the negative effect of their insensitive mothering was magnified if: (1) the quality of the nonmaternal care also was poor, (2) the infant spent more than 10 hours a week in care, or (3) the infant had experienced more than one child care arrangement within his or her first 15 months (Belsky, 2005; NICHD Early Child Care Research Network, 1997). Interestingly, in a different study, infants with difficult temperaments were *more* likely to have secure attachment with their mother with *more* out-of-home care (McKim, Cramer, Stuart, & O'Connor, 1999). Perhaps when mothers got a break from these difficult infants, they were able to provide care to their infants in their homes with more enthusiasm.

The nature of an infant's attachment to caregivers is influenced by the relationships we have described, but it is also influenced by the infant's biological predispositions and by the larger cultural context in which the attachment relationship develops. We describe both of these influences in this section.

THE BIOLOGY OF ATTACHMENT

As we have seen throughout this book, researchers are uncovering many links between behavior and biology. In the study of attachment, they have looked for neurochemical explanations for the development of adaptive and maladaptive behaviors. Later in this chapter, you will read about children who were reared in situations marked by severe neglect in orphanages in Romania (Fries, Ziegler, Kurian, Jacoris, & Pollak, 2005). Many of these children continued to have problems forming secure attachment relationships with their adoptive parents even after they were adopted into families that loved them very much. Fries et al. (2005) found that 3 years after these children had been adopted, they had different hormonal responses to social interaction than other children.

Oxytocin is a chemical that has been linked with a positive feeling that arises in connection with warm social interactions. Children raised by their parents from birth experience a rise in oxytocin after interacting with their parents, but previously neglected children do not demonstrate a similar rise in oxytocin following interaction with their parents. Many also produce very low levels of vasopressin, a neurochemical linked with the ability to recognize individuals as being familiar (Carter, 2005). This may help to explain why children reared in deprived situations sometimes will run to any available adult when they are distressed. What is not yet clear from this research is whether these chemical responses are set for life or whether they can change with life experience.

Researchers also have identified differences in the way that children in the different attachment categories react to stress. Being under stress affects the release of cortisol by the hormonal system, activates the fight-or-flight response of the sympathetic nervous system, and interferes with the functioning of the immune system (Pietromonaco & Powers, 2015). An insecure attachment has been associated with impaired functioning of all three of these systems. For instance, infants who are ambivalently attached are uncertain of their caregiver's response when they need help, so they become hypervigilant and their stress response system overreacts to potential threats. Those who are avoidantly attached rely on strategies that minimize distress and distance themselves from others, so their system underreacts in the face of threat. It is infants who are securely attached who expect others to be available and responsive who can respond to distress in a flexible and effective way, turning to others when they need to. A secure attachment helps them regulate their emotions and thus their physiological response to stress (Gander & Buchheim, 2015). In this way, a secure attachment style helps infants develop strategies that will help them regulate affect and develop self-control.

ATTACHMENT AND CULTURE

Remember that Bowlby (1969) thought that attachment behaviors were adaptive behaviors that helped ensure the survival of infants. This would suggest that attachment should be seen in cultures all over the world, and quite a few cross-cultural studies have tested this premise. Many have focused on one of two questions: (1) Is the proportion of secure versus insecure attachments in infants similar from one culture to another? (2) What does a "securely attached" infant look like to parents in different cultures?

In regard to the first question, cross-cultural research has found that the proportion of infants who are classified by the Strange Situation as having a secure attachment does not differ very much from one country to another (Posada & Jacobs, 2001; van Ijzendoorn & Sagi-Schwartz, 2008). Secure infants typically account for about two-thirds of the infants in a study. What is more likely to differ, however, is the proportion of infants in the different categories of insecure attachment.

In American and Northern European cultures, the most common insecure category is avoidant attachment, but in Israel, Korea, and Japan, it is the anxious/ambivalent attachment category (Jin, Jacobvitz, Hazen, & Jung, 2012; Svanberg, 1998). Table 10.5 shows a comparison of secure, avoidant, and resistant attachment types in the United States, Japan, Korea, and a larger international sample of infants. Disorganized/disoriented attachment, which is not included in this table, was found in 9% of infants in Korea, compared to 15% in North American and European samples (Jin et al., 2012; Lyons-Ruth & Jacobvitz, 2008). In Japan, research on attachment has been complicated because the Japanese concept of *amae*, an emotional interdependence between a caregiver and child encouraged by the Japanese culture, is not identical to the Western concept of attachment (Rothbaum, Kakinuma, Nagaoka, & Azuma, 2007). This has led Nakagawa, Lamb, and Miyaki (1992) to question whether a

TABLE 10.5

Distributions of infant–mother attachment classification in diverse cultures. Although there are similar percentages of securely attached infants in many cultures, the type of anxious/avoidant or resistant attachment differs between countries.

	Avoidant A	Secure B	Resistant C
Sapporo, Japan	0 (0%)	41 (68%)	19 (32%)
Baltimore, USA	22 (21%)	70 (67%)	13 (12%)
Global Sample	423 (21%)	1,294 (65%)	273 (14%)
Taegu, Korea	1 (1%)	66 (78%)	18 (21%)

SOURCE: Jin, Jacobvitz, Hazen, & Jung (2012).

measure such as the Strange Situation, which has been used primarily with middle-class Western samples, is valid as a cross-cultural measure. We return to this issue of cross-cultural validity later in the section.

This leads us to our second question. Rather than asking where children in different cultures fall in Ainsworth's classification scheme, we can ask what parents in different cultures think a securely attached infant looks like. In the United States, mothers are more likely to associate secure attachment in their infants with autonomy and self-determination. In other words, a child is seen as secure if she can move away from her mother and play independently. Mothers in Japan are more likely to see their children as secure if they show behaviors that put them into harmony with others by being accommodating, well-behaved, and cooperative (Rothbaum et al., 2007). In addition, Japanese mothers are more likely to see their children's demands for attention (such as crying every hour through the night even though all their needs have already been met) as a need for closeness or interdependence, whereas American mothers tend to see this behavior as testing the limits and asserting one's self.

Likewise, although sensitive mothering is related to secure attachment in most cultures, the definition of sensitivity may vary. For example, Carlson and Harwood (2003) found that Puerto Rican mothers were more likely than mothers in Boston to be physically controlling of their infants. In the United States, this type of physical control has been seen as insensitive, but for Puerto Rican parents, physical control is positive because it leads to respectful behavior on the part of the child, which is highly valued in this culture. This reminds us that recognizing what a "good mother" does must be seen in a cultural context (Keller, 2013). Being intrusive in a Western culture can be interpreted as a mother being insensitive to her infant's need to be a separate and autonomous individual who has wishes of his own, but being directive and controlling is exactly what a good mother is expected to do in other cultures.

In Chapter 5, we described how a new mother might be quite isolated following the birth of her baby, but that would not be the case in many non-Western cultures. While Western cultures often rely on a dyadic relationship model (one that focuses on mother and infant), other cultures may rely on a social network model. The Efe in Zaire pass a newborn among a group of women who hold, carry, and even nurse her. Foragers in the Congo Basin Rainforest raise their children collectively and by the time an infant is only a couple of weeks old, he may routinely interact with 20 different caregivers each day (Keller, 2013). Through these early social interactions, infants are being socialized to fit into the collective social network structure of their culture. Attachment research has not always recognized or respected cultural differences in the socialization goals and caregiving strategies because these differences do not easily fit how we conceptualize or measure attachment. For instance, the concept of stranger anxiety is not meaningful in a culture in which infants are routinely handled by 20 or more caregivers. This research reminds us of how difficult it is to search for universal developmental processes when they can take so many forms as we move from one culture to another.

ATTACHMENT BEYOND INFANCY

Early attachment experiences are very important for later development. In this section, we examine the long-term effects of attachment security in infancy, and also look at other factors that limit or change the impacts of early attachment on later development. We then look at the nature of attachment relationships as children move through middle childhood and adolescence.

Long-Term Outcomes of Infant Attachment

Research has documented long-term effects of attachment security in infancy, as Bowlby's concept of internal working models would predict. As we described, in their early years, the relationship that securely attached infants have with their parents serves to soothe and

TABLE 10.6

Internal working models. Think about how having each type of internal working model of attachment would affect a child's approach to and interaction with new people.

Type of Attachment	Internal Working Model
Secure	I can trust and rely on others. I am lovable, capable, significant, and worthwhile. My world is safe.
Anxious Avoidant	Other people are unavailable and rejecting. I have to protect myself. If I deny my needs, I will not be rejected. If I do what is expected of me, I will not be rejected. If I take care of others and deny my own needs, I will be loved.
Anxious Ambivalent/ Resistant	Others are unpredictable, sometimes loving and protective, sometimes hostile and rejecting. I don't know what to expect—I am anxious and angry. I cannot explore—I may miss an opportunity for love and affection. If I can read others and get them to respond, I will get my needs met.
Disorganized/ Disoriented	My caregiver, at times, seems overwhelmed by me and, at other times, seems very angry with me. Others are abusive—neglectfully, physically, emotionally, and/or sexually. I am unable to get my needs met. I don't know how to protect myself.

SOURCE: Public Health Agency of Canada (2003).

modulate their reactions to frightening or other arousing events. This soothing is then internalized so that an older child or adolescent is able to soothe himself when needed. On the other hand, attachment insecurity and disorganization in infancy is related to later externalizing behavior problems such as aggression and oppositional behavior (Fearon, Bakermans-Kranenburg, van Ijzendoorn, Lapsley, & Roisman, 2010) and internalizing problems such as anxiety and depression (Groh, Roisman, van Ijzendoorn, Bakermans-Kranenburg, & Fearon, 2012). Table 10.6 provides examples of what is going on in the minds of children with different types of internal working models.

One reason that security of attachment in infancy can predict later outcomes is because there is a good deal of continuity of attachment styles over time. Several factors contribute to this continuity. For most people, their families do not change drastically, so characteristics of parenting remain stable over time and the patterns of attachment and adaptation that develop in infancy continue to be reinforced by later experiences. Also, as we have already described, children usually continue to behave in ways that cause their later relationships to replicate their earlier ones. However, what happens when a child's life circumstances *do* change? Ample evidence shows that new life circumstances can change a secure attachment to an insecure one and vice versa (Weinfield, Whaley, & Egeland, 2004).

For instance, parents who experience stressful life events often show declines in the quality of their parenting, and this can result in a less secure attachment. Moss et al. (2005) studied attachment in children at age 3½ and assessed their attachment again 2 years later. Although the majority of children maintained the same attachment style, they found that children whose attachment style changed from secure to insecure and/or disorganized/disoriented were more likely to have experienced events such as parental hospitalization or death, decreased quality of mother-child interaction, and decreased marital satisfaction of their parents.

It is also possible that parents whose lives become more stable as their children get older are able to develop more secure attachments with them (Moss, Cyr, Bureau, Tarabulsy, & Dubois-Comtois, 2005). If, for instance, the child's parents take part in a parenting intervention designed for parents of infants with insecure attachments, these programs can and do change parenting patterns and allow for changes in attachment over time (for example, see Bernard et al., 2012). This means that infants' earliest attachment experiences do not doom infants who begin with insecure attachment nor are they a guarantee for those who begin with secure attachment. Even though insecurely attached infants are at an increased risk for psychological problems compared to securely attached infants, a variety of factors, including having a positive relationship with some other caring adult or the child's own characteristics, can help promote positive development. We will return to a description of protective factors such as these in Chapter 15 when we talk about resilient children.

Even if attachment style remains consistent, Alan Sroufe and his colleagues have found that later experiences interact with early attachment relationships to help determine adult functioning. In 1974 and 1975, they recruited 257 low-income pregnant women for a longitudinal study. The children of these women were studied from birth through age 26 (Sroufe, Carlson, & Shulman, 1993). In early research reports, Sroufe and his colleagues reported straightforward effects of secure attachment in infancy on later development. Securely attached infants became children who were more competent in their interactions with peers, were more self-reliant, and had better self-control (Sroufe et al., 1993).

However, as the children got older, the picture became more complicated. For example, while the researchers did not find a *direct* link between early attachment and the ability to have intimate, romantic relationships in early adulthood, there was an indirect link, mediated through subsequent experiences in the person's life. Although secure attachment in infancy prepared the child for later positive peer relationships, the child's history with peer relationships independently predicted some aspects of adult relationships more clearly than early attachment history. Further, the researchers found that the combination of early attachment and later experiences with peers was even more predictive of some aspects of later romantic relationships. Research such as this suggests that each stage provides the foundation for the next stage, but experiences at each successive stage also can change the nature and direction of a child's development (Van Ryzen, Carlson, & Sroufe, 2012).

ATTACHMENT IN CHILDHOOD AND ADOLESCENCE

As children get older, they no longer need a caregiver to be physically close in order to feel secure, but they do need to have a sense that the caregiver is available to them in times of distress. As early as 1 year of age, children begin developing a **secure base script** which is their expectation for how their distress will be met with care, concern, and support. It includes the idea that if a child is in distress, he can approach someone for help who will be available and supportive, and the child will experience relief as the result of being close to this person (Waters & Waters, 2006). A securely attached child expects support, while an insecurely attached child does not.

A child's secure base script can be assessed by asking children to complete stories about what they would do in various situations when they need help (Psouni & Apetroaia, 2014). Research with 7- to 12-year-old children found consistency on the measure of a secure base script across situations (for instance, the child's idea of how a parent would help if the child did poorly on an exam and how a parent would help if the child was injured) and consistency across relationships (that is, the expectations the child has for a parent and for a peer) (Psouni & Apetroaia, 2014). Having a positive secure base script in times of distress enables a child to respond in an adaptive way.

Although most people would not question the continuing importance of attachment relationships for preschoolers and school-age children, the question of adolescent attachment to

T ☐ F ☐ If a child has developed an insecure attachment to a parent, that child can still become securely attached later in her life. **True**

Secure base script The expectation that a child develops that distress will or will not be met with care, concern, and support.

TRUE/FALSE VIDEO ▲

T ☐ F ☐ Teens who are securely attached to their friends are also likely to be securely attached to their parents. **True**

parents has been more controversial. Contrary to what some people think, parents remain important people in the lives of most adolescents, and the attachment relationship that began in childhood continues to be important to their well-being. Adolescents may not require their parents' physical presence to feel secure, but a sense that their parents are committed to them and their well-being continues to form a secure base that allows the adolescent to explore a widening world of social relationships and experiences (Gorrese & Ruggieri, 2012). At the same time, as relationships with peers become more intimate and more supportive, peers also begin to function as a type of attachment relationship. At one time, we thought of parent and peer relations as being in competition. It was assumed that as the importance of one of these relationships went up, the importance of the other would necessarily need to decrease. However, we now know that adolescents can maintain positive, high-quality relationships with both their parents and their peers, just as the idea of internal working models for relationships would suggest. A recent review of the literature on parent and peer attachment found that adolescents who report a secure relationship with their parents also tend to report a secure attachment with their close friends (Gorrese & Ruggieri, 2012).

Internal working models continue to influence our significant relationships in late adolescence as we develop committed romantic relationships. In a romantic relationship, we use our partner as a safe haven in times of stress and as a secure base for exploring the environment, and we even show separation distress when away from our partner for a significant period of time (Furman & Collins, 2009; Shaver & Mikulincer, 2014). These are all characteristics of a secure attachment we carry forward from early parent-child relationships. However, in a romantic relationship, each partner becomes an attachment figure for his or her partner. You can see how adolescent and adult attachment styles relate to Ainsworth's types of attachment described for infants in **Active Learning: Romantic Attachment Styles**.

Active LEARNING

Romantic Attachment Styles

The following table includes the descriptions used in Hazan and Shaver's (1987) research to describe romantic relationships. You should be able to recognize which of these descriptions fits the descriptions of three of the different infant attachment categories described earlier in this chapter. Review that information, if you need to, then read each description and match it to the correct infant attachment category. Ainsworth's categories are *secure, anxious avoidant,* and *anxious ambivalent/resistant*.

Romantic Relationship Descriptions	Attachment Category
I find that others are reluctant to get as close as I would like. I often worry that my partner doesn't really love me or won't want to stay with me. I want to merge completely with another person, and this desire sometimes scares people away.	1.
I find it relatively easy to get close to others and am comfortable depending on them and having them depend on me. I don't often worry about being abandoned or about someone getting too close to me.	2.
I am somewhat uncomfortable being close to others; I find it difficult to trust them completely, difficult to allow myself to depend on them. I am nervous when anyone gets too close, and often, love partners want me to be more intimate than I feel comfortable being.	3.

Answers: Box 1—anxious ambivalent/resistant; Box 2—secure; Box 3—anxious avoidant.

Hazan and Shaver found that the percentage of adults in their sample who fell into each of these categories was very similar to the percentages found in infant attachment research conducted in the United States. The respondents' perception of the quality of their relationship with their parents (and the parents' relationship with each other) was the best predictor of a respondent's romantic attachment style, but these researchers were careful to say that relationships are complex and personality variables such as attachment styles are not enough, on their own, to explain romantic attachment. Their results do, however, point to an apparent continuity in the quality of personal relationships over time.

CHECK YOUR UNDERSTANDING

1. What is an internal working model?
2. What are Ainsworth's four types of attachment?
3. What effect does non-parental care have on an infant's attachment to parents?
4. What differences in attachment categories has cross-cultural research found?
5. How does the quality of an infant's attachment affect relationships later in childhood and adolescence?
6. What is a secure base script?

ATTACHMENT DISORDERS

10.6 What is an attachment disorder?

Most children develop secure attachments to their caregivers and some have insecure attachments to specific caregivers, but only a rare few have such difficulty in all of their attachment relationships that they require intervention (Balbernie, 2010). The DSM-5 recognizes two such conditions, reactive attachment disorder (RAD) and disinhibited social engagement disorder (APA, 2013). Both are based on experiences during infancy, such as abuse and neglect, which interfere with the formation of secure relationships.

A child with **reactive attachment disorder (RAD)** is not able to form any attachment. The child is withdrawn from caregivers and shows disturbance in both social and emotional functioning (APA, 2013). A child with **disinhibited social engagement disorder** is indiscriminate in whom he goes to. He does not seem to have any special relationship with his caregiver, and his behavior is the same whether he is interacting with a stranger or someone he knows well (APA, 2013). It has been suggested that this type of indiscriminate attachment is actually adaptive for children who have been abandoned or mistreated because children who have no effective parenting may do best when they approach a range of adults for help (Balbernie, 2010). Part of the problem is that these children do not change their behavior even when adopted into caring families, and this can cause problems if the adoptive parents do not understand the roots of this unusual behavior.

Reactive attachment disorder (RAD) A disorder marked by inability to form attachments to caregivers.

Disinhibited social engagement disorder An attachment disorder in which children approach strangers indiscriminately, not differentiating between attachment figures and other people.

CAUSES OF ATTACHMENT DISORDER

The diagnosis of reactive attachment disorder was developed in part in response to the observations made in the 1960s by Tizard and her colleagues of children raised in orphanages in England (Tizard & Rees, 1975; Zeanah, Smyke, Koga, Carlson, & Bucharest Early Intervention Project Core Group, 2005). These children were raised with multiple and changing caretakers rather than a few people who knew and understood each child well. When Tizard observed the children at age 4, only one-third had formed secure attachments to a caregiver.

Romanian orphans. The terrible conditions in Romanian orphanages created lasting problems, even for children who were eventually adopted. The inability of these children to form emotional attachments was one of the most serious ones.

Much of the more recent research has focused on children raised in deplorable conditions found in orphanages in Romania. In the 1980s, the country's leader, Nicolae Ceausescu, wanted to increase the population so he abolished access to contraception and abortion and forced women to continue having children beyond the ability of their families to care for them. As a result, over 100,000 children were sent to Romanian orphanages that were not prepared to care for their physical, mental, or emotional needs (Kaler & Freeman, 1994). One study reported that an individual child would be cared for by as many as 17 different caregivers at different times in a single week, all of whom were caring for many infants at the same time (Zeanah et al., 2005). After reading earlier in this chapter about how an infant forms a secure attachment with a caregiver, you can see why these children could not form attachments. They never had the consistent, sensitive, or responsive caregiving necessary for this bond to form.

PREVENTION AND TREATMENT OF ATTACHMENT DISORDERS

One group of researchers developed a foster care program that could accommodate some of the institutionalized children from Romania (Smyke et al., 2012). They later compared the incidence of reactive attachment disorder in those who remained in the institutions to those in foster care and to a control group who had never been institutionalized. Institutionalized infants and toddlers between the ages of 6 and 30 months had more signs of RAD than the control group. However, for those who were then moved into foster care, the incidence of RAD declined to the same level as the noninstitutionalized control group. The researchers also assessed the children for indications of disinhibited social engagement disorder and found that these behaviors also declined, but in this case remained higher than the level of the control group. It appears that moving infants to a more secure environment improves attachment, but there may be limits to the improvement achieved, at least in the early years of a child's life. Families that adopt children with attachment disorders need to recognize that much hard work will be needed to try to reverse the negative effect of the child's earlier experiences.

Although the eventual outcome for many Romanian orphans who were adopted was positive, it is much better to try to prevent attachment disorders in high-risk populations, such as children living in poverty or in abusive families, than to try to fix the problem after it occurs. Bakermans-Kranenburg, van IJzendoorn, and Juffer (2003) found that the most effective approaches focused on developing the mother's sensitivity to her baby. As maternal sensitivity increased, so did infant-mother attachment. Although only a few programs to date have targeted the sensitivity of both mothers and fathers, those that did found an even greater effect than those that intervened only with the mother.

CHECK YOUR UNDERSTANDING

1. What is the difference between reactive attachment disorder and disinhibited social engagement disorder?

2. What are some causes of attachment disorders?

CONCLUSION

From early infancy onward, we must all learn to understand, express, and control our emotions. In this chapter, we have shown how our emotional experiences develop within the context of our close relationships with other people. Through our earliest attachment relationships, we develop our basic understandings about emotions, and we carry this knowledge with us into later relationships. At each stage of development, we add new levels of understanding and experience that build on each other to shape the nature of our feelings about others and about ourselves. In the next chapter, we see how emotional, cognitive, and even language development all contribute as the infant begins to develop a first sense of self, which leads eventually to the adolescent's ongoing development of identity.

CHAPTER SUMMARY

Test your understanding of the content.
Take the practice quiz at **edge.sagepub.com/levine3e**

10.1 What is emotion and how do biology and culture shape our emotions?

The experience of an **emotion** includes your body's physiological reaction to a situation, your interpretation of the situation, communication of the feeling to another person, and your own actions in response to the feeling. Within the first year of life, all infants show the **basic emotions**: happiness, sadness, fear, anger, interest, and disgust. Children need to learn the **emotional display rules** for their culture so they know when and how they can show various emotions. **Social referencing** is the process by which children check with others to see how to react in an emotionally ambiguous situation. We share other people's feelings when we have **empathy** for them, which can lead to feelings of **sympathy** which motivates us to help others. **Self-conscious emotions** that rely on self-awareness, including pride, **shame**, and **guilt**, do not develop until the preschool years or beyond.

10.2 What is temperament?

Temperament is the general way in which we respond to experiences in the world, such as being timid or fearless. Infant temperaments have been characterized as **easy**, **difficult**, or **slow to warm**. Mary Rothbart defined temperament as biologically based differences in reactivity and self-regulation. **Goodness of fit** describes the match between the temperament of an infant and the level of demand placed on the infant by the environment. Temperament is usually a stable characteristic of the individual, although it can change.

10.3 How do children learn to regulate and control their emotions?

Infants cannot regulate their emotional impulses, but they begin to develop self-soothing techniques, such as thumb sucking. Parents help infants develop emotional control by soothing them when upset, providing a predictable environment, and modeling self-control. Whether a parent has an **emotion coaching** or an **emotion dismissing** style influences how children learn to deal with their emotions. **Effortful control** allows children to consciously control their behavior so they can **delay gratification** when necessary or desirable. Self-control plays an important role in the development of **emotional intelligence**.

10.4 Describe how normal emotions develop and some emotional problems that children and adolescents experience.

What infants and children fear changes with their age. Fear, **anxiety**, sadness, and anger are normal emotions but when children's emotions become unmanageable, they can develop into disorders such as **anxiety disorders**, *phobias*, and **major depression**, and antisocial behavior, including **oppositional defiant disorder**, **disruptive mood dysregulation disorder**, or a **conduct disorder**.

10.5 What is attachment and why is it important for development?

Attachment is a strong emotional bond with a particular person that provides a sense of security. It is adaptive because it provides children the **secure base for exploration** necessary for exploring the environment. Bowlby described four stages in the development of attachment: **preattachment**, **attachment in the making**, **clear-cut attachment**, and **goal-corrected partnership** (or formation of reciprocal relationships). Children develop an **internal working model** of relationships that they carry into new relationships. Ainsworth described four types of attachment based on how an infant behaves in the **Strange Situation**. Infants can be classified as **secure, anxious avoidant, anxious ambivalent/resistant,** or **disorganized/disoriented**. Sensitive and responsive caretaking is related to a secure attachment. Infants can develop qualitatively different attachments to the adults in their lives, and can form a secure attachment to more than one person so high–quality child care does not harm children's attachment to their parents.

Attachment security affects the functioning of the hormonal, neurological, and immune systems of the body so it affects the way an individual responds to stress. Although the percentage of infants with secure attachment does not differ much among Western cultures, the ways that sensitive parenting and security in infancy are defined do differ.

There is a fair amount of continuity in attachment styles, but an attachment style can change if a child's situation changes significantly. Children develop a **secure base script** that determines their expectations for new relationships. Peers, and later romantic partners, become objects of attachment as children move into adolescence then adulthood. Adolescents can be securely attached to both parents and peers.

10.6 What is an attachment disorder?

A **reactive attachment disorder** (withdrawal from emotional connections to all people) or **disinhibited social engagement disorder** (indiscriminately attaching to anyone) can occur in children who have been abused early in their lives or deprived of consistent, sensitive caregiving. Treatment can help, but full recovery is difficult.

KEY TERMS

Strengthen your understanding of these key terms with mobile-friendly eFlashcards at **edge.sagepub.com/levine3e**

practice
AND
apply
WHAT YOU'VE LEARNED

edge.sagepub.com/levine3e

chapter 11

IDENTITY
The Self, Gender, and Moral Development

©iStockphoto.com/mikeuk

Master these objectives using an online action plan at **edge.sagepub.com/levine3e**

TEST YOUR KNOWLEDGE

Test your knowledge of child development by deciding whether each of the following statements is *true* or *false,* and then check your answers as you read the chapter.

1. **T ☐ F ☐:** Young children develop a sense of self in about the same way in cultures around the world.

2. **T ☐ F ☐:** Children's self-esteem is extraordinarily high in early childhood.

3. **T ☐ F ☐:** Programs that help build students' self-esteem not only improve their grades but also help reduce delinquency, drug use, and adolescent pregnancy.

4. **T ☐ F ☐:** The self-esteem of most adolescents remains high and stable from mid-adolescence through early adulthood.

5. **T ☐ F ☐:** By comparison to other ethnic and racial groups, Asian American adolescents have the lowest self-esteem.

6. **T ☐ F ☐:** Today most parents do not reinforce gender-specific stereotypes and treat their sons and daughters in very similar ways.

7. **T ☐ F ☐:** Most lesbian, gay, bisexual, and transgender (LGBT) adolescents are optimistic about their future.

8. **T ☐ F ☐:** Because we learn to imitate the behaviors that we see, children raised by homosexual couples are much more likely to become homosexual themselves when they become adults.

9. **T ☐ F ☐:** For African Americans, a strong identification with their ethnic group is linked with fewer problem behaviors at school.

10. **T ☐ F ☐:** Your moral values and beliefs are the best predictor of what you will actually do when faced with a moral dilemma.

Correct answers: (1) F, (2) T, (3) F, (4) T, (5) T, (6) F, (7) T, (8) F, (9) T, (10) F

▲ **VIDEO: Watch as students answer some of these questions and the authors respond.**

If you were asked to describe yourself, what would you say? Take a minute to make a list of terms that you would use. You will use this list later as a point of comparison with the descriptions that we typically find for preschoolers, school-age children, and teenagers and when we discuss self-esteem. In this chapter, we look at many aspects of the "self" and how those different aspects change as the individual moves through childhood and adolescence. We start by looking at the self-concept, the totality of how you describe yourself and your relationships. Next, we look at self-esteem, or how you evaluate and feel about those characteristics. We also discuss several important aspects of a person's sense of who she is: her gender identity, ethnic and racial identity, and moral identity.

DEVELOPMENT OF SELF-CONCEPT

11.1 How does the sense of self that develops in infancy become identity in adolescence?

The modern study of the self began back in the 1890s, when William James (1892/1992) wrote about two aspects of the self: the "I" self and the "me" self. Just as

FIGURE 11.1

Ratio of personal-to-social statements in self-descriptions in two cultures. This figure shows the mean personal-to-social ratio of statements in the self-descriptions of young Euro-American and Chinese children. Euro-American children who live in an individualistic culture use more personal than social descriptions compared to Chinese children who live in a collectivist culture.

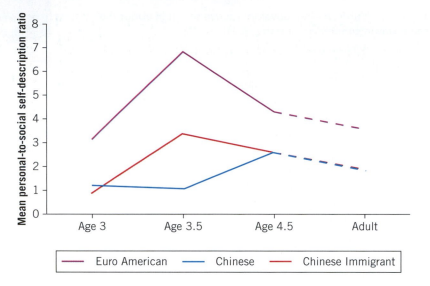

SOURCE: Wang (2006).

Cultural values. Children are socialized into the values of their cultures, and these values become part of how they see themselves. Children in individualistic cultures (such as the United States) often take great pride in individual achievement and success, while children in collectivist cultures (such as China) are more likely to see themselves as embedded in a rich network of social relationships that take precedence over individual needs or accomplishments.

the word *I* is used as the subject or actor in a sentence (for example, "I am reading this book"), James conceptualized *I* as the self that experiences or acts on the world. The word *me* is used as the object in a sentence (for example, "Look at me!"), and for James this second aspect was the self that we can think about and define with characteristics such as being a hard worker or an outgoing person. Both of these aspects of self change throughout childhood and adolescence.

Building on these ideas, sociologist Charles Cooley (1902/1964) suggested that our sense of self is largely a reflection of how other people see us, what he termed a *looking-glass self*. Cooley proposed that first we form a picture of ourselves and our characteristics, and then we see how others react to us and base our self-concept on our interpretation of the reactions of others. In other words, our sense of self is the product of our interaction with others in our social world.

SELF-CONCEPT AND CULTURE

Recall our discussion of individualistic and collectivist cultures from Chapter 1. As we saw, individualistic cultures place a high value on the role of the individual and individual achievement. In the United States, an individualistic culture, we tend to see people as separate, autonomous individuals who choose their own paths in life. In contrast, collectivist cultures conceptualize the self as part of a group, and the goals of that group take priority over individual accomplishments. Read these self-descriptions from two 6-year-old children:

> I am a wonderful and very smart person. A funny and hilarious person. A kind and caring person. A good-grade person who is going to go to [a prestigious university]. A helpful and cooperative girl.

> I'm a human being. I'm a child. I like to play cards. I'm my mom and dad's child, my grandma and grandpa's grandson. I'm a hard working good child. (Wang, 2006, p. 182)

Can you guess which description came from an American child and which came from a Chinese child? Euro-American children typically include more traits and abilities ("I'm smart," "I am funny") in their descriptions, while Chinese children include more situational descriptions ("I play with my friend after school") and overt behaviors ("I like to play cards"). Euro-American children also are more likely to include positive evaluations like "beautiful" or "smart" while Chinese children use less evaluative descriptions like "work hard." Euro-American children place more emphasis on the personal aspects of their lives, and Chinese children place more emphasis on the social aspects of theirs (Wang, 2006). Do you feel that the self-description you wrote at the beginning of this chapter reflects the values of your culture?

In all societies, individuals define themselves both in terms of individual characteristics and in terms of their relationships to others, but the *ratio* of personal-to-social references is different between the groups, with Euro-American children using more personal references relative to the number of social references Chinese children use (Raeff, 2004). Figure 11.1 shows that these cultural differences appear early in development and persist into adulthood. One important implication of these cultural differences is that the way you embody and enact those characteristics that are valued by your society has a significant impact on how you feel about yourself, that is, your self-esteem.

T ☐ F ☐ Young children develop a sense of self in about the same way in cultures around the world. **False**

THE SELF IN INFANTS AND TODDLERS

How early in development does a sense of self emerge? Psychoanalyst Margaret Mahler argued that infants are not born with a sense that they have a self that is separate from those who take care of them (Mahler, Pine, & Bergman, 1975). Babies must develop this sense, and they appear to do it in two stages. The first understanding of self is based on the infant's growing ability to make things happen (similar to William James's "I" self): "I make this mobile move" or "I make my mommy smile." The baby's *intention* to make things happen reflects her awareness that she is the agent of change. Rochat (2001) has argued that this first understanding then leads to a new concept of "me" when the child can begin to think *about* herself. Self-awareness means that the child is the object of her own perceptions and thoughts, similar to James's "me" self (Gallup, Anderson, & Shillito, 2002). This second type of awareness begins to develop in the second year of life. Four ways in which this new sense of self is expressed are mirror self-recognition, use of the pronouns *I* and *you*, visual perspective taking, and possessiveness. All four develop at about the same time, somewhere near the child's second birthday (Rochat, 2015).

Vanessa Davies/Dorling Kindersley/Getty Images

That's me! Shortly before their second birthday, toddlers in Western cultures begin to recognize their own image in the mirror. Prior to this, they may have been fascinated by the baby in the mirror, but now they know who that baby is—they are looking at themselves.

Mirror Self-Recognition

The classic experiment that has been carried out to determine whether a toddler has physical self-awareness is the mirror self-recognition task. In this task, the toddler's parent pretends to wipe the toddler's nose, but secretly puts rouge or lipstick on the Kleenex and marks the child's nose. The child is then placed in front of a mirror. If the child realizes that the image in the mirror is really himself and not another child, he will touch his own nose when he sees the funny red mark on it. Children at 1 year of age will not do this. Instead, they react as if their mirror image were another child with whom they can interact. It is not until sometime between 18 and 24 months that children in Western societies understand that the mirror image is a reflection of themselves and they touch their own nose (Broesch, Callaghan, Henrich, Murphy, & Rochat, 2011; Gallup et al., 2002). However, culture affects the age at which toddlers develop this understanding and recognize their own mirror image. Toddlers raised in cultures that value autonomy and individualism recognize themselves earlier than ones from collectivist cultures that value relationships over individuality (Kärtner, Keller, Chaudhary, & Yovsi, 2012).

Use of Pronouns

You may hear toddlers say something like "Daddy, pick you up, pick you up!" when what they mean is "Daddy, pick me up!" Using *I* and *you* appropriately is not something that can be learned by imitation. The child hears Daddy say, "I'll pick you up," so he imitates what he hears. Only when the child understands that *I* and *me* are different from *you* does he become able to use the pronouns correctly and say "Pick me up!"

Before this time, many resort to the strategy of referring to themselves by name—for example, "Joseph do it!" The child's understanding of pronouns increases when parents use a combination of pronouns and the child's name in their speech (Smiley, Chang, & Allhoff, 2011). This seems to help the child to understand that "That's Sylvie's book" and "That's your book" mean the same thing. They must make the link that when someone else says "you" they mean Sylvie, but when Sylvie herself says "you" she means the other person.

Infants begin to understand terms such as *my* and *mine* as early as 12 months of age, and they can begin to use personal pronouns like *my* and *mine* between the ages of 15 and 18 months (Saylor, Ganea, & Vazquez, 2011). The ability to use both *I/me* and *you* correctly is linked with mirror self-recognition (Lewis & Ramsay, 2004). The developing sense of self is shown as both abilities develop during the middle of the second year.

Visual Perspective-Taking

Visual perspective-taking The understanding that other people can see an object from a point of view that is different from one's own.

If you ask a toddler to show you her drawing, she may hold it up so that she can see it, but you cannot. She assumes that because she can see it, you must be able to see it as well. In Chapter 7, you learned that Piaget described this as egocentric behavior, because the child cannot see the situation from someone else's point of view. The child must develop an understanding that you and she are separate people with different points of view to develop what is called **visual perspective-taking**. This ability develops in toddlers between 18 and 24 months of age (Moll & Tomasello, 2006). Ricard, Girouard, and Gouin Décairie (1999) found that developing this ability to see from another's perspective was linked with the ability to use *I* and *you* correctly. Perspective-taking ability is also linked with culture. Individuals growing up in collectivist cultures, which value interdependence more than individualism, generally have a greater ability to take the perspective of others than those from individualistic cultures, whose focus is more on the self (Wu & Keysar, 2007).

Possessiveness

Two-year-olds are entering what Erik Erikson (1963) referred to as the stage of *autonomy versus shame and doubt*. Being "autonomous" means that you are independent and have some control over what happens to you. Toddlers assert their autonomy, or separation of self from others, through two of their favorite commands: "No!" and "Mine!" Their ability to do this is linked to the ability to recognize themselves in a mirror (Rochat, 2015).

As they develop a clearer sense of themselves as separate from those around them, toddlers are motivated to defend their own way of doing things and what they think belongs to them. In one study, Levine (1983) found that 2-year-old boys who recognized themselves in a mirror and were able to understand and use *I* and *you* accurately were more likely than those with a less clear sense of self to claim toys when interacting with an unfamiliar peer. Caregivers who deal with toddlers should see this toy claiming not as selfishness but as a first expression of the child's understanding that "I have a self that is different from yours."

It's mine! Possessiveness is another component of toddlers' growing sense of self. Once they know that they are a separate individual, they also understand that there are things that belong to them.

PhotoAlto/Sigrid Olsson/Getty Images

THE SELF IN PRESCHOOLERS

For Erikson, the toddler is trying to become autonomous in relation to his parents; that is, he is becoming a separate self. For the preschooler, the self becomes tied to what the child can do. If you recall Erikson's stages of psychosocial development described in Chapter 2, Erikson (1963) describes the central issue of this stage as *initiative versus guilt*. Preschoolers try to initiate activity; that is, they want to do things, to create, and to make things happen. However, they may fail at these attempts to do things by themselves, and that can lead to guilty feelings that they have done something wrong, especially if parents are impatient with their failed attempts. The child's definition of self as "what I do" is reflected in Susan Harter's (1999) illustration of a preschooler's self-description:

> I'm 3 years old and I live in a big house with my mother and father. . . . I have blue eyes and a kitty that is orange. . . . I know all of my ABC's, listen: A, B, C, D, E, F, G, H, J, L, K, O, M, P, Q, X, Z. I can run real fast. . . . I can count up to 100. . . . I can climb to the top of the jungle gym, I'm not scared! I'm never scared! I'm always happy. . . . I'm really strong. I can lift this chair, watch me! (p. 37)

Can you list the characteristics that make up this description? It includes physical description (blue eyes), possessions (a kitty), abilities (knowing ABCs, climbing, lifting a chair), feelings (never scared), and some basic information—the child's age and where he lives. Are these similar

"I can do it myself!" During the preschool years, children struggle with becoming autonomous and being able to do things by themselves. Parents can support this growing autonomy by being patient with their children's attempts.

Westend61/Getty Images

to the way you described yourself in the beginning of the chapter? In all likelihood, there are some major differences.

At this age, children also begin to develop a more coherent set of memories about their lives, which is referred to as *autobiographical memory*. Although autobiographical memories are based on our unique life experiences, the content also reflects cultural differences. In individualistic cultures, memories focus more on events that have significance for the individual, such as getting a desired toy, while in collectivist cultures they highlight the interconnectedness of the individual to others, such as family vacations (Ross & Wang, 2010; Wang, 2008).

The way parents talk with their children about what happens in their lives also has an effect on the way children remember their lives. When parents guide their children in discussions about events, children are better able to remember details about their lives and may even understand them in more complex ways (Haden, 2003). Memory for the events in one's life plays an important role in the development of a self-concept (Prebble, Addis, & Tippett, 2013).

THE SELF IN SCHOOL-AGE CHILDREN

As children enter middle childhood, they become able to think about themselves in more complex ways. Erikson (1963) describes this developmental period as a conflict of *industry versus inferiority*. Erikson saw middle childhood as the time when children set aside childhood fantasies and begin the work that is needed to learn the "industry" of their society. In most modern societies, this means going to school to prepare for adult life. Erikson also saw that this is an age when children begin to compare themselves to others and don't always come out on top. In carrying out this social comparison, they can think, "I am better than Joe at arithmetic but not as good as Arina at reading." This reflects a new ability to coordinate two or more concepts at the same time. While younger children can only think of one thing at a time, older children can keep more than one thing in their minds—their own performance and someone else's performance—in order to compare them (Harter, 2006b). This is, of course, exactly what Piaget would say that children of this age are able to do cognitively.

While young children tend to see themselves in an all-or-nothing way ("I'm never scared! I'm always happy"), children between 8 and 11 years of age are refining their self-concepts to include shades of gray; for example, "I get sad *if* there is no one to do things with" (Harter, 2006b, p. 527). They can also experience more than one feeling at a time; for example, "I was happy that I got a present *but* mad that it wasn't what I wanted" (Harter, 2006b, p. 527).

THE SELF IN ADOLESCENTS

It is not surprising that the physical, cognitive, and social changes that occur during adolescence are reflected in changes in the self-concept. In particular, the cognitive changes that occur during the stage of formal operations are reflected in how the adolescent can think about the self. Self-descriptions become more abstract (Harter, 1999) and contain more psychological attributes (Martins & Calheiros, 2012). Adolescents also can incorporate contradictory traits in their self-descriptions. They now understand that they can show different characteristics in different situations but that these differences are all part of a unitary whole. For example, an adolescent might say, "I am usually a pretty friendly, outgoing person, but I really clam up when I am around adults." Adolescents have the cognitive ability to pull these divergent pieces of the self together into a coherent whole.

Erikson described the developmental crisis of adolescence as *identity versus role confusion*. According to Erikson (1963, 1968), in order for development to proceed in an optimal way, the young person must figure out and become comfortable with who he is but also must think about the person he wants to become as he moves from adolescence into young adulthood. An important part of this process of identity development is "trying on" different identities,

Teen identities. *As part of the process of identity development, adolescents may "try on" different identities like "skater," "brain,"or "jock."*

and that helps explain some of the behaviors we associate with adolescence. Teenagers experiment with new activities or associate with new friends, and sometimes they even take on new identities (Cross & Fletcher, 2009). An adolescent who has held conventional views and attitudes may flirt briefly with the Goth culture or begin spending time with the hipsters or the stoners at school. Most of the time, adolescents settle on a positive identity, one that is approved by society, but sometimes the identity that the adolescent adopts is one that parents or other adults would not approve of, or what Erikson (1963) called a **negative identity**. Choosing to be a druggie or burnout provides the adolescent with a ready-made identity with a clearly defined set of attitudes, values, and behaviors that go with it and these may clearly state to parents, "I am not you."

When adolescents are able to develop a strong sense of their own identity, they are in a good place to deal with the next developmental issue that emerges in early adulthood: *intimacy versus isolation*. Individuals with a strong sense of identity are able to enter into an intimate relationship and to connect their identity with another individual without losing their own sense of self in the process.

Marcia's Identity Statuses

The Canadian developmental psychologist James Marcia extended Erikson's work on identity development by describing the process by which adolescents work toward achieving an identity. According to Marcia (1966; see also Kroger, Martinussen, & Marcia, 2010; Luyckx, Goossens, Soenens, & Beyers, 2006; Meeus, van de Schoot, Keijsers, Schwartz, & Branje, 2010), identity achievement requires adolescents to engage in a period of active *exploration* of the alternatives available to them (a process he has also labeled *crisis*), followed by a personal investment in the choices they make, a process he calls *commitment*. By combining these two processes, Marcia named and described the four identity statuses shown in Table 11.1.

Identity Diffusion. If you talk with some adolescents about their future, it becomes clear they haven't spent much time thinking about it and, what is more, they don't seem overly concerned about it. Adolescents who experience **identity diffusion** feel both a lack of crisis (or the perceived need to explore alternatives) and a lack of commitment to a future identity.

Identity Foreclosure. Some adolescents make a firm commitment to an identity even before they have engaged in an active process of exploration. How can you feel that you already know who you will become in the future without having actively looked for an identity? You may have grown up in a family in which everyone expected you to become a doctor, a teacher, or a police officer, and these expectations became an unquestioned part of the way you saw yourself. In this case, you would have foreclosed (or cut off) other possibilities. In many parts of the world, **identity foreclosure** is the norm because choices are limited. For

Negative identity An identity that is in direct opposition to an identity that parents or other adults would support.

Identity diffusion A lack of interest in developing an identity.

Identity foreclosure Commitment to an identity without any exploration of possibilities.

TABLE 11.1

Marcia's identity statuses. According to Marcia, identity development during adolescence reflects two processes: exploration of the alternatives available and commitment to an identity. Where an individual is on these two processes determines the adolescent's identity status.

		Crisis (exploration)	
		Low	High
Commitment	Low	Identity Diffusion	Identity Moratorium
	High	Identity Foreclosure	Identity Achievement

example, Bedouin Arab youth, who live in a more collective and authoritarian society, had higher levels of foreclosure than urban Arab youth (Dwairy, 2004). In another study, higher rates of foreclosure were found among the Cameroonian Nso youth than among German youth. The authors of this study speculated that children and teens in more collectivist societies may find a satisfactory identity by adopting elements of their identity from their parents. In other words, the type of identity may fit the nature of the society in which the children live (Busch & Hofer, 2011).

Identity moratorium A time of exploration in search of identity, with no commitment made yet.

Identity Moratorium. Adolescents in the status of **identity moratorium** are actively exploring alternatives that can shape their future identity so, in Marcia's terms, they are in a state of crisis. However, they are not yet ready to commit to a specific choice. For example, you may remain undeclared in your major in college as you try out different subjects or even take time off from school to explore and define your interests before making a commitment to one.

Identity achievement The choice of an identity following exploration of the possibilities.

Identity Achievement. Finally, adolescents who have actively explored the alternatives and who are now ready to commit to one of the possible identities are in the status of **identity achievement**.

Although movement between statuses is possible, the process of identity formation is *not* as dynamic as we might expect it to be. Stability within a status category over the course of a longitudinal study can be as high as 59%, which means that almost 6 out of 10 participants do not change their status over the course of the study (Meeus et al., 2010). Where movement does occur, it is likely to be in the direction of identity achievement (Meeus, 2011). But even adolescents who have an achieved identity status can have new experiences that shake up their commitment to an identity and push them back into a state of moratorium. Having a close relationship with someone who has different attitudes or values than you have, traveling to a part of the world you have never seen before and experiencing a new culture, or coming to college and being exposed to new ideas—any of these experiences could shake up a previously solid commitment to an identity.

One question has been whether teens must create distance from their parents in order to develop their own identity. It appears that the opposite is true. Teens are more likely to develop a committed identity when they have warm and supportive relationships with their parents (Crocetti, Branje, Rubini, Koot, & Meeus, 2016). Relationship with parents affect the development of identity, but development of identity then allows teens to have more supportive relationships with both parents and siblings.

Keep in mind that Marcia's process of exploring and committing can apply to any aspect of identity development, not just the choice of a future occupation (Bergh & Erling, 2005). Later in this chapter, we see how Marcia's ideas have been applied to the development of an ethnic or racial identity. People are likely to change at least some aspects of their identity even during adulthood. Significant life events such as the birth of a child, a divorce, or a change in health can motivate you to reevaluate your identity.

Rites of passage. The Xhosa circumcision ceremony in southern Africa, the quinceañera in the Latin American tradition, and the Bar Mitzvah in the Jewish tradition are all cultural ceremonies intended to do the same thing: acknowledge the transition of a young person from the status of child to that of adult.

Look again at Table 11.1. Where would you place yourself in it? Where were you a year ago? Where do you think you'll be a year from now?

Adolescent Rites of Passage

In many cultures, identity development is promoted for adolescents through rituals called **rites of passage**. Rites of passage are designed to provide the individual with an experience that marks his or her movement from childhood to adulthood, while simultaneously announcing this change to the community. Many rites are based on religious beliefs, and some are explicitly linked to the sexual maturation of the adolescent. In the United States, several traditional rites of passage may already be familiar to you. In the Jewish tradition, boys at age 13 and girls at age 12 or 13 celebrate the *Bar Mitzvah* or *Bat Mitzvah* (which means "son, or daughter, of the commandment" in Hebrew). In this ceremony, the boy or girl may lead a religious service to display all he or she has learned in his or her religious education. A party follows to celebrate the child's acceptance as an adult member of the community, with the responsibility to carry out the religious commandments. A rite of passage that has come to the United States from Latin America is called the *quinceañera*. In this tradition, girls are given a special party to mark their 15th birthday (Alomar & Zwolinski, 2002). The girl dresses in an elaborate dress, possibly white, and is attended by a number of her friends. The high point of the event is a Catholic Mass of thanksgiving. Traditionally, the quinceañera announces that the girl is of marriageable age; in other words, she is no longer a child but has become a young woman.

In other parts of the world, rites of passage take a variety of forms that may not be familiar to you. In Bali it is believed that teeth are symbols of bad impulses, such as greed and jealousy, so they are filed down to make the person more beautiful, both physically and spiritually (Bali Travel Guidebook, 2002). Young people are considered to be adults after taking part in this ceremony.

In some cultures, the rites of passage are explicitly connected to the sexual maturation of adolescence. For example, the Navajo Kinaaldá ceremony is held the summer after a girl has her first menstrual period (Markstrom & Iborra, 2003). In southern Africa, traditional Zulu and Xhosa boys undergo circumcision during a ritual to mark their movement into manhood. The boys are supposed to perform an act of bravery, following which they are taken to a seclusion lodge where a circumcision ceremony takes place. They must show their manhood by not reacting to the pain. After the ceremony, the boys are painted with white chalk to show their purity. They are instructed by an elder on their adult responsibilities, including sexual responsibility. When the wounds are finally healed, they wash off the white chalk, and a great ceremony marks the end of their childhood and the beginning of their manhood (Mandela, 1994).

Reflect on the importance of any ritual that may have marked your movement from childhood to adulthood as you were growing up by answering the questions posed in **Active Learning: Rites of Passage**.

Rites of passage Rituals that publicly mark a change in status from child to adult.

Rites of Passage

Have you experienced anything you might consider a ritual that marked your movement to adulthood? In your religion, there may be rituals that happen in adolescence that mark a new level of responsibility and understanding. Although the United States has few formal rituals, you can probably think of important events that translate into the concept "I am an adult now." A common and meaningful one is receiving a driver's license. In our mobile society, being able to get from place to place on one's own is central to adulthood. What other events can you think of that are linked to public acknowledgement of a new maturity? Could you create a new rite of passage that would be meaningful to you and would symbolize the movement from childhood to adolescence in your community?

CHECK YOUR UNDERSTANDING

1. How does self-concept differ between cultures?
2. Which behaviors show that toddlers have begun developing a sense of self?
3. How does the sense of self differ between preschool and school-age children?
4. What are Marcia's identity statuses?

DEVELOPMENT OF SELF-ESTEEM

11.2 How does self-esteem change from preschool through adolescence?

Self-esteem How people feel about characteristics they associate with themselves.

We began this chapter by talking about self-concept, or how you describe yourself. Now we turn our attention to **self-esteem,** or how you *feel* about those characteristics. Sometimes people confuse these terms, but they are distinct, and it is important that you understand that distinction. Remember that list of characteristics you wrote about yourself at the beginning of the chapter? Use it now in **Active Learning: The Difference Between Self-Concept and Self-Esteem** to examine the difference between self-concept and self-esteem.

The Difference Between Self-Concept and Self-Esteem

In the column labeled "Self-Concept," make a list of seven characteristics that describe you. They can include anything you think is important, such as physical characteristics (height, weight, or body build), skills and abilities (good student, athletic), or personality characteristics (shy, curious). After you complete your list, go back and circle a number to indicate for each characteristic how much you like or dislike this characteristic in yourself.

Self-Concept	Self-Evaluation							
	Like	5	4	3	2	1	Dislike
	Like	5	4	3	2	1	Dislike
	Like	5	4	3	2	1	Dislike
	Like	5	4	3	2	1	Dislike
	Like	5	4	3	2	1	Dislike
	Like	5	4	3	2	1	Dislike
	Like	5	4	3	2	1	Dislike

If you are like most people, you will find some variability in your self-evaluation. There are some things (probably a lot of things) that you like about yourself and some things that are important aspects of your self-concept that you don't like very much. If you look carefully at the characteristics that you included in your self-concept, you also can understand how someone else with the same list of characteristics could end up with a different level of self-esteem. For instance, you may describe yourself as a very tall person, but you could love or hate that about yourself. Or you may see yourself as a very trusting person, but you could like that you always think the best of everyone or hate that you are so trusting that people frequently take advantage of you.

Remember that these self-evaluations occur in a cultural context. Is there anything on your list of characteristics that you like and your culture values that would *not* be seen as positively in another culture? For example, being self-assertive might be positive in an individualistic culture like that in the United States, but negative in a more collectivist culture.

When we talk about how we feel about our own general self-worth, we are talking about what is called **global self-esteem**. But as you saw when you did the preceding **Active Learning** exercise, there usually are some characteristics that we like about ourselves and some that we don't particularly like. Susan Harter (2012) has developed a model of self-esteem that identifies five separate dimensions relevant to the way children and adolescents feel about themselves. They are:

Global self-esteem The feelings you have about your own general self-worth.

1. Scholastic competence—feeling you are doing well at school
2. Social competence—feeling you know how to make friends
3. Behavioral conduct—feeling you act the way you are supposed to act
4. Athletic competence—feeling you are good at sports
5. Physical appearance—liking the way you look

Research has found that as children get older, they are better able to integrate these five dimensions into one overall assessment of global self-esteem (Harter, 2012).

SELF-ESTEEM DURING CHILDHOOD

Social comparison Comparing one's own performance or characteristics to those of other people.

If you look back at the self-description of the 3-year-old that appeared earlier in this chapter, you may be struck by how very positive and optimistic it was. This 3-year-old claimed he knew *all* of his ABCs (although he clearly did not), could run *fast*, climb to the *top* of the jungle gym, and was *never* scared. Another example of this unrealistic self-appraisal comes from a little girl who was asked whether she knew how to swim. "Yes" was her reply, but when she set out across the pool she sank like a stone. Where does this unbounded optimism come from?

Preschoolers are not yet able to compare themselves to others, a process called **social comparison**, which will emerge during the school years. Without a standard of comparison, almost everything they do can be the "best" in their eyes (Harter, 2012), but as children move from early childhood into middle childhood, their confidence in their own abilities often declines (Harter, 2006a; Jacobs, Lanza, Osgood, Eccles, & Wigfield, 2002). Several factors contribute to this. First, as children increasingly compare themselves to their peers, their self-evaluations become more realistic and drop from the inflated levels of early childhood. Second, the constant feedback that children in elementary school receive from their teachers helps them develop a more accurate appraisal of their ability. When younger children receive feedback on their success or failure at a particular task, that information has little effect on their expectations for future success (Davis-Kean, Jager, & Collins, 2009). In contrast, older children take in this information and use it to change their predictions for their future behavior. This means that over time children's conceptions of self become more realistic. Third, children during middle childhood often participate in a variety of organized activities in which they are evaluated. They may be taking music lessons or gymnastics, playing organized sports, or participating in competitive activities such as the chess club or the debate team at school. In all these situations, they clearly see when someone else can do more or less than they can.

Self-esteem movement School-based programs designed to boost students' self-esteem, with the goal of eventually improving their academic performance.

High self-esteem has been associated with a number of positive developmental outcomes, and low self-esteem with a number of negative ones. For instance, students who have higher self-esteem tend to do better in school than students with lower self-esteem (Baumeister, Campbell, Krueger, & Vohs, 2003). Based on this observed relationship, school systems developed a number of programs designed to boost students' self-esteem, with the goal of eventually improving their academic performance. Collectively, these efforts are referred to as the **self-esteem movement**. To learn how successful or unsuccessful these programs have been, read **Journey of Research: The Self-Esteem Movement.**

JOURNEY OF *Research*

The Self-Esteem Movement

The self-esteem movement had its roots in the efforts of California state assemblyman John Vasconcellos, who created the California Task Force to Promote Self-Esteem and Personal and Social Responsibility in 1986 (Mecca, Smelser, & Vasconcellos, 1989). The foreword to an edited volume titled *The Social Importance of Self-Esteem* produced by the members of the task force says that the data and testimony from public hearings they held led to "a consensus that a primary factor affecting how well or how poorly an individual functions in society is self-esteem" (p. vii). Social problems as wide-ranging as alcohol and drug abuse, crime, and even child abuse were attributed to low self-esteem.

As a result of this conclusion, a number of school-based programs designed to boost students' self-esteem were created. However, over the years, critics charged that these were largely "feel good" programs that had little or no impact on actual school performance. While such programs emphasized the uniqueness and the value of the individual, the praise they offered was not tied to specific achievements or accomplishments (and was specifically *not* tied to academic performance). Despite an expenditure of millions of dollars on these programs, research has failed to find any significant positive outcomes from them (Baumeister et al., 2003; Twenge, 2006).

Roy F. Baumeister and his colleagues (2003) pointed out that these programs may have failed because we got it backward. Self-esteem and positive outcomes may be correlated, but remember that we can't determine the direction of an effect from a correlation. Children who are good students often feel good about themselves (that is, they have high self-esteem), but the question is whether feeling good about yourself makes you a good student. Imagine for a moment what would happen if you felt *great* about yourself but were required to take a test on matrix algebra when you had never studied matrix algebra. Although in theory the direction of the effect can move in either direction, most evidence supports the idea that high self-esteem is primarily an *outcome* that results from performing well rather than being the *cause* of good performance (Baumeister et al., 2003). High self-esteem also has not been found to "prevent children from smoking, drinking, taking drugs, or engaging in early sex" (Baumeister et al., 2003, p. 1), which were other goals of the self-esteem movement.

The failure of self-esteem enhancement programs to produce the hoped-for outcomes does not mean we shouldn't promote high self-esteem among children. We want children to feel good about themselves. Rather, it means we need to help children base their esteem on actual achievement rather than on empty praise.

If the self-esteem movement simply failed to deliver the expected results, that would have been disappointing but not necessarily harmful. However, some critics of the movement have charged that these programs have contributed to an increase in narcissism in recent generations that is marked by a need to be admired, arrogant attitudes, and a lack of empathy for others (Twenge, 2006). Whether self-esteem programs actually help make people narcissistic has not yet been resolved (Trzesniewski, Donnellan, & Robins, 2008), but the findings are clear that simply boosting self-esteem will not be a solution to the myriad of problems children may experience.

T ☐ F ☐ Programs that help build students' self-esteem not only improve their grades but also help reduce delinquency, drug use, and adolescent pregnancy. **False**

TRUE/FALSE VIDEO ▲

SELF-ESTEEM DURING ADOLESCENCE

Think of a time in your life when you were dealing with many changes all at the same time, and chances are that you may remember feeling overwhelmed, with little confidence in your ability to handle things in a competent way. Now think about all the changes that young teens are going through: changes in their bodies, their schools, their friends. The transition into early adolescence is notoriously hard on a teen's self-esteem. Physical, social, and environmental factors come together in a way that is challenging for many (Finkenauer, Engels, Meeus, & Oosterwegel, 2002; Huang, 2010).

As young adolescents go through the rapid physical changes of puberty, they can feel clumsy and awkward and often become self-conscious about their appearance. At this same time, adolescents are moving from elementary school to middle school or junior high school. A number of researchers have noted a developmental mismatch between the demands of the middle or junior high school environment and the characteristics of young adolescents (Akos, Rose, & Orthner, 2015; Fenzel, 2000). Middle school teachers have higher academic expectations for their students than teachers in elementary school have, so grades often decline after the transition, lowering the students' perception of their own academic competence. The school environment becomes more competitive and places more emphasis on assessment, increasing the social comparison between students at a time when students are already particularly sensitive about negative social comparisons.

Consequently, young adolescents may need more help and support from their teachers, but in middle or junior high school they have different teachers for each of their subjects, so they have less opportunity to get to know their teachers well and for their teachers to know them. When there is a good fit with the adolescent's needs, for instance when young teens perceive their teachers to be supportive while promoting competence and autonomy, they tend to be more engaged in school and to have higher academic motivation (Wang & Eccles, 2013).

The cognitive changes of adolescence also affect self-esteem. Adolescents' ability to think hypothetically allows them to think not only about their real selves (the characteristics they currently have), but also about their **ideal self** (the characteristics they aspire to have in the future). The impact this comparison has on self-esteem depends on both the discrepancy between the two selves and the importance of the domain for the individual (Harter, 2006). For instance, there might be a relatively small discrepancy between your current weight and your ideal weight, but if the domain of physical appearance is very important to you, even a small discrepancy can have a large impact on your self-esteem. This domain is so important to most teens that body image can account for between 45% and 70% of the variance or difference in global self-esteem among adolescents (Wichstrøm & von Soest, 2016).

Fortunately the negative impact of the physical, social, and cognitive changes that accompany the transition into adolescence is relatively short-lived for most adolescents, and may not be as great as we have thought them to be (Huang, 2010). For most teens, the decline that typically occurs in early adolescence is followed by a recovery of self-esteem that tends to remain stable throughout the remainder of middle adolescence and into early adulthood (Erol & Orth, 2011; Impett, Sorsoli, Schooler, Henson, & Tolman, 2008). See Figure 11.2.

Ideal self The characteristics one aspires to in the future.

T ☐ F ☐ The self-esteem of most adolescents remains high and stable from mid-adolescence through early adulthood. **True**

FIGURE 11.2

Age-related changes in adolescent self-esteem. For the majority of adolescents—as many as 87%, according to the results of the study shown in this figure—self-esteem is relatively high by mid-adolescence and remains high through early adulthood. However, about 6% of adolescents begin with low self-esteem which remains low over the course of years. About 7% of the study participants reported low self-esteem as teenagers but rebounded after they finished high school.

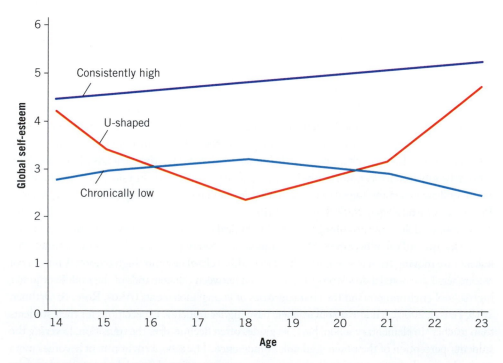

SOURCE: Birkeland, Melkevik, Holsen, & Wold (2012).

Gender differences in self-esteem appear fairly early in adolescence and persist through adulthood. Girls and women tend to have lower global self-esteem than boys and men (Rentzsch, Wenzler, & Schütz, 2016). While a recent analysis of 115 studies found that the gender difference in global self-esteem was quite small, it was much larger in the areas of athletic and appearance self-esteem (Gentile et al., 2009). The largest differences were in early adolescence when girls had significantly lower appearance self-esteem than boys. However, women had higher self-esteem in relation to behavioral conduct and moral-ethical domains, which may reflect earlier maturation in adolescent girls. There were no differences in academic self-esteem.

Research that looked at differences in self-esteem by race or ethnicity has found that African American adolescents on average score higher than White students, who are very similar to Hispanics. Asian American students had the lowest self-esteem (Bachman, O'Malley, Freedman-Doan, Trzesniewski, & Donnellan, 2011). To understand these results, we should remember that in collectivist cultures, often found in Asia, children are socialized to be modest so showing high self-esteem would not be socially acceptable. By contrast, in individualistic cultures, the expression of high self-esteem is valued and encouraged. However, the researchers note that differences *within* any of these groups are greater than the differences between them so there is a big range in the way teens think about themselves within all ethnic and racial groups.

> T ☐ F ☐ By comparison to other ethnic and racial groups, Asian American adolescents have the lowest self-esteem.
> **True**

MEDIA, SELF-CONCEPT, AND SELF-ESTEEM

We have known for a long time that parents and peers are important sources of self-esteem, but more recently we have begun paying attention to media as another source. As social comparison becomes an increasingly important element in building children's self-concept and self-esteem, images they see on television and in movies, in advertising, and online are another standard against which they can compare themselves. Unfortunately, the unrealistic images they see there can lead them to feel dissatisfied with their body (Martins & Harrison, 2012; Murnen, Smolak, Mills, & Good, 2003; Wonderlich, Ackard, & Henderson, 2005). Women and girls are almost universally portrayed as unrealistically thin, and being repeatedly exposed to this **thin ideal** can be damaging to girls' self-esteem. Girls as young as 6 or 7 years of age express their desire to be thinner (Dohnt & Tiggemann, 2006), and the situation is not much better for boys (Murnen et al., 2003) because the images of super heroes and super athletes are no more realistic for them than the images that girls see. These images can lead to body dissatisfaction in boys tied to a desire to be bigger, stronger, and more muscular.

Thin ideal The idea promoted by media images that it is best for girls and women to be thin.

Women are frequently portrayed in movies, video games, ads, and television shows as dependent upon men and secondary to them, while male characters are independent and in charge of the situation. Minority characters are frequently portrayed as criminals, sex objects, and people of lower status (Martins & Harrison, 2012). One recent study of 7- to 12-year olds found that television viewing was negatively related to self-esteem in White and Black girls and Black boys, but not in White boys (Martins & Harrison, 2012). One explanation for this finding is that exposure to the negative portrayal of women in general and Black men in particular lowers the self-esteem of these groups, while the positive portrayal of White men boosts the self-esteem of White boys.

The typical U.S. child between ages 8 and 18 spends an average of 7 hours a day with entertainment media (Rideout, Foehr, & Roberts, 2010). Simply the amount of time spent with entertainment media would make it a powerful influence on a child's self-concept, but another reason media exposure is such a strong influence is that the more time spent with media, the less time the child has to engage in other positive, productive activities that contribute to building self-esteem (Martins & Harrison, 2012). Encouraging children to take part in activities they enjoy and are good at, such as sports, cultural or artistic activities, or hobbies, helps those in middle childhood build a positive self-concept based on diverse aspects of the self, not just on physical appearance.

1. How does self-esteem differ from self-concept?
2. What was wrong with the approach of the self-esteem movement?
3. How does self-esteem differ by gender and ethnic/racial groups?
4. In what ways does media exposure affect self-concept and self-esteem?

GENDER IDENTITY

11.3 How does gender identity develop for most children and how does it develop for LGBT children and teens?

"It's a boy!" "It's a girl!" When an infant is born, the first announcement made is the sex of the baby because one of the most central aspects of our identity is our gender. Your sex, that is, whether you are a boy or a girl biologically, is determined by genes, hormones, and physical body parts. However, the concept of gender includes all the roles and stereotypes that your society connects with being a boy or a girl. Whether you are a boy or a girl determines much about what your experiences in life will be. Take a minute to think about what you associate with the concept of "boy" and the concept of "girl."

In this section, we describe five theories that seek to explain how gender identity develops. We then look at gender stereotyping and its effects. Finally, we examine the identity development of lesbian, gay, bisexual, and transgender (LGBT) children and teens.

THEORIES OF GENDER DEVELOPMENT

Numerous theories have contributed ideas about how children develop their concept of gender and their own gender identity. We describe here the approach of five theories, as well as the research that has been guided by them: behaviorism, social cognitive theory, cognitive developmental theory, gender schema theory, and the gender self-socialization model. Table 11.2 introduces you to the basic mechanisms for each theory.

TABLE 11.2

Theories of gender development. This table introduces five theories of gender development by describing the mechanism by which each says we develop our gender identity.

Theory	Mechanisms for Developing Gender Identity
Behaviorism	Gender-consistent behavior is reinforced by others.
Social Cognitive Theory	Children imitate gender-consistent behavior they see others perform.
Cognitive Developmental Theory	Identity is determined by cognitive growth in stages: Gender identity Gender stability Gender constancy
Gender Schema Theory	Gender concepts are learned from society's norms for each gender.
Gender Self-Socialization Model	Gender is defined by each individual.

Behaviorism and Social Cognitive Theories

As we learned in Chapter 2, a central concept of the theory of behaviorism is reinforcement, those environmental responses that cause a behavior to continue or be repeated. For behaviorists, gender identity results from direct and indirect reinforcement of gender roles and activities. Parents today may claim they do not discriminate between boys and girls and that all the observed differences between the sexes have biological origins, but considerable research shows that parents do, in fact, reinforce sex-typed play activities and household chores for their children (Berenbaum, Martin, Hanish, Briggs, & Fabes, 2008). While both boys and girls receive positive reinforcement for gender-appropriate behavior, boys receive more active discouragement for behaviors and activities that are defined as feminine than girls do for masculine activities. At least one reason for this is that feminine boys are expected to stay that way into adulthood, while masculine girls are expected to outgrow these characteristics (Sandnabba & Ahlberg, 1999). Fathers are more likely than mothers to respond negatively to cross-gender activities (Bussey & Bandura, 1999). In one study, young children believed that their parents would disapprove of cross-gender play, especially for boys, even if the parents claimed they did not hold gender stereotypes (Freeman, 2007). Children thus may be picking up on their parents' unconscious attitudes about gender roles.

The central concept of social cognitive theory is the role that imitation plays in shaping behavior. Children are exposed every day to numerous examples of gender roles and activities that they can imitate. Even when their parents do not demonstrate strongly differentiated gender roles, children still see these stereotypical roles portrayed in the world around them and in the media. As just one example, in a study of superhero cartoons, male superheroes outnumbered females 2 to 1, and the male superheroes were rated as more likely to show anger while the female superheroes were more concerned about their appearance (Baker & Raney, 2007). Young boys who watch superhero cartoons more often are more likely to show male stereotyped play and weapons play than those who do not (Coyne, Linder, Rasmussen, Nelson, & Collier, 2014). Although both boys and girls imitate what they see, the question remains as to why girls are more likely to imitate girls while boys imitate boys. Kohlberg's cognitive developmental theory addresses this question.

Cognitive Developmental Theory

Lawrence Kohlberg (1966) was the first theorist to examine the development of gender identity through the lens of cognitive theory. As a follower of Piaget, he believed that children's understanding of gender goes through stages as they mature. When they are younger, they do not understand that gender is a characteristic that is stable and permanent. He found that young children believed that gender could change over time ("I'm a boy, but I can be a mommy when I grow up") or because of changes in appearance, such as a hairstyle or clothing.

The first stage Kohlberg described, called **gender identity**, begins at about age 2. In this stage children can identify gender— "I am a girl, and you are a boy"—but their concept of gender relies on external appearance. They may believe that if a girl were to wear a tie, she might become a boy. As toddlers learn these gender

DEVELOPMENT IN ACTION VIDEO ▲

Gender identity Stage when children can identify gender but their concept of gender relies on external appearance.

T ☐ F ☐ Today most parents do not reinforce gender-specific stereotypes and treat their sons and daughters in very similar ways.
False

Vanessa Vick/Photo Researchers, Inc.

What is gender-appropriate behavior? How do you think this boy's peers or parents would react if they saw him playing with dolls? What would their response communicate to him?

Gender stability Stage when children understand that their gender will remain stable over time, but aren't sure that it won't change if they do activities usually performed by the other gender.

Gender constancy The stage at which children understand that one's gender remains constant despite external changes.

labels, there is some evidence that their play becomes more gender stereotyped (Zosuls et al., 2009). The second stage, called **gender stability**, begins at age 3 when children understand that their gender is constant over time—that is, a girl will become an adult woman, and a boy will become an adult man. However, they are still not clear that a girl playing with trucks does not become a boy or that a boy playing with dolls doesn't become a girl. Finally, in the third stage, called **gender constancy**, 5-year-old children understand that gender remains constant even with external changes; for example, a boy with long hair is still a boy and a girl with short hair is still a girl (Halim & Ruble, 2010). Ruble and her colleagues found support for these ideas, including the fact that children who had achieved gender constancy were less likely to be rigid in their adherence to gendered characteristics (Halim et al., 2014; Ruble et al., 2007). They asked the children questions such as "Is it wrong for boys to wear nail polish?" or "Would it be OK for a boy to wear nail polish if he didn't get into trouble and nobody laughed?" to determine how rigidly the children held gender role standards. They found that before children have gender constancy, when there is still some question in their minds as to whether they can turn into the other sex, they are more likely to have rigid standards. Therefore, preschool children often have more rigid adherence to gender stereotypes than school-age children. Once the children are clear that they will forever be a boy or a girl, they are more flexible about external things like clothing, hairstyles, and nail polish. A boy may or may not want to wear nail polish, but he knows that he will still be a boy if he does. **Active Learning: Kohlberg's Cognitive Developmental Theory of Gender Development** is designed to show you how to test these concepts with a young child.

Active LEARNING

Kohlberg's Cognitive Developmental Theory of Gender Development

To identify the level of gender concept a child has reached according to Kohlberg's cognitive developmental theory, interview a child between the ages of 2 and 6 and ask the questions in the first column. The information in the second column will later help you identify the child's stage of gender identity. You will read the questions differently if you are interviewing a boy or a girl. When interviewing a boy, you will substitute

ACTIVE LEARNING VIDEO ▲

Younger children are guided by appearance, while older children understand that gender does not change with appearance or activity.

"boy" where it says (same sex) and "girl" where it says (other sex) and when interviewing a girl you will substitute "girl" for (same sex) and "boy" for (other sex). You can also ask the child the names of male and female friends and substitute their names, instead of asking the child directly about himself or herself.

Questions for the Child	Stage of Gender Development
1. Are you a girl or a boy? *Follow-up question*: Whatever the child answers, follow up by asking the opposite. For example, if the child says she is a girl, ask whether she is a boy.	Gender identity
2. When you were a baby, were you a boy, or a girl, or sometimes a boy and sometimes a girl?	Gender stability
3. When you grow up, will you be a man, a woman, or sometimes a man and sometimes a woman?	Gender stability
4. If you went into the other room and put on (other-sex) clothes, would you then really be a boy or really be a girl? *Follow-up question (if correct)*: Why did you say you would really be a (same sex)? Is it because you didn't want to be a (other sex) or because you can't change from a (same sex) to a (other sex)?	Gender constancy
5. When you grow up, if you do the work that (other sex) do, will you really be a man or really be a woman?	Gender constancy
6. If a boy wore nail polish, would he become a girl? If a girl had really short hair, would she become a boy? If a boy played with baby dolls, would he become a girl? If a girl played with trucks, would she become a boy?	Gender constancy
7. If you really wanted to be a (other sex), could you be?	Gender constancy

SOURCE: Arthur, Bigler, & Ruble (2009, p. 444).

If the child can answer only Question 1 correctly, she is in the gender identity stage. If she can answer only the first three questions correctly, she is in the gender stability stage. If she can answer at least the first four correctly, she demonstrates gender constancy. Children who answer some but not all questions correctly within a stage are still working on the understanding in that stage. If possible, compare your results with those of classmates who interviewed children who were younger or older than the child you interviewed.

To prepare for this activity or if you do not have access to a child, watch the video of this Active Learning.

Sandra Bem believed that much of what Kohlberg found about the stages of gender understanding was based on children's ignorance of the real physical differences between the sexes. In raising her own child, she made sure that he did know the difference. She tells the following story to illustrate the idea that when children understand the physical differences, they are not as affected by the superficial differences, such as length of hair. Because Bem was trying to raise her son not to be gender stereotyped, she accepted his request to go to school with barrettes in his hair. One of his buddies told him, "You're a girl, because only girls wear barrettes." Her son decided to show him in no uncertain terms that he was a boy, not a girl, so he pulled down his pants, but his friend replied, "Everybody has a penis; only girls wear barrettes!" (Bem, 1989, p. 662). Without the knowledge of physical differences between the sexes, his friend had to rely on superficial characteristics like barrettes to determine his friend's gender.

Gender and avatars. How would what you say be different if you were communicating with people you didn't know but who each used one of these avatars? Most people find it easier to communicate with someone else when they know the person's gender.

©iStockphoto.com/Bluebearry
©iStockphoto.com/nickyларson974
©iStockphoto.com/Askold Romanov

Gender Schema Theory

In Chapters 2 and 7, we described a schema as a way that we organize our understanding of the world, and gender is one important schema that guides the way that we see the world. Most people find it easier to navigate social relationships when they can categorize others as "male" or "female." For example, when people were asked to evaluate the images that other people chose to represent themselves for their online interactions, most people preferred avatars that had clear indicators of being male or female rather than ones that were difficult to categorize in terms of gender (Nowak & Rauh, 2008). See examples in Figure 11.3.

However, a gender schema contains more than simply whether someone is male or female. It also contains all the things that an individual connects with each gender, such as expected behaviors, abilities, and occupations. Sandra Bem believed that gender development does not follow stages based on cognitive development, as Kohlberg said. Instead, she believed that gender concepts are learned from your particular society. Children's self-concepts are formed in part by what characteristics are assigned to their gender. In many Western cultures, a boy is likely to have "strong" but not "nurturing" in his self-description, while a girl is likely to have the opposite. Parents will exclaim how strong their little boy is or "what an arm" he has when he throws a ball. Little girls are unlikely to hear this. Rather, parents may talk with excitement about how their little girl is so loving to her dolls, a real "little mommy." As children learn what is expected for their gender, they try to fill those expectations (Hyde, 2014).

Defining gender roles and gender-based activities may be more difficult than it appears. When we try to classify roles and activities as either masculine or feminine, we imply that masculinity and femininity are polar opposite: You are either masculine or you are feminine. In 1974, Sandra L. Bem proposed a different way of thinking about masculinity and femininity that she called **androgyny**. Bem believed that individuals can be both masculine and feminine, for example, calling upon assertiveness when needed and submissiveness when that is appropriate. She believed that having that flexibility would lead to better adjustment. Although a great deal of research was generated by Bem's ideas in the 1970s and 1980s, the research carried out then and in subsequent years has shown that it is masculine traits (not androgynous ones) that are associated with psychological well-being for both males and females (see, for example, Castlebury & Durham, 1997; Johnson et al., 2006; Lau, 1989; Whitley, 1983; Woo & Oei, 2006). Remember we said earlier in this chapter that self-esteem is affected by a person's perceptions of whether they have characteristics that are valued by their society. It makes sense then that in a society that values traits it defines as masculine, such as assertiveness and independence, individuals who see themselves as more masculine will have higher self-esteem and well-being.

Androgyny The idea that both sexes can have characteristics that are traditionally considered masculine and traditionally considered feminine.

Masculine and feminine traits. Which traits that are associated with masculine and feminine roles might this female construction worker and male preschool teacher need to be effective at their jobs?

Of course, our gender schema for masculine and feminine will be different from one culture to another or from one situation to another. Can you think of some situation in which it would be more acceptable for a boy to show some traits typically associated with femininity than others, or think of situations in which it would be acceptable for girls to display masculine traits? Perry and Pauletti (2011) describe the range of gender identities, including those who show same-gender typing across most domains, those who have a mix of gender-typed characteristics, and those who are mostly cross-gender-typed.

Gender Self-Socialization Model

A more recent model of gender identity development, called the **gender self-socialization model**, has eliminated any predefined characteristics of masculinity, femininity, or androgyny. Instead, this approach looks at children's and teens' own individual experiences and ideas of gender consistency and pressure. Tobin et al. (2010) describe gender identity as one's thoughts and feelings about belonging to one's gender. For example, they believe that gender identity cannot be assessed by asking whether someone believes him- or herself to be nurturing or aggressive because these characteristics may not fit neatly into that person's gender stereotypes. Instead, they ask, "Do you feel you are a typical girl?" or "Do you like being a boy?" (p. 604). They describe five dimensions of gender identity:

Gender self-socialization model An approach to gender identity development that is based on each individual's own ideas of gender consistency and pressure.

1. Membership knowledge—knowledge of one's membership in a gender category

2. Gender contentedness—satisfaction with one's gender

3. Felt pressure for gender conformity—expectations experienced from self and others for adhering to gender stereotypes

4. Gender typicality—self-perceived similarity to others of the same gender

5. Gender centrality—the importance of gender relative to one's other identities; e.g., ethnic or racial identity (Tobin et al., 2010, p. 608)

Each of these dimensions interacts with all of the others to influence an individual's gender identity. Children who are content with their gender role report a higher sense of global self-worth. Those who are not content report greater distress in their relationships with peers, and peers see these children as being depressed, anxious, and self-deprecating (Carver et al., 2003).

Think about how you would characterize yourself on each of the five dimensions. You are likely to have a clear idea of your basic gender, the first dimension, but your answers to the others will vary from those of other students in your class. Trying **Active Learning: Going Against Gender Stereotypes** will give you a chance to push the boundaries of your own self-defined gender identity to see how you and others respond when you do so.

Active LEARNING

Going Against Gender Stereotypes

To experience for yourself how strongly gender stereotypes affect our behavior, choose an activity that goes against your own stereotype for your gender. First, you need to identify the behavior that you are going to "try on." It could be a leisure activity, a household task, or the use of media. We realize that students today may already have a good deal of gender flexibility, but for this activity choose something you associate with the opposite gender that you *don't* routinely do. Men might want to learn to braid hair or knit, or they might purchase and read fashion or bridal magazines. Women might want to learn how to change the oil in their car, mow the lawn, or use a snowblower (be sure you learn from someone who will make sure that you do this safely). Keep a diary record of how you feel taking on this new role, and make note of any resistance that you receive from others if they observe your behavior. How comfortable do you feel, and how likely are you to continue your new behavior beyond this brief experiment? If you have learned a new skill, how do you feel about your ability to do something that you never knew how to do before?

IDENTITY IN LESBIAN, GAY, BISEXUAL, AND TRANSGENDER (LGBT) CHILDREN AND TEENS

Sexual orientation
Sexual attraction to same- or opposite-sex partners

In this section, we look at two important issues related to gender and identity. We first examine the role that **sexual orientation**, or preference for a same- or opposite-sex partner, plays in identity development. Second, we discuss the development of transgender children whose gender identity does not match their physical sex.

Lesbian, Gay, and Bisexual [LGB] Children and Teens

About 3.5% of the adults in the United States self-identify as gay, lesbian, or bisexual. Slightly more identify as bisexual than as lesbian or gay, and women are substantially more likely to describe themselves as bisexual. The estimated percentage of the population who report any lifetime same-sex sexual behavior rises to about 8.2%, while 11% acknowledge some attraction to an individual of the same sex (Gates, 2011).

The topic of sexual orientation is a very complex one. Research by Savin-Williams (2014) has shown that sexual orientation is more a continuum than a category. Individuals may define themselves as "mostly gay," for example, and may have sex with men, but still sometimes have sexual fantasies about women. We will likely need more complex and differentiated conceptualization of sexual orientation to adequately cover the range of human experiences. It is also a mistake to assume sexual questioning happens at only one point in time and then is resolved (Diamond, 2006). It is more likely that individuals return to and reexamine their sexual orientation from time to time in their lives. In fact, a term currently in use is *LGBQ*, which stands for lesbian, gay, bisexual, and *questioning*.

Adults who identify as gay or lesbian often recall that they began to feel they were somehow different from their same-sex peers at some point during childhood (Savin-Williams & Cohen, 2015). They may have engaged in cross-sex-typed behaviors (for example, girls playing masculine competitive sports, boys playing with feminine dolls) or have had cross-sex-typed interests. At around age 10, when many children have their first romantic attraction, these children found themselves being drawn to someone of the same sex, and this experience can trigger a period of sexual questioning, often before the child even enters puberty (Carver et al., 2004).

Adolescents may take the next step of exploring a same-sex relationship before finally adopting a gay, lesbian, or bisexual identity in late adolescence. However, this type of sexual exploration is not uncommon in adolescence and does not occur only among young people who are homosexual. In one study, most youth who had taken part exclusively in same-sex behavior still identified themselves as heterosexual (Mustanski et al., 2014), but for gay and lesbian youth, same-sex sexual experience often confirms their identity. In another study, half the gay and bisexual men surveyed said they had fully accepted their sexual identities and had a homosexual romance or homosexual experiences during high school or college (Savin-Williams & Cohen, 2015).

Once young people have settled on a sexual orientation, they need to integrate their sexual orientation into their identity. An important part of that process involves disclosing this information to others (Savin-Williams & Cohen, 2015). Young people today seem to be taking this step at younger ages than they did in the past (Riley, 2010). The first disclosure is still likely to be to a friend or a sibling, but with regard to disclosure to parents, it is much more likely that young people will disclose to their mother, who they expect to be more accepting, before disclosing to their father (Savin-Williams & Ream, 2003). Although there is relatively little information on how this disclosure affects the parent-child relationship in the long run, what information there is indicates that after an initial period of adjustment, most parent-child relationships rebound, and some even improve (Savin-Williams & Ream, 2003). Not surprisingly, acceptance and support from family members and friends is associated with better adjustment and mental health outcomes for the individual following disclosure of his or her sexual orientation (D'Augelli, 2003; Perrin-Wallqvist & Lindblom, 2015). Disclosing their orientation is most often a relief for these youth, but it also is the beginning of an alternative lifestyle that has its own rewards and risks (Riley, 2010).

Being gay, lesbian, or bisexual is still not easy in many places in the world. It is illegal in many countries and even punishable by death in Saudi Arabia, the Sudan, Somalia, and Iran (BBC News, 2014). Within the United States, LGB youth report higher levels of bullying and harassment, including threats or attacks with a knife on school property. They are more likely to experience dating violence and forced sexual intercourse. It is not surprising then that these youth experience emotional difficulties at a higher rate than heterosexual youth. In a large survey of high school students in New York City, LGB youth reported higher levels of use of alcohol and drugs compared to heterosexual students (Seil, Desai, & Smith, 2014). They were more likely to be depressed and even suicidal. Among LGB youth who said that they were not connected to an adult at school, 45% reported that they had thought about suicide and 31% had made an attempt. In a different study, lesbian, gay, and bisexual youth were 5 times more likely than heterosexual youth to have attempted suicide in the 12 months prior to the study, but this risk was less for adolescents in supportive environments (Hatzenbuehler, 2011). When LGB teens are in a supportive environment and are not subject to bullying, their well-being is much higher (CDC, 2014g).

Sexual orientation. When teens have support from their peers, regardless of their sexual preference, the process of developing a gender identity in adolescence becomes easier.

RosaIreneBetancourt 1 / Alamy

The good news is that support for and acceptance of LGB students has increased in recent years. In a national online survey, gay and straight teens reported that school-based gay-straight alliance programs are increasing, more school staff are supportive, and there are more anti-bullying policies that specifically protect LGB students (Gay, Lesbian & Straight Education Network, 2013). There is also more instructional material that includes the role of LGB adults in history and society. At this point, these changes are more likely to be found in high schools than middle schools and in urban than rural areas (Gay, Lesbian & Straight Education Network, 2013). And, despite the challenges and concerns LGBT adolescents have, many show a good deal of optimism and hope for the future. In a 2012 survey of more than 10,000 LGBT adolescents, three-quarters of the survey respondents said they know things will get better for them in the future, and 83% said they believe they will be happy (Human Rights Campaign, 2012), although many feel that they will need to leave their community to realize their hopes and dreams for the future.

Gay and lesbian teens are often asked to explain their sexual orientation to others. To see what that experience might be like, try **Active Learning: The Heterosexual Questionnaire**.

T ☐ F ☐ Most lesbian, gay, bisexual, and transgender (LGBT) adolescents are optimistic about their future. **True**

Active LEARNING

The Heterosexual Questionnaire

When gay, lesbian, and bisexual young people come out, they are often asked questions that are nearly impossible to answer. Advocates for Youth (2008) developed the following activity to help create greater understanding of their experiences (adapted from Rochlin, 1977). Regardless of your sexual orientation, try to answer the Heterosexual Questionnaire from the point of view of a heterosexual, then reflect on the questions posed at the end of the questionnaire.

The Heterosexual Questionnaire

Please answer the following questions as honestly as possible.

1. What do you think caused your heterosexuality?

2. When and how did you first decide you were heterosexual?

3. Is it possible that your heterosexuality is just a phase you may grow out of?

4. Is it possible that your heterosexuality stems from a fear of others of the same sex?

5. If you have never slept with a member of your own sex, is it possible that you might be gay if you tried it?

6. If heterosexuality is normal, why are so many mental patients heterosexual?

7. Why do you heterosexual people try to seduce others into your lifestyle?

8. Why do you flaunt your heterosexuality? Can't you just be who you are and keep it quiet?

9. The great majority of child molesters are heterosexual. Do you consider it safe to expose your children to heterosexual teachers?

10. With all the societal support that marriage receives, the divorce rate is spiraling. Why are there so few stable relationships among heterosexual people?

11. Why are heterosexual people so promiscuous?

12. Would you want your children to be heterosexual, knowing the problems they would face, such as heartbreak, disease, and divorce?

Reflection Questions

1. Did you find the questions hard to answer? Were some harder than others? Which ones were especially difficult? What, specifically, was so difficult about these questions?

2. How did the questions make you feel?

3. What does it say about our society that gay, lesbian, and bisexual youth are asked similar questions?

4. What can you do in the future if you hear someone asking a homosexual youth such questions?

Our thoughts about the causes of homosexuality have changed substantially over the years. The evolution of our understanding is described in **Journey of Research: Explanations for Homosexuality**.

JOURNEY OF *Research*

Explanations for Homosexuality

Homosexuality as a sexual orientation is as old as human history, but attempts to understand and explain it in a scientific manner are far more recent. In the late 1800s, Karl Heinrich Ulrichs proposed a scientific theory of homosexuality that claimed that there was a biological basis for it (Kennedy, 1997), but this view was quickly overshadowed by a psychoanalytic explanation that then dominated the field for many years (Bieber et al., 1962).

The psychoanalytic explanation is based on a family dynamic that includes a dominant or seductive mother and a weak, hostile, or distant father, but the research that tested this idea often relied on the accounts of people who were already troubled enough that they were seeking help from a therapist, used small samples or single-subject designs, or did not have a comparison group. The fact that these studies were conducted by clinicians who already subscribed to the notion that a neurotic family was a root cause of homosexuality further compromised the scientific value of this work. It also is hard to disentangle the fact that the distancing of a father from a child who is exhibiting some cross-gender traits could be a response to the child's gender orientation rather than the cause of it (Isay, 1996).

The idea that homosexuality was pathological persisted until 1973, when the *Diagnostic and Statistical Manual of Mental Disorders* of the American Psychiatric Association officially excluded homosexuality as a disorder (Spitzer, 1981). However, there continues to be debate within our society about whether homosexuality is "normal" or "natural" and about whether people can make a voluntary decision to adopt a heterosexual orientation.

(Continued)

(Continued)

Although no single explanation for homosexuality has received universal support, there is more support for biological causes than social ones (Bailey et al., 2016). If social influences were dominant, you would expect that children raised by homosexual parents would be more likely to be homosexual themselves, but this is not the case (Patterson, 2013). Several biological causes have been explored, including prenatal influences and genetic influences.

One line of evidence for the importance of prenatal hormones rests on a small number of cases between 1960 and 2000 in which young boys who had malformed penises or had lost their penis through surgical accidents were surgically reassigned as female and given female genitalia. The bodies of these individuals had produced normal male hormones during prenatal development and as adults, despite the change in genitalia, they were attracted to women. In other words, their gender orientation was influenced by their hormones rather than their changed body type (Bailey et al., 2016).

Having older, biological brothers also increases the odds of homosexuality in later-born boys. It has been proposed that the prenatal development of the first male fetus may produce an immune reaction in the mother that results in antibodies that act on the sexual differentiation of the brain of males in subsequent pregnancies (Blanchard, 2008). Of course this explanation does not explain homosexuality in first-born males.

Research on twins has found that genes play a role, but are not the entire story. Studies of the concordance rate for homosexuality between monozygotic and dizygotic twins have shown that about one-third of the variation in sexual orientation is due to genes, one-quarter is due to shared environmental effects, and the rest is due to different experiences had by the twins (Bailey et al., 2016).

Bailey et al. (2016) reviewed a large number of studies on causes of homosexuality and concluded that there is clearer evidence for biological effects for gay men than for gay women, although they also admit that women's sexual orientation is just less understood than that of men. Regarding the effect of the social environment, it may not affect the occurrence of male homosexuality, but it is likely to affect its expression; that is, in less accepting environments, gay men are more likely to hide or deny their attraction to men but there will still be gay men.

This area of research still has many unanswered questions, and in all likelihood, the best possible explanation will include a complex set of interacting biological and social factors.

T ☐ F ☐ Because we learn to imitate the behaviors that we see, children raised by homosexual couples are much more likely to become homosexual themselves when they become adults. **False**

Natal gender The sex assigned to an individual at birth based on physical characteristics

Transgender Identification with a gender other than the one with which an individual was born.

Transgender, Transsexual, and Gender Nonconforming Children and Teens

Being heterosexual, gay, lesbian, and bisexual is defined by a person's choice of partners, but transgender, transsexual, and gender nonconforming individuals develop a gender identity that does not match their assigned or **natal gender**. These children and teens may feel that they are a boy trapped in a girl's body, or vice versa, and some feel they do not conform to either gender. The term **transgender** indicates an identification with a gender other than your natal gender. A **transsexual** is someone who has or is planning to become the other sex, possibly but not always, including hormonal or surgical interventions to make this transition (APA, 2013). And the term **gender nonconforming** is used for individuals who do not identify or conform to gender norms for either males or females. The term **cisgender** is used to indicate people who do identify with their natal sex. Estimating the number of transgender individuals has been difficult, but in a national sample of New Zealand teens, 1.2% reported being transgender while 4% reported questioning their gender. Only 40% of those identifying as transgender had disclosed their identity to anyone (Clark et al., 2014). The causes of transgender identity are not known. To date, studies of monozygotic and dizygotic twins have provided evidence for the role of genes, while studies looking at the effects of the environment have been inconclusive (Diamond, 2013).

Dissatisfaction with one's natal gender can start early in life. As early as age 2, some children express a desire to be a different sex (Steensma, Kreukels, de Vries, & Cohen-Kettenis, 2013). These children avoid clothing, games, and playmates of their natal gender. Some express negative feelings about their own genitals and wish they had those of the other sex. Not all of these children continue to feel this way as they get older, but the more extreme their early preferences are, the more likely these preferences will continue into adolescence (Steensma et al., 2013). The period between ages 10 and 13 appears to be pivotal in the development of a variant gender identity. As preteens begin to experience the changes of puberty, their gender identity seems to consolidate as typical or variant and remains that way. A significant percent of those who do not persist in a transgender identity eventually identify themselves as gay or lesbian (APA, 2013). As puberty begins to change their bodies, transgender teens may hide their breasts or penis. They may use hormone suppressors to stop the progression of the changes of puberty and may request gender reassignment surgery (APA, 2015), although in most cases surgery is not performed before age 18 (Hembree et al., 2009). While many transgender teens have this identity before puberty, there are some who showed little evidence of a transgender identity in childhood but developed one in adolescence (APA, 2015; Clark et al., 2014).

Transsexual Someone who has or is planning to become the other sex, possibly but not always, including biological treatments to make this transition.

Gender nonconforming Individuals who do not identify or conform to gender norms for either males or females.

Cisgender Individuals who identify with their natal gender.

Transgender identity can begin early in life. Although Jazz Jennings was born a male as shown in this photo at age 3, beginning at a very young age she strongly identified as a girl as shown in the second photo when she was 5 years old.

Tasia Wells/Contributor/WireImage/Getty Images

Which bathroom to use? The issue of whether transgender people should use the bathroom designated for their natal gender or their preferred gender affects this transgender man. Where is he most likely to be comfortable and where are others most likely to be comfortable with him?

Gender dysphoria A diagnosis in the DSM-5 that is made when an individual is distressed about his or her preference to be different from his or her natal gender.

Being transgender is no longer considered a disorder as it once was. In the DSM-5, a diagnosis of **gender dysphoria** is made only if the individual is distressed about his or her variant gender identity (APA, 2013). Many transgender children and adolescents do not experience distress about their identity, but when they do, it is most likely because of teasing, harassment, and attacks by peers and possibly by adults as well. In a large national study, 78% of transgender children reported being the victim of harassment, 35% reported physical assault, and 12% experienced sexual violence in the school environment. As a result, 15% of transgender children and teens reported leaving school (Grant et al., 2011). Although the majority of transgender teens reported that they had a parent who cared for them, felt safe in their neighborhood and school, and were not depressed or suicidal, there was an increased likelihood that they had been bullied and a higher percentage of these teens were depressed or suicidal than their cisgender peers (Clark et al., 2014).

As transgender people have become more public about who they are, society has had mixed reactions. For instance, the issue of whether they should use public bathrooms based on their natal sex or on their preferred sex became a national debate when North Carolina passed a bill in 2016 requiring transgender people to use public bathrooms that match their natal sex. Shortly thereafter the federal government issued a directive that public schools should provide these students with access to bathrooms and other facilities consistent with the sex matching their gender identity (Davis & Apuzzo, 2016). In one survey, 46% of Americans thought that transgender people should use the bathroom corresponding to their natal sex while 41% thought they should be able to use the bathroom of the sex they identify with (Salvanto, Backus, Dutton, & DePinto, 2016). Transgender youth must deal with all of society's conflicting reactions to them on a daily basis.

Treatment approaches for children with gender dysphoria are controversial. Some therapists encourage the child to accept his or her given body, while others support the child's variant gender identity. Overall, it is most important for the child and family to have support as they deal with their exploration of the child's gender identity. For adolescents, there is generally agreement that treatment should support the teen's chosen gender identity, including the use of puberty suppressing medication when this is the path the adolescent and his or her parents choose. The involvement of families is crucial in the treatment of these children and teens because their acceptance is central to the child's well-being (APA, 2015).

CHECK YOUR UNDERSTANDING

1. What do behaviorism and social cognitive theory tell us about gender development in early childhood?
2. Describe the stages in Kohlberg's cognitive developmental theory of gender development.
3. What are gender schemas?
4. How do lesbian, gay, and bisexual teens differ in their gender identity from transgender teens?

ETHNIC AND RACIAL IDENTITY

11.4 How do ethnic and racial identity affect development?

Developing a gender identity is a basic task that all children must deal with, but all children also need to develop a sense of their **ethnic and racial identity**, consisting of their attitudes toward the ethnic and racial groups to which they feel they belong (Marks, Szalacha, Lamarre, Boyd, & Coll, 2007). Although there is some overlap between the terms *ethnicity* and *race*, ethnicity generally refers to a group of people that have a nationality or culture in common, while race tends to refer to physical characteristics that differ between groups of people, such as skin color. These concepts overlap, so we examine them together.

Byrd (2012) has described steps children take in developing a basic ethnic and racial identity that are based on cognitive development and are similar to the steps in developing a gender identity. Although children are aware of differences in people's appearance, they do not generally identify people by race until age 4 or 5. After they become aware of racial and ethnic categories, they are then able to self-identify with the groups to which they belong. Children label the ethnic group they belong to by ages 6 to 8; understand that differences are based on biological features, as well as social features such as speech patterns and lifestyle, by age 7 to 8; and develop **racial** and **ethnic constancy**, or the understanding that race and ethnicity remain the same across time and in different settings, between ages 8 to 10 (Byrd, 2012). By the time children enter middle childhood, they have the cognitive capacity to begin to form a coherent racial and ethnic identity (Byrd, 2012).

The formation of your racial and ethnic identity is affected by society's attitudes toward the group with which you identify. Although many believe that racism is no longer an issue in the United States, those who experience it have a very different perception. In a variety of studies, between 49% and 90% of African American adolescents report having had experiences of racial discrimination in the form of harassment, poor treatment in public settings, or others' assumptions of lower ability or more violent behavior (Cooper, McLoyd, Wood, & Hardaway, 2008). Perhaps in response to these experiences, African American parents are more likely than parents of other ethnicities and races to teach their children about their race and ethnicity, a process called *ethnic* or *racial socialization* (Else-Quest & Morse, 2015). Adolescents in all ethnic and racial groups are more likely to explore and commit to an ethnic identity when they have been taught in this way by their parents.

Jean Phinney has built on Marcia's identity statuses, described earlier in this chapter, to develop a theory of ethnic and racial identity status development. She describes four identity statuses based on the individual's exploration of and commitment to an ethnic or racial identity. Table 11.3 shows the four types of ethnic identity, with a description and example of statements that correspond to each one.

Progress toward achieving a clear racial and ethnic identity has been associated with a number of positive outcomes for adolescents, including higher scores on measures of self-esteem, mastery, psychological adjustment, social and peer interactions, school performance, and family relations, and lower levels of depression (Crocetti, Rubini, & Meeus, 2008; Mandara, Gaylord-Harden, Richards, & Ragsdale, 2009; Seaton, Scottham, & Sellers, 2006; Smith & Silva, 2011; Umaña-Taylor, Gonzales-Backen, & Guimond, 2009). African American teens tend to have a stronger racial and ethnic identity than many other groups, perhaps because of their parents' racial and ethnic socialization, as we described earlier (Else-Quest & Morse, 2015). The benefits of these socialization practices are shown by research that has found that a strong positive connection to their racial and ethnic group reduced the impact of discrimination on academic self-concept and school achievement among African American adolescents and was associated with resistance to problem behaviors such as skipping classes, lying to parents about their whereabouts, bringing alcohol or drugs to school, and cheating on exams (Wang & Huguley, 2012; Wong, Eccles, & Sameroff, 2003).

Ethnic and racial identity A person's attitudes toward the racial and ethnic groups to which they feel they belong.

Racial and ethnic constancy The understanding that appears between 8 and 10 years of age that race and ethnicity remain the same across time and in different situations.

T ☐ F ☐ For African Americans, a strong identification with their ethnic group is linked with fewer problem behaviors at school. **True**

TABLE 11.3

Phinney's stages of ethnic/racial identity development.

Stage	Description	Comment
Diffuse Ethnic Identity	Little or no interest in one's ethnic identity	"My past is just there; I have no reason to worry about it. I'm American now."
Ethnic Identity Foreclosure	Commitment to an identity based on parents' or others' input rather than one's own exploration	"I don't go looking for my culture. I just go by what my parents say and do, and what they tell me to do, the way they are."
Moratorium	Exploration of ethnic identity without a clear commitment	"There are a lot of non-Japanese around me and it gets pretty confusing to try and decide who I am." "I think people should know what Black people had to go through to get to where we are now."
Achieved Ethnic Identity	Commitment to one's ethnic identity based on an exploration of its meaning to the individual	"People put me down because I'm Mexican, but I don't care anymore. I can accept myself more." "I used to want to be White, because I wanted long flowing hair. And I wanted to be real light. I used to think being light was prettier, but now I think there are pretty dark-skinned girls and pretty light-skinned girls. I don't want to be White now. I'm happy being Black."

SOURCES: Adapted from Phinney (1989) and Phinney, Jacoby, & Silva (2007).

Finding an ethnic identity. Sharing family traditions—whether it is celebrating Kwanzaa, enjoying a birthday party with a piñata, or having a large Italian family dinner—helps children and adolescents form a sense of their ethnic identity. What family traditions did your family share while you were growing up?

1. What is ethnic constancy?
2. How do children develop a racial and ethnic identity?
3. What impact can a strong racial and ethnic identity have on adolescent development?

MORAL IDENTITY

11.5 What factors influence a child's development of a moral identity?

Earlier in this chapter, we said that your self-concept included all the ways you think about and describe yourself. Would you describe yourself as honest or trustworthy? As caring and compassionate? As respectful and patient toward others? All of these are characteristics of your self-concept that are rooted in moral development. In this section, we examine development of a moral identity, or the degree to which being a moral person is part of one's sense of self (Hardy & Carlo, 2011). This aspect of identity also is related to self-esteem. If being honest or caring is central to your self-concept, your self-esteem suffers if you lie or act in an uncaring fashion. However, if honesty is not central to your sense of identity, lying may have little or no effect on your self-esteem.

Morality is the individual's understanding of right and wrong. It includes both what we think and what we do. The form that moral thought and behavior take changes throughout childhood. We have long believed that young children's morality is primarily determined by other people. Toddlers do what is right because they will be rewarded if they do or punished if they don't, but there is recent research showing that even within the first year infants have a sense of what is right and what is wrong (Hamlin, 2013). In this section, we describe how different theories and research have connected moral development with the influences of the environment, cognitive development, and emotional development. In addition, understanding morality is not the same as behaving in a moral fashion, so we examine the development of moral thought but also the development of moral behavior. Finally, we will look at some recent evidence for an innate moral sense.

THE ROLE OF THE ENVIRONMENT

Children's moral judgment and moral behavior are influenced by many aspects of the environment in which they grow up. Parents, peers, and media all affect the way children think about right and wrong, whether through direct or indirect mechanisms. The theory of behaviorism offers an explanation for how children learn right from wrong through the direct mechanism of operant conditioning. According to this theory, when a child does something good, like helping a friend, he may receive praise from an adult or a positive reaction from the friend. This reinforcement makes it more likely the child will behave this way again. It follows that when the child does something bad, like taking a toy away from a friend, he is likely to be scolded by an adult and receive a negative reaction from his friend. He will associate negative consequences with this behavior, and that should make it less likely that the behavior will occur again in the future.

Social cognitive theory adds a more indirect learning mechanism for moral development. Children will imitate what they see others do, especially if the other person's behavior receives reinforcement. Although they are not directly reinforced for their own behavior, they learn what is good behavior and what is bad from what they see. For example, young children imitate both the aggressive behavior and helping behavior they see when they watch television

Developing a conscience. From the expression on this child's face, it looks like he knows he is doing something wrong. Do you think that internalized moral values are causing his concern, or does he simply fear that he will be punished if his misbehavior is discovered?

shows. When high-quality prosocial television programs and DVDs were substituted for more aggression-laden programming for a sample of 3- to 5-year-old children, social competence scores increased and angry/aggressive/oppositional behavior decreased. The effects were particularly strong for boys from low-income families (Christakis et al., 2013).

The biggest question in the development of morality is how children move from responding to external consequences, such as rewards and punishments, to internalizing a moral sense of right and wrong so that they do what is right even if no one is around. Some of the theories that have attempted to explain how this happens emphasize the role of cognitive development, and others emphasize the role of emotional development, while another approach sees the origins of morality in innate preferences.

THE ROLE OF COGNITIVE DEVELOPMENT

Cognitive theories link the development of moral thought to the development of thought in general. It has been argued that young children learn the basic rules of right and wrong by first grade. This **moral knowledge** is based on their understanding of what is considered right or wrong in the context of their culture. For example, *do unto others as you would have them do to you*, or *honesty is the best policy* are moral principles many cultures endorse. **Moral judgment** is the way we reason about moral issues and reach conclusions. For example, two children may know it is wrong to take a cookie without asking. They have the same moral knowledge. However, the reason they don't take a cookie differs based on their stage of cognitive development. A young child doesn't take the cookie because she knows she will be punished if she does. A child at a higher level of moral judgment understands that taking the cookie is wrong because it breaks trust with a parent.

To test some of his ideas about moral development, Piaget (1965) posed moral dilemmas to children of different ages to see how they would respond. He described their resulting judgments as falling into three stages: premoral, heteronomous morality, and autonomous morality. Piaget believed that before the age of 4, young children were **premoral**; that is, they were unable to consider issues in terms of their morality.

Piaget described the moral thought of children from ages 4 through 7 as **heteronomous morality**. *Heteronomous* means "subject to external controls and impositions" (Heteronomous, n.d.). In this stage, young children base their judgments on adult authority. Because they do not really understand why moral rules should be followed, their behavior often is not consistent from one situation to another (Lapsley, 2006). Another aspect of this second level of moral thought is described as **immanent justice** or "the existence of automatic punishments which emanate from things themselves" (Piaget, 1965, p. 251). For example, in one moral dilemma, Piaget told a story about a boy who stole apples and ran away, but then fell through a rotten bridge. He asked children whether the boy would have fallen if he had not stolen the apples. A child in the heteronomous stage will say that the boy would not have fallen into the water if he had not stolen the apples. Falling into the water was a punishment for what he did. One difficulty with this kind of thinking is that children who have experienced a negative event, such as being hospitalized for an illness, may believe it is a punishment for something bad that they did.

Moral knowledge Understanding of right and wrong.

Moral judgment The way people reason about moral issues.

Premoral The inability to consider issues on the basis of their morality.

Heteronomous morality Moral judgments based on the dictates of authority.

Immanent justice The belief that unrelated events are automatic punishment for misdeeds.

©iStockphoto.com/YouraPechkin

In fact, many adults still show this kind of thinking when they ask, "What did I do to deserve this?" if something terrible happens to them. It is as if they think they are being punished for something they did earlier that really has no connection with the bad event that happened.

By age 7 or 8, children have generally moved on to the third stage known as **autonomous morality** in which they are aware of the rules and realize that they must adhere to them to maintain their interaction with others. In Piaget's words, they come to understand that "everyone must play the same" (1965, p. 44). The issue of fairness to all becomes central as children become less egocentric and more aware of others' points of view. Piaget believed that children's play contributes to moral development because everything must be negotiated between peers, not handed down from adults, so children must figure out together how to play fair and treat each other decently if they want to continue playing.

Lawrence Kohlberg built upon Piaget's ideas on moral development. Kohlberg used a similar technique of presenting a series of moral dilemmas to children and young adults of different ages and came up with stages based on their responses to these dilemmas. His most famous story is titled "Heinz and the Drug":

> In Europe, a woman was near death from a rare form of cancer. There was one drug that the doctors thought might save her, a form of radium that a druggist in the same town had recently discovered. The druggist was charging $2,000, ten times what the drug cost him to make. The sick woman's husband, Heinz, went to everyone he knew to borrow the money, but he could only get together about half of what [the drug] cost. He told the druggist that his wife was dying, and asked him to sell it cheaper or let him pay later. But the druggist said, "No." So, Heinz got desperate and broke into the man's store to steal the drug for his wife. Should the husband have done that? Why? (Kohlberg, 2005, p. 214)

Some people read this dilemma and immediately say that Heinz should definitely break in to get the drug, while others say it would be wrong to do so. In fact, Kohlberg was less interested in what people thought they would do than in understanding how they came to their decision. Someone who said that he would break in because his wife would be angry at him if he did not would be at quite a different level of moral thought than someone who said he would break in because human life is sacred. Likewise, someone who said he would not break in because he might get caught and sent to jail would be at a different level than someone who said he would not break in because it is important to respect another person's property.

Based on these different types of reasoning, Kohlberg described three levels of moral judgment: preconventional, conventional, and postconventional. Two stages were found within each level, and these are described in Table 11.4. We describe here the broad outlines of the three major levels.

The first level, **preconventional moral judgment**, is most characteristic of young children. It is marked by self-interest and motivation based on rewards and punishments. In some circumstances we all continue to think in these terms. For example, if you are driving faster than the speed limit and you hit the brakes when you see a police car, you

Autonomous morality When children are aware of the rules and realize that they must adhere to them to maintain their interaction with others, rather than because an adult has told them what to do.

Preconventional moral judgment Moral judgment that is marked by self-interest and motivation based on rewards and punishments.

Postconventional moral thought. Members of the organization Greenpeace believed their moral beliefs about the environment were more important than existing law when they attempted to block a Russian oil tanker from offloading its cargo of oil from the Arctic.

©AP Photo/Robin Utrecht/REX

TABLE 11.4

Kohlberg's stages of moral development. In addition to the three levels of moral development described in this chapter, Kohlberg further broke each level into two stages. This table provides a description about how thinking about moral development changes at each of these stages.

Levels	Stages	Description (the basis for moral judgment)
I. Preconventional (under age 9)	1. Heteronomous morality	Obeying the word of authorities and fear of punishment
	2. Individualism, instrumental purpose, and exchange	Fairness—believing everyone's self-interest must be taken into account
II. Conventional (most adolescents and adults)	3. Mutual interpersonal expectations and conformity	Desiring to be seen as "good" by others by meeting their expectations, including being caring, loyal, and grateful
	4. Social system and conscience	Considering the good of society as a whole, maintaining societal order for the good of all
III. Postconventional (some adults older than 20–25)	5. Social contract and individual rights	Understanding that the rules of society may differ for different groups but that some values, such as life and liberty, are universal
	6. Universal ethical principles	Following self-chosen principles involving equal rights even when they conflict with society's rules

SOURCE: Adapted from Kohlberg (1987).

are not thinking about the underlying reasons for the speed limit (such as safety or conserving gasoline). You hit your brakes because you don't want to get an expensive speeding ticket.

Conventional moral judgment Moral reasoning that moves beyond self-interest to take into account the good of others.

In the second level, **conventional moral judgment** moves beyond self-interest to take into account the good of those around you. In the first substage, a person bases moral decisions on the moral expectations of important people in his life. At this stage, "trust, loyalty, respect, and gratitude" are central values (Kohlberg, 1987, p. 284). In the second substage, a person makes decisions based more on the expectations of society as a whole. Laws are to be followed because society would break down if everyone disobeyed them. In this stage, a person might respond to the Heinz dilemma by saying that he should not break in because if everyone did things like this, social order would break down.

Postconventional moral judgment Moral judgements that move beyond society as the defining factor of what is moral or right and are based on universal principles that apply to all people.

In the third level, **postconventional moral judgment** moves beyond society as a defining factor of what is moral or right. Kohlberg says that a person in this stage believes in the human rights of all people, so moral judgments are based on universal principles that apply to all. Often these principles will correspond with society's rules, but when they don't, the person still chooses to follow the principles. For example, members of the organization Greenpeace broke the law in May 2014, when they tried to block a Russian oil tanker from offloading its cargo of oil from the Arctic. All were arrested but they felt that their moral principles were more important than the rules of their society. One protestor said, "This tanker is the first sign of a reckless new push to exploit the Arctic, a place of incredible beauty which is melting before our eyes" (Vidal, 2014, para. 7). You can read about another situation in which an individual chose to break the law on behalf of what he believed was a higher moral purpose in **Journey of Research: Kohlberg's Life History and His Theory.**

JOURNEY OF *Research*

Kohlberg's Life History and His Theory

Many times individuals' life experiences influence the theories they develop and the research they carry out. Lawrence Kohlberg has a life history that is clearly connected to his research. Kohlberg served with the U.S. Merchant Marines after World War II. After his service, he volunteered to help sail ships that would move Jewish refugees out of Europe to the British-controlled territory of Palestine. In doing so, he was breaking British law, which made it illegal for these refugees to enter Palestine. He was captured and held in Cyprus until the Jewish fighting force known as the Haganah liberated him. Kohlberg's research in later years focused on how people make decisions about what is right and wrong. As was described previously, the highest level in Kohlberg's theory is one in which a person develops universal moral principles that may or may not conform to what a particular country or group of people believes is right. Can you see how his life experiences shaped his theoretical ideas? (Adapted from Levine, 2002).

Although these stages are usually described in terms of children's development, Kohlberg believed that even adults may remain in the first stage of moral judgment, and many do not move beyond the stage of conventional moral judgment.

Gender Differences in Moral Thought

When Kohlberg did his original research, he studied only boys. When he did include girls, they tended to perform at a lower level of moral reasoning than the boys. Carol Gilligan believed that this was because Kohlberg's theory was gender-biased and reflected a masculine view of morality. Gilligan argued that women do not have a lower level of morality than men, but rather have a different way of thinking about moral issues. Her idea was that women base their moral judgments more on what she called the *principle of care* while men base their judgments more on impersonal, abstract justice, which she believed was the basis for Kohlberg's stages. Although Gilligan did much of her research using real-life moral dilemmas, she also used hypothetical dilemmas, such as the following fable, called The Porcupine and the Moles, that she used with children:

> It was growing cold and a Porcupine was looking for a home. He found a most desirable cave, but saw it was occupied by a family of Moles. "Would you mind if I shared your home for the winter?" the Porcupine asked the Moles. The generous Moles consented, and the Porcupine moved in. But the cave was small, and every time the Moles moved around they were scratched by the Porcupine's sharp quills. The Moles endured this discomfort as long as they could. Then at last they gathered courage to approach their visitor. "Pray leave," they said, "and let us have our cave to ourselves once again." "Oh no!" said the Porcupine. "This place suits me very well."

After telling this fable, Gilligan would then ask, "What should the moles do? Why?" (Gilligan, 1987, p. 14).

Gilligan (1987) believed that girls and women would be more likely to respond in terms of everyone's needs: "Cover the porcupine with a blanket [so that the moles will not be stuck and the porcupine will have shelter]" or "Dig a bigger hole" (p. 7). Boys would be more likely to respond in terms of absolute right and wrong: "The porcupine has to go definitely. It's the moles' house" (p. 7).

Although several studies have reported such gender differences, the majority have found that both boys and girls think about morality from both the justice and the care perspectives (Jaffee & Hyde, 2000; Walker, 2006). Neither boys nor girls are consistent in the perspective that they bring to resolving moral dilemmas, with the nature of the dilemma itself being the determining factor in which perspective they adopt (Walker & Frimer, 2009). In fact, Kohlberg's original findings that men were more moral than women also have not been borne out. In more recent research, the only gender differences found in Kohlberg's stages of moral reasoning have tended to favor girls, although these differences vary from country to country (Gibbs, Basinger, Grime, & Snarey, 2007). The major conclusion we can draw at the present time is that there is no clear gender difference in moral reasoning.

Cultural Differences in Moral Thought

Kohlberg believed that the same stages of moral development that he found in the United States would be found in cultures around the world. A review of studies carried out in 75 different countries found evidence for the universality of the move from preconventional to conventional morality (Gibbs et al., 2007). However, the universality of the move from conventional to postconventional moral reasoning has been much more controversial. Some have argued that the postconventional stage is reflective of Western and urban values. For example, in one study that compared Korean and British children, the researchers found that a concept that Koreans refer to as *chung* could not be scored according to Kohlberg's method. *Chung* is a central value in Korean society that translates as an emotional bond between people in which "the boundary between individuals was dimmed and a sense of one-ness, same-ness, affection, comfort, acceptance and so forth emerged" (Baek, 2002, p. 387). One example of how *chung* affects moral judgment comes from the response of a 16-year-old Korean adolescent when asked whether Heinz should steal the drug for his wife even if he didn't love her:

TRUE/FALSE VIDEO ▲

> "Even though he doesn't love her, he should steal the drug. It is said that husband and wife live together based on *chung* rather than love. They (Heinz and his wife) might also have *chung* between them since they have been together for a long time" (Baek, 2002, p. 384).

The concept of *chung* seems to represent a high level of moral reasoning, but it does not fit very well into Kohlberg's idea of postconventional morality.

Moral Thought and Moral Action

People often believe their behavior mirrors their values. In other words, they adopt a trait approach to understanding morality (Doris, 2002). They see themselves as a moral person and believe they act based on that morality. However, a substantial amount of research has shown there is only a moderately strong link between moral identity and moral behavior (Hardy & Carlo, 2011), suggesting that morality is more statelike than traitlike because any number of situational factors affect how likely it is that we will behave in accordance with our moral values or beliefs.

T ☐ F ☐ Your moral values and beliefs are the best predictor of what you will actually do when faced with a moral dilemma. **False**

When you are given a hypothetical moral dilemma, you are largely free from the situational constraints that might influence your actual behavior, but real life is filled with them. For example, divinity students were told they were going to give a practice sermon. Some were told to talk about the Good Samaritan who helped another person who was suffering, while others were given unrelated topics. Then some students were told they were going to be late for their sermon, and some were not. On the way to deliver the sermon, each divinity student saw a man who appeared to be in pain and needed help. What do you think determined whether a student stopped to give help? The students' actual behavior was determined less by whether they had just been thinking about compassion and the Good Samaritan than it was by whether they were going to be late to give their sermon or not (Darley & Batson, 1973).

Social Domain Theory

According to **social domain theory**, moral behavior is constructed from an individual's interactions with the environment. There are three domains of social knowledge—moral, social-conventional, and personal—and the way we decide whether a behavior is moral or not is different for each of these domains. The moral domain involves judgment about "justice, welfare and rights" and how people ought to be treated (Smetana, 2006, p. 120). Issues in the moral domain are obligatory (that is, everyone must obey these rules), generalizable (that is, the rules apply at all times and in all places), and independent of authority (that is, you need to obey these rules even if there is no one else around to see what you are doing). Violation of moral rules is considered a serious offense (Smetana, 2006). The social-conventional domain is based on social expectations and these issues differ from one culture to another (Turiel, 2006). The personal domain includes issues that affect the individual, but not others, and thus are matters of personal choice (Smetana, 2006). Whereas Piaget and Kohlberg describe moral development as moving from concern for oneself (personal) in early childhood, to concern for society (social-conventional) in middle childhood, to concern for universal moral principles (moral) in adolescence, social domain theory sees all three of these aspects developing independently starting in early childhood.

Similar to the way that Kohlberg and Piaget conducted their research, work on social domain theory also has frequently used hypothetical dilemmas to explore how children reason about situations that involve the different domains and researchers are most interested in the reasons the child gives for his or her answers. Nucci (2008) provides this example of how a 4-year-old girl thought about a moral issue and a conventional issue that happened at her preschool:

Social domain theory A theory of moral development based on three domains of social knowledge—moral, social-conventional, and personal—with different ways of deciding what is moral in each of them.

Moral issue (physical injury)

Interviewer:	Did you see what happened?
Girl:	Yes. They were playing and John hit him too hard.
Interviewer:	Is that something you are supposed to do or not supposed to do?
Girl:	Not so hard to hurt.
Interviewer:	Is there a rule about that?
Girl:	Yes.
Interviewer:	What is the rule?
Girl:	You're not to hit hard.
Interviewer:	What if there were no rule about hitting hard, would it be all right to do then?
Girl:	No.
Interviewer:	Why not?
Girl:	Because he could get hurt and start to cry.

Conventional issue

Interviewer:	Did you see what just happened?
Girl:	Yes. They were noisy.
Interviewer:	Is that something you are supposed to or not supposed to do?
Girl:	Not do.
Interviewer:	Is there a rule about that?
Girl:	Yes. We have to be quiet.
Interviewer:	What if there were no rule, would it be all right to do then?
Girl:	Yes.
Interviewer:	Why?
Girl:	Because there is no rule.

We can see from this example that even a young child understands the difference between a moral issue which should be respected under any circumstance and a social-conventional issue that is based upon a rule that can be changed. As children get older, the criteria they use to make these judgments become more abstract (Smetana, 2006). Of course, not all issues are easily classified into one of these three domains. In ambiguous situations, how the individual makes a decision is influenced by context, culture, and age, as well as the salience of the issue (Smetana, 2006).

THE ROLE OF EMOTIONAL DEVELOPMENT

Emotions enter into the development of morality in two ways. First, we don't want to do what we think is wrong because we will feel guilty about it, and that is a very uncomfortable emotion. Second, we want to do what is right because we will feel good about doing it. These emotions are the result of our *conscience,* an autonomous inner guiding system that is based on our understanding of moral rules (Kochanska & Aksan, 2006).

Grazyna Kochanska and her colleagues have shown a link between conscience and moral behavior. They found that when a mother is responsive to her infant it leads to the toddler's willingness to comply with the parent's guidance and rules. In preschoolers, these rules become internalized to form the basis for the child's conscience. In turn, children who develop an effective internal conscience are much less likely to engage in disruptive and negative behavior (Kochanska, Barry, Aksan, & Boldt, 2008; Hardy & Carlo, 2011).

The central role of emotions in moral development is shown in the following simple example: A young child bumps her head as she emerges from a play structure. The teacher says, "Oooh, ouch! That must hurt. Should we put some ice on it?" This example demonstrates the two basic aspects of emotional response that underlie **prosocial behavior** that helps and supports other people: empathy and sympathy. The teacher is experiencing *empathy* when he says, "Oooh, ouch!" It is almost as if he too were experiencing the hurt. Even newborns seem to experience this type of emotional sharing. When they hear other babies crying, they are likely to start crying themselves (Geangu et al., 2010). However, unlike a newborn, the teacher is able to manage his own emotional response to react with concern for the child. This response is called *sympathy* (Eisenberg, Spinrad, & Sadovsky, 2006). If you feel empathy for other people, it is likely to lead to sympathy for their plight. You also are more likely to want to do something to help them and less likely to want to hurt them. Although prosocial behaviors that help and support other people can result from empathy and sympathy, they

Prosocial behavior Actions that help and support other people.

also can result from guilt. In a recent study of older children, the likelihood of sharing with a peer was affected in some children by their ability to be sympathetic and for others by their anticipation of feeling guilty if they did not share (Ongley & Malti, 2014).

Anger is an emotion that has the opposite effect and can lead to **antisocial behaviors** that hurt other people physically or emotionally. The use of aggression by children at different ages is related to the level of their moral understanding. We are less concerned by a preschooler who pushes a friend away to get to a toy than we are by a teenager who uses the Internet to destroy another teen's reputation; this is in part because we don't expect the preschooler to understand how her behavior is hurtful to the other child, while the teenager usually has a good idea of the damage he is doing.

Antisocial behavior Actions that hurt other people, physically or emotionally

THE ROLE OF INNATE PROCESSES

The theory of core knowledge that we discussed in Chapter 7 proposes that certain types of knowledge and understanding of the world are built into the brain prenatally. Could one of these be a sense of morality? Several researchers have attempted to show that this is so through research with infants during the first year of life. In research by Hamlin, Wynn, and Bloom (2007), 10-month-old infants were shown the scenes in Figure 11.4. Each scene begins with the red circle trying to get to the top of the hill and not succeeding. In the first scenario, the yellow triangle arrives and pushes the circle so it gets to the top successfully. In the second scenario, the blue square pushes the circle back down the hill so it never reaches the top. After the infants saw these scenes, the yellow triangle and the blue square were put in front of them. The researchers found that the infants were more likely to point to or touch the "helper" triangle than the "hinderer" square. Results were consistent for other scenarios including one in which an animal puppet is trying to open a box with a toy inside and one

---

FIGURE 11.4

Helpers and hinderers. In each of these photos, the red circle character has been shown trying and failing to get to the top of the hill. In the first scene, the yellow triangle helps by pushing the circle successfully to the top. In the second photo, the blue square hinders the circle by pushing it back down to the bottom of the hill. Infants like the helper more than the hinderer, showing very early moral judgment.

SOURCE: Hamlin, Wynn, & Bloom (2007).

figure opens the box and another slams it closed (Hamlin, 2013). These researchers believe that life experiences then build on this early understanding in all the ways we have described in our discussion of the role of the environment, emotion, and cognition in the development of morality, but that a basic sense of morality is innate, not learned.

Moral thought and moral behavior are likely to result from a combination of all the factors we have mentioned: inborn tendencies, cognitive and emotional development, and the influence of aspects of the environment, including media, parents, and peers.

PROMOTING MORAL DEVELOPMENT

Service learning Educational programs that involve students in direct community service and also reflection about their experiences to learn from them.

Although there have been many different programs designed to promote moral development in children and teens, we have chosen one specific type to give as an example of the type of intervention that can be successfully implemented. **Service learning** is a program in which children provide community service and then reflect upon their experiences to learn from them. Service learning programs have been used as early as kindergarten and on through adolescence and research on these programs has shown that participants increase their moral awareness, including empathy, understanding, altruism, giving, and caring (Leming, 2001). It is essential, however, that these programs provide an opportunity for structured reflection to guide children's thinking about moral and ethical issues if they are going to learn from them (Conway, Amel, & Gerwien, 2009).

One example of program effectiveness comes from a group of middle school students in Australia whose service learning involved work with the Red Cross and a local nursing home. When interviewed before the activity, many dismissed the likelihood that the experience would have much of an impact on them. However, afterward their reflective responses about what they had gotten from the experience included: "Understanding because you need to know how people feel and what they think" and "There are values in everything. I just didn't realise it before" (Lovat & Clement, 2016, p. 123). Service learning provides an opportunity for students to look beyond themselves and to clarify the values that make up their sense of morality.

CHECK YOUR UNDERSTANDING

1. How does the environment affect children's moral development?
2. Compare Piaget's and Kohlberg's stages of moral development.
3. What support is there for Gilligan's theory of gender differences in moral reasoning?
4. Describe how moral thought relates to moral action.
5. What role do emotions play in the development of moral thought and behavior?
6. What evidence supports the idea that infants are born with a moral sense?

CONCLUSION

In this chapter, we have looked at an essential aspect of development: the development of the self. Children and adolescents develop a sense of who they are as individuals (self-concept) as well as how they feel about themselves (self-esteem). Three important aspects of the sense of self that develop throughout childhood and adolescence are gender identity, racial and ethnic identity, and moral identity. By the end of adolescence, most young people have a complex concept of their own identity that combines all the elements we described in this chapter, as well as their hopes and aspirations for who they will become as adults.

CHAPTER SUMMARY

Test your understanding of the content.
Take the practice quiz at **edge.sagepub.com/levine3e**

11.1 How does the sense of self that develops in infancy become identity in adolescence?

Infants have little self-awareness, but within the first 2 years of life they develop the ability to recognize themselves in a mirror, to use the pronouns *I* and *you* correctly, and to understand that other people see the world differently than they do (**visual perspective taking**). They also become possessive of their toys. Preschoolers think about themselves in very concrete ways: possessions, size, and abilities. School-age children begin to make **social comparisons**, in which they compare themselves to others. Adolescents develop a differentiated self that takes into account their characteristics at various times and in different situations. **Rites of passage** in different cultures mark the transition from childhood to an adult identity in that culture. According to Marcia, two processes are involved in forming an identity: exploring the possibilities and making a commitment. The four identity statuses he identified are **foreclosure** (no exploration, commitment made), **identity diffusion** (no exploration, no commitment), **moratorium** (exploration in process, no commitment), and **identity achievement** (exploration completed, commitment made).

11.2 How does self-esteem change from preschool through adolescence?

Preschoolers tend to have high **self-esteem** because they do not compare themselves to other people. When school-age children begin to use social comparisons, self-esteem often declines. In early adolescence, self-esteem may drop with the physical changes of puberty and the new social and cognitive demands of middle school, but later in adolescence self-esteem often improves as a sense of identity develops and remains high through the transition to adulthood. Teens can now imagine their **ideal self** and compare reality with that ideal. Even a small discrepancy between the real and ideal self can negatively impact self-esteem if it is in an area that is important to the teen.

11.3 How does gender identity develop for most children and how does it develop for LGBT children and teens?

Behavioral theories emphasize reinforcement and imitation of gender-appropriate behaviors. Cognitive developmental theory ties gender identity development to Piaget's stages of cognitive development. Gender schema theory emphasizes the development of ideas associated with each gender based on societal expectations and experiences. The gender self-socialization model examines gender identity by looking at children's and teens' own individual experiences and ideas of gender consistency and pressure to conform.

Lesbian, gay, and bisexual teens identify with their **natal gender** but are attracted to partners of the same sex. **Transgender** children experience their gender as opposite from their natal sex. Their identification with a different sex may begin as early as age 2 or it may not begin until adolescence. LGBT children and teens experience harassment at a high level, which can negatively affect their well-being, so family acceptance is crucial to their positive development. Support for and acceptance of LGBT students has increased in recent years, so many are optimistic about their futures.

11.4 How do ethnic and racial identity affect development?

At first, children may not think specifically about their **ethnic and racial identity**. During adolescence, ethnicity may become more meaningful, and teens may engage in an ethnic identity search, exploring the meaning of their ethnicity. Finally, they reach a clear understanding and acceptance of their ethnic identity. Those adolescents with a strong sense of ethnic identity are more able to resist problem behaviors and more likely to have higher self-esteem.

11.5 What factors influence a child's development of a moral identity?

Children learn what is right and what is wrong from the reinforcements they receive from the environment, while also learning what to do by imitation. Piaget and Kohlberg describe the development of moral judgment as a series of stages similar to Piaget's stages of cognitive development. For Piaget, these stages are **premoral**, **heteronomous morality**, and **autonomous morality**. Kohlberg's levels are **preconventional**, **conventional**, and **postconventional**. For both theories, the progression is from judgments based on others' rules to internalized rules. The emotions of empathy and guilt play a role in influencing children to behave in moral ways. According to **social domain theory**, moral behavior is based on three domains of social knowledge—moral, social-conventional, and personal—and the way we decide whether a behavior is moral or not is different for each of these domains. Finally, some aspects of **moral judgment** may be innate, as demonstrated by research with infants.

KEY TERMS

Strengthen your understanding of these key terms with
mobile-friendly eFlashcards at **edge.sagepub.com/levine3e**

Give your students the SAGE edge!

SAGE edge offers a robust online environment featuring an impressive array of free tools and resources for review, study, and further exploration, keeping both instructors and students on the cutting edge of teaching and learning. Learn more at **edge.sagepub.com/levine3e**

practice AND apply

WHAT YOU'VE LEARNED

edge.sagepub.com/levine3e

chapter 12

SOCIAL DEVELOPMENT

Social Cognition and Peer Relationships

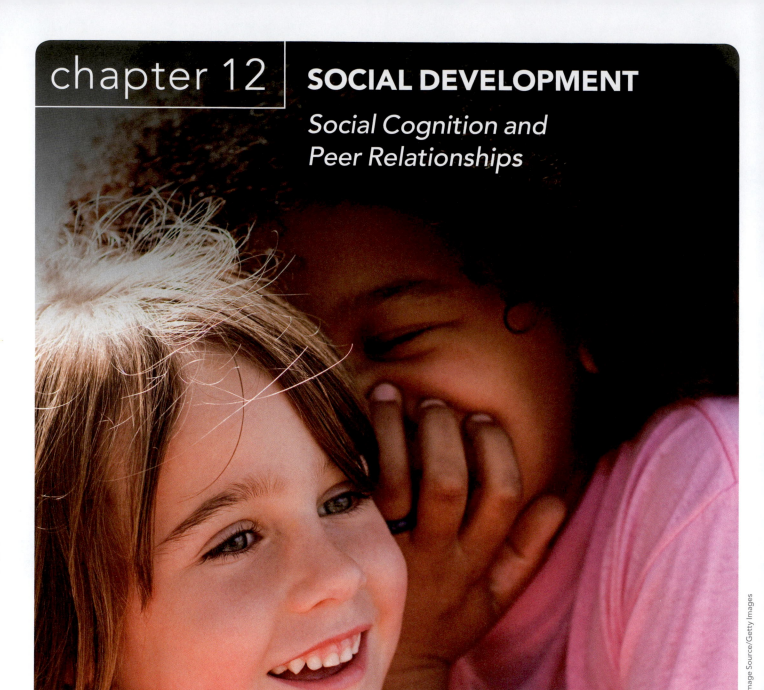

Image Source/Getty Images

LEARNING QUESTIONS

12.1 What is theory of mind and how does it develop from infancy through adolescence?

12.2 How is play important for children's development?

12.3 How do peer relationships change during middle childhood?

12.4 What types of peer relationships are important during adolescence?

12.5 How do bullying and school violence impact children and adolescents?

Master these objectives using an online action plan at **edge.sagepub.com/levine3e**

TEST YOUR KNOWLEDGE

Test your knowledge of child development by deciding whether each of the following statements is *true* or *false,* and then check your answers as you read the chapter.

1. T ☐ F ☐: Infants and toddlers do not understand what other people are thinking.

2. T ☐ F ☐: If a child chooses to play alone, even when there are other children available to play with him, there is no reason for concern.

3. T ☐ F ☐: Preschoolers are not likely to maintain a friendship for more than a few weeks.

4. T ☐ F ☐: It is important for children to play because they have fun when they are playing, but the real learning happens in the classroom.

5. T ☐ F ☐: Being rejected by peers doesn't bother some children.

6. T ☐ F ☐: Recess is an important part of education and should not be taken away for disciplinary reasons.

7. T ☐ F ☐: In general, for adolescents, the more friends they have, the better.

8. T ☐ F ☐: Most adolescents say that they feel a good deal of peer pressure to do things that they know they shouldn't do.

9. T ☐ F ☐: Anti-bullying programs that use peer mediation or peer mentors to reduce bullying in schools have actually increased the amount of bullying that occurs.

10. T ☐ F ☐: Adolescents are much less likely to be victims of violence while in school now than they were 20 years ago.

Correct answers: (1) F, (2) T, (3) F, (4) F, (5) T, (6) T, (7) F, (8) F, (9) T, (10) T

▲ **VIDEO: Watch as students answer some of these questions and the authors respond.**

I n this chapter, we explore the social world of children and adolescents. We begin by discussing how the development of social cognition affects how children understand their social world and influences the kinds of social interactions they are able to have with others. We then look at a central aspect of children's social development: their movement from total dependence on parents into the world of peers. We examine the nature of peer relationships in childhood and adolescence, how these relationships change over time, and why they are crucial for development.

SOCIAL COGNITION: THEORY OF MIND

12.1 What is theory of mind and how does it develop from infancy through adolescence?

When we study **social cognition,** we are looking at the ways children use the cognitive processes described in Chapter 7 to understand their social world. One important aspect of social cognition that develops in childhood is called *theory of mind,* which

Social cognition The way we use cognitive processes to understand our social world.

refers to the ability "to understand self and others as agents who act on the basis of their mental states (i.e., beliefs, desires, emotions, intentions)" (Astington & Filippova, 2005, p. 211). Children actively construct their ideas about what happens in their own and other people's minds and they become better at doing this as they get older (Peterson, Wellman, & Slaughter, 2012). For example, if you ask a child why she took her friend's toy away, she may answer, "Because I *wanted* it!" She explains her behavior in terms of her own mental state of *wanting* the toy. It takes children longer to understand that the other child is now crying because he, too, *wanted* it. Over time, as we understand more and more about the motives, emotions, and thoughts of others, we all become pretty accomplished mind readers. See **Active Learning: Mind Reading and Mindblindness** to experience what it might be like if you did not have a theory of mind.

Active LEARNING

Mind Reading and Mindblindness

Simon Baron-Cohen (1995) presents the following scenario in his book *Mindblindness*: "John walked into the bedroom, walked around, and walked out" (p. 1). Think about how you might try to explain this behavior. What could possibly be going on to make this happen?

Write down your ideas about what John might be doing. Next, underline each word in your explanation that reflects something about his possible mental state—for example, *wanted, heard, wanted to know, looked for, was confused*. After you do this, try to write an explanation for John's behavior that does *not* include anything about his mental state. It is hard for us to do. Here is one attempt by Baron-Cohen: "Maybe John does this every day, at this time: he just walks into the bedroom, walks around, and walks out again" (p. 2). Not very satisfactory, is it? Most of us automatically put ideas about others' thoughts into our explanations for their behavior.

Mindblindness The inability to understand and theorize about other people's thoughts.

It is hard for us even to imagine what it would be like if we did not have theories about what goes on in other people's minds. Baron-Cohen describes **mindblindness** as the inability to understand and theorize about other people's thoughts. This is a characteristic of many people who have autism spectrum disorders. To remind yourself about the characteristics of autism spectrum disorders, see Chapters 6 and 9.

Theory of mind can be broken down into six types of understanding that children seem to master in the following order:

1. Diverse desires—different people may like and want different things.

2. Diverse beliefs—different people can hold different beliefs about the same thing.

3. Knowledge access—people who see something also know about it; if they do not see, then they do not know.

4. False belief—people do things based on what they think, even if they are mistaken.

5. Hidden emotion—people can deliberately conceal emotions by facial expression management.

6. Sarcasm—in order to be humorous, people sometimes say the opposite of what they really mean. (Slaughter, 2015, p. 170)

Some aspects of theory of mind develop even during the first year of life. For instance, young infants appear to understand other people's intentions or desires, rather than just their actions. In one study, babies saw someone repeatedly reach over a barrier to retrieve an object (see Figure 12.1). When the barrier was removed, they looked longer when the person reached in the same way they had just seen (indirect reach in the figure), as if there were still a barrier, than if the person reached directly to get the object (Wellman, 2014). Based on the idea that infants will look longer at something that is surprising, researchers concluded that the infants seemed to understand that the person intended to get the object and the most efficient way to do that would be to use the direct route. Using the indirect reach when there was no barrier would be surprising to them if they understood that the person's desire was to obtain the object.

This growing understanding of others' intentions also helps the child's early language learning. Children have a primitive understanding of what an adult is thinking when the adult says "doll" while *looking* at an object. The child understands that the adult is labeling

> **T ☐ F ☐** Infants and toddlers do not understand what other people are thinking. **False**

FIGURE 12.1

Infant understanding of intentional action. Infants looked longer at the third event than the second. They appeared to understand that the person intended to get the object, showing an early comprehension of theory of mind.

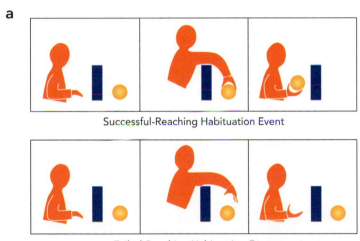

Successful-Reaching Habituation Event

Failed-Reaching Habituation Event

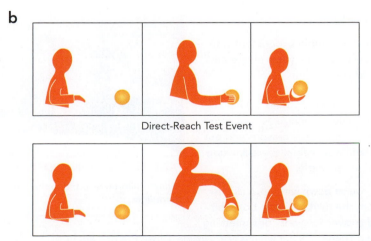

Direct-Reach Test Event

Indirect-Reach Test Event

SOURCE: Wellman (2014).

that object rather than something else. There is evidence that the ability to follow an adult's gaze leads to the development of another important aspect of theory of mind: the ability to use language to describe internal states (Brooks & Meltzoff, 2015). In describing internal states, children seem to progress from an understanding of wants and desires ("she wants that cookie") to an understanding of beliefs ("he believes the cookie is over there") (Tardif & Wellman, 2000).

Understanding that different people can have different beliefs about the same thing is the second step in the development of theory of mind. There is evidence that young children have some ability to understand that other people can believe something that the child knows is untrue, which is called a **false belief**. A classic experiment designed to test whether children understand that what goes on in someone else's mind might be different from what is going on in their own is called the **false belief paradigm**. In these experiments, a child views a scene something like this: A doll named Louise is shown that a piece of candy is hidden in a certain drawer in a toy kitchen. Louise then leaves, and the experimenter takes the candy and moves it into the refrigerator. When Louise returns, she wants the candy. The child is asked where she thinks Louise will look for it. A child who doesn't understand that others can have false beliefs will say that Louise will look in the refrigerator. The child knows where the candy is and, if she doesn't yet understand false beliefs, it seems to her that Louise must know that, too. Children who understand that others may have false beliefs understand that Louise will look first in the drawer where she last saw the candy.

By age 4, most children can respond based on an understanding of false beliefs, and recent research has indicated that younger children can carry out similar tasks successfully when verbal responses are not required. For example, 2-year-olds watched while an adult saw a puppet place a ball in a particular box. Then a phone rang and the adult turned away while the puppet moved the ball to a different location. When the adult went to retrieve the ball, these toddlers looked toward the box that the adult would have falsely believed still contained the ball (Southgate, Senju, & Csibra, 2007). Similar results have been found for even younger infants (Scott & Baillargeon, 2009). You can determine for yourself whether a young child has developed an understanding of false beliefs that he or she can express verbally by following the instructions in **Active Learning: False Beliefs**.

False belief The understanding that someone else may believe something that a child knows to be untrue.

False belief paradigm An experimental task used to assess a child's understanding that others may believe something the child knows to be untrue.

Active LEARNING

False Beliefs

Try the following simple experiment with a child between 3 and 4 years of age and another child who is older.

1. Before you see each child, take a box a child would recognize as containing crayons. Remove the crayons and put something else inside: short drinking straws, for example.

2. When you sit down with the child, ask her what she thinks is in the box. She should answer "crayons" or something like that. Then show her what is really inside. Close the box again.

3. Ask her the following: "If [name of a friend] came into the room right now, what would she think is inside this box?"

ACTIVE LEARNING VIDEO ▲

Watch children respond to the false belief paradigm.

If the child replies "crayons" (or whatever she said the first time), then she has demonstrated a good understanding that a friend may believe something different from what she herself does. If she replies that her friend would know that it is not crayons but is instead whatever you have put in the box, then she does not understand that her friend could have a false belief. Instead, she thinks her friend knows everything that she herself knows despite the fact that her friend never saw that you had replaced the crayons with some other objects (adapted from Flavell, 1999).

To prepare for this activity or if you do not have access to a child, watch the video of this Active Learning.

The ability to understand what others are thinking is a skill affected by children's experiences. When parents discuss thoughts, wants, and emotions with their children, the children are more likely to develop a theory of mind at a younger age (Slaughter, 2015). Children with siblings also tend to develop theory of mind more quickly than those with no siblings. The type of interaction that goes on between siblings, including playing tricks, comforting, and arguing, gives children experience with what is in other people's minds on a daily basis (McAlister & Peterson, 2013).

Although children in many different cultures develop theory of mind at about the same age, the way in which it develops differs (Ahn & Miller, 2012; Shahaeian, Peterson, Slaughter, & Wellman, 2011). The order in which theory of mind concepts develop is slightly different in collectivist cultures such as Iran and China where children are encouraged to obtain knowledge but not to express opinions that challenge their elders' points of view and disrupt family harmony. Consequently, the first understanding of theory of mind for these children is that others can know things that they do not or vice versa. Children in individualist cultures such as Australia and the United States are more often encouraged to express their own opinions and they learn that others can have different opinions before they understand that they can have different knowledge (Shahaeian et al., 2011).

Even after young children have developed a theory of mind, their understanding is still limited. For example, children between 2 and 5 years of age observed a researcher try to retrieve a stuffed animal from a container. She turned a crank, which didn't work, and said "Whoops, I didn't mean to do that!" She then opened the door on the container and successfully retrieved the animal, saying "There!" Children who were 3 years old and older were much less likely to imitate the first action in order to get the toy out, while 2-year-olds were just as likely to perform the mistaken action as the intentional action, showing less understanding that the researcher did not intend to do the first action (Gardiner, Greif, & Bjorklund, 2011).

It is not until middle childhood that children begin to understand that two people might interpret the same event differently. This new understanding was demonstrated in

Digital Vision/Thinkstock

"Mind reading" in childhood. This young child is beginning to understand that you must know what someone else is thinking in order to interact effectively with him (called *theory of mind*). He has picked up all the signals his father is sending indicating that his father likes what the child is feeding him and he should continue.

one study in which children were presented with stories about sibling conflict such as the following:

> Peter and Helen are brother and sister. It is Halloween, and they are both taking costumes for the contest at school. The winner of the contest gets a really cool prize. Before they go to school, Peter realizes that he is missing one piece for his costume. He asks Helen: "Can you bring your bat to school for me? I have lots of other stuff that I need to carry." Helen says sure. Helen finds a baseball bat and a hairy rubber bat. She grabs the hairy rubber bat to take for Peter. Helen and Peter go to school. When the contest is starting, Helen gives Peter the hairy rubber bat. Peter is wearing a baseball player costume so he needs the baseball bat not a hairy rubber bat. "Oh no," Peter says, "You ruined my costume, you jerk!" (Ross, Recchia, & Carpendale, 2005, p. 591)

The children were asked who Peter thought was to blame and then who Helen thought was to blame and to explain each person's perspective. Finally, they were asked whether it made sense that they had different points of view. By age 7 or 8 children were able to see that the two characters would have different ideas about who was at fault and that both views were valid.

Anyone who has played poker will know that understanding theory of mind gets even more complicated. A good poker player understands that not only does she have to intuit what the other players are thinking ("I have a good hand"), but she also has to keep in mind that the other players are trying to figure out what she is thinking. If she wants to bluff the others, she must make them think that she has different cards than she really does. In other words, she is thinking about their thinking about her thinking. This ability, called **recursive thinking**, has been found in children as young as 7 (Sher, Koenig, & Rustichini, 2014). Examples of recursive thinking are shown in Figure 12.2.

So far we have seen that social cognition becomes more complex as children develop. A second important issue involves individual differences in how children interpret what other people think. Although the ability to understand what others are thinking is most often linked with popularity among peers and a greater ability to cooperate and interact in a

Recursive thinking The ability to think about other people thinking about your thinking.

FIGURE 12.2

Recursive thinking. Pictures like this have been used to test whether participants can describe the recursive thinking process shown in each image. For instance, in the first picture, the boy is thinking about the girl and her father. In the second picture, the boy is thinking that he is thinking about himself. In the third picture, the boy is thinking about a girl thinking about what her father is thinking about her mother.

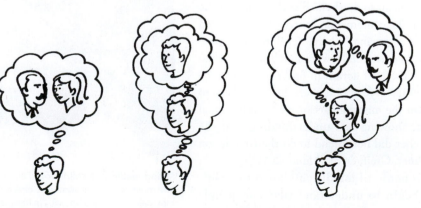

SOURCE: Oppenheimer (1986).

positive fashion with others (Slaughter, Imuta, Peterson, & Henry, 2015), there are children who have a tendency to interpret others' intentions to be hostile rather than benign. This is called a **hostile attributional bias**. An attribution is the explanation or cause that we give to behavior. If you are nice to me, I can attribute it to my belief that you are a kind person or, if I have a hostile attributional bias, I might attribute it to my assumption that you want something from me. In one study, children were presented with an ambiguous situation such as the following: A peer breaks a child's new radio while the child is out of the room, or a child overhears a friend talking about a birthday party to which she has not been invited. They were then presented with four possibilities, two attributing hostility (for example, "My friend wanted to get back at me for something") and two that did not (for example, "My friend did it by accident" or "My friend will invite me later") (Crick, Grotpeter, & Bigbee, 2002, p. 1137). Children who had more hostile attributions in response to these stories tended to be more aggressive in the eyes of their peers. As we see from this example, social understanding is important for social relationships, yet there is more to social relationships than just social cognition. In the next sections, we explore the nature of children's relationships with their peers.

Hostile attributional bias
A tendency to interpret the innocent behavior of others as intentionally hostile rather than benign.

CHECK YOUR UNDERSTANDING

1. What is theory of mind?
2. Describe the false belief paradigm.
3. What is recursive thinking?
4. How can theory of mind promote both positive and negative social behavior?

PEER RELATIONSHIPS IN INFANCY AND EARLY CHILDHOOD

12.2 How is play important for children's development?

The world of peers becomes increasingly important as children grow older. In this section, we discuss the earliest types of social interactions infants and toddlers have with their peers. We then describe the important role of play with peers in promoting physical, cognitive, emotional, and social development in early childhood.

INFANTS AND TODDLERS: FROM PARENT TO PEER

It has become clear that infants are biologically "programmed" to be social from their earliest days of life. From Chapters 5 and 6 you'll remember that infants imitate facial expressions, prefer to look at faces rather than inanimate objects, respond to voices, and to touch. Their cry draws others to care for them and their first social smiles strengthen the bond that is already developing between parent and infant. The nature of children's early attachment relationships with their parents becomes the foundation for their ability to engage successfully with other children.

As you learned in Chapter 10, infants develop either secure or insecure attachment relationships with their parents, and these early attachments have consequences for their ability to form relationships with other children their own age, their peers. Toddlers and preschoolers who have secure attachments to their parents are more responsive to peers (McElwain, Holland, Engle, & Ogolsky, 2014). In a large study carried out by the National

Institute of Child Health and Human Development (NICHD), children who had secure attachments to their mothers at age 3 were more likely to have high-quality friendships in third grade, while insecurely attached children became increasingly withdrawn from their peers (Booth-LaForce & Oxford, 2008; McElwain, Booth-LaForce, Lansford, Wu, & Dyer, 2008). It appears that children who have secure attachments to their parents have a higher sense of self-worth, and this translates into more confident interactions with peers (Booth-LaForce et al., 2006). The quality of relationships that children develop with peers will further affect many aspects of their life.

From infancy onward, there is something qualitatively different and special about children's interactions with other children their own age. When a child interacts with adults and even older children, it is the older people who are largely in charge of the interactions, both because they are more powerful and because they can keep the interaction going in spite of the young child's lesser social abilities. Peer interactions are different because children must work out how to maintain the relationship themselves, at their own level of social and cognitive functioning. The other reason that the relationship between peers is special is because peers are often more fun and exciting (Dunn, 2004). Mom and Dad will tire of "chase me" games long before two toddlers do. Preschoolers may share a deep interest in dinosaurs that the adults in their lives encourage but do not necessarily share. Teens can often share secrets with each other that they don't want to share with their parents.

What is the youngest age at which children are able to interact in a meaningful way with peers? While most people are very aware that preschoolers are able to play with other children, they often believe infants and toddlers are not yet capable of real peer relationships. However, there is some evidence that even before age 2 infants can form relationships with other children. Babies are often very interested when they see other babies, smiling at them and trying to touch them (Hay, Caplan, & Nash, 2009). Near the end of their first year of life, infants want to be near other young children, seek them out, and engage in a number of behaviors such as offering their toys, that are meant to draw them into a social interaction (Williams, Ontai, & Mastergeorge, 2010). By their second year, infants bring reciprocity into their peer interactions as they match their own behavior to what other children are doing. As they become capable of moving around, they interact by imitating each other—for example, "I see you jump, it looks like fun, so I jump too." By 20 to 24 months of age, imitation becomes mutual (Eckerman & Peterman, 2001). For example, "You jump, then I jump, then you jump, then I jump, both of us laughing the whole time."

As the children develop language, they add this new ability to their interactions. Language allows them to begin to coordinate their activities in a more cooperative way, planning what they will do together, or solving problems as they arise (Eckerman & Didow, 1996). Language also indicates that children are developing the ability to use symbols, and this ability leads to pretend play. Now, instead of using just their bodies, as with the previous example of imitative jumping, they can begin to arrange a tea party with pretend tea and cookies, or engage in other make-believe games.

All relationships have their conflicts, and toddlers' relationships with peers are no exception. Adults who work with toddlers know "Mine!" and "No!" are two of their favorite words. Especially when these words are linked with hitting or biting, adults are not likely to see them in a positive light. However, being able to use these words

Early social interactions. Toddlers' first interactions are often imitations of each other. Can you see how the imitative play of these two children as they follow each other on this play equipment might lead to turn taking and eventually cooperative interaction as they develop more social skills?

reflects some positive aspects of toddlers' development. Claiming toys indicates a developing sense of self as an individual as we described in Chapter 11 (Levine, 1983; Rochat, 2011). In addition, conflicts are not just about possessing objects. They also reflect a new social awareness. Research has shown that toddler conflicts are reciprocal in nature (Hay, Hurst, Waters, & Chadwick, 2011)—that is, "If you take my toy, the next time I see you, I will take yours." This becomes part of the way that children learn how to make friends. If you want someone to play with you, you will not succeed if you take his toy

PRESCHOOLERS AND THE ROLE OF PLAY

Play is the hallmark of preschool peer interaction. In make-believe play, children take on different identities as they create a whole world of their own. As adults, we must appreciate the social skill this takes. One researcher has likened it to the level of coordination that must be achieved by a jazz quartet in which individual players improvise and the others must react (Dunn, 2004). Children must learn to control their own impulses and understand others' intentions. At this stage, imitation is no longer enough to maintain an interaction. Instead the children develop complementary roles: "You be the mommy, and I'll be the baby." Judy Dunn (2004) believes that taking part in shared make-believe in which children can express and explore their feelings, including their fears, dreams, and disappointments, becomes the basis for the development of the trust and closeness that are essential to relationships among older children.

The ability to play with peers originates in part from the play that infants and toddlers engage in with adults. Parents from many different cultures engage in fantasy play with their young children (Haight, Black, Ostler, & Sheridan, 2006), and this play is associated with the development of social skills in children's interactions with peers. For example, Lindsey and Mize (2000) studied play between parents and their 3- to 6-year-old children. They found that children who engaged in more pretend play with their parents that was mutually responsive (that is, parent and child each responded effectively to each other's cues) had higher social competence with peers in their preschools. By age 3, children turn their attention from play with parents to play with peers.

What is play? See **Active Learning: What Is Play?** to try to define the characteristics of play for yourself.

Active LEARNING

What Is Play?

Read the following descriptions of two play situations with 4-year-olds in two different cultures.

Scenario #1. In the following translated dialogue, a 4-year-old boy (Dagiwa) and girl (Hoyali) in Papua New Guinea are pretending to be doctors taking care of patients, which are represented first by the visiting anthropologist's feet and then by a tree stump:

Dagiwa: (addresses foot-patient) Are you also sick?

Hoyali: Hold this one (takes foot in hands and places it down on ground). I am letting it stay here.

Dagiwa: Has this one also been sick, eh?

Hoyali: Yes, this one has been sick.

(Continued)

(Continued)

Dagiwa:	(pretends to give the foot-patient an injection) The injection is finished.
	(Dagiwa leaves Hoyali and focuses his attention on a small banana stump . . . which is treated as if it is a new patient. Hoyali moves to join him.)
Dagiwa:	Is this one ill?
Hoyali:	I am giving it an injection. (adapted from Goldman & Smith, 1998)

Scenario #2. In this second example, a group of 4-year-olds is interacting in a day care center in the United States.

Elisha and Max are in their make-believe library in their day care center pretending to read a book about building castles. Elisha counts the blocks as she hands them to Max, who repeats the numbers as he places each block in the structure. Max is growing impatient, however, and says that he will be the castle's "big green dragon." Elisha responds, "OK, I will be the princess with a purple dress, but let's finish making the castle." Juan joins them and wants to play. Max agrees and offers Juan a role as the prince. But Juan wants to be the green dragon. Much negotiating takes place. Finally, Juan agrees to assume this role, but he insists on wearing a gold crown (Bellin & Singer, 2006, p. 101).

Based on these scenarios, answer these questions:

1. How would you define play based on these two examples? What are the characteristics that make this play rather than some other kind of activity?

2. What cognitive, language, social, and emotional abilities must children have to be able to play in these ways?

3. Finally, how does this play help children develop physically, cognitively, linguistically, socially, and emotionally? What are they learning in each of these domains?

You will find answers to these questions as you continue reading this section of the chapter.

What definition of play did you come up with? Perhaps the chief characteristic of play is that it is fun. Children are actively and fully involved in the "private reality" that makes up their play (Segal, 2004, p. 38). Other characteristics that have been proposed include the following:

1. Play is done for its own sake, not for any outside goal or purpose.

2. Even when it is an imitation of adult work, play is marked as being different through signals such as exaggeration of activities, role reversals, or laughing.

3. Play is voluntary and spontaneous (Burghardt, 2004, p. 294).

Some have argued that play is a universal human behavior, though it is not unique to humans, as anyone with a puppy knows. Even children who must work at an early age find ways to play while they are working (Drewes, 2005). For example, fantasy play was found among both low-income and middle-class Brazilian children regardless of their ethnic group and location within the country (Gosso, Morais, & Otta, 2007). In 2013, the United Nations Committee on the Rights of the Child (CRC) affirmed its long-time commitment to the importance of play for children's development around the world. As a part of this reaffirmation, the CRC said, "Play and recreation are essential to the health and well-being of children and promote the development of creativity, imagination, self-confidence, self-efficacy, as well as physical, social, cognitive and emotional strength and skills. They contribute to all aspects of learning . . ." (p. 4).

Play is such a central aspect of children's lives that difficulties with play often indicate larger problems in the child's life. When children have the opportunity to play but are unable to do so, it can be an indication of a variety of behavioral problems. In the DSM-5, one characteristic of autism spectrum disorder is a "lack of shared social play and imagination (e.g., age-appropriate flexible pretend play) and, later, insistence on playing by very fixed rules" (APA, 2013, p. 54). Other children who are highly stressed and anxious may have the cognitive and social abilities to play, but may experience **play disruption**, an inability to play because their emotions are preventing the kind of free expression linked with the fun of play (Scarlett, Naudeau, Salonius-Pasternak, & Ponte, 2005).

We next discuss how play promotes physical, cognitive, social, and emotional development in children. Although we have presented these different aspects of development in separate chapters, remember that they all interact and play is a good example of the ways that they do this. Although we include the topic of play in this chapter on social development, it has important connections to all the other aspects of development.

Physical Development

Play contributes directly to physical development in several ways. One way in which this happens is through **physical activity play**, the type of play that involves large muscle activity. Physical activity play goes through three stages (Smith, 2010). In infants we see patterns of activity called **rhythmic stereotypies**. These consist of repeated large muscle movements that have no purpose, such as kicking the legs or waving the hands. The development of these behaviors seems to be guided by neuromuscular maturation. Infants engage in these types of movements shortly before they gain voluntary control of the specific body parts they are exercising (Smith, 2010).

Toddlers take part in **exercise play**. This type of play involves large muscle movement, such as running or jumping in the context of play, and not surprisingly peaks at age 4 or 5 and declines as children enter school. The function of exercise play may be to train the muscles and to build strength and endurance (Smith, 2010). The age range when exercise play is most prevalent is also the period of time in development when the muscles and bones in arms and legs are growing very rapidly (Smith, 2010).

The third type of physical activity play is **rough-and-tumble play**. Common games throughout the world, especially for boys, are based on this type of play (Storli & Sandseter, 2015). This type of play increases during the early school years and continues, although at a greatly reduced level, into early adolescence. These activities not only promote physical strength and endurance, they may also affect brain development. In rats, the greatest amount of neuronal growth was found during times in their lives when the rats were most involved with rough-and-tumble play and exploration (Haight & Black, 2001). The function of rough-and-tumble play changes from childhood

Play disruption An inability to play because the child's emotions are preventing the kind of free expression linked with the fun of play.

Physical activity play The type of play that involves large muscle activity.

Rhythmic stereotypies Repeated large muscle movements that have no purpose, such as kicking the legs or waving the hands, usually seen in infants.

Exercise play Play in young children that involves large muscle movement, such as running or jumping.

Rough-and-tumble play Play that looks like fighting or wrestling, where the goal is not to hurt or win, but to have fun.

Rough-and-tumble play. Play can promote physical development in children. This type of rough-and-tumble play builds strength and coordination, and also helps establish a hierarchy within the peer group without the need to resort to real fights or struggles.

to adolescence. For younger children (especially boys), taking part in same-sex rough-and-tumble play is associated with emotional expressiveness and emotion regulation, as well as being liked by peers (Lindsey, 2013, 2014). In adolescents, it becomes a safe way to establish social dominance within the peer group (Pelligrini, 2003).

Emotional Development

In the psychoanalytic tradition of Sigmund Freud, play is seen as the expression of the child's inner emotional conflicts (Scarlett et al., 2005). Children play out in fantasy what is bothering them in real life. For example, a child may become the "mean mother" with her dolls to express her frustration with parental discipline she has experienced. This fantasy gives the child some sense of control that helps her deal with real situations in which she feels helpless, as all children do at some times when dealing with the powerful adults in their lives. It also allows her to express in play certain emotions that might be unacceptable in real life, such as anger at a baby sibling (Haight et al., 2006). Play is associated with the expression, regulation, and understanding of emotions. Research has shown that children who spend more time in fantasy play have a better understanding of their own emotions as well as those of others (Lindsey & Colwell, 2003).

Play therapy A way to help children work through difficult feelings with the help of an adult who is trained to understand play as a type of communication.

While play normally helps children express their feelings and deal with them, when children have more severe emotional difficulties, they may use play to reenact traumatic scenes over and over again with little emotional relief (Haight et al., 2006). **Play therapy** developed as a way to help children work through difficult feelings with the help of an adult such as a psychologist, psychiatrist, or social worker who is trained to understand play as a type of communication.

Many children, especially young children, are unlikely to be able to sit and talk with a therapist about their feelings as adults do. Instead they present their thoughts and emotions in symbolic form through their play. As their thoughts and feelings become clear in their play, the therapist helps the children manage them in more adaptive ways. One example was provided by Jones and Landreth (2002) in a study on play therapy for children with chronic, insulin-dependent diabetes. These children often suffer from anxiety as they experience frightening symptoms, such as diabetic coma, along with many mystifying and painful interventions from doctors and nurses. In one case, a child was experiencing stomachaches every day. Over five sessions of play therapy, he acted out battle scenes, which initially used play soldiers but eventually came to involve doctors and nurses as the "bad guys" who would never go away, because "they just keep coming back!" (Jones & Landreth, 2002, p. 127). After expressing his feelings in this symbolic way, he was able to talk about the "anxiousness" in his stomach. When the therapist clarified that "feeling worried or nervous" could be experienced as a stomachache, the boy was able to move on to a less conflicted and less compulsive type of play, and his stomachaches did not return.

A meta-analysis of studies on the efficacy of play therapy found that this type of treatment was generally very helpful to children and resulted in changes in their maladaptive behavior (Bratton, Ray, & Rhine, 2005). Treatment was especially effective when parents were involved in the treatment so that they too could begin to understand what their child was communicating to them through play. When parents can see more clearly how things appear from their child's point of view, they are better able to help the child resolve conflicts rather than acting them out in negative ways, such as fighting with other children or experiencing stomachaches.

Fotosearch/Royalty-Free/Getty Images

Play therapy. This 6-year-old girl is participating in a play therapy session. Games help her express her inner world in a secure space.

Social Development

Play with other children is intrinsically social, so it is no surprise that it has been linked with the development of social skills and the formation of friendships. In the 1930s, Mildred Parten (1932) described the following six levels of play, still used by researchers and those who work with children, based on the level of social skills a child is capable of using with peers.

1. Unoccupied behavior—looking around at whatever occurs, but engaging in no activity.

2. Onlooker behavior—watching others play.

3. Solitary independent play—engaging actively with toys that are different from those being used by other children.

4. Parallel play—playing next to, but not in interaction with each other, often using the same type of materials, for example, blocks or dolls.

5. Associative play—playing with other children, sharing toys, and interacting, but with no overall organization of the group to achieve a common goal.

6. Cooperative play—playing as part of a group that has a common goal such as building a building, creating a make-believe scene such as "house" with assigned roles, or playing sports.

Unoccupied behavior Looking around at whatever occurs, but engaging in no activity.

Onlooker behavior Watching other children play.

Solitary independent play Engaging actively with toys that are different from those being used by other children.

Parallel play Playing next to a peer with the same type of materials, but not interacting with the other child.

Associative play Sharing toys and interacting with peers, but without a common goal.

Cooperative play Play with peers that has a common goal.

Parten's stages of social play. As children develop social skills, they move from solitary play (first photo) to parallel play (second photo) and eventually to cooperative play (third photo).

Many studies have provided support for Parten's idea that children become more inter-active and more cooperative with age and that the tendency to take part in more socially interactive play reflects better social adjustment (Coplan & Arbeau, 2009; Fantuzzo, Bulotsky-Sheare, Fusco, & McWayne, 2005). For examples of studies that use Parten's stages, see Dyer and Moneta (2006) and Freeman and Somerindyke (2001).

Whereas unoccupied and onlooker activities have been linked to immaturity and lack of social skills, solitary independent play, such as when a child plays alone but imaginatively with dolls or creates block buildings, has been linked with positive development, autonomy, and maturity (Luckey & Fabes, 2005). The meaning of solitary play is in part determined by the reason behind it. Some children may prefer to play alone because they can be in control of what happens and can create what they have in mind without interference. Others prefer play with objects rather than with people, and this type of social disinterest has not clearly been linked to any long-term problems for these children (Coplan & Armer, 2007). However, children may be found playing alone because they have been rejected by others, are too shy to approach them, or lack the social skills to initiate contact with them, and these causes are more likely to be connected with later difficulties. For example, children who are shy and anxious in new social situations are more likely to have difficulties such as academic prob-lems and low self-esteem, particularly if their shyness is combined with lower verbal skills, overprotective parents, and/or the lack of a high quality friendship (Coplan & Armer, 2007).

For the stage of parallel play, contrary to what Parten proposed, research has not con-sistently shown that it is a higher level of social interaction than solitary play. Parallel play is prevalent throughout the preschool years and may be more related to the nature of the school curriculum than to the children's social skills. In one study, children were more likely to engage in parallel play if the school provided many activities that promoted an individ-ual task orientation rather than less structured or more cooperative activities (Provost & LaFreniere, 1991). To test yourself on your understanding of Parten's stages of play, see **Active Learning: Parten's Stages of Social Play**.

T ☐ F ☐ If a child chooses to play alone, even when there are other children available to play with him, there is no reason for concern. **True**

Active LEARNING

Parten's Stages of Social Play

Next to each level of Parten's play scale, write the number of the description that best matches it:

Unoccupied Behavior _____	1. Francisco and Martha decide to play house and agree that Devorah will be the baby.
Onlooker Behavior _____	2. Keisha sucks her thumb while gazing randomly around the room.
Solitary Independent Play ____	3. Isaac and Cho each work on a puzzle, occasionally looking at each other's work.
Parallel Play _____	4. Ted builds a tower with blocks.
Associative Play _____	5. Agata is new in class. She watches the children play with great interest.
Cooperative Play _____	6. Sadie and Sabine play in the sandbox, talking with each other, and exchanging the tools and cups they need for their individual sand castles.

Answers: Unoccupied behavior—2; Onlooker behavior—5; Solitary independent play—4; Parallel play—3; Associative play—6; Cooperative play—1

Play and social development are inextricably linked, so researchers have difficulty determining which comes first, play or social competence. While play undoubtedly contributes to social development, children whose social development is more advanced probably also make better playmates. Some research has shown that preschool children who were more likely to engage in fantasy play were also more likely to demonstrate theory of mind, the ability to understand what others are thinking. However, in a review of this research, Lillard et al. (2013) conclude that there is limited evidence for a direct relationship between play and theory of mind. Rather, it may be a third factor, such as parents talking more with their child about states of mind, which underlies the development of both.

By the age of 3, children begin to show preferences for specific playmates and friendships develop. **Friendship** has been defined as a mutual relationship, meaning both people must agree that they have a friendship. It is marked by companionship, closeness, and affection (Dunn, 2004). Although preschoolers are notoriously fickle, many form friendships that last months or even years (Dunn, 2004). Preschool children who are friends are more comfortable with each other, have more fun when they play together, and are more able to resolve conflicts and show sympathy and support for each other. Their interactions are more complex than those found among preschoolers who are not friends (Dunn, 2004).

However, friendships at this age are not based on sophisticated qualities that will enter into relationships at an older age, such as how trustworthy the friend is. Preschoolers are more attracted to another child who enjoys the same kinds of play activities that they do. Rubin, Lynch, Coplan, Rose-Krasnor, and Booth (1994) studied the role of play in the formation of friendship. They brought groups of four previously unacquainted 7-year-olds together to play and then asked the children which child they liked to play with most. The children were drawn to those who shared their same play style. A child who took part in fantasy play preferred to play with another child who also played this way, while a child who liked to build things (constructive play) preferred playing with another who also liked this activity.

Cognitive Development

Play has increasingly been seen by some as something that simply takes time from the "important work" of childhood, or in other words, academic learning (Pellegrini, 2005). For example, several years ago the U.S. government wanted to narrow the focus of the Head Start preschool program for disadvantaged children to one outcome: literacy. While literacy is definitely a core skill all children should have, this narrow focus ignores the developmental need that preschoolers have to learn through exploration and play (Zigler & Bishop-Josef, 2006). As Joan Almon (2003) of the Alliance for Childhood said, "The child's love of learning is intimately linked with a zest for play" (p. 18).

Educators in early childhood programs continue to feel pressure to focus on academic achievement to prepare children to do well on standardized tests and to make a choice between play-based, child-centered programs and academic, teacher-directed programs. To reconcile these divergent approaches to early education, Kyle Snow (n.d.), director of the National Association for the Education of Young Children's Center for Applied Research, has proposed that we think of preschool environments as shown in Figure 12.3 on the next page. Rather than thinking about play *versus* learning, we can think about ways to incorporate learning into play so we have play *and* learning.

Discovery learning is an example of an approach that focuses on allowing children to discover new information and understanding without the teacher's direct involvement. The advantage of including discovery learning in preschool is illustrated by research in which children were shown a novel toy with four different interesting results. For example, one tube squeaked, a second one had a hidden mirror, and so on. For one group of 4-year-olds, the experimenter acted as though she discovered the first tube could squeak by accident and seemed surprised and delighted by what she discovered. With the second group, she acted

Friendship A mutual relationship marked by companionship, closeness, and affection.

T ☐ F ☐
Preschoolers are not likely to maintain a friendship for more than a few weeks. **False**

TRUE/FALSE VIDEO ▲

T ☐ F ☐ It is important for children to play because they have fun when they are playing, but the real learning happens in the classroom. **False**

Discovery learning An approach to teaching that emphasizes allowing children to discover for themselves new information and understanding.

FIGURE 12.3

The combination of play and direct instruction. Rather than thinking of the preschool environment as being either play centered or teacher directed, we can look at the different ways those two approaches can be combined. For instance, the type of play that is called *scaffolding guided* is high on both the dimension of an active child and the dimension of an active teacher. If you were choosing a preschool for your young child, which balance would you prefer? Why?

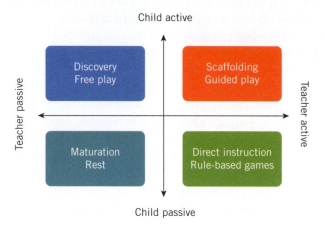

SOURCE: Snow (n.d.)

more like a traditional teacher and told the children to watch her as she showed them how to make the first tube squeak. Both groups were then allowed to play with the toy on their own (Bonawitz et al., 2011). All the children could repeat what they saw the researcher do, but the first group played with new toy longer and discovered more of its features than the group that had received instruction on how to use the toy. The researchers concluded that direct instruction made the children less curious and less likely to discover new information on their own. Of course, we also want learning to be efficient, and direct instruction does accomplish that, so that is why a balanced approach that offers opportunities for discovery learning but also some elements of direct instruction may be best.

Jean Piaget (1962) described a developmental sequence of play based on a child's cognitive maturity. He hypothesized that the nature of children's play would change as the level of their thinking changed. You can review Piaget's stages of cognitive development in Chapter 7. Based on this sequence, he proposed three levels of play:

Practice play Performing a certain behavior repetitively for the mere pleasure of it.

1. **Practice play**—performing a certain behavior repetitively for the mere pleasure of it, for example, jumping back and forth over a puddle for no purpose other than the enjoyment of doing so. An infant in the sensorimotor stage of development is capable of practice play such as dropping a ball over and over again just to see it happen.

Symbolic/sociodramatic play Using symbolic representations and imagination for play.

2. **Symbolic/sociodramatic play**—using symbolic representations and imagination for play, for example, pretending to talk on the telephone. Toddlers begin to use symbols in play at the end of the sensorimotor period, and preschoolers in the preoperational stage of cognition develop fantasy play to a much greater extent.

Games with rules Making up rules for a game or playing games with preestablished rules.

3. **Games with rules**—making up rules for a game or playing games with preestablished rules, such as baseball or soccer. This type of play is developed most clearly in the stage of concrete operations. Piaget argued that younger children try to fit reality to their own purposes through fantasy, while older children begin to fit themselves into the larger reality of the social world around them by following rules.

Sara Smilansky (1968) added a stage after practice play, which she labeled **constructive play**, consisting of building or making something for the purposes of play. While practice play begins in infancy when, for example, babies shake a rattle over and over, both symbolic/sociodramatic and constructive play develop during early childhood as children develop the cognitive abilities necessary to pretend, plan, and carry out different scenarios. Young children are not very good at games with rules, as anyone who has ever tried to play a board game such as Candyland or Chutes and Ladders with a preschooler soon finds out. They are interested in winning but don't understand the nature of rules and that these rules apply equally to all players. On the other hand, Piaget believed that children stopped fantasy play when they began taking part in games with rules, but children report that they continue pretend play through age 12 and some continue on into adulthood (Lillard, Pinkham, & Smith, 2011).

Fantasy play. Fantasy play plays a big role in many children's lives in early childhood and beyond. What skills are these boys practicing when they play at being Vikings?

Constructive play Building or making something for the purposes of play.

Symbolic/sociodramatic play, also referred to as fantasy play, appears in widely diverse cultures around the world as children move from infancy to early childhood, with the content of their play reflecting the culture in which it is embedded. For example, in one study, American children based their play on toys and the ideas they represented, so a toy rocket might trigger fantasy play about a trip into outer space. By contrast, Chinese children tended not to use objects, but rather based their pretend play on social interactions, such as pretending to address a guest or interacting with a shopkeeper (Haight, Wang, Fung, Williams, & Mintz, 1999).

In Chapter 7, we discussed Vygotsky's concept of private speech, which is when young children talk out loud to direct themselves. Fantasy play seems to promote self-talk more than other activities do. In one study, researchers observed children's play with their mothers. They found that children often incorporated what their mothers had said during play when they talked to themselves during their own private fantasy play (Haight & Miller, 1992). If you have spent time with preschoolers, you have most likely seen the way they talk to themselves as they make-believe, giving voice to different characters and having whole conversations all by themselves. In one study, almost all the mothers who were interviewed reported that that their 3- to 5-year-olds used private speech during their fantasy play, and the preschoolers were more likely to engage in private speech while they were playing than when they were problem solving (Winsler, Feder, Way, & Manfra, 2006)

The way that fantasy play can facilitate cognitive development is shown by its use as an intervention strategy to help young children learn preacademic skills. Together with colleagues, Dorothy Singer developed a program called *My Magic Story Car* in which parents and caregivers of low-income children are taught to use fantasy play to help their children develop the skills necessary for school (Bellin & Singer, 2006). For example, in the Trip to Mars game, the parent or caregiver helps children teach Martian children about life on Earth by creating a book explaining it in their own words. The children then fly to Mars and pretend to teach the Martian children how to use the book. Clearly, children should and do respond with more enthusiasm to this way of learning literacy than by using worksheets to learn letters. Research has shown this program to be successful in improving young children's school readiness.

We have made the argument that play supports children's development in physical skills, emotional expression, social skills, cognitive abilities, and motivation for learning. Clearly, play should be available for the benefit of all children. However, there are children for whom play may be limited because of disabilities. In the next section, we discuss one program designed to help all children play.

Playgrounds That Accommodate Children (and Adults) With Disabilities

Amy Jaffe Barzach's life changed after she saw a little girl in a wheelchair watching other children play on a playscape, unable to join in. If you imagine the usual playground available to children, you will quickly realize that children who cannot walk or who have other physical limitations would never be able to get to the slide or play on a swing. Barzach believed that play should be every child's right, and she set out to make it so. She developed a program called Boundless Playgrounds© that creates playgrounds accessible to all children, regardless of their physical and mental conditions. One such playground was established at an army base. Barzach realized that typical playscapes also limit the interaction that parents with disabilities can have playing with their children in these places. In the Boundless Playground on the army base, soldiers who were missing limbs or who were in wheelchairs were able to join in the fun with their children, creating a priceless opportunity to cement the bonds that may have been threatened when a parent who has been gone for a long time returns to his or her family but is very changed.

DEVELOPMENT IN ACTION VIDEO ▲

Fotosearch/Royalty-Free/Getty Images

Don Smetzer/The Image Bank/Getty Images

A universal playground. This playground has been specifically designed to be accessible to all children and adults—both those with disabilities and those without. Look at the photo on the right carefully. What accommodations can you see? The young boy in the second photo has a chance to play that he would not have had on a normal playground with all its steps, uneven surfaces, and monkey bars raised up high.

1. How do infants and toddlers develop peer relationships?
2. Describe the process of play therapy.
3. What are Parten's levels of play?
4. What characterizes friendships between preschoolers?
5. Why is play important for cognitive development in early childhood?

PEER RELATIONSHIPS IN MIDDLE CHILDHOOD

12.3 How do peer relationships change during middle childhood?

Peers become increasingly important during middle childhood. In this section, we look at the nature and impact of friendships, and the importance of status within the peer group and social acceptance by peers during this period of development.

SCHOOL-AGE CHILDREN AND FRIENDSHIPS

As children enter school, two aspects of peer interaction become important: close friendships and general acceptance or rejection within the peer group. Children between the ages of 6 and 12 begin to value having a best friend. Friends spend time together, like to do the same kinds of things, and increasingly offer each other emotional support. Another important aspect of peer relationships is **social status,** or the general acceptance or rejection of an individual within the peer group. Researchers have used a technique called **sociometry** to study peer acceptance. In this technique, researchers ask children to nominate the children they like the most or like the least (Poulin & Dishion, 2008). The choices of all the children are then combined to determine the overall level of social acceptance or rejection of each child in the peer group. Figure 12.4 shows how the dimensions of peer acceptance and peer rejection can be combined to describe different social statuses of individual children.

Children who receive a lot of nominations from the peer group for "like most" and few nominations for "like least" are classified as **popular children.** Those who receive a lot of nominations for "like least" and few for "like most" are classified as **rejected.** Children who receive a number of nominations close to the median for the group are classified as **average,** and those who receive relatively few nominations in either category are classified as **neglected.** The final group is a particularly interesting one. Some children receive both a large number of nominations for "like most" from some peers and a large number of nominations for "like least" from other peers. They are classified as **controversial** children (Coie, Dodge, & Coppotelli, 1982).

There are two ways a child becomes popular within the peer group. **Popular-prosocial children** are high on desirable characteristics, such as helpfulness and athletic or academic competence, and low on aggression, while **popular-antisocial children** are usually the "tough boys" who combine social manipulation with athletic ability and aggression in order to get their own way. This second group is described by peers as stuck-up, bullies, and not caring about school, but they also are seen as influential leaders and are admired for this characteristic (de Bruyn & Cillessen, 2006; Rodkin, Farmer, Pearl, & Van Acker, 2000).

In a similar way, we now distinguish two groups of rejected children. **Rejected-aggressive children** are rejected by their peers because they are aggressive, annoying, or

Social status The level of peer acceptance or peer rejection of an individual in the peer group.

Sociometry A research technique used to assess a child's social status within the peer group.

Popular children Children who receive a lot of nominations as "like most" and few as "like least" on a sociometric measure.

Rejected children Children who receive a lot of nominations as "like least" and few as "like most" on a sociometric measure.

Average children Children who receive a number of nominations for "like most" and "like least" that is close to the median in the peer group on a sociometric measure.

Neglected children Children who receive relatively few nominations either as "like most" or as "like least" on a sociometric measure.

Controversial children Children who receive both a large number of nominations for "like most" and a large number of nominations for "like least" from peers on a sociometric measure.

Popular-prosocial children Children who are popular among peers because they are low on aggression and have a number of desirable characteristics.

Popular-antisocial children Children who are popular with peers by combining prosocial behavior with social manipulation.

Rejected-aggressive children Children who are rejected by peers because they are aggressive, annoying, or socially unskilled.

Determining sociometric status. After asking peers who they like the best (peer acceptance) and who they like the least (peer rejection), this information can be combined to produce the five sociometric status groups used in sociometric research.

Peer Acceptance

	HIGH	
Controversial		Popular
	Average	
Rejected		Neglected
	LOW	

Peer Rejection — HIGH / LOW

Popular children = High on peer acceptance, low on peer rejection
Rejected children = High on peer rejection, low on peer acceptance
Controversial children = High on peer acceptance, high on peer rejection
Neglected children = Low on peer acceptance, low on peer rejection
Average children = Average level of peer acceptance and peer rejection

SOURCE: Coie, Dodge, & Coppotelli (1982). © 1982 American Psychological Association.

socially unskilled (Sandstrom & Zakriski, 2004). For instance, they may annoy potential playmates by trying to enter a game other children are already playing by disrupting it. **Rejected-withdrawn children** are socially withdrawn and anxious (Juvonen, 2013). A child who is very shy, nervous, or depressed is not a very appealing playmate for the other children and may be rejected for these reasons.

Research on popularity and peer rejection has been focused largely on the personal characteristics of the individual child, but the context of peer relationships also influences who will be popular and who will be rejected. The characteristics that are seen as desirable can vary from one peer group to another. For example, although children can be rejected by peers for being either aggressive or withdrawn, withdrawn children are more likely to be rejected in groups that are more aggressive, and aggressive children are more likely to be rejected in groups that are more withdrawn (Mikami, Lerner, & Lun, 2010). Children, like adults, also tend to accept and form friendships with others they perceive to be similar to themselves. Therefore, African American children are more likely to be rejected when the majority of their classmates are White, and White children are more likely to be rejected when many of their classmates are African American (Mikami et al., 2010).

Some children who are not popular with their peers may still have friendships that are able to soften the negative effects of rejection or neglect by the peer group. Having one good friend can be enough to save a child from loneliness and to buffer the child from the physiological experience of stress experienced by rejected children who do not have a close friend (Peters, Riksen-Walraven, Cillessen, & de Weerth, 2011). However, the friendships that unpopular children do have tend to be less stable and less supportive than those of their more accepted peers, and they are often less able to resolve conflicts in their peer relationships (Dunn, 2004b; Lansford et al., 2006). On the other hand, there are children who are widely accepted by the group as a whole who do not have a close friend and who describe themselves as lonely (Dunn, 2004b).

You may wonder how stable peer status is (that is, how likely it is that a child will remain in one category over time). The popular and rejected statuses are the most stable categories. Studies that examined peer status over intervals from 6 months to several years have found

Rejected-withdrawn children Children who are rejected by peers because they are socially withdawn and anxious

that about 50% of popular and rejected children retained their peer status over time, but neglected and controversial children were more likely to change their status (Cillessen, 2011). We can easily understand why popular children retain their popular status over time. They regularly receive positive feedback from their peers, which should make it more likely they will continue to engage in those behaviors that contribute to their popularity. However, rejected children also tend to maintain their status across various groups of peers and over time (Peets, Hodges, Kikas, & Salmivalli, 2007). That is more difficult to understand because we would think negative feedback from peers would lead to a change in their behavior, but being aggressive is a characteristic that often contributes to peer rejection and, as you learned in Chapter 11, having high levels of aggression tends to be a fairly stable characteristic across childhood, so rejected-aggressive children continue to show the very behaviors that alienate their peers. Those who are rejected-withdrawn are not aggressive but they may not have many opportunities to engage with peers and to develop their social skills. Those who do are the children who move out of the rejected status over time (Haselager, Cillessen, Van Lieshout, Riksen-Walraven, & Hartup, 2002).

Both peer rejection and lack of friends are related to difficulties in adulthood, while both peer acceptance and having a good friend are related to better outcomes. In one study, preadolescents who had friends were more likely to have a high sense of self-worth when they became adults. Preadolescents who were rejected by their peer group were more likely to have trouble with the law later in life, probably because rejected children are more likely to seek out and form friendships with deviant peers who in turn are more likely to engage in criminal behavior (Juvonen, 2013).

You gotta have friends! Popular children are liked by many of their peers, while rejected and neglected children are not. However, close individual friendships are as important as social status for children's well-being.

Finally, the effects of peer rejection may be mediated by how sensitive the child is to rejection. All children experience rejection at some time in their lives, but some children respond more strongly than others. **Active Learning: Rejection Sensitivity** gives you an opportunity to better understand how this affects a child's peer relationships.

Active LEARNING

Rejection Sensitivity

In the Children's Rejection Sensitivity Questionnaire (Downey, Lebolt, Rincon, & Freitas, 1998), children are given several scenarios and asked to imagine how they would feel if these things happened to them. Begin by reading these two examples from the questionnaire.

1. Imagine you are the last to leave your classroom for lunch one day. As you're running down the stairs to get to the cafeteria, you hear some kids whispering on the stairs below you. You wonder if they are talking about you.

How NERVOUS would you feel, RIGHT THEN, about whether or not those kids were badmouthing you?

Not nervous					Very, very nervous
1	2	3	4	5	6

How MAD would you feel, RIGHT THEN, about whether or not those kids were badmouthing you?

Not mad					Very, very mad
1	2	3	4	5	6

Do you think they were saying bad things about you?

Yes!!!					No!!!
1	2	3	4	5	6

2. Imagine you're back in your classroom, and everyone is splitting up into groups to work on a special project together. You sit there and watch lots of other kids getting picked. As you wait, you wonder if the kids will want you for their group.

How NERVOUS would you feel, RIGHT THEN, about whether or not they will choose you?

Not nervous					Very, very nervous
1	2	3	4	5	6

How MAD would you feel, RIGHT THEN, about whether or not they will choose you?

Not mad					Very, very mad
1	2	3	4	5	6

Do you think the kids in your class will choose you for their group?

Yes!!!   No!!!

1   2   3   4   5   6

Questions:

1. Why did these researchers ask children both about how nervous they would be in each situation and whether or not they would be mad about what happened?

2. How does being nervous versus getting mad affect a child's relationship with peers?

3. What might be the consequence over time of a child expecting to be rejected by peers, but this not happening?

4. Think about a time when you wanted to get together with someone and he or she said no. How did you interpret this response? What did you do? How did this affect your relationship with that person?

A child who doesn't notice rejection or doesn't care very much about it is less likely to be negatively affected by it than a child who has a high level of **rejection sensitivity**. People who are particularly sensitive to rejection are more likely to interpret others' responses to them as hostile and a sign that the person doesn't like or respect them. They become either angry or anxious. When social rejection makes a child feel anxious, it can lead to social anxiety and a withdrawal from future social situations. When the response is anger, however, it can lead to aggression directed toward others (London, Downey, Bonica, & Paltin, 2007).

Rejection sensitivity is associated with experiences of rejection from parents. When children experience rejection from either parents or peers, they begin to expect they will be rejected and may start to see it even when it is not there (London et al., 2007; Rudolph & Zimmer-Gembeck, 2014). This can create a vicious cycle that perpetuates a child's rejection by potential friends. In one study, children who became more accepted by their peers reduced their rejection sensitivity over time (London et al., 2007). Finally, rejection-sensitive children who were able to control the expression of their emotions had better long-term outcomes in adulthood (Ayduk et al., 2000). It appears that children who act aggressively or in a highly anxious and withdrawn manner may drive peers further away, but a child who can control these responses is less likely to do so.

Gender and Play

Gender segregation, the tendency of children to play and become friends with other children of the same gender, begins in preschool (Martin & Fabes, 2001). By age 3, boys are already showing a preference for playing with children of their own gender (Fabes, Gaertner, & Popp, 2006). Although plenty of play involves both boys and girls, the preference for same-sex play interaction has been found in many cultures and even among nonhuman primates (Fouts, Hallam, & Purandare, 2013; Golombok & Hines, 2002; Maccoby, 2002). Although it begins at a young age, it becomes even stronger in middle childhood, especially for boys (Munroe & Romney, 2006).

One of the reasons why boys and girls play separately may be because they have different styles of play. Many girls do not like the rough kind of play preferred by many boys. Although both boys and girls are cooperative with friends, boys' friendships are more likely to also include competition and dominance, while girls' friendships are more likely to include self-disclosure and agreement (Zarbatany, McDougall, & Hymel, 2000). Another possible

T ☐ F ☐ Being rejected by peers doesn't bother some children. **True**

Rejection sensitivity The extent to which a child is affected by peer rejection.

Gender segregation A preference for playing with other children of the same gender.

reason is that boys do not respond to girls' style of communication during play, which is more likely to be in the form of suggestions rather than commands. When girls realize they can't influence boys as play partners, they turn to partners who *will* respond: other girls (Ayres & Leve, 2006). Another gender difference related to play is that many girls prefer to interact in pairs or small groups, while boys are more likely to interact in large groups and involve themselves in organized games or projects (Markovits, Benenson, & Dolenszky, 2001). This difference in group size means that boys and girls engage in different types of social interactions. Large groups involve cooperation, competition, conflict, and coordination, while small groups allow for intimate connection, with attention to the individual needs and feelings of the participants (Ayres & Leve, 2006; Maccoby, 2002).

To examine the question of whether gender or play preference determines who boys and girls choose to play with, try **Active Learning: Gender Play Preferences**.

Active LEARNING

Gender Play Preferences

Interview a child between the ages of 4 and 8 using the following procedure, based on the *Playmate and Play Style Preferences Structured Interview* developed by Alexander and Hines (1994):

ACTIVE LEARNING VIDEO ▲

Children demonstrate whether they prefer to play with a child of the same sex, or one who likes to play with the same kinds of toys that they do.

1. Prepare materials: Take four blank cards or pieces of paper. On two cards draw a plain stick figure. On the third card, draw a "female" stick figure (for example, with a skirt and long hair) and on the fourth card draw a "male" stick figure (for example, with a cap and bow tie). Then on separate cards draw a few gender-stereotyped toys, such as a baby doll and a toy truck, and a few gender-neutral toys, such as a slide and a puzzle. (You could also glue pictures of toys from magazines or print pictures from the Internet, if you prefer.)

2. After reassuring the child that there are no right or wrong answers to these questions, carry out the following series of activities:

   a. Show the child the two plain stick figures, one paired with a male gender-typed toy and the other with a female gender-typed toy. Explain that each figure is a child and the toy shows what that child likes to play with. Then ask the child to pick which figure he or she would want to play with. Do this with several gender-typed toy pairs.

   b. Then use the female and male stick figures with gender-neutral toys and ask which figure he or she would choose to play with.

   c. Finally, pair the gendered figures with opposite sex-typed toys (e.g., the male with the baby doll, the female with the toy truck) and ask the child to choose the playmate they'd prefer.

Did the child prefer to play with a figure who was using toys stereotyped for his or her own gender? Did the child prefer to play with a child of his or her own gender? When forced to choose, did he or she select a child of the same gender or the child who played with the gender-stereotyped toy? Alexander and Hines (1994) found that boys consistently chose the activity regardless of whether a boy or a girl was playing with it, perhaps rejecting boys who play outside of the accepted range of activities. Younger girls (4–5 years old) chose to play with girls, regardless of the supposed toy preference of the figure. Older girls (6–8 years old) chose the activity over the gender of the figure.

To prepare for this activity or if you do not have access to a child, watch the video of this Active Learning.

Other differences in play styles between boys and girls have been found in both Western and non-Western cultures. It is generally the case that boys play in larger groups and farther from home than girls and engage in more physical play (Gosso & Carvahlo, 2013; Munroe & Romney, 2006). In many cultures, it has been found that boys' play is more likely to be exploratory than girls' play, perhaps because adults put more limitations on where girls can go on their own. For fourth-grade children in Bulgaria, Taiwan, and the United States, boys spent more time in free play and with computer games, while girls did more adult-chosen activities, chores, extracurricular activities, and reading (Newman et al., 2007). Girls also tend to engage in more make-believe play (Drewes, 2005).

The Importance of Recess

Within the school context, free play with peers is most likely to occur during recess. We have seen that play in early childhood promotes all aspects of development and this continues to be the case in middle childhood. However, similar to the situation with free play in preschool classrooms that we described earlier in this chapter, in recent years there has been an increasing tendency to eliminate or decrease the amount of time allotted to recess to make room for increased hours of academic instruction. The American Academy of Pediatricians (AAP) has reacted to this trend with a statement in support of recess:

> Recess is a necessary break in the day for optimizing a child's social, emotional, physical, and cognitive development. In essence, recess should be considered a child's personal time, and it should not be withheld for academic or punitive reasons. (Council on School Health, 2013b, p. 186)

Specifically, the AAP stated that recess is important for social development in middle childhood:

> Peer interactions during recess are a unique complement to the classroom. The lifelong skills acquired for communication, negotiation, cooperation, sharing, problem solving, and coping are not only foundations for healthy development but also fundamental measures of the school experience. (Council on School Health, 2013, p. 186)

However, the opportunity to have play time at recess during the school day has consequences not just for social development, but also for physical and cognitive development. For physical development, the decrease in the opportunity for physical play during recess may be one of the factors contributing to the obesity problem among American children (Story, Kaphingst, & French, 2006). Availability of recess helps children to reach the recommended 60 minutes per day of physical activity (CDC, 2015e), and children who had the recommended amount of recess time had lower body mass index than those who did not (Fernandes & Sturm, 2011).

T ☐ F ☐ Recess is an important part of education and should not be taken away for disciplinary reasons. **True**

For cognitive development and academic achievement, research by Pellegrini (2005) has demonstrated that children become less attentive to their schoolwork the longer they go without a break. When they are allowed some free time for play during the school day, they return to their academic tasks with increased attention. One theory is that children have limited attention spans and go into cognitive overload after working continually on their academic tasks (Smith, 2010). Play helps children maintain their attention as a result of letting off steam during recess, and research has shown that children who have at least one recess during the day have better behavior while they are in class (Barros, Silver, & Stein, 2009). The AAP concludes: recess is a "crucial and necessary component of a child's development" that offers cognitive, social, emotional, and physical benefits (as cited in Murray & Ramstetter, 2013, p. 183).

CHECK YOUR UNDERSTANDING

1. What are the different social status groups seen in childhood?
2. How does rejection sensitivity affect a child's relationship with peers?
3. How are the play experiences of boys and girls different?
4. Why is recess an important part of a child's school day?

ADOLESCENTS: THE WORLD OF PEERS

12.4 What types of peer relationships are important during adolescence?

Although peers are important during middle childhood, peer relationships become an increasingly important context for development during adolescence. These relationships take a variety of forms, from individual friendships to association with large groups of adolescents who share reputations and interests. In this section, we also discuss the emergence of romantic relationships during adolescence and the dangers of bullying.

FRIENDSHIPS

Almost all adolescents can report having at least one close friend, and adolescents who have high-quality peer relationships enjoy better emotional adjustment (Demir & Urberg, 2004). Although adolescent friendships are not always stable, they tend to become more stable with age as teens continue to learn how to negotiate, to compromise, and to be more sensitive to the needs of others (Brown & Klute, 2003). While friendships are important to adolescents, this is a case where more is not necessarily better (Pescosolido & Levy, 2002). The benefits that we normally associate with friendships may not be forthcoming from a large group that lacks closeness and, as the number of friends increases, so does the strain that results from having a sense of obligation to a great many people (Falci & McNeely, 2009).

Adolescent girls generally have smaller, more exclusive friendship networks than boys, and boys are more willing to admit new members to their friendship group than girls are (Baines & Blatchford, 2008). Girls consider intimacy, loyalty, and commitment as important qualities in their relationships, whereas boys are more likely to base their friendships on qualities such as status or achievement (Vaquero & Kao, 2008). Girls say that within their friendships they can share their problems and will be understood and cared for by their friends, while boys are more likely to feel that sharing problems is "weird" and a waste of time (Rose et al., 2012). However, because girls do more intimate sharing and disclosing in

T ☐ F ☐ In general, for adolescents, the more friends they have, the better. **False**

their relationships, they understandably are more concerned about a possible betrayal by a friend who might share this personal information with others, and this becomes one of the potential emotional costs of maintaining intimate relationships with friends.

Some other characteristics of adolescent friendships are that both equality and reciprocity are expected. Adolescents are likely to select as friends people who they see as similar to themselves, so close friendships are usually same-gender friendships (with a strong preference for friends from the same ethnic or racial background) (Brown & Klute, 2003; Hafen, Laursen, Burk, Kerr, & Stattin, 2011). Of course, peer groups include more members of the opposite sex as the adolescent becomes older and begins dating (Hebert, Fales, Nangle, Papadakis, & Grover, 2013). Beyond similarity in demographic characteristics such as age, gender, and ethnicity, there also is evidence for similarity among friends in attitudes, values, and activity preferences (including engaging in antisocial behavior) (Hafen et al., 2011; Solomon & Knafo, 2007).

Denise Kandel (1978) proposed two explanations for why friends tend to be so similar to each other: selection and influence. People tend to seek out friendships with people with whom they have things in common. Think of a time when you were in a new setting, such as your first year of college or when you went to summer camp as a child. If you didn't know anyone in that setting, you probably gravitated first toward people whom you saw as somewhat similar to yourself. Why? Because it is easier to initiate conversations when there is something in common to talk about. However, once a relationship has formed and as you do things together, you develop even more things in common with your friends and your attitudes and preferences begin to influence each other. Friendships are more likely to be maintained over time when this happens (Hafen et al., 2011). This process is often pleasant and positive, but it also means that teens can play a role in initiating friends into risky or problem behaviors, including sexual behavior (Baumgartner, Valkenburg, & Peter, 2011; Rew, Carver, & Li, 2011), smoking (Kobus, 2003), substance use (Dishion & Owen, 2002), and delinquency (Hafen et al., 2011). Peers do this by establishing the norms for the peer group (that is, what is expected or accepted within the group), but also through their direct modeling of these behaviors. We talk about peer pressure later in this chapter, but for now you can use **Active Learning: Friends—Similar or Different?** to explore the similarities between you and your own friends during adolescence.

Best friends. Friendships between teenage girls are marked with intimacy and disclosure. Friends also usually share a number of personal qualities.

Blend Images - Peathegee Inc/Brand X Pictures/Getty Images

Active LEARNING

Friends—Similar or Different?

Think about your two best friends during your freshman or sophomore year of high school, and circle on the chart on the next page whether they were *similar to* or *different from* you on each of the following characteristics.

(Continued)

(Continued)

	Friend #1		Friend #2	
Attitude toward school achievement	Similar	Different	Similar	Different
Level of participation in school activities	Similar	Different	Similar	Different
Hobbies or interests (for example, music, drama, video games, collections)	Similar	Different	Similar	Different
Religious values or beliefs	Similar	Different	Similar	Different
Attitude toward smoking	Similar	Different	Similar	Different
Attitude toward drinking	Similar	Different	Similar	Different
Crowd you were identified with (for example, populars, brains, jocks)	Similar	Different	Similar	Different
How shy or outgoing you were	Similar	Different	Similar	Different
Other characteristics that were important to you:				
1.	Similar	Different	Similar	Different
2.	Similar	Different	Similar	Different
3.	Similar	Different	Similar	Different

In what ways was the similarity between you and your friends beneficial to you? In what ways were any differences beneficial? Were there any differences that caused stress or tension in your relationship? Can you think of any way that either you or your friend changed over time as the result of your friendship?

CLIQUES AND CROWDS

Cliques Small groups of friends who spend time together and develop close relationships.

Crowds Large, reputation-based groups that are based on a shared stereotype but whose members do not necessarily spend time together.

Peers can influence each other even when they are not immediate friends. Small groups of friends who spend time together and develop close friendships are called **cliques**, but teens are also influenced by **crowds**, which are larger groups of adolescents in which membership is based on an individual's abilities, interests, or activities (Brown & Klute, 2006).

Cliques are most common during early adolescence, and membership in most cliques is fairly stable at least in the short-term (Rubin, Bowker, McDonald, & Menzer, 2013). Within a clique, the members can hold different roles. A leader often emerges, some are core members, and still others are "wannabes" who hang around the periphery of the clique. Some adolescents are members of more than one clique at a time and link the cliques together (Brown & Klute, 2006). And, of course, some adolescents are not a member of any clique. They may have friendships with individual peers or they may be socially isolated. Young adolescents who were not part of any clique at age 11 to 13 experienced loneliness that made them more prone to depression by age 14 (Witvliet, Brendgen, Van Lier, Koot, & Vitaro, 2010). Although cliques can be an important source of social support, they also can use techniques like ridicule or the threat of being ostracized to control their members. For boys, clique membership has been linked to increased externalizing behavior as groups of friends influence and reward each other's negative behaviors (Witvliet, van Lier, Brendgen, Koot, & Vitaro, 2010).

Brown and Klute (2006) describe crowds as large, reputation-based groups that share a common identity among peers but whose members do not necessarily spend time together. Think for a minute about the crowds that you would recognize at your high school. Some common adolescent crowds include the brains, jocks, skaters, populars, farmers, nerds, and druggies. In multiethnic communities, there also may be crowds identified by ethnic labels, although this isn't always the case. The number of different crowds and how easily recognizable they are differs from one school setting to another. Even though a teen probably does not know all the people in a particular crowd, they more often form friendships with others in the same crowd rather than with peers in different crowds because they do have some characteristics in common with their crowd members (Bagwell & Schmidt, 2011) and, as we've said, similarity is an important characteristic of most friendships.

One advantage of being part of a crowd is that it gives you a type of ready-made identity among your peers. As adolescents get older and develop a stronger sense of their own identity, crowds (just like cliques) become less important to them. **Active Learning: Recognizing a Crowd When You See One** gives you a chance to reflect on the crowd structure at your high school.

Teen crowds. Teenage crowds are groups of teens who share a similar taste in fashion, music, and activities. Although the members of a particular crowd may not know each other or spend time together, their peers see them as a part of an identifiable crowd. Would you have found the crowd these students represent at your high school?

Active LEARNING

Recognizing a Crowd When You See One

Although most people report that they did not belong to just one clique or crowd in high school, most people are perceived this way. Name some of the different crowds that existed in your high school. What determined who belonged in which group? How were these groups similar to and different from each other in how they dressed, what music they listened to, how they spent their time, their attitudes toward school, and other things you can think of? How did the crowds relate to each other? Did they do some things together or have some values in common?

ACTIVE LEARNING VIDEO ▲

Teens discuss their understanding of what a crowd is and talk about the types of crowds that exist in their schools.

If you have classmates who came from a different type of school than you attended, it would be interesting for you to compare notes. The number and types of crowds in a given school vary by the size of school; its ethnic and socioeconomic composition; rural, urban, or suburban location; and a variety of other characteristics. Some of the crowds you were familiar with at your high school might not even exist in other high schools.

To see teenagers respond to this activity, watch the video of this Active Learning, available at the student website.

PEER PRESSURE

We associate the concept of peer pressure with adolescents, but evidence of the effects of peer pressure has been found even in 4-year-old children. For example, Haun and Tomasello (2011) found that 4-year-old children were more likely to give answers they knew to be wrong when the three other peers in their group had given those answers before them.

Peer pressure Influence exerted by peers to get others to comply with their wishes or expectations.

T ☐ F ☐ Most adolescents say that they feel a good deal of peer pressure to do things they know they shouldn't do. **False**

Peer pressure can be direct (for instance, when peers use direct rewards or punishment for compliance) or more subtle (for instance, through modeling or by establishing group norms for behavior), and it can be an intentional attempt to influence the behavior of another person or quite unintentional. Reports from adolescents support the idea that peer pressure, when it does occur, is more likely to be subtle rather than direct. For instance, in a study conducted in Scotland of peer pressure to begin using drugs during the preteen years, most participants said they were able to be friends with others preteens who did use drugs without feeling threatened or pressured in any way (McIntosh, MacDonald, & McKeganey, 2006). One 13-year-old girl described her experience in this way:

Interviewer: So you've got a few pals who smoke hash?

Respondent: Aye [Yes].

Interviewer: Are you ever around when they're smoking it?

Respondent: Aye. Some of us do and some dinnae [don't].

Interviewer: And is that OK with you? Are you happy to be with them when they're smoking it?

Respondent: Aye it's no problem. It's an unpleasant smell but ah [I] don't mind.

Interviewer: But what about them, do they mind you being there when they're smoking hash?

Respondent: No. It's up to you if you want tae [to] or no. They never say anything.

The nature of the peer pressure on individual experiences largely depends on the nature of the peer group itself, with deviant groups supporting deviance and well-functioning groups supporting positive and adaptive behaviors. Despite the concerns of parents or other adults that peers are a constant source of pressure for adolescents to behave in negative ways (for example, to be sexually active, to use drugs, to engage in delinquent behavior), they are just as likely to influence each other away from these types of behaviors (Brown, Bakken, Ameringer, & Mahon, 2008). So, although peers can devalue academic achievement and draw adolescents away from their schoolwork, having high-achieving peers can and does exert a positive influence on an adolescent's own academic achievement (Robnett & Leaper, 2013; Véronneau & Dishion, 2011). Peers also are an important source of support for health-promoting behaviors such as having a good diet and engaging in exercise (Cappella & Hwang, 2015). Again we see how selection and influence work together. For example, it is more likely that young adolescents who are aggressive or prone to deviance will gravitate toward other adolescents with similar inclinations (selection), and over time the norms that evolve within that group will reinforce antisocial behavior by group members (influence).

Susceptibility to peer pressure typically peaks in early adolescence and then decreases as adolescents get older (McIntosh et al., 2006; Sumter, Bokhorst, Steinberg, & Westenberg, 2009). However, we should remember that there is not one, but many, peer groups influencing an adolescent's behavior and that other people in an adolescent's life, including adults and siblings, are other sources of influence.

Burger/Phanie/Photo Researchers, Inc.

Peer pressure. Peer pressure can be direct, or it can be subtle. The group norms that develop within a clique are one way that pressure is exerted on friends to adopt similar attitudes and behaviors.

For example, in one study, White teens were most influenced by peers to use or not use cigarettes and alcohol, but Black teens were most influenced by their siblings (Rowan, 2016). Our understanding of the relative influence that parents and peers have on adolescents has changed over time, and these changes are described in **Journey of Research: The Influence of Parents and Peers**.

JOURNEY OF *Research*

The Influence of Parents and Peers

Adolescents have qualitatively different relationships with their parents and their peers. For a long time, the field has debated the relative influence of these two relationships on adolescents. Must adolescents break away from parents and follow peers before they can successfully become adults?

Historically it was assumed that parents were the primary influence on adolescent development and decision making. The goal of adolescents was to grow up and become adults, just like their parents. However, as a separate teen culture evolved following World War II, the perception that came to dominate our thinking was that adults and peers were in two separate worlds, with little or no meeting ground in the middle. Adolescents were lured away from their parents' world by their peers. Kandel and Lesser (1972) popularized what became known as the *hydraulic model,* based on the assumption that there was a fixed amount of influence available so that increases in peer influence would necessarily mean that there would be compensating decreases in the influence of parents. The portrayal of adolescents as torn between two opposing forces continued to influence our thinking about adolescence for decades.

In 1998, Judith Harris challenged many of these assumptions with the publication of her controversial book *The Nurture Assumption: Why Children Turn Out the Way They Do.* Although she never claims that parents have no effect on their children, Harris puts forth very strong arguments for the idea that their influence has been significantly overestimated and that peers are the primary force in the process of socialization. In a 1995 article in *Psychological Review,* she says, "What GS [group socialization] theory implies is that children would develop into the same sort of adults if we left them in their

George Marks/Retrofile/Getty Images

Teens in the 1950s. In the 1950s, the goal of many teenagers was to be as much like an adult as they possibly could be.

(Continued)

(Continued)

homes, their schools, their neighborhoods, and their cultural or subcultural groups, but switched all the parents around" (p. 461). At the conclusion of this article, she says, "The home environment has no lasting effects on psychological characteristics. The shared environment that leaves permanent marks on children's personalities is the environment they share with their peers" (pp. 482–483).

Harris's ideas represent an extreme position on the relative influence of parents and peers, and they have their supporters as well as critics (see, for example, Vandell, 2000). Most contemporary research has walked the middle ground, finding that parents exert more influence than peers with regard to some areas of adolescent development, while peers exert more influence in other areas. For instance, peers have greater influence in areas related to the peer culture (for example, hairstyles, music preference, leisure activities), but parents continue to have the greater influence in more enduring aspects of adolescent development (for example, educational and career plans, religiosity, and personal values) (Brown, 2004; Wang, Peterson, & Morphey, 2007). And parents and peers jointly influence adolescents in still other areas. You may be surprised to learn that although peers are influential in whether young teens smoke, parents are as well and their effect is more enduring throughout adolescence (Liao, Huang, Huh, Pentz, & Chou, 2013).

ROMANTIC RELATIONSHIPS IN ADOLESCENCE

Adolescent romantic relationships are related to many of the developmental tasks of adolescence. They play an important role in the development of identity (including a sexual identity), influence the process of individuation from the family of origin, change the nature of peer relationships, and lay the groundwork for future intimate relationships. Romantic relationships first emerge in adolescence, although the desire to have a boyfriend or girlfriend may begin before that.

Although romance seems to occupy a prominent place in the thoughts of many adolescents, there actually has been relatively little research done on the topic (Furman & Collins, 2009). This is especially true when we compare the body of research on romantic relationships in adolescence to the body of research on adolescent sexual behavior described in Chapter 6. One of the reasons is the fact that we do not have a commonly accepted definition of what a romantic relationship is. For example, in one study, teens were asked "On average, how often do you go out with a date?" (Child Trends, 2015b), while another study asked "Have you ever dated, hooked up with or otherwise had a romantic relationship with another person?" (Lenhart, Anderson, & Smith, 2015). In the first study 60% of 8th graders, 44% of 10th graders, and 38% of 12th graders reported that they had never dated. In the second study, 80% of teens age 13 to 14 (8th–9th grade) and 56% of teens age 15 to 17 (10th-12th grade) reported never having been in a romantic relationship. The differences between these two studies may have resulted from the different definitions of romantic relationships, but also from how the questions were asked; that is, " . . . how often do you . . . " versus "Have you ever . . . "

Many studies simply allow the participants to decide for themselves whether they are in (or have had) a romantic relationship (Karney, Beckett, Collins, & Shaw, 2007). The problem with this approach is illustrated in one national longitudinal study in which participants were asked to name up to three people with whom they had had a romantic relationship. The researchers found that a large percentage of the named relationships were not reciprocated (in other words, the person who was named as someone the adolescent had a romantic relationship with did *not* include that adolescent on *his* or *her* list of romantic partners) (Karney et al., 2007).

Another challenge in doing research on romantic relationships is that the nature of these relationships changes a great deal over a relatively short amount of time. What a young adolescent wants from a romantic relationship and what makes that relationship satisfying or not is quite different from what an older adolescent wants. Younger adolescents place more importance on superficial characteristics such as physical appearance or having fun together, but older adolescents place a greater value on qualities such as commitment, trust, and intimacy as they search for someone who could become a life partner (Montgomery, 2005; Shulman & Kipnis, 2001). Also, various aspects of dating have a different impact on adolescents depending on their age. While having an intimate and exclusive dating relationship can be problematic in an early adolescent relationship, these same qualities are part of a strong romantic relationship in late adolescence (Karney et al., 2007).

Although adolescent romantic relationships differ in a number of ways, there is a general developmental pattern that describes how adolescents move into these relationships. Teens begin the process by getting together in mixed-gender groups to do things such as going to parties or hanging out. After they become comfortable with one another in these mixed-sex groups, individuals begin to find romantic partners, but often these partners are not from the same group and rarely does friendship precede romance (Kreager, Molloy, Moody, & Feinberg, 2016). Romantic partners may begin to influence each other in ways that separate them from their same-sex friends. For example, DeLay et al. (2016) found that teens became more similar to romantic partners and less like their friends in drinking behavior over time.

The availability of social media and dating sites has influenced a number of aspects of romantic relationships for adolescents. Although most teens who date say they have only dated people they first met face to face, about half of teens use these sites for flirting and for the early exchanges that are a part of a new relationship (Lenhart et al., 2015). Starting a relationship online carries its own risks. Twice as many girls (35%) as boys (16%) have blocked someone who they felt was flirting in a way that made them uncomfortable. Once a relationship has been established, most teens use texting and phoning, in addition to time together, to maintain that relationship. When a relationship ends, the majority break up with their partner in person, but breakups can also happen online, sometimes by simply changing their relationship status on Facebook. Although social media can make teens feel closer to their romantic partner, about one in four teens say it also can make them feel jealous or unsure of their relationships. While teens may like using social media to publicly express their love for their partner, the majority also feel that the public scrutiny of their personal relationships is at times disturbing (Lenhart et al., 2015).

Of course not all societies allow young men and women to find a romantic partner by mixing together or dating. Choosing a dating partner based on attraction, love, and personal needs is characteristic of individualistic societies such as the United States, but in collectivist societies such as India, teens' connection to their families plays a larger role. In India, parents and children examine potential marital partners in terms of how they will fit in with the family. About 90% of marriages are arranged by parents or other older family members. Children are encouraged to be practical in their choices rather than focusing exclusively on romance (Bejanyan, Marshall, & Ferenczi, 2014).

Where do adolescents get their ideas about what a romantic relationship is like? They learn from observing their parents'

Romantic relationships. Couples in romantic relationships are often similar in age, race, and attractiveness, among other factors. Why do you suppose they are also similar in their level of risk-taking behavior?

relationship and from endless discussions of the topic of romance with peers. These discussions create the norms or expectations within the peer group for what will happen in a relationship. The other important source of information on romantic relationships for adolescents is the media. Research by Ward and Friedman (2006) found that "sexy" primetime and talk shows influence teens to see romance in a stereotypical way, with men as sexual predators and women as sex objects, and with both sexes using manipulation and deceit to get the partner they desire. By contrast, marital relationships are often shown as having few serious conflicts and almost none that cannot be resolved easily through a bit of frank communication between the partners (Karney et al., 2007). Both types of portrayals distort the quality of relationships most couples experience and may leave adolescents unprepared for the reality they encounter when they find themselves in these situations. In a longitudinal study of older adolescents, girls who watched reality shows that were centered on romance later talked more with peers about sexuality, and boys who watched these shows thought there was an unrealistically high level of sexual activity among teens in the real world (Verdenbosch & Eggermont, 2011). In a slightly older sample, college undergraduates who saw more romance media were more likely to have unrealistic ideas about relationships, including the belief that "I will feel an instant sense of oneness and indivisibility with my romantic soul mate" and "People who have a close relationship can sense each other's needs as if they could read each other's minds" (Holmes, 2007, paras. 12, 13).

You can use **Active Learning: Romance as Seen on TV** to take a closer look at how romance is portrayed on a current television program.

Active LEARNING

Romance as Seen on TV

Watch a television program that focuses on the romantic relationship of a young couple. If you cannot find one specifically about adolescents, watching a program about young adults will do for this activity. Choose a show you know to be popular among adolescents, but it is best to stay away from what purports to be "reality television."

As you watch it, make notes concerning the subtle, hidden messages about romantic relationships that are embedded in the program. Are they portrayed as blissful or as a constant source of conflict? Are they based on honesty or deceit and manipulation? How are any conflicts or disagreements resolved? How easy or difficult is it to resolve them? What are the rewards or benefits of being in this relationship? Does each partner benefit to the same extent? If there is sexual behavior in the program, does it occur in a committed relationship or a casual one?

Compare your observations with those of classmates who watch other programs. Do you see any patterns or themes in how romantic relationships are portrayed across different programs?

Researchers have been interested in understanding how romantic relationships are similar to or different from adolescents' other relationships. Friendships and romantic relationships have many qualities in common. Both relationships are voluntary, and adolescents enter or leave them at will. In both, adolescents spend time together, confide in each other, provide social support, and share intimacy, but romantic relationships have an intensity and level of affection (as well as the potential for a sexual component of the relationship) that makes them different from other peer relationships (Furman & Collins, 2009). There also is a good deal of similarity in the quality of peer and romantic relationships. Adolescents with high-quality peer relationships are more likely to enjoy a high-quality relationship with their romantic partner, and likewise those with maladaptive peer relationships are more likely to have problematic romantic relationships (Karney et al., 2007; Kiesner, Kerr, & Stattin, 2004). Like peers, romantic partners are often similar to the adolescent on a number of characteristics, including age, race, ethnicity, attractiveness, academic interest, level of risk-taking behavior, and plans for attending college (Furman & Collins, 2009; Karney et al., 2007). While boys are more likely to prefer partners who are within a year of their own age, girls often prefer partners who are slightly older.

The quality of early family relationships is also related to the quality of romantic relationships in adolescence (Karney et al., 2007; Laursen, Furman, & Mooney, 2006). You'll remember from Chapter 10 that attachment theory proposes that our early relationships form the basis for an internal working model of close relationships that we carry forward with us into future relationships (Shaver & Mikulincer, 2014). Research evidence supports this expectation of continuity in the quality of relationships from early childhood through adolescence (Karney et al., 2007; Laursen et al., 2006). Some of the characteristics of secure attachment that we described in Chapter 10 for children and their parents are also found in romantic relationships. A romantic partner is a secure base in times of stress and partners are often upset when separated for a significant period of time (Furman & Collins, 2009; Shaver & Mikulincer, 2014), but in a romantic relationship *both* partners experience security and separation anxiety toward each other.

Unfortunately, we also see continuity among adolescents who have been victims of abuse while growing up (Karney et al., 2007). Physical or sexual abuse during childhood places an adolescent at an increased risk of either experiencing or perpetrating violence within an intimate relationship during adolescence. Although survivors of abuse are more likely to engage in high-risk sexual behaviors as they get older (Hornor, 2010), this replication of violence in intimate relationships is not inevitable. Adolescents who are at risk in this way can benefit from intervention programs designed to help them develop healthy and happy relationships.

The prevalence of dating violence among teens is difficult to assess because many teens do not report it, and studies often define dating violence in different ways, but according to the Centers for Disease Control and Prevention (2014j), 22% of women and 15% of men recalled experiencing some form of partner violence when they were between the ages of 11 and 17. More than 9% of high school students report being physically hurt by someone they considered a boyfriend or girlfriend in the previous 12 months (CDC, 2014i). The incidence of psychological abuse is even higher, with 30% of heterosexual youth and 22% of homosexual youth between the ages of 12 and 21 reporting they had experienced psychological abuse from an intimate partner in the previous 18 months (National Institute of Justice, 2011). The earlier teens initiate sexual relationships and the more partners they have, the more likely they are to experience intimate partner victimization (Halpern, Spriggs, Martin, & Kupper, 2009).

Experiencing violence at the hands of someone you consider an intimate partner violates the expectations that we have for this type of relationship. Adolescents who have been victims of dating violence are more likely to suffer depression, experience eating disorders, and consider or attempt suicide (CDC, 2014j). They are also more likely to be revictimized in early adulthood (Halpern et al., 2009). On the other hand, adolescents who had high-quality relationships and fewer partners had happier relationships in early adulthood. They were better able to resolve conflict and provide and receive support in their adult relationships (Madsen & Collins, 2011).

In conclusion, adolescents' experiences with romantic relationships should not be dismissed as unimportant (Meier & Allen, 2009). What teens learn in their early relationships can have an impact on their ability to form positive and long-lasting relationships in adulthood.

1. How are friendships in adolescence different from friendships in middle childhood?
2. How are the friendships of adolescent girls and boys different?
3. What is the difference between a clique and a crowd?
4. How much and what type of peer pressure do most adolescents experience?
5. How do friendships and family relationships relate to an adolescent's romantic relationship?

BULLYING, CYBERBULLYING, AND SCHOOL VIOLENCE

12.5 How do bullying and school violence impact children and adolescents?

Although peers usually are positive influences and an important source of support and companionship during childhood and adolescence, there is a darker side of peer relationships that includes bullying, harassment, intimidation, and violence. We look at what constitutes bullying, the characteristics of bullies and their victims, and the consequences of this behavior for both. We examine programs that have been used to decrease the incidence of bullying to see how effective they have been. Finally, we look at violence in schools.

WHAT IS BULLYING?

Bullying Being exposed repeatedly and over time to negative actions on the part of peers, including physical bullying, verbal bullying, and/ or emotional bullying.

Cyberbullying The use of electronic technologies, including e-mails, text messages, digital images, webpages (including social network sites), blogs, or chat rooms, to socially harm others.

Bullying has attracted increasing interest since the 1990s when several highly publicized cases of bullying led to tragic consequences that came to the attention of the public. In some cases, the bullying resulted in the suicide of the victim, and in others the victims struck back violently through school shootings. **Bullying** occurs when a victim is "exposed repeatedly and over time to negative actions on the part of one or more other students" (Olweus, 2003, p. 12). A wide range of behaviors are considered bullying, including physical bullying such as hitting, pinching, or punching; verbal bullying such as name-calling or teasing; and emotional bullying such as threatening or intimidating someone.

Recently a new form of bullying called **cyberbullying** has appeared. Cyberbullying involves the use of electronic technologies, including e-mails, text messages, digital images, webpages (including social media), blogs, and chat rooms, to harm others. A particularly hurtful form of cyberbullying is known as *sexting*, which is the distribution of embarrassing photos. Teens sometimes exchange nude or seminude pictures with their boyfriend or girlfriend, but after the relationship ends, those photos can become ammunition in a vicious campaign of hurt and retribution when they are forwarded to others within the peer group or made available to the public.

Cyberbullying differs from other forms of bullying in ways that make it particularly damaging (Kowalski & Limber, 2007). First, electronic messages can be sent instantaneously to a large number of people, which means that the impact can be even greater than face-to-face bullying. Second, although a victim can try to avoid a bully at school or in the neighborhood, he or she can't hide from cyberbullying, which can "get you" at any time and in any place. Finally, the anonymity of being a cyberbully means that adolescents might say things electronically that they would not say to another person's face because they do not see the hurt that it is causing their victim that might otherwise make them stop. In fact, more than half

Bullying and Cyberbullying. Bullying can take different forms, including physical, verbal, and psychological abuse. Intimidating or threatening someone is a type of psychological bullying, even if the bully never carries out any threats to physically harm the person. Cyberbullying takes this problem to a new level because it can involve so many more people.

of students who report that they have been a victim of cyberbullying say they do not know who the bully was (Kowalski & Limber, 2007).

PREVALENCE OF BULLYING

One of the difficulties with trying to estimate the prevalence of bullying is that the estimate a researcher gets depends on how bullying is defined, whether the definition includes the fact that the behavior is repeated or not, and the time period used for the research. For instance, you can easily understand that the estimate you get would differ depending on whether you asked students to report on whether they had been bullied in the past 30 days or during the entire past school year. Despite these difficulties, the rates of bullying in the United States are fairly consistent from one study to another (Carney & Merrell, 2001). According to the National Center for Education Statistics (2015a), about 22% of students ages 12 to 18 reported having been bullied at school during the 2013 school year. This is a decrease from 32% in 2007 and 28% in 2011 (Bidwell, 2015). Figure 12.5 shows the different types of bullying they reported.

With almost all U.S. adolescents having access to the Internet and 88% of American teens between the ages of 13 and 17 having, or having access to, a mobile phone (Lenhart, 2015), there is a great potential for many adolescents to participate in—or to be the victim of—cyberbullying. According to the National Center for Education Statistics, approximately 7% of students between the ages of 12 and 18 reported being cyberbullied during the 2013 school year (Robers, Zhang, Morgan, & Musu-Gillette, 2015). In about three-quarters of the cases, the cyberbullying happened once or twice during the year. Females were victims almost twice as often as males (9% versus 5%). About one-fourth of the victims said they had told an adult about what had happened, with girls reporting this information 3 times as frequently as males.

Since research on bullying began in Scandinavia in the 1960s, the topic has been studied in a number of countries. Large differences in the self-reported rates of victimization have been found, ranging from 9% of students in Norway and Sweden, to 22% of students in Japan and the United States and 42% of students in Italy. The number of children who self-identify as bullies also varies, from 7% in Scandinavia, to 28% of Italian primary school

FIGURE 12.5

Bullying at school. This figure shows the percentage of U.S. students ages 12 to 18 who reported being bullied at school during the 2013 school year, by type of bullying and sex of the victim.

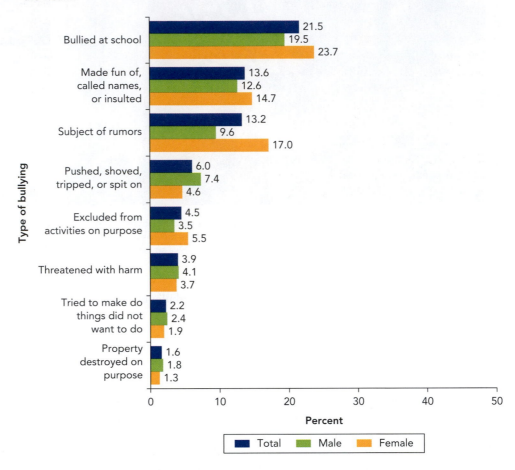

NOTE: "At school" includes the school building, on school property, on a school bus, or going to and from school. Bullying types do not sum to totals because students could have experienced more than one type of bullying. Students who reported experiencing more than one type of bullying at school were counted only once in the total for students bullied at school.

SOURCE: National Center for Education Statistics (2015a).

students and 52% of Japanese elementary school students (Borntrager et al., 2009). The picture that emerges suggests that in many settings and across a number of cultures, the threat of being victimized by a bully is a significant concern for many school-age children and adolescents.

CHARACTERISTICS OF BULLIES AND VICTIMS

There is not just one type of bully. In one study, three types were identified: (1) bullies who are popular and have good social intelligence that they can use to manipulate their peer group in order to achieve dominance (2) bullies who are popular but average in social intelligence, and (3) bullies who are unpopular and have lower levels of social intelligence who often have the hostile attribution bias we described earlier, causing them to see hostile intent in ordinary social interactions (Peeters, Cillessen, & Scholte, 2010). Although both boys and girls can be bullies as well as victims, more bullies are male than female and more victims are female (Faris & Felmlee, 2014; Olweus, 2003). Boys bully others in different ways than girls do. Male bullies tend to use physical intimidation, and female bullies tend to use emotional and psychological intimidation (Wang et al., 2009). The incidence of bullying peaks in the middle school years (Grades 6–8) and then decreases through adolescence. At all ages, there is far more emotional and psychological bullying than physical bullying (Harris, 2004; Olweus, 2003; Wang et al., 2009).

Bullies often engage in deviant behaviors, such as smoking, drinking, carrying a weapon, stealing, or damaging property (Hay, Meldrum, & Mann, 2010). They also tend to have lower academic achievement, school adjustment, and bonding to the school environment (Demaray & Malecki, 2003; Harris, 2004; Sassu, Elinoff, Bray, & Kehle, 2004). Family characteristics include an insecure attachment to their parents (Eliot & Cornell, 2009), a lack of parental supervision, the use of punitive discipline, and family violence that models aggression as a way to resolve disputes (MacNeil & Newell, 2004). Parents of bullies may be uninvolved in their children's lives, and the child may feel unloved and uncared for (Demaray & Malecki, 2003).

Bullies appear to select as their targets children who are not accepted by their same-gender classmates so they will not have others who stand by them (Veenstra, Lindenberg, Munniksma, & Dijkstra, 2010). In particular, bullies are likely to select children described as "anxious-solitary," whose vulnerabilities and fears are apparent to others, rather than children who are simply unsociable (Ladd, Kochenderfer-Ladd, Eggum, Kochel, & McConnell, 2011). However, you may be surprised to learn that bullies also target popular children. Bullying can be used to move up the social ladder, so bullies may target social rivals in order to gain greater status. The results for these popular children may be just as negative as for the isolated children who are targeted, but this type of bullying is often passed off as "drama" by adults and other children, thereby minimizing the pain that the popular children experience (Faris & Felmlee, 2014).

CONSEQUENCES OF BULLYING

Being a victim of bullying has serious emotional, psychological, and physical consequences for a child or an adolescent. Victims report feeling anxious and depressed and often have a poor self-concept (Sassu et al., 2004). Because victims often feel as though they have no friends, this sense of loneliness and powerlessness can contribute to thoughts of suicide or even a suicide attempt (Sassu et al., 2004). Being the victim of bullying also affects children's ability to be successful in school because victimization is associated with absenteeism, a lack of participation in extracurricular events (Harris, 2004), and a decline in academic performance (MacNeil & Newell, 2004). On the other hand, a victim's response could take the form of violence against others.

There are also long-term effects of being either the bully or the victim later in adulthood. Victims are at greater risk for internalizing disorders such as depression and anxiety, while bullies are at greater risk of externalizing disorders and criminal behavior, particularly violent crime and use of illegal drugs. A victim can also become a bully and vice versa. These bully-victims are at increased risk for all of the difficulties found in each group. The more frequently children are involved either as victim or bully, the more likely they are to have negative outcomes in adulthood (Klomek, Sourander, & Elonheimo, 2015). One study in the United States and the United Kingdom found that peer bullying in childhood had even more detrimental effects to mental health than maltreatment by parents (Lereya, Copeland, Costello, & Wolke, 2015).

INTERVENTIONS

As adults, we could hope that a victim of bullying would tell an adult in school what is happening to him, but about half of children who say they have been bullied have not told a teacher (Carroll-Lind & Kearney, 2004; Fekkes, Pijpers, & Verloove-Vanhorick, 2005). Many students think that administrators or teachers may not believe them, are not interested in stopping bullying, or that reporting it will make the situation worse rather than better (Carroll-Lind & Kearney, 2004; Cortes & Kochenderfer-Ladd, 2014; deLara, 2012). In cases where the adults within a school are seen by students as being more supportive, children are more likely to say that they would seek help if they were victims of a bully (Eliot, Cornell, Gregory, & Fan, 2010). Because victimization can make people distrustful of other people, this likely contributes to the child's unwillingness to tell others what is happening. And, finally, some victims don't report what has happened because they claim that being bullied simply didn't bother them (Harris, 2004).

Bullying involves more than the interaction between a bully and a victim. To fully understand what happens—and why it happens—we need to look at the social context in which it occurs. Dan Olweus (2003) has provided such a description with the *bullying circle* (see Figure 12.6). As you can see, in addition to victim and bully, there are others who are passive or possible supporters of what is happening and others who are defenders or possible defenders of the victim, as well as curious onlookers. One goal of anti-bullying programs is to empower students so they can move in the direction of becoming someone who effectively acts as a defender in the face of bullying.

Public concern about bullying has increased, and all 50 states now have anti-bullying legislation, although there is no national legislation that treats bullying as a problem shared by all parts of the country (USDHHS, 2015c). It is tempting to say that the solution is to get the bullies out of schools. That is the goal of *zero-tolerance programs* in which any student who is found to be bullying another is automatically suspended or expelled from

---

FIGURE 12.6

The bullying circle. The bullying circle shows that bullying involves more than just a bully and a victim. A number of others are involved to a greater or lesser extent.

A. Students Who Bully
These students want to bully, start the bullying, and play a leader role.

B. Followers or Henchmen
These students are positive toward the bullying and take an active part, but don't usually initiate it and do not play a lead role.

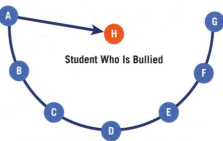

C. Supporters or Passive Bullies
These students actively and openly support the bullying, for example, through laughter or calling attention to the situation, but they don't join in.

D. Passive Supporters or Possible Bullies
These students like the bullying but do not show outward signs of support.

E. Disengaged Onlookers
These students do not get involved and do not take a stand, nor do they participate actively in either direction. (They might think or say: "It's none of my business," or "Let's watch and see what happens.")

F. Possible Defenders
These students dislike the bullying and think they should help the student who is being bullied but do nothing.

G. Defenders
They dislike the bullying and help or try to help the student who is being bullied.

school (Borgwald & Theixos, 2013). As appealing as this approach may sound, these programs have faced a number of problems. Because they require an automatic response, it may inhibit both students and teachers from reporting what has happened. These programs tend to focus on overt bullying, so one unintended consequence is that bullying has become more hidden and secretive, especially because students can now use online bullying and remain somewhat anonymous. Another consequence is that the punished students spend more time at home, and bullies have often been bullied and mistreated at home. They become more likely to drop out of school and are more likely to become involved in criminal activity. Finally, there is no evidence that these widespread zero-tolerance programs have decreased the incidence of bullying (Borgwald & Theixos, 2013), which is the primary goal of these programs.

Other types of anti-bullying programs that have been developed and implemented in U.S. schools include the following:

- Traditional programs such as the Olweus Bullying Prevention Program, which seeks to reduce the opportunities for bullying to occur while removing the rewards for it when it does happen (Olweus, 2003)

- Programs that increase social competence while reducing antisocial behavior such as aggression

- Programs that teach students how to respond to conflict

- Restorative justice programs that try to restore a relationship between the victim and the bully through techniques such as reconciliation or peer mediation (Ferguson, San Miguel, Kilburn, & Sanchez, 2007)

A review of anti-bullying programs (Ttofi & Farrington, 2011) found that on average these programs decreased bullying by 20% to 23% and reduced victimization by 17% to 20%. This review also identified the program elements that contributed to effectiveness. They included programs that were longer and more intensive, involved the parents, and included more playground supervision. Perhaps surprisingly, this study found that peer-based interventions such as peer mediation, peer mentors, or bystander intervention programs actually increased victimization. The overall atmosphere of a school may either promote or discourage bullying, so schools that have clear rules that are enforced and that offer support to students have the lowest levels of bullying (Gregory et al., 2010).

SCHOOL VIOLENCE

School violence is another threat to the well-being of children and adolescents. Horrifying and tragic events such as the mass school shootings that have taken place in recent years have focused attention on the dangers that children can face while in school. Although even one child killed at school is too many, as Figure 12.7 shows, schools are safe places for most children and adolescents and have become safer in recent years as the overall rates of school violence have fallen (Robers et al., 2015). It is important to recognize that child homicides and suicides are much more likely to occur outside of school than inside one. In 2011-2012, there were 1,199 homicides involving children between the ages of 5 and 18 and 1,184 (98.7%) of them occurred outside of school. Only fifteen occurred at school. During the same period, there were 1,568 suicides and 99.7% of them occurred outside of school. Five occurred at school (Robers et al., 2015).

Although school-related deaths are rare, school violence also includes assaults (with or without weapons), physical fights, threats, bullying, and gang violence. In 2013, 55 students per 1,000 were victims of crimes while at school, and 30 students per 1,000 were victims away from school. According to the Centers for Disease Control and Prevention (2015m), in

T ☐ F ☐ Anti-bullying programs that use peer mediation or peer mentors to reduce bullying in schools have actually increased the amount of bullying that occurs. **True**

T ☐ F ☐ Adolescents are much less likely to be victims of violence while in school now than they were 20 years ago. **True**

TRUE/FALSE VIDEO ▲

FIGURE 12.7

Violent victimization of children in and outside of school, 1991–2013. Victimization rates for children age 12 to 18 have declined substantially in recent years according to the U.S. Department of Justice.

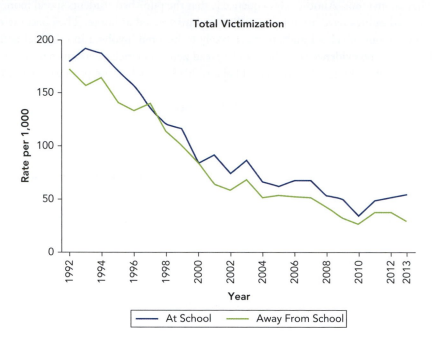

SOURCE: Robers, Zhang, Morgan, & Musu-Gillette (2015).

a nationally representative sample of youth in Grades 9 through 12 conducted in 2013, 8.1% reported they had been in a physical fight on school property during the previous year, 7.1% said they did not go to school one or more days in the past 30 days because they did not feel safe at school, and 6.9% said they had been threatened with or injured by a weapon on school property in the past year.

Efforts to reduce school violence have included providing services that are designed to help individual children who are at risk of perpetrating violence and conducting school-wide interventions designed to change the school climate in a more positive direction. There also are broad-based community interventions designed to reduce violence in the community in which an individual school is located. In **Active Learning: School Violence from a Student's Perspective**, you can compare your own experience of school violence with those of classmates.

Active LEARNING

School Violence From a Student's Perspective

Begin by thinking about your own experience with violence in your elementary, middle, and high school. You may have been a victim yourself, witnessed school violence, or simply have heard about it occurring in your school or to people you knew. Next, talk with several friends and/or classmates who came from different high schools and compare your experiences. This activity will be most effective if the members of each group have had experiences in different types of schools. Violence on average is greater in middle school and high school than in elementary school and in urban schools than in suburban or rural

schools. Fewer than half of public schools report a violent crime each year, and only 10% report a serious violent crime (National Youth Violence Prevention Resource Center, 2008), but in your discussion, remember to think about a full range of violent behavior, including threats of violence, assaults, and bullying in addition to other more clearly criminal acts. Also discuss what, if any, efforts were made by your schools to reduce school violence or to improve the school climate.

CONCLUSION

In this chapter, we have seen how children's thinking about social concepts plays a role in how they manage their relationships with other people. Children develop their social worlds through the kinds of interactions they experience but also by how they make sense out of those experiences. Young children first learn about social interaction from their relationships with their parents, but they must develop the social, emotional, and cognitive skills necessary to develop and maintain many kinds of relationships throughout their lives. Increasingly, peers become important, but parents continue to play a central role even in adolescence. The network of social relationships becomes more complex as romantic partners enter the mix. While most social relationships are positive and enhance development, those that involve threats, intimidation, and violence are detrimental to both victim and perpetrator. The good news is that both bullying and school violence have decreased in recent years.

CHAPTER SUMMARY

Test your understanding of the content.
Take the practice quiz at **edge.sagepub.com/levine3e**

12.1 What is theory of mind and how does it develop from infancy through adolescence?

Theory of mind refers to the ability to understand that people act on the basis of their mental states, including beliefs, desires, emotions, and intentions. Even young infants can understand another's intentions, but they do not completely understand **false beliefs,** when someone believes something the child knows to be false. **Recursive thinking** is an even more sophisticated understanding that others can think about how you are thinking. By middle childhood, children understand that different people might understand the same event in different ways. While theory of mind is important for cooperation and prosocial behavior, some children have a **hostile attributional bias** and tend to interpret others' innocent behavior as having aggressive intentions.

12.2 How is play important for children's development?

Play is self-chosen activity that is done for its own sake because it is fun. Mildred Parten described the social stages of play based on children's developing ability to coordinate their activity with a peer: **unoccupied behavior, onlooker behavior, solitary independent play, parallel play, associative play,** and **cooperative play.** Piaget described stages of play as based on cognitive levels of understanding: **practice play, symbolic/ sociodramatic play,** and **games with rules.** Through physical activity, play promotes health and cognitive development. It allows for emotional expression, emotional regulation, and emotional understanding. Play also develops social skills and friendships. Play is one of the best ways to learn because children remain enthusiastic about what they are learning. Recess is important during the school day to recharge energy for learning and because free play supports development.

12.3 How do peer relationships change during middle childhood?

After children enter school, their **social status** among peers becomes important. **Sociometry** is a measure of peer acceptance. Based on nominations by peers, children can be classified as **popular, rejected, average, neglected,** or **controversial.** Children can become popular because of prosocial or antisocial characteristics. Likewise, children can be rejected because they are aggressive or socially withdrawn. Certain child characteristics are associated with different statuses, and there are different developmental outcomes for children in different statuses. Although the rejected status places a child at risk, some children have a low level of **rejection sensitivity,** so being rejected by peers may not distress them. In middle childhood, **gender segregation** results in children playing with peers of the same gender. Boys and girls have qualitatively different experiences within these same-sex groups.

12.4 What types of peer relationships are important during adolescence?

Adolescents spend an increasing amount of time with peers, and relationships become reciprocal and more intimate (especially for girls). There is a great deal of similarity between adolescent friends, and both selection and influence contribute to this similarity. Friends form **cliques,** and individual adolescents are placed within different **crowds** by their peers. Although peers exert **peer pressure,** the pressure is often subtle and is more likely to be for positive rather than negative behavior.

Adolescents become more resistant to peer pressure as they get older. There has been debate over the relative influence of parents and peers, but it appears that peers have more influence in certain areas while parents have greater influence in others. Romantic relationships first emerge in adolescence. Adolescents' ideas about the nature of romantic relationships are influenced by their observation of their parents' relationship, conversations with friends, and the media. Teens with secure attachment relationships with their parents and high-quality friendships are more likely to form positive romantic relationships, while those who have suffered abuse are more likely to experience abuse in their romantic relationships. Adolescent romance allows teens to learn how to handle intimate relationships, and this is related to the nature of their intimate relationships in early adulthood.

12.5 How do bullying and school violence impact children and adolescents?

Bullying is a threat to the well-being of a number of children and adolescents, and **cyberbullying** is a particularly vicious form of bullying. Bullies may be popular and socially skilled or unpopular and socially unskilled. Bullying may reflect the bullies' sense of inadequacy or it may come from their drive for status in their peer group. Victims of bullies may feel anxious or depressed and may react by withdrawing from peers or striking out against them. Programs designed to reduce bullying have only had a small effect on reducing the incidence of bullying and could be improved. Both bullying and violence have decreased within schools in recent years, but there is still room for improvement to ensure every child feels safe.

KEY TERMS

Strengthen your understanding of these key terms with mobile-friendly eFlashcards at **edge.sagepub.com/levine3e**

Give your students the SAGE edge!

SAGE edge offers a robust online environment featuring an impressive array of free tools and resources for review, study, and further exploration, keeping both instructors and students on the cutting edge of teaching and learning. Learn more at **edge.sagepub.com/levine3e**

practice AND apply
WHAT YOU'VE LEARNED

edge.sagepub.com/levine3e

Squaredpixels/E+/Getty Images
©iStockphoto.com/Xavier Arnau
Gary Schultz/Design Pics/Getty Images
Zero Creatives/Cultura/Getty Images

PART V

CONTEXTS FOR DEVELOPMENT

chapter 13 | FAMILIES

LEARNING QUESTIONS

13.1 What constitutes a family?

13.2 What are the roles individuals in a family fill and how have these roles changed?

13.3 How do parents socialize their children?

13.4 What interventions are used to improve family life?

Master these objectives using an online action plan at **edge.sagepub.com/levine3e**

TEST YOUR KNOWLEDGE

Test your knowledge of child development by deciding whether each of the following statements is *true* or *false,* and then check your answers as you read the chapter.

1. **T ☐ F ☐:** The incidence of stepfamilies in the United States has not changed much from 1900 to today.

2. **T ☐ F ☐:** The majority of women who are single but living with the father of their baby when their baby is born are likely to marry the baby's father shortly after the baby's birth.

3. **T ☐ F ☐:** Couples who marry today have a lower risk of getting divorced than couples who married in the 1970s and 1980s (the Baby Boomers).

4. **T ☐ F ☐:** Children living in stepfamilies have significantly more adjustment and behavior problems than children in intact families.

5. **T ☐ F ☐:** Adolescents who have mothers who are employed are more likely to drink alcohol, smoke, use drugs, become sexually active, or commit delinquent acts.

6. **T ☐ F ☐:** Children who grow up without siblings tend to be more self-centered, maladjusted, lonely, and neurotic than children who have siblings.

7. **T ☐ F ☐:** Good parenting is good parenting, so the same parenting strategies work equally well for all children.

8. **T ☐ F ☐:** More than half of American adolescents say they eat a meal together as a family five or more times a week.

9. **T ☐ F ☐:** Mother-daughter relationships are the closest family relationship during adolescence, and father-daughter relationships have the greatest amount of conflict.

10. **T ☐ F ☐:** A good deal of parent-adolescent conflict is normal in families with adolescents.

Correct answers: (1) T, (2) F, (3) T, (4) F, (5) F, (6) F, (7) F, (8) T, (9) F, (10) F

▲ **VIDEO: Watch as students answer some of these questions and the authors respond**

I n this chapter, we examine the influence that families have on children's development. We begin by exploring the diversity among types of families that exist in American society, with a focus on the children who live within them. We examine issues of divorce, single parenting, coparenting, noncustodial parents, stepfamilies, and the role of grandparents, gay and lesbian parents, adoptive parents, and foster families. We then look at the dynamic nature of families and at the roles and functions filled by the individuals in the family. All families socialize their children to meet the expectations of the society in which they live. We discuss the many ways in which they do that. Finally, we describe various interventions that can help the family be the best possible context for the development of children.

WHAT CONSTITUTES A FAMILY?

13.1 **What constitutes a family?**

The primary context for development is the family. In this section, we look at the diverse forms that families take. We look at how those forms change from one cultural setting to another, and how they have changed through history.

DIFFERING CULTURAL DEFINITIONS

"Few would dispute that the family is the basic social unit in the organization of human society and a primary context for the development and socialization of society's children" (McLoyd, Hill, & Dodge, 2005, p. 3), yet the definition of **family** may differ widely from one cultural setting to another. Before reading on, write down your thoughts about what makes a family. Think about how a family is created and who its members might be. The following examples illustrate some of the diversity in the forms that families can take in different cultures. Some may be family forms that you have not encountered before.

For instance, in an area in southern India, a woman marries all of her husband's brothers, and her children are each assigned to one of the brothers, not necessarily the biological father (Coontz, 2000). In Micronesia, an Ifaluk family consists of two sets of parents: biological and adoptive. Anyone can ask a pregnant woman for permission to adopt her baby. The baby will live with its biological mother until age 3 when it will move in with the adoptive family. Both families are involved with the child's upbringing (DeLoache & Gottlieb, 2000). Would these family forms be included in your definition of a family?

Families differ in many ways within the United States as well. Many people think of a family as being a husband and wife living with their biological and/or adopted children, or what is called a **nuclear family,** but a family can have a number of different structures. There are single-parent families, multigenerational families, families with two same-sex partners, and families formed by divorce or remarriage. We can also talk about **extended families,** which include nuclear family members as well as other relatives such as grandparents, aunts, uncles, or cousins. Stephanie Coontz (2000) has said that the major difference between current and earlier levels of diversity in family types is not "the *existence* of diversity but . . . its increasing *legitimation*" (Coontz, 2000, p. 28). In other words, diverse forms of family life have always existed, but it has taken time for them to be recognized as acceptable ways to raise children.

THE AMERICAN FAMILY TODAY

We are often tempted to think of "the good old days" as a time when families stayed together and life was much better for children, so we begin with some perspective on what families are like now and what they were like in the last 150 years. The divorce rate has risen dramatically in the past century, but we must remember that divorce is only one way in which a marriage is dissolved. In earlier times, marital desertion, in which one parent simply ran away, was more common than it is today (Duncan, 1994). Beverly Schwartzberg (2004) describes many marriages in the 1850s as "'fluid marriage,' for they demonstrate that the seemingly rigid marriage contract contained many escape clauses" (pp. 573–574). Husbands and wives would simply disappear and might remarry even without a prior divorce, which was very difficult to obtain at the time.

It may also surprise you to learn that the incidence of stepfamilies in this country has probably not risen very much from the early 1900s. While stepfamilies today are most likely the result of divorce, in earlier times they could be the result of abandonment and remarriage as we have described, or they could result from parental death and remarriage of the remaining parent. In the years between 1901 and 1910, 22.6% of children under age 18 experienced the death of either their mother or their father (Chadwick & Heaton, 1987). In 1915, over 600 pregnant women died for every 100,000 births (compared to 12 per 100,000 births in 2003) (Hoyert, 2007), and the average life expectancy for a man was 46 years. "In 2000 it was more likely that 20-year-olds would have a *living grandmother* than it was that 20-year-olds in 1900 would have a *living mother*" (Coleman, Ganong, & Warzinik, 2007, p. 34). In a mostly agricultural society, it was considered essential to have two parents present to raise children, so remarriage following the death of a parent was very common. It was not until 1970 that the number of marriages that were ended by divorce outnumbered the number ended by death (Fischer, Hout, & Stiles, 2006).

Family Any two or more individuals living together who are related by birth, marriage, or adoption.

Nuclear family A family consisting of a husband, a wife, and their biological and/or adopted children.

Extended family A family structure that includes nuclear family members and other relatives, such as grandparents, aunts, uncles, and cousins.

T ☐ F ☐ The incidence of stepfamilies in the United States has not changed much from 1900 to today. **True**

CHILDREN'S LIVING ARRANGEMENTS

Today, children grow up in a variety of family structures. Figure 13.1 shows how many American children 17 years of age or younger live in each of several different family forms. As the figure shows, in the 1960s, 73% of all children lived in a family with two married parents in their first marriage. By the 1980s, that percentage had fallen to 61% of all children, and today it is 46%, or less than half (Pew Research Center, 2015). Because each type of living arrangement has different consequences for children's growth and well-being, we discuss the different structures separately in the following sections. Before we do that, though, it is important to note that not only has the family structure in which children grow up changed, but so has the stability of their living arrangements. One recent study estimated that about one-third of children younger than age 6 would experience a major change in family structure over a 3-year period due to parental divorce, separation, marriage, cohabitation, or death (Laughlin, 2014). This means that any statistic about family structure reflects a particular point in time when the research was carried out. This is one reason why the percentage you see in this chapter for mothers who are single when they give birth and the percentage of children who live in single-parent families is different.

Single-Parent Families

Today, one-third of American children live in a single-parent household (Child Trends, 2015b). This group includes parents who have never married, as well as those who are divorced or widowed. A single-parent household is the living arrangement for two-thirds of African American children, 4 out of 10 Hispanic or Latino children, and one-quarter of non-Hispanic White children (The Annie E. Casey Foundation, 2015). Single parents come from all backgrounds and a wide variety of circumstances, but if you were asked to describe the typical single parent, what would your description look like? Is this parent male or female? Is this parent a teenager? Was this parent *ever* married? Is this parent employed or do the parent and children live in poverty or on public assistance? According to recent statistics from the U.S. Census, a single parent is more likely to be a mother than a father (84% female versus 16% male), was married at one point in time (only 34.2% of single mothers and 20.0% of single fathers were never married), is employed (79.5% of mothers and 90% of fathers are employed either full or part time) (Grall, 2011), and does not live in poverty (although 40% of single mothers and 22% of single fathers do) (U.S. Census Bureau, 2014b). Also, only 8% of births to unmarried mothers occur to women under the age of 18 (Edin & Kefalas, 2005). How accurate were your ideas of what the typical single parent is like?

Figure 13.2 shows the increase in the number of children born to unmarried mothers in the United States in recent years. In 2015, 40.3% of births in the United States were to unmarried women. This percentage differs by racial and ethnic groups: 70.9% of African American mothers, 52.9% of Hispanic mothers, and 29.2% of non-Hispanic White mothers were unmarried at the time of their child's birth (Child Trends, 2015b). This does not, of course, mean that the mother is the only adult in the household. In the case of about 60% of

FIGURE 13.1

Children's household living arrangements. This figure shows recent percentages of children living in different family arrangements in the United States. The percent of children living with two married parents has fallen dramatically since the 1960s, while the percent living with a single parent has increased substantially.

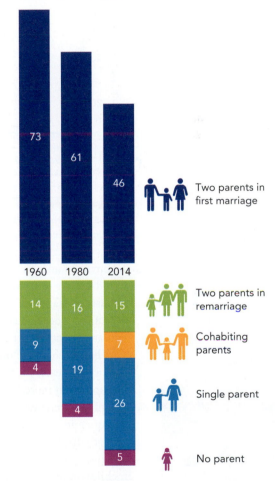

For children, growing diversity in family living arrangements

% of children living with . . .

SOURCE: Pew Research Center (2015).

FIGURE 13.2

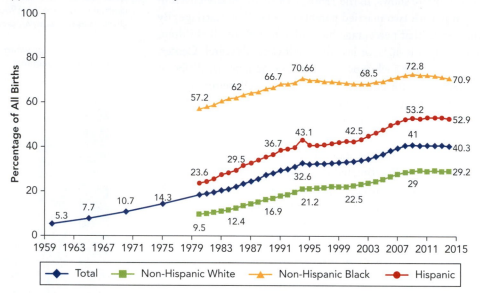

Statistics on the rise in number of unmarried mothers in the United States. This figure shows the dramatic rise in the number of births to single mothers in the United States since 1960. Although more than 4 in every 10 births in the United States in 2015 were to an unmarried mother, the rate appears to have stabilized in recent years.

SOURCE: Child Trends (2015a).

TRUE/FALSE VIDEO ▲

the births to unmarried women aged 25 and older, the woman is cohabiting with a partner (Child Trends, 2015a). Although many unmarried women in this situation plan eventually to marry the father of their child, one large-scale study found that 1 year after the birth only 10% of the mothers had actually married the father and only 20% of the fathers maintained regular contact with the child (McLanahan & Carlson, 2004).

Whether there are one or two parents in a household is important because of the living situation it creates for the child. When there is only a single wage earner in the family, families are much more likely than two-parent families to fall below the poverty line. While 13% of children under the age of 6 living with married parents live in low-income families, 46% of children residing with a single parent do (Jiang, Ekono, & Skinner, 2015). Poverty has both direct and indirect effects on children. A lack of adequate financial resources while growing up has been associated with a number of cognitive, social, and emotional problems in children, but it also increases parental stress and reduces parenting skill which, in turn, affects child well-being (Amato, 2005). We have discussed the impact of poverty on different aspects of children's development throughout this book, and you will read a more extensive discussion of the impact of poverty on development in Chapter 15.

Divorce

You may have heard the statistic that half of all marriages in the United States end in divorce. The number of divorces that occur each year or the number of children affected by a parental divorce is difficult to determine for a number of reasons, but a recent analysis of divorce statistics found that the rate was substantially different for different age segments of the U.S. population (Amato, 2012; Kennedy & Ruggles, 2014). Figure 13.3 shows the divorce rate for Baby Boomers (those married in the 1970s and 1980s) and younger cohorts married in the 1990s and 2000s. Baby boomers, who began divorcing at a historically high rate earlier in their marriages, continue to divorce at a higher rate than younger couples, while younger cohorts are on track to have lower rates throughout their marriage. Several changes in how

FIGURE 13.3

A cohort comparison of divorce risk. Different birth cohorts have different levels of risk for experiencing a divorce. People married in the 1970s and 1980s have had higher rates of divorce at each point in their marriage. By comparison, younger couples appear to be on track to have a lower risk at each of these points in their marriage.

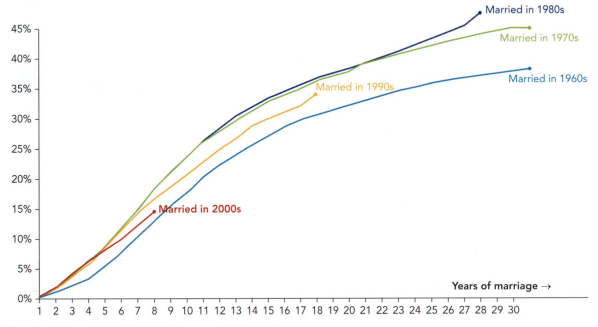

SOURCE: The Survey of Income and Program Participation, U.S. Census Bureau.

and when people are marrying likely account for this cohort difference. Young people are marrying at later ages today, and we know that couples who marry at later ages are less likely to experience a divorce. More couples today are living together rather than getting married, so when they separate this does not added to the divorce statistics (Kennedy & Ruggles, 2014). And, as young people feel less social pressure to marry, they can be more selective about who they choose as a marriage partner. Table 13.1 shows several other characteristics that lower the risk of a divorce for an individual. Wilcox (2011) summarized this information by saying, "If you are a reasonably well-educated person with a decent income, come from an intact family and are religious, and marry after age 25 without having a baby first, your chances of divorce are very low indeed" (p. 74).

The earliest research on divorce tended to treat it as a single event. Children from divorced families and children from intact families were compared, and there appeared to be many negative outcomes for children from divorced families. However, current thinking defines divorce as a process that unfolds over time rather than as one event (Amato, 2010; Dowling & Elliott, 2012). After the divorce, there will likely be a number of changes that affect the children in the family, including residential moves, changes in the family's financial resources, new caretakers, custody changes, parental dating relationships, cohabitation, step-parents, new siblings, and more that may be disruptive and distressing for the children. All of these factors play a role in how children fare following a divorce.

Of course the age of the child at the time of the divorce is another factor to consider. For infants and toddlers, research has focused on the effect of a parental divorce on attachment security. As the concept of an internal working model for relationships would predict, people who were younger when their parents divorced were more likely to have an insecure attachment to their parents than people whose parents divorced when they were older, with the highest level of insecurity for those who experienced parental divorce during the first few years of life (Fraley & Heffernan, 2013). One factor related to attachment for infants is the nature of

TABLE 13.1

Your chances of divorce may be much lower than you think. Almost everyone has heard that the national divorce rate is almost 50% of all marriages. This is basically true for the married population as a whole, but for many individuals, the actual chances of divorce are far below 50/50. The background characteristics of people entering a marriage, such as their age at marriage, amount of education, and annual income, have major implications for their risk of divorce. Here are some percentage-point decreases in the risk of divorce or separation during the first ten years of marriage, based on various personal and social factors:

Factors	Percent Decrease in Risk of Divorce
Annual income over $90,000 (vs. under $25,000)	30
Having a baby 7 months or more after marriage (vs. before marriage)	24
Marrying over 25 years of age (vs. under 18)	24
Family of origin intact (vs. divorced parents)	14
Religious affiliation (vs. none)	14
College (vs. high school dropout)	25

SOURCE: Wilcox (2011). © The National Marriage Project and the Institute for American Values. Reprinted with permission; all rights reserved.

the custody arrangements with the two parents. While continuing contact with a noncustodial parent is usually good for a child, frequent and long out-of-home visits with a noncustodial parent may be stressful for an infant who is in the process of forming an attachment (George, Solomon, & McIntosh, 2011). In one study, infants who had frequent overnight visits with their fathers were more likely to be insecurely attached than those who only had contact during the day or who had fewer than one overnight visit per week (McIntosh, Smyth, Kelsher, Wells, & Long, 2010). However, more frequent overnights were not related to adjustment problems at older ages, and none of this means that noncustodial fathers should not have contact with their infants. Instead, the recommendation is that visits be frequent, short, and on a regular basis in a setting that is familiar to the infant (Ram, Finzi, & Cohen, 2002).

Preschool children cannot understand what is happening during a divorce and their bewilderment can lead to anxiety (Clarke-Stewart & Brentano, 2006). They also do not understand the permanence of the situation and may hope for reconciliation between their parents. Often preschool children regress in their behavior when they are under stress, and we see this in less mature play behavior, more acting out and temper tantrums, and the reappearance of earlier behaviors such as bedwetting (Cohen & the American Academy of Pediatrics Committee on Psychosocial Aspects of Child and Family Health, 2002). Nightmares may become more common. Preschoolers also may feel guilty, as though the divorce was their fault, so they need to be reassured that this was an adult decision, not something they caused. Like younger children, preschoolers may also experience separation anxiety because they believe that because one parent has left, the other could also abandon them.

While school-aged children can better understand the situation, this does not necessarily ease their pain or reduce their feelings of guilt, anxiety, or sadness (Clarke-Stewart & Brentano, 2006). Younger school-aged children are more likely to be anxious and depressed, while older ones may not directly show their grief and sadness, but rather express their feelings through anger (Clarke-Stewart & Brentano, 2006). They may blame one parent or the other, or be angry about the impact that the divorce has on their lives, such as making them move to a new school.

Adolescence is a time for becoming more independent of parents, a task that is easier when the parents are in a position to give both support and control to their teens. When parents are embroiled in the emotional conflicts of a divorce, parenting becomes much more difficult. Adolescents may respond by acting out as a way to express their disappointment with their parents. They may increase their dating and social involvement, perhaps as an attempt to find a supportive relationship outside the family (Hartman, Magalhães, & Mandich, 2011). This may help to explain why the rate of teen pregnancy is twice as high in divorced families as in married families (Martin et al., 2004). Depression, delinquent behavior, and substance abuse are also more likely to occur for these teens than for teens in intact families (Cohen et al., 2002).

One of the most important factors associated with parental divorce that negatively impacts children is ongoing high levels of conflict between the parents. When a parent resorts to criticizing the other parent, it is particularly damaging to the child's self-esteem and emotional well-being (Baker & Ben-Ami, 2011). When the parent says, "Your other parent doesn't love you," the child may hear, "You are not worth loving." Recently, attention has been given to what is called **constructive conflict.** There is evidence that when parents disagree, but handle it in a positive way (for example, they are affectionate despite their disagreement, resolve conflict through problem solving, and remain emotionally supportive of each other), it is associated with positive emotional development in the children in the family (McCoy, Cummings, & Davies, 2009). In fact, when high levels of family conflict are resolved by divorce, children's functioning often improves (Strohschein, 2005; Yu, Pettit, Lansford, Dodge, & Bates, 2010)

Constructive conflict
Family conflict that is resolved in a positive way using affection, problem solving, and emotional support.

As parents deal with the stress of decreased income that often accompanies divorce, the emotional distress from the breakup of their relationship (including depression and anger), changes in work situations, and more, their parenting skills often suffer and children's well-being also declines. Parents who are highly stressed often provide less positive support for the child, use less effective communication, and provide less monitoring and control over the child's behavior (Greene, Sullivan, & Anderson, 2008; Martinez & Forgatch, 2002). However, when parents can maintain positive parenting, the effects of divorce on the child are lessened (Bastaits & Mortelmans, 2016). Sometimes during or following a divorce, children become more concerned with their parents' emotional needs than their own as they become a parental confidant or mediator between their parents (Jurkovic, Thirkield, & Morrell, 2001; Martin et al., 2004). At other times, they take on responsibility for managing the household by caring for siblings, shopping, or cleaning for the family (Jurkovic et al., 2001). These children may appear to be doing well and the added responsibility can contribute to the development of competence and maturity in older children, but it can be an overwhelming burden for younger children that is associated with depression later in life (Jurkovic et al., 2001; Schier, Herke, Nickel, Egle, & Hardt, 2015).

Family conflict. What would it feel like to be this boy, listening to his parents fight?

Research has examined numerous aspects of the well-being of children following a parental divorce. Many studies have found that academic achievement suffers, with the biggest impact on school completion. Children from single-parent families formed by divorce are twice as likely as those with two parents to leave school before high school graduation (Martin et al., 2004). They are less than half as likely to attend college (Elliott, 2009) and when they do enter college they have significantly lower grade point averages and are less likely to continue into their second year (Soria & Linder, 2014).

AB Studio/Photolibrary/Getty Images

Peopleimages.com/DigitalVision/Getty Images

A child's view of divorce. When parents of school-age children divorce, it is important that parents help them understand that they are still loved by both parents and they will be cared for by them.

Research also has examined both externalizing and internalizing behavior problems. Children from divorced and single-parent families, especially boys, have generally been found to have more externalizing behavior problems, like being "disobedient, aggressive, demanding and lacking in self-control" both in early childhood and later in life (Martin et al., 2004, p. 284; see also Ehrenberg, Regev, Lazinski, Behrman, & Zimmerman, 2014). About 20% to 25% of children of divorce experience high levels of behavior problems, compared to 10% of children in intact families (Greene, Anderson, Hetherington, Forgatch, & DeGarmo, 2003). To a lesser extent, parental divorce is associated with internalizing behavior problems, such as anxiety and depression (Ehrenberg et al., 2014; Franic, Middeldorp, Dolan, Ligthart, & Boomsma, 2010; Kim, 2011).

Another effect of divorce that cannot be assessed until the children have reached adulthood is the adult child's ability to be involved in and committed to a long-term intimate relationship. Children of divorce are at greater risk than children from two-parent families of experiencing a divorce themselves (Wauterickx, Gouwy, & Bracke, 2006; Wolfinger, 2011). In a number of studies, young adults whose parents had divorced were more wary of intimate relationships (Burns & Dunlop, 2002) and more likely to have many short-term relationships (Jónsson, Njardvik, Ólafsdóttir, & Grétarsson, 2000). Once they were married, they were less satisfied with their marriage (Jacquet & Surra, 2004). However, it is important to keep in mind that, although more children of divorced parents experience these problems, the majority of them do succeed in creating committed relationships.

Although the problems described do exist, the average differences between children of divorce and children in intact families are small, and most children from divorced families score within the normal range of functioning on many measures (Amato & Anthony, 2014; American Psychological Association [APA], 2004; Ehrenberg et al., 2014). In trying to understand the large and complex body of research on divorce and its effects on children, we should remember that we cannot assume that any differences we observe between children from divorced and intact families are necessarily *caused* by the divorce.

Most psychologists today would agree that rather than asking *whether* divorce affects children, we should try to understand *how* and *under what circumstances* divorce affects children (Amato, 2010) and identify ways we can help children cope with this experience. When parents are able to disengage from each other while continuing to provide warm and consistent parenting for their children, children's cognitive and social development are less likely to be negatively affected in the long term (APA, 2004; Ehrenberg et al., 2014). We talk about coparenting following a divorce later in this chapter. As part of that process, parents can encourage their children to talk about how they are feeling, reassure them that both parents still love them and that the divorce is not their fault, and help them to stay in contact with both parents. Keeping up with child support payments also helps reduce financial hardship, one of the greatest sources of stress during the divorce process (American Academy of Matrimonial Lawyers, 2009; Nemours Foundation, 2013).

Noncustodial Parents

Following a divorce, most children continue to reside with their mothers, but one in six resides with a custodial father (Grall, 2016). However, when a father does not reside in the same household as his children, we should not assume that he is not part of their lives.

There are a variety of ways in which a nonresident father can sustain a relationship with them. Much of the research that has been done on noncustodial fathers has looked at the amount of face-to-face contact the father has with his children (for example, the frequency of contact or the length of time they spend together) or the provision of financial support to the family. Much less of it has looked at the quality of the relationship maintained despite the physical separation (Dunn, Cheng, O'Connor, & Bridges, 2004). One explanation for why there is so much variability in the outcomes for children of divorce is that simple measures of paternal contact may not be enough to assess the impact of nonresident fathers on their children's development. To do this, we need to look at the *quality* of the relationship that is maintained over time (Stone, 2006).

Skyping to keep in touch. In 2011, British courts began using contact through Facetime or Skype as part of their custody rulings.

The amount of contact that children have with nonresident fathers varies greatly. In one 14-year-long study, following a divorce, 38% of fathers were consistently highly involved with their children, 32% had little contact, another 23% had a pattern of declining contact, and a smaller group of 8% increased contact over time (Cheadle, Amato, & King, 2010). However, there is some evidence that more recent cohorts of fathers are maintaining more frequent contact with their children following divorce than was the case in the past (Dunn, 2004a). Even if a noncustodial parent lives at a distance from the child, they are often now able to use Skype and Facetime to interact with their child on a regular basis so the way we think about and measure "contact" between a noncustodial father and his child or children will need to change as technology changes.

In a study of young adolescents in which about half the sample resided with their father and the other half lived apart, the adolescents were asked to describe the perceived quality of their relationship with their father on a number of dimensions (Munsch, Woodward, & Darling, 1995). When adolescents who lived with their father and adolescents who lived apart but who still had contact with him were asked to describe the quality of their relationship with their father, there were surprisingly few differences between their perceptions. Because maintaining contact with a child a father no longer resides with takes effort, noncustodial fathers need to hear the message that they can be—and often are—important people in the lives of their children, an idea that research continues to support (Dunn et al., 2004; Mandel & Sharlin, 2006). In one study, it was the father's perception of his role as a noncustodial parent that was the most important factor related to the ongoing quality of his relationships with his children (Stone, 2006). Fathers with a clearer understanding of how to continue to be a father to their children despite not living with them were more likely to have a high quality relationship with their children.

There is considerably less research on noncustodial mothers, but people often make negative

Noncustodial fathers. Many fathers remain important people in their children's lives, even if they don't live with them. When noncustodial fathers understand this, they are more likely to work at maintaining a relationship with their children following a divorce.

assumptions about why a mother would not have custody of her children (Bemiller, 2010). They assume she is selfish, incompetent, or unfit, but it is more likely that she has voluntarily relinquished custody to the children's father because she is unable to financially support the children, has physical or emotional problems, or the child has asked to reside with someone else (Bemiller, 2010). There are several ways in which children's relationship with a non-custodial mother could be considered more positive than the relationship with noncustodial fathers. Noncustodial mothers are seen as maintaining greater emotional involvement in the lives of their children, even when they live apart, and as being more sensitive to their child's needs, more effective at providing support and comfort, and are more knowledgeable about the child's day-to-day activities (Gunnoe & Hetherington, 2004). There also is some evidence that the relationship with a noncustodial mother plays a bigger role in the child's postdivorce adjustment (Gunnoe & Hetherington, 2004).

Coparenting

Coparenting Sharing parenting responsibilities between two or more people.

The term **coparenting** refers to the sharing of parenting responsibilities between two or more people. Although we often think of coparenting in terms of how a couple handles parenting responsibilities following a divorce or separation, it is something that is routinely done by married couples, as well as by parents who have never married and by single parents who share parental responsibilities with any other person. Of course, what coparenting looks like can be quite different from one of these situations to another. We provide a good deal of information on parenting styles later in this chapter and have looked at coparenting by divorced and separated parents, so in this section we will focus more on how coparenting is handled by couples that have never married.

We have already said that divorced fathers who live apart from their children typically have relatively high levels of involvement in their children's life at first, but that this involvement declines over time (Cheadle et al., 2010). Given the large number of situations in which a child's parents have never married, we can ask whether contact between *unmarried* fathers and their children follows the same pattern. Although many unmarried mothers live with the father of their baby at the time their baby is born, two-thirds will no longer be living with him by the child's fifth birthday (Goldberg & Carlson, 2015). When researchers looked at patterns of coparenting within a group of almost 1,200 unmarried couples, they found four distinct patterns of father involvement. Over a period of 6 years, involvement decreased for 20% of the fathers, but 41% maintained a consistently high level of involvement, and 13% moved from low involvement to high involvement over this period. Another

Kidstock/Blend Images/ Getty Images

Coparenting. When two parents are not available, parenting may be shared with another adult or family member.

25% of these fathers had little involvement with their child when the child was 3 years old, and the level remained low beyond that point (Goldberg & Carlson, 2015).

What characteristics predicted which fathers would continue to coparent their child and which would not? Having a strong, positive relationship with the baby's mother before the birth of the baby was one factor that predicted which fathers would remain involved with the child. While you might expect that it would be older parents or those with more income or education who would be most likely to stay involved, it was race that was the strongest predictor, with Black fathers maintaining the highest levels of coparenting. The researchers hypothesize that the fact that being unmarried at the time of a baby's birth is a more typical occurrence in the Black population made it less likely that the men would disengage from their children even when they were not married to the child's mother (Goldberg & Carlson, 2015). The fathers were likely to stay involved with their children even if the mother later had a child with a different partner. However, when the father had a child with a different woman, involvement was more likely to decline, suggesting that he disengaged from the first child to invest his time and energy in the child born in his current relationship. A different type of coparenting has been found in other research on African American families, in which up to 97% of mothers identified another adult or family member (for example, a mother's mother or grandmother) as someone who acted as a coparent (Gonzalez, Jones, & Parent, 2014).

Coparents must maintain communication with each other, but this can be difficult to do if there is a lot of conflict between the parents (Ganong, Coleman, Feistman, Jamison, & Stafford Markham, 2012). Fortunately coparents today do not necessarily need to communicate face-to-face to arrange schedules or coordinate activities. Electronic communication, including text and e-mails, can reduce some these negative exchanges between parents. While electronic communication gives them a chance to carefully consider the wording in their messages and edit out some of the hostility before sending, it also can lead to misunderstandings if the communications are not clear. When coparents keep their focus on their children and their well-being, it benefits the children in many ways.

Stepfamilies and Blended Families

Three out of four divorced people eventually remarry, so many children who have experienced a parental divorce later face the challenge of entering **stepfamilies.** In fact, one out of every three American children will live in a stepfamily at some point during their childhood or adolescence (Braithwaite, Schrodt, & DiVerniero, 2009). One definition of a stepfamily is that it is a family with two adults in a formal or informal marriage where at least one of the adults has children from a previous relationship and there also may be children from the current union (Howden, 2007). The new families that are formed may be very complex, as the following example shows:

> A "his," "hers," and "ours" family. The father has one biological son (11), and the mother has two biological children, a boy, 16, and girl, 13, who all live in the same household. They have an "ours" three-year-old daughter. Shared parenting arrangements see children moving in and out for five and four days each week. The whole stepfamily is together on two separate nights each week. One ex-partner has re-partnered and has two young adult stepchildren. (Howden, 2007, para. 15)

The cartoon in Figure 13.4 shows that confusion may arise in other situations as well. Try **Active Learning: Diagram Your Family** to see how complex your own family is by using a genogram to diagram these relationships.

A family undergoes transformations as a couple becomes parents, a marriage goes through a divorce, and a new stepfamily emerges. Within a

Stepfamilies Families in which there are two adults and at least one child from a previous relationship of one of the adults; there also may be biological children of the couple.

FIGURE 13.4

Stepfamilies are complicated. Children may become confused when they deal with all the complexity they find in their family structures.

"When you say you want to speak to my parents, do you mean my mommy and her new husband or my daddy and his new wife or my mommy and my daddy?"

stepfamily, *boundary ambiguity*, or lack of clarity regarding who is in and who is out of the family system, can become an issue (Stewart, 2005). People may need to redefine or clarify their roles and relationships within the stepfamily. In this process, it is not uncommon for children to show dislike or challenging behavior to a new stepparent (Ganong, Coleman, & Jamison, 2011). They may feel they are being disloyal to their biological parent if they like their new stepparent, may continue to hold the fantasy that their parents will get back together, or they may simply resent the attention that their parent now pays to their new partner (Hetherington & Kelly, 2002). Strained relationships between stepparent and stepchild undoubtedly contribute to the fact that 60% to 67% of remarried couples experience a

Active LEARNING

Diagram Your Family

A genogram is a mapping of your biological family; however, many families are much more complex than a simple genogram would indicate. Try the following activity to map your family.

Using circles for females and squares for males, put yourself in the middle of a page. Draw your family relationships around you. Put horizontal solid lines to indicate marriages, and use dashed lines to indicate cohabiting, committed relationships. A horizontal line with a ——//—— indicates a divorce or separation. Put an X over anyone who has died. Put vertical or slanted solid lines to show biological children, and use dashed lines to show adoption, steprelations, or other nonbiological parent-child relationships (adapted from Gerlach, 2010). Does your family look like the traditional nuclear family or more like the multigenerational stepfamily shown in Figure 13.5?

FIGURE 13.5

Genogram for a nuclear family.

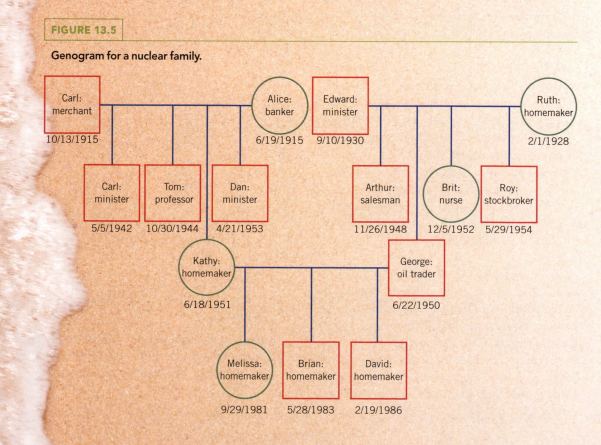

Genogram for a multigenerational stepfamily.

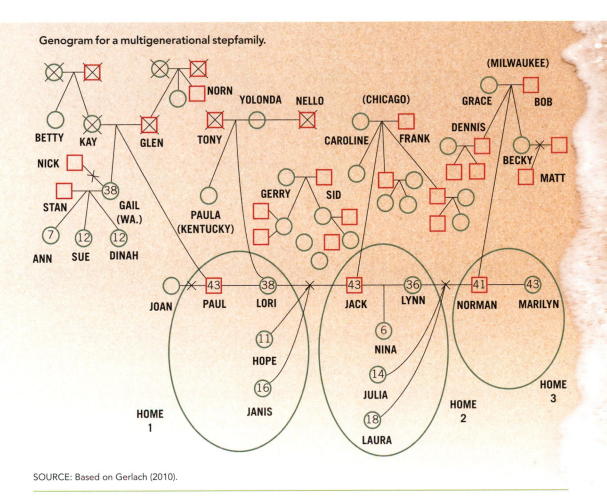

SOURCE: Based on Gerlach (2010).

second divorce (Divorce Statistics, 2012). However, if the stepparent can ride out this period of adjustment, which lasts for 5 to 7 years on average, a better relationship may ultimately develop (Amato, 2005). On a positive note, if a parent's second marriage is better than the first, it provides the child with a new model of what a loving relationship can be.

Families add or lose traditions when a family structure changes, and this requires adaptation on everyone's part (Moriarty & Wagner, 2004). For example, if everyone had gathered at a grandparent's home to celebrate Thanksgiving each year, the death of that grandparent would make the family decide whether someone else will assume that role or whether the tradition will be abandoned or transformed in some way. Stepfamilies also need to renegotiate family traditions. In blended families, do they adopt the traditions of one family or the other? Do they try to combine elements from both traditions and create a hybrid? Or do they develop new traditions that are unique to the new blended family? This type of adjustment is part of the restabilization process that stepfamilies go through.

For many years, stepfamilies were studied using a deficit comparison model that compared them to intact families and found them lacking. For example, academic performance is somewhat lower for children from divorced families, and remarriage of a parent does not increase academic performance of the children over the level they achieved in a single-parent family (Tillman, 2007). However, for many aspects of development, no conclusive differences have been found (Clarke-Stewart & Brentano, 2006; Pasley & Moorefield, 2004). Although overall adjustment and well-being of children in stepfamilies is slightly lower on average than that of children in well-functioning biological families, individual differences are very large, which means that many children in stepfamilies are thriving (Clarke-Stewart & Brentano, 2006; Dunn, 2002). The most important factors that relate

T ☐ F ☐ Children living in stepfamilies have significantly more adjustment and behavior problems than children in intact families. **False**

to children's well-being in stepfamilies are the number of transitions and stresses a child has been exposed to and the quality of the parent-child relationship (Amato, 2005; Dunn, 2002). Parents and others need to be open to listening to children's thoughts and feelings about their complicated family lives. Frequently engaging in everyday conversation is associated with stepparents' satisfaction with their stepchildren and stepchildren's satisfaction with their stepparents (Schrodt, Soliz, & Braithwaite, 2008).

Grandparents Raising Grandchildren

There are a number of reasons why a grandparent might be raising his or her grandchildren. In some cultures, multigenerational families are the normative family form. According to the 2010 U.S. Census, almost 7.8 million children under the age of 18 live with their grandparents or other relatives, and for more than 2.7 million children, their grandparent is the person primarily responsible for their care (Ellis & Simmons, 2014). Grandparents may fill in the gaps in child care in single-parent and divorced families or when both parents work outside the home (Bengtson, 2001; Dunn, Fergusson, & Maughan, 2006). In other cases, substance abuse, mental illness, incarceration, or some problem in the lives of adult children prevent them from caring for their children and the responsibility falls entirely to a grandparent (Dunifon, 2013).

Grandparents are sometimes named as the primary caretaker of their grandchildren by child welfare agencies, but in many cases these are informal arrangements. Without a formal arrangement, grandparents may not receive services that are available to families who have a formal placement (Collins, 2011; Robinson & Wilks, 2006). They also may not be able to give permission for the child's medical care or may have difficulty enrolling the child in school (American Association of Retired Persons [AARP], 2012; Robinson & Wilks, 2006).

Being a grandparent raising young grandchildren has been called a "time disordered" role (Backhouse & Graham, 2013, p. 442). Grandparents understandably may feel conflicted about their new role. At a time in their lives when most were looking forward to retirement with less responsibility and more leisure time, they find themselves taking on the full-time care of their grandchildren. Although most say they get joy and satisfaction from being able to do this and believe that it is what is best for the grandchildren, they also may feel anger, frustration, or resentment about this unanticipated change in their lives. Grandparents also may feel guilty because they feel that they failed as parents the first time with their own child and now question their ability to do a better job with their grandchildren (Backhouse & Graham, 2013). Custodial grandparents feel socially isolated from others their age who are enjoying a traditional retirement, but also are isolated by age from the young parents of their grandchildren's peers. In addition to these concerns, the grandchildren they are caring for may have a number of physical or behavioral problems that are the product of their life circumstances prior to coming to live with their grandparents. Many custodial grandparents feel that the social welfare system does not provide the services and support they need to meet these challenges (Backhouse & Graham, 2013; Collins, 2011).

Although these grandparent-headed families are marginalized, there are some programs specifically designed to help them. For example, in Hartford, Connecticut, a program

Shestock/Blend Images/Getty Images

Grandparents raising their grandchildren. Grandparents are often involved in the care of their grandchildren and sometimes are the ones who raise them. What issues arise when a grandparent becomes a child's major caregiver?

called Generations provides help to 24 families in which grandparents are raising their grandchildren (Community Renewal Team, 2013). Housing is provided with rent on a sliding scale, along with free after-school child care on a campus separated from the dangerous neighborhood that surrounds it. A variety of services are offered both to the grandparents and the children. Not only does this program benefit the families involved, but it also saves taxpayers the money that otherwise would be spent placing the children in foster care.

Gay and Lesbian Parents

According to the 2014 U.S. Census, there are nearly 783,000 same-sex couples living in the United States, and an estimated 17% of same-sex households include children under the age of 18. The majority of children in households with gay or lesbian parents were born when one of the parents was in a heterosexual marriage. The children of parents who came out following a divorce say that dealing with their parents' sexual orientation was not as stressful as dealing with how others reacted to it (Sasnsett, 2015). If the quality of the child's relationship with the parent was good, the child was likely to be doing well. Children born into a gay or lesbian family are likely to experience less stress than those who have a parent who comes out when the child is older. Gay and lesbian couples are increasingly having children through pregnancy or adoption (Elliott & Umberson, 2004).

In 2005, the American Psychological Association released a comprehensive review of the research literature on gay and lesbian parenting and its effects on children. Based on its review of 59 published studies on the subject, the authors of the report concluded:

> [T]here is no evidence to suggest that lesbian women or gay men are unfit to be parents or that psychosocial development among children of lesbian women or gay men is compromised relative to that among offspring of heterosexual parents. Not a single study has found children of lesbian or gay parents to be disadvantaged in any significant respect relative to children of heterosexual parents. Indeed, the evidence to date suggests that home environments provided by lesbian and gay parents are as likely as those provided by heterosexual parents to support and enable children's psychosocial growth. (APA, 2005, p. 15)

In 2012, the American Psychological Association reaffirmed its position based on its continued monitoring of research in this area. While parents in lesbian households report more parenting stress than parents in heterosexual households, there were no differences in children's general health, emotional difficulties, coping behavior, and learning behavior (Bos, Knox, van Rijn-van Gelderen, & Gartrell, 2016). Although children adopted into sexual minority families report that they feel different and are sometimes subjected to subtle, everyday slights or indignities by their peers, they see their families in a positive light and have developed coping strategies that give them resilience in the face of these challenges (Farr, Crain, Oakley, Cashen, & Garber, 2016).

Although the report from the American Psychological Association came from the premiere professional organization in the field of

Laura Doss/Image Source/Getty Images

Growing up with two dads. Children who grow up with gay parents are likely to be as happy and well-adjusted as children of heterosexual parents. It is the quality of the parent-child relationship (rather than the parents' sexual orientation) that is important to the child.

psychology, almost immediately critics found problems with its conclusions, based primarily on the methodology used for the studies in the review (Marks, 2012; Regneurus, 2012). Most had relied on samples that were not necessarily representative of the population, but rather were ones that were convenient and accessible to the researcher.

A more recent longitudinal study using a large, random sample of adults ages 18 through 39 who grew up in diverse family forms came to a different conclusion. It concluded that children do best when raised in continually married mother-father relationships because about one-quarter of the large number of comparisons made in this study were "suboptimal" (p. 764) for adult children of LGBT parents (Regnerus, 2012). However, this study also had methodological issues that may have biased the results and the conclusions drawn from them. First, many of the children raised in gay and lesbian families had experienced a number of other stressful family events in their lives (for example, a contentious divorce or custody fight between heterosexual parents prior to the formation of the LGBT family), and second, these adult children grew up in a nontraditional family at a historical time when these family forms were less common, and probably less accepted, than they are in today's society (Regnerus, 2012).

Open adoptions Adoptions in which the children and their biological and adoptive families have access to each other.

The fact that most children residing with lesbian or gay parents have lived in other family structures as they grew up makes it extremely difficult to determine which of the observed effects are attributable only to the child's time in a lesbian or gay family. Paul Amato (2012) joined the debate by saying that "if differences exist between children with gay/lesbian and heterosexual parents, they are likely to be small or moderate in magnitude" (p. 772). This may be the best conclusion we can draw about research on children in gay and lesbian families at this time.

Adoptive Families

Approximately 120,000 children are adopted in the United States each year (American Academy of Child and Adolescent Psychiatry, 2015). In 2007, about 40% of them were interracial adoptions (Vandivere, Malm, & Radel, 2009) and in 2015, there were almost 5,700 intercountry adoptions (U.S. Department of State, 2015). Professionals who study and work with adoptive families point to the importance of developing a "family story." Parents can begin to tell children, in simple terms and in a loving context, the story of their adoption, even before they can really understand it. This sets the stage to fill in details as the child grows and is able to understand more. Especially during adolescence, when teens are dealing with identity issues, adoptees need to know as much as their adoptive parents can tell them about their birth parents (Rampage et al., 2003). When the details are difficult, the adoptive parents walk a fine line between "honoring the birthparent and acknowledging hardships and limitations" (Rampage et al., 2003, p. 217). This is important because when adopted children have honest information about their birth parents and reassurance that their bond with their adoptive parents is real and strong, they can go on to develop a positive identity. Respecting the child's cultural origins is especially important for those children who have been adopted from another country.

Purestock/Getty Images

Multicultural adoptive family. About 14% of U.S. adoptions involve children who come from another country. Whenever an adoptive child's cultural background is different from the adoptive parents, it is important that the parents try to honor the child's cultural heritage.

Most adoptions today are **open adoptions,** in which the child and the birth and adoptive families have access to each other, although the amount of information shared and the frequency of contact between the adopted child and the child's biological parents is very variable (Siegel, 2012). In one study, adoptive parents were interviewed about their attitudes surrounding their open adoption of an infant at the time of the adoption and 20 years later. None regretted having an open adoption, and nearly half wished it was even more open (Siegel, 2013). For the adopted children, it was satisfaction with the amount of contact adoptees have—rather than a specific amount or type of contact—that was associated with better outcomes as adoptees moved into adulthood (Grotevant, McRoy, Wrobel, & Ayers-Lopez, 2013). Of course, contact with birth parents is based on their ability to provide adequate, nonabusive care. No child should be visiting a birth parent who is neglectful or abusive without direct supervision.

Foster Families

Currently there are almost 400,000 children in foster care in the United States (Adoption and Foster Care Analysis and Reporting System, 2013). Children must be removed from their homes for their own well-being if they have been abused or neglected, or if their parents are unable to care for them because of mental or physical illness, incarceration, substance abuse, or if a parent dies (American Academy of Child and Adolescent Psychiatry [AACAP], 2005). When there are no alternative caregivers within the family, these children are likely to be placed in the **foster care** system with a family that receives financial support from the state. One of the ways in which foster care is different from the other living arrangements we have discussed is that it is never intended to be a permanent situation for the child or adolescent. Children go into care with all the stress that brought them there in the first place, but also with the anxiety of living with a family that they don't know, possibly needing to change schools and losing contact with friends, and having unanswered questions about when or whether they will have to move again, either to return to their own family, to be moved to another foster home, or even to be adopted.

The issues involved with foster care differ for children of different ages. The temporary nature of a foster care placement is particularly challenging for infants and toddlers who need consistent care to promote development. Toddlers may reject their temporary caregivers which can, in turn, elicit rejection from even well-meaning foster parents. When children experience a lack of commitment from caregivers, they are more likely to see themselves negatively and may develop problem behaviors (Dozier, Zeanah, & Bernard, 2013). Foster parents must not only be committed to an infant or toddler in their care, but also be ready to support the child's return to the birth parents. Participation in supervised visits with the child's parents can help to ensure a smooth transition between homes at a later time.

When 20 children in foster care were asked to provide advice to children who were just entering foster care, they said new foster children had to be prepared for the fact that this situation might be quite different from other places they had lived (Mitchell, Kuczynski, Tubbs, & Ross, 2010). They also said that it would take time to adapt to new foster families but that it gets easier as time passes. At least some of the children recognized that a new placement could mean that there will be new opportunities. Regarding how to best handle the emotions that come along with this transition, the children recommended that children new to the foster care system try to stay calm, remain respectful, and have a positive attitude. Keeping some item that has sentimental value to them can also be helpful. The children were advised to begin building a relationship with their foster parents, and that included expressing their likes and dislikes.

Despite efforts to provide a safe, supportive, and nurturing environment for foster children, they remain at elevated risk of later developmental problem. A study conducted in Sweden compared youth who left long-term foster care after age 17 to youth who had not been in foster care (Berlin, Vinnerljung, & Hjern, 2011). The former foster care youth had a 6 to 11 times greater risk of suicide attempts, substance abuse, serious criminality, and public welfare dependency. However, these researchers determined that half the risk for psychosocial problems could be attributed to the poor school performance of the foster youth. We can

Foster care The temporary placement of children in a family that is not their own because of unhealthy situations within their birth family.

understand how being in the foster care system can have a negative effect on the educational process. A child in foster care often has to change schools and school records can be lost, days are missed, and the new school setting may be uncomfortable for the child. These disruptions are reflected in the fact that only 50% of American children who have been in foster care either graduate high school or pass the General Educational Development (GED) test and fewer than 2% go on to college (Bruskas, 2008).

To help older foster youth successfully transition out of care, Congress passed the Fostering Connections to Success and Increasing Adoptions Act in 2008 that allows states to provide support for foster children beyond age 18. In passing this legislation, Congress recognized that families in the United States today often help their adolescents move into adulthood with both financial and emotional support, so this new act continues the role of government in providing care until foster adolescents reach age 21 if they are in school, in employment training, or employed at least 80 hours per month (Courtney, 2009). Currently 22 states and Washington, DC have extended foster care beyond age 18 (National Conference of State Legislatures, 2016).

CHECK YOUR UNDERSTANDING

1. How has the number of children living with two married parents changed in recent years?
2. What factors reduce the risk of a couple experiencing a divorce?
3. What are some of the challenges that stepfamilies face?
4. What has the research on children growing up in gay and lesbian families found?

FAMILY ROLES AND RELATIONSHIPS

13.2 What are the roles individuals in a family fill and how have these roles changed?

In the last section, we looked at different types of family structures. Regardless of family structure, all families change as children grow and relationships evolve. In this section, we look at the nature of family systems and how the different systems function and change over time.

FAMILY SYSTEMS

Families are dynamic systems made up of the individuals within them and within this dynamic system, relationships develop and change over time. A system is always more than just the sum of its parts. Just as when you listen to a song, you can identify individual notes and instruments but the song itself is something more than those different pieces, a family system is more than the individuals within it. Families also are embedded in the larger context of society and a culture that shapes both their form and their function. In Chapter 2, we described Bronfenbrenner's ecological systems theory, which illustrated all the different levels of influence on children and families.

The family system is composed of the adult relationship, the parent-child relationship, and the sibling relationship. These relationships, or subsystems, all interact with each other. That means that when we discuss a mother's relationship with her child we must keep in mind that this relationship is influenced by the mother's relationship with her partner and with her other children, as well as by external factors such as parental employment, community characteristics, and external supports or stresses.

For example, a family therapist might see a family in which the presenting problem is their toddler's negative behaviors, including a great deal of crying and whining. The therapist may see that both mother and father respond to the toddler's negative behavior with anxiety, frustration, and anger. As she gets to know the family better, she realizes that there was conflict between the couple before the birth of the toddler. When therapy helps the parents to resolve conflicts with each other in a more positive way, it can result in less negative behavior from the toddler, and this then allows the parents to create a more secure attachment with the child. In this case, the marital subsystem interacted with the parent-child subsystem resulting in difficult behavior in the child, and intervening with one subsystem affected the other (Frankel, Umemura, Jacobvitz, & Hazen, 2015).

THE CHANGING ROLES OF MOTHERS AND FATHERS

Two of the most significant changes that have occurred in recent years that affect families and how they function have been the number of mothers who are working outside the home and the new role that fathers have assumed in childcare. We look in detail at these two changes in this section and discuss their impact on children's development and well-being.

Maternal Employment

One of the biggest changes in the American family in recent history has been the movement of mothers into the world of work outside the family home, as illustrated in Figure 13.6. In 2014, the labor force participation rate of mothers with children under the age of 18 was 70.1%, compared to 92.8% of all fathers with children under 18. For married mothers with children under 18, the rate was 67.8% (U. S. Bureau of Labor Statistics, 2015). Mothers with younger children are less likely to be in the labor force than mothers with older ones.

A major issue for families has become how to manage the balance between work and family life. Mothers and fathers tend to manage this stress in different ways. A recent study of almost 4,000 executives found that when fathers felt a conflict between their work and family responsibilities and needed to spend time away from their families, they often fell back on the idea that they are good financial providers for their family. Women, however, were more likely to experience guilt in the same situation and to feel they were not living up to the cultural expectations for a mother (Groysberg & Abrahams, 2014).

For middle-class couples with fewer financial resources, it may be even more important to find adaptive strategies that help manage the strain created in dual-earner families. Couples who see themselves as having done that successfully say they try to create a partnership in which both members equally share housework, childcare, and the emotional work involved with parenting (Zimmerman, Haddock, Current, & Ziemba, 2003). Despite these intentions, however, even these families admit that wives continue to be the ones who bear the majority of the responsibility for childcare and for organizing and managing the family's schedule. And, although both partners value the other's work and life goals, husbands' jobs are still given the priority by their wives.

Although the American public has become more accepting of mothers working outside the home, there is still concern about the effects of maternal employment on infants and young children. In a survey conducted by the Pew Research Center in 2009, only 11% of the respondents said that a woman with young children should work full time. Despite these continuing concerns in the minds of many people, a meta-analysis of 69 studies examining the effect of maternal employment on children's academic achievement and behavior problems found that "maternal employment per se was rarely associated with later outcomes" (Lucas-Thompson, Goldberg, & Prause, 2010, p. 933). This means that they did not detect differences between children with employed versus at-home mothers, with one exception: Teachers rated children of employed mothers as having higher achievement and fewer internalizing problems, and this effect was stronger for families who were socioeconomically disadvantaged. As we found for the influence of nonmaternal childcare on attachment to

FIGURE 13.6

Workforce participation by U.S. mothers. Until quite recently, the number of mothers employed outside the home increased steadily over the last 3 decades. Mothers with the youngest children typically have had the lowest rates of labor force participation.

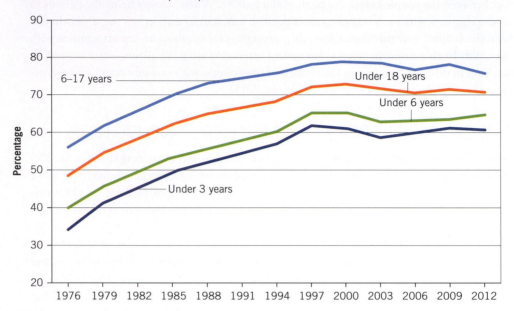

SOURCE: U.S. Department of Labor (n.d.).

the mother in Chapter 10, research has shown that children's outcomes are determined much more by their relationship with their mother than by whether she is employed (Stein, Malmberg, Leach, Barnes, & Sylva, 2013).

Research on the effect of maternal employment on adolescents has largely focused on the fact that adolescents with employed mothers often spend time at home without adult supervision and this might give them the opportunity to get into trouble. The good news for working mothers is that there is accumulating evidence that maternal employment has "only a small and indirect effect on delinquency" (Vander Ven, Cullen, Carrozza, & Wright, 2001, p. 252). Aughinbaugh and Gittleman (2003) also found little association between maternal employment and adolescents' decision to drink alcohol, smoke, use drugs, become sexually active, or commit delinquent acts. Perhaps not surprisingly, when adolescents are supervised at a distance (for example, by phone), do not associate with delinquent peers, and feel an attachment to school, they are less likely to become involved in delinquency (Vander Ven et al., 2001). Taking part in after-school activities also reduces the likelihood of delinquency (Mahatmya & Lohman, 2011).

An analysis of 4 decades of research has looked at whether maternal employment has a differential effect on sons and daughters (Goldberg, Prause, Lucas-Thompson, & Himsel, 2008). A number of previous studies have suggested that there are some benefits of maternal employment for girls, but perhaps some risks for boys. In this study, several analyses showed a trend toward a benefit for girls. The authors suggest that a mother who is employed outside of the household provides girls with a role model for achievement, allows their daughters more independence than nonemployed mothers, and endorses more egalitarian gender role attitudes. Each of these differences could promote a girl's feeling of competence. Any negative effect of maternal employment for boys could be attributed to too much independence for boys who are active and require more supervision or guidance than girls. Again, it must be noted, however, that these gender differences, when found, were relatively small.

T ☐ F ☐
Adolescents who have mothers who are employed are more likely to drink alcohol, smoke, use drugs, become sexually active, or commit delinquent acts. **False**

The effect of maternal employment also has different consequences in families at different socioeconomic levels. It has no effect or slight beneficial effects on cognitive development for young adolescents from economically disadvantaged families, while those from more advantaged families show some detrimental effects (Ruhm, 2008). Low-income mothers are more likely to rely on grandparents or other relatives who have an emotional investment in the child to care for them after school, and these relatives may provide a level of attention and stimulation similar to what the mother herself would provide if she were available, while adolescents of more educated and affluent mothers may lose the benefit of having more after-school time with her. Mothers from all socioeconomic groups use organized after-school activities, especially sports, to occupy this time for their adolescents, although more affluent mothers rely more on lessons than other mothers (Lopoo, 2007).

The Changing Role of Fathers

When we look at how the role of fathers has changed in the United States, we find that married fathers are more involved with their children than in the past (Coltrane, 2004), and an increasing numbers of men are the primary caretakers of their children while their wives work outside the home (Livingston, 2014). Although the majority of stay-at-home fathers are unable to work because of illness or disability, or are unable to find employment, the number of fathers who are at home full time for the primary reason of caring for home and family has shown a fourfold increase since 1989 (Livingston, 2014). As Figure 13.7 shows, those who have chosen to stay at home now comprise 21% of stay-at-home fathers. Even when fathers work outside the home, they were the primary caregivers for almost 3 million preschoolers during the hours that their mothers worked (U.S. Census Bureau, 2008b). Research has shown that fathers with positive parenting skills and more involvement with their children foster greater cognitive skills, self-control, and empathy and less gender stereotyping in both preschoolers and adolescents (Coltrane, 2004).

Of course some differences in the parenting by mothers and fathers persist. On average, mothers spend more time with their infants and young children than fathers do, and they are more involved in caregiving activities. Mothers are often found to be more sensitive to their young children, especially their daughters, than fathers (Lovas, 2005; Schoppe-Sullivan et al., 2006). By contrast, fathers' role with children has been described as moving the child away from the protection of the mother into the wider world of social relationships. Fathers engage in more physical play with their children than mothers, but this is not a universal role for fathers. Fathers have been found to be more playful than mothers in France, Switzerland, Italy, and India, but not in Germany, Sweden, or Taiwan (Lewis & Lamb, 2003).

Ariel Skelley/Blend Images/Getty Images

Stay-at-home dads. A number of fathers either are full-time caregivers for their children or have primary care when their partner works. Children experience many benefits when fathers with positive parenting skills are more involved.

FIGURE 13.7

Growth in the number of stay-at-home fathers in the United States. Although the majority of stay-at-home fathers are disabled or unemployed, since 1989 a growing number say they are there by choice. In 2012, 21% said they were at home primarily so they could care for their family.

% of stay-at-home fathers who say they are not working because they are . . .

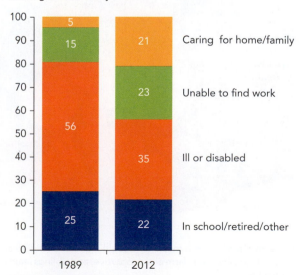

SOURCE: Livingston (2014).

RELATIONSHIPS WITH SIBLINGS

Siblings occupy a special place in a child's social world. They are the longest-lasting relationship that you will have in your life, on average lasting longer than parent-child relationships or marital relationships. Some of the functions they fill overlap with those of parents, and others overlap with those of peers, but the combination of roles they fill is unique. Older siblings may act as caregivers to their younger siblings and it is within the sibling relationship that we learn much of what we know about social relationships. They are sources of support in times of distress, as well as being playmates, confidantes, and sometimes even "partners in crime" who influence each other to engage in delinquent behaviors (Richmond, Stocker, & Rienks, 2005, p. 556; see also Stormshak, Comeau, & Shepard, 2004).

About 80% of children in the United States have at least one sibling, but it is not simply a question of how many siblings you have because who those siblings are makes a difference. Sister-sister relationships are different from brother-brother relationships or sister-brother relationships, siblings who are quite a few years apart in age have a different type of relationship than siblings who are born close together, and finally, there are qualitatively different relationships with stepsiblings, half-siblings, and adoptive siblings.

One of the unique characteristics of sibling relationships is that they can be marked *both* by closeness and by conflict (Buist &Vermande, 2014; Howe, Rinaldi, Jennings, & Petrakos, 2002). The sibling relationship can contain levels of jealousy and rivalry that are not usually seen in more discretionary relationships, like those between peers, but to varying degrees there also is a sense of obligation in the sibling relationship. There is an expectation that siblings will be there to provide support and resources to each other in times of need (Kramer, 2011).

Sibling relationships often reflect the quality of the relationship between parents and their children. For example, a warmer relationship with parents was related to more positive sibling relationships (McHale, Whiteman, Kim, & Crouter, 2007), although siblings can sometimes compensate for difficulties in relationships with the parents. A warm relationship with a sibling can help children deal with stress in their lives, even when their relationship with their mother is not warm (Gass, Jenkins, & Dunn, 2007).

Shared and Nonshared Environments

Nonshared environment
The different experiences that siblings in the same family have in that environment.

The assumption underlying much of the research on siblings has been that siblings share the same environment and that what is different between them is their degree of genetic similarity. That is why we have sometimes studied siblings by comparing identical twins to fraternal twins. Increasingly, however, we have realized that each child in the family actually has many different experiences both within the family and in their experiences outside of the family. This has led us to an interest in understanding the impact of the **nonshared environment** (Plomin, 2011).

How important is the effect of nonshared influences? It is so great that one group of researchers concluded that children growing up in the same family are not very similar to each other (Hetherington, Reiss, & Plomin, 1994). If we take out the effects that we can attribute to the genetics they share, siblings are no more similar to each other than almost any two other children chosen at random (Turkheimer & Waldron, 2000). It is almost as though they were reared in completely different environments.

She's my sister! There is much more to sibling relationships than sibling rivalry. Most relationships are warm and supportive, and siblings learn a great deal from each other.

How can that be? Previously we had assumed that things like the quality of the parents' marital relationship, the neighborhood the children grew up in, and the family's socioeconomic status equally affected all children in a family, but are these really the same thing for all children in the family? You were born into a family at a certain point in your family's life history, but each of your siblings was born at a different point in that timeline. Your family's financial circumstances may have been better or worse by the time they were born. Your parents' relationship may have gotten stronger or become more troubled by that time. You may have moved to a better or worse neighborhood. Any of these changes mean that the family environment that you experienced in your early childhood would not necessarily be the same environment that your siblings experienced later. And as children get older, they have increasing opportunities to select their own experiences outside of the family. If you chose to play soccer, join the band, and hang out with the cool kids, did all of your siblings make the same choices, or did they pick different activities, have different interests, and choose different friends than you did? **Active Learning: Examining Nonshared Environments** allows you to continue thinking about ways in which you and your siblings grew up in separate worlds even though you grew up in the same family.

Active LEARNING

Examining Nonshared Environments

For this activity, choose one of your siblings as your focus. You might want to choose the sibling that you feel is most different from you, but you don't need to do this. We apologize to only children for not being able to include them in this activity. We suggest that you do not write any personal identifying information in your textbook if you might sell it at some time in the future.

For each item, write a brief description (just words or phrases) of your experiences and the experiences of your sibling as you see them. Then think about how these differences may have affected the two of you.

Event/Experience	You	Your Focus Sibling
Family Interactions—the amount of each given by your parents: • Affection • Control/strictness • Responsibility		
Academic Success		
Social Relationships • Number of close friends • Quality of friendships (supportive, conflictual, etc.) • Peer group you spent time with (jocks, brains, populars, druggies, nerds, etc.)		
Participation in Activities (list which ones) • At school • In the community • Lessons • Work (If "yes," at what age?)		

(Continued)

(Continued)

Event/Experience	You	Your Focus Sibling
Major Family Life Events (residential moves, major changes in finances, serious illness/injury of family members, parental separation or divorce, etc.). For each event, indicate the age at which this occurred for you and your sibling.		

Based on this comparison, what did you conclude about the nature of the shared environment between you and your sibling? In what ways did you have environments that were not shared that may have contributed to differences between you and your sibling?

Birth Order

There have been several broad descriptions of differences between siblings by birth order, based on the idea that children have different experiences and play different roles in the family depending on whether they were born first, in the middle, or last. Personality research describes firstborn children as high achievers who behave responsibly, middle children as more socially skilled and popular, and youngest as the spoiled, rebellious, and artistic ones (Eckstein et al., 2010). However, the evidence for these differences is mixed, at best. One of the problems with this research is that birth order is confounded with family size, which is further confounded with other family characteristics such as ethnicity, education, and wealth (Hartshorne, 2009). The best we can say is that any effect of birth order on personality characteristics is extremely small and not consistent across studies.

Differential Parental Treatment

Parents are often quick to say that they treat all the children in their family the same, but the children themselves often disagree. Although parents may *love* their children the same, the way they actually treat their children can be quite variable. This really shouldn't be surprising given that children within the same family differ by age and gender, as well as by a number of personality and temperament characteristics (Plomin, Asbury, & Dunn, 2001). However, siblings who are treated in a less favorable way—or *perceive* that they are treated less favorably—show lower levels of adjustment and have more conflicted sibling relationships (Jensen & Whiteman, 2014; Jensen, Whiteman, Fingerman, & Birditt, 2013; Siennick, 2013) and can even be at an increased risk of engaging in delinquent activities (Jensen & Whiteman, 2014; Scholte, Engles, de Kemp, Harakeh, & Overbeek, 2007).

Of course, in one situation, differential treatment between siblings is almost inevitable, and that is in the case of stepsiblings (Baham, Weimer, Braver, & Fabricius, 2008). Each parent in the family likely has a qualitatively different relationship with his or her biological children and his or her stepchildren; plus, each stepsibling has a different biological parent who comes into the mix. Under these complex circumstances, it is not surprising if rivalries or conflicts develop.

The impact of differential parental treatment of siblings is lessened if a child who receives less attention or is treated more harshly sees the differential treatment as legitimate or justified. For instance, when one of the siblings in a family has a developmental disability or other condition that necessitates the special treatment by the parents, the healthy sibling usually recognizes and accepts that difference in parental treatment (Schuntermann, 2007).

ONLY CHILDREN

American families have gotten smaller in recent years for a number of reasons. Women may choose to remain childless, couples marry and begin their childbearing at later ages, and the cost of raising children continues to climb. In 2010, there were over 15 million one-child households in the United States (U.S. Census Bureau, 2012a). There are a number of negative ideas about what only children are like (Mancillas, 2006). If only children have their parents' exclusive attention, won't they be selfish or totally dependent on others when they grow up? If they don't have social interactions with siblings, won't they lack communication or social skills?

The good news for only children is that, contrary to the popular stereotype, research has failed to support these negative predictions. Rather, it has found that only children share many of the advantages that firstborn children enjoy: They show high achievement, good adjustment, strong character, and positive social relationships (Falbo, 2012). That also suggests that they are *not* unique. They instead look like other children who have had the same advantage of having parent-child relationships that support positive development and high achievement.

TRUE/FALSE VIDEO ▲

T ☐ **F** ☐ Children who grow up without siblings tend to be more self-centered, maladjusted, lonely, and neurotic than children who have siblings. **False**

CHECK YOUR UNDERSTANDING

1. Explain why we describe a family as a system.
2. What are the effects of maternal employment on children?
3. What are some differences in how mothers and fathers parent?
4. How is the sibling relationship different from other relationships?

SOCIALIZATION IN CHILDHOOD AND ADOLESCENCE

13.3 How do parents socialize their children?

We have talked about several different types of families and relationships within families thus far, but what is the *function* of a family? Families provide children with many things, including the basic necessities of life, love, education, supervision, and control, and parents are the first teachers and the models of what social relationships are like. In a process called *socialization,* parents teach children how to interact in appropriate ways according to the rules and norms of their society (Damon, 2006). The main goal of socialization is the **internalization** of these social norms. We now look at how parents try to promote their children's ability to understand society's expectations for their behavior, to act on this understanding, and to make those values a part of how to guide their own behavior.

The way we have thought about this process has changed over time, reflecting changes in both our philosophical beliefs about the nature of children and families and our growing understanding of the factors that influence child development. **Journey of Research: Changing Views of Parenting** describes some of these changes.

Internalization The process by which individuals adopt the attitudes, beliefs, and values held by their society.

JOURNEY OF *Research*

Changing Views of Parenting

Parents have received just about every type of advice possible with regard to childrearing. Philosopher Thomas Hobbes portrayed children as sinful by nature and in need of firm discipline. Freud portrayed childhood as a critical time in which parents' handling of eating, sleeping, and bodily functions would make a lasting impression on the child's development. In the early 20th century, John Watson, the father of behaviorism, warned parents against showing too much affection toward their children because it would make them overly dependent on their parents. Watson advocated maintaining a strict schedule and treating even very young children like young adults, but the research on attachment in the 1940s and 1950s advocated for parents being sensitive and responsive to the needs of their children rather than making them adhere to a strict schedule. Dr. Benjamin Spock popularized an approach to parenting that struck a middle ground between Freud's leniency and Watson's unresponsiveness, and his ideas remained popular through the 1970s. In the 1960s, the influential research on parenting by Diana Baumrind emphasized both parental warmth and firm control of children. We elaborate on her ideas just a bit later in this chapter.

Whether we think of children as fragile or resilient, as in need of a firm hand or of tolerance, all of these different approaches to parenting share one thing in common: They all assume that what parents do makes their children the type of people they become. This is called a **parent effects model** because it assumes that parents are responsible for the characteristics that we see in their children.

Parent effects model
A model of parenting effects that assumes that parents cause the characteristics that we see in their children.

However, it became clear that in some cases, it was characteristics of the child that seemed to be driving the process and determining the parenting style that the parents used. This idea is called a **child effects model**. Stop for a minute and think about what characteristics of a child would be so powerful that they could determine a parent's parenting style. Did you think about the child's age and gender? Of course both of these child characteristics influence how parents treat different children. For instance, as infants become toddlers and begin to do more things on their own, their growing independence affects their parents, who react by exerting greater control over their child's behavior. And when children become adolescents, parents typically respond to their growing maturation by granting them greater autonomy. The child's gender is another important characteristic that elicits different types of parenting behavior. Parents often exercise more control over their daughters and show more warmth and affection to them, while granting greater autonomy to (or exercising less control over) their sons. Another situation in which the child can drive the parenting process is when the child has some extreme characteristics that parents react to. As an example, children who are extremely defiant or oppositional evoke harsher and more controlling behavior from their parents than children who are more obedient or compliant.

Child effects model
A model that assumes it is the characteristics of the child that determine the parenting style parents use.

The model of parenting used most often today is the **transactional model,** in which the influence moves in both directions as part of an ongoing process. Parents do influence their children's behavior, but children also influence their parents' behavior. Parents respond to characteristics of their children (for example, age, gender, temperament) and exert effort to shape their behavior, but children are not passive recipients of these efforts. Their responses to these efforts feed back and influence future parenting behaviors, as parents try to adapt to changing characteristics of their child. For instance, a child's oppositional behavior can result in parents escalating their efforts to forcefully control the child's misbehavior, which in turn can provoke greater misbehavior on the part of the child. Fortunately, this process can (and usually does) work in a positive direction.

Transactional model
A model of parenting effects that assumes that influence moves from parent to child but also from child to parent in a reciprocal process.

When a child or an adolescent behaves in a responsible or competent way, parents are likely to respond by granting more autonomy or relinquishing some parental control, which in turn gives the child or adolescent the new opportunity to continue developing autonomy as he or she moves toward greater maturity.

Finally, parenting research has increasingly recognized the role that context plays in influencing parental behavior. Parenting styles research has begun looking at the powerful influence of cultural values, expectations, and customs on parenting styles, as well as how parents adapt their parenting style to the characteristics of the communities and neighborhoods in which they live. This is another situation where, as we described in Chapter 10, the best situation is one in which there is a *goodness of fit* between the characteristics of the environment and the characteristics of the child.

As you read about parenting strategies and styles on the following pages, try to identify which of these differing views are reflected in the research.

PARENTING STRATEGIES AND TECHNIQUES

There are many different techniques that parents use to teach their children appropriate behavior. Which specific technique they choose will vary, of course, based on a number of factors including the parent's own personality characteristics, the way the parent was raised, the parent's understanding of the nature of child development, and the characteristics of the child.

Positive Discipline

There are a number of discipline strategies that parents use to help children learn from their experiences, develop a sense of competence, and build their self-esteem. **Inductive discipline** sets clear limits for children, gives consequences for negative behavior, and provides explanations to the child about why the behavior was wrong and what he might do to fix the situation (Hoeve et al., 2009). Induction can be further divided into **self-oriented induction** which asks the child to think about the consequences that the child might experience as a result of his behavior—for example, "Put the cookie back [setting limits], or you will ruin your appetite for dinner [explaining why]," and **other-oriented induction** in which the child focuses on the consequences of the child's behavior for someone else—for example, "Look how sad Joey looks when you said that mean thing to him. Can you help him feel better?" (Gibbs, 2014).

In many situations, parents influence their children's behavior simply because children recognize and respect their parents' authority (Gibbs, 2014). When using the **command strategy,** parents simply state what should be done. They do not make any overt threats of punishment, but the child responds to the legitimate authority that the parent has to make this request—for example, "It is time to turn off your computer and get ready for bed."

You'll remember that according to social cognitive theory, behavior changes through the processes of modeling and imitation, and we are more likely to want to imitate models we like or admire. In the technique of **relationship maintenance,** parents try to create a positive relationship with their child so that they will have a greater influence on the child's behavior or be a more attractive model for the child to imitate. When parents display affection toward a child, praise the child for things she has done well in the past, or show that they understand how the child feels, it helps motivate the child to comply with what the parents want the child to do (Grusec, Goodnow, & Kuczynski, 2000).

Inductive discipline A parenting technique that involves setting clear limits for children and explaining the consequences for negative behavior, why the behavior was wrong, and what the child might do to fix the situation.

Self-oriented induction A parenting technique in which the child is asked to think about the consequences that the child might experience as a result of his behavior.

Other-oriented induction A parenting technique in which the child thinks about consequences of the child's behavior for someone else.

Command strategy A parenting technique in which the parent does not make any overt threats of punishment, but the child responds to the legitimate authority that the parent has to make a request of the child.

Relationship maintenance A parenting technique in which the parents try to create a positive relationship with their child so that they will have a greater influence on the child's behavior.

What are the outcomes of each of these strategies? The use of inductive discipline has been related to reduced problem behavior, such as aggression (Choe et al., 2013), and greater empathy which results in more prosocial behavior in children. Induction is seen by adolescents as a more appropriate discipline strategy than alternatives such as power assertion or **love withdrawal** (Padilla-Walker & Carlo, 2004). When induction is paired with parental expression of disappointment in the adolescent, it is particularly effective because the parental disappointment expresses the idea that the parent knows the adolescent could do better (Patrick & Gibbs, 2012).

Although inductive discipline is beneficial to children in Western cultures, the same may not be true in all cultures. You can see how a discipline strategy that gives children the opportunity to make choices within certain limits and tells them how they can rectify a situation if they do something wrong fits well with cultural values that emphasize choice, independence, and self-motivation. The same would not be as effective for children in a culture that emphasizes interdependence, behavior that is proper in the eyes of others, and a hierarchical family structure. For instance, in Japan if a child misbehaves, rather than reprimanding the child, the mother is likely to apologize for the child's behavior to anyone who saw what happened (Miyake & Yamazaki, 1995). The mother's apology preserves the social harmony with others while also preserving her close emotional bond with the child.

Negative Discipline

In contrast to these types of positive discipline, **power assertion** is a technique that relies on the parents' superior power to compel the child to do what the parents want her to do. Power assertion may use physical or nonphysical threats of punishment. Another approach is **psychological control** which uses psychological or emotional manipulation to get the child to comply with what the parent wants (Cui, Morris, Criss, Houltberg, & Silk, 2014). The manipulation might involve making the child feel guilty for what she has done, threatening to withdraw love unless the child does what the parent wants, or invalidating the child's feelings. In this case, parental love and acceptance is always dependent upon the child's behavior. For instance, a parent might say, "I'm not speaking to you until you apologize." The child is then pressured to make decisions based upon what his parents want and need, rather than on his own wants and needs (Oudekerk, Allen, Hessel, & Molloy, 2015).

While some power assertion or psychological control may be necessary from time to time to get the child's attention, it is the more positive approaches that help the child internalize ideas about what is good and bad behavior (Choe, Olson, & Sameroff, 2013; Hoffman, 2000; Kristjánsson, 2004). A steady reliance on psychological control has been associated with an increased incidence of depression and higher levels of aggression in children (Cui et al., 2014), and problems establishing and maintaining friendships as well as romantic relationships in adolescence (Oudekerk et al., 2015).

Cultural expectations affect how the child perceives these parental behaviors. As an example, African American parents are more likely than Anglo American parents to use power assertion as a discipline technique. Parental power assertion usually makes children feel angry, resentful, and disconnected from the parent and can lead to a number of negative behaviors (Kim & Kochanska, 2015). Physical punishment has been linked with an increased level of bullying and fighting (Ohene, Ireland, McNeely, & Borowsky, 2006) and an increased likelihood of delinquency in adolescents (Hoeve et al., 2009). However, whereas Anglo American parents often combine power assertion with love withdrawal, in African American families, power assertion more often occurs in the context of a loving and warm relationship and in this context, it does not have the same negative consequences for the children. In fact, in this cultural context, strong control is often linked with better outcomes for these children, perhaps because exerting strong parental control is more often seen by African American parents and their children as a legitimate role for parents (Lansford, Deater-Deckard, Dodge, Bates, & Pettit, 2004).

Love withdrawal A parenting technique in which parents threaten to withhold their love until a child conforms to the parents' expectations for his behavior.

Power assertion A disciplinary technique that emphasizes control of the child's behavior through physical and nonphysical punishment.

Psychological control The use of psychological or emotional manipulation to get a child to comply with what the parent wants.

Despite the evidence that power assertion in the form of physical punishment can have negative effects, many parents continue to rely on spanking as a way to try to control their child's behavior. Statistics on the use of spanking vary dramatically from one study to the next, but in a 2013 Harris Interactive Poll of American parents, two-thirds of the parents said they have spanked their children. The good news is that this was down from 80% in 1995, and younger parents were less likely to have spanked their children than older parents. This change is positive because there is no evidence that spanking is a positive socialization practice (Gershoff, 2013). When children are spanked, they become angry and resentful. This emotional distress gets in the way of hearing their parent's message about correct behavior and they are less likely to internalize the values that the parent is trying to instill in them.

Power assertion. This father is reprimanding his son, but in the cultural context of a warm, positive relationship this reprimand is not likely to have a negative effect on the child's subsequent behavior.

Why then do so many parents continue to rely on spanking? Because it can be an effective way to immediately stop a behavior. However, there are several reasons why it is not a good long-term strategy for changing a child's behavior. First, while spanking can be an effective way to stop a behavior, it does not help children understand how to control themselves in the long run. Second, because parents may be out of control themselves when they spank their children, they model exactly the opposite of what they want their children to learn. And third, physical punishment can cross a line and become abusive, and abuse is clearly linked with negative outcomes for children. The impact of child abuse is covered in detail in Chapter 15.

You might wonder whether some parents are more strict and punitive with their children because their children are more difficult to control. In that case, the parents' punitive behavior would be a response to the child's behavior rather than the cause of later problems. This is a very reasonable question to ask, but parents' use of spanking is more likely to precede and escalate children's aggressive behavior rather than the other way around (Gershoff, 2013; MacKenzie, Nichlas, Waldfogel, & Brooks-Gunn, 2013). The most important factor determining whether parents are likely to use power assertion with their children was whether they themselves were raised that way (Hoeve et al., 2009).

Parents are not always consistent in the way they discipline their children. Even parents who usually use positive discipline strategies may resort to using power assertion when they are under stress, especially when they are in a bad mood; when they believe the child's bad behavior was deliberate rather than accidental; or when the child has done something hurtful to others rather than commit some minor infraction of the rules (Critchley & Sanson, 2006).

PARENTING STYLES

Next we examine different parenting styles that are based, in part, on the techniques and strategies that parents use as part of the socialization process. Diana Baumrind (1971, 2013) took dimensions that had appeared repeatedly in previous research on parenting and combined them to describe four different parenting styles.

The first dimension is parental acceptance/responsiveness, and the second is parental demandingness/control. Parents can be high or low on each of these dimensions. Parents who are high on **acceptance/responsiveness** show a good deal of warmth and affection in their relationship with their child and provide a lot of praise and encouragement. In contrast, parents who are low on this dimension can be cool and even rejecting and they

Acceptance/ responsiveness A dimension of parenting that measures the amount of warmth and affection in the parent-child relationship.

FIGURE 13.8

Baumrind's parenting styles. By combining two important dimensions of parenting—acceptance/responsiveness and demandingness/control— Diana Baumrind described four different parenting styles.

		Acceptance/Responsiveness	
		High	Low
Demandingness/Control	High	Authoritative	Authoritarian
	Low	Permissive	Disengaged

Demandingness/control A dimension of parenting that measures the amount of restrictiveness and structure that parents place on their children.

Authoritative parents Parents who combine high levels of control with a good deal of warmth and encouragement, together with reasonable expectations and explanation of the parents' rules.

Authoritarian parents Parents who combine high levels of control and low levels of warmth, and who expect compliance from the child.

Permissive parents Parents who provide a great deal of warmth and acceptance but few, if any, rules or restrictions.

Disengaged parents Parents who do not set limits or rules for their children and are not emotionally connected to them.

Parenting styles Fairly regular and consistent patterns of interacting with children.

are more likely to criticize or punish the child than to praise him. Parents who are high on the **demandingness/control** dimension promote and expect appropriate mature behavior from their children and will step in to control their misbehavior (Baumrind, Larzelere, & Owens, 2010). In contrast, parents who are low on this dimension impose much less structure and fewer limits on their children. If we combine these two dimensions, we get the four distinct parenting styles shown in Figure 13.8.

Authoritative parents combine high levels of control with a good deal of warmth and encouragement. Although they do make demands on their children, their expectations are reasonable and appropriate for the child's age and are directed at specific behaviors they want the child to change (Baumrind, 2013). A hallmark of this style is that they are willing to provide rationales for their rules and expectations and are open to listening to their children's point of view (Heath, 2005). Sometimes they are even persuaded by their children to be flexible about the rules because the situation warrants it. Overall, these parents treat their children with respect and respond to their child's unique characteristics.

Authoritarian parents are high on control and often have a large number of rules that they expect their children to obey. These parents highly value unquestioning compliance from their children. They feel no obligation to explain the reasons for their rules and are generally unyielding about the rules themselves. They are not sensitive to the feelings of their children and are, therefore, considered low on the dimension of acceptance/responsiveness. The most negative aspect of this kind of parenting is discipline that is arbitrary, harsh, and demanding (Baumrind et al., 2010).

Permissive parents provide a great deal of warmth and acceptance to their children, but this acceptance is coupled with few, if any, rules or restrictions. Children are free to express their ideas and opinions (often having an equal say with parents in decision making in the family), and parents usually do little monitoring or restricting of the child's activities.

Disengaged parents provide neither control nor warmth to their children (Baumrind, 2013). They do not make demands for good behavior or set rules or limits, and they also are not emotionally connected to their children. Some parents in this category are so consumed with problems in their own lives that they appear to have nothing left to give to their relationship with their children.

These brief descriptions provide a good sense of these different parenting styles, but parents do not always fit neat, clear-cut textbook descriptions. Even the most authoritarian parent might relent and show some flexibility occasionally, and even the most permissive parent might have to draw the line at some point and stop a child's misbehavior. However, **parenting styles** are fairly regular and consistent patterns that play themselves out in a variety of situations. It would not be surprising if, as you read these descriptions, some parents you know came to mind for at least a couple of them.

Consequences of Parenting Styles

A great deal of research has been done on the consequences of each of these different parenting styles. In this section we describe what this research has shown, but bear in mind that most of the research has been done on White, middle-class children from Western cultures. Because the characteristics of different cultures influence which parenting styles parents use and the consequences for children, we will describe some of those cultural differences in the next section of the chapter.

Baumrind's research has continued for over 45 years. In both the original and the current longitudinal research, children raised by authoritative parents have been found to be "the most self-reliant, self-controlled, explorative, and content" (Baumrind, 1971, p. 1; see also Baumrind et al., 2010). The positive achievement orientation that Baumrind (1967) found in preschool children raised by authoritative parents continues to be reflected in the academic achievement of older children and adolescents (Pinquart, 2015).

Compared to children raised with the other parenting styles, children raised by authoritative parents are more likely to be seen as outgoing; as leaders (Baumrind, 1991); as more cooperative with peers, siblings, and adults (Denham, Renwick, & Holt, 1991); and as more empathetic and altruistic (Aunola et al., 2000). They also have been found to have higher self-esteem (McClun & Merrell, 1998), to be more self-reliant (Steinberg, Mounts, Lamborn, & Dornbusch, 1991), and are less likely to use substances (Adamczyk-Robinette, Fletcher, & Wright, 2002; Fletcher & Jefferies, 1999; Gray & Steinberg, 1999).

In comparison, children raised by authoritarian parents are more likely to be defiant, resentful, and withdrawn (Baumrind, 2013). Two of the most destructive aspects associated with authoritarian parenting are verbal hostility and intrusive control (Baumrind et al., 2010). Baumrind described the situation as one in which children feel trapped and angry, but are afraid to protest because of the possible negative consequences. Authoritarian parents often rely on physical punishment, so they model aggressive behaviors for their children. This may help explain why authoritarian parenting has been associated with a child becoming a bully (Baldry & Farrington, 2000). A child who has, in effect, been bullied by authoritarian parents may vent the resulting anger and frustration he or she feels on other weaker victims. Children of authoritarian parents have lower self-esteem (Martinez & Garcia, 2008; Rudy & Grusec, 2006), lower psychosocial maturity (Mantzicopoulos & Oh-Hwang, 1998), a lower level of moral reasoning (Boyes & Allen, 1993), and are more likely to have both externalizing and internalizing behavior problems (Fletcher, Walls, Cooks, Madison, & Bridges, 2008). The picture that emerges suggests that across a range of developmental outcomes, authoritarian parenting has negative repercussions for child development.

Children raised by permissive parents were described as "the least self-reliant, explorative, and self-controlled" (Baumrind, 1971, p. 2). Permissive parents are the other extreme on the dimension of control, although they combine permissiveness with a good deal of warmth and affection. Parents may choose this style with the best of intentions, but the child outcomes are not particularly positive. Adolescents who had experienced permissive parenting as preschoolers were less autonomous, perhaps as a result of having a less solid grounding in appropriate expectations and controls in their early years (Baumrind et al., 2010). Nijhof and Engels (2007) describe children of permissive parents as "self-centered, impulsive and aggressive" (p. 711), as having poor social skills, and as feeling unworthy of the love of another person.

Children with disengaged parents have the worst outcomes. Both young children and young adolescents who are raised by parents who are less warm and less involved have been found to be more angry and defiant (Miller, Cowan, Cowan, Hetherington, & Clingempeel, 1993). In middle childhood, they have lower levels of academic achievement (Murray, 2012) and as adolescents, they score more poorly than peers on measures of psychosocial development (self-reliance, work orientation, social competence), school achievement (grade point average, school orientation), internalized distress (psychological and somatic symptoms), and problem behavior such as drug use and delinquency (Lamborn, Mounts, Steinberg, & Dornbusch, 1991).

Table 13.2 summarizes the parent behaviors and child outcomes for each of these styles of parenting.

TABLE 13.2

Parenting styles and their outcomes. Research over the last 45 years has linked the four parenting styles described by Diana Baumrind with certain outcomes for children.

Parenting Style	Parent Behaviors	Child Outcomes
Authoritative	High levels of control and a good deal of warmth and encouragement. Inductive discipline.	Outgoing, leaders, more cooperative, more empathetic and altruistic, higher self-esteem, more self-reliant and less likely to use substances.
Authoritarian	High on control and not sensitive to the feelings of their children. Discipline that is arbitrary, harsh, and demanding.	Defiant, resentful, and withdrawn, bullying, lower self-esteem, lower psychosocial maturity, lower level of moral reasoning, more likely to have both externalizing and internalizing behavior problems.
Permissive	Warmth and acceptance coupled with few, if any, rules or restrictions. Little monitoring or discipline.	Least self-reliant, explorative, and self-controlled, less autonomous, self-centered, impulsive, and aggressive. Poor social skills, and feeling unworthy of the love of another person.
Disengaged	Neither control nor warmth. Minimal discipline.	More angry and defiant, lower levels of academic achievement, lower psychosocial maturity and school achievement, more internalized distress and problem behavior such as drug use and delinquency.

You are likely to have some reaction when you see the photo in **Active Learning: How Parents React.** This active learning will help you to better understand how parents with different parenting styles would deal with this situation. How would you react?

Active LEARNING

How Parents React

Imagine that a parent comes into the living room to find this scene. Now think about each parenting style that Diana Baumrind has identified. Describe what you think an authoritative parent would say and do. Next do the same for an authoritarian parent, a permissive parent, and a disengaged parent. Now imagine that you are one of these children and think about what you would learn from the response of each type of parent. In the long run, which type of response is likely to be most effective in making you want to behave differently in the future? Why?

©iStockphoto.com/BanksPhotos

Parenting in Cultural Context

Parenting is not something that happens in a vacuum. It happens in a context—whether a cultural, socioeconomic, or familial context—and it reflects the values and beliefs found in that context (Davidov, Grusec, & Wolfe, 2012; Lansford et al., 2005). As an example, research in Southern European and Latin American countries has not always found the same negative effects of permissive parenting as found in the United States and for some outcomes, children with permissive parents did even better than children with authoritative parents (Calafat, García, Juan, Becoña, & Fernández-Hermida, 2014; Garcia & Gracia, 2009). Authoritarian parenting in collectivist cultures such as Egypt, Iran, India, and Pakistan teaches children to inhibit the expression of their own wants and needs in accordance with their culture's expectations and is not associated with lower self-esteem in these children (Rudy & Grusec, 2006). The more authoritarian style adopted by many African American parents emphasizes important values in that culture, such as respect for authority and an obligation to family (Jambunathan, Burts, & Pierce, 2000). It has been suggested that when physical discipline is the cultural norm, as it is in many of these African American families, children understand and accept it and consequently it is not as likely to lead to the aggressiveness typically seen in children living in cultures where it is associated with parental rejection (Lansford & Deater-Deckard, 2012).

Research with Latino families has failed to find a consistent parenting style, perhaps because Baumrind's parenting types do not characterize Latino parenting very well (Jambunathan et al., 2000). Although Latino families are not a singular group, whether their country of origin is Mexico, Cuba, Puerto Rico, or a country in Central or South America, there are several shared cultural values that influence how parents raise their children (Halgunseth, Ispa, & Rudy, 2006). The first is *familismo*, which includes a strong desire to maintain family ties, to be loyal to the family, and to give the needs of the family priority over one's own needs, together with a belief that one's family will be available to provide instrumental and emotional support when it is needed. The second is *respeto*, which requires that individuals fulfill the expectations for their social roles and maintain harmonious interpersonal relationships through respect of themselves and others. The third is *educación*, which is a broader concept than academics. It involves "training in responsibility, morality and interpersonal relationships" (Halgunseth et al., 2006, p. 1286).

We see these cultural values reflected in several specific parenting behaviors. Latino parents engage in more physical guidance of young children, more parental direction and modeling for school-age children, and more rule setting and monitoring for adolescents. All of these behaviors have been associated with good outcomes for their children (Halgunseth et al., 2006). Because of the position of respect that Latino fathers occupy within the family, it is the father's responsibility to set the family rules. Although there are more rules in Latino families, adolescents are less willing to confront their fathers about the rules and suffer greater distress when there is conflict within the family (Crean, 2008). Because cultural values can change as families become more acculturated to their new countries, the role of fathers in Latino families in the United States may be undergoing some change. There is some evidence that Latino fathers in the United States are becoming more nurturant and less authoritarian than they were in the past (Jambunathan et al., 2000).

Although Chinese parents are more controlling than Euro-American parents, their children typically do well in school. When children reach school age, Chinese mothers provide the drive for their children's efforts to succeed in school, but do this in the context of the warm, supportive, and physically close relationship that was established when the child was much younger. Another important concept in Chinese culture is *guan*, which literally means "to govern" but can also mean "to care for" or even "to love" (Yi, 2013). The close monitoring and correcting of a child's behavior is seen by both parent and child as fulfilling parental responsibilities to the child and in the child's best interest. All of these findings remind us to be careful to take cultural norms into consideration whenever we discuss parenting approaches. Good parenting does not look the same in all cultures.

T ☐ F ☐ Good parenting is good parenting, so the same parenting strategies work equally well for all children. **False**

Congruence of Parenting Styles

Much of the research on parenting has looked at mothers' parenting styles (Winsler, Madigan, & Aquilino, 2005), but once researchers began to look at fathers' parenting styles as well, the issue of how much agreement there was between mothers and fathers arose. Several consistent differences between mothers and fathers have been found. Mothers are more likely than fathers to use an authoritative style, and fathers are more likely than mothers to use an authoritarian style (Russell, Hart, Robinson, & Olsen, 2003; Winsler et al., 2005).

Within the same family, the congruence between parents' styles is only modest. In one study, there was fairly high agreement between parents who were permissive, moderate agreement between parents in families where one parent was authoritarian, and no agreement in families where one parent was authoritative (Winsler et al., 2005). What can explain these differences? Being a permissive parent is often an intentional choice by parents who want to create a specific type of child rearing environment, so these parents may discuss and reach agreement on this philosophy of child rearing. In other families, one parent may adopt a style that balances the style of the other parent. If one parent is authoritarian, it may be more important that the second parent balance that style by being authoritative or even permissive. However, if one parent is authoritative, it may matter less which style the second parent adopts.

Fortunately, children can adapt to the fact that their parents have different styles of interacting with them, and, of course, children sometimes try to use these differences to their own advantage. When children want something from their parents, they often have a pretty good idea of which parent to approach and just how to frame that request to increase the chance that they will get what they want. The one potential problem with this is if the lack of agreement between parents becomes a source of conflict within the family.

In conclusion, the relationship between parenting behaviors and children's outcomes is complex and multidimensional. In addition to considering the direction of the effect, we need to consider characteristics of both the children and the situation. Cultural values, neighborhood characteristics, and socioeconomic status will have an impact on these outcomes, but it is clear that one reason that we see the variations that we do is because parents try to adjust and adapt their parenting to find what works best for their children. **Active Learning: Exploring Your Parents' Style** guides you in connecting the experiences you have had with your own parents to the ideas presented here.

Active LEARNING

Exploring Your Parents' Style

Based on what you have learned about parenting styles, reflect on how you were parented while you were growing up by answering these questions:

- What style of parenting did each of your parents use? Did they use the same or different styles?
- Can you identify any values associated with your socioeconomic or cultural background that were reflected in their parenting style?
- If you have siblings, were there any differences in the styles your parents used with your siblings? Can you think of reasons why they may have treated siblings differently?
- How did your parents' parenting style affect you?
- Did their parenting style change as you grew older? If so, *how* did it change?
- What would you do differently with your own children? What would you do the same? Why?

CHANGES IN RELATIONSHIPS DURING ADOLESCENCE

Adolescence is a time of great change, so it is not surprising that these changes are reflected in changes in adolescents' relationships with their parents. Although most adolescents maintain their attachment to their parents, a renegotiation of that relationship occurs (Collins & Laursen, 2004). Both warmth and control from parents will look different in adolescence than it did earlier in childhood.

Increasing Autonomy

Developing autonomy, or a sense that you are your own person, is a central task of adolescence. As this happens, adolescents are less willing than children to accept the unilateral authority of their parents, so decision making within the family moves toward becoming more of a shared process in most families (Hill, Bromell, Tyson, & Flint, 2007). If parents try to exercise the same type of strict behavioral control they used in childhood, this approach can backfire and result in adolescent misconduct and rebelliousness. On the other hand, if parents relinquish some control and replace it with monitoring and tracking of their adolescent's activities, the teen is more likely accept it as legitimate and to comply with parents' expectations (Darling, Cumsille, & Martínez, 2008).

Other changes in the parent-adolescent relationship that have consistently been found include the fact that adolescents spend less time with their parents (Brown, 2004). There is, however, a daily opportunity for family members to be together, and that is family mealtime. Although the popular perception is that families no longer eat together, national surveys have found that more than half of families surveyed report that they have three to five meals together each week (Fiese & Schwartz, 2008). In one study, 58% of adolescents reported having dinner with their family at least five times a week (National Center on Addiction and Substance Abuse at Columbia University, 2006) and most teens report enjoying meals with their families and eat more healthfully when they share family meals (Neumark-Sztainer, 2008). Although these meals last only 20 minutes on average, evidence has shown that families who share meals have children who are less likely to be obese or have other eating disorders, less likely to use drugs and alcohol,

and more likely to succeed in school (Fiese & Schwartz, 2008). The positive effects of family mealtime were attributed to its ability to strengthen family relationships and build communication between members. However, the use of media, such as texting, watching television, or playing videogames, can interfere with the closeness that family meals can foster. Of course, mealtime is not the only way that parents connect with their teens and may be as much an indicator of overall family functioning as a factor in and of itself. It is important for parents to connect with their children and teens in all the various ways possible, even if it is difficult to have family dinners on a regular basis (Meier & Musick, 2012). **Active Learning: Family Mealtime** will guide you in thinking about your own family's experiences with mealtimes.

T ☐ F ☐ More than half of American adolescents say they eat a meal together as a family five or more times a week.
True

Ariel Skelley/Blend Images/Getty Images

Family dinnertime. Families exchange more than food when they sit down to meals together. Family members have a chance to share the events of the day and spend time together.

Active LEARNING

Family Mealtime

Think about your own family when you were a child and a teenager. How often did your family eat together? Did the frequency of eating together change from childhood to adolescence, and if it did, how did it change? When you ate together, remember what types of things were discussed and what the atmosphere was. What interfered with your family eating together: job responsibilities, sports, or other extracurricular activities? Was the TV on in the room on a regular basis? Were there rules about use of individual media, such as cell phones, at the table? If so, what impact did this have on family interaction? What kind of food was served—homemade, frozen, or fast food? Now consider your own experience in light of the general findings that connect family dinners with positive outcomes. How does your experience fit or not fit with this research? What does this activity tell you about your own experience, but also what does it tell you about how the research might be refined so that it could capture other pertinent issues?

T ☐ F ☐
Mother-daughter relationships are the closest family relationship during adolescence, and father-daughter relationships have the greatest amount of conflict. **False**

Adolescents also report they feel less emotional closeness to their parents as they move through adolescence but, despite this emotional distancing, parents remain important people in the lives of most adolescents (Shearer, Crouter, & McHale, 2005; Smetana, Metzger, & Campione-Barr, 2004; Steinberg & Silk, 2002). There are some consistent differences that appear between adolescents' relationships with their mother and with their father. Adolescents report spending less time with their father than with their mother, and report feeling closer to their mother than their father (Galambos & Kotylak, 2012; Shearer et al., 2005; Steinberg & Silk, 2002). Father-daughter relationships are typically the most distant parent-adolescent relationship (Shearer et al., 2005). Although mother-daughter relationships are the closest, they also are the ones marked by more conflict, particularly around the time of puberty (Steinberg & Silk, 2002). In fact, mothers of both sons and daughters are more likely to experience conflict with their adolescents than fathers do, perhaps because they spend more time in contact with their children (Shearer et al., 2005). However, one review of studies on parent-adolescent relationships found differences between parents' interactions with sons and daughters in only about 40% of studies (Russell & Saebel, 1997), so these gender differences may not be as great as is commonly believed.

Parent-Adolescent Conflict

Although many believe that adolescents' relationships with their parents are marked by significant amounts of conflict, there is little research support for this idea. While it is not unusual to find some level of conflict in most American families, there is a good deal of variability from one family to another (Smetana, 2011). The idea that adolescence is a time of conflict and alienation between adolescents and their families probably describes no more than 20% of families (Johnston, Walters, & Olesen, 2005). The *frequency* of conflict is highest in early adolescence and then declines as adolescents move into middle and late adolescence, but the *intensity* of conflict, when it does occur, tends to increase across adolescence (Laursen, Coy, & Collins, 1998; De Goede, Branje, & Meeus, 2009; Van Doorn, Branje, & Meeus, 2011). In **Active Learning: Sources of Parent-Adolescent Conflict,** you can explore the kinds of issues that cause conflict in families.

T ☐ F ☐ A good deal of parent-adolescent conflict is normal in families with adolescents. **False**

Active LEARNING

Sources of Parent-Adolescent Conflict

In 1994, Brian K. Barber conducted research in which he asked 1,828 White, Black, and Hispanic families of adolescents to rank order the frequency of conflict in their family about each of the topics below. Go through the list and rank from 1 (most frequent) to 10 (least frequent) how often you think other families with adolescents have conflict about each of these topics. Then go through the list again and think back to your own experiences when you were in middle adolescence (about 14 to 16 years of age) and rank how often you had conflict with your parents about each of these topics (again with 1 for the most frequent topic of conflict down to 10 for the least frequent topic of conflict). When you are done, you can check your rankings against Barber's results below.

Topics of Conflict	In Most Families	In My Family
	1 = most frequent 10 = least frequent	
How the adolescent dresses		
The adolescent's boyfriend/girlfriend		
The adolescent's friends		
How late the adolescent stays out at night		
Helping around the house		
The adolescent's sexual behavior		
The adolescent's drinking, smoking, or drug use		
Money		
School		
Getting along with other family members		

This is the rank ordering of actual conflict from Barber's (1994) sample: (1) helping around the house (most frequent), (2) family relations, (3) school, (4) how the adolescent dresses, (5) money, (6) how late the adolescent stays out, (7) the adolescent's friends, (8) the adolescent's boyfriend/girlfriend, (9) substance use, (10) sexual behavior (least frequent) (p. 379).

Many people believe that conflict between adolescents and their parents typically focuses on explosive issues like adolescent sexuality or substance use, but when conflict occurs between parents and teens, it is much more likely to occur around ordinary, everyday events like homework, curfews, loud music, and messy rooms (Eisenberg et al., 2008; Smetana, 2011; Van Doorn et al., 2011). It would not be surprising if you identified these mundane issues as the most frequent sources of conflict in your family, even if you thought that *other families* were fighting about the big things.

It seems that issues that create conflict between adolescents and their parents have not changed much over the last few decades. A 2008 study found that the four most frequent sources of conflict between adolescents and their parents were cleaning chores, getting along with family, respect/manners, and school issues, and the least frequent sources of conflict

B2M Productions/Photodisc/Getty Images

It's all a matter of how you see it. One thing that contributes to conflict between adolescents and their parents is the different ways that they define issues. To this teen, a messy room is a matter of personal choice and is nobody's business but her own, but to her parents, it may be seen as a violation of social conventions.

were friends and dating and smoking or alcohol (Eisenberg et al., 2008). These findings are very similar to what Barber reported 14 years earlier.

Despite the way it might feel to families when it is happening, conflict is *not* necessarily bad during adolescence (Smetana, 2011). In individualistic societies, some level of conflict is an inevitable part of the individuation and identity development that normally occur during adolescence (Adams & Laursen, 2001). The challenge for parents of adolescents is to find the right balance between granting teens the autonomy they want and maintaining the connectedness or attachment that they need. Doing this is tricky because the right balance in early adolescence isn't the same as it will be in middle or late adolescence, so parents must be responsive to the developmental changes in their child. Conflict that takes place in the context of a warm, supportive family environment can foster personal growth (Smetana, 2011). Having a warm, supportive relationship with parents can reduce problem behaviors and enhance mental well-being, for both male and female adolescents (Hair, Moore, Garrett, Ling, & Cleveland, 2008).

The amount and type of conflict families will tolerate will differ from one cultural context to another. In countries with more collectivist values, such as India, adolescents' conflict with their parents is handled in a different way. As we saw with Western samples, conflicts in Indian families also are most likely to be about minor things, like homework and household chores (Kapadia, 2008). However, Indian culture emphasizes honoring parents and maintaining harmony within the family. Consequently, adolescents are more likely to compromise to meet their parents' expectations and demands rather than believe that they should decide for themselves what is best for them. Similar patterns for resolving parent-adolescent differences have been found in other collectivist cultures, such as Mexico and Korea (Phinney, Kim-Jo, Osorio, & Vilhjalmsdottir, 2005).

Parents would be relieved to know that although conflict does cause some disruption in the parent-adolescent relationship, its effects are usually temporary. Most families successfully weather their children's transition through adolescence without conflict doing any serious harm to the quality of their relationship (Shearer et al., 2005). In fact, parents of adolescents report that their relationship with their adolescent children becomes closer during the process and that there are more positive changes than negative ones (Shearer et al., 2005). Families are able to handle moderate levels of conflict because patterns of positive interactions have been laid down throughout childhood (McGue, Elkins, Walden, & Iacono, 2005). The relationship changes from one that is parent dominated to one that is more egalitarian, but the love, support, and responsiveness that were central to the earlier parent-child relationship remain strong as the child becomes an adolescent (Van Doorn et al., 2011).

CHECK YOUR UNDERSTANDING

1. Explain why spanking is not an effective way to change a child's behavior.
2. Which parenting style is associated with the best child outcomes for children in the United States and why is it effective?
3. Explain whether it is necessary for both parents in a family to adopt the same parenting style.
4. What are the typical causes of parent-adolescent conflict?

INTERVENTIONS FOR A BETTER FAMILY LIFE

13.4   What interventions are used to improve family life?

Ecological theory tells us that children and their families are affected by influences at many different levels, from broad cultural expectations, to government policies, to the neighborhoods in which they live, and to their own individual, even internal, experiences in life. When a family is struggling, intervention may occur at any of these levels, and support can be provided to families at different points in the development of the family. Some programs pick high-risk populations and try to intervene to prevent the development of problems, while other programs respond to problems that already exist. We obviously cannot describe all of these programs, but we give you a few examples to illustrate these approaches.

At the level of government, some of the social policies that influence families include those that are concerned with economic security, child care, education, health care, and reproductive rights (Hartman, 2003). For example, in Chapter 5 we described the Family and Medical Leave Act (FMLA) which allows workers up to 12 weeks of unpaid leave, with the guarantee that the parent can return to the same or a comparable job when they need to care for a newborn, adopt, or take a child into foster care, or to care for a family member with a serious health problem (U.S. Department of Labor, 2010). Since its passage in 1993, the act has been amended to extend leave for certain circumstances related to children and spouses on active military duty, and now recognizes same-sex partners as spouses under this law (Department of Labor, 2016).

While this is an improvement from when there was no job protection for parents who had children, it does not cover all workers. The provisions of the FMLA only apply to people who work in companies with at least 50 employees and the worker must have been employed for at least 1,250 hours for 1 year before the leave is taken. This is much less protection than governments in other countries offer. In France, parents can take off 16 to 26 weeks at 100% of their current salary, and they may take up to 2 years of unpaid leave (Stebbins, 2001). In Sweden, parents can share more than 12 months of paid leave to care for a new baby (Duvander & Andersson, 2006). Figure 13.9 shows a comparison between countries on the duration of paid maternity leave and the payment rate provided by that country's laws. As you can see, the United States is the only country with no provision for paid family leave.

Wraparound program A comprehensive set of services offered to families to strengthen them or reunite them.

Intervention for families can also come at the level of the community. One example is the Safe Start Promising Approaches program sponsored by the U.S. Department of Justice. This ongoing program was originally set up in 11 communities to help families with children ages 6 and younger who had been exposed to violence. As a **wraparound program,** it included services from the justice system, health and mental health care providers, and other human services (Arteaga & Lamb, 2008). Through this program, new screening protocols were used by police, schools, and others involved with children to identify more children who had been exposed to violence. As a result, children experienced less exposure to violence and fewer

Family therapy. Family therapy often helps children and adolescents by helping the family understand and change interactions within the whole family unit.

©iStockphoto.com/CEFutcher

FIGURE 13.9

Paid maternity leave, 2015. Do you see where the United States falls in this international comparison of the duration of paid maternity leave and percent of salary paid to new parents? American workers are not guaranteed any paid leave. That is why there is no bar next to the entry for the United States on this chart.

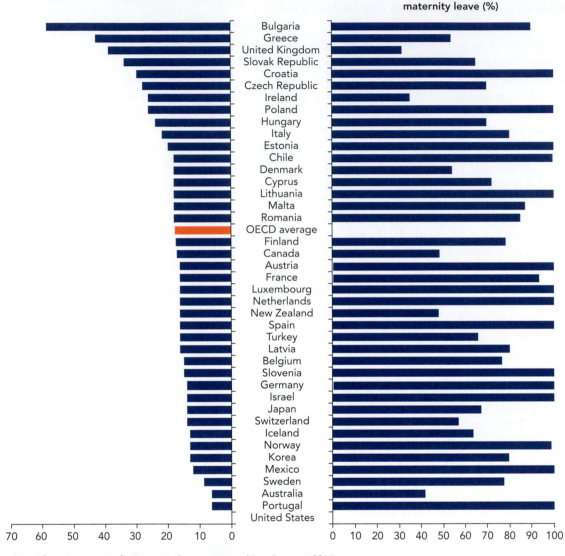

SOURCE: Adapted from Organisation for Economic Co-operation and Development (2016).

psychological symptoms and parents experienced less stress and showed a better understanding of the effects of violence on their children (Hyde, Lamb, Arteaga, & Chavis, 2008).

Interventions at the level of the individual family may consist of family therapy for those with identified difficulties. Often it is the child who presents with a problem, but the therapist meets with the whole family or with various combinations of family members, such as father and daughter or parents and one son (Fox, 2006). The therapist might be a psychiatrist, psychologist, social worker, or marriage and family therapy counselor. Family therapy typically begins with a family history, a discussion of the nature of the problem, and an evaluation of the family's strengths and possible barriers to treatment (Eyberg, Nelson, & Boggs, 2008). Interventions can include teaching parenting skills, helping parents understand their children's behavior, or helping parents with their own emotional problems. Therapists also may help families reflect on their interactions or may coach the families while they interact.

Another type of family-based program targets those families whose children are at high risk for developing psychological and behavioral problems and attempts to intervene *before* those problems emerge. For example, a program for preschool children with behavioral problems such as aggression and impulsivity provided an 8-week intervention the summer before the children began school. The goal of the program was to help the children develop skills to make a successful transition into kindergarten. In the classroom, trained educators used a behavior modification program to teach the children to follow instructions, complete tasks, comply with teacher instructions, and interact in a positive and cooperative way with peers. During this time, the children's parents received training on how to use the same behavioral management strategies with their children at home to reduce the problem behaviors (Graziano, Slavec, Hart, Garcia, & Pelham, 2014). All of the measures of school readiness, including emotional regulation and executive functioning, improved by the end of the intervention and these improvements were maintained at a 6-month follow up.

The authors of the book *From Neurons to Neighborhoods* conclude that interventions with families work best when they consist of "empowering parents as the true experts with respect to their own child's and family's needs and . . . building a strong, mutually respectful, working partnership in which parents and professionals relate comfortably in a collaborative effort to achieve family-driven objectives" (Shonkoff & Phillips, 2000, p. 366). To find and evaluate intervention programs available to families in your community, try **Active Learning: Finding Community Resources.**

Active LEARNING

Finding Community Resources

Most communities have a number of programs available that can assist families and children, but locating these services when you need them is not always easy. Find an intervention program in your own community that provides therapeutic services to children and families. You might look for information on programs that is posted on public bulletin boards or included in flyers handed out at a physician's office, or by searching the Internet. If you do a web search, remember to include the name of your community in your search terms so that you find a local program. Particularly in larger communities, there may be a local guide to community resources published by a social services agency.

Answer as many of these questions as you can:

- Who provides the services? (This could be a community hospital, an agency or organization, a school, or a private service provider, such as a counselor or psychologist.)

- What types of family problems or concerns are addressed through this program?

- What types of services are provided? (This could include group counseling, workshops, individual sessions, online delivery, or some other type of delivery.)

- Is there a charge for receiving services? If so, what is it? Is there a sliding scale (that is, does the amount that is charged depend on the income level of the family)?

CHECK YOUR UNDERSTANDING

1. How do the provisions of the Family and Medical Leave Act in the United States compare to laws in other countries?

2. What is a wraparound program?

3. What are important characteristics of a successful program to help families?

CONCLUSION

In this chapter, we have examined some of the types of families found in modern American society, examining the strengths and weaknesses of each, and discovered that when parents and other caregivers maintain warm and supportive relationships and provide appropriate supervision, the type of family structure seems to matter less for children's well-being. However, the strategies parents use to socialize their children and the parenting styles that they adopt have important consequences for their children. We have also shown some of the cultural differences that exist in family types and family interactions. While there is both continuity and change in the nature and quality of parent-child relations as children get older, parents remain important people in the lives of most adolescents. Siblings also play an important role in children's lives, but it is important to remember that children with no siblings are not at a disadvantage. When family relationships are strained and families are struggling and not functioning in an optimal way, interventions at a variety of levels can help the family recover, but it is important that these interventions are based on collaboration with and respect for the families who participate.

CHAPTER SUMMARY

Test your understanding of the content.
Take the practice quiz at **edge.sagepub.com/levine3e**

13.1 What constitutes a family?

A **family** is the basic social unit for socializing children, but it takes different forms from one culture to another. A **nuclear family** consists of a husband, wife, and their biological and/or adopted children, but there are many other family structures. The number of single-parent families in the United States has increased substantially in recent years and single parents face their own unique challenges. The divorce rate in the United States is high, but may be declining for younger cohorts. It takes time for everyone in a family to adjust following a divorce and it affects different children differently. Conflict between parents is related to poorer child outcomes, but **constructive conflict** can reduce the negative effects. The differences between children in divorced, versus intact families are small. Noncustodial parents continue to be important people in the lives of their children. **Coparenting** occurs in married, divorced, and separated couples, as well as in couples that have never married, and families in which parenting is shared with another person. Grandparents sometimes raise their grandchildren, which can be challenging for older adults. Children raised by gay or lesbian parents are as well-adjusted as children in other types of families. Having a family story helps adopted children develop a sense

of identity, and both children and adoptive parents often prefer having an **open adoption**. **Foster care** is a temporary living arrangement, so it may be difficult for foster children and foster parents to bond.

13.2 What are the roles individuals in a family fill and how have they changed?

Families are dynamic systems made up of the individuals and relationships within them. Today more mothers are employed in the workforce, and fathers are more involved with caretaking of their children. Despite changes in roles, parents' roles continue to differ. Mothers are often more responsive to the emotional needs of their children while fathers engage in play and encourage exploration. Models of parenting have included the **parent effects model** and the **child effects model,** but a **transactional model** is the one used most often today. Sibling relationships are unique, embodying both closeness and conflict. Siblings are not as similar as we might think because of the impact of their **nonshared environment.** Differential treatment of siblings can create problems unless the child who is not receiving the preferential treatment understands the reasons for it. Although only children do not have siblings, they are as likely to be as well-adjusted and happy as children with siblings.

13.3 How do parents socialize their children?

Parents use a variety of positive and negative discipline techniques to socialize their children, including **inductive discipline, command strategies, relationship maintenance techniques, power assertion,** and **psychological control.** The effectiveness of any particular strategy depends in large part on the values of the culture in which the child lives. In the United States, inductive discipline is associated with greater empathy and power assertion is associated with bullying, fighting, and delinquency. Based on the amount of parental **acceptance/responsiveness** and the amount of parental **demandingness/control,** we can describe four styles of parents: **authoritative parents, authoritarian parents, permissive parents,** and **disengaged parents.** In the United States, authoritative parenting is associated with a number of positive characteristics, and children raised by disengaged parents do the worst. However, the same styles are not equally effective in other cultures. As adolescents become more autonomous, parents need to balance autonomy granting with connectedness. Although conflict becomes more common in adolescence, it is usually about mundane, everyday issues and is not damaging to adolescents' relationship with their parents.

13.4 What interventions are used to improve family life?

Programs to promote better family life can be implemented at the national, community, or family level, and they can aim to prevent problems or to help families recover from problems. At the family level, intervention may include family therapy. Effective programs empower parents to advocate for their children and to build a working relationship with professionals.

KEY TERMS

Strengthen your understanding of these key terms with mobile-friendly eFlashcards at **edge.sagepub.com/levine3e**

Acceptance/responsiveness 525
Authoritarian parents 526
Authoritative parents 526
Child effects model 522
Command strategy 523
Constructive conflict 503
Coparenting 506
Demandingness/control 526
Disengaged parents 526
Extended family 498
Family 498
Foster care 513
Inductive discipline 523
Internalization 521
Love withdrawal 524

Nonshared environment 518
Nuclear family 498
Open adoptions 512
Other-oriented induction 523
Parent effects model 522
Parenting styles 526
Permissive parents 526
Power assertion 524
Psychological control 524
Relationship maintenance 523
Self-oriented induction 523
Stepfamilies 507
Transactional model 522
Wraparound program 535

Give your students the SAGE edge!

SAGE edge offers a robust online environment featuring an impressive array of free tools and resources for review, study, and further exploration, keeping both instructors and students on the cutting edge of teaching and learning. Learn more at **edge.sagepub.com/levine3e**

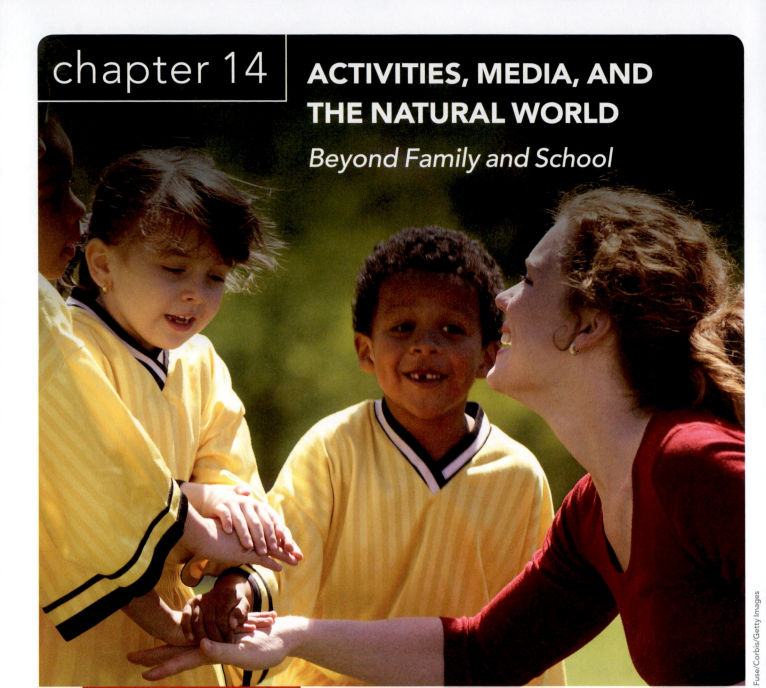

chapter 14

ACTIVITIES, MEDIA, AND THE NATURAL WORLD

Beyond Family and School

LEARNING QUESTIONS

14.1 What does the daily life of children and teens around the world look like?

14.2 How does unstructured time, including time spent in the natural world and with electronic media, affect children's development?

14.3 How do structured activities contribute to positive youth development?

14.4 What relationships beyond immediate family and peers are important for social development?

Master these objectives using an online action plan at **edge.sagepub.com/levine3e**

TEST YOUR KNOWLEDGE

Test your knowledge of child development by deciding whether each of the following statements is *true* or *false*, and then check your answers as you read the chapter.

1. **T ☐ F ☐:** When children diagnosed with ADHD play outdoors, their symptoms are reduced.

2. **T ☐ F ☐:** Most families do not have any rules related to the amount of time children spend watching television.

3. **T ☐ F ☐:** Babies 8 to 16 months of age who watch videotapes designed to improve cognitive development (like *Baby Einstein* videos) have larger vocabularies than babies who don't watch these videos.

4. **T ☐ F ☐:** Children who watch educational television when they are preschoolers do better in English, math, and science in high school.

5. **T ☐ F ☐:** The least hostile and aggressive children who play violent video games get into more fights than the most hostile and aggressive children who don't.

6. **T ☐ F ☐:** Girls who watch more educational shows are more likely than other girls to take part in relational aggression.

7. **T ☐ F ☐:** Adolescents who are narcissistic are more likely to take selfies, and the more selfies they post online, the more narcissistic they become.

8. **T ☐ F ☐:** Many children and teens these days are overscheduled, spending most of their time after school in multiple organized activities, like sports and music lessons.

9. **T ☐ F ☐:** Children who participate in organized sports develop skills they use to keep them physically active throughout their lifetime.

10. **T ☐ F ☐:** Formal mentoring programs have a significant impact on most of the adolescents who participate in them.

Correct answers: (1) T, (2) T, (3) F, (4) T, (5) T, (6) T (7) T, (8) F, (9) F, (10) F

▲ **VIDEO: Watch as students answer some of these questions and the authors respond.**

I n this chapter, we explore the context of children's lives, focusing on what they do with the time they spend outside of school. Children and teens spend their days in many different environments and with many different people. Having free time to play or hang out with friends is important for development, and electronic media use plays a growing role both for time with friends and time alone. Many structured activities, like sports and the arts, promote positive youth development. These types of activities often help to connect children and adolescents to nonparental adults who become important in their lives.

THE DAILY LIVES OF CHILDREN AND ADOLESCENTS

14.1 What does the daily life of children and teens around the world look like?

The lives of children and adolescents contain much more than school and family. The majority of children and teens have some amount of time that is discretionary because they decide for themselves how to spend it. The ways in which young people spend their leisure time vary between cultures and reflect their cultural values. In Taiwan, academics outside of school make up a relatively large portion of the day, and many activities for Taiwanese children are chosen and/or directed by adults (Newman et al., 2007). By comparison, American children are more likely to choose their own activities, and the one area they choose more than children in most other cultures is sports. In general, American youth do far less homework and have much more free time. Larson (2004) describes three ways in which they use this free time: (1) playing or "hanging out" with others in unstructured activities; (2) using media, such as television, video games, and computers; and (3) engaging in structured activities, such as sports, drama or musical productions, or interest-based clubs. Table 14.1 shows the daily activities of children and adolescents and the time devoted to them in different regions of the world. Try **Active Learning: The Daily Life of a U.S. Teen** to see how an adolescent you know uses his or her time and how much of that is leisure time. You can then compare your results to the averages shown in Table 14.1.

TABLE 14.1

Average daily time use of adolescents in 45 studies.

Activity	Nonindustrial, Unschooled Populations	Postindustrial, Schooled Populations		
		United States	Europe	East Asia
Household Labor	5–9 hours	20–40 minutes	20–40 minutes	10–20 minutes
Paid Labor	0.5–8 hours	40–60 minutes	10–20 minutes	0–10 minutes
Schoolwork	0 (unschooled population)	3.0–4.5 hours	4.0–5.5 hours	5.5–7.5 hours
Total Work Time	6–9 hours	4–6 hours	4.5–6.5 hours	6–8 hours
TV Viewing	Insufficient data	1.5–2.5 hours	1.5–2.5 hours	1.5–2.5 hours
Talking	Insufficient data	2–3 hours	Insufficient data	45–60 minutes
Sports	Insufficient data	30–60 minutes	20–80 minutes	0–20 minutes
Structured Voluntary Activities	Insufficient data	10–20 minutes	10–20 minutes	0–10 minutes
Total Free Time	4–7 hours	6.5–8 hours	5.5–7.5 hours	4.0–5.5 hours

NOTE: The estimates in the table are averaged across a 7-day week, including weekdays and weekends. Time spent in maintenance activities like eating, personal care, and sleeping is not included. The data for nonindustrial, unschooled populations come primarily from rural peasant populations in developing countries.

SOURCE: Larson (2004).

Active LEARNING

The Daily Life of a U.S. Teen

Ask a teenager to keep a journal reporting what she is doing every hour for 2 days (one school day and one weekend day). You might want to give her two sheets of paper divided into the hours of the day so she can note when she wakes up and goes to sleep (so you'll know how much time she was awake) and with one block of space for each hour. If you are not able to interview a teen, think back to a typical day when you were in high school and describe for each hour what you were likely to be doing.

In either case, for each hour, decide whether you would classify the activity as school, paid work, or leisure time. Total the number of waking hours and divide the number of leisure hours by the total number of waking hours to find the percentage of time that was "leisure time." For example, the teen below has a total of 18 hours in her day. She has 7 hours of leisure time, including sports, hanging out, dinner, and TV time. Therefore, seven-eighteenths or .39 (almost 40%) of her day was spent in leisure activity.

8 a.m.	9 a.m.	10 a.m.	11 a.m.	12 p.m.	1 p.m.	2 p.m.	3 p.m.	4 p.m.
school	school	school	school	school	school	hanging out with friends	sports	sports
5 p.m.	6 p.m.	7 p.m.	8 p.m.	9 p.m.	10 p.m.	11 p.m.	12 a.m.	1 a.m.
homework	dinner with family	homework	TV with family	TV	homework	TV/ Facebook/ phone	homework	sleep

Next try to categorize each leisure hour as one of the following: media use, structured activities like sports or school clubs, hanging out with friends, or interacting with family. Calculate the percentage of time spent on each type of activity by totaling the number of hours you decided are spent in leisure activities and dividing the number of hours in each type of leisure activity by the total number of leisure hours. For example, if you decide that the teen spent 6 hours in leisure activities and 2 of those hours were spent hanging out, divide 2 hours (time spent hanging out) by 6 hours (the total leisure time) to get 33% or one-third of the teen's leisure time. The teen shown in the chart above spends 3 hours watching TV; therefore .43 or slightly more than 40% of her leisure time is spent watching TV.

American teens have been found to spend 40% to 50% of their day in leisure activities, compared with 25% to 35% for East Asians, and 35% to 45% for Europeans (Larson, 2004). The particular type of activity that occurs during these leisure hours has an effect on teens' development, as we see later in this chapter.

CHECK YOUR UNDERSTANDING

1. How do U.S. children and teens spend most of their free time?
2. How do children around the world differ in their use of free time?

UNSTRUCTURED TIME

14.2 How does unstructured time, including time spent in the natural world and with electronic media, affect children's development?

Children today are less likely than children in previous generations to go outside to play with their friends because of parents' concerns for safety, the amount of time children spend using media, and their participation in adult-organized activities. Children are less likely to be able to roam their neighborhoods safely as more and more open space is developed, with more traffic as a result. Parents are also less likely to be home monitoring their children's behavior because both parents are working or there is only a single parent to manage the home. In 2011, about 11% of children between ages 5 and 14 spent unsupervised time after school in their homes (Laughlin, 2013).

Jack Hollingsworth/Digital Vision/Thinkstock

Hanging out at the mall. Children and teens need some unstructured time to spend in activities that they choose. Although too much unsupervised time is associated with problem behaviors, some time to "hang out" and enjoy being with friends is a positive thing for young people.

Parents of teens are especially concerned about risky or negative behaviors that can result from their unsupervised time spent with peers. These concerns may be well founded. When teens spend unstructured time socializing with peers away from adult supervision, the likelihood of criminal behavior, teen sexuality and pregnancy, and drug and alcohol use increases (Mahoney, Stattin, & Lord, 2004). When teens have delinquent friends, the more free time they have to hang out with them, the more likely they are to take part in criminal behavior (Svensson & Oberwittler, 2010).

However, even those who argue for the value of structured activities acknowledge that children and teens need some unstructured time. Just as younger children need free time to play, adolescents need time to just "hang out." Unstructured time with peers allows adolescents to develop an identity separate from their parents and to learn how to manage themselves with their peers, and that may include experimentation with somewhat risky behaviors. The challenge is to provide teens with an appropriate balance of freedom and structured time so that they develop a sense of self-direction while minimizing risk (Osgood, Anderson, & Shaffer, 2005). As teens get older, parents increasingly allow them to spend time away from home in unstructured time with peers, but this is truer for boys than for girls and for Anglo American than for African American teens (Osgood et al., 2005).

CHILDREN AND THE NATURAL WORLD

"Those who contemplate the beauty of the earth find reserves of strength that will endure as long as life lasts."

—Rachel Carson (1998, p. 100), *The Sense of Wonder*

DEVELOPMENT IN ACTION VIDEO ▲

As we have said, children today are less likely to just go out and play. As a consequence, they are more cut off from the natural world than past generations. In this section, we examine the role that experiencing nature plays in children's healthy development. This involves giving children regular opportunities to experience the land, water, and living things in green environments, such as parks, forests, and gardens.

In his book, *Last Child in the Woods: Saving Our Children From Nature-Deficit Disorder,* Richard Louv (2008) focused attention on the consequences of separating children from the natural world. Louv proposed a campaign he called "Leave No Child Inside" (Charles, Louv, Bodner, Guns, & Stahl, 2009). Subsequently, President Obama began the America's Great Outdoors Initiative, designed to bring people of all ages back to the natural world. After listening to more than 100,000 people, and conducting 21 sessions with children and teens, the initiative's leaders proposed four goals for America's youth:

1. Make the outdoors relevant to today's young people: Make it inviting, exciting, and fun.

2. Ensure that all young people have access to outdoor places that are safe, clean, and close to home.

3. Empower and enable youth to work and volunteer in the outdoors.

4. Build on a base of environmental and outdoor education, both formal and informal (America's Great Outdoors, 2011).

According to survey research by the Outdoor Foundation (2014), all this attention may be having a positive effect. The steep decline in outdoor participation that took place between 2006 and 2010 did not continue after that year and in 2014, 64% of 6- to 12-year-olds and 60% of 13- to 17-year-olds took part in outdoor recreation at least once during the year and many of these children spent a great deal of time outdoors. The most popular outdoor activities were biking and running, followed by fishing (21%), camping (20%), and hiking (12%). Researchers have begun to focus their attention on the effects of engagement with and isolation from the natural world on children, looking at a broad range of types of contact, from play in green spaces to therapy using horseback riding.

As you might imagine, when children are outdoors in green spaces they engage in more physical activity and this has been related to reduced levels of obesity (Bell, Wilson, & Liu, 2008; Cleland et al., 2008; McCurdy, Winterbottom, Mehta, & Roberts, 2010). A study carried out in eight European cities found that a higher level of obesity among low-income children was linked to their limited access to green spaces in which to play (Evans, Jones-Rounds, Belojevic, & Vermeylen, 2012). Activity level is only one contributor to obesity; diet is the other. The natural world has been brought to thousands of children through school gardens, and there is some evidence that activity in these gardens increases their likelihood of choosing and enjoying healthy vegetables (Parmer, Salisbury-Glennon, Shannon, & Struempler, 2009).

Children and nature. This girl's fascination with this butterfly will likely encourage her interest in the natural world as well as her willingness to protect it.

School gardens. Can you see why these children might be more likely to want to eat vegetables they planted themselves?

Several studies have shown that time spent in nature can renew and revive the ability to focus attention (Berman, Jonides, & Kaplan, 2008). It also may allow for unstructured reflection, which often results in effective problem solving. Several studies by Frances Kuo and Andrea Taylor have shown that exposure to natural outdoor environments can even reduce the attention-deficit symptoms of ADHD and is related to increased self-discipline in inner-city girls (Kuo & Taylor, 2004; Taylor & Kuo, 2009; Taylor & Kuo, 2011).

As you know if you have spent time at an ocean beach or taken a walk through the woods, the natural environment can be relaxing. Even children in rural areas who experience more life stress have lower levels of distress and higher self-worth when they have more access to natural environments in and around their homes. Although this access can be related to income, the relation between natural environment and stress relief was found to be independent of the effect of income (Wells & Evans, 2003). Children who spend more time in parks and playgrounds and have a home garden are also less likely to have behavior problems (Flouri, Midouhas, & Joshi, 2014). The evidence from this emerging area of research suggests that public policy can work to ensure that everyone, regardless of income, has access to green space and the natural environment.

Finally, experience with nature, as well as parents' attitudes toward nature, promotes children's positive attitudes toward the natural world, including their enjoyment of it and their wish to protect it (Cheng & Monroe, 2012). Although there is a growing body of research that links children's well-being and access to and engagement with natural environments, the reasons behind this relation still need to be explored. It is also not yet clear whether a nearby park, a natural view out of a window, or indoor plants are sufficient to bring about these outcomes. There is a long way to go to understand the effects of nature on children's development, but it is important that we explore these effects now that children have less and less exposure to the natural world. Try **Active Learning: Encouraging Children and Teens to Engage With Nature** to see what resources are available in your community.

T ☐ F ☐ When children diagnosed with ADHD play outdoors, their symptoms are reduced. **True**

Active LEARNING

Encouraging Children and Teens to Engage With Nature

There are many ways that young people can be involved with the natural world. Take this opportunity to look online for sources of outdoor activities in your community.

1. Go to https://mapofplay.kaboom.org/ to find playgrounds in your area. You will have to allow the website to access your location.

2. Go to www.discovertheforest.org/?m=1#map to find parks, nature visitor centers, and other wildlife areas near you. You will have to put in your zip code. When you find a visitor center near you on the map above, click on the icon to get details about the programs offered for children and their families.

3. You can also use Facebook to keep up with ideas and activities that connect youth and their families with the great outdoors at www.facebook.com/discovertheforest/

ELECTRONIC MEDIA USE

One of the reasons why children and adolescents are spending less time in the natural environment is that electronic media use is taking up more and more time in their lives. Although TV content, movies, and videos still make up the majority of children's screen time (Nielsen, 2014), the content of media and the ways in which it is received are rapidly changing. For more than 50 years, TV and movies were the only screen media available, but media use has been revolutionized in the 21st century with the introduction of handheld media devices, such as smartphones and tablets. Now the world of the Internet—including information, entertainment, and communication—is constantly available. In this section, we look at the effects of electronic media use. We begin by taking a look at how much and what type of media American children and teens are using.

Even the youngest children are using many different types of media. While 34% of children under age 2 do not watch any screen-based programming, 66% do watch TV sometimes and 43% watch TV, including recorded programming, every day for an average of almost an hour a day (Rideout, 2013; Rideout & Hamel, 2006). Mobile media has greatly increased the use of screens by infants. In one study, 65% of children under age 3 used one or more forms of mobile media on a typical day (Levine, Bowman, Kachinsky, Sola, & Waite, 2015) and most begin using it during the first year of life (Kabali et al., 2015). Many parents offer media to infants to keep them busy, and those with fussier babies are more likely to use media as a way to quiet the baby (Radesky, Silverstein, Zuckerman, & Christakis, 2014). Until recently, the American Academy of Pediatrics recommended that children under 2 years of age not use any electronic media, but in 2015 they realized that this had become unrealistic. They now recommend that parents set appropriate limits on viewing based in part on whether the use of media helps or hinders participation in other activities. Parents can monitor the content of what young children see, and limit their own use of media (Brown, Shifrin, & Hill, 2015), but should remember that young children learn the most from live interaction with people, and that no educational media improves on playing and interacting with an infant or toddler.

Based on a national sample of 8- to 18-year-olds in 2009, the Kaiser Family Foundation (KFF) found that children watched an average of almost 4.5 hours of TV and videos or DVDs per day, some of it on handheld devices such as cell phones (Rideout, Foehr, & Roberts, 2010). This compares to 1 hour and 45 minutes of physical activity per day and 40 minutes of reading books, magazines, and newspapers. In almost half of homes, the television was always on and rules set by parents for media use tended to monitor content, but did not limit the amount of time (Rideout et al., 2010). In those families that did have rules about media use, children used media an average of almost 3 hours less per day. A reduction of just 1 hour per day is the equivalent of 365 hours in 1 year, or more than 2 full weeks, so it is not an inconsequential amount of time to shift to other activities. In the KFF study, 71% of children had a TV in their bedroom, and these children spent significantly more time watching TV and less time reading than those who did not have their own TVs, although the average amount of time spent reading for both groups was less than 1 hour per day. Although the statistics give a clear impression of extensive media use by children and teens, averages hide the fact that significant numbers of children used media only infrequently. For example, 21% of those surveyed by the Kaiser Family Foundation reported watching no TV on an average day (Rideout et al., 2010).

There are also large racial and ethnic differences in the use of electronic media. Although there were no differences in the amount of time spent reading print material (30–40 minutes per day) in the KFF study, and no differences in the amount of time spent doing school work online (16–20 minutes per day), overall Asian American, Black, and Hispanic 8- to 18-year-olds spent 50% more time per day (13 hours) using electronic media, including mobile media, than White youth did (8.5 hours) and Asian American children spent about twice as much time (almost 3 hours per day) using computers for entertainment purposes than other groups (Lenhart, 2015; Rideout et al., 2010).

Media consumption increases dramatically as children move into early adolescence, to an average of almost 9 to 12 hours a day for all media combined (Rideout et al., 2010; Rideout, Lauricella, & Wartella, 2011). Television viewing peaks in early adolescence and decreases as adolescents get older when other forms of media become more prominent (see Figure 14.1). In 2014, 80% of teens 14 to 17 years old reported having their own smartphone and most used it

T ☐ F ☐ Most families do not have any rules related to the amount of time children spend watching television.
True

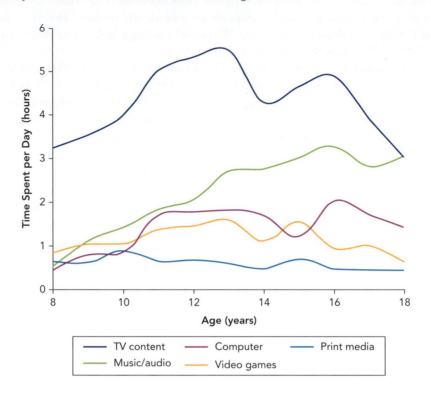

FIGURE 14.1

Time spent with each medium by age. Media use increases rapidly in early adolescence, especially for TV content, which then levels off as teens get older.

SOURCE: Rideout et al. (2010)

for social networking and watching videos (Nielsen, 2015). Almost all teens report that they go online every day, and 24% report that they are online "almost constantly" (Lenhart, 2015).

Not only are children and teens using more different forms of media than in the past, they are also more likely to use several of these forms at the same time, a process described in Chapter 7 as multitasking. In 2010, the Kaiser Family Foundation found that children and teens were using media on average for almost 7.5 hours per day. Because they used more than one media source at a time, this accounted for 10 hours and 45 minutes of media content daily (Rideout et al., 2010). As we will see later in this chapter, all of this multitasking of electronic media may have implications for children's developing ability to focus intensely and for long periods of time on just one thing, such as reading a book or doing a homework assignment and we have already discussed in Chapter 7 that multitasking by using cellphones while driving increases the chances of having an accident enormously.

The amount, type, and content of media used have consequences in many areas of development. Next, we will review the evidence concerning the impact that media use has on

Multitasking. When we split our attention between different tasks (for example, reading a book while watching TV), we lower our capacity to process information, and we retain less information. However, many of us still do it anyway, don't we?

children's physical, cognitive, and social development and on their self-concept. We conclude this section with a discussion about media literacy, or how children and their parents can be taught to better understand the effects of media and how to use it most effectively to promote rather than harm their development.

Media and Physical Development

There has been a good deal of research that has linked television viewing with obesity (for example, Crespo et al., 2001). Television viewing is related both directly and indirectly with body weight (Boulos, Vikre, Oppenheimer, Chang, & Kanarek, 2012). Viewing directly affects weight because the more time children spend watching television, the less time they have for physical activities, the more advertisements promoting high-calorie but low-nutrition foods they see (Ferguson, Muñoz, & Medrano, 2012), and the more mindless eating they do while watching television (Boulos et al., 2012). Television also promotes obesity in indirect ways. Beyond the advertisements in television programs, product placement of food within shows promotes particular brands of food in a less obvious way, and we now treat losing great amounts of weight as entertainment and a competition rather than as a lifelong challenge (Boulos et al., 2012). Whether it is from reduced exercise or changes in eating habits, there is a growing body of evidence that watching more television appears to be related to greater problems with weight as children grow and develop, so limiting their television viewing should be helpful and healthful under any circumstances.

It is ironic that watching television contributes to obesity in children, while at the same time promoting the concept of thinness as the ideal for everyone, especially girls and women. Messages from the media are implicated in the increase in body dissatisfaction and eating disorders that we see among girls and increasingly among boys (Grabe, Ward, & Hyde, 2008). In Chapter 6 we described some factors, such as early puberty, that may underlie the development of anorexia nervosa or bulimia, but that list needs to include the influence of images in movies, in magazines, and on TV that promote the thin ideal, described in Chapter 11. The relation between thin ideal messages and eating disorders in teenage girls has been well documented (Keel & Forney, 2013; López-Guimerà, Levine, Sánchez-Carracedo, & Fauquet 2010). The impact of television on bulimic symptoms was demonstrated on the island of Fiji. Before television was introduced, 3% of girls had such symptoms. Three years after TV was introduced, 15% of girls used vomiting to control weight. Although there could be other variables that changed along with the introduction of TV on the island, it does appear that the introduction of the Western thin ideal affected Fiji women's traditional idea of the beauty of a more rounded body (Walcott, Pratt, & Patel, 2003).

Media, Cognitive Development, and Academic Achievement

Not all television viewing has the same effect on children's development. There is evidence that educational TV improves cognitive functioning and academic performance for some children, while entertainment TV makes academic performance worse. In this section, we first describe how electronic media affects cognitive development for infants and toddlers. We then examine how educational media and entertainment media have different effects on cognitive development and academic achievement of children and teens.

TV viewing and obesity. There is an association between the amount of TV children watch and their weight. Whether it is because children eat while they are watching TV or because watching TV keeps them from being more physically active is still an open question, but both factors are probably at work.

© Mark Richards/Corbis

Effects of media on infants and toddlers. Although educational TV has been shown to promote cognitive development in older children, there is no evidence that TV of any kind is helpful for infants (Kirkorian, Wartella, & Anderson, 2008). The research evidence shows that infants and toddlers learn much more effectively from real-life interaction than from on-screen programs (Anderson & Pempek, 2005; DeLoache et al., 2010; Krcmar, Grela, & Lin, 2007). In one study, babies age 8 to 16 months who watched videotapes designed specifically to improve cognitive development, such as the *Baby Einstein* videos, actually had smaller vocabularies than those who did not (Zimmerman, Christakis, & Meltzoff, 2007). One reason is that parents talk less to their children when watching these programs with them and the more they watch TV programming with their babies, the less language they use during free play when the TV is off (Lavigne, Hanson, & Anderson, 2015; Pempek, Demers, Hanson, Kirkorian, & Anderson, 2011). In one study, 1-year-olds who watched an educational video designed to promote language development did not have better language development than babies who did not watch the video. What did predict vocabulary use and understanding was how much adults read to the infants (Robb, Richert, & Wartella, 2009). In another study, parent engagement with the baby and the video determined how much the baby learned from watching the video. The more engaged the parent was, the more the baby learned (Fender, Richert, Robb, & Wartella, 2010).

In addition to programming specifically directed at infants and toddlers, children under age 3 are exposed on average to 5½ hours a day of background TV (Lapierre, Piotrowski, & Linebarger, 2012). More than one-third of families with young children have the TV on all or most of the time, even if no one is watching it (Rideout, 2013), and simply having a TV playing in the background can be detrimental to young children's cognitive development. Although toddlers usually will not continue to watch shows they don't understand, TV is designed to grab a viewer's attention with techniques that work on young children as well as on adults. Infants and toddlers will look at background TV over 25 times during a 30-minute show, disrupting the play and social interactions that are crucial for optimal cognitive development in the early years (Schmidt, Pempek, Kirkorian, Lund, & Anderson, 2008). The more adult-focused background TV they are exposed to at age 1, the lower children's cognitive functioning at age 4 (Barr, Lauricella, Zack, & Calvert, 2010).

Today, even toddlers are focusing their attention on iPads and other mobile devices. The number of children under age 2 who have used these devices jumped from 10% in 2011 to 38% in 2013 (Rideout, 2013). You might think that toddlers would learn more from interacting with touch-screens than simply watching videos, but research has shown that for children under age 3, tasks learned via touchscreens do not generalize to an understanding of or ability to perform the same task with real objects (Moser et al., 2015). What does it mean for cognitive development when a 2-year-old can assemble a six-piece puzzle on a screen but has no idea what a real puzzle is? Researchers are only beginning to examine the effects of this new use of media by infants and toddlers.

The American Academy of Pediatrics (2011b) reminds parents that "Unstructured playtime is more valuable for the developing brain than any electronic media exposure. Even for infants as young as 4 months of age, solo play allows a child to think creatively, problem-solve, and accomplish tasks with minimal parent interaction" (p. 1043). In other words, infants do not have to be entertained all the time, either by parents or by media.

T ☐ F ☐ Babies 8 to 16 months of age who watch videotapes designed to improve cognitive development (like *Baby Einstein* videos) have larger vocabularies than babies who don't watch these videos.
False

TRUE/FALSE VIDEO ▲

Peopleimages/E+/Getty Images

Media use in infancy. Despite marketing claims to the contrary, there is no evidence that exposure to media is helpful for infants' cognitive development. Why do you think products such as educational DVDs for babies remain popular with parents?

Effects of educational media. From age 2 on, educational (but not entertainment) TV does seem to affect learning in a positive way. For example, research on *Sesame Street* has found even greater positive effects on preacademic skills when children watched beginning at ages 2 and 3 rather than at age 4 (Wright, Huston, Scantlin, & Kotler, 2001). Although there are many educational programs on television, *Sesame Street* has included a research component since the very beginning of its programming and, as a result, has more research on its effectiveness than any other program. See **Journey of Research: Educational TV and *Sesame Street*** for additional information about the history and effectiveness of *Sesame Street*.

JOURNEY OF *Research*

Educational TV and *Sesame Street*

In the decade following World War II, the number of TV sets in American homes quickly grew from 44,000 to over 8,000,000 by the late 1950s (Levine & Waite, 2002). Educational programs for children at that time often filmed a teacher leading activities typical of a preschool or kindergarten. The teachers were not trained actors, and surveys at that time showed that children greatly preferred commercial TV to these early attempts at educational programming (Lemish, 2007).

In the 1960s, research by Joan Ganz Cooney for the Carnegie Corporation found that preschoolers were watching a great deal of television every day (Friedman, 2006) and the vast majority of American homes had a television, regardless of their income level. Cooney and her colleagues believed that a different kind of TV show could be used to engage and teach young children, especially those being raised in poverty, to help get them ready for school. She created the Children's Television Workshop (CTW, now called the Sesame Workshop) to achieve this goal.

Bringing together top educators, psychologists, and television producers, CTW used the latest research available at that time to determine how children would best learn from this relatively new medium (Lemish, 2007). From the observation that children are greatly attracted to commercials, CTW developed a show that would use the same techniques found in commercials, such as short segments, bright colors, and music, but with educational rather than commercial goals in mind. With the addition of Jim Henson's Muppets, this show became *Sesame Street,* which first aired in 1969 (Friedman, 2006; Williams-Rautiolla, 2008).

Today, the U.S. version of *Sesame Street* is watched by about 8 million people each week, but *Sesame Street* has gone far beyond the borders of the United States. Twenty versions of the show appear in 150 countries around the world (Sesame Street Workshop, 2014). In each version, *Sesame Street* staff members from the United States work together with local producers, artists, and actors to create a program appropriate for that culture.

Sesame Street sets very specific goals based on research-supported knowledge about children's development. For example, it has been shown that children learn more from TV when they interact with an adult about what they've seen, so *Sesame Street* has designed segments that will engage parents as well as their preschoolers (Wright et al., 2001). To this end, many celebrities, actors, and musicians, including Jimmy Kimmel, Michelle Obama, Ellen DeGeneres, and Garth Brooks, have done guest segments on *Sesame Street,* and the program often features parodies of programs adults watch, such as *Upside Downton Abbey, The Hungry Games: Catching Fur,* and *Game of Chairs.* Children ages 3 and 4 are not going to understand these jokes, but their parents will. The idea has been to

(Continued)

(Continued)

Getty Images /Handout /Getty Images News

Sesame Street around the world. In November 2014, Sesame Street celebrated its 45th anniversary. It now appears in 120 countries around the world. In each country, the cast of Muppets is adapted to the local culture and its important issues. This is Kami from South Africa who is living with HIV.

encourage parents to watch with their children so they can discuss and reinforce what the show teaches.

Sesame Street is designed to teach preacademic skills that prepare children for reading, writing, and arithmetic but the show teaches much more than that. "Social, moral and affective" teaching goals have guided the programming throughout *Sesame Street*'s history (Mielke, 2001, p. 84). For example, diversity has always been a central value, with characters from all backgrounds represented in the cast. *Sesame Street* also has not shied away from the big issues that impact children's lives. For instance, in 2002 Sesame Street in South Africa introduced Kami, a Muppet who is living with HIV.

The show's commitment to educating all children has been shown when the producers in Bangladesh sent their fleet of rickshaws to bring TVs linked to power generators to children who have no electricity (Gordian, 2012).

There is much research evidence that watching *Sesame Street* does make a difference for young children who would otherwise be unprepared to enter school. These children were more prepared to learn to read and to do arithmetic, and this seemed to be truly a result of watching the show and not a result of other variables, such as how educated their parents were or how much their parents read to them. This advantage continued even through high school. Children who watched Sesame Street at age 5 had higher grades in English, math, and science in high school (Huston, Anderson, Wright, Linebarger, & Schmitt, 2001; Schmidt & Anderson, 2007). You might wonder how watching one TV series could have such a long-term effect. Longitudinal research has shown that watching *Sesame Street* is related not only to preacademic skills but also to a greater sense of competence, less aggression, and more motivation for academic achievement (Huston et al., 2001). When children begin school more prepared, they can build on success rather than feeling defeated by failure.

Sesame Street remains a major force in children's educational television. Today, *Sesame Street* has a website with podcasts, computer games, and other activities and ideas for parents and caregivers to help children develop all types of abilities that will help when they enter school.

T ☐ **F** ☐ Children who watch educational television when they are preschoolers do better in English, math, and science in high school. **True**

Effects of entertainment media. Although *educational* TV has been shown to have a positive effect on children's cognitive development and school achievement, *entertainment* TV, which is the majority of viewing for school-age children, appears to have a negative effect. Particularly in the early years, when children are learning to read, school achievement declines as the amount of entertainment TV viewing increases (Schmidt & Anderson, 2007). Other recreational media, such as video games, are also linked with poorer school performance.

Several explanations have been proposed for this link. The simplest is that children and teens may be spending their time using media in place of doing homework (Van Evra, 2004; Weis & Cerankosky, 2010). This idea found support from a national survey in which light TV viewers spent more time each day doing homework, while children who spent more time using media spent less time doing work for school (Rideout, Roberts, & Foehr, 2005). Shin (2004) found that the more TV 6- to 13-year-olds watched, the less leisure reading, homework, and studying they did, but several studies have found this relationship only for entertainment TV, not educational TV (Ennemoser & Schneider, 2007; Huston, Wright, Marquis, and Green, 1999). There is growing support for the idea that time spent on recreational media is cutting into time that could be spent—perhaps could be *better* spent—doing homework.

A second possible reason for a link between media use and lower academic performance is that many children and teens are using a variety of types of media *while* they are doing their homework. Almost one-third of 8- to 18-year-olds said they multitask most of the time while doing homework (Rideout et al., 2010). Also, as we discussed in Chapter 7, older children's academic performance can be affected by the distraction of background TV even if they are not actively watching it.

A third possible reason for a link between media use and poor academic performance is that children are having more difficulty focusing attention on just one thing in depth because they are used to the attention-grabbing techniques used on television. Television programs grab and hold our attention by taking advantage of a natural tendency we have to respond automatically to "novel, moving, meaningful, or surprising" stimuli, which is called the **orienting response** (Diao & Sundar, 2004, p. 539). Our minds are designed to react, or orient, to anything new in the environment so we can evaluate what our response to it should be. Television uses editing to make us attend to the images on the screen. "Jump cuts" (shifting from one scene to another) are used to provide motion, novelty, and surprise that keep attracting our attention. However, throughout the years, as people got used to these scene shifts, they became less novel and surprising. TV programs, and in particular commercials, which are designed to make the viewer pay attention to their product, had to pick up the pace to keep grabbing the viewer's attention. You can examine the pacing of programming for yourself in **Active Learning: The Pace of TV.**

Orienting response The tendency to pay attention automatically to novel, moving, meaningful, or surprising stimuli.

Active LEARNING

The Pace of TV

While you are watching your favorite television show, place a check mark on a sheet of paper each time there is a shift from one scene or point of view to another. Note the name and type of show, and the time you start and finish. In a different place on your paper, record the same information on pacing during the commercials, making note of when the commercial started and finished. See if there is a difference when you average the number of jump cuts per minute for the show and the commercial.

Finally, watch a children's television show to compare the number of jump cuts or scene shifts shown to children. You may be surprised at how many jump cuts are found. Each one is designed to capture your attention by activating your orienting response so that you do not turn away from the TV. Compare your findings with those of others in your class. Were there differences in pacing between different types of shows or between the adult- and child-oriented shows? Did violent shows have more or fewer jump cuts than nonviolent shows? Becoming aware of the techniques used in media to affect you in this and a variety of ways is the beginning of what is known as *media literacy*.

There is evidence that watching a lot of entertainment TV is related to attention difficulties (Lillard & Peterson, 2011; Nikkelen, Valkenburg, Huizinga, & Bushman, 2014). Longitudinal studies have found that the amount of TV that preschoolers, school-age children, and teens watch is associated with attention problems later in their lives (Johnson, Cohen, Kasen, & Brook, 2007; Landhuis, Poulton, Welch, & Hancox, 2007; Zimmerman & Christakis, 2007). Shin (2004) found that children who watched more TV were more impulsive and this impulsiveness contributed to poorer school performance.

Although it is clear that TV viewing and attention problems are correlated, the question of causality remains unanswered. Does TV viewing shorten children's attention span, or do children with short attention spans like to watch TV? The studies mentioned previously suggest that TV viewing comes before the development of attention problems, but Acevedo-Polakovich, Lorch, and Milich (2007) argue that children with severe attention problems that result in a diagnosis of attention-deficit/hyperactivity disorder choose to watch more TV than other children because TV is one of the few things that will hold their attention. Gentile, Swing, Lim, and Khoo (2012) addressed the problem of direction of causation in a large-scale, longitudinal study focused on video games that was carried out in Singapore. They found that children with attention problems played more video games, but that playing video games contributed to even greater attention problems later on, so causality moves in both directions.

Media and Social Development

Different forms of media have very different effects on social development. In this section, we discuss the impact of video games and television on aggression and prosocial behavior. We then discuss social media, texting, and other ways children and teens incorporate media into their social relationships.

Aggression and prosocial behavior. The study of media's impact on aggression began with Albert Bandura's study described in Chapter 2, in which children watched a film showing an adult attacking a Bobo doll. Since that time, a clear and consistent picture has emerged, namely that watching violence or playing violent video games promotes aggression in young viewers (Comstock & Scharrer, 2003; Gentile, 2003; Gentile, Linder, & Walsh, 2003; Kirsh, 2012). Christakis and Zimmerman (2007) found that viewing violent television at ages 2 to 5 was linked with greater aggression at ages 7 to 10. Gentile, Coyne, and Walsh (2011) found that third- through fifth-grade children who were exposed to more violent media early in the school year showed higher levels of physical, verbal, and relational aggression 5 months later. This relationship has been found for teens as well. Over a 2-year period, the pattern of aggression shown by high school students in Germany followed the same pattern as their use of violent media. In this case, teens who reduced their use of violent media also showed decreased aggression (Krahé, Busching, & Möller, 2012).

Violent video games increase aggressive tendencies even more than TV because players are acting out the violence rather than just viewing it (Polman, de Castro, & van Aken, 2008). In a review of studies on violent video games, Anderson et al. (2010) concluded that they increase the player's actual aggression, raise arousal levels, increase aggressive thoughts and feelings, and decrease prosocial behavior. When the player identifies with and acts out the role of the "shooter," and when there is more blood in the game, these effects appear to be even stronger (Barlett, Harris, & Bruey, 2008; Konijn, Bijvank, & Bushman, 2007). Although there is some evidence that children who are already more hostile and aggressive are more likely than others to be further affected by playing violent video games, it appears that even children who do not fit this profile become more violent. In one study, the least hostile children who played video games got into more fights than the most hostile children who did not. When parents limited the amount of time and controlled the content of the video games their children played, children had lower levels of aggression (Gentile & Anderson, 2003).

Clearly not all media are violent, and research has shown that viewing other types of programming can be related to children's prosocial behavior such as sharing and cooperation.

TRUE/FALSE VIDEO ▲

T ☐ F ☐ The least hostile and aggressive children who play violent video games get into more fights than the most hostile and aggressive children who don't. **True**

In a classic study, children were assigned to watch either Batman and Superman cartoons or *Mr. Rogers' Neighborhood*, an educational program that emphasized kindness and caring, over a period of 4 weeks. The researchers found that watching Batman and Superman increased aggressive behavior for children who were already more aggressive, while watching *Mr. Rogers' Neighborhood* increased prosocial behavior (Friedrich & Stein, 1973). In a more recent study, 4-year-old children who watched more educational programming were more prosocial in their interactions 2 years later (Ostrov, Gentile, & Crick, 2006). However, even educational programs have their risks. Girls who watched more educational shows were also more likely than other girls to take part in relational aggression (for example, "*We* don't want to play with *you!*"). The authors speculate that even educational shows model this type of behavior, although they usually show the characters making up by the end of the show. They speculate that preschool children do not understand the storyline in the same way that adults do. They don't connect the positive resolution at the end of the program with the earlier aggression, so they only see the relational aggression as a model to imitate.

Violent video games. Research has found that playing violent video games brings out aggressive tendencies in children who are already aggressive and also in those who are not.

BISP/Newscom

T ☐ F ☐ Girls who watch more educational shows are more likely than other girls to take part in relational aggression. **True**

Using media for communication. Teens are avid users of electronic media for communication and the forms of communication are increasing exponentially. Teens stay in touch with friends by contacting them online, using instant messaging, e-mailing, text messaging, blogging, playing interactive games together, and viewing online social networking sites such as Facebook, Instagram, and Snapchat. The devices they use are shown in Figure 14.2. In a survey by the Center for the Digital Future in 2014, teens reported that texting (76% of those surveyed), the Internet (61%), and social networking or video sharing (55%) were important for maintaining social relationships (Center for the Digital Future, 2015). Almost

FIGURE 14.2

Teens, phone, computer and console access. Most teens have access to more than one of these types of mobile media. How does their use contribute to the prevalence of multitasking?

% of all teens who have access to the following:

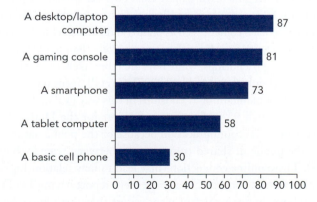

SOURCE: Lenhart (2015).

FIGURE 14.3

Sex differences in media use. Girls like to use visual social media, sharing photos and videos with friends, while boys are more interested in video games. What explanations can you offer for these differences?

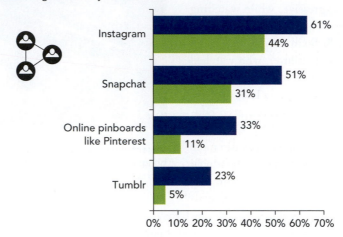

Girls Dominate Visually Oriented Social Media Platforms
Percent of girls and boys who use . . .

Instagram — 61% / 44%
Snapchat — 51% / 31%
Online pinboards like Pinterest — 33% / 11%
Tumblr — 23% / 5%

0% 10% 20% 30% 40% 50% 60% 70%

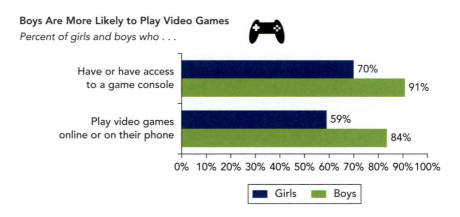

Boys Are More Likely to Play Video Games
Percent of girls and boys who . . .

Have or have access to a game console — 70% / 91%
Play video games online or on their phone — 59% / 84%

0% 10% 20% 30% 40% 50% 60% 70% 80% 90% 100%

■ Girls   ■ Boys

SOURCE: Lenhart (2015).

all teens who have cell phones use them to text other people and typically they exchange about 30 texts per day, with girls texting more than boys (Lenhart, 2015).

As shown in Figure 14.3, girls are more likely than boys to use social media, particularly applications that provide visual content such as photos and videos, while boys are more likely to play videogames (Lenhart, 2015). Also girls are more likely than boys to use social and other media to maintain existing friendships, while boys are more likely to use them for flirting and for making new friends (Lenhart & Madden, 2007). Overall, teens report an enhanced sense of well-being as a result of maintaining friendships in this way (Valkenburg & Peter, 2007).

Social networking, which 93% of teens use (Center for the Digital Future, 2015), is changing the nature of social communication because of the public nature of each person's "friends" list and the public or shared conversations between friends (Subrahmanyam & Greenfield, 2008). These online connections may lead to new relationships, as "friends of a friend" make contact with each other. On average teens report having 145 Facebook friends, more for girls than boys, but one-third of teens report they don't know how many friends they have (Lenhart, 2015). Instagram, used to share photos and videos, is also used by more than half of teens, again more by girls than boys (Lenhart, 2015).

FIGURE 14.4

Internet safety for children. The Federal Trade Commission provides these guidelines to help parents talk with their children about staying safe while exploring the internet. What other advice would you give to children and teens?

Socializing Online

Kids share pictures, videos, thoughts, plans, and their whereabouts with friends, family, and sometimes, the world at large. Socializing online can help kids connect with others, but it's important to help your child learn how to navigate these spaces safely.

Oversharing

Some pitfalls that come with online socializing are sharing too much information, or posting pictures, videos, or words that can damage a reputation or hurt someone's feelings. Applying real-world judgment and sense can help minimize those downsides.

What can you do?

Remind your kids that online actions have consequences.

The words kids write and the images they post have consequences offline.

- **Kids should post only what they're comfortable with others seeing.** Parts of your children's profiles may be seen by a broader audience than you—or they—are comfortable with, even if they use privacy settings. Encourage your kids to think about the language they use online, and to think before posting pictures and videos, or altering photos posted by someone else. Employers, college admissions officers, coaches, teachers, and the police may view these posts.
- **Remind kids that once they post it, they can't take it back.** Even if they delete the information from a site, they have little control over older versions that may be saved on other people's devices and may circulate online. And a message that's supposed to disappear from a friend's phone? There's software that lets them keep it.

Tell kids to limit what they share.

- **Help your kids understand what information should stay private.** Tell them why it's important to keep some things—about themselves, family members, and friends—to themselves. Information like their Social Security number, street address, phone number, and family financial information is private and should stay that way.
- **Talk to your teens about avoiding sex talk online.** Teens who don't talk about sex with strangers online are less likely to come in contact with predators. In fact, researchers have found that predators usually don't pose as children or teens, and most teens who are contacted by adults they don't know find it creepy. Teens should not hesitate to ignore or block them, and trust their gut when something feels wrong.
- **Send group messages with care.** Suggest that your kids think about who needs to see their message before sending to multiple people.

Limit access to your kids' profiles.

- **Use privacy settings.** Many social networking sites, chat, and video accounts have adjustable privacy settings, so you and your kids can restrict who has access to kids' profiles. Talk to your kids about the importance of these settings, and your expectations for who should be allowed to view their profile.
- **Review your child's friends list.** Suggest that your kids limit online "friends" to people they actually know. Ask about who they're talking to online.

Cyberbullying

Cyberbullying is bullying or harassment that happens online. It can happen in an email, a text message, an online game, or on a social networking site. It might involve rumors or images posted on someone's profile or circulated for others to see.

What can you do?

Help prevent cyberbullying.

- **Talk to your kids about bullying.** Tell your kids that they can't hide behind the words they type and the images they post or send. Bullying is a lose-lose situation: Hurtful messages make the target feel bad, and they make the sender look bad. Often they can bring scorn from peers and punishment from authorities.
- **Tell your kids to talk to you about bullying, too.** Ask your kids to let you know if an online message or image makes them feel threatened or hurt.
- **Recognize the signs of a cyberbully.** Cyberbullying often involves mean-spirited comments. Check out your kid's social networking pages from time to time to see what you find. Could your kid be the bully? Look for signs of bullying behavior, such as creating mean images of another kid.
- **Help stop cyberbullying.** Most kids don't bully, and there's no reason for anyone to put up with it. If your kids see cyberbullying happening to someone else, encourage them to try to stop it by telling the bully to stop, and by not engaging or forwarding anything. One way to help stop bullying online is to report it to the site or network where you see it.

What to do about a cyberbully.

- **Don't react to the bully.** If your child is targeted by a cyberbully, keep a cool head. Remind your child that most people realize bullying is wrong. Tell your child not to respond in kind. Instead, encourage your kid to work with you to save the evidence and talk to you about it. If the bullying persists, share the record with school officials or local law enforcement.
- **Protect your child's profile.** If your child finds a profile that was created or altered without their permission, contact the site to have it taken down.
- **Block or delete the bully.** Delete the bully from friends lists or block their user name, email address, and phone number.

Social media not only makes it easy to stay in touch with friends and family, but also promotes community involvement, creativity and growth of ideas, connections with new people from diverse backgrounds, and identity development (O'Keeffe, Clarke-Pearson, & Council on Communications Media, 2011). Students and schools use social media for group projects and to reinforce in-class learning. Social networking sites can create groups of people with common interests who may help each other. One study found that teens with cancer often used their websites to make contact with others who have cancer and to share information about their disease (Suzuki & Beale, 2006). Teens have also used an online peer advice bulletin board to share information about general and sexual health and development. In this anonymous setting, they may feel freer to ask questions they would be too embarrassed to ask their parents or even their friends (Suzuki & Calzo, 2004).

There are also risks for teens using social media, such as the cyberbullying we discussed in Chapter 12. Teens can also put themselves at risk by their own online behavior. About 20% of teens report that they have exchanged nude or seminude pictures or videos of themselves, an activity known as **sexting**. Although the teen may think of this as harmless flirtation, in many states the practice is illegal and can lead to child pornography charges or school suspension (O'Keeffe et al., 2011). In addition, the individual loses control of the image so it can be widely distributed without his or her permission or even knowledge, causing the teen a great deal of humiliation or embarrassment.

Sexting Sending nude or seminude pictures of oneself online.

Another risk of online communication is the presence of online predators. A study of online predators determined that most are adult men who create relationships with teenagers by developing trust over a long period of time (Wolak, Finkelhor, Mitchell, & Ybarra, 2008). Teens who eventually meet with the adult in person believe that they are having a romantic, sexual relationship with someone who cares for them. Most of the crimes that result from these contacts are statutory rapes rather than forced rapes, meaning the adult has sex with someone who is legally too young to be able to give consent. Clearly teens need to be better educated about the potential dangers of relationships with adults that are created through electronic communications, but it is often difficult for parents to know how to monitor the safety of their children's interactions online, especially when teens are more familiar with the online landscape than they are. The Federal Trade Commission provides information to help parents protect their children online as shown in Figure 14.4.

Media and Self-Concept

As we discussed in Chapter 11, children and teens are vulnerable to many influences as they develop their self-concept and build their self-esteem. The way they see themselves and the way they value themselves is certain to be affected by the media they use for so many hours each day. In this section, we discuss how television relates to self-concept and self-esteem for young children and for minority and LGBT youth. We then discuss the phenomenon of the "selfie," and how it relates to self-concept and narcissism.

Television, self-concept, and self-esteem. For many years, Fred Rogers (better known by his television name of Mr. Rogers) made it his goal to make children feel "special" and to enhance their self-esteem through his television program *Mr. Rogers' Neighborhood.* This is a tribute to Mr. Rogers, written after his death in 2003.

Mr. Rogers: A Personal Tribute

Fred Rogers was a remarkable man whose show *Mister Rogers' Neighborhood* impacted millions of children over 33 years. Although his program did not have the high "production values" found in *Sesame Street,* his personal touch reached children in a very comforting way. When he was awarded the Presidential Medal of Freedom in 2002, he said, "The whole idea . . . is to look at the television camera and present as much love as you possibly could to a person who needs it" (as cited in McFeatters, 2002, para. 2).

When my son was 3 years old, we sat together comfortably watching Mr. Rogers on TV. At the end of the show, my son turned to me and said, "Mom, I think he knows my name." I was so moved by his sense that his "friend" on TV knew him personally that I told my sister about what he'd said. My sister is a freelance writer and subsequently interviewed Fred Rogers about a book he had written. He agreed to the interview, but only on the condition that she allow him to find out about her as well. So they talked and they wrote several letters to each other. She eventually wrote to Mr. Rogers about what my son had said about him. He replied, "How perceptive your 3-year-old nephew is! When he said, 'I think he knows my name,' little did he know that *name* and *nature* are the exact same word in Old Testament Hebrew. I've spent much of my professional life trying to know the nature of children like your nephew. Please give him a hug for me when you see him" (F. M. Rogers, personal communication, June 12, 1989).

Research has confirmed the wisdom of Mr. Rogers's approach. Several studies have shown that watching *Mr. Rogers' Neighborhood* increases positive peer interactions, the ability to deal with fear and anger, and the ability to delay gratification among young children (Cantor, Sparks, & Hoffner, 1988; Coates, Pusser, & Goodman, 1976; Friedrich & Stein, 1973). (Adapted from Levine, 2003).

Fred Rogers's legacy lives on through a new show based on a favorite character from his original program: *Daniel Tiger's Neighborhood*. This show is dedicated to the same principles of social-emotional growth for young children that Mr. Rogers developed in his original program.

Although self-esteem can be raised by shows such as *Mr. Rogers' Neighborhood* and *Daniel Tiger's Neighborhood*, we know that there are many ways in which TV can be harmful to the self-esteem of children and teens. We have already discussed the research showing that even young girls begin to have lower self-esteem when they are constantly exposed to the thin ideal shown on television and in magazines. Media can affect children's self-concept in another way by limiting the options they see for their lives. Harrison (2006) has argued that television shows and movies are less diverse than real life. People from minority groups are underrepresented and are often portrayed in negatively stereotyped ways. Diversity is also absent in other ways. The types of stories told tend to show the same types of characters with the same types of goals over and over again. If you think of cartoons, Wile E. Coyote, who is mainly unintelligent and aggressive, has only one goal in life: to catch the Road Runner. Shows for teens can be just as limited, showing little complexity in either character or plot. As children watch hours of these programs, do they become so focused on these few characteristics that they define themselves according to these few possibilities as well?

Mr. Rogers and Daniel Tiger. The classic show Mr. Rogers' Neighborhood and the new spin-off Daniel Tiger's Neighborhood are designed to promote social-emotional growth in young children.

FIGURE 14.5

TV viewing and self-complexity. Research conducted by Harrison (2006) found that the more hours per week that teens watched television, the less complex their self-images. This may reflect the stereotypical portrayal of characters and plots in many television shows.

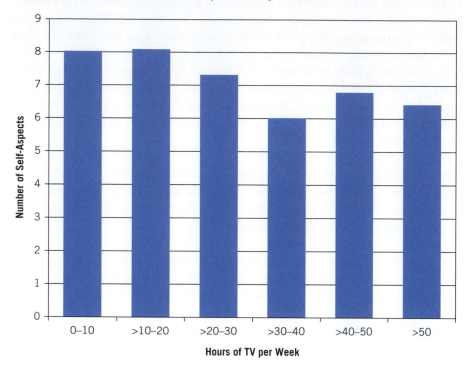

SOURCE: Harrison (2006).

Self-complexity The number of different ways in which an individual defines herself.

Harrison argued that a positive self-concept relies to some extent on **self-complexity**—that is, the number of different ways in which an individual defines herself. For example, an individual with high self-complexity might see herself as someone who is an attractive person, a fairly good athlete, an excellent student, and a good friend (most of the time). Someone with low self-complexity might tie her identity to her appearance and little else. Harrison found that the more television teens watched, the less complex their self-image was (see Figure 14.5). These limitations can cause trouble for teens when they experience stressful situations. For example, a boy whose identity is limited to being "a loving boyfriend" may become distraught when his girlfriend breaks up with him. Another boy with a more complex identity who is also very proud of his achievements in academics may be able to turn to this aspect of himself when faced with a breakup with his girlfriend.

When minorities are presented in the media, they are often shown in a negative light. For example, African American characters are often characterized by criminality, lack of intelligence, laziness, or inappropriate behavior (Tyree, 2011; Ward, 2004). Latino characters are 4 times as likely as others to be represented as domestic workers. They, too, are associated with crime and stereotypes, such as having a "hot temper" (Rivadeneyra, Ward, & Gordon, 2007). These portrayals are likely to affect minority youth, who are greater consumers of media than nonminorities (Rivadeneyra et al., 2007; Ward, 2004).

The more media Latino teens viewed, the lower their social and body self-esteem was, and this relationship was strongest for women and for those who more closely identified with Latino culture (Rivadeneyra et al., 2007). For African American teens, only two types of programming, sports and music videos, were related to lower self-esteem. In general, those who identified with Black characters on TV tended to have higher self-esteem, while those who identified with White characters had lower self-esteem. Finally, these relationships held only for those who reported themselves to be less religious. It appears that African American teens' background, the kind of programming they watch, and the reactions they have to TV all play a role in the way TV viewing is related to their self-concept (Ward, 2004).

A report from the Gay and Lesbian Alliance Against Defamation (GLAAD) found that 4.4% of the characters scheduled to appear in prime-time network drama and comedies during the 2012–2013 season were identified as gay, lesbian, bisexual, or transgender (Moore, 2012), an increase from 2.9% in the 2011–2012 television season. There is some indication the portrayal of homosexual characters in the media may be moving through the same stages of acceptance that minority characters have moved through in the past (Raley & Lucas, 2006). A number of

Selfies. Many teens take and post selfies. When is it fun and when is there reason for concern?

years ago, Clark (1969) proposed that portrayals move from nonrepresentation (the group is excluded) to ridicule (the group is portrayed but primarily as objects of derisive humor) to regulation (the group is portrayed in limited but socially acceptable roles) to respect (the group is shown in the both positive and negative roles). In 2006, Raley and Lucas concluded that TV shows had moved through Clark's first stage and were in the second stage (with much of the ridicule written for the gay characters to say about themselves) and that they were moving into the third and even the fourth stage of portrayal. As the GLAAD report indicates, the number of portrayals continues to increase, and progress toward the fourth stage of portrayal continues. This is particularly important to adolescent viewers who may be dealing with gender identity issues but who lack real life role models and turn to the media for information about how to conduct themselves.

"Selfies" and narcissism. More than 90% of teens take photos of themselves with their mobile phone or other device and post those photos online for others to see. These are called **selfies**. Recall our discussion in Chapter 7 about the imaginary audience in adolescence and you may see that the selfie is another way that teens think about others looking at and thinking about them (Uhls, 2015).

Research on this topic has addressed the question whether those who take and post selfies are more narcissistic than those who don't; in other words, are they people who have an inflated view of their own importance and seek admiration from others? In one study of people 18 to 34 years of age, results showed that narcissistic individuals are, in fact, more likely to take selfies and the more they post selfies online the more narcissistic they become (Halpern, Valenzuela, & Katz, 2016). We do not yet know what impact selfies will have on children and teens, but there is reason for some concern. It is important that parents discuss some of the dangers, including the risk of having an accident when taking a selfie while driving, or the consequences of posting inappropriate content. They can also promote interest in taking photos of and showing interest in other people and not just themselves (Uhls, 2015).

Selfies Photos of oneself taken with a mobile device and posted online.

T ☐ F ☐
Adolescents who are narcissistic are more likely to take selfies, and the more selfies they post online, the more narcissistic they become. **True**

Helping Children and Adolescents Use Media Wisely

Good advice to parents regarding TV viewing can be very simple: Think about whether you want your child to act like the characters he or she sees on TV and let that guide your selection of programs (Franklin, Rifkin, & Pascual, 2001). There are three ways in which parents can interact with children around TV: (1) by providing active mediation and guidance, which means talking with the child about what she is watching; (2) by setting limitations on what the child watches; and (3) by viewing programs with the child (Nathanson, 1999).

Although putting some limits on viewing has a positive effect, evidence also suggests that too much limitation might make the programs "forbidden fruit" and therefore even more appealing to children. Viewers between ages 8 and 22 reported being *more* attracted to programs that were given restrictive ratings (Bushman, 2006; Bushman & Cantor, 2003). However, as we reported earlier, many families report that they have no rules for their children regarding the amount of TV their children watch, and over 70% of children have TV and/or other media in their bedrooms, where no direct parental supervision occurs (Rideout et al., 2010).

This suggests that parents need to find a comfortable medium between being overly restrictive and having no restrictions at all. When parents watched shows containing violence with children without commenting on the show's content, children's aggression increased, possibly because it appeared to them that the parents tacitly approved of the messages they were seeing. We might speculate that giving children unfettered access to TV in the bedroom may also give the clear message of parental acceptance of all TV content (Barkin et al., 2006).

Media literacy The skills to understand the underlying purposes and messages of media.

Media literacy is the ability to understand the underlying purposes and messages of media presentations. Teaching media literacy to children and teens can help them become more savvy consumers of media content. Although even a single lesson can be effective, training that includes actual production of media helps teens learn how messages are created and transmitted through media (Banerjee & Greene, 2007).

One example of how media tries to manipulate viewers is the way smoking is portrayed in movies and on TV. Teens can be greatly affected by what they see in this regard. Even controlling for parent and peer smoking, those teens who watched the most smoking in media were 2.6 times more likely to start smoking than those who watched shows that had the lowest level of smoking (Wills, Sargent, Stoolmiller, Gibbons, & Gerrard, 2008). One way to reduce the influence on teen smoking would be to have the movie industry reduce the amount of smoking portrayed or to provide warning labels to indicate that smoking is shown in the movie, similar to the warnings that movies contain sex, violence, or adult language. In fact, the film industry has responded to these concerns. Some of the major companies have instituted specific policies to decrease tobacco use on screen. In 2010, the most popular movies contained less than half as much smoking as in 2005 (Glantz et al., 2011). However, in 2015 smoking still occurred in 38% of movies rated G, PG, or PG-13 and in 72% of R-rated movies (Smoke Free Movies, 2015) and in February, 2016 a class-action lawsuit was brought against the Motion Picture Association of America stating that the industry has known that smoking in movies rated G, PG, and PG-13 is related to smoking by children and teens and seeking to ban smoking from movies with these ratings (Gardner, 2016).

Another approach would be to use media education to teach children and teens about why movies contain so much smoking. Smoking-related media education has been successful at increasing reflective thinking about tobacco use and reducing susceptibility to smoking advertisements (Brown & Bobkowski, 2011; Pinkleton, Austin, Cohen, Miller, & Fitzgerald, 2007). *Blowing Smoke* was the name of one project designed to teach sixth and eighth graders about smoking in movies (Bergsma & Ingram, 2001). The researchers found that most children initially believed that smoking in movies was a random event with no particular purpose. *Blowing Smoke* taught the children that when they see smoking in films, it represents a form of advertising, sometimes even including brand names. In the past, tobacco companies paid for such placement of their product in films or gave free tobacco products to actors and others involved with the film. By helping children understand the motivation behind showing people smoking in movies and helping them think critically about it, children's tendency to want to emulate admired movie stars when they smoke can be changed (Bergsma & Ingram, 2001). Try **Active Learning: Cigarettes in the Movies** to see how much smoking there is in the movies and TV programs that you watch and to think about how you might talk with children about what you see.

Active LEARNING

Cigarettes in the Movies

In the next week, notice how many characters in movies and TV shows that you watch smoke cigarettes. Do you see the same amount of smoking occurring in real life as you see in these programs? Can you explain why the directors of the show would choose to have each character smoke? What, if anything, does it convey about the person? Can you think of any reasons, besides artistic ones, for the decision to have a character smoke?

Some resources concerning media literacy include websites from the American Academy of Pediatrics' Safety Net and the Center for Media Literacy.

Another successful media education program targeted the influence of media on teen sexuality. Teens presented five lessons to their peers on topics such as "Using sex to sell." Compared to a control group, teens who took part in the program were more likely to report that "sexual depictions in the media are inaccurate and glamorized" (Pinkleton, Austin, Chen, & Cohen, 2012, p. 469).

CHECK YOUR UNDERSTANDING

1. Why are children less likely to just go out and play today than in the past?
2. What positive effects can experience with nature have on children?
3. How well do infants and toddlers learn from educational TV?
4. How does use of violent media affect children?
5. What is self-complexity and how does media content affect its development?
6. What is media literacy and how can we promote it in children and adolescents?

STRUCTURED TIME

14.3 How do structured activities contribute to positive youth development?

Some people have blamed the loss of unstructured playtime on the increase in organized activities, such as team sports, for children and teens. What were once just informal pick-up games now are activities that are highly structured by adults. Fifty-seven percent of children between 6 and 18 years of age take part in at least one after-school activity (U.S. Census Bureau, 2014a). In this section, we look at the amount of time that children and adolescents spend in organized activities and the impact that different types of organized activities have on development.

THE AMOUNT OF SCHEDULED TIME

Although some people claim that children are doing too much, research has shown that relatively few children appear to be overscheduled with organized activities. Figure 14.6 gives an overview of the amount of time that children and teens spend in after-school activities. According to Mahoney, Harris, and Eccles (2006), about 40% of children ages 5 to 18 do

T ☐ F ☐ Many children and teens these days are overscheduled, spending most of their time after school in multiple organized activities, like sports and music lessons. **False**

not participate in *any* organized, out-of-school activity, and most of those who do participate spend 10 hours a week or less on them. Not surprisingly, adolescents tend to be involved in more activities than younger children. In one national survey, 92.4% of American teens took part in at least one activity, 27.1% took part in one to three activities, 31.4% took part in four to six activities, and 33.9% participated in seven or more activities (Substance Abuse and Mental Health Services Administration, Office of Applied Studies, 2007). However, Mahoney et al. (2006) found that only a small percentage (between 3% and 6%) of youth, ages 5 to 18, report spending more than 20 hours a week in organized activities. These authors conclude that only 1 in 10 children could be described as overscheduled. It is true that 1 in 10 still might be too many, but overscheduling doesn't seem to be a typical pattern for children. Perhaps more important, when children and adolescents ages 9 through 19 were asked to describe *why* they participated in activities such as sports, after-school programs, clubs, and religious youth groups, the reasons they gave included enjoyment and excitement, encouragement and support from parents and friends, opportunities to challenge themselves and build skills, and social interactions with others. Mahoney et al. (2006) point out that in most cases it appears that children and adolescents have their own internal motivations for seeking out and participating in these experiences. Involvement in these activities is related to a number of positive outcomes for teens, including higher levels of achievement in school (high school graduation rates and entrance to college), lower levels of substance abuse, and better overall psychological adjustment (Mahoney et al., 2006).

For the relatively small number of children and adolescents who are overscheduled, often by well-intentioned parents, there is a price to pay. In an interview, David Elkind (2007a, 2007b), the author of *The Power of Play* and *The Hurried Child*, said, "It may be intuitively clear to parents that they have to push kids because it's a very competitive world, but they may be doing more harm than good because they may not be nourishing the kinds of abilities and skills that are most necessary in today's world" (as cited in Joiner, 2007, para. 9). Elkind reminds us of what we said earlier in this chapter: Children acquire important skills such as creativity and innovation during free, unstructured playtime.

Mixed outcomes for teens' healthy development have been found for structured activities, so it is clear that these activities must be carefully planned if they are going to be beneficial rather than potentially harmful. Although such involvement is correlated with positive social

FIGURE 14.6

Weekly hours that White and Black youth (ages 5–18) spend in organized and nonorganized activities. Looking at this chart, do you think that American youth are overscheduled with organized activities or not?

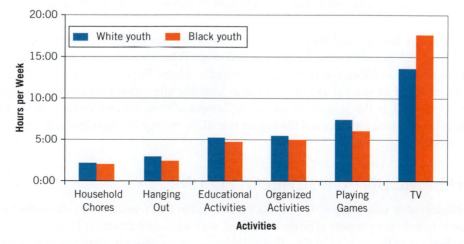

SOURCE: Mahoney, Harris, & Eccles (2006).

and academic development, it also has been linked with higher rates of alcohol use in high school (Mahoney et al., 2006). To be beneficial, programs should occur during times when the teens would otherwise be hanging out with friends without adult supervision, usually the hours directly after the school day is over. Most problematic behavior for teens, including crime and sexuality, occurs between the hours of 3 and 6 in the afternoon (Osgood et al., 2005) so activities scheduled during that time period are likely to be more successful in preventing trouble for teens.

In the next section, we describe a relatively recent way of thinking about how activities contribute to the development of children and adolescents. After that we examine the nature and outcomes of two particular types of extracurricular activity that engage many young people: sports and the arts.

POSITIVE YOUTH DEVELOPMENT

In Chapter 1, we introduced a new way of thinking about development that adds a great deal to our understanding of the role that activities play in the lives of young people. This approach is called *positive youth development (PYD)* because its primary focus is on finding ways to help young people reach their full potential. Although PYD does not deny that many young people face various challenges, it does not focus on adolescence as a time of deficit and stress. Instead PYD sees adolescence as a time full of potential and growth and strives to identify the people, contexts, circumstances, and activities that use that potential to help youth grow in the most healthy and positive way (Sanders & Munford, 2014; Youth. gov, n.d.). When organizations and communities give adolescents the chance to exercise leadership, build their skills, and engage in positive and productive activities, youth develop the building blocks they need to grow into healthy, happy, self-sufficient adults. Goals for

Joyce Munsch

Organized activities. Children and adolescents get many benefits from participating in organized sports and activities, but the activities they participate in should be ones that the children enjoy, and adults need to be careful not to put too much pressure on them to perform. What organized activities influenced you when you were growing up, and in what ways did they impact your development?

positive youth development have been described as the five Cs: competence, confidence, connection, care and compassion, and character—all of which lead to a sixth C: contribution to the community (Erdem et al., 2016). When Roeser and Peck (2003) looked at patterns of involvement in positive activities in a group of adolescents who were at risk of academic failure, they found that vulnerable youth who were involved in high levels of both school and community sports activities were twice as likely to graduate high school and go on to college as students who did not have this level of involvement.

Developmental assets
Common sense positive experiences and qualities that help young people become caring, responsible adults.

The Search Institute in Minneapolis has identified a set of 40 **developmental assets** for each age group from age 3 through 18. It defines a developmental asset as "common sense, positive experiences and qualities that help influence choices young people make and help them become caring, responsible adults" (Search Institute, 2012, para. 1). *Constructive use of time* is one of the sets of assets the Search Institute has identified. This asset includes creative activities such as lessons or practice in music, theater, or other arts; youth programs in the community; membership in a religious institution; and not spending time outside the home just hanging out with friends for more than 2 nights a week.

When the Search Institute looked at students' level of participation in each of these activities, they found that only 21% of the youth surveyed participated in creative activities at the level the Search Institute considers adequate to support youth development, but 57% participated in youth programs, 58% participated in a religious community, and 51% did not spend more than 2 days a week outside of their home just hanging out with friends. These numbers suggest that for many young people, there still is room in their lives for higher levels of participation in constructive activities in their community that support their positive development, and there is particularly room for more adolescents to find creative outlets through the arts.

Obviously, activities such as these will vary in quality and that can affect the outcome for the youth involved. Successful programs all seem to have the following three characteristics: (1) positive interaction with an adult that continues for at least 1 year, (2) development of real-world life skills, and (3) involvement in and leadership of activities valued by the child's community (Mueller et al., 2011; Ramey & Rose-Krasnor, 2012). Parents should consider the extent to which programs meet these criteria when helping their children and adolescents choose how they spend their time.

Jose Luis Pelaez/Corbis/VCG/Getty Images

Developmental assets. A relationship with a supportive and caring adult is one of the developmental assets identified by the Search Institute as a way to promote positive youth development.

ORGANIZED SPORTS

Approximately 38 million children and teens in the United States take part in organized sports every year. That number includes about three-quarters of all families with school-age children (Mickalide & Hansen, 2012). The kind of experience children have in sports can vary widely. They can participate in highly structured, adult-supervised, competitive activities, or they can play in informal activities organized by the children themselves that only loosely follow a set of rules. They can join team sports like football, basketball, or hockey, or pursue individual sports like track, swimming, or gymnastics. All of these types of sports can help them achieve similar health benefits.

Participation in sports has been linked with many positive benefits. It helps children reach the recommended daily 60 minutes of moderate or vigorous activities. It also benefits self-esteem, higher competence, and confidence; promotes better social skills; and children who participate in sports have less depression compared to those who do not (Eime, Young,

FIGURE 14.7

Sports-Related Injuries. One in five children who go to an emergency room for treatment is there because of a sports-related injury. What do you think places children in the 12- to 15-year-old age group at the greatest risk of suffering a concussion?

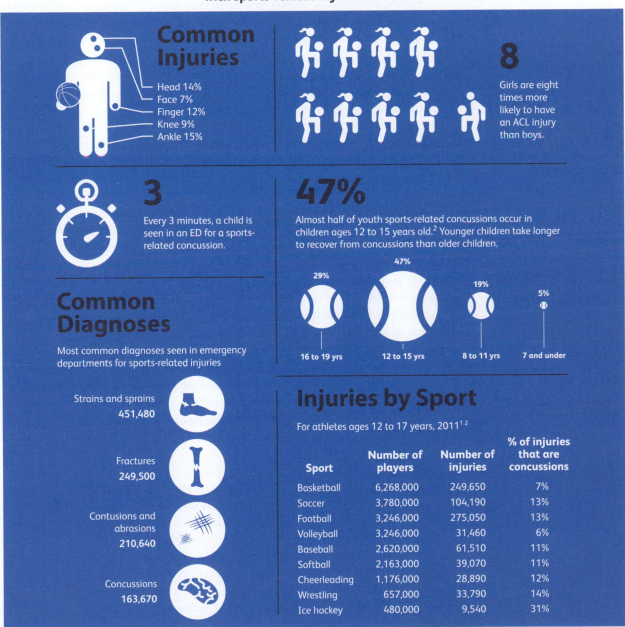

1.35 Million
Number of children seen in emergency departments with sports-related injuries in 2012

Common Injuries

Head 14%
Face 7%
Finger 12%
Knee 9%
Ankle 15%

8
Girls are eight times more likely to have an ACL injury than boys.

3
Every 3 minutes, a child is seen in an ED for a sports-related concussion.

47%
Almost half of youth sports-related concussions occur in children ages 12 to 15 years old.[2] Younger children take longer to recover from concussions than older children.

29% — 16 to 19 yrs
47% — 12 to 15 yrs
19% — 8 to 11 yrs
5% — 7 and under

Common Diagnoses

Most common diagnoses seen in emergency departments for sports-related injuries

Strains and sprains
451,480

Fractures
249,500

Contusions and abrasions
210,640

Concussions
163,670

Injuries by Sport

For athletes ages 12 to 17 years, 2011[1,2]

Sport	Number of players	Number of injuries	% of injuries that are concussions
Basketball	6,268,000	249,650	7%
Soccer	3,780,000	104,190	13%
Football	3,246,000	275,050	13%
Volleyball	3,246,000	31,460	6%
Baseball	2,620,000	61,510	11%
Softball	2,163,000	39,070	11%
Cheerleading	1,176,000	28,890	12%
Wrestling	657,000	33,790	14%
Ice hockey	480,000	9,540	31%

To learn more about youth sports safety, visit www.safekids.org

SAFE K:DS WORLDWIDE™

Founding Sponsor

SOURCE: Ferguson, Green, & Hansen (2013).

Harvey, Charity, & Payne, 2013). However, children need to be developmentally ready to participate in particular sports. Between the ages of 6 and 9, posture and balance improve, and by ages 10 to 12, most children are ready for sports like football or basketball that depend upon more complex skills (DiFiori et al., 2014), but chronological age alone is not a good indicator of a child's readiness to participate in a particular sport. Other factors, such as the skill set of an individual child and the child's motivation to participate, also need to figure into the decision.

Sports Safety

Safety in sports is essential: In 2012, about 1.35 million children under the age of 19 were injured seriously enough while playing sports that they required treatment in an emergency room (Ferguson, Green, & Hansen, 2013). Figure 14.7 shows the risk of various sports-related injuries. This risk increases as children get older, and at all ages it is greater for boys than girls (Wier, Miller, & Steiner, 2009). One-third of all children who play team sports suffer injuries that are serious enough to keep them off the field at least for a while, and some of these injuries have consequences that will last for the rest of their lives (Mickalide & Hansen, 2012).

Unfortunately, about one-third of child athletes believe they should play even while injured and almost half the coaches are pressured by the parents of injured children to let the players back into the game (Mickalide & Hansen, 2012). Parents also may not be fully aware of the level of risk to which their children are exposed. In a nationally representative sample of parents, 86% agreed with the statement that injuries are "just part of the game", with fathers less likely than mothers to think that injuries could be avoided (Hart Research Associates, 2011, p. 5). Perhaps this finding is not surprising. If parents believed the risk of injury were high, they would be unlikely to allow their child to participate at all.

There are several ways to reduce the risk of injury when children are playing sports. Competitors should be fairly equally matched in size and weight. Adults should be sure players have a reasonable level of skills to participate safely and are matched by skill level, where appropriate. Children must use the right safety equipment for their sports and they should warm up before practice or a game to prepare their bodies for the activity. Preparation helps reduce the risk of injury during the game itself, and practice helps children develop the skills they need to play well in addition to improving their physical condition so they play safely. Although many people believe that it is in the intensity of actual games that children are injured, most injuries actually occur during practice; therefore, it is just as important for children to take the preventive steps of warming up, wearing protective gear, and drinking plenty of fluids during practice as it is for a game (SafeKids USA, 2015).

Concussions

We have recently become more aware of the long-term effects of one particular type of sports injury: concussion. Concussions are traumatic brain injuries that change the way the brain functions and may result in headache, memory loss, and confusion (Mayo Clinic, 2014a). A sharp blow to the head makes the brain shake inside the skull, causing the injury. More than 160,000 children are seen in emergency rooms for sports-related concussions each year (Ferguson et al., 2013). Almost half of those concussions occur in children ages 12 to 15 (see Figure 14.8). Also, in sports that both boys and girls play, such as soccer, lacrosse, and basketball, girls are proportionately more likely to suffer a concussion than boys (Ferguson et al., 2013). The reason for this gender difference is not clear. A biomechanical difference may make females more vulnerable, or it could be something to do with the way the game itself is played. Did you know that women lacrosse players are not required to wear helmets, while male players are (Ferguson et al., 2013)?

It is not always easy to tell whether someone has had a concussion because victims do not always lose consciousness (Mickalide & Hansen, 2012). If concussion is suspected, the child or adolescent should be seen by a qualified heath care professional experienced in evaluating concussions to determine whether the child can return to normal daily activities (CDC,

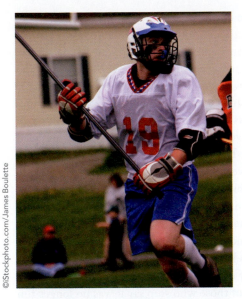

Gender differences on the lacrosse field. Both of these adolescents are about to begin a game of lacrosse. Female players are more likely to suffer a concussion than boys during a game. From these pictures, can you see some reasons why girls might be more vulnerable to injury in this sport?

FIGURE 14.8

Who is at risk of concussion? What do you think contributes to younger adolescents' and girls' higher risk of suffering a concussion while playing sports? When studying the second figure, remember that more boys than girls play competitive sports, so boys suffer a greater number of total concussions, but for any individual child, the risk is greater for females than for males.

29%
47%
19%
5%

16 to 19 years   12 to 15 years   8 to 11 years   7 and under

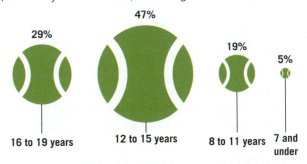

SOURCE: Ferguson et al. (2013).

n.d.). Under no condition should the player return to the sport or recreational activity on the same day the injury occurred. Following a concussion, a child's or teen's brain needs time to heal. The American Academy of Pediatrics recommends that skilled athletic trainers be on the sidelines of contact sports such as football to intervene immediately with any injury, and especially with concussions, which may not be obvious to the untrained adult (AAP, 2015).

Increasing evidence suggests that concussions can have long-term effects on cognitive function, motor skills, and mental health issues such as depression (Broglio et al., 2011). Despite all of this evidence, almost half of coaches believe that children can "see stars" from head impact without any negative effects (Mickalide & Hansen, 2012). When asked, the majority agree that they need more training in how to prevent sports injuries, but many are unable to get it due to the expense, lack of time, or unavailability of local training programs (Mickalide & Hansen, 2012). As of 2013, 48 states and the District of Columbia had enacted legislation intended to educate coaches, parents, and children about concussions and how to prevent them, although the state laws vary in their rigor and implementation (Ferguson et al., 2013).

We may think of organized sports as a way to keep children physically active and to set a pattern of lifelong physical activity, but 70% of children drop out of organized sports by the age of 13 (Engle, 2004). About one-quarter of those who stop say it was no longer fun for them, while another 16% say they stopped because they or their parents were concerned about the possibility of injuries (Mickalide & Hansen, 2012). Perhaps we could improve the retention rate if we listened more to what children are telling us about their experiences. Emphasizing skills, teamwork, and fun (rather than winning) may be a good way to put the spontaneity and joy back into organized sports for children and teens.

T ☐ F ☐ Children who participate in organized sports develop skills they use to keep them physically active throughout their lifetime. **False**

CREATIVE ACTIVITIES

Creative activities, such as painting, music, dance, and drama, are avenues for the expression of thoughts and emotions for people of all ages. Creative activities are also a very important part of positive youth development, helping children and adolescents express themselves and become involved with their peers both within and outside of their schools, with the supervision of caring and often skilled adults.

Some researchers have also claimed that involvement in the arts, especially music, has broad effects on children's intelligence. These claims were based on one study that showed that college students who listened to classical music consequently did better on a task assessing spatial intelligence (Rauscher, Shaw, & Ky, 1993), but this small and temporary effect has *not* been replicated by other researchers (Pietschnig, Voracek, & Formann, 2010).

Teens in the arts. What benefits do you think these teens may get from involvement in this play?

However, you'll remember from Chapter 8 that there is evidence for physiological changes in the brains of people who play instruments. When Ellen Winner and her colleagues examined abilities and brain function of children involved with musical training, they found that changes do occur, but they are very specific to the skills associated with playing music. For example, young musicians showed improved finger dexterity and rhythmic abilities, along with further development in the corresponding parts of the brain, but they did not show any evidence of a broad increase in intelligence or unrelated abilities (Hyde et al., 2009). Winner concludes, "If you are trying to bring up a young Einstein, it might be better to invest in mathematics and physics tutoring rather than daily violin practice" (Hatva, 2010, para. 5).

Art enrichment programs have helped low-income preschoolers become more prepared for school (Brown, Benedett, & Armistead, 2010), and helped English-language learners to further develop their reading ability (Rieg & Paquette, 2009). The advantages may come in a variety of ways. The nonverbal as well as verbal aspects of arts education may be particularly helpful to children who are learning a new language, as well as for those whose language development has not been fostered effectively at home. In addition, the arts provide opportunities for children to develop socioemotional and self-regulation skills they need for adjustment to school. Finally, the arts can reflect the cultural diversity of children involved in the program, promoting pride and self-confidence.

Researchers have also examined teens' involvement with performance in theater productions. Acting requires skills that are similar to, but more sophisticated than, those used by young children during fantasy play. In Chapter 12, we found that fantasy play in younger children is associated with a higher level of theory of mind and more empathy for other people. In a similar way, older children and teens who received acting training over the course of a year showed gains in these same areas (Goldstein & Winner, 2012). In theater programs, teens learn valuable lessons about understanding and managing emotions and find new ways to deal with frustration and to celebrate success together with others (Larson & Brown, 2007).

Creating a play or a musical program is an effective way to bring students from many different backgrounds together with a common goal. This helps to create strong bonds and a positive group identity, while the students draw on a variety of talents. Often they gain a new respect for the people they work with, regardless of their background. The public recognition that comes from a performance serves as a source of pride for those who take part in it. Dutton (2001) has found that goals of positive youth development, including exploration in a safe environment, a sense of connection to others, making a contribution to something worthwhile, and a feeling of competence, are all enhanced by involvement in the arts.

THE WORLD OF WORK

As children reach adolescence, paid work takes over some of what was leisure time in childhood. In 2015, 34% of U.S. teens ages 16 to 19 were in the labor force. Most teens take part in paid employment of some kind at some point in their adolescence, whether it is informal work for family, neighbors, or friends or more formal employment. They are most likely to work during the summer months when they are not in school. Youth in the United States are 30% more likely to be employed than youth in other developed countries (Rauscher, 2011).

Unless the work the teen is doing is specifically tied to the development of school-related skills, the evidence that employment promotes positive development for teenagers is mixed. Some research shows that teens who work have higher earnings 4 years after high school, but are less likely to succeed in higher education (Casey, Ripke, & Huston, 2005). In another study, teens who worked more than 20 hours per week were more likely to decrease their involvement in school and to become involved in problem behaviors, while teens who worked less than 20 hours did not differ academically or socially from those who did not work (Monahan, Lee, & Steinberg, 2011).

The effect of work appears to be different for teens from low-income and minority families.

Adolescent employment. Most teens work to have extra money. What do you think are the benefits and the drawbacks of teen employment?

Jamie Kingham/Image Source/Getty Images

TABLE 14.2

Adolescent patterns of employment during the school year. These four patterns reflect different approaches taken by teens who work at paid employment. Teens from low income families were most likely to fall into the Most Invested group, while those from families with higher incomes were more likely to be Steady or Occasional workers.

Average Intensity	Duration (Grades 10–12)	
	High (22 of 24 months)	Low (10–12 of 24 months)
Work More Than 20 Hours a Week	**Most Invested** (26%)	**Sporadic** (18%)
Work 20 Hours a Week or Less	**Steady** (25%)	**Occasional** (24%)

SOURCE: Mortimer (2010).

For these students, working may not be a choice, but rather a necessity to help their families or to save for their future education. Their added income may help them pay for extra educational expenses, such as field trips, that add to their academic interest and achievement (Lee & Staff, 2007). For teens from urban, low-income families, a transition from teen jobs, such as mowing lawns and babysitting, to adult-type jobs after age 16 was related to a lower high school dropout rate (Entwisle, Alexander, & Olson, 2005). Whereas Anglo American and Asian American students with highly educated parents did more poorly in school when they worked more hours for pay, this relation did not hold for Hispanic and African American students (Bachman, Staff, O'Malley, & Freedman-Doan, 2013).

Mortimer (2010) has argued that employment does not in itself produce positive or negative effects, but rather teens from different backgrounds and with different types of motivation choose different types of employment that have different consequences for their development. In a national longitudinal study, four patterns of teen employment were identified as shown in Table 14.2. Those teen workers who were identified as steady or occasional workers came from higher socioeconomic status and were more invested in school. Their work was seen as a sideline or as a way to make money for further education. These adolescents were more likely to graduate college. The teens who were most invested, working continuously for more than 20 hours per week, came from lower socioeconomic status and saw their jobs as opportunities for learning job-related skills that would help them later in life. They were more likely to attend community colleges and vocational schools and to move quickly into career jobs. Those who worked sporadically, that is, they worked more than 20 hours per week but were not consistently employed, had the most problem behaviors and were most likely to be unemployed after finishing high school. Therefore, although work itself affects teens' development, the nature of the work they take on is shaped by the students' pre-existing background and motivations. The research reminds us that we must be careful when we attribute certain effects, such as school dropout, to work itself.

CHECK YOUR UNDERSTANDING

1. What are developmental assets?
2. What are some positive and negative effects of participation in team sports?
3. What abilities are strengthened through participation in music and theater productions?
4. What benefits and risks does paid employment have for teens?

THE ROLE OF IMPORTANT NONPARENTAL ADULTS

14.4 What relationships beyond immediate family and peers are important for social development?

As we have explored the kinds of activities in which children and teens are involved, it is clear that these activities often involve adults other than the child's parents, including coaches, teachers, and employers. Young people's connection with adults who promote growth is an essential aspect of the positive youth development concept we described earlier. Although research on social relations has largely focused on the relationships that children and adolescents have with parents and peers, if we simply ask children or adolescents to name the people who are important to them, they spontaneously include on their lists a wide range of relatives and nonrelated adults (Chang, Greenberger, Chen, Heckhausen, & Farruggia, 2010; Farruggia, Bullen, & Davidson, 2013). Adolescents report that they have the most frequent contact with a favorite teacher (Rishel et al., 2007), but people such as coaches, youth leaders, clergy and nonparental relatives also appear on many lists.

Most research has relied upon self-reports from adolescents about the characteristics of their social networks, but when both parents and adolescents report on the strength of the adolescent's relationship with other people, parents tended to underestimate the influence of extended family members and to overestimate the influence of unrelated adults, such as coaches, teachers, or clergy, who knew the adolescent in a formal or professional capacity (Rishel et al., 2007). Although people in these formal roles are devoted to working with young people, their time is often spread across many individuals, so their impact on any single adolescent may be diluted. Also, the role they play is more limited than the role that a relative, who may have contact with the child throughout the child's life, might play. An adolescent may seek out the help of a teacher for a school-related problem but would be less likely to go to that person for help with a personal issue or general concerns (Beam et al., 2002).

Girls are more likely than boys to report that they have a nonparental adult whom they consider to be a very important person in their lives, but the percentage of very important people who were relatives is similar for boys (48%) and girls (52%) (Greenberger et al., 1998). Girls also report greater enjoyment and greater psychological intimacy in the relationship (Rishel et al., 2007). Although it is most likely that the adult will be the same gender as the adolescent, boys had more cross-gender relationships than girls.

Nonparental adults provide a unique context for development because they represent an adult point of view but are often less judgmental than parents (Darling, Hamilton, & Shaver, 2003). They also are important sources of social support when the adolescent is trying to cope with a stressful experience (Munsch & Blyth, 1993), as well as support for educational achievement (Farruggia et al., 2013), personal development, and trying new things (Chen et al., 2003). Nonparental adults are seen as role models, companions, teachers, guides, and confidants by

Rana Faure/Fuse/Getty Images

Relationships with nonparental adults. Many children and adolescents have adults other than their parents who are important to them. Many young people participate in sports, and for them, their coaches can be one of those very important adults in their lives.

adolescents (Chen et al., 2003; Munsch & Blyth, 1993). On occasion they are sources of more tangible support, such as financial assistance. Beam, Chen, and Greenberger (2002) found that these relationships do not compensate for a troubled parent-teen relationship, but rather become a unique source of support in their own right.

COACHES

Connecting children and adolescents to positive adult role models is often considered one of the benefits of participating in organized sports. For many young people, their coach becomes one of the important nonparental adults in their lives. Most adults who volunteer their time to coach organized youth activities have the children's best interests at heart, but many lack experience working with children and may not have a good understanding of child development. An adult coach might push a young player to perform at a higher level, thinking it will help the child develop skills or inspire a sense of accomplishment, yet the child may just want to have fun and spend some time with friends. When children participating in sports programs were asked what they *liked* about their coaches, they said their coach was nice, was fair, and "teaches us good things" (for boys) or "helps us play better" (for girls). However, when asked what they *liked least,* they said the coach "gets mad and yells at us," "works us too hard," "does not let me play enough" (for boys), or "doesn't teach us much" (for girls) (Humphrey, 2003, p. 58). Coaches thus may not understand how young players see their well-intended efforts to motivate them.

Coaches also influence children's motivation to take part in sports. In a study of 9- to 13-year-old basketball players, Smith, Smoll, and Cumming (2009) found that girls had higher *mastery motivation* (the desire to accomplish a goal or develop a skill) and boys had higher *ego motivation* (the desire to do better than others to get recognition and status). However, both boys and girls were affected over the course of a school year by the motivational climate created by their coaches. When children perceived that their coach "made players feel good when they improved a skill," for example, they developed higher mastery motivation, while coaches who "paid most attention to the best players" fostered higher ego motivation among the young athletes (Smith et al., 2009, p. 177).

The Coach Effectiveness Training program (CET) was developed to help coaches create the best possible experiences for young athletes. To replace the overemphasis on winning that is common in children's sports programs, coaches were taught to reward children for their efforts and improvements in skills. When this well-researched program has been implemented, it has resulted in a higher evaluation of the coaches by the team members, more enjoyment of the team as a group, an increase in self-esteem, less anxiety, and less likelihood of dropping out of the sport (APA, 2003).

NATURAL MENTORS

Mentor A trusting relationship between a young person and a nonparental adult who provides guidance intended to promote positive development.

Natural mentor A mentoring relationship between an adult and child that develops spontaneously rather than through a formal program.

Mentors are nonparental adults who have a trusting emotional relationship with a young person and offer guidance intended to promote the young person's positive development (DuBois & Karcher, 2013). We first describe the effects of having a **natural mentor** who becomes involved with a child spontaneously. We then discuss more formal mentorships.

Children and teens are more likely to have a natural mentor than a formal mentor relationship. In a number of studies, between 53% and 85% of young people reported having a natural mentor (Spencer, 2010). These relationships develop gradually over time, unlike formal mentorships that begin when the particular program begins. In fact, many adolescents report having known their natural mentor all of their lives (Spencer, 2010). Having a natural mentor has been associated with higher levels of educational attainment for at-risk African American students, lower levels of anxiety and depression among adolescent mothers, lower levels of reported use of marijuana and nonviolent delinquency, and higher levels of attachment to school (Hurd, Sánchez, Zimmerman, & Caldwell, 2012; Hurd & Zimmerman, 2010;

Zimmerman, Bingenheimer, & Notaro, 2002). Rural African American adolescents were less aggressive when they had natural mentors who were supportive both emotionally and by providing real advice about issues in the adolescent's life (Kogan, Brody, & Chen, 2011). The natural mentor directly reduces the risk of problem behavior by monitoring and sanctioning the behavior of the adolescent and also has an indirect effect because the support that this relationship provides helps the adolescent resist pressure from peers to engage in negative behaviors.

We often think about the importance of nonparental adult mentors for teens who have few other sources of support. However, teens who already have many resources are more likely to have a natural mentor than teens without those resources. When those with few resources do develop a mentoring relationship with an adult, they are more likely to reap benefits than other teens, particularly if that mentor is a teacher (Erickson, McDonald, & Elder, 2009). A relationship with a nonfamilial mentor may be particularly important for specific aspects of development, such as health practices (DuBois & Silverthorn, 2005). One reason for this may be that family members often share similar attitudes and behaviors, but a nonfamilial mentor can model and encourage the young person to adopt new attitudes and behaviors that are more beneficial. Also nonfamilial mentors often are professionals, such as teachers, counselors, or coaches, who are particularly strong role models for educational goals.

Active Learning: Relationships With Nonparental Adults gives you an opportunity to think about the people who have filled the role of natural mentor in your life and the impact they have had on your development.

Active LEARNING

Relationships With Nonparental Adults

Think about the relationships other than your relationship with your parents and your friends that were important to you while you were a teenager. Was there someone who was particularly influential, perhaps someone you would call a natural mentor? Were there different people who filled this role as you moved through childhood and adolescence, or did a single relationship continue throughout this time? What kinds of things did you do with this person that made the relationship an important one to you? Were these the same types of things that you did with your parents and/or friends, or were there unique functions they filled that you did not get from other relationships?

MENTORSHIP PROGRAMS

There are also over 3 million children and teens in the United States who are in formal mentoring relationships (MENTOR, 2012). These are established through programs in schools and through organizations such as Boys and Girls Clubs, or Big Brothers Big Sisters. The characteristics of a successful mentoring relationship sound very similar to those that make for the most positive parent-child relationship: closeness and warmth, consistency, and structure. Note that this description is similar to the description of authoritative parenting in Chapter 13. Mentoring relationships that focus on the child's developmental needs and interests and include a long-term commitment of at least a year are the ones most likely to result in positive outcomes (Erdem, DuBois, Larose, De Wit, & Lipman, 2016; Grossman, Chan, Schwartz, & Rhodes, 2012). When mentors also interact with the child's parents or peers, the positive effects increase. However, when relationships fall short on these factors, they are often linked with a *decrease* in well-being for the child or teen, so it is important for mentors to fully understand the commitment they are making to their protégé.

As appealing as mentor programs sound, research has shown only small effects in many cases (Rhodes & DuBois, 2006). In a review of the effectiveness of 55 formal mentoring programs, the youth were worse off after participation in 10% of the programs, there was no impact either positive or negative in one-third, and in the remainder there was a benefit for the youth, although it was usually small (DuBois, 2007). Mentoring programs are most effective when they include intensive and ongoing training and support for the mentors, parent interaction, and clear guidelines for the duration of the relationship and how often the mentor and protégé will meet (DuBois, Holloway, Valentine, & Cooper, 2002). Knowing these findings, a number of mentoring programs with children have made forming mentor-mentee relationships for at least a year a priority. In one program, the average length of the relationship was almost 4 years (Higley, Walker, Bishop, & Fritz, 2016).

CHECK YOUR UNDERSTANDING

1. What role do nonparental adults play in an adolescent's life?
2. How do family members and nonfamily adults provide different types of support?
3. What characteristics foster success for a formal mentoring program?

CONCLUSION

We have seen that children and teens spend their leisure time in a variety of ways. Unstructured time allows children to play or just hang out with friends while structured extracurricular activities build skills and strengthen peer relationships and often help to connect children and adolescents to nonparental adults who are important in their lives. Children of all ages spend a considerable amount of time using media, including television, computers, smartphones, gaming technology, and many other new technologies. This use of media can contribute to a decrease in children's contact with the natural world. It is important that we continue to examine the entire context of children's lives to understand and help children use all the resources available to them and their families in the most positive way.

CHAPTER SUMMARY

Test your understanding of the content.
Take the practice quiz at **edge.sagepub.com/levine3e**

14.1 What does the daily life of children and teens around the world look like?

In cultures in which children are not required to work to help feed their families, leisure time is spent in many different ways. In Asia, parents require their children to do more academic work. In the United States, children are more likely to take part in unstructured play and participate in structured activities such as sports or the arts, and use electronic media.

14.2 How does unstructured time, including time spent in the natural world and with electronic media, affect children's development?

Unstructured play promotes creativity and imagination for children. For teens, too much unsupervised time may lead to problem behaviors, but some amount of autonomy is necessary for developing identity. Relatively few children have too many structured activities in their lives, despite some fears that this is a problem. There has been much concern about the decrease in children's involvement in the natural world. Researchers have found evidence that interaction with the natural world is related to lower rates of obesity, an enhanced ability to pay attention, reduced stress, and a greater willingness to protect nature. One reason for the decline in outdoor activity is increasing use of electronic media. Heavy TV viewing can promote obesity because of lack of physical activity or overeating in front of the TV. Paradoxically, it also can promote eating disorders because of images of ultrathin models. For cognitive development, no positive effects of TV viewing have been found for children under age 2. For older children, educational TV and other educational media can promote positive cognitive and social development, but entertainment TV has a negative effect on academic achievement. Violent media promotes aggressive thoughts and behavior, while prosocial messages in the media can have a positive effect. Social networking can enhance friendships, but there is a danger of adult predators when children and teens talk with people they don't know. Media can constrict **self-complexity** for teens, and minority children may be hurt by stereotypes shown in the media. It is important to teach **media literacy** to help children understand how the media is trying to manipulate their thinking in subtle ways.

14.3 How do structured activities contribute to positive youth development?

Positive youth development focuses on using positive activities to link into the great potential young people have for change and growth. Well-supervised activities provide opportunities for achievement, socialization with peers and adults, and excitement shared with a group. However, organized sports may cause injuries, and children may be pressured to win. Many drop out by age 13. Creative activities promote interpersonal skills and social cognitive abilities.

14.4 What relationships beyond immediate family and peers are important for social development?

Many children and adolescents have nonparental adults (both relatives and unrelated adults such as teachers, coaches, and clergy) who are important in their lives. These adults can function as **natural mentors**. Having a mentor can benefit children's development or even act as a protective factor for those at risk. The Coach Effectiveness Training program (CET) helps coaches do the best job of promoting the welfare of the children and teens under their supervision. Having a **mentor** through a formal mentoring program has not made a substantial impact on many of the children and adolescent protégés. Programs are more likely to be effective when they do a good job of training the mentors, continue for at least 1 year, and involve parents in the program.

KEY TERMS

Strengthen your understanding of these key terms with mobile-friendly eFlashcards at **edge.sagepub.com/levine3e**

Developmental assets   566
Media literacy   562
Mentor   574
Natural mentor   574

Orienting response   553
Self-complexity   560
Selfies   561
Sexting   558

Give your students the SAGE edge!

SAGE edge offers a robust online environment featuring an impressive array of free tools and resources for review, study, and further exploration, keeping both instructors and students on the cutting edge of teaching and learning. Learn more at **edge.sagepub.com/levine3e**

chapter 15

HEALTH, WELL-BEING, AND RESILIENCE

LEARNING QUESTIONS

15.1 What is stress, and how do we cope with it?

15.2 How do physical illnesses and mental disorders affect children's development?

15.3 What are other threats to the health and well-being of children and adolescents?

15.4 What are effects of poverty, homelessness, trauma, maltreatment, and racial discrimination on the development of children and adolescents?

15.5 What factors contribute to resilience in children faced with great adversity?

Master these objectives using an online action plan at **edge.sagepub.com/levine3e**

TEST YOUR KNOWLEDGE

Test your knowledge of child development by deciding whether each of the following statements is *true* or *false,* and then check your answers as you read the chapter.

1. **T ☐ F ☐:** The best way to define "being healthy" is to say that you don't have any illnesses.

2. **T ☐ F ☐:** When you are trying to deal with a stressful situation, you should try to ignore your emotional response and focus on solving the problem.

3. **T ☐ F ☐:** A lack of sleep can contribute to weight gain.

4. **T ☐ F ☐:** Because children are still growing, they are more resistant to the effects of environmental toxins than adults.

5. **T ☐ F ☐:** Rates of adolescent smoking and alcohol consumption are at their lowest levels in more than 40 years.

6. **T ☐ F ☐:** Once families live in poverty, they are unlikely to move out of it.

7. **T ☐ F ☐:** In the United States, one child dies from child abuse or neglect every 4 days.

8. **T ☐ F ☐:** Almost all sexual abuse of children is perpetrated by adult male strangers.

9. **T ☐ F ☐:** Adults who were abused as children are likely to become abusive parents themselves.

10. **T ☐ F ☐:** Children who are able to rise above great adversity like poverty or child abuse have a number of unique abilities.

Correct answers: (1) F, (2) F, (3) T, (4) F, (5) T, (6) F, (7) F, (8) F, (9) F, (10) F

▲ **VIDEO:** Watch as students answer some of these questions and the authors respond.

==H==ealth is more than the absence of illness. It is a general state of well-being that includes not only physical well-being but also mental and social well-being. In this chapter, we describe some common threats to children's health and well-being and review some recommendations that can help ensure that children are healthy. Physical and emotional well-being are affected by stress so we first look at how children and adolescents learn to cope with the stress that they experience. For most children, their stress is the normal stress that everyone experiences (for example, taking an important test or starting a new school), but for others the stress is traumatic. We then examine children's health by describing a number of common and chronic illnesses and mental disorders as well as accidents and injuries that threaten children's well-being. Other issues discussed in this chapter include how growing up in poverty, experiencing trauma, being homeless or a victim of child abuse or neglect, or experiencing racism can affect a child's development and well-being. Despite these hardships, the chapter concludes with a look at how resilient children and adolescents can be and at some of the factors that help build that resilience.

> **T ☐ F ☐** The best way to define "being healthy" is to say that you don't have any illnesses. **False**

STRESS AND COPING

15.1 What is stress, and how do we cope with it?

Increasingly, the field of child development has recognized that facing adversity while growing up can produce a stress response that undermines the developing brain and the functioning of the cardiovascular system, immune system, and metabolic control system (Center on the Developing Child at Harvard University, 2010). These developmental disruptions have lifelong consequences for the physical and mental well-being of an individual. Adversity comes in many forms—from day-to-day hassles that are resolved in minutes to long-term stressors that persist over months or even years, to catastrophic events that change everything in a child's world in a matter of minutes. However, child development researchers also have identified effective ways children can cope with these stressors, and we continue to learn the sources of the strengths that enable them to overcome these challenges.

WHAT IS STRESS?

Stress Anything that places excessive demands on our ability to cope.

Stress is a normal and inevitable part of life. In the broadest sense, stress is anything that places excessive demands on our ability to cope. Think of all the experiences that fit this definition. They include short-term experiences like riding on a roller coaster or long-term situations like growing up in poverty. They can be events that occur repeatedly over time, like child abuse, or a single occurrence like living through a tornado. Positive as well as negative experiences, or even perceived threats that actually pose little or no real danger, can cause stress.

When you experience stress, your hypothalamus sends signals to your adrenal gland which then produces high levels of cortisol, a hormone that prepares your body to deal with threats in the environment. That is why your heart races, you breathe more rapidly, and you begin to sweat (APA, 2016c). All of these physiological reactions evolved as a part of the **fight-or-flight response** that was meant to protect us from real, physical threats in the environment. When we are dealing with short-term sources of stress, this response works the way it should—it energizes us just when we need it so we can deal with a real and immediate threat. The trouble occurs when stress becomes long-term or chronic. When stress continues over time and the body tries to maintain this elevated level of readiness, it can take a toll on us physically. Chronic stress can result in physical symptoms, such as fatigue, headaches, and stomach upsets, or emotional consequences such as anxiety and depression (APA, 2016c). The production of large amounts of cortisol over a long period of time lowers the body's immune response and this increases the likelihood of illness (National Scientific Council on the Developing Child, 2005/2014).

Fight-or-flight response The body's physiological response to threat.

A study conducted by Kaiser Permanente in the 1990s identified the types of adverse experiences that occur in childhood and described how those cumulative experiences create a pathway that can lead to illness, disability, and even early death (Felitti et al., 1998) (see Figure 15.1). Seven categories of adverse childhood experiences (ACEs) were identified: psychological, physical, or sexual abuse; living with individuals who were substance abusers, mentally ill, or had been in prison; and witnessing domestic violence. The number of ACEs experienced showed a graded relationship to the number of adult health risk behaviors and diseases that were studied, meaning that the greater the number, the greater the risk of a poor outcome. The risks included alcoholism; drug abuse; depression; suicide; smoking; having numerous sexual partners; severe obesity; adult diseases that affect the heart, lungs, and liver; and cancer. Reducing a child's exposure to any of these risk factors and helping them have a safe and stable environment to grow up in reduces their lifetime risk.

The stress response also affects brain development and a child's ability to learn. Persistent high levels of cortisol can cause brain cells to die or can reduce the connections between areas of the brain that are essential for learning and memory (National Scientific Council on the

FIGURE 15.1

Adverse childhood experiences (ACEs). Researchers have found that as the number of adverse experiences during childhood increases, so does the negative impact that they have on a person's ability to function well in adulthood. This figure illustrates the pathway by which these early experiences affect lifelong health and functioning.

**Mechanism by Which Adverse Childhood Experiences
Influence Health and Well-being Throughout the Lifespan**

SOURCE: Centers for Disease Control and Prevention (2016). Adverse childhood experiences presentation graphics.

Developing Child, 2005/2014). Prolonged exposure to stressful situations also can make neural systems overreactive or slow to shut down throughout the remainder of the individual's life. Infants who are under chronic stress may become children and adults who are overly anxious and fearful. Because infants' brains are plastic or changeable, the good news is that many of the effects of stress early in life can be reversed with sensitive caregiving, but without intervention, the maladaptive stress response can severely limit the child's growth and development.

Throughout our lives, which experiences we consider to be stressful can be pretty subjective. Some people find speaking before a crowd to be energizing and even fun, but others are nearly paralyzed with fright at the prospect of having to take the stage. The types of things children and adolescents experience as stressful change as a function of their age (Humphrey, 2004). For young children, being separated from their parents is a stressful experience, and dealing with new things in their environment can also be difficult. When children get older and enter school, the need to make new friends and deal with situations that test their competence can be stressful. For adolescents, social experiences are important, so peer rejection can be stressful, and all adolescents need to cope with the changes in their bodies as they go through puberty.

Stressful or fun? How do you imagine this young girl is feeling as she looks out at the audience she is about to face? How we react to various situations that challenge us can be very variable from one person to another. How do you feel about speaking in public?

One source of stress for children that is often overlooked is their response to their parents' level of stress. In a national survey conducted by the American Psychological Association (2010a), 69% of the parents thought that their stress level had little or no impact on their children, but only 14% of the children said that their parents' stress didn't bother them. Children who report that their parents are often stressed report more stress themselves, as well as more sadness, anxiety, and frustration.

To examine your own experiences with stress, try **Active Learning: Stress and Coping.**

Active LEARNING

Stress and Coping

Write down three events in your life you have experienced as stressful. Next to each event, write the age at which it occurred and then write how you coped with each one. Were different kinds of experiences stressful at different ages? How did you cope with the stress you felt? Did you cope in different ways at different ages? How successful have your coping methods been in reducing your stress?

Now look at the sources of stress in your life at present. How do you cope with this stress? If possible, compare your experiences with classmates. Which sources of stress are common and which are unique? Do your classmates have coping methods that might be useful for you?

Normative Stress and Non-Normative Stress

Normative stress Stress that is predictable and that most individuals go through, and which requires a moderate and relatively brief response.

Most of the stress that we experience is **normative stress.** This type of stress is caused by things that happen to everyone (or almost everyone), is often something we can anticipate and prepare for, and does not overwhelm our ability to cope. For example, starting kindergarten, middle school, or college is a normative event, even though it usually creates some amount of stress. Going through puberty, learning to drive, and dating someone you like are other examples. We deal with these experiences with a positive stress response in which the physiological reaction is mild or moderate in intensity and relatively brief in duration (Shonkoff et al., 2012). Such experiences give children a chance to build coping skills and develop confidence in their ability to deal with challenges that they will continue to face as they grow.

Non-normative stress Stress that results from a relatively rare occurrence that often overwhelms the individual.

By contrast, **non-normative stress** is the result of a relatively rare occurrence that creates a great deal of stress which often overwhelms the individual, at least for a period of time. The death of a parent, a serious illness or hospitalization, and living through a natural disaster are all examples of non-normative stress. We discuss this type of stress later in the chapter when we talk about trauma as a threat to child development.

COPING

Coping Conscious effort made to master, tolerate, or reduce stress.

When faced with stressful situations, we do what we can to reduce that stress and return ourselves to a more balanced physiological state. **Coping** is the conscious effort we make to regulate our emotions, thoughts, and behaviors when we are challenged by stressful situations (Compas, Connor-Smith, Saltzman, Thomsen, & Wadsworth, 2001). One way of categorizing the strategies is to divide them into problem-focused or emotion-focused strategies.

Problem-focused strategies are designed to change the situation in a way that reduces your stress, while **emotion-focused strategies** are designed to reduce or manage the emotional distress you are feeling. Table 15.1 provides examples of each of these strategies. For instance, you could try to improve a stressful situation by finding information you can use to change the situation, learning some new skills, or mobilizing social support for assistance. Problem-focused strategies are most effective when the situation is one that you can realistically change or control. However, sometimes situations are beyond your control, and in those situations, you can reduce some of the stress by using emotion-focused strategies like sharing your feelings with trusted friends or changing your perception of the situation (Zimmer-Gembeck & Skinner, 2008). In most situations, people use a combination of strategies as part of their coping efforts. Look back at your answers to **Active Learning: Stress and Coping.** Which types of coping methods have you used, problem-focused and/or emotion-focused strategies? Why do you think you used each type in each situation?

We said that the types of things that children find stressful change with age, but so do the ways they try to cope. Young children tend to rely on problem-focused approaches when they are in distress. For example, if they don't want to be separated from their parents, they run after them or wave to them to come back. When they use emotion-focused strategies, those strategies are pretty simple and direct, such as reassuring themselves that their mother will come back or hugging a blanket for comfort. Older children and adolescents begin to use metacognitive abilities to identify what type of coping is most likely to work for them

T ☐ F ☐ When you are trying to deal with a stressful situation, you should try to ignore your emotional response and instead focus on solving the problem. **False**

Problem-focused strategies Coping strategies that focus on changing or improving a stressful situation.

Emotion-focused strategies Coping strategies designed to reduce or manage emotional distress.

TABLE 15.1

Coping strategies. This table contains examples of strategies that children and adolescents might use to cope with stress.

Problem-Focused Coping Strategies (efforts to change the source of the stress or one's relationship to it)	
Strategy	Example
Active coping—taking action to remove the source of the stress or soften its effect	I put more time and effort into overcoming this problem.
Planning—thinking about the best way to handle the situation	I think about what I can do, step by step, to make the situation better.
Seeking instrumental social support—seeking advice, assistance, or information from others	I talk to others who have the same problem to get some advice from them.
Restraint coping—waiting for the right opportunity to take action	I make myself be patient until it is the right time to act.
Emotion-Focused Coping Strategies (attempts to manage or regulate the emotions caused by the situation)	
Strategy	Example
Expressing or venting feelings—releasing the emotions surrounding the situation	When I get upset, I just let it all out because it makes me feel better.
Seeking emotional support—seeking moral support, sympathy, or understanding	I talk to my best friend because she is always there for me when I need her.
Accepting the situation—realizing that one must accommodate the situation because it can't be changed	I just learn how to live with those things I can't change.
Positive reframing or reappraisal—viewing the stressful situation in a more positive way	I realize that what has happened to me is really all for the best in the long run.

SOURCE: Carver, Scheier, & Weintraub (1989).

James Lauritz/Photodisc/Getty Images

Emotion-focused coping. This child might find flying stressful. Her stuffed animals help her feel comforted so she can cope with the stress.

DEVELOPMENT IN ACTION VIDEO ▲

(Skinner & Zimmer-Gembeck, 2007). Although adolescents have the ability to do this, a national study of tweens and teens found that a large number of them still rely on behaviors that may make themselves feel better but don't improve the situation that is causing the stress (APA, 2010b). They report using sedentary behaviors that include listening to music, playing video games, or watching television. Although this may help them manage feelings of distress, it does not change the situation for the better.

Ways to Help Children Cope With Stress

There are a number of things that parents and people who work with children and adolescents can do to help them deal with stress in their lives. First, they need to simply watch for signs of stress. These will differ with the age of the child. A young child might regress to more immature behavior (for example, thumb sucking or beginning to wet himself again after he has been toilet trained). Routine patterns of eating, sleeping, and leisure activities can be disrupted for children or adolescents at any age. Older children and adolescents might begin having trouble at school because they can't concentrate or pay attention. There may be changes in their emotions. Children may become more aggressive than usual, or more clingy or withdrawn. They may have vague physical complaints about headaches or upset stomachs. Any of these changes should prompt a concerned adult to ask the child how she is feeling and if something is bothering her. Disclosure is the necessary first step for getting social support in a time of stress, and we can encourage children to take this step.

Next, we can help children or adolescents think about problem-solving strategies that might work for them, or we can help them reappraise the stressful situation if it has been blown out of proportion. If stress is chronic, there are other behavior management strategies that can be helpful. Getting enough rest, eating a healthy diet, and getting some exercise all help in coping with stress (Mayo Clinic, 2014b). **Active Learning: Finding Resources to Cope With Stress** gives you the opportunity to explore some of the resources available to you on your campus if you are dealing with a good deal of stress.

Active LEARNING

Finding Resources to Cope With Stress

You may be well aware of the fact that being a college student can be stressful. Other people also recognize this, which is why most colleges and universities offer a wide range of services to their students to help them cope. These services are usually free of charge.

Go to your college's home page and search for terms like *student workshops* or *counseling services* to see what your campus offers. On one campus, searching for the term *counseling services* found this information on the webpage for University Counseling Services:

- Counseling services—Individual Counseling, Couples Counseling, Group Counseling, Psychiatric Consultation, and Urgent Care

- Group therapy—Relationship Support, Gay/Lesbian/Bisexual Support, Men's Support, Making Peace with Your Body (body image, eating disorders), Saying Goodbye to Shy, First-Year College Experience

- Personal improvement workshops—Choice or Chance: Career Development, Improving Your Sleep, Building Self-Esteem, Overcoming Procrastination, Public Speaking Anxiety Workshop

If you know you are experiencing a high level of stress, you may want to look into the services that your college offers to help prevent future health problems.

With this general understanding of what stress is and how we cope with it, we next discuss the impact of some major causes of stress for many children and adolescents: threats to physical health and well-being, mental disorders, poverty and homelessness, child abuse, and racial discrimination.

CHECK YOUR UNDERSTANDING

1. What is the difference between normative and non-normative stress?
2. What is the difference between problem-focused and emotion-focused coping?
3. What are some ways we can help children and adolescents cope with stress?

PHYSICAL ILLNESS AND MENTAL DISORDERS

15.2 How do physical illnesses and mental disorders affect children's development?

We have already discussed some important topics related to health in earlier chapters. For instance, in Chapter 6, you learned how both malnourishment and obesity threaten children's health in different ways. In the following sections of this chapter we look at some common and chronic illnesses that affect children and adolescents. We also review information that was covered earlier in this book regarding mental health and mental disorders that affect many children. As you will learn, there is much that can be done to help promote the well-being of children with these conditions and to support their families.

COMMON ILLNESSES

The immune systems of young children are still developing, so they are not as resistant to common germs as older children and adults. That is why physicians recommend that young children be immunized to protect them against 14 common diseases, including measles, mumps, whooping cough, polio, and rubella or German measles (CDC, 2015h). Many of these diseases have been greatly reduced or nearly eliminated in the United States in recent years, but if parents do not continue to immunize their children, the diseases will be able to regain a foothold in the population. For example, whooping cough, which was virtually eradicated in the United States, recently made a resurgence in an area of California where vaccination rates were low (Atwell et al., 2013). Some vaccinations are given at an older age. In Chapter 6, you learned about the vaccine that is available for young adolescents that can protect against the human papillomavirus (HPV) which can lead to genital warts or cancer if it doesn't clear the body on its own.

Although some parents have concerns about the safety of vaccines, all formulas go through clinical trials before they are put into general use, and the Centers for Disease Control continually monitors vaccines for effectiveness and safety. Parents need to understand that preventable diseases have serious health consequences for children who are not protected by a vaccine. As an example, mumps is usually a relatively mild disease that causes fever, headaches, and swelling of the salivary glands in the cheeks and jaw, but it can lead to meningitis, encephalitis, deafness, or even death (CDC, 2015h).

While immunizations offer protection against many contagious diseases, they do not protect against common illnesses such as diarrhea, sore throats, or colds. It is not unusual for young children to get these illnesses. In countries with inadequate sanitation and few medical resources, pneumonia and diarrhea are among the most common causes of childhood deaths (World Health Organization, 2013). Fortunately, most common childhood illnesses are self-limiting (that is, they resolve without needing any medical intervention), but when a symptom is severe or long-lasting, parents need to consult a physician. Because infants are not able to tell us what they are feeling, adults have an extra obligation to watch for and correctly interpret these symptoms of illness when they occur in young children.

When children first enter school or child care, they have contact with many new people and are exposed to new illnesses. Their risk of getting these illnesses can be reduced with simple, but important, prevention strategies, such as thoroughly washing their hands and covering their mouth and nose when they sneeze. The best way to protect a child from the flu is to have the child vaccinated with the influenza vaccine, but once a child catches a cold or the flu, there isn't much that can be done to treat or speed up the progress of the illness. The Food and Drug Administration (2008) strongly recommends that children under the age of 2 not be given over-the-counter cough and cold medicines because these medications do not make the cold go away sooner but do have some potentially serious side effects. Keeping children well hydrated and allowing plenty of rest can make them more comfortable as the illness runs its course.

CHRONIC ILLNESSES

In contrast to common illnesses which usually run their course without medical intervention, chronic illnesses are ones that are long-lasting, do not resolve spontaneously, and cannot be

How to help prevent spreading colds and the flu. These photos show two precautions children are taught to help prevent the spread of illness: coughing or sneezing into the crook of their arm instead of into their hand or the air and frequently washing their hands.

cured completely in most cases (Compas, Jaser, Dunn, & Rodriguez, 2012). Chronic illnesses in children and adolescents include conditions such as asthma (the most common chronic illness), diabetes, sickle cell anemia, cancer, HIV/AIDS, cystic fibrosis, epilepsy, congenital heart problems, cerebral palsy, and seizure disorders. By one estimate, 25% of children in the United States live with a chronic illness (Compas et al., 2012). The recent increase in the number of children living with chronic illness is attributable, at least in part, to the fact that many diseases that in the past would have been fatal are now treatable (Halfon & Newacheck, 2010). This means that many children are now *living with*, rather than *dying from*, chronic illnesses.

Because families are systems, a chronic illness or disability in one family member affects everyone in the family. Parents experience stress because of their concern for the well-being of their child. The medical expenses associated with the child's illness are another source of stress. Parents understandably may feel disappointment or a sense of grief at the loss of the life they had imagined for their child. The need for constant vigilance concerning a child's medical condition can place a tremendous strain on a marriage, and caregiver burnout is a real possibility if parents don't make time to meet some of their own needs. Healthy siblings may resent that they don't get the same amount of time or attention from their parents that their ill sibling does (Boyse, Boujaoude, & Laundy, 2010; Malone & Price, 2012). Although siblings may experience feelings of sadness, anxiety, and guilt, they also can develop greater empathy, interpersonal sensitivity, and maturity as the result of this experience (Malone & Price, 2012; O'Brien, Duffy, & Nicholl, 2009). One promising family intervention helps healthy siblings develop coping skills and facilitates problem-solving communication in parents, while strengthening family time and routines for the entire family (Giallo & Gavidia-Payne, 2008). One strength of this approach is that the focus is not just on the sick child, but on the whole family and the supports it needs.

Of course the child suffers from whatever pain, discomfort, or limitations the condition brings with it. When hospitalization is required, being in a strange environment, often separated from their parents, is stressful to children, especially younger ones who cannot fully understand all that is happening to them. Fortunately, more hospitals and medical offices now offer families the services of professionals such as pediatric psychologists and child life specialists.

Pediatric psychologists provide therapeutic interventions to help with the emotional and behavioral difficulties that children experience in connection with medical conditions. They also can help children deal with painful and frightening medical procedures (APA, 2016b). **Child life specialists** are experts in child development who promote optimal development in children by providing information, support, and guidance to children and family members who are dealing with serious health threats (Child Life Council, n.d.). To do this, they use a variety of techniques, including play that prepares children for medical procedures and opportunities for self-expression. They also help families understand the medical procedures that are being used to treat their children.

How a child copes with a chronic illness depends on several factors, including the age and temperament of the child and the nature of the illness itself. When children are in stressful situations, they often seek social support from peers, but this support may not be easily available to chronically ill

Pediatric psychologists
Child psychologists who provide therapeutic interventions for children with medical disorders.

Child life specialists
Experts in child development who promote optimal development in children in medical settings.

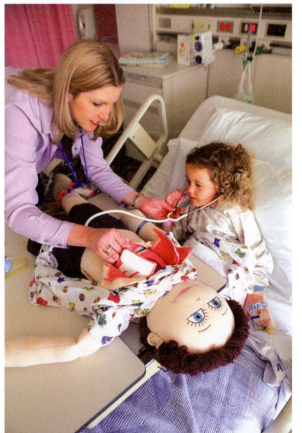

Spencer Grant/Photo Researchers, Inc.

The work of a child life specialist. A child life specialist uses play and age-appropriate communication to prepare children for upcoming hospital procedures and to develop coping strategies for what they must face. They also help children deal with their feelings and keep families involved in the child's care.

children. Peers may avoid the sick child, mistakenly fearing that the child is contagious. It also is difficult for school-age children to establish and maintain friendships if they are frequently absent from school or cannot participate in the same activities as other children. And, frankly, sometimes peers can just be mean, especially if medical procedures disfigure a child or change the child's appearance. At a time when adolescents would ordinarily be developing autonomy and independence from parents, an adolescent with a chronic illness may still need a great deal of parental monitoring and supervision. As a result, a teen may rebel against the medical regime that is essential to his or her health. For instance, a diabetic teenager who eats what everyone else does may temporarily feel more normal, but this rebellion can take a serious toll on her health.

Many chronic illnesses run in families. How much do you know about your own health history? You are routinely asked for this information when you see a new physician. **Active Learning: Creating a Personal Health History** will help you compile this information.

Active LEARNING

Creating a Personal Health History

You can use this activity to track down information from your childhood that you may not have or to ask questions about your family's health history that you have never discussed with your parents before. It is important that you know about your family's medical history because major illnesses such as arthritis, diabetes, hypertension (high blood pressure), heart disease, or conditions such as major depression, alcoholism, or other substance abuse problems that have affected your parents, grandparents, and siblings can increase your risk for these illnesses or conditions.

The Surgeon General of the United States maintains a webpage at https://familyhistory .hhs.gov/FHH/html/index.html where you can compile a detailed family health history. You also can create a personal health history by finding answers to these general questions:

- What childhood illnesses did you have (for example, mumps, rubella or German measles, chicken pox, rheumatic fever, or strep throat)? At which age did you have each illness, and how severe was it?

- Are you current with your immunizations (for example, tetanus, polio, rubella, and diphtheria)? Find out the date that you received each immunization, and remember that immunizations need to be updated from time to time.

- What are the names and dates of any surgical procedures you have had?

- What are the dates and reasons for any hospitalizations?

- What allergies (if any) do you have?

- What medications do you take (both by prescription and over the counter), and what is the amount and frequency of using them?

MENTAL HEALTH AND MENTAL DISORDERS

According to the Centers for Disease Control and Prevention (2015g), in any one year, between 13% and 20% of children and adolescents in the United States experience a mental health disorder. In Chapter 1, we introduced the idea of *developmental psychopathology,* which describes psychological disorders as distortions of normal developmental pathways. For that reason, we have included a number of mental health disorders in our discussions of typical development throughout this text. For example, eating disorders appeared with the discussion of nutrition, and reactive attachment disorder appeared as part of our discussion of attachment.

Table 15.2 provides a summary of the mental disorders we have discussed in earlier chapters that affect a number of children and adolescents. You will read about posttraumatic stress disorder and substance use disorder later in this chapter.

TABLE 15.2

Childhood mental disorders. These brief descriptions will remind you of a number of childhood mental disorders that have been described in earlier chapters. Two additional disorders (posttraumatic stress disorder and substance use disorder) are covered later in this chapter. You can use the chapter reference to return to any of these topics to refresh your memory about each one.

Mental Disorder (Chapter)	Description
Autism Spectrum Disorder (Chapters 6 and 9)	A pervasive impairment in social communication and interaction, and restricted or repetitive behaviors, interests or activities, with a degree of impairment that can run from mild to severe.
Schizophrenia (Chapter 6)	A rare but serious mental disorder that is diagnosed by two or more of these symptoms: delusions, hallucinations, disorganized speech, disorganized or catatonic behavior, or negative symptoms such as reduced expression of emotion and reduction in self-motivated behavior.
Eating Disorders (Chapter 6)	• *Anorexia nervosa*—An eating disorder in which individuals intentionally restrict their food intake to a point that may become life threatening. • *Bulimia nervosa*—An eating disorder characterized by eating binges followed by self-induced vomiting or the excessive use of laxatives.
Attention-Deficit/ Hyperactivity Disorder (Chapter 7)	A disorder marked by extreme difficulty with inattention, distractibility, impulsivity, or a combination of these.
Intellectual Disability (Chapter 8)	Intellectual impairment that begins early in life and includes deficits in intellectual, social, and adaptive functioning.
Specific Learning Disorder (Chapters 8 and 9)	Performance that is substantially below the average on an appropriate test of skill that cannot be better explained by another problem. There are "specifiers" within the category for difficulties within the various academic domains (e.g., reading [dyslexia], writing, and arithmetic).
Communication Disorders (Chapter 9)	• *Language disorder*—A disorder in which a child's understanding and use of language is significantly below his or her nonverbal intelligence. • *Speech sound disorder*—Difficulty producing or using sounds at an age-appropriate level. • *Childhood-onset fluency disorder or stuttering*— Difficulty with fluency and time patterning of speech. • *Social or pragmatic communication disorder*— Difficulty with appropriate use of both verbal and nonverbal communication.
Attachment Disorders (Chapter 10)	• *Reactive attachment disorder (RAD)*—A disorder in which the child is unable to form any attachment, is withdrawn from caregivers, and shows disturbance in both social and emotional functioning. • *Disinhibited social engagement disorder*—A disorder in which a child approaches strangers indiscriminately, not differentiating between attachment figures and other people.

(Continued)

(Continued)

Mental Disorder (Chapter)	Description
Major Depression (Chapter 10)	A condition marked by feelings of worthlessness and hopelessness, a lack of pleasure, sleep and appetite disturbances, and possibly suicidal thoughts.
Anxiety Disorders (Chapter 10)	• *Generalized anxiety disorder*—Vague but persistent worry that something bad is about to happen. • *Panic disorder*—A sudden, intense feeling of terror and dread accompanied by physical sensations such as heart palpitations, chest pain, and nausea. • *Separation anxiety disorder*—Developmentally inappropriate and excessive distress when away from a loved one, usually a parent or other caregiver, to whom the child is attached. • *Social anxiety disorder (social phobia)*—Unusual or excessive fear of being scrutinized and evaluated in social situations.
Disruptive Mood Dysregulation Disorder (Chapter 10)	Severe and frequent temper tantrums that are out of proportion to the situation.
Oppositional Defiant Disorder (Chapter 10)	A persistent pattern of behavior marked by defiant, disobedient, and hostile behavior toward authority figures.
Conduct Disorder (Chapter 10)	A repetitive and persistent pattern of behavior in which the basic rights of others or major age-appropriate social norms or rules are violated.
Posttraumatic Stress Disorder (Chapter 15)	Re-experiencing a traumatic event through intrusive thoughts, distressing dreams, flashbacks, or extreme reactions in situations similar to the original trauma.
Substance Use Disorder (Chapter 15)	Use of drugs that is marked by cravings, social impairment, risky use, and tolerance build-up and withdrawal symptoms.

Often the symptoms of these disorders are not unlike behavior that many people exhibit from time to time. The difference is that the behaviors, thoughts, and feelings are more extreme, last longer than most people experience, and cause significant distress and/or disruption to the lives of the children and adolescents who experience them. For many of these disorders, early onset in childhood has a worse prognosis for later well-being, but children can be flexible and resilient and this may help them have a better chance for recovery.

Treatment for these disorders may include psychiatric medicines and psychosocial interventions with the child and the family. However, in 2012 less than half of children with mental disorders received treatment (NIMH, n.d.) and part of the reason is the stigma connected with having a mental disorder. When children with mental disorders experience discrimination and negative attitudes from others, it may become part of their self-concept and add to the problems associated with their disorder. There is some evidence that school-based programs can increase children's and teens' understanding of mental disorders and decrease their avoidance of others who have these disorders (Milin et al., 2016; Murman et al., 2014).

CHECK YOUR UNDERSTANDING

1. Why is it important for parents to immunize their children?
2. How does a chronic illness affect all members in a family?
3. What is *developmental psychopathology*?

OTHER THREATS TO HEALTH AND WELL-BEING

15.3 **What are other threats to the health and well-being of children and adolescents?**

In this section, we cover several threats to the day-to-day well-being of children and adolescents. Inadequate sleep has increasingly affected the functioning of children and teens. Toxins in their environment can put them at risk for a number of serious health conditions, including asthma and cancer, and accidents and injuries are a threat to children at any age. Teens make decisions about the use of alcohol, tobacco, and illicit drugs that also can become threats to their well-being.

SLEEP DEFICIT

Children and adolescents need an adequate amount of sleep to support their physical and cognitive development, but many are getting less sleep than they did in the past (Astill, Van der Heijden, Van Ijzendoorn, & Van Someren, 2012). Only 9% of adolescents get the optimal amount of sleep (9 hours or more each night), while almost two-thirds report

FIGURE 15.2

Adolescent sleep habits. Only about 9% of adolescents in Grades 9 through 12 report getting what is considered an optimal amount of sleep each night. What do you think accounts for this sleep deficit for so many young people? What suggestions would you make to improve the situation?

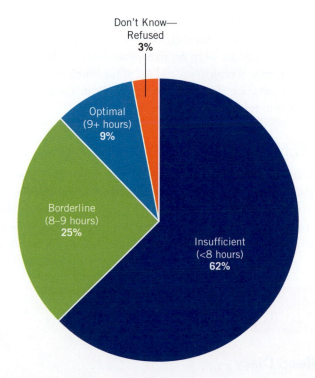

NOTE: Percentages do not add up to 100% due to rounding.

SOURCE: Garber et al. (2013).

getting fewer than 8 hours (see Figure 15.2; Garber et al., 2013). Although younger children sleep about the same amount of time every day, both on school days and on weekends, as children get older, there is more "catch-up sleeping" on weekends as they try to make up for sleep lost during the week (Garmy, Nyberg, & Jakobsson, 2012; Olds et al., 2010). Because an inadequate amount of sleep or poorer quality sleep lowers academic performance, increases levels of depression and anxiety, and increases the rate of car accidents, sleep deficit is now considered a public health issue (Colten & Altevogt, 2006; Short, Gradisar, Lack, & Wright, 2013).

Teens can improve the quality of their sleep by avoiding video games and other screen-based activities near bedtime, but even with these measures, their internal biological clock makes it difficult for them to fall asleep earlier and leads to poorer sleep quality when they do finally get to sleep (Hasler & Clark, 2013). Consequently, many communities are discussing what time school should start for adolescents. When one high school started classes 1 hour later, teens got more sleep each night and the rate of teen car crashes declined by 16.5% (Danner & Phillips, 2008). At another school, a mere 25-minute delay in the start of school significantly lowered daytime sleepiness, depressed mood, and caffeine consumption (Boergers, Gable, & Owens, 2014).

For younger children, having a television in the bedroom and watching more than 2 hours of television a day have been associated with getting less sleep (Garmy et al., 2012). If parents understand the importance of adequate amounts of sleep for their children, these are things a family can control.

In addition to sleep duration (that is, the number of hours of sleep you get a night), sleep quality matters. Do you fall asleep quickly, stay asleep through the night, and feel rested when you wake up? Younger children do well on these measures (Astill et al., 2012; Simola, Liukkonen, Pitkäranta, Pirinen, & Aronen, 2012), but as they get older, sleep problems occur more often (Garmy et al., 2012). Sleep problems are also associated with some very serious problems. In one study, a persistent pattern of sleep problems over a 4-year period from preschool to school age was associated with a 16-fold increase in the risk of psychosocial symptoms, especially aggression, problems with social interactions, and anxious/depressed mood (Simola et al., 2014). Insufficient sleep has even been connected with being overweight (Olds et al., 2010). When you are sleep deprived, your body produces *more* of the hormone *ghrelin* that tells you when it is time to eat and *less* of the hormone *leptin* that tells you when to stop eating. Sleep deprivation also slows your metabolism. You can use **Active Learning: Keeping a Sleep Diary** to track your own sleep habits.

ENVIRONMENTAL TOXINS AND THREATS

Because children are still growing and because they eat and drink more in proportion to their body size than adults, they are even more vulnerable than adults to environmental toxins (U.S. Environmental Protection Agency, 2012). According to the World Health Organization, as much as 24% of all disease, and one-third of the disease burden on children, is the result of environmental factors (Prüss-Üstün & Corvalán, 2006). Some environmental

T ☐ F ☐ A lack of sleep can contribute to weight gain. **True**

T ☐ F ☐ Because children are still growing, they are more resistant to the effects of environmental toxins than adults. **False**

Active LEARNING

Keeping a Sleep Diary

As a college student, you know it can be difficult to get an adequate amount of sleep. The National Sleep Foundation has developed this sleep diary so that people can track their sleep for a week to identify habits and patterns that may be interfering with their ability to get the optimal amount of sleep each night.

Complete in Morning	Day 1	Day 2	Day 3	Day 4	Day 5	Day 6	Day 7
Start date: __/__/__							
Day of week:	____	____	____	____	____	____	____
I went to bed last night at:	PM / AM	PM / AM	PM / AM	PM / AM	PM / AM	PM / AM	PM / AM
I got out of bed this morning at:	AM / PM	AM / PM	AM / PM	AM / PM	AM / PM	AM / PM	AM / PM
Last night I fell asleep: Easily / After some time / With difficulty	☐☐☐	☐☐☐	☐☐☐	☐☐☐	☐☐☐	☐☐☐	☐☐☐
I woke up during the night: # of times							
# of minutes							
Last night I slept a total of:	Hours	Hours	Hours	Hours	Hours	Hours	Hours
My sleep was disturbed by: List mental or physical factors including noise, lights, pets, allergies, temperature, discomfort, stress, etc.							
When I woke up for the day, I felt: Refreshed / Somewhat refreshed / Fatigued	☐☐☐	☐☐☐	☐☐☐	☐☐☐	☐☐☐	☐☐☐	☐☐☐
Notes: Record any other factors that may affect your sleep (i.e. hours of work shift, or monthly cycle for women).							

Complete at the End of Day	Day 1	Day 2	Day 3	Day 4	Day 5	Day 6	Day 7
Day of week:	____	____	____	____	____	____	____
I consumed caffeinated drinks in the: (M)orning, (A)fternoon, (E)vening, (N/A) — M / A / E / NA							
How many?	____	____	____	____	____	____	____
I exercised at least 20 minutes in the: (M)orning, (A)fternoon, (E)vening, (N/A)							
Medications I took today:							
Took a nap? (circle one)	Yes No	Yes No	Yes No	Yes No	Yes No	Yes No	Yes No
If Yes, for how long?							
During the day, how likely was I to doze off while performing daily activities: No chance, Slight chance, Moderate chance, High chance							
Throughout the day, my mood was… Very pleasant, Pleasant, Unpleasant, Very unpleasant							
Approximately 2-3 hours before going to bed, I consumed: Alcohol / A heavy meal / Caffeine / Not applicable	☐☐☐☐	☐☐☐☐	☐☐☐☐	☐☐☐☐	☐☐☐☐	☐☐☐☐	☐☐☐☐
In the hour before going to sleep, my bedtime routine included: List activities including reading a book, using electronics, taking a bath, doing relaxation exercises, etc.							

What did you learn from your sleep diary that can help improve the amount and quality of your sleep?

SOURCE: National Sleep Foundation (n.d.).

hazards that have been identified to date include asbestos, dioxin, household chemicals, lead, mercury, molds, pesticides, radon, and secondhand smoke.

Children are frequently exposed to pesticides in their homes, at school, and on the playground through rodent and insect control products, household chemicals and cleaning products, lawn and garden products, and pet products. These are even present in the food we eat (Egeghy et al., 2007). To lower this risk, some families choose to eat organic foods. In 2010, U.S. consumers spent $26.7 billion on organic foods (Smith-Spangler et al., 2012). While a controlled study showed that eating organic foods did reduce the presence of insecticides in children's urine, children are exposed to more pesticides in and around their homes than from their diet (Bradman et al., 2015). For this reason, it is important that adults store pesticides where children cannot get to them, keep all pesticides in their original containers, and follow the warnings on the containers for their use (U.S. Environmental Protection Agency, 2012).

Lead is another environmental toxin that has negative effects on children's development. While childhood deaths from lead poisoning are extremely rare today, blood lead levels in even the moderate range are associated with lower IQ scores and shortened attention spans. Chronic lead poisoning in early childhood has even been associated with violent and criminal behaviors later in life (Godwin, 2009; Jusko et al., 2008; Surkan et al., 2007; Zhang et al., 2013).

Lead paint on children's toys. Paint used on some children's toys that are imported from other countries such as this baby book exceed the permitted level of lead for such products. Babies like to put things in their mouth, but doing so with this book could have very negative consequences.

The risk of exposure to lead was greatly reduced when the federal government eliminated lead as an ingredient in household paint and in motor fuel (Federal Interagency Forum on Child and Family Statistics, 2009), but the risk that remains is not evenly distributed across the population. Many older houses still have surfaces covered in old lead-based paint and there are millions of metric tons of lead from motor fuels in the soil around homes near roadways. This places children who live in older housing and in traffic-congested areas at the greatest risk of exposure to lead in the environment (Godwin, 2009). Additional sources of lead exposure include certain candies produced in Mexico and the paint used on some imported toys, primarily ones manufactured in China (Godwin, 2009). These sources are of particular concern because the products are marketed specifically for children.

In 2014 the city of Flint, Michigan, changed its water source to save money, but the water from the new source was so toxic that it corroded the lead pipes that brought water into people's homes. In the period of about a year, the number of children in the area with above average levels of lead in their blood doubled (Wang, 2015). The city has since reverted to a safer water source, but there is some evidence that the effects of lead on health, behavior, and cognitive development are irreversible. While Flint's story gained a great deal of attention, there are many other cities in which children's lead levels are unacceptably high (Rosner & Markowitz, 2016). The Centers for Disease Control (2016g) estimates that at least 4 million families are living in situations that expose children to unacceptable levels of lead.

Environmental factors also play a role in several chronic illnesses that affect a significant number of children each year. The most common chronic illness among children in the United States is **asthma,** which is caused by an inflammation of the bronchial airways that results in chest tightness, coughing and wheezing, and shortness of breath. More than half of all cases are caused by allergies, but exposure to secondhand smoke also poses a risk. Even a mother smoking during her pregnancy has been associated with an increased risk, possibly as a result of stunted growth of the lungs prenatally (Jaakola & Gissler, 2007). As the number of adult smokers has decreased in recent years, so has the percentage of young children exposed to secondhand smoke (U.S. Environmental Protection Agency, 2011), but air pollutants such as ozone, particulates, nitrogen dioxide, and sulfur dioxide can trigger an asthmatic attack and they remain an ongoing risk.

The number of children who have asthma has increased substantially in recent years (see Figure 15.3), with the greatest increase among African American children (Federal Interagency Forum on Child and Family Statistics, 2015). Most children who have asthma develop their first symptoms before the age of 5, with boys being more vulnerable than girls, although this gender

Asthma The most common chronic illness in childhood, in which a child's airways constrict, making it difficult to breathe.

Childhood asthma. This boy has asthma and must use an inhaler when he has difficulty breathing. Asthma is the most common chronic illness among children in the United States.

FIGURE 15.3

Asthma risk in the United States. Until recently, the percentage of children in the United States who have asthma has increased from year to year. In 2013, about 8% of children currently had asthma, a slight decrease from the previous year.

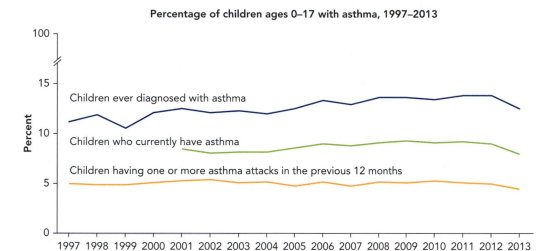

Percentage of children ages 0–17 with asthma, 1997–2013

NOTE: Children are identified as ever diagnosed with asthma by asking parents, "Has a doctor or other health professional EVER told you that your child has asthma?" If the parent answers YES to this question, they are then asked (1) "Does your child still have asthma?" and (2) "During the past 12 months, has your child had an episode of asthma or an asthma attack?" The question "Does your child still have asthma?" was introduced in 2001 and identifies children who currently have asthma.

SOURCE: National Center for Health Statistics, National Health Interview Survey, as cited in Federal Interagency Forum on Child and Family Statistics (2015).

difference disappears in older age groups (National Institutes of Health, 2014). Asthma places more limits on children's activity than any other disease (Mayo Clinic, 2010), and asthma attacks were responsible for 10.5 million missed days of school in 2008 (CDC, 2013a).

The **hygiene hypothesis** has been proposed as a possible explanation for the recent increase in asthma and allergies. According to this hypothesis, as our environment has become cleaner, it has lowered our exposure to germs and, as a result, our immune system is now less able to differentiate between harmful substances and less harmful irritants. Consequently, it overreacts to harmless irritants like pollen. Support for this idea came from a research finding that children from Amish farm families had lower rates of asthma, hay fever, and allergies than are found in most population studies (Holbreich, Genuneit, Weber, Braun-Fahrlander, & von Mutious, 2012; Holbreich et al., 2012). These researchers argued that early exposure to the variety of allergens found on a farm, together with growing up in a larger family, strengthens the immune system and that provides the protective effect.

As intuitive as this sounds, the hypothesis does not have unequivocal support. Some countries with high rates of infections that expose children to a variety of microbes also have high rates of asthma, so exposure on its own does not seem to provide the protection predicted by the hygiene hypothesis. Also, the overall rate of asthma is declining in some Western countries even though there is no evidence they are less clean than in the past (Brooks, Pearce, & Douwes, 2013). The role that early exposure to allergens plays in the development of asthma and allergies remains under investigation, but many researchers think that it is the interaction of a genetic vulnerability and exposure to an environmental trigger, most often early in life, that produces the symptoms (National Institutes of Health, 2014).

A child's diet also may play a role with asthma. Diets that are higher in fresh fruits, green vegetables, and other dietary sources of antioxidants (substances which can prevent or slow cell damage caused by molecules called free radicals) are associated with a lower incidence of asthma (Protudjer, Severhuysen, Ramsey, Kozyrskyi, & Becker, 2012). This is

Hygiene hypothesis The idea that living in a germ-free environment is causing our immune systems to become more reactive to allergens.

FIGURE 15.4

Incidence and mortality rates of childhood cancer in the United States, 1992–2009. The number of cases of diagnosed cancer in children has gone up over time, but fortunately with better treatment, the death rate from the disease has gone down.

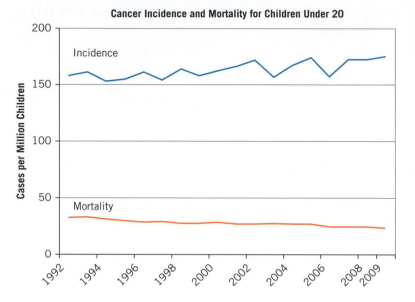

Cancer Incidence and Mortality for Children Under 20

SOURCE: U.S. Environmental Protection Agency (2015).

a relatively new area of investigation and we will undoubtedly learn more about the impact of diet as it continues.

Cancer remains the number one cause of death by disease during childhood. About 15,000 children between birth and age 19 receive this diagnosis each year. The causes of childhood cancer are still poorly understood, but there is evidence that exposure to toxins, such as radiation and pesticides, may be one factor that contributes to some types of childhood cancer (U.S. Environmental Protection Agency, 2013). Recent statistics on childhood cancers contain both good news and bad news. As you can see from Figure 15.4, the good news is that the number of fatalities due to childhood cancer has decreased over the last 30 years, but the bad news is that the incidence of childhood cancers has continued to climb during that same period (U.S. Environmental Protection Agency, 2015). Research will need to continue to identify the environmental conditions associated with this increase.

Exposure to toxins in childhood may not result in negative health outcomes until later in life. For instance, exposure to the ultraviolet rays in sunlight is one such risk. Even a few serious sunburns during childhood can increase a person's risk of getting skin cancer later in life (CDC, 2016h). Preventing burns is a much better strategy than dealing with them afterwards. Avoiding being out in the midday sun when ultraviolet rays are the most harmful, wearing clothing that covers exposed skin, wearing a hat and sunglasses, and using sunscreen with at least sun-protection factor of (SPF) 15 and UVA and UVB protection are all important protection against getting too much sun.

Kidstock/Blend Images/Getty Images

Sunscreen. Protection from ultraviolet rays with sunscreen is important for all children.

There are a number of national organizations that provide information, help, and support to people dealing with many of the health-related issues we have discussed to this point. You can use **Active Learning: Finding Local Sources of Support** to find the resources that these organizations offer to families in your area of the country.

Active LEARNING

Finding Local Sources of Support

Because childhood illness imposes a burden on all members in a family, they often need to locate sources of help and support in their community. This activity will let you find some of those resources in your own community. Begin by visiting the home page for some of these national organizations. On their home page, read about the mission of the organization, then follow these links to find information on local resources:

- American Academy of Allergy, Asthma, and Immunity—From their website at www. aaaai.org/conditions-and-treatments/library/at-a-glance/childhood-asthma, you can select "Find an Allergist/Immunologist." By providing a city and state, you will receive a list of specialists in your area who treat allergies and asthma.

- American Diabetes Association—From their website at www.diabetes.org/living-with -diabetes/parents-and-kids/, you can click on "In My Community" to bring up a menu that includes links for local diabetes education programs, upcoming diabetes expos, camps for children with diabetes, and meal planning advice for parents.

- American Cancer Society—From their website at www.cancer.org/, you can click on "Find local ACS" and by entering your zip code, you will find "Local Programs and Services." They include Support Groups, Health Care Services and Screening, Information and Referral Services, and more.

- Anxiety and Depression Association of America—On their home page at www.adaa. org/, there is a drop-down menu for "Find Help." From that menu, you can find a licensed mental health provider who specializes in anxiety, depression, obsessive-compulsive disorders, and PTSD; a local support group; and self-help publications.

There are many other organizations in your community that offer help for specific health challenges. Take a few minutes to search for one that has relevance for you or someone you know.

ACCIDENTS

Although the number of fatal injuries to children has decreased dramatically in recent years (see Figure 15.5), unintentional injury remains the leading cause of death and disability for children in the United States between birth and age 19 (Gilchrist, Ballesteros, & Parker, 2012). More than 20 children die each day from injuries and for each death, many more children are hospitalized or require medical treatment for nonfatal injuries. The rate of nonfatal injuries is highest among children ages 1 to 4, followed by the rate for adolescents (Child Trends, 2014). Except for infancy, when rates are similar, boys have a higher rate of nonfatal injuries than girls and are more likely to die as the result of an accidental injury (Borse et al., 2008). The rate is highest among American Indian/Alaskan natives and lowest among Asians/Pacific Islanders (Child Trends, 2014).

Several societal changes have helped reduce fatal and nonfatal childhood accidents. Laws requiring that children be restrained while riding in a motor vehicle have made the greatest

FIGURE 15.5

Unintentional injury deaths among U.S. children, 1981–2012. The number of fatal childhood unintentional injuries has fallen dramatically in recent years. The largest portion of this decline is attributable to a reduction in the number of fatalities from motor vehicle accidents.

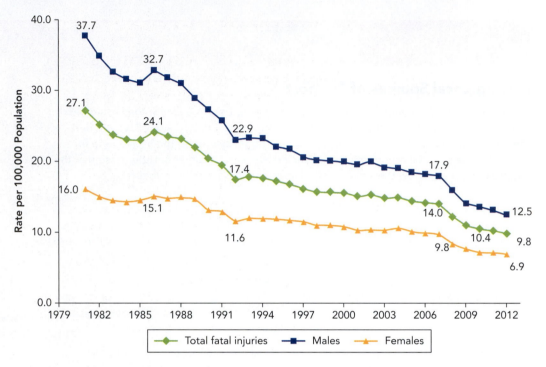

SOURCE: Child Trends (2014).

contribution to the decrease in accidental fatalities (Child Trends, 2014). Additionally, school and community programs that promote bicycle safety, accident awareness, and injury prevention in organized sports for children, along with governmental screening of children's toys for health and safety hazards, have all helped to reduce the risk of preventable accidents, but there remains considerable room for improvement.

As Figure 15.6 shows, the cause of fatal accidents changes throughout childhood and adolescence. In the first year of life, infants are particularly vulnerable to suffocation, which accounts for more than 80% of the accidental deaths at this age (Child Trends, 2014). As children get older, motor vehicle accidents pose an increasing risk and by adolescence, they account for two-thirds of all accidental deaths.

ALCOHOL, SMOKING, AND ILLICIT DRUGS

As children move into adolescence, they begin to make lifestyle choices that directly affect their health and well-being, including their decisions about the use of substances. Monitoring the Future is a survey that has been collecting data on behaviors, attitudes, and values from almost 50,000 8th, 10th, and 12th grade students on an annual basis since the 1970s. In their most recent report, they found that the level of smoking and alcohol consumption by their participants in 2015 were at the lowest levels since the survey began (Johnston, O'Malley, Miech, Bachman, & Schulenberg, 2016). Despite the decrease, alcohol remains the most used substance by adolescents, while marijuana remains the most widely used illicit drug.

TRUE/FALSE VIDEO ▲

T ☐ F ☐ Rates of adolescent smoking and alcohol consumption are at their lowest levels in more than 40 years.
True

FIGURE 15.6

Cause of fatal injuries by child age. The cause of fatal injuries changes substantially at different points in development. While suffocation is a significant risk in infancy, at each succeeding age, motor vehicle accidents become an increasingly significant risk.

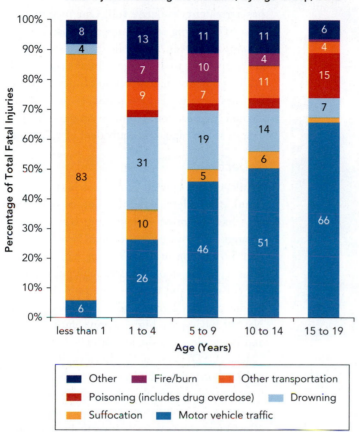

Fatal Injuries: Leading Mechanisms, by Age Group, 2012

SOURCE: Child Trends (2014).

Although there was little change in the reported use of marijuana by adolescents, there was continued movement toward greater acceptance of its use and a decline in the perceived risk of using the drug. There also was a decline in the perceived risk of using prescription drugs such as amphetamines and sedatives for nonmedical reasons. Now we will look more closely at the use of each of these substances.

Alcohol

For many young people, much of their alcohol consumption occurs in the form of binge drinking, which is defined as five or more drinks within a 2-hour period for men, or four or more drinks for women (National Institute on Alcohol Abuse and Alcoholism, 2004). About 90% of the alcohol young people consume is in the form of binge drinking (Naimi et al., 2003).

Binge drinking places a young person at risk in a number of ways, including increased risks of motor vehicle accidents, injuries, and fighting. In Chapter 6, we discussed the long-term effects of heavy alcohol use during adolescence on cognitive development, including impairments in memory, attention, spatial skills, and executive functioning (Squeglia et al., 2009). In addition, heavy drinkers are more impulsive and less able to delay gratification, so older teens who drink act similar to younger teens who do not (Sullivan et al., 2016). Of course alcohol addiction later in life is also a risk. Early onset of heavy drinking

©iStockphoto.com/wundervisuals

Alcopops. Alcopops are sweet, fruity alcoholic drinks that are marketed primarily to young drinkers and women. Some products contain the alcohol equivalent of a binge drinking episode in a single serving. Although these products have declined in popularity since their introduction, for many adolescents they are a gateway to stronger liquors.

is particularly problematic because young adolescents are still immature in their decision-making skills and may not fully appreciate the consequences of their decision to start drinking. Those who start drinking at a young age also have a longer period of exposure to alcohol compared to adolescents who wait to start drinking, so their alcohol consumption has a greater cumulative toll. One incentive for adolescents to start drinking at a younger age has been the marketing of *alcopops,* sweet, fruity alcoholic drinks that are particularly appealing to underage drinkers (Alcohol Justice, 2015). Although their bright colors and fruity taste make them seem harmless, many of these products contain as much as 14% alcohol. Because some come in single-serve 16- to 24- ounce cans, a single can is the equivalent of 4.7 standard drinks.

Tobacco

While a single episode of binge drinking or of driving while drunk can be lethal, the decision to smoke may be the one that has the most serious long-term consequences. The Centers for Disease Control and Prevention (2016k) estimate that 5.6 million of today's teens will die early from conditions related to smoking. Although rates of smoking are similar for males and females, the rate differs substantially by ethnic and racial group, with Native Americans and Alaska Natives having the highest prevalence, followed by Whites and Hispanics, and the lowest prevalence among Asians and Blacks (USDHHS, 2012). Because it is so difficult to stop smoking once the habit has been established, efforts designed to prevent young people from starting to smoke seem the wisest course. As we discussed in Chapter 14, any prevention effort must compete with advertising that continues to portray smoking as pleasurable.

Factors that help to reduce teen smoking include raising the price of tobacco products, limiting the areas where smoking is allowed, promoting media messages and community and school programs that encourage a tobacco-free lifestyle, and limiting advertising and availability of tobacco products (CDC, 2016k). Until recently, the legal age for buying cigarettes in all states has been 18, but Hawaii and California have recently raised that age to 21 (NPR, 2016). Because most people who smoke begin smoking during their teen years, limiting teens' legal access to cigarettes is designed to prevent young people from starting to smoke and this will eventually reduce the number of tobacco-related deaths and the cost of health care associated with tobacco use.

The Monitoring the Future survey recently began asking about e-cigarettes, battery-powered devices that use heat to vaporize a liquid or create a mist that the user inhales. A wide range of flavored liquids, both with and without nicotine, are available for use in inhalers. Between 2011 and 2012, the number of teens who had used e-cigarettes doubled, from just under 5% to 10% (CDC, 2016k), and by 2015, Monitoring the Future reported that adolescents were using e-cigarettes at a higher level than traditional tobacco cigarettes (Johnston et al., 2016).

Although e-cigarettes may help current smokers quit, the concern regarding adolescent use has centered on the question of whether e-cigarettes will become a gateway for them to the use of regular tobacco products. As of the end of 2015, 48 states had laws that prohibit the sale of e-cigarettes or vaping devices to teens 18 and younger (National Conference of State Legislatures, 2015). Most adolescents who report having used e-cigarettes said they did so to see what it was like, and one-third said they use e-cigarettes because they taste good. Although only a minority reported using nicotine in their inhaler (Johnston et al., 2016), a survey of 40,000 middle school and high school students found that use of e-cigarettes was associated with a greater likelihood of using conventional cigarettes (Dutra & Glantz, 2014). This study concluded that e-cigarettes do not discourage, and may even encourage, cigarette smoking. Although adolescents perceive e-cigarettes to be safe (Johnston et al., 2016), none of the 7,700 flavors of vapor liquids available have been evaluated by the Food and Drug Administration for safety (American Lung Association, 2016).

Illicit Drugs

The illicit drugs that adolescents use include hallucinogens, tranquilizers, cocaine or crack, heroin, methamphetamines, and more. The effect of the drug depends on the particular substance used, its frequency, and dosage. Although many teens believe that smoking marijuana is not harmful, in Chapter 6 we described the effects of marijuana usage on the developing adolescent brain. Marijuana has been associated with decreases in several aspects of cognitive functioning, but any substance that affects physical or cognitive functioning can have collateral damage for health. For example, if reaction time is slowed, teens put themselves and others at risk when they get behind the wheel and drive. If decision making is impaired, they put themselves and others at risk when they engage in unprotected sex or take foolish dares.

The rate of teen addiction to prescription drugs, particularly opioids such as oxycodone and fentanyl, has increased greatly in the past 10 years. In 2014, there were 5 times as many youth addicted to prescription drugs as to heroin (American Society of Addiction Medicine, 2016). The rise in use of opioids is connected to a spike in the number of deaths due to overdose. Considering all age groups, 78 Americans die of an overdose of opioid drugs every day (CDC, 2016j).

When teens use any of these substances, including alcohol, to excess or develop significant life problems as a result of their use, they may be diagnosed with a **substance use disorder (SUD)**. SUD is marked by cravings and use of more of the substance than intended; problems with peers, at home, or in school; risky use of the substance even when teens know it is causing problems in their lives; and the build-up of tolerance to the substance so the individual needs more and more of the substance and experiences withdrawal symptoms when they stop using it (APA, 2013).

Substance use disorder (SUD) Use of drugs that is marked by cravings, social impairment, risky use, tolerance build-up and withdrawal symptoms.

The sooner the problem is identified, the easier it is to get treatment for the problem. Because there are a number of treatment options, one should be tailored to the specific needs of the individual, and it should focus on the whole person, not just the person's drug use (National Institutes of Health, n.d.). Involvement of the adolescent's family is an essential part of the process. Programs help strengthen family communication and educate family members on ways that they can support the adolescent during treatment and recovery. Although relapses frequently occur, behavioral therapies that increase the adolescent's motivation to resist drugs and build refusal skills are the ones that have the best chance at success.

CHECK YOUR UNDERSTANDING

1. Why is a sleep deficit associated with weight gain?
2. In what ways are poorer children more likely to be exposed to lead in their environment?
3. What is the cause of asthma according to the hygiene hypothesis?
4. What is the recent trend in fatal childhood unintentional injuries?
5. What are recent trends in adolescent use of cigarettes, alcohol, and illicit drugs?

CHALLENGES TO POSITIVE CHILD DEVELOPMENT

15.4 What are effects of poverty, homelessness, trauma, maltreatment, and racial discrimination on the development of children and adolescents?

Many children and adolescents grow up in situations that put their physical, cognitive, and social-emotional development at risk. In this section, we discuss several important ones, including poverty, homelessness, trauma, and child maltreatment. Children and adolescents also can be the victims of racial stereotyping, prejudice, and discrimination. We discuss the consequences of each of these challenges and describe some ways to reduce their negative impact on development.

POVERTY

According to the U.S. Census Bureau, one in five U.S. children—or more than 15 million children—lived in poverty in 2014 (Children's Defense Fund, 2015). As Figure 15.7 shows, Black and Hispanic children are the groups most likely to live in poverty and in all ethnic and racial groups, children under the age of 5 are more likely than older children to live in poverty. As we discussed in Chapter 13, children are more likely to live in poverty if they are living in a single-parent household. We should note, however, that single parenthood and poverty do not need to coexist. Although they do in the United States, in other countries far fewer single-parent households fall below the poverty line. For example, Sweden and Denmark have higher rates of out-of-wedlock births than the United States, but a far lower rate of childhood poverty because these countries have economic and social policies that support all families. Wage equality, paid family leave, and publicly subsidized child care provide help to keep single-parent families in those countries out of poverty (Coontz & Folbre, 2002).

FIGURE 15.7

Percent of children living in poverty in the United States. More than 15 million children lived in poverty in 2014 in the United States. Children under the age of 5 were more likely than older children to live in poverty, and Black children and Hispanic families had the highest proportions of poor children.

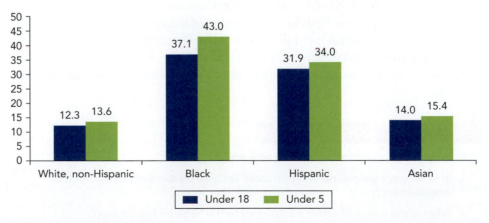

SOURCE: Children's Defense Fund (2015).

Of course, poverty is not a static condition. Families move in and out of poverty as their circumstances change. By one estimate, in any particular year, individuals living in poverty have a 1 in 3 chance of moving out of poverty. In most cases, people experience periods of poverty that last 1 to 4 years (Allhusen et al., 2005). However, chronically poor children have worse outcomes than those who have brief periods of economic disadvantage, and those with even brief experiences of poverty do worse than those who never experience it (Allhusen et al., 2005). Children also seem to do worse if they live in poverty early in their childhood rather than later. One explanation for this is that poverty affects both the neural wiring and the physical structures of a child's brain, both of which are developing at a faster rate in early childhood and are therefore more vulnerable to the effects of negative experiences. The structural differences that have been identified so far can affect language development, self-regulation, working memory, and academic achievement (Hair, Hanson, Wolfe, & Pollak, 2015; Lempinen, 2012).

The impact of poverty on physical development begins before birth. Lack of adequate health services and poor maternal nutrition contribute to prenatal problems, low birth weight, and premature birth (Strully, Rehkopf, & Xuan, 2010). As we described in Chapter 5, both low birth weight and prematurity are risk factors for later health problems and cognitive limitations. Many of these problems can be overcome when the family later has access to adequate resources, but a positive outcome is less likely if the family continues to live in poverty.

Poverty reduces both a family's material and nonmaterial investments in their children's development (Aber, Morris, & Raver, 2012). It also creates enormous ongoing stress for parents, which can affect their physical and mental health. Depression is more common in low-income families, and depressed parents are much less able to care for their children in ways that support their optimal growth. Low-income parents also are less likely to provide a cognitively stimulating environment and are less likely to talk with their children than mothers who are better off economically (Chazan-Cohen et al., 2009; Hart & Risley, 1995; Leffel & Suskind, 2009). The result can be a lower level of language development in the children, which has an important impact on later academic achievement.

Other life circumstances associated with poverty, such as living in a dangerous neighborhood with high levels of noise, crowding, and substandard housing, are also linked to behavioral problems in poor children (Aber et al., 2012). Parents who have to deal with these living conditions are more likely to be highly punitive and less warm toward their children, a pattern of parenting that has been linked with childhood behavioral problems (Bradley, Corwyn, McAdoo, & Garcia Coll, 2001). Both externalizing problems, such as aggression, and internalizing problems, such as depression, are elevated in poor children and increase the longer the child lives in poverty (Allhusen et al., 2005).

At a time when the U.S. economy is showing signs of recovery from the recent economic recession, some encouraging information comes from research showing that when income relative to family needs increases in low-income families, child outcomes improve. A large study carried out by the National Institute of Child Health and Human Development followed children from birth to age 3 (Dearing, McCartney, & Taylor, 2001). Although increases in income for middle- and upper-income families did not affect children's abilities at age 3, increases in income for low-income families had a large effect. Children's language abilities, readiness for school, and social behaviors all improved, even reaching the same level as that for children in families who were not deprived. It was also true that poor families who became poorer had children with even worse outcomes. These same results were found when these children were retested at age 9 (Allhusen et al., 2005). In a separate study, antisocial behavior was found to decrease in 4- to 7-year-olds when their families moved out of poverty and to increase the longer the families remained in poverty (MacMillan, McMorris, & Kruttschnitt, 2004).

> T ☐ F ☐ Once families live in poverty, they are unlikely to move out of it. **False**

In the mid-1990s, the U.S. Department of Housing and Urban Development began an experiment called the Moving to Opportunity program in which they gave housing vouchers to 4,600 randomly selected families living in high-poverty housing developments. With the vouchers, the selected families were able to move to better neighborhoods (Chetty, Hendren, & Katz, 2015). When researchers looked at the effects of improving neighborhood quality for these low-income families, they found that the children who moved to better neighborhoods while they were young had better outcomes than those who remained in their original neighborhood. As young adults, they earned an average of 31% more than young adults in the comparison group and were more likely to attend college, continued to live in better neighborhoods themselves, and were less likely to become single parents. Note that this was true only for children who moved before the age of 13. Those children who moved to better neighborhoods at later ages did not benefit, and in some ways may have been harmed by the disruption caused by their move. The conclusion drawn from this research was that it was the length of time that children were removed from poor neighborhoods that was responsible for the better outcomes.

There are some nonfinancial factors that are linked with better outcomes for children who grow up in low-income families. Firm parental discipline in the context of a relationship that is warm and responsive is associated with more positive outcomes (Berlin et al., 2009; Kim & Kochansha, 2015). Attending an early education program, such as Head Start, also helps. However, direct financial aid to low-income families may be the most direct and effective way to improve the lot of children in those families. Several programs that directly reduce poverty by providing child allowances or tax credits for poor families have yielded significant increases in academic achievement and reductions in behavioral problems for children in those families (Dahl & Lockner, 2008; Duncan, Huston, & Weisner, 2007; Gennetian & Miller, 2000).

HOMELESSNESS

According to the National Center on Family Homelessness (2014), in 2013 1 in every 30 children in the United States (or nearly 2.5 million children) was homeless, and more than half (51%) of those children were under the age of 6. Homeless families share many stresses and risks with families living in poverty. Their children often go hungry, do not have necessary access to medical care, and miss many educational opportunities.

Homeless families try to cope by moving in with family members, doubling up with other families or friends, staying in motel rooms, or sleeping in cars or public spaces. If emergency shelters are available to the family, they often are crowded, noisy, and at times unsafe so they are considered a last resort for many families. Because their living arrangements are temporary, homeless families move frequently from one situation to another and these moves often mean that children must change schools. An estimated 40% of homeless children attend two different schools in a year, and 28% attend three or more school (Bassuk et al., 2011). Siblings may be separated from their parents and from each other if they are sent to live with friends or relatives. Problems are compounded because families

John Moore/Getty Images News/Getty Images

Homelessness. One outcome of poverty can be homelessness. The mother cuddling her daughter in this photo searched for work for 6 months and then was unable to pay her rent, so the family lost their house.

who become homeless often are dealing with other serious family issues such as parental substance abuse, family violence, or mental health issues, but have limited access to services that meet their needs.

Because homelessness is a complex, multifaceted challenge for families, a variety of services, including medical services, substance recovery services, job training, and child care for working families, are needed to improve the lives of these children. The U.S. Interagency Council on Homelessness (2014) has proposed a comprehensive plan to address the issue. The plan includes a coordinated system to assess the needs of homeless families and connect them to temporary housing and appropriate assistance tailored to the family's needs with the goal that "no family will be without shelter, and homelessness will be a rare and brief occurrence" (p. 1). In addition to coordinated federal efforts, an economic recovery and the greater availability of affordable housing options will help many families move out of homelessness.

TRAUMA

Recent years have seen a rapidly growing research interest in trauma and how it affects physical and mental well-being (Aldwin, 2012). According to the American Psychological Association (2016a), a traumatic event "threatens injury, death, or the physical integrity of self or others and also causes horror, terror, or helplessness at the time it occurs" (para. 3). Traumatic events include, but are not limited to, exposure to domestic violence, physical or sexual abuse, neglect, motor vehicle accidents, natural disasters, school violence, medical trauma, terrorism, refugee and war zone trauma, suicides, and other traumatic losses. Estimates of a child's risk of trauma exposure vary depending on the sample of children examined and the methods used in the study, but in some studies more than two-thirds of children report experiencing a traumatic event by age 16 and 25% report such experiences before age 4 (APA, 2016a; Grasso, Ford, & Briggs-Gowan, 2013). A child's reaction to a traumatic event is affected by the exact nature of the experience, whether the child was in any way prepared for it, how the child perceives the threat, how long it lasts, the severity of the incident, the child's age or gender, and whether the child has a personal history of other traumatic experiences, as well as the child's personality characteristics, coping abilities, and pretrauma psychological health (Skuse, Bruce, Dowdney, & Mrazek, 2011).

Following a traumatic event, children may feel that their world is neither secure nor predictable (Aldwin, 2012). Almost all will suffer some immediate reactions, which might include the development of new fears, separation anxiety, sleep disturbances or nightmares, loss of interest in normal activities, lack of concentration, anger, sadness, or somatic complaints (such as stomachaches or headaches) (American Psychological Association Presidential Task Force on Posttraumatic Stress Disorder and Trauma in Children and Adolescents, 2008). Some, however, continue to reexperience the trauma through intrusive thoughts, distressing dreams, flashbacks, or extreme reactions to situations that resemble the original traumatizing event (Aldwin, 2012), all of which are characteristics of **posttraumatic stress disorder (PTSD)**. **Active Learning: Intrusive Thoughts** gives you a bit of the experience of what having an intrusive thought might feel like.

Posttraumatic stress disorder (PTSD) Reexperiencing a traumatic effect through intrusive thoughts, distressing dreams, flashbacks, or extreme reactions in situations similar to the original trauma.

Aris Messinis/AFP/Getty Images

Traumatic experiences. This young child has just experienced the trauma of making a crossing from Syria to Turkey with her family to escape the war raging in her home country. However the trauma is not over for her because she will now live in a crowded refugee camp that will be her family's temporary home. Children need a great deal of resilience and extraordinary support from others to recover from such trauma.

Active LEARNING

Intrusive Thoughts

Sit quietly for several minutes with your eyes closed and think about anything you want, except do *not* think about the green rabbit on this page.

©George Doyle and Ciaran Griffin/
Stockbyte/Thinkstock

Were you able to keep this rabbit out of your mind? People with PTSD often try very hard not to think about the traumatic events they have experienced. In fact, some actually develop amnesia for those events, but for many, the more they try to keep the memories and thoughts out of their minds, the more these thoughts and emotions intrude in a way that is out of their control. This has been likened to a messy closet, with toys and clothes falling out. When items are examined and put back in a more orderly way, the closet can be kept closed and only opened when you choose to take something out. In a similar way, examining and understanding your thoughts, emotions, and memories allows you to put them in the past so you can fully engage in your current life (adapted from Vickers, 2005).

Children are helped when their parents maintain a warm relationship with them throughout the trauma and when the parents themselves are coping effectively (Hamblen & Barnett, 2009). One therapeutic approach called *cognitive behavioral therapy*, described in Chapter 10, has been shown to be effective in many cases (Lenz & Hollenbaugh, 2015). The child is helped to develop the skills necessary to manage the stress associated with the traumatizing event (Lenz & Hollenbaugh, 2015). For instance, the child and the child's parents are educated about stress and the consequences of it. The child learns relaxation techniques that help the child feel prepared to cope with the stress and to cognitively reframe the situation as one that is manageable. The child is encouraged to tell the story of his or her trauma in the child's own words with the goal of understanding and managing emotions and increasing communication and cohesiveness between all members of the family.

While this approach is useful with older children and adolescents, young children do not have the verbal or cognitive abilities that it requires (Aldwin, 2012; Lenz & Hollenbaugh, 2015). Play therapy, described in Chapter 12, or art therapy may be more helpful for this age group. There are also school-based interventions. Many behaviors preschool children show as a result of the experience of trauma can be disruptive when they are with other children. Preschoolers and children in kindergarten have a very high rate of expulsion and suspension from school—13 times the national average for older children (Giliam & Shahar, 2006)—and some who are expelled may be suffering the aftereffects of trauma.

A new program called Head Start Trauma Smart is designed to identify and help children whose difficulties are related to experiences of trauma. It is based on a program called ARC, which stands for attachment, self-regulation, and competency. Identified children meet individually with therapists trained in this approach. In addition, all of the adults who work with the children, from parents and teachers to bus drivers, are taught about the ways trauma affects both brain development and behavior. As you learned earlier in this chapter, the persistent high levels of cortisol produced as part of the stress response can cause brain cells to die or can reduce the connections between areas of the brain that are essential for learning and memory (National Scientific Council on the Developing Child,

2005/2014). They learn to help children talk about their feelings rather than getting out of control. If children need help calming down, they can use "breathing stars" made from file folders to help them concentrate on just breathing to relax, or they can go to "calming corners" where there are sensory items that may help soothe them. Once the child is more relaxed, the adult can help the child find a better solution to the problem. The main point is to help the child to take control of his or her own feelings and behavior (Bornstein, 2014; Smith, 2013). As adults learn to see these children as *troubled* rather than as *trouble*, they become more capable of making a warm connection with them, which is essential to helping the children manage their feelings and form relationships.

CHILD MALTREATMENT

Stop for a moment and count slowly to 10. In the time it took you to count to 10, it is likely that another report of suspected child maltreatment was made. In 2013, an estimated 3.5 million reports of suspected abuse or neglect involving 6.4 million children were made to child protection agencies in the United States (USDHHS, 2015b).

Maltreatment is the broad, overarching term that covers both abuse and neglect. It includes any act by a parent or caregiver that results in harm or potential harm to a child. **Abuse** more specifically includes deliberate and intentional words and actions that cause physical, sexual, or psychological harm or potential harm to a child. **Neglect** is the failure to provide for the basic physical, emotional, medical, or educational needs of a child or failure to protect the child from harm or potential harm (CDC, 2014d). In the sections that follow, we describe how the Child Protective Services system deals with reports of suspected maltreatment, who are its victims and perpetrators, and what can be done to help victims and families.

Child Protective Services (CPS)

Before we describe the current child protective services system, you can read about the history of efforts to protect children from abuse and neglect in **Journey of Research: Child Protective Legislation.**

Cathy Malchiodi/www.cathymalchiodi.com

Dealing with the aftermath of a disaster. Children can experience posttraumatic stress disorder following a traumatic event. As shown in this child's drawing of the events of September 11, 2001, art therapy can help children relive the experience in a way that allows them to deal with their emotions and control some of their anxiety as they talk about their experience.

Maltreatment Any act committed by a parent or caregiver that results in harm or potential harm to a child; incudes abuse and neglect.

Abuse Deliberate and intentional words and actions that cause physical, sexual, or psychological harm or potential harm to a child.

Neglect Failure to provide for the basic physical, emotional, medical, or educational needs of a child or to protect the child from harm or potential harm.

JOURNEY OF *Research*

Child Protective Legislation

Throughout much of human history, children were considered the property of their parents and their parents were free to do whatever they wanted to do to them. Children who were sickly, disabled, deformed, or simply unwanted could be killed, abandoned, or sold into servitude or slavery (Krug, Dahlberg, Mercy, Zwi, & Lozano, 2002). As long as children were seen as property, society chose not to interfere with decisions made by individual families about how they treated their children. Today we think of children

(Continued)

(Continued)

as individuals who need to be nurtured and protected, but the view of children in the 1800s was that they needed hard work and strict discipline if they were to be kept on the straight and narrow path and to grow up to be honest, moral people (Bagnell, 2001).

A pivotal event in the history of child protection in the United States occurred in 1873, when a church worker became aware of a 9-year-old girl named Mary Ellen who was being horribly mistreated by her family (Miller-Perrin & Perrin, 1999). When the church worker tried to have Mary Ellen removed from her home, she found that there was no legal precedent for doing this, and the authorities refused to act. Being persistent, the church worker next turned to the American Society for the Prevention of Cruelty to Animals (ASPCA) for help, arguing that as a member of the animal kingdom, Mary Ellen deserved at least the same protection that would be offered to a mule that was being mistreated. With the help of the ASPCA, Mary Ellen was removed from her abusive home and placed in foster care (Miller-Perrin & Perrin, 1999). The following year, in 1874, the Society for Prevention of Cruelty to Children was formed with the mission of protecting children from abuse and maltreatment (Miller-Perrin & Perrin, 1999). However, the case of Mary Ellen did not lead directly to broadly based efforts to protect children.

That had to wait for almost another 100 years. In the 1960s, Dr. Henry Kempe, a pediatrician in Denver, Colorado, found evidence in the X-rays of some children he treated of broken bones and fractures in different stages of healing, indicating that whatever had caused them had happened repeatedly over a period of time. It was Dr. Kempe and some of his colleagues who published the groundbreaking article "The Battered Child Syndrome" in 1962 and began a campaign to raise awareness not only among doctors but also among the general public of a situation that had remained hidden behind the closed doors of private homes before this (Leventhal, 2003).

Even with the growing recognition that child abuse existed and might be widespread, it took more than another decade before the United States passed comprehensive legislation intended to protect children from abuse. In 1974, Public Law 93–247, the Child Abuse Prevention and Treatment Act—CAPTA, was enacted by Congress. This legislation established a way to report cases of suspected abuse or neglect to child protection agencies and for tracking the disposition of those cases. The act has been amended several times, most recently in 2010, but it remains the foundation for our efforts to identify and protect children who are being mistreated, and to provide support to families so that children can safely remain in their homes with their parents.

The Child Abuse Prevention and Treatment Act (CAPTA) maintains a toll-free hotline in each state to receive reports of suspected maltreatment. Figure 15.8 shows how a report of suspected maltreatment moves through the Child Protection Services (CPS) system. Calls made to the hotline are evaluated to determine whether the report is covered by the laws regarding child abuse and neglect. If it is, the report is referred to a local CPS agency for investigation of the allegations (USDHHS, 2015b). Following the investigation, a determination is made as to whether the allegations are *substantiated* (an official decision that a child has been mistreated) or *indicated* (when there is enough evidence to support the allegation that a child has been maltreated but not enough to support a formal substantiation), or are *unsubstantiated* (when there is not enough evidence to support the allegation). Children can be removed from the family if they are considered to be in imminent danger, or services can be provided to the family to prevent further maltreatment. As you see in Figure 15.8, services also can be offered by CPS to families even when a report is not substantiated.

FIGURE 15.8

How the CPS system works. This figure shows how a report made to Child Protective Services moves through the system. The figure includes the statistics for 2014 at each step of the process.

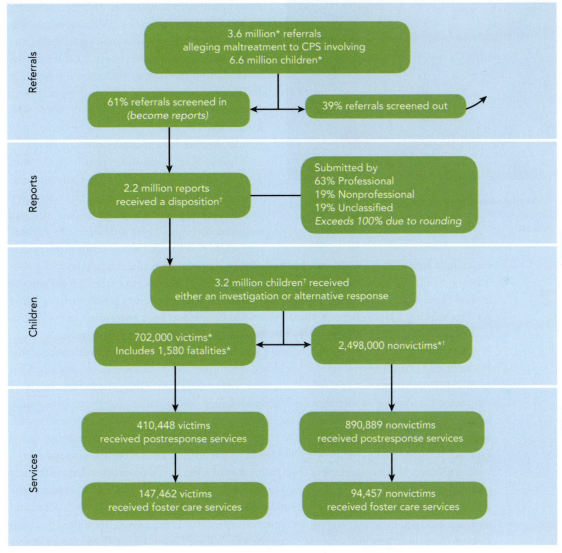

Referrals

3.6 million* referrals alleging maltreatment to CPS involving 6.6 million children*

61% referrals screened in (become reports)

39% referrals screened out

Reports

2.2 million reports received a disposition†

Submitted by
63% Professional
19% Nonprofessional
19% Unclassified
Exceeds 100% due to rounding

Children

3.2 million children† received either an investigation or alternative response

702,000 victims*
Includes 1,580 fatalities*

2,498,000 nonvictims*¹

Services

410,448 victims received postresponse services

890,889 nonvictims received postresponse services

147,462 victims received foster care services

94,457 nonvictims received foster care services

* Indicates a nationally estimated number.

† Please refer to the report Child Maltreatment 2014 http://www.acf.hhs.gov/programs/cb/research-data-technology/statistics-research/child-maltreatment for information regarding how the estimates were calculated. Average 1.83 children per referral.

¹ The estimated number of unique nonvictims was calculated by subtracting the unique count of estimated victims from the unique count of estimated children.

SOURCE: USDHHS (2015b).

The balance between child protection and family preservation is a central concern of child welfare agencies (Roberts, 2002), so agencies are reluctant to remove children from their homes unless they are clearly in danger. In 2013, approximately 3.1 million children who were considered at risk of abuse and neglect received prevention services that were intended to keep the family together while protecting the child from further harm. Services can help parents better understand the developmental needs of their children, and provide childcare or employment and housing referrals (USDHHS, 2015b).

As you read in the **Journey of Research: Child Protective Legislation,** when the public first realized the magnitude of the child abuse and neglect problem, there was a great deal of outrage over the ways in which children had been let down by the system, so the original

Physical child abuse. Child abuse has immediate consequences such as those seen in the child above, but it also has many long-term, psychological consequences for its victims.

Mandatory reporters
Individuals who work with children who are required by law to report suspicions of child maltreatment to authorities.

legislation was intended to uncover every possible case in which abuse was occurring. To this end, any concerned citizen, including a family's neighbors, relatives, or friends, can report suspicions to authorities, who then are responsible for conducting an investigation. Although there was initially some concern that making a false report would become a way for disgruntled neighbors or vindictive ex-spouses to harass a parent, in 2013 only two-tenths of 1% of all reports were found to be intentionally false, and people who knowingly file false reports can be prosecuted (Child Welfare Information Gateway, 2015).

Three-fifths of reports typically come from professionals who work with children and families. These professionals are considered **mandatory reporters** under the law and are required to report their suspicions to authorities (USDHHS, 2015b). Mandatory reporters include health care providers, teachers, child care providers, social workers, and police officers. Failure by a professional to report a suspicion of maltreatment carries a legal penalty (either a fine or imprisonment). However, all states protect mandatory reporters from being sued for making a report because their reports are assumed to have been made in good faith (Crosson-Tower, 2003). The identity of the reporter is not disclosed to the family.

One consequence of the original decision to cast a wide net to uncover any maltreatment that was occurring is that the system must screen and investigate over 3 million reports annually. This takes a tremendous amount of time and resources, and in 2013, fewer than one in five cases were substantiated following an investigation. We could change the legislation to make reporting maltreatment more difficult, but that would mean more cases of abuse or neglect would go undetected. So far we have not been willing to make this trade-off, so we continue to have a broad-based approach designed to discover as many families in which maltreatment is occurring as possible.

Our estimate of the magnitude of child maltreatment reflects only those cases that are actually reported to protective services, so we need to remember that they represent only a portion of the actual cases that occur. Based on a nationally representative sample of over 4,500 children and adolescents, David Finkelhor and his colleagues estimated that 1 out of every 10 children had been a victim of maltreatment during the previous year (Finkelhor, Turner, Ormrod, & Hamby, 2009).

Types of Maltreatment

The incidence of neglect (the failure to provide for the physical, emotional, medical, and educational needs of children) is much higher than the incidence of abuse. In 2013:

- 79.5% of victims suffered from neglect.
- 18% suffered physical abuse.
- 9% suffered sexual abuse.
- 8.7% suffered psychological maltreatment.
- 2.3% suffered medical neglect.
- An additional 10% of victims experienced such "other" types of maltreatment as abandonment or parental drug addiction.

A child can suffer from more than one type of maltreatment, which is why these numbers total to more than 100%.

In this same year, there were 1,484 child fatalities in the United States (USDHHS, 2015b). While this is a 12.7% decrease since 2009, it still means that on average four children die *each day* as the result of abuse or neglect (Child Welfare Information Gateway, 2015). Children under the age of 4 were at the greatest risk of dying at the hands of their own parents. Almost three-quarters of the childhood fatalities reported to CPS involve children younger than age 3 (USDHHS, 2015b). The risk of a boy suffering a fatality is almost double that of a girl. In a sample of cases taken from 33 states, researchers found that in 12.1% of the child fatalities the family had received services intended to keep the family together in the 5 years prior to the child's death, and in another 1.3% of the fatalities, the child had been in foster care but was reunited with his or her family prior to the child's death (Sedlak et al., 2010).

Victims and Perpetrators

Some children have a greater risk of becoming a victim of maltreatment than others. The child's age is one important risk factor. Figure 15.9 shows that younger children are at a greater risk than older children. Having a disability is another risk factor. Thirteen percent of child victims have a physical, behavioral, or mental disability (USDHHS, 2015b). African American children are at relatively greater risk than White or Hispanic children (14.6 per 1,000 children versus 8.5 and 8.1 children, respectively). Boys and girls are at similar risk of becoming a victim of the different types of maltreatment (USDHHS, 2015b), with the exception that the risk of being a victim of sexual abuse is 4 times greater for girls than for boys. Because cases of sexual abuse are different in several ways from other types of child maltreatment, we discuss this topic separately a little later in the chapter.

In 2013, one or both parents were responsible for the maltreatment of 91.4% of the victims (USDHHS, 2015b), but in 12.5% of these cases, at least one of the perpetrators was not a parent (Child Welfare Information Gateway, 2015). In most of these cases, the nonparental perpetrator was a male relative of the victim or the parent's male partner. Female perpetrators were more often responsible for neglect (females were responsible for 86% of victims of neglect), and males were more often responsible for abuse (males were responsible for 62% of the victims of abuse).

> **T ☐ F ☐** In the United States, one child dies from child abuse or neglect every 4 days. **False**

FIGURE 15.9

Maltreatment by age of victim. The youngest children are the ones at greatest risk of becoming a victim of child maltreatment. Infants account for almost one-quarter of all victims, and children under the age of 3 account for almost half. What do you think explains this vulnerability of very young children?

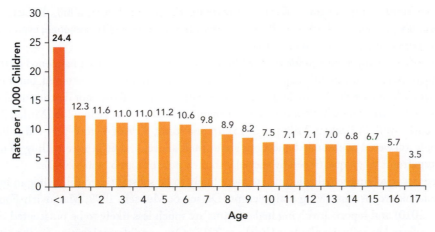

SOURCE: U.S. Department of Health and Human Services (2015b).

Child abuse and neglect certainly can occur at any socioeconomic level in society, but low-income families are at greater risk of being reported (Laskey et al., 2012). Some of this difference may be a reporting bias (that is, people may be more likely to report a poorer family to Child Protective Services), but it also is likely that maltreatment actually occurs more frequently in poorer families (USDHHS, 2015b). As we have seen, a number of circumstances associated with being poor can contribute to this increased risk. Poorer families, in general, are exposed to more life stressors, and increased stress makes it more likely that parents could lose control and strike out at their children. And of course, fewer financial resources can result in living conditions that represent neglect. When the economy takes a downturn, reports of both abuse and neglect typically increase (Freisthler, Merritt, & LaScala, 2006). Parents who have substance abuse problems are both more likely to be living in marginal conditions and more likely to be abusing or neglecting the children in their households. Finally, it is much more likely that low-income families will be in contact with agencies such as welfare agencies, probation services, or public health clinics that are mandatory reporters of suspected abuse or neglect.

Sexual Abuse

Although we know that many cases of child maltreatment are never detected or reported to authorities, the problem of underreporting is even greater for cases of sexual abuse (American Academy of Child and Adolescent Psychiatry, 2012). Contrary to what some people think, most children who are sexually abused were victimized by someone they know (Cromer & Goldsmith, 2010; Finkelhor et al., 2005), 12.2% of the perpetrators were women (USDHHS, 2015b), and 23% of the perpetrators were under the age of 18 (National Child Traumatic Stress Network [NCTSN], 2009). The victims often have been threatened with harm to themselves or their family if they disclose what has happened, which lowers the chance of the child telling someone about the abuse, and, if the perpetrator is known to the victim, the child may be afraid of getting that person in trouble (NCTSN, 2009).

T ☐ F ☐ Almost all sexual abuse of children is perpetrated by adult male strangers. **False**

Although both boys and girls might fear that they won't be believed or won't receive help if they disclose their abuse, boys have some additional issues tied to our cultural expectations for males. In interviews with male survivors of childhood sexual abuse, they describe the societal demands for acceptable masculine behavior as "strength, silence, and stoicism" (Sorsoli, Kia-Keating, & Grossman, 2008, p. 342). Males are raised to believe that they shouldn't be weak and shouldn't allow themselves to be victims and, if they have been victimized, that they should keep it to themselves. Such attitudes work against the chance that a boy will disclose to someone that sexual abuse has happened, but disclosure is the necessary first step in protecting the child from further abuse and getting him access to therapeutic services. A retrospective study conducted in Australia found that men were significantly less likely to disclose the abuse around the time it occurred (26% for men versus 64% for females) and took significantly longer to disclose to anyone (O'Leary & Barber, 2008). In fact, some of the study participants took over 20 years to discuss their abuse with someone, even if they were experiencing a great deal of distress.

Because so many adults go for years without disclosing the abuse that happened to them, it seemed that it would be difficult to get children to admit they had been abused, but it turns out that children are neither in denial about the reality of their abuse, nor do they need specific suggestions about what happened to get them to talk about it (Allnook & Miller, 2013; Jackson, Newall, & Backett-Milburn, 2015). In one study, 83% of 4- to 8-year-old children willingly answered open-ended questions about their abuse, and 66% were willing to name the perpetrator when questioned by specially trained police (Lamb et al., 2003).

Reports involving female victims are more likely to be substantiated following an investigation than reports involving male victims (Dersch & Munsch, 1999; Maikovich-Fong & Jaffee, 2010) and reports involving male victims are much less likely to be prosecuted if the case is referred to a district attorney (Edelson, 2013). One possible explanation for the gender difference in substantiation is that more reports with female victims come from mandatory reporters (Dersch & Munsch, 1999). Because mandatory reporters have a better understanding of what is necessary for Child Protective Services to substantiate a report, their reports in general are substantiated at a higher rate than reports from members of the general public. This suggests that mandatory reporters may need additional training in recognizing the signs of sexual abuse in male children so these cases also are reported to CPS.

Sexual abuse occurs in families from all ethnic and racial backgrounds and at all socioeconomic levels. It occurs in countries around the world, in many different cultures, with rates that average below 10% for boys and between 10% and 20% for girls. However, rates as high as 50% to 60% have been found in some studies in South Africa (Pereda, Guilera, Forns, & Gómez-Benito, 2009). Children are at greatest risk of becoming a victim of sexual abuse between the ages of 7 and 13, although 20% of sexually abused children experience the abuse before the age of 8 (Darkness to Light, 2015). Children living with two married biological parents have the lowest risk, while children living with a single parent or with a stepparent have a greater risk, and children who do not live with either biological parent (such as those in foster care) are at the greatest risk (Darkness to Light, 2015).

Of great concern worldwide is the sexual exploitation of young people for prostitution and pornography. For example, estimates are that 200,000 girls from Nepal are currently working in brothels in India (Crawford & Kaufman, 2008), but this is not a problem that happens only in less developed countries. "U.S. children are being sold for sex not only on the streets, by pimps, but via craigslist and at truck stops across the country" (Kotrla, 2010, p. 182). It is difficult to estimate the occurrence of sex trafficking because the crime is by its very nature clandestine, but current estimates are that more than 100,000 children are being trafficked within the United States (Kotrla, 2010). The children who are most vulnerable to this type of abuse are those who have run away from home or who have been forced to leave.

The Impact of Child Abuse and Neglect

Experiencing maltreatment during childhood has been associated with a number of physical, behavioral, and mental health problems, but the specific outcomes differ for different types of abuse and for neglect. They include a range of physical and mental health problems in childhood and through adulthood.

Sexual abuse negatively impacts the physical health of the survivor in a number of ways, including gastrointestinal and gynecologic symptoms, cardiopulmonary symptoms, and obesity (Irish, Kobayashi, & Delahanty, 2010). It also has been associated with higher rates of depression, anxiety disorders, antisocial behavior, substance abuse, conduct disorders, and attempted suicides (Irish et al., 2010; Maniglio, 2015; Putnam, 2003). Children who have been sexually abused at younger ages may show age-inappropriate sexual knowledge or engage in sexualized behaviors (Irish et al., 2010; Putnam, 2003). Survivors of more severe sexual abuse are more likely to engage in high-risk sexual behaviors as they get older, including having more frequent one-night stands or having sex under the influence of alcohol (Hornor, 2010; Negriff, Schneiderman, & Trickett, 2015). In general, the outcomes are poorer for survivors who suffered more severe abuse (for example, the abuse began at a younger age, if the abuse involved penetration or attempted penetration, or if there was little or no support following the child's disclosure of the abuse) (Hornor, 2010; Lacelle, Hébert, Lavoie, Vitaro, & Tremblay, 2012).

The consequences of physical abuse are not as clear (Fergusson, Boden, & Horwood, 2008). Although some research has found reports of suicidal thoughts, depression, antisocial behavior, and substance abuse, other studies have not found differences in these outcomes between physically abused children and matched control samples of children who were not abused. In a study of 16,000 adults who had experienced physical abuse while growing up, the researchers found that although physical abuse occurs more often to boys than to girls, the health-related outcomes as an adult seemed to be worse for girls (Thompson, Kingree, & Desai, 2004).

Parents and other caregivers can be investigated for psychological and emotional abuse, but this type of abuse is much more difficult to define and investigate than physical or sexual

Words can hurt. Psychological and emotional abuse, including verbal abuse, may not leave physical wounds on a child, but they create lasting damage that affects the child's physical, social, and emotional well-being. Despite the harm done, we have been slow to recognize it for the threat that it is and to provide interventions to stop it.

©iStockphoto.com/MachineHeadz

abuse because there is no physical evidence of the harm done. However, that does not mean that no harm has been done. The effects have been described as "unseen wounds" (Spinazzola et al., 2014, p. S18). In a study that defined psychological maltreatment as caregiver-inflicted bullying, terrorizing, coercive control, severe insults, debasement, threats, overwhelming demands, shunning, and/or isolation, the effect of psychological maltreatment was as great or greater than the effect of physical or sexual abuse for a number of the outcomes measured (Spinazzola et al., 2014). When psychological maltreatment co-occurred with physical or sexual abuse, the damaging effect was even stronger. Despite how often psychological maltreatment occurs and the significant consequences it can have for the child, it is rarely the focus of interventions offered by Child Protective Services.

Few studies have examined the long-term impact of neglect on children's development. It is very difficult to study the effects of neglect on child outcomes because neglect co-occurs with other life circumstances that also place a child at risk. One study of young children with substantiated reports of neglect found that 17% had been born to a teenage mother, 40% had high blood-lead levels, almost two-thirds of the mothers had received inadequate prenatal care, 45% had been homeless, and almost two-thirds lived in poverty. Neglected children experienced even higher levels of these risk factors than children who had suffered physical abuse. While victims of neglect had lower academic achievement, there was no similar significant association between abuse and academic outcomes (Fantuzzo, Perlman, & Dobbins, 2011). A study of adolescents who had experienced neglect found that they were more likely to have had one-night stands with sexual partners, and neglected females were more likely to get pregnant than females who had experienced other types of maltreatment (Negriff et al., 2015), findings that are perhaps not surprising given the lack of parental supervision that is frequently found in neglectful families.

Although it isn't surprising to learn that being a victim of abuse or neglect has later negative repercussions for children, it is important to understand the nature and the magnitude of those repercussions. Although these experiences increase a child's risk of suffering from mental and psychosocial problems, one estimate of the magnitude of the effect was that childhood sexual abuse accounted for 13% of the mental health problems experienced by the participants in the study and childhood physical abuse accounted for 5% of the mental health problems (Fergusson et al., 2008). So, although abuse contributes to an increased risk of problems, it is not the sole cause of these negative outcomes.

The research conducted by Fergusson and his colleagues (2008) is particularly important because it controlled for a number of other life experiences that are known to be associated with the same negative mental health and psychosocial outcomes associated with physical and sexual abuse. For instance, we know that children who grow up in families that are unstable, who are not securely attached to their caregivers, who live in poverty, or who live in difficult and dangerous environments are more prone to these types of mental health problems. When Fergusson et al. (2008) controlled for these factors within their sample, the relationship between childhood physical abuse and later mental health problems became statistically nonsignificant. By contrast, the relationship between childhood sexual abuse and mental health outcomes was reduced in strength but remained statistically significant. This type of analysis helps us understand how the factors that often co-occur with maltreatment contribute to the negative outcomes seen in these children. The fact that sexual abuse often occurs over a period of years and escalates in its severity over time is another possible explanation for why its effect on developmental outcomes is larger than the effect for physical abuse which may be more easily detected and stopped.

What can we take from this research on child outcomes? First, as traumatic as childhood experiences of abuse are, this research highlights the fact that many children find some way to recover from them. While it is extremely important that we continue to do whatever we can to prevent abuse from occurring and to stop it when it does, children have a great deal of resilience, and with appropriate help they can and do recover. Second, it reminds us that most children who are the victims of abuse are not dealing with a singular problem. They often are faced with multiple threats to their healthy development. The fact that inadequate parenting, domestic violence, poverty, and abuse occur together is not surprising, but these life circumstances multiply the amount of stress that a child faces. Remember what you learned at the beginning of this chapter about the cumulative effect of adverse childhood experiences (ACEs). Children who have fewer developmental challenges are more likely to overcome them and have a more positive prognosis for their future.

One consequence of abuse that you have probably heard about is the idea that abused children grow up to become abusive parents. It is not as simple as that. When we look at the histories of parents who have abused their children, it is true that many of them were victims of abuse themselves, but most estimates are that about 30% of children with a history of abuse perpetuate the cycle with their own children. This would mean that 70% (or over two-thirds) manage to find some way to break the cycle and do not repeat the pattern with their own children (Kim, 2009). It is encouraging to know that many adults who have experienced the pain of abuse manage to overcome these experiences to become positive, effective parents themselves.

Preventing child maltreatment can be expensive, but the cost of letting it occur is many times greater. A 2012 estimate of the total lifetime economic burden from 1 year of fatal and nonfatal child maltreatment in the United States was approximately $124 billion (Fang, Brown, Florence, & Mercy, 2012). Beyond the monetary cost, however, there is the incalculable pain and suffering and loss of quality of life for the victims.

RACIAL STEREOTYPING, PREJUDICE, AND DISCRIMINATION

A group of teenagers presented a skit in which an African American teen enters a store and is harassed by the store owner, who clearly assumes that the teen is going to steal something. When the students watching this skit were asked to write their responses to it, the Anglo American students indicated that they thought this was ridiculous and inaccurate, but the African American students in the class wrote "this happens all the time." Although there are many who believe that racism is no longer an issue in the United States, those who experience it have a very different perception. In a variety of studies, between 49% and 90% of African American adolescents report having had experiences of racial discrimination involving harassment, poor treatment in public settings, or assumptions of lower ability or more violent behavior (Cooper, McLoyd, Wood, & Hardaway, 2008).

Racism has been defined as "a pervasive system of advantage based on race" (Tatum, 1997, p. 92). There are three aspects: **stereotypes,** which are fixed beliefs about a particular racial group; **prejudice,** which is negative attitudes about that group; and **discrimination,** which is negative behavior directed at that group (Cooper et al., 2008). Racism can be overt, meaning it is openly accepted and acted on, or it can be covert. When it is covert, it is not acknowledged, and the individual who carries the racist attitudes may not even be aware of them but continues to be affected by them.

We also find racism in the way that institutions are created and operate. For example, in a large study carried out in Baltimore, African American youth applied more often for jobs but had lower rates of employment, even when they had the same socioeconomic status and academic achievement as their Anglo American peers (Entwisle, Alexander, & Olson, 2000).

T ☐ F ☐ Adults who were abused as children are likely to become abusive parents themselves. **False**

TRUE/FALSE VIDEO ▲

Racism A pervasive system of advantage and disadvantage based on race.

Stereotypes Conclusions made about someone based solely on the group with which he or she is identified.

Prejudice Negative attitudes toward individuals based on their race, ethnicity, religion, or other factors.

Discrimination Negative behavior directed at people on the basis of their race, ethnicity, religion, or other factors.

The result of institutional racism is to provide fewer opportunities for African American youth, which then has an impact on later achievement and economic well-being.

Children's perception that they are being treated unfairly because of their race is linked with lower levels of self-esteem; higher levels of depression, anxiety, and behavioral problems; and increased substance use (Pachter & Garcia Coll, 2009). Discrimination experienced in school can interfere with students' willingness to engage in academic pursuits, and substance abuse or violence may become a way to avoid or fight against feelings of a lack of control over their lives (Cooper et al., 2008).

Two issues associated with racism are how those who suffer racism can overcome its effects, and how society can prevent racism. We address these two questions separately. In relation to overcoming the effects, some teens who experience discrimination develop an attitude of "no one is going to stand in the way of my success" and take enormous pride in their ability to overcome adversity. Several factors contribute to the ability to take this approach. First, parental warmth and support and positive social support from others in their lives play a role in helping minority teens maintain their self-esteem in the face of negative events. Second, through a process called **racial socialization,** minority parents teach their children about discrimination so that they may prepare them with ideas and tactics that can help them deal with it. In addition, parents promote positive racial identification by instilling pride for their children's ethnic and racial heritage. Both parental support and racial socialization improve the outcomes for children who have experienced racial discrimination (Brody et al., 2006; Cooper et al., 2008; Sellers, Copeland-Linder, Martin, & Lewis, 2006).

The second issue regarding racial discrimination is how society can reduce or eliminate it. It was long assumed that racial discrimination was learned from adults and that children do not naturally develop these attitudes. However, research has shown that a variety of factors, including the cognitive limitations of young children, contribute to a natural tendency to differentiate among people on the basis of surface features such as skin color. Consequently, children's ideas about groups of people become increasingly stereotypical and prejudiced up to age 4 or 5, but beginning at about age 7, children develop cognitive skills that enable them to classify others on multiple dimensions (Levy & Hughes, 2009). With these skills, they can see that people may belong to a certain ethnic or racial group and yet have characteristics that are not stereotypically associated with that group. Role-taking ability and empathy develop as children move beyond the preschool years, and these abilities also contribute to less stereotyping and prejudice.

Racial socialization
Efforts by minority parents to teach their children about discrimination, prepare them to deal with these experiences, and teach them to take pride in their heritage.

Interventions that have been used and evaluated in schools to reduce stereotyping include multicultural education, cooperative learning experiences, and antibias social cognitive skills training (Pfeifer, Brown, & Juvonen, 2007). In multicultural education, children are introduced to positive ideas about racial or ethnic groups other than their own through learning about the history, values, beliefs, cultural traditions, and perspectives of people from different cultural backgrounds. These programs are often carried out in schools in which there is little diversity in the student body. The results have been disappointing because little change has been found in students' racial attitudes (Pfeifer et al., 2007). In fact, the focus on racial differences may make children think that these are the most important differences between people (Levy & Hughes, 2009).

A different approach encourages interaction among children of different races and

Breaking down discrimination. Racial discrimination is reduced when multiracial groups work together toward a common goal. Sports teams are one type of group that can make this happen. Have you been involved in activities that helped break down barriers between people from different backgrounds?

backgrounds through cooperative learning experiences. In these programs, multiracial groups of students must work together on a learning project to ensure that everyone in the group masters the material. Groups compete with one another, and rewards are given for group, not individual, performance. These programs have been more successful than multicultural education in promoting cross-race friendships that seem to last beyond the particular group project in which the students are involved (Pfeifer et al., 2007).

A third approach, antibias programs, focuses specifically on prejudice and discrimination and their effects rather than on information about ethnic or racial groups. These programs are often combined with education designed to promote role-taking skills and empathy. Many have been found to be successful in changing children's prejudiced attitudes, especially when the children were in integrated schools where they had the opportunity to interact with children from different backgrounds (Pfeifer et al., 2007).

CHECK YOUR UNDERSTANDING

1. Under what conditions is poverty most harmful to children?
2. Explain how cognitive behavioral therapy helps children cope with traumatic stress.
3. What must mandatory reporters do if they suspect that child maltreatment is occurring?
4. Why are male victims of sexual abuse less likely than female victims to disclose that they are being abused?
5. What is racial socialization and how does it prepare children to deal with discrimination?

RESILIENCE

15.5 What factors contribute to resilience in children faced with great adversity?

Throughout this chapter, we have described a number of experiences that challenge the growth and development of children and adolescents. At this point you may be thinking that it is amazing that children who experience such great adversity can thrive and grow up to be what Emmy Werner (2005) has described as "competent, confident, and caring adults" (p. 98). Throughout this discussion of threats to children's well-being, we have tried to point out the essential **resilience** or self-righting tendency that children have. We always hope that children are spared these types of challenges, but they do have the ability to face challenges, cope with them, learn from the experiences, and then use what they have learned in the future. **Journey of Research: Invincible, Invulnerable, and Resilient** describes how our understanding of children's ability to cope with developmental challenges has changed over the years.

Resilience The ability to bounce back from adversity or to thrive despite negative life circumstances.

JOURNEY OF *Research*

Invincible, Invulnerable, and Resilient

An important and interesting shift occurred in the field of child development in the 1970s. Prior to that time, psychologists and psychiatrists had primarily focused on understanding circumstances that threatened or disrupted the developmental process, using what is known as a *deficit model* or *risk perspective*. They wanted to understand the factors

(Continued)

(Continued)

(for example, environmental circumstances or individual characteristics) that placed a child at risk for less-than-optimal development. With that understanding, they hoped to be able to intervene in ways that would prevent problems or correct ones that already existed.

A change in perspective emerged in the 1970s and 1980s when several researchers caught people's attention with stories of children who had overcome great adversity and went on to become extraordinary individuals in the process. In one of the most widely known studies, Emmy Werner (1992) followed a cohort of almost 700 children on the island of Kauai from birth until they were in their 30s. Almost one-third of the children were initially considered to be at high risk due to their life circumstances. They had difficult births, lived in poverty, had parents who were alcoholic or suffered from mental illness, or experienced parental divorce or discord, and many of them had multiple risk factors. But as Werner and Smith (1985) tracked these high-risk children over time, they found that one-third of them had very good outcomes by the time they entered adulthood. With the advent of this type of research on resilience, the focus in the field began to shift from what could go wrong in development to what could go right. What helps a child recover or bounce back from adversity?

Protective personal characteristics that have been identified in resilience research include having an active, outgoing personality that engages other people (both adults and peers); having good communication and problem-solving skills; having a talent or an ability that attracts other people; and having faith in one's own ability to make good things happen (Werner, 2005). These children also are emotionally stable and not easily upset. Often they make good use of whatever resources are available to them, and they form warm, emotional bonds with alternative caregivers when their own parents are unavailable to provide support. Another important protective factor is the ability to take advantage of major life transitions as opportunities to redirect one's life (Werner, 2005). Entering into a supportive marriage, returning to school, and entering military service are all opportunities for a second chance, and resilient individuals seize those opportunities.

The next shift in perspective came with the advent of the *positive youth development* perspective. This approach was discussed in Chapter 14, when we looked at the impact of participating in positive community-based activities as a way to build strengths in children and adolescents. It seeks to understand circumstances that promote optimal development rather than just to identify circumstances that place a child at risk or even protect a child from harm. We could think of *protective factors* as factors that are at work when a child is already at risk for some negative developmental outcome, but the developmental assets framework adopted by the positive youth development perspective presumes that assets work in *any* circumstance for *any* child, whether there is risk or not, to maximize the child's positive potential for growth. From this perspective, the goal is not surviving in the face of adversity or protecting children from risk, but rather finding ways to help all children thrive regardless of their life situation. Sesma, Mannes, and Scales (2005) sum up this approach by saying, "The concept of thriving encompasses not only the relative absence of pathology, but also more explicit indicators of healthy and even optimal development" (p. 288).

FACTORS THAT BUILD RESILIENCE

When research on resilience first entered the literature, and later entered the mind of the public, the portrayal of resilient children suggested that they were remarkable—even heroic—in some way. Words like *invulnerable* and *invincible* were used to describe them, as though nothing could harm them (Masten, 2001). But as research on these children has matured, the picture that emerges is quite different from that of a superhero over-coming impossible odds. Anne Masten (2001), a researcher who has studied resilience for many years, has concluded that resilience is the product of what she calls "ordinary magic" (p. 227). She says, "The greatest surprise of resilience research is the ordinariness of the phenomena. Resilience appears to be a common phenomenon that results in most cases from the operation of basic human adaptational systems" (Masten, 2001, p. 227). Those systems include "connection to competent and caring adults in the family and community, cognitive and self-regulation skills, positive views of self, and motivation to be effective in the environment" (Masten, 2001, p. 234).

We have discussed each of these characteristics at some point in this book. Recall what you have learned about the role of attachment, effective parenting, self-esteem, self-regulation, and a drive to master the environment and consider their effect on the course of development. These are aspects of development that we get right most of the time, and that try to reassert themselves when things go wrong. Thinking about the "power of the ordinary" leads us to the conclusion that "resilience does not come from rare and special qualities, but from the everyday magic of ordinary, normative human resources in the minds, brains, and bodies of children, in their families and relationships, and in their communities" (Masten, 2001, p. 235), but these adaptational systems need to be nurtured so they will be available to children when they are needed. Rather than thinking of resilience as a trait that the child *has*, it may be more helpful to think of it as a process, or something the individual is able *to do* in the face of adversity to change the situation for the better (Luthar, 2000).

Characteristics of the child's family and their wider social environment play an important role in this process (Luthar, 2000). The child may have the capacity to reach out to others and engage them, but supportive individuals need to be available in the child's environment and be willing to respond. Emmy Werner (2005) summarized the process by saying that the resilient children in her study "had relied on sources of support within the family and community that *increased* their competence and efficacy, *decreased* the number of stressful life events they subsequently encountered, and *opened up* new opportunity for them" (author's emphasis, p. 99). The Center on the Developing Child (2016) at Harvard University describes resilience as the result of a combination of factors, noting that neither individual characteristics nor social environment alone can ensure positive outcomes for children who experience prolonged periods of toxic stress. Rather there must be "an interaction between biology and environment that builds a child's ability to cope with adversity and overcome threats to healthy development" (para. 4).

Active Learning: Resilience gives you a chance to think about where and when you have seen this process at work in your own experience.

T ☐ F ☐ Children who are able to rise above great adversity like poverty or child abuse have a number of unique abilities. **False**

Active LEARNING

Resilience

Children and adolescents may experience many types of traumatic events or life circumstances, such as poverty, a natural disaster, child abuse, or a difficult parental divorce. Think about someone you know who appears to be doing well despite difficult life experiences that could have put that person at risk for emotional disturbance, criminal behavior, or other negative outcomes. If there have been potentially traumatic events or circumstances in your life, you can reflect on your own experiences.

Then think about what factors in that person's life may have contributed to his or her apparent resilience. For example, one young teenager was part of a tough, inner-city

(Continued)

(Continued)

gang and was headed for trouble. Instead he ended up going to college. He attributes his change in direction and resilience to the guidance of his stepfather who got him into football, where he found a different way to succeed, a positive group of peers, and a reason to do well in school. His resilience came from the interest of a caring adult, plus his own talents. The factors you see for the individual you describe may come from the outside, such as loving support from one individual; they may come from the child, such as a lively intelligence or social skills; or, most likely, they may come from a combination of the two.

One of the greatest challenges to our understanding of the concept of resilience is the great variability that we see in child outcomes. For example, many Romanian orphans who are adopted by well-functioning families showed an incredible amount of recovery when their life circumstances change (Masten, 2001), but some continued to show serious pathology despite their improved living conditions. As we have already pointed out, most children who are abused while growing up do not perpetuate that pattern with their own children, but some do (Jaffee et al., 2013). Children of mothers who are clinically depressed have a high incidence of psychiatric disorders themselves, but a sizeable proportion are able to function adequately in their own lives (Goldstein & Brooks, 2005). Although children growing up in poverty are likely to have psychological and academic difficulties that could limit their achievements, the list of children who have been able to overcome their early experiences of poverty includes people who have been successful in all fields of endeavor, and includes several presidents of the United States.

What research on resilience shows us is that recovery is possible, even if it is not inevitable. As of now, we have not identified all the critical factors, and the course of development is so complex that it is unlikely that we will ever be able to devise a formula for resilience that can correct every possible negative trajectory. What is important, however, is that work continues within the field to identify and understand the complex interactions between the individual and his or her environment that help children reach their full and unique potential whatever their life circumstances happen to be.

CHECK YOUR UNDERSTANDING

1. How did Emmy Warner's research change the perspective of the field about development?
2. What are some characteristics that help to make a child resilient in the face of adversity?
3. What environmental factors interact with personal characteristics to develop resilience?

CONCLUSION

As children grow, they not only face a multitude of risk factors, but also have many factors that help protect them from risk. In this chapter, we have discussed some of the experiences that may challenge children, including illness, mental disorders, poverty and homelessness, racial discrimination, and child abuse. Any child who experiences these problems will be affected by them, and usually the greater the number of risk factors children experience, the less likely it is that they will emerge with the physical, cognitive, social, and emotional skills they need for a successful life. However, many children are able to cope well and show remarkable resilience. As a society and as individuals, we owe it to all our children to do whatever we can to improve their chances.

As you finish this course in child development, you are now armed with some tools that will help you make a difference, whether you work with an individual child, have your own children, teach in a classroom, develop programs for families or neighborhoods, advocate for children in the courts or the government, or carry out research to continue to add to our body of knowledge about children and their development. We hope that what you have learned will become the basis for your work (and play) with children in the future and that you have gained a solid foundation of knowledge to build on in the future.

CHAPTER SUMMARY

Test your understanding of the content.
Take the practice quiz at **edge.sagepub.com/levine3e**

15.1 What is stress, and how do we cope with it?

Stress is anything that places excessive demands on our ability to cope. Our body responds with a **fight-or-flight response** that prepares us to deal with a threat. Children may experience **normative stress** that most children go through, or they may experience **non-normative stress** when they experience unusual distressing events. As the number of stress events increases, so does the risk of a number of health problems. What is seen as stressful differs from one person to another. Children can use **problem-focused strategies** and **emotion-focused strategies** to cope with the stress.

15.2 How do physical illnesses and mental disorders affect children's development?

Immunizations can protect children from many common illnesses and are safe and effective. Young adolescents can receive a vaccine to protect them from HPV. When a child has a chronic illness, such as asthma, every member in a family is affected, not just the ill child. Symptoms of mental disorders are similar to behaviors that all people exhibit from time to time, but are more extreme, last longer, and cause significant distress and disruption in the lives of the children and adolescents who experience them. Treatment for these disorders can help put children back on a positive developmental path.

15.3 What are other threats to the health and well-being of children and adolescents?

Many children and adolescents have a sleep deficit or poor quality sleep. Environmental toxins such as lead or pesticides put children's health at risk, and may play a role in childhood cancer. The **hygiene hypothesis** suggested that living in a germ-free environment may be a cause of **asthma** because it reduces resistance to common allergens. Rates of injury and death from accidents in childhood and adolescence have been decreasing but still pose a risk to many young people. Adolescents are smoking, drinking, and using illicit drugs at a lower rate than in the past, but for those who continue to use these substances, these behaviors can have negative effects on health. Some teens develop a **substance use disorder.**

15.4 What are effects of poverty, homelessness, trauma, maltreatment, and racial discrimination on the development of children and adolescents?

Poverty is associated with school failure, health problems, and behavior problems. The longer and the earlier that a child lives in poverty, the worse the outcomes tend to be. However, when income increases for low-income families, child outcomes often improve. Homelessness is a complex problem that requires a multifaceted solution. Experiencing traumatic stress leaves children feeling their world is not secure or predictable, and may cause intrusive thoughts or **posttraumatic stress disorder (PTSD)**. Child **maltreatment** includes **abuse** and **neglect**. **Mandatory reporters** are required to report suspected abuse and neglect to child protective services, but private citizens also can report in most states. Following an investigation, services may be offered to the family, or the child may be removed from the home. Infants and young children are more likely to be the victims of abuse, and parents are most likely to be the perpetrators. Sexual abuse is more clearly linked to negative outcomes than physical abuse or neglect, and when it is paired with psychological or emotional abuse, the damaging effects are even stronger. Sexual exploitation of children, including sex trafficking, is a major concern around the world. **Racism** includes **stereotypes, prejudice,** and **discrimination.** Parents can help to prepare their children to deal with discrimination through **racial socialization.** Schools have used multicultural education, cooperative learning experiences, and antibias social cognitive skills training to reduce racism.

15.5 What factors contribute to resilience in children faced with great adversity?

Resilient children often have a number of positive characteristics that attract others to them. They also are able to take advantage of major life transitions as opportunities to change the direction of their life and overcome adversity. **Resilience** is a process in which the child's characteristics interact with the environment. Having a supportive and caring adult in that environment is particularly important.

KEY TERMS

Strengthen your understanding of these key terms with mobile-friendly eFlashcards at **edge.sagepub.com/levine3e**

Abuse   607
Asthma   594
Child life specialists   587
Coping   582
Discrimination   615
Emotion-focused strategies   583
Fight-or-flight response   580
Hygiene hypothesis   595
Maltreatment   607
Mandatory reporters   610
Neglect   607
Non-normative stress   582

Normative stress   582
Pediatric psychologists   587
Posttraumatic stress disorder (PTSD)   605
Prejudice   615
Problem-focused strategies   583
Racial socialization   616
Racism   615
Resilience   617
Stereotypes   615
Stress   580
Substance use disorder (SUD)   601

Give your students the SAGE edge!

SAGE edge offers a robust online environment featuring an impressive array of free tools and resources for review, study, and further exploration, keeping both instructors and students on the cutting edge of teaching and learning. Learn more at **edge.sagepub.com/levine3e**

Glossary

A-not-B task   A test for object permanence in which an object is hidden under cloth A and then moved under cloth B.

Ability grouping   An educational approach that places students of similar ability in learning groups so they can be taught at a level that is most appropriate for their level of understanding.

Abortion   A medical procedure that uses medicine or surgery to remove an embryo or fetus and placenta from a woman's uterus.

Abuse   Deliberate and intentional words and actions that cause physical, sexual, or psychological harm or potential harm to a child.

Academic mind-sets   Deeply held beliefs that influence our behaviors in academic settings.

Accelerated program   A type of program that allows gifted students to move through the standard curriculum but more quickly than is typical.

Acceptance/responsiveness   A dimension of parenting that measures the amount of warmth and affection in the parent-child relationship.

Accommodation   Changing mental schemas so they fit new experiences.

Active gene-environment interaction   When one's genetic endowment becomes a driving force for children to seek out experiences that fit their genetic endowments.

Active labor   The second phase in the first stage of labor in which contractions become longer, stronger, and more frequent and the cervix dilates to 4 centimeters.

Adolescent growth spurt   The period of rapid increase in height and weight that occurs in early adolescence.

Amniocentesis   A test to look for genetic abnormalities prenatally, in which a physician uses a long, thin needle to extract amniotic fluid, which is then tested.

Amnion   The inner fetal membrane that surrounds the fetus and is filled with amniotic fluid.

Anal stage   Freud's second stage during which toddlers' sexual energy is focused on the anus.

Analytical intelligence   The type of intelligence that is the one closest to "g" or general intelligence and the one prized highly in most schools.

Androgyny   The idea that both sexes can have characteristics that are traditionally considered masculine and traditionally considered feminine.

Anorexia nervosa   A condition in which individuals become obsessed with their weight and intentionally restrict food intake to a point that it may become life threatening.

Antisocial behavior   Actions that hurt other people, physically or emotionally

Anxiety   A vague fear of events that may or may not occur.

Anxiety disorder   A level of anxiety that is severe, lasts a long time, and interferes with normal functioning.

Anxious ambivalent/resistant attachment   An attachment classification in which the infant is reluctant to move away from his mother to explore and is very distressed when she leaves, but when she returns, he approaches her but also angrily resists her attempt to pick him up.

Anxious avoidant attachment   An attachment classification in which the infant is not distressed when her mother leaves, is as comfortable with the stranger as with her mother, and does not rush to greet her mother when she returns.

Apgar Scale   An assessment of a newborn's overall condition at 1 minute and 5 minutes after birth that is based on the newborn's activity level, pulse, grimace, appearance, and respiration.

Applied behavior analysis (ABA)   Application of principles of behaviorism to change behavior of individuals with a range of difficulties, including autism spectrum disorder.

Applied research   Research that has the primary goal of solving problems or improving the human condition.

Archival records   Data collected at an earlier date that are used for research purposes.

Assimilation Fitting new experiences into existing mental schemas.

Associative play Sharing toys and interacting with peers, but without a common goal.

Asthma The most common chronic illness in childhood, in which a child's airways constrict, making it difficult to breathe.

Attachment An emotional bond to a particular person.

Attachment in the making The stage from 6 weeks to 6 to 8 months in which infants develop stranger anxiety, differentiating those they know from those they don't.

Attention-deficit/hyperactivity disorder (ADHD) A disorder marked by extreme difficulty with inattention, impulsivity, or a combination of both.

Attrition The loss of participants over the course of a longitudinal study.

Authentic assessment A testing procedure that focuses on the process used in solving complex, real-life problems rather than the product that results from the process.

Authoritarian parents Parents who combine high levels of control and low levels of warmth, and who expect compliance from the child.

Authoritative parents Parents who combine high levels of control with a good deal of warmth and encouragement, together with reasonable expectations and explanation of the parents' rules.

Autism spectrum disorder A disorder characterized by pervasive impairment in social communication and interaction and by restricted or repetitive behaviors, interests, or activities. Severity is classified by how much support the individual needs to function effectively.

Autobiographical memory A coherent set of memories about one's life.

Automaticity The process by which skills become so well practiced that you can do them without much conscious thought.

Autonomous morality When children are aware of the rules and realize that they must adhere to them to maintain their interaction with others, rather than because an adult has told them what to do.

Average children Children who receive a number of nominations for "like most" and "like least" that is close to the median in the peer group on a sociometric measure.

Axons The parts of a nerve cell that conduct impulses away from the cell body.

Balanced reading approach An approach to teaching reading that combines elements of the whole language approach (which emphasizes comprehension and meaning) with elements of the phonics approach (which emphasizes decoding of words).

Basic emotions An automatic and unlearned set of emotions that arise early in development and have a biological basis.

Basic research Research that has the primary goal of adding to our body of knowledge rather than having immediate direct application.

Behavioral genetics Research to determine the degree of genetic basis for a behavior, a trait, or an ability.

Behaviorism The theory developed by John B. Watson that focuses on environmental control of observable behavior.

Big-C creativity The type of creativity that transforms a culture by impacting the way we think or live our lives.

Blastocyst A hollow ball of cells that consists of the inner cell mass (which becomes the embryo) and an outer ring of cells (which becomes the placenta and chorion).

Broca's area The part of the brain that is involved in the physical production of speech.

Bulimia nervosa An eating disorder characterized by eating binges, followed by purging (for example, self-induced vomiting or the excessive use of laxatives) to get rid of the food.

Bullying Being exposed repeatedly and over time to negative actions on the part of peers, including physical bullying, verbal bullying, and/or emotional bullying.

Canalization The degree to which the expression of a gene is influenced by the environment.

Case study An in-depth study of a single individual or small group of individuals which uses multiple methods of study.

Centration Focusing on only one aspect of a situation.

Cephalocaudal development A principle whereby development proceeds from the head region down through the body.

Cerebral palsy A chronic condition that appears early in development and primarily involves problems with body movement and muscle coordination.

Cervix The narrow, lower end of the uterus.

Checklist A prepared list of behaviors, characteristics, or judgments observers use to assess a child's development.

Child effects model A model that assumes it is the characteristics of the child that determine the parenting style parents use.

Child life specialists Experts in child development who promote optimal development in children in medical settings.

Child-directed speech Speech that is tailored to fit the sensory and cognitive capabilities of infants and children so that it holds their attention; includes speaking in a higher pitch with exaggerated intonation and a singsong rhythm and using a simplified vocabulary.

Childhood-onset fluency disorder or stuttering Difficulty with fluency and time patterning of speech.

Chorion The outer fetal membrane that surrounds the fetus and gives rise to the placenta.

Chorionic villus sampling (CVS) A test to look for genetic abnormalities prenatally, in which a small tube is inserted either through the vagina and cervix or through a needle inserted in the abdomen, and a sample of cells is retrieved from the chorion for testing.

Chromosome disorders Disorders that result when too many or too few chromosomes are formed or when there is a change in the structure of the chromosome caused by breakage.

Chromosomes The strands of genes that constitute the human genetic endowment.

Chronosystem In ecological systems theory, the dimension of time, including one's age and the time in history in which one lives.

Cisgender Individuals who identify with their natal gender.

Circular reaction An infant's repetition of a reflexive action that results in a pleasurable experience.

Classical conditioning The process by which a stimulus (the unconditioned stimulus) that naturally evokes a certain response (the unconditioned response) is paired repeatedly with a neutral stimulus. Eventually the neutral stimulus becomes the conditioned stimulus and evokes the same response, now called the conditioned response.

Classification The ability to organize objects into hierarchical conceptual categories.

Clear-cut attachment The stage from 6 to 8 months to 18 months to 2 years, when an infant develops separation anxiety when a person he is attached to leaves him.

Clinical interview An interview strategy in which the interviewer can deviate from a standard set of questions to gather additional information.

Cliques Small groups of friends who spend time together and develop close relationships.

Coercive family environment A pattern of family interaction in which parents and children mutually train each other so that the child becomes increasingly aggressive and the parents become less effective in controlling the child's behavior.

Cognitive behavioral therapy A therapeutic approach based on changing maladaptive thoughts and behaviors to deal with problem-focused goals.

Cognitive development Changes in the way children think, understand, and reason as they grow older.

Cognitive flexibility The ability to switch focus as needed to complete a task.

Cognitive processing theory The theory that learning language is a process of "data crunching," in which the actual process of learning words and their meanings relies on the computational ability of the human brain.

Cohort effect Differences between groups in a cross-sectional or sequential study that are attributable to the fact that the participants have had different life experiences.

Collaborative learning An educational strategy that allows groups of students who are at different ability levels to work together on a common goal.

Collectivism The cultural value that emphasizes obligations to others within your group.

Colostrum The thick, yellowish substance filled with antibodies and nutrients that is produced from a woman's breasts after she gives birth before milk is produced.

Command strategy A parenting technique in which the parent does not make any overt threats of punishment, but the child responds to the legitimate authority that the parent has to make a request of the child.

Concordance rate The degree to which a trait or an ability of one individual is similar to that of another; used to examine similarities between twins and among adopted children and their biological and adoptive parents.

Concrete operations The third stage in Piaget's theory in which children between 6 and 12 years of age develop logical thinking but still cannot think abstractly.

Conduct disorder A persistent pattern of behavior marked by violation of the basic rights of others or of major age-appropriate social norms or rules.

Connectionist or neural network model In this model of memory, the process is envisioned as a neural network that consists of concept nodes that are interconnected by links.

Conservation The understanding that a basic quantity of something (amount, volume, mass) remains the same regardless of changes in appearance.

Constraints Assumptions language learners make that limit the alternative meanings that they attribute to new words.

Constructive conflict Family conflict that is resolved in a positive way using affection, problem solving, and emotional support.

Constructive play Building or making something for the purposes of play.

Constructivism The idea that humans actively construct their understanding of the world, rather than passively receiving knowledge.

Control group The group in an experiment that does not get the special treatment and provides a baseline against which the experimental group can be compared.

Controversial children Children who receive both a large number of nominations for "like most" and a large number of nominations for "like least" from peers on a sociometric measure.

Conventional moral judgment Moral reasoning that moves beyond self-interest to take into account the good of others.

Convergent thinking Finding one correct solution for a problem.

Cooing Soft vowel sounds, such as *ooh* and *aah*.

Cooperative play Play with peers that has a common goal.

Coparenting Sharing parenting responsibilities between two or more people.

Coping Conscious effort made to master, tolerate, or reduce stress.

Corpus callosum The band of fibers that connects the two hemispheres of the brain.

Correlational research design Research design that measures the strength and direction of the relationship between two or more variables that are not created by the experimenter.

Couvade A sympathetic pregnancy in which a man experiences a variety of symptoms associated with pregnancy or childbirth while his partner is pregnant.

Creative intelligence The ability to generate ideas and to deal successfully with novelty (sometimes referred to as divergent thinking).

Creativity Thinking that is novel and that produces ideas that are of value.

Critical period A period of time during which development is occurring rapidly and the organism is especially sensitive to damage, which often is severe and irreversible.

Cross-sectional design A research design that uses multiple groups of participants who represent the age span of interest to the researcher.

Crowds Large, reputation-based groups that are based on a shared stereotype but whose members do not necessarily spend time together.

Crystallized intelligence What we already know and can draw on to solve problems.

Culture The system of behaviors, norms, beliefs, and traditions that form to promote the survival of a group that lives in a particular environmental niche.

Cyberbullying The use of electronic technologies, including e-mails, text messages, digital images, webpages (including social network sites), blogs, or chat rooms, to socially harm others.

Decenter The ability to think about more than one aspect of a situation at a time.

Delay of gratification The ability to wait until later to get something desirable.

Demandingness/control A dimension of parenting that measures the amount of restrictiveness and structure that parents place on their children.

Dendrites The portions of a neuron that receive impulses from other neurons.

Dependent variable The outcome of interest to the researcher that is measured at the end of an experiment.

Depression with peripartum onset A major depression that occurs in the last month of pregnancy or the first couple of months after birth.

Developmental assets Common sense positive experiences and qualities that help young people become caring, responsible adults.

Developmental bilingual programs Programs in which English language learners receive instruction in core subjects in their native language until they have the language skills to be instructed in English.

Developmental cognitive neuroscience The study of the relation between cognitive development and the development of the brain.

Developmental coordination disorder (DCD) A condition in which delays in reaching motor milestones interfere with daily living or academic performance.

Developmental psychopathology An approach that sees mental and behavioral problems as distortions of normal developmental processes rather than as illnesses.

Developmental theory A model of development based on observations that allows us to make predictions.

Deviation IQ A measure of intelligence that is based on the individual's deviation from the norms for a given test.

Dialogic reading A technique used to facilitate early literacy, in which an adult and a child look at a book together while the adult asks questions and encourages a dialogue, followed by switching roles so the child asks questions of the adult.

Difficult temperament A child's general responsiveness marked by more negative mood, intense responses, slow adaptation to change, and irregular patterns of eating, sleeping, and elimination.

Discourse skills The ability to understand whether a story or information someone is hearing makes logical sense.

Discovery learning An approach to teaching that emphasizes allowing children to discover for themselves new information and understanding.

Discrimination Negative behavior directed at people on the basis of their race, ethnicity, religion, or other factors.

Disengaged parents Parents who do not set limits or rules for their children and are not emotionally connected to them.

Disequilibrium A state of confusion in which your schemas do not fit your experiences.

Disinhibited social engagement disorder An attachment disorder in which children approach strangers indiscriminately, not differentiating between attachment figures and other people.

Disorganized/disoriented attachment An attachment classification in which behavior is unpredictable and odd and shows no coherent way of dealing with attachment issues, often linked with parental abuse or neglect.

Disruptive mood dysregulation disorder (DMDD) Severe and frequent temper tantrums that are out of proportion with the situation.

Divergent thinking The ability to find as many possible solutions to a problem as possible, rather than the one "correct" solution.

Dizygotic (DZ) twins Twins formed when a woman produces two ova or eggs, which are fertilized by two sperm; genetically DZ twins are as similar as any siblings.

Dominant genes Genes that are usually expressed in the phenotype.

Doula A trained, knowledgeable companion who supports a woman during her labor and delivery.

Drive reduction The idea that human behavior is determined by the motivation to satisfy or reduce the discomfort caused by biological needs or drives.

Dynamic assessment A testing procedure that uses a test-intervene-test procedure to assess the examinee's potential to change.

Dynamic systems theory The theory that all aspects of development interact and affect each other in a dynamic process over time.

Dyslexia A learning disorder marked by difficulty reading as a result of problems with decoding written language.

Early labor The first phase in the first stage of labor in which contractions are usually not painful but the cervix begins to thin out and dilate.

Easy temperament A child's general responsiveness marked by positive mood, easy adaptation to change, and regularity and predictability in patterns of eating, sleeping, and elimination.

Echolalia When children repeat what has been said to them instead of responding appropriately.

Effect size A statistical measure of how large the difference is between groups being compared.

Effortful control The ability to consciously control one's behavior.

Ego The part of the personality that contends with the reality of the world and controls the basic drives.

Egocentric speech A limitation of young children's communication due to their inability to take the perspective of other people into account.

Egocentrism The inability to see or understand things from someone else's perspective.

Elaboration A memory strategy that involves creating extra connections, like images or sentences, that can tie information together.

Embryo The developing organism from conception to the end of the second month of a pregnancy.

Embryonic stage The prenatal stage that lasts from 2 weeks to 2 months postconception.

Emergent literacy   The set of skills that develop before children begin formal reading instruction that provide the foundation for later academic skills.

Emotion   The body's physiological reaction to a situation, your cognitive interpretation of the situation, communication to another person, and your own actions.

Emotion coaching   A parental style that teaches children how to understand their emotions and deal with them.

Emotion dismissing   A parental style that teaches children to ignore their feelings.

Emotion schemas   All the associations and interpretations that an individual connects to a certain emotion.

Emotional display rules   Culturally determined norms for when, how, and to whom emotions should, or should not, be shown.

Emotion-focused strategies   Coping strategies designed to reduce or manage emotional distress.

Emotional intelligence   The ability to understand and control one's emotions, to understand the emotions of others, and to use this understanding in human interactions.

Empathy   Sharing the feelings of other people.

Encoding processes   The transformation processes through which new information is stored in long-term memory.

Endocrine disruptors   Chemicals that interfere with the functioning of the hormonal systems of the body.

English as a second language (ESL) pull-out programs   Programs in which students are taught English in a separate classroom.

Enrichment approach   An educational approach for gifted children in which the curriculum is covered but in greater depth, breadth, or complexity than is done in a typical classroom.

Epigenetics   A system by which genes are activated or silenced in response to events or circumstances in the individual's environment.

Equifinality   The principle by which different developmental pathways may result in the same outcome.

Equilibration   An attempt to resolve uncertainty to return to a comfortable cognitive state.

Ethnic and racial identity   A person's attitudes toward the racial and ethnic groups to which they feel they belong.

Ethnography   A qualitative research technique in which a researcher lives with a group of people as a participant observer, taking part in the group's everyday life while observing and interviewing people in the group.

Ethology   The study of the adaptive value of animal and human behavior in the natural environment.

Evocative gene-environment interaction   When children's genetic endowment causes them to act in a way that draws out or "evokes" certain responses from those around them.

Executive function   The ability of the brain to coordinate attention and memory, and control behavioral responses for the purpose of attaining a certain goal.

Exercise play   Play in young children that involves large muscle movement, such as running or jumping.

Exosystem   Settings that the child never enters but that affect the child's development nevertheless, such as the parents' place of work.

Expectancy effects   The effect that the expectations of others can have on one's self-perception and behavior.

Experience-dependent brain development   Development that occurs in response to specific learning experiences.

Experience-expectant brain development   Development that occurs when we encounter experiences that our brain expects as a normal event.

Experimental group   The group in an experiment that gets the special treatment that is of interest to the researcher.

Experimental research design   A research design in which an experimental group is administered a treatment and the outcome is compared with a control group that does not receive the treatment.

Expressive language   The written or spoken language that we use to convey our thoughts, emotions, or needs.

Extended family   A family structure that includes nuclear family members and other relatives, such as grandparents, aunts, uncles, and cousins.

Externalizing (or other directed) behaviors   Behaviors, such as aggressive or destructive behavior, in which the child or adolescent "acts out" on the environment.

Extinction   In operant conditioning, the process by which a behavior stops when it receives no response from the environment.

Extrinsic motivation   Motivation that depends on receiving an incentive or reward from the environment.

False belief   The understanding that someone else may believe something that a child knows to be untrue.

False belief paradigm   An experimental task used to assess a child's understanding that others may believe something the child knows to be untrue.

False memories Memory for something you thought happened but did not.

Fast mapping A process by which children apply constraints and their knowledge of grammar to learn new words very quickly, often after a single exposure.

Fertilization The union of a father's sperm and a mother's egg to produce a zygote.

Fetal alcohol spectrum disorders (FASDs) A range of impairments in a child resulting from consumption of alcohol during a pregnancy.

Fetal alcohol syndrome (FAS) A condition in the child resulting from heavy or binge consumption of alcohol during a pregnancy; associated with characteristic facial features, small stature, and a small head, as well as cognitive deficits and trouble controlling behavior and regulating emotions.

Fetal stage The prenatal stage that lasts from Week 9 postconception until birth.

Fetus The developing organism from the end of the eighth week postconception until birth.

Fight-or-flight response The body's physiological response to threat.

Fine motor skills Skills that involve small movements, mostly of the hands and fingers, but also of the lips and tongue.

Fluid intelligence Intelligence that allows us to quickly and effectively solve novel problems for which we have little training.

Flynn effect The increase in intelligence test scores that has occurred over time, necessitating the renorming of the tests.

Food insecurity A situation in which food is often scarce or unavailable, causing people to overeat when they do have access to food.

Formal operations Piaget's fourth stage in which people 12 and older think both logically and abstractly.

Foster care The temporary placement of children in a family that is not their own because of unhealthy situations within their birth family.

Friendship A mutual relationship marked by companionship, closeness, and affection.

Functional behavioral assessment Identification of reinforcements that are maintaining undesirable behavior in order to change them and reduce the behaviors.

Fuzzy trace theory The theory that there are two memory systems: a systematic, controlled memory for exact details, and an automatic, intuitive memory for the gist, or meaning, of events.

Games with rules Making up rules for a game or playing games with preestablished rules.

Gender constancy The stage at which children understand that one's gender remains constant despite external changes.

Gender dysphoria A diagnosis in the DSM-5 that is made when an individual is distressed about his or her preference to be different from his or her natal gender.

Gender identity Stage when children can identify gender but their concept of gender relies on external appearance.

Gender nonconforming Individuals who do not identify or conform to gender norms for either males or females.

Gender segregation A preference for playing with other children of the same gender.

Gender self-socialization model An approach to gender identity development that is based on each individual's own ideas of gender consistency and pressure.

Gender stability Stage when children understand that their gender will remain stable over time, but aren't sure that it won't change if they do activities usually performed by the other gender.

Gene A segment of DNA on a chromosome that creates proteins that are the basis for the body's development and functioning.

Gene therapy Treatment of genetic disorders through implanting or disabling specific genes.

Generalist genes Genes that affect many, apparently distinct cognitive abilities.

Generalize To draw inferences from the findings of research on a specific sample about a larger group or population.

Genetic-epistemology Piaget's theory that cognitive development of knowledge is based on both genetics (from biology) and epistemology (a philosophical understanding of the nature of knowledge).

Genital stage Freud's fifth and final stage in which people 12 and older develop adult sexuality.

Genome The complete sequence of bases that make up the genetic instructions of an organism.

Genotype The genes that are present at a particular location on the chromosome.

Germinal stage The prenatal stage that lasts from conception to 2 weeks postconception.

Gifted (or talented) children   Children and youth who exhibit high performance capability in intellectual, creative, and/or artistic areas; possess an unusual leadership capacity; or excel in specific academic fields.

Global self-esteem   The feelings you have about your own general self-worth.

Goal-corrected partnership   The stage of development of attachment from 18 months on, when toddlers create reciprocal relationships with their mothers.

Goodness of fit   How well a child's temperamental characteristics match with the demands of the child's environment.

Grey matter   The neurons and synapses that make up the brain.

Gross motor skills   Skills that involve the large muscle groups of the body—for example, the legs and arms.

Guilt   Feelings children have when they think about the negative aspects of something they have done, particularly moral failures.

Habituation   The reduction in the response to a stimulus that is repeated.

Hemispheres   The two halves of the brain.

Heritability   A measure of the extent to which genes determine a particular behavior or characteristic.

Heteronomous morality   Moral judgments based on the dictates of authority.

Hostile attributional bias   A tendency to interpret the innocent behavior of others as intentionally hostile rather than benign.

Hygiene hypothesis   The idea that living in a germ-free environment is causing our immune systems to become more reactive to allergens.

Hypothesis   A prediction, often based on theoretical ideas or observations, that is tested by the scientific method.

Hypothetico-deductive reasoning   The ability to form hypotheses about how the world works and to reason logically about these hypotheses.

Id   According to psychoanalytic theory, the part of personality that consists of the basic drives, such as sex and hunger.

Ideal self   The characteristics one aspires to in the future.

Identity achievement   The choice of an identity following exploration of the possibilities.

Identity diffusion   A lack of interest in developing an identity.

Identity foreclosure   Commitment to an identity without any exploration of possibilities.

Identity moratorium   A time of exploration in search of identity, with no commitment made yet.

Imaginary audience   The belief that one is the center of other people's attention much of the time.

Immanent justice   The belief that unrelated events are automatic punishment for misdeeds.

Immersion programs   Programs in which English language learners are taught academic subjects in English.

Implicit associations test   A measure of a person's automatic, unconscious associations between different concepts.

Imprinting   In ethology, the automatic process by which animals attach to their mothers.

Incremental theories   Theories in which development is a result of continuous quantitative changes.

Independent variable   The variable in an experiment that the researcher manipulates.

Individualism   The cultural value that emphasizes the importance of the individual with emphasis on independence and reliance on one's own abilities.

Inductive discipline   A parenting technique that involves setting clear limits for children and explaining the consequences for negative behavior, why the behavior was wrong, and what the child might do to fix the situation.

Infant mortality   The rate of infant death within the first year of life.

Infant states   Different levels of consciousness used to regulate the amount of stimulation an infant receives; states range from crying to deep sleep.

Infantile amnesia   An adult's inability to remember experiences that happened before they were about 3 years of age.

Infertility   The inability to conceive within 1 year of frequent, unprotected sex.

Information processing speed   The efficiency with which one can perform cognitive tasks.

Inhibitory control   The ability to stay on task and ignore distractions.

Inner cell mass   A solid clump of cells in the blastocyst, which later develops into the embryo.

Intellectual disability   A type of intellectual impairment that begins early in life and includes deficits in intellectual, social, and adaptive functioning.

Intelligence   Those qualities that help us adapt successfully so that we achieve our goals in life.

Intelligence quotient or IQ   Originally a measure of intelligence calculated based on the ratio of a child's mental age to chronological age, largely replaced now by the deviation IQ.

Interactionism   A theory of language development that proposes that the child's biological readiness to learn language interacts with the child's experiences with language in the environment to bring about the child's language development.

Internal working model   Mental representations of the particular attachment relationships that a child has experienced that shape expectations of future relationships

Internalization   The process by which individuals adopt the attitudes, beliefs, and values held by their society.

Internalizing (or self-directed) behaviors   Behaviors in which a child's emotions are turned inward and become hurtful to themselves.

Interview   A data collection technique in which an interviewer poses questions to a respondent.

Intrinsic motivation   Motivation that comes from inside the person, such as a feeling of pride for a job well done.

Intuitive thought   According to Piaget, the beginning forms of logic developing during the preoperational stage.

Kangaroo care   A practice where the baby is placed in skin-to-skin contact with the parent's bare chest or breasts and draped with a blanket.

Knowledge telling   A style of writing (typical of younger children) in which the writer proceeds with little or no evidence of planning or organization of ideas, with the goal of telling as much as she knows about a topic.

Knowledge transforming   A type of writing in which the goal is to convey a deeper understanding of a subject by taking information and transforming it into ideas that can be shared with a reader.

Language   A system of symbols used to communicate with others or in our thinking.

Language disorder   A disorder in which a child's understanding and use of language is significantly below his nonverbal intelligence.

Latency stage   Freud's fourth stage, involving children ages 6 to 12, when the sex drive goes underground.

Long-term memory   The capacity for nearly permanent retention of memories.

Longitudinal design   A research design that follows one group of individuals and gathers data from them at several points in time.

Love withdrawal   A parenting technique in which parents threaten to withhold their love until a child conforms to the parents' expectations for his behavior.

Low birth weight   A full-term infant who weighs less than 5 pounds, 8 ounces.

Macrosystem   Cultural norms that guide the nature of the organizations and places that make up one's everyday life.

Major depression   A condition marked by feelings of worthlessness and hopelessness, a lack of pleasure, sleep and appetite disturbances, and possibly suicidal thoughts.

Maltreatment   Any act committed by a parent or caregiver that results in harm or potential harm to a child; incudes abuse and neglect.

Mandatory reporters   Individuals who work with children who are required by law to report suspicions of child maltreatment to authorities.

Media literacy   The skills to understand the underlying purposes and messages of media.

Menarche   A girl's first menstrual period.

Mental age   The age level at which a child is performing on a test of mental ability.

Mentor   A trusting relationship between a young person and a nonparental adult who provides guidance intended to promote positive development.

Mesosystem   The interaction among the various settings in the microsystem, such as a child's school and home.

Meta-analysis   A statistical procedure that combines data from different studies to determine whether there is a consistent pattern of findings across studies.

Metacognition   The ability to think about and monitor one's own thoughts and cognitive activities.

Metalinguistic abilities   The abilities to think about and talk about language.

Microgenetic design   A research design that involves frequent observations of participants during a time of change or transition.

Microsystem   In ecological theory, the face-to-face interaction of the person in her immediate settings, such as home, school, or friendship groups.

Mindblindness   The inability to understand and theorize about other people's thoughts.

Miscarriage (or spontaneous abortion) The natural loss of a pregnancy before the fetus reaches a gestational age of 20 weeks.

Molecular genetics Research focused on the identification of particular genes to identify how these genes work within the cell.

Monozygotic (MZ) twins Formed when a woman produces one egg that is fertilized by one sperm and the resulting ball of cells then splits to form two individuals with the same genes.

Moral judgment The way people reason about moral issues.

Moral knowledge Understanding of right and wrong.

Morpheme The smallest unit in a language that has meaning.

Morphology The way words are formed from the sounds of a language and how these words are related to other words.

Motor schema Infants' understanding of the world through their action on it.

Multifactorial inheritance disorders Disorders that result from many genes in interaction with environmental influences.

Multifinality The principle by which the same pathways may lead to different developmental outcomes.

Multitasking Doing several different activities at the same time, often involving several forms of media.

Mutations Changes in the formation of genes that occur as cells divide.

Mutual exclusivity constraint An assumption made by language learners that there is one (and only one) name for an object.

Myelination The process of laying down a fatty sheath of myelin on the neurons.

Natal gender The sex assigned to an individual at birth based on physical characteristics

Nativism A theory of language development that hypothesizes that human brains are innately wired to learn language and that hearing spoken language triggers the activation of a universal grammar.

Natural mentor A mentoring relationship between an adult and child that develops spontaneously rather than through a formal program.

Natural or "quasi" experiment Research in which the members of the groups are selected because they represent different "treatment" conditions.

Nature The influence of genetic inheritance on development.

Negative correlation A correlation in which increases in one variable are associated with decreases in another variable.

Negative identity An identity that is in direct opposition to an identity that parents or other adults would support.

Negative reinforcement In operant conditioning, a response that makes a behavior more likely to happen again because it removes an unpleasant stimulus.

Neglect Failure to provide for the basic physical, emotional, medical, or educational needs of a child or to protect the child from harm or potential harm.

Neglected children Children who receive relatively few nominations either as "like most" or as "like least" on a sociometric measure.

Neurons The cells that make up the nervous system of the body.

Neuropsychology The study of the interaction of the brain and behavior.

Neurotransmitters Chemicals that transmit nerve impulses across a synapse from one nerve cell to another.

Niche-picking The process by which people express their genetic tendencies by finding environments that match and enhance those tendencies.

Non-normative stress Stress that results from a relatively rare occurrence that often overwhelms the individual.

Nonshared environment The different experiences that siblings in the same family have in that environment.

Norm The average or typical performance of an individual of a given age on a test.

Normative stress Stress that is predictable and that most individuals go through, and which requires a moderate and relatively brief response.

Nuclear family A family consisting of a husband, a wife, and their biological and/or adopted children.

Nucleotide An organic molecule that contains one of the four bases with a phosphate group and a sugar molecule.

Nurture The influence of learning and the environment on children's development.

Obesity Being 20% or more over an individual's ideal body weight.

Object permanence The understanding that objects still exist when an infant does not see them.

Observer bias   The tendency for an observer to notice and report events that the observer is expecting to see.

Onlooker behavior   Watching other children play.

Open adoptions   Adoptions in which the children and their biological and adoptive families have access to each other.

Operant conditioning   The process that happens when the response that follows a behavior causes that behavior to happen more.

Operationalize   To define a concept in a way that allows it to be measured.

Operations   Mental actions that follow systematic, logical rules.

Oppositional defiant disorder   A persistent pattern of behavior marked by defiant, disobedient, and hostile behavior toward authority figures.

Oral stage   Freud's first stage in which the infant's sexual drive is centered on the mouth area.

Organogenesis   The process in prenatal development by which all of the major organ systems of the body are laid down.

Orienting response   The tendency to pay attention automatically to novel, moving, meaningful, or surprising stimuli.

Other-oriented induction   A parenting technique in which the child thinks about consequences of the child's behavior for someone else.

Overregularization   A type of grammatical error in which children apply a language rule to words that don't follow that rule or pattern (for example, adding an *s* to make the plural of an irregular noun like *foot*).

Ovulation   The release of a mature egg from an ovary.

Ovum   An unfertilized egg.

Parallel play   Playing next to a peer with the same type of materials, but not interacting with the other child.

Parent effects model   A model of parenting effects that assumes that parents cause the characteristics that we see in their children.

Parenting styles   Fairly regular and consistent patterns of interacting with children.

Passive gene-environment interaction   A situation in which a child's family shares his own genetically determined abilities and interests.

Pediatric psychologists   Child psychologists who provide therapeutic interventions for children with medical disorders.

Peer pressure   Influence exerted by peers to get others to comply with their wishes or expectations.

Peer review   A process by which professional peers critique research and make suggestions for improvement prior to its publication or dissemination.

Perceptual bias   The tendency to see and understand something in the way you expect it to be.

Permissive parents   Parents who provide a great deal of warmth and acceptance but few, if any, rules or restrictions.

Personal fable   The belief (often held by teenagers) that you are in some way unique and different from all other people.

Phallic stage   Freud's third stage in which children 3 to 6 years of age overcome their attraction to the opposite-sex parent and begin to identify with the same-sex parent.

Phenotype   The genetically-based characteristics that are actually shown in one's body.

Phobia   An irrational fear of something specific that is so severe that it interferes with day-to-day functioning.

Phoneme   The smallest distinct sound in a particular language.

Phonics (or basic skills) approach   An approach to teaching reading that starts with basic elements like letters and phonemes and teaches children that phonemes can be combined into words before moving on to reading as a whole.

Phonological awareness   The understanding that words are made up of a combination of individual sounds.

Phonology   The study of the sounds of a language.

Physical activity play   The type of play that involves large muscle activity.

Physical development   Biological changes that occur in the body and brain, including changes in size and strength, integration of sensory and motor activities, and development of fine and gross motor skills.

Placenta   The organ that supports a pregnancy by bringing oxygen and nutrients to the embryo from the mother through the umbilical cord and carrying away fetal waste products.

Plasticity   The ability of an immature brain to change in form and function.

Play disruption   An inability to play because the child's emotions are preventing the kind of free expression linked with the fun of play.

Play therapy   A way to help children work through difficult feelings with the help of an adult who is trained to understand play as a type of communication.

Pleasure principle The idea that the id seeks immediate gratification for all of its urges to feel pleasure.

Pleiotropic effects The many different influences any single gene may have.

Polygenic inheritance Numerous genes that may interact together to promote any particular trait or behavior.

Popular children Children who receive a lot of nominations as "like most" and few as "like least" on a sociometric measure.

Popular-antisocial children Children who are popular with peers by combining prosocial behavior with social manipulation.

Popular-prosocial children Children who are popular among peers because they are low on aggression and have a number of desirable characteristics.

Population A set that includes everyone in a category of individuals that researchers are interested in studying (for example, all toddlers, all teenagers with learning disabilities).

Positive correlation A correlation in which increases in one variable are associated with increases in another variable.

Positive youth development (PYD) An approach to finding ways to help all young people reach their full potential.

Postconventional moral judgment Moral judgements that move beyond society as the defining factor of what is moral or right and are based on universal principles that apply to all people.

Postformal operations The cognitive ability to consider multiple perspectives and bring together seemingly contradictory information.

Posttraumatic stress disorder (PTSD) Reexperiencing a traumatic effect through intrusive thoughts, distressing dreams, flashbacks, or extreme reactions in situations similar to the original trauma.

Power assertion A disciplinary technique that emphasizes control of the child's behavior through physical and nonphysical punishment.

Practical intelligence The ability to solve everyday problems by changing ourselves or our behavior to fit the environment better, changing the environment, or moving to a different environment in which we can be more successful.

Practice play Performing a certain behavior repetitively for the mere pleasure of it.

Pragmatics The rules that guide how we use language in social situations.

Preattachment The stage of development of attachment from birth to 6 weeks, in which infant sensory preferences bring infants into close connection with parents.

Precocious puberty A condition in which pubertal changes begin at an extraordinarily early age (as young as 6 or 7 years of age).

Preconventional moral judgment Moral judgment that is marked by self-interest and motivation based on rewards and punishments.

Prejudice Negative attitudes toward individuals based on their race, ethnicity, religion, or other factors.

Premature (or preterm) A birth that occurs before a gestational age of 37 weeks.

Premoral The inability to consider issues on the basis of their morality.

Preoperational stage Piaget's second stage of development, in which children ages 2 to 7 do not yet have logical thought and instead think magically and egocentrically.

Prepubescence The period before puberty when hormonal changes begin.

Primary sex characteristics Physical characteristics directly involved in reproduction.

Private speech Talking to oneself, often out loud, to guide one's own actions.

Problem-focused strategies Coping strategies that focus on changing or improving a stressful situation.

Processing capacity The amount of information an individual can think about at one time.

Proprioception The sense of knowing where the parts of one's body are located in space without the need to look at them.

Prosocial behavior Actions that help and support other people.

Proximodistal Development that proceeds from the central axis of the body toward the extremities.

Pruning The deterioration and disappearance of synapses that are not used.

Psychoanalytic theory Freud's theory in which the way we deal with biological urges moves us through a series of stages that shape our personalities.

Psychological control The use of psychological or emotional manipulation to get a child to comply with what the parent wants.

Psychosexual stages Freud's idea that at each stage sexual energy is invested in a different part of the body.

Psychosocial stages Erikson's stages based on a central conflict to be resolved involving the social world and the development of identity.

Puberty The physical changes that occur in adolescence and make an individual capable of sexual reproduction.

Punishment Administering a negative consequence or taking away a positive reinforcement to reduce the likelihood of an undesirable behavior occurring.

Qualitative changes Changes in the overall nature of what you are examining.

Quantitative changes Changes in the amount or quantity of what you are measuring.

Questionnaire A written form of a survey.

Racial socialization Efforts by minority parents to teach their children about discrimination, prepare them to deal with these experiences, and teach them to take pride in their heritage.

Racial and ethnic constancy The understanding that appears between 8 and 10 years of age that race and ethnicity remain the same across time and in different situations.

Racism A pervasive system of advantage and disadvantage based on race.

Random assignment Assigning participants to the experimental and control groups by chance so that the groups will not systematically differ from each other.

Range of reaction The range of potential outcomes for any given genotype.

Reactive attachment disorder (RAD) A disorder marked by inability to form attachments to caregivers.

Reality principle The psychoanalytic concept that the ego has the ability to deal with the real world and not just drives and fantasy.

Recast Repeating what children say but in a more advanced grammar to facilitate language learning.

Receptive language The ability to understand words or sentences.

Recessive genes Genes that are generally not expressed in the phenotype unless paired with another recessive gene.

Recursive thinking The ability to think about other people thinking about your thinking.

Reflexes Patterned, involuntary motor responses that are controlled by the lower brain centers.

Rehearsal Repeating information to remember it.

Reinforcement A response to a behavior that causes that behavior to happen more.

Rejected children Children who receive a lot of nominations as "like least" and few as "like most" on a sociometric measure.

Rejected-aggressive children Children who are rejected by peers because they are aggressive, annoying, or socially unskilled.

Rejected-withdrawn children Children who are rejected by peers because they are socially withdawn and anxious

Rejection sensitivity The extent to which a child is affected by peer rejection.

Relationship maintenance A parenting technique in which the parents try to create a positive relationship with their child so that they will have a greater influence on the child's behavior.

Reliability The ability of a measure to produce consistent results.

Representative sample A group of participants in a research study who have individual characteristics in the same distribution that exists in the population.

Resilience The ability to bounce back from adversity or to thrive despite negative life circumstances.

Reversibility The ability to reverse mental operations.

Rhythmic stereotypies Repeated large muscle movements that have no purpose, such as kicking the legs or waving the hands, usually seen in infants.

Rites of passage Rituals that publicly mark a change in status from child to adult.

Rough-and-tumble play Play that looks like fighting or wrestling, where the goal is not to hurt or win, but to have fun.

Sample bias Changes in the makeup of the sample in a longitudinal or sequential study that make the sample less representative over time.

Scaffolding The idea that more knowledgeable adults and children support a child's learning by providing help to move the child just beyond his current level of capability.

Schema A cognitive framework that places concepts, objects, or experiences into categories or groups of associations.

Schizophrenia A psychotic disorder marked by disorganized thinking, hallucinations, and delusions.

Scientific method The process of formulating and testing hypotheses in a rigorous and objective manner.

Scientific thinking   The type of thinking that scientists use when they set out to test a hypothesis.

Scripts   Memory for the way common occurrences in one's life, such as grocery shopping, take place.

Secondary sex characteristics   Physical characteristics associated with gender that do not directly affect the sex organs.

Secure attachment   A strong, positive emotional bond with a person who provides comfort and a sense of security.

Secure base for exploration   The use of a parent to provide the security that an infant can rely on as she explores the environment.

Secure base script   The expectation that a child develops that distress will or will not be met with care, concern, and support.

Selective attention   Tuning in to certain things while tuning out others.

Self-complexity   The number of different ways in which an individual defines herself.

Self-conscious emotions   Emotions that depend on awareness of oneself, such as pride, guilt, and shame.

Self-efficacy   A belief in our ability to influence our own functioning and life circumstances.

Self-esteem   How people feel about characteristics they associate with themselves.

Self-esteem movement   School-based programs designed to boost students' self-esteem, with the goal of eventually improving their academic performance.

Self-fulfilling prophecy   The process by which expectations or beliefs lead to behaviors that help ensure that you fulfill the initial prophecy or expectation.

Self-oriented induction   A parenting technique in which the child is asked to think about the consequences that the child might experience as a result of his behavior.

Selfies   Photos of oneself taken with a mobile device and posted online.

Semantic bootstrapping   The use of conceptual categories to create grammatical categories.

Semantics   The study of the meanings of words.

Sensorimotor stage   Piaget's first stage in which infants learn through their senses and their actions on the world.

Sensory memory   The capacity for information that comes in through our senses to be retained for a very brief period of time in its raw form.

Separation anxiety   Distress felt when separated from a parent.

Sequential design   A research design that uses multiple groups of participants and follows them over a period of time, with the beginning age of each group being the ending age of another group.

Service learning   Educational programs that involve students in direct community service and also reflection about their experiences to learn from them.

Sexting   Sending nude or seminude pictures of oneself online.

Sexual orientation   Sexual attraction to same- or opposite-sex partners

Sexually transmitted disease (STD)   A pathology that can result from a sexually transmitted infection.

Sexually transmitted infection (STI)   An infection caused by a microorganism that is transmitted by direct sexual contact.

Shaken baby syndrome   Shaking a baby so hard that the baby's brain bounces against the inside of the skull, causing bruising, bleeding or swelling in the brain.

Shame   A feeling that occurs as a result of personal failure or when children attribute their bad behavior to an aspect of themselves that they believe they cannot change.

Shaping behavior   Reinforcing behaviors to become progressively more like the desired behavior.

Single gene disorders   Genetic disorders caused by a single recessive gene or mutation.

Slow-to-warm temperament   A general responsiveness marked by a slow adaptation to new experiences and moderate irregularity in eating, sleeping, and elimination.

Small-c creativity   The type of creativity we use in everyday life to solve problems and adapt to change.

Social cognition   The way we use cognitive processes to understand our social world.

Social cognitive theory   The theory that individuals learn by observing others and imitating their behavior.

Social or pragmatic communication disorder   Difficulty with appropriate use of both verbal and nonverbal communication.

Social comparison   Comparing one's own performance or characteristics to those of other people.

Social domain theory   A theory of moral development based on three domains of social knowledge—moral, social-conventional, a and personal—with different ways of deciding what is moral in each of them.

Social-emotional development Changes in the ways we connect to other individuals and express and understand emotions.

Social policy Policies that to are intended to promote the welfare of individuals in a society.

Social promotion Promoting a child who has not mastered grade-level material to keep the child in a class with same-age peers.

Social referencing Using the reaction of others to determine how to react in ambiguous situations.

Social status The level of peer acceptance or peer rejection of an individual in the peer group.

Social-emotional development Changes in the ways we connect to other individuals, and express and understand emotions.

Socialization The process of instilling the norms, attitudes, and beliefs of a culture in its children.

Sociobiology The application of principles of evolution to the development of social behavior and culture.

Socioeconomic status A person's social standing based on a combined measure of income, education, and occupation.

Sociometry A research technique used to assess a child's social status within the peer group.

Solitary independent play Engaging actively with toys that are different from those being used by other children. ·

Specific learning disorder (SLD) Persistent difficulty with learning that is substantially below the average and cannot be better explained by another problem. Specific areas of difficulty include reading, writing, and arithmetic.

Speech sound disorder Difficulty producing or using sounds at an age-appropriate level.

Spermarche The beginning of production of viable sperm.

Stage theories Theories of development in which each stage in life is seen as qualitatively different from the ones that come before and after.

Standardized test A test that is administered and scored in a standard or consistent way for all examinees.

Stepfamilies Families in which there are two adults and at least one child from a previous relationship of one of the adults; there also may be biological children of the couple.

Stereotype threat The anxiety that results when individuals feel they are behaving in ways that confirm negative stereotyped expectations of a group with which they identify.

Stereotypes Conclusions made about someone based solely on the group with which he or she is identified.

Stores model The idea that information is processed through a series of mental locations (sensory to short-term to long-term memory "stores").

Strange Situation Mary Ainsworth's experimental procedure designed to assess security of attachment in infants.

Stranger anxiety Fearfulness that infants develop at about 6 months of age toward people they do not know.

Stress Anything that places excessive demands on our ability to cope.

Substance use disorder (SUD) Use of drugs that is marked by cravings, social impairment, risky use, tolerance build-up and withdrawal symptoms.

Sudden infant death syndrome (SIDS) The death of an apparently healthy infant; the rate of SIDS peaks between the ages of 1 month and 4 months.

Superego Freud's concept of the conscience or sense of right and wrong.

Survey A data collection technique that asks respondents to answer a common set of questions.

Sustained attention Maintaining focus over time.

Symbolic/sociodramatic play Using symbolic representations and imagination for play.

Sympathy Concern for others' welfare that often leads to helping or comforting them.

Synapse The place where the axon from one neuron meets the dendrite of another neuron.

Synaptogenesis The development of new synapses.

Syntactic bootstrapping The use of syntax to learn the meaning of new words (semantics).

Syntax The grammar of a language.

Taxonomic constraint An assumption language learners make that two objects that have features in common can have a name in common, but that each object also can have its own individual name.

Telegraphic speech A stage in language development in which children only use the words necessary to get their point across and omit small words that are not necessary (for example, *Go bye-bye*).

Temperament The general emotional style an individual displays in responding to events.

Teratogens Agents that can disrupt prenatal development and cause malformations or termination of the pregnancy.

Theory of core knowledge   The theory that basic areas of knowledge are innate and built into the human brain.

Theory of mind   The ability to understand self and others as agents who act on the basis of their mental states, such as beliefs, desires, emotions, and intentions.

Theory of multiple intelligences   Gardner's idea that there are a number of different types of intelligence that are all relatively independent of each other.

Thin ideal   The idea promoted by media images that it is best for girls and women to be thin.

Three-ring model of giftedness   A conception of giftedness as the intersection of above average intellectual ability, creativity, and task commitment.

Transactional model   A model of parenting effects that assumes that influence moves from parent to child but also from child to parent in a reciprocal process.

Transgender   Identification with a gender other than the one with which an individual was born.

Transition   The third phase in the first stage of labor in which contractions come in rapid succession and last up to 90 seconds each, with little or no pause between them, and which ends when the cervix has dilated 10 centimeters.

Transitional bilingual education programs   Programs for English language learners in which students receive some instruction in their native language while they also receive concentrated instruction in learning English.

Transitional probability   The likelihood that one particular sound will follow another one to form a word.

Transsexual   Someone who has or is planning to become the other sex, possibly but not always, including biological treatments to make this transition.

Triarchic theory   Sternberg's idea that intelligence represents a balance of analytical, creative, and practical abilities.

Trophoblast   The outer ring of cells in the blastocyst that later develops into the support system for the pregnancy.

Two-way immersion programs   Programs in which children who are native speakers of English and children who are not work together in a classroom where both English and the children's other native language are used.

Ultrasound   A prenatal test that uses high-frequency sound waves to create an image of the developing embryo's size, shape and position in the womb.

Unconscious mind   The part of the mind that contains thoughts and feelings about which we are unaware.

Undernutrition   A deficiency of calories or of one or more essential nutrients.

Universal grammar   A hypothesized set of grammatical rules and constraints proposed by Chomsky that is thought to underlie all languages and that is hardwired in the human brain.

Unoccupied behavior   Looking around at whatever occurs, but engaging in no activity.

Validity   The ability of a research tool to accurately measure what it purports to measure.

Variable   A characteristic that can be measured and that can have different values.

Violation of expectation   Research based on the finding that babies look longer at unexpected or surprising events.

Visual acuity   The ability to see things in sharp detail.

Visual perspective-taking   The understanding that other people can see an object from a point of view that is different from one's own.

Vocabulary burst   The rapid growth of a child's vocabulary that often occurs in the second year.

Wernicke's area   The part of the brain that has to do with understanding the meaning in speech.

White matter   The myelin-coated axons that connect neurons in the brain.

Whole language instruction   A way to teach reading that emphasizes understanding the meaning of words from the context in which they appear.

Whole object bias   An assumption made by language learners that a word describes an entire object, rather than just some portion of it.

Working (or short-term) memory   The memory system that stores information for only a brief time to allow the mind to process information and move it into long-term memory.

Wraparound program   A comprehensive set of services offered to families to strengthen them or reunite them.

Zone of proximal development   According to Vygotsky, this is what a child cannot do on her own but can do with a little help from someone more skilled or knowledgeable.

Zygote   A fertilized egg.

References

Abbott, R., & Burkitt, E. R. (2015). *Child development and the brain: An introduction*. Bristol, UK: Policy Press.

AbdelMalik, P., Husted, J., Chow, E. C., & Bassett, A. S. (2003). Childhood head injury and expression of schizophrenia in multiply affected families. *Archives of General Psychiatry, 60*(3), 231–236. doi: 10.1001/archpsyc.60.3.231

Aber, L., Morris, P., & Raver, C. (2012). Children, families and poverty: Definitions, trends, emerging science and implications for policy. *SRCD Social Policy Report, 26*(3), 1–21.

Abreu-Villac, Y., Seidler, F. J., Tate, C. A., Cousins, M. M., & Slotkin, T. A. (2004). Prenatal nicotine exposure alters the response to nicotine administration in adolescence: Effects on cholinergic systems during exposure and withdrawal. *Neuropsychopharmacology, 29*, 879–890.

Abrutyn, S., & Mueller, A. S. (2014). Are suicidal behaviors contagious? Using longitudinal data to examine suicide suggestion. *American Sociological Review, 79*(2), 211–27.

Acevedo-Polakovich, I. D., Lorch, E. P., & Milich, R. (2007). Comparing television use and reading in children with ADHD and non-referred children across two age groups. *Media Psychology, 9*, 447–472.

Achiron, R., Lipitz, S., & Achiron, A. (2001). Sex-related differences in the development of the human fetal corpus callosum: In utero ultrasonographic study. *Prenatal Diagnosis, 21*, 116–120.

Adamczyk-Robinette, S. L., Fletcher, A. C., & Wright, K. (2002). Understanding the authoritative parenting-early adolescent tobacco use link: The mediating role of peer tobacco use. *Journal of Youth and Adolescence, 31*(4), 311–318.

Adams, R., & Laursen, B. (2001). The organization and dynamics of adolescent conflict with parents and friends. *Journal of Marriage and Family, 63*(1), 97–110.

ADHD Educational Institute. (2013). *Aetiology of ADHD*. Retrieved from http://www.adhd-institute.com/What-is -ADHD/Aetiology.aspx

Adolph, K. E., & Berger, S. E. (2006). Motor development. In W. Damon & R. Lerner (Series Eds.), & D. Kuhn & R. S. Siegler (Vol. Eds.), *Handbook of child psychology: Vol. 2: Cognition, perception and language* (6th ed., pp. 161–213). New York: John Wiley & Sons.

Adolph, K. E., Kretch, K. S., & LoBue, V. (2014). Fear of heights in infants? *Current Directions in Psychological Science, 23*(1), 60–66.

Adoption and Foster Care Analysis and Reporting System. (2010). *Adoption and Foster Care Analysis and Reporting System (AFCARS) FY data (October 1, 2009–September 30, 2010)*. Retrieved from http://www.acf.hhs.gov/programs/cb/stats_research/afcars/tar/report18.htm

Adoption and Foster Care Analysis and Reporting System. (2013). *Preliminary FY 2012 estimates as of November 2013. The AFCARS Report, No. 20*. Retrieved from http://www.acf.hhs.gov/sites/default/files/cb/afcarsreport20.pdf

Advocates of Youth. (2008). *The Heterosexual Questionnaire*. Retrieved from http://www.advocatesforyouth.org/publications/223-lessons

Agache, A., Leyendecker, B., Schäfermeier, E., & Schölmerich, A. (2014). Paternal involvement elevates trajectories of life satisfaction during transition to parenthood. *European Journal of Developmental Psychology, 11*(2), 259–277.

Agras, W. S., Bryson, S., Hammer, L. D., & Kraemer, H. C. (2007). Childhood risk factors for thin body preoccupation and social pressure to be thin. *Journal of the American Academy of Child and Adolescent Psychiatry, 46*(2), 171–178.

Ahn, S., & Miller, S. A. (2012). Theory of mind and self-concept: A comparison of Korean and American children. *Journal of Cross-Cultural Psychology, 43*(5), 671–686. doi: 10.1177/0022022112441247

Ahrens, K., DuBois, D. L., Lozano, P., & Richardson, L. P. (2010). Naturally acquired mentoring relationships and young adult outcomes among adolescents with learning disabilities. *Learning Disabilities Research & Practice, 25*(4), 207–216. doi:10.1111/j.1540-5826.2010.00318.x

AIDSinfo. (2015). *HIV and women Preventing mother-to-child transmission of HIV during childbirth*. Retrieved from https://aidsinfo.nih.gov/education-materials/fact-sheets/24/70/preventing-mother-to-child-transmission-of-hiv-during-childbirth

Ainsworth, M. D. S. (1979). Infant-mother attachment. *American Psychologist, 34*(10), 932–937.

Ainsworth, M. D. S., & Bell, S. M. (1970). Attachment, exploration and separation: Illustrated by the behavior of one-year-olds in a strange situation. *Child Development, 41*(1), 49–67.

Ainsworth, M. D. S., Blehar, M. C., Waters, E., & Wall, S. (1978). *Patterns of attachment*. Hillsdale, NJ: Erlbaum.

Ainsworth, M. D. S., & Bowlby, J. (1989). An ethological approach to personality development. *American Psychologist, 46*(4), 333–341.

Akers, K. G., Martinez-Canabal, A., Restivo, L., Yiu, A. P., De Cristofaro, A., Hsiang, H., . . . Frankland, P. W. (2014). Hippocampal neurogenesis regulates forgetting during adulthood and infancy. *Science, 344*(6184), 598–602. doi: 10.1126/science.1248903

Akhgarnia, G. (2011). *Overconnectivity in brain found in autism*. San Diego State University News Center. Retrieved from http://newscenter.sdsu.edu/sdsu_newscenter/news.aspx?s=73005

Akos, P., Rose, R. A., & Orthner, D. (2015). Sociodemographic moderators of middle school transition effects on academic achievement. *The Journal of Early Adolescence, 35*(2), 170–198. doi:10.1177/0272431614529367

Alamargot, D., & Chanquoy, L. (2001). Development of expertise in writing. In G. Rijlaarsdam (Series Ed.), D. Alamargot & L. Chanquoy, *Studies in writing: Vol 9. Through the models of writing* (pp. 185–218). Norwell, MA: Kluwer Academic.

Albert, M., & McCaig, L. F. (2014). *Injury-related emergency department visits by children and adolescents: United States, 2009–2010. NCHS data brief, No. 150*. Hyattsville, MD: National Center for Health Statistics.

Alberts, A., Elkind, D., & Ginsberg, S. (2007). The personal fable and risk-taking in early adolescence. *Journal of Youth and Adolescence, 36*, 71–76.

Alcañiz, L. (1997-2016). *Traditional Hispanic beliefs and myths about pregnancy*. Retrieved from http://www.babycenter.com/0_traditional-hispanic-beliefs-and-myths-about-pregnancy_3653769.bc?showAll=true

Alcohol Justice. (2015). *Alcopops: Sweet, cheap, and dangerous to youth*. Retrieved from http://alcoholjustice.org/images//reports/AlcopopsReportFinalWeb.pdf

Aldrich, P. (2001). The intellectually gifted child. In C. Green-Hernandez, J. K. Singleton, & D. Z. Aronzon (Eds.), *Primary care pediatrics* (pp. 223–228). New York: Lippincott.

Aldwin, C. M. (2012). *Stress, coping, and development: An integrative perspective* (2nd ed.). New York: Guilford Press.

Alexander, G. M., & Hines, M. (1994). Gender labels and play styles: Their relative contribution to children's selection of playmates. *Child Development, 65*, 869–879.

Alexander-Passe, N. (2006). How dyslexic teenagers cope: An investigation of self-esteem, coping and depression. *Dyslexia: An International Journal of Research and Practice, 12*(4), 256–275.

Alfaro, E. C., Umaña-Taylor, A. J., & Bámaca, M. Y. (2006). The influence of academic support on Latino adolescents' academic motivation. *Family Relations, 55*, 279–291.

Alford, S., & Hauser, D. (2009). *Adolescent sexual health in Europe and the U.S.—Why the difference?* (3rd ed.). Washington, DC: Advocates for Youth.

Alijotas-Reig, J., & Garrido-Gimenez, C. (2013). Current concepts and new trends in the diagnosis and management of recurrent miscarriage. *Obstetrical & Gynecological Survey, 68*(6), 445–466. doi:10.1097/OGX.0b013e31828aca19

Ali, M. M., & Dwyer, D. S. (2009). Estimating peer effects in adolescent smoking behavior: A longitudinal analysis. *Journal of Adolescent Health, 45*(4), 402–408.

Allen, J. P., Seitz, V., & Apfel, N. H. (2007). The sexually mature teen as a whole person: New directions in prevention and intervention for teen pregnancy and parenthood. In J. L. Aber, S. J. Bishop-Josef, S. M. Jones, K. T. McLearn, & D. A. Phillips (Eds.), *Child development and social policy: Knowledge for action* (pp. 185–200). Washington, DC: American Psychological Association.

Allhusen, V., Belsky, J., Booth-LaForce, C., Bradley, R., Brownell, C. A., Burchinal, M., . . . Weinraub, M. (2005). Duration and developmental timing of poverty and children's cognitive and social development from birth through third grade. *Child Development, 76*(4), 795–810.

Allnook, D., & Miller, P. (2013). *No one noticed, no one heard: A study of disclosures of childhood abuse.* Retrieved from https://www.nspcc.org.uk/services-and-resources/research-and-resources/2013/no-one-noticed-no-one-heard/

Alloway, T. (2010). *Improving working memory: Supporting students' learning.* Thousand Oaks, CA: Sage.

Alloway, T., Gathercole, S., & Pickering, S. J. (2006). Verbal and visuospatial short-term and working memory in children: Are they separable? *Child Development, 77*(6), 1698–1716.

Almendrala, A. (2014, May 19). *The U.S. is the only developed nation with a rising maternal mortality rate.* Retrieved from http://www.huffingtonpost.com/2014/05/19/us-maternal-mortality-rate_n_5340648.html

Almon, J. (2003). The vital role of play in early childhood education. In S. Olfman (Ed.), *All work and no play: How educational reforms are harming our preschoolers* (pp. 17–42). Westport, CT: Praeger.

Alomar, L., & Zwolinski, M. (2002). Quinceañera! A celebration of Latina womanhood. *Voices: The Journal of New York Folklore, 28.* Retrieved from http://www.nyfolklore.org/pubs/voic28-3-4/onair.html

Amato, P. R. (2005). The impact of family formation change on the cognitive, social, and emotional well-being of the next generation. *The Future of Children, 15*(2), 75–96. doi:10.1353/foc.2005.0012

Amato, P. R. (2010). Research on divorce: Continuing trends and new developments. *Journal of Marriage and Family, 72*, 650–666.

Amato, P. R. (2012). The well-being of children with gay and lesbian parents. *Social Science Research, 41*(4), 771–774.

Amato, P. R., & Anthony, C. J. (2014). Estimating the effects of parental divorce and death with fixed effects models. *Journal of Marriage and Family, 76*(2), 370–386.

Ambert, A. (1997). *Parents, children and adolescents.* New York: Haworth Press.

America's Future Workforce. (2013). *School to Work Opportunities Act of 1994.* Retrieved from http://americasfutureworkforce.org/2013/10/26/opportunities/

America's Great Outdoors. (2011). *America's great outdoors: A promise to future generations.* Retrieved from http://www.americasgreatoutdoors.gov/

American Academy of Child and Adolescent Psychiatry. (2005). *Foster care.* Retrieved from http://www.aacap.org/cs/root/facts_for_families/foster_care

American Academy of Child and Adolescent Psychiatry. (2012). *Child sexual abuse.* Retrieved from http://www.aacap.org/cs/root/facts_for_families/child_sexual_abuse

American Academy of Child and Adolescent Psychiatry. (2015). *The adopted child.* Retrieved from https://www.aacap.org/AACAP/Families_and_Youth/Facts_for_Families/FFF-Guide/The-Adopted-Child-015.aspx

American Academy of Matrimonial Lawyers. (2009). *Ten tips for divorcing parents.* Retrieved from http://www.aaml.org/go/library/publications/stepping-back-from-anger/ten-tips-for-divorcing-parents/

American Academy of Pediatrics. (n.d.). *Fetal alcohol spectrum disorders program.* Retrieved from http://www.aap.org/en-us/advocacy-and-policy/aap-health-initiatives/fetal-alcohol-spectrum-disorders-toolkit/Pages/Frequently-Asked-Questions.aspx#ques2

American Academy of Pediatrics. (2001). Organized sports for children and preadolescents. *Pediatrics, 107*(6), 1459–1462.

American Academy of Pediatrics. (2004). *Caring for your school-age child: Ages 5 to 12* (Rev. ed., E. L. Schor, ed.). New York: Bantam.

American Academy of Pediatrics. (2005). The changing concept of sudden infant death syndrome: Diagnostic coding shifts, controversies regarding the sleeping environment, and new variables to consider in reducing risk. *Pediatrics, 116*, 1245–1255.

American Academy of Pediatrics. (2006a). Child life services. *Pediatrics, 118*(4), 1757–1763.

American Academy of Pediatrics. (2006b). *Choking prevention and first aid for infants and children.* Elk Grove Village, IL: Author.

American Academy of Pediatrics. (2007). Childhood: Growing pains. *Healthy Children, 24–25.*

American Academy of Pediatrics. (2009a). *Caring for your baby and young child: Birth to age 5* (5th ed.). New York: Bantam.

American Academy of Pediatrics. (2009b). Policy statement. *Pediatrics, 123*(1), 188.

American Academy of Pediatrics. (2009c). Recommendations for preventive pediatric health care. *Pediatrics, 96*, 373–374.

American Academy of Pediatrics. (2011a). ADHD: Clinical practice guideline for the diagnosis, evaluation, and treatment of attention-deficit/hyperactivity disorder in children and adolescents. *Pediatrics, 128*(5), 1007–1022. doi: 10.1542/peds.2011–2654

American Academy of Pediatrics. (2011b). Media use by children younger than 2 years. *Pediatrics, 128*(5), 1040–1045. doi: 10.1542/peds.2011-1753.

American Academy of Pediatrics. (2011c). SIDS and other sleep-related infant deaths: Expansion of recommendations for a safe infant sleeping environment. *Pediatrics, 128*(5), e1341–e1367. doi: 10.1542/peds.2011-2285

American Academy of Pediatrics. (2012). *AAP reaffirms breastfeeding guidelines.* Retrieved from https://www.aap.org/en-us/about-the-aap/aap-press-room/pages/aap-reaffirms-breast-feeding-guidelines.aspx

American Academy of Pediatrics. (2013a). *Common food allergies.* Retrieved from http://www.healthychildren.org/English/healthy-living/nutrition/pages/Common-Food-Allergies.aspx

American Academy of Pediatrics. (2013b). Policy statement: The crucial role of recess in school. *Pediatrics, 131*(1), 183–188.

American Academy of Pediatrics. (2015). *The American Academy of Pediatrics tackles youth football injuries.* Retrieved from https://www.aap.org/en-us/about-the-aap/aap-press-room/pages/Youth-Football-Injuries.aspx

American Academy of Pediatrics Committee on Bioethics. (2001). Ethical issues with genetic testing in pediatrics. *Pediatrics, 107*(6), 1451–1455.

American Academy of Pediatrics Committee on Drugs. (2001). The transfer of drugs and other chemicals into human milks. *Pediatrics, 108*(3), 776–789.

American Association of Retired Persons. (2012). *Grandfacts.* Retrieved from http://www.aarp.org/relationships/friends-family/grandfacts-sheets/

American Congress of Obstetricians and Gynecologists. (2007). *You and your baby: Prenatal care, labor and delivery, and postpartum care.* Retrieved from http://www.acog.org/publications/patient_education/ab005.cfm

American Congress of Obstetricians and Gynecologists. (2010, reaffirmed 2015). *Smoking cessation during pregnancy. ACOG Committee Opinion (No. 471).* Retrieved from http://www.acog.org/Resources-And-Publications/Committee-Opinions/Committee-on-Health-Care-for-Underserved-Women/Smoking-Cessation-During-Pregnancy

American Congress of Obstetricians and Gynecologists. (2013). *Frequently asked questions: Ultrasound exams.* Retrieved from http://www.acog.org/~/media/For%20Patients/faq025.pdf?dmc=1&ts=20140613T0856481728

American Congress of Obstetricians and Gynecologists. (2015). Marijuana use during pregnancy and lactation. Committee Opinion, No. 637. *Obstetrics and Gynecology, 126*, 234–238.

American Diabetes Association. (2008). *American Diabetes Association recognizes World Diabetes Day.* Retrieved from http://www.diabetes.org/newsroom/press-releases/2008/recognizes-world-diabetes-day.html

American Diabetes Association. (2013). Economic costs of diabetes in the U.S. in 2012. *Diabetes Care, 36*(4), 1033–1046. http://dx.doi.org/10.2337/dc12-2625

American Foundation for Suicide Prevention and Suicide Prevention Resource Center. (2011). *After a suicide: A toolkit for schools.* Newton, MA: Education Development Center, Inc.

American Lung Association. (2016). *Myths and facts about e-cigarettes.* Retrieved from http://www.lung.org/stop-smoking/smoking-facts/myths-and-facts-about-e-cigs.html

American Medical Association. (2008). *Prenatal screening questionnaire.* Retrieved from http://www.ama-assn.org/ama1/pub/upload/mm/464/ped_screening.pdf

American Optometric Association. (2013). *Infant vision: Birth to 24 months.* Retrieved from http://www.aoa.org/patients-and-public/good-vision-throughout-life/childrens-vision/infant-vision-birth-to-24-months-of-age

American Pregnancy Association. (2015). *Exercising while pregnant: Safety, benefits & guidelines.* Retrieved from http://americanpregnancy.org/pregnancy-health/exercise-during-pregnancy/

American Pregnancy Association. (2016). *Epidural anesthesia.* Retrieved from http://americanpregnancy.org/labor-and-birth/epidural/

American Psychiatric Association. (2013). *Diagnostic and statistical manual of mental disorders* (5th ed.). Washington, DC: Author.

American Psychological Association. (n.d.). *PsycINFO.* Retrieved from http://www.apa.org/pubs/databases/psycinfo/psycinfo-printable-fact-sheet.pdf

American Psychological Association. (2003). *When psychologists teach coaches how to coach, young athletes feel better and play longer*. Retrieved from http://www.apa.org/research/action/coach.aspx

American Psychological Association. (2004). *Briefing sheet: An overview of the psychological literature on the effects of divorce on children*. Retrieved from http://www.apa.org/about/gr/issues/cyf/divorce.aspx

American Psychological Association. (2005). *Lesbian and gay parenting*. Washington, DC: Author.

American Psychological Association. (2010). *APA survey raises concern about health impact of stress on children and families*. Retrieved from https://www.apa.org/news/press/releases/2010/11/stress-in-america.aspx

American Psychological Association. (2012). *APA on children raised by gay and lesbian parents*. Retrieved from http://www.apa.org/news/press/response/gay-parents.aspx

American Psychological Association. (2014). *Mental health and abortion*. Retrieved from http://www.apa.org/pi/women/programs/abortion/

American Psychological Association. (2015). *Guidelines for psychological practice with transgender and gender nonconforming people*. Retrieved from http://www.apa.org/practice/guidelines/transgender.pdf

American Psychological Association. (2016a). *Children and trauma. Update for mental health professionals*. Retrieved from http://www.apa.org/pi/families/resources/children-trauma-update.aspx

American Psychological Association. (2016b). *Society of Pediatric Psychology*. Retrieved from http://www.apa.org/about/division/div54.aspx

American Psychological Association. (2016c). *Stress effects on the body*. Retrieved from http://www.apa.org/helpcenter/stress-body.aspx

American Psychological Association Division of Educational Psychology. (2014). *Research in brain function and learning*. Retrieved from http://www.apa.org/education/k12/brain-function.aspx?itcm=1

American Psychological Association Presidential Task Force on Posttraumatic Stress Disorder and Trauma in Children and Adolescents. (2008). *Children and trauma: An update for mental health professionals*. Washington, DC: Author.

American Social Health Association. (2015). *Herpes and pregnancy*. Retrieved from http://www.ashasexualhealth.org/stdsstis/herpes/herpes-and-pregnancy/

American Society of Addiction Medicine. (2016). *Opioid addiction: 2016 facts and figures*. Retrieved from http://www.asam.org/docs/default-source/advocacy/opioid-addiction-disease-facts-figures.pdf

American Speech-Language-Hearing Association. (n.d.). *Social language use (pragmatics)*. Retrieved from http://www.asha.org/public/speech/development/Pragmatics/

Anderson, C. A., Shibuya, A., Ihori, N., Swing, E. L., Bushman, B. J., Sakamoto, A., . . . Saleem, M. (2010). Violent video game effects on aggression, empathy, and prosocial behavior in Eastern and Western countries: A meta-analytic review. *Psychological Bulletin, 136*(2), 151–173.

Anderson, C. M., Rodriguez, B. J., & Campbell, A. (2015). Functional behavior assessment in schools: Current status and future directions. *Journal of Behavioral Education, 24*(3), 338–371. doi:10.1007/s10864-015-9226-z

Anderson, D. I., Roth, M. B., & Campos, J. J. (2005). Reflexes. In *Encyclopedia of human development*. Thousand Oaks, CA: Sage. Retrieved from http://www.sage-ereference.com/humandevelopment/Article_n517.html

Anderson, D. R., & Hanson, K. G. (2013). What researchers have learned about toddlers and television. *Zero to Three, 33*(4), 4–10.

Anderson, D. R., Levin, S. R., & Lorch, E. P. (1977). The effects of TV program pacing on the behavior of preschool children. *Educational Communication & Technology, 25*(2), 159–166.

Anderson, D. R., & Pempek, T. A. (2005). Television and very young children. *American Behavioral Scientist, 48*(5), 505–522.

Anderson, J. R., Van Ryzin, M. J., & Doherty, W. J. (2010). Developmental trajectories of marital happiness in continuously married individuals: A group-based modeling approach. *Journal of Family Psychology, 24*, 587–596.

Andreou, G., & Karapetsas, A. (2004). Verbal abilities in low and highly proficient bilinguals. *Journal of Psycholinguistic Research, 33*(5), 357–364.

Ankrum, J. W., Genest, M. T., & Belcastro, E. G. (2014). The power of verbal scaffolding: 'Showing' beginning readers how to use reading strategies. *Early Childhood Education Journal, 42*(1), 39–47. doi:10.1007/s10643-013-0586-5

Annie E. Casey Foundation. (2015a). *About us*. Retrieved from http://www.aecf.org/about/

Annie E. Casey Foundation. (2015b). *Children in single-parent families by race*. Retrieved from http://datacenter.kidscount.org/data/tables/107-children-in-single-parent-families-by#detailed/1/any/false/36/10,168,9,12,1,13,185/432,431

Anobile, G., Stievano, P., & Burr, D. C. (2013). Visual sustained attention and numerosity sensitivity correlate with math achievement in children. *Journal of Experimental Child Psychology, 116*(2), 380–391. doi: 10.1016/j.jecp.2013.06.006

Anxiety and Depression Association of America. (2014). *Understand the facts*. Retrieved from http://www.adaa.org/understanding-anxiety

The ARC. (2015). *Intellectual disability*. Retrieved from http://www.thearc.org/learn-about/intellectual-disability

Arcelus, J., Mitchell, A. J., Wales, J., & Nielson, S. (2011). Mortality rates in patients with anorexia nervosa and other eating disorders. A meta-analysis of 36 studies. *Archives of General Psychiatry, 68*(7), 724–731.

Armbruster, B. B., Lehr, F., & Osborn, J. M. (2001). *Putting reading first: The research building blocks for teaching children to read*. Washington, DC: National Institute for Literacy.

Armstrong, T. (2009). *Multiple intelligences in the classroom*. Alexandria, VA: Association for Supervision and Curriculum Development.

Arnold, D. H., Fisher, P. H., & Doctoroff, G. L. (2002). Accelerating math development in Head Start classrooms. *Journal of Educational Psychology, 94*(4), 762–770.

Aro, T., Poikkeus, A., Laakso, M., Tolvanen, A., & Ahonen, T. (2015). Associations between private speech, behavioral self-regulation, and cognitive abilities. *International Journal of Behavioral Development, 39*(6), 508–518. doi:10.1177/0165025414556094

Arteaga, S. S., & Lamb, Y. (2008). Expert review of key findings on children exposed to violence and their families from the Safe Start Demonstration Project. *Best Practices in Mental Health: An International Journal, 4*(1), 99–107.

Arthur, A. E., Bigler, R. S., & Ruble, D. N. (2009). An experimental test of the effects of gender constancy on sex typing. *Journal of Experimental Child Psychology, 104*(4), 427–446. doi:10.1016/j.jecp.2009.08.002

Artman, L., Cahan, S., & Avni-Babad, D. (2006). Age, schooling and conditional reasoning. *Cognitive Development, 21*(2), 131–145. doi:10.1016/j.cogdev.2006.01.004

Asato, M. R., Sweeney, J. A., & Luna, B. (2006). Cognitive processes in the development of TOL performance. *Neuropsychologia, 44*(12), 2259–2269.

Ashiabi, G. S., & O'Neal, K. K. (2008). A framework for understanding the association between food insecurity and children's developmental outcomes. *Child Development Perspectives, 2*(2), 71–77.

Association for Psychological Science. (n.d.). *Registered replication reports*. Retrieved from http://www.psychologicalscience.org/index.php/replication

Astill, R. G., Van der Heijden, K. B., Van Ijzendoorn, M. H., & Van Someren, E. J. (2012). Sleep, cognition, and behavioral problems in school-age children: A century of research meta-analyzed. *Emotional Bulletin, 138*(6), 1109–1138.

Astington, J. W., & Filippova, E. (2005). Language as the route into other minds. In B. F. Malle & S. D. Hodges (Eds.), *Other minds* (pp. 209–222). New York: Guilford Press.

Atwell, J. E., Otterloo, J. V., Zipprich, J., Winter, K., Harriman, K., Salmon, D. A., Halsey, N. A., & Omer, S. B. (2013). Nonmedical vaccine exemptions and pertussis in California, 2010. *Pediatrics, 132*, 624–630.

Aud, S., Hussar, W., Kena, G., Bianco, K., Frohlich, L., Kemp, J., & Tahan, K. (2011a). *The Condition of Education 2011* (NCES 2011-033). U.S. Department of Education, National Center for Education Statistics. Washington, DC: U.S. Government Printing Office.

Aud, S., Kewal Ramani, A., & Frohlich, L. (2011b). *America's youth: Transitions to adulthood (NCES 2012-026)*. U.S. Department of Education, National Center for Education Statistics. Washington, DC: Government Printing Office.

Auerbach, J., Berger, A., Atzaba-Poria, N., Arbelãe, S., Cypin, N., Friedman, A., & Landau, R. (2008). Temperament at 7, 12, and 25 months in children at familial risk for ADHD. *Infant and Child Development, 17*(4), 321–338. doi:10.1002/icd.579

Aughinbaugh, A., & Gittleman, M. (2003). *Maternal employment and adolescent risky behavior*. U.S. Bureau of Labor Statistics Working Paper #366.

Aunola, K., Stattin, H., & Nurmi, J. (2000). Parenting styles and adolescents' achievement strategies. *Journal of Adolescence, 23*(2), 205–222.

Avenevoli, S., Swendsen, J., He, J., Burstein, M., & Merikangas, K. R. (2015). Major depression in the national comorbidity survey–Adolescent supplement: Prevalence, correlates, and treatment. *Journal of the American Academy of Child & Adolescent Psychiatry, 54*(1), 37–44. doi:10.1016/j.jaac.2014.10.010

Ayduk, O., Mendoza-Denton, R., Mischel, W., Downey, G., Peake, P. K., & Rodriguez, M. (2000). Regulating the interpersonal self: Strategic self-regulation for coping with rejection sensitivity. *Journal of Personality and Social Psychology, 79*(5), 776–792.

Ayres, M., & Leve, L. D. (2006). Gender identity and play. In D. P. Fromberg & D. Bergen (Eds.), *Play from birth to twelve: Contexts, perspective, and meanings* (pp. 41–46). New York: Routledge.

Azevedo, F. A., Carvalho, L. R., Grinberg, L. T., Farfel, J. M., Ferretti, R. E., Leite, R. E., Filho, W. J., Lent, R., & Herculano-Houzel, S. (2009). Equal numbers of neuronal and nonneuronal cells make the human brain an isometrically scaled-up primate brain. *Journal of Comparative Neurology, 513*, 532–541.

Bachman, J. G., O'Malley, P. M., Freedman-Doan, P., Trzesniewski, K. H., & Donnellan, M. B. (2011). Adolescent self-esteem: Differences by race/ethnicity, gender and age. *Self-Identity, 10*(4), 445–473, doi:10.1080/15298861003794538

Bachman, J. G., Staff, J., O'Malley, P. M., & Freedman-Doan, P. (2013). Adolescent work intensity, school performance, and substance use: Links vary by race/ethnicity and socioeconomic status. *Developmental Psychology, 49*(11), 2125–2134. doi:10.1037/a0031464

Backhouse, J., & Graham, A. (2013). Grandparents raising their grandchildren: Acknowledging the experience of grief. *Australian Social Work, 66*(3), 440–454. doi:10.1080/0312407X.2013.817595

Baek, H. (2002). A comparative study of moral development of Korean and British children. *Journal of Moral Education, 31*(4), 373–391.

Bafunno, D., & Camodeca, M. (2013). Shame and guilt development in preschoolers: The role of context, audience and individual characteristics. *European Journal of Developmental Psychology, 10*(2), 128–143.

Bagnell, K. (2001). *The little immigrants: The orphans who came to Canada*. Toronto, ON. Canada: Dundurn Press.

Bagwell, C. L., & Schmidt, M. E. (2011). *Friendships in childhood and adolescence*. New York: Guilford.

Baham, M. E., Weimer, A. A., Braver, S. L., & Fabricius, W. V. (2008). Sibling relationships in blended families. In J. Pryor (Ed.), *The international handbook of stepfamilies* (pp. 175–207). Hoboken, NJ: Wiley & Sons.

Bailey, J. A., Hill, K. G., Hawkins, J. D., Catalano, R. F., & Abbott, R. D. (2008). Men's and women's patterns of substance use around pregnancy. *Birth: Issues in Perinatal Care, 35*(1), 50–59.

Bailey, J. M., Vasey, P. L., Diamond, L. M., Breedlove, S. M., Vilain, E., & Epprecht, M. (2016). Sexual orientation, controversy, and science. *Psychological Science in the Public Interest,17*(2), 45–101. doi:10.1177/1529100616637616

Bailey, R. (2005). Physical development and growth. In N. Salkind (Ed.), *Encyclopedia of human development* (pp. 1001–1008). Thousand Oaks, CA: Sage.

Baillargeon, R. (2008). Innate ideas revisited: For a principle of persistence in infants' physical reasoning. *Perspectives on Psychological Science, Special Issue: From Philosophical Thinking to Psychological Empiricism, 3*(1), 2–13.

Baillargeon, R., Li, J., Ng, W., & Yuan, S. (2009). An account of infants' physical reasoning. In A. Woodward & A. Needham (Eds.), *Learning and the infant mind* (pp. 66–116). New York: Oxford University Press.

Baillargeon, R., Needham, A., & DeVos, J. (1992). The development of young infants' intuitions about support. *Early Development & Parenting, 1*(2), 69–78.

Baillargeon, R., Spelke, E. S., & Wasserman, S. (1985). Object permanence in five-month-old infants. *Cognition, 20*(3), 191–208.

Baker, A. L., & Ben-Ami, N. (2011). To turn a child against a parent is to turn a child against himself: The direct and indirect effects of exposure to parental alienation strategies on self-esteem and well-being. *Journal of Divorce & Remarriage, 52*(7), 472–489.

Baker, K., & Raney, A. A. (2007). Equally super? Gender-role stereotyping of superheroes in children's animated programs. *Mass Communication and Society, 10*(1), 25–41.

Bakermans-Kranenburg, M. J., van IJzendoorn, M. H., & Juffer, F. (2003). Less is more: Meta-analyses of sensitivity and attachment interventions in early childhood. *Psychological Bulletin, 129*(2), 195–215.

Baines, E., & Blatchford, P. (2009). Sex differences in the structure and stability of children's playground social networks and their overlap with friendship relations. *British Journal of Developmental Psychology, 27*(3), 743–760. doi:10.1348/026151008X371114.

Balbernie, R. (2010). Reactive attachment disorder as an evolutionary adaptation. *Attachment & Human Development, 12*(3), 265–281.s

Baldry, A. C., & Farrington, D. P. (2000). Bullies and delinquents: Personal characteristics and parental styles. *Journal of Community & Applied Social Psychology, 10*(1), 17–31.

Bali Travel Guidebook. (2002). *Royal Odalan and tooth filing ceremony (Mepandes)*. Retrieved from http://www.klubkokos.com/guidebook/royal_odalan.htm

Balkin, R., Heard, C., Lee, S., & Wines, L. A. (2014). A primer for evaluating test bias and test fairness: Implications for multicultural assessment. *Journal of Professional Counseling: Practice, theory, and research, 41*(1), 42–52.

Ballard, W., Hall, M. N., & Kaufmann, L. (2010). Do dietary interventions improve ADHD symptoms in children? *Journal of Family Practice, 59*(4), 234–235.

Bandstra, E. S., Morrow, C. E., Mansoor, E., & Accornero, V. H. (2010). Prenatal drug exposure: Infant and toddler outcomes. *Journal of Addictive Disorders, 29*(2), 245–258.

Bandura, A. (1986). *Social foundations of thought and action*. Englewood Cliffs, NJ: Prentice Hall.

Bandura, A., Caprara, G. V., Barbaranelli, C., Pastorelli, C., & Regalia, C. (2001). Sociocognitive self-regulatory mechanisms governing transgressive behavior. *Journal of Personality and Social Psychology, 80*(1), 125–135.

Bandura, A., Ross, D., & Ross, S. A. (1963). Imitation of film-mediated aggressive models. *Journal of Abnormal and Social Psychology, 66*(1), 3–11.

Banerjee, S. C., & Greene, K. (2007). Antismoking initiatives: Effects of analysis versus production media literacy interventions on smoking-related attitude, norm, and behavioral intentions. *Health Communication, 22*, 37–48.

Barac, R., & Bialystok, E. (2012). Bilingual effects on cognitive and linguistic development: Role of language, cultural background, and education. *Child Development, 83*, 413–422.

Barbash, F. (2015). *Sleepy face, sad face or shocked face: The emoji identity crisis*. Retrieved from https://www.washingtonpost.com/news/morning-mix/wp/2015/06/12/why-we-cant-agree-what-emoji-mean/

Barber, B. K. (1994). Cultural, family, and personal contexts of parent-adolescent conflict. *Journal of Marriage and Family, 56*(2), 375–386.

Barker, L. (2006). Teaching evolutionary psychology: An interview with David M. Buss. *Teaching of Psychology, 33*(1), 69–76.

Barker, R. D., & Wright, H. F. (1951). *One boy's day: A specimen record of behavior*. New York: Harper.

Barkin, S., Ip, E., Richardson, I., Klinepeter, S., Finch, S., & Krcmar, M. (2006). Parental media mediation styles for children aged 2 to 11 years. *Archives of Pediatrics & Adolescent Medicine, 160*(4), 395–401.

Barkley, R. A. (1991). *Attention deficit and hyperactivity disorder—A clinical workbook*. New York: Guilford Press.

Barkley, R. A. (2006). Attention-deficit/hyperactivity disorder. In D. A. Wolfe & E. J. Mash (Eds.), *Behavioral and emotional disorders in adolescents* (pp. 91–152). New York: Guilford Press.

Barkley, R. A. (2008). *ADHD in adults: What the science says*. New York: Guilford Press.

Barlett, C. P., Harris, R. J., & Bruey, C. (2008). The effect of the amount of blood in a violent video game on aggression, hostility, and arousal. *Journal of Experimental Social Psychology, 44*(3), 539–546.

Barnes, S. K. (2010). Sign language with babies: What difference does it make? *Dimensions of Early Childhood, 38*(1), 21–30.

Barnhart, R. D., Davenport, M. J., Epps, S. B., & Nordquist, V. M. (2003). Developmental coordination disorder. *Physical Therapy, 83*, 722–731.

Baron-Cohen, S. (1995). *Mindblindness*. Cambridge, MA: MIT Press.

Barr, R., Lauricella, A., Zack, E., & Calvert, S. L. (2010). Infant and early childhood exposure to adult-directed and child-directed television programming: Relations with cognitive skills at age four. *Merrill-Palmer Quarterly, 56*(1), 21–48. doi:10.1353/mpq.0.0038

Barrett, J. R. (2007). Shift in the sexes: Are endocrine disruptors changing birth ratios? *Environmental Health Perspectives, 115*(6), A312.

Barros, R. M., Silver, E. J., & Stein, R. E. K. (2009). School recess and group classroom behavior. *Pediatrics, 123*(2), 431–436.

Bartlett, E. E. (2004). The effect of fatherhood on the health of men: A review of the literature. *Journal of Men's Health and Gender, 1*(2–3), 159–169.

Bassuk, E. L., Murphy, C., Coupe, N. T., Kenney, R. R., & Beach, C. A. (2011). *America's youngest outcasts: 2010*. Needham, MA: National Center on Family Homelessness.

Basten, U., Hilger, K., & Fiebach, C. J. (2015). Where smart brains are different: A quantitative meta-analysis of functional and structural brain imaging studies on intelligence. *Intelligence, 51*, 10–27. doi:10.1016/j.intell.2015.04.009

Bastaits, K., & Mortelmans, D. (2016). Parenting as mediator between post-divorce family structure and children's well-being. *Journal of Child and Family Studies, 25*(7), 2178–2188. doi:10.1007/s10826-016-0395-8

Bauer, K., Laska, M., Fulkerson, J., & Neumark-Sztainer, D. (2011). Longitudinal and secular trends in parental encouragement for healthy eating, physical activity, and dieting throughout the adolescent years. *Journal of Adolescent Health, 49*(3), 306–311. doi: 10.1016/j.jadohealth.2010.12.023

Bauer, P. J. (2007). Recall in infancy: A neurodevelopmental account. *Current Directions in Psychological Science, 16*(3), 142–146.

Bauer, P. J., & Leventon, J. S. (2013). Memory for one-time experiences in the second year of life: Implications for the status of episodic memory. *Infancy, 18*(5), 755–781. doi: 10.1111/infa.12005

Baumeister, R. F., Campbell, J. D., Krueger, J. I., & Vohs, K. D. (2003). Does high self-esteem cause better performance, interpersonal success, happiness, or healthier lifestyles? *Psychological Science in the Public Interest, 4*(1), 1–44.

Baumgartner, S. E., Valkenburg, P. M., & Peter, J. (2011). The influence of descriptive and injunctive peer norms on adolescents' risky sexual online behavior. *Cyberpsychology, Behavior, and Social Networking, 14*(12), 753–758. doi: 10.1089/cyber.2010.0510

Baumrind, D. (1967). Child care practices anteceding three patterns of preschool behavior. *Genetic Psychology Monographs, 75*(1), 43–88.

Baumrind, D. (1971). Current patterns of parental authority. *Developmental Psychology Monograph, 4*(1), Part 2, 1–103.

Baumrind, D. (1991). Effective parenting during the early adolescent transition. In P. A. Cowan & E. M. Hetherington (Eds.), *Family transitions* (pp. 111–163). Hillsdale, NJ: Erlbaum.

Baumrind, D. (2013). Authoritative parenting revisited: History and current status. In R. E. Larzelere, A. Morris, & A. W. Harrist (Eds.), *Authoritative parenting: Synthesizing nurturance and discipline for optimal child development* (pp. 11–34). Washington, DC: American Psychological Association. doi: 10.1037/13948–000

Baumrind, D., Larzelere, R. E., & Owens, E. B. (2010). Effects of preschool parents' power assertive patterns and practices on adolescent development. *Parenting: Science and Practice, 10*(3), 157–201. doi:10.1080/15295190903290790

BBC News. (2014). *Where is it illegal to be gay?* Retrieved from http://www.bbc.com/news/world-25927595

Beam, M. R., Chen, C., & Greenberger, E. (2002). The nature of adolescents' relationships with their 'very important' nonparental adults. *American Journal of Community Psychology, 30*(2), 305–325.

Bear, M. F., Connors, B. W., & Paradiso, M. A. (2007). *Neuroscience: Exploring the brain* (3rd ed.). Baltimore, MD: Lippincott, Williams & Wilkins.

Bearce, K., & Rovee-Collier, C. (2006). Repeated priming increases memory accessibility in infants. *Journal of Experimental Child Psychology, 93*(4), 357–376. doi: 10.1016/j.jecp.2005.10.002

Beasley, N. M. R., Hall, A., Tomkins, A. M., Donnelly, C., Ntimbwa, P., Kivuga, J., . . . Bundy, D. A. P. (2000). The health of enrolled and non enrolled children of school age in Tanga, Tanzania. *Acta Tropica, 76*(3), 223–229.

Beaudet, A. L. (2013). The utility of chromosomal microarray analysis in developmental and behavioral pediatrics. *Child Development, 84*(1), 121–132.

Beesdo, K., Knappe, S., & Pine, D. S. (2009). Anxiety and anxiety disorders in children and adolescents: Developmental issues and implications for DSM-V. *Psychiatric Clinics of North America, 32*(3), 483–524.

Beilock, S. L., Gunderson, E. A., Ramirez, G., & Levine, S. C. (2010). Female teachers' math anxiety affects girls' math achievement. *Proceedings of the National Academy of Sciences of the United States of America, 107*(5), 1860–1863.

Bejanyan, K., Marshall, T. C., & Ferenczi, N. (2014). Romantic ideals, mate preferences, and anticipation of future difficulties in marital life: A comparative study of young adults in India and America. *Frontiers in Psychology, 5,* Article1355, 1-10. doi:10.3389/fpsyg.2014.01355

Bell, J. F., Wilson, J. S., & Liu, G. C. (2008). Neighborhood greenness and 2-year changes in body mass index of children and youth. *American Journal of Preventive Medicine, 5*(6), 547–553.

Bell, S. M., & Ainsworth, M. D. (1972). Infant crying and maternal responsiveness. *Child Development, 43*(4), 1171–1190.

Bellin, H. F., & Singer, D. G. (2006). My magic story car: Video based play intervention to strengthen emergent literacy of at-risk preschoolers. In D. G. Singer, R. M. Golinkoff, & K. Hirsh-Pasek (Eds.), *Play=learning* (pp. 101–123). New York: Oxford University Press.

Belsky, J. (2005). Attachment theory and research in ecological perspective. In K. E. Grossmann, K. Grossmann, & E. Waters (Eds.), *Attachment from infancy to adulthood: The major longitudinal studies* (pp. 71–97). New York: Guilford Press.

Belsky, J., Burchinal, M., McCartney, K., Vandell, D. L., Clarke-Stewart, K. A., Owen, M. T., & the NICHD Early Child Care Research Network. (2007). Are there long-term effects of early child care? *Child Development, 78*(2), 681–701.

Belsky, J., Houts, R. M., & Fearon, R. (2010). Infant attachment security and the timing of puberty: Testing an evolutionary hypothesis. *Psychological Science, 21*(9), 1195–1201.

Belsky, J., & Kelly, J. (1994). *The transition to parenthood: How a first child changes a marriage.* New York: Delacorte Press.

Belsky, J., Steinberg, L. D., Houts, R. M., Friedman, S. L., DeHart, G., Cauffman, E., . . . NICHD Early Child Care Research Network. (2007). Family rearing antecedents of pubertal timing. *Child Development, 78*(4), 1302–1321.

Bem, S. L. (1974). The measurement of psychological androgyny. *Journal of Consulting and Clinical Psychology, 42*(2), 155–162.

Bem, S. L. (1989). Genital knowledge and gender constancy in preschool children. *Child Development, 60*(3), 649–662.

Bem, S. L., & Lewis, S. A. (1975). Sex role adaptability: One consequence of psychological androgyny. *Journal of Personality and Social Psychology, 31*(4), 634–643.

Bemiller, M. (2010). Mothering from a distance. *Journal of Divorce & Remarriage, 51*(3), 169–184.

Ben-Joseph, E. P. (2014). *First day of life.* Retrieved from http://kidshealth.org/parent/pregnancy_center/childbirth/first_day.html#

Bengtson, V. L. (2001). Beyond the nuclear family: The increasing importance of multigenerational bonds [The Burgess Award Lecture]. *Journal of Marriage and Family, 63,* 1–16.

Bengtsson, S. L., Nagy, Z., Skare, S., Forsman, L., Forssberg, H., & Ullén, F. (2005). Extensive piano practicing has regionally specific effects on white matter development. *Nature Neuroscience, 8*(9), 1148–1150.

Benight, C. C., & Bandura, A. (2004). Social cognitive theory of posttraumatic recovery: The role of perceived self-efficacy. *Behaviour Research and Therapy, 42,* 1129–1148.

Benner, A. D., & Mistry, R. S. (2007). Congruence of mother and teacher educational expectations and low-income youth's academic competence. *Journal of Educational Psychology, 99*(1), 140–153.

Bera, A., Ghosh, J., Singh, A. K., Hazra, A., Mukherjee, S., & Mukherjee, R. (2014). Effect of kangaroo mother care on growth and development of low birthweight babies up to 12 months of age: A controlled clinical trial. *Acta Paediatrica, 103*(6), 643–650. doi:10.1111/apa.12618

Berenbaum, S. A., Martin, C. L., Hanish, L. D., Briggs, P. T., & Fabes, R. A. (2008). Sex differences in children's play. In J. B. Becker, K. J. Berkley, N. Gear, E. Hampson, & J. P. Herman (Eds.), *Sex differences in the brain from genes to behavior* (pp. 275–290). New York: Oxford University Press.

Bergelson, E., & Swingley, D. (2012). At 6-9 months, human infants know the meanings of many common nouns. *Proceedings of the National Academy of Sciences, 109*(9), 3253–3258.

Berger, U., Weitkamp, K., & Strauss, B. (2009). Weight limits, estimations of future BMI, subjective pubertal timing and physical appearance comparisons among adolescent girls as precursors of disturbed eating behaviour in a community sample. *European Eating Disorders Review, 17*(2), 128–136. doi:10.1002/erv.898

Bergh, S., & Erling, A. (2005). Adolescent identity formation: A Swedish study of identity status using the EOM-EIS-II. *Adolescence, 40*(158), 377–396.

Bergsma, L., & Ingram, M. (2001). *Blowing smoke—Project evaluation final report.* Retrieved from http://www.scenesmoking.org/research/BlowingSmoke.pdf

Berk, L. E., Mann, T. D., & Ogan, A. T. (2006). Make-believe play: Wellspring for development of self-regulation. In D. G. Singer, R. M. Golinkoff, & K. Hirsh-Pasek (Eds.), *Play=learning* (pp. 74–100). New York: Oxford University Press.

Berlin, L. J., Ispa, J. M., Fine, M. A., Malone, P. S., Brooks-Gunn, J., Brady-Smith, C., . . . & Bai, Y. (2009). Correlates and consequences of spanking and verbal punishment for low-income White, African American, and Mexican American toddlers. *Child Development, 80*(5), 1403–1420. doi:10.1111/j.1467-8624.2009.01341.x

Berlin, M., Vinnerljung, B., & Hjern, A. (2011). School performance in primary school and psychosocial problems in young adulthood among care leavers from long term foster care. *Children and Youth Services Review, 33*(12), 2489–2497.

Berman, M. G., Jonides, J., & Kaplan, S. (2008). The cognitive benefits of interacting with nature. *Psychological Science, 19*(12), 1207–1212.

Bernard, J. (1972). *The future of marriage.* New Haven, CT: Yale University Press.

Bernard, K., Dozier, M., Bick, J., Lewis-Morrarty, E., Lindhiem, O., & Carlson, E. (2012). Enhancing attachment organization among maltreated children: Results of a randomized clinical trial. *Child Development, 83*(2), 623–636.

Berti, A. E., Garattoni, C., & Venturini, B. (2000). The understanding of sadness, guilt, and shame in 5-, 7-, and 9-year-old children. *Genetic, Social, and General Psychology Monographs, 126*(3), 293–318.

Best, C. C., & McRoberts, G. W. (2003). Infant perception of non-native consonant contrasts that adults assimilate in different ways. *Language and Speech, 46*(2–3), 183–216.

Bezerra Alves, J. G., Russo, P. C., & Alves, G. V. (2013). Facial responses to basic tastes in breastfeeding and formula-feeding infants. *Breastfeeding Medicine, 8*(2), 235–236. doi:10.1089/bfm.2012.0092

Bialystok, E. (2001). *Bilingualism in development: Language, literacy, and cognition.* New York: Cambridge University Press.

Bialystok, E., Craik, F. I. M., Green, D. W., & Gollan, T. H. (2009). Bilingual minds. *Psychological Science in the Public Interest, 10*(3), 89–129.

Bianchi, S. M., Robinson, J. P., & Milkie, M. A. (2006). *Changing rhythms of American family life.* New York: Russell Sage Foundation.

Biddle, B. J., & Berliner, D. C. (2002). Small class size and its effects. *Educational Leadership, 59*(5), 12–23.

Bidwell, A. (2015, March 15). *School bullying, cyberbullying continue to drop.* Retrieved from http://www.usnews.com/news/blogs/data-mine/2015/05/15/school-bullying-cyber-bullying-continue-to-drop

Bieber, L., Dince, P., Drellich, M., Grand, H., Gundlach, R., Kremer, M.,. . . . Bieber, T. (1962). *Homosexuality: A psychoanalytic study of male homosexuals.* New York: Basic Books.

Biggs, M., Gould, H., & Foster, D. (2013). Understanding why women seek abortions in the US. *BMC Women's Health, 1329,* doi:10.1186/1472-6874-13-29.

Biggs, S. N., Lushington, K., Martin, A. J., van den Heuvel, C., & Kennedy, J. D. (2013). Gender, socioeconomic, and ethnic differences in sleep patterns in school-aged children. *Sleep Medicine, 14*(12), 1304–1309. doi:10.1016/j.sleep.2013.06.014

Binder, E. B., Bradley, R. G., Liu, W., Epstein, M. P., Deveau, T. C., Mercer, K. B.,. . . . Ressler, K. J. (2008). Association of *FKBP5* polymorphisms and childhood abuse with risk of post-traumatic stress disorder symptoms in adults. *JAMA, 299*(11), 1291–1305.

Bingham, A., & Pennington, J. L. (2007). As easy as ABC: Facilitating early literacy enrichment experiences. *Young Exceptional Children, 10*(2), 17–29.

Birkeland, M. S., Melkevik, O., Holsen, I., & Wold, B. (2012). Trajectories of global self-esteem development during adolescence. *Journal of Adolescence, 35*(1), 43–54.

Bittner, A., Egger, H. L., Erkanli, A., Costello, E. J., Foley, D. L., & Angold, A. (2007). What do childhood anxiety disorders predict? *Journal of Child Psychology and Psychiatry, 48*(12), 1174–1183.

Black, M. H., Smith, N., Porter, A. H., Jacobsen, S. J., & Koebnick, C. (2012). Higher prevalence of obesity among children with asthma. *Obesity, 20,* 1041–1047.

Black, M. M., Hess, C. R., & Berenson-Howard, J. (2000). Toddlers from low-income families have below normal mental, motor, and behavior scores on the Revised Bayley Scales. *Journal of Applied Developmental Psychology, 26*(6), 655–666.

Blackwell, G. L. (2010). A little help along the way. *Outlook, 104*(1), 16–19.

Blair, C., & Razza, R. P. (2007). Relating effortful control, executive function, and false belief understanding to emerging math and literacy ability in kindergarten. *Child Development, 78*(2), 647–663. doi:10.1111/j.1467-8624.2007.01019.x

Blair, C., Zelazo, P. D., & Greenberg, M. T. (2005). The measurement of executive function in early childhood. *Developmental Neuropsychology, 28*(2), 561–571.

Blakemore, S. J., & Choudhury, S. (2006). Development of the adolescent brain: Implications for executive function and social cognition. *Journal of Child Psychology and Psychiatry, 47*(3), 296–312.

Blanchard, R. (2008). Review and theory of handedness, birth order, and homosexuality in men. *Laterality, 13*(1), 51–70.

Blascovich, J. (2004). Psychophysiological measures. In M. Lewis-Beck, A. Bryman, & T. Liao (Eds.), *Encyclopedia of social science research methods* (pp. 882–884). Thousand Oaks, CA: Sage. doi: http://dx.doi.org/10.4135/9781412950589.n772

Blasi, C. H., & Bjorklund, D. F. (2003). Evolutionary developmental psychology: A new tool for better understanding human ontogeny. *Human Development, 46,* 259–281.

Blumberg, S. J., Zablotsky, B., Avila, R. M., Colpe, L. J., Pringle, B. A., & Kogan, M. D. (2016). Diagnosis lost: Differences between children who had and who currently have an autism spectrum disorder diagnosis. *Autism, 20*(7), 783–795. doi: 10.1177/1362361315607724

Blumenthal, H., Leen-Feldner, E. W., Babson, K. A., Gahr, J. L., Trainor, C. D., & Frala, J. L. (2011). Elevated social anxiety among early maturing girls. *Developmental Psychology, 47*(4), 1133–1140.

Boake, C. (2002). From the Binet-Simon to the Wechsler-Bellevue: Tracing the history of intelligence testing. *Journal of Clinical and Experimental Neuropsychology, 24*(3), 383–405.

Bobo, J. K., Klepinger, D. H., & Dong, F. B. (2006). Changes in the prevalence of alcohol use during pregnancy among recent and at-risk drinkers in the NLSY cohort. *Journal of Women's Health, 15*(9), 1061–1070.

Boelema, S. R., Harakeh, Z., Ormel, J., Hartman, C. A., Vollebergh, W. M., & van Zandvoort, M. E. (2013). Executive functioning shows differential maturation from early to late adolescence: Longitudinal findings from a TRAILS study. *Neuropsychology, 28*(2), 177–187. doi: 10.1037/neu0000049

Boergers, J., Gable, C. J., & Owens, J. A. (2014). Later school start time is associated with improved sleep and daytime functioning in adolescents. *Journal of Developmental and Behavioral Pediatrics, 35*(1), 11–17. doi: 10.1097/DBP.0000000000000018

Boets, B., Op de Beeck, H. P., Vandermosten, M., Scott, S. K., Gillebert, C. R., Mantini, D. . . . Ghesquière, P. (2013). Intact but less accessible phonetic representations in adults with dyslexia. *Science, 342*(6163), 1251–1254.

Bohannon, J. N., & Bonvillian, J. D. (2005). Theoretical approaches to language acquisition. In J. B. Gleason (Ed.), *The development of language* (6th ed., pp. 230–291). Boston: Pearson.

Boksa, P. (2008). Maternal infection during pregnancy and schizophrenia. *Journal of Psychiatry & Neuroscience, 33*(3), 183–185.

Bonawitz, E., Shafto, P., Gweon, H., Goodman, N. D., Spelke, E., & Schulz, L. (2011). The double-edged sword of pedagogy: Instruction limits spontaneous exploration and discovery. *Cognition, 120*(3), 322–330. doi: 10.1016/j.cognition.2010.10.001

Bone and Joint Initiative (2013-2015). *Sports injuries – Children and adolescents.* Retrieved from http://www.boneandjointburden.org/2013-report/workforce-implications/vii3d

Booth-LaForce, C., Oh, W., Kim, A. H., Rubin, K. H., Rose-Krasnor, L., & Burgess, K. (2006). Attachment, self-worth, and peer-group functioning in middle childhood. *Attachment & Human Development, 8*(4), 309–325.

Booth-LaForce, C., & Oxford, M. L. (2008). Trajectories of social withdrawal from Grades 1 to 6: Prediction from early parenting, attachment, and temperament. *Developmental Psychology, 44*(5), 1298–1313.

Borgwald, K., & Theixos, H. (2013). Bullying the bully: Why zero-tolerance policies get a failing grade. *Social Influence, 8*(2–3), 149-160. doi:10.1080/15534510.2012.724030

Bornstein, D. (2014). *Teaching children to calm themselves. The New York Times.* Retrieved from http://opinionator.blogs.nytimes.com/2014/03/19/first-learn-how-to-calm-down/?_php=true&_type=blogs&_r=0

Bornstein, M. H., Hahn, C., Bell, C., Haynes, O. M., Slater, A., Golding, J., . . . ALSPAC Study Team. (2006). Stability in cognition across early childhood: A developmental cascade. *Psychological Science, 17*(2), 151–158.

Bornstein, M. H., Hahn, C., & Wolke, D. (2013). Systems and cascades in cognitive development and academic achievement. *Child Development, 84*(1), 154–162.

Borntrager, C., Davis, J. L., Bernstein, A., & Gorman, H. (2009). A cross-national perspective on bullying. *Child & Youth Care Forum, 38*(3), 121–134.

Borse, N. N., Gilchrist, J., Dellinger, A. M., Rudd, R. A., Ballesteros, M. F., & Sleet, D. A. (2008). *CDC childhood injury report: Patterns of unintentional injuries among 0–19 year olds in the United States, 2000–2006.* Atlanta, GA: Centers for Disease Control and Prevention, National Center for Injury Prevention and Control.

Bos, H. W., Knox, J. R., van Rijn-van Gelderen, L., & Gartrell, N. K. (2016). Same-sex and different-sex parent households and child health outcomes: Findings from the National Survey of Children's Health. *Journal of Developmental and Behavioral Pediatrics, 37*(3), 179–187. doi:10.1097/DBP.0000000000000288

Bosma, H., & Gerlsma, C. (2003). From early attachment relations to the adolescent and adult organization of self. In J. Valsiner & K. J. Connolly (Eds.), *Handbook of developmental psychology* (pp. 450–488). Thousand Oaks, CA: Sage.

Bouchard, S. (2011). Could virtual reality be effective in treating children with phobias? *Expert Review of Neurotherapeutics, 11*(2), 207–213. doi: 10.1586/ern.10.196.

Bouchard, S., Weiderhold, B. K., & Bossé, J. (2014). Arachnophobia and fear of other insects: Efficacy and lessons learned from treatment process. In B. K. Weiderhold & S. Bouchard (Eds.), *Advances in virtual reality and anxiety disorders* (pp. 119–144). New York: Springer.

Bouchez, C. (2008). *Childbirth options: What's best?* Retrieved from http://www.webmd.com/baby/features/childbirth-options-whats-best

Boulet, S., Schieve, L., & Boyle, C. (2011). Birth weight and health and developmental outcomes in U.S. children, 1997–2005. *Maternal & Child Health Journal, 15*(7), 836–844. doi:10.1007/s10995-009-0538-2

Boulos, R., Vikre, E., Oppenheimer, S., Chang, H., & Kanarek, R. B. (2012). ObesiTV: How television is influencing the obesity epidemic. *Physiology & Behavior, 107*(1), 146–153.

Bosse, M. (2015). Learning to read and spell: How children acquire word orthographic knowledge. *Child Development Perspectives, (9)*4, 201–268. doi:10.1111/cdep.12133

Bowden, V., Greenberg, C., & Donaldson, N. (2000). Developmental care of the newborn. *Online Journal of Clinical Innovations, 3*(7), 1–77.

Bower, B. (2005). Investing on a whiff. *Science News, 167*(23), 356–357.

Bowlby, J. (1958). The nature of the child's tie to his mother. *International Journal of Psycho-Analysis, 39,* 350–373.

Bowlby, J. (1969). *Attachment and loss: Vol. 1. Attachment.* New York: Basic Books.

Bowman, S. A., Gortmaker, S. L., Ebbeling, C. B., Pereira, M. A., & Ludwig, D. S. (2004). Effects of fast food consumption on energy intake and diet quality among children in a national household survey. *Pediatrics, 113*(1, pt. 1), 112–118.

Bowman, L. L., Levine, L. E., Waite, B. M., & Gendron, M. (2010). Can students really multitask? An experimental study of instant messaging while reading. *Computers & Education, 54*(4), 927–931.

Boyce, P., Condon, J., Barton, J., & Corkindale, C. (2007). First-time fathers' study: Psychological distress in expectant fathers during pregnancy. *Australian & New Zealand Journal of Psychiatry, 41*(9), 718–725.

Boyd, R. (2008). Do people only use 10 percent of their brains? *Scientific American.* Retrieved from http://www.scientificamer ican.com/article.cfm?id=people-only-use-10-percent-of-brain

Boyes, M. C., & Allen, S. G. (1993). Styles of parent-child interaction and moral reasoning in adolescence. *Merrill-Palmer Quarterly, 39*(4), 551–570.

Boyse, K., Boujaoude, L., & Laundy, J. (2010). *Children with chronic conditions.* University of Michigan Health System. Retrieved from http://www.med.umich.edu/yourchild/top ics/chronic.htm

Bradley, R. H., & Corwyn, R. F. (2002). Socioeconomic status and child development. *Annual Review of Psychology, 53,* 371–399.

Bradley, R. H., Corwyn, R. F., McAdoo, H. P., & Garcia Coll, C. (2001). The home environments of children in the United States: Part I. Variations by age, ethnicity, and poverty status. *Child Development, 72*(6), 1844–1867.

Bradman, A., Quirós-Alcalá, L., Castorina, R., Schall, R. A., Camacho, J., Holland, N. T.,. . . . Eskenazi, B. (2015). Effect of organic diet intervention on pesticide exposures in young children living in low-income urban and agricultural communities. *Environmental Health Perspectives, 123*(10), 1086–1093. doi:10.1289/ehp.1408660

Brainerd, C. J., & Reyna, V. F. (2004). Fuzzy-trace theory and memory development. *Developmental Review, 24*(4), 396–439.

Braithwaite, D. O., Schrodt, P., & DiVeniero, R. (2009). Stepfamilies. In H. T. Reis & S. Sprecher (Eds.), *Encyclopedia of human relationships* (pp. 1595–1598). Thousand Oaks, CA: Sage.

Branum, A. M., & Lukacs, S. L. (2009). Food allergy among children in the United States. *Pediatrics, 124*(6), 1549–1555.

Bratton, S. C., Ray, D., & Rhine, T. (2005). The efficacy of play therapy with children: A meta-analytic review of treatment outcomes. *Professional Psychology: Research and Practice, 36*(4), 376–390.

The Brazelton Institute. (n.d.). *The Newborn Behavioral Observations system: What is it?* Retrieved from http://www.brazelton-institute.com/clnbas.html

Bregman, E. O. (1934). An attempt to modify the emotional attitudes of infants by conditioned response technique. *Journal of Genetic Psychology, 45,* 169–198.

Bregman, J. (2005). Apgar Score. *Encyclopedia of human development.* Thousand Oaks, CA: Sage. Retrieved from http://www.sage-erefer ence.com/humandevelopment/Article_n

Breier, J., Simos, P. G., & Fletcher, J. M. (2002). Abnormal activation of tempoparietal language areas during phonetic analysis in children with dyslexia. *Neuropsychology, 17,* 610–621.

Brennan, A., Marshall-Lucette, S., Ayers, S., & Ahmed, H. (2007). A qualitative exploration of the Couvade syndrome in expectant fathers. *Journal of Reproductive & Infant Psychology, 25*(1), 18–39.

Brenoff, A. (2016). *14 teen slang terms decoded for middle-age parents. The Huffington Post.* Retrieved from http://www.huffingtonpost.com/entry/14-teen-slang-terms-decoded-for-con fused-middle-age-parents_us_56c49aaee4b0b 40245c88cec

Brisch, K. H., Bechinger, D., Betzler, S., Heinemann, H., Kächele, H., Pohlandt, F., . . . Buchheim, A. (2005). Attachment quality in very low-birthweight premature infants in relation to maternal attachment representations and neurological development. *Parenting: Science and Practice, 5*(4), 311–331.

Britsch, B., Callahan, N., & Peterson, K. (2010). The power of partnerships. *Outlook, 104*(1), 13–15.

Brody, G. H., Chen, Y., Murry, V. M., Ge, X., Simons, R. L., Gibbons, F. X., . . . Cutrona, C. E. (2006). Perceived discrimination and the adjustment of African-American youths: A five year longitudinal analysis with contextual moderation effects. *Child Development, 77*(5), 1170–1189.

Brody, L. E. (2005). The study of exceptional talent. *High Ability Studies, 16*(1), 87–96.

Brody, L. R., & Hall, J. A. (2008). Gender and emotion in context. In M. Lewis & J. Haviland (Eds.), *Handbook of emotions* (3rd ed., pp. 395–408). New York: Guilford.

Broesch, T., Callaghan, T., Henrich, J., Murphy, C., & Rochat, P. (2011). Cultural variations in children's mirror self-recognition. *Journal of Cross-Cultural Psychology, 42*(6), 1018–1029.

Broglio, S. P., Eckner, J. T., Martini, D., Sosnoff, J. J., Kutcher, J. S., & Randolph, C. (2011). Cumulative head impact burden in high school football. *Journal of Neurotrauma, 28*(10), 2069–2078.

Bronfenbrenner, U. (1975). Reality and research in the ecology of human development. *Proceedings of the American Philosophical Society, 119*(6), 439–469.

Bronfenbrenner, U. (1977). Toward an experimental ecology of human development. *American Psychologist, 32*(7), 513–531.

Bronfenbrenner, U. (1986). Ecology of the family as a context for human development: Research perspectives. *Developmental Psychology, 22*(6), 723–742.

Brooks, C., Pearce, N., & Douwes, J. (2013). The hygiene hypothesis in allergy and asthma: An update. *Current Opinion in Allergy & Clinical Immunology, 13*(1), 70–77.

Brooks, R., & Meltzoff, A. N. (2015). Connecting the dots from infancy to childhood: A longitudinal study connecting gaze following, language, and explicit theory of mind. *Journal of Experimental Child Psychology, 130,* 67–78. doi:10.1016/j.jecp.2014.09.010

Brophy, J. E. (1983). Research on the self-fulfilling prophecy and teacher expectations. *Journal of Educational Psychology, 75*(5), 631–661.

Brophy-Herb, H. E., Lee, R. E., Nievar, M. A., & Stollak, G. (2007). Preschoolers' social competence: Relations to family characteristics, teacher behaviors and classroom climate. *Journal of Applied Developmental Psychology, 28*(2), 134–148.

Browder, D. M., Wakeman, S. Y., Spooner, F., Ahlgrim-Delzell, L., & Algozzine, B. (2006). Research on reading instruction for individuals with significant cognitive disabilities. *Exceptional Children, 72*(4), 392–408.

Brown, A., Shifrin, D. L., & Hill, D. L. (2015). Beyond 'turn it off': How to advise families on media use. *AAP News.* Retrieved from http://preschool.uen.org/docs/AAPNews-2015-Brown-54.pdf

Brown, A. S., & Susser, E. (2008). Prenatal nutritional deficiency and risk of adult schizophrenia. *Schizophrenia Bulletin, 34*(6), 1054–1063.

Brown, B., Bakken, J. P., Ameringer, S. W., & Mahon, S. D. (2008). A comprehensive conceptualization of the peer influence process in adolescence. In M. J. Prinstein & K. A. Dodge (Eds.), *Understanding peer influence in children and adolescents* (pp. 17–44). New York: Guilford Press.

Brown, B. B. (2004). Adolescents' relationships with peers. In R. M. Lerner & L. Steinberg (Eds.), *Handbook of adolescent psychology* (pp. 363–394). Hoboken, NJ: Wiley.

Brown, B. B., & Klute, C. (2003). Friendships, cliques, and crowds. In G. R. Adams & M. D. Berzonsky (Eds.), *Blackwell handbook of adolescence* (pp. 330–348). Malden, MA: Blackwell.

Brown, E. D., Benedett, B., & Armistead, M. E. (2010). Arts enrichment and school readiness for children at risk. *Early Childhood Research Quarterly, 25,* 112–124.

Brown, J. D., & Bobkowski, P. S. (2011). Older and newer media: Patterns of use and effects on adolescents' health and well-being. *Journal of Research on Adolescence, 21*(1), 95–113. doi:10.1111/j.1532-7795.2010.00717.x

Brown, S. L., & Ronau, R. R. (2012). Students' perceptions of single-gender science and mathematics classroom experiences. *School Science and Mathematics, 112*(2), 66–87.

Browne, J. V. (2005). Preterm infants. *Encyclopedia of human development.* Thousand Oaks, CA: Sage. Retrieved from http://www.sage-eref erence.com/humandevelopment/Article_n496.html

Bruder, C. E. G., Piotrowski, A., Gijsbers, A. A. C. J., Andersson, R., Erickson, S., Diaz de Stahl, T., . . . Dumanski, J. P. (2008). Phenotypically concordant and discordant monozygotic twins display different DNA copy-number-variation profiles. *The American Journal of Human Genetics, 82*(3), 763–771.

Brunton, P. J., & Russell, J. A. (2008). The expectant brain: Adapting for motherhood. *Nature Reviews Neuroscience, 9*(1), 11–25.

Bruskas, D. (2008). Children in foster care: A vulnerable population at risk. *Journal of Child and Adolescent Psychiatric Nursing, 21,* 70–77.

Brüske, I., Flexeder, C., & Heinrich, J. (2014). Body mass index and the incidence of asthma in children. *Current Opinion in Allergy and Clinical Immunology, 14*(2),155–160.

Bryant, G. A., & Barrett, H. C. (2007). Recognizing intentions in infant-directed speech. *Psychological Science, 18*(8), 746–751.

Buckley, K. W. (1989). *Mechanical man: John Broadus Watson and the beginnings of behaviorism.* New York: Guilford Press.

Buist, K. L., & Vermande, M. (2014). Sibling relationship patterns and their associations with child competence and problem behavior. *Journal of Family Psychology, 28*(4), 529–537. doi: 10.1037/a0036990

Bull, R., & Lee, K. (2014). Executive functioning and mathematics achievement. *Child Development Perspectives, 8*(1), 36–41.

Burdi, A. R., Huelke, D. F., Snyder, R. G., & Lowrey, G. H. (1969). Infants and children in the adult world of automobile safety design: Pediatric and anatomical considerations for design of child constraints. *Journal of Biomechanics, 2,* 267–280.

Burghardt, G. M. (2004). Play and the brain in comparative perspective. In R. L. Clements & L. Fiorentino (Eds.), *The child's right to play—A global approach* (pp. 293–308). Westport, CT: Praeger.

Burns, A., & Dunlop, R. (2002). Parental marital quality and family conflict: Longitudinal effects on adolescents from divorcing and non-divorcing families. *Journal of Divorce & Remarriage, 37*(1–2), 57–74.

Burt Solorzano, C. M., & McCartney, C. R. (2010). Obesity and the pubertal transition in girls and boys. *Reproduction, 140*(3), 399–410.

Busch, H., & Hofer, J. (2011). Identity, prosocial behavior, and generative concern in German and Cameroonian Nso adolescents. *Journal of Adolescence, 34*(4), 629–638. doi:10.1016/j.adolescence.2010.09.009

Bushman, B. J. (2006). Effects of warning and information labels on attraction to television violence in viewers of different ages. *Journal of Applied Social Psychology, 36*(9), 2073–2078. doi:10.1111/j.0021-9029.2006.00094.x

Bushman, B. J., & Cantor, J. (2003). Media ratings for violence and sex. *American Psychologist, 58*(2), 130–141.

Bussey, K., & Bandura, A. (1999). Social cognitive theory of gender development and differentiation. *Psychological Review, 106*(4), 676–713.

Butte, N. F., Fox, M. K., Briefel, R. R., Siega-Riz, A. M., Dwyer, J. T., Deming, D. M., & Reidy, K. C. (2010). Nutrient intakes of U.S. infants, toddlers, and preschoolers meet or exceed dietary reference intakes. *Journal of the American Dietetic Association, Supplement, 110,* S27–S37.

Butterworth, G. (2003). Pointing is the royal road to language for babies. In S. Kita (Ed.), *Pointing: Where language, culture, and cognition meet* (pp. 9–33). Mahwah, NJ: Erlbaum.

Byers-Heinlein, K., Burns, T. C., & Werker, J. F. (2010). The roots of bilingualism in newborns. *Psychological Science, 21*(3), 343–348.

Byrd, C. M. (2012). The measurement of racial/ethnic identity in children: A critical review. *Journal of Black Psychology, 38*(1), 3–31. doi:10.1177/0095798410397544

Cacciatore, J. (2009). Appropriate bereavement practice after the death of a Native American child. *Families in Society, 90*(1), 46–50.

Cadoret, R. J., Yates, W. R., Troughton, E., Woodworth, G., & Steward, M. A. (1995). Genetic-environmental interaction in the genesis of aggressivity and conduct disorders. *Archives of General Psychiatry, 52*(11), 916–924.

Calafat, A., García, F., Juan, M., Becoña, E., & Fernández-Hermida, J. (2014). Which parenting style is more protective against adolescent substance use? Evidence within the European context. *Drug and Alcohol Dependence, 138,* 185–192. doi: 10.1016/j.drugalcdep.2014.02.705

Calhoun, F., & Warren, K. (2006). Fetal alcohol syndrome: Historical perspectives. *Neuroscience and Biobehavioral Reviews, 31,* 168–171.

Camilli, G., Vargas, S., & Yurecko, M. (2003, May 8). Teaching children to read: The fragile link between science and federal education policy. *Education Policy Analysis Archives, 11*(15), 1–51. Retrieved from http://epaa.asu.edu/epaa/v11n15/

Camos, V., & Barrouillet, P. (2011). Developmental change in working memory strategies: From passive maintenance to active refreshing. *Developmental Psychology, 47*(3), 898–904. doi: 10.1037/a0023193

Campbell, S. B., Shaw, D. S., & Gilliom, M. (2000). Early externalizing behavior problems: Toddlers and preschoolers at risk for later maladjustment. *Development and Psychopathology, 12,* 467–488.

Campbell, S. B., Spieker, S., Burchinal, M., Poe, M. D., & NICHD Early Child Care Research Network. (2006). Trajectories of aggression from toddlerhood to age 9 predict academic and social functioning through age 12. *Journal of Child Psychology and Psychiatry, 47*(8), 791–800.

Canals, J., Hernández-Martínez, C., Esparó, G., & Fernández-Ballart, J. (2011). Neonatal Behavioral Assessment Scale as a predictor of cognitive development and IQ in full-term infants: A 6-year longitudinal study. *Acta Paediatrica, 100*(10), 1331–1337.

Cannon, J. S., Lipscomb, S., & Public Policy Institute of California. (2011). *Early grade retention and student success: Evidence from Los Angeles.* San Francisco: Public Policy Institute of California.

Cano, F., & Cardelle-Elawar, M. (2004). An integrated analysis of secondary school students' conceptions and beliefs about learning. *European Journal of Psychology of Education, 19*(2), 167–187.

Cantor, J., Sparks, G. G., & Hoffner, C. (1988). Calming children's television fears: Mr. Rogers vs. The Incredible Hulk. *Journal of Broadcasting and Electronic Media, 32*(3), 271–288.

Cappella, E., & Hwang, S. H. (2015). Peer contexts in schools: Avenues toward behavioral health in early adolescence. *Behavioral Medicine, 41*(3), 80–89. doi:10.1080/08964289.2015.1034646

Carbo, M. (1996). Whole language vs. phonics: The great debate. *Principal, 75,* 36–38.

Carlson, V. J., & Harwood, R. L. (2003). Attachment, culture, and the caregiving system: The cultural patterning of everyday experiences among Anglo and Puerto Rican mother-infant pairs. *Infant Mental Health Journal, 24*(1), 53–73.

Carney, A. B., & Merrell, K. W. (2001). Bullying in schools: Perspectives on understanding and preventing an international problem. *School Psychology International, 22*(3), 364–382.

Carpenter, S. K. (2012). Testing enhances the transfer of learning. *Current Directions in Psychological Science, 21,* 279–283.

Carranza, J., Gonzalez-Salinas, D., & Ato, E. (2013). A longitudinal study of temperament continuity through IBQ, TBAQ and CBQ. *Infant Behavior & Development, 36*(4), 749–761.

Carroll-Lind, J., & Kearney, A. (2004). Bullying: What do students say? *Kairaranga, 5,* 19–24.

Carson, R. (1998). *The sense of wonder.* New York: Harper Collins.

Carter, C. S. (2005). The chemistry of child neglect: Do oxytocin and vasopressin mediate the effects of early experience? *Proceedings of the National Academy of Sciences, 102*(51), 18247–18248.

Carter, D. B., & Levy, G. D. (1988). Cognitive aspects of early sex role development: The influence of gender schemas on preschoolers' memories and preferences for sex-typed toys and activities. *Child Development, 59,* 782–792.

Cartwright, K. B., Galupo, M., Tyree, S. D., & Jennings, J. (2009). Reliability and validity of the Complex Postformal Thought Questionnaire: Assessing adults' cognitive development. *Journal of Adult Development, 16*(3), 183–189. doi:10.1007/s10804-009-9055-1

Carver, C. S., Scheier, M. F., & Weintraub, J. K. (1989). Assessing coping strategies: A theoretically based approach. *Journal of Personality and Social Psychology, 56*(2), 267–283.

Carver, K., Joyner, K., & Udry, J. R. (2003). National estimates of adolescent romantic relationships. In P. Florsheim (Ed.), *Adolescent romantic relations and sexual behavior: Theory, research, and practical implications* (pp. 23–56). Mahwah, NJ: Erlbaum.

Carver, P. R., Egan, S. K., & Perry, D. G. (2004). Children who question their heterosexuality. *Development Psychology, 40*(1), 43–53.

Carver, P. R., Yunger, J. L., & Perry, D. G. (2003). Gender identity and adjustment in middle childhood. *Sex Roles, 49*(3-4), 95–109.

Casalin, S. Luyten, P., Vliegen, N., & Neurs, P. (2012). The structure and stability of temperament from infancy to toddlerhood: A one-year prospective study. *Infant Behavior & Development, 35*(1), 94–108.

Casey, D. M., Ripke, M. N., & Huston, A. C. (2005). Activity participation and the well-being of children and adolescents in the context of welfare reform. In J. L. Mahoney, R. W. Larson, & J. S. Eccles (Eds.), *Organized activities as contexts of development* (pp. 65–84). Mahwah, NJ: Erlbaum.

Caspi, A., Lynam, D., Moffitt, T. E., & Silva, P. A. (1993). Unraveling girls' delinquency: Biological, dispositional, and contextual contributions to adolescent misbehavior. *Developmental Psychology, 29,* 19–30.

Caspi, A., McClay, J., Moffitt, T. E., Mill, J., Martin, J., Craig, I. W., . . . Poulton, R. (2002). Role of genotype in the cycle of violence in maltreated children. *Science, 297*(5582), 851–854.

Caspi, A., Sugden, K., Moffit, T., Taylor, A., Craig, I. W., Harrington, H., . . . Poulton, R. (2003). Influence of life stress on depression: Moderation by a polymorphism in the 5-HTT gene. *Science, 301,* 386–389.

Castlebury, F. D., & Durham, T. W. (1997). The MMPI-2 GM and GF scales as measures of psychological well-being. *Journal of Clinical Psychology, 53,* 879–893.

Cattell, R. B. (1963). Theory of fluid and crystallized intelligence: A critical experiment. *Journal of Educational Psychology, 54,* 1–22.

Causey, K., Gardiner, A., & Bjorklund, D. F. (2008). Evolutionary developmental psychology and the role of plasticity in ontogeny and phylogeny. *Psychological Inquiry, 19*(1), 27–30.

CBS News. (2015). *Doctors call for warnings on pot use during pregnancy.* Retrieved from http://www.cbsnews.com/news/pot-use-during-pregnancy-a-risk-needs-warnings/

Ceci, S. J., & Bruck, M. (1995). *Jeopardy in the courtroom: A scientific analysis of children's testimony.* Washington, DC: American Psychological Association.

Ceci, S. J., Bruck, M., & Loftus, E. F. (1998). On the ethics of memory implantation research. *Applied Cognitive Psychology, 12*(3), 230–240.

Celce-Murcia, M., & Olshtain, E. (2001). *Discourse and context in language teaching: A guide for language teachers.* New York: Cambridge University Press.

Center for Public Education. (2005). *Teacher quality and student achievement: Key lessons learned.* Retrieved from http://www.education.com/reference/article/Ref_Key_lessons_findings

Center for the Digital Future Report (2015). *The digital future report: Surveying the digital future - Year 13.* Retrieved from http://www.digitalcenter.org/wp-content/uploads/2013/06/2015-Digital-Future-Report.pdf

Center on the Developing Child at Harvard University. (2010). *The foundations of lifelong health are built in early childhood.* Retrieved from http://www.developingchild.harvard.edu

Center on the Developing Child at Harvard University. (2016). *Resilience.* Retrieved from http://developingchild.harvard.edu/science/key-concepts/resilience/

Centers for Disease Control and Prevention. (n.d.). *Know your concussion ABCs.* Retrieved from http://www.cdc.gov/concussion/pdf/TBI_factsheets_PARENTS-508-a.pdf

Centers for Disease Control and Prevention. (2005). *Intellectual disability.* Retrieved from http://www.cdc.gov/ncbddd/dd/mr2.htm

Centers for Disease Control and Prevention. (2007). *What do we know about tobacco use and pregnancy?* Retrieved from http://www.cdc.gov/reproductivehealth/TobaccoUsePregnancy/index.htm

Centers for Disease Control and Prevention. (2008a). *Birth defects: Data and statistics.* Retrieved from http://www.cdc.gov/ncbddd/birthdefects/data.html

Centers for Disease Control and Prevention. (2008b). *STDs and pregnancy—CDC fact sheet.* Retrieved from http://www.cdc.gov/std/STDFact-STDs&Pregnancy.htm

Centers for Disease Control and Prevention. (2009). *Eliminating perinatal HIV transmission.* Retrieved from http://www.cdc.gov/actagainstaids/ottl/pdf/ottl_curriculum.pdf

Centers for Disease Control and Prevention. (2012). Estimated HIV incidence in the United States 22007-2010. *HIV Surveillance Supplemental Report 2012, 17(4).*

Centers for Disease Control and Prevention. (2013a). *Asthma facts—CDC's National Asthma Control Program grantees.* Atlanta, GA: Department of Health and Human Services, Centers for Disease Control and Prevention.

Centers for Disease Control and Prevention. (2013b). *Infertility FAQs.* Retrieved from http://www.cdc.gov/reproductive health/Infertility/index.htm

Centers for Disease Control and Prevention. (2013c). *Sexually transmitted infections among young Americans.* Retrieved from http://www.cdc.gov/nchhstp/newsroom/2013/SAM-Infographic-2013.html?s_cid=nchhstp-nr-sam-008

Centers for Disease Control and Prevention. (2014a). *Assisted reproductive technology.* Retrieved from http://www.cdc.gov/art/index.html

Centers for Disease Control and Prevention. (2014b). *Births: Final data for 2014.* Retrieved from http://www.cdc.gov/nchs/data/nvsr/nvsr64/nvsr64_12.pdf

Centers for Disease Control and Prevention. (2014c). *Breastfeeding report card United States/2014.* Retrieved from http://www.cdc.gov/breastfeeding/pdf/2014breastfeedingreportcard.pdf

Centers for Disease Control and Prevention. (2014d). *Child maltreatment: Definitions.* Retrieved from http://www.cdc.gov/violenceprevention/child maltreatment/definitions.html

Centers for Disease Control and Prevention. (2014e). *During pregnancy.* Retrieved from http://www.cdc.gov/pregnancy/during.html

Centers for Disease Control and Prevention. (2014f). *Fetal alcohol spectrum disorders (FASDs).* Retrieved from http://www.cdc.gov/ncbddd/fasd/data.html

Centers for Disease Control and Prevention. (2014g). *LGBT youth.* Retrieved from http://www.cdc.gov/lgbthealth/youth.htm

Centers for Disease Control and Prevention. (2014h). *Reported STDs in the United States.* Retrieved from http://www.cdc.gov/nchhstp/newsroom/docs/std-trends-508.pdf

Centers for Disease Control and Prevention. (2014i). *Tobacco use and pregnancy.* Retrieved from http://www.cdc.gov/Reproductivehealth/TobaccoUsePregnancy/index.htm

Centers for Disease Control and Prevention. (2014j). *Understanding teen dating violence.* Retrieved from http://www.cdc.gov/violenceprevention/pdf/teen-datingviolence-2014-a.pdf

Centers for Disease Control and Prevention. (2014k). Youth risk behavior surveillance — United States, 2013. *Morbidity and Mortality Weekly Report, 63*(SS04);1–168.

Centers for Disease Control and Prevention. (2015a). *Cervical cancer facts.* Retrieved from http://www.cdc.gov/cancer/cervical/statistics/

Centers for Disease Control and Prevention. (2015b). *Childhood obesity facts.* Retrieved from http://www.cdc.gov/healthyschools/obesity/facts.htm

Centers for Disease Control and Prevention. (2015c). *Genital HSV infections.* Retrieved from http://www.cdc.gov/std/tg2015/herpes.htm#a11

Centers for Disease Control and Prevention. (2015d). *HIV among pregnant women, infants and children.* Retrieved from http://www.cdc.gov/hiv/group/gender/pregnantwomen/index.html

Centers for Disease Control and Prevention. (2015e). *How much physical activity do children need?* Retrieved from http://www.cdc.gov/physicalactivity/basics/children/index.htm

Centers for Disease Control and Prevention. (2015f). *HPV vaccine is recommended for boys.* Retrieved from http://www.cdc.gov/features/hpvvaccineboys/

Centers for Disease Control and Prevention. (2015g). Mental health surveillance among children — United States, 2005–2011. *Morbidity and Mortality Weekly Report, 62*(02), 1–35.

Centers for Disease Control and Prevention. (2015h). *Parent's guide to childhood immunization.* Retrieved from http://www.cdc.gov/vaccines/parents/tools/parents-guide/downloads/parents-guide-508.pdf

Centers for Disease Control and Prevention. (2015i). *PLAY Study findings (Project to Learn About ADHD in Youth).* Retrieved from http://www.cdc.gov/ncbddd/adhd/play2.html

Centers for Disease Control and Prevention. (2015j). *Sexual risk behaviors: HIV, STD, & teen pregnancy prevention.* Retrieved from http://www.cdc.gov/healthyyouth/sexualbehaviors/

Centers for Disease Control and Prevention. (2015k). *Suicide.* Retrieved from http://www.cdc.gov/violenceprevention/pdf/suicide-datasheet-a.pdf

Centers for Disease Control and Prevention. (2015l). *Teen vaccine coverage: 2014 National Immunization Survey-Teen (NIS-Teen).* Retrieved from http://www.cdc.gov/vaccines/who/teens/vaccination-coverage.html

Centers for Disease Control and Prevention. (2015m). *Understanding school violence.* Retrieved from http://www.cdc.gov/violenceprevention/pdf/school_violence_fact_sheet-a.pdf

Centers for Disease Control and Prevention. (2015n). *Youth suicide.* Retrieved from http://www.cdc.gov/violenceprevention/suicide/youth_suicide.html

Centers for Disease Control and Prevention. (2016a). *About teen pregnancy.* Retrieved from http://www.cdc.gov/teenpregnancy/about/

Centers for Disease Control and Prevention. (2016b). *Autism spectrum disorders: ASD.* Retrieved from http://www.cdc.gov/ncbddd/autism/data.html

Centers for Disease Control and Prevention. (2016c). *Distracted driving.* Retrieved from http://www.cdc.gov/motorvehiclesafety/distracted_driving/

Centers for Disease Control and Prevention. (2016d). *Facts about microcephaly.* Retrieved from http://www.cdc.gov/ncbddd/birthdefects/microcephaly.html

Centers for Disease Control and Prevention. (2016e). *Genital HPV infection - Fact sheet.* Retrieved from http://www.cdc.gov/std/hpv/stdfact-hpv.htm

Centers for Disease Control and Prevention. (2016f). *HIV among youth.* Retrieved from http://www.cdc.gov/hiv/group/age/youth/

Centers for Disease Control and Prevention. (2016g). *Lead.* Retrieved from http://www.cdc.gov/nceh/lead/

Centers for Disease Control and Prevention. (2016h). *Skin cancer.* Retrieved from http://www.cdc.gov/cancer/skin/basic_info/children.htm

Centers for Disease Control and Prevention. (2016i). *Symptoms, diagnosis, and treatment.* Retrieved from http://www.cdc.gov/zika/symptoms/

Centers for Disease Control and Prevention. (2016j). *Understanding the epidemic.* Retrieved from http://www.cdc.gov/drugoverdose/epidemic/index.html

Centers for Disease Control and Prevention. (2016k). *Youth and tobacco use.* Retrieved from http://www.cdc.gov/tobacco/data_statistics/fact_sheets/youth_data/tobacco_use/index.htm#background

Centers for Disease Control and Prevention. (2016l). *Zika and sexual transmission.* Retrieved from http://www.cdc.gov/zika/transmission/sexual-transmission.html

Centers for Disease Control and Prevention, Division of Nutrition and Physical Activity. (2007). *Does breastfeeding reduce the risk of pediatric overweight? Research to Practice Series No. 4.* Atlanta, GA: Author.

Central Intelligence Agency. (2014). *World fact book.* Retrieved from https://www.cia.gov/library/publications/the-world-factbook/rankorder/2223rank.html

Chaddock-Heyman, L., Hillman, C. H., Cohen, N. J., & Kramer, A. F. (2014). The relation of childhood physical activity to brain health, cognition, and scholastic achievement: III. The importance of physical activity and aerobic fitness for cognitive control and memory in children. *Monographs of the Society for Research in Child Development, 79*(4), 25–50. doi:10.1111/mono.12129

Chadwick, B. A., & Heaton, T. B. (1987). *Statistical handbook on the American family.* Phoenix, AZ: Oryx Press.

Chang, E. S., Greenberger, E., Chen, C., Heckhausen, J., & Farruggia, S. P. (2010). Nonparental adults as social resources in the transition to adulthood. *Journal of Research on Adolescence, 20*(4), 1065–1082. doi:10.1111/j.1532-7795.2010.00662.x

Chang, S., & Piacentini, J. (2002). Childhood obsessive-compulsive disorder and tic disorders. In D. T. Marsh & M. A. Fristad (Eds.),

Handbook of serious emotional disturbance (pp. 266–283). New York: Wiley.

Chaplin, T. M., & Aldao, A. (2013). Gender differences in emotion expression in children: A meta-analytic review. *Psychological Bulletin, 139*(4), 735–765.

Charles, C., Louv, R., Bodner, L., Guns, B., & Stahl, D. (2009). Children and nature 2009: A report on the movement to reconnect children to the natural world. *Children & Nature Network*. Retrieved from http://www.childrenandnature.org/downloads/CNNMovement2009.pdf

Charlesworth, L., Wood, J., & Viggiani, P. (2011). Middle childhood. In E. D. Hutchison (Ed.), *Dimensions of human behavior: The changing life course* (4th ed., pp. 175–226). Thousand Oaks, CA: Sage.

Chawarska, K., Lin, A., Paul, R., & Volkmar, F. (2007). Autism spectrum disorder in the second year: Stability and change in syndrome expression. *Journal of Child Psychology and Psychiatry, 48*(2), 128–138.

Chazan-Cohen, R., Raikes, H., Brooks-Gunn, J., Ayoub, C., Pan, B. A., Kisker, E. E., . . . Fuligni, A. S. (2009). Low-income children's school readiness: Parent contributions over the first five years. *Early Education and Development, 20*(6), 958–977. doi:10.1080/10409280903362402

Cheadle, J. E., Amato, P. R., & King, V. (2010). Patterns of nonresident father contact. *Demography, 47*(1), 205–225.

Chen, C., Greenberger, E., Farruggia, S., Bush, K., & Dong, Q. (2003). Beyond parents and peers: The role of important non-parental adults (VIPs) in adolescent development in China and the United States. *Psychology in the Schools, 40*(1), 35–50.

Cheng, J., & Monroe, M. C. (2012). Connection to nature: Children's affective attitude toward nature. *Environment and Behavior, 44*(1), 31–49.

Chess, S., & Thomas, A. (1999). *Goodness of fit: Clinical applications from infancy through adult life.* Philadelphia: Brunner/Mazel.

Chess, S., Thomas, A., & Birch, H. G. (1965). *Your child is a person: A psychological approach to childhood without guilt.* New York: Viking Press.

Chetty, R., Hendren, N., & Katz, L. F. (2015). The effects of exposure to better neighborhoods on children: New evidence from the Moving to Opportunity experiment. *National Bureau of Economic Research Working Paper #21156.* Retrieved from http://www.nber.org/papers/w21156.

Chew, S. L. (2006). Seldom in doubt but often wrong: Addressing tenacious student misconceptions. In D. S. Dunn & S. L. Chew (Eds.), *Best practices for teaching introduction to psychology* (pp. 211–223). Mahwah, NJ: Erlbaum.

Child Care Aware of America. (2013). *Child/staff ratios.* Retrieved from http://www.naccrra.org/about-child-care/state-child-care-licensing/child/staff-ratios

Child Life Council. (n.d.). *What is a child life specialist?* Retrieved from http://www.childlife.org/The%20Child%20Life%20Profession/

Child Trends. (2010). *High school dropout rates.* Retrieved from http://www.childtrendsdatabank.org/alphalist?q=node/162

Child Trends. (2012). *Births to unmarried women.* Retrieved from http://www.childtrendsdatabank.org/sites/default/files/75_Births_to_Unmarried_Women.pdf

Child Trends. (2013a). *High school dropout rates.* Retrieved from http://www.childtrends.org/?indicators=high-school-dropout-rates

Child Trends. (2013b). *Physical development and daily health.* Publication #2013-09. Bethesda, MD: Author.

Child Trends. (2014). *Unintentional injuries.* Retrieved from http://www.childtrends.org/wp-content/uploads/2014/10/122_Unintentional_Injuries.pdf

Child Trends. (2015a). *Births to unmarried women.* Bethesda, MD: Author.

Child Trends. (2015b). *Dating.* Retrieved from http://www.childtrends.org/?indicators=dating

Child Trends. (2015c). *Late or no prenatal care.* Retrieved from http://www.childtrends.org/wp-content/uploads/2014/07/25_Prenatal_Care.pdf

Child Welfare Information Gateway. (2015). *Child maltreatment 2013: Summary of key findings.* Washington, DC: U.S. Department of Health and Human Services, Children's Bureau.

Children's Defense Fund. (2015). *Child poverty in America, 2014: National analysis.* Retrieved from http://www.childrensdefense.org/library/poverty-report/child-poverty-in-america-2014.pdf

Choe, D., Olson, S. L., & Sameroff, A. J. (2013). The interplay of externalizing problems and physical and inductive discipline during childhood. *Developmental Psychology, 49*(11), 2029–2039. doi: 10.1037/a0032054

Chomsky, N. (1968). *Language and mind.* New York: Harcourt, Brace & World.

Chowdhury, R., Sinha, B., Sankar, M. J., Taneja, S., Bhandari, N., Rollins, N. . . . Martines, J. (2015). Breastfeeding and maternal health outcomes: A systematic review and meta-analysis. *Acta Paediatrica, 104*(Suppl 467), 96–113. doi:10.1111/apa.13102

Christakis, D. A., Garrison, M. M., Herrenkohl, T., Haggerty, K., Rivara, F. P., Zhou, C., & Liekweg, K. (2013). Modifying media content for preschool children: A randomized controlled trial. *Pediatrics, 131*(3), 431–438. doi:10.1542/peds.2012-1493

Christakis, D. A., & Zimmerman, F. J. (2007). Violent television viewing during preschool is associated with antisocial behavior during school age. *Pediatrics, 120*(5), 993–999.

Chye, T. T., Teng, T. K., Hao, T. H., & Seng, J. T. C. (2008). *The new art and science of pregnancy and childbirth: What you want to know from your obstetrician.* Hackensack, NJ: World Scientific.

Cianciolo, A. J., & Sternberg, R. J. (2004). *Intelligence: A brief history.* Malden, MA: Blackwell.

Cicchetti, D., & Toth, S. L. (2009). The past achievements and future promises of developmental psychopathology: The coming of age of a discipline. *Journal of Child Psychology and Psychiatry, 50*(1–2), 16–25.

Cillessen, A H. N. (2011). Sociometric methods. In K. H. Rubin, W. M. Bukowsi, & B. Laursen (Eds.), *Handbook of peer interactions, relationships, and groups* (pp. 82–99). New York: Guilford Press.

Cingel, D. P., & Krcmar, M. (2014). Understanding the experience of imaginary audience in a social media environment: Implications for adolescent development. *Journal of Media Psychology: Theories, Methods, and Applications, 26*(4), 155–160. doi:10.1027/1864-1105/a000124

Clark, C. (1969). Television and social controls: Some observation of the portrayal of ethnic minorities. *Television Quarterly, 9*(2), 18–22.

Clark, M. A., & Fox, M. K. (2009). Nutritional quality of the diets of U.S. public school children and the role of the school meal programs. *Journal of the American Dietetic Association, 109*(2 Supplement), S44–S56.

Clark, T. C., Lucassen, M. G., Bullen, P., Denny, S. J., Fleming, T. M., Robinson, E. M., & Rossen, F. V. (2014). The health and well-being of transgender high school students: Results from the New Zealand Adolescent Health Survey (Youth'12). *Journal of Adolescent Health, 55*(1), 93–99. doi:10.1016/j.jadohealth.2013.11.008

Clarke-Stewart, A., & Brentano, C. (2006). *Divorce: Causes and consequences.* New Haven, CT: Yale University Press.

Cleland, V., Crawford, D., Baur, L. A., Hume, C., Timperio, A., & Salmon, J. (2008). A prospective examination of children's time spent outdoors, objectively measured physical activity and overweight. *International Journal of Obesity, 32,* 1685–1693.

Coates, B., Pusser, H. E., & Goodman, I. (1976). The influence of "Sesame Street" and "Mister Rogers' Neighborhood" on children's social behavior in the preschool. *Child Development, 47*(1), 138–144.

Cobb, R. J., & Davila, J. (2009). Internal working models and change. In J. H. Obegi & E. Berant (Eds.), *Attachment theory and research in clinical work with adults* (pp. 209–233). New York: Guilford Press.

Coe, C. L., & Lubach, G. R. (2008). Fetal programming: Prenatal origins of health and illness. *Current Directions in Psychological Science, 17*(1), 36–41.

Cohen, G. J., & the American Academy of Pediatrics Committee on Psychosocial Aspects of Child and Family Health. (2002). Helping children and families deal with divorce and separation. *Pediatrics, 110,* 1019–1023.

Cohen, L. B., Chaput, H. H., & Cashon, C. H. (2002). A constructivist model of infant cognition. *Cognitive Development, 17*(3–4), 1323–1343.

Coie, J. D., Dodge, K. A., & Coppotelli, H. (1982). Dimensions and types of social status: A cross-age perspective. *Developmental Psychology, 18*(4), 557–570.

Cole, M., & Cagigas, X. E. (2010). Cognition. In M. H. Bornstein (Ed.), *Handbook of cultural developmental science* (pp. 127–142). New York: Psychology Press.

Coleman, M., Ganong, L. H., & Warzinik, K. (2007). *Family life in twentieth century America.* Westport, CT: Greenwood Press.

College Board. (2008). *2008 college bound seniors—Total group profile report.* Retrieved from http://professionals.collegeboard.com/profdownload/Total_Group_Report.pdf

College Board. (2013). *2013 SAT® report on college & career readiness.* New York: Author.

Collins, W. A., & Laursen, B. (2004). Parent-adolescent relationships and influences. In R. M. Lerner & L. Steinberg (Eds.), *Handbook of adolescent psychology* (2nd ed., pp. 331–361). Hoboken, NJ: Wiley.

Collins, W. L. (2011). A strengths-based support group to empower African American grandmothers raising grandchildren. *Social Work & Christianity, 38*(4), 453–466.

Colombo, J., & Mitchell, D. W. (2009). Infant visual habituation. *Neurobiology of Learning and Memory, 92*(2), 225–234.

Coltrane, S. (2004). Fathering. In M. Coleman & L. H. Ganong (Eds.), *Handbook of contemporary families* (pp. 224–243). Thousand Oaks, CA: Sage.

Community Renewal Team. (2013). *Grandparents raising grandchildren.* Retrieved from http://www.crtct.org/en/need-help/housing-a-shelters/grandparentgrandchildren

Compas, B. E., Banez, G. A., Malcarne, V., & Worsham, N. (1991). Perceived control and coping with stress: A developmental perspective. *Journal of Social Issues, 47*(4), 23–34.

Compas, B. E., Connor-Smith, J. K., Saltzman, H., Thomsen, A. H., & Wadsworth, M. E. (2001). Coping with stress during childhood and adolescence: Problems, progress, and potential in theory and research. *Psychological Bulletin, 127*, 87–127.

Compas, B. E., Jaser, S. S., Dunn, M. J., & Rodriguez, E. M. (2012). Coping with chronic illness in childhood and adolescence. *Annual Review of Clinical Psychology, 8*, 455–480. http://doi.org/10.1146/annurev-clinpsy-032511-143108

Comstock, G., & Scharrer, E. (2003). Meta-analyzing the controversy over television violence and aggression. In D. A. Gentile (Ed.), *Media violence and children* (pp. 205–226). Westport, CT: Praeger.

Conboy, B. T., & Kuhl, P. K. (2011). Impact of second-language experience in infancy: Brain measures of first- and second-language speech perception. *Developmental Science, 14*(2), 242–248.

Condon, E., Crepinsek, M., & Fox, M. (2009). School meals: Types of foods offered to and consumed by children at lunch and breakfast. *Journal of the American Dietetic Association, 109*(2), S67–S78.

Conway, J. M., Amel, E. L., & Gerwien, D. P. (2009). Teaching and learning in the social context: A meta-analysis of service learning's effects on academic, personal, social, and citizenship outcomes. *Teaching of Psychology, 36*(4), 233–245.

Cooley, C. H. (1964). *Human nature and the social order.* New York: Schocken Books. (Original work published in 1902 by Scribner)

Coontz, S. (2000). Historical perspectives on family diversity. In D. H. Demo, K. R. Allen, & M. A. Fine (Eds.), *Handbook of family diversity* (pp. 15–31). New York: Oxford University Press.

Coontz, S., & Folbre, N. (2002). *Marriage, poverty and public policy.* Retrieved from https://contemporaryfamilies.org/wp-content/uploads/2013/10/2002_Briefing_Coontz_Marriage-poverty-and-public-policy.pdf

Cooper, J. J. (2016). *California lawmakers vote to raise smoking, vaping age to 21.* Retrieved from http://abcnews.go.com/Health/wireStory/california-lawmakers-vote-raising-smoking-age-21-37538583

Cooper, S. M., McLoyd, V. C., Wood, D., & Hardaway, C. R. (2008). Racial discrimination and mental health. In S. M. Quintana & C. McKown (Eds.), *Handbook of race, racism, and the developing child* (pp. 278–312). Hoboken, NJ: Wiley.

Copeland, W., Shanahan, L., Miller, S., Costello, E., Angold, A., & Maughan, B. (2010). Outcomes of early pubertal timing in young women: A prospective population-based study. *American Journal of Psychiatry, 167*(10), 1218–1225.

Coplan, R. J., & Armer, M. (2007). A "multitude" of solitude: A closer look at social withdrawal and nonsocial play in early childhood. *Child Development Perspectives, 1*(1), 26–32.

Correll, S. J. (2004). Constraints into preferences: Gender, status, and emerging career aspirations. *American Sociological Review, 69*(1), 93–113.

Cortes, K. I., & Kochenderfer-Ladd, B. (2014). To tell or not to tell: What influences children's decisions to report bullying to their teachers? *School Psychology Quarterly, 29*(3), 336–348.

Costello, J., & Angold, A. (2011). Contributions from epidemiology. In J. Garber, P. R. Costanzo, & T. J. Strauman (Eds.), *Depression in adolescent girls: Science and prevention* (pp. 25–34). New York: Guilford Press.

Côté, S., Tremblay, R. E., Nagin, D. S., Zoccolillo, M., & Vitaro, F. (2002). Childhood behavioral profiles leading to adolescent conduct disorder: Risk trajectories for boys and girls. *American Academy of Child & Adolescent Psychiatry, 41*(9), 1086–1094.

Côté, S. M., Vaillancourt, T., LeBlanc, J. C., Nagin, D. S., & Tremblay, R. E. (2006). The development of physical aggression from toddlerhood to pre-adolescence: A nationwide longitudinal study of Canadian children. *Journal of Abnormal Child Psychology, 34*(1), 71–85.

Courage, M. L., & Howe, M. L. (2004). Advances in early memory development research: Insights about the dark side of the moon. *Developmental Review, 24*(1), 6–32.

Courage, M. L., Reynolds, G. D., & Richards, J. E. (2006). Infants' attention to patterned stimuli: Developmental change from 3 to 12 months of age. *Child Development, 77*(3), 680–695.

Courtney, M. E. (2009). The difficult transition to adulthood for foster youth in the US: Implications for the state as corporate parent. *Society for Research in Child Development Social Policy Report, 23*(1), 3–11, 14–18.

Cox, K. (2016). *Hands-on learning activities & printables to inspire young minds.* Retrieved from www.prekinders.com

Cox, M., Paley, B., Payne, C. C., & Burchinal, M. (1999). The transition to parenthood: Marital conflict and withdrawal and parent-infant interactions. In M. J. Cox & J. Brooks-Gunn (Eds.), *Conflict and cohesion in families: Causes and consequences* (pp. 87–104). Mahwah, NJ: Erlbaum.

Coyne, S. M., Linder, J. R., Rasmussen, E. E., Nelson, D. A., & Collier, K. M. (2014). It's a bird! It's a plane! It's a gender stereotype!: Longitudinal associations between superhero viewing and gender stereotyped play. *Sex Roles, 70*(9–10), 416–430. doi:10.1007/s11199-014-0374-8

Crain, W. (2005). *Theories of development: Concepts and applications* (5th ed.). Upper Saddle River, NJ: Pearson Prentice Hall.

Crawford, J. (1995). *Bilingual education: History, politics, theory and practice.* Los Angeles: Bilingual Educational Services.

Crawford, M., & Kaufman, M. R. (2008). Sex trafficking in Nepal: Survivor characteristics and long-term outcomes. *Violence Against Women, 14*(8), 905–916.

Crean, H. F. (2008). Conflict in the Latino parent-youth dyad: The role of emotional support from the opposite parent. *Journal of Family Psychology, 22*(3), 484–493.

Crespo, C. J., Smit, E., Troiano, R. P., Bartlett, S. J., Macera, C. A., & Andersen, R. E. (2001). Television watching, energy intake, and obesity in US children: Results from the third National Health and Nutrition Examination Survey, 1988–1994. *Archives of Pediatrics and Adolescent Medicine, 155*(3), 360–365.

Creswell, K. G., Wright, A. G., Toxel, W. M., Ferrell, R. E., Flory, J. D., & Manuck, S. B. (2015). OXTR polymorphism predicts social relationships through its effects on social temperament. *Social Cognitive and Affective Neuroscience, 10*(6). 869–876. doi: 10.1093/scan/nsu132

Crick, N. R., Grotpeter, J. K., & Bigbee, M. A. (2002). Relationally and physically aggressive children's intent attributions and feelings of distress for relational and instrumental peer provocations. *Child Development, 73*(4), 1134–1142.

Criss, M. M., & Shaw, D. S. (2005). Sibling relationships as contexts for delinquency training in low-income families. *Journal of Family Psychology, 19*(4), 592–600.

Critchley, C. R., & Sanson, A. V. (2006). Is parent disciplinary behavior enduring or situational? A multilevel modeling investigation of individual and contextual influences on power assertive and inductive reasoning behaviors. *Journal of Applied Developmental Psychology, 27*(4), 370–388.

Crocetti, E., Branje, S., Rubini, M., Koot, H. M., & Meeus, W. (2016). Identity processes and parent-child and sibling relationships in adolescence: A five-wave multi-informant longitudinal study. *Child Development,* 1–19.

Crocetti, E., Rubini, M., & Meeus, W. (2008). Capturing the dynamics of identity formation in various ethnic groups: Development and validation of a three-dimensional model. *Journal of Adolescence, 31*(2), 207–222.

Crockenberg, S., & Leerkes, E. (2003). Infant negative emotionality, caregiving, and family relationships. In A. C. Crouter & A. Booth (Eds.), *Children's influence on family dynamics* (pp. 57–78). Mahwah, NJ: Erlbaum.

Cromer, L., & Goldsmith, R. (2010). Child sexual abuse myths: Attitudes, beliefs, and individual differences. *Journal of Child Sexual Abuse, 19*(6), 618–647.

Cromwell, S. (1998). *The bilingual education debate: Part I.* Retrieved from http://www.education-world.com/a_curr/curr047.shtml

Cross, J., & Fletcher, K. L. (2009). The challenge of adolescent crowd research: Defining the crowd. *Journal of Youth and Adolescence, 38*(6), 747–764.

Crosson-Tower, C. (2003). *The role of educators in preventing and responding to child abuse and neglect.* Washington, DC: U.S. Department of Health and Human Services, Office on Child Abuse and Neglect.

Csikszentmihalyi, M. (1998). Reflections on the field. *Roeper Review: A Journal on Gifted Education, 21*(1), 80–81.

Cui, L., Morris, A. S., Criss, M. M., Houltberg, B. J., & Silk, J. S. (2014). Parental psychological control and adolescent adjustment: The role of adolescent emotion regulation. *Parenting, Science and Practice, 14*(1), 47–67. doi.org/10.1080/15295192.2014.880018

Cullen, F. T., Blevins, K. R., Trager, J. S., & Gendreau, P. (2005). The rise and fall of boot camps: A case study in common-sense corrections. *Journal of Offender Rehabilitation, 40*(3/4), 53–70.

Cummings, C. M., Caporino, N. E., & Kendall, P. C. (2014). Comorbidity of anxiety and depression in children and adolescents: 20 years after. *Psychological Bulletin, 140*(3), 816–845. doi: 10.1037/a0034733

Cummings, E. M., Goeke-Morey, M., & Papp, L. (2003). Children's responses to everyday marital conflict tactics in the home. *Child Development, 74*, 1918–1929.

Cunningham, F. G., Bangdiwala, S., Brown, S. S., Dean, T. M., Frederiksen, M., Rowland Hogue, C. J., . . . Zimmet, S. C. (2010).

National Institutes of Health Consensus Development Conference Statement: Vaginal birth after cesarean: New insights. *Obstetrics & Gynecology, 115*(6), 1279–1295.

Cunningham, F. G., Leveno, K. J., Bloom, S. L., Spong, C. Y., Dashe, J. S., Hoffman, B. L., ... Sheffield, J. S. (2014). *Williams Obstetrics* (24th ed.). New York: McGraw Hill.

Cunningham, J., & Scarlett, W. G. (2004). Children's humor. In W. G. Scarlett, S. Naudeau, D. Salonius-Pasternak, & I. Ponte (Eds.), *Children's play* (pp. 93–109). Thousand Oaks, CA: Sage.

Curry, P., De Amicis, L., & Gilligan, R. (2011). *The effect of cooperative learning on inter-ethnic relations in schools.* Paper presented at the 2011 Society for Research on Educational Effectiveness Conference, Washington, DC.

Curtis, N. M., Ronan, K. R., & Borduin, C. M. (2004). Multisystemic treatment: A meta-analysis of outcome studies. *Journal of Family Psychology, 18*(3), 411–419.

Curtiss, S. (1977). *Genie: A psycholinguistic study of a modern day "wild child."* New York: Academic Press.

Cvencek, D., Meltzoff, A. N., & Greenwald, A. G. (2011). Math-gender stereotypes in elementary school children. *Child Development, 82*(3), 766–779.

D'Augelli, A. R. (2003). Lesbian and bisexual female youth aged 14 to 21: Developmental challenges and victimization experiences. *Journal of Lesbian Studies, 7*(4), 9–29.

Dahl, A., & Kim, L. (2014). Why is it bad to make a mess? Preschoolers' conceptions of pragmatic norms. *Cognitive Development, 32,* 12–22. doi:10.1016/j.cogdev.2014.05.004

Dahl, G. B., & Lochner, L. (2008). *The impact of family income on child achievement: Evidence from the Earned Income Tax Credit* (NBER Working Paper No. 14599). Cambridge, MA: National Bureau of Economic Research.

Dahlgreen, W. (2015). *What do emoji really mean?* Retrieved from https://yougov.co.uk/news/2015/06/10/are-we-all-using-emojis-wrong/

Dai, D. Y. (2006). There is more to aptitude than cognitive capacities: Comment. *American Psychologist, 61*(7), 723–724.

Damon, W. (2006). Socialization and individuation. In G. Handel (Ed.), *Childhood socialization* (pp. 3–9). New Brunswick, NJ: Aldine Transaction.

Daniel, E., & Balog, L. F. (2009). Early female puberty: A review of research on etiology and implications. *Health Educator, 41*(2), 47–53.

Danner, F., & Phillips, B. (2008). Adolescent sleep, school start times, and teen motor vehicle crashes. *Journal of Clinical Sleep Medicine, 4*(6), 533–535.

Darke, K., Clewell, B., & Sevo, R. (2002). Meeting the challenge: The impact of the National Science Foundation's program for women and girls. *Journal of Women and Minorities in Science and Engineering, 8*(3–4), 285–303.

Darkness to Light. (2015). *Child sexual abuse statistics: Risk factors.* Retrieved from http://www.d2l.org/atf/cf/%7B64AF78C4-5EB8-45AA-BC28-F7EE2B581919%7D/Statistics_4_Risk_Factors.pdf

Darley, J. M., & Batson, C. (1973). "From Jerusalem to Jericho": A study of situational and dispositional variables in helping behavior. *Journal of Personality and Social Psychology, 27*(1), 100–108.

Darling, N., Cumsille, P., & Martínez, M. L. (2008). Individual differences in adolescents' beliefs about the legitimacy of parental authority and their own obligation to obey: A longitudinal investigation. *Child Development, 79*(4), 1103–1118.

Darling, N., Hamilton, S. F., & Shaver, K. H. (2003). Relationships outside the family: Unrelated adults. In G. R. Adams & M. D. Berzonsky (Eds.), *Blackwell handbook of adolescence* (pp. 349–370). Malden, MA: Blackwell.

Darrah, J., Law, M., & Pollock, N. (2001). Innovations in practice. Family-centered functional therapy: A choice for children with motor dysfunction. *Infants & Young Children: An Interdisciplinary Journal of Early Childhood Intervention, 13*(4), 79–87.

Darwin, C. R. (1859). *On the origin of species.* London: John Murray.

Darwin, C. R. (1877). A biographical sketch of an infant. *Mind: A Quarterly Review of Psychology and Philosophy, 2*(7), 285–294.

David, J. L. (2008). What research says about grade retention. *Educational Leadership, 65*(6), 83–84.

Davidov, M., Grusec, J. E., & Wolfe, J. L. (2012). Mother's knowledge of their children's evaluations of discipline: The role of type of discipline and misdeed, and parenting practices. *Merrill-Palmer Quarterly, 58*(3), 314–340. doi:10.1353/mpq.2012.0018

Davidson, T. (2003). Developmental coordination disorder. In E. Thackery & M. Harris (Eds.), *Gale Encyclopedia of Mental Disorders* (Volume 2, pp. 301–303). Detroit, MI: Thomson.

Davidson Institute for Talent Development. (2004). *Gifted-friendly parenting strategies.* Retrieved from http://www.davidsongifted.org/db/Articles_id_10284.aspx

Davies, G., Tenesa, A., Payton, A., Yang, J., Harris, S. E., Liewald, D., . . . Deary, I. J. (2011). Genome-wide association studies establish that human intelligence is highly heritable and polygenic. *Molecular Psychiatry, 16*(10), 996–1005. doi:10.1038/mp.2011.85

Davies, P. G., Spencer, S. J., Quinn, D. M., & Gerhardstein, R. (2002). Consuming images: How television commercials that elicit stereotype threat can restrain women academically and professionally. *Personality and Social Psychology Bulletin, 28*(12), 1615–1628.

Davis, B. E., Moon, R. Y., Sachs, H. C., & Ottolini, M. C. (1998). Effects of sleep position on infant motor development. *Pediatrics, 102*(5), 1135–1140.

Davis, B. G. (1993). *Tools for teaching.* San Francisco: Jossey-Bass.

Davis, E. P., & Sandman, C. A. (2010). The timing of prenatal exposure to maternal cortisol and psychosocial stress is associated with human infant cognitive development. *Child Development, 81*(1), 131–148.

Davis, E. P., Glynn, L. M., Waffarn, F., & Sandman, C. A. (2011). Prenatal maternal stress programs infant stress regulation. *Journal of Child Psychology and Psychiatry, 52*(2), 119–129.

Davis, J. H., & Apuzzo, M. (2016). U.S. directs public schools to allow transgender access to restrooms. *The New York Times.* Retrieved from http://www.nytimes.com/2016/05/13/us/politics/obama-administration-to-issue-decree-on-transgender-access-to-school-restrooms.html?_r=0

Davis, L., Mohay, H., & Edwards, H. (2003). Mothers' involvement in caring for their premature infants: An historical overview. *Journal of Advanced Nursing, 42*(6), 578–586.

Davis-Kean, P. E., Jager, J., & Collins, W. A. (2009). The self in action: An emerging link between self-beliefs and behaviors in middle childhood. *Child Development Perspectives, 3*(3), 184–188.

Daxinger, L., & Whitelaw, E. (2012). Understanding transgenerational epigenetic inheritance via the gametes in mammals. *Nature Reviews Genetics, 13*(3), 153–162. doi: 10.1038/nrg3188

Day, N. L., Goldschmidt, L., & Thomas, C. A. (2006). Prenatal marijuana exposure contributes to the prediction of marijuana use at age 14. *Addiction, 101*(9), 1313–1322.

Dayton, C. J., Walsh, T. B., Oh, W., & Volling, B. (2015). Hush now baby: Mothers' and fathers' strategies for soothing their infants and associated parenting outcomes. *Journal of Pediatric Health Care, 29*(2), 145–155.

de Baulny, H. O., Abadie, V., Feillet, F., & de Parscau, L. (2007). Management of phenylketonuria and hyperphenylalaninemia. *Journal of Nutrition, 137,* 1561S–1563S.

de Bruyn, E. H., & Cillessen, A. N. (2006). Popularity in early adolescence: Prosocial and antisocial subtypes. *Journal of Adolescent Research, 21*(6), 607–627.

de Cos, P. L. (2001). *California's public schools: What experts say about their mission and functions.* Sacramento, CA: California Research Bureau.

De Genna, N. M., Cornelius, M. D., Goldschmidt, L., & Day, N. L. (2015). Maternal age and trajectories of cannabis use. *Drug & Alcohol Dependence, 156,* 199–206. doi:10.1016/j.drugalcdep.2015.09.014

De Goede, I. A., Branje, S. T., & Meeus, W. J. (2009). Developmental changes in adolescents' perceptions of relationships with their parents. *Journal of Youth and Adolescence, 38*(1), 75–88.

de Groot, M. J., Hoeksma, M., Blau, N., Reijngoud, D. J., & van Spronsen, F. J. (2010). Pathogenesis of cognitive dysfunction in phenylketonuria: Review of hypotheses. *Molecular Genetics and Metabolism, 99,* S86–S89.

de Haan, M. (2007). *Infant EEG and event-related potentials.* New York: Psychology Press.

De Houwer, A., Bornstein, M. H., & Putnick, D. L. (2014). A bilingual-monolingual comparison of young children's vocabulary size: Evidence from comprehension and production. *Applied Psycholinguistics, 35*(6), 1189–1211. doi:10.1017/S0142716412000744

Dearing, E., McCartney, K., & Taylor, B. A. (2001). Change in family income-to-needs matters more for children with less. *Child Development, 72*(6), 1779–1793.

DeCasper, A. J., & Spence, M. J. (1986). Prenatal maternal speech influences newborns' perception of speech sounds. *Infant Behavior & Development, 19*(2), 133–150.

deLara, E. W. (2012). Why adolescents don't disclose incidents of bullying and harassment. *Journal of School Violence, 11*(4), 288–305.

DeLay, D., Laursen, B., Bukowski, W. M., Kerr, M., & Stattin, H. (2016). Adolescent friend similarity on alcohol abuse as a function of participation in romantic relationships: Sometimes a new love comes between old friends. *Developmental Psychology, 52*(1), 117–129. doi:10.1037/a0039882

DeLeersnyder, J., Boiger, M., & Mesquita, B. (2013). Cultural regulation of emotion: Individual, relational and structural sources. *Frontiers of Psychology, 4*(Article 55). doi:10.3389/fpsyg.2013.00055

DeLeersnyder, J., Mesquita, B., & Kim H. (2011). Where do my emotions belong? A study of immigrants' emotional acculturation. *Personality and Social Psychology Bulletin, 37,* 451–463.

DeLoache, J. S., Chiong, C., Sherman, K., Islan, N., Vanderborght, M., Troseth, G. L., . . . O'Doherty, K. (2010). Do babies learn from baby media? *Psychological Science, 21*(11), 1570–1574.

DeLoache, J. S., & Gottlieb, A. (2000). *A world of babies.* New York: Cambridge University Press.

Demaray, M. K., & Malecki, C. K. (2003). Perceptions of the frequency and importance of social support by students classified as victims, bullies, and bully/victims in an urban middle school. *School Psychology Review, 32*(3), 471–489.

Demetriou, A., Christou, C., Spanoudis, G., & Platsidou, M. (2002). The development of mental processing: Efficiency, working memory, and thinking. *Monographs of the Society for Research in Child Development, 67*(1, Serial No. 268).

Demir, M., & Urberg, K. A. (2004). Friendship and adjustment among adolescents. *Journal of Experimental Child Psychology, 88*(1), 68–82.

Demuth, K. (1990). Subject, topic, and Sesotho passive. *Journal of Child Language, 17*(1), 67–84.

Denham, S. A., Renwick, S. M., & Holt, R. W. (1991). Working and playing together: Predictions of preschool social-emotional competence from mother-child interaction. *Child Development, 62*(2), 242–249.

Denney, J. M., Culhane, J. F., & Goldenberg, R. L. (2008). Prevention of preterm birth. *Women's Health, 4*(6), 625–638.

Dennis, C. (2002). Breastfeeding initiation and duration: A 1990-2000 literature review. *Journal of Obstetric, Gynecologic & Neonatal Nursing, 31*(1), 12–32. doi:10.1111/j.1552-6909.2002.tb00019.x

Dennissen, J. J. A., Asendorpf, J. B., & van Aken, M. A. G. (2008). Childhood personality predicts long-term trajectories of shyness and aggressiveness in the context of demographic transitions in emerging adulthood. *Journal of Personality, 76*(1), 67–99.

Deoni, S. C., Mercure, E., Blasi, A., Gasston, D., Thomson, A., Johnson, M., . . . Murphy, D. G. (2011). Mapping infant brain myelination with magnetic resonance imaging. *Journal of Neuroscience, 31*(2), 2106–2110.

Deoni, S. L., O'Muircheartaigh, J., Elison, J. T., Walker, L., Doernberg, E., Waskiewicz, N., . . . Jumbe, N. L. (2016). White matter maturation profiles through early childhood predict general cognitive ability. *Brain Structure & Function, 221*(2), 1189–1203. doi:10.1007/s00429-014-0947-x

Dersch, C. A., & Munsch, J. (1999). Male victims of sexual abuse: An analysis of substantiation of Child Protective Services reports. *Journal of Child Sexual Abuse, 8*(1), 27–48.

Desmarais, C., Sylvestre, A., Meyer, F., Bairati, I., & Rouleau, N. (2008). Systematic review of the literature on characteristics of late-talking toddlers. *International Journal of Language & Communication Disorders, 43*(4), 361–389.

Desrochers, J. E., & Houck, G. (2013). *Depression in children and adolescents: Guidelines for school practice.* Silver Spring, MD, & Bethesda, MD: National Association of School Nurses & National Association of School Psychologists.

Desrochers, S. (2008). From Piaget to specific Genevan developmental models. *Child Development Perspectives, 2*(1), 7–12.

Detterman, D. K., & Thompson, L. A. (1997). What is so special about special education? *American Psychologist, 52*(10), 1082–1090.

Diamond, A. (2006). The early development of executive functions. In E. Bialystok & F. I. M. Craik (Eds.), *Lifespan cognition: Mechanisms of change* (pp. 70–95). Oxford, UK: Oxford University Press.

Diamond, A., Barnett, W., Thomas, J., & Munro, S. (2007). Preschool program improves cognitive control. *Science, 318*(5855), 1387–1388. doi:10.1126/science.1151148

Diamond, L. M. (2006). What we got wrong about sexual identity development: Unexpected findings from a longitudinal study of young women. In A. M. Omoto & H. S. Kurtzman (Eds.), *Sexual orientation and mental health: Examining identity and development in lesbian, gay, and bisexual people* (pp. 73–94). Washington, DC: American Psychological Association.

Diamond, M. (2013). Transsexuality among twins: Identity, concordance, transition, rearing and orientation. *International Journal of Transgenderism, 14*(1), 24–38.

Diao, F., & Sundar, S. S. (2004). Orienting response and memory for web advertisements: Exploring effects of pop-up window and animation. *Communication Research, 31*, 537–567.

Dick, D. M., & Rose, R. J. (2004). Behavior genetics: What's new? What's next? In J. Lerner & A. E. Alberts (Eds.), *Current directions in developmental psychology* (pp. 3–10). Upper Saddle River, NJ: Pearson Prentice Hall.

Diego, M. A., Hernandez-Reif, M., Field, T., Friedman, L., & Shaw, K. (2001). HIV adolescents show improved immune function following massage therapy. *International Journal of Neuroscience, 106*, 35–45.

DiFiori, J. P., Benjamin, H. J., Brenner, J., Gregory, A., Jayanthi, N., Landry, G. L., & Luke, A. (2014). Overuse injuries and burnout in youth sports: A position statement from the American Medical Society for Sports Medicine. *Clinical Journal of Sports Medicine, 24*(1), 3–20.

Dilworth-Bart, J. E., Khurshid, A., & Vandell, D. L. (2007). Do maternal stress and home environment mediate the relation between early income-to-need and 54-months attentional abilities? *Infant and Child Development, 16*(5), 525–552.

Dingfelder, S. F. (2005). Fighting children's fears, fast. *Monitor on Psychology, 36*(7), 90.

Diorio, J., & Meaney, M. J. (2007). Maternal programming of defensive responses through sustained effects on gene expression. *Journal of Psychiatry and Neuroscience, 32*(4), 275–284.

DiPietro, J. A., Bornstein, M. H., Costigan, K. A., Pressman, E. K., Hahn, C., Painter, K., . . . Yi, L. J. (2002). What does fetal movement predict about behavior during the first two years of life? *Developmental Psychobiology, 40*(4), 358–371.

DiPietro, J. A., Caulfield, L., Costigan, K. A., Merialdi, M., Nguyen, R. H. N., Zavaleta, N., & Gurewitsch, E. D. (2004). Fetal neurobehavioral development: A tale of two cities. *Developmental Psychology, 40*(3), 445–456.

Dishion, T. J., & Owen, L. D. (2002). A longitudinal analysis of friendships and substance use: Bidirectional influence from adolescence to adulthood. *Developmental Psychology, 38*(4), 480–491.

Dittmann, M. (2005). Adolescent development and severity of criminal punishment. *Monitor on Psychology, 36*(6), 28. Retrieved from http://www.apa.org/monitor/jun05/adolescent.aspx

Divorce Statistics. (2012). *Divorce statistics and divorce rate in the USA.* Retrieved from http://www.divorcestatistics.info/divorce-statistics-and-divorce-rate-in-the-usa.html

Dodge, K. A., Coie, J. D., & Lynam, D. (2006). Aggression and antisocial behavior in youth. In N. Eisenberg, W. Damon, & R. M. Lerner (Eds.), *Handbook of childhood psychology: Vol. 3. Social, emotional and personality development* (6th ed., pp. 719–788). Hoboken, NJ: John Wiley & Sons.

Dohnt, H. K., & Tiggemann, M. (2006). Body image concerns in young girls: The role of peers and media prior to adolescence. *Journal of Youth and Adolescence, 35*(2), 141–151.

Dombrowski, S. C., Noonan, K., & Martin, R. P. (2007). Low birth weight and cognitive outcomes: Evidence for a gradient relationship in an urban, poor, African American birth cohort. *School Psychology Quarterly, 22*(1), 26–43.

Donat, D. J. (2006). Reading their way: A balanced approach that increases achievement. *Reading & Writing Quarterly, 22*(4), 305–323.

Donnellan, M., Trzesniewski, K., Conger, K., & Conger, R. (2007). A three-wave longitudinal study of self-evaluations during young adulthood. *Journal of Research in Personality, 41*(2), 453–472.

Doris, J. M. (2002). *Lack of character: Personality and moral behavior.* New York: Cambridge University Press.

Dowling, E., & Elliott, D. (2012). Promoting positive outcomes for children experiencing change in family relationships. In S. Roffey (Ed.), *Positive relationships: Evidence based practice across the world* (pp. 109–126). New York: Springer Science and Business Media.

Downey, G., Lebolt, A., Rincón, C., & Freitas, A. L. (1998). Rejection sensitivity and children's interpersonal difficulties. *Child Development, 69*(4), 1074–1091.

Dozier, M., Zeanah, C. H., & Bernard, K. (2013). Infants and toddlers in foster care. *Child Development Perspectives, 7*(3), 166–171. doi:10.1111/cdep.12033

Dr. Seuss Enterprises. (n.d.) Biography. Retrieved from http://www.seussville.com/#/author

Drewes, A. A. (2005). Play in selected cultures: Diversity and universality. In E. Gil & A. A. Drewes (Eds.), *Cultural issues in play therapy* (pp. 26–71). New York: Guilford Press.

Drews, F. A., Yazdani, H., Godfrey, C. N., Cooper, J. M., & Strayer, D. L. (2009). Text messaging during simulated driving. *Human Factors, 51*(5), 762–770.

Drouin, M., & Davis, C. (2009). R u txting? Is the use of text speak hurting your literacy? *Journal of Literacy Research, 41*(1), 46–67.

DuBois, D. L. (2007). Effectiveness of mentoring program practices. Alexandria, VA: MENTOR.

DuBois, D. L., & Karcher, M. J. (2013). Youth mentoring in contemporary perspective. In D. L. DuBois & M. J. Karcher (Eds.), *Handbook of youth mentoring* (pp. 3–14). Thousand Oaks, CA: Sage.

DuBois, D. L., Holloway, B. E., Valentine, J. C., & Cooper, H. (2002). Effectiveness of mentoring programs for youth: A meta-analytic review. *American Journal of Community Psychology, 30*(2), 157–197.

DuBois, D. L., & Silverthorn, N. (2005). Characteristics of natural mentoring relationships and adolescent adjustment: Evidence from a national study. *Journal of Primary Prevention, 26*(2), 69–92.

Duckworth, A. L., Quinn, P. D., & Tsukayama, E. (2012). What No Child Left Behind leaves behind: The roles of IQ and self-control in predicting standardized achievement test scores and report card grades. *Journal* of *Educational Psychology, 104*(2), 439–451. doi:10.1037/a0026280

Duckworth, A. L., Quinn, P. D., Lynam, D. R., Loeber, R., & Stouthamer-Loeber, M. (2011). Role of test motivation in intelligence testing. *Proceedings of The National Academy of Sciences of the United States of America, 108*(19), 7716–7720. doi:10.1073/pnas.1018601108

Duckworth, A. L., & Seligman, M. E. P. (2005). Self-discipline outdoes IQ in predicting academic performance of adolescents. *Psychological Science, 16*(12), 939–944.

Duff, F. J., & Clarke, P. J. (2011). Practitioner review: Reading disorders: What are the effective interventions and how should they be implemented and evaluated? *Journal of Child Psychology and Psychiatry, 52*(1), 3–12.

Duffy, P. M. (2014). *Parenting your delinquent, defiant, or out-of-control teen.* Oakland, CA: New Harbinger Publications.

Dumontheil, I. (2014). Development of abstract thinking during childhood and adolescence: The role of rostrolateral prefrontal cortex. *Developmental Cognitive Neuroscience, 10*, 57–76. doi:10.1016/j.dcn.2014.07.009

Duncan, G. J., Huston, A. C., & Weisner, T. S. (2007). *Higher ground: New hope for the working poor and their children.* New York: Russell Sage.

Duncan, R. M., & Cheyne, J. A. (2002). Private speech in young adults: Task difficulty, self-regulation, and psychological predication. *Cognitive Development, 16*, 889–906.

Duncan, S. W. (1994). Economic impact of divorce on children's development: Current findings and policy implications. *Journal of Clinical Child Psychology, 23*, 444–457.

Dunifon, R. (2013). The influence of grandparents on the lives of children and adolescents. *Child Development Perspectives, 7*(1), 55–60.

Dunn, J. (2002). The adjustment of children in stepfamilies: Lessons from community studies. *Child and Adolescent Mental Health, 7*(4), 154–161.

Dunn, J. (2004a). Annotation: Children's relationships with their nonresident fathers. *Journal of Child Psychology & Psychiatry & Allied Disciplines, 45*(4), 659–671.

Dunn, J. (2004b). *Children's friendships.* Malden, MA: Blackwell.

Dunn, J. (2005). Naturalistic observation of children and their families. In S. Greene & D. Hogan (Eds.), *Researching children's experience: Methods and approaches* (pp. 87–101). Thousand Oaks, CA: Sage.

Dunn, J., Cheng, H., O'Connor, T. G., & Bridges, L. (2004). Children's perspectives on their relationships with their nonresident fathers: Influences, outcomes and implications. *Journal of Child Psychology and Psychiatry, 45*(3), 553–566.

Dunn, J., Fergusson, E., & Maughan, B. (2006). Grandparents, grandchildren, and family change. In A. Clarke-Stewart & J. Dunn (Eds.), *Families count* (pp. 299–318). New York: Cambridge University Press.

Dupler, D. (2014). Psychophysiology. In L. J. Fundukian (Ed.), *The Gale encyclopedia of alternative medicine, Vol. 3* (4th ed., pp. 1982–1984). Farmington Hills, MI: Gale.

Dush, C. K., Taylor, M. G., & Kroeger, R. A. (2008). Marital happiness and psychological well-being across the life course. *Family Relations, 57*(2), 211–226. doi:10.1111/j.1741-3729.2008.00495.x

Dutra, L. M., & Glantz, S. A. (2014). Electronic cigarettes and conventional cigarette use

among U.S. adolescents: A cross-sectional study. *JAMA Pediatrics, 168*(7), 610–617.

Dutton, S. E. (2001). Urban youth development—Broadway style: Using theatre and group work as vehicles for positive youth development. *Social Work with Groups, 23*(4), 39–58.

Duvander, A., & Andersson, G. (2006). Gender equality and fertility in Sweden: A study on the impact of the father's uptake of parental leave on continued childbearing. *Marriage and Family Review, 39*(1), 121–142.

Dwairy, M. (2004). Individuation among Bedouin versus urban Arab adolescents: Ethnic and gender differences. *Cultural Diversity and Ethnic Minority Psychology, 10*(4), 340–350. doi:10.1037/1099-9809.10.4.340

Dyer, S., & Moneta, G. B. (2006). Frequency of parallel, associate, and cooperative play in British children of different socioeconomic status. *Social Behavior and Personality, 34*(5), 587–592.

Eckerman, C. O., & Didow, S. M. (1996). Nonverbal imitation and toddlers' mastery of verbal means of achieving coordinated action. *Developmental Psychology, 32*(1), 141–152.

Eckerman, C. O., & Peterman, K. (2001). Peers and infant social/communicative development. In G. Bremner & A. Fogel (Eds.), *Blackwell handbook of infant development* (pp. 326–350). Malden, MA: Blackwell.

Eckstein, D., Aycock, K. J., Sperber, M. A., McDonald, J., Van Wiesner, V., Watts, R. E., & Ginsburg, P. (2010). A review of 200 birth-order studies: Lifestyle characteristics. *Journal of Individual Psychology, 66*(4), 408–434.

Edelson, M. G. (2013). Why have all the boys gone? Gender differences in prosecution acceptance of child sexual abuse cases. *Sexual Abuse: Journal of Research and Treatment, 25*(5), 461–481.

Edin, K., & Kefalas, M. (2005). *Promises I can keep: Why poor women put motherhood before marriage.* Berkeley and Los Angeles: University of California Press.

Education Week. (2004). *Reading.* Retrieved from http://www.edweek.org/rc/issues/reading/

Egeghy, P. P., Sheldon, D. M., Stout, E. A., Cohen-Hubal, N. S., Tulve, L. J., Melnyk, M. K., . . . Coan, A. (2007). *Important exposure factors for children: An analysis of laboratory and observational field data characterizing cumulative exposure to pesticides* (EPA Report 600/R-07/013). Washington, DC: Environmental Protection Agency.

Egger, H. (2009). Toddler with temper tantrums: A careful assessment of a dysregulated preschool child. In C. A. Galanter & P. S. Jensen (Eds.), *DSM-IV-TR casebook and treatment guide for child mental health* (pp. 365–384). Arlington, VA: American Psychiatric Publishing.

Ehrenberg, M., Regev, R., Lazinski, M., Behrman, L. J., & Zimmerman, J. (2014). Adjustment to divorce for children. In L. Grossman & S. Walfish (Eds.), *Translating psychological research into practice* (pp. 1–7). New York: Springer.

Eigsti, I., Zayas, V., Mischel, W., Shoda, Y., Ayduk, O., Dadlani, M. B., . . . Casey, B. J. (2006). Predicting cognitive control from preschool to late adolescence and young adulthood. *Psychological Science, 17*(6), 478–484.

Eime, R. M., Young, J. A., Harvey, J. T., Charity, M. J., & Payne, W. R. (2013). A systematic review of the psychological and social benefits of participation in sport for children and adolescents: Informing development of a conceptual model of health through sport. *The International Journal of Behavioral Nutrition and Physical Activity, 10*, 1–21. doi: 10.1186/1479-5868-10-98.

Eisenberg, N., Hofer, C., Spinrad, T. L., Gershoff, E. T., Valiente, C., Losoya, S. H., . . . Maxon, E. (2008). Understanding mother-adolescent conflict discussions: Concurrent and across-time prediction from youths' dispositions and parenting: III. Descriptive analyses and correlations. *Monographs of the Society for Research in Child Development, 73*(2), 54–80.

Eisenberg, N., Hofer, C., & Vaughan, J. (2007). Effortful control and its socioemotional consequences. In J. J. Gross (Ed.), *Handbook of emotion regulation* (pp. 287–306). New York: Guilford Press.

Eisenberg, N., Spinrad, T. L., & Sadovsky, A. (2006). Empathy-related responding in children. In M. Killen & J. Smetana (Eds.), *Handbook of moral development* (pp. 517–549). Mahwah, NJ: Erlbaum.

Elam, K. K., Harold, G. T., Neiderhiser, J. M., Reiss, D., Shaw, D. S., Natsuaki, M. N., . . . Leve, L. D. (2014). Adoptive parent hostility and children's peer behavior problems: Examining the role of genetically informed child attributes on adoptive parent behavior. *Developmental Psychology, 50*(5), 1543–1552. doi:10.1037/a0035470

Elbert, T., Pantev, C., Wienbruch, C., Rockstroh, B., & Taub, E. (1995). Increased cortical representation of the fingers of the left hand in string players. *Science, 270*(5234), 305–307.

Eliot, L. (1999). *What's going on in there? How the brain and mind develop in the first five years of life.* New York: Bantam Books.

Eliot, M., & Cornell, D. (2009). Bullying in middle school as a function of insecure attachment and aggressive attitudes. *School Psychology International, 30*(2), 201–214.

Eliot, M., Cornell, D., Gregory, A., & Fan, X. (2010). Supportive school climate and student willingness to seek help for bullying and threats of violence. *Journal of School Psychology, 48*(6), 533–553.

Elkind, D. (2007a). *The hurried child.* Cambridge, MA: DaCapo.

Elkind, D. (2007b). *The power of play.* Cambridge, MA: DaCapo.

Elkind, D., & Bowen, R. (1979). Imaginary audience behavior in children and adolescents. *Developmental Psychology, 15*(1), 38–44.

Elliott, S., & Umberson, D. (2004). Recent demographic trends in the US and implications for well-being. In J. Scott, J. Treas, & M. Richards (Eds.), *The Blackwell companion to the sociology of families* (pp. 34–53). Malden, MA: Blackwell.

Elliott, W. (2009). Children's college aspirations and expectations: The potential role of children's development accounts (CDAs). *Children and Youth Services Review, 31*, 274–283.

Ellis, B. J., & Essex, M. J. (2007). Family environments, adrenarche, and sexual maturation: A longitudinal test of a life history model. *Child Development, 78*(6), 1799–1817.

Ellis, R. R., & Simmons, T. (2014). *Coresident grandparents and their grandchildren: 2012.* Current Population Reports, P20-576. Washington, DC: U.S. Census Bureau.

Else-Quest, N. M., Hyde, J. S., & Linn, M. C. (2010). Cross-national patterns of gender differences in mathematics: A meta-analysis. *Psychological Bulletin, 136*(1), 103–127.

Else-Quest, N. M. & Morse, E. (2015). Ethnic variations in parental ethnic socialization and adolescent ethnic identity: A longitudinal study. *Cultural Diversity and Ethnic Minority Psychology, 21*(1), 54–64.

Ely, R. (2005). Language and literacy in the school years. In J. B. Gleason (Ed.), *The development of language* (6th ed., pp. 396–443). Boston: Pearson.

Engelmann, J. B., & Pogosyan, M. (2013). Emotion perception across cultures: The role of cognitive mechanisms. *Frontiers in Psychology, 4*(Article 118). doi:10.3389/fpsyg.2013.00118.

Engle, M. (2004). Kids and sports. *New York University Child Study Center Letter, 9*(1), 1–7.

Ennemoser, M., & Schneider, W. (2007). Relations of television viewing and reading: Findings from a 4-year longitudinal study. *Journal of Educational Psychology, 99*(2), 349–368.

Entwisle, D. R., Alexander, K. L., & Olson, L. S. (2000). Early work histories of urban youth. *American Sociological Review, 65*(2), 279–297.

Entwisle, D. R., Alexander, K. L., & Olson, L. S. (2005). Urban teenagers: Work and dropout. *Youth & Society, 37*(1), 3–32.

Erdem, G., DuBois, D. L., Larose, S., De Wit, D., & Lipman, E. L. (2016). Mentoring relationships, positive development, youth emotional and behavioral problems: Investigation of a mediational model. *Journal of Community Psychology, 44*(4), 464–483. doi:10.1002/jcop.21782

Erickson, L. D., McDonald, S., & Elder, G. R. (2009). Informal mentors and education: Complementary or compensatory resources? *Sociology of Education, 82*(4), 344–367.

Erikson, E. H. (1963). *Childhood and society* (2nd ed.). New York: W. W. Norton.

Erikson, E. H. (1968). *Identity, youth and crisis.* New York: W. W. Norton.

Erol, R. Y., & Orth, U. (2011). Self-esteem development from age 14 to 30 years: A longitudinal study. *Journal of Personality and Social Psychology, 101*(3), 607–619.

Ersoy, B., Balkan, C., Gunay, T., & Egemen, A. (2005). The factors affecting the relation between the menarcheal age of mother and daughter. *Child: Care, Health and Development, 31*(3), 303–308.

Erus, G., Battapady, H., Satterthwaite, T. D., Hakonarson, H., Gur, R. E., Davatzikos, C., & Gur, R. C. (2015). Imaging patterns of brain development and their relationship to cognition. *Cerebral Cortex, 25*(6), 1676–1684. doi:10.1093/cercor/bht425

Espinoza, P., da Luz Fontes, A., & Arms-Chavez, C. J. (2014). Attributional gender bias: Teachers' ability and effort explanations for students' math performance. *Social Psychology of Education, 17*(1), 105–126. doi:10.1007/s11218-013-9226-6

Essex, M. J., Boyce, W. T., Hertzman, C., Lam, L. L., Armstrong, J. M., Neumann, S. M. A., & Kobor, M. S. (2013). Epigenetic vestiges of early developmental adversity: Childhood stress exposure and DNA methylation in adolescence. *Child Development, 84*(1), 58–75.

Evans, G. W., Jones-Rounds, M. L., Belojevic, G., & Vermeylen, F. (2012). Family income and childhood obesity in eight European cities: The mediating roles of neighborhood characteristics and physical activity. *Social Science & Medicine, 75*(3), 477–481.

Evins, A. E., Green, A. I., Kane, J. M., & Murray, R. M. (2012). The effect of marijuana use on the risk for schizophrenia. *Journal of Clinical Psychiatry, 73*(11), 1463–1468.

Eyberg, S. M., Nelson, M. M., & Boggs, S. R. (2008). Evidence-based psychosocial treatments for children and adolescents with disruptive behavior. *Journal of Clinical Child and Adolescent Psychology, 37*, 215–237.

Eyer, D. (1992). *Mother-infant bonding: A scientific fiction.* New Haven, CT: Yale University Press.

Fabes, R. L., Gaertner, B. M., & Popp, T. K. (2006). Getting along with others: Social competence in early childhood. In K. McCartney & D. Phillips (Eds.), *Blackwell handbook of early childhood development* (pp. 297–316). Malden, MA: Blackwell.

Faden, V., Ruffin, B., Newes-Adeyi, G., & Chen, C. (2010). The relationship among pubertal stage, age, and drinking in adolescent boys and girls. *Journal of Child & Adolescent Substance Abuse, 19*(1), 1–15.

Fagan, J. F., Holland, C. R., & Wheeler, K. (2007). The prediction, from infancy, of adult IQ and achievement. *Intelligence, 35*(3), 225–231.

Fahlman, S. E. (n.d.). *Smiley lore :-).* Retrieved from http://www.cs.cmu.edu/~sef/sefSmiley.htm

FairTest. (2010). *2010 College bound seniors average SAT scores.* Retrieved from http://fairtest.org/2010-collegebound-seniors-average-sat-scores

FairTest. (2016). *Colleges and universities that do not use SAT/ACT scores for admitting substantial numbers of students into bachelor degree programs.* Retrieved from http://www.fairtest.org/university/optional

Falbo, T. (2012). Only children: An updated review. *Journal of Individual Psychology, 68*(1), 38–49.

Falci, C. D., & McNeely, C. (2009). Too many friends: Social integration, network cohesion and adoescent depressive symptoms. *Social Forces, 87*(4), 2031–2062.

Fan, J., Gu, X., Guise, K. G., Liu, X., Fossella, J., Wang, H., & Posner, M. I. (2009). Testing the behavioral interaction and integration of attentional networks. *Brain and Cognition, 70*(2), 209–220.

Fancy, S. P., Harrington, E. P., Yuen, T. J., Silbereis, J. C., Zhao, C., Baranzini, S. E., & Rowitch, D. H. (2011). Axin2 as regulatory and therapeutic target in newborn brain injury and remyelination. *Nature Neuroscience, 14*(8), 1009–1016.

Fang, X., Brown, D. S., Florence, C. S., & Mercy, J. A. (2012). The economic burden of child maltreatment in the United States and implications for prevention. *Child Abuse & Neglect, 36*(2), 156–165. doi:10.1016/j.chiabu.2011.10.006

Fantuzzo, J. W., Bulotsky-Sheare, R., Fusco, R. A., & McWayne, C. (2005). An investigation of preschool classroom behavioral adjustment problems and social-emotional school readiness competencies. *Early Childhood Research Quarterly, 20*(3), 259–275. doi: 10.1016/j.ecresq.2005.07.001

Fantuzzo, J. W., Perlman, S. M., & Dobbins, E. K. (2011). Types and timing of child maltreatment and early school success: A population-based investigation. *Children and Youth Services Review, 33*(8), 1404–1411.

Faris, R., & Felmlee, D. (2014). Casualties of social combat: School networks of peer victimization and their consequences. *American Sociological Review, 79*(2), 228–257.

Farmer, R. L., Floyd, R. G., Reynolds, M. R., & Kranzler, J. H. (2014). IQs are very strong but imperfect indicators of psychometric "g": Results from joint confirmatory factor analysis. *Psychology in the Schools, 51*(8), 801–813.

Farr, R. R., Crain, E., Oakley, M., Cashen, K., & Garber, K. (2016). Microaggressions, feelings of difference, and resilience among adopted children with sexual minority parents. *Journal of Youth & Adolescence, 45*(1), 85–104.

Farroni, T., Massaccesi, S., Pividori, D., & Johnson, M. (2004). Gaze following in newborns. *Infancy, 5*(1), 39–60.

Farroni, T., Menon, E., & Johnson, M. H. (2006). Factors influencing newborns' preference for faces with eye contact. *Journal of Experimental Child Psychology, 95*(4), 298–308.

Farruggia, S. P., Bullen, P., & Davidson, J. (2013). Important nonparental adults as an academic resource for youth. *Journal of Early Adolescence, 33*(4), 498–522. doi:10.1177/0272431612450950

Fasko, D. Jr. (2006). Creative thinking and reasoning. In J. C. Kaufman & J. Baer (Eds.), *Creativity and reason in cognitive development* (pp. 159–176). New York: Cambridge University Press.

Fast, I. (1985). Infantile narcissism and the active infant. *Psychoanalytic Psychology, 2*(2), 153–170.

Fay-Stammbach, T., Hawes, D. J., & Meredith, P. (2014). Parenting influences on executive function in early childhood: A review. *Child Development Perspectives, 8*(4), 258–264. doi:10.1111/cdep.12095

Fearon, R. P., Bakermans-Kranenburg, M. J., van IJzendoorn, M. H., Lapsley, A-M., & Roisman, G. I. (2010). The significance of insecure attachment and disorganization in the development of children's externalizing behavior: A meta-analytic study. *Child Development, 81*(2), 435–456.

Federal Interagency Forum on Child and Family Statistics. (2009). *America's children: Key national indicators of well-being.* Washington, DC: U.S. Government Printing Office.

Federal Interagency Forum on Child and Family Statistics. (2013). *High school academic course-taking.* Retrieved from http://www.childstats.gov/americaschildren/edu3.asp

Federal Interagency Forum on Child and Family Statistics. (2015). *America's children: Key national indicators of well-being, 2015.* Washington, DC: U.S. Government Printing Office.

Feinberg, M. E., Reiss, D., Neiderhiser, J. M., & Hetherington, E. M. (2005). Differential association of family subsystem negativity on siblings' maladjustment: Using behavior genetic methods to test process theory. *Journal of Family Psychology, 19*(4), 601–610.

Feld, S., & Schieffelin, B. B. (1998). Hard words: A functional basis for Kaluli discourse. In D. Brenneis & R. K. S. Macauley (Eds.), *The matrix of language* (pp. 56–74). Boulder, CO: Westview Press.

Feldman, R., Rosenthal, Z., & Eidelman, A. I. (2014). Maternal-preterm skin-to-skin contact enhances child physiologic organization and cognitive control across the first 10 years of life. *Biological Psychiatry, 75*(1), 56–64. doi:10.1016/j.biopsych.2013.08.012

Feldman, R., Weller, A., Zagoory-Sharon, O., & Levine, A. (2007). Evidence for a neuroendocrinological foundation of human affiliation: Plasma oxytocin levels across pregnancy and the postpartum period predict mother-infant bonding. *Psychological Science, 18*(11), 965–970. doi:10.1111/j.1467-9280.2007.02010.x

Felitti, J. J., Anda, R. F., Mordenberg, D., Williamson, D. V., Spitz, A. M., Edwards. V.,. . . .Marks, J S. (1998). Relationship of childhood abuse and household dysfunction to many of the leading causes of death in adults: The Adverse Childhood Experiences (ACE) Study. *American Journal of Preventative Medicine, 14*(4), 245–258. http://dx.doi.org/10.1016/S0749-3797(98)00017-8

Fender, J. G., Richert, R. A., Robb, M. B., & War-tella, E. (2010). Parent teaching focus and toddlers' learning from an infant DVD. *Infant & Child Development, 19*(6), 613–627. doi: 10.1002/icd.713

Feng, X., Keenan, K., Hipwell, A. E., Henneberger, A. K., Rischall, M. S., Butch, J., . . . Babinski, D. E. (2009). Longitudinal associations between emotion regulation and depression in preadolescent girls: Moderation by the care-giving environment. *Developmental Psychology, 45*(3), 798–808.

Fenzel, L. M. (2000). Prospective study of changes in global self-worth and strain during the tran-sition to middle school. *Journal of Early Adoles-cence, 20*(2), 93–116.

Ferguson, A. N., & Bowey, J. A. (2005). Global pro-cessing speed as a mediator of developmental changes in children's auditory memory span. *Journal of Experimental Child Psychology, 91*(2), 89–112. doi:10.1016/j.jecp.2004.12.006

Ferguson, B., Graf, E., & Waxman, S. R. (2014). Infants use known verbs to learn novel nouns: Evidence from 15- and 19-month-olds. *Cognition, 131*(1), 139–146. doi:10.1016/j.cognition.2013.12.014

Ferguson, C. J., Muñoz, M. E., & Medrano, M. R. (2012). Advertising influences on young children's food choices and parental influence. *Journal of Pediatrics, 160*(3), 452–455.

Ferguson, C. J., San Miguel, C., Kilburn, J. C., & Sanchez, P. (2007). The effectiveness of school-based anti-bullying programs: A meta-analytic review. *Criminal Justice Review, 32*(4), 401–414.

Ferguson, R. W., Green, A., & Hansen, L. M. (2013). *Game changers: Stats, stories and what communities are doing to protect young athletes.* Washington, DC: Safe Kids Worldwide.

Ferguson, T. J., Stegge, H., Miller, E. R, & Olsen, M. E. (1999). Guilt, shame, and symptoms in children. *Developmental Psychology, 35*(2), 347–357.

Fergusson, D. M., Boden, J. M., & Horwood, L. J. (2008). Exposure to childhood sexual and physical abuse and adjustment in early adult-hood. *Child Abuse & Neglect, 32*(6), 607–619.

Fernald, A. (1985). Four-month-olds prefer to listen to motherese. *Infant Behavior and Develop-ment, 8*, 181–195.

Fernald, A., Marchman, V. A., & Weisleder, A. (2013). SES differences in language processing skill and vocabulary are evident at 18 months. *Developmental Science, 16*(2), 234–248. doi:10.1111/desc.12019

Fernald, A., Pinto, J. P., Swingley, D., Weinberg, A., & McRoberts, G. W. (2001). Rapid gains in speed of verbal processing by infants in the 2nd year. In M. Tomasello & E. Bates (Eds.), *Language development: The essential readings* (pp. 49–56). Malden, MA: Blackwell.

Fernald, A., & Weisleder, A. (2015). Twenty years after "meaningful differences," it's time to reframe the "deficit" debate about the impor-tance of children's early language experience. *Human Development, 58*(1), 1–4.

Fernandes, M., & Sturm, R. (2011). The role of school physical activity programs in child body mass trajectory. *Journal of Physical Activity & Health, 8*(2), 174–181.

Fernyhough, C., & Fradley, E. (2005). Private speech on an executive task: Relations with task difficulty and task performance. *Cognitive Development, 20*(1), 103–120.

Ferrari, P. F., & Rizzolatti, G. (2014). Mirror neuron research: The past and the future. *Philosophi-cal Transactions of the Royal Society B: Biological Sciences, 369*(1644), 2013.0169. http://doi.org/10.1098/

Field, T. (2007). *The amazing infant.* Malden, MA: Blackwell.

Field, T. (2010). Touch for socioemotional and physical well-being: A review. *Developmental Review, 30*, 367–383.

Field, T., Diego, M., & Hernandez-Reif, M. (2007). Massage therapy research. *Developmental Review, 27*(1), 75–89.

Fiese, B. H., & Schwartz, M. (2008). Reclaiming the family table: Mealtime and child health and well-being. *Society for Research in Child Development Social Policy Report, 22*(4), 3–9, 13–18.

Fifer, W. P., Monk, C. E., & Grose-Fifer, J. (2004). Pre-natal development and risk. In G. Bremner & A. Fogel (Eds.), *Blackwell handbook of infant devel-opment* (pp. 505–542). Malden, MA: Blackwell.

Figueiredo, B., Costa, R., Pacheco, A., & Pais, Á. (2009). Mother-to-infant emotional involvement at birth. *Maternal and Child Health Journal, 13*(4), 539–549. Doi:10.1007/s10995-008-0312-x

Filippova, E., & Astington, J. (2010). Children's understanding of social-cognitive and social-communicative aspects of discourse irony. *Child Development, 81*(3), 913–928.

Finer, L., & Zolna, M. (2011). Unintended preg-nancy in the United States: Incidence and dis-parities, 2006. *Contraception, 84*(5), 478–485.

Finkelhor, D., & Hashima, P. Y. (2001). The victim-ization of children and youth: A comprehen-sive overview. In S. O. White (Ed.), *Handbook of youth and justice* (pp. 48–78). New York: Klu-wer Academic.

Finkelhor, D., Ormrod, R., Turner, H., & Hamby, S. L. (2005). The victimization of children and youth: A comprehensive, national survey. *Child Maltreatment, 10*(1), 5–25.

Finkelhor, D., Turner, H., Ormrod, R., & Hamby, S. L. (2009). Violence, abuse, and crime exposure in a national sample of children and youth. *Pediatrics, 124*(5), 1411–1423.

Finkenauer, C., Engels, R. C. M. E., Meeus, W., & Oosterwegel, A. (2002). Self and identity in early adolescence: The pains and gains of knowing who and what you are. In T. M. Brinthaupt & R. P. Lipka (Eds.), *Understand-ing early adolescent self and identity: Applications and interventions* (pp. 25–56). Albany: State University of New York Press.

Finn, A. S., Sheridan, M. A., Kam, C. L. H., Hin-shaw, S., & D'Esposito, M. (2010). Longitudi-nal evidence for functional specialization of the neural circuit supporting working memory in the human brain. *Journal of Neuroscience, 30*(33), 11062–11067.

First Candle. (2015). *Grieving families.* Retrieved from http://www.firstcandle.org/grieving-families/

Firth, N., Frydenberg, E., & Greaves, D. (2008). Perceived control and adaptive coping: Pro-grams for adolescent students who have learn-ing disabilities. *Learning Disability Quarterly, 31*(3), 151–165.

Firth, N., Greaves, D., & Frydenberg, E. (2010). Coping styles and strategies: A comparison of adolescent students with and without learning disabilities. *Journal of Learning Disabilities, 43*(1), 77–85.

Fischer, C. S., Hout, M., & Stiles, J. (2006). How Americans lived: Families and life courses in flux. In C. S. Fischer & M. Hout (Eds.), *Century of difference* (pp. 57–95). New York: Russell Sage.

Flanagan, D., Mascolo, J., & Hardy-Braz, S. (2006–2012). *Standardized testing.* Retrieved from http://www.education.com/reference/article/standardized-testing

Flavell, J. H. (1999). Cognitive development: Chil-dren's knowledge about the mind. *Annual Review of Psychology, 50*, 21–45.

Flavell, J. H., Miller, P. H., & Miller, S. A. (2002). *Cognitive development* (4th ed.). Upper Saddle River, NJ: Prentice Hall.

Fletcher, A. C., & Jefferies, B. C. (1999). Parental mediators of associations between perceived authoritative parenting and early adolescent substance use. *Journal of Early Adolescence, 19*(4), 465–487.

Fletcher, A. C., Walls, J. K., Cook, E. C., Madi-son, K. J., & Bridges, T. H. (2008). Parenting style as a moderator of associations between maternal disciplinary strategies and child well-being. *Journal of Family Issues, 29*(12), 1724–1744. doi: 10.1177/0192513X08322933

Fletcher, G. E., Zach, T., Pramanik, A. K., & Ford, S. P. (2009). Multiple births. *E-Medicine.* Retrieved from http://www.emedicine.com/ped/TOPIC2599.HTM

Fletcher, J., & Branen, L. (n.d.). *Erik Erikson's psycho-social stages: Application for children's eating skills development.* Retrieved from http://www.cals.uidaho.edu/feeding/forparents/pdfs/2_1%20Erikson.pdf

Flouri, E., Midouhas, E., & Joshi, H. (2014). The role of urban neighbourhood green space in chil-dren's emotional and behavioural resilience. *Jour-nal of Environmental Psychology, 40*, 179–186.

Flynn, E., Pine, K., & Lewis, C. (2006). The micro-genetic method: Time for change? *The Psychol-ogist, 19*(3), 152–155.

Flynn, J. R. (2007). *What is intelligence? Beyond the Flynn effect.* New York: Cambridge University Press.

Foerde, K., Knowlton, B. J., & Poldrack, R. A. (2006). Modulation of competing memory sys-tems by distraction. *Proceedings of the National Academy of Sciences, 103*(31), 11778–11783.

Fogel, A. (2002). *Infancy* (4th ed.). Belmont, CA: Wadsworth.

Fogel, A. (2011). Theoretical and applied dynamic systems research in developmental science. *Child Development Perspectives, 5*(4), 267–272. doi:10.1111/j.1750-8606.2011.00174.x

Fombonne, E., Zakarian, R., Bennett, A., Meng, L., & McLean-Heywood, D. (2005). Pervasive developmental disorders in Montreal, Quebec, Canada: Prevalence and links with immuniza-tions. *Pediatrics, 118*(1), 139–150.

Fonagy, P., Target, M., & Gergely, G. (2006). Psy-choanalytic perspectives on developmental psychology. In D. J. Cohen & D. Cicchetti (Eds.), *Developmental psychopathology: Theory and method* (Vol. 1, pp. 701–749). Hoboken, NJ: Wiley.

Food and Drug Administration. (2008). *OTC cough and cold products: Not for infants and children under 2 years of age.* Retrieved from http://www.fda.gov/ForConsumers/ConsumerUpdates/ucm048682.htm

Food Research and Action Center. (2010). *School breakfast program.* Retrieved from http://frac.org/federal-foodnutrition-programs/school-breakfast-program/

Forhan, S., Gottlieb, S., Sternberg, M., Xu, F., Datta, S., McQuillan, G., . . . Markowitz, L. (2009). Prevalence of sexually transmitted infections among female adolescents aged 14 to 19 in the United States. *Pediatrics, 124*(6), 1505–1512. doi:10.1542/peds.2009-0674

Fortin, N. M., Oreopoulos, P., & Phipps, S. (2015). Leaving boys behind: Gender disparities in high academic achievement. *Journal of Human Resources, 50*(3), 549–579.

Fouts, H. N., Hallam, R. A., & Purandare, S. (2013). Gender segregation in early-childhood social play among the Bofi foragers and Bofi farmers in Central Africa. *American Journal of Play, 5*(3), 333–356.

Fox, B. (2001). The formative years: How parenthood creates gender. *Canadian Review of Sociology and Anthropology, 28*(4), 373–390.

Fox, G. (2006). Development in family contexts. In L. Combrinck-Graham (Ed.), *Children in family contexts* (pp. 26–50). New York: Guilford Press.

Fraley, R., & Heffernan, M. E. (2013). Attachment and parental divorce: A test of the diffusion and sensitive period hypotheses. *Personality and Social Psychology Bulletin, 39*(9), 1199–1213.

Franceschini, S., Gori, S., Ruffino, M., Pedrolli, K., & Facoetti, A. (2012). A causal link between visual spatial attention and reading acquisition. *Current Biology, 22*, 814–819.

Franic, S., Middeldorp, C. M., Dolan, C. V., Ligthart, L., & Boomsma, D. I. (2010). Childhood and adolescent anxiety and depression: Beyond heritability. *Journal of the American Academy of Child and Adolescent Psychiatry, 49*, 820–829.

Frank, D. A., Augustyn, M., Knight, W. G., Pell, T., & Zuckerman, B. (2001). Growth, development, and behavior in early childhood following prenatal cocaine exposure: A systematic review. *Journal of the American Medical Association, 285*(12), 1613–1625.

Frank-Briggs, A. (2011). Attention deficit hyperactivity disorder (ADHD). *Journal of Pediatric Neurology, 9*(3), 291–298.

Frankel, L. A., Umemura, T., Jacobvitz, D., & Hazen, N. (2015). Marital conflict and parental responses to infant negative emotions: Relations with toddler emotional regulation. *Infant Behavior & Development, 40*, 73–83. doi:10.1016/j.infbeh.2015.03.004

Franklin, B., Jones, A., Love, D., Puckett, S., Macklin, J., & White-Means, S. (2012). Exploring mediators of food insecurity and obesity: A review of the recent literature. *Journal of Community Health, 37*(1), 253–264.

Franklin, J., Rifkin, L., & Pascual, P. (2001). Serving the very young and the restless. In D. G. Singer & J. L. Singer (Eds.), *Handbook of children and the media* (pp. 507–520). Thousand Oaks, CA: Sage.

Freeman, N. K. (2007). Preschoolers' perceptions of gender appropriate toys and their parents' beliefs about genderized behaviors: Miscommunication, mixed messages, or hidden truths? *Early Childhood Education Journal, 34*(5), 357–366.

Freeman, N. K., & Somerindyke, J. (2001). Social play at the computer: Preschoolers scaffold and support peers' computer competence. *Information Technology in Childhood Education Annual, 12*, 203–213.

Freisthler, B., Merritt, D. H., & LaScala, E. A. (2006). Understanding the ecology of child maltreatment: A review of the literature and directions for future research. *Child Maltreatment, 11*(3), 263–280.

Freud, A. (1965). *Normality and pathology in childhood.* New York: International Universities Press.

Freud, S. (1953). Two encyclopedia articles (1922): (a) Psycho-analysis. In *Collected papers* (Vol. V, pp. 107–130). London: Hogarth Press.

Freud, S. (1959). Character and anal erotism (1908). In *Collected papers* (Vol. II, pp. 45–50). London: Hogarth Press.

Frey, N. (2005). Retention, social promotion, and academic redshirting: What do we know and need to know? *Remedial and Special Education, 26*(6), 332–346.

Friedman, A. M., Ananth, C. V., Prendergast, E., D'Alton, M. E., & Wright, J. D. (2015). Variation in and factors associated with use of episiotomy. *Journal of the American Medical Association, 313*(2), 197–199. doi: 10.1001/jama.2014.14774

Friedman, H. S., & Martin, L. R. (2011). *The longevity project: Surprising discoveries for health and long life from the landmark eight-decade study.* New York: Hudson Street Press.

Friedman, H. S., Tucker, J. S., Schwartz, J. E., Martin, L. R., Tomlinson-Keasey, C., Wingard, D. L., & Criqui, M. H. (1995). Childhood conscientiousness and longevity. *Journal of Personality & Social Psychology, 68*, 696–703.

Friedman, M. J. (2006). *Sesame Street educates and entertains internationally.* Retrieved from http://www.america.gov/st/washfile-english/2006/April/20060405165756jmnamdeirf0.4207117.html

Friedman, S. L., & Boyle, D. E. (2008). Attachment in U.S. children experiencing nonmaternal care in the early 1990s. *Attachment and Human Development, 10*(3), 225–261.

Friedrich, L. K., & Stein, A. H. (1973). Aggressive and prosocial television programs and the natural behavior of preschool children [Special issue]. *Monographs of the Society for Research in Child Development, 38*(4, Serial No. 151).

Fries, A. B. W., Ziegler, T. E., Kurian, J. R., Jacoris, S., & Pollak, S. D. (2005). Early experience in humans is associated with changes in neuropeptides critical for regulating social behavior. *Proceedings of the National Academy of Sciences, 102*(47), 17237–17240.

Frith, U. (2003). *Autism: Explaining the enigma.* Malden, MA: Blackwell.

Froschl, M., & Sprung, B. (2008). A positive and pro-active response to young boys in the classroom. *Exchange: The Early Childhood Leaders' Magazine, 182*, 34–36.

Fry, D. P. (2005). Rough-and-tumble social play in humans. In A. D. Pellegrini & P. K. Smith (Eds.), *The nature of play* (pp. 54–85). New York: Guilford Press.

Fuhs, M. W., & Day, J. D. (2011). Verbal ability and executive functioning development in preschoolers at Head Start. *Developmental Psychology, 47*(2), 404–416.

Furman, W., & Collins, W. A. (2009). Adolescent romantic relationships and experiences. In K. H. Rubin, W. M. Bukowski, & B. Laursen (Eds.), *Handbook of peer interactions, relationships, and groups* (pp. 341–360). New York: Guilford Press.

The Future of Children. (2010). *About the Future of Children.* Retrieved from http://futureofchildren.org/futureofchildren/about/

Gaillard, V., Barrouillet, P., Jarrold, C., & Camos, V. (2011). Developmental differences in working memory: Where do they come from? *Journal of Experimental Child Psychology, 110*(3), 469–479.

Galambos, N. L., & Kotylak, L. A. (2012). Transformations in parent-child relationships from adolescence to adulthood. In B. Laursen & W. A. Collins (Eds.), *Relationship pathways: From adolescence to young adulthood* (pp. 23–42). Thousand Oaks, CA: Sage.

Galan, H. L., & Hobbins, J. C. (2003). Intrauterine growth restriction. In J. S. Scott, R. S. Gibbs, B. Y. Karlan, & A. F. Haney (Eds.), *Danforth's obstetrics and gynecology* (9th ed., pp. 203–217). Philadelphia: Lippincott.

Galanaki, E. P. (2012). The imaginary audience and the personal fable: A test of Elkind's theory of adolescent egocentrism. *Psychology, 3*(6), 457–466.

Galler, J. R., Bryce, C. P., Waber, D. P., Hock, R. S., Harrison, R., Eaglesfield, G. D., & Fitzmaurice, G. (2012). Infant malnutrition predicts conduct problems in adolescents. *Nutritional Neuroscience, 15*(4), 186–192.

Galler, J. R., Bryce, C., Waber, D. P., Zichlin, M. L., Fitzmaurice, G. M., & Eaglesfield, D. (2012). Socioeconomic outcomes in adults malnourished in the first year of life: A 40-year study. *Pediatrics, 130*(1), e1–e7.

Gallup, G. G., Anderson, J. R., & Shillito, D. J. (2002). The mirror test. In M. Bekoff, C. Allen, & G. M. Burghardt (Eds.), *The cognitive animal: Empirical and theoretical perspectives on animal cognition* (pp. 325–334). Cambridge, MA: MIT Press.

Gander, M., & Buchheim, A. (2015). Attachment classification, psychophysiology and frontal EEG asymmetry across the lifespan: A review. *Frontiers in Human Neuroscience, 9* (Article 79), 1–16.

Ganger, J., & Brent, M. R. (2004). Reexamining the vocabulary spurt. *Developmental Psychology, 40*(4), 621–632.

Ganley, C. M., & Vasilyeva, M. (2011). Sex differences in the relation between math performance, spatial skills, and attitudes. *Journal of Applied Developmental Psychology, 32*(4), 235–242.

Ganong, L. H., Coleman, M., Feistman, R., Jamison, T., & Stafford Markham, M. (2012). Communication technology and postdivorce coparenting. *Family Relations, 61*(3), 397–409.

Ganong, L. H., Coleman, M., & Jamison, T. (2011). Patterns of stepchild–stepparent relationship development. *Journal of Marriage and Family, 73*(2), 396–413. doi: 10.1111/j.1741–3737.2010.00814.x

Garan, E. M. (2001). Beyond the smoke and mirrors. *Phi Delta Kappan, 82*(7), 500–506.

Garber, A. K., Park, J., Brindis, C. D., Vaughn, B., Barry, M., Guzman, L., & Berger, A. (2013). *Adolescent health highlights: Physical development and daily health habits.* Child Trend Publication #2013-09. Bethesda, MD: Child Trends.

Garber, J., & Weersing, V. R. (2010). Comorbidity of anxiety and depression in youth: Implications for treatment and prevention. *Clinical Psychology, 17*(4), 293–306. doi.org/10.1111/j.1468-2850.2010.01221.x

Garces, E., Thomas, D., & Currie, J. (2002). Longer-term effects of Head Start. *American Economic Review, 9*(4), 999–1012.

García, F., & Gracia, E. (2009). Is always authoritative the optimum parenting style? Evidence from Spanish families. *Adolescence, 44*(173), 101–131.

Gardephe, C. D., & Ettlinger, S. (1993). *Don't pick up the baby or you'll spoil the child and other old wives' tales about pregnancy and parenting.* San Francisco: Chronicle Books.

Gardiner, A. K., Greif, M. L., & Bjorklund, D. F. (2011). Guided by intention: Preschoolers' imitation reflects inferences of causation. *Journal of Cognition and Development, 12*(3), 355–373. doi:10.1080/15248372.2010.542216

Gardner, E. (2016, February 26). Hollywood's rating system blamed in class action lawsuit for smoking-related deaths. *The Hollywood Reporter*. Retrieved from http://www.hollywoodreporter.com/thr-esq/hollywoods-rating-system-blamed-class-869950

Gardner, H. (1975). *The shattered mind: The person after brain damage*. New York: Knopf.

Gardner, H. (1976). *The shattered mind*. New York: Vintage Books.

Gardner, H. (1993). *Frames of mind: The theory of multiple intelligences*. New York: Basic Books.

Gardner, H. (1999). *Intelligence reframed*. New York: Basic Books.

Gardner, H. (2006). On failing to grasp the core of MI theory: A response to Visser et al. *Intelligence, 34*(5), 503–505. doi:10.1016/j.intell.2006.04.002

Gardner, H. (2011). *Frames of mind: The theory of multiple intelligences*. New York: Basic Books.

Gardner, H., & Connell, M. (2000). Response to Nicholas Allix. *Australian Journal of Education, 44*, 288–293.

Gardner, H., & Moran, S. (2006). The science of multiple intelligences theory: A response to Lynn Waterhouse. *Educational Psychologist, 41*(4), 227–232.

Gardner, H., & Traub, J. (2010). A debate on "multiple intelligences." In D. Gordon (Ed.), *Cerebrum 2010: Emerging ideas in brain science* (pp. 34–61). Washington, DC: Dana Press.

Gardner, R. M., Stark, K., Friedman, B. N., & Jackson, N. A. (2000). Predictors of eating disorder scores in children ages 6 through 14: A longitudinal study. *Journal of Psychosomatic Research, 49*(3), 199–205.

Gargiulo, R. M. (2012). *Special education in contemporary society: An introduction to exceptionality* (4th ed.). Thousand Oaks, CA: Sage.

Garmy, P., Nyberg, P., & Jakobsson, U. (2012). Sleep and television and computer habits of Swedish school-age children. *Journal of School Nursing, 28*, 469–476.

Gartner, L. M., Morton, J., Lawrence, R. A., Naylor, A. J., O'Hare, D., Schanler, R. J., & Eidelman, A. I. (2005). Breastfeeding and the use of human milk. *Pediatrics, 115*(2), 496–506.

Gartstein, M. A., & Iverson, S. (2014). Attachment security: The role of infant, maternal, and contextual factors. *International Journal of Psychology and Psychological Therapy, 14*(2), 261–276.

Garven, S., Wood, J. M., Malpass, R. S., & Shaw, J. S. (1998). More than suggestion: The effect of interviewing techniques from the McMartin Preschool case. *Journal of Applied Psychology, 83*(3), 347–359.

Gaskins, I. W., & Pressley, M. (2007). Teaching metacognitive strategies that address executive function processes within a schoolwide curriculum. In L. Meltzer (Ed.), *Executive function in education: From theory to practice* (pp. 261–286). New York: Guilford Press.

Gass, K., Jenkins, J., & Dunn, J. (2007). Are sibling relationships protective? A longitudinal study. *Journal of Child Psychology and Psychiatry, 48*(2), 167–175.

Gates, G. J. (2011). *How many people are lesbian, gay, bisexual, and transgender?* Los Angeles: The Williams Institute.

Gathercole, S. E., Pickering, S. J., Ambridge, B., & Wearing, H. (2004). The structure of working memory from 4 to 15 years of age. *Developmental Psychology, 40*(2), 177–190.

Gathwala, G., Singh, B., & Balhara, B. (2008). KMC facilitates mother baby attachment in low birth weight infants. *Indian Journal of Pediatrics, 75*(1), 43–47.

Gauvain, M., & Parke, R. D. (2010). Socialization. In M. H. Bornstein (Ed.), *Handbook of cultural developmental science* (pp. 239–258). New York: Psychology Press.

Gay, P. (1999). Sigmund Freud. *Time*. Retrieved from http://205.188.238.181/time/time100/scientist/

Gay, Lesbian & Straight Education Network. (2013). *The 2013 National School Climate Survey – Executive Summary*. Retrieved from http://www.glsen.org/sites/default/files/NSCS_ExecSumm_2013_DESIGN_FINAL.pdf

Ge, X., Brody, G. H., Conger, R. D., Simons, R. L., & Murry, V. M. (2002). Contextual amplification of pubertal transition effects on deviant peer affiliation and externalizing behavior among African-American children. *Developmental Psychology, 38*(1), 42–54.

Geangu, E., Benga, O., Stahl, D., & Striano, T. (2010). Contagious crying beyond the first days of life. *Infant Behavior & Development, 33*(3), 279–288. doi: 10.1016/j.infbeh.2010.03.004

Gennetian, L., & Miller, C. (2000). *Reforming welfare and rewarding work: Final report on the Minnesota Family Investment Program: Vol. 2. Effects on children*. New York: MDRC. Retrieved from http://www.mdrc.org/publications/206/full.pdf

Gentile, D. A. (2003). Introduction. In D. A. Gentile (Ed.), *Media violence and children* (pp. ix–xi). Westport, CT: Praeger.

Gentile, D. A., & Anderson, C. A. (2003). Violent video games: The newest media violence hazard. In D. A. Gentile (Ed.), *Media violence and children* (pp. 131–152). Westport, CT: Praeger.

Gentile, D. A., Coyne, S., & Walsh, D. A. (2011). Media violence, physical aggression, and relational aggression in school age children: A short-term longitudinal study. *Aggressive Behavior, 37*(2), 193–206.

Gentile, D. A., Linder, J. R., & Walsh, D. A. (2003). *Looking through time: A longitudinal study of children's media violence consumption at home and aggressive behaviors at school*. Paper presented at the Biennial Conference of the Society for Research in Child Development (April, 2003), Tampa, Florida. ERIC Document ED474790.

Gentile, D. A., Swing, E. L., Lim, C., & Khoo, A. (2012). Video game playing, attention problems, and impulsiveness: Evidence of bidirectional causality. *Psychology of Popular Media Culture, 1*(1), 62–70.

George, C., Solomon, J., & McIntosh, J. (2011). Divorce in the nursery: On infants and overnight care. *Family Court Review, 49*(3), 521–528.

Geraerts, E., Bernstein, D. M., Merckelbach, H., Linders, C., Raymaekers, L., & Loftus, E. F. (2008). Lasting false beliefs and their behavioral consequences. *Psychological Science, 19*(8), 749–753. doi:10.1111/j.1467-9280.2008.02151.x

Gerard, M. (2004). What's a parent to do? Phonics and other stuff. *Childhood Education, 83*(3), 159–160.

Gerlach, P. K. (2010). *Make a family map (genogram) to see who you all are*. Retrieved from http://sfhelp.org/sf/basics/geno.htm

Gernsbacher, M. A., Dawson, M., & Goldsmith, H. H. (2005). Three reasons not to believe in an autism epidemic. *Current Directions in Psychological Science, 14*(2), 55–58.

Gershoff, E. (2013). Spanking and child development: We know enough now to stop hitting our children. *Child Development Perspectives, 7*(3), 133–137.

Gettler, L. T., McDade, T. W., & Kuzawa, C. W. (2011). Cortisol and testosterone in Filipino young adult men: Evidence for co-regulation of both hormones by fatherhood and relationship status. *American Journal of Human Biology, 23*, 609–620.

Ghetti, S., & Angelini, L. (2008). The development of recollection and familiarity in childhood and adolescence: Evidence from the dual-process signal detection model. *Child Development, 79*(2), 339–358.

Ghoting, S. N., & Martin-Díaz, P. (2006). *Early literacy storytimes @ your library: Partnering with caregivers for success*. Chicago: American Library Association.

Giallo, R., & Gavidia-Payne, S. (2008). Evaluation of a family-based intervention for siblings of children with a disability or chronic illness. *Australian e-Journal for the Advancement of Mental Health, 7*(2), 1–13.

Gibbs, J. C. (2014). *Moral development and reality* (3rd ed.). New York: Oxford University Press.

Gibbs, J. C., Basinger, K. S., Grime, R. L., & Snarey, J. R. (2007). Moral judgment development across cultures: Revisiting Kohlberg's universality claims. *Developmental Review, 27*(4), 443–500.

Gibson, E. J., & Walk, R. D. (1960). The 'visual cliff.' *Scientific American, 202*(4), 64–71.

Giedd, J. N. (2004). Structural magnetic resonance imaging of the adolescent brain. *Annals of the New York Academy of Sciences, 1021*, 77–85.

Gielen, U. P., & Jeshmaridian, S. S. (1999). Lev S. Vygotsky: The man and the era. *International Journal of Group Tensions, 28*(3/4), 273–301.

Gilbert, S. F. (2000). *Developmental biology*. Sunderland, MA: Sinauer.

Gilchrist, J., Ballesteros, M. F., & Parker, E. M. (2012). Vital signs: Unintentional injury deaths among persons aged 0–19 Years — United States, 2000–2009. *Morbidity and Mortality Weekly Report, 61*. Centers for Disease Control and Prevention.

Gilliam, W. S. (2005). *Prekindergartners left behind: Expulsion rates in state prekindergarten systems*. Retrieved from http://childstudycenter.yale.edu/faculty/pdf/Gilliam05.pdf

Gilliam, W. S. (2008). *Implementing policies to reduce the likelihood of preschool expulsion*. Retrieved from http://medicine.yale.edu/childstudy/zigler/350_34772_PreKExpulsionHVioris-Brief2.pdf

Gilliam, W. S., & Shahar, G. (2006). Preschool and child care expulsion and suspension: Rates and predictors in one state. *Infants & Young Children, 19*(3), 228–245. doi:10.1097/00001163-200607000-00007

Gilligan, C. (1987). *Adolescent development reconsidered*. 10th Annual Konopka Lecture. Retrieved from http://www.konopka.umn.edu/peds/ahm/prod/groups/med/@pub/@med/documents/asset/med_21792.pdf

Ginn, J. D. (2008). *At issue: Bilingual education*. Detroit, MI: Thomson-Gale.

Gjerdingen, D. K., & Center, B. A. (2005). First-time parents' postpartum changes in employment, childcare, and housework responsibilities. *Social Science Research, 34*, 103–116.

Glantz, S. A., Mitchell, S., Titus, K., Polansky, J. R., Kaufmann, R. B., & Bauer, U. E. (2011). *Smoking in top-grossing movies—United States, 2010*. Centers for Disease Control and Prevention. Retrieved from http://www.cdc

.gov/mmwr/preview/mmwrhtml/mm6027a1. htm?s_cid=mm6027a1_w

Glaser, S. (1993). Intelligence testing. *Congressional Quarterly Researcher, 3,* 649–672.

Gleason, J. B. (2005). The development of language: An overview and a preview. In J. B. Gleason (Ed.), *The development of language* (6th ed., pp. 1–38). Boston: Pearson.

Godwin, H. A. (2009). Lead exposure and poisoning in children. *UCLA Institute of the Environment and Sustainability, Southern California Environmental Report Card, Spring 2009.* Retrieved from http://www.environment.ucla.edu/report card/article3772.html

Gogate, L., Maganti, M., & Bahrick, L. E. (2015). Cross-cultural evidence for multimodal motherese: Asian Indian mothers' adaptive use of synchronous words and gestures. *Journal of Experimental Child Psychology, 129,* 110–126. doi:10.1016/j.jecp.2014.09.002

Gogtay, N., Giedd, J. N., Lusk, L., Hayashi, K. M., Greenstein, D., Vaituzis, A. C., . . . Thompson, P. M. (2004). Dynamic mapping of human cortical development during childhood through early adulthood. *Proceedings of the National Academy of Sciences, 101*(21), 8174–8179.

Goldberg, J. S., & Carlson, M. J. (2015). Patterns and predictors of coparenting after unmarried parents part. *Journal of Family Psychology, 29*(3), 416–426. doi:10.1037/fam0000078

Goldberg, R. J., Higgins, E. L., Raskind, M. H., & Herman, K. L. (2003). Predictors of success in individuals with learning disabilities: A qualitative analysis. *Learning Disabilities Research and Practice, 18*(4), 222–236.

Goldberg, W. A., Prause, J., Lucas-Thompson, R., & Himsel, A. (2008). Maternal employment and children's achievement in context: A meta-analysis of four decades of research. *Psychological Bulletin, 134*(1), 77–108.

Goldenberg, C., & Wagner, K. (2015). Bilingual education. Reviving an American tradition. *American Educator, 39,* 28–32, 44.

Goldfield, B. A., & Snow, C. E. (2005). Individual differences—Implications for the study of language acquisition. In J. B. Gleason (Ed.), *The development of language* (6th ed., pp. 292–323). Boston: Pearson.

Goldman, L., & Smith, C. (1998). Imagining identities: Mimetic constructions in Huli child fantasy play. *Journal of the Royal Anthropological Institute, 4*(2), 207–234.

Goldsmith, H. H., Lemery, K. S., Aksan, N., & Buss, K. A. (2000). Temperamental substrates of personality. In V. J. Molfese & D. L. Molfese (Eds.), *Temperament and personality development across the life span* (pp. 1–32). Mahwah, NJ: Erlbaum.

Goldstein, J. R. (2011). A secular trend toward earlier male sexual maturity: Evidence from shifting ages of male young adult mortality. *PLoS ONE, 6*(8), e14826. doi: 10.1371/journal. pone.0014826

Goldstein, S., & Brooks, R. B. (2005). The future of children today. In S. Goldstein & R. B. Brooks (Eds.), *Handbook of resilience in children* (pp. 397–400). New York: Springer.

Goldstein, T. R., & Winner, E. (2012). Enhancing empathy and theory of mind. *Journal of Cognition and Development, 13*(1), 19–37.

Golombok, S., & Hines, M. (2002). Sex differences in social behavior. In P. K. Smith & C. H. Hart (Eds.), *Blackwell handbook of childhood social development* (pp. 117–136). Malden, MA: Blackwell.

Gonzalez, M., Jones, D., & Parent, J. (2014). Coparenting experiences in African American families: An examination of single mothers and their nonmarital coparents. *Family Process, 53*(1), 33–54. doi:10.1111/famp.12063

Good, C., Johnsrude, I., Ashburner, J., Henson, R. N., Friston, K. J., & Frackowiak, R. S. (2001). Cerebral asymmetry and the effects of sex and handedness on brain structure: A voxel-based morphometric analysis of 465 normal adult human brains. *NeuroImage, 14*(3), 685–700.

Good, C., Aronson, J., & Inzlicht, M. (2003). Improving adolescents' standardized test performance: An intervention to reduce the effects of stereotype threat. *Journal of Applied Developmental Psychology, 24*(6), 645–662.

Good, C., Aronson, J., & Harder, J. A. (2008). Problems in the pipeline: Stereotype threat and women's achievement in high-level math courses. *Journal of Applied Developmental Psychology, 29*(1), 17–28.

Goodwin, C. J. (2005). *A history of modern psychology* (2nd ed.). Hoboken, NJ: Wiley.

Gopnik, A., Meltzoff, A. N., & Kuhl, P. K. (1999). *The scientist in the crib.* New York: William Morrow.

Gordian, G. (2012). *Sisimpur celebrates anniversary of USAID with ambassador to Bangladesh.* Retrieved from http://www.sesa meworkshop.org/our-blog/tag/bangladesh/

Gorrese, A., & Ruggieri, R. (2012). Peer attachment: A meta-analytic review of gender and age differences and associations with parent attachment. *Journal of Youth and Adolescence, 41*(5), 650–672.

Gosso, Y., & Carvalho, A. (2013). Play: The cultural context. *Encyclopedia on Early Childhood Development.* Retrieved from http://www. child-encyclopedia.com/sites/default/files/ textes-experts/en/774/play-and-cultural-con text.pdf

Gosso, Y., Morais, M. L. S., & Otta, E. (2007). Pretend play of Brazilian children: A window into different cultural worlds. *Journal of Cross-Cultural Psychology, 38*(5), 539–558.

Gottfredson, L. (1998). The general intelligence factor. *Scientific American Presents, 9*(4), 24–29.

Gottman, J. (2001). Meta-emotions, children's emotional intelligence, and buffering children from marital conflict. In C. D. Ryff & B. Singer (Eds.), *Emotion, social relationships, and health* (pp. 23–39). Oxford: Oxford University Press.

Gouin, K., Murphy, K., Shah, P. S., & Knowledge Synthesis Group on Determinants of Low Birth Weight and Preterm Births. (2011). Effects of cocaine use during pregnancy on low birthweight and preterm birth: Systematic review and meta-analyses. *American Journal of Obstetrics and Gynecology, 204*(4), 340, e1–12.

Gould, S. J. (1996). *The mismeasure of man.* New York: W. W. Norton.

Governors' Highway Safety Association. (2014). *Distracted driving laws.* Retrieved from http:// www.ghsa.org/html/stateinfo/laws/cell-phone_laws.html

Grabe, S., Ward, L. M., & Hyde, J. S. (2008). The role of the media in body image concerns among women: A meta-analysis of experimental and correlational studies. *Psychological Bulletin, 134*(3), 460–476.

Grady, D. (2007). Promising dystrophy drug clears early test. *The New York Times.* Retrieved from http://www.nytimes .com/2007/12/27/health/27drug.html

Grall, T. (2011). *Custodial mothers and fathers and their child support: 2009.* Washington, DC: U.S. Department of Commerce, Economics and Statistics Administration.

Grall, T. (2016). *Custodial mothers and fathers and their child support: 2013.* Retrieved from http://www.census.gov/content/dam/Cen sus/library/publications/2016/demo/P60-255.pdf

Granic, I., & Patterson, G. R. (2006). Toward a comprehensive model of antisocial development: A dynamic systems approach. *Psychological Review, 113*(1), 101–131.

Grant, J. M., Mottet, L. A., Tanis, J., Harrison, J., Herman, J. L., & Keisling, M. (2011). *Injustice at every turn: A report of the National Transgender Discrimination Survey.* Washington: National Center for Transgender Equality and National Gay and Lesbian Task Force, 2011. Retrieved from http://endtransdiscrimination. org/PDFs/NTDS_Report.pdf

Grasso, D. J., Ford, J. D., & Briggs-Gowan, M. J. (2013). Early life trauma exposure and stress sensitivity in young children. *Journal of Pediatric Psychology, 38*(1), 94–103. doi:10.1093/jpepsy/ jss101

Gray, L., Watt, L., & Blass, E. M. (2000). Skin-to-skin contact is analgesic in healthy newborns. *Pediatrics, 105*(1), e14.

Gray, M. R., & Steinberg, L. (1999). Unpacking authoritative parenting: Reassessing a multidimensional construct. *Journal of Marriage and Family, 61,* 574–587.

Graziano, P. A., Slavec, J., Hart, K., Garcia, A., & Pelham, W. E. (2014). Improving school readiness in preschoolers with behavior problems: Results from a summer treatment program. *Journal of Psychopathology and Behavioral Assessment, 36*(4), 555–569. doi: 10.1007/ s10862-014-9418-1

Green, E. J., Fazio-Griffith, L., & Parson, J. (2015). Treating children with psychosis: An integrative play therapy approach. *International Journal of Play Therapy, 24*(3), 162–176. doi:10.1037/a0039026

Green, J., & Hotelling, B. A. (2014). Healthy birth practice #3: Bring a loved one, friend, or doula for continuous support. *Journal of Perinatal Education, 23*(4), 194–197. doi:10.1891/1058-1243.23.4.194

Greenberg, L. S. (2015). *Emotion-focused therapy: Coaching clients to work through their feelings* (2nd ed.). Washington, DC: American Psychological Association. doi:10.1037/14692-015

Greenberger, E., Chen, C., & Beam, M. R. (1998). The role of "very important" nonparental adults in adolescent development. *Journal of Youth and Adolescence, 27*(3), 321–343.

Greene, A. (2004). *From first kicks to first steps: Nurturing your baby's development from pregnancy through the first year of life.* New York: McGraw-Hill.

Greene, S. M., Anderson, E. R., Hetherington, E. M., Forgatch, M. S., & DeGarmo, D. S. (2003). Risk and resilience after divorce. In F. Walsh (Ed.), *Normal family processes* (3rd ed., pp. 96–120). New York: Guilford Press.

Greene, S. M., Sullivan, K., & Anderson, E. R. (2008). Divorce and custody. In M. Hersen & A. M. Gross (Eds.), *Handbook of clinical psychology: Vol. 2. Children and adolescents* (pp. 833–855). Hoboken, NJ: Wiley.

Greenfield, P. M., Keller, H., Fuligni, A., & Maynard, A. (2003). Cultural pathways through universal development. *Annual Review of Psychology, 54,* 461–490.

Greenough, W. T., Black, J. E., & Wallace, C. S. (1987). Experience and brain development. *Child Development, 58*(3), 539–559.

Greenwald, A. G., & Nosek, B. A. (2001). Health of the Implicit Association Test at age 3. *Zeitschrift Für Experimentelle Psychologie, 48*(2), 85–93. doi:10.1026//0949-3946.48.2.85

Greenwald, A. G., Poehlman, A. T., Uhlmann, E. L., & Banaji, M. R. (2009). Understanding and using the Implicit Association Test: III. Meta-analysis of predictive validity. *Journal of Personality and Social Psychology, 97*, 17–41.

Gregory, A., Cornell, D., Fan, X., Sheras, P., Shih, T., & Huang, F. (2010). Authoritative school discipline: High school practices associated with lower bullying and victimization. *Journal of Educational Psychology, 102*(2), 483–496.

Grigorenko, E. L., & Dozier, M. (2013). Introduction to the special section on genomics. *Child Development, 84*(1), 6–16.

Groh, A. M., Roisman, G. I., van IJzendoorn, M. H., Bakermans-Kranenburg, M. J., & Fearon, R. (2012). The significance of insecure and disorganized attachment for children's internalizing symptoms: A meta-analytic study. *Child Development, 83*(2), 591–610.

Gross, M. M. (2006). Exceptionally gifted children: Long-term outcomes of academic acceleration and nonacceleration. *Journal for the Education of the Gifted, 29*(4), 404–429.

Grossman, J. B., Chan, C. S., Schwartz, S. O., & Rhodes, J. E. (2012). The test of time in school-based mentoring: The role of relationship duration and re-matching on academic outcomes. *American Journal of Community Psychology, 49*(1–2), 43–54.

Grotevant, H. D., McRoy, R. G., Wrobel, G. M., & Ayers-Lopez, S. (2013). Contact between adoptive and birth families: Perspectives from the Minnesota/Texas Adoption Research Project. *Child Development Perspectives, 7*(3), 193–198. doi: 10.1111/cdep.12039

Groysberg, B. & Abrahams, R. (2014). Manage your work, manage your life. *Harvard Business Review, 92*(3), 58–66.

Gruber, K. J., Cupito, S. H., & Dobson, C. F. (2013). Impact of doulas on healthy birth outcomes. *Journal of Perinatal Education, 22*(1), 49–58. doi:10.1891/1058-1243.22.1.49

Grusec, J. E. (1992). Social learning theory and developmental psychology: The legacies of Robert Sears and Albert Bandura. *Developmental Psychology, 28*(5), 776–786.

Grusec, J. E., Goodnow, J. J., & Kuczynski, L. (2000). New directions in analyses of parenting contributions to children's acquisition of values. *Child Development, 71*(1), 205–211.

Guglielmi, R. S. (2008). Native language proficiency, English literacy, academic achievement, and occupational attainment in limited-English-proficient students: A latent growth modeling perspective. *Journal of Educational Psychology, 100*(2), 322–342.

Gunnar, M. R. (2007). Stress effects on the developing brain. In D. Romer & E. F. Walker (Eds.), *Adolescent psychopathology and the developing brain: Integrating brain and prevention science* (pp. 127–147). New York: Oxford University Press.

Gunnoe, M. L., & Hetherington, E. M. (2004). Stepchildren's perceptions of noncustodial mothers and noncustodial fathers: Differences in socioemotional involvement and associations with adolescent adjustment problems. *Journal of Family Psychology, 18*(4), 555–563.

Guo, Y., Connor, C. M., Tompkins, V., & Morrison, F. J. (2011). Classroom quality and student engagement: Contributions to third-grade reading skills. *Frontiers in Psychology, 2*, (Article 157).

Gurung, R. A. R. (2005). How do students really study (and does it matter)? *Teaching of Psychology, 32*(4), 239–241.

Gupta, R. S., Springston, E. E., Warrier, M. R., Smith, B., Kumar, R., Pongracic, J., & Holl, J. L. (2011). The prevalence, severity, and distribution of childhood food allergy in the United States. *Pediatrics 128*(1), e9–17.

Gustafson, G. E., Wood, R. M., & Green, J. A. (2000). Can we hear the causes of infants' crying? In R. G. Barr, B. Hopkins, & J. A. Green (Eds.), *Crying as a sign, a symptom, & a signal: Clinical emotional and developmental aspects of infant and toddler crying* (pp. 8–22). New York: University Press.

Gutman, A., Dautriche, I., Crabbé, B., & Christophe, A. (2015). Bootstrapping the syntactic bootstrapper: Probabilistic labeling of prosodic phrases. *Language Acquisition: A Journal of Developmental Linguistics, 22*(3), 285–309. doi:10.1080/10489223.2014.971956

Guttmacher Institute. (2012). *Facts on American teens' sexual and reproductive health.* Retrieved from http://www.guttmacher.org/pubs/fb_ATSRH.html

Guttmacher Institute. (2014). *American teens' sexual and reproductive health.* Retrieved from http://www.guttmacher.org/pubs/FB-ATSRH.html

Ha, S., Sohn, I.-J., Kim, N., Sim, H. J., & Cheon, K.-A. (2015). Characteristics of brains in autism spectrum disorder: Structure, function and connectivity across the lifespan. *Experimental Neurobiology, 24*(4), 273–284. doi.org/10.5607/en.2015.24.4.273

Hackshaw, A., Rodeck, C., & Boniface, S. (2011). Maternal smoking in pregnancy and birth defects: A systematic review based on 173,687 malformed cases and 11.7 million controls. *Human Reproduction Update, 17*(5), 589–604.

Haden, C. A. (2003). Joint encoding and joint reminiscing: Implications for young children's understanding and remembering of personal experiences. In R. Fivush & C. A. Haden (Eds.), *Autobiographical memory and the construction of a narrative self* (pp. 49–69). Mahwah, NJ: Erlbaum.

Hafen, C. A., Laursen, B., Burk, W. J., Kerr, M., & Stattin, H. (2011). Homophily in stable and unstable adolescent friendships: Similarity breeds constancy. *Personality and Individual Differences, 51*(5), 607–612.

Haight, W. L., & Black, J. E. (2001). A comparative approach to play: Cross-species and cross-cultural perspectives of play in development. *Human Development, 44*, 228–234.

Haight, W. L., Wang, X., Fung, H., Williams, K., & Mintz, J. (1999). Universal, developmental, and variable aspects of young children's play: A cross-cultural comparison of pretending at home. *Child Development, 70*(6), 1477–1488.

Haight, W., & Miller, P. J. (1992). The development of everyday pretend play: A longitudinal study of mothers' participation. *Merrill-Palmer Quarterly, 38*(3), 331–349.

Haight, W., Black, J., Ostler, T., & Sheridan, K. (2006). Pretend play and emotion learning in traumatized mothers and children. In D. G. Singer, R. M. Golinkoff, & K. Hirsh-Pasek (Eds.), *Play=learning* (pp. 209–230). New York: Oxford University Press.

Hair, E. C., Moore, K. A., Garrett, S. B., Ling, T., & Cleveland, K. (2008). The continued importance of quality parent-adolescent relationships during late adolescence. *Journal of Research on Adolescence, 18*(1), 187–200.

Hair, N. L., Hanson, J. L., Wolfe, B. L., & Pollak, S. D. (2015). Association of child poverty, brain development, and academic achievement. *JAMA Pediatrics, 169*(9), 822–829. doi:10.1001/jamapediatrics.2015.1475

Halfon, N., & Newacheck, P. W. (2010). Evolving notions of childhood chronic illness. *Journal of the American Medical Association, 303*, 665–666.

Halgunseth, L. C., Ispa, J. M., & Rudy, D. (2006). Parental control in Latino families: An integrated review of the literature. *Child Development, 77*(5), 1282–1297.

Halim, M. L., & Ruble, D. (2010). Gender identity and stereotyping in early and middle childhood. In J. C. Chrisler & D. R. McCreary (Eds.), *Handbook of gender research in psychology* (pp.495–525). New York: Springer.

Halim, M. L., Ruble, D. N., Tamis-LeMonda, C. S., Zosuls, K. M., Lurye, L. E., & Greulich, F. K. (2014). Pink frilly dresses and the avoidance of all things 'girly': Children's appearance rigidity and cognitive theories of gender development. *Developmental Psychology, 50*(4), 1091–1101. doi:10.1037/a0034906

Hall, D. M. (2008). Feminist perspectives on the personal and political aspects of mothering. In J. C. Chrisler, C. Golden, & P. D. Rozee (Eds.), *Lectures on the psychology of women* (4th ed., pp. 58–79). Boston, MA: McGraw-Hill.

Halle, C., Dowd, T., Fowler, C., Rissel, K., Hennessy, K., MacNevin, R., & Nelson, M. A. (2008). Supporting fathers in the transition to parenthood. *Contemporary Nurse, 31*(1), 57–70.

Halpern, C. T., Spriggs, A. L., Martin, S. L., & Kupper, L. L. (2009). Patterns of intimate partner violence victimization from adolescence to young adulthood in a nationally representative sample. *Journal of Adolescent Health, 45*(5), 508–516.

Halpern, D., Valenzuela, S., & Katz, J. E. (2016). 'Selfie-ists' or 'Narci-selfiers'?: A cross-lagged panel analysis of selfie taking and narcissism. *Personality and Individual Differences, 97*, 98–101. doi:10.1016/j.paid.2016.03.019

Hamblen, J., & Barnett, E. (2009). *PTSD in children and adolescents.* U.S. Department of Veterans' Affairs. Retrieved from http://www.ptsd.va.gov/professional/pages/ptsd_in_children_and_adolescents_overview_for_professionals.asp

Hamblin, J. (2016). Concerns about folate causing autism are premature. Retrieved from http://www.theatlantic.com/science/archive/2016/05/on-folate-and-autism/482307/

Hamilton, B. E., Martin, J. A., Osterman, M. J. K., & Curtin, S. C. (2015). Births: Preliminary data for 2014. *National Vital Statistics Reports, 64*(6), 1–18.

Hamilton, B. E., Martin, J. A., Osterman, M. J. K., & Curtin, S. C., & Mathews, T. J. (2015). Births: Final data for 2014. *National Vital Statistics Reports, 64*(12), 1–63.

Hamilton, M. A., & Hamilton, S. F. (1997). *Learning well at work: Choices for quality.* Washington, DC: U.S. Department of Education/U.S. Department of Labor.

Hamilton, S. F., & Hamilton, M. A. (1999). *Building strong school-to-work systems: Illustrations of key components.* Washington, DC: U.S. Department of Education/U.S. Department of Labor.

Hamlin, J. K. (2013). Moral judgment and action in preverbal infants and toddlers: Evidence for an innate moral core. *New Directions in Psychological Science, 22*(3), 186–193.

Hamlin, J. K., Wynn, K., & Bloom, P. (2007). Social evaluation in preverbal infants. *Nature, 450*(7169), 557–559. doi:10.1038/nature06288

Hanrahan, C. (2006). Sleep. In K. Krapp & J. Wilson (Eds.), *Gale encyclopedia of children's health: Infancy through adolescence* (Vol. 4, pp. 1676–1680). Detroit, MI: Gale.

Hansen, M. B., & Markman, E. M. (2009). Children's use of mutual exclusivity to learn labels for parts of objects. *Developmental Psychology, 45*(2), 592–596.

Hansen, T. (2012). Parenthood and happiness: A review of folk theories versus empirical evidence. *Social Indicators Research, 108*(1), 29–64. doi: 10.1007/s11205–011–9865-y

Hardy, S. A., & Carlo, G. (2011). Moral identity: What is it, how does it develop, and is it linked to moral action? *Child Development Perspectives, 5*, 212–218.

Harkness, S., Johnston Mavridis, C., Ji Liu, J., & Super, C. M. (2015). In L. A. Jensen (Ed.), *The Oxford handbook of human development and culture* (pp. 271–291). New York: Oxford University Press.

Harlow, H. F. (1958). The nature of love. *American Psychologist, 13*(12), 673–685.

Harris Interactive. (2013). *Four in five Americans believe parents spanking their children is sometimes appropriate.* Retrieved from http://www.theharrispoll.com/health-and-life/Four_in_Five_Americans_Believe_Parents_Spanking_Their_Children_is_Sometimes_Appropriate.html

Harris, J. R. (1995). Where is the child's environment? A group socialization theory of development. *Psychological Review, 102*(3), 458–489.

Harris, J. R. (1998). *The nurture assumption: Why children turn out the way they do.* New York: Free Press.

Harris, S. (2004). Bullying at school among older adolescents. *Prevention Researcher, 11*(3), 12–14.

Harrison, D., Beggs, S., & Stevens, B. (2012). Sucrose for procedural pain management in infants. *Pediatrics, 130*(5), 918–925. doi:10.1542/peds.2011-3848

Harrison, K. (2006). Scope of self: Toward a model of television's effects on self-complexity in adolescence. *Communication Theory, 16*(2), 251–279.

Hart Research Associates. (2011). *A national survey of parents' knowledge, attitudes, and self-reported behaviors concerning sports safety.* Washington, DC: Safe Kids Worldwide.

Hart, B., & Risley, T. R. (1995). *Meaningful differences in the everyday experience of young American children.* Baltimore, MD: Paul H. Brookes.

Harter, S. (1999). *The construction of the self.* New York: Guilford Press.

Harter, S. (2006a). The development of self-esteem. In M. H. Kernis (Ed.), *Self-esteem issues and answers: A sourcebook of current perspectives* (pp. 144–150). New York: Psychology Press.

Harter, S. (2006b). The self. In N. Eisenberg, W. Damon, & R. M. Lerner (Eds.), *Handbook of child psychology: Vol. 3. Social, emotional, and personality development* (6th ed., pp. 505–570). Hoboken, NJ: Wiley.

Harter, S. (2012). *The construction of the self: Developmental and sociocultural foundations* (2nd ed.). New York: Guilford Press.

Hartman, A. (2003). Family policy: Dilemmas controversies, and opportunities. In F. Walsh (Ed.), *Normal family processes* (3rd ed., pp. 635–662). New York: Guilford Press.

Hatfield, H. (2016). Home DNA tests: Buyer beware. *WebMD Magazine.* Retrieved from http://www.webmd.com/a-to-z-guides/features/home-dna-tests-buyer-beware

Hartman, L. R., Magalhães, L., & Mandich, A. (2011). What does parental divorce or marital separation mean for adolescents? A scoping review of North American literature. *Journal of Divorce & Remarriage, 52*(7), 490–518. doi:10.1080/10502556.2011.609432

Hartshorne, J. K. (2010). How birth order affects your personality. *Scientific American.* Retrieved from http://www.scientificamerican.com/article/ruled-by-birth-order/

Haselager, G. T., Cillessen, A. N., Van Lieshout, C. M., Riksen-Walraven, J. A., & Hartup, W. W. (2002). Heterogeneity among peer-rejected boys across middle childhood: Developmental pathways of social behavior. *Developmental Psychology, 38*(3), 446–456.

Hasler, B. P., & Clark, D. B. (2013). Circadian misalignment, reward related brain function, and adolescent alcohol involvement. *Alcoholism: Clinical and Experimental Research, 37*(4), 558–565. doi: 10.1111/acer.12003

Hatva, E. (2010). Cognitive and brain consequences of learning in the arts. *APS Observer, 23*(6). Retrieved from http://www.psychologicalscience.org/index.php/publications/observer/2010/july-august-10/cognitive-and-brain-consequences-of-learning-in-the-arts.html

Hatzenbuehler, M. L. (2011). The social environment and suicide attempts in lesbian, gay, and bisexual youth. *Pediatrics, 127*(5), 896–903.

Haun, D. M., & Tomasello, M. (2011). Conformity to peer pressure in preschool children. *Child Development, 82*(6), 1759–1767.

Havighurst, S. S., Wilson, K. R., Harley, A. E., & Prior, M. R. (2009). Tuning in to kids: An emotion-focused parenting program—Initial findings from a community trial. *Journal of Community Psychology, 37*(8), 1008–1023. doi:10.1002/jcop.20345

Haworth, C. M. A., Kovas, Y., Harlaar, N., Hayiou-Thomas, M. E., Petrill, S. A., Dale, P. S., & Plomin, R. (2009). Generalist genes and learning disabilities: A multivariate genetic analysis of low performance in reading, mathematics, language and general cognitive ability in a sample of 8000 12-year-old twins. *Journal of Child Psychology and Psychiatry, 50*(10), 1318–1325.

Hay, C., Meldrum, R., & Mann, K. (2010). Traditional bullying, cyber bullying, and deviance: A general strain theory approach. *Journal of Contemporary Criminal Justice, 26*(2), 130–147. doi: 10.1177/1043986209359557

Hay, D. F., Caplan, M., & Nash, A. (2009). The beginnings of peer relations. In K. H. Rubin, W. M. Bukowski, & B. Laursen (Eds.), *Handbook of peer interactions, relationships, and groups* (pp. 121–142). New York: Guilford Press.

Hay, J. F., Pelucchi, B., Estes, K., & Saffran, J. R. (2011). Linking sounds to meanings: Infant statistical learning in a natural language. *Cognitive Psychology, 63*(2), 93–106.

Hayne, H. (2004). Infant memory development: Implications for childhood amnesia. *Developmental Review, 24*(1), 33–73.

Hazan, C., & Shaver, P. (1987). Romantic love conceptualized as an attachment process. *Journal of Personality and Social Psychology, 52*(3), 511–524.

Head Start. (n.d.). *Head Start Family and Child Experiences Survey (FACES).* Retrieved from http://www.acf.hhs.gov/opre/research/project/head-start-family-and-child-experiences-survey-faces

Head Start. (2010). *Head Start program fact sheet fiscal year 2010.* Retrieved from https://eclkc.ohs.acf.hhs.gov/hslc/data/factsheets/fHeadStartProgr.htm

Health Resources and Services Administration. (n.d.). *Prenatal services.* Retrieved from http://mchb.hrsa.gov/programs/womeninfants/prenatal.html

Heath, P. (2005). *Parent-child relations: History, theory, research, and context.* Upper Saddle River, NJ: Pearson.

Hebert, K. R., Fales, J., Nangle, D. W., Papadakis, A. A., & Grover, R. L. (2013). Linking social anxiety and adolescent romantic relationship functioning: Indirect effects and the importance of peers. *Journal of Youth and Adolescence, 42*(11), 1708–1720. doi: 10.1007/s10964–012–9878–0

Heckman, J. J. (2011). The economics of inequality. *American Educator, 35*(1), 31–35, 47.

Heisler, E. J. (2012). *The U.S. infant mortality rate: International comparisons, underlying factors, and federal programs.* Washington, DC: Congressional Research Service.

Hembree, W. C., Cohen-Kettenis, P., Delemarre-van de Waal, H. A., Gooren, L. J., Meyer, W. J., Spack, N., ...Montori, V. M. (2009). Endocrine treatment of transsexual persons: An endocrine society clinical practice guideline. *Journal of Clinical Endocrinology & Metabolism, 94*(9), 3132–3154

Hennessey, B. A. (2007). Promoting social competence in school-aged children: The effects of the Open Circle Program. *Journal of School Psychology, 45*(3), 349–360.

Hennessey, B. A. (2015). If I were Secretary of Education: A focus on intrinsic motivation and creativity in the classroom. *Psychology of Aesthetics, Creativity, and the Arts, 9*(2), 187–192. doi:10.1037/aca0000012

Hennighausen, K. H., & Lyons-Ruth, K. (2010). Disorganization of attachment strategies in infancy and childhood. Centre of Excellence for Early Childhood Development. Retrieved from http://www.enfant-encyclopedie.com/pages/PDF/Hennighausen-Lyons-RuthANGxp_rev.pdf

Herman-Giddens, M. E. (2013). The enigmatic pursuit of puberty in girls. *Pediatrics, 132*(6), 1125–1126. doi: 10.1542/peds.2013–3058

Herman-Giddens, M. E., Steffes, J., Harris, D., Slora, E., Hussey, M., Dowshen, S. A., ... Reiter, E. O. (2012). Secondary sexual characteristics in boys: Data from the pediatric research in office settings network. *Pediatrics, 130*(5), e1058–e1068. doi: 10.1542/peds.2011-3291

Herrnstein, R. J., & Murray, C. (1994). *The bell curve: Intelligence and class structure in American life.* New York: Free Press.

Herschensohn, J. (2007). *Language development and age.* New York: Cambridge University Press.

Heteronomous. (n.d.). Retrieved September 2, 2016, from http://www.merriam-webster.com/dictionary/heteronomous

Hetherington, E. M. (1991). Presidential address: Families, lies and videotapes. *Journal of Research on Adolescence, 1*(4), 323–348.

Hetherington, E. M., & Kelly, J. (2002). *For better or for worse: Divorce reconsidered.* New York: W W. Norton & Company.

Hetherington, E. M., Reiss, D., & Plomin, R. (Eds.). (1994). *Separate social words of siblings: The impact of nonshared environment on development.* Hillsdale, NJ: Erlbaum.

Hickman, G. R., Bartholomew, M., Mathwig, J., & Heinrich, R. S. (2008). Differential developmental pathways of high school dropouts and graduates. *Journal of Educational Research*, *102*(1), 3–14.

Higley, E., Walker, S. C., Bishop, A. S., & Fritz, C. (2016). Achieving high quality and long-lasting matches in youth mentoring programmes: A case study of 4Results mentoring. *Child & Family Social Work, 21*(2), 240–248. doi:10.1111/cfs.12141

Hill, C., Corbett, C., & St. Rose, A. (2010). *Why so few? Women in science, technology, engineering and mathematics*. Washington, DC: AAUW. Retrieved from http://www.aauw.org/learn/research/upload/whysofew.pdf

Hill, J. L., Brooks-Gunn, J., & Waldfogel, J. (2003). Sustained effects of high participation in early intervention for low-birth-weight premature infants. *Developmental Psychology, 39*(4), 730–744.

Hill, N. E., Bromell, L., Tyson, D. F., & Flint, R. (2007). Developmental commentary: Ecological perspectives on parental influences during adolescence. *Journal of Clinical Child and Adolescent Psychiatry, 36*(3), 367–377.

Hillman, C. H., Buck, S. M., Themanson, J. R., Pontifex, M. B., & Castelli, D. M. (2009). Aerobic fitness and cognitive development: Event-related brain potential and task performance indices of executive control in preadolescent children. *Developmental Psychology, 45*(1), 114–129.

Hinde, E. R., & Perry, N. (2007). Elementary teachers' application of Jean Piaget's theories of cognitive development during social studies curriculum debates in Arizona. *The Elementary School Journal, 108*(1), 63–79.

Hindman, A. H., & Morrison, F. J. (2011). Family involvement and educator outreach in Head Start. *Elementary School Journal, 111*(3), 359–386. doi:10.1086/657651

Hines, M. (2006). Prenatal testosterone and gender-related behaviour. *European Journal of Endocrinology, 155*, S115–S121.

Hiscock, H. (2006). The crying baby. *Australian Family Physician*, 35(9), 680–684.

Hiscock, H., Cook, F., Bayer, J., Le, H. N., Mensah, F., Cann, W. . . . James-Roberts, I. S. (2014). Preventing early infant sleep and crying problems and postnatal depression: A randomized trial. *Pediatrics, 133*(2), e346–e354.

Hiss, W. C., & Franks, C. W. (2014). *Defining promise: Optional standardized testing policies in American college and university admissions*. Arlington, VA: National Association for College Admission Counseling.

Hoeve, M., Dubas, J. S., Eichelsheim, V. I., van der Laan, P. H., Smeenk, W., & Gerris, J. R. M. (2009). The relationship between parenting and delinquency: A meta-analysis. *Journal of Abnormal Child Psychology, 37*(6), 749–775.

Hoff, E., & Naigles, L. (2002). How children use input to acquire a lexicon. *Child Development, 73*(2), 418–433.

Hoffman, M. L. (2000). *Empathy and moral development: Implications for caring and justice*. New York: Cambridge University Press.

Holbreich, M., Genuneit, J., Weber, J., Braun-Fahrlander, C., Waser, M., & von Mutius, E. (2012). Amish children living in northern Indiana have a very low prevalence of allergic sensitization. *Journal of Allergy and Clinical Immunology, 129*(6), 1671–1673.

Holbreich, M., Genuneit, J., Weber, J., Braun-Fahrlander, C., & von Mutius, E. (2012). The prevalence of asthma, hay fever and allergic sensitization in Amish children. *Journal of Allergy and Clinical Immunology, 129*(2), Supplement, Page AB130. doi: 10.1016/j.jaci.2011.12.433

Hollich, G., Golinkoff, R. M., & Hirsh-Pasek, K. (2007). Young children associate novel words with complex objects rather than salient parts. *Developmental Psychology, 43*(5), 1051–1061.

Holmes, E., Sasaki, T., & Hazen, N. L. (2013). Smooth versus rocky transitions to parenthood: Family systems in developmental context. *Family Relations, 62*(5), 824–837. doi:10.1111/fare.12041

Honein, M. A., Paulozzi, L. J., & Erickson, J. D. (2001). Continued occurrence of Accutane-exposed pregnancies. *Teratology, 64*(3), 142–147.

Hopkins, B., & Johnson, S. P. (2005). *Prenatal development of postnatal functions*. Westport, CT: Praeger.

Hopson, J. L. (1998). Fetal psychology: Your baby can feel, dream and even listen to Mozart in the womb. *Psychology Today, 31*, 44–48.

Hornor, G. (2010). Child sexual abuse: Consequences and implications. *Journal of Pediatric Health Care, 24*(6), 358–364.

Houdé, O., Pineau, A., Leroux, G., Poirel, N., Perchey, G., Lanoë, C., . . . Mazoyer, B. (2011). Functional magnetic resonance imaging study of Piaget's conservation-of-number task in preschool and school-age children: A neo-Piagetian approach. *Journal of Experimental Child Psychology, 110*(3), 332–346. doi:10.1016/j.jecp.2011.04.008

Howden, M. (2007). *Stepfamilies: Understanding and responding effectively*. Australian Family Relationships Clearinghouse Briefing No. 6.

Howe, M. L. (2015). Memory development. In L. Liben & U. Müller (Eds.), *Handbook of child psychology and developmental science, Vol. 2* (7th ed., pp. 203–249). Hoboken, NJ: Wiley.

Howe, N., Rinaldi, C. M., Jennings, M., & Petrakos, H. (2002). 'No! The lambs can stay out because they got cozies!': Constructive and destructive sibling conflict, pretend play, and social understanding. *Child Development, 73*(5), 1460–1473. doi:10.1111/1467-8624.00483

Hoyert, D. L. (2007). *Maternal mortality and related concepts*. National Center for Health Statistics. *Vital and Health Statistics, Series 3*, Number 33.

Hoyland, A., Dye, L., & Lawton, C. L. (2009). A systematic review of the effect of breakfast on the cognitive performance of children and adolescents. *Nutrition Research Reviews, 22*, 220–243.

Huang, B. H. (2014). The effects of age on second language grammar and speech production. *Journal of Psycholinguistic Research, 43*(4), 397–420. doi:10.1007/s10936-013-9261-7

Huang, C. (2010). Mean-level change in self-esteem from childhood through adulthood: Meta-analysis of longitudinal studies. *Review of General Psychology, 14*(3), 251–260.

Hubel, D. H., & Wiesel, T. N. (1965). Comparison of the effects of unilateral and bilateral eye closure on cortical unit responses in kittens. *Journal of Neurophysiology, 28*, 1029–1040.

Huizink, A. C., & Mulder, E. J. H. (2006). Maternal smoking, drinking or cannabis use during pregnancy and neurobehavioral and cognitive functioning in human offspring. *Neuroscience & Biobehavioral Reviews, 30*(1), 24–41.

Huelke, D. F. (1998). An overview of anatomical considerations of infants and children in the adult world of automobile safety design. *Annual Proceedings of the Association for the Advancement of Automotive Medicine, 42*, 93–113.

The Human Rights Campaign. (2012). *Growing up LGBT in America: HRC Youth Survey Report key findings*. Washington, DC: Author.

Humphrey, J. H. (2003). *Child development through sport*. New York: Haworth Press.

Humphrey, J. H. (2004). *Childhood stress in contemporary society*. New York: Haworth Press.

Hunt, J. M. (1988). Relevance to educability: Heritability or range of reaction. In S. G. Cole & R. G. Demaree (Eds.), *Applications of interactionist psychology: Essays in honor of Saul B. Sells* (pp. 59–108). Hillsdale, NJ: Erlbaum.

Hurd, N. M., Sánchez, B., Zimmerman, M. A., & Caldwell, C. H. (2012). Natural mentors, racial identity, and educational attainment among African American adolescents: Exploring pathways to success. *Child Development, 83*(4), 1196–1212.

Hurd, N. M., & Zimmerman, M. A. (2010). Natural mentoring relationships among adolescent mothers: A study of resilience. *Journal of Research on Adolescence, 20*(3), 789–809.

Huston, A. C., Anderson, D. R., Wright, J. C., Linebarger, D. L., & Schmitt, K. L. (2001). *Sesame Street* viewers as adolescents: The recontact study. In S. M. Fisch & R. T. Truglio (Eds.), *"G" is for growing—Thirty years of research on children and* Sesame Street (pp. 131–146). Mahwah, NJ: Erlbaum.

Huston, A. C., Wright, J. C., Marquis, J., & Green, S. B. (1999). How young children spend their time: Television and other activities. *Developmental Psychology, 35*(4), 912–925.

Hyde, J. (2014). Gender similarities and differences. *Annual Review of Psychology, 65*, 373–398. doi:10.1146/annurev-psych-010213-115057

Hyde, K. L., Lerch, J., Norton, A., Forgeard, M., Winner, E., Evans, A. C., & Schlaug, G. (2009). Musical training shapes structural brain development. *Journal of Neuroscience, 29*(10), 3019–3025.

Hyde, M. M., Lamb, Y., Arteaga, S. S., & Chavis, D. (2008). National evaluation of the Safe Start Demonstration Project: Implications for mental health practice. *Best Practices in Mental Health, 4*(1), 108–122.

Hyde, T. E., & Gengenbach, M. S. (2007). *Conservative management of sports injuries*. Sudbury, MA: Jones & Bartlett.

Igualada, A., Bosch, L., & Prieto, P. (2015). Language development at 18 months is related to multimodal communicative strategies at 12 months. *Infant Behavior & Development, 39*, 42–52. doi:10.1016/j.infbeh.2015.02.004

Impett, E. A., Sorsoli, L., Schooler, D., Henson, J. M., & Tolman, D. L. (2008). Girls' relationship authenticity and self-esteem across adolescence. *Developmental Psychology, 44*(3), 722–733.

Institute of Education Sciences. (n.d.). *ERIC: Education Resources Information Center*. Retrieved from http://ies.ed.gov/ncee/projects/eric.asp

Institute of Education Sciences. (2007). *Intervention: Dialogic reading*. Retrieved from http://ies.ed.gov/ncee/wwc/reports/early_ed/dial_read/

International Dyslexia Association. (2014). *DSM-5 Changes in diagnostic criteria for specific learning disabilities (SLD): What are the Implications?* Retrieved from http://www.cdl.org/articles/dsm-5-changes-in-diagnostic-criteria-for-specific-learning-disabilities-sld-what-are-the-implications%E2%80%A8/

Ip, S., Chung, M., Raman, G., Chew, P., Magula, N., DeVine, D., ... Lau, J. (2007). *Breastfeeding and maternal and infant health* outcomes in developed countries. Evidence Report-Technology Assessment No. 153. AHRQ Publication No. 07-E007. Rockville, MD: Agency for Health Care Research and Quality.

Ireson, J., Hallam, S., & Plewis, I. (2001). Ability grouping in secondary schools: Effects on pupils' self-concepts. *British Journal of Educational Psychology, 71*(2), 315–326.

Irish, L., Kobayashi, I., & Delahanty, D. L. (2010). Long-term physical health consequences of childhood sexual abuse: A meta-analytic review. *Journal of Pediatric Psychology, 35*(5), 450–461.

Irwin, J. R., Moore, D. L., Tornatore, L. A., & Fowler, A. E. (2012). Expanding on early literacy. *Children & Libraries: The Journal of the Association for Library Service to Children, 10*(2), 20–28.

Isaacs, J. B. (2012). *Starting school at a disadvantage: The school readiness of poor children.* Brookings Institution. Retrieved from http://www.brookings.edu/~/media/research/files/papers/2012/3/19%20school%20disadvantage%20isaacs/0319_school_disadvantage_isaacs.pdf

Isay, R. A. (1996). Psychoanalytic therapy with gay men: Developmental considerations. In R. P. Cabaj & T. S. Stein (Eds.), *Textbook of homosexuality and mental health* (pp. 451–469). Washington, DC: American Psychiatric Association.

Ito, T., Ando, H., Suzuki, T., Ogura, T., Hotta, K., Imamura, Y. . . . Handa, H. (2010). Identification of a primary target of thalidomide teratogenicity. *Science, 327*(5971), 1345–1350.

Iverson, J. M., Capirci, O., Volterra, V., & Goldin-Meadow, S. (2008). Learning to talk in a gesture-rich world: Early communication in Italian vs. American children. *First Language, 28*(2), 164–181.

Iverson, J. M., & Goldin-Meadow, S. (2005). Gesture paves the way for language development. *Psychological Science, 16*, 368–371.

Izard, C. E. (2007). Basic emotions, natural kinds, emotion schemas and a new paradigm. *Perspectives on Psychological Science, 2*(3), 260–280.

Jaakola, J. K., & Gissler, M. (2007). Are girls more susceptible to the effects of prenatal exposure to tobacco smoke on asthma? *Epidemiology, 18*, 573–576.

Jack, F., MacDonald, S., Reese, E., & Hayne, H. (2009). Maternal reminiscing style during early childhood predicts the age of adolescents' earliest memories. *Child Development, 80*(2), 496–505.

Jack, R. E., Blais, C., Scheepers, C., Schyns, P. G., & Caldara, R. (2009). Cultural confusions show that facial expressions are not universal. *Current Biology, 19*(18), 1543–1548.

Jackson, K. M., & Nazar, A. M. (2006). Breastfeeding, the immune response, and long-term health. *Journal of the American Osteopathic Association, 106*(4), 203–207.

Jackson, S., Newall, E., & Backett-Milburn, K. (2015). Children's narratives of sexual abuse. *Child & Family Social Work, 20*(3), 322–332. doi:10.1111/cfs.12080

Jacobs, B. A., & Lefgren, L. (2004). Remedial education and student achievement: A regression continuity analysis. *The Review of Economics and Statistics, 86*(1), 226–244.

Jacobs, J. E., Davis-Kean, P., Bleeker, M., Eccles, J. S., & Malanchuk, O. (2005). I can, but I don't want to: The impact of parents, interests, and activities on gender differences in math. In A. Gallagher & J. Kaufman (Ed.), *Gender differences in mathematics* (pp. 246–263). New York: Cambridge University Press.

Jacobs, J. E., Lanza, S., Osgood, D. W., Eccles, J. S., & Wigfield, A. (2002). Changes in children's self-competence and values: Gender and domain differences across grades one though twelve. *Child Development, 73*(2), 509–527. doi:10.1111/1467-8624.00421

Jacquet, S. E., & Surra, C. A. (2004). Parental divorce and premarital couples: Commitment and other relationship characteristics. *Journal of Marriage and Family, 63*(3), 627–638.

Jaffee, S., & Hyde, J. S. (2000). Gender differences in moral orientation: A meta-analysis. *Psychological Bulletin, 126*(5), 703–726.

Jaffee, S. R., Bowes, L., Ouellet-Morin, I., Fisher, H. L., Moffitt, T. E., Merrick, M. T., & Arseneault, L. (2013). Safe, stable, nurturing relationships break the intergenerational cycle of abuse: A prospective nationally representative cohort of children in the United Kingdom. *Journal of Adolescent Health, 53*(4, Suppl), S4–S10. doi: 10.1016/j.jadohealth.2013.04.007

Jambunathan, S., Burts, D. C., & Pierce, S. (2000). Comparisons of parenting attitudes among five ethnic groups in the United Sates. *Journal of Comparative Family Studies, 31*(4), 395–406.

James, K. H., & Engelhardt, L. (2012). The effects of handwriting experience on functional brain development in pre-literate children. *Trends in Neuroscience and Education, 1*(1), 32–42. doi.org/10.1016/j.tine.2012.08.001

James, W. (1990). *The principles of psychology.* Cambridge, MA: Harvard University Press. (Original work published in 1890)

James, W. (1992). The self. In W. James (Ed.), *Psychology: Briefer course* (pp. 174–209). New York: Library Classics of the United States. (Original work published in 1892)

Jauk, E., Benedek, M., Dunst, B., & Neubauer, A. C. (2013). The relationship between intelligence and creativity: New support for the threshold hypothesis by means of empirical breakpoint detection. *Intelligence, 41*(4), 212–221. doi:10.1016/j.intell.2013.03.003

Jay, T., & Janschewitz, K. (2012). The science of swearing. *APS Observer, 25*(5). Retrieved from http://www.psychologicalscience.org/index.php/publications/observer/2012/may-june-12/the-science-of-swearing.html

Jensen, A. C., & Whiteman, S. D. (2014). Parents' differential treatment and adolescents' delinquent behaviors: Direct and indirect effects of difference-score and perception-based measures. *Journal of Family Psychology, 28*(4), 549–559. doi: 10.1037/a0036888

Jensen, A. C., Whiteman, S. D., Fingerman, K. L., & Birditt, K. S. (2013). 'Life still isn't fair': Parental differential treatment of young adult siblings. *Journal of Marriage And Family, 75*(2), 438–452.

Jepsen, J., & Martin, H. (2006). *Born too early: Hidden handicaps of premature children.* London: Karnac Books.

Jiang, Y., Ekono, M., & Skinner. C. (2015). *Basic facts about low-income children: Children under 18 years, 2013.* New York: National Center for Children in Poverty, Mailman School of Public Health, Columbia University.

Jimerson, S. R., & Ferguson, P. (2007). A longitudinal study of grade retention: Academic and behavioral outcomes of retained students through adolescence. *School Psychology Quarterly, 22*(3), 314–339.

Jin, M., Jacobvitz, D., Hazen, N., & Jung, S. (2012). Maternal sensitivity and infant attachment security in Korea: Cross-cultural validation of the Strange Situation. *Attachment & Human Development, 14*(1), 33–44.

Johnson, H. D., McNair, R., Vojick, A., Congdon, D., Monacelli, J., & Lamont, J. (2006). Categorical and continuous measurement of sex-role orientation: Differences in associations with young adults' reports of well-being. *Social Behavior and Personality, 34*(1), 59–76. doi:10.2224/sbp.2006.34.1.59

Johnson, J. G., Cohen, P., Kasen, S., & Brook, J. S. (2007). Extensive television viewing and the development of attention and learning difficulties during adolescence. *Archives of Pediatrics & Adolescent Medicine, 16*(5), 480–486.

Johnson, K. (2000). *Do small classes influence academic achievement? What the National Assessment of Education Progress shows* [Center for Data Analysis Report #00–07]. Washington, DC: Heritage Foundation.

Johnson, V. E., & de Villiers, J. G. (2009). Syntactic frames in fast mapping verbs: Effects of age, dialect, and clinical status. *Journal of Speech, Language, and Hearing Research, 52*(3), 610–622.

Johnston, J. R., Walters, M. G., & Olesen, N. W. (2005). Is it alienating parenting, role reversal or child abuse? A study of children's rejection of a parent in child custody disputes. *Journal of Child Custody, 5*, 191–218.

Johnston, L. D., O'Malley, P. M., Miech, R. A., Bachman, J. G., & Schulenberg, J. E. (2016). *Monitoring the Future: National survey results on drug use, 1975–2015: Overview, key findings on adolescent drug use.* Ann Arbor, MI: Institute for Social Research, The University of Michigan.

Joiner, L. L. (2007). The road to stress is paved with good parental intentions. *Gannett News Service, USA Today.* Retrieved from http://www.usatoday.com/news/education/2007-08-15-kids-scheduling_N.htm

Jones, C. (2014). New law tackles high school football collisions head on. *SF Gate.* Retrieved from http://www.sfgate.com/preps/article/New-California-law-limits-schools-full-contact-5636585.php

Jones, E. G., Renger, R., & Kang, Y. (2007). Self-efficacy for health-related behaviors among deaf adults. *Research in Nursing & Health, 30*(2), 185–192.

Jones, E. M., & Landreth, G. (2002). The efficacy of intensive individual play therapy for chronically ill children. *International Journal of Play Therapy, 11*(1), 117–140.

Jones, M. C. (1924). A laboratory study of fear: The case of Peter. *Pedagogical Seminary, 31*, 308–315.

Jones, P. (1995). Contradictions and unanswered questions in the Genie case: A fresh look at the linguistic evidence. *Language & Communication, 15*(3), 261–280.

Jónsson, F. H., Njardvik, U., Ólafsdóttir, G., & Grétarsson, S. J. (2000). Parental divorce: Long-term effects on mental health, family relations and adult sexual behavior. *Scandinavian Journal of Psychology, 41*(2), 101–105.

Joo, M. (2010). Long-term effects of Head Start on academic and school outcomes of children in persistent poverty: Girls vs. boys. *Children and Youth Services Review, 32*(6), 807–814. doi:10.1016/j.childyouth.2010.01.018

Jorde, L. B., Carey, J. C., Bamshad, M. J., & White, R. L. (2006). *Medical genetics* (3rd ed.). St. Louis, MO: Mosby.

Joseph, J. (2001). Separated twins and the genetics of personality differences: A critique. *American Journal of Psychology, 114*(1), 1–30.

Josselyn, S. A., & Frankland, P. W. (2012). Infantile amnesia: A neurogenic hypothesis. *Learning & Memory, 19*(9), 423–433.

Jurkovic, G. J., Thirkield, A., & Morrell, R. (2001). Parentification of adult child of divorce: A multidimensional analysis. *Journal of Youth and Adolescence, 30*(2), 245–257.

Jusko, T. A., Henderson, C. R., Lanphear, B. P., Dory-Slechta, D. A., Parsons, P. J., & Canfield, R. L. (2008). Blood lead concentrations < 10 µg/dL and child intelligence at 6 years of age. *Environmental Health Perspectives, 116*(2), 243–248.

Jussim, L., & Harber, K. D. (2005). Teacher expectations and self-fulfilling prophecies: Knowns and unknowns, resolved and unresolved controversies. *Personality and Social Psychology Review, 9*(2), 131–155. doi:10.1207/s15327957pspr0902_3

Juster, F. T., Ono, H., & Stafford, F. (2004). *Changing times of American youth: 1981-2003.* Ann Arbor, MI: Institute for Social Research, University of Michigan. Retrieved from http://www.umich.edu/news/Releases/2004/Nov04/teen_time_report.pdf

Jung, C. (2015, October 18). Overselling breastfeeding. *New York Times*, p. SR1. Retrieved from http://www.nytimes.com/2015/10/18/opinion/sunday/overselling-breast-feeding.html?_r=0

Juvonen, J. (2013). Peer rejection among children and adolescents: Antecedents, reactions, and maladaptive pathways. In C. DeWall (Ed.), *The Oxford handbook of social exclusion* (pp. 101–110). New York: Oxford University Press.

Kabali, H. K., Irigoyen, M. M., Nunez-Davis, R., Budacki, J. G., Mohanty, S. W., Leister, K. P., & Bonner, R. L. (2015). Exposure and use of mobile media devices by young children. *Pediatrics, 136*, 1044–1050. doi: 10.1542/peds.2015-2151

Kagan, J. (2008). In defense of qualitative changes in development. *Child Development, 79*(6), 1606–1624.

Kahn, M. (2002). *Basic Freud: Psychoanalytic thought for the twenty first century.* New York: Basic Books.

Kail, R. V., & Ferrer, E. (2007). Processing speed in childhood and adolescence: Longitudinal models for examining developmental change. *Child Development, 78*(6), 1760–1770.

Kalb, C. (2005, February 27). When does autism start? *Newsweek*, pp. 45–47, 50–53. Retrieved from http://www.newsweek.com/when-does-autism-start-122297

Kaler, S. R., & Freeman, B. J. (1994). Analysis of environmental deprivation: Cognitive and social development in Romanian orphans. *Journal of Child Psychology and Psychiatry, 35*(4), 769–781.

Kaltiala-Heino, R., Kosunen, E., & Rimpela, M. (2003). Pubertal timing, sexual behaviour and self-reported depression in middle adolescence. *Journal of Adolescence, 26*, 531–545.

Kam, K. (2014). *The top 7 pregnancy myths.* Retrieved from http://www.webmd.com/baby/guide/top-7-pregnancy-myths

Kamii, C., Rummelsburg, J., & Kari, A. (2005). Teaching arithmetic to low-performing, low-SES first graders. *Journal of Mathematical Behavior, 24*(1), 39–50.

Kanazawa, S. (2015). Breastfeeding is positively associated with child intelligence even net of parental IQ. *Developmental Psychology, 51*(12), 1683–1689. doi.org/10.1037/dev0000060

Kandel, D. B. (1978). Homophily, selection, and socialization in adolescent friendships. *American Journal of Sociology, 84*(2), 427–436.

Kandel, D. B., & Lesser, G. S. (1972). *Youth in two worlds.* San Francisco: Jossey-Bass.

Kaneshiro, N. K., & Zieve, D. (2011). *Shaken baby syndrome.* Retrieved from http://www.nlm.nih.gov/medlineplus/ency/article/000004.htm

Kanner, L. (1949). Problems of nosology and psychodynamics of early infantile autism. *American Journal of Orthopsychiatry, 19*, 416–426.

Kapadia, S. (2008). Adolescent-parent relationships in Indian and Indian immigrant families in the US: Intersections and disparities. *Psychology and Developing Societies, 20*, 257–275.

Kaplan, S. (1995). The restorative benefits of nature: Toward an integrative framework. *Journal of Environmental Psychology, 15*(3), 169–182.

Kaplow, J. B., Gipson, P. Y., Horwitz, A. G., Burch, B. N., & King, C. A. (2014). Emotional suppression mediates the relation between adverse life events and adolescent suicide: Implications for prevention. *Prevention Science, 15*(2), 177–185. doi:10.1007/s11121-013-0367-9

Kaplowitz, P. B. (2008). Link between body fat and the timing of puberty. *Pediatrics, 121*(Supplement No. 3), S208–S217.

Kapoun, J. (1998). Teaching undergrads WEB evaluation: A guide for library instruction. *C&RL News.* Retrieved from http://www.ala.org/ala/mgrps/divs/acrl/publications/crlnews/1998/jul/teachingundergrads.cfm

Karmiloff, K., & Karmiloff-Smith, A. (2001). *Pathways to language.* Cambridge, MA: Harvard University Press.

Karney, B. R., Beckett, M. K., Collins, R. L., & Shaw, R. (2007). *Adolescent romantic relationships as precursors of healthy adult marriages: A review of theory, research, and programs.* Santa Monica, CA: RAND Corporation. (Technical report TR-488-ACF prepared by the RAND Labor and Population Program for the U.S. Department of Health and Human Services).

Karpouzis, F., & Bonello, R. (2012). Nutritional complementary and alternative medicine for pediatric attention-deficit/hyperactivity disorder. *Ethical Human Psychology and Psychiatry, 14*(1), 41–60.

Kärtner, J., Keller, H., Chaudhary, N., & Yovsi, R. D. (2012). The development of mirror self-recognition in different sociocultural contexts. *Monographs of The Society for Research in Child Development, 77*(4), 37–65.

Kärtner, J. (2015). The autonomous developmental pathway: The primacy of subjective mental states for human behavior and experience. *Child Development, 86*(4), 1298–1309. doi:10.1111/cdev.12377

Karuza, E. A., Newport, E. L., Aslin, R. N., Starling, S. J., Tivarus, M. E., & Bavelier, D. (2013). The neural correlates of statistical learning in a word segmentation task: An fMRI study. *Brain and Language, 127*(1), 46–54. doi:10.1016/j.bandl.2012.11.007

Kasthuri, N., & Lichtman, J. W. (2010). Neurocartography. *Neuropsychopharmacology, 35*, 342–343.

Katz, C., Bolton, S., Katz, L. Y., Isaak, C., Tilston-Jones, T., & Sareen, J. (2013). A systematic review of school-based suicide prevention programs. *Depression and Anxiety, 30*(10), 1030–1045.

Katz, V. L. (2003). Prenatal care. In J. S. Scott, R. S. Gibbs, B. Y. Karlan, & A. F. Haney (Eds.), *Danforth's obstetrics and gynecology* (9th ed., pp. 1–33). Philadelphia: Lippincott.

Kavšek, M. (2004). Predicting later IQ from infant visual habituation and dishabituation: A meta-analysis. *Journal of Applied Developmental Psychology, 25*(3), 369–393.

Kayyal, M. H., & Russell, J. A. (2013). Americans and Palestinians judge spontaneous facial expressions of emotion. *Emotion, 13*(5), 891–904.

Keel, P. K., & Forney, K. J. (2013). Psychosocial risk factors for eating disorders. *International Journal of Eating Disorders, 46*, 433–439.

Keller, H. (2013). Attachment and culture. *Journal of Cross-Cultural Psychology 44*(2), 175-194.

Kelly, Y., Sacker, A., Gray, R., Kelly, J., Wolke, D., & Quigley, M. A. (2009). Light drinking in pregnancy, a risk for behavioural problems and cognitive deficits at 3 years of age? *International Journal of Epidemiology, 38*, 129–140.

Kemp, N., & Bryant, P. (2003). Do beez buzz? Rule-based and frequency-based knowledge in learning to spell plurals. *Child Development, 74*(1), 63–74.

Kena, G., Musu-Gillette, L., Robinson, J., Wang, X., Rathbun, A., Zhang, J., ... Dunlop-Velez, E. (2015). *The condition of education 2015* (NCES 2015-144). Washington, DC: U.S. Department of Education, National Center for Education Statistics.

Kendall-Tackett, K. (2014). Social connectedness versus mothers on their own. In D. Narvaez, K. Valentino, A. Fuentes, J. J. McKenna, & P. Gray (Eds.), *Ancestral landscapes in human evolution: Culture, childrearing and social wellbeing* (pp. 104–107). New York: Oxford University Press.

Kendler, K. S., Gardner, C., & Dick, D. M. (2011). Predicting alcohol consumption in adolescence from alcohol-specific and general externalizing genetic risk factors, key environmental exposures, and their interaction. *Psychological Medicine, 41*(7), 1507–1516. doi:10.1017/S003329171000190X

Kenneady, L. M., & Intercultural Development Research Association. (2004). *Good for nothing: In grade retention.* Retrieved from http://www.idra.org/IDRA_Newsletter/June_-_July_2004%3A_Self-Renewing_Schools%E2%80%A6Leadership/Good_for_Nothing_In_grade_Retention

Kennedy, H. (1997). Karl Heinrich Ulrichs: First theorist of homosexuality. In V. A. Rosario (Ed.), *Science and homosexualities* (pp. 26–45). New York: Routledge.

Kennedy, S., & Ruggles, S. R. (2014). Breaking up is hard to count: The rise of divorce in the United States, 1980-2010. *Demography, 51*(2), 587–598.

Kennell, J. H., & Klaus, M. H. (1979). Early mother–infant contact: Effects on the mother and the infant. *Bulletin of the Menninger Clinic, 43*(1), 69–78.

Kenney-Benson, G. A., Pomerantz, E. M., Ryan, A. M., & Patrick, H. (2006). Sex differences in math performance: The role of children's approach to schoolwork. *Developmental Psychology, 42*(1), 11–26.

Kessenich, M. (2003). Developmental outcomes of premature, low birth weight, and medically fragile infants. *Newborn & Infant Nursing Reviews, 3*(3), 80–87.

KidsHealth. (2008). *10 things that might surprise you about being pregnant.* Retrieved from http://kidshealth.org/parent/preg nancy_newborn/pregnancy/pregnancy.html

Kiesner, J., Kerr, M., & Stattin, H. (2004). "Very important persons" in adolescence: Going beyond in-school, single friendships in the study of peer homophily. *Journal of Adolescence*, *27*, 545–560.

Kim, J. (2009). Type-specific intergenerational transmission of neglectful and physically abusive parenting behaviors among young parents. *Children and Youth Services Review*, *31*(7), 761–767.

Kim, H. (2011). Consequences of parental divorce for child development. *American Sociological Review*, *76*(3), 487–511.

Kim, K. H. (2005). Can only intelligent people be creative? A meta-analysis. *Journal of Secondary Gifted Education*, *16*(2–3), 57–66.

Kim, K. H. (2008). Meta-analyses of the relationship of creative achievement to both IQ and divergent thinking test scores. *Journal of Creative Behavior*, *42*(2), 106–130.

Kim, S., & Kochanska, G. (2015). Mothers' power assertion; children's negative, adversarial orientation; and future behavior problems in low-income families: Early maternal responsiveness as a moderator of the developmental cascade. *Journal of Family Psychology*, *29*(1), 1–9. doi:10.1037/a0038430

Kim, Y. S., Leventhal, B. L., Koh, Y. J., Fombonne, E., Laska, E., Lim, E. C., . . . Grinker, R. R. (2011). Prevalence of autism spectrum disorders in a total population sample. *American Journal of Psychiatry*, *168*(9), 904–912.

Kim-Cohen, J., Caspi, A., Taylor, A., Williams, B., Newcombe, R., Craig, I. W., & Moffitt, T. E. (2006). MAOA, maltreatment, and gene-environment interaction predicting children's mental health: New evidence and a meta-analysis. *Molecular Psychiatry*, *11*(10), 903–913.

Kinsbourne, M. (2009). Development of cerebral lateralization in children. In C. R. Reynolds & E. Fletcher-Janzen (Eds.), *Handbook of clinical child neuropsychology* (3rd ed., pp. 47–66). New York: Springer.

Kirk, E., Howlett, N., Pine, K. J., & Fletcher, B. (2013). To sign or not to sign? The impact of encouraging infants to gesture on infant language and maternal mind-mindedness. *Child Development*, *84*(2), 574–590. doi:10.1111/j.1467-8624.2012.01874.x

Kirkorian, H. L., Wartella, E. A., & Anderson, D. R. (2008). Children and electronic media. *The Future of Children*, *18*(1), 39–62.

Kirsh, S. J. (2012). *Children, adolescents, and media violence: A critical look at the research* (2nd ed.). Thousand Oaks, CA: Sage.

Kirschner, F., Paas, F., & Kirschner, P. A. (2009). A cognitive load approach to collaborative learning: United brains for complex tasks. *Educational Psychology Review*, *21*(1), 31–42.

Kisilevsky, B. S., Hains, S. J., Lee, K., Xie, X., Huang, H., Ye, H. H., . . . ,Wang, Z. (2003). Effects of experience on fetal voice recognition. *Psychological Science*, *14*(3), 220–224. doi:10.1111/1467-9280.02435

Klahr. A. M., Rueter, M. A., McGue, M., Iacono, W. G., & Burt, S. A. (2011). The relationship between parent-child conflict and adolescent antisocial behavior: Confirming shared environmental mediation. *Journal of Abnormal Child Psychology*, *39*(5), 683–694.

Kleber de Oliveira, W., Cortez-Escalante, J., De Oliveira, W. T., Ikeda do Carmo, G. M., Henriques, C., Coelho, G., & Araújo de França, G. (2016). Increase in reported prevalence of microcephaly in infants born to women living in areas with confirmed Zika virus transmission during the first trimester of pregnancy — Brazil, 2015. *Mortality and Morbidity Weekly Report*, *65*, 242–247. doi.org/10.15585/mmwr.mm6509e2

Klemm, W. R. (2013). Why writing by hand could make you smarter. *Psychology Today*. Retrieved from https://www.psychology-today.com/blog/memory-medic/201303/why-writing-hand-could-make-you-smarter

Klomek, A. B., Sourander, A., & Elonheimo, H. (2015). Bullying by peers in childhood and effects on psychopathology, suicidality, and criminality in adulthood. *The Lancet Psychiatry*, *2*(10), 930–941. doi:10.1016/S2215-0366(15)00223-0

Klug, W. S., Cummings, M. R., Spencer, C. A., & Palladino, M. A. (2016). *Concepts of genetics*. Essex, UK: Pearson.

Kobak, R., Rosenthal, N., & Serwik, A. (2005). The attachment hierarchy in middle childhood: Conceptual and methodological issues. In K. A. Kerns & R. A. Richardson (Eds.), *Attachment in middle childhood* (pp. 71–89). New York: Guilford Press.

Kobus, K. (2003). Peers and adolescent smoking. *Addiction*, *98*, 37–55.

Kochanska, G., & Aksan, N. (2006). Children's conscience and self-regulation. *Journal of Personality*, *74*(6), 1587–1617.

Kochanska, G., Barry, R. A., Aksan, N., & Boldt, L. J. (2008). A developmental model of maternal and child contributions to disruptive conduct: The first six years. *Journal of Child Psychology and Psychiatry*, *49*(11), 1220–1227.

Kogan, S. M., Brody, G. H., & Chen, Y. (2011). Natural mentoring processes deter externalizing problems among rural African American emerging adults: A prospective analysis. *American Journal of Community Psychology*, *48*(3–4), 272–283.

Kohlberg, L. (1966). A cognitive-developmental analysis of children's sex-role concepts and attitudes. In E. E. Maccoby (Ed.), *The development of sex differences* (pp. 82–173). Palo Alto, CA: Stanford University Press.

Kohlberg, L. (1987). The development of moral judgment and moral action. In L. Kohlberg (Ed.), *Child psychology and childhood education* (pp. 259–328). White Plains, NY: Longman.

Kohlberg, L. (2005). Moral stages and moralization: The cognitive developmental approach. In C. Lewis & J. G. Bremner (Eds.), *Developmental psychology II: Social and language development* (Vol. 5, pp. 201–231). Thousand Oaks, CA: Sage.

Kokko, K., & Pulkkinen, L. (2005). Stability of aggressive behavior from childhood to middle age in women and men. *Aggressive Behavior*, *31*(5), 485–497.

Kokko, K., Tremblay, R. E., Lacourse, E., Nagin, D. S., & Vitaro, F. (2006). Trajectories of prosocial behavior and physical aggression in the middle childhood: Links to adolescent school dropout and physical violence. *Journal of Research on Adolescence*, *16*(3), 403–428.

Koniak-Griffin, D., Spears, G. V., & Stein, J. A. (2010). Substance use during and after pregnancy: Patterns and predictors of use in Latina and African American adolescents. *Journal of Obstetric, Gynecologic & Neonatal Nursing*, *39*, S89–S90. doi:10.1111/j.1552-6909.2010.01123_4.x

Konijn, E. A., Bijvank, M. N., & Bushman, B. J. (2007). I wish I were a warrior: The role of wishful identification in the effects of violent video games on aggression in adolescent boys. *Developmental Psychology*, *43*(4), 1038–1044.

Kopp, C. B., and Krakow, J. B. *Child Development: Development in social context*. Upper Saddle River, NJ: Pearson.

Korkman, M., Kirk, U., & Kemp, S. (2016). *NEPSY®-Second edition*. Retrieved from http://www.pearsonclinical.com/psychology/products/100000584/nepsy-second-edition-nepsy-ii.html#tab-details

Kotila, L. E., Schoppe-Sullivan, S. J., & Kamp Dush, C. M. (2013). Time parenting activities in dual-earner families at the transition to parenthood. *Family Relations*, *62*(5), 795–807.

Kotrla, K. (2010). Domestic minor sex trafficking in the United States. *Social Work*, *55*(2), 181–187.

Kovács, Á. M., & Mehler, J. (2009). Cognitive gains in 7-month-old bilingual infants. *Proceedings of the National Academy of Sciences of the United States of America*, *106*(16), 6556–6560.

Kovas, Y., & Plomin, R. (2007). Learning abilities and disabilities: Generalist genes, specialist environments. *Current Directions in Psychological Science*, *16*(5), 284–288.

Kowalski, R. M., & Limber, S. P. (2007). Electronic bullying among middle school students. *Journal of Adolescent Health*, *41*(6 Supplement), S22–S30.

Kowlessar, O., Fox, J. R., & Wittkowski, A. (2015). First-time fathers' experiences of parenting during the first year. *Journal of Reproductive and Infant Psychology*, *33*(1), 4–14. doi:10.1080/02646838.2014.971404

Krahé, B., Busching, R., & Möller, I. (2012). Media violence use and aggression among German adolescents: Associations and trajectories of change in a three-wave longitudinal study. *Psychology of Popular Media Culture*, *1*(3), 152–166.

Krähenbühl, S., & Blades, M. (2006). The effect of interviewing techniques on young children's responses to questions. *Child: Care, Health & Development*, *32*(3), 321–331.

Kramer, L. (2011). Supportive sibling relationships. In J. Caspi (Ed.), *Sibling development: Implications for mental health practitioners* (pp. 41–58). New York: Springer Publishing Company.

Krashen, S. (2009). Anything but reading. *Knowledge Quest*, *37*(5), 18–25.

Krcmar, M., Grela, B., & Lin, K. (2007). Can toddlers learn vocabulary from television? An experimental approach. *Media Psychology*, *10*(1), 41–63.

Kreager, D. A., Molloy, L. E., Moody, J., & Feinberg, M. E. (2016). Friends first? The peer network origins of adolescent dating. *Journal of Research on Adolescence*, *26*(2), 257–269. doi:10.1111/jora.12189

Kretch, K. S., & Adolph, K. E. (2013). Cliff or step? Posture-specific learning at the edge of a drop-off. *Child Development*, *84*(1), 226–240. doi:10.1111/j.1467-8624.2012.01842.x

Kristensen, P., & Bjerkedal, T. (2007). Explaining the relation between birth order and intelligence. *Science*, *316*(5832), 1717.

Kristjánsson, K. (2004). Empathy, sympathy, justice and the child. *Journal of Moral Education*, *33*(3), 291–305. doi:10.1080103057242042000733064

Kristjansson, B., Petticrew, M., MacDonald, B., Krasevec, J., Janzen, L., Greenhalgh, T., . . . Welch, V. (2007). School feeding for improving the physical and psychosocial health of disadvantaged students. *Cochrane Database of Systematic Reviews*, *1*, Art. No. CD004676.

Krogstad, J. M. (2016). *Rise in English proficiency among U.S. Hispanics is driven by the young*. Pew Research Center. Retrieved from http://www.pewresearch.org/fact-tank/2016/04/20/rise-in-english-proficiency-among-u-s-hispanics-is-driven-by-the-young/

Krogstad, J., & Gonzalez-Barrera, A. (2015). *A majority of English-speaking Hispanics in the U.S. are bilingual*. Pew Research Center. Retrieved from http://www.pewresearch .org/fact-tank/2015/03/24/a-majority-of-english-speaking-hispanics-in-the-u-s-are-bilingual/

Kronk, C. M. (1994). Private speech in adolescents. *Adolescence, 29*(116), 781–804.

Krug, E. G., Dahlberg, L., Mercy, J., Zwi, A., & Lozano, R. (2002). *World report on violence and health*. Geneva, Switzerland: World Health Organization.

Kuhl, P. K. (2010). Brain mechanisms in early language acquisition. *Neuron, 67*(5), 713–727. http://doi.org/10.1016/j.neuron.2010.08.038

Kuhl, P. K., Conboy, B. T., Padden, D., Nelson, T., & Pruitt, J. (2005). Early speech perception and later language development: Implications for the "critical period." *Language Learning and Development, 1*(3 & 4), 237–264.

Kuhn, D. (2009). Adolescent thinking. In R. M. Lerner & L. Steinberg (Eds.), *Handbook of adolescent psychology. Vol. 1: Individual bases of adolescent development* (3rd ed., pp. 152–186). Hoboken, NJ: Wiley.

Kuo, F. E., & Taylor, A. (2004). A potential natural treatment for attention-deficit/hyperactivity disorder: Evidence from a national study. *American Journal of Public Health, 94*(9), 1580–1586.

Kutscher, M. (2008). *ADHD—Living without brakes*. Philadelphia: Jessica Kingsley.

Lablanc, L., Richardson, W., & McIntosh, J. (2005). The use of applied behavioural analysis in teaching children with autism. *International Journal of Special Education, 20*(1), 13–34.

Labouvie-Vief, G. (2006). Emerging structures of adult thought. In J. A. Arnett & J. L. Tanner (Eds.), *Emerging adults in America: Coming of age in the 21st century* (pp. 59–84). Washington, DC: American Psychological Association.

Lacelle, C., Hébert, M., Lavoie, F., Vitaro, F., & Tremblay. R. E. (2012). Sexual health in women reporting a history of child sexual abuse. *Child Abuse & Neglect, 36*, 247–259.

Ladd, G. W., Kochenderfer-Ladd, B., Eggum, N. D., Kochel, K. P., & McConnell, E. M. (2011). Characterizing and comparing the friendships of anxious-solitary and unsociable preadolescents. *Child Development, 82*(5), 1434–1453.

LaGravenese, R. (Director). (2007). *Freedom writers* [Motion picture]. United States: Paramount.

Laird, J. A., & Feldman, S. S. (2004). Evaluation of the Summerbridge Intervention Program: Design and preliminary findings. In G. D. Borman & M. Boulay (Eds.), *Summer learning: Research, policies, and programs* (pp. 199–229). Mahwah, NJ: Erlbaum.

Lamb, M. E., Sternberg, K., Orbach, Y., Esplin, P., Stewart, H., & Mitchell, S. (2003). Age differences in children's responses to open ended invitations in the course of forensic interviews. *Journal of Consulting and Clinical Psychology, 71*, 926–934.

Lamborn, S. D., Mounts, N. S., Steinberg, L., & Dornbusch, S. M. (1991). Patterns of competence and adjustment among adolescents from authoritative, authoritarian, indulgent, and neglectful families. *Child Development, 62*(5), 1049–1065.

Lammas, C., & Poland, G. (2014). *Motor skills: The handbook for referrers*. Halton, UK: Bridgewater Community Health Care.

Landhuis, C. E., Poulton, R., Welch, D., & Hancox, R. J. (2007). Does childhood television viewing lead to attention problems in adolescence? Results from a prospective longitudinal study. *Pediatrics, 120*(3), 532–537.

Landrum, T. J., & Kauffman, J. M. (2006). Behavioral approaches to classroom management. In C. M. Evertson & C. S. Weinstein (Eds.), *Handbook of classroom management: Research, practice and contemporary issues* (pp. 47-72). Mahwah, NJ: Erlbaum.

Lane, J. (1994). *History of genetics timeline*. Retrieved from http://www.accessexcellence.org/AE/AEPC/WWC/1994/genetic stln.php

Laney, C., Morris, E. K., Bernstein, D. M., Wakefield, B. M., & Loftus, E. F. (2008). Asparagus, a love story: Healthier eating could be just a false memory away. *Experimental Psychology, 55*(5), 291–300. doi:10.1027/1618-3169.55.5.291

Lange, N., Travers, B. G., Bigler, E. D., Prigge, M. B., Froehlich, A. L., Nielsen, J. A., ... Lainhart, J. E. (2015). Longitudinal volumetric brain changes in autism spectrum disorder ages 6-35 years. *Autism Research, 8*, 82–93.

Language and Reading Research Consortium. (2015). The dimensionality of language ability in young children. *Child Development, 86*(6), 1948–1965.

Lansford, J. E., Chang, L., Dodge, K. A., Malone, P. S., Oburu, P., Palmérus, K., & Quinn. N. (2005). Physical discipline and children's adjustment: Cultural normativeness as a moderator. *Child Development, 76*(6), 1234–1246. doi: 10.1111/j.1467–8624.2005.00847.x

Lansford, J. E., Deater-Deckard, K., Dodge, K. A., Bates, J. E., & Pettit, G. S. (2004). Ethnic differences in the link between physical discipline and later adolescent externalizing behaviors. *Journal of Child Psychology and Psychiatry 45*(4), 801–812.

Lansford, J. E., Putallaz, M., Grimes, C. L., Schiro-Osman, K. A., Kupersmidt, J. B., & Coie, J. D. (2006). Perceptions of friendship quality and observed behaviors with friends: How do sociometrically rejected, average, and popular girls differ? *Merrill-Palmer Quarterly, 52*(4), 694–720.

Lany, J., & Saffran, J. R. (2010). From statistics to meaning: Infants' acquisition of lexical categories. *Psychological Science, 21*(2), 284–291.

Lapierre, M. A., Piotrowski, J. T., & Linebarger, D. L. (2012). Background television in the homes of U.S. children. *Pediatrics, 130*(5), 839–846.

Lapsley, D. K. (2006). Moral stage theory. In M. Killen & J. Smetana (Eds.), *Handbook of moral development* (pp. 37–66). Mahwah, NJ: Erlbaum.

Larson, J. P. (2002). Genetic counseling. In D. S. Blachfeld & J. L. Longe (Eds.), *Gale encyclopedia of medicine* (Vol. 3), (2nd ed., pp. 1429–1431). Detroit, MI: Gale.

Larson, R. (2004). How U.S. children and adolescents spend time: What it does (and doesn't) tell us about their development. In J. Lerner & A. E. Alberts (Eds.), *Current directions in developmental psychology* (pp. 134–144). Upper Saddle River, NJ: Pearson Prentice Hall.

Larson, R. W., & Brown, J. R. (2007). Emotional development in adolescence: What can be learned from a high school theater program? *Child Development, 78*(4), 1083–1099.

Laskey, A., Stump, T., Perkins, S., Zimet, G., Sherman, S., & Downs, S. (2012). Influence of race and socioeconomic status on the diagnosis of child abuse: A randomized study. *Journal of Pediatrics, 160*(6), 1003–1008.

Latzman, R. D., Naifeh, J. A., Watson, D., Vaidya, J. G., Heiden, L. J., Damon, J. D., . . . Young, J. (2011). Racial differences in symptoms of anxiety and depression among three cohorts of students in the Southeastern United States. *Psychiatry: Interpersonal and Biological Processes, 74*, 332–348.

Lau, S. (1989). Sex role orientation and domains of self-esteem. *Sex Roles, 2*, 415–422.

Laughlin, L. (2013). Who's minding the kids? Child care arrangements: Spring 2011. *Current Population Reports*, P70-135. Washington, DC: U.S. Census Bureau.

Laughlin, L. (2014). A child's day: Living arrangements, nativity, and family transitions: 2011. *Current Population Reports*, P70-139. Washington, DC: U.S. Census Bureau.

Laursen, B., Coy, K. C., & Collins, W. (1998). Reconsidering changes in parent–child conflict across adolescence: A meta-analysis. *Child Development, 69*(3), 817–832. doi: 10.2307/1132206

Laursen, B., Furman, W., & Mooney, K. A. (2006). Predicting interpersonal competence and self-worth from adolescent relationships and relationship networks: Variable-centered and person- centered perspectives. *Merrill-Palmer Quarterly, 52*(3), 572–600.

Lauw, M. M., Havighurst, S. S., Wilson, K. R., Harley, A. E., & Northam, E. A. (2014). Improving parenting of toddlers' emotions using an emotion coaching parenting program: A pilot study of Tuning in to Toddlers. *Journal of Community Psychology, 42*(2), 169–175. doi:10.1002/jcop.21602

Lavelli, M., Pantoja, A. P. F., Hsu, H.-C., Messinger, D., & Fogel, A. (2005). Using microgenetic designs to study change processes. In D. M. Teti (Ed.), *Handbook of research methods in developmental science* (pp. 40–65). Oxford, UK: Blackwell. doi: 10.1002/9780470756676.ch3

Lavigne, H. J., Hanson, K. G., & Anderson, D. R. (2015). The influence of television coviewing on parent language directed at toddlers. *Journal of Applied Developmental Psychology, 36*, 1–10.

Law, K. L., Stroud, L. R., LaGasse, L. L., Niaura, R., Liu, J., & Lester, B. (2003). Smoking during pregnancy and newborn neurobehavior. *Pediatrics, 111*(6), 1318–1323.

LD OnLine. (2008a). *Celebrity quiz*. Retrieved from http://www.ldonline.org/article/5938

LD OnLine. (2008b). *LD basics: What is a learning disability?* Retrieved from http://www.ldonline.org/ldbasics/whatisld

Le, H. (2000). Never leave your little one alone—Raising an Ifaluk child. In J. DeLoache & A. Gottlieb (Eds.), *A world of babies* (pp. 199-222). New York: Cambridge University Press.

Lebedeva, G. C., & Kuhl, P. K. (2010). Sing that tune: Infants' perception of melody and lyrics and the facilitation of phonetic recognition in songs. *Infant Behavior and Development, 33*(4), 419–430.

Lecanuet, J., Graniere-Deferre, C., & DeCasper, A. (2005). Are we expecting too much from prenatal sensory experiences? In B. Hopkins & S. P. Johnson (Eds.), *Prenatal development of postnatal functions* (pp. 31–49). Westport, CT: Praeger.

Lecce, S., Demicheli, P., Zocchi, S., & Palladino, P. (2015). The origins of children's metamemory: The role of theory of mind. *Journal of Experimental Child Psychology, 131*, 56–72.

Lee, G. Y., & Kisilevsky, B. S. (2014). Fetuses respond to father's voice but prefer mother's voice after birth. *Developmental Psychobiology, 56*(1), 1–11. doi:10.1002/dev.21084

Lee, J. C., & Staff, J. (2007). When work matters: The varying impact of work intensity on high school dropout. *Sociology of Education, 80*(2), 158–178.

Lee, M. D., MacDermid, S. M., Dohring, P. L., & Kossek, E. E. (2005). Professionals becoming parents: Socialization, adaptation and identity transformation. In E. E. Kossek & S. J. Lambert (Eds.), *Work and life integration: Organization, cultural and individual perspectives* (pp. 287–317). Mahwah, NJ: Erlbaum.

Leerkes, E. M., & Crockenberg, S. C. (2006). Antecedents of mothers emotional and cognitive responses to infant distress: The role of family, mother, and infant characteristics. *Infant Mental Health Journal, 27*(4), 405–428. doi:10.1002/imhj.20099

Leffel, K., & Suskind, D. (2013). Parent-directed approaches to enrich the early language environments of children living in poverty. *Seminars in Speech & Language, 34*(4), 267–277. doi:10.1055/s-0033-1353443

Legg, S., & Hutter, M. (2007). *A collection of definitions of intelligence.* Technical Report IDSIA-07-07. Retrieved from http://arxiv.org/pdf/0706.3639.pdf

LeHalle, H. (2006). Cognitive development in adolescence: Thinking freed from concrete constraints. In S. Jackson & L. Goossens (Eds.), *Handbook of adolescent development.* New York: Psychology Press.

Lehman, E. B., & Erdwins, C. J. (2004). The social and emotional adjustment of young, intellectually gifted children. In S. M. Moon (Ed.), *Social/emotional issues, underachievement, and counseling of gifted and talented students* (pp. 1–8). Thousand Oaks, CA: Corwin.

Lehman, J. D. (2005). *Understanding marriage, family, and intimate relationships.* Springfield, IL: Charles C. Thomas.

Lehmann, C. (2004). Brain studies could affect death penalty case outcome. *Psychiatric News, 39*(24), 10–34.

Leming, J. S. (2001). Integrating a structured ethical reflection curriculum into high school community service experiences: Impact on students' sociomoral development. *Adolescence, 36*(141), 33–45.

Lemish, D. (2007). *Children and television: A global perspective.* Oxford, UK: Blackwell.

Lempinen, E. W. (2012). Poverty can harm early brain development, researchers say. *Science, 337*(6093), 428.

Lenhart, A. (2015). *Mobile access shifts social media use and other online activities.* Pew Research Center. Retrieved from http://www.pewinternet.org/2015/04/09/mobile-access-shifts-social-media-use-and-other-online-activities/

Lenhart, A., Anderson, M., & Smith, A. (2015). *Teens, technology and romantic relationships.* Pew Research Center. Retrieved from http://www.pewinternet.org/2015/10/01/teens-technology-and-romantic-relationships/

Lenhart, A., & Madden, M. (2007). *Social networking websites and teens: An overview.* Pew Research Center. Retrieved from http://www.pewinternet.org/PPF/r/198/report_display.asp

Lenroot, R. K., Greenstein, D. K., Gogtay, N., Wallace, G. L., Clasen, L. S., Blumenthal, J. D., . . . Giedd, J. N. (2007). Sexual dimorphism of brain developmental trajectories during childhood and adolescence. *NeuroImage, 36,* 1065–1073.

Lenz, A. S., & Hollenbaugh, K. M. (2015). Meta-analysis of trauma-focused cognitive behavioral therapy for treating PTSD and co-occurring depression among children and adolescents. *Counseling Outcome Research and Evaluation, 6*(1), 18–32. doi:10.1177/2150137815573790

Lereya, S. T., Copeland, W. E., Costello, E. J., & Wolke, D. (2015). Adult mental health consequences of peer bullying and maltreatment in childhood: Two cohorts in two countries. *The Lancet Psychiatry, 2*(6), 524–531. doi:10.1016/S2215-0366(15)00165-0

Lerner, R. M. (2002). *Concepts and theories of human development* (3rd ed.). Mahwah, NJ: Erlbaum.

Lester, B. M., Tronick, E., Nestler, E., Abel, T., Kosofsky, B., Kuzawa, C. W., . . . Wood, M. A. (2011). Behavioral epigenetics. *Annals of the New York Academy of Sciences, 1226,* 14–33. http://doi.org/10.1111/j.1749-6632.2011.06037.x

Leventhal, J. M. (2003). Test of time: "The battered child syndrome" 40 years later. *Clinical Child Psychology and Psychiatry, 8*(4), 543–545.

Levine, L. E. (1983). Mine: Self-definition in 2-year-old boys. *Developmental Psychology, 19*(4), 544–549.

Levine, L. E. (2002). Kohlberg, Lawrence (1927–1987). In N. J. Salkind (Ed.), *Child development* (pp. 225–226). New York: Macmillan Reference USA.

Levine, L. E. (2003). Mr. Rogers: The nature of the man. *Clio's Psyche, 10,* 24.

Levine, L. E., Bowman, L. L., Kachinsky, K., Sola, A., & Waite, B. M. (2015). *Infants, toddlers and mobile media use.* Poster presented at the 27th annual convention of the Association for Psychological Science, New York.

Levine, L. E., & Waite, B. M. (2000). Television viewing and attentional abilities in fourth and fifth grade children. *Journal of Applied Developmental Psychology, 21*(6), 667–679.

Levine, L. E., & Waite, B. M. (2002). Television and the American child. *Clio's Psyche, 9*(1), 24–26.

LeVine, R. A., Dixon, S., LeVine, S., Richman, A., Leiderman, P. H., Keefer, C. H., & Brazelton, T. B. (1994). *Child care and culture: Lessons from Africa.* Cambridge, UK: Cambridge University Press.

Levy, S. R., & Hughes, J. M. (2009). Development of racial and ethnic prejudice among children. In T. D. Nelson (Ed.), *Handbook of prejudice, stereotyping, and discrimination* (pp. 23–42). New York: Psychology Press.

Lew-Williams, C., Pelucchi, B., & Saffran, J. R. (2011). Isolated words enhance statistical language learning in infancy. *Developmental Science, 14*(6), 1323–1329. doi:10.1111/j.1467-7687.2011.01079.x

Lew-Williams, C., & Saffran, J. R. (2012). All words are not created equal: Expectations about word length guide infant statistical learning. *Cognition, 122*(2), 241–246. doi:10.1016/j.cognition.2011.10.007

Lewin, T. (2013, October 28). New milestone emerges: Baby's first iPhone app. *The New York Times,* p. A17. Retrieved from http://www.nytimes.com/2013/10/28/us/new-milestone-emerges-babys-first-iphone-app.html

Lewis, C., & Lamb, M. E. (2003). Fathers' influences on children's development: The evidence from two-parent families. *European Journal of Psychology of Education, 18*(2), 211–228.

Lewis, M., & Ramsay, D. (2004). Development of self-recognition, personal pronoun use, and pretend play during the 2nd year. *Child Development, 75*(6), 1821–1831. doi:10.1111/j.1467-8624.2004.00819.x

Lewis, S., Stumbitz, B., Miles, L., & Rouse, J. (2014). *Maternity protection in SMEs: An international review.* Geneva: International Labour Office.

Li, P., Legault, J., & Litcofsky, K. A. (2014). Neuroplasticity as a function of second language learning: Anatomical changes in the human brain. *Cortex, 58,* 301–324. doi:10.1016/j.cortex.2014.05.001

Li, R., Darling, N., Maurice, E., Barker, L., & Grummer-Strawn, L. M. (2005). Breastfeeding rates in the United States by characteristics of the child, mother, or family: The 2002 National Immunization Survey. *Pediatrics, 115*(1), e31–e37.

Liao, Y., Huang, Z., Huh, J., Pentz, M. A., & Chou, C. (2013). Changes in friends' and parental influences on cigarette smoking from early through late adolescence. *Journal of Adolescent Health, 53*(1), 132–138. doi:10.1016/j.jadohealth.2013.01.020

Lidz, C. (2003). Dynamic assessment (learning potential testing, testing the limits). In R. Fernández-Ballesteros (Ed.), *Encyclopedia of psychological assessment* (pp. 338–345). London: Sage.

Lickenbrock, D. M., & Braungart-Rieker, J. M. (2015). Examining antecedents of infant attachment security with mothers and fathers: An ecological systems perspective. *Infant Behavior and Development, 39,* 173–187.

Lillard, A. S., & Peterson, J. (2011). The immediate impact of different types of television on young children's executive function. *Pediatrics, 128*(4), 644–649. doi:10.1542/peds.2010-1919

Lillard, A. S., Lerner, M. D., Hopkins, E. J., Dore, R. A., Smith, E. D., & Palmquist, C. M. (2013). The impact of pretend play on children's development: A review of the evidence. *Psychological Bulletin, 139*(1), 1–34. doi:10.1037/a0029321

Lillard, A., Pinkham, A. M., & Smith, E. (2011). Pretend play and cognitive development. In U. Goswami (Ed.), *The Wiley-Blackwell handbook of childhood cognitive development* (2nd ed.) (pp. 285–311). Malden, MA: Wiley-Blackwell.

Lim, M. M., & Young, L. J. (2006). Neuropeptidergic regulation of affiliative behavior and social bonding in animals. *Hormones and Behavior, 50*(4), 506–517.

Lim, M. M., Wang, Z., Olazábal, D. E., Ren, X., Terwilliger, E. F., & Young, L. J. (2004). Enhanced partner preference in a promiscuous species by manipulating the expression of a single gene. *Nature, 429,* 754–757.

Limosin, F., Rouillon, F., Payan, C., Cohen, J. M., & Strub, N. (2003). Prenatal exposure to influenza as a risk factor for adult schizophrenia. *Acta Psychiatrica Scandinavica, 107*(5), 331–335.

Lindberg, S. M., Hyde, J. S., Petersen, J. L., & Linn, M. C. (2010). New trends in gender and mathematics performance: A meta-analysis. *Psychological Bulletin, 136*(6), 1123–1135. doi:10.1037/a0021276

Lindsey, E. W. (2014). Physical activity play and preschool children's peer acceptance: Distinctions between rough-and-tumble and exercise play. *Early Education and Development, 25*(3), 277–294. doi:10.1080/10409289.2014.890854

Lindsey, E. W., & Colwell, M. J. (2003). Preschoolers' emotional competence: Links to pretend and physical play. *Child Study Journal, 33*(1), 39–52.

Lindsey, E. W., & Colwell, M. J. (2013). Pretend and physical play: Links to preschoolers' affective social competence. *Merrill-Palmer Quarterly, 59*(3), 330–360. doi:10.1353/mpq.2013.0015

Lindsey, E. W., & Mize, J. (2000). Parent-child physical and pretense play: Links to children's social competence. *Merrill-Palmer Quarterly, 46*(4), 565–591.

Lips, H. M. (2006). *A new psychology of women* (3rd ed.). New York: McGraw-Hill.

Lipsitt, L., & Rovee-Collier, C. (2012). The psychophysics of olfaction in the human newborn: Habituation and cross-adaptation. In G. M. Zucco, R. S. Herz, & B. Schall (Eds.), *Olfactory cognition: From perception and memory to environmental odours and neuroscience* [e-book] (pp. 221–235). Amsterdam, Netherlands: John Benjamins Publishing Company.

Livingston, G. (2014). *Growing number of dads home with the kids: Biggest increase among those caring for family.* Washington, DC: Pew Research Center's Social and Demographic Trends Project.

Livingston, G. (2016, September 26). Among 41 Nations, U.S. is the Outlier When it Comes to Paid Parental Leave. Retrieved November 2, 2016, from http://www.pewresearch.org/fact-tank/2016/09/26/u-s-lacks-mandated-paid-parental-leave/

Loeb, S. (2007). Race, SES and achievement gaps. In H.F. Ladd & E.B. Fiske (Eds.), *Handbook of research in education finance and policy* (pp. 499-518). London: Routledge.

Loehlin, J. C., Horn, J. M., & Willerman, L. (1997). Heredity, environment and IQ in the Texas Adoption Project. In R. J. Sternberg & E. L. Grigorenko (Eds.), *Intelligence, heredity, and environment* (pp. 105–125). New York: Cambridge University Press.

Logsdon, M. C., Wisner, K., & Shanahan, B. (2007). Evidence on postpartum depression: 10 publications to guide nursing practice. *Issues in Mental Health Nursing, 28,* 445–451.

López-Guimerà, G., Levine, M. P., Sánchez-Carracedo, D., & Fauquet, J. (2010). Influence of mass media on body image and eating disordered attitudes and behaviors in females: A review of effects and processes. *Media Psychology, 13*(4), 387–416. doi:10.1080/15213269.2010.525737

London, B., Downey, G., Bonica, C., & Paltin, I. (2007). Social causes and consequences of rejection sensitivity. *Journal of Research on Adolescence, 17*(3), 481–506.

Long, J. M., Mareno, N., Shabo, R., & Wilson, A. H. (2012). Overweight and obesity among White, Black, and Mexican American children: Implications for when to intervene. *Journal for Specialists in Pediatric Nursing, 17*(1), 41–50.

Lonigan, C. (2006). Development, assessment, and promotion of preliteracy skills. *Early Education and Development, 17*(1), 91–114.

Lonigan, C. J., Purpura, D. J., Wilson, S. B., Walker, P. M., & Clancy-Menchetti, J. (2013). Evaluating the components of an emergent literacy intervention for preschool children at risk for reading difficulties. *Journal of Experimental Child Psychology,114*(1), 111–130.

Lopoo, L. M. (2007). While the cat's away, do the mice play? Maternal employment and the after-school activities of adolescents. *Social Science Quarterly, 88*(5), 1357–1373. doi:10.1111/j.1540-6237.2007.00506.x

Lord, C., Risi, S., DiLavore, P. S., Shulman, C., Thurm, A., & Pickles, A. (2006). Autism from 2 to 9 years of age. *Archives of General Psychiatry, 63*(6), 694–701.

Lorence, J., & Dworkin, A. G. (2006). Elementary grade retention in Texas and reading achievement among racial groups: 1994–2002. *Review of Policy Research, 23*(5), 999–1033.

Lorenz, K. (1988). *Here am I—Where are you? The behavior of the graylag goose.* New York: Harcourt Brace Jovanovich.

Louv, R. (2008). *Last child in the woods: Saving our children from nature-deficit disorder.* Chapel Hill, NC: Algonquin Books.

Lovas, G. S. (2005). Gender and patterns of emotional availability in mother-toddler and father-toddler dyads. *Infant Mental Health Journal, 26*(4), 327–353.

Lovat, T. T., & Clement, N. (2016). Service learning as holistic values pedagogy. *Journal of Experiential Education, 39*(2), 115–129.

Love, J. M., Kisker, E. E., Ross, C., Constantine, J., Boller, K., Brooks-Gunn, J., ... Vogel, C. (2005). The effectiveness of Early Head Start for 3-year-old children and their parents: Lessons for policy and programs. *Developmental Psychology, 41*(6), 885–901.

Love, K. M., & Murdock, T. B. (2007). Stepfamilies. In N. J. Salkind (Ed.), *Encyclopedia of human development* (pp. 1220–1222). Thousand Oaks, CA: Sage.

Loveless, T. (2013). How well are American students learning? *Brown Center Report on American Education, 3*(2).

Lowe, W. (2007). "I finally got real parents, and now they are gonna die"—A case study of an adolescent with two HIV-positive parents. *Families, Systems, and Health, 25*(2), 227–233.

Luby, J. L. (2010). Preschool depression: The importance of identification of depression early in development. *Current Directions in Psychological Science, 19*(2), 91–95.

Luby, J. L., Si, X., Belden, A. C., Tandon, M., & Spitznagel, E. (2009). Preschool depression: Homotypic continuity and course over 24 months. *Archives of General Psychiatry, 66*(8), 897–905.

Lucas, S. R. (1999). *Tracking inequality. Stratification and mobility in American high schools.* New York: Teachers College Press.

Lucas-Thompson, R. G., Goldberg, W. A., & Prause, J. (2010). Maternal work early in the lives of children and its distal associations with achievement and behavior problems: A meta-analysis. *Psychological Bulletin, 136*(6), 915–942.

Luckey, A. J., & Fabes, R. A. (2005). Understanding nonsocial play in early childhood. *Early Childhood Education Journal, 33*(2), 67–72.

Luhmann, M., Hofmann, W., Eid, M., & Lucas, R. E. (2012). Subjective well-being and adaptations to life-events: A meta-analysis on differences between cognitive and affective well-being. *Journal of Personality and Social Psychology, 102,* 592–615. doi: 10.1037/a0025948.

Luna, B., Paulsen, D. J., Padmanabhan, A., & Geier, C. (2013). The teenage brain: Cognitive control and motivation. *Current Directions in Psychological Science, 22*(2), 94–100.

Luthar, S. S. (2000). The construct of resilience: A critical evaluation and guidelines for future work. *Child Development, 71*(3), 543–562.

Luyckx, K., Goossens, L., Soenens, B., & Beyers, W. (2006).Unpacking commitment and exploration: Preliminary validation of an integrative model of late adolescent identity formation. *Journal of Adolescence, 29*(3), 361–378.

Lyman, R. D., & Barry, C. T. (2006). The continuum of residential treatment care for conduct-disordered youth. In W. M. Nelson, III, A. J. Finch, & K. J. Hart (Eds.), *Conduct disorders: A practitioner's guide to comparative treatments* (pp. 259–297). New York: Spring.

Lyons-Ruth, K., & Jacobvitz, D. (2008). Attachment disorganization: Genetic factors, parenting contexts, and developmental transformation from infancy to adulthood. In J. Cassidy & P. R. Shaver (Eds.), *Handbook of attachment: Theory, research, and clinical applications* (2nd ed., pp. 666–697). New York: Guilford Press.

Ma, H., Unger, J. B., Chou, C., Sun, P., Palmer, P. H., Zhou, Y., . . . Johnson, C. A. (2008). Risk factors for adolescent smoking in urban and rural China: Findings from the China seven cities study. *Addictive Behaviors, 33*(8), 1081–1085.

Maccoby, E. E. (2002). Gender and group process: A developmental perspective. *Current Directions in Psychological Science, 11*(2), 54–58.

MacDorman, M. F. (2013). QuickStats: Infant mortality rates, by race and Hispanic ethnicity of mother—United States, 2000, 2005, and 2009. *Morbidity and Mortality Weekly Report.* Retrieved from http://www.cdc.gov/mmwr/preview/mmwrhtml/mm6205a6.htm

MacDorman, M.F, Hoyert, D. L., & Mathews, T. J. (2013). Recent declines in infant mortality in the United States, 2005–2011. *NCHS Data Brief, 120,* 1–7. Retrieved from http://www.cdc.gov/nchs/data/databriefs/db120.htm

MacDorman, M. F., Mathews, T. J., & Declercq, E. (2014). Trends in out-of-hospital births in the United States, 1990–2012. *NCHS data brief,* No. 144. Hyattsville, MD: National Center for Health Statistics.

MacKenzie, M. J., Nicklas, E., Waldfogel, J., & Brooks-Gunn, J. (2013). Spanking and child development across the first decade of life. *Pediatrics, 132,* e1118–e1125.

MacMillan, R., McMorris, B. J., & Kruttschnitt, C. (2004). Linked lives: Stability and change in maternal circumstances and trajectories of antisocial behavior in children. *Child Development, 75*(1), 205–220.

MacNeil, G. A., & Newell, J. M. (2004). School bullying: Who, why, and what to do. *Prevention Researcher, 11*(3), 15–17.

Madon, S., Guyll, M., Willard, J., & Scherr, K. (2011). Self-fulfilling prophecies: Mechanisms, power, and links to social problems. *Social and Personality Psychology Compass, 5*(8), 578–590.

Madsen, S. D., & Collins, W. (2011). The salience of adolescent romantic experiences for romantic relationship qualities in young adulthood. *Journal of Research on Adolescence, 21*(4), 789–801.

Mah, V. K., & Ford-Jones, E. L. (2012). Spotlight on middle childhood: Rejuvenating the "forgotten years." *Paediatrics & Child Health, 17*(2), 81–83.

Mahatmya, D., & Lohman, B. (2011). Predictors of late adolescent delinquency: The protective role of after-school activities in low-income families. *Children and Youth Services Review, 33*(7), 1309–1317. doi:10.1016/j.childyouth.2011.03.005

Mahler, M. S., Bergman, A., & Pine, F. (2000). *The psychological birth of the human infant: Symbiosis and individuation.* New York: Basic Books.

Mahler, M. S., Pine, F., & Bergman, A. (1975). *The psychological birth of the human infant.* New York: Basic Books.

Mahoney, J. L., Harris, A. L., & Eccles, J. S. (2006). Organized activity participation, positive youth development, and the over-scheduling hypothesis. *Society for Research in Child Development Social Policy Report, 20*(4), 3–30.

Mahoney, J. L., Stattin, H., & Lord, H. (2004). Unstructured youth recreation centre participation and antisocial behaviour development: Selection influences and the moderating role of antisocial peers. *International Journal of Behavioral Development, 28*(6), 553–560.

Maikovich-Fong, A., & Jaffee, S. R. (2010). Sex differences in childhood sexual abuse characteristics and victims' emotional and behavioral problems: Findings from a national sample of youth. *Child Abuse & Neglect, 34*(6), 429–437.

Makel, M. C., Plucker, J. A., & Hegarty, B. (2012). Replications in psychology research: How often do they really occur? *Perspectives on Psychological Science, 7*(6), 537–542. doi:10.1177/1745691612460688

Malanga, C. J., & Kosofsky, B. E. (2003). Does drug abuse beget drug abuse? Behavioral analysis of addiction liability in animal models of prenatal drug exposure. *Developmental Brain Research, 147*(1–2), 47–57.

Malik, A. B., & Turner, M. E. (2015). *Neuropsychological evaluation.* Retrieved from http://emedicine.medscape.com/article/317596-overview#a1

Malina, R. M., Bouchard, C., & Oded, B. (2004). *Growth maturation and physical activity.* Champaign, IL: Human Kinetics.

Malone, A., & Price, J. (2012). The significant effects of childhood cancer on siblings. *Cancer Nursing Practice, 11*(4), 26–31.

Mampe, B., Friederici, A. D., Christophe, A., & Wermke, K. (2009). Newborns' cry melody is shaped by their native language. *Current Biology, 19*(23), 1994–1997.

Management of Acute Malnutrition in Infants Project. (2009). *Management of Acute Malnutrition in Infants (MAMI) Project: Summary report.* Retrieved from http://www.actionagainsthunger.org/publication/2009/10/summary-report-management-acute-malnutrition-infants-mami-project

Mandara, J., Gaylord-Harden, N. K., Richards, M. H., & Ragsdale, B. L. (2009). The effects of changes in racial identity and self-esteem on changes in African American adolescents' mental health. *Child Development, 80*(6), 1660–1675.

Mandel, S., & Sharlin, S. A. (2006). The non-custodial father: His involvement in his children's lives and the connection between his role and the ex-wife's, child's and father's perception of that role. *Journal of Divorce & Remarriage, 45*(1/2), 79–95.

Mandela, N. (1994). *Long walk to freedom.* Boston: Little, Brown.

Mancillas, A. (2006). Challenging the stereotypes about only children: A review of the literature and implications for practice. *Journal of Counseling & Development, 84*(3), 268–275.

Maniglio, R. (2015). Significance, nature, and direction of the association between child sexual abuse and conduct disorder: A systematic review. *Trauma, Violence, & Abuse, 16*(3), 241–257. doi:10.1177/1524838014526068

Manlove, J., Terry-Humen, E., Papillo, A. R., Franzetta, K., Williams, S., & Ryan, S. (2002). Preventing teenage pregnancy, childbearing, and sexually transmitted diseases: What the research shows, *Child Trends Research Brief, American Teens Series.* Washington, DC: Child Trends and the Knight Foundation.

Mann, M. B., Pearl, P. T., & Behle, P. D. (2004). Effects of parent education on knowledge and attitudes. *Adolescence, 39*(154), 355–360.

Mantzicopoulos, P. Y., & Oh-Hwang, Y. (1998). The relationship of psychosocial maturity to parenting quality and intellectual ability for American and Korean adolescents. *Contemporary Educational Psychology, 23*(2), 195–206.

March of Dimes. (2003). *Understanding the behavior of term infants.* Retrieved from https://www.marchofdimes.org/nursing/modnemedia/othermedia/states.pdf

March of Dimes. (2008a). *Genetic counseling.* Retrieved from http://www.marchofdimes.com/pnhec/4439_15008.asp

March of Dimes. (2008b). *Your baby right after birth.* Retrieved from http://www.marchofdimes.org/baby/newborn-care-in-the-delivery-room.aspx

March of Dimes. (2014). *Premature babies cost employers $12.7 billion annually.* Retrieved from http://www.marchofdimes.org/news/premature-babies-cost-employers-127-billion-annually.aspx

March of Dimes. (2015). *Genetic counseling.* Retrieved from http://www.marchofdimes.org/pregnancy/genetic-counseling.aspx

Marchetta, C. M., Denny, C. H., Floyd, R. L., Cheal, N. E., Sniezek, J. E., & McKnight-Eily, L. R. (2012). Alcohol use and binge drinking among women of childbearing age — United States, 2006–2010. *Mortality and Morbidity Weekly Report, 61*, 534–538.

Marcia, J. E. (1966). Development and validation of ego-identity status. *Journal of Personality and Social Psychology, 3*(5), 551–558.

Mareschal, D., & Shultz, T. R. (1999). Development of children's seriation: A connectionist approach. *Connection Science, 11*(2), 149–186.

Markman, E. M. (1990). Constraints children place on word meanings. *Cognitive Science, 14*(1), 57–77.

Markovits, H., Benenson, J., & Dolensky, E. (2001). Evidence that children and adolescents have internal models of peer interactions that are gender differentiated. *Child Development, 72*(3), 879–886.

Marks, L. (2012). Same-sex parenting and children's outcomes: A closer examination of the American psychological association's brief on lesbian and gay parenting. *Social Science Research, 41*(4), 735–751.

Marks, A. K., Szalacha, L. A., Lamarre, M., Boyd, M. J., & Coll, C. G. (2007). Emerging ethnic identity and interethnic group social preferences in middle childhood: Findings from the Children of Immigrants Development in Context (CIDC) study. *International Journal of Behavioral Development, 31*(5), 501–513.

Markstrom, C. A., & Iborra, A. (2003). Adolescent identity formation and rites of passage: The Navajo Kinaalda ceremony for girls. *Journal of Research on Adolescence, 13*(4), 399–425.

Marlier, L., & Schaal, B. (2005). Human newborns prefer human milk: Conspecific milk odor is attractive without postnatal exposure. *Child Development, 76*, 155–168.

Marsh, H. W., Seaton, M., Trautwein, R., Ludtke, O., Hau, K. T., O'Mara, A. J., & Craven, R. G. (2008). The big-fish-little-pond-effect stands up to critical scrutiny: Implications for theory, methodology, and future research. *Educational Psychology Review, 20*(3), 319–350.

Martin, C. L., & Fabes, R. A. (2001). The stability and consequences of young children's same-sex peer interactions. *Developmental Psychology, 37*(3), 431–446. doi:10.1037/0012–1649.37.3.431

Martin, D. C., Mark, B. L., Triggs-Raine, B. L., & Natowicz, M. R. (2007). Evaluation of the risk for Tay-Sachs disease in individuals of French Canadian ancestry living in New England. *Clinical Chemistry, 53*, 392–398

Martin, J. A., Hamilton, B. E., Ventura, S. J., Osterman, M. J., Kirmeyer, S., Mathews, T. J., & Wilson, E. C. (2011). Births: Final data for 2009. *National Vital Statistics Reports, 60*(1), 1–70.

Martin, J. A., Hamilton, B. E., & Osterman, M. J. K. (2012). Three decades of twin births in the United States, 1980-2009. *NCHS Data Brief, No. 80.* Retrieved from http://www.cdc.gov/nchs/data/databriefs/db80.pdf

Martin, J. A., Hamilton, B. E., Osterman, M. J. K., Curtin, S. C., & Mathews, T. J. (2013). Births: Final data for 2012. *National Vital Statistics Reports, 62*(9). Hyattsville, MD.: National Center for Health Statistics.

Martin, J. A., Osterman, M. J. K., & Sutton, P. D. (2010). Are preterm births on the decline in the United States? Recent data from the National Vital Statistics System. *NCHS Data Brief, No. 39.* Hyattsville, MD: National Center for Health Statistics.

Martin, J., & Sokol, B. (2011). Generalized others and imaginary audiences: A neo-Meadian approach to adolescent egocentrism. *New Ideas In Psychology, 29*(3), 364–375.

Martin, M. T., Emery, R. E., & Peris, T. S. (2004). Single-parent families—Risk, resilience and change. In M. Coleman & L. H. Ganong (Eds.), *Handbook of contemporary families* (pp. 282–301). Thousand Oaks, CA: Sage.

Martinez, C. R., & Forgatch, M. S. (2002). Adjusting to change: Linking family structure transitions with parenting and boys' adjustment. *Journal of Family Psychology, 16*, 107–117.

Martinez, I., & Garcia, J. F. (2008). Internalization of values and self-esteem among Brazilian teenagers from authoritative, indulgent, authoritarian, and neglectful homes. *Family Therapy, 35*(1), 43–59.

Martino, W., & Kehler, M. (2006). Male teachers and the "boy problem": An issue of recuperative masculinity politics. *McGill Journal of Education, 41*(2), 113–131.

Martins, A., & Calheiros, M. M. (2012). Construction of a self-complexity scale for adolescents. *Psychological Assessment, 24*(4), 973–982.

Martins, C., & Gaffan, E. A. (2000). Effects of early maternal depression on patterns of infant-mother attachment: A meta-analytic investigation. *Journal of Child Psychology and Psychiatry, 41*(6), 737–746.

Martins, N., & Harrison, K. (2012). Racial and gender differences in the relationship between children's television use and self-esteem: A longitudinal panel study. *Communication Research, 39*(3), 338–357.

Mash, E. J., & Hunsley, J. (2007). Assessment of child and family disturbance. In E. J. Mash & R. A. Barkley (Eds.), *Assessment of childhood disorders* (pp. 3–50). New York: Guilford Press.

Maslova, E., Bhattacharya, S., Lin, S. W., & Michels, K. B. (2010). Caffeine consumption during pregnancy and risk of preterm birth: A meta-analysis. *American Journal of Clinical Nutrition, 92*(5), 1120–1132.

Masten, A. S. (2001). Ordinary magic: Resilience process in development. *American Psychologist, 56*(3), 227–238.

Matsumoto, D. (1992). American-Japanese cultural differences in the recognition of universal facial expressions. *Journal of Cross-Cultural Psychology, 23*(1), 72–84.

Matsumoto, D. (2006). Are cultural differences in emotion regulation mediated by personality traits? *Journal of Cross-Cultural Psychology, 37*(4), 421–437.

Matsumoto, D., & Juang, L. (2004). *Culture and psychology* (3rd ed.). Belmont, CA: Wadsworth/Thomson.

Maughan, B., Collishaw, S., & Stringaris, A. (2013). Depression in childhood and adolescence. *Journal of the Canadian Academy of Child and Adolescent Psychiatry / Journal De L'académie Canadienne De Psychiatrie De L'enfant Et De L'adolescent, 22*(1), 35–40.

Mavroveli, S., Petrides, K. V., Sangareau, Y., & Furnham, A. (2009). Exploring the relationships between trait emotional intelligence and objective socio-emotional outcomes in childhood. *British Journal of Educational Psychology, 79*(2), 259–272. doi:10.1348/000709908X368848

Mavroveli, S., & Sánchez-Ruiz, M. J. (2011). Trait emotional intelligence influences on academic achievement and school behaviour. *British Journal of Educational Psychology, 81*(1), 112–134. doi:10.1348/2044-8279.002009

May, P. A., Blankenship, J., Marais, A., Gossage, J., Kalberg, W. O., Joubert, B., . . . Seedat, S. (2013). Maternal alcohol consumption producing fetal alcohol spectrum disorders (FASD): Quantity, frequency, and timing of drinking. *Drug and Alcohol Dependence, 133*(2), 502–512. doi:10.1016/j.drugalcdep.2013.07.013

Mayes, S. D., Mathiowetz, C., Kokotovich, C., Waxmonsky, J., Baweja, R., Calhoun, S. L., & Bixler, E. O. (2015). Stability of disruptive mood dysregulation disorder symptoms (irritable-angry mood and temper outbursts) throughout childhood and adolescence in a general population sample. *Journal of Abnormal Child Psychology, 43*(8), 1543–1549. doi:10.1007/s10802-015-0033-8

Maynard, A. E. (2008). What we thought we knew and how we came to know it: Four decades of cross-cultural research from a Piagetian point of view. *Human Development, 51*, 56–65.

Maynard, A. E., & Greenfield, P. M. (2003). Implicit cognitive development in cultural tools and children: Lessons from Maya Mexico. *Cognitive Development, 18*(4), 489–510.

Mayo Clinic. (2009). *Sudden infant death syndrome (SIDS)*. Retrieved from http://www.mayoclinic.com/print/sudden-infant-death-syndrome/DS00145/DSECTION=all&METHOD=print

Mayo Clinic. (2010). *Childhood asthma*. Retrieved from http://www.mayoclinic.com/health/childhood-asthma/DS00849

Mayo Clinic. (2014a). *Concussion*. Retrieved from http://www.mayoclinic.org/diseases-conditions/concussion/basics/definition/con-20019272

Mayo Clinic. (2014b). *Stress relief*. Retrieved from http://www.mayoclinic.org/healthy-lifestyle/stress-management/basics/stress-relief/hlv-20049495

Mayo Clinic. (2015a). *Antidepressants: Safe during pregnancy?* Retrieved from http://www.mayoclinic.org/healthy-lifestyle/pregnancy-week-by-week/in-depth/antidepressants/art-20046420

Mayo Clinic. (2015b). *Pregnancy and exercise: Baby, let's move!* Retrieved from http://americanpregnancy.org/pregnancy-health/exercise-during-pregnancy/

Mayo Foundation for Medical Education and Research. (n.d.). *Genetic testing*. Retrieved from http://www.mayoclinic.org/tests-procedures/genetic-testing/multimedia/genetic-disorders/sls-20076216

Maxwell, L. A. (2014). U.S. school enrollment hits majority-minority milestone. *Education Week, 34*(1), 1, 12, 14–15.

McAlister, A. R., & Peterson, C. C. (2013). Siblings, theory of mind, and executive functioning in children aged 3–6 years: New longitudinal evidence. *Child Development, 84*(4), 1442–1458. doi:10.1111/cdev.12043

McCabe, L. A., & Brooks-Gunn, J. (2007). With a little help from my friends? Self-regulation in groups of young children. *Infant Mental Health Journal, 28*(6), 584–605.

McCarthy, F., O'Keeffe, L., Khashan, A., North, R., Poston, L., McCowan, L., . . . Kenny, L. (2013). Association between maternal alcohol consumption in early pregnancy and pregnancy outcomes. *Obstetrics & Gynecology, 122*(4), 830–837. doi:10.1097/AOG.0b013e3182a6b226

McClain, M., & Pfeiffer, S. (2012). Identification of gifted students in the United States today: A look at state definitions, policies, and practices. *Journal of Applied School Psychology, 28*(1), 59–88.

McCleery, J., Akshoomoff, N., Dobkins, K., & Carver, L. (2009). Atypical face versus object processing and hemispheric asymmetries in 10-month-old infants at risk for autism. *Biological Psychiatry, 66*(10), 950–957. doi:10.1016/j.biopsych.2009.07.031

McClellan, J., & Stock, S. (2013). Practice parameter for the assessment and treatment of children and adolescents with schizophrenia. *Journal of the American Academy of Child & Adolescent Psychiatry, 52*(9), 976–990.

McClelland, M. M., Acock, A. C., Piccinin, A., Rhea, S. A., & Stallings, M. C. (2013). Relations between preschool attention span-persistence and age 25 educational outcomes. *Early Childhood Research Quarterly, 28*(2), 314–324.

McClun, L. A., & Merrell, K. W. (1998). Relationship of perceived parenting styles, locus of control orientation, and self-concept among junior high age students. *Psychology in the Schools, 35*(4), 381–390.

McClure, M. M., & Fitch, R. H. (2005). Hormones. In N. J. Salkind (Ed.), *Encyclopedia of human development* (pp. 646–649). Thousand Oaks, CA: Sage.

McCoy, K., Cummings, E. M., & Davies, P. T. (2009). Constructive and destructive marital conflict, emotional security and children's prosocial behavior. *Journal of Child Psychology and Psychiatry, 50*(3), 270–279.

McCurdy, L., Winterbottom, K., Mehta, S., & Roberts, J. (2010). Using nature and outdoor activity to improve children's health. *Current Problems in Pediatric and Adolescent Health Care, 40*(5), 102–117.

McDonell, M. G., & McClellan, J. M. (2007). Early-onset schizophrenia. In E. J. Mash & R. A. Barkley (Eds.), *Assessment of childhood disorders* (pp. 526–550). New York: Guilford Press.

McElwain, N. L., Booth-LaForce, C., Lansford, J. E., Wu, X., & Dyer, W. J. (2008). A process model of attachment-friend linkages: Hostile attribution biases, language ability, and mother-child affective mutuality as intervening mechanisms. *Child Development, 79*(6), 1891–1906.

McFeatters, A. (2002). Fred Rogers gets Presidential Medal of Freedom. *Post-Gazette*. Retrieved from http://www.post-gazette.com/ae/200 20710fredrogersp1.asp

McGhee, P. E. (1979). *Humor: Its origin and development*. San Francisco: Freeman.

McGivern, R. F., Andersen, J., Byrd, D., Mutter, K. L., & Reilly, J. (2002). Cognitive efficiency on a match to sample task decreases at the onset of puberty in children. *Brain and Cognition, 50*, 73–89.

McGue, M., Elkins, I., Walden, B., & Iacono, W. G. (2005). Perceptions of the parent-adolescent relationship: A longitudinal investigation. *Developmental Psychology, 41*(6), 972–984.

McGuffin, P., Riley, B., & Plomin, R. (2001). Genomics and behavior: Toward behavioral genomics. *Science, 291*(5507), 1232–1249.

McHale, S. M., Kim, J., Whiteman, S., & Crouter, A. C. (2004). Links between sex-typed time use in middle childhood and gender development in early adolescence. *Developmental Psychology, 40*(5), 868–881.

McHale, S. M., Whiteman, S. D., Kim, J., & Crouter, A. C. (2007). Characteristics and correlates of sibling relationships in two-parent African American families. *Journal of Family Psychology, 21*(2), 227–235.

McIntosh, J., MacDonald, F., & McKeganey, N. (2006). Why do children experiment with illegal drugs? The declining role of peer pressure with increasing age. *Addiction Research & Theory, 14*(3), 275–287. doi:10.1080/16066350500330465

McIntosh, J., Smyth, B., Kelaher, M., Wells, Y., & Long, C. (2010). *Post-separation parenting arrangements and developmental outcomes for infants and children*. Canberra, Australia: Attorney General's Department.

McKeachie, W., & Sims, B. (2004). Review of *Educational Psychology: A century of contributions* [A project of Division 15 (Educational Psychology) of the American Psychological Association]. *Educational Psychology Review, 16*(3), 283–298.

McKim, M. K., Cramer, K. M., Stuart, B., & O'Connor, D. L. (1999). Infant care decisions and attachment security: The Canadian Transition to Child Care Study. *Canadian Journal of Behavioural Science, 31*(2), 92–106.

McKown, D., & Weinstein, R. S. (2008). Teacher expectations, classroom context, and the achievement gap. *Journal of School Psychology, 46*(3), 235–261.

McLanahan, S., & Carlson, M. S. (2004). Fathers in fragile families. In M. E. Lamb (Ed.), *The role of the father in child development* (4th ed., pp. 368–396). Hoboken, NJ: Wiley.

McLoyd, V. C. (2000). Childhood poverty. In A. E. Kazdin (Ed.), *Encyclopedia of psychology* (pp. 251–257). New York: Oxford University Press.

McLoyd, V. C., Hill, N. E., & Dodge, K. A. (2005). Ecological and cultural diversity in African American family life. In V. C. McLoyd, N. E. Hill, & K. A. Dodge (Eds.), *African American family life* (pp. 3–20). New York: Guilford Press.

McMahon, R. J., & Kotler, J. S. (2006). Conduct problems. In D. A. Wolfe & E. J. Mash (Eds.), *Behavioral and emotional disorders in adolescents* (pp. 153–225). New York: Guilford Press.

Mead, S. (2006). The evidence suggests otherwise: The truth about boys and girls. *Education Sector, 23*(3). Retrieved from http://www.educationsector.org/usr_doc/ESO_BoysAndGirls.pdf

Meadows, S. (2006). *The child as thinker: The development and acquisition of cognition in childhood* (2nd ed.). London, UK: Routledge.

Meaney, M. J. (2004). The nature of nurture: Maternal effects and chromatin remodeling. In J. T. Cacioppo & G. G. Bentson (Eds.), *Essays in social neuroscience* (pp. 1–14). Cambridge, MA: MIT Press.

Meaney, M. J. (2010). Epigenetics and the biological definition of gene x environment interactions. *Child Development, 81*, 41–79.

Mecca, A. M., Smelser, N. J., & Vasconcellos, J. (1989). *The social importance of self-esteem.* Berkeley: University of California Press.

Mechelli, A., Crinion, J. T., Noppeney, U., O'Doherty, J., Ashburner, J., Frackowiak, R. S., & Price, C. J. (2004). Structural plasticity in the bilingual brain: Proficiency in a second language and age at acquisition affect grey-matter density. *Nature, 431*(7010), 757. doi:10.1038/431757a

Meeker, J. (2012). Exposure to environmental endocrine disruptors and child development. *Archives of Pediatrics & Adolescent Medicine, 166*(10), 952–958.

Meeus, W. (2011). The study of adolescent identity formation 2000–2010: A review of longitudinal research. *Journal of Research on Adolescence, 21*(1), 75–94.

Meeus, W., van de Schoot, R., Keijsers, L., & Branje, S. (2012). Identity statuses as developmental trajectories: A five-wave longitudinal study in early-to-middle and middle-to-late adolescents. *Journal of Youth & Adolescence, 41*(8), 1008–1021.

Meeus, W., van de Schoot, R., Keijsers, L., Schwartz, S. J., & Branje, S. (2010). On the progression and stability of adolescent identity formation: A five-wave longitudinal study in early-to-middle and middle-to-late adolescence. *Child Development, 81*(5), 1565–1581.

Mehta-Lee, S., Bernstein, P. S., Harrison, E. A., & Merkatz, I. R. (2013). Preconception and prenatal care. In W. R. Cohen & P. August (Eds.), *Obstetric medicine: Management of medical disorders in pregnancy* (6th ed., pp. 3–24). People's Medical Publishing House–USA Ltd.

Meier, A., & Allen, G. (2009). Romantic relationships from adolescence to young adulthood: Evidence from the National Longitudinal Study of Adolescent Health. *Sociological Quarterly, 50*(2), 308–335.

Meier, A., & Musick, K. (2012). Is the family dinner overrated? *The New York Times.* Retrieved from http://www.nytimes.com/2012/07/01/opinion/sunday/is-the-family-dinner-overrated.html?_r=0

Mejia, B., & Carcamo, C. (2016). As more Latino kids speak only English, parents worry about chatting with grandma. *Los Angeles Times.* Retrieved from http://www.latimes.com/local/california/la-me-latino-immigrants-english-fluency-20160422-story.html

Melo, I., Katz, L., Coutinho, I., & Amorim, M. M. (2014). Selective episiotomy vs. implementation of a non-episiotomy protocol: A randomized clinical trial. *Reproductive Health, 11*, 66. doi.org/10.1186/1742-4755-11-66

Mendle, J., Turkheimer, E., & Emery, R. E. (2007). Detrimental psychological outcomes associated with early pubertal timing in adolescent girls. *Developmental Review, 27*(2), 151–171. doi:10.1016/j.dr.2006.11.001

Menéndez, R. (Director). (1988). *Stand and deliver* [Motion picture]. United States: American Playhouse.

Menken, K., & Solorza, C. (2014). No child left bilingual: Accountability and the elimination of bilingual education programs in New York City schools. *Educational Policy, 28*(1), 96–125.

Menn, L., & Stoel-Gammon, C. (2005). Phonological development: Learning sounds and sound patterns. In J. B. Gleason (Ed.), *The development of language* (6th ed., pp. 39–61). Boston: Pearson.

Mennella, J. A., Griffin, C. E., & Beauchamp, G. K. (2004). Flavor programming during infancy. *Pediatrics, 113*(4), 840–845.

Mensah, F. K., Bayer, J. K., Wake, M., Carlin, J. B., Allen, N. B., & Patton, G. C. (2013). Early puberty and childhood social and behavioral adjustment. *Journal of Adolescent Health, 53*(1), 118–124. doi:10.1016/j.jadohealth.2012.12.018

MENTOR. (2012). *National Mentoring Partnership.* Retrieved from http://www.mentoring.org/

Merck Manual. (2008). *Function and dysfunction of the cerebral lobes.* Retrieved from http://www.merck.com/mmpe/sec16/ch210/ch210a.html#sec16-ch210-ch210a-313

Merikangas, K. R., He, J., Burstein, M., Swanson, S. A., Avenevoli, S., Cui, L., Benjet, K. G., & Swendsen, J. (2010). Lifetime prevalence of mental disorders in U.S. adolescents: Results from the National Comorbidity Survey Replication-Adolescent Supplement (NCS-A). *Journal of the American Academy of Child & Adolescent Psychiatry, 49*(10), 980–989. doi:10.1016/j.jaac.2010.05.017

Merrell, K. W., Cohn, B. P., & Tom, K. M. (2011). Development and validation of a teacher report measure for assessing social-emotional strengths of children and adolescents. *School Psychology Review, 40*(2), 226–241.

Merriam, S. (2009). *Qualitative research: A guide to design and implementation.* San Francisco: Jossey-Bass.

Metcalfe, J., & Finn, B. (2013). Metacognition and control of study choice in children. *Metacognition and Learning, 8*(1), 19–46. doi: 10.1007/s11409-013-9094-7

Metz, T., & Stickrath, E. (2015). Marijuana use in pregnancy and lactation: A review of the evidence. *American Journal of Obstetrics and Gynecology, 213*(6), 761-778.

Mickalide, A. D., & Hansen, L. M. (2012). *Coaching our kids to fewer injuries: A report on youth sports safety.* Washington, DC: Safe Kids Worldwide. Retrieved from http://www.safekids.org/assets/docs/safety-basics/sports/2012-sports.pdf

Mielke, K. W. (2001). A review of research on the educational and social impact of *Sesame Street.* In S. M. Fisch & R. T. Truglio (Eds.), *"G" is for growing—Thirty years of research on children and Sesame Street* (pp. 83–96). Mahwah, NJ: Erlbaum.

Mikami, A. Y., Lerner, M. D., & Lun, J. (2010). Social context influences on children's rejection by their peers. *Child Development Perspectives, 4*(2), 123–130.

Milin, R., Kutcher, S., Lewis, S. P., Walker, S., Wei, Y., Ferrill, N., & Armstrong, M. A. (2016). Impact of a mental health curriculum on knowledge and stigma among high school students: A randomized controlled trial. *Journal of the American Academy of Child & Adolescent Psychiatry, 55*(5), 383–391. doi:10.1016/j.jaac.2016.02.018

Miller, A. M., & Harwood, R. L. (2002). The cultural organization of parenting: Change and stability of behavior patterns during feeding and social play across the first year of life. *Parenting: Science and Practice, 2*(3), 241–272.

Miller, N. B., Cowan, P. A., Cowan, C. P., Hetherington, E. M., & Clingempeel, W. G. (1993). Externalizing in preschoolers and early adolescents: A cross-study replication of a family model. *Developmental Psychology, 29*(1), 3–18.

Miller-Perrin, C. L., & Perrin, R. D. (1999). *Child maltreatment: An introduction.* Thousand Oaks, CA: Sage.

Mischel, W., & Ayduk, O. (2004). Willpower in a cognitive-affective processing system: The dynamics of delay of gratification. In R. F. Baumeister & K. D. Vohs (Eds.), *Handbook of self-regulation: Research, theory, and applications* (pp. 99–129). New York: Guilford Press.

Mischel, W., Ayduk, O., Berman, M. G., Casey, B. J., Gotlib, I. H., Jonides, J., . . . Shoda, Y. (2011). 'Willpower' over the life span: Decomposing self-regulation. *Social Cognitive and Affective Neuroscience, 6*(2), 252–256. doi:10.1093/scan/nsq081

Mitchell, A. W. (2005). *Stair steps to quality: A guide for states and communities developing quality rating systems for early care and education.* Fairfax, VA: National Child Care Information Center.

Mitchell, M. B., Kuczynski, L., Tubbs, C. Y., & Ross, C. (2010). We care about care: Advice by children in care for children in care, foster parents and child welfare workers about the transition into foster care. *Child and Family Social Work, 15*, 176–185.

Miyake, K., & Yamazaki, K. (1995). Self-conscious emotions, child rearing, and child psychopathology in Japanese culture. In J. P. Tangney & K. W. Fischer (Eds.), *Self-conscious emotions: The psychology of shame, guilt, embarrassment, and pride* (pp. 488–504). New York: Guilford Press.

Moats, L. (2007). *Whole-language high jinks: How to tell when "scientifically-based reading instruction" isn't.* Washington, DC: Thomas B. Fordham Institute.

Moffitt, T. E., & Caspi, A. (2001). Childhood predictors differentiate life-course persistent and adolescence-limited antisocial pathways among males and females. *Development and Psychopathology, 13*(2), 355–375.

Moffitt, T. E., & Caspi, A. (2005). Life-course persistent and adolescence-limited antisocial males: Longitudinal followup in adulthood. In D. M. Stoff & E. J. Susman (Eds.), *Developmental psychobiology of aggression* (pp. 161–186). New York: Cambridge University Press.

Moll, H., & Tomasello, M. (2006). Level I perspective-taking at 24 months of age. *British Journal of Developmental Psychology, 24*(3), 603–613.

Möller, E. L., Majdandžić, M., & Bögels, S. M. (2014). Fathers' versus mothers' social referencing signals in relation to infant anxiety and avoidance: A visual cliff experiment. *Developmental Science, 17*(6), 1012–1028.

Monahan, K. C., Lee, J. M., & Steinberg, L. (2011). Revisiting the impact of part-time work on adolescent adjustment: Distinguishing between selection and socialization using propensity score matching. *Child Development, 82*(1), 96–112.

Montgomery, M. J. (2005). Psychosocial intimacy and identity: From early adolescence to emerging adulthood. *Journal of Adolescent Research, 20*(3), 346–374.

Moon, C., Lagercrantz, H., & Kuhl, P. (2013). Language experienced in utero affects vowel perception after birth: A two-country study. *Acta Paediatrica, 102*(2), 156–160.

Moore, F. (2102, October 5). *GLAAD's 'Where We Are On TV' report finds LGBT television characters at record high.* Huffington Post. Retrieved from http://www.huffingtonpost.com/2012/10/05/glaads-where-we-are-on-tv-report-gay-characters_n_1942313.html

Moore, K. L., & Persaud, T. V. N. (2003). *The developing human: Clinically oriented embryology* (7th ed.). Philadelphia: W. B. Saunders.

Moore, K. L., Persaud, T. V. N., & Tochia, M. G. (2013). *The developing human: Clinically oriented embryology* (9th ed.). Philadelphia: Elsevier.

Moore, M., & Meltzoff, A. N. (2008). Factors affecting infants' manual search for occluded objects and the genesis of object permanence. *Infant Behavior & Development, 31*(2), 168–180.

Moran, E. (2000). *Dick and Jane readers*. In S. Pendergast & T. Pendergast (Eds.), *St. James encyclopedia of popular culture* (Vol. 1, pp. 700–701). Detroit, MI: St. James Press.

Morgan, D. L. (2014). *Integrating qualitative and quantitative methods: A pragmatic approach*. Thousand Oaks, CA: Sage.

Morgan, S., Koren, G., & Bozzo, P. (2013). Is caffeine consumption safe during pregnancy? *Canadian Family Physician, 59*(4), 361–362.

Moriarty, P. H., & Wagner, L. D. (2004). Family rituals that provide meaning for single-parent families. *Journal of Family Nursing, 10*(2), 190–210.

Mortimer, J. T. (2010). The benefits and risks of adolescent employment. *The Prevention Researcher, 17*(2), 8–11.

Moser, A., Zimmermann, L., Dickerson, K., Grenell, A., Barr, R., & Gerhardstein, P. (2015). They can interact, but can they learn? Toddlers' transfer learning from touchscreens and television. *Journal of Experimental Child Psychology, 137*, 137–155.

Moser, S. E., West, S. G., & Hughes, J. N. (2012). Trajectories of math and reading achievement in low-achieving children in elementary school: Effects of early and later retention in grade. *Journal of Educational Psychology, 104*(3), 603–621.

Moss, E., Cyr, C., Bureau, J., Tarabulsy, G. M., & Dubois-Comtois, K. (2005). Stability of attachment during the preschool period. *Developmental Psychology, 41*(5), 773–783.

Mounts, N. S., & Steinberg, L. (1995). An ecological analysis of peer influence on adolescent grade point average and drug use. *Developmental Psychology, 31*(6), 915–922.

Moustafa, M. (2001). Contemporary reading instruction. In T. Loveless (Ed.), *The great curriculum debate* (pp. 247–267). Washington, DC: The Brookings Institution Press.

Müller, R., Shih, P., Keehn, B., Deyoe, J. R., Leyden, K. M., & Shukla, D. K. (2011). Underconnected, but how? A survey of functional connectivity MRI studies in autism spectrum disorders. *Cerebral Cortex, 21*(10), 2233–2243. doi:10.1093/cercor/bhq296

Mueller, M., Phelps, E., Bowers, E. P., Agans, J. P., Urban, J., & Lerner, R. M. (2011). Youth development program participation and intentional self-regulation skills: Contextual and individual bases of pathways to positive youth development. *Journal of Adolescence, 34*(6), 1115–1125.

Murnen, S. K., Smolak, L., Mills, J., & Good, L. (2003). Thin, sexy women and strong, muscular men: Grade-school children's responses to objectified images of women and men. *Sex Roles, 49*(9–10), 427–437.

Munroe, R. L., & Romney, A. K. (2006). Gender and age differences in same-sex aggregation and social behavior: A four-culture study. *Journal of Cross-Cultural Psychology, 37*, 3–19.

Munsch, J., & Blyth, D. A. (1993). An analysis of the functional nature of adolescents' supportive relationships. *Journal of Early Adolescence, 13*(2), 132–153.

Munsch, J., Woodward, J., & Darling, N. (1995). Children's perceptions of their relationships with coresiding and non-custodial fathers. *Journal of Divorce & Remarriage, 23*(1–2), 39–54.

Muris, P., Merckelbach, H., Gadet, B., & Moulaert, V. (2000). Fears, worries and scary dreams in 4- to 12-year-old children: Their content, developmental pattern, and origins. *Journal of Clinical Child Psychology, 29*(1), 43–52.

Murman, N. M., Buckingham, K. E., Fontilea, P., Villanueva, R., Leventhal, B., & Hinshaw, S. P. (2014). Let's Erase the Stigma (LETS): A quasi-experimental evaluation of adolescent-led school groups intended to reduce mental illness stigma. *Child & Youth Care Forum, 43*(5), 621–637. doi:10.1007/s10566-014-9257-y

Murray, A. (2012). The relationship of parenting style to academic achievement in middle childhood. *The Irish Journal of Psychology, 33*(4), 137–152. doi:10.1080/03033910.2012.724645

Murray, R., & Ramstetter, C. (2013). The crucial role of recess in school. *Pediatrics, 131*(1), 183–188. doi: 10.1542/peds.2012-2993

Murphy, T. P., Laible, D. J., Augustine, M., & Robeson, L. (2015). Attachment's links with adolescents' social emotions: The roles of negative emotionality and emotion regulation. *The Journal of Genetic Psychology, 176*(5), 315–329. doi:10.1080/00221325.2015.1072082

Mustanski, B., Birkett, M., Greene, G. J., Rosario, M., Bostwick, W., & Everett, B. G. (2014). The association between sexual orientation, identity and behavior across race/ethnicity, sex, and age in a probability sample of high school students. *American Journal of Public Health, 104*(2), 237–244.

Muzzatti, B., & Agnoli, F. (2007). Gender and mathematics: Attitudes and stereotype threat susceptibility in Italian children. *Developmental Psychology, 43*(3), 747–759.

Myers, B. J. (1984). Mother-infant bonding: Rejoinder to Kennell and Klaus. *Developmental Review, 4*(3), 283–288.

Myers, S. M., & Plauche Johnson, C. (2007). Management of children with autism spectrum disorder. *Pediatrics, 120*(5), 1162–1182. doi:10.1542/peds.2007-2362

Nagy, E., Pilling, K., Orvos, H., & Molnar, P. (2013). Imitation of tongue protrusion in human neonates: Specificity of the response in a large sample. *Developmental Psychology, 49*(9), 1628–1638. doi:10.1037/a0031127

Naigles, L. R., Hoff, E., Vear, D., Tomasello, M., Brandt, S., Waxman, S. R., & Childers, J. B. (2009). Flexibility in early verb use: Evidence from a multiple-N dairy study: VII. General discussion. *Monographs of the Society for Research in Child Development, 74*(2), 91–104.

Naimi, T. S., Brewer, R. D., Mokdad, A., Clark, D., Serdula, M. K., & Marks, J. S. (2003). Binge drinking among U.S. adults. *Journal of the American Medical Association, 289*(1), 70–75.

Nakagawa, M., Lamb, M. E., & Miyaki, K. (1992). Antecedents and correlates of the Strange Situation behavior of Japanese infants. *Journal of Cross-Cultural Psychology, 23*(3), 300–310.

Narine, L., Krishnakumar, A., Roopnarine, J. L., & Logie, C. (2013). A multilevel analysis of the role of parental and community variables on young children's health. *Journal of Pediatric Psychology, 38*(10), 1144–1154.

Nathanson, A. I. (1999). Identifying and explaining the relationship between parental mediation and children's aggression. *Communication Research, 26*, 124–143.

The Nation's Report Card. (2012). *Top stories in NAEP long-term trend assessments 2012*. Retrieved from http://www.nationsreportcard.gov/ltt_2012/

National Assessment of Educational Progress (NAEP, 2012) *The nation's report card: Writing 2011 (NCES 2012–470)*. Retrieved from http://nces.ed.gov/nationsreportcard/pubs/main2011/2012470.aspx

National Association for Gifted Children. (2013). *State definitions of giftedness*. Retrieved from http://www.nagc.org/sites/default/files/Advocacy/State%20definitions%20(8-1-13).pdf

National Cancer Institute. (2006). *Gene therapy for cancer: Questions and answers*. Retrieved from http://www.cancer.gov/cancertopics/factsheet/Therapy/gene

National Cancer Institute. (2010). *Human papillomavirus (HPV) vaccines*. Retrieved from http://www.cancer.gov/cancertopics/factsheet/Prevention/HPV-vaccine

National Center for Chronic Disease Prevention and Health Promotion. (2011). *Teen pregnancy: Improving the lives of young people and strengthening communities by reducing teen pregnancy*. Washington, DC: U.S. Government Printing Office.

National Center for Education Statistics. (2004). *Trends in educational equity for girls and women: 2004* [NCES 2000–021]. U.S. Department of Education. Washington, DC: U.S. Government Printing Office.

National Center for Education Statistics. (2013). Institutional retention and graduation rates for undergraduate students (NCES 2013-037). Retrieved from http://nces.ed.gov/programs/coe/indicator_cva.asp

National Center for Education Statistics. (2015a). *Fast facts: Bullying*. Retrieved from https://nces.ed.gov/fastfacts/display.asp?id=719

National Center for Education Statistics. (2015b). *The nation's report card: 2015 Mathematics and reading assessments*. Retrieved from http://www.nationsreportcard.gov/reading_math_2015/#?grade=4

National Center for Education Statistics (2016). *Children and youth with disabilities*. Retrieved from http://nces.ed.gov/programs/coe/indicator_cgg.asp

National Center for Environmental Health. (2011). *Asthma in the US: Growing every year*. Retrieved from http://www.cdc.gov/VitalSigns/pdf/2011-05-vitalsigns.pdf

National Center for HIV/AIDS, Viral Hepatitis, STD and TB Prevention. (n.d.). *AIDS trends*. Retrieved from http://www.cdc.gov/hiv/pdf/statistics_surveillance_aidstrends.pdf

National Center for HIV/AIDS, Viral Hepatitis, STD, and TB Prevention. (2011). *HIV among youth*. Retrieved from http://www.cdc.gov/hiv/youth/pdf/youth.pdf

National Center for Learning Disabilities. (2010). *LD explained*. Retrieved from http://www.ncld.org/ld-basics/ld-explained

National Center for Learning Disabilities. (2014). *The state of learning disabilities: Facts, trends and emerging issues* (3rd ed.). New York: Author.

National Center on Addiction and Substance Abuse at Columbia University. (2006). *The importance of family dinners III*. Retrieved from http://www.casacolumbia.org./addiction-research/reports/importance-of-family-dinners-2006

National Center on Family Homelessness. (2014). *America's youngest outcasts: A report card on child homelessness*. Waltham, MA: Author.

National Child Traumatic Stress Network. (2009). *Child sexual abuse fact sheet*. Retrieved from http://nctsn.org/nctsn_assets/pdfs/caring/ChildSexualAbuseFactSheet.pdf

National Commission on Writing. (2004). *Writing: A ticket to work . . . or a ticket out.* Retrieved from http://www.writing commission.org/prod_downloads/writingcom/writing-ticket-to-work.pdf

National Conference of State Legislatures. (2015). *Alternative nicotine products/Electronic cigarettes.* Retrieved from http://www.ncsl.org/research/health/alternative-nicotine-products-e-cigarettes.aspx

National Conference of State Legislatures. (2016). *Fostering connections act: State action.* Retrieved from http://www.ncsl.org/research/human-services/fostering-connections-state-action.aspx

National Dissemination Center for Children with Disabilities. (2011a). *Intellectual disability.* Retrieved from http://nichcy.org/disability/specific/intellectual#def

National Dissemination Center for Children with Disabilities. (2011b). *Learning disabilities.* Retrieved from http://nichcy.org/disability/specific/ld#def

National Head Start Association. (2014). *2014 Head Start fact sheet – national.* Retrieved from https://www.nhsa.org/files/resources/national_fact_sheet_-_2014.pdf

National Heart, Lung, and Blood Institute. (2007). *What is sickle-cell anemia?* Retrieved from http://www.nhlbi.nih.gov/health/dci/Diseases/Sca/SCA_WhatIs.html

National Human Genome Research Institute. (2007). *A guide to your genome.* Retrieved from http://www.genome.gov/Pages/Education/AllAbouttheHumanGenomeProject/GuidetoYourGenome07.pdf

National Human Genome Research Institute. (2010). *An overview of the human genome project.* Retrieved from http://www.genome.gov/12011239

National Human Genome Research Institute. (2011a). *Chromosome abnormalities.* Retrieved from http://www.genome.gov/11508982#6

National Human Genome Research Institute (2011b) ELSI research priorities and possible research topics. Retrieved from http://www.genome.gov/27543732

National Human Genome Research Institute. (2011c). *Frequently asked questions about genetic disorders.* Retrieved from http://www.genome.gov/19016930

National Human Genome Research Institute (2011d). *Learning about Down syndrome.* Retrieved from http://www.genome.gov/19517824

National Human Genome Research Institute. (2012). *International HapMap Project.* Retrieved from https://www.genome.gov/10001688/

National Human Genome Research Institute. (2013a). *Learning about Klinefelter syndrome.* Retrieved from http://www.genome.gov/19519068

National Human Genome Research Institute. (2013b). *Learning about Turner syndrome.* Retrieved from http://www.genome.gov/19519119

National Human Genome Research Institute (2016). All about the Human Genome Project. Retrieved from https://www.genome.gov/10001772/

National Institute of Alcohol Abuse and Alcoholism. (2004). *NIAAA Council approves definition of binge drinking.* Retrieved from http://pubs.niaaa.nih.gov/publications/Newsletter/winter2004/Newsletter_Number3.pdf

National Institute of Child Health and Human Development. (2006). *Phenylketonuria (PKU).* Retrieved from http://www.nichd.nih.gov/health/topics/phenylketonuria.cfm

National Institute of Child Health and Human Development. (2010). *Back to Sleep public education campaign.* Retrieved from http://www.nichd.nih.gov/sids/

National Institute of Child Health and Human Development. (2012). *What causes learning disabilities?* Retrieved from http://www.nichd.nih.gov/health/topics/learning/conditioninfo/pages/causes.aspx

National Institute on Alcohol Abuse and Alcoholism. (n.d.). *Drinking levels defined.* Retrieved from https://www.niaaa.nih.gov/alcohol-health/overview-alcohol-consumption/moderate-binge-drinking

National Institute on Drug Abuse. (2015). *Monitoring the Future 2015 Survey results.* Retrieved from https://www.drugabuse.gov/related-topics/trends-statistics/infographics/monitoring-future-2015-survey-results

National Institute on Deafness and Other Communication Disorders. (2013). *Cochlear implants.* Retrieved from http://www.nidcd.nih.gov/health/hearing/pages/coch.aspx

National Institute for Environmental Health Sciences. (2016). *Endocrine disruptors.* Retrieved from http://www.niehs.nih.gov/health/topics/agents/endocrine/

National Institute of Justice. (2011). *Prevalence of teen dating violence.* Retrieved from http://www.nij.gov/nij/topics/crime/intimate-partner-violence/teen-dating-violence/prevalence.htm

National Institute of Mental Health (n.d.). Use of mental health services and treatment among children. Retrieved from http://www.nimh.nih.gov/health/statistics/prevalence/use-of-mental-health-services-and-treatment-among-children.shtml

National Institute of Mental Health. (2009). *The diagnosis of autism spectrum disorders.* Retrieved from http://www.nimh.nih.gov/health/publications/autism/complete-index.shtml#pub3

National Institute of Mental Health. (2014). *Major depression among adolescents.* Retrieved from http://www.nimh.nih.gov/health/statistics/prevalence/major-depression-among-adolescents.shtml

National Institute of Neurological Disorders and Stroke. (2008). *Autism fact sheet.* Retrieved from http://www.ninds.nih.gov/disorders/autism/detail_autism.htm

National Institute of Neurological Disorders and Stroke. (2015). *Cerebral palsy: Hope through research.* Retrieved from http://www.ninds.nih.gov/disorders/cerebral_palsy/detail_cerebral_palsy.htm#179323104

National Institutes of Health. (n.d.). *Principles of adolescent substance use disorder treatment: A research-based guide.* Washington, DC: Author.

National Institutes of Health. (2014). *What causes asthma?* Retrieved from http://www.nhlbi.nih.gov/health/health-topics/topics/asthma/causes

National Institutes of Health. (2015a). *Infant–newborn development.* Retrieved from https://www.nlm.nih.gov/medlineplus/ency/article/002004.htm

National Institutes of Health. (2015b). *Research on back sleeping and SIDS.* Retrieved from www.nichd.nih.gov/sts/campaign/science/Pages/backsleeping.aspx

National Partnership for Women and Families. (2016). *State paid family leave insurance laws.* Retrieved from http://www.nationalpartnership.org/research-library/work-family/paid-leave/state-paid-family-leave-laws.pdf

National Reading Panel. (2000). Alphabetics Part II: Phonics instruction. In *Report of the National Reading Panel: Teaching children to read: An evidence-based assessment of the scientific research literature on reading and its implications for reading instruction: Reports of the subgroups.* Rockville, MD: NICHD Clearinghouse.

National Research Council. (2011). *Adverse effects of vaccines: Evidence and causality.* Washington, DC: National Academies Press.

National Scientific Council on the Developing Child. (2005/2014). *Excessive stress disrupts the architecture of the developing brain: Working Paper 3.* (Updated ed.). Retrieved from http://www.developingchild.harvard.edu

National Sleep Foundation. (n.d.). Sleep diary. Retrieved from https://sleepfoundation.org/sleep-diary/SleepDiaryv6.pdf

National Sleep Foundation. (2013). *Children and sleep.* Retrieved from http://www.sleepfoundation.org/article/sleep-topics/children-and-sleep

National Society of Genetic Counselors. (n.d.). *Understanding and collecting your family history.* Retrieved from http://nsgc.org/p/cm/ld/fid=52

National Student Clearinghouse Research Center. (2015). *Snapshot report: Degree attainment.* Retrieved from https://nscresearchcenter.org/wp-content/uploads/SnapshotReport15-DegreeAttainment.pdf

National Writing Project. (2014). *Writing, technology, and teens.* Retrieved from http://www.nwp.org/cs/public/print/resource/2432

National Youth Violence Prevention Resource Center. (2008). *School violence fact sheet.* Retrieved from http://www.safeyouth.org/scripts/facts/school.asp

Natsuaki, M. N., Biehl, M. C., & Ge, X. (2009). Trajectories of depressed mood from early adolescence to young adulthood: The effects of pubertal timing and adolescent dating. *Journal of Research on Adolescence, 19*(1), 47–74.

Neber, H., Finsterwald, M., & Urban, N. (2001). Cooperative learning with gifted and high-achieving students: A review and meta-analyses of 12 studies. *High Ability Studies, 12*(2), 199–214.

Negriff, S., Schneiderman, J. U., & Trickett, P. K. (2015). Child maltreatment and sexual risk behavior: Maltreatment types and gender differences. *Journal of Developmental and Behavioral Pediatrics, 36*(9), 708–716. doi:10.1097/DBP.0000000000000204

Neisser, U., Boodoo, G., Bouchard, T. J., Boykin, A. W., Brody, N., Ceci, S. J., . . . Urbina, S. (1996). Intelligence: Knowns and unknowns. *American Psychologist, 51*(2), 77–101.

Neitzel, J., & Bogin, J. (2008). *Steps for implementation: Functional behavior assessment.* Chapel Hill, NC: The National Professional Development Center on Autism Spectrum Disorders, Frank Porter Graham Child Development Institute, The University of North Carolina.

Nelson, C. (1999). How important are the first 3 years of life? *Applied Developmental Science, 3*(4), 235–238.

Nelson, K. (2014). Events, narratives, memory: What develops. In C. A. Nelson (Ed.), *Memory and affect in development: The Minnesota Symposia on Child Psychology* (Vol. 26, pp. 1–24). New York: Psychology Press.

Nelson, K. (2015). Making sense with private speech. *Cognitive Development, 36,* 171–179. doi:10.1016/j.cogdev.2015.09.004

Nemours Foundation. (2013). *Tips for divorcing parents.* Retrieved from http://kidshealth.org/parent/emotions/feelings/divorce.html#

Neonatology on the Web. (2007). *Incubators for infants.* Retrieved from http://www.neonatology.org/classics/portroyal.html

Neppl, T. K., Donnellan, M., Scaramella, L. V., Widaman, K. F., Spilman, S. K., Ontai, L. L., & Conger, R. D. (2010). Differential stability of temperament and personality from toddlerhood to middle childhood. *Journal of Research on Personality, 44*(3), 386–396.

Neuman, S. B., Kaefer, T., Pinkham, A., & Strouse, G. (2014). Can babies learn to read? A randomized trial of baby media. *Journal of Educational Psychology, 106*(3), 815–830.

Neumark-Sztainer, D. (2008). Family meals in adolescents: Findings from Project EAT. *Society for Research in Child Development Social Policy Reports, 22*(4), 11.

Neville, H. J., Stevens, C., Pakulak, E., Bell, T. A., Fanning, J., Klein, S., & Isbella, E. (2013). Family-based training program improves brain function, cognition, and behavior in lower socioeconomic status preschoolers. *Proceedings of the National Academy of Sciences of the United States of America, 110,* 12138–12143.

Newcombe, N. S. (2011). Three families of isms. *Child Development Perspectives, 5*(3), 171–172.

Newcombe, N. S., Sluzenski, J., & Huttenlocher, J. (2005). Preexisting knowledge versus on-line learning: What do young infants really know about spatial location? *Psychological Science, 16*(3), 222–227.

Newman, H. H. (1932). *Evolution, genetics, and eugenics.* Chicago: University of Chicago Press.

Newman, J., Bidjerano, T., Özdogru, A. A., Kao, C., Özköse-Biyik, C., & Johnson, J. J. (2007). What do they usually do after school? A comparative analysis of fourth-grade children in Bulgaria, Taiwan, and the United States. *Journal of Early Adolescence, 27,* 431–456.

Newman, M. G., Llera, S. J., Erickson, T. M., Przeworski, A., & Castonguay, L. G. (2013). Worry and generalized anxiety disorder: A review and theoretical synthesis of evidence on nature, etiology, mechanisms, and treatment. *Annual Review of Clinical Psychology, 9,* 275–297 doi:10.1146/annurev-clinpsy-050212-185544

Ng, F. F., Tamis-LeMonda, C., Yoshikawa, H., & Sze, I. N. (2015). Inhibitory control in preschool predicts early math skills in first grade: Evidence from an ethnically diverse sample. *International Journal of Behavioral Development, 39*(2), 139–149. doi:10.1177/0165025414538558

Nicholas, J., & Geers, A. E. (2007). Will they catch up? The role of age at cochlear implantation in the spoken language development of children with severe to profound hearing loss. *Journal of Speech, Language, and Hearing Research, 50*(4), 1048–1062.

Nield, L. S., Cakan, N., & Kamat, D. (2007). A practical approach to precocious puberty. *Clinical Pediatrics, 46*(4), 299–306.

Nielsen. (2015). *Grow and tell: As children age from toddlers to teens, their media palate changes.* Retrieved from http://www.nielsen.com/us/en/insights/news/2015/grow-and-tell-as-children-age-from-toddlers-to-teens-their-media-palate-changes.html

Nijhof, K. S., & Engels, R. C. M. E. (2007). Parenting styles, coping strategies, and the expression of homesickness. *Journal of Adolescence, 30*(5), 709–720.

Nikčević, A. V., & Nicolaides, K. H. (2014). Search for meaning, finding meaning and adjustment in women following miscarriage: A longitudinal study. *Psychology & Health, 29*(1), 50–63. doi:10.1080/08870446.2013.823497

Nikkelen, S. C., Valkenburg, P. M., Huizinga, M., & Bushman, B. J. (2014). Media use and ADHD-related behaviors in children and adolescents: A meta-analysis. *Developmental Psychology, 50*(9), 2228–2241. doi:10.1037/a0037318

Nikolaidis, A., Baniqued, P. L., Kranz, M. B., Scavuzzo, C. J., Barbey, A. K., Kramer, A. F., & Larsen, R. J. (2016). Multivariate associations of fluid intelligence and NAA. *Cerebral Cortex* (Epub ahead of print).

Nikulina, V., Widom, C. S., & Czaja, S. (2010). The role of childhood neglect and childhood poverty in predicting mental health, academic achievement and crime in adulthood. *American Journal of Community Psychology, 48,* 309–321.

Nisbett, R. E., Aronson, J., Blair, C., Dickens, W., Flynn, J., Halpern, D. F., & Turkheimer, E. (2012). Intelligence: New findings and theoretical developments. *American Psychologist, 67*(2), 130–159.

Nock, M. K., Green, J. G., Hwang, I., McLaughlin, K. A., Sampson, N. A., Zaslavsky, A. M., & Kessler, R. C. (2013). Prevalence, correlates, and treatment of lifetime suicidal behavior among adolescents: Results from the National Comorbidity Survey Replication Adolescent Supplement. *JAMA Psychiatry, 70*(3), 300–310. doi:10.1001/2013.jamapsychiatry.55

Nomaguchi, K. M., & Milkie, M. A. (2003). Costs and rewards of children: The effect of becoming a parent on adults' lives. *Journal of Marriage and Family, 65*(2), 356–374.

Nomi, T. (2010). The effects of within-class ability grouping on academic achievement in early elementary years. *Journal of Research on Educational Effectiveness, 3*(1), 56–92.

Nomikou, I., Rohlfing, K. J., & Szufnarowska, J. (2013). Educating attention: Recruiting, maintaining, and framing eye contact in early natural mother-infant interactions. *Interaction Studies, 14*(2), 240–267.

Nordenbæk, C., Jørgensen, M., Kyvik, K. O., & Bilenberg, N. (2014). A Danish population-based twin study on autism spectrum disorders. *European Child & Adolescent Psychiatry, 23*(1), 35–43. doi:10.1007/s00787-013-0419-5

Nosek, B. A., Smyth, F. L., Sriram, N. N., Lindner, N. M., Devos, T., Ayala, A., . . . Greenwald, A. G. (2009). National differences in gender–science stereotypes predict national sex differences in science and math achievement. *Proceedings of The National Academy of Sciences of The United States of America, 106*(26), 10593–10597. doi:10.1073/pnas.0809921106

Nowak, K., & Rauh, C. (2008). Choose your "buddy icon" carefully: The influence of avatar androgyny, anthropomorphism and credibility in online interactions. *Computers in Human Behavior, 24,* 1473–1493.

NPR. (2016). *California raises age of tobacco purchases to 21 and tightens vaping rules.* Retrieved from http://www.npr.org/sections/health-shots/2016/05/05/476872674/california-raises-age-of-tobacco-purchase-to-21-and-tightens-vaping-rules

Nsamenang, A. B. (2015). Indigenous Social Science at the intersection with human development: Implications for and lessons from African ecoculture. In L. A. Jensen (Ed.), *The Oxford handbook of human development and culture* (pp. 61–78). New York: Oxford University Press.

Nsamenang, A. B., & Lo-oh, J. L. (2010). Afrique noir. In M. H. Bornstein (Ed.), *Handbook of cultural developmental science* (pp. 383–407). New York: Psychology Press.

Nucci, L. P. (2008). Social cognitive domain theory and moral education. In L. P. Nucci & D. Narvaez (Eds.), *Handbook of moral and character education* (pp. 291–309). New York: Routledge.

Nugent, J. K. (2013). The competent newborn and the Neonatal Behavioral Assessment Scale: T. Berry Brazelton's legacy. *Journal of Child and Adolescent Psychiatric Nursing, 26*(3), 173–179. doi:10.1111/jcap.12043

Nwaru, B., Erkkola, M., Ahonen, S., Kaila, M., Haapala, A., Kronberg-Kippilä, C., . . . Virtanen, S. (2010). Age at the introduction of solid foods during the first year and allergic sensitization at age 5 years. *Pediatrics, 125*(1), 50–59 doi:10.1542/peds.2009-0813

O'Brien, I., Duffy, A., & Nicholl, H. (2009). Impact of childhood chronic illnesses on siblings: A literature review. *British Journal of Nursing, 18*(22), 1358–1365.

O'Connor, T. G., & Croft, C. M. (2001). A twin study of attachment in preschool children. *Child Development, 72,* 1501–1511.

O'Keefe, L. (2014). Parents who read to their children nurture more than literary skills. *AAP News.* Retrieved from http://aapnews.aappublications.org/content/early/2014/06/24/aapnews.20140624-2.full.pdf+html

O'Keeffe, G., & Clarke-Pearson, K., & Council on Communications Media. (2011). The impact of social media on children, adolescents, and families. *Pediatrics, 127*(4), 800–804. doi:10.1542/peds.2011-0054

O'Leary, P., & Barber, J. (2008). Gender differences in silencing following childhood sexual abuse. *Journal of Child Sexual Abuse, 17*(2), 133–143.

O'Mara, D. A., & Waller, A. (2003). What do you get when you cross a communication aid with a riddle? *The Psychologist, 16*(2), 78–80.

O'Mea, M. L. (2013). Implementing applied behavior analysis for effective orientation and mobility instruction of students with multiple disabilities. *Journal of Visual Impairment & Blindness, 107*(1), 65–70.

Oatley, K., Keltner, D., & Jenkins, J. M. (2006). *Understanding emotions* (2nd ed.). Malden, MA: Blackwell.

Odegard, T. N., & Toglia, M. P. (2013). Children as eyewitnesses: Historical background, and factors affecting children's eyewitness testimony. In R. E. Holliday, & T. A. Marche (Eds.), *Child forensic psychology: Victim and eyewitness memory* (pp. 95–118). New York: Palgrave Macmillan.

Ogbuanu, C. A., Probst, J., Laditka, S. B., Liu, J., Baek, J., & Glover, S. (2009). Reasons why women do not initiate breastfeeding: A southeastern state study. *Women's Health Issues: Official Publication of the Jacobs Institute of Women's Health, 19*(4), 268–278. http://doi.org/10.1016/j.whi.2009.03.005

Ohene, S., Ireland, M., McNeely, C., & Borowsky, I. W. (2006). Parental expectations, physical punishment, and violence among adolescents who score positive on a psychosocial screening test in primary care. *Pediatrics, 117,* 441–447.

Olds, S. B., London, M. L., & Ladewig, P. A. (2002). *Maternal-newborn nursing: A family and community-based approach* (6th ed.). Upper Saddle River, NJ: Prentice Hall.

Olds, T., Maher, C., Blunden, S., & Matricciani, L. (2010). Normative data on the sleep habits of Australian children and adolescents. *Sleep, 33*(10), 1381–1388.

Ollendick, T. H., Grills, A. E., & Alexander, K. L. (2014). Fears, worries, and anxiety in children and adolescents. In C. A. Essau, F. Petermann, C. A. Essau, & F. Petermann (Eds.), *Anxiety disorders in children and adolescents: Epidemiology, risk factors and treatment* (pp. 1–35). New York: Psychology Press.

Olson, S. L., Bates, J. E., Sandy, J. M., & Lanthier, R. (2000). Early developmental precursors of externalizing behavior in middle childhood and adolescence. *Journal of Abnormal Child Psychology, 28*(2), 119–133.

Olweus, D. (2003). A profile of bullying at school. *Educational Leadership, 60*(6), 12–17.

Ongley, S. F., & Malti, T. (2014). The role of moral emotions in the development of children's sharing behavior. *Developmental Psychology, 50*(4), 1148–1159. doi: 10.1037/a0035191

Oppenheimer, L. (1986). Development of recursive thinking: Procedural variations. *International Journal of Behavioral Development, 9*(3), 401–411.

Organisation for Economic Co-operation and Development. (2009). *Equally prepared for life? How 15-year-old boys and girls perform in school.* Washington, DC: Author.

Organisation for Economic Co-operation and Development. (2016). Key characteristics of parental leave systems. Retrieved from https://www.oecd.org/els/soc/PF2_1_Parental_leave_systems.pdf

Orzack, S. H., Stubblefield, J. W., Akmaev, V. R., Colls, P., Munné, S., Scholl, T., Steinsaltz, D., & Zuckerman, J. E. (2015). The human sex ratio from conception to birth. *Proceedings of the National Academy of Sciences of the United States of America, 112*(16), E2102–E2111. doi:10.1073/pnas.1416546112

Osgood, D. W., Anderson, A. L., & Shaffer, J. N. (2005). Unstructured leisure in the after-school hours. In J. L. Mahoney, R. W. Larson, & J. S. Eccles (Eds.), *Organized activities as contexts of development* (pp. 45–64). Mahwah, NJ: Erlbaum.

Ostrov, J. M., Gentile, D. A., & Crick, N. R. (2006). Media exposure, aggression and prosocial behavior during early childhood: A longitudinal study. *Social Development, 15*(4), 612–627.

Østvik, L., Eikeseth, S., & Klintwall, L. (2012). Grammatical constructions in typical developing children: Effects of explicit reinforcement, automatic reinforcement and parity. *Analysis of Verbal Behavior, 28*(1), 73–82.

Oudekerk, B. A., Allen, J. P., Hessel, E. T., & Molloy, L. E. (2015). The cascading development of autonomy and relatedness from adolescence to adulthood. *Child Development, 86*(2), 472–485. doi:10.1111/cdev.12313

Outdoor Foundation. (2012). *Outdoor recreation participation report 2012.* Retrieved from http://www.outdoorfoundation.org/pdf/ResearchParticipation2012.pdf

Pachter, L. M., & Garcia Coll, C. (2009). Racism and child health: A review of the literature and future directions. *Journal of Developmental and Behavioral Pediatrics, 30*, 255–263.

Padilla-Walker, L. M., & Carlo, G. (2004). "It's not Fair!" Adolescents' constructions of appropriateness of parental reactions. *Journal of Youth and Adolescence, 33*(5), 389–401.

Pagan, J. L., Rose, R. J., Viken, R. J., Pulkkinen, L., Kaprio, J., & Dick, D. M. (2006). Genetic and environmental influences on stages of alcohol use across adolescence and into young adulthood. *Behavior Genetics, 36*(4), 483–497.

Pahlke, E., & Hyde, J. S. (2016). The debate over single-sex schooling. *Child Development Perspectives, 10*(2), 81–86.

Pajares, F. (2002). *Overview of social cognitive theory and of self-efficacy.* Retrieved from http://www.emory.edu/EDUCATION/mfp/eff.html

Pajares, F. (2005). Self-efficacy during childhood and adolescence. In F. Pajares, & T. C. Urdan (Eds.), *Self-efficacy beliefs of adolescents* (pp. 339–367). Charlotte, NC: Information Age.

Pajares, F., & Schunk, D. H. (2002). Self and self-belief in psychology and education: An historical perspective. In J. Aronson (Ed.), *Improving academic achievement* (pp. 5–21). New York: Academic Press.

Palm, G. (2014). Attachment theory and fathers: Moving from 'being there' to 'being with.' *Journal of Family Theory & Review, 6*(4), 282–297. doi:10.1111/jftr.12045

Palusci, V. J., Crum, P., Bliss, R., & Bavolek, S. J. (2008). Changes in parenting attitudes and knowledge among inmates and other at-risk populations after a family nurturing program. *Children and Youth Services Review, 30*(1), 79–89.

Pan, B. A. (2005). Semantic development. In J. B. Gleason (Ed.), *The development of language* (6th ed., pp. 112–147). Boston: Pearson.

Panel Study of Income Dynamics. (2015a). *The Panel Study of Income Dynamics – PSID – is the longest running longitudinal household survey in the world.* Retrieved from https://psidonline.isr.umich.edu/

Panel Study of Income Dynamics. (2015b). *The Panel Study of Income Dynamics – Studies.* Retrieved from https://psidonline.isr.umich.edu/Studies.aspx

Panfile, T. M., & Laible, D. J. (2012). Attachment security and child's empathy: The mediating role of emotion regulation. *Merrill-Palmer Quarterly, 58*(1), 1–21. doi:10.1353/mpq.2012.0003

Pang, W. (2015). Promoting creativity in the classroom: A generative view. *Psychology of Aesthetics, Creativity, and the Arts, 9*(2), 122–127. doi:10.1037/aca0000009

Papadakis, A. A., Prince, R. P., Jones, N. P., & Strauman, T. J. (2006). Self-regulation, rumination, and vulnerability to depression in adolescent girls. *Development and Psychopathology, 18*(3), 815–829.

Papert, S. (1999). Jean Piaget. *Time.* Retrieved from http://content.time.com/time/magazine/article/0,9171,990617,00.html

Parent, A. S., Teilmann, G., Juul, A., Skakkebaek, N. E., Toppari, J., & Bourguignon, J. P. (2003). The timing of normal puberty and the age limits of sexual precocity: Variations around the world, secular trends, and changes after migration. *Endocrine Reviews, 24*(5), 668–693.

Park, H., Choi, B. S., Lee, S. J., Son, I., Seol, I., & Lee, H. J. (2014). Practical application of kangaroo mother care in preterm infants: Clinical characteristics and safety of kangaroo mother care. *Journal of Perinatal Medicine, 42*(2), 239–245. doi:10.1515/jpm-2013-0066

Parker, K., & Wang, W. (2013). *Modern parenthood: Roles of moms and dads converge as they balance work and family.* Washington, DC: Pew Research, Social & Demographic Trends. Retrieved from http://www.pewsocialtrends.org/2013/03/14/modern-parenthood-roles-of-moms-and-dads-converge-as-they-balance-work-and-family/

Parks, S. E., Annest, J. L., Hill, H. A., & Karch, D. L. (2012). *Pediatric abusive head trauma: Recommended definitions for public health surveillance and research.* Atlanta, GA: Centers for Disease Control and Prevention.

Parmer, S. M., Salisbury-Glennon, J., Shannon, D., & Struempler, B. (2009). School gardens: An experiential learning approach for a nutrition education program to increase fruit and vegetable knowledge, preference, and consumption among second-grade students. *Journal of Nutrition Education and Behavior, 41*(3), 212–217.

Parten, M. (1932). Social participation among preschool children. *Journal of Abnormal and Social Psychology, 27*(3), 243–269.

Pasley, K., & Moorefield, B. S. (2004). Stepfamilies changes and challenges. In M. Coleman & L. H. Ganong (Eds.), *Handbook of contemporary families* (pp. 317–330). Thousand Oaks, CA: Sage.

Patrick, R. B., & Gibbs, J. C. (2012). Inductive discipline, parental expression of disappointed expectations, and moral identity in adolescence. *Journal of Youth and Adolescence, 41*(8), 973–983.

Patterson, C. J. (2006). Children of lesbian and gay parents. *Current Directions in Psychological Science, 15*(5), 241–244.

Patterson, C. J. (2013). Children of lesbian and gay parents: Psychology, law, and policy. *Psychology of Sexual Orientation and Gender Diversity, 1*(S), 27–34. doi:10.1037/2329-0382.1.S.27

Patterson, G. R., & Yoerger, K. (2002). A developmental model for early- and late-onset delinquency. In J. B. Reid, G. R. Patterson, & J. Snyder (Eds.), *Antisocial behavior in children and adolescents: A developmental analysis and model for intervention* (pp. 147–172). Washington, DC: American Psychological Association.

Patterson, G. R., Dishion, T. J., & Yoerger, K. (2000). Adolescent growth in new forms of problem behavior: Macro- and micro-peer dynamics. *Prevention Science, 1*(1), 3–13.

Paul, R., Chawarska, K., Fowler, C., Cicchetti, D., & Volkmar, F. (2007). 'Listen my children and you shall hear': Auditory preferences in toddlers with autism spectrum disorders. *Journal of Speech, Language, and Hearing Research, 50*(5), 1350–1364. doi:10.1044/1092-4388(2007/094)

Paulson, A., & Teicher, S. A. (2006). Move to single-sex classes fans debate. *Christian Science Monitor.* Retrieved from http://www.csmonitor.com/2006/1026/p02s01-legn.html

Pavlov, I. P. (1927). *Conditioned reflexes: An investigation of the physiological activity of the cerebral cortex.* Retrieved from http://www.ivanpavlov.com/lectures/ivan_pavlov-lecture_002.htm

PDR Staff. (2016). *Physicians' desk reference* (70th ed.). PDR Network, LLC.

Pearson, P. D. (2004). The reading wars. *Educational Policy, 18*(1), 216–252.

Peeters, M., Cillessen, A. N., & Scholte, R. J. (2010). Clueless or powerful? Identifying subtypes of bullies in adolescence. *Journal of Youth and Adolescence, 39*(9), 1041–1052. doi:10.1007/s10964-009-9478-9

Peets, K., Hodges, E. E., Kikas, E., & Salmivalli, C. (2007). Hostile attributions and behavioral strategies in children: Does relationship type matter? *Developmental Psychology, 43*(4), 889–900.

Pellegrini, A. D. (1987). Rough-and-tumble play: Developmental and educational significance. *Educational Psychologist, 22*(1), 23–43.

Pellegrini, A. D. (2003). Perceptions and functions of play and real fighting in early adolescence. *Child Development, 74*(5), 1522–1533.

Pellegrini, A. D. (2005). *Recess—Its role in education and development*. Mahwah, NJ: Erlbaum.

Pellegrini, A.D., & Smith, P. K. (1998). Physical activity play: The nature and function of a neglected aspect of play. *Child Development, 69,* 557–598

Pelucchi, B., Hay, J. F., & Saffran, J. R. (2009). Statistical learning in a natural language by 8-month-old infants. *Child Development, 80*(3), 674–685.

Pempek, T. A., Demers, L. B., Hanson, K. G., Kirkorian, H. L., & Anderson, D. R. (2011). The impact of infant-directed videos on parent-child interaction. *Journal of Applied Developmental Psychology, 32*(1), 10–19.

Pereda, N., Guilera, G., Forns, M., & Gómez-Benito, J. (2009). The international epidemiology of child sexual abuse: A continuation of Finkelhor (1994). *Child Abuse & Neglect, 33*(6), 331–342.

Perrin-Wallqvist, R., & Lindblom, J. (2015). Coming out as gay: A phenomenological study about adolescents disclosing their homosexuality to their parents. *Social Behavior and Personality, 43*(3), 467–480. doi:10.2224/sbp.2015.43.3.467

Perry, D. F. (2014). *Can preschool expulsion be prevented? A growing body of research says Yes!* Retrieved from http://psychologybenefits.org/2014/12/23/can-preschool-expulsion-be-prevented-a-growing-body-of-research-says-yes/#_ftnref6

Perry, D. G., & Pauletti, R. E. (2011). Gender and adolescent development. *Journal of Research on Adolescence, 21*(1), 61–74. doi:10.1111/j.1532-7795.2010.00715.x

Perry, S. B. (1998). Clinical implications of a dynamic systems theory. *Neurology Report, 22*(1), 4–10.

Persad, M. D., & Mensinger, J. L. (2008). Maternal breastfeeding attitudes: Association with breastfeeding intent and socio-demographics amojng urban primiparas. *Journal of Community Health, 33*(2), 53–60.

Pescosolido, B. A., & Levy, J. A. (2002). The role of social networks in health, illness, disease and healing. In J. Levy & B. Pescosolido (Eds.), *Social networks and health* (Vol. 8, pp. 3–25). Elsevier Science.

Peter J. Peterson Foundation. (2013). *Americans spend over twice as much per capita on healthcare as the average developed country.* Retrieved from http://pgpf.org/Chart-Archive/0006_health-care-oecd

Peters, E., Riksen-Walraven, J., Cillessen, A. N., & de Weerth, C. (2011). Peer rejection and HPA activity in middle childhood: Friendship makes a difference. *Child Development, 82*(6), 1906–1920.

Peterson, C. (2002). Children's long-term memory for autobiographical events. *Developmental Review, 22*(3), 370–402.

Peterson, C. C., Wellman, H. M., & Slaughter, V. (2012). The mind behind the message: Advancing theory-of-mind scales for typically developing children, and those with deafness, autism, or Asperger syndrome. *Child Development, 83*(2), 469–485. doi:10.1111/j.1467-8624.2011.01728.x

Peterson-Kaiser Health System Tracker. (2015). *How does infant mortality in the U.S. compare to other countries?* Retrieved from http://www.healthsystemtracker.org/chart-collection/how-does-infant-mortality-in-the-u-s-compare-to-other-countries

Petitto, L. A., Katerelos, M., Levy, B. G., Gauna, K., Tétreault, K., & Ferraro, V. (2001). Bilingual signed and spoken language acquisition from birth: Implications for the mechanisms underlying early bilingual language acquisition. *Journal of Child Language, 28*(2), 453–496.

Petrill, S. A., & Deater-Deckard, K. (2004). The heritability of general cognitive ability: A within-family adoption design. *Intelligence, 32*(4), 403–409. doi:10.1016/j.intell.2004.05.001

Petrovich, G. D., & Gallagher, M. (2007). Control of food consumption by learned cues: A forebrain—hypothalamic network. *Physiology & Behavior, 91*(4), 397–403. doi:10.1016/j.physbeh.2007.04.014

Petrzela, N. M. (2010). Before the Federal Bilingual Education Act: Legislation and lived experience in California. *Peabody Journal of Education, 85,* 406–424.

Pew Research Center. (2009). *The harried life of the working mother.* Retrieved from http://www.pewsocialtrends.org/2009/10/01/the-harried-life-of-the-working-mother/

Pew Research Center. (2015). *Parenting in America: Outlook, worries, aspirations are strongly linked to financial situation.* Washington, DC: Author.

Pfeifer, J. H., Brown, C. S., & Juvonen, J. (2007). Prejudice reduction in schools—Teaching tolerance in schools: Lessons learned since *Brown v. Board of Education* about the development and reduction of children's prejudice. *SRCD Social Policy Report, 21*(2), 3–13, 16–17, 20–23.

Pfeiffer, S. I. (2012). Current perspectives on the identification and assessment of gifted students. *Journal of Psychoeducational Assessment, 30*(1), 3–9.

Phan, H. P., & Ngu, B. H. (2016, March). Sources of self-efficacy in academic contexts: A longitudinal perspective. *School Psychology Quarterly.* doi:10.1037/spq0000151

Phinney, J. S. (1989). Stages of ethnic identity development in minority group adolescents. *Journal of Early Adolescence, 9*(1–2), 34–49.

Phinney, J. S., Jacoby, B., & Silva, C. (2007). Positive intergroup attitudes: The role of ethnic identity. *International Journal of Behavioral Development, 31*(5), 478–490. doi:10.1177/0165025407081466

Phinney, J. S., Kim-Jo, T., Osorio, S., & Vilhjalmsdottir, P. (2005). Autonomy and relatedness in adolescent-parent disagreements: Ethnic and developmental factors. *Journal of Adolescent Research, 20*(1), 8–39.

Phinney, J. S., & Ong, A. D. (2007). Conceptualization and measurement of ethnic identity: Current status and future directions. *Journal of Counseling Psychology, 54*(3), 271–281. doi:10.1037/0022-0167.54.3.271

Piaget, J. (1926). *The language and thought of the child.* New York: Harcourt, Brace.

Piaget, J. (1952/1963). *The origins of intelligence in children.* New York: W. W. Norton.

Piaget, J. (1954). *The construction of reality in the child.* New York: Basic Books.

Piaget, J. (1955/1973). *The language and thought of the child.* New York: Meridian Books.

Piaget, J. (1962). *Play, dreams and imitation in childhood.* New York: W. W. Norton.

Piaget, J. (1965). *The moral judgment of the child.* New York: Free Press.

Piaget, J. (1969). *The child's conception of the world.* Totowa, NJ: Littlefield, Adams.

Piaget, J. (1999). The stages of intellectual development of the child. In A. Slater & D. Muir (Eds.), *Blackwell reader in developmental psychology* (pp. 35–42). Malden, MA: Blackwell.

Piaget, J., & Inhelder, B. (1956). *The child's conception of space.* London: Routledge.

Pietromonaco, P. R., & Powers, S. I. (2015). Attachment and health-related physiological stress processes, *Current Opinion in Psychology, 1,* 34–39. DOI: 10.1016/j.copsyc.2014.12.001

Pietschnig, J., Voracek, M., & Formann, A. K. (2010). Mozart effect–Shmozart effect: A meta-analysis. *Intelligence, 38*(3), 314–323.

Pinkleton, B. E., Austin, E., Chen, Y., & Cohen, M. (2012). The role of media literacy in shaping adolescents' understanding of and responses to sexual portrayals in mass media. *Journal of Health Communication, 17*(4), 460–476. doi:10.1080/10810730.2011.635770

Pinkleton, B. E., Austin, E. W., Cohen, M., Miller, A., & Fitzgerald, E. (2007). A statewide evaluation of the effectiveness of media literacy training to prevent tobacco use among adolescents. *Health Communication, 21,* 23–34.

Pinquart, M. (2015). Associations of parenting styles and dimensions with academic achievement in children and adolescents: A meta-analysis. *Educational Psychology Review, 28,* 475–493. doi:10.1007/s10648-015-9338-y

Pinquart, M., & Teubert, D. (2010). A meta-analytic study of couple interventions during the transition to parenthood. *Family Relations, 59*(3), 221–231. doi: 10.1111/j.1741–3729.2010.00597.x

Piper, P. S. (2000). Better read that again: Web hoaxes and misinformation. *Searcher, 8*(8), 40–49.

Planty, M., Provasnik, S., & Daniel, B. (2007). *High school course taking: Findings from the condition of education 2007* [NCES 2007–065]. U.S. Department of Education. Washington, DC: National Center for Education Statistics.

Plucker, J. A., & Callahan, C. M. (2014). Research on giftedness and gifted education: Status of the field and considerations for the future. *Exceptional Children, 80*(4), 390–406.

Plomin, R. (2011). Commentary: Why are children in the same family so different? Non-shared environment three decades later. *International Journal of Epidemiology, 40*(3), 582–592. doi:10.1093/ije/dyq144

Plomin, R. (2013). Child development and molecular genetics: 14 years later. *Child Development, 84*(1), 104–120.

Plomin, R., Asbury, K., & Dunn, J. (2001). Why are children in the same family so different? Non-shared environment a decade later. *Canadian Journal of Psychiatry, 46,* 225–233.

Plomin, R., DeFries, J. C., Craig, I. W., & McGuffin, P. (2003). Behavioral genomics. In R. Plomin, J. C. DeFries, I. W. Craig, & P. McGuffin (Eds.), *Behavioral genetics in the postgenomic era* (pp. 531–540). Washington, DC: American Psychological Association.

Plomin, R., & Petrill, S. A. (1997). Genetics and intelligence: What's new? *Intelligence, 24*(1), 53–77.

Plomin, R., & Simpson, M. A. (2013). The future of genomics for developmentalists. *Development and Psychopathology, 25*(4, part 2), 1263–1278. doi:10.1017/S0954579413000606

Poehner, M. E. (2007). Beyond the test: L2 dynamic assessment and the transcendence of mediated learning. *Modern Language Journal, 91*(3), 323–340.

Poh, H. L., Koh, S. L., & He, H. (2014). An integrative review of fathers' experiences during pregnancy and childbirth. *International Nursing Review, 61*(4), 543–554. doi:10.1111/inr.12137

Pollet, T. V. (2007). Genetic relatedness and sibling relationship characteristics in a modern society. *Evolution and Human Behavior, 28*(3), 176–185.

Polman, H., de Castro, B. O., & van Aken, M. A. G. (2008). Experimental study of the differential effects of playing versus watching violent video games on children's aggressive behavior. *Aggressive Behavior, 34*(3), 256–264.

Ponitz, C. C., McClelland, M. M., Matthews, J. S., & Morrison, F. J. (2009). A structured observation of behavioral self-regulation and its contribution to kindergarten outcomes. *Developmental Psychology, 45*(3), 605–619.

Pool, M. M., Koolstra, C. M., & van der Voort, T. H. A. (2003). Distraction effects of background soap operas on homework performance: An experimental study enriched with observational data. *Educational Psychology, 23*(4), 361–380.

Porath, A. J., & Fried, P. A. (2005). Effect of prenatal cigarette and marijuana exposure on drug use among offspring. *Neurotoxicology and Teratology, 27*(2), 267–277.

Porter, N. (2012). *High turnover among early childhood educators in the United States.* Retrieved from http://www.childresearch.net/projects/ecec/2012_04.html

Porter, R. (Ed.) (2013). *Merck Manual Home Health Handbook.* Retrieved from http://www.merckmanuals.com/home

Posada, G., & Jacobs, A. (2001). Child–mother attachment relationships and culture. *American Psychologist, 56*(10), 821–822. doi:10.1037/0003-066X.56.10.821

Posner, M. I., Rothbart, M. K., & Sheese, B. E. (2007). Attention genes. *Developmental Science, 10*(1), 24–29.

Posner, R. B. (2006). Early menarche: A review of research on trends in timing racial differences, etiology and psychosocial consequences. *Sex Roles, 54*(5/6), 315–322.

Poti, J. M., Duffey, J. J., & Popkin, B. M. (2014). The association of fast food consumption with poor dietary outcomes and obesity among children: Is it the fast food or the remainder of the diet? *American Journal of Clinical Nutrition, 99*(1), 162–171.

Poulin F., & Dishion, T. (2008). Methodological issues in the use of peer sociometric nominations with middle school youth. *Social Development [serial online], 17*(4), 908–921.

Powell, L., & Nguyen, B. (2013). Fast-food and full-service restaurant consumption among children and adolescents: Effect on energy, beverage, and nutrient intake. *JAMA Pediatrics, 167*(1), 14–20.

Powers, K. (2005). Authentic assessment. In S. Lee (Ed.), *Encyclopedia of school psychology* (pp. 36–38). Thousand Oaks, CA: Sage.

Prebble, S. C., Addis, D., & Tippett, L. J. (2013). Autobiographical memory and sense of self. *Psychological Bulletin, 139*(4), 815–840. doi:10.1037/a0030146

Preissler, M. A., & Bloom, P. (2007). Two-year-olds appreciate the dual nature of pictures. *Psychological Science, 18*(1), 1–2.

Preissler, M. A., & Carey, S. (2004). Do both pictures and words function as symbols for 18- and 24-month-old children? *Journal of Cognition and Development, 5*(2), 185–212.

Prince, J. B., Wilens, T. E., Spencer, T. J., & Biederman, J. (2015). Pharmacotherapy of ADHD in adults. In R. Barkley (Ed.), *Attention-deficit hyperactivity disorder* (4th ed., pp. 826–860). New York: Guilford.

Protudjer, J. L., Sevenhuysen, G. P., Ramsey, C. D., Kozyrskyj, A. L., & Becker, A. B. (2012). Low vegetable intake is associated with allergic asthma and moderate-to-severe airway hyperresponsiveness. *Pediatric Pulmonology, 47*(12), 1159–1169.

Provost, M. A., & LaFreniere, P. J. (1991). Social participation and peer competence in preschool children: Evidence for discriminant and convergent validity. *Child Study Journal, 21*(1), 57–72.

Prüss-Üstün, A., & Corvalán, C. (2006). *Preventing disease through healthy environments. Towards an estimate of the environmental burden of disease.* Geneva, Switzerland: World Health Organization.

Psouni, E., & Apetroaia, A. (2014). Measuring scripted attachment-related knowledge in middle childhood: The Secure Base Script Test. *Attachment & Human Development, 16*(1), 22–41. doi:10.1080/14616734.2013.804329

Public Broadcasting Service. (2001). *Timeline: The bilingual education controversy.* Retrieved from http://www.pbs.org/kcet/publicschool/roots_in_history/bilingual.html

Public Health Agency of Canada. (2003). *Infant attachment: What professionals need to know.* Retrieved from http://www.phac-aspc.gc.ca/mh-sm/mhp-psm/pub/fc-pc/prof_know-eng.php

Puma, M., Bell, S., Cook, R., Heid, C., Broene, P., Jenkins, F., Mashburn, A., & Downer, J. (2102). *Third grade follow-up to the Head Start Impact Study Final Report, OPRE Report #2012-45.* Washington, DC: Office of Planning, Research and Evaluation, Administration for Child and Families, U.S. Department of Health and Human Services.

Punch, S. (2012). Studying transnational children: A multi-sited, longitudinal, ethnographic approach. *Journal of Ethnic & Migration Studies, 38*(6), 1007–1023.

Putnam, F. W. (2003). Ten-year research update review: Child sexual abuse. *Journal of the American Academy of Child and Adolescent Psychiatry, 42*(3), 269–278.

Quee, P. J., Meijer, J. H., Islam, M., Aleman, A., Alizadeh, B. Z., Meijer, C. J., & van den Heuvel, E. R. (2014). Premorbid adjustment profiles in psychosis and the role of familial factors. *Journal of Abnormal Psychology, 123*(3), 578–587. doi: 10.1037/a0037189

Quiocho, A. M. L., & Daoud, A. M. (2006). Dispelling myths about Latino parent participation in school. *Educational Forum, 70*(3), 255–267.

Raby, K. L., Lawler, J. M., Shlafer, R. J., Hesemeyer, P. S., Collins, W. A., & Sroufe, L. A. (2015). The interpersonal antecedents of supportive parenting: A prospective, longitudinal study from infancy to adulthood. *Developmental Psychology, 51*(1), 115–123. doi:10.1037/a0038336

Radesky, J. S., Silverstein, M., Zuckerman, B., & Christakis, D. A. (2014). Infant self-regulation and early childhood media exposure. *Pediatrics, 133*(5), e1172–e1178. doi: 10.1542/peds.2013-2367

Raeff, C. (2004). Within culture complexities: Multifaceted and interrelated autonomy and connectedness characteristics in late adolescent selves. In M. E. Mascolo & J. Li (Eds.), *Culture and developing selves: Beyond dichotomization* (pp. 61-78). San Francisco: Jossey-Bass.

Raley, A. B., & Lucas, J. L. (2006). Stereotype or success? Prime-time television's portrayals of gay male, lesbian, and bisexual characters. *Journal of Homosexuality, 51*(2), 19–38.

Ram, A., Finzi, R., & Cohen, O. (2002). The non-custodial parent and his infant. *Journal of Divorce & Remarriage, 36*(3–4), 41–55.

Ramey, H. L., & Rose-Krasnor, L. (2012). Contexts of structured youth activities and positive youth development. *Child Development Perspectives, 6*(1), 85–91.

Rampage, C., Eovaldi, M., Ma, C., & Weigel-Foy, C. (2003). Adoptive families. In F. Walsh (Ed.), *Normal family processes* (3rd ed., pp. 210–232). New York: Guilford Press.

Rampersaud, G. C., Pereira, M. A., Girard, B. L., Adams, J., & Metzl, J. D. (2005). Breakfast habits, nutritional status, body weight, and academic performance in children and adolescents. *Journal of the American Dietetic Association, 105*(5), 743–760.

Ramsey-Rennels, J. L., & Langlois, J. H. (2007). How infants perceive and process faces. In A. Slater & M. Lewis (Eds.), *Introduction to infant development* (pp. 191–215). New York: Oxford University Press.

Ratjen, F., & Döring, G. (2003). Cystic fibrosis. *Lancet, 361*(9358), 681–689.

Rattan, A., Savani, K., Chugh, D., & Dweck, C. S. (2015). Leveraging mindsets to promote academic achievement: Policy recommendations. *Perspectives on Psychological Science, 10*(6), 721–726. doi:10.1177/1745691615599383

Rauscher, E. (2011). Producing adulthood: Adolescent employment, fertility, and the life course. *Social Science Research, 40*(2), 552–571. doi:10.1016/j.ssresearch.2010.09.002

Rauscher, F. H., Shaw, G. L., & Ky, K. N. (1993). Music and spatial task performance. *Nature, 365*(6447), 611.

Raver, C., Blair, C., & Willoughby, M. (2013). Poverty as a predictor of 4-year-olds' executive function: New perspectives on models of differential susceptibility. *Developmental Psychology, 49*(2), 292–304. doi: 10.1037/a0028343

Read, S. C., Carrier, M., Boucher, M., Whitley, R., Bond, S., & Zelkowitz, P. (2014). Psychosocial services for couples in infertility treatment: What do couples really want? *Patient Education and Counseling, 94*(3), 390–395. doi:10.1016/j.pec.2013.10.025

Reading Rockets. (2015). *Inference.* Retrieved from http://www.readingrockets.org/strategies/inference

Reagan-Steiner, S., Yankey, D., Jeyarajah, J., Elam-Evans, L. D., Singleton, J. A., Curtis, C. R., MacNeil, J., Markowitz, L. E., & Stokley, S. (2015). National, regional, state, and selected local area vaccination coverage among adolescents aged 13-17 years – United States, 2014. *Morbidity and Mortality Weekly Report, 64*(29), 784–792. Retrieved from http://www.cdc.gov/mmwr/preview/mmwrhtml/mm6429a3.htm#tab1

Reed, R. K. (2005). *Birthing fathers: The transformation of men in American rites of birth.* New Brunswick, NJ: Rutgers University Press.

Reef, S., & Redd, S. (2008). *Congenital rubella syndrome.* In Centers for Disease Control and Prevention (Ed.), *Manual for the surveillance of vaccine-preventable diseases* (4th ed.).

Reeves, J. (2006). Recklessness, rescue and responsibility: Young men tell their stories of the transition to fatherhood. *Practice, 18*(2), 79–90.

Regnerus, M. (2012). How different are the adult children of parents who have same-sex relationships? Findings from the New Family Structures Study. *Social Science Research, 41*(4), 752–770.

Reif, A., Rosler, M., Freitag, C. M., Schneider, M., Eujen, A., Kissling, C., . . . Retz, W. (2007). Nature and nurture predispose to violent behavior: Serotonergic genes and adverse childhood environment. *Neuropsychopharmacology*, *32*(11), 2375–2383.

Reis, S. M. (2004). Series introduction. In R. J. Sternberg (Ed.), *Definitions and conceptions of giftedness* (pp. ix–xxi). Thousand Oaks, CA: Corwin.

Reis, S. M., & Renzulli, J. S. (2010). Is there still a need for gifted education? An examination of current research. *Learning & Individual Differences, 20*(4), 308–317.

Ren, W., Lui, S., Deng, W., Li, F., Li, M., Huang, X., . . . Gong, Q. (2013). Anatomical and functional brain abnormalities in drug-naive first-episode schizophrenia. *The American Journal of Psychiatry, 170*(11), 1308–1316. doi:10.1176/appi.ajp.2013.12091148

Rentzsch, K., Wenzler, M. P., & Schütz, A. (2016). The structure of multidimensional self-esteem across age and gender. *Personality and Individual Differences, 88,* 139–147. doi:10.1016/j.paid.2015.09.012

Renzulli, J. S. (1998). Three-ring conception of giftedness. In S. M. Baum, S. M. Reis, & L. R. Maxfield (Eds.), *Nurturing the gifts and talents of primary grade students.* Mansfield Center, CT: Creative Learning Press.

Renzulli, J. S. (2005). The three-ring conception of giftedness: A developmental model for promoting creative productivity. In R. J. Sternberg & J. E. Davidson (Eds.), *Conceptions of giftedness* (pp. 246–279). New York: Cambridge University Press.

RESOLVE: The National Fertility Association. (2014). *Fast facts about infertility.* Retrieved from http://www.resolve.org/about/fast-facts-about-fertility.html

Rew, L., Carver, T., & Li, C. (2011). Early and risky sexual behavior in a sample of rural adolescents. *Issues in Comprehensive Pediatric Nursing, 34*(4), 189–204. doi:10.3109/01460862.2011.619861

Reynolds, C. R. (2000). Why is psychometric research on bias in mental testing so often ignored? *Psychology, Public Policy, and Law, 6*(1), 144–150.

Reynolds, B. M., & Juvonen, J. (2011). The role of early maturation, perceived popularity, and rumors in the emergence of internalizing symptoms among adolescent girls. *Journal of Youth and Adolescence, 40*(11), 1407–1422. doi:10.1007/s10964–010–9619–1

Rhodes, J. E., & DuBois, D. L. (2006). Understanding and facilitating the youth mentoring movement. *Social Policy Report, 20*(3), 1–19.

Ricard, M., Girouard, P. C., & Gouin Décarie, T. (1999). Personal pronouns and perspective taking in toddlers. *Journal of Child Language, 26*(3), 681–697.

Richmond, M. K., Stocker, C. M., & Rienks, S. L. (2005). Longitudinal associations between sibling relationship quality, parental differential treatment, and children's adjustment. *Journal of Family Psychology, 19*(4), 550–559.

Rideout, V. (2013). Zero to eight: Children's media use in American 2013. Common Sense Media. Retrieved from http://www.commonsensemedia.org/research/zero-to-eight-childrens-media-use-in-america-2013

Rideout, V., Foehr, U. G., & Roberts, D. F. (2010). *Generation M²: Media in the lives of 8- to 18-year-olds. A Kaiser Family Foundation Study.* Retrieved from http://www.kff.org/ent media/upload/8010.pdf

Rideout, V., & Hamel, E. (2006). *The media family: Electronic media in the lives of infants, toddlers, preschoolers and their parents.* Retrieved from http://www.kff.org/entmedia/upload/7500.pdf

Rideout, V., Lauricella, A., & Wartella, E. (2011). *Children media, and race – Media use among White, Black, Hispanic, and Asian American children.* Retrieved from http://web5.soc.northwestern.edu/cmhd/wp-content/uploads/2011/06/SOCconfReportSingleFinal-1.pdf

Rideout, V., Roberts, D. F., & Foehr, U. G. (2005). *Executive summary: Generation M: Media in the lives of 8–18 year-olds.* Retrieved from http://www.kff.org/entmedia/7250.cfm

Rieg, S. A., & Paquette, K. R. (2009). Using drama and movement to enhance English language learners' literacy development. *Journal of Instructional Psychology, 36*(2), 148–154.

Riley, B. H. (2010). GLB adolescent's 'Coming out'. *Journal of Child and Adolescent Psychiatric Nursing, 23*(1), 3-10. doi:10.1111/j.1744-6171.2009.00210.x

Rishel, C. W., Cottrell, L., Cottrell, S., Stanton, B., Gibson, C., & Bougher, K. (2007). Exploring adolescents' relationships with non-parental adults using the Non-Parental Adult Inventory (N.P.A.I.). *Child & Adolescent Social Work Journal, 24*(5), 495–508.

Rivadeneyra, R., Ward, L. M., & Gordon, M. (2007). Distorted reflections: Media exposure and Latino adolescents' conceptions of self. *Media Psychology, 9*(2), 261–290.

Robb, M. B., Richert, R. A., & Wartella, E. A. (2009). Just a talking book? Word learning from watching baby videos. *British Journal of Developmental Psychology, 27*(1), 27–45. doi:10.1348/026151008X320156

Robers, S., Zhang, J., & Truman, J. (2012). *Indicators of school crime and safety: 2011* (NCES 2012-002/NCJ 236021). Washington, DC: National Center for Education Statistics.

Robers, S., Zhang, A., Morgan, R. E., & Musu-Gillette, L. (2015). *Indicators of school crime and safety: 2014* (NCES 2015-072/NCJ 248036). Washington, DC: National Center for Education Statistics.

Roberts, D. (2002). *Shattered bonds: The color of child welfare.* New York: Basic Civitas Books.

Robinson, J., Cox, G., Malone, A., Williamson, M., Baldwin, G., Fletcher, K., & O'Brien, M. (2013). A systematic review of school-based interventions aimed at preventing, treating, and responding to suicide-related behavior in young people. *Crisis: The Journal of Crisis Intervention and Suicide Prevention, 34*(3), 164–182. doi:10.1027/0227-5910/a000168

Robinson, J. L., Zahn-Waxler, C., & Emde, R. N. (1994). Patterns of development in early empathic behavior: Environmental and child constitutional influences. *Social Development, 3*(2), 125–145.

Robinson, M. M., & Wilks, S. E. (2006). "Older but not wiser": What custodial grandparents want to tell social workers about raising grandchildren. *Social Work & Christianity, 33*(2), 164–177.

Robinson-Riegler, G., & Robinson-Riegler, B. (2008). *Cognitive psychology: Applying the science of the mind.* Boston: Pearson/Allyn & Bacon.

Rochat, P. (2001). Origins of self-concept. In G. Bremner & A. Fogel (Eds.), *Blackwell handbook of infant development* (pp. 191–212). Malden, MA: Blackwell.

Rochat, P. (2015). Layers of awareness in development. *Developmental Review, 38,* 122–145. doi:10.1016/j.dr.2015.07.009

Rogers, J. M. (2009). Tobacco and pregnancy. *Reproductive Toxicology, 28*(2), 152–160.

Rochlin, M. (2008). *Heterosexual questionnaire— Handout: A lesson plan from Creating Safe Space for GLBTQ Youth: A Toolkit.* Adapted for use by Advocates for Youth. Retrieved from http://www.advocatesforyouth.org/index.php?option=com_content&task=view&id=223&Itemid=129 (Original work published in 1977).

Rodkin, P. C., Farmer, T. W., Pearl, R., & Van Acker, R. (2000). Heterogeneity of popular boys: Antisocial and prosocial configurations. *Developmental Psychology, 36*(1), 14–24.

Rodriguez, E. T., & Tamis-LeMonda, C. S. (2011). Trajectories of the home learning environment across the first 5 years: Associations with children's vocabulary and literacy skills at prekindergarten. *Child Development, 82*(4), 1058–1075.

Rodriguez, E. T., Tamis-LeMonda, C. S., Spellmann, M. E., Pan, B. A., Raikes, H., Lugo-Gil, J., & Luze, G. (2009). The formative role of home literacy experiences across the first three years of life in children from low-income families. *Journal of Applied Developmental Psychology, 30*(6), 677–694.

Roeser, R. W., & Peck, S. C. (2003). Patterns and pathways of educational achievement across adolescence: A holistic developmental perspective. *New Directions for Child and Adolescent Development, 2003*(101), 39–62.

Rogers, J. M. (2009). Tobacco and pregnancy. *Reproductive Toxicology, 28*(2), 152–160.

Rohde, T. E., & Thompson, L. A. (2007). Predicting academic achievement with cognitive ability. *Intelligence, 35,* 83–92.

Rose, A., & Rudolph, K. D. (2006). A review of sex differences in peer relationship processes: Potential trade-offs for the emotional and behavioral development of girls and boys. *Psychological Bulletin, 132,* 98–131.

Rose, A. J., Schwartz-Mette, R. A., Smith, R. L., Asher, S. R., Swenson, L. P., Carlson, W., & Waller, E. M. (2012). How girls and boys expect disclosure about problems will make them feel: Implications for friendships. *Child Development, 83*(3), 844–863.

Rose, S. A., Feldman, J. F., Jankowski, J. J., & Van Rossem, R. (2012). Information processing from infancy to 11 years: Continuities and prediction of IQ. *Intelligence, 40*(5), 445–457. doi:10.1016/j.intell.2012.05.007

Rosenstein, D., & Oster, H. (2005). Differential facial responses to four basic tastes in newborns. In P. Ekman & E. L. Rosenberg (Eds.), *What the face reveals: Basic and applied studies of spontaneous expression using the facial action coding system (FACS)* (2nd ed., pp. 302–327). New York: Oxford University Press.

Rosenthal, R., & Jacobson, L. (1968). *Pygmalion in the classroom: Teacher expectation and pupils' intellectual development.* New York: Rinehart & Winston.

Rosenzweig, M. R., Breedlove, S. M., & Watson, N. V. (2005). *Biological psychology* (4th ed.). Sunderland, MA: Sinauer.

Rosner, D., & Markowitz, G. (2016, February 13). It's not just Flint. There's an ugly history of lead poisoning and the poor in the US. *Mother Jones.* Retrieved from http://www.motherjones.com/environment/2016/02/flint-lead-poisoning-america-toxic-crisis

Ross, H. S., Recchia, H. E., & Carpendale, J. I. M. (2005). Making sense of divergent interpretations of conflict and developing an interpretive understanding of mind. *Journal of Cognition and Development, 6*(4), 571–592.

Ross, M., & Wang, Q. (2010). Why we remember and what we remember: Culture and autobiographical memory. *Perspectives on Psychological Science, 5*(4), 401–409. doi:10.1177/1745691610375555

Rossin-Slater, M. (2015). Promoting health in early childhood. *The Future of Children, 25*(1), 35–64.

Rothbart, M. K. (1981). Measurement of temperament in infancy. *Child Development, 52,* 569–578.

Rothbart, M. K. (2007). Temperament, development, and personality. *Current Directions in Psychological Science, 16*(4), 207–212.

Rothbart, M. K., Ahadi, S. A., Hershey, K. L., & Fisher, P. (2001). Investigations of temperament at three to seven years: The Child's Behavior Questionnaire. *Child Development, 72*(5), 1394–1408.

Rothbart, M., & Bates, J. (2006). Temperament. In N. Eisenberg, W. Damon, & L. M. Richard (Eds.), *Handbook of child psychology: Vol. 3, Social, emotional, and personality development* (6th Ed., pp. 99–166). Hoboken, NJ: Wiley.

Rothbaum, R., Kakinuma, M., Nagaoka, R., & Azuma, H. (2007). Attachment and *amae*: Parent-child closeness in the United States and Japan. *Journal of Cross-Cultural Psychology, 38,* 465–486.

Rovee-Collier, C. (1999). The development of infant memory. *Current Directions in Psychological Science, 8*(3), 80–85.

Rowan, Z. R. (2016). Social risk factors of black and white adolescents' substance use: The differential role of siblings and best friends. *Journal of Youth and Adolescence, 45*(7), 1482–1496. doi:10.1007/s10964-016-0473-7

Rowe, D. C. (2003). Assessing genotype-environment interactions and correlations in the postgenomic era. In R. Plomin, J. C. DeFries, I. W. Craig, & P. McGuffin (Eds.), *Behavioral genetics in the postgenomic era* (pp. 71–86). Washington, DC: American Psychological Association.

Rowe, M. L. (2008). Child-directed speech: Relation to socioeconomic status, knowledge of child development and child vocabulary skill. *Journal of Child Language, 35*(1), 185–205.

Rowe, M. L., & Goldin-Meadow, S. (2009). Differences in early gesture explain SES disparities in child vocabulary size at school entry. *Science, 323*(5916), 951–953.

Rubia, K., Alegria, A., & Brinson, H. (2014). Imaging the ADHD brain: Disorder-specificity, medication effects and clinical translation. *Expert Review of Neurotherapeutics, 14*(5), 519–538. doi:10.1586/14737175.2014.907526

Rubin, K. H., Lynch, D., Coplan, R., Rose-Krasnor, L., & Booth, C. L. (1994). "Birds of a feather . . .": Behavioral concordances and preferential personal attraction in children. *Child Development, 65*(6), 1778–1785.

Rubin, K. H., Bowker, J. C., McDonald, K. L., & Menzer, M. (2013). Peer relationships. In P. D. Zelazo (Ed.), *The Oxford handbook of developmental psychology* (Vol. 2, pp. 242–275). Oxford, UK: Oxford University Press.

Ruble, D. N., Taylor, L. J., Cyphers, L., Greulich, F. K., Lurye, L. E., & Shrout, P. E. (2007). The role of gender constancy in early gender development. *Child Development, 78*(4), 1121–1136.

Rudolph, J., & Zimmer-Gembeck, M. J. (2014). Parent relationships and adolescents' depression and social anxiety: Indirect associations via emotional sensitivity to rejection threat. *Australian Journal of Psychology, 66*(2), 110–121. doi:10.1111/ajpy.12042

Rudy, D., & Grusec, J. E. (2006). Authoritarian parenting in individualist and collectivist groups: Associations with maternal emotion and cognition and children's self-esteem. *Journal of Family Psychology, 20*(1), 68–78.

Rueda, M., Posner, M. I., & Rothbart, M. K. (2005). The development of executive attention: Contributions to the emergence of self-regulation. *Developmental Neuropsychology, 28*(2), 573–594. doi: 10.1207/s15326942dn2802_2

Ruhm, C. J. (2008). Maternal employment and adolescent development. *Labour Economics, 15*(5), 958–983. doi:10.1016/j.labeco.2007.07.008

Rumbaut, R. G., Massey, D. S., & Bean, F. D. (2006). Linguistic life expectancies: Immigrant language retention in Southern California. *Population and Development Review, 32*(3), 447–460 doi: 10.111/j.1728-4457.2006.00132.x

Rumberger, R. W. (2013). *Poverty and high school dropouts.* Retrieved from http://www.apa .org/pi/ses/resources/indicator/2013/05/pover ty-dropouts.aspx

Russell, A., Hart, C. H., Robinson, C. C., & Olsen, S. F. (2003). Children's sociable and aggressive behavior with peers: A comparison of the US and Australia, and contributions of temperament and parenting styles. *International Journal of Behavioral Development, 27*(1), 74–86.

Russell, A., & Saebel, J. (1997). Mother-son, mother-daughter, father-son, and father-daughter: Are they distinct relationships? *Developmental Review, 17*(2), 111–147.

Ryan, R. M., Fauth, R. C., & Brooks-Gunn, J. (2006). Childhood poverty: Implications for school readiness and early childhood education. In B. Spodek & O. Saracho (Eds.), *Handbook of research on the education of young children* (2nd ed., pp. 323–346). Mahwah, NJ: Erlbaum.

Ryder, J. F., Tunmer, W. E., & Greaney, K. T. (2008). Explicit instruction in phonemic awareness and phonemically based decoding skills as an intervention strategy for struggling readers in whole language classrooms. *Reading & Writing, 21*(4), 349–369.

Sabeti, P. (2008) Natural selection: Uncovering mechanisms of evolutionary adaptation to infectious disease. *Nature Education 1*(1),13.

Sachs, J. (2005). Communication development in infancy. In J. B. Gleason (Ed.), *The development of language* (6th ed., pp. 39–61). Boston: Pearson.

Sadock, B. J., & Sadock, V. A. (2008). *Kaplan & Sadock concise textbook of clinical psychiatry* (3rd ed.) Philadelphia: Lippincott, Williams & Wilkins.

Safdar, S., Friedlmeier, W., Matsumoto, D., Yoo, S. H., Kwantes, C. T., Kakai, H., & Shigemasu, E. (2009). Variations of emotional display rules within and across cultures: A comparison between Canada, USA, and Japan. *Canadian Journal of Behavioural Science, 41*(1), 1–10. doi:10.1037/a0014387

SafeKids USA. (2015). *Sports and recreation safety fact sheet.* Retrieved from https://www. safekids.org/sites/default/files/documents/ skw_sports_fact_sheet_feb_2015.pdf Sahin, N. H., & Gungor, I. (2010). Prevention of congenital anomalies and the roles of healthcare professionals. In E. Pereira & J. Soria (Eds.), *Handbook of prenatal diagnosis: Methods, issues, and health impacts* (pp. 1–39). Hauppauge, NY: Nova Science Publishers.

Sajjad, A., Tharner, A., Kiefte-de Jong, J. C., Jaddoe, V. W., Hofman, A., Verhulst, F. C., . . . Roza, S. J. (2015). Breastfeeding duration and non-verbal IQ in children. *Journal of Epidemiology and Community Health, 69*(8), 775–781. doi:10.1136/jech-2014-204486

Sakai, T., Demura, S., & Fujii, K. (2012). Relationship between body composition and BMI in preschool children. *Sport Sciences for Health, 7*(1), 5–12.

Saleh, M., Lazonder, A. W., & De Jong, T. (2005). Effects of within-class ability grouping on social interaction, achievement, and motivation. *Instructional Science, 33*(2), 105–119. doi: 10.1007/s11251-004-6405-z

Sales, J. M., & Fivush, R. (2005). Social and emotional functions of mother-child reminiscing about stressful events. *Social Cognition, 23*(1), 70–90.

Salkind, N. J. (2004). *Introduction to theories of human development.* Thousand Oaks, CA: Sage.

Salmela-Aro, K. (2012). Transition to parenthood and positive parenting: Longitudinal and intervention approaches. *European Journal of Developmental Psychology, 9*(1), 21–32. doi:10. 1080/17405629.2011.607584

Salvanto, A., Backus, F., Dutton, S., & DePinto, J. (2016). CBS/NYT poll: Americans divided over transgender bathroom laws, SCOTUS nomination. *CBS News.* Retrieved from http://www .cbsnews.com/news/cbs-poll-americans-divid ed-over-transgender-bathroom-laws-supreme- court/

Sameroff, A. (2010). A unified theory of development: A dialectic integration of nature and nurture. *Child Development, 81*(1), 6–22.

Sammons, W. A. H., & Lewis, J. M. (1985). *Premature babies: A different beginning.* St. Louis, MO: Mosby.

Samra, N. M., El Taweel, A., & Cadwell, K. (2013). Effect of intermittent kangaroo mother care on weight gain of low birth weight neonates with delayed weight gain. *Journal of Perinatal Education, 22*(4), 194–200. doi:10.1891/1058-1243.22.4.194

Sanders, J., & Munford, R. (2014). Youth-centred practice: Positive youth development practices and pathways to better outcomes for vulnerable youth. *Children and Youth Services Review, 46*, 160–167. doi:10.1016/j. childyouth.2014.08.020

Sandnabba, N. K., & Ahlberg, C. (1999). Parents' attitudes and expectations about children's cross-gender behavior. *Sex Roles, 40*(3–4), 249–263.

Sandstrom, M. J., & Zakriski, A. L. (2004). Understanding the experience of peer rejection. In J. B. Kupersmidt & K. A. Dodge (Eds.), *Children's peer relations: From development to intervention* (pp. 101–118). Washington, DC: American Psychological Association.

Sankar, M. J., Sinha, B., Chowdhury, R., Bhandari, N., Taneja, S., Martines, J., & Bahl, R. (2015). Optimal breastfeeding practices and infant and children mortality: A systematic review and meta-analysis. *Acta Paediatrica, 104*(467), 3–13. doi: 10.1111/apa.13147.

Sann, C., & Streri, A. (2007). Perception of object shape and texture in human newborns: Evidence from cross-modal transfer tasks. *Developmental Science, 10*(3), 399–410.

Sasnett, S. (2015). Are the kids all right? A qualitative study of adults with gay and lesbian parents. *Journal of Contemporary Ethnography, 44*(2), 196–222. doi:10.1177/0891241614540212

Sassu, K. A., Elinoff, M. J., Bray, M. A., & Kehle, T. J. (2004). *Bullies and victims: Information for parents.* Retrieved from http://www.nasp online.org/resources/handouts/revisedPDFs/ bulliesvictims.pdf

Sato, Y., Sogabe, Y., & Mazuka, R. (2010). Discrimination of phonemic vowel length by Japanese infants. *Developmental Psychology, 46*(1), 106–119.

Sauve, K., & Bartlett, D. (2010). *Dynamic systems theory: A framework for exploring readiness to change in children with cerebral palsy.* Publication KC#2010-02. CanChild Centre for Childhood Disability Research, McMaster University. Retrieved from http://www.canchild.ca/en/canchildresources/resources/KC_Dynamic_Systems_Theory.pdf

Savin-Williams, R. C. (2014). An exploratory study of the categorical versus spectrum nature of sexual orientation. *Journal of Sex Research, 51*(4), 446–453. doi:10.1080/00224499.2013.871691

Savin-Williams, R. C., & Cohen, K. M. (2015). Developmental trajectories and milestones of lesbian, gay, and bisexual young people. *International Review of Psychiatry, 27*(5), 357–366. doi:10.3109/09540261.2015.1093465

Savin-Williams, R. C., & Ream, G. L. (2003). Sex variations in the disclosure to parents of same-sex attractions. *Journal of Family Psychology, 17*(3), 429–438.

Sawyer, A. P., Miller-Lewis, L. R., Searle, A. K., Sawyer, M. G., & Lynch, J. W. (2015). Is greater improvement in early self-regulation associated with fewer behavioral problems later in childhood? *Developmental Psychology, 51*(12), 1740–1755. doi:10.1037/a0039829

Sax, L. (2007). The boy problem: Many boys think school is stupid and reading stinks—Is there a remedy? *School Library Journal, 53*(9), 40–43.

Saxbe, D. E., & Repetti, R. L. (2009). Brief report: Fathers' and mothers' marital relationship predicts daughters' pubertal development two years later. *Journal of Adolescence, 32*(2), 415–423.

Saxe, G. B., & Moylan, T. (1982). The development of measurement operations among the Oksapmin of Papua New Guinea. *Child Development, 53*(5), 1242–1248.

Saygin, Z. M., Norton, E. S., Osher, D. E., Beach, S. D., Cyr, A. B., Ozernov-Palchik, O., Yendiki, A., Fischl, B., Gaab, N., & Gabrieli, J. D. E. (2013). Tracking the roots of reading ability: White matter volume and integrity correlate with phonological awareness in prereading and early-reading kindergarten children. *Journal of Neuroscience, 33*(33), 13251–13258.

Sayler, M. F., & Brookshire, W. K. (2004). Social, emotional and behavior adjustment of accelerated students, students in gifted classes, and regular students in eighth grade. In S. M. Moon (Ed.), *Social/emotional issues, underachievement, and counseling of gifted and talented students* (pp. 9–19). Thousand Oaks, CA: Corwin.

Saylor, M. M., Ganea, P. A., & Vazquez, M. D. (2011). What's mine is mine: Twelve-month olds use possession pronouns to identify referents. *Developmental Science, 14*(4), 859–864.

Scafidi, T., & Bui, K. (2010). Gender similarities in math performance from middle school through high school. *Journal of Instructional Psychology, 37*(3), 252–255.

Scarlett, W. G., Naudeau, S., Salonius-Pasternak, D., & Ponte, I. (2005). *Children's play.* Thousand Oaks, CA: Sage.

Scarr, S. (1992). Developmental theories for the 1990s: Development and individual differences. *Child Development, 63*, 1–19.

Scarr, S., & McCartney, K. (1983). How people make their own environments: A theory of genotype environment effects. *Child Development, 54*(2), 424–435.

Schalet, A. T. (2011). Beyond abstinence and risk: A new paradigm for adolescent sexual health. *Women's Health Issues, 21*(3 Suppl), S5–7. doi:10.1016/j.whi.2011.01.007

Schier, K., Herke, M., Nickel, R., Egle, U. T., & Hardt, J. (2015). Long-term sequelae of emotional parentification: A cross-validation study using sequences of regressions. *Journal of Child and Family Studies, 24*(5), 1307–1321. doi:10.1007/s10826-014-9938-z

Schmader, T. (2010). Stereotype threat deconstructed. *Current Directions in Psychological Science, 19*(1), 14–18.

Schmidt, L. A., & Tasker, S. L. (2000). Childhood shyness: Determinants, development and "depathology." In W. R. Crozier (Ed.), *Shyness: Development, consolidation and change* (pp. 30–46). New York: Routledge.

Schmidt, M. E., & Anderson, D. R. (2007). The impact of television on cognitive development and educational achievement. In N. Pecora, J. P. Murray, & E. A. Wartella (Eds.), *Children and television: Fifty years of research* (pp. 65–84). Mahwah, NJ: Erlbaum.

Schmidt, M. E., Pempek, T. A., Kirkorian, H. L., Lund, A. F., & Anderson, D. R. (2008). The effects of background television on the toy play behavior of very young children. *Child Development, 79*(4), 1137–1151.

Schneider, W., Kron, V., Hünnerkopf, M., & Krajewski, K. (2004). The development of young children's memory strategies: First findings from the Würzburg Longitudinal Memory Study. *Journal of Experimental Child Psychology, 88*(2), 193–209. doi: 10.1016/j.jecp.2004.02.004

Schneider, W. (2002). Memory development in childhood. In U. Goswami (Ed.), *Blackwell handbook of childhood cognitive development* (pp. 236–256). Malden, MA: Blackwell.

Schneider, W. (2015). Memory development from early childhood through emerging adulthood. New York: Springer.

Scholte, R. H. J., Engels, R. C. M. E., de Kemp, R. A. T., Harakeh, Z., & Overbeek, G. (2007). Differential parental treatment, sibling relationships and delinquency in adolescence. *Journal of Youth and Adolescence, 36*(5), 661–671.

Scholz, J., Klein, M. C., Behrens, T. E. J., & Johansen-Berg, H. (2009). Training induces changes in white matter architecture. *Nature Neuroscience, 12*(11), 1370–1371. http://doi.org/10.1038/nn.2412

Schoppe-Sullivan, S. J., Diener, M. L., Mangelsdorf, S. C., Brown, G. L., McHale, J. L., & Frosch, C. A. (2006). Attachment and sensitivity in family context: The roles of parent and infant gender. *Infant and Child Development, 15*(4), 367–385.

Schrodt, P., Soliz, J., & Braithwaite, D. O. (2008). A social relations model of everyday talk and relational satisfaction in stepfamilies. *Communication Monographs, 75*(2), 190–217.

Schuh, J. M., & Eigsti, I-M. (2012). Working memory, language skills, and autism symptomatology. *Behavioral Sciences, 2*, 207–218.

Schuett, V. (2008). What is PKU? *National PKU News.* Retrieved from http://pkunews.org/about/intro.htm

Schuntermann, P. (2007). The sibling experience: Growing up with a child who has pervasive developmental disorder or mental retardation. *Harvard Review of Psychiatry, 15*(3), 93–108.

Schwartzberg, B. (2004). "Lots of them did that": Desertion, bigamy, and marital fluidity in late-nineteenth-century America. *Journal of Social History, 37*(3), 573–600.

Schwarz, E. B., & Nothnagle, M. (2015). The maternal health benefits of breastfeeding. *American Family Physician, 91*(9), 602–604.

ScienceMuseum. (n.d.). Who am I? Retrieved from http://www.sciencemuseum.org.uk/whoami/findoutmore/yourgenes/whydoscientistsstudygenes/howdoscientistslookatchromosomes

Scott, R. M., & Baillargeon, R. (2009). Which penguin is this? Attributing false beliefs about object identity at 18 months. *Child Development, 80*(4), 1172–1196.

Seal of Biliteracy. (2016). *State laws regarding the seal of biliteracy.* Retrieved from http://sealofbiliteracy.org/

Search Institute. (2012). *What kids need: Developmental assets.* Retrieved from http://www.search-institute.org/developmental-assets

Seaton, E. K., Scottham, K., & Sellers, R. M. (2006). The status model of racial identity development in African American adolescents: Evidence of structure, trajectories, and well-being. *Child Development, 77*(5), 1416–1426. doi:10.1111/j.1467-8624.2006.00944.x

Sedgh, G., Singh, S., Shah, I. H., Åhman, E., Henshaw, S. K., & Bankole, A. (2012). Induced abortion: Incidence and trends worldwide from 1995 to 2008. *The Lancet, 379*(9816), 625–632. doi: 10.1016/S0140-6736(11)61786-8

Sedlak, A. J., Mettenburg, J., Basena, M., Petta, I., McPherson, K., Greene, A., & Li, S. (2010). *Fourth National Incidence Study of Child Abuse and Neglect (NIS–4): Report to Congress.* Washington, DC: U.S. Department of Health and Human Services, Administration for Children and Families.

Segal, M. (2004). The roots and fruits of pretending. In E. F. Zigler, D. G. Singer, & S. J. Bishop-Josef (Eds.), *Children's play— The roots of reading* (pp. 33–48). Washington, DC: Zero to Three Press.

Segal, N. (2012). *Born together – reared apart: The landmark Minnesota Twin Study.* Cambridge, MA: Harvard University Press.

Segal, N. (2013). Personality similarity in unrelated look-alike pairs: Addressing a twin study challenge. *Personality and Individual Differences, 54*, 23–28.

Segui-Gomez, M. (2000). Drive air bag effectiveness by severity of the crash. *American Journal of Public Health, 90*(10), 1575–1581.

Seil, K. S., Desai, M. M., & Smith, M. V. (2014). Sexual orientation, adult connectedness, substance use, and mental health outcomes among adolescents: Findings from the 2009 New York City Youth Risk Behavior survey. *American Journal of Public Health, 104*(10), 1950–1956. doi:10.2105/AJPH.2014.302050

Seligman, M. P., & Csikszentmihalyi, M. (2000). Positive psychology: An introduction. *American Psychologist, 55*(1), 5–14. doi:10.1037/0003-066X.55.1.5

Sellers, R. M., Copeland-Linder, N., Martin, P. P., & Lewis, L. (2006). Racial identity matters: The relationship between racial discrimination and psychological functioning in African-American adolescents. *Journal of Research on Adolescence, 16*(2), 187–216.

Semrud-Clikeman, M. (2014). *Research in brain function and learning.* Retrieved from http://www.apa.org/education/k12/brain-function.aspx?item=1

Sénéchal, M., Ouellette, G., Pagan, S., & Lever, R. (2012). The role of invented spelling on learning to read in low-phoneme awareness kindergartners: A randomized-control-trial study. *Reading & Writing, 25*(4), 917–934.

Seo, Y., Abbott, R. D., & Hawkins, J. D. (2008). Outcome status of students with learning disabilities at ages 21 and 14. *Journal of Learning Disabilities, 41*(4), 300–314.

Sesame Street Workshop. (2014). *Sweeping the clouds away for 43 years—and counting.* Retrieved from http://www.sesameworkshop.org/what-we-do/our-initiatives/sesame-street/

Sesma, A., Mannes, M., & Scales, P. C. (2005). Positive adaptation, resilience, and the developmental asset framework. In S. Goldstein & R. B. Brooks (Eds.), *Handbook of resilience in children* (pp. 281–296). New York: Springer.

Setliff, A. E., & Courage, M. L. (2011). Background television and infants' allocation of their attention during toy play. *Infancy, 16*(6), 611–639. doi: 10.1111/j.1532-7078.2011.00070.x

Shahaeian, A., Peterson, C. C., Slaughter, V., & Wellman, H. M. (2011). Culture and the sequence of steps in theory of mind development. *Developmental Psychology, 47*(5), 1239–1247. doi: 10.1037/a0023899

Shamir-Essakow, G., Ungerer, J. A., & Rapee, R. M. (2005). Attachment, behavioral inhibition, and anxiety in preschool children. *Journal of Abnormal Child Psychology, 33*(2), 131–143.

Shanahan, T. (2004). Critiques of the National Reading Panel report. In P. McCardle & V. Chhabra (Eds.), *The voice of evidence in reading research* (pp. 235–265). Baltimore, MD: Brooks.

Sharfi, K, & Rosenblum, S. (2014). Activity and participation characteristics of adults with learning disabilities - A systematic review. *PLoS ONE 9*(9), e106657. doi:10.1371/journal.pone.0106657

Shaver, K. (2012). *Female dummy makes her mark on male-dominated crash tests.* Retrieved from http://www.washingtonpost.com/local/trafficandcommuting/female-dummy-makes-her-mark-on-male-dominated-crash-tests/2012/03/07/gIQANBLjaS_story.html

Shaver, P. R., & Mikulincer, M. (2014). Attachment bonds in romantic relationships. In M. Mikulincer & P. R. Shaver (Eds.), *Mechanisms of social connection: From brain to group* (pp. 273–290). Washington, DC: American Psychological Association.

Shaw, D. S., Owens, E. B., & Giovannelli, J. (2001). Infant and toddler pathways leading to early externalizing disorders. *Journal of the American Academy of Child and Adolescent Psychiatry, 40*(1), 36–43.

Shaw, P., Greenstein, D., Lerch, J., Clasen, L., Lenroot, R., Gogtay, N., Evans, A., Rapoport, J., & Giedd, J. (2006). Intellectual ability and cortical development in children and adolescents. *Nature, 440*, 676– 679.

Shayer, M., & Ginsburg, D. (2009). Thirty years on—a large anti-Flynn effect? (II): 13- and 14-year-olds. Piagetian tests of formal operations norms 1976-2006/7. *British Journal of Educational Psychology, 79*(3), 409–418.

Shea, A. K., & Steiner, M. (2008). Cigarette smoking during pregnancy. *Nicotine and Tobacco Research, 10*(2), 267–278.

Shearer, C. L., Crouter, A. C., & McHale, S. (2005). Parents' perceptions of changes in mother-child and father-child relationships during adolescence. *Journal of Adolescent Research, 20*(6), 662–684.

Sher, I., Koenig, M., & Rustichini, A. (2014). Children's strategic theory of mind. *Proceedings of the National Academy of Sciences of the United States of America, 111*(37), 13307–13312. doi:10.1073/pnas.1403283111

Shield, B. M., & Dockrell, J. E. (2003). The effects of noise on children at school: A review. *Journal of Building Acoustics, 10*(2), 97–106.

Shih, J.H., Eberhart, N., Hammen, C., & Brennan, P. A. (2006). Differential exposure and reactivity to interpersonal stress predict sex differences in adolescent depression. *Journal of Clinical Child and Adolescent Psychology, 35*, 103–115.

Shin, N. (2004). Exploring pathways from television viewing to academic achievement in school age children. *Journal of Genetic Psychology, 165*(4), 367–381.

Shonkoff, J. P., Garner, A. S., & Committee on Psychosocial Aspects of Child and Family Health, Committee on Early Childhood, Adoption and Department Care, and Section on Development and Behavioral Pediatrics. (2012). The lifelong effects of early childhood adversity and toxic stress. *Pediatrics, 129*(1), e232–246.

Shonkoff, J. P., & Phillips, D. A. (2000). *From neurons to neighborhoods: The science of early childhood development.* Washington, DC: National Academy Press.

Shuford, J. A. (2008). *What is the difference between sexually transmitted infection (STI) and sexually transmitted disease (STD)?* Retrieved from http://www.medinstitute.org/public/132.cfm

Short, M. A., Gradisar, M., Lack, L. C., & Wright, H. R. (2013). The impact of sleep on adolescent depressed mood, alertness and academic performance. *Journal of Adolescence, 36*(6), 1025–1033. doi: 10.1016/j.adolescence.2013.08.007

Shulman, S., & Kipnis, O. (2001). Adolescent romantic relationships: A look from the future. *Journal of Adolescence, 24*(3), 337–351. doi:10.1006/jado.2001.0409

Sicherer, S. H., Mahr, T., & the American Academy of Pediatrics Section on Allergy and Immunology. (2010). Management of food allergy in the school setting. *Pediatrics, 126*(6), 1232–1239.

Siegel, D. H. (2012). Growing up in open adoption: Young adults' perspectives. *Families in Society, 93*(2), 133–140.

Siegel, D. H. (2013). Open adoption: Adoptive parents' reactions two decades later. *Social Work, 58*(1), 43–52. doi: 10.1093/sw/sws053

Siennick, S. E. (2013). Still the favorite? Parents' differential treatment of siblings entering young adulthood. *Journal of Marriage and Family, 75*(4), 981–994.

Silberglitt, B., Jimerson, S. R., Burns, M. K., & Appleton, J. J. (2006). Does the timing of grade retention make a difference? Examining the effects of early versus later retention. *School Psychology Review, 35*(1), 134–141.

Silvén, M., Voeten, M., Kouvo, A., & Lundén, M. (2014). Speech perception and vocabulary growth: A longitudinal study of Finnish-Russian bilinguals and Finnish monolinguals from infancy to three years. *International Journal of Behavioral Development, 38*(4), 323–332. doi:10.1177/0165025414533748

Sim, L. A., Homme, J. H., Lteif, A. N., Vande Voort, J. L., Schak, K. M., & Ellingson, J. (2009). Family functioning and maternal distress in adolescent girls with anorexia nervosa. *International Journal of Eating Disorders, 42*(6), 531–539. doi:10.1002/eat.20654

Simcock, G., & Hayne, H. (2002). Breaking the barrier? Children fail to translate their preverbal memories into language. *Psychological Science, 13*(3), 225–231.

Simola, P. P., Liukkonen, K. K., Pitkäranta, A. A., Pirinen, T. T., & Aronen, E. T. (2012). Psychosocial and somatic outcomes of sleep problems in children: A 4-year followup study. *Child: Care, Health and Development, 40*(1), 60–67. doi: 10.1111/j.1365–2214.2012.01412.x

Simpson, J. L. (2007). Causes of fetal wastage. *Clinical Obstetrics and Gynecology, 50*(1), 10–30.

Simpson, R., de Boer-Ott, S., Griswold, D., Myles, B. S., Byrd, S. E., Ganz, J., . . . Garriott, L. (2005). *Autism spectrum disorders: Interventions and treatments for children and youth.* Thousand Oaks, CA: Corwin.

Singer, D. G., & Revenson, T. A. (1996). *A Piaget primer* (Rev. ed.). New York: Penguin Books.

Singh, A. S., Mulder, C., Twisk, J. W., van Mechelen, W., & Chinapaw, M. J. (2008). Tracking of childhood overweight into adulthood: A systematic review of the literature. *Obesity Review, 9*(5), 474–88.

Sirois, S., & Jackson, I. R. (2012). Pupil dilation and object permanence in infants. *Infancy, 17*, 61–78. doi:10.1111/j.1532-7078.2011.00096.x

Skafida, V. (2012). Juggling work and motherhood: The impact of employment and maternity leave on breastfeeding duration: A survival analysis on growing up in Scotland. *Maternal and Child Health Journal, 16*(2), 519–527.

Skinner, B. F. (1953). *Science and human behavior.* New York: Macmillan.

Skinner, B. F. (1991). *Verbal behavior.* Acton, MA: Copley. (Original work published in 1957)

Skinner, E. A., & Zimmer-Gembeck, M. J. (2007). The development of coping. *Annual Review of Psychology, 58*, 119–144. doi:10.1146/annurev.psych.58.110405.085705

Skinner, M. K., Haque, C. M., Nilsson, E., Bhandari, R., & McCarrey, J. R. (2013). Environmentally induced transgenerational epigenetic reprogramming of primordial germ cells and the subsequent germ line. *PLoS ONE, 8*(7), 1–15. doi: 10.1371/journal.pone.0066318

Skogerbø, A., Kesmodel, U., Denny, C., Kjaersgaard, M., Wimberley, T., Landrø, N., & Mortensen, E. (2013). The effects of low to moderate alcohol consumption and binge drinking in early pregnancy on behaviour in 5-year-old children. *BJOG: An International Journal of Obstetrics & Gynaecology, 120*(9), 1042–1050. doi:10.1111/1471-0528.12208.

Skuse, D., Bruce, H., Dowdney, L., & Mrazek, D. (2011). *Child psychology and psychiatry: Frameworks for practice.* Hoboken, NJ: Wiley.

Slater, A., Field, T., & Hernandez-Reif, M. (2007). The development of the senses. In A. Slater & M. Lewis (Eds.), *Introduction to infant development.* New York: Oxford University Press.

Slaughter, V. (2015). Theory of mind in infants and young children: A review. *Australian Psychologist, 50*, 169–172.

Slaughter, V., Imuta, K., Peterson, C. C., & Henry, J. D. (2015). Meta-analysis of theory of mind and peer popularity in the preschool and early school years. *Child Development, 86*(4), 1159–1174. doi:10.1111/cdev.12372

Slotkin, T. A. (2008). If nicotine is a developmental neurotoxicant in animal studies, dare we recommend nicotine replacement therapy in pregnant women and adolescents? *Neurotoxicology and Teratology, 30*(1), 1–19.

Smetana, J. (2006). Social-cognitive domain theory: Consistencies and variations in children's moral and social judgments. In M. Killen & J. Smetana, *Handbook of moral development*, (pp. 119–153). Mahwah, NJ: Erlbaum.

Smetana, J. (2011). *Adolescents, families, and social development: How teens construct their worlds*. Malden, MA: Wiley-Blackwell.

Smetana, J. G., Metzger, A., & Campione-Barr, N. (2004). African American late adolescents' relationships with parents: Developmental transitions and longitudinal patterns. *Child Development, 75*(3), 932–947.

Smilansky, S. (1968). *The effects of sociodramatic play on disadvantaged preschool children*. New York: Wiley.

Smiley, P. A., Chang, L. K., & Allhoff, A. K. (2011). Can Toddy give me an orange? Parent input and young children's production of I and you. *Language Learning and Development, 7*(2), 77–106. doi:10.1080/15475441.2010.499495

Smith, A. (2013). *Head Start Trauma Smart: Creating trauma-informed Head Start communities*. Retrieved from http://www.saintlukeshealthsystem.org/sites/default/files/files/Head%20Start%20Trauma%20Smart%20Article-Summer%202013%20Magazine(1).pdf

Smith, B. H., & Shapiro, C. J. (2015). Combined treatments for ADHD. In R. Barkley (Ed.), *Attention- deficit hyperactivity disorder* (4th ed., pp. 686–704). New York: Guilford.

Smith, C. L., Diaz, A., Day, K. L., & Bell, M. A. (2015). Infant frontal electroencephalogram asymmetry and negative emotional reactivity as predictors of toddlerhood effortful control. *Journal of Experimental Child Psychology, 142*, 262–273. doi:10.1016/j.jecp.2015.09.031

Smith, P. K. (2010). *Children and play*. Malden, MA: Wiley-Blackwell.

Smith, R. E., Smoll, F. L., & Cumming, S. P. (2009). Motivational climate and changes in young athletes' achievement goal orientations. *Motivation and Emotion, 33*(2), 173–183. doi:10.1007/s11031-009-9126-4

Smith, T. B., & Silva, L. (2011). Ethnic identity and personal well-being of people of color: A meta-analysis. *Journal of Counseling Psychology, 58*, 42–60.

Smith-Spangler, C., Brandeau, M., Hunter, G., Bavinger, J., Pearson, M., Eschbach, P., . . . Bravata, D. (2012). Are organic foods safer or healthier than conventional alternatives?: A systematic review. *Annals of Internal Medicine, 157*(5), 348–366.

Smoke Free Movies. (2015). *Who's accountable?* Retrieved from http://smokefreemovies.ucsf.edu/whos-accountable

Smyke, A., Zeanah, C., Gleason, M., Drury, S., Fox, N., Nelson, C., & Guthrie, D. (2012). A randomized controlled trial comparing foster care and institutional care for children with signs of reactive attachment disorder. *American Journal of Psychiatry, 169*(5), 508–514.

Snow, K. (n.d.). *Research news you can use: Debunking the play vs. learning dichotomy*. National Association for the Education of Young Children. Retrieved from http://www.naeyc.org/content/research-news-you-can-use-play-vs-learning

Snow, R. F. (1981, June/July). Martin Couney. *American Heritage Magazine, 32*(4). Retrieved from http://www.americanheritage.com/articles/magazine/ah/1981/4/1981_4_90.shtml

Snowling, M. J. (2012). Changing concepts of dyslexia: Nature, treatment and comorbidity. *Journal of Child Psychology and Psychiatry, 53*(9), e1–e3. doi:10.1111/j.1469-7610.2009.02197.x

Snowling, M. J., & Hulme, C. (2011). Evidence-based interventions for reading and

language difficulties: Creating a virtuous circle. *British Journal of Educational Psychology, 81*, 1–23.

Soares de Oliveira-Szejnfeld, P., Levine, D., de Oliveira Melo, A. S., Amorim, M. M. R., Batista, A. G. M., Chimelli, L.,, . . . & Tovar-Moll, F. (2016). Congenital brain abnormalities and Zika virus: What the radiologist can expect to see prenatally and postnatally, *Radiology, 281*(1), 203–218

Sobralske, M. C., & Gruber, M. E. (2009). Risks and benefits of parent/child bed sharing. *Journal of the American Academy of Nurse Practitioners, 21*, 474–479.

Society for Neuroscience. (2007). *The adolescent brain: Brain Briefings*. Retrieved from http://www.sfn.org/index.aspx?pagename=brainBriefings_Adolescent_brain

Society for Research in Child Development. (2012). *Ethical standards in research*. Retrieved from http://www.srcd.org/about-us/ethical-standards-research

Solomon, S., & Knafo, A. (2007). Value similarity in adolescent friendships. In T. C. Rhodes (Ed.), *Focus on adolescent behavior research* (pp. 133–155). Hauppauge, NY: Nova Science.

Somers, M., Aukes, M. F., Ophoff, R. A., Boks, M. P., Fleer, W., de Visser, K. L., . . . Sommer, I. E. (2015). On the relationship between degree of hand-preference and degree of language lateralization. *Brain & Language, 144*, 10–15. doi:10.1016/j.bandl.2015.03.006

Sorhagen, N. S. (2013). Early teacher expectations disproportionately affect poor children's high school performance. *Journal of Educational Psychology,105*(2), 465–477. doi:10.1037/a0031754

Soria, K. K., & Linder, S. (2014). Parental divorce and first-year college students' persistence and academic achievement. *Journal of Divorce & Remarriage, 55*(2), 103–116.

Sorsoli, L., Kia-Keating, M., & Grossman, F. K. (2008). "I keep that hush-hush": Male survivors of sexual abuse and the challenges of disclosure. *Journal of Counseling Psychology, 55*(3), 333–345.

Southgate, V., Senju, A., & Csibra, G. (2007). Action anticipation through attribution of false belief by 2-year-olds. *Psychological Science, 18*(7), 587–592.

Sowden, P. T., & Barrett, P. (2006). Psychophysiological methods. In G. M. Breakwell, C. Fife-Schaw, S. Hammond & J. Smith (Eds.), *Research methods in psychology* (3rd ed., pp. 146–159). London: Sage.

Sparks, B. F., Friedman, S. D., Shaw, D. W., Aylward, E. H., Echelard, D., Artru, A. A., . . . Dager, S. R. (2002). Brain structural abnormalities in young children with autism spectrum disorder. *Neurology, 29*(2), 184–192. doi:10.1212/WNL.59.2.184

Specialist Schools and Academies Trust. (2011). *Premature births*. Retrieved from http://complexld.ssatrust.org.uk/uploads/prem-birth-briefing%20APRIL%202011.pdf

Spelke, E. S. (2000). Core knowledge. *American Psychologist, 55*(11), 1233–1243.

Spelke, E. S., & Kinzler, K. D. (2007). Core knowledge. *Developmental Science 10*(1), 89–96.

Spencer, J. P., Austin, A., & Schutte, A. R. (2012). Contributions of dynamic systems theory to cognitive development. *Cognitive Development, 27*(4), 401–418. doi:10.1016/j.cogdev.2012.07.006

Spencer, J. P., Clearfield, M., Corbetta, D., Ulrich, B., Buchanan, P., & Schöner, G. (2006). Moving toward a grand theory of development: In

memory of Esther Thelen. *Child Development, 77*(6), 1521–1538.

Spencer, J. P., Perone, S., & Buss, A. (2011). Twenty years and going strong: A dynamic systems revolution in motor and cognitive development. *Child Development Perspectives, 5*, 260–266.

Spencer, J. P., Vereijken, B., Diedrich, F., & Thelen, E. (2000). Posture and the emergence of manual skills. *Developmental Science, 3*, 216–233.

Spencer, R. (2010). Naturally occurring mentoring relationships involving youth. In T. D. Allen & L. T. Eby (Eds.), *The Blackwell handbook of mentoring: A multiple perspectives approach* (pp. 99–118). Malden, MA: Wiley-Blackwell.

Spinazzola, J., Hodgdon, H., Liang, L., Ford, J. D., Layne, C. M., Pynoos, R., . . . Kisiel, C. (2014). Unseen wounds: The contribution of psychological maltreatment to child and adolescent mental health and risk outcomes. *Psychological Trauma: Theory, Research, Practice, and Policy, 6*(Suppl 1), S18–S28. doi:10.1037/a0037766

Spitz, H. H. (1999). Beleaguered Pygmalion: A history of the controversy over claims that teacher expectancy raises intelligence. *Intelligence, 27*(3), 199–234.

Spitzer, R. L. (1981). The diagnostic status of homosexuality in DSM-III: A reformulation of the issues. *American Journal of Psychiatry, 138*, 210–215.

Sprenger, M. (2013). *The developing brain: Building language, reading, physical, social, and cognitive skills from birth to age eight*. New York: Skyhorse Publishing.

Sprengelmeyer, R., Perrett, D. I., Fagan, E. C., Cornwell, R. E., Lobmaier, J. S., Sprengelmeyer, A., . . . Young, A. W. (2009). The cutest little baby face: A hormonal link to sensitivity to cuteness in infant faces. *Psychological Science, 20*(2), 149–154.

Squeglia, L. M., Jacobus, J., & Tapert, S. F. (2009). The influence of substance use on adolescent brain development. *Journal of Clinical EEG & Neuroscience, 40*(1), 31–38.

Sroufe, L. A. (1997). *Emotional development*. Cambridge, UK: Cambridge University Press.

Sroufe, L. A. (2005). Attachment and development: A prospective, longitudinal study from birth to adulthood. *Attachment and Human Development, 7*(4), 349–367.

Sroufe, L. A. (2009). The concept of development in developmental psychopathology. *Child Development Perspectives, 3*, 178–183.

Sroufe, L. A., Carlson, E., & Shulman, S. (1993). Individuals in relationships: Development from infancy through adolescence. In D. C. Funder, R. D. Parke, C. Tomlinson-Keasey, & K. Widaman (Eds.), *Studying lives through time* (pp. 315–342). Washington, DC: American Psychological Association.

Sroufe, L. A., Egeland, B., Carlson, E., & Collins, W. A. (2005). Placing early attachment experiences in developmental context. In K. E. Grossmann, K. Grossmann, & E. Waters (Eds.), *Attachment from infancy to adulthood* (pp. 48–70). New York: Guilford Press.

St. James-Roberts, I. (2007). Helping parents to manage infant crying and sleeping: A review of the evidence and its implications for services. *Child Abuse Review, 16*(1), 47–69.

Stebbins, L. F. (2001). *Work and family in America: A reference handbook*. Santa Barbara, CA: ABC-CLIO.

Steele, C. M., & Aronson, J. (1995). Stereotype threat and the intellectual test performance of

African-Americans. *Journal of Personality and Social Psychology, 69*, 797–811.

Steensma, T. D., Kreukels, B. C., de Vries, A. C., & Cohen-Kettenis, P. T. (2013). Gender identity development in adolescence. *Hormones and Behavior, 64*(2), 288–297.

Steffens, M. C., Jelenec, P., & Noack, P. (2010). On the leaky math pipeline: Comparing implicit math-gender stereotypes and math withdrawal in female and male children and adolescents. *Journal of Educational Psychology, 102*(4), 947–963. doi:10.1037/a0019920

Stein, A., Malmberg, L., Leach, P., Barnes, J., & Sylva, K. (2013). The influence of different forms of early childcare on children's emotional and behavioural development at school entry. *Child: Care, Health and Development, 39*(5), 676–687. doi:10.1111/j.1365-2214.2012.01421.x

Steinberg, L., Mounts, N. S., Lamborn, S. D., & Dornbusch, S. M. (1991). Authoritative parenting and adolescent adjustment across varied ecological niches. *Journal of Research on Adolescence, 1*(1), 19–36.

Steinberg, L., & Silk, J. S. (2002). Parenting adolescents. In M. H. Bornstein (Ed.), *Handbook of parenting* (2nd ed., pp. 103–133). Mahwah, NJ: Erlbaum.

Steinhausen, H. C. (2009). The heterogeneity of causes and courses of attention-deficit/hyperactivity disorder. *Acta Psychiatrica Scandinavica, 120*(5), 392–399.

Stephen Wiltshire Gallery. (2012). *Stephen Wiltshire MBE – Biography*. Retrieved from http://www.stephenwiltshire.co.uk/biography.aspx

Stern, M., Karraker, K., McIntosh, B., Moritzen, S., & Olexa, M. (2006). Prematurity stereotyping and mothers' interaction with their premature and full-term infants during the first year. *Journal of Pediatric Psychology, 31*(6), 597–607.

Sternberg, R. J. (2002a). Beyond *g*: The theory of successful intelligence. In R. J. Sternberg & E. L. Grigorenko (Eds.), *The general factor of intelligence: How general is it?* (pp. 447–479). Mahwah, NJ: Erlbaum.

Sternberg, R. J. (2002b). Raising the achievement of all students: Teaching for successful intelligence. *Educational Psychology Review, 14*(4), 383–393.

Sternberg, R. B. (2003a). Creative thinking in the classroom. *Scandinavian Journal of Educational Research, 47*(3), 325–338.

Sternberg, R. J. (2003b). Our research program validating the triarchic theory of successful intelligence: Reply to Gottfredson. *Intelligence, 31*(4), 399–413.

Sternberg, R. J. (2009). The Rainbow and Kaleidoscope Projects: A new psychological approach to undergraduate admissions. *European Psychologist, 14*(4), 279–287. doi:10.1027/1016-9040.14.4.279

Sternberg, R. J. (2012). Intelligence in its cultural context. In M. J. Gelfand, C. Ciu, Y. Hong, M. J. Gelfand, C. Ciu, & Y. Hong (Eds.), *Advances in culture and psychology* (Vol. 2, pp. 205–248). New York: Oxford University Press.

Sternberg, R. J., Castejón, J. L., Prieto, M. D., Hautamäki, J., & Grigorenko, E. L. (2001). Confirmatory factor analysis of the Sternberg Triarchic Abilities Test in three international samples: An empirical test of the triarchic theory of intelligence. *European Journal of Psychological Assessment, 17*(1), 1–16.

Sternberg, R. J., Jarvin, L., & Grigorenko, E. L. (2011). *Explorations in giftedness*. Cambridge, UK: Cambridge University Press

Stewart, S. D. (2005). Boundary ambiguity in stepfamilies. *Journal of Family Issues, 26*(7), 1002–1029.

Stice, E., & Shaw, H. (2004). Eating disorder prevention programs: A meta-analytic review. *Psychological Bulletin, 130*(2), 206–227.

Stiefel Laboratories. (2008). *Contraception counseling referral program*. Retrieved from http://www.soriatane.com/media/ContraceptCounseling.pdf

Stiles, J. (2009). On genes, brains and behavior: Why should developmental psychologists care about brain development? *Child Development Perspectives, 3*, 196–202.

Stone, G. (2006). An exploration of factors influencing the quality of children's relationships with their father following divorce. *Journal of Divorce & Remarriage, 46*(1/2), 13–28.

Storey, A. E., Walsh, C. J., Quinton, R. L., & Wynne-Edwards, K. E. (2000). Hormonal correlates of paternal responsiveness in new and expectant fathers. *Evolution and Human Behavior, 21*(2), 79–95.

Storli, R., & Sandseter, E. H. (2015). Preschool teachers' perceptions of children's rough-and-tumble play (R&T) in indoor and outdoor environments. *Early Child Development and Care, 185*, 11–12. doi:10.1080/03004430.2015.1028394

Stormshak, E. A., Comeau, C. A., & Shepard, S. A. (2004). The relative contribution of sibling deviance and peer deviance in the prediction of substance use across middle childhood. *Journal of Abnormal Child Psychology, 32*(6), 635–649. doi: 10.1023/B:JACP.0000047212.49463.c7

Story, M., Kaphingst, K. M., & French, S. (2006). The role of schools in obesity prevention. *The Future of Children, 16*(1), 109–142.

Stowe, L. A., & Sabourin, L. (2005). Imaging the processing of a second language: Effects of maturation and proficiency on the neural processes involved. *International Review of Applied Linguistics in Language Teaching, 43*(4), 329–353.

Strayer, D. L., Drews, F. A., & Crouch, D. J. (2006). Fatal distraction? A comparison of the cell phone driver and the drunk driver. *Human Factors, 48*(2), 381–391.

Strohschein, L. (2005). Parental divorce and child mental health trajectories. *Journal of Marriage and Family, 67*(5), 1286–1300.

Strully, K. W., Rehkopf, D. H., & Xuan, Z. (2010). Effects of prenatal poverty on infant health: State earned income tax credits and birth weight. *American Sociological Review, 75*(4), 534–562. http://doi.org/10.1177/0003122410374086

Stuewig, J., Tangney, J. P., Kendall, S., Folk, J. B., Meyer, C. R., & Dearing, R. L. (2015). Children's proneness to shame and guilt predict risky and illegal behaviors in young adulthood. *Child Psychiatry and Human Development, 46*(2), 217–227. doi:10.1007/s10578-014-0467-1

Sturm, L. (2004). *Temperament in early childhood: A primer for the perplexed*. Retrieved from http://www.zero tothree.org/site/DocServer/v0124–4a.pdf?docID=1761&AddInterest=1158

Suarez, E. C. (2004). C-reactive protein is associated with psychological risk factors of cardiovascular disease in apparently healthy adults. *Psychosomatic Medicine, 66*, 684–691.

Subotnik, R. F., Olszewski-Kubilius, P., & Worrell, F. C. (2011). Rethinking giftedness and gifted education: A proposed direction forward based on psychological science. *Psychological Science in the Public Interest, 12*(1), 3–54.

Subrahmanyam, K., & Greenfield, P. (2008). Online communication and adolescent relationships. *The Future of Children, 18*(1), 119–146.

Substance Abuse and Mental Health Services Administration. (2009). *Depression takes its toll*. Retrieved from http://www.samhsa.gov/samhsanewsletter/Volume_17_Number_3/YouthAdultDepression.aspx

Substance Abuse and Mental Health Services Administration. (2012). *2012 national strategy for suicide prevention: How you can play a role in preventing suicide*. Retrieved from http://www.surgeongeneral.gov/library/reports/national-strategy-suicide-prevention/factsheet.pdf

Substance Abuse and Mental Health Services Administration, Office of Applied Studies. (2007). *The NSDUH Report: Youth activities, substance use, and family income*. Rockville, MD: Author.

Sudfeld, C. R., McCoy, D. C., Fink, G., Muhihi, A., Bellinger, D. C., Masanja, H., . . . Fawzi, W. W. (2015). Malnutrition and its determinants are associated with suboptimal cognitive, communication, and motor development in Tanzanian children. *Journal of Nutrition, 145*(12), 2705–2714 10p. doi:10.3945/jn.115.215996

Sullivan, E. V., Brumback, T., Tapert, S. F., Fama, R., Prouty, D., Brown, S. A., . . . Pfefferbaum, A. (2016). Cognitive, emotion control, and motor performance of adolescents in the NCANDA study: Contributions from alcohol consumption, age, sex, ethnicity, and family history of addiction. *Neuropsychology, 30*(4), 449–473. doi:10.1037/neu0000259

Sullivan, G. M., & Feinn, R. (2012). Using effect size—or why the *P* value is not enough. *Journal of Graduate Medical Education, 4*(3), 279–282. doi:10.4300/JGME-D-12-00156.1

Sullivan, R. M., & Toubas, P. (1998). Clinical usefulness of maternal odor in newborns: Soothing and feeding preparatory responses. *Biology of the Neonate, 74*(6), 402–408.

Sumter, S. R., Bokhorst, C. L., Steinberg, L., & Westenberg, P. M. (2009). The developmental pattern of resistance to peer influence in adolescence: Will the teenager ever be able to resist? *Journal of Adolescence, 32*(4), 1009–1021.

Surkan, P. J., Zhang, A., Trachtenberg, F., Daniel, D. B., McKinlay, S., & Bellinger, D. C. (2007). Neuropsychological function in children with blood lead levels <10 µg/dL. *Neurotoxicology, 28*(6), 1170–1177.

Suzuki, L. K., & Beale, I. I. (2006). Personal Web home pages of adolescents with cancer: Self-presentation, information dissemination, and interpersonal connection. *Journal of Pediatric Oncology Nursing, 23*(3), 152–161.

Suzuki, L. K., & Calzo, J. P. (2004). The search for peer advice in cyberspace: An examination of online teen bulletin boards about health and sexuality. *Journal of Applied Developmental Psychology, 25*(6), 685–698.

Svanberg, P. O. G. (1998). Attachment, resilience and prevention. *Journal of Mental Health, 7*(6), 543–578.

Svensson, R., & Oberwittler, D. (2010). It's not the time they spend, it's what they do: The interaction between delinquent friends and unstructured routine activity on delinquency: Findings from two countries. *Journal of Criminal Justice, 38*(5), 1006–1014.

Symonds, W. C., Schwartz, R. B., & Ferguson, R. (2011). *Pathways to prosperity: Meeting the challenge of preparing young Americans for the 21st century*. Cambridge, MA: Pathways to Prosperity Project, Harvard University Graduate School of Education.

Szyf, M., & Bick, J. (2013). DNA methylation: A mechanism for embedding early life experiences in the genome. *Child Development, 84*(1), 49–57.

Takishima-Lacasa, J. Y., Higa-McMillan, C. K., Ebesutani, C., Smith, R. L., & Chorpita, B. F. (2014). Self-consciousness and social anxiety in youth: The Revised Self-Consciousness Scales for Children. *Psychological Assessment, 26*(4), 1292–1306. doi:10.1037/a0037386

Talwar, V., & Lee, K. (2011). A punitive environment fosters children's dishonesty: A natural experiment. *Child Development, 82*(6), 1751–1758. doi:10.1111/j.1467-8624.2011.01663.x

Tamis-LeMonda, C. S., Bornstein, M. H., & Baumwell, L. (2001). Maternal responsiveness and children's achievement of language milestones. *Child Development, 72*(3), 748–767.

Tamis-LeMonda, C. S., Cristofaro, T. N., Rodriguez, E. T., & Bornstein, M. H. (2006). Early language development: Social influences in the first years of life. In L. Balter & C. S. Tamis-LeMonda (Eds.), *Child psychology: A handbook of contemporary issues* (2nd ed., pp. 79–108). New York: Psychology Press.

Tanaka, J. W., Wolf, J. M., Klaiman, C., Koenig, K., Cockburn, J., Herlihy, L., . . . Schultz, R. T. (2010). Using computerized games to teach face recognition skills to children with autism spectrum disorder: The Let's Face It! program. *Journal of Child Psychology and Psychiatry, 51*(8), 944–952. doi:10.1111/j.1469-7610.2010.02258.x

Tandon, R., Gaebel, W., Barch, D. M., Bustillo, J., Gur, R. E., Heckers, S., . . . Carpenter, W. (2013). Definition and description of schizophrenia in the DSM-5. *Schizophrenia Research, 150*(1), 3–10. doi: 10.1016/j.schres.2013.05.028

Tang, G., Gudsnuk, K., Kuo, S., Cotrina, M. L., Rosoklija, G., Sosunov, A. . . ., & Sulzer, D. (2014). Loss of mTOR-dependent macroautophagy causes autistic-like synaptic pruning deficits. *Neuron, 83*, 1–13. doi.org/10.1016/j.neuron.2014.07.040

Tanner, K. D. (2012). Promoting student metacognition. *Life Sciences Education, 11*, 113–120.

Tardif, T., & Wellman, H. M. (2000). Acquisition of mental state language in Mandarin- and Cantonese-speaking children. *Developmental Psychology, 36*(1), 25–43.

Task Force on Sudden Infant Death Syndrome. (2011). SIDS and other sleep-related infant deaths: Expansion of recommendations for a safe infant sleeping environment. *Pediatrics, 128*, 1030–1039.

Tatum, B. D. (1997). Racial identity development and relational theory: The case of black women in white communities. In B. Jordan (Ed.), *Women's growth in diversity* (pp. 91–106). New York: Guilford Press.

Taylor, A., & Kuo, F. (2009). Children with attention deficits concentrate better after walk in the park. *Journal of Attention Disorders, 12*(5), 402–409.

Taylor, A., & Kuo, F. (2011). Could exposure to everyday green spaces help treat ADHD? Evidence from children's play settings. *Applied Psychology: Health and Well-Being, 3*(3), 281–303. doi:10.1111/j.1758-0854.2011.01052.x

Tawia, S. (2013). Breastfeeding, brain structure and function, cognitive development and educational attainment. *Breastfeeding Review, 21*(3), 15–20.

Tenenbaum, H. R., & Ruck, M. D. (2007). Are teachers' expectations different for racial minority than for European American students?: A meta-analysis. *Journal of Educational Psychology, 99*(2), 253–273.

Terlecki, M. S., Newcombe, N. S., & Little, M. (2008). Durable and generalized effects of spatial experience on mental rotation: Gender differences in growth patterns. *Applied Cognitive Psychology, 22*(7), 996–1013.

Texas Education Agency. (2004). *Foundations of reading: Effective phonological awareness instruction and progress monitoring.* Retrieved from http://www.meadowscenter.org/vgc/downloads/primary/guides/PA_Guide.pdf

Thaler, N. S., Goldstein, G., Pettegrew, J. W., Luther, J. F., Reynolds, C. R., & Allen, D. N. (2013). Developmental aspects of working and associative memory. *Archives of Clinical Neuropsychology, 28*(4), 348–355. doi:10.1093/arclin/acs114

Thelen, E. (1989). Self-organization in developmental processes: Can systems approaches work? In M. R. Gunnar & E. Thelen (Eds.), *Systems and development: The Minnesota Symposia on child psychology* (pp. 77–117). Hillsdale, NJ: Erlbaum.

Thelen, E., Corbetta, D., Kamm, K., Spencer, J. P., Schneider, K., & Zernicke, R. F. (1993). The transition to reaching: Mapping intention and intrinsic dynamics. *Child Development, 64*(4), 1058–1098.

Thelen, E., & Smith, L.B. (2006) Dynamic systems theories. In W. Damon & R. M. Lerner (Eds.), *Handbook of child psychology, Volume 1, Theoretical models of human development* (6th ed., pp. 258–312). Hoboken, NJ: Wiley.

Thomas, A., & Chess, S. (1977). *Temperament and development.* New York: Brunner/Mazel.

Thomason, M. E., Grove, L. E., Lozon, T. J., Vila, A. M., Ye, Y., Nye, M. J., . . . Romero, R. (2015). Age-related increases in long-range connectivity in fetal functional neural connectivity networks in utero. *Developmental Cognitive Neuroscience, 11*, 96–104. doi:10.1016/j.dcn.2014.09.001

Thompson, M. P., Kingree, J. B., & Desai, S. (2004). Gender differences in long-term health consequences of physical abuse of children: Data from a nationally representative survey. *American Journal of Public Health, 94*(4), 599–604.

Tiedemann, J. (2000). Parents' gender stereotypes and teachers' beliefs as predictors of children's concept of their mathematical ability in elementary school. *Journal of Educational Psychology, 92*(1), 144–151.

Tillman, K. H. (2007). Family structure pathways and academic disadvantage among adolescents in stepfamilies. *Sociological Inquiry, 77*, 383–424.

Tinbergen, N. (1963). On aims and methods of ethology. *Zeitschrift für Tierpsychologie, 20*, 410–433.

Tison, J., Chaudhary, N., & Cosgrove, L. (2011). *National phone survey on distracted driving attitudes and behaviors.* (Report No. DOT HS 811 555). Washington, DC: National Highway Traffic Safety Administration.

Tither, J. M., & Ellis, B. J. (2008). Impact of fathers on daughters' age at menarche: A genetically and environmentally controlled sibling study. *Developmental Psychology, 44*(5), 1409–1420.

Tizard, B., & Rees, J. (1975). The effect of early institutional rearing on the behavior problems and affectional relationships of four-year-old children. *Journal of Child Psychology, Psychiatry, and Allied Disciplines, 27*, 61–73.

Tobin, D. D., Menon, M., Menon, M., Spatta, B. C., Hodges, E. E., & Perry, D. G. (2010). The intrapsychics of gender: A model of self-socialization. *Psychological Review, 117*(2), 601–622. doi:10.1037/a0018936

Toga, A. W., & Thompson, P. M. (2005). Genetics of brain structure and intelligence. *Annual Review of Neuroscience, 28*, 1–23. doi:10.1146/annurev.neuro.28.061604.135655

Tokolahi, E. (2014). Developmental coordination disorder: The domain of child and adolescent mental health occupational therapists? *New Zealand Journal of Occupational Therapy, 61*(1), 21–25.

Torff, B. (1996). How are you smart? Multiple intelligences and classroom practices. *The NAMTA Journal, 21*(2), 31–43.

Tracy, J. L., & Robins, R. W. (2008). The nonverbal expression of pride: Evidence for cross-cultural recognition. *Journal of Personality and Social Psychology, 94*(3), 516–530.

Tracy, J. L., Robins, R. W., & Lagattuta, K. H. (2005). Can children recognize pride? *Emotion, 5*(3), 251–257.

Trautwein, U., Ludtke, O., Marsh, H. W., Koller, O., & Baumert, J. (2006). Tracking, grading, and student motivation: Using group composition and status to predict self-concept and interest in ninth-grade mathematics. *Journal of Educational Psychology, 98*(4), 788–806.

Trevarthen, C. (1991). Reviewed work(s): *Developmental psychology in the Soviet Union* by Jaan Valsiner. *Soviet Studies, 43*(1), 183–187.

Trzaskowski, M., Shakeshaft, N. G., & Plomin, R. (2013). Intelligence indexes generalist genes for cognitive abilities. *Intelligence, 41*(5), 560–565. doi:10.1016/j.intell.2013.07.011

Trzesniewski, K. H., Donnellan, M. B., & Robins, R. W. (2008). Do today's young people really think they are so extraordinary? An examination of secular changes in narcissism and self-enhancement. *Psychological Science, 19*, 181–188.

Tsai, K. M., Park, H., Liu, L. L., & Lau, A. S. (2012). Distinct pathways from parental cultural orientation to young children's bilingual development. *Journal of Applied Developmental Psychology, 33*(5), 219–226. doi:10.1016/j.appdev.2012.07.002

Ttofi, M. M., & Farrington, D. P. (2011). Effectiveness of school-based programs to reduce bullying: A systematic and meta-analytic review. *Journal of Experimental Criminology, 7*(1), 27–56.

Tu, M. T., Lupien, S. J., & Walker, C. (2005). Measuring stress responses in postpartum mothers: Perspectives from studies in human and animal populations. *Stress: The International Journal on the Biology of Stress, 8*(1), 19–34.

Tucker-Drob, E. M., Rhemtulla, M., Harden, K. P., Turkheimer, E., & Fask, D. (2011). Emergence of a gene x socioeconomic status interaction on infant mental ability between 10 months and 2 years. *Psychological Science, 22*(1), 125–133. doi:10.1177/0956797610392926

Tulsky, D. S., Carlozzi, N. E., Chevalier, N., Espy, K. A., Beaumont, J. L., & Mungas, D. (2013). National Institutes of Health Toolbox Cognition Battery (NIH Toolbox CB): Validation for children between 3 and 15 years: V. NIH Toolbox Cognition Battery (CB): Measuring working memory. *Monographs of the Society for Research in Child Development, 78*(4), 70–87. doi: 10.1111/mono.12035

Turiel, E. (2006). Thought, emotions, and social interactional processes. In M. Killen & J. Smetana (Eds.), *Handbook of moral development* (pp. 7–36). Mahwah, NJ: Erlbaum.

Turkheimer, E., & Waldron, M. (2000). Nonshared environment: A theoretical, methodological, and quantitative review. *Psychological Bulletin, 126*(1), 78–108.

Turkheimer, E., Haley, A., Waldron, M., D'Onofrio, B., & Gottesman, I. I. (2003). Socioeconomic status modifies heritability of IQ in young children. *Psychological Science, 14*(6), 623–628.

Turlecki, G., & Meaney, M. J. (2016). Effects of the social environment and stress on glucocorticoid receptor gene methylation: A systematic review. *Biological Psychiatry, 79*(2), 87–96. doi10.1016/j.biopsych.2014.11.022

Turns, B. A., & Kimmes, J. (2014). 'I'm NOT the problem!' Externalizing children's 'problems' using play therapy and developmental considerations. *Contemporary Family Therapy, 36*(1), 135–147. doi:10.1007/s10591-013-9285-z

Tuteur, A. (2016, April 30). Why is American home birth so dangerous? *The New York Times.* Retrieved from http://www.nytimes.com/2016/05/01/opinion/sunday/why-is-american-home-birth-so-dangerous.html?_r=0

Twenge, J. M. (2006). *Generation me: Why today's young Americans are more confident, assertive, entitled—and more miserable than ever before.* New York: Free Press.

Twenge, J. M., Campbell, W., & Foster, C. A. (2003). Parenthood and marital satisfaction: A meta-analytic review. *Journal of Marriage and Family, 65*(3), 574–583. doi:10.1111/j.1741-3737.2003.00574.x

Twenge, J. M., & Nolen-Hoeksema, S. (2002). Age, gender, race, socioeconomic status, and birth cohort differences on the Children's Depression Inventory: A meta-analysis. *Journal of Abnormal Psychology, 111*, 578–588.

Tyree, T. (2011). African American stereotypes in reality television. *Howard Journal of Communications, 22*(4), 394–413. doi:10.1080/10646175.2011.617217

Tyrka, A. R., Graber, J. A., & Brooks-Gunn, J. (2000). The development of disordered eating: Correlates and predictors of eating problems in the context of adolescence. In A. J. Sameroff, M. Lewis, & S. Miller (Eds.), *Handbook of developmental psychopathology* (2nd ed., pp. 607–624). New York: Plenum Press.

Tyson, J. E., Nehal, A. P., Langer, J., Green, C., & Higgins, R. D. (2008). Intensive care for extreme prematurity—Moving beyond gestational age. *New England Journal of Medicine, 358*, 1672–1681.

Tzuriel, E., & Egozi, G. (2010). Gender differences in spatial ability of young children: The effects of training and processing strategies. *Child Development, 81*, 1417–1430.

U.S. Bureau of Labor Statistics. (2015a). *College enrollment and work activity of 2014 high school graduates* [Press release]. Retrieved from http://www.bls.gov/news.release/pdf/hsgec.pdf

U.S. Bureau of Labor Statistics. (2015b). *Occupational outlook handbook.* Retrieved from http://www.bls.gov/ooh/

U.S. Census Bureau. (2008a). *Current population survey (CPS)—Definitions and explanations.* Retrieved from http://www.census.gov/population/www/cps/cpsdef.html

U.S. Census Bureau. (2008b). *Father's day: June 15, 2008.* Retrieved from http://www.census.gov/newsroom/releases/pdf/cb08-ff09.pdf

U.S. Census Bureau. (2011a). *Back to school: 2011–2012.* Document CB11-FF.15. Retrieved from http://www.census.gov/newsroom/releases/pdf/cb11ff-15_school.pdf

U.S. Census Bureau. (2011b). *Half of young children in the U.S. are read to at least once a day, Census Bureau Reports.* Retrieved from http://www.census.gov/newsroom/releases/archives/children/cb11-138.html

U.S. Census Bureau. (2012a). *Family households by number of own children under 18 years of age: 2000 to 2010.* Retrieved from http://www.census.gov/compendia/statab/2012/tables/12s0064.pdf

U.S. Census Bureau. (2012b). *Historical poverty tables: Families.* Retrieved from http://www.census.gov/hhes/www/poverty/data/historical/families.html

U.S. Census Bureau. (2014a). *Nearly 6 out of 10 children participate in extracurricular activities, Census Bureau reports.* Retrieved from http://www.census.gov/newsroom/press-releases/2014/cb14-224.htm

U.S. Census Bureau. (2014b). *Poverty.* Retrieved from http://www.census.gov/topics/income-poverty/poverty.html

U.S. Bureau of Labor Statistics. (2015). *Employment characteristics of families summary.* Retrieved from http://www.bls.gov/news.release/famee.nr0.htm

U.S. Department of Agriculture. (2012). *Dietary guidelines consumer brochure.* Retrieved from http://www.choosemyplate.gov/print-materials-ordering/dietary-guidelines.html

U.S. Department of Agriculture. (2016). *WIC Program: Overview.* Retrieved from http://www.ers.usda.gov/topics/food-nutrition-assistance/wic-program.aspx

U.S. Department of Education. (2006). *Secretary Spellings announces more choices in single sex education.* Retrieved from http://www.ed.gov/news/pressreleases/2006/10/10242006.html

U.S. Department of Education. (2012). *Gender equity in education: A data snapshot.* Retrieved from http://www2.ed.gov/about/offices/list/ocr/docs/gender-equity-in-education.pdf

U.S. Department of Education, Office of English Language Acquisition, Language Enhancement, and Academic Achievement for Limited English Proficient Students. (2015). *The biennial report to Congress on the implementation of the Title III State Formula Grant Program. School years 2010– 12.* Washington, DC: Author.

U.S. Department of Energy Genome Programs. (2008). *Genomics and its impact on science and society. The human genome project and beyond (2008).* Retrieved from http://www.ornl.gov/sci/techresources/Human_Genome/publicat/primer2001/primer11.pdf

U.S. Department of Energy Genome Programs. (2012). *Human Genome Project information.* Retrieved from http://www.ornl.gov/sci/techresources/Human_Genome/home.shtml

U.S. Department of Health and Human Services. (2005a). *Code of federal regulations.* Retrieved from http://www.hhs.gov/ohrp/humansubjects/guidance/45cfr46.htm

U.S. Department of Health and Human Services. (2005b). *U.S. Surgeon General releases advisory on alcohol use in pregnancy* [press release]. Retrieved from http://www.surgeongeneral.gov/pressreleases/sg02222005.html

U.S. Department of Health and Human Services. (2010). *Head Start impact study: Final report.* Washington, DC: Author.

U.S. Department of Health and Human Services. (2012). *Preventing tobacco use among youth and young adults: A report of the Surgeon General.* Atlanta, GA: U.S. Department of Health and Human Services, Centers for Disease Control and Prevention, National Center for Chronic Disease Prevention and Health Promotion, Office on Smoking and Health.

U.S. Department of Health and Human Services. (2014). *Breastfeeding.* Retrieved from http://www.womenshealth.gov/breastfeeding/breastfeeding-benefits.html

U.S. Department of Health and Human Services. (2015a). *About Early Head Start.* Retrieved from http://eclkc.ohs.acf.hhs.gov/hslc/tta-system/ehsnrc/about-ehs#about

U.S. Department of Health and Human Services. (2015b). *Child maltreatment 2013.* Available from http://www.acf.hhs.gov/sites/default/files/cb/cm2013.pdf

U.S. Department of Health and Human Services. (2015c). *Policies and laws.* Retrieved from http://www.stopbullying.gov/laws/index.html

U.S. Department of Health and Human Services. (2015d). *Preterm birth.* Retrieved from http://www.cdc.gov/reproductivehealth/maternalinfanthealth/pretermbirth.htm

U.S. Department of Health and Human Services. (2015e). *Sexually-transmitted infections, pregnancy and breastfeeding.* Retrieved from http://www.womenshealth.gov/publications/our-publications/fact-sheet/sti-pregnancy-breastfeeding.html

U.S. Department of Health and Human Services. (2016). *Checklist of foods to avoid during pregnancy.* Retrieved from http://www.foodsafety.gov/risk/pregnant/chklist_pregnancy.html

U.S. Department of Labor. (n.d.). *Facts over time: Women in the labor force.* Retrieved from http://www.dol.gov/wb/stats/facts_over_time.htm

U.S. Department of Labor. (2010). *Fact Sheet #28: The Family and Medical Leave Act of 1993.* Retrieved from http://www.dol.gov/whd/regs/compliance/whdfs28.htm

U.S. Department of Labor. (2015). *Need time? An employee's guide to the Family and Medical Leave Act.* Retrieved from https://www.dol.gov/whd/fmla/employeeguide.pdf

U.S. Department of Labor. (2016). *Family and Medical Leave Act: Overview.* Retrieved from http://www.dol.gov/whd/fmla/

U.S. Department of State. (2015). *Intercountry adoptions: Statistics.* Retrieved from https://travel.state.gov/content/adoptionsabroad/en/about-us/statistics.html

U.S. Environmental Protection Agency. (2011). *Health effects of exposure to secondhand smoke.* Retrieved from http://www.epa.gov/smokefre/healtheffects.html

U.S. Environmental Protection Agency. (2012). *Ten tips to protect children from chemical and lead poisoning.* Retrieved from http://www.epa.gov/pesticides/factsheets/child-ten-tips.htm

U.S. Environmental Protection Agency. (2013). *Childhood cancer. America's children and the environment* (3rd ed.). Retrieved from http://www.epa.gov/sites/production/files/2015-06/documents/health-childhood-cancer.pdf

U.S. Environmental Protection Agency. (2015). *Health: Childhood cancer. America's children and the environment.* Retrieved from http://www.epa.gov/ace/health-childhood-cancer

U.S. Food and Drug Administration. (2008a). *FDA releases recommendations regarding use of over-the-counter cough and cold products.* Retrieved from http://www.fda.gov/NewsEvents/Newsroom/PressAnnouncements/2008/ucm116839.htm

U.S. Food and Drug Administration. (2008b). *OTC cough and cold products: Not for infants and children under 2 years of age.* Retrieved from http://www.fda.gov/ForConsumers/ConsumerUpdates/ucm048682.htm

U.S. Interagency Council on Homelessness. (2014). *Family connection.* Washington, DC: Author.

U.S. National Library of Medicine. (2010a). *X chromosome.* Retrieved from http://ghr.nlm.nih.gov/chromosome=X

U.S. National Library of Medicine. (2010b). *Y chromosome*. Retrieved from http://ghr.nlm.nih.gov/chromosome/Y

U.S. National Library of Medicine. (2015a). *Cystic fibrosis*. Retrieved from http://ghr.nlm.nih.gov/condition/cystic-fibrosis

U.S. National Library of Medicine. (2015b). *Intellectual disability*. Retreieved from https://www.nlm.nih.gov/medlineplus/ency/article/001523.htm

U.S. National Library of Medicine. (2016a). *Abortion*. Retrieved from https://www.nlm.nih.gov/medlineplus/abortion.html

U.S. National Library of Medicine. (2016b). *Miscarriage*. Retrieved from https://www.nlm.nih.gov/medlineplus/ency/article/001488.htm

U.S. National Library of Medicine. (2016c). *Premature infant*. Retrieved from https://www.nlm.nih.gov/medlineplus/ency/article/001562.htm

UC San Diego Center for Functional MRI. (2016). *What is fMRI?* Retrieved from http://fmri.ucsd.edu/Research/whatisfmri.html

Uddin, L. Q. (2015). The influence of brain state on functional connectivity in autism. *EBioMedicine, 2*(12), 1840–1841. doi.org/10.1016/j.ebiom.2015.11.017

Uhls, Y. T. (2015). *The science of selfies*. Retrieved from https://www.commonsensemedia.org/blog/the-science-of-selfies#

Umaña-Taylor, A. J., Gonzales-Backen, M. A., & Guimond, A. B. (2009). Latino adolescents' ethnic identity: Is there a developmental progression and does growth in ethnic identity predict growth in self-esteem? *Child Development, 80*(2), 391–405.

Unicode Consortium. (1991-2015). *The Unicode Consortium*. Retrieved from http://unicode.org/consortium/consort.html

United Nations Committee on the Rights of the Child (CRC). (2013). General comment No. 17 (2013) on the right of the child to rest, leisure, play, recreational activities, cultural life and the arts (art. 31). United Nations: Author.

United Nations International Children's Emergency Fund. (2015). *Breastfeeding*. Retrieved from http://www.unicef.org/nutrition/index_24824.html

University of Calgary. (n.d.). *Visual acuity*. Retrieved from http://www.ucalgary.ca/pip369/mod9/vision/acuity

Uro, G., & Barrio, A. (2013). *English language learners in America's great city schools: Demographics, achievement, and staffing*. Washington, DC: Council of the Great City Schools.

Vaglio, S. (2009). Chemical communication and mother-infant recognition. *Communicative and Integrative Biology, 2*(3), 279–281.

Valkenburg, P. M., & Peter, J. (2007). Online communication and adolescent well-being: Testing the stimulation versus the displacement hypothesis. *Journal of Computer-Mediated Communication, 12*(4), 1169–1182.

Van, P. (2012). Conversations, coping, & connectedness: A qualitative study of women who have experienced involuntary pregnancy loss. *Omega: Journal of Death and Dying, 65*(1), 71–85.

van den Bergh, L., Denessen, E., Hornstra, L., Voeten, M., & Holland, R. W. (2010). The implicit prejudiced attitudes of teachers: Relations to teacher expectations and the ethnic achievement gap. *American Educational Research Journal, 47*(2), 497–527. doi:10.3102/0002831209353594

van der Veer, R. (2007). *Lev Vygotsky*. New York: Continuum.

Van Doorn, M. D., Branje, S. T., & Meeus, W. J. (2011). Developmental changes in conflict resolution styles in parent-adolescent relationships: A four-wave longitudinal study. *Journal of Youth and Adolescence, 40*(1), 97–107.

Van Evra, J. (2004). *Television and child development* (3rd ed.). Mahwah, NJ: Erlbaum.

van Ijzendoorn, M. H., & Sagi-Schwartz, A. (2008). Cross-cultural patterns of attachment: Universal and contextual dimensions. In J. Cassidy & P. R. Shaver (Eds.), *Handbook of attachment: Theory, research, and clinical applications* (2nd ed., pp. 880–905). New York: Guilford Press.

van Jaarsveld, C. H. M., Fidler, J. A., Simon, A. E., & Wardle, J. (2007). Persistent impact of pubertal timing on trends in smoking, food choice, activity, and stress in adolescence. *Psychosomatic Medicine, 69*(8), 798–806.

Van Ryzen, M. J., Carlson, E. A., & Sroufe, L. A. (2012). Attachment discontinuity in a high-risk sample. *Attachment & Human Development, 13*(4), 381–401.

Vance, E. (2007). Cuteness: We know it when we see it. *Observer, 20*(6), 8.

Vandell, D. (2000). Parents, peer groups, and other socializing influences. *Developmental Psychology, 36*(6), 699–710.

Vandenbosch, L., & Eggermont, S. (2011). Temptation Island, The Bachelor, Joe Millionaire: A prospective cohort study on the role of romantically themed reality television in adolescents' sexual development. *Journal of Broadcasting & Electronic Media, 55*(4), 563–580. doi:10.1080/08838151.2011.620663

Vander Ven, T. M., Cullen, F. T., Carrozza, M. A., & Wright, J. P. (2001). Home alone: The impact of maternal employment on delinquency. *Social Problems, 48*(2), 236–257.

VanderBerg, K. A. (2007). Individualized developmental care for high risk newborns in the NICU: A practice guideline. *Early Human Development, 83*(7), 433–442.

Vandivere, S., Malm, K., & Radel, L. (2009). *Adoption USA: A chartbook based on the 2007 National Survey of Adoptive Parents*. Washington, DC: U.S. Department of Health and Human Services, Office of the Assistant Secretary for Planning and Evaluation.

Vann, M. R. (2016). *Is anxiety heredity?* Retrieved from http://www.everydayhealth.com/news/is-anxiety-hereditary/

Vaquero, E., & Kao, G. (2008). Do you like me as much as I like you? Friendship reciprocity and its effects on school outcomes among adolescents. *Social Science Research, 37*(1), 55–72.

Vargas, J. S. (2005). *A brief biography of B.F. Skinner*. Retrieved from http://www.bfskinner.org/BFSkinner/AboutSkinner.html

Varnhagen, C. K., McFall, G., Pugh, N., Routledge, L., Sumida-MacDonald, H., & Kwong, T. E. (2010). Lol: New language and spelling in instant messaging. *Reading and Writing, 23*(6), 719–733.

Vasilyeva, M., Huttenlocher, J., & Waterfall, H. (2006). Effects of language intervention on syntactic skill levels in preschoolers. *Developmental Psychology, 42*(1), 164–174.

Vasilyeva, M., Waterfall, H., & Huttenlocher, J. (2008). Emergence of syntax: Commonalities and differences across children. *Developmental Science, 11*(1), 84–97.

Vaughan, B. S., March, J. S., & Kratochvil, C. J. (2012). The evidence-based pharmacological treatment of paediatric ADHD. *International Journal of Neuropsychopharmacology, 15*(1), 27–39.

Veenstra, R., Lindenberg, S., Munniksma, A., & Dijkstra, J. (2010). The complex relation between bullying, victimization, acceptance, and rejection: Giving special attention to status, affection, and sex differences. *Child Development, 81*(2), 480–486.

Venezia, A., & Jaeger, L. (2013). Transitions from high school to college. *Future of Children, 23*(1), 117–136.

Venkatesh, S. (2008). *Gang leader for a day: A rogue sociologist takes to the streets*. New York: Penguin Press.

Verstraeten, K., Vasey, M. W., Raes, F., & Bijttebier, P. (2009). Temperament and risk for depressive symptoms in adolescence: Mediation by rumination and moderation by effortful control. *Journal of Abnormal Child Psychology, 37*(3), 349–361. doi:10.1007/s10802-008-9293-x

Vialle, W., Ashton, T., Carlon, G., & Rankin, F. (2001). Acceleration: A coat of many colours. *Roeper Review, 24*(1), 14–19.

Vickers, B. (2005). Cognitive model of the maintenance and treatment of post-traumatic stress. *Clinical Child Psychology and Psychiatry, 10*(2), 217–234.

Vidal, J. (2014, May 14). Dutch arrest 44 Greenpeace activists blocking Russian Arctic oil tanker. *The Guardian*. Retrieved from http://www.theguardian.com/environment/2014/may/01/greenpeace-russian-arctic-oil-tanker

Visser, B. A., Ashton, M. C., & Vernon, P. A. (2006). Beyond "g": Putting multiple intelligences theory to the test. *Intelligence, 34*(5), 487–502.

Visu-Petra, L., Cheie, L., & Benga, O. (2008). Short-term memory performance and metamemory judgments in preschool and early school-age children: A quantitative and qualitative analysis. *Cognitie, Creier, Comportament/Cognition, Brain, Behavior, 12*(1), 71–101.

Viswanathan M., Visco, A. G., Hartmann, K., Wechter, M. E., Gartlehner, G., Wu, J. M., . . . Lohr, K. N. (2006). *Cesarean delivery on maternal request*. Rockville, MD: Agency for Healthcare Research and Quality. Evidence Report/Technology Assessment.

Viterbori, P., Usai, M. C., Traverso, L., & De Franchis, V. (2015). How preschool executive functioning predicts several aspects of math achievement in Grades 1 and 3: A longitudinal study. *Journal of Experimental Child Psychology, 140*, 38–55. doi:10.1016/j.jecp.2015.06.014

Vogt Yuan, A. (2007). Gender differences in the relationship of puberty with adolescents' depressive symptoms: Do body perceptions matter? *Sex Roles, 57*(1/2), 69–80. doi:10.1007/s11199-007-9212-6

Volkmar, F. R., & Tsatsanis, K. (2002). Psychosis and psychotic conditions in childhood and adolescence. In D. T. Marsh & M. A. Fristad (Eds.), *Handbook of serious emotional disturbance* (pp. 266–283). New York: Wiley.

Volkarsky, K. B. (2010). *Diet quality of American school-age children*. New York: Nova Science.

Volpe, J. J. (2009). Cerebellum of the premature infant: Rapidly developing, vulnerable, clinically important. *Journal of Child Neurology, 24*(9), 1085–1104.

Von Drehle, D. (2007, July 26). The myth about boys. *Time*. Retrieved from http://www.time.com/time/magazine/article/0,9171,1647452,00.html

Vrugt, A., & Oort, F. J. (2008). Metacognition, achievement goals, study strategies and academic achievement: Pathways to achievement. *Metacognition and Learning, 30*, 123–146.

Vygotsky, L. S. (1962/1986). *Thought and language.* Cambridge, MA: MIT Press. (Original work published in 1934)

Vygotsky, L. S. (1978). *Mind in society: The development of higher psychological processes* (M. Cole, V. John-Steiner, S. Scribner & E. Souberman., Eds.) (A. R. Luria, M. Lopez-Morillas & M. Cole [with J. V. Wertsch], Trans.) Cambridge, Mass.: Harvard University Press. (Original manuscripts [ca. 1930-1934])

Waddington, C. H. (1942). Canalization of development and the inheritance of acquired characters. *Nature, 150*, 563–564.

Wadhwa, P. D. (2005). Psychoneuroendocrine processes in human pregnancy influence fetal development and health. *Psychoneuroendocrinology, 30*(8), 724–743.

Wahlstrom, D., White, T., & Luciana, M. (2010). Neurobehavioral evidence for changes in dopamine system activity during adolescence. *Neuroscience and Biobehavioral Reviews, 34*(5), 631–648. doi: 10.1016/j.neubiorev.2009.12.007

Wakefield, A. J., Murch, S. H., Anthony, A., Linnell, J., Casson, D. M., Malik, M., . . . Walker-Smith, J. A. (1998). Ileal-lymphoid-nodular hyperplasia, non-specific colitis, and pervasive developmental disorder in children. *Lancet, 351*(9103), 637–641.

Walcott, D. D., Pratt, H. D., & Patel, D. R. (2003). Adolescents and eating disorders: Gender, racial, ethnic, sociocultural, and socioeconomic issues. *Journal of Adolescent Research, 18*(3), 223–243.

Walker, L. J. (2006). *Gender and morality.* In M. Killen & J. G. Smetana (Eds.), *Handbook of moral development* (pp. 93–115). Mahwah, NJ: Erlbaum.

Walker, L. J., & Frimer, J. A. (2009). "The song remains the same": Rebuttal to Sherblom's re-envisioning of the legacy of the care challenge. *Journal of Moral Education, 38*(1), 53–68.

Walker, S. K. (2005). Use of parenting newsletter series and other child-rearing information sources by mothers of infants. *Family and Consumer Sciences Research Journal, 34*(2), 153–172.

Walum, H., Westberg, L., Henningsson, S., Neiderhiser, J. M., Reiss, D., Igl, W., . . . Lichtenstein, P. (2008). Genetic variation in the vasopressin receptor 1a gene (AVPR1A) associates with pair-bonding behavior in humans. *Proceedings of the National Academy of Sciences, 105*(37), 14153–14156.

Wang, A., Peterson, G. W., & Morphey, L. (2007). Who is more important for early adolescents' developmental choices? Peers or parents? *Marriage & Family Review, 42*(2), 95–122.

Wang, M., & Eccles, J. S. (2013). School context, achievement motivation, and academic engagement: A longitudinal study of school engagement using a multidimensional perspective. *Learning and Instruction, 28*, 12–23. doi:10.1016/j.learninstruc.2013.04.002

Wang, M., & Huguley, J. P. (2012). Parental racial socialization as a moderator of the effects of racial discrimination on educational success among African American adolescents. *Child Development, 83*(5), 1716–1731. doi:10.1111/j.1467-8624.2012.01808.x

Wang, Q. (2006). Culture and the development of self-knowledge. *Current Directions in Psychological Science, 15*(4), 182–187.

Wang, Q. (2008). Being American, being Asian: The bicultural self and autobiographical memory in Asian Americans. *Cognition, 107*(2), 743–751.

Wang, Y. (2015, December 15). In Flint, Mich., there's so much lead in children's blood that a state of emergency is declared. *The Washington Post.* Retrieved from https://www.washingtonpost.com/news/morning-mix/wp/2015/12/15/toxic-water-soaring-lead-levels-in-childrens-blood-create-state-of-emergency-in-flint-mich/

Ward, L. M. (2004). Wading through the stereotypes: Positive and negative associations between media use and black adolescents' conception of self. *Developmental Psychology, 40*(2), 284–294.

Ward, L. M., & Friedman, K. (2006). Using TV as a guide: Associations between television viewing and adolescents' sexual attitudes and behavior. *Journal of Research on Adolescence, 16*(1), 133–156.

Wasserman, J. D. (2012). A history of intelligence assessment: The unfinished tapestry. In D. P. Flanagan & P. L. Flanagan (Eds.), *Contemporary intellectual assessment* (pp. 3–55). New York: Guilford.

Waterhouse, L. (2006). Multiple intelligences, the Mozart effect, and emotional intelligence: A critical review. *Educational Psychologist, 41*(4), 207–225.

Waters, H. S., & Waters, E. (2006). The attachment working models concept: Among other things, we build script-like representations of secure base experiences. *Attachment & Human Development, 8*, 185–198.

Watson, J. B. (1928). *Psychological care of infant and child.* New York: W. W. Norton.

Watson, J. B. (1994). Psychology as the behaviorist views it. *Psychological Review, 101*(2), 248–253. (Original work published in 1913)

Watson, J. B., & Rayner, R. (1920). Conditioned emotional reactions. *Journal of Experimental Psychology, 3*(1), 1–14.

Watson, J. D. (2003). *DNA: The secret of life.* New York: Knopf.

Wauterickx, N., Gouwy, A., & Bracke, P. (2006). Parental divorce and depression: Long-term effects on adult children. *Journal of Divorce & Remarriage, 45*(3–4), 43–68.

Waxman, S., Fu, X., Arunachalam, S., Leddon, E., Geraghty, K., & Song, H. (2013). Are nouns learned before verbs? Infants provide insight into a long-standing debate. *Child Development Perspectives, 7*(3), 155–159. doi:10.1111/cdep.12032

Weatherspoon, L. J., Venkatesh, S., Horodynski, M. A., Stommel, M., & Brophy-Herb, H. E. (2013). Food patterns and mealtime behaviors in low-income mothers and toddlers. *Journal of Community Health Nursing, 30*(1), 1–15.

Wechsler, D. (2014). *Wechsler Intelligence Scale for Children* (5th ed.). San Antonio, TX: Pearson.

Weems, C. F. (2008). Developmental trajectories of childhood anxiety: Identifying continuity and change in anxious emotion. *Developmental Review, 28*(4), 488–502.

Weersing, V. R., & Brent, D. A. (2010). Treating depression in adolescents using individual cognitive-behavioral therapy. In J. R. Weisz & A. Kazdin (Eds.), *Evidence-based psychotherapies for children and adolescents* (2nd ed., pp. 126–139). New York: Guilford Press.

Weichold, K., Silbereisen, R. K., & Schmitt-Rodermund, E. (2003). Short-term and long-term consequences of early versus late physical maturation in adolescents. In C. Hayward (Ed.), *Gender differences at puberty* (pp. 241–276). Cambridge, UK: Cambridge University Press.

Weil, L. G., Fleming, S. M., Dumontheil, I., Kilford, E. J., Weil, R. S., Rees, G., . . . Blakemore, S. (2013). The development of metacognitive ability in adolescence. *Consciousness and Cognition: An International Journal, 22*(1), 264–271. doi:10.1016/j.concog.2013.01.004

Weinfield, N. S., Whaley, G. J. L., & Egeland, B. (2004). Continuity, discontinuity, and coherence in attachment from infancy to late adolescence: Sequelae of organization and disorganization. *Attachment and Human Development, 6*(1), 73–97.

Weintraub, S., Bauer, P. J., Zelazo, P., Wallner-Allen, K., Dikmen, S. S., Heaton, R. K., . . . Gershon, R. C. (2013). National Institutes of Health Toolbox Cognition Battery (NIH Toolbox CB): Validation for children between 3 and 15 years: I. NIH Toolbox Cognition Battery (CB): Introduction and pediatric data. *Monographs of The Society for Research in Child Development, 78*(4), 1–15. doi:10.1111/mono.12031

Weis, R., & Cerankosky, B. C. (2010). Effects of video-game ownership on young boys' academic and behavioral functioning: A randomized, controlled study. *Psychological Science, 21*(4), 463–470.

Weisberg, M. (2016). *Zika vaccines are in the works, but still years away.* Retrieved from http://www.livescience.com/53659-zika-virus-vaccine-research.html.

Weisleder, A., & Fernald, A. (2013). Talking to children matters: Early language experience strengthens processing and builds vocabulary. *Psychological Science, 24*(11), 2143–2152. doi:10.1177/0956797613488145

Weisman, O., Zagoory-Sharon, O., & Feldman, R. (2014). Oxytocin administration, salivary testosterone, and father-infant social behavior. *Progress in Neuro-Psychopharmacology & Biological Psychiatry, 49*, 47–52. doi: 10.1016/j.pnpbp.2013.11.006

Weiss, R. E. (2014). *Why labor is good for babies.* Retrieved from http://pregnancy.about.com/cs/laborbirth/a/aa042300a.htm

Weitz, T., Moore, K., Gordon, R., & Adler, N. (2008). You say "regret" and I say "relief": A need to break the polemic about abortion. *Contraception, 78*(2), 87–89. doi: 10.1016/j.contraception.2008.04.116

Wellman, H. (2014). *Making minds: How theory of mind develops.* New York: Oxford University Press.

Wells, N. M., & Evans, G. W. (2003). Nearby nature: A buffer of life stress among rural children. *Environment and Behavior, 35*(3), 311–330.

Wenger, A., & Fowers, B. J. (2008). Positive illusion in parenting: Every child is above average. *Journal of Applied Social Psychology, 38*(3), 611–634.

Wenig, M. (2007, August 28). The benefits of yoga for kids. *Yoga Journal.* Retrieved from http://www.yogajournal.com/article/family/yoga-kids/

Werner, E. E. (1992). The children of Kauai: Resiliency and recovery in adolescence and adulthood. *Journal of Adolescent Health, 13*(4), 262–268.

Werner, E. E. (2005). What can we learn about resilience from large-scale longitudinal studies? In S. Goldstein & R. B. Brooks (Eds.), *Handbook of resilience in children* (pp. 91–106). New York: Springer.

Werner, E. E., & Smith, R. S. (1985). *Vulnerable but invincible: A study of resilient children.* New York: McGraw-Hill.

Wertsch, J. V. (1985). *Vygotsky and the social formation of mind*. Cambridge, MA: Harvard University Press.

Westerveld, M., Sass, K. J., Chelune, G. J., Hermann, B. P., Barr, W. B., Loring, D. W., . . . Spencer, D. D. (2000). Temporal lobectomy in children: Cognitive outcome. *Journal of Neurosurgery, 92*(1), 24–30.

Westling, E., Andrews, J. A., Hampson, S. E., & Peterson, M. (2008). Pubertal timing and substance use: The effects of gender, parental monitoring and deviant peers. *Journal of Adolescent Health, 42*(6), 555–563.

Whitehurst, G. J., & Chingos, M. M. (2011). *Class size: What research says and what it means for state policy*. Washington, DC: The Brookings Institute.

Whitley, B. E. (1983). Sex role orientation and self-esteem: A critical meta-analytic review. *Journal of Personality and Social Psychology, 44*(4), 765–778.

Whitman, A. (1980, September 17). Jean Piaget dies in Geneva at 84. *The New York Times*. Retrieved from http://www.nytimes.com/learning/general/onthisday/bday/0809.html

Wichstrøm, L., & von Soest, T. (2016). Reciprocal relations between body satisfaction and self-esteem: A large 13-year prospective study of adolescents. *Journal of Adolescence, 47*, 16–27. doi:10.1016/j.adolescence.2015.12.003

Wier, L., Miller, A., & Steiner, C. (2009). Sports injuries in children requiring hospital emergency care, 2006. *HCUP Statistical Brief #75*. Rockville, MD: Agency for Healthcare Research and Quality. Retrieved from http://www.hcup-us.ahrq.gov/reports/statbriefs/sb75.jsp

Wilcox, W. B. (2011). *The state of our unions: Marriage in America 2011*. Charlottesville: University of Virginia.

Williams, J. F., Smith V. C., and the Committee on Substance Abuse. (2015). Fetal alcohol spectrum disorders. *Pediatrics, 136*(5), e1395–e1406.

Williams, S., Mastergeorge, A. M., & Ontai, L. L. (2010). Caregiver involvement in infant peer interactions: Scaffolding in a social context. *Early Childhood Research Quarterly, 25*(2), 251–266.

Williamson, D. M., Abe, K., Bean, C., Ferré, C., Henderson, Z., & Lackritz, E. (2008). Current research in preterm birth. *Journal of Women's Health, 17*(10), 1545–1549.

Williams-Rautiolla, S. (2008). *Cooney, Joan Ganz*. The Museum of Broadcast Communications. Retrieved from http://www.museum.tv/archives/etv/C/htmlC/cooneyjoan/cooneyjoan.htm

Willis, J. O., Dumont, R., & Kaufman, A. S. (2011). Factor-analytic models of intelligence. In R. J. Sternberg & S. Kaufman (Eds.), *The Cambridge handbook of intelligence* (pp. 39–57). New York: Cambridge University Press.

Wills, T. A., Sargent J. D., Stoolmiller, M., Gibbons, F. X., & Gerrard, M. (2008). Movie smoking exposure and smoking onset: A longitudinal study of mediation processes in a representative sample of U.S. adolescents. *Psychology of Addictive Behaviors, 22*(2), 269–277.

Wilson, E. O. (1975). *Sociobiology: The new synthesis*. Cambridge, MA: Harvard University Press.

Wilson, K. R., Havighurst, S. S., & Harley, A. E. (2014). Dads Tuning in to Kids: Piloting a new parenting program targeting fathers' emotion coaching skills. *Journal of Community Psychology, 42*(2), 162–168. doi:10.1002/jcop.21601

Wilson, L. (2014). Environmental exposure: Educating the childbirth educator. *International Journal of Childbirth Education, 29*(1), 32–40.

Windsor, J., Benigno, J. P., Wing, C. A., Carroll, P. J., Koga, S. F., Nelson, C. A., . . . Zeanah, C. H. (2011). Effect of foster care on young children's language learning. *Child Development, 82*(4), 1040–1046.

Winickoff, J., Friebely, J., Tanski, S., Sherrod, C., Matt, G., Hovell, M., & McMillen, R. (2009). Beliefs about health effects of "thirdhand" smoke and home smoking bans. *Pediatrics, 123*(1), e74–e79. doi:10.1542/peds.s008-2184

Winn, W. (2004). Cognitive perspectives in psychology. In D. H. Jonassen (Ed.), *Handbook of research for educational communications and technology* (2nd ed., pp. 79–112). New York: Simon & Schuster.

Winsler, A., Feder, M., Way, E. L., & Manfra, L. (2006). Maternal beliefs concerning young children's private speech. *Infant and Child Development, 15*(4), 403–420. doi:10.1002/icd.467

Winsler, A., Madigan, A. L., & Aquilino, S. A. (2005). Correspondence between maternal and paternal parenting styles in early childhood. *Early Childhood Research Quarterly, 20*(1), 1–12.

Winsler, A., & Naglieri, J. (2003). Overt and covert verbal problem-solving strategies: Developmental trends in use, awareness, and relations with task performance in children aged 5 to 17. *Child Development, 74*(3), 659–678.

Witvliet, M., Brendgen, M., Van Lier, P. C., Koot, H. M., & Vitaro, F. (2010). Early adolescent depressive symptoms: Prediction from clique isolation, loneliness, and perceived social acceptance. *Journal of Abnormal Child Psychology, 38*(8), 1045–1056.

Witvliet, M., van Lier, P. C., Brendgen, M., Koot, H. M., & Vitaro, F. (2010). Longitudinal associations between clique membership status and internalizing and externalizing problems during late childhood. *Journal of Clinical Child and Adolescent Psychology, 39*(5), 693–704.

Wolak, J., Finkelhor, D., Mitchell, K. J., & Ybarra, M. L. (2008). Online "predators" and their victims: Myths, realities and implications for prevention treatment. *American Psychologist, 63*(2), 111–128.

Wolfe, D. A., & Mash, E. J. (Eds.). (2006). *Behavioral and emotional disorders in adolescents: Nature, assessment, and treatment*. New York: Guilford Press.

Wolfinger, N. H. (2011). More evidence for trends in the intergenerational transmission of divorce: A completed cohort approach using data from the General Social Survey. *Demography, 48*, 581–592.

Wolters Kluwer Health. (2009). *Professional guide to diseases* (9th ed.). Philadelphia: Lippincott, Williams & Wilkins.

Wonderlich, A. L., Ackard, D. M., & Henderson, J. B. (2005). Childhood beauty pageant contestants: Associations with adult disordered eating and mental health. *Eating Disorders: The Journal of Treatment & Prevention, 13*(3), 291–301.

Wong, C. A., Eccles, J. S., & Sameroff, A. (2003). The influence of ethnic discrimination and ethnic identification on African American adolescents' school and socioemotional adjustment. *Journal of Personality, 71*(6), 1197–1232.

Woo, M., & Oei, T. P. S. (2006). The MMPI-2 gender-masculine and gender-feminine scales: Gender roles as predictors of psychological health in clinical patients. *International Journal of Psychology, 41*(5), 413–422.

Woodward, A. L. (2009). Infants' grasp of others' intentions. *Current Directions in Psychological Science, 18*(1), 53–57.

Woollett, K., & Maguire, E. A. (2011). Acquiring "the Knowledge" of London's layout drives structural brain changes. *Current Biology, 21*(24-2), 2109–2114. http://doi.org/10.1016/j.cub.2011.11.018

The World Bank. (2015). *Adolescent fertility rate (births per 1,000 women ages 15–19)*. Retrieved from http://data.worldbank.org/indicator/SP.ADO.TFRT

World Fact Book. (2015). *Sex ratio*. Retrieved from https://www.cia.gov/library/publications/the-world-factbook/fields/2018.html

World Health Organization. (2013). *New plan to address pneumonia and diarrhoea could save 2 million children annually*. Retrieved from http://www.who.int/mediacentre/news/releases/2013/pneumonia_diarrhoea_plan_20130412/en/

World Health Organization. (2014). *Rubella*. Retrieved from http://www.who.int/mediacentre/factsheets/fs367/en/

World Health Organization. (2016). *Endocrine disrupting chemicals (EDCs)*. Retrieved from http://www.who.int/ceh/risks/cehemerging2/en/

Wörmann, V., Holodynski, M., Kärtner, J., & Keller, H. (2014). The emergence of social smiling: The interplay of maternal and infant imitation during the first three months in cross-cultural comparison. *Journal of Cross-Cultural Psychology, 45*(3), 339–361. doi:10.1177/0022022113509134

Wright, J. C., Huston, A. C., Scantlin, R., & Kotler, J. (2001). The Early Window Project: *Sesame Street* prepares children for school. In S. M. Fisch & R. T. Truglio (Eds.), *"G" is for growing—Thirty years of research on children and* Sesame Street (pp. 97–114). Mahwah, NJ: Erlbaum.

Wu, C. S., Jew, C. P., & Lu, H. D. (2011). Lasting impacts of prenatal cannabis exposure and the role of endogenous cannabinoids in the development brain. *Future Neurology, 6*(4), 459–480.

Wu, S., & Keysar, B. (2007). The effect of culture on perspective taking. *Psychological Science, 18*(7), 600–606.

Xu, H., Wen, L., Rissel, C., & Baur, L. (2013) Smoking status and factors associated with smoking of first-time mothers during pregnancy and postpartum: Finding from the Healthy Beginnings Trial. *Maternal & Child Health Journal, 17*(6), 1151–1157.

Yatvin, J. (2002). Babes in the woods: The wanderings of the National Reading Panel. *Phi Delta Kappan, 83*(5), 364–369.

Yi, C. (2013). *The psychological well-being of East Asian youth*. New York: Springer.

Youth.gov. (n.d.). *Positive youth development*. Retrieved from http://youth.gov/youth-topics/positive-youth-development

Yu, T., Pettit, G. S., Lansford, J. E., Dodge, K. A., & Bates, J. E. (2010). The interactive effects of marital conflict and divorce on parent-adult children's relationships. *Journal of Marriage and Family, 72*(2), 282–292.

Zarbatany, L., McDougall, P., & Hymel, S. (2000). Gender-differentiated experience in the peer culture: Links to intimacy in preadolescence. *Social Development, 9*(1), 62–79.

Zeanah, C. H., Smyke, A. T., Koga, S. F., Carlson, E., & Bucharest Early Intervention Project Core Group. (2005). Attachment in institutionalized and community children in Romania. *Child Development, 76*(5), 1015–1028.

Zelazo, D. (2006). The Dimensional Change Card Sort (DCCS): A method of assessing executive function in children. *Nature Protocols, 1,* 297–301.

Zelazo, P. D., Anderson, J. E., Richler, J., Wallner-Allen, K., Beaumont, J. L., & Weintraub, S. (2013). National Institutes of Health Toolbox Cognition Battery (NIH Toolbox CB): Validation for children between 3 and 15 years: II. NIH Toolbox Cognition Battery (CB): Measuring executive function and attention. *Monographs of The Society for Research in Child Development, 78*(4), 16–33. doi:10.1111/mono.12032

Zeleznikow, L., & Zeleznikow, J. (2015). Supporting blended families to remain intact: A case study. *Journal of Divorce & Remarriage, 56*(4), 317–335. doi:10.1080/10502556.2015.1025845

Zeller, M. H., Reiter-Purtill, J., & Ramey, C. (2008). Negative peer perceptions of obese children in the classroom environment. *Obesity, 16*(4), 755–762. doi:10.1038/oby.2008.4

Zentner, M., & Bates, J. E. (2008). Child temperament: An integrative review of concepts, research programs, and measures. *European Journal of Developmental Science, 2*(1-2), 7–37.

Zevenbergen, A. A., & Whitehurst, G. J. (2003). Dialogic reading: A shared picture book reading intervention for preschoolers. In A. van Kleeck, S. A. Stahl, & E. B. Bauer (Eds.), *On reading books to children: Parents and teachers* (pp.177–202). Mahwah, NJ: Erlbaum.

Zhai, F., Brooks-Gunn, J., & Waldfogel, J. (2014). Head Start's impact is contingent on alternative type of care in comparison group. *Developmental Psychology, 50*(12), 2572–2586. doi:10.1037/a0038205

Zhang, N., Baker, H. W., Tufts, M., Raymond, R. E., Salihu, H., & Elliott, M. R. (2013). Early childhood lead exposure and academic achievement: Evidence from Detroit public schools, 2008–2010. *American Journal of Public Health, 103*(3), e72–e77.

Zhang, T., & Meaney, M. J. (2010). Epigenetics and the environmental regulation of the genome and its function. *Annual Review of Psychology, 61,* 439–466.

Zhou, Q., Hofer, C., Eisenberg, N., Reiser, M., Spinrad, T. L., & Fabes, R. A. (2007). The developmental trajectories of attention focusing, attentional and behavioral persistence, and externalizing problems during school-age years. *Developmental Psychology, 43*(2), 369–385.

Zigler, E., & Bishop-Josef, S. J. (2006). The cognitive child versus the whole child: Lessons from 40 years of Head Start. In D. G. Singer, R. M. Golinkoff, & K. Hirsh-Pasek (Eds.), *Play=learning* (pp. 15–35). New York: Oxford University Press.

Zimmer-Gembeck, M. J., & Skinner, E. A. (2008). Adolescents coping with stress: Development and diversity. *Prevention Researchers, 15*(4), 3–7.

Zimmerman, F. J., & Christakis, D. A. (2007). Associations between content types of early media exposure and subsequent attentional problems. *Pediatrics, 120*(5), 986–992.

Zimmerman, F. J., Christakis, D. A., & Meltzoff, A. N. (2007). Associations between media viewing and language development in children under age two years. *Journal of Pediatrics, 151,* 364–368.

Zimmerman, M. A., Bingenheimer, J. B., & Notaro, P. C. (2002). Natural mentors and adolescent resiliency: A study with urban youth. *American Journal of Community Psychology, 30*(2), 221–243.

Zimmerman, T. S., Haddock, S. A., Current, L. R., & Ziemba, S. (2003). Intimate partnership: Foundation to the successful balance of family and work. *American Journal of Family Therapy, 31*(2), 107–124.

Zosuls, K. M., Ruble, D. N., Tamis-LeMonda, C. S., Shrout, P. E., Bornstein, M. H., & Greulich, F. K. (2009). The acquisition of gender labels in infancy: Implications for gender-typed play. *Developmental Psychology, 45*(3), 688–701. doi:10.1037/a0014053

Author Index

Subject Index